Film Study

An Analytical Bibliography

VOLUME 3

Frank Manchel

Rutherford • Madison • Teaneck
Fairleigh Dickinson University Press
London and Toronto: Associated University Presses

Associated University Presses
440 Forsgate Drive
Cranbury, NJ 08512

Associated University Presses
25 Sicilian Avenue
London WC1A 2QH, England

Associated University Presses
P.O. Box 488, Port Credit
Mississauga, Ontario
Canada L5G 4M2

The paper used in this publication meets the requirements
of the American National Standard for Permanence of Paper
for Printed Library Materials Z39.48-1984.

Library of Congress Cataloging-in-Publication Data

Manchel, Frank.
    Film study: an analytical bibliography / Frank Manchel.
        p.   cm.
    ISBN 0-8386-3413-3 (v. 3: alk. paper)
    1. Motion pictures—Bibliography.   2. Motion pictures—Study and teaching.   I. Title.
Z5784.M9M34   1990
[PN1994]
016.79143—dc20   85-45026
                                                                            CIP

Contents of Volume 3

TOD BROWNING	1762
JAMES CAGNEY	1762
FRANK CAPRA	1762
MAURICE CHEVALIER	1764
CLAUDETTE COLBERT	1765
GARY COOPER	1765
JOSEPH COTTON	1765
JOAN CRAWFORD	1765
MICHAEL CURTIZ	1766
BETTE DAVIS	1766
OLIVIA DE HAVILLAND	1767
MARLENE DIETRICH	1767
WALT DISNEY	1767
MELVYN DOUGLAS	1769
W. C. FIELDS	1770
ROBERT FLOREY	1771
ERROL FLYNN	1771
HENRY FONDA	1771
JOHN FORD	1772
CLARK GABLE	1772
JUDY GARLAND	1773
CARY GRANT	1774
JEAN HARLOW	1774
HOWARD HAWKS	1774
SUSAN HAYWARD	1777
EDITH HEAD	1777
KATHARINE HEPBURN	1777
WILLIAM HOLDEN	1778
LESLIE HOWARD	1778
AL JOLSON	1778
BORIS KARLOFF	1778
HENRY KING	1779
HEDY LAMARR	1780
WALTER LANTZ	1780
PETER LAWFORD	1780
MERVYN LEROY	1780
CAROLE LOMBARD	1781
MYRNA LOY	1781
ERNST LUBITSCH	1781
BELA LUGOSI	1782
THE LUNTS	1782
IDA LUPINO	1782
ROUBEN MAMOULIAN	1782
FREDRIC MARCH	1782
THE MARX BROTHERS	1783

Film Study

Chapter 7: Approaching the History of Film

It is only very thoughtless and presumptuous people who can erect laws and an esthetic for cinema proceeding from premises of some incredible virgin-birth of this art! Let Dickens and the whole ancestral array, going back as far as the Greeks and Shakespeare, be superfluous reminders that both Griffith and our cinema prove our origins to be not solely as of Edison and his fellow inventors, but as based on an enormous cultured past; each part of this in its own moment of world history has moved forward the great art of cinematography. Let this past be a reproach to those thoughtless people who have displayed arrogance in reference to literature, which has contributed so much to this apparently unprecedented art and is, in the first and most important place, the art of viewing.

Sergei Eisenstein, FILM FORM: ESSAYS IN FILM THEORY

Throughout this book, we have been exploring, under various topics, the nature and shape of film history. Whether talking about the links between film and literature, or about the importance of the period from 1913 to 1919, a fundamental assumption has been that a historical examination of the relevant data extends our understanding of the world of film, and the world on film. It is axiomatic that films are a product of the age in which they are made, and nothing makes this more striking than the study of film in its historical context. But film history is more than just a study of the past.[1]

First, film history is the study of the medium's COMPLETE past, which requires the study of EVERY significant event--political, social, economic, cultural, technological, or intellectual--that has occurred since the origins of film. The fact

---

[1] My broad perspective on historiography has been shaped by *Mark A. Stoler and Marshall True, EXPLORATIONS IN AMERICAN HISTORY: A SKILLS APPROACH, Vols.1 & 2 (New York: Alfred A. Knopf, 1987). My broad overview on the study of film history is based upon the following material: *Robert C. Allen and Douglas Gomery, FILM HISTORY: THEORY AND PRACTICE (New York: Alfred A. Knopf, 1985); Robert C. Allen, "Film History: The Narrow Discourse," 1977 FILM STUDIES ANNUAL (West Lafayette: Purdue University, 1978):9-16; Edward Buscombe, "A New Approach to Film History," ibid., PART II, pp.1-8; ___, "Introduction: Metahistory of Films," FILM READER 4 (1979):11-5; ___, Notes on Columbia Pictures Corp., 1926-41," SCREEN 16 (Autumn 1975):65-82; Charles Altman, "Towards a Historiography of American Film," CINEMA JOURNAL 16:2 (Spring 1977):1-25; *Andre Bazin, WHAT IS CINEMA? Volume 1, ed. Hugh Gray (Berkeley: University of California Press, 1968), pp.23-40; Edward Branigan, "Color and Cinema: Problems in the Writing of History," FILM READER 4 (1979):16-34; Mary Beth Haralovich, "The Social History of Film: Heterogeneity and Mediation," WIDE ANGLE 8:2 (1986):4-13; Michael T. Isenberg, "Toward a Historical Methodology for Film Scholarship," THE ROCKY MOUNTAIN SOCIAL SCIENCE JOURNAL 12:1 (January 1975):45-57; Vance Kepley, "Griffith's BROKEN BLOSSOMS and the Problem of Historical Specificity," QUARTERLY REVIEW OF FILM STUDIES 3:1 (Fall 1977):37-48; Geoffrey Nowell-Smith, "Facts About Films and Facts of Films," ibid., pp.272-5; Gerald Mast, "Film History and Film Histories," ibid., 1:3 (August 1976):297-314; ___, "What Isn't Cinema," CRITICAL INQUIRY 1:2 (December 1974):373-93; Pauline Kael, "Circles and Squares," FILM QUARTERLY 16:3 (Spring 1963):12-26, Rpt. *Pauline Kael, I LOST IT AT THE MOVIES (Boston: Little, Brown, and Company, 1965), pp.264-88, *Gerald Mast and Marshall Cohen, eds., FILM THEORY AND CRITICISM: INTRODUCTORY READINGS, 3rd ed. (New York: Oxford University Press, 1985), pp.541-52; Myron O. Lounsbury, "'The Gathered Light': History, Criticism and THE RISE OF THE AMERICAN FILM," QUARTERLY REVIEW OF FILM STUDIES 5:1 (Winter 1980):49-85; and Ron Mottram, "Fact and Affirmation: Thoughts on the Methodology of Film History and the Relation of Theory to Historiography," QUARTERLY REVIEW OF FILM STUDIES 5:3 (Summer 1980):335-47.

that no one can produce a comprehensive history is neither surprising nor alarming. Comprehensiveness has always been more an ideal than a reality. Moreover, historical inquiry requires an emphasis on investigating and interpreting particulars, rather than on collecting unlimited data. Second, as the historians Mark A. Stoler and Marshall True point out, "History is also a way of thinking and a way of interpreting the present as well as the past."[2] For example, Jeanne Thomas Allen explains that "changing definitions of what film is, from a purely artistic construct governed by its own internal history and development to an industrial commodity, allow us to understand the shift from documentary actualities or topical films to dramatic fictional narratives early in the twentieth century."[3] Those changing definitions reveal how specific cultural conditions shape movies into cultural artifacts that represent important values of their respective societies at specific times in history. By examining a film's box-office popularity, for example, social film historians identify what specific audiences needed, wanted, or desired. The results are constantly being re-evaluated. Every generation produces its share of "revisionist historians"--scholars who seek to reassess commonly held notions of historical events and causes--and who profess their objectivity about methodology and interpretations. But so long as we are part of the historical continuum, we will never stand apart from what is being analyzed. What is discouraging is that ninety years into the history of film, the profession is still having difficulty putting film history on a sensible methodological footing.

What constitutes good film history is a major concern for film scholars. For example, between 1972 and 1974 the annual Congress of the FEDERATION INTERNATIONAL DES ARCHIVES DU FILM held three separate symposia on film history, each time trying to decide on how to deal with the history of film. Eileen Bowser, who chaired the 1974 symposium, writes,

> With the distance of time and other experiences, our ideas of films, their meanings, and their place in our cultural history undergo a strange transformation. What once seemed unimportant details stand out as revealing facts. Some films considered great in their time sink into mere pretensions. Films that were seen and forgotten sometimes leap to the eye with new force. Films of our own recent past may give us discomfort, or embarrassment, yet seen thirty years later take on a style not noticed or not valued formerly.[4]

Bowser and her colleagues were arguing not only for reliable techniques that could assimilate significant data, but also for reliable perspectives on film that did not isolate aesthetic analyses from other significant political, cultural, social, and economic events of the age in which films were produced.

A major problem is that much of what has previously been reported about film history is highly suspect. According to Douglas Gomery, "The history of film must be written from the ground-up--monograph by monograph."[5] Thomas R. Cripps notes that "The central paradox is found in the close interlocking of the film buff's

---

[2]   Stoler and True, Volume 1., p.v.

[3]   Jeanne Thomas Allen, "Film History: A Revisionist Perspective," JOURNAL OF THE UNIVERSITY FILM AND VIDEO ASSOCIATION 35:4 (Fall 1983):6.

[4]   Eileen Bowser, "Introduction: Symposium on the Methodology of Film History," CINEMA JOURNAL 14:2 (Winter 1974-75):2.

[5]   Douglas Gomery, "Books: THE DREAM THAT KICKS and HISTORY MUST ANSWER TO MAN, WIDE ANGLE 4:3 (1980):81.

enthusiasms with a contempt for the scholar's discipline."[6] Symptomatic of the problem is a case, cited by Edward Buscombe, in which a popular film historian

> manages to combine a complete innocence of historiography with an utter disregard for the normal conventions of scholarship. It is indeed astounding to find that a book which presumably has claims to being the standard work on the subject contains no references at all and makes mention of a mere twenty or so printed works in the bibliography. Less surprising, perhaps, is its adherence to a historical "method" which mixes "facts" (this film made money, that one introduced a new technique) with idiosyncratic aesthetic judgments (Stroheim's FOOLISH WIVES leaves "a sour taste in the mouth") and generalizations of doubtful value ("The difference between the two media [silent and sound film] is literally [sic] the difference between painting and photography." What can this mean?) It's not that this kind of thing continues to appear but that its claims to authority are boosted by the fact that it is published by an established press and favorably reviewed in an established film journal by another acknowledged "authority". . . .[7]

The problem of finding a suitable methodology go beyond a single book or critical journal. Robert C. Allen observes that a majority of general film histories organize their historical interpretations as narratives ("a chronological arrangement of events in a cause-effect relationship").[8] These "stories", he ironically explains,

> present the reader with a serious obstacle to getting at the historical arguments behind their narratives. In many of them, the quantity and quality of evidence used as the foundation of the historical narrative are difficult to determine from the text itself or from references in footnotes and bibliographies. One standard criterion for judging the merits of any historical argument is the extent to which its conclusions are supported by relevant evidence. The absence of footnotes and detailed bibliographic references in survey film histories frequently makes it impossible to trace conclusions back to their evidentiary sources. Compounding this problem is the fact that, unlike survey works in other historical disciplines, survey film histories are not based on mountains of more narrowly focused books, specialized monographs, journal articles, and other pieces of primary research, which have been accumulated, scrutinized, and critiqued over a period of years if not decades.[9]

Vladimir Petric is another scholar appalled at the amount of inaccurate and insufficient analytical documentation in studies of film history. For example, in reviewing the material in series like CLASSIC FILM SCRIPTS and MODERN FILM SCRIPTS, he found that

> no less than 90 percent of their breakdown of the visual and auditory structure is inaccurate, and therefore useless for serious film study. Similarly, many

---

[6]   Thomas Cripps, "The Future Film Historian: Less Art and More Craft," CINEMA JOURNAL 14:2 (Winter 1974-75):42.

[7]   "Introduction: Metahistory of Films," p.11.

[8]   Allen and Gomery, p.44.

[9]   Allen and Gomery, p.46.

inaccurate descriptions of sequences from great films have passed on from one history to another for decades without being checked or corrected.[10]

While scholars like Petric are arguing for the importance of a historiography and historical accuracy that emphasizes cinematic language and filmic structure, other's are pointing out the significance of an institutional setting. For example, Calvin Pryluck emphasizes the importance of an interpretive framework that demonstrates the constraints imposed on filmmakers as they attempt to create significant products for the marketplace. He notes that

> The writing and teaching of film history is [sic] more than merely the chronicling of the development of the film form or merely the analysis of institutional forces which impinge on film development or merely the detailing of the individuals who influence the development. The development of film forms is the result of individuals working within a confluence of forces which constrain and facilitate the production of certain kinds of films at particular moments in history.[11]

Geoffrey Nowell-Smith adds still another perspective to the concerns that scholars have with existing approaches to film history. He observes that

> History claims to concern itself with facts. It's raison d'etre is indeed the belief that the past can be dismembered and put together again in factual form. (Theory also has to do with facts, though in a different way.) In my opinion, there is also such a thing as the fact of style, and within the context of this fact there are stylistic facts, which are as amenable to investigation as facts of any other kind. The question, therefore arises, Why has historiography on the whole abstained from dealing with these facts?[12]

Each of these scholars, in his own way, is appealing to the film community to rethink its traditional approach to the study of film history. Instead of relying so heavily on the accumulation of "facts," film historians argue, these scholars should not only be more accurate in collecting and selecting their facts, but also should focus on the causal relationships between film and its historical contexts. What the current generation of film scholars are preoccupied with is questions of why this rather than that, why then rather than later, why here rather than there.[13]

At the heart of their arguments is the reasonable assumption that the way we approach film history determines our understanding of this medium. For example, if the historian believes that one person, an AUTEUR, is responsible for a work of art, then data about studios, genres, economic systems, and technological breakthroughs

---

[10]   Vladimir Petric, "From a Written Film History to a Visual Film History," CINEMA JOURNAL 14:2 (Winter 1974-75):21.

[11]   Calvin Pryluck, "The Aesthetic Relevance of the Organization of Film Production," CINEMA JOURNAL 15:2 (Spring 1978):6.

[12]   Nowell-Smith, p.273.

[13]   Lest anyone assume that the new scholasticism is going unchallenged, Myron O. Lounsbury writes, "The emerging professionalism of film studies has not been without its skeptics; ironically, some of the harshest language has been uttered by respected critics and historians who gained their reputation as film scholars before the recent profusion of academic literature on the medium." Among the people cited are Ernest Callenbach, Richard Dyer MacCann, and William K. Everson. See Lounsbury, pp.50-1.

are relegated to secondary status. On the other hand, if the historian argues that the history of film is determined by technological breakthroughs, then data on star systems, genres, political upheavals, and AUTEURS are subordinated to a survey of specific techniques evolving over a period of time. As Jeanne Thomas Allen explains, the current trend in studying film history is to place film in a broader social context "than the internal or autonomous history of an art form with particular stylistic and technical properties, although knowing that history is a fundamental step in understanding film as a social practice."[14]

One way to become more critical of historical methodology is to question the assumptions that film historians make in writing their general film histories. As Yon Barna insists, "The key approach in any research is to question the data."[15] To aid in that process, Robert C. Allen summarizes six basic questions that perceptive readers ask of film historians.[16] First, how has the author defined and limited the purpose and scope of the historical investigation? It is important to know not only what is being studied, but also why. Second, how does the author assess historical change, and what is the basis for the conclusions presented? By answering these questions, the reader can recognize that there is a formula used in arriving at explanations for historical changes. Third, how does the author interpret historical stasis, and what is the basis for that assumption? As Allen states, "The massive changes that have occurred in the cinema since its initial development in the late nineteenth century disguise the fact that some aspects of film history have remained remarkably resistant to change for long periods."[17] How has the author accounted for this historical equilibrium in the presence of notable changes? Fourth, are the author's conclusions and explanations logical? Is there a clear link between what we are asked to accept and the evidence presented? Fifth, has the author identified the sources for the explanations? The reader has a right to know what sources were used and whether the historian's analysis is original or based upon the interpretations of others. Sixth, is the evidence presented convincing? Quotations, footnotes, and bibliographical references by themselves do not constitute historical facts. Not only can material be taken out of context, but it can also be misinterpreted. Finally, Allen raises the important issue of how the times in which authors lived and their cultural backgrounds influenced their judgment and perspective.

These types of questions are uppermost in the minds of current film scholars. Gerald Mast, for example, in his analysis of several popular film histories, sought answers to two basic concerns:

First, what are the significant questions that have been raised about the history of the cinema? What theories of significance, of cinema, of art, and of history underlie each of these questions? Second, what kinds of documentation do each of these questions require? What are the rules of evidence and of selection in applying these documents to the significant questions?[18]

The answers that Mast reports are useful to explore. In brief, he found that most historians are interested in one of three types of history: film masterpieces, the social history of film, or the significant types of institutions and inventions that shaped film content and style. Each of these three approaches relies on different forms of

---

[14]   "Film History: A Revisionist Perspective," p.7.

[15]   Yon Barna, "Next Steps in Film History Research," CINEMA JOURNAL 14:2 (Winter 1974-75):38.

[16]   Allen and Gomery, pp.48-51.

[17]   Allen and Gomery, p.49.

[18]   Mast, pp.298-9.

documentation, and each has its own set of limitations. For example, those who study
the history of film as art concentrate on identifying film masterpieces. Their basic
assumption is that the purpose of film is, in fact, to produce masterpieces. Thus for
them, studying film history is studying how film classics are made. It follows,
therefore, that the primary resources in such film histories are the films themselves.
"The sole fact that concerns the historian in this kind of investigation," explains
Mast, "is that however the work got to be what it is, it is what it is."[19]

As many scholars point out, the "masterpiece" approach has two fundamental
limitations. One, films rarely remain the same as they were at the time of release.
Mast uses silent films as an example. Not only is there a problem finding a suitable
projector that runs at silent speed, but some people forget that silent films were never
silent[20] nor that were they exclusively black-and-white prints.[21] Moreover, as
discussed in Chapter 2, many films have been re-edited, censored, or mutilated over
a period of time. Thus the possibility of seeing silent films with their original
content, length, or color[22] is indeed rare. Even further, there is the problem of the
availability of the silent films themselves. Douglas Gomery estimates that "nearly half
of the theatrical-length motion pictures made in the United States are lost
forever."[23] And when it comes to documenting the problems related to the production
of films, Robert C. Allen reminds us that "The business records of all but a few
early companies have long since been lost, thrown away, or burned."[24]

The second fundamental limitation of the masterpiece approach relates to what
Janet Staiger calls "the Politics of Film Canons."[25] As discussed in Chapter 3, the
problem is how to determine the criteria for selection in the "classic" category.[26]
Most scholars agree that such judgments are subjective and interpretive.
Consequently, Mast makes a valid point in challenging the criteria used by a number
of current historians and asking:

Is a film a significant work of art because it was immensely popular, expanding
the audience and impact of cinema (a criterion that would embrace THE BIRTH
OF A NATION and JAWS, but not INTOLERANCE and CITIZEN KANE)? Or
because it developed and expanded the tools, language, and expressive

[19]   Mast, p.299.

[20]   Richard Schickel, "The Silents Weren't Just Voiceless Talkies," NEW YORK TIMES
        MAGAZINE (November 28, 1971):32-3, 54, 57, 59-60, 62, 64.

[21]   Mast, p.299.

[22]   For more information, see "Colour Problem," SIGHT AND SOUND 30:1 (Winter
        1980-81):12-3; Harlan Jacobson, "Old Pix Don't Die, They Fade Away," VARIETY
        (July 9, 1980):1; and Paul Spehr, "The Color Film Crisis," AMERICAN FILM 5:2
        (November 1979):56-61.

[23]   Allen and Gomery, p.29.

[24]   "Film History: The Narrow Discourse," p.10.

[25]   Janet Staiger, "The Politics of Film Canons," CINEMA JOURNAL 24:3 (Spring
        1985):4-23.

[26]   In 1988, Congress passed the National Film Preservation Act. A year later,
        representatives from thirteen organizations met at th University of California
        at Los Angeles to determine what films should be classified as film classics.
        For more information, see Aljean Harmetz, "25 Films to Become US Treasures," NEW
        YORK TIMES C (July 17, 1989):13.

possibilities of the art (a criterion that would embrace THE BIRTH OF A NATION, NAPOLEON, and CITIZEN KANE, but not CITY LIGHTS, and BRINGING UP BABY)? Or because it influenced other films and the direction of cinema history (a criterion that would embrace THE BIRTH OF A NATION, CITIZEN KANE, and BREATHLESS, but not MEET ME IN ST. LOUIS, SINGIN' IN THE RAIN, and VERTIGO)? Or because it espoused some noble or complex political or moral philosophy (a criterion that would embrace CITY LIGHTS and CITIZEN KANE, but not THE BIRTH OF A NATION, METROPOLIS, and TRIUMPH OF THE WILL)? Or because of critical and historical consensus (as if artistic quality could be determined democratically, by means of a vote)? Or because it moved the historian and was therefore significant? Or because it fulfilled some theoretical mission or criterion that the historian valued?[27]

Such questions illustrate the fact that historians using the film masterpiece approach not only make different assumptions about the relevance of technology, business, and social influences on the art of the film, but they also have very different criteria when evaluating the same films.

The one common thread among many masterpiece historians is a belief in AUTEURISM, the idea that one person (generally the director) is responsible for the work of art. The underlying assumption is that there is a dichotomy between art and industry. But that just isn't true, as Buscombe, restating a point made earlier in this book, points out:

One might suppose that a little common sense would tell us that such a distinction is nonsense, that all film is both industry AND art, in some sense. Even the lowest, most despised products (choose your own examples) are made with some kind of art. Do they not share the same language as the acknowledged masterpieces: do they not tell a story, try to affect the spectators' emotions? They may do it more or less effectively, but isn't this a difference of degree, not of kind? Conversely, in the making of the most spiritual and sublime films grubby bank notes change hands. The film stock on which the masterpiece is recorded may come from the same batch used to shoot the potboiler on the adjoining stage.[28]

At the core of Buscombe's objections is the belief that film history should not pattern itself after other traditional art histories in which the authors ignore the business or technological end of the process. Not only does he see film functioning as an art AND as an industry, but he also faults film critics and historians for not appreciating the fact that film grows out of an industrial environment.

The same reservations can be made about the assumptions used by historians studying the social history of film, or the types of institutions and inventions that shaped film content and style. While both groups downplay film aesthetics, they differ considerably about causal relationships and how the cinema interacts with society. For example, in his analysis of what's wrong with the study of film history, Buscombe argues that AUTEURISM and technological approaches take too much for granted. Nothing is a "given." The technological evolution of film did not occur in a vacuum. The film industry was "not just part of the economic system," he writes, "but [it was part of] a group of institutions embodying a set of learned practices carrying with them an ideology."[29] The social historian studying how movies interact with society would be interested in why a particular studio (e.g., Warner Bros.) produced a certain type of film (e.g., LITTLE CAESAR), rather than another type (e.g.,

---

[27]   Mast, p.300.

[28]   "Notes," p.66.

[29]   "A New Approach to Film History," p.5.

GRAND HOTEL), and why one style was more prevalent at that studio than at another studio. "In other words," Buscombe concludes, "history needs to ascertain not only causes, but a hierarchy of causes."[30] Mary Beth Haralovich takes another tack. She argues that many social film histories are too narrow in their focus. "In order to avoid reductionist or reflectionist analysis," she writes, "the two essential factors which must inform the social history of film are the heterogeneity of social relations and the many levels of mediation between film texts and social processes."[31] This form of history stresses the importance of avoiding a consensus that obscures cultural hegemony (a complex set of relationships that collectively reflect a nation's worldview). what Haralovich wants is a social history that accents the complexity of social life and reminds us that people take an active role in their relationships with their social institutions.

Charles F. Altman, in his study of approaches to film history, finds not three, but thirteen schools of thought, "each depending on a different hypothesis about the fundamental determinants of cinema production and distribution, each proposing its own canon, its own periodization."[32] Under the general category of production (the determinants of the film image), he lists ten approaches: technology, technique, personality, film and the other arts, chronicle, social, studio, AUTEUR, genre, and ritual. In addition to providing a representative bibliography, Altman summarizes the mode of historical interpretation, gives a specific example of how the approach works, and explains the dangers in such an approach. A case in point is the technology approach. Not only is this methodology the first employed in film history (i.e., chronicling who invented what, where, and when), but it also represents a simplistic causal interpretation of film history (i.e., an apparatus produces an image) that currently is undergoing considerable rethinking. Some revisionist historians are arguing that ideology, rather than scientific curiosity, is the explanation for the types of inventions that gave birth to film. Other revisionist historians insist that the way to study the history of film technology is to use a theoretical production/distribution/feedback loop (including factors like AUTEURISM, image, audience, ideology, industry, and society) instead of a linear model consisting of a film author who produces an image that is sent to the audience.[33] The problem with many histories of film technology is that they are too narrow in scope.

Altman's remaining three schools of historical interpetation, subsumed under the general category of distribution (the delivery of the image), are legal, industrial, and sociological. The treatment for them is the same as for those approaches discussed under production. In all thirteen cases, Altman matter-of-factly divides eighty years of film history into nine periods. Before he concludes his useful overview, however, he makes it clear that such a periodization of film history is very misleading and a manifestation "of a hopeless confusion of methods." So long as we recognize that each approach defines its own periodization, he argues, we can be conscious of the arbitrary nature of film history. The best way to insure intelligent decisions, Altman insists, is to identify "theories of coherence" and "modes of historical explanation."[34]

---

[30]   "A New Approach to Film History," p.8.

[31]   Haralovich, p.13.

[32]   Altman, pp.1-2.

[33]   Altman, pp.3-4.

[34]   Altman, pp.1-2. For a critical reaction to Altman's ideas, see "Film History: A Revisionist Perspective," pp.7-9.

Such perceptions expose us to the differences between A history of film and THE history of film. The latter is unattainable; there is just too much material and no reasonable way to assimilate and to analyze it. The former is possible. Film histories based on reasonable assumptions result in sensible film chronicles that focus on the formation and influence of such factors as economic organizations, star systems, film masterpieces, narrative development, and film theories. Although many general film histories indicate that all factors work simultaneously in the world of film, most surveys are concerned with charting the changes and historical stases of specific factors that influence the present perception of the phenomenon known as film. Each study grows out of a film historian's curiosity for knowing more about the causal links between the past and the present.

Before describing how this chapter will approach a study of film history, it seems sensible to recall how our study of the past has helped our study of film as a work of art, an industry, and a form of mass communication. For example, in Chapter 2, in examining film genres, we explored how theatrical films about the Vietnam War retained or rejected ideological values that were first developed in movies about World War I.[35] Particular attention was paid to the differences between history on film, and history in film and to the way war movies function in society. Questions were raised about how a series of shots on celluloid was edited to create specific effects for a multitude of reasons and then manipulated by producers, distributors, and exhibitors. Among the benefits gained from this perspective on film history was an awareness of how films about the past--e.g., ALL QUIET ON THE WESTERN FRONT (1930), WILSON (1944), and APOCALYPSE NOW (1979)--became persuasions to restructure the present. The evidence presented did more than identify a link between the ambience of the times and the products produced. It taught us about the values of the filmmakers, the influence of political and economic events on the film industry, and the various ways in which audiences and intellectuals receive films.

Our study of the past also explored the impact of technology on the nature of film. For example, in Chapter 3, in investigating film stereotypes, we identified the importance of projectors, sound, color, screen sizes, and television on the content of films and on the careers of film stars, directors, and producers. Referring to Biblical epics like DAVID AND BATHSHEBA (1951), THE TEN COMMANDMENTS (1956), BEN HUR (1959), and SOLOMON AND SHEBA (1960), we highlighted how a technological struggle to find a screen process that would compete successfully with the novelty of television enriched our understanding of why such films were made and what they represented. Especially meaningful was the ability to anchor the discussion in both a historical and an institutional context. Not only did we see some of the effects that the times were having on the industry (the historical context), but we also saw the effect that the technology was having on the medium (the institutional context).

Moreover, our study of the past drew meaningful parallels between film conventions of the past and the present, and their relationship to human history. It is worth remembering, for example, that we are not the first Americans to complain bitterly about film stereotyping of minorities. Demeaning characterizations, ethnic exploitation, and racial discrimination are "contemporary" issues. They are, nonetheless, the offspring of racial problems that existed before the birth of the movies or the founding of this nation. In short, our study of the past demonstrates that a study of film history is indispensable for educating us about how the present film structure evolved and what the processes are by which films are made, distributed, exhibited, and received.

---

[35] For a useful introduction to the complex relationship between product differentiation and expansion of the American film industry in early film history, see Robert Anderson, "The Role of the Western Film Genre in Industry Competition, 1907-1911," JOURNAL OF THE UNIVERSITY FILM ASSOCIATION 31:2 (Spring 1979):19-26.

A second vital point to recall before moving on to the priorities of this chapter is that there is no one valid interpretation of the meaning of the past. Contrary to what some people believe, there is no indisputable historical truth. In the words of Stoler and True, there are no SINGLE statements of fact.

It is important for you to realize that interpretations can be analyzed, changed, and contradicted. Indeed, historians do this all the time. They often reach DIFFERENT conclusions based on their evaluation of the SAME evidence, because history involves more than the discovery of past facts. Historians must put these facts together into a coherent pattern, assess their interrelationship, and reach some conclusions. These tasks are always speculative, seldom easy, and never foolproof; mistakes can be made. Moreover, every historian is a product of a particular time and tends to interpret the past in light of his or her experiences . . . In the final analysis, history is a subjective, interpretive discipline.[36]

Let us be very clear on this point. Stoler and True are not saying that one opinion is just as good as another. Rather, they are stressing the need for historians to defend their selections and interpretations of facts within the context of the period analyzed. Evidence, not assertion, is the stuff of good histories.

Given the enormity of the task and the intellectual dangers involved, the reader may rightly ask, "Why then do film historians attempt general surveys about the nature and scope of film?" The simple answer is that it is exciting and challenging. The more academic response is that they are raising important questions and collecting valuable data for more reliable interpretations of film history. That is what film history is all about. Every historian is trying to make some sense of what happened at a particular time and place, why it happened, and what the consequences were. Working with primary and secondary sources, for example, social and industrial film historians form educated hypotheses about what possibly could have caused a number of Eastern European immigrant Jewish retailers to become the first film moguls, why Hollywood (rather than Florida or New York) emerged as the production capital of the world, and how distribution became the cornerstone of the contemporary film scene. Historians investigating the art of film struggle with the role of social and commercial influences in the process of creative filmmaking. As film historians thread their way through a web of conflicting opinions and controversial documents, they decide what is "historical fact," and what is insignificant information. Although there are those scholars who stress their objectivity in developing their historical arguments, Robert C. Allen speaks for many contemporary scholars when he writes that "Because the historian's job requires selection, interpretation, appraisal, and judgment, he or she is never totally 'objective.'"[37]

Where then does one start a history of film? And what basic assumptions about the role of technology, aesthetics, industry, economics, politics, and society are appropriate in weaving together a tapestry on the evolution and development of the movies? Before getting all tangled up in controversial historical threads relating to origins and authorship, let me reaffirm the fact that the discipline of film is in the throes of a major shift in historical research. Where once it was fashionable to ask questions and downplay documentation, the present generation of film scholars and educators is focusing on specific events, dates, and issues. Moreover, there is a greater demand for evidence than at any other time in film history. It's as if every assertion taken for granted in the sweeping film histories of the past is being given a microscopic analysis. When the first edition of this book appeared in 1973, only the rarest of film chronicles made passing reference to footnotes and bibliographies.

---

[36]   Stoler and True, p.82.

[37]   Allen and Gomery, pp.8-9.

Almost none cited archival material, early film journals, authentic screenplays, corporate records, and legal documentation. Now footnoting these basic sources is almost standard operating procedure in scholarly publications. Hopefully, the major film texts will soon follow. Thus, at the outset of this general overview of film history, I want to make it clear that EVERYTHING that follows is suspect and in need of careful scrutiny. Hardly a month passes without a noteworthy article in a leading film journal pointing out the fallacy in assertions about the evolution of the narrative form, the contributions of a particular film pioneer, or the significance of a neglected film. My purpose, therefore, in synthesizing the general notions about film history is to allow other serious students to choose how these assumptions about the past can be clarified, corrected, or corroborated.

The object of this chapter is to outline the general history of film, while suggesting materials to be referred to for the study of film history. Unlike previous chapters, it takes a sweeping look at the phenomenon of film. The historical method used is a synthesis of Altman's thirteen classifications relating to distribution and production. My basic assumption is that a study of the past reveals important insights about the interrelationship between the past and the present. After studying thousands of documents and films produced over ninety years of film history, I am persuaded to conclude that no one person, event, or work functions in isolation. A framework exists in which the contributions of film critics, historians, and other intellectuals can be studied as an ongoing process toward investigating and interpreting a significant phenomenon of the twentieth century. While I will draw upon the data presented throughout this book, my primary sources for the sweeping picture of film history are the most significant general film histories published in the English

---

[38]   Maurice Bardeche and Robert Brasillach, THE HISTORY OF MOTION PICTURES, Trans. Iris Barry (New York: W. W. Norton, 1938, New York: Arno Press, 1970); *Frank E. Beaver, ON FILM: A HISTORY OF THE MOTION PICTURE (New York: McGraw-Hill Book Company, 1983); *Thomas W. Bohn and Richard L. Stromgren, LIGHT AND SHADOWS: A HISTORY OF MOTION PICTURES, 3rd ed. (Palo Alto: Mayfield Publishing Company, 1987); *David Bordwell, Janet Staiger, and Kristin Thompson, THE CLASSICAL HOLLYWOOD CINEMA: FILM STYLE & MODE OF PRODUCTION TO 1960 (New York: Columbia University Press, 1985); *Kevin Brownlow, THE PARADE'S GONE BY (Berkeley: University of California Press, 1968); *Alan Casty, DEVELOPMENT OF THE FILM: AN INTERPRETIVE HISTORY (New York: Harcourt Brace Jovanovich, 1973); *Charles Champlin, THE MOVIES GROW UP 1940-1980 (Athens: Swallow Press, 1981); *David A. Cook, A HISTORY OF NARRATIVE FILM (New York: W. W. Norton and Company, 1981); *Jack C. Ellis, A HISTORY OF FILM, 2nd ed. (Englewood Cliffs: Prentice-Hall, 1985); William K. Everson, AMERICAN SILENT FILM (New York: Oxford University Press, 1978); *John L. Fell, A HISTORY OF FILMS (New York: Holt, Rinehart and Winston, 1979); *Louis Giannetti and Scott Eyman, FLASHBACK: A BRIEF HISTORY OF FILM (Englewood Cliffs: Prentice-Hall, 1986); Robert Grau, THE THEATRE OF SCIENCE (New York: Broadway Publishing Company, 1914); *Benjamin B. Hampton, A HISTORY OF THE AMERICAN FILM INDUSTRY FROM ITS BEGINNINGS TO 1931, With a New Introduction by Richard Griffith (New York: Dover Publications, 1970); Charles Higham, THE ART OF THE AMERICAN FILM 1900-1971 (Garden City: Doubleday and Company, 1973); *Lewis Jacobs, THE RISE OF THE AMERICAN FILM: A CRITICAL HISTORY, With an Essay Experimental Cinema in America 1921-1947 (New York: Teachers College Press, 1967); *Arthur Knight, THE LIVELIEST ART: A PANORAMIC HISTORY OF THE MOVIES, rev. ed. (New York: Macmillan Publishing Company, 1978); William Luhr, ed., WORLD CINEMA SINCE 1945 (New York: Ungar Publishing Company, 1987); *Gerald Mast, A SHORT HISTORY OF THE MOVIES, 4th ed. (New York: Macmillan Publishing Company, 1985); James Monaco, AMERICAN FILM NOW: THE PEOPLE, THE POWER, THE MONEY, THE MOVIES (New York: Oxford University Press, 1979); *Terry Ramsaye, A MILLION AND ONE NIGHTS: A HISTORY OF THE MOTION PICTURE THROUGH 1925, New edition (New York: Touchstone, 1986); David Robinson, THE HISTORY OF WORLD CINEMA, Revised and expanded edition (New York: Stein and Day, 1981); *Eric

language.[38] Despite all the limitations suggested by scholars like Allen, Altman, Buscombe, Gomery, Haralovich, Mast, Petric, and Pryluck, these historical investigations represent the collective thinking of my young discipline. I do not intend to minimize the authors' failings. But thanks to their efforts, we now have the ability to move beyond a stage of popularizing and identifying a new and remarkable form of mass communication to an interpretation of what film means to the twentieth century.

Obviously, the best illustrative material for a history of film is the film itself. Usually 16mm prints are recommended. However, the reader should consider the advantages of videodiscs and videotapes: availability, accessibility, and cost. I have, therefore, suggested some videodiscs and videotapes within the course of this chapter.

In deciding what films to mention, what personalities to highlight, and what events to stress, I again rely on consensus rather than on personal choices. This approach allows for a grouping of movies in a chronological order, while offering information about the historical and artistic conditions, trends, innovations, and major figures that bear on them.

The periodization that follows also represents the consensus of general surveys. Film history, although relatively short, includes a number of significant periods and trends. It is useful to present a brief overview of general pre-film history and then investigate major film periods starting with the pioneer years of motion pictures (1896-1914), and then going on to American films (1914-1918), the Scandinavian tradition (1906-1927), the great German silent films (1919-1927), Soviet films (1896-1929), Hollywood in the 1920s (1920-1927), experimentation in France (1921-1930), the beginnings of sound films (1927-1941), the French, German, British, and Soviet feature film (1929-1940), the documentary film in Britain and America (1929-1940), World War II and the film industry (1940-1945), the new realism in Italian and British films (1945-1952), France after World War II (1945-1955), Hollywood in the postwar years (1945-1955), the transition years (1955-1970), and the Contemporary cinema. The remainder of the chapter contains short introductory comments on the periods, as well as an annotated list of books[39] and films that help illustrate the development of film.[40]

Informed readers will readily detect the limitations of my strategy, sensing the problems with synthesis and condensation. Given the scope of this project, it is impossible to flesh out every aspect of the artistic, social, political, and economic variables that contribute to the production of a specific film, let alone the structure and nature of a national or international film industry. Moreover, it does not seem

---

Rhode, A HISTORY OF THE CINEMA: FROM ITS ORIGINS TO 1970 (New York: Hill and Wang, 1976); Paul Rotha with Richard Griffith, THE FILM TILL NOW: A SURVEY OF WORLD CINEMA, 3rd ed. (New York: Twayne Publishers, 1963); *Thomas Sobchack and Vivian C. Sobchack, AN INTRODUCTION TO FILM, 2nd ed. (Boston: Little, Brown, and Company, 1987); and Basil Wright, THE LONG VIEW (London: Secker and Warburg, 1974). In addition, a valuable aid is the fiftieth anniversary issue of AMERICAN CINEMATOGRAPHER 50:1 (January 1969), which deals with the history of the film industry.

[39] Except in rare instances, books by and about stars will be listed but not annotated. In addition, books recently published but not received in time to do an honest analysis, will be noted in the Bibliography sections.

[40] In addition to my list of annotated bibliographies in this chapter, see John L. Fell, "A Film Student's Guide to the Reference Shelf," CINEMA JOURNAL 9:1 (Fall 1969):43-8; Richard Dyer MacCann, "Appendix II--Reference Works for Film Study," ibid., 14:2 (Winter 1974/75):72-9; and Richard C. Vincent, "An Introduction to Film Bibliographies," JOURNAL OF THE UNIVERSITY FILM ASSOCIATION 28:3 (Summer 1976):39-43.

necessary. The value of this exercise lies in alerting serious students to the possiblities for interpreting and appreciating film history. What is unique is the opportunity to review thousands of scholarly sources in one unified chapter. The test of its success will be in what ways and to what extent it leads to a better understanding of the strengths and weaknesses of the study of film history.

BOOKS

REFERENCE BOOKS

Allan, Elkan, ed. A GUIDE TO WORLD CINEMA. Detroit: Gale Research Company, 1985. Illustrated. 682pp.

A collation of 7,200 capsule film reviews and stills from the insightful programmes of the National Film Theatre from 1950 to 1984, this highly interesting publication demonstrates the imagination and eclecticism of one of the world's leading film institutions. The entries are alphabetically arranged by the movie's English title (and foreign title when appropriate), and include thumbnail comments as well as the name of the director. An index of directors is included.   Recommended for special collections.

Allen, Nancy. FILM STUDY COLLECTIONS: A GUIDE TO THEIR DEVELOPMENT AND USE. New York: Fredrich Ungar Publishing Company, 1979. 194pp.

Authored by a University of Illinois communications librarian concerned about the proliferation of film literature, this practical guide offers a helpful description of the material segregated by form and content. For example, the section on periodicals is broken down into core collection, trade magazines, new periodicals, foreign language periodicals, related areas, and indexes examined for journals frequently cited. Other sections include evaluations of printed material, nonprint material, scripts, bookstores and film memorabilia dealers, major U. S. archives, reference services, instruction to library users, cataloging and classification of film study material, a survey of film study libraries, and two appendexes with publishers' addresses and libraries holding screenplays.   Two admitted limitations to the guide are its exclusively English language orientation and its over-reliance on the American Film Institute's 1978 edition of GUIDE TO COLLEGE COURSES IN FILM AND TELEVISION. More serious drawbacks relate to the shallow bibliographies, the weak introductory material, and the poor annotations. Overall, Allen's sensible organization and thoughtful advice on how to construct film libraries outweigh the manual's sometimes simplistic tone and general information. Three indexes on topics, collections, and works cited conclude the effort. Worth browsing.

Armour, Robert A. FILM: A REFERENCE GUIDE. Westport: Greenwood Press, 1980. 251pp.

In eleven well-organized chapters, the Armour sets out to answer numerous questions about American popular films. Nearly 1,500 books are described and evaluated in extended essays relating to film history, production, criticism, genres, and the related arts, as well as film and society, major actors and directors and other production personnel, major films, international influences on American films, and reference works. The results are mixed. On the one hand, the selection of books, while not exhaustive, is quite good and the idea of discussing them in the context of specific topics is very useful. On the other hand, both the prose and the evaluations are disappointing and inadequate. The most annoying aspect is having to coordinate the comments in the chapter with the full bibliographical entry at the end of the chapter.   Other drawbacks relate to outdated entries and minor factual errors.   Two appendexes--a selected chronology of American films and events, and research collections--plus two indexes--author and subject--are included. Well worth browsing.

Batty, Linda. RETROSPECTIVE INDEX TO FILM PERIODICALS, 1930-1971. New York: R. R. Bowker, 1971. 425pp.

"The purpose of this volume," explains Batty, "is to allow the retrieval of information contained in important English-language periodicals devoted to the serious study of film." Of the nineteen periodicals indexed, one began publishing in the thirties (SIGHT AND SOUND, 1932); one, in the forties (HOLLYWOOD QUARTERLY, the predecessor of QUARTERLY REVIEW OF FILM, RADIO AND TELEVISION, 1945); six, in the fifties (FILM CULTURE, 1955; FILM QUARTERLY, 1958; FILMS AND FILMING, 1954; FILMS IN REVIEW, 1950; and THE VILLAGE VOICE, 1955); and eleven in the sixties (AFFS NEWSLETTER, the predecessor of FILM SOCIETY REVIEW, 1965; CINEASTE, 1967; CINEMA, 1963; CINEMA JOURNAL, 1961; FILM COMMENT, 1962; FILM HERITAGE, 1965; FILM LIBRARY QUARTERLY, 1967; FILM SOCIETY REVIEW, 1965; MOVIE, 1962; TAKE ONE, 1966; and VISION, the predecessor of FILM COMMENT, 1962). Thus, the claim that this is a retrospective index on film periodicals from 1930 to 1971 is somewhat inappropriate. The book itself is divided into three separate categories: individual films, subjects, and book review citations. For example, the film section lists the film title, followed by country of origin and the director's name. Under each film title, titles of articles are arranged alphabetically by author (when known), along with information about the periodical title, volume, number, date, pages, the inclusion of illustrations, and the type of publication (e.g., script extract, interview). What hurts this pioneering venture is that it provides less information than is available in contemporary publications like AN INDEX TO CRITICAL FILM REVIEWS and THE NEW FILM INDEX. Moreover, there are no indexes for quick access to the information in the major sections, and there is no attempt to cross-reference the entries. Worth browsing.

Bawden, Liz-Anne, ed. THE OXFORD COMPANION TO FILM. New York: Oxford University Press, 1976. Illustrated. 767pp.

A highly controversial reference book covering the silent era to 1970, this overly ambitious attempt to catalog "any query which might occur to the amateur of film in the course of reading or film-going" is a mixture of interesting and frequently misleading information. The entries highlight what can go wrong in trying to be all things to all people.[41] Approach with caution.

BIBLIOGRAPHY: FIAF MEMBERS PUBLICATIONS. Edited annually by the Canadian Film Archives. Ottawa: Canadian Film Institute.

This is a useful annual bibliography of books, periodicals, and other relevant printed material published by members of the International Federation of Film Archives.[42]

---

[41]   For a list of extended problems, see Larry Swindell, "References, Please: On Film Encyclopedias," AMERICAN FILM 2:3 (December-January 1977):80-1, and Robin Wood, "Book Review: THE OXFORD COMPANION TO FILM," FILM COMMENT 12:6 (November-December 1976):62-4.

[42]   See Appendix V for a list of resources for scholarship. Some useful articles are collected in a special survey conducted by FILM QUARTERLY and discussed in a special issue, "Our Resources for Film Scholarship," FILM QUARTERLY 16:2 (Winter 1962-63);29-50. For comments on film scholarship, see Ronald Gottesman, "Film Culture: The State of the Art," QUARTERLY REVIEW OF FILM STUDIES 2:2 (May

Blum, Daniel, SCREEN WORLD. New York: Crown Publishers, Inc., published annually.

Emphasizing mainly the credits for the yearly American releases, this handsomely illustrated review includes annual obituaries, box-office stars, and an invaluable index. Since 1969, the annual publication has been under the editorship of John Willis. Recommended for special collections.

*Blum, Eleanor. BASIC BOOKS IN THE MASS MEDIA: AN ANNOTATED SELECT BOOKLIST COVERING GENERAL COMMUNICATIONS, BOOK PUBLISHING, BROADCASTING, FILM, MAGAZINES, NEWSPAPERS, ADVERTISING, INDEXES, AND SCHOLARLY AND PROFESSIONAL PERIODICALS. Urbana: University of Illinois Press, 1972. 252pp.

A revised and updated version of REFERENCE BOOKS IN THE MASS MEDIA, this highly subjective and less-than-impressive publication contains information on almost 670 reference books. The entries are descriptive rather than evaluative. After an examination of the film material, one wonders just who the targeted audience is. Many classic books were omitted, names were misspelled, and questions arise about the classification of key books in other categories. Two appendexes--subject and author-title--are included. Approach with extreme caution.

Bowles, Stephen E., ed. INDEX TO CRITICAL FILM REVIEWS IN BRITISH AND AMERICAN FILM PERIODICALS TOGETHER WITH INDEX TO CRITICAL REVIEWS OF BOOKS ABOUT FILM. Two volumes. New York: Burt Franklin and Company, 1974. 782pp.

An impressive compendium of over 20,000 critical reviews of 6,000 films (from the silent era to the early-1970s) and over 3,000 reviews of 1,200 film books (from 1930 to 1972), this valuable cross-referenced guide draws information from twenty-nine film publications. The major section on films has the titles arranged with information on the director, the length of the review, the availability of credits in the review, name of reviewer, and the journal's volume number, date, and review pages. The entries proved to be reliable and accessible. The film reviews take up all of the first volume and a good portion of the second. Where the film guide suffers is in its selectivity and in its failure to indicate what version of a specific film property is being reviewed. The book review sections also could benefit from a wider scope. A number of invaluable indexes (directors, film reviewers, book authors, book reviewers, and subject index to books) are included. Recommended for special collections.

Brady, Anna, et al. UNION LIST OF FILM PERIODICALS: HOLDINGS OF SELECTED AMERICAN COLLECTIONS. Westport: Greenwood Press, 1984. 317pp.

1977):212-26; Jerzy Toeplitz, "Film Scholarship: Past and Prospective," FILM QUARTERLY 16:3 (Spring 1963):27-37; Jay Leyda, "Waiting Jobs," ibid., 16:2 (Winter 1962-63):29-33; "A Note on Progress," ibid., 21:4 (Summer 1968):28-33; Iris Barry, "The Film Library and How It Grew," ibid., 22:4 (Summer 1969):19-27; Ernest Callenbach, "Notes on Film Scholarship, Criticism, Methodology, and What Are We Doing Here Anyway?" ibid., 28:2 (Winter 1974-75):1-3; Richard Dyer MacCann, "Film Scholarship: Dead or Alive?" JOURNAL OF THE UNIVERSITY FILM ASSOCIATION 28 (Winter 1976):3-4; Don Fredrickson, "Film Study, Literary Criticism, and Science: A Polemical Response to Richard Dyer MacCann," ibid., pp.21-9; and George Mitchell, "The Library of Congress," FILMS IN REVIEW 4:8 (October 1953):417-21.

*Brenner, Debbie, and Gary Hill. CREDITS: VOLUME I--BY FILM TITLE, '85-'86 Edition. Wallington: Magpie Press, 1985. 331pp.

*Brenner, Debbie, and Gary Hill. CREDITS: VOLUME II--BY PRODUCTION CATEGORY, '85-'86 Edition. Wallington: Magpie Press, 1985. 329pp.

*Brenner, Debbie, and Gary Hill. CREDITS: VOLUME III--BY INDIVIDUAL, '85-'86 Edition. Wallington: Magpie Press, 1985. 397pp.

Bukalski, Peter. FILM RESEARCH: A CRITICAL BIBLIOGRAPHY WITH ANNOTATIONS AND INDEX. Boston: G. K. Hall, 1972. 215pp.
    One of the pioneering efforts in modern film bibliographies, this guide suffers from poor annotations and weak introductory chapters. The primary bibliography is subdivided into fourteen categories, including film history, production, genre, sociology, film scripts, particular films, personalities, education, film-related works, careers, bibliographies, and selected works in foreign languages. The author's once-useful contributions to the field have now been surpassed by a number of bibliographies, leaving this work a reminder of how far we have come in the past two decades. No index is included. Worth browsing.

*Carey, Gary. LOST FILMS. New York: Museum of Modern Art, 1970. Illustrated. 91pp.
    Based mainly upon an exhibit Carey set up for the Museum of Modern Art, this nicely produced text presents an invaluable list of thirty presumably missing silent films, complete with plot synopses, cast and credit listings, and marvelous stills. Academicians will probably be most interested in the several Victor Sjostrom movies (including Garbo's THE DIVINE WOMAN) and a Lon Chaney film (one of two movies directed by Tod Browning). The major fault of the book is its limited critical commentary.[43] An index is provided. Well worth browsing.

Chaneles, Sol. COLLECTING MOVIE MEMORABILIA. New York: Arco Publishing Company, 1977. Illustrated. 176pp.
    Intended for neophyte collectors, this nostalgic guide offers information not only on the history of film posters, curios, and photographs, but also on shopping techniques applicable to a number of "Memory Lane," "Silver Screen," or "Memorabilia" shops around the United States. Nine chapters, handsomely illustrated, cover such topics as black-and-white movie stills; color photographs and negatives; posters, lobby cards, and inserts; "3-D": decorative memorabilia, curios, and knicknacks; fan magazines; press books; moviebooks: novelizations, big little books, scrapbooks, and books about the movies; sound tracks and other movie music; and archives, special collectors and collections, museums, libraries, and shows. Typical of the style and content are the following comments on black-and-white stills: "Even the best preserved glossy stills, like certain types of glazed vases will, if they are originals, show some minor crackling in the glossy finish. The gloss finish on photographs is produced on the surface of the paper by a process of very slow heating after prolonged immersion in cold water. In time, impurities in the air and

---

[43]   For information on reconstructing controversial prints, see Gosta Werner, "A Method of Constructing Lost Films," CINEMA JOURNAL 14:2 (Winter 1974-75):11-5.

changes in the humidity cause cracking in the gloss, and this is the only way to be certain that the still is an original made for a first release movie. Duplicates, or 'dupes' as they are called, are generally less valuable than originals--even when well made." An index is included. Well worth browsing.

COPYRIGHT ENTRIES (CUMULATIVE SERIES): MOTION PICTURES 1960-69. Washington: Library of Congress (USGPO), 1971.

In what appears to be an exhaustive listing, this valuable catalog of the 1960s accounts for every movie (including TV films for TV series) produced in America. The preface explains the three-fold purpose of the volume: "(1) to provide correct index volumes to the legal profession, publishers, authors, and others interested in copyright, (2) to meet the administrative needs of the copyright office, and (3) to make available, for other research uses, the information on record in the copyright office, much of which is not available elsewhere." Included in the catalog is information on more than 30,000 scripts (more than 11,000 deal with nonfiction films), date released (including copyright TV movie commercials) for each title, cast and director credits, running time, silent or sound, film mm, series title, and copyright date. Well worth browsing.

*Coster, Patience, ed. FILM AND TELEVISION YEARBOOK 1987. London: British Film Institute, 1987. Illustrated. 344pp.

Initiated in 1983, this annual publication is not only a summary of the events occurring each year at the British Film Institute, but also a wonderful compilation of information about British films, movie theaters, film societies, publications, and awards. The material is accurate and well-organized. An index is included. Recommended for special collections.

Council of the London Film Society. THE FILM SOCIETY PROGRAMMES: 1925-1939. Introduction by George Amberg. New York: Arno Press, 1972. 456pp.

This complete edition of the London Film Society's program notes represents an assortment of intellectual attempts to chronicle the rise of Soviet films, the demise of Germany's major film era, rare AVANT-GARDE experiments, the coming of sound, and the revolutionary use of color. The notes include brief biographical information and historical background material plus complete credits. It is an important contribution to film scholarship. An index is included. Recommended for special collections.

*Cowie, Peter, ed. INTERNATIONAL FILM GUIDE. New York: A. S. Barnes and Company, published annually.

Since 1963, this excellent guide to current films produced all over the world has been issued annually. It contains significant, valuable, and handy information on awards, festivals, film archives, film schools, surveys of theatrical film releases around the globe (the largest section), book reviews, film magazines, and film memorabilia. An index to advertisers and film reviewed is included. Recommended for special collections.

Dyment, Alan R. THE LITERATURE OF THE FILM: A BIBLIOGRAPHIC GUIDE TO FILM AS ART AND ENTERTAINMENT. New York: White Lion, 1976. 398pp.

This disappointing reference tool contains over 1,300 entries on English-language books about film published between 1936 and 1970. The presumption is that Leonard's THE FILM INDEX includes all relevant earlier publications. In fact, Dyment adapts, with minor modifications, Leonard's categories as his own. Not only have Rehrauer and other bibliographers provided a more comprehensive set of information, but the author's descriptive annotations and limited research in the field disqualify him as a serious contender in the bibliographical arena. A name index is included. Worth browsing.

*Ebert, Roger. ROGER EBERT'S MOVIE HOME COMPANION 1987 EDITION. Kansas City: Andrews, McMeel and Parker, 1986. 640pp.

An entertaining guide to over 600 movies released since 1970, this provocative collection of witty and controversial reviews is packed with information, sarcasm, and occasional sexist remarks. For example, in reviewing AGAINST ALL ODDS, the pop critic comments that "What we need are more no-good, double-dealing broads who can cross their legs and break your heart." More often, however, the brief essays contain a number of literary and scholarly allusions that reveal a perceptive mind at work. In addition to the critical synopses, the entries include Ebert's mainstream ratings (e.g., four stars equals a great film; one star, a poor one), the movie's MPAA rating (e.g., G, PG, PG-13, and R), the running time, date of release, and the major cast and credits. Other sections include the critic's ten favorite films--e.g., TAXI DRIVER (1976), and NOTORIOUS (1946)--and why, a basic video library, and thirteen films for Halloween--BLOOD SIMPLE (1985), GREMLINS (1984), and POLTERGEIST (1982), a glossary, and an index. Well worth browsing.

*Editors of FILM IN REVIEW, et al. 500 BEST AMERICAN FILMS TO BUY, RENT OR VIDEOTAPE. New York: Pocket Books, 1985. 509pp.

Working with the National Film Board of Review, the editors of FILMS IN REVIEW have put together a basic videocassette library list that contains the standard information--e.g., year of release, production company, b/w or color, major cast credits, director, running time (of original release, not necessarily that of the videocassette), availability, and a synopsis with critical commentary. The upbeat tone of the reviews plus the generally top-notch selections make this an enjoyable book to peruse. An appendix breaking down the films into categories (e.g., adventure or Biblical) is included. Well worth browsing.

Ellis, Jack C., Charles Derry, and Sharon Kern. THE FILM BOOK BIBLIOGRAPHY, 1940-1975. Metuchen: The Scarecrow Press, 1979. 752pp.

Growing out of a 1976 seminar on film historiography taught at Northwestern University, this book complements Harold Leonard's THE FILM INDEX (1941) and Edward Perry-Richard Dyer MacCann's THE NEW FILM INDEX (1975). The 5,400 classified entries are arranged by subject. The ten basic categories are "Reference"; "Film Technique and Technology"; "Film Industry"; "Film History"; "Film Classifications"; "Biography, Analysis, and Interview"; "Individual Films"; "Film Theory and Criticism"; "Film and Society"; and "Film and Education." Each of these categories is then subdivided. For example, Reference has six sections: General Reference Works (encyclopedias, glosseries, annuals, directories), Filmographies (international, national, persons, subjects), Discographies, Bibliographies, Awards and Film Festivals, and Film Institutions (archives, libraries, museums). Each citation contains an author listing, title, publication information, and page or leaf numbers. Annotations appear mainly as means of providing a reference for the name index or clarifying the content of a book where the title may be misleading. Except for the Biography, Analysis, and Interview and Individual Films categories, the material is presented chronologically. Moreover, the entries are accurate and valuable. A Title and Name Index are included. Recommended for special collections.

Emmens, Carol A. FAMOUS PEOPLE ON FILM. Metuchen: The Scarecrow Press, 1977. Illustrated. 355pp.

"The aim of this guide," writes Emmens, "is to list all the non-theatrical films on famous people available in the United States by major distributor. . . ." Each entry contains a filmography with the following information: title of film, running time, b/w or color, production or release date, producer and distributor, grade level, and annotation. Except for the weak annotations, the format works very well. Especially helpful are the selective theatrical film section, the title index, and the subject index. Well worth browsing.

*Essoe, Gabe. THE BOOK OF MOVIE LISTS. Westport: Arlington House, 1981. Illustrated. 240pp.
       A fun book to flip through, this exercise contains fifteen chapters packed with movie nostalgia. Essoe's love for his subject is obvious not only in his focus, but also in his attitude toward the material. Consider the contents: "Critic's Choice Or: Some Best, Some Worsts . . . And How You Can't Please Everybody," "Somebody Up There Likes Me Or: Jeez! Lookit My Oscar!", "Great Expectations Or: Howcum Our Golden Goose Laid an Egg at the Box Office?", "Forbidden Fruit Or: How Much Cleaveage Can You Show in a Family Film?", and "The Groove Tube Or: How Movies and TV Became Reluctant Bedfellows." Among my favorite lists are the one-liners about Ronald Reagan as President. For example, Johnny Carson quipped, "Reagan's in the news again. He's at the ranch chopping wood--he's building the log cabin he was born in." An index is included to find information quickly. (If you enjoy this book, you might also pick up Essoe's companion volume, THE BOOK OF TV LISTS.) Recommended for special collections and for gifts.

Fawcett, Marion, et al. AN INDEX TO FILMS IN REVIEW 1950-1959. New York: The The National Board of Review, 1961. AN INDEX TO FILMS IN REVIEW 1960-1964. New York: The National Board of Review, 1966. AN INDEX TO FILMS IN REVIEW 1965-1969. New York: National Board of Review, 1972.
       These three handy references give a good cross-index to this invaluable magazine that belongs in every library interested in serious film study. The first publication divided its contents into a number of categories (e.g., film history and film festivals), thereby making it difficult to locate specific information quickly. Thankfully, that format was changed to a strictly alphabetical listing in the second volume. Each entry offers information on volume, number, and page, as well as the type of material (i.e., book review, career article). Moreover, each volume is more complete than the previous one. Sandra Lester is responsible for the last index. Recommended for special collections.

FILM DAILY YEAR BOOK OF MOTION PICTURES. New York: Available on Microfilm, 18 reels from Arno Press.
       This outstanding, comprehensive, and definitive record to date of the history of motion pictures is available on microfilm from 1918 to 1925. The first four years are available in two volumes from Arno Press, as is the 1970 Yearbook. Highly recommended for special collections.

*Garbicz, Adam, and Jacek Klinowski. CINEMA, THE MAGIC VEHICLE: A GUIDE TO ITS ACHIEVEMENT. New York: Schocken Books, 1983. Volume One: THE CINEMA THROUGH 1949. 551pp. Volume Two: THE CINEMA IN THE FIFTIES. 551pp.
       A sweeping attempt at a panoramic look at motion picture history, this ambitious directory takes a "film-by-film" approach. "Our main concern," Garbicz and Klinowski write, "is the aesthetic standard of a film." Following a short introduction-synopsis of what they consider to be the most important events in film history, the highly subjective critics offer a chronological listing of films, which they divide into three categories: movies of the first, second, and third ranks. For example, INTOLERANCE (1916) is placed at the highest rank; THE KID (1921), second rank; and WAY DOWN

EAST (1920), the lowest rank. Each year lists films in rank order, giving the year of production, rather than release date. Preceding each entry are the screen credits, followed by a paragraph of plot summary and concluding with a brief critical commentary. The number of films critiqued in any one year ranges from one to twenty. If you're looking for controversy, oversimplifications, and stimulating material, your search may be over. Each volume contains an index of directors and an index of films. Well worth browsing.

*Gerlach, John C., and Lana Gerlach. THE CRITICAL INDEX: A BIBLIOGRAPHY OF ARTICLES ON FILM IN ENGLISH, 1946-1973. New York: Teachers College Press, 1974. 726pp.
    The opening volume in the Teachers College Press New Humanistic Research series contains more than 5,000 entries compiled from twenty-two American, British, and Canadian film periodicals, as well as sixty general sources. The study covers directors, producers, performers, screenwriters, cinematographers, specific films, and 175 topics related to history, aesthetics, economics, film and society, and genres. An extensive opening section carefully explains how to use the resource guide, which includes two major sections arranged alphabetically by name and topic. Two indexes--author and film--add to the editors' well thought out organization. Particularly interesting are a number of appendexes describing the purpose and method of the selection of articles for inclusion, a wealth of supplementary bibliographies (including a discussion of the editors' own limitations in this bibliography), a list of magazines not indexed, and an essay on criticism. Highly recommended for special collections.

*Geduld, Harry M., and Ronald Gottesman. AN ILLUSTRATED GLOSSARY OF FILM TERMS. New York: Holt, Rinehart and Winston, 1973. Illustrated. 179pp.
    Well organized and extremely useful, this is the best approach to finding out the definitions of technical terms are used by filmmakers and critics. Geduld and Gottesman perceptively aim their language toward film buffs and novices, rather than to experts who would not only know the material, but would also take advantage of much more technical reference books. The definitions supplied are jargon-free and replete with illustrations and/or specific examples in particular films. Moreover, Geduld and Gottesman take pains to cross-reference their entries to maximize the book's effectiveness. Highly recommended for undergraduates.[44]

*Gottesman, Ronald, and Harry M. Geduld, eds. GUIDEBOOK TO FILM: AN ELEVEN-IN-ONE REFERENCE. New York: Holt, Rinehart and Winston, Inc., 1972. 230pp.
    This useful but sketchy book contains brief descriptive comments about a number of areas in film study: books and periodicals, museums and archives, equipment and supplies, distributors, bookstores, publishers, sources for stills, film schools, and theses up to 1969. The gentle annotations do little more than indicate contents and eschew any critical evaluations. Worth browsing.

*Graham, Peter, ed. A DICTIONARY OF THE CINEMA, 2nd ed. New York: A. S. Barnes & Company, 1968.

---

[44] For another effective and inexpensive but more technical approach, see *John Mercer, ed., MONOGRAPH NO. 2: GLOSSARY OF FILM TERMS, Rev. ed., UNIVERSITY FILM ASSOCIAION (Summer 1979).

This useful volume contains 620 terse annotations plus a handy index to over 5000 movie titles. For quick, helpful, and usually accurate information, this was a good source book in its day. Worth browsing.

*Halliwell, Leslie. THE FILMGOER'S COMPANION: AN INTERNATIONAL ENCYCLOPEDIA. 6th ed. New York: Hill and Wang, 1978. Illustrated. 825pp.
     One of the best available resources to date and getting better with each expanded and revised edition. There are more than 10,000 entries on films, filmmakers, themes, and technical jargon. The information is generally accurate and the scope is impressive. Highly recommended.

*Halliwell, Leslie. FILM GUIDE, 4th ed. New York: Charles Scribner's Sons, 1983. 1,585pp.
     A compendium containing more than 14,000 entries on English-language sound films, this handy reference book offers information about running time, date of release, color or other process, production company, synopsis and review, writer, original source, director, cinematographer, designer, and cast. The entries also include a selective listing of silent and foreign films. In addition to being generally reliable, the size of the print provides for easier reading; in comparison to the Maltin and Scheuer annual publications. In addition, there is an index of alternative titles, English-language titles of foreign films, and original titles of foreign-language films listed in English. A few particularly interesting sections, however, come at the end of the book, where Halliwell gives a succinct explanation of the effect that various screen shapes, including TV, have on film; and a hard-hitting commentary titled, "The Decline and Fall of the Movie," in which he candidly admits that "this essay is a deliberate hatchet job by a disappointed fan who has turned devil's advocate." Recommended for special collections.

Haun, Harry. THE MOVIE QUOTE BOOK. New York: Harper & Row, 1980. 415pp.
     "This book," explains Haun, "celebrates a time when movies had something to say--and what was said was worth remembering, worth holding on to." Organized by subject matter (e.g., adolescence, adultery, and curtain speeches) and effectively cross-referenced, the collection provides over 4,000 quotations from more than 500 movies. For example, Joan Crawford's reply to Jan Sterling in FEMALE ON THE BEACH (1955): "I know it's considered noble to accept apologies, but I'm afraid I'm not the noble type." I particularly enjoyed Oscar Levant's wry observation in HUMORESQUE (1946): "I envy people who drink. At least they know what to blame everything on." A filmography of the movies cited is included at the back of the book. Recommended for special collections and fun gifts.

Heide, Robert, and John Gilman. STARSTRUCK: THE WONDERFUL WORLD OF MOVIE MEMORABILIA. Garden City: Doubleday and Company, 1986. Illustrated. 245pp.
     With more than 400 intriguing illustrations to demonstrate the appeal of movie memorabilia, this coffee-table publication offers useful information on collecting posters, stills, lobby cards, props, costumes, and assorted ephemera. The charm of this book in comparison to its rival editions lies in its anecdotal approach to the subject. Heide and Gilman are well-known aficionados of American popular culture and lace their discussion of the movie-merchandising market not only with insights on what to buy but also with amusing stories about the novelties themselves. The book's sixteen major sections cover a number of areas: e.g., "What Is Movie Memorabilia?"; "The Silents--Fabulous Faces in the Dark"; "Kenneth Anger, Film Mystic, Valentino, Collector Extraordinaire"; "Garbo, Harlow and Lombard"; "Movie Fan Mags"; "The Movie Musicals; Blondes at Fox--Temple, Henie, Faye and Grable"; "Movie Star Sheet Music"; "We're Off to See the Wizard"; "Gone With the Wind"; "Queen Betty and Queen Joan"; "Ronald Reagan--the Movie Star President"; "Monroemania and Deanabilia";

and "Epilogue--Save a Picture Palace." Most notable about this guide is the enormous pleasure the authors take in their information-gathering efforts. A listing of memorabilia sources, a bibliography, and an index are included. Well worth browsing.

*Henderson, Kathy. FIRST STAGE: PROFILES OF THE NEW AMERICAN ACTORS. New York: William Morrow and Company, 1985. Illustrated. 159pp.

A lightweight, profusely illustrated introduction to twenty successful and versatile performers, the breezy prose is incidental to the more than 160 entertaining pictures of talents like Kevin Bacon, Matthew Broderick, Glenn Close, Gregory Hines, Mary Beth Hurt, William Hurt, Judith Ivey, Kevin Kline, John Lithgow, John Malkovich, Mandy Patinkin, Pamela Reed, Eric Roberts, John Shea, Meryl Streep, Sigourney Weaver, Peter Weller, JoBeth Williams, and Treat Williams. An index is included. Well worth browsing.

Herx, Henry, and Tony Zaza, eds. THE FAMILY GUIDE TO MOVIES ON VIDEO: THE MORAL AND ENTERTAINMENT VALUES OF 5,000 MOVIES ON TV AND VIDEOCASSETTE. New York: Crossroads, 1988. 331pp.

Compiled by the managers of the media review and educational services for the United States Catholic Conference (USCC), Department of Communication, this comprehensive resource book provides summaries, evaluations, and "family-oriented" ratings of the major studio releases and important independent films available on video or on broadcast or cable TV. The unique compilation dealing with the past fifty years of movie history reflects a consensus of parents, clergymen, industry professionals, and films buffs that constitute an interdenominational review board. Films are classified as A-I--general patronage; A-II--adults and adolescents; A-III--adults; A-IV--adults, with reservations ("this refers to certain movies which are not morally offensive in themselves but do require some analysis and explanation to avoid mistaken interpretations and false conclusions"); and O--morally offensive. Examples of how the USCC applies its ratings are A-I: ABE LINCOLN IN ILLINOIS (1940), LADY AND THE TRAMP (1955), SOUNDER (1972); A-II: ABSENCE OF MALICE (1981), THE AFRICAN QUEEN (1951), THE KILLING FIELDS (1984); A-III: ACCIDENT (1967), JESUS CHRIST SUPERSTAR (1973), KING OF HEARTS/LE ROI DE COEUR) (1966); A-IV: AFTER HOURS (1985), JOHNNY GOT HIS GUN (1971), KRAMER VS. KRAMER (1979); O: THE LAST PICTURE SHOW (1971), LIFE OF BRIAN (1979), and LITTLE SHOP OF HORRORS (1986). The USSC classifications system, an offshoot of the National Legion of Decency, originated in 1936, and since 1969 has provided a broad spectrum of capsule moral judgments on motion pictures. The opinions are stated crisply, clearly, and unambiguously. Well worth browsing.

*Jordan, Thurston C., Jr., ed. GLOSSARY OF MOTION PICTURE TERMINOLOGY. Menlo Park: Pacific Coast Publishers, 1968. Illustrated. 64pp.

Written by a member of the personnel department of 20th Century-Fox, this book, modeled after the employee's manual, presents succinct definitions of over 500 terms. It has been surpassed by Mercer's 1978 revised University Film and Video publication. Worth browsing.

*Kaplan, Mike, ed. VARIETY: INTERNATIONAL MOTION PICTURE MARKETPLACE 1982-1983. Garland Publishing, 1982. 430pp.

Divided into three sections, this unique publication offers speedy access to vital information about the global film industry. Section 1--"The Companies"--is a listing first by country and then by company of the world's principal filmmaking firms. Almost all of the entries include the company name, address, telephone number, cable address, telex number, names of the major executives, and types of services provided by the firms. In certain areas like exhibition, Kaplan includes the number of theaters;

in dealing with studios, the types of facilities are included. Section 2--"Classified Indexes--identifies the company by the activities it provides. The breakdown begins by country (the U. S. is subdivided by states) and within each country alphabetically by name. The author makes access to this information readily available by listing the major categories in a special Table of Contents. Section 3--"Names and Numbers"--offers an alphabetical listing of the names and numbers contained in the two previous sections. The directory identifies the name of the executive, nation working in, company affiliation, and telephone number. Regrettably, the volatile nature of the industry makes some of the information obsolete. Hopefully, Kaplan will find a way to update the information regularly and quickly. Recommended for special collections.

Kaplan, Mike, ed. VARIETY: INTERNATIONAL SHOWBUSINESS REFERENCE. New York: Garland Publishing, 1981. 1135pp.

A potpourri of information from the "Bible" of the entertainment world, this seventy-five-year retrospective selects material on "the basis of possible reference need, judged by the queries which the publication receives daily for specific showbusiness information." The seventeen categories include "Biographies"; "Distributor Code"; "Film Credits 1976-1980"; "Oscars; All-Time Film Rental Champs"; "Festivals, Markets, and Conventions 1981"; "TV Credits 1976-1980"; "Emmys"; "Top 50 Nielsen-Rated TV Shows"; "Broadway Play Credits 1976-1980"; "Plays Abroad Credits 1976-1980"; "Tonys"; "Pulitzer Prizes (which are not arranged in subcategories)"; "Long-Running Broadway Plays"; "Grammys"; "Platinum Records 1976-1980"; and "Necrology 1976-1980." The largest section deals with the biographies of almost 6,000 performers, directors, technicians, composers, executives, journalists, musicians, and writers. Kaplan plans to update the book periodically. Well worth browsing.

*Kaplan, Mike, ed. VARIETY PRESENTS THE COMPLETE BOOK OF MAJOR U. S. SHOWBUSINESS AWARDS. New York: Garland Publishing, 1985. 564pp.

A useful updating of five major entertainment awards--Oscars, Emmys, Tonys, Grammys, and Pulitzer Prize plays--from Kaplan's earlier VARIETY: INTERNATIONAL SHOWBUSINESS REFERENCE, this well-organized book offers basic information on winners and nominees in the specific categories from the inception of the award, through honors presented in 1983. Each award is given an individual section and chronologically arranged. Except for the Pulitzer Prizes (which have no subdivisions), the sections are subdivided by various categories in each year. In addition, an alphabetized master index lists the data necessary for locating specific people and titles. Among the entertaining information are the answers to Gloria Steinem's Emmy nomination, how many Oscars Edith Head received, whether Ronald Reagan had any award nominations, and Norman Mailer's single award nomination. Recommended for special collections.

Karney, Robyn, ed. THE MOVIE STARS STORY. New York: Crescent Books, 1986. Illustrated. 288pp.

A companion volume to the lavish studio history series also published by Crescent Books, this charming coffee-table collection of over 700 illustrations in black and white and color is light on information but wonderful on visual delights. Representative selections of 500 stars from the silent era to the present are profiled in eight chapters divided by decades. The commentaries are unpretentious, nostalgic, and gossipy. A name index is included. Recommended as a gift for film buffs.

*Katz, Ephraim. THE FILM ENCYCLOPEDIA. New York: Thomas Y. Crowell Company, 1979. 1,266pp.

An impressive one-volume work on world cinema, this valuable guide offers a good balance of American, British, and international topics that goes beyond the range of its competitors. The entries not only contain expected information (e.g., personal and professional details) but also include (where appropriate) references to important publications. That is not to say that important omissions do not occur (e.g., Louis de Rochemont) nor that there are not occasional errors. Hopefully, future additions will add to the book's considerable value. Highly recommended for general collections.

*Kone, Grace Ann, ed. 8MM FILM DIRECTORY: A COMPREHENSIVE DESCRIPTIVE INDEX. New York: Comprehensive Service Corporation, 1969-70. 532pp.
    This handy guide to almost all 8mm films, regardless of length or subject matter, comes complete with dates, distributors, and other pertinent information. Also listed and detailed are 8mm film equipment and distributors. It serves as a reminder of the extensive interest in 8mm film during the late 1960s and early 1970s. Worth browsing.

Lahue, Kalton C. COLLECTING CLASSIC FILMS. New York: Hastings House, 1970. Illustrated. 159pp.
    Because there are so many missing entries, this first comprehensive guide to the hobby of collecting old films should be skimmed rather than owned. It deals with film sizes, copyrights, projectors, purchasing, storage and care, and film music. Several indexes are included. Worth browsing.

Langman, Larry. ENCYCLOPEDIA OF AMERICAN FILM COMEDY. New York: Garland Publishing Company, 1987. Illustrated. 639pp.
    The first comprehensive work incorporating information on major American comedians, comedy teams, directors, character performers, comedy series, and screenwriters in a single volume, this welcome study also comments on a variety of comedy genres--e.g., screwball comedy, war comedies, and romantic comedies--as well as providing thumbnail film critiques. The format stresses accessibility rather than depth or debate. The subject matter arrangement, alphabetically listed, begins each personality's entry with dates of birth and death (when appropriate), a short synopsis of the individual's total output, and concludes with a filmography. Individual film entries include title, year of release, distributing company, director, screenwriter(s), and featured players. Cross-references are capitalized and deal with personalities, series, and topics that are listed elsewhere in the book. Well worth browsing.

Leonard, Harold, ed. THE FILM INDEX--A BIBLIOGRAPHY, VOLUME I, THE FILM AS ART. New York: The Museum of Modern Art, 1941. Illustrated. 723pp. New York: Arno Press, 1970.
    One of the best reference books ever compiled, this valuable index to film writing--books, periodicals, and newspapers--is a remarkable example of compilation and annotation. It still remains an outstanding tribute not only to its editors, but to the New York City Writers Program of the 1930s. Leonard began the undertaking by submitting a prospectus to the Federal Writers' Project in 1935. Nearly a year later the proposal was accepted and work began on what was to be a three-volume film bibliography for scholars. Twenty-five trained people pooled their talent over the next three years to produce America's first significant film bibliography. But in 1939, Congress sharply reduced the resources of the Works Project Administration (WPA, the agency responsible for the Federal Writers' Project), and Leonard's staff was forced to concentrate its efforts on just this one volume. It is divided into two major categories: "History and Technique," and "Types of Film." These in turn are subdivided into numerous subdivisions. For example, the former includes "General

Works," "Criticism and Aesthetics (The World of the film," "The Screen and the Stage," "The Art of film criticism, Aesthetics of film"), "History" ("General History," "Pre-screen History," "The American film," "The Foreign Film"), "Technique" ("Survey of Film Crafts," "Acting," "Actors," "Editing," "Make-up," "Music" ("Silent Era," "Sound Era"), "Photography" ("General," "Trick Photography"), "Production Effects" ("Aerial Scenes," "Underwater Scenes," "War Scenes," "Miscellaneous Production Effects"), "Set Design," "Sound" ("General," "Early Sound Effects and Recording Devices"), "Writing" ("Silent Era," "Sound Era"), and "Writing--Scenarios" ("Continuities," "Treatments," "Unproduced Scenarios"). An extended general index is included. Recommended for all collections.

Leonard, Harold, ed. THE FILM INDEX--A BIBLIOGRAPHY: THE FILM AS INDUSTRY, VOLUME 2. White Plains: Kraus International Publications, 1985. Illustrated. 587pp.

Organized into nine major sections dealing with the industrial and commercial aspects of film, this splendid publication is a boon to film scholarship. It is the second of the three-part series initially planned by Leonard for the the Writers' Program of the Work Projects Administration in the City of New York, 1935-1940. When the project came to an abrupt halt in 1943, the materials for Volumes 2 and 3 were stored in the archives of the Museum of Modern Art. Scholars owe a debt of gratitude to the publishers for making this invaluable document available after a forty-year hiatus. The contents include major sections on advertising and publicity, associations and organizations, distribution, exhibition, finance, history, jurisprudence, labor relations, and production. The general index is available in the companion volume THE FILM IN SOCIETY. Recommended for all collections.

Leonard, Harold, ed. THE FILM INDEX--A BIBLIOGRAPHY: THE FILM IN SOCIETY, VOLUME 3. White Plains: Kraus International Publications, 1985. 527pp.

The final volume of this superb reference trilogy contains an impressive collection of material on seven major topics: censorship, cultural aspects, education, Hollywood, moral and religious aspects, social and political aspects, and special applications. As in the previous volumes, the entries are arranged alphabetically by author or anonymous title in the various categories. The wealth of information relating to many important publications on film through 1935, is considerable. No scholarly library should be without this indispensable three-volume set.

*Levine, Michael. HOW TO REACH ANYONE WHO'S ANYONE. Los Angeles: Price/Stern/Sloan, 1980. No pagination.

If you want to know how to contact over 3,000 celebrities and hope to get your letter answered, this is the book to get. Levine makes no guarantees, but he does give accurate information and promises to help if you run into problems. Well worth browsing.

Library of Congress. MOTION PICTURES FROM THE LIBRARY OF CONGRESS PAPER PRINT COLLECTION 1912-1939. Washington, D.C.: Library of Congress, Copyright Office, 1951.

Together with a valuable index, this publication offers information on films copyrighted during this period. In 1953, two further publications continued the work, covering the periods 1940-1949 and 1950-1959. Well worth browsing.

*Limbacher, James L. A REFERENCE GUIDE TO AUDIOVISUAL INFORMATION. New York: R. R. Bowker and Company, 1972. 197pp.

"This reference guide," explains Limbacher, "was developed to aid the librarian in finding the material which both he and the public he serves need. The term 'audiovisual' has been construed to include basically motion pictures, filmstrips, disc recordings, tapes, theater, music, dance, and television." To that end, Limbacher divides his useful work into two major sections: books and periodicals. The entries appear in alphabetical order by title, followed by publication information and a brief description of the contents. Information is also available on prices, addresses of publishers, and basic books for a personal library. Regrettably, the proofreading problems, weak annotations, imbalance among the various topics, and ill-advised attempt to be comprehensive in such a limited format create serious credibility concerns. A subject index, a glossary, and a selected bibliography are included. Approach with caution.

Limbacher, James L., ed. FEATURE FILMS: A DIRECTORY OF FEATURE FILMS ON 16MM AND VIDEOTAPE AVAILABLE FOR RENTAL, SALE, AND LEASE. EIGHTH EDITION. New York: R. R. Bowker Company, 1985. 734pp.
By far the best and most comprehensive source of information about theatrical films for rent, sale, or lease, this book cross-references information available from countless catalogues on over 22,200 movies. The new edition updates all aspects of the earlier volumes--a director's index, a foreign-language index, a list of film reference works, and a complete list of film companies and distributors by alphabetical code and classified by geographical districts. "Feature" films are defined as 16mm or as running more than forty-eight minutes. The one notable omission is the reference to 8mm films, the explanation being that so few are now in distribution or for sale. Each alphabetically arranged feature film entry includes information about leading performers, director, year of release, production company, running time, sound or silent, format, and rental/sale/lease source. There are omissions and even errors relating to dates and running times. Nevertheless, there is no single source more valuable for renting 16mm films at present. Moreover, there are several hundred documentaries listed and a serials index. Limbacher adds new information at various intervals in SIGHTLINES, published by the Educational Film Library Asociation. Highly recommended for special collections.

*Lyon, Christopher, and Susan Doll, eds. THE INTERNATIONAL DICTIONARY OF FILMS AND FILMMAKERS: VOLUME I--FILMS. Chicago: St. James Press, 1984. 553pp.
The first of five volumes in this commendable series, this guide offers a fascinating reference source for many of the most widely studied films. The selections represent the choices of more than 115 scholars in America, Britain, and Western Europe. The criteria for inclusion required that films be works of "art" and demonstrate formal and technical aspects of the medium: "(1) technical innovation resulting in the enhancement of film's expressive potential; (2) formal innovation in terms of structural techniques or narrative strategies now recognized as contributions to the language of film; (3) generic significance through initiating a genre, being an especially mature or successful example of one, or involving an innovative synthesis of established genres; (4) significance as a prime example of a major filmmaker's characteristic themes, style, or concerns; (5) ideological or cultural significance, a criterion intended as leavening for the first four in that it allowed consideration of films relatively undistinguished in artistic and technical terms which nevertheless retain exceptional interest as social documents or cultural artifacts." Over 600 entries, alphabetically arranged, include information on the English-language title (and foreign, when appropriate), the production company, b/w or color, film format (e.g., 35mm), running time, release date and place, cast and credits, where filmed and cost, awards won, bibliography, and a critical plot analysis. One may quibble about favorite films missing from the book (e.g., ANNIE HALL,) but not about the scholarly and stimulating approach. The two major problems here and in successive volumes are that article citations rarely have page references (and in some cases, only the name of the author and date of publication in a journal), and the discussion of British film history tends to ignore contemporary scholarly evaluations.

Moreover, there are no director and performer indexes for cross-referencing (these appear in a fifth volume). One major problem that surfaces frequently throughout the series is that bibliographic entries tend to be difficult to locate and, at times, are wrong. Either a date or a journal reference is wrong. My guess is that in dealing with such voluminous information, the editors were overwhelmed by the material. Nevertheless, the ground-breaking effort by distinguished scholars to amass important information compensates for the initial errors in this first attempt. Highly recommended for special collections.

*Lyon, Christopher, and Susan Doll, eds. THE INTERNATIONAL DICTIONARY OF FILMS AND FILMMAKERS: VOLUME II--DIRECTORS/FILMMAKERS. Chicago: St. James Press, 1984. 620pp.
    This volume deals with over 500 people "considered to have had the principal creative responsibility for a substantial body of work, whether or not they pursued filmmaking within an established film industry." The entries, alphabetically arranged, provide brief critical-biographical profiles, concluding with bibliographies. The material lacked the depth and freshness of the entries in Volume 1 and seemed far more subjective and vague than necessary. Regrettably, no film and personality indexes are available for cross-referencing. Well worth browsing.

MacCann, Richard Dyer, and Edward S. Perry. THE NEW FILM INDEX: A BIBLIOGRAPHY OF MAGAZINE ARTICLES IN ENGLISH, 1930-1970. New York: E. P. Dutton, 1975. 522pp.
    The long-awaited sequel to Leonard's THE FILM INDEX (1941), this ambitious volume covering 12,000 annotated entries divided into 278 separate sections has a number of strengths and a few weaknesses. On the positive side, the classification system follows closely the format used in the original publication. The two notable exceptions are that only magazine articles are indexed (Leonard included film books) and no short film reviews commonly found in most film periodicals are cataloged. The authors point out that "The 1941 INDEX . . . appears to have been quite selective, with lengthy descriptions of items deemed especially important. The present work is intended to be more exhaustive, with brief annotations. We have in fact omitted any descriptive note when the title seemed self-explanatory (or in a few cases, when we could not find and check the article itself)." The major sections include "Introduction and Reference," "Motion-Picture Arts and Crafts," "Film Theory and Criticism," "Film History," "Biography," "Motion Picture Industry," "Film and Society," "Nonfiction Films," and "Case Histories of Film Making." In addition, there is an extensive Subject Index to the INDEX itself. The in-depth coverage of thirty-eight important periodicals adds to the book's comprehensiveness, particularly the inclusion of small but important journals like CINEMA STUDIES and THE SILENT PICTURE. It would have been preferrable if journals like AMERICAN CINEMATOGRAPHER, CINEMA PROGRESS, PHOTOPLAY, and NEW THEATRE AND FILM had also been included in the index. On the negative side, many people will have difficulty locating information quickly about specific film titles, books, articles, and studios because of the single subject index. Except for that one annoying weakness, this is a welcome addition to reference shelves. Recommended for special collections.

*Maltin, Leonard, ed. THE WHOLE FILM SOURCEBOOK. New York: New American Library, 1983. 454pp.
    A practical and useful guide to important material, this inexpensive resource is the best buy for quick answers to reference questions. Fifteen authors pool their collective insights to provide SELECTIVE leads to three general areas: education and careers, access to films, and research and reference. The section on education is subdivided into Todd McCarthy's "The Hollywood Dream: 1983," covering a career in movies; Louis Black and Warren Spector's useful commentaries on how to choose a film school; Thomas Zummer's tips on grantsmanship; and Lawrence Haverhill and Rene

L. Ash's primer on unions and guilds. Not only is the section sensibly organized, but it is also expertly presented. The material on accessing films is very impressive, thanks to Gary Bordzuk's overview of 16mm distributors; Mark Schlesinger's discussion of the nature of distribution and production; Audrey E. Kupferberg's review of how film archives function; Adam Reilly's treatment of specialized film exhibitions; and Rob Edelman's roundup on selected film festivals home and abroad. Much of the information cannot easily be found elsewhere. Unfortunately, section three on research and reference falls short of its predecessors, mainly because Carol Epstein's selective bibliographies of film books are inadequate, given the wealth of material available. On the other hand, Ron Magliozzi's excellent annotations of film periodicals, Anthony Slide's skillful summary of the nature of film research, Judith Kass's research on film bookstores, and the valuable Maltin-Kass-Slide wrap-up on photo services in the United States are first-rate. Here is a book that, with few exceptions, uses good judgment, intelligent organization, and outstanding researchers. No index is included. Recommended for general collections.

Manvell, Roger, et al. THE INTERNATIONAL ENCYCLOPEDIA OF FILM. New York: Crown Publishers, 1972. Illustrated. 574pp.

If I had to choose one book to own in my library, this text would be it. Not enough praise can be given to the editors, who have combined scholarship, production design, and information in order to synthesize intelligently the world of film condensed while maintaining both depth and breadth. This classic work covers the international history of movies from an aesthetic and industrial perspective. The alphabetically arranged entries, numbering more than a thousand and including biographies, national film histories, general topics, and technical terms, are followed by an extensive bibliography, an index of title changes, an index of films, and an index of names. That is not to say that omissions and flaws are absent. These predictable problems in a work of this magnitude do not mar the value or achievement of such an undertaking. Highly recommended for special collections.

*Marill, Alvin H. MOVIES MADE FOR TELEVISION: THE TELEFEATURE AND THE MINI-SERIES 1964-1986. New York: New York Zoetrope, 1987. Illustrated. 576pp.

An updated and expanded version of the 1980 illustrated reference book, this valuable guide, covering more than 2,100 films produced for TV, abandons its original chronology by season (e.g., 1964-65) in favor of alphabetically arranged entries and a cross-indexed chronology at the end. The useful annotations provide information on cast and production credits, plot summary, release date, production company, and running time. Many of the annotations provide insights into the unique contributions of a specific series or the TV debuts of noted performers. Moreover, Marill makes it clear in his introduction how the made-for-TV movie has evolved from the mid-1960s to the present: "Within its restricted time limits and perhaps the scaled down scope for outdoor dramas, and on perhaps a quarter of the budget, the television movie, even without the increasingly broadened theatrical (and cable) parameters that allow for nudity, profanity, and explicit mayhem, has proved an equal in popularity to its elder brother (or sister) being unreeled at the local twin theater or tenplex or 16-plex." Especially useful for researchers are the alphabetically arranged indexes on producers, directors, writers, and actors. Hopefully, this study will be updated frequently. Recommended for special collections.

*Mast, Gerald, ed. THE MOVIES IN OUR MIDST: DOCUMENTS IN THE CULTURAL HISTORY OF FILM IN AMERICA. Chicago: University of Chicago Press, 1982. Illustrated. 766pp.

"There are many ways to write a history of film," Mast states. "This collection suggests an attempt by film history to 'write itself.'" Using dozens of documents from 1882 to 1977, Mast assembles a fascinating chronicle that captures the evolving attitudes of experts and the general public toward the phenomenon of film. The two specific criteria for inclusion in the anthology are that the material be relevant and representative and that they be social documents. This strategy allows Mast not only to make comparisons between important artifacts like THE MOTION PICTURE PRODUCTION CODE of 1930 and the Motion Picture Association's OFFICAL CODE OBJECTIVES of 1968, but also enables him to include examples of significant court decisions dealing with patent fights (e.g., Circuit Court of Appeals, Second Circuit, EDISON v. AMERICAN MUTOSCOPE COMPANY in 1902), censorship (e.g., United States Supreme Court, MUTUAL FILM CORP. v. INDUSTRIAL COMMISSION OF OHIO (in 1915), and United States Supreme Court, JOSEPH BURSTYN, INC., v. WILSON, COMMISSIONER OF NEW YORK ET AL. in 1952), and the structure of the film industry itself (e.g., United States Supreme Court, UNITED STATES v. PARAMOUNT PICTURES, INC. in 1947). This splendid collection includes much more than "primary" documents dealing with court decisions and congressional hearings, and pronouncements by the motion picture producers and distributors, film pioneers, and inventors. There are also "secondary" documents recording the feelings of the people who attended the nickelodeons, reporters who covered the activities of censorship bodies, and critics who reviewed the premieres of landmark movies. Finally, there are "reflective" documents written by personalities who look back on their involvement in the history of film or academics who challenge longstanding myths about Hollywood.

Collectively, the documents address six major social issues, "defined as the central problems in the cultural history of American film": (1) technology and invention, (2) economics and industry, (3) the industry's ties to national political issues and federal regulating bodies, (4) movies as a barometer of public opinion and morality, (5) the issue of censorship, and (6) the social influence of Hollywood. Mast knows that these social issues vary in importance with different stages of American film history, and thus he alters the type of material included in the book's seven major chapters. For example, the opening section on film beginnings examines the writings of inventors, along with some historical observations and a leading court case. On the other hand, the coming of sound and events in the thirties get two full sections with a multitude of perspectives relating to the six major social issues.

This rare collection is an invaluable reference source. A good bibliography is included. Highly recommended for special collections.

Mehr, Linda Harris, ed. MOTION PICTURES, TELEVISION AND RADIO: A UNION CATALOGUE OF MANUSCRIPT AND SPECIAL COLLECTIONS IN THE WESTERN UNITED STATES. Boston: G. K. Hall, 1977. 201pp.

Recognizing the need for a comprehensive bibliography describing the scope of primary film source materials in America, Mehr takes the first step toward achieving this noteworthy goal. The sponsorship for this Union Catalogue comes from the Film and Television Study Center, a non-profit cultural organization located in California. As such, the organization limited the scope of the publication to materials available in eleven states on the West Coast: Arizona, California, Colorado, Idaho, Montana, Nevada, New Mexico, Oregon, Utah, Washington, and Wyoming. The book locates, identifies, and describes institutions, libraries, museums, and historical societies that contain materials on radio, television, and film. Alphabetically arranged by institution, the entries contain information on production and/or personal papers of directors, writers, producers, actors, cinematographers, costume designers, art directors, composers, publicists, editors, inventors; screenplays, television scripts and radio scripts; advertising material, including posters, lobby cards, press books and programs; production and publicity stills and candid photos; clipping files; scrapbooks; oral histories; musical scores; artwork; animation material; costume designs, costumes; props and equipment. Particularly helpful are two detailed indexes on general matters (name, title, subject) and occupations. Well worth browsing.

*Mercer, John. THE INFORMATIONAL FILM. Champaign: Stipes Publishing Company, 1981. Illustrated. 200pp.

Targeted for people interested in media design and film production courses, this unusual book takes a cursory look at the kind of learning films produce rather than their specific content. Eight general chapters in stilted prose explore the history and use of various film types (e.g., educational, instructional, theatrical, and training) in the classroom. Two appendexes--a course outline on the informational film, and a list of useful organizations--plus an extensive bibliography and an index are included. Well worth browsing.

*Monaco, James. WHO'S WHO IN AMERICAN FILM NOW. Updated edition. New York: New York Zoetrope, 1987. 389pp.

A unique reference book and a decided improvement over the original 1981 publication, this guide lists more than 11,000 creative and technical personnel in the American filmmaking community. They are listed alphabetically, followed by a chronological filmography. Monaco divides his perfunctory entries into thirteen major categories: writers, producers, directors, performers, production designers, costume designers, cinematographers, sound personnel, choreographers, stunt people, musicians, special effects people, and editors. No attempt is made to be all-inclusive. While each category has minor variations in the criteria for selection, all share in insisting that the participants exert a significant effect on American filmmaking. The largest number of people listed are the writers. The most enjoyable section was the introductory material dealing with costs--e.g., how much general extras are paid per day ($90), the basic rate for an actor hired for a week on TV ($1,319), and the highest priced male actors today (Sylvester Stallone and Dustin Hoffman). Regrettably, no cross-referencing information is provided. Worth browsing.

*THE MOTION PICTURE ANNUAL: 1988--COVERING FILMS OF 1987. Evanston: Cinebooks, 1988. Illustrated. 305pp.

An entertaining and welcome addition to film annuals, this premiere edition contains entries on 433 American releases in 1987. A sample entry is MANON OF THE SPRING. It includes star rating (***1/2), 1987 (U. S. release year), France (country made in), 113minutes (running time), Renn-Films (production company), Orion Classics (releasing company), c (color or black and white), MANON DES SOURCES (foreign title), AKA: JEAN DE FLORETTE 2 (alternate title), complete cast credits (with names of roles played in film), synopsis and critical appraisal, content advisory (nudity and adult situations), production credits, genre (drama), parental recommendation, and MPAA rating. The book itself is divided into seven major categories: films by star rating, parental recommendation, and genre, 1987 film reviews, people to watch, obituaries, and awards. The writing is clear, the observations stimulating, and the photographs adequate. Well worth browsing.

Munden, Kenneth W., ed. THE AMERICAN FILM INSTITUTE CATALOG OF MOTION PICTURES PRODUCED IN THE UNITED STATES: FEATURE FILMS 1921-30. New York: R. R. Bowker Company, 1971. Two volumes.

One of the most valuable and scholarly works yet published, this comprehensive and almost perfect national filmography is just the beginning of a series on every motion picture filmed in the United States since 1893. Volume One contains over 6,600 entries that are numerically arranged, beginning with 0001, "with the prefix F2 identifying the series of volumes describing feature films and the volume number of the present work within that series." Most entries provide production and cast credits, the film genre, the source of the film, and a description of the action. Volume Two contains a set of indexes on credits, literary and dramatic sources, subject, and national productions. Highly recommended for special collections.

NEW YORK TIMES FILM REVIEWS, 1913-1968. 6 Volumes. New York: Arno Press and The New York Times, 1970. Published Semi-annually.

No matter how controversial the film reviewers of the TIMES continue to be, this excellent reference source on the most powerful popular film force in motion picture history represents invaluable guidance to the cinematic taste, values, and opinions of twentieth-century America. Students will find it helpful for titles, credits, plots, and social revelations. Recomended for special collections.

Oumano, Ellen. MOVIES FOR A DESERT ISLE: FORTY-TWO WELL-KNOWN FILM LOVERS IN SEARCH OF THEIR FAVORITE MOVIE. New York: St. Martin's Press, 1987. 271pp.

Parish, James Robert, and Michael R. Pitts. FILM DIRECTORS: A GUIDE TO THEIR AMERICAN FILMS. Metuchen: The Scarecrow Press, 1974. Illustrated. 436pp.

A compendium of data on over 500 American and foreign film directors, this volume offers information on individuals who have made feature-length films (at least forty minutes long or over four reels). The entries, alphabetically arranged and ranging from the silent era to the early 1970s, provide details about the director's date and place of birth (and death when appropriate), followed by a chronological filmography indicating film title, producer or distributor, and release date. Regrettably, there is no index to cross-reference film titles with directors. Well worth browsing.

*Park, James, ed. THE FILM YEARBOOK: VOLUME 6. New York: St. Martin's Press, 1987. Illustrated. 192pp.

Not to be confused with the British Film Institute's FILM AND TELEVISION YEARBOOK, this highly entertaining reference work offers a journalistic overview of the key trends and films of the year. The idea originated in 1981 and is getting better with each new edition. A feature article introduces and reviews the big events, while subsequent chapters comment on the best and worst films of the year, the major awards, the year's best quotes, new books, and obituaries. A high point is the attractive mixture of color and b/w stills. No index is provided. Well worth browsing.

Parlato, Salvatore, Jr. SUPERFILMS: AN INTERNATIONAL GUIDE TO AWARD-WINNING EDUCATIONAL FILMS. Metuchen: The Scarecrow Press, 1976. Illustrated. 365pp.

Encompassing nearly 1,500 productions from 1935 to 1975, and dealing with a vast range of movies that have been honored independently at 259 American film festivals, this reference book describes 16mm live and animated short educational films that have "been rated by evaluators who, however uneven in expertise, are strengthened in their credibility by the very diversity of their composition, by the public nature of the festivals, and by the on-going (usually annual) nature of their operations." The guide is divided into six parts: (1) a list of subject index classifications; (2) a programming section (topical index); (3) an alphabetically arranged annotation section; (4) an alphabetically arranged list of film festivals, events, and competitions; (5) a company-title index; and (6) film distribution rental sources. What weakens this otherwise novel idea is the weak, terse annotating. Worth browsing.

Pate, Michael. THE FILM ACTOR: ACTING FOR MOTION PICTURES AND TELEVISION. New York: A. S. Barnes and Company, 1970. Illustrated. 245pp.

Based upon his professional acting career, Pate's fascinating and very helpful technical discussion of general film techniques is a first-rate handbook for novices. The book is divided into three main sections, with the greatest emphasis placed on screen terminology. For those who want specific help, the author provides twenty practical exercises and diagrams that should assist in developing one's confidence prior to shooting actual scenes. An index is included. Well worth browsing.

Parish, James Robert, et al. FILM ACTORS GUIDE: WESTERN EUROPE. Metuchen: The Scarecrow Press, 1977. Illustrated. 606pp.

Parish, James Robert, et al. FILM DIRECTORS GUIDE: WESTERN EUROPE. Metuchen: The Scarecrow Press, 1976. Illustrated. 300pp.

Perry, Jeb H. VARIETY OBITS: AN INDEX TO OBITUARIES IN "VARIETY," 1905-1978. Metuchen: The Scarecrow Press, 1980. 311pp.
Focusing on 15,000 people who worked in film, television, radio, vaudeville, and minstrelsy, this unique guide tries to fill in the gaps provided by other necrologies. This summary of the obituaries published in the "Bible" of the entertainment industry since its inception in 1905, is one of the most important sources of information on a range of professionals (performers, directors, writers, producers, designers, composers, editors, animators, sound technicians, cinematographers, special effects artists, choreographers, inventors, stage managers, stunt people, set decorators, cosmetologists, lighting designers, and make-up artists). Each alphabetically arranged entry contains professional and real names, age at the time of death, the date of death, and principal professional title (e.g., director or producer), and the location of the obituary entry in VARIETY. Recommended for special collections.

Pickard, R. A. E. DICTIONARY OF 1000 BEST FILMS. New York: Association Press, 1971. Illustrated. 496pp.
Arranged alphabetically, this interesting book gives a short, critical summary of "the most famous films produced in the United States and abroad since 1903," together with terse critical synopses, major credits, and cast listings. What hurts this nostalgic study are the highly subjective annotations and the poor format that excludes cross-referencing indexes. The limited illustrations only add to the author's problems. Worth browsing.

*Pratt, Douglas. THE LASER VIDEO DISC COMPANION: A GUIDE TO THE BEST (AND WORST) LASER VIDEO DISCS. New York: New York Zoetrope, 1988. 447pp.
An invaluable resource for collectors and instructors, this well-researched guide contains information on over 2,000 discs released in the United States, and over 1,900 Japanese discs released commercially in the U. S. from 1979 to the present. Pratt's useful introduction explains not only the history of the laserdisc format, but also the variety of functions the format provides, and why it is superior, in many ways, to the Beta and VHS formats. An alphabetically arranged list of more than 1,200 feature films, musical programs, imports, and educational/interactive programs provides outstanding thumbnail reviews. The book concludes with nine appendexes, covering such topics as videodisc producers and retailers, a bibliography, and fifty top-selling discs. Recommended for special collections.

Quinlan, David. QUINLAN'S ILLUSTRATED DIRECTORY OF FILM STARS. New York: Hippocrene Books, 1986. Illustrated. 460pp.
An updated edition of an earlier book, this ordinary guide to over 1,700 stars offers little that cannot be found in more detail in reference works like Vinson's THE INTERNATIONAL DICTIONARY OF FILMS AND FILMMAKERS: VOLUME III--ACTORS AND ACTRESSES. The major values of Quinlan's scheme are found in the useful

snapshots that accompany the alphabetically arranged entries, with their brief annotations and filmographies that run through the end of 1985. No indexes for cross-referencing are available. Worth browsing.

Ragan, David. WHO'S WHO IN HOLLYWOOD 1900-1976. New Rochelle: Arlington House, 1976. 864pp.

A bulky compilation dealing with 20,000 American performers from the early days of store-front theaters, to cineplexes of the 1970s, this reference book provides an adequate overview of the stars, but nothing novel or impressive. The material is divided into two sections: the living and the deceased. In the former, the alphabetically arranged entries include some film credits, a kind word or two, and frequently information about their marital status. What's more, they often omit the important in favor of the trivial. For example, the John Huston entry lists him as a character actor and director, without mentioning that he was also an extremely important writer. More space is devoted to the silent screen star Bessie Love, than to Deborah Kerr, George Segal, and Anthony Quinn. The section on the deceased is a much-abbreviated, alphabetically arranged collection of names, dates, and film titles. Why the dead deserve less discussion than the living is never satisfactorily explained. Approach with caution.

Rehrauer, George. CINEMA BOOKLIST. Three volumes. Metuchen: The Scarecrow Press, 1974. Volume One, 473pp. Volume Two, 470pp. Volume Three, 473pp.

All of the material in this outstanding undertaking is included in Rehrauer's superb film bibliography for Macmillan. Worth studying in this work are the comprehensive format, alphabetizing and numbering thousands of books (e.g., hardbound, paperback, and pamphlets), and indexing them by author and subject. Highly recommended for special collections.

Rehrauer, George. THE MACMILLAN FILM BIBLIOGRAPHY. Two volumes. New York: Macmillan Publishing, 1982. Volume 1, 969pp. Volume 2, 532pp.

Unquestionably the best film bibliography of its type, this outstanding research project offers a comprehensive reference guide for almost every researcher in film studies. Volume 1, which deals with the bibliographic annotations of close to 7,000 books, is alphabetically arranged by book titles and includes information about the author, publisher, and date and place of publication. Volume 2 is a superbly arranged work that includes three indexes. First is the Subject Index, a selected guide alphabetically listing personalities, films, and general topics that appear in Volume 1. Each of the three major categories is examined separately. Although the guide directs attention mainly to books, there are references to a few periodicals as well. The personality entries refer you to books providing information on the person in question. The film title entries provide additional information on release dates, director, and principal performer. The second major index in Volume 2 is the author index, which alphabetically lists the writer's name, title of film book(s), and the review number(s) in Volume 1. The final index, dealing with Scripts, alphabetically lists the title and director's last name in parentheses. The few gliches (e.g., several misspellings, entries with no annotations, and sporadic cross-referencing) hopefully will be clarified in future editions. What makes this extraordinary effort so commendable are the author's perceptive comments and extensive breadth of the field. Highly recommended for all libraries.

Rehrauer, George. THE SHORT FILM: AN EVALUATIVE SELECTION OF 500 RECOMMENDED FILMS. New York: Macmillan Publishing Company, 1975. Illustrated. 199pp.

A worthwhile sourcebook of good 16mm films from the 1930s to the mid-1970s, this guide relies on the collective judgments of individuals and groups who have used short subjects in their classrooms. The selections included were also based upon the recommendations gleaned primarily from thirty-six film reference books. Each entry, alphabetically listed, contains information on release date, producer or distributor, running time, type of film (e.g., animation and no dialogue), b/w or color, brief description, suggested audience, suggested areas of use, and recommended sources for further information. A subject index is included. Recommended for special collections.

*Roberts, James R., ed. ACADEMY PLAYERS DIRECTORY. 2 Volumes. Los Angeles: Academy of Motion Picture Arts and Sciences, 1972. Published annually.
     This is a handy source of information about the members of the Academy of Motion Picture Arts and Sciences. Volume One deals with women and children; Volume 2, men. Worth browsing.

*Robertson, Patrick. MOVIE FACTS AND FEATS: A GUINNESS RECORD BOOK. New York: Sterling Publishing Company, 1980. Illustrated. 288pp.
     One of the most audacious books yet published on film, this reference work takes on a host of controversial issues in film history. Robertson offers no documentation, but states, without reservation, who made the first this or that, where and when, and why other claims are incorrect. There's no way of knowing the validity of claims that Chaplin insisted on 342 takes for a particular scene in CITY LIGHTS (1931) or that all the Nazi concentration camp guards in THE BIG RED ONE (1980) were Jews. On the other hand, assertions that the "first motion pictures were taken with a camera patented in Britain by the French-born Louis Aime Augustin Le Prince," the "first public demonstration of motion pictures took place at the Edison laboratories at West Orange, NJ, on 22 May 1891," and that it is possible to provide accurate worldwide feature film production figures from 1906 to 1945 (with no indication of the sources) are debatable at best. If you're not bothered by claims being represented as facts, this is fun to read. A general index is included. Worth browsing.

*Roud, Richard, ed. CINEMA: A CRITICAL DICTIONARY--THE MAJOR FILM-MAKERS. Two volumes. New York: The Viking Press, 1980. 1,136pp.
     This extraordinary guide contains alphabetically arranged essays, varying from 300 words to eighteen pages, written by forty of film's most prominent authors (e.g., Noel Burch, Gary Carey, Carlos Clarens, Richard Corliss, Arlene Croce, James Damico, Molly Haskell, Penelope Houston, Tom Milne, James Monaco, Edward Perry, Vlada Petric, Donald Richie, David Robinson, Andrew Sarris, John Russell Taylor, and Robin Wood) on 234 noted personalities (mostly directors). In addition, there are intelligent evaluations of important eras in specific national cinemas, the evolution of the documentary, and the development of the American AVANT-GARDE. Some directors like Alfred Hitchcock and Carl Theodor Dreyer get multiple evaluations. Roud deserves considerable credit not only for his own seventeen critical entries but also for the idea and its execution. The essays themselves are hard-hitting, incisive, and extremely subjective, requiring a good background in film studies to appreciate the individual criteria applied to specific personalities like Howard Hawks, Ernst Lubitsch, and Francois Truffaut. The major drawback is the book's title, which suggests more than the contents deliver. Particularly disappointing are the matter-of-fact evaluations of British filmmakers, who are in need of more critical interpretations. On the other hand, what's in most of this wonderful anthology cannot be found anywhere else. An index of names and titles is included. Highly recommended.

Rowan, Bonnie G., with David Culbert. SCHOLAR'S GUIDE TO WASHINGTON, D. C. FILM AND VIDEO COLLECTION. Washington, D. C., Smithsonian Institution Press, 1980. 282pp.

Part of the Scholar Guide series operated by the Woodrow Wilson International Center for Scholars at the Smithsonian Institute, this sourcebook for academicians who wish to study in the nation's capital offers invaluable information on film and video collections, referral services, and film/TV programs. Each of the crucial entries includes addresses, phone numbers, office hours, brief descriptions, and name of the program director. In addition, there are ten appendexes that answer almost any question the visitor to Washington needs answered on this type of program. A bibliography and six indexes ("Type," "Content," "Production Date," "Organizational," "Foreign Productions," and "Name Collections") are provided. Recommended for special collections.

*Sadoul, Georges. DICTIONARY OF FILMS. Trans., ed., and updated Peter Morris. Berkeley: University of California Press, 1972. 432pp.

A valuable guide to the distinguished French film critic's judgments on 1,000 notable films produced in more than fifty countries over a seventy-year history, this reference book benefits considerably from Morris's scholarly research and the addition of fifteen percent new material (three hundred additional film citations). Each film is alphabetically entered under its original-language title (the one exception being Chinese films), with cross references to all known release titles. The entries include a list of credits, the running time (or length for silent films), color or black and white, a brief paragraph of plot synopsis, and a critical paragraph evaluation. Well worth browsing.

Schuster, Mel, ed. MOTION PICTURE PERFORMERS: A BIBLIOGRAPHY OF MAGAZINE AND PERIODICAL ARTICLES, 1900-1969. Metuchen: The Scarecrow Press, 1971. 702pp.

In this massive collection of entries that favors fan magazine gossip, Schuster arranges his information on the 2,900 stars alphabetically by the player's name and then chronologically by the article. No attention is paid to critical reviews of specific performances, nor is there any serious attempt to balance the silent and sound eras. The guide's appeal is limited by the editor's decisions on what to include and what to omit. Well worth browsing.

Schuster, Mel., ed. MOTION PICTURE PERFORMERS: A BIBLIOGRAPHY OF MAGAZINE AND PERIODICAL ARTICLES, SUPPLEMENT No. 1 1970-1974. Metuchen: The Scarecrow Press, 1976. 783pp.

A valuable addition to the project, this volume provides information on 2,600 performers not covered in the earlier bibliography and significantly broadens the scope of the work. Interestingly, Schuster is not altogether pleased with his new approach, stating that the title of his work has become somewhat of a "misnomer" in that his guide now offers "material on many performers whose involvement with the motion picture medium is very limited or nonexistent." Other new feature include the incorporation of entries from CUMULATED DRAMATIC INDEX 1909-1949. Well worth browsing.

*Skorman, Richard, et al. OFF-HOLLYWOOD MOVIES: A FILM LOVER'S GUIDE. New York: Harmony Books, 1989. Illustrated. 370pp.

Smith, John M., and Tim Cawkwell, eds. THE WORLD ENCYCLOPEDIA OF THE FILM. New York: World Publishing, 1972. Illustrated. 444pp.

A useful reference work for students interested in brief statistics on key directors, technicians, and players, this nuts-and-bolts book contains more than 2,000 biographical entries on many of the most creative film people in cinematic history. Given the role played by the British Film Institute, it is somewhat surprising that the book's bias is toward Americans and the sound era rather than toward a more international perpspective and a stronger balance between the silent and sound eras. Moreover, Smith and Cawkwell point out that the book's focus is primarily on directors, and thus their credits are more complete than those given for other artists. Particularly useful is the inclusion of foreign film titles alongside their English titles in the extensive film title index. Except for omitting personalities like Dustin Hoffman and Oscar Homolka, this encyclopedia offers an easy and generally reliable guide to who's who up to 1970. Recommended for special collections.

*Smith, Marsha, and Amy Schewel, eds. THE ACTOR'S BOOK OF MOVIE MONOLOGUES. New York: Penguin Books, 1987. 240pp.

Steele, Robert. THE CATALOGING AND CLASSIFICATION OF CINEMA LITERATURE. Metuchen: The Scarecrow Press, Inc., 1967. 133pp.
An interesting book that attempts to present more precise information about the flood of publications on the cinema than is available elsewhere, this unique publication discusses various classification principles and their related problems. Individual chapters are devoted to analyzing schemes of the Canadian Film Institute Library Service, of the Academy of Motion Picture Arts and Sciences, of the Museum of Modern Art Library, and of the Library of Congress Classification. Steele's thoughtful observations extend our understanding of the classification processes and should prove helpful to modern librarians. A bibliography and index are included. Well worth browsing.

*Steinberg, Try Corbett. REEL FACTS: THE MOVIE BOOK OF RECORDS. New York: Vintage, 1978. 496pp.
A compendium of lists, statistics, and surveys, this delightful and fascinating resource mixes many different aspects of the film industry. "Some of the entries, like the Academy's technical awards," Steinberg explains, "stress the practical side of filmmaking. Other entries, like the studios' incomes, emphasize the financial. Still other sections, like the New York Film Festival programs, remind us of the personal and creative elements. And still other selections, like the annual box-office champs, record the social and popular appeal films exert." Especially appealing is the author's range of data. Not only are we given information on what the industry prizes (e.g., awards and salaries) but also what the critics and the public condemns (e.g., HARVARD LAMPOON's "Movie Worsts"). Unfortunately, there are no indexes to cross-reference the fascinating material. Well worth browsing.

Stewart, William T., Arthur F. McClure, and Ken D. Jones. INTERNATIONAL FILM NECROLOGY. New York: Garland Publishing, 1980. 328pp.
Anyone who reads a mere handful of biographies of a film personality soon encounters significant problems with birth and death dates. In large measure, the problem is as much the fault of the personalities themselves, as the misinformation sloppily supplied by publicists for journalistic obituaries. Thanks to the authors of this useful reference book, dates and birthplaces of people in the film industry should be more accurate in future obituary notices. The major source for the 12,000 alphabetically arranged entries is from the generally reliable statistics files at the California Department of Public Health in Sacramento, which contain death certificates for individuals who have died in that state since 1905. The current necrology contains professional and real names, film occupation, birth date, place of birth, date of death, and age at time of death. One drawback is that the listings are not as international as expected, being heavily biased toward Americans. Recommended for special collections.

Thorpe, Frances, ed. INTERNATIONAL DIRECTORY OF FILM AND TV DOCUMENTATION CENTRES. Chicago: St. James Press, 1988. 140pp.

A valuable but flawed resource guide, this useful directory is the third edition of the original 1976 publication FIAF DIRECTORY AND TV DOCUMENTATION SOURCES. To its credit, the book contains the best discriptions of what 104 archives around the world contain. Where this edition falters is in acts of omission--e.g., no mention of Indiana University's Black Film Center, Edison National Historic Site, and Brandeis University's National Center for Jewish Film--and minor editing problems--e.g., incomplete phone number for the Museum of Broadcasting. More careful pre-publication efforts will result in this book's becoming an indispensible research tool. An index is included. Well worth browsing.

*Truitt, Evelyn Mack. WHO WAS WHO ON THE SCREEN: ILLUSTRATED EDITION. New York: R. R. Bowker Company, 1984. Illustrated. 438pp.

A condensed version of the third edition of this book, the useful biographical dictionary lists nearly 3,100 film personalities (mainly American, British, French, and German) who died between 1905 and 1982. To be included, the individual had to appear on screen. Entries are alphabetically arranged and include a terse profile and extensive screen credits. In an effort to be consistent when dealing with dates of film releases, the sensible author relies on FILM DAILY (through 1970) and on the INTERNATIONAL PICTURE ALMANAC (1971 through 1981). Moreover, Truitt reduces perennial problems with identifying foreign film releases by listing the retitled or translated American film title. For the most part, the result is a comprehensive, functional, and reliable reference tool. A selected bibliography is included. Recommended for special collections.

Turner, Roland, ed. THE ANNUAL OBITUARY 1980. New York: St. Martin's Press, 1981. Illustrated. 885pp.

A valuable bibliographical reference, this first edition lists 450 celebrities who died during 1980. Each entry, chronologically arranged, contains information about the person's occupation, date and place of birth and death, an extended obituary, a snapshot picture, and a listing of sources for additional information. At the front of the book is an alphabetical index of entrants. An index listing the deceased by professions is also included. Well worth browsing.

VARIETY FILM REVIEWS, 1913-1970. Nine volumes. New York: Arno Press, 1972.

A major contribution to film scholarship, this publication provides one of the most complete records to date of commercial filmmaking. Among the features of the reviews are cast and production credits, running times, and synopses. Highly recommended for special collections.

*Vinson, James, Christopher Lyon, and Greg S. Faller, eds. THE INTERNATIONAL DICTIONARY OF FILMS AND FILMMAKERS: VOLUME III--ACTORS AND ACTRESSES. Chicago: St. James Press, 1986. 670pp.

The third volume in this ambitious five-volume project states that the performers selected represent "as wide a spectrum as possible, from stars associated with the birth of the industry in both old and new worlds, through the studio products of the early sound period and the international period following World War II, to the current cinema." The same set of highly qualified authors contribute over 600 entries, alphabetically arranged, with the by-now standard profiles, professional roles, and bibliographies. A spotcheck of celebrities reveals a surprising set of omissions (e.g., Woody Allen, Chester Conklin, and Rex Ingram), a wonderful sensitivity to the performers' unique talents, and an uneven depth in the bibliographical material. Regrettably, the series continues to ignore the need for current cross-referencing aids. Well worth browsing.

*Vinson, James, and Greg S. Faller, eds. THE INTERNATIONAL DICTIONARY OF FILMS AND FILMMAKERS: VOLUME IV--WRITERS AND PRODUCTION ARTISTS. Chicago: St. James Press, 1987. 484pp.

A valuable addition to film scholarship, this handy guide to over 500 creative individuals includes information on screenwriters, producers, art directors, cinematographers, costume designers, composers, editors, choreographers, stuntmen and second unit directors, special effects and sound technicians, makeup artists, and animators. Each entry includes a short biography, a filmography, and a bibliography. The selections are accurate, informative, and well-written. Vinson and Faller are planning a fifth volume, which will include comprehensive indexing to the entire collection. Highly recommended for special collections.

Weaver, John T., ed. FORTY YEARS OF SCREEN CREDITS 1929-1969. Two volumes. Metuchen: The Scarecrow Press, 1970. 1,458pp.

This extensive, alphabetically arranged coverage of nearly 4,000 performers' credits includes the players' year of birth (and death when appropriate), a chronological subarrangement of film titles, plus a listing of Oscar nominations and awards. Unfortunately, it is not always accurate, and there are still too many omissions. Worth browsing.

*Weaver, Kathleen, ed. FILM PROGRAMMER'S GUIDE TO 16MM RENTALS. Third edition. Albany: Reel Research, 1980. 288pp.

This computerized compilation of 14,000 titles is a practical guide to a wide range of international productions from the start of film history to the late 1970s. The main title directory includes information on theatrical releases and short subjects. Alphabetically arranged by title, each entry includes data on the director, year of release, running time, sound or silent, explicit rental prices, and names of distributors. Some entries also include names of the major personalities. Other smaller sections are devoted to documentaries, early films, and newsreels. The major drawbacks of this otherwise unique directory are that the listings are selective rather than comprehensive, and the amount of information is not as comprehensive as the Limbacher listings (although this guide is broader in scope than Limbacher's work). Given the field, this is a commendable effort that needs updating and expansion. Recommended for special collections.

Wheaton, Christopher D., and Richard B. Jewell. PRIMARY CINEMA RESOURCES: AN INDEX TO SCREENPLAYS, INTERVIEWS AND SPECIAL COLLECTIONS AT THE UNIVERSITY OF SOUTHERN CALIFORNIA. Boston: G. K. Hall, 1975. 312pp.

An important study that describes various parts of the University of Souhtern California's Cinema Library, Department of Special Collections, it is divided into a number of categories dealing with screenplays and related materials, interviews on tape, and unique material contributed to the library by individuals. A Titles Index and an Individuals Index, each with its own introductory material, facilitate research efforts by providing interesting information and valuable cross-referencing. For example, the introduction to the Title Index points out that USC's Cinema Library owns more than 3,000 scripts of Hollywood movies. What makes this so impressive is that up to the late 1970s, less than 25 percent of the ninety-five Oscar-winning screenplays had been published, and only 7 percent of the scripts honored by the Screen Writers' Guild since 1948 were available for public consumption. We are then provided data on when specific films were released, who the writer(s) were, what studio did the script, and, when appropriate, the name of the donor who gave the script to the Cinema Library. Other sections identify screenwriters alphabetically, including scripts and taped interviews available at USC. Overall, this is a highly useful reference tool. Recommended for special collections.

*Young, William C. AMERICAN THEATRICAL ARTS: GUIDE TO MANUSCRIPTS AND SPECIAL COLLECTIONS IN THE UNITED STATES AND CANADA. Chicago: The American Library Association, 1971. 168pp.

This listing and description of existing repositories and collections of film scripts and related documents will be updated annually in the JOURNAL OF THEATRE DOCUMENTATION. The alphabetically arranged entries, grouped by states, review the collections of over 135 groups and indicate in a second section the subjects and personalities found in the various collections. Well worth browsing.

DIRECTORS

*Bergan, Ronald. A-Z OF MOVIE DIRECTORS. New York: Proteus, 1982. Illustrated. 160pp.

In thumbnail sketches of more than 350 Hollywood directors, this film buff effort provides basic information mixed with provocative judgments.[45] Consider the entry for John Huston. The bibliographical material glosses over the legendary director's traumatic early years in Hollywood by stating that "After writing screenplays for a number of successful Warner Bros. dramas, he made an astonishingly assured debut with THE MALTESE FALCON. . . ." Aside from omitting that this was Huston's directorial debut and that nearly a decade of bad scripts and a year's flight from Hollywood in the early 1930s set the stage for that debut, the sentence is fine. Each entry, alphabetically arranged, contains a precis of a director's works, critical judgments, the director's date of birth (and death), country of origin (and naturalization), and filmography (with dates) of the subject's most notable movies. The writing is crisp and entertaining. Well worth browsing.

*Braudy, Leo, and Morris Dickstein, eds. GREAT FILM DIRECTORS. New York: Oxford University Press, 1978. 778pp.

A fascinating collection chronicling the career of twenty-three important directors in film history, this anthology provides eighty articles that also touch on film theory and film appreciation. The AUTEURIST approach, Braudy and Dickstein tell us, has spawned two major traditions in film history: the image of the flamboyant genius and the tale of the retiring professional craftsman. "Both extremes," they explain, ". . . involve the interaction of publicity and personal temperament at a particular stage of film history. The categories are further complicated by the overlapping myth of commercial pressure, a tyranny exerted on genius and professional alike--the conformist studios, the doltish producers, and the struggle to achieve great projects that should have found funding immediately. Only the hack, goes the story--the director on studio contract--is immune from pressure, because he has no art in his soul." Braudy and Dickstein attempt to set the record straight. Each of their twenty-three sections begins with a critical-biographical commentary, followed generally by four essays. The choices are intended to highlight the types of analytical and popular attention the director has attained. The emphasis is on contrasting the subject with peers rather than with focusing on a specific work. What is particularly refreshing is the internal cross-referencing that emerges from these rich selections and the feeling they collectively provide for the art of film.

The directors, alphabetically arranged, are Michelangelo Antonioni, Ingmar Bergman, Robert Bresson, Luis Bunuel, Frank Capra, Charles Chaplin, Carl Theodor Dryer, Sergei Eisenstein, Federico Fellini, Robert Flaherty, John Ford, Jean-Luc Godard, D. W. Griffith, Howard Hawks, Alfred Hitchcock, Buster Keaton, Akira

---

[45]   For an interesting review of books on directors, see Isabel Quigley, "The Directorate," ENCOUNTER 37:1 (July 1971):63-7.

Kurosawa, Fritz Lang, Jean Renoir, Roberto Rossellini, Josef von Sternberg, Francois Truffaut, and Orson Welles. The authors of the essays are equally well-known: i.e., Andre Bazin, David Thomson, Raymond Durgnat, Satyajit Ray, John Baxter, Andrew Sarris, Robin Wood, Pauline Kael, Roy Armes, Stanley Kauffmann, Otis Ferguson, Jame Agee, Manny Farber, Lindsay Anderson, Penelope Houston, Gerald Mast, Donald Richie, Tony Richardson, Francois Truffaut, Luis Bunuel, Graham Greene, Siegfried Kracauer, Susan Sontag, Dwight Macdonald, John Grierson, Edward Perry, Robert Warshow, Michael Roemer, and Carlos Fuentes. Recommended for special collections.

*Chell, David. MOVIEMAKERS AT WORK. Redmond: Microsoft Press, 1987. Illustrated. 358pp.

*Coursodon, Jean-Pierre, with Pierre Sauvage, eds. AMERICAN DIRECTORS. Two volumes. New York: McGraw-Hill Book Company, 1983. Volume 1, 456pp. Volume 2, 424pp.
   A reflective and stimulating collection of essays on more than 100 American film directors from the early days of sound to the present, these companion volumes articulate modern day attitudes about AUTEURISM. Directors who died or who were otherwise inactive after 1940 are excluded, as are foreign directors who occasionally made films in America. A brief filmography precedes the critical notes (generally about four pages) in each of the alphabetically arranged entries.   Volume 1 contains fifty-nine essays (more than half written by Coursodon) on directors like Lloyd Bacon, Busby Berkeley, Clarence Brown, Frank Capra, George Cukor, Roy Del Ruth, John Ford, Byron Haskin, Fritz Lang, Ernst Lubitsch, Douglas Sirk, Preston Sturges, and William Wyler. Volume 2, containing fifty-eight essays, takes a look at more recent directors like Robert Aldrich, Woody Allen, John Cassavetes, Brian DePalma, Clint Eastwood, George Roy Hill, Arthur Penn, and Charles Walters. One wonders why Ida Lupino is included in Volume 2, not Volume 1, and why there is a shocking absence of both endnotes and a bibliography. Otherwise, this set of subjective evaluations is a welcome addition to reference shelves. An index is included. Well worth browsing.

Dixon, Wheeler W. THE "B" DIRECTORS: A BIOGRAPHICAL DIRECTORY. Metuchen: The Scarecrow Press, 1985. Illustrated. 595pp.
   A valuable guide to more than 350 American directors, spanning the years from 1929 to the present, this book provides a useful feature filmography for all the entries. The directors are listed alphabetically, followed by a chronological listing of their films (titles of major pictures are in bold face), the producing company, the film's date of release/and or copyright, any additional role the director played (e.g., screenwriter or performer), and a brief note about the director's career. Although far from complete, the directory is a good beginning to the upgrading of the status of many "B" movies that Dixon argues were the "works of serious artists who saw that only by working in the depths of poverty row could they hope to accomplish the sort of films the majors would never let them make." Among the examples the author provides are Robert Aldrich, Budd Boetticher, Nicholas Ray, and Edgar G. Ulmer. Regrettably, two filmographies dealing with feature films and serials cited in the book do not contain page numbers for easy cross-referencing. A bibliography is included. Well worth browsing.

*Ebert, Roger. A KISS IS STILL A KISS: ROGER EBERT AT THE MOVIES. Kansas City: Andrews, McMeel and Parker, 1984. 256pp.

Finler, Joel W. THE MOVIE DIRECTORS STORY. New York: Crescent Books, 1985. Illustrated. 272pp.

A beautifully designed coffee-table book that is a companion volume to THE MOVIE STARS STORY, this account of 140 popular mainstream filmmakers is divided into three major sections. Chapter One--1920 to 1939--contains forty short essays on directors from Dorothy Arzner to Sam Wood. Following a brief overview of the period, each alphabetically arranged entry includes information on the director's date of birth and death (when appropriate), a critical-biographical essay, and a smattering of handsome and rare illustrations. The research is good, but the amount of information is limited. Chapter Two--1940 to 1959--contains fifty essays on directors from Anthony Asquith to Fred Zinnemann. Chapter Three--1960 to 1985--contains fifty-four essays ranging from Robert Aldrich to Peter Yates. Especially praiseworthy are the consistently high quality of the illustrations and the book's layout. Special credit goes to Robyn Karney, who was the editor for both volumes. An appendix listing Oscar nominations and awards for directors, an index of directors, and an index of other personnel are included. Recommended for special collections and friends.

Fleming, Alice. THE MOVIEMAKERS. New York: St. Martin's Press, 1973. Illustrated. 184pp.

Geared for secondary school students, this weak overview of American film history focuses on eleven film directors and charts the growth and development of an art form and industry as if they were the outcome of a handful of artists working in a vacuum. The patronizing prose is offensive, and the poor design of the book prevents it from doing justice to the subject. The directors covered are Edwin S. Porter, D. W. Griffith, Mack Sennett, Cecil B. DeMille, Robert Flaherty, Ernst Lubitsch, Frank Capra, John Ford, Walt Disney, Alfred Hitchcock, and Stanley Kubrick. Particularly nonsensical, given the level at which the book is aimed, is the bibliography that includes mostly academic works. An index is included. Approach with caution.

Geduld, Harry M., ed. FILM MAKERS ON FILM MAKING. Bloomington: Indiana University Press, 1967. 302pp.

An uneven collection of thirty directors' comments about their individual work, this anthology runs into trouble mainly because much of its contents is available elsewhere and because some of the material doesn't deserve republication. The book is divided into two parts; Section one includes Hepworth, Porter, Sennett, Griffith, Chaplin and Vertov. Section two, dealing with the sound period, has Hitchcock, Cocteau, Bergman, and Kurosawa. Approach with caution.

*Gelmis, Joseph, THE FILM DIRECTOR AS SUPERSTAR. New York: Doubleday and Company, 1970. Illustrated. 316pp.

This is one of the few collections of interviews that emphasizes film mavericks as well as popular mainstream directors. Another unique feature of this anthology is that Gelmis did the interviews himself rather than editing work done by others. The result is a coherent set of questions and responses that portray American filmmaking with its strengths and weaknesses. Collectively, the sixteen people queried give us a number of intriguing insights into the business aspect of filmmaking, offer good advice to beginners, and provide some juicy gossip. Among the best chapters are those dealing with Roger Corman, Robert Downey, Brian DePalma, Norman Mailer, Andy Warhol, and John Cassavetes. The book's primary drawbacks are that the interviews and filmographies are too brief, and no index is available for cross-referencing. Worth browsing.

*Giannetti, Louis. MASTERS OF THE AMERICAN CINEMA. Englewood Cliffs: Prentice-Hall, 1981. Illustrated. 466pp.

Higham, Charles, and Joel Greenberg. THE CELLULOID MUSE: HOLLYWOOD
DIRECTORS SPEAK. Chicago: Henry Regency, 1969. Illustrated. 268pp.
     A mixed bag of interviews with fifteen directors, this unusual anthology stresses
the autobiographical nature of filmmaking. The project grew out of the research
Higham and Greenberg did for their study on Hollywood in the forties. Since they
could not capture the flavor of movie folklore and memorabilia in the book on the
1940s, the authors decided to publish the interviews in essay form. The directors,
alphabetically arranged, are Robert Aldrich, Curtis Bernhardt, George Cukor, John
Frankenheimer, Alfred Hitchcock, Fritz Lang, Rouben Mamoulian, Jean Negulesco,
Irving Rapper, Mark Robson, Jacques Tourneur, King Vidor, and Billy Wilder.
Filmographies and an index are included. Well worth browsing.

Hochman, Stanley, ed. A LIBRARY OF FILM CRITICISM: AMERICAN FILM
DIRECTORS. New York: Frederick Ungar Publishing Company, 1974. 590pp.
     The first book in a projected series, this unique anthology contains information
about sixty-five internationally known directors from the silent and sound eras, up
to the mid-1960s. Each of the alphabetically arranged entries includes sizable
quotations from specialized film periodicals and general publications about the
director's reputation and specific works. For example, John Ford's entry has excerpts
from such periodicals as CLOSE UP, CINEMA, LITERARY DIGEST, THE FILM
CRITICISM OF OTIS FERGUSON, NEW THEATRE, THE HISTORY OF MOTION
PICTURES, NEW YORK TIMES, FILM ESSAYS, SIGHT AND SOUND, FILMS IN
REVIEW, THE IMMEDIATE EXPERIENCE, THE LIVELIEST ART, NOVELS INTO FILM,
CONFESSIONS OF A CULTIST, A WORLD ON FILM, KISS KISS BANG BANG, and
THE NAME ABOVE THE TITLE. The chronologically arranged observations are
well-chosen and extremely informative. Filmographies and a general index are
included. Highly recommended for special collections.

Kantor, Bernard R., et al., eds. DIRECTORS AT WORK: INTERVIEWS WITH
AMERICAN FILM-MAKERS. New York: Funk and Wagnalls, 1970. 442pp.
     This is a pleasant collection of interviews with Richard Brooks, George Cukor,
Norman Jewison, Elia Kazan, Stanley Kramer, Richard Lester, Jerry Lewis, Elliot
Silverstein, Robert Wise, and William Wyler. The major weakness is that the emphasis
is more on sociability, than on critical discussions. Worth browsing.

*Koszarski, Richard, ed. GREAT AMERICAN FILM DIRECTORS IN PHOTOGRAPHS.
New York: Dover Publications, 1984. Illustrated. 108pp.
     This welcome gallery of portraits--primarily "work shots" taken on location and
designed for publicity purposes--offers an eighty year chronology of many of
America's greatest directors. The nearly 200 strikingly reproduced photographs are
arranged to highlight the social and technological context in which directors like
Edwin S. Porter, D. W. Griffith, Mack Sennett, Cecil B. DeMille, Victor Fleming,
Busby Berkeley, Arch Oboler, Steven Spielberg, and William Wyler worked. Adding
to the superb concept are detailed captions explaining the significance of the
illustrations. An index is provided. Recommended for special collections and gifts for
friends.

*Koszarski, Richard, ed. HOLLYWOOD DIRECTORS 1914-1940. New York: Oxford
University Press, 1976. Illustrated. 364pp.
     An uneven compilation of fifty essays allegedly written by directors (e.g., Edwin
S. Porter, Alice Guy-Blache, Mack Sennett, and John Ford), performers (e.g.,
Charles Chaplin, Harold Lloyd, Buster Keaton, and Harry Langdon), and other

creative people during their working days in the film industry, this anthology is more of a curiosity piece than an important contribution to film scholarship. The major problem is Koszarski's presumed innocence in assuming that the essays were honest representations of what the film pioneers actually felt about their day-to-day assignments and challenges. More likely, as Douglas Gomery points out, we have no reason to believe that the powerful film moguls who controlled the movie industry during the times in question permitted anything to be written or published that did not meet the approval of their tightly controlled studios.[46] Issues of validity aside, Koszarski's opening chapter, plus his brief introductory remarks preceding each of the essays on the silent and sound periods provide a general introduction to material that is interesting to peruse, but foolish to ponder. A general index is included. Worth browsing.

*Koszarski, Richard, ed. HOLLYWOOD DIRECTORS 1941-1976. New York: Oxford University Press, 1977. Illustrated. 426pp.

A follow-up volume to the 1976 publication, this anthology continues Koszarski's interest in material written by important personalities in the development of the film industry. The danger that such material will pass for fact has already been noted, although there is every reason to believe that the current volume is a bit more reliable than the earlier collection. Following a brief introduction by Koszarski, we're given another set of fifty essays, mostly by directors (e.g., Orson Welles, Rouben Mamoulian, King Vidor, John Huston, Robert Rossen, Frank Capra, William Wyler, Jean Renoir, and Michael Curtiz), who offer a variety of opinions on filmmaking. The quality of the essays varies, with few providing any incisive comments. A general index is included. Worth browsing.

*Lambray, Maureen. THE AMERICAN FILM DIRECTORS, Volume 1. New York: Rapoport Press, 1976. Illustrated. 179pp.

An interesting attempt to define the "American" director, this beautifully produced picture book is about eighty-two, men each of whom has made more than three feature films and has finished a significant portion of his work in America or American studios. Interestingly, Lambray points out that she "never had the chance to preplan the photograph of any director with the exception of one. They would tell me to meet them at a specific place--and I would never know whether it was their home, office, set or whatever." The results are very impressive. Each director's filmography, with an appropriate quotation by the director, is listed opposite a striking black-and-white portrait of the subject. Among the celebrities included are Robert Aldrich, Woody Allen, Bob Fosse, Gordon Parks, and Melvin Van Peebles. Regrettably, the pictures are presented in no apparent order and without an index to locate specific personalities. Well worth browsing.

Lloyd, Ronald. AMERICAN FILM DIRECTORS: THE WORLD AS THEY SEE IT. New York: Franklin Watts, 1976. Illustrated. 143pp.

Geared for secondary school students, this lively account of six directors offers a simple introduction to American film history. The premise is that these original artists did much more than provide us with escapist entertainment. By analyzing their collective works, Lloyd attempts to prove that men like John Ford, Orson Welles, Howard Hawks, Alfred Hitchcock, Arthur Penn, and Stanley Kubrick gave us insights about ourselves and the world we inhabit. The Hitchcock and Kubrick sections appear to strain the point. On the other hand, there is a good overview of new directors emerging in the late 1960s: e.g., Peter Bogdanovich, Francis Ford Coppola, and

---

[46] Douglas Gomery, "Books: HOLLYWOOD DIRECTORS, 1914-1940," WIDE ANGLE 1:4 (1977):76.

Robert Altman. An attractive set of illustrations and an index are included. Well worth browsing.

*McBride, Joseph, ed. FILMMAKERS ON FILMMAKING: THE AMERICAN FILM INSTITUTE SEMINARS ON MOTION PICTURES AND TELEVISION. Los Angeles: J. P. Tarcher, 1983. Illustrated. 215pp.
     Two years after The American Film Institute (AFI) was established in 1967, the controversial organization opened its Center for Advanced Film Studies in Los Angeles. One of the benefits of the conservatory was to gain access to some of the most important creative personnel in the film and television community. Many of the visitors agreed to participate in an oral history program loosely termed "Dialogue on Film." The transcripts of those AFI seminars were initially printed on looseleaf paper and distributed to the membership with a looseleaf binder for monthly additions. Then the transcripts were bound into individual booklets. Eventually, they began appearing regularly in AMERICAN FILM. Some of the more interesting ones are reprinted and edited in these two companion volumes. Volume One contains twelve transcripts of chatty discussions with Hal Wallis, Richard Zanuck and David Brown, Ingmar Bergman, Billy Wilder and I. A. L. Diamond, Sidney Poitier, Lucille Ball, James Wong Howe, Leonard Rosenman, Polly Platt, Verna Fields, Anthea Sylbert, and Sue Mengers. It also includes an irritating set of short quotations about the film industry by celebrities, a bibliography, and an index. Worth browsing.

*McCrindle, Joseph F., ed. BEHIND THE SCENES: THEATER AND FILM INTERVIEWS FROM "THE TRANSATLANTIC REVIEW." New York: Holt, Rinehart and Winston, 1971. 341pp.

*Oumano, Ellen. FILM FORUM: THIRTY-FIVE TOP FILMMAKERS DISCUSS THEIR CRAFT. New York: St. Martin's Press, 1985. 331pp.

Phillips, Gene D. THE MOVIE MAKERS: ARTISTS IN AN INDUSTRY.   Chicago: Nelson-Hall Company, 1973. Illustrated. 249pp.
     A coffee-table book on thirteen AUTEURS, this breezy set of essays looks better than it reads. The work is divided into two major sections on filmmakers in America and Britain. The former deals with James Wong Howe, Charles Chaplin, Howard Hawks, George Cukor, George Stevens, Fred Zinnemann, and Stanley Kubrick. The British section discusses Carol Reed, David Lean, Joseph Losey, Bryan Forbes, John Schlesinger, and Ken Russell. One can, of course, quibble with Kubrick being in the American section and Losey being in the British section. For each personality, Phillips offers a bit of career history, a heavy dose of plot summaries, and a simplistic analysis of the films mentioned. A filmography concludes each of the highly subjective sections. A bibliography, endnotes, and an index are included. Worth browsing.

Quinlan, David. THE ILLUSTRATED GUIDE TO FILM DIRECTORS. Totowa: Barnes and Noble Books, 1983. Illustrated. 334pp.
     Consisting of 550 short career studies and lengthy filmographies of internationally known directors, this adequate reference guide shows a bias toward American and British artists. The alphabetically arranged entries include information on dates of films, awards received, professional and actual names, and dates of birth (and death when appropriate), as well as terse critical evaluations. Regrettably, there is no cross-referencing or title index to locate specific information, and the illustrations are less than promised by the title. A poor bibliography is included. Worth browsing.

Rhode, Eric. TOWER OF BABEL: SPECULATIONS ON THE CINEMA. Philadelphia: Chilton Books, 1966. 214pp.

A series of uneven essays on eleven directors, this highly theoretical study strives to relate the artist's work to his cultural roots. Rhodes's premise is that the director's vision of his world is found in "the fruitful clash between temperament and ideology." Rhode believes that "Without a temperament capable of carrying out this labour [a director's struggle to understand his subject], a temperament that refuses compromise or complicity, . . . [his] style [the method an artist uses to arrange his vision] would never come into being." The eleven directors, chronologically presented, are Jean Vigo, Robert Bresson, Sergei Eisenstein, Humphrey Jennings, and Fritz Lang (the German period: 1919-33), Jacques Rivette, Federico Fellini, Alain Resnais, Max Ophuls, Andrzej Wajda, and Satyajit Ray. Unless one has a good background in their works, this book is tough going. An index is included. Well worth browsing.

*Sadoul, Georges. DICTIONARY OF FILMMAKERS. Trans., ed., and updated Peter Morris. Berkeley: University of California Press, 1972. 288pp.

In the original edition, the distinguished French author focused on 1,000 directors, screenwriters, cinematographers, art directors, composers, producers, and inventors "who have contributed something to the artistic industry of the cinema." The entries represented personalities from sixty nations and contained over 20,000 dates and film titles. The entries, alphabetically arranged, included a critical evaluation followed by an abridged filmography. Entries related to major directors (e.g., Cecil B. DeMille and Joseph Losey) also offered quotations from significant interviews, statements, or critical essays.

This English translation not only maintains that information, but also includes revisions and corrections from the original publication. Additional entries, minor revisions in style (e.g., the individual's professional and real names are included, certain personalities have been cross-referenced), and expanded filmographies all add considerably to the book's worth. Whether one agrees with Sadoul's assessment of the filmmakers is less important than the opportunity to gain access to his critical and historical perspectives. Almost no attention is paid to performers. Highly recommended for special collections.

*Sarris, Andrew, ed. INTERVIEWS WITH FILM DIRECTORS. New York: The Bobbs-Merrill Company, 1967. Illustrated. 478pp.

The best directors' anthology yet available, it includes statements from forty of the screen's most talented men, including Antonioni, Fellini, Bunuel, Chaplin, Dreyer, Eisenstein, Godard, Hawks, Losey, and von Sternberg. Sarris also provides a brief introduction to most of the directors, plus a filmography following each interview. Recommended for special collections.

Schickel, Richard. THE MEN WHO MADE THE MOVIES: INTERVIEWS WITH FRANK CAPRA, GEORGE CUKOR, HOWARD HAWKS, ALFRED HITCHCOCK, VINCENTE MINNELLI, KING VIDOR, RAOUL WALSH, AND WILLIAM WELLMAN. New York: Atheneum, 1975. Illustrated. 308pp.

Growing out of Schickel's splendid 1973 TV series in which he captured the flavor and talents of the eight famous directors, this valuable publication contains wonderful excerpts from each of the programs. Each section includes a brief introduction followed by the subject's comments on each of his important films. The attractive illustrations add to the book's appeal. An index is included. Highly recommended for special collections.

Schuster, Mel. MOTION PICTURE DIRECTORS: A BIBLIOGRAPHY OF MAGAZINE AND PERIODICAL ARTICLES, 1900-1972. Metuchen: The Scarecrow Press, 1973. 418pp.

Using full runs of 340 magazines (listed in an appendix), this guide provides useful information on more than 2,300 creative people in the international film community. The alphabetically arranged entries contain biographical and career information not readily available and often quite interesting. Recommended for special collections.

Singer, Michael, ed. FILM DIRECTORS: A COMPLETE GUIDE. Beverly Hills: Lone Eagle Publishing, 1983. Published Annually.

A useful resource guide that lists directors alphabetically, this book also contains screen credits chronologically arranged, along with a cross-referencing of film titles, Oscar and Emmy nominees and winners, date and place of birth, professional and actual names, and how the individual can be contacted.   An index of directors is included. Well worth browsing.

Thompson, Frank. BETWEEN ACTION AND CUT: FIVE AMERICAN DIRECTORS. Metuchen: The Scarecrow Press, 1985. Illustrated. 320pp.

Wakeman, John, ed. WORLD FILM DIRECTORS, VOLUME ONE, 1890-1945. New York: H. W. Wilson Company, 1987. 1247pp.

INTRODUCTORY BOOKS TO FILM HISTORY

*Allen, Robert C., and Douglas Gomery. FILM HISTORY: THEORY AND PRACTICE. New York: Alfred A. Knopf, 1985. Illustrated. 276pp.

A valuable introduction to the study of film history, this pioneering book places its subject matter within the general field of historical research, orients the reader to specific problems historians face, surveys the standard approaches to examining film history, and offers examples of the various types of film history conducted. The emphasis is on training more discriminating readers and qualified film historians. The impetus for this effort arises out of the authors' frustrations as film teachers and their view that most available survey books remain "silent as to the process by which historical questions are posed, research conducted, evidence analyzed, and generalizations drawn." No definitive answer is given to the question of what is the best way to study and write film history. Instead, Allen and Gomery stress that each approach has its strengths and weaknesses. But they do insist that studying film history requires active, not passive, readers. Pointing out that film is a multifaceted phenomenon, involving aesthetics, economics, cultural products, and technology, the authors study each of these facets of film history, resulting in a controversial summary of the methodologies, problems, and advantages most widespread in contemporary film history surveys. The major problem is that the otherwise astute authors only occasionally examine film in the context of society itself. Although we are never allowed to forget that film is influenced by political, social, intellectual, and economic factors, the book's specific focus is on the importance of studying film as an industrial phenomenon.

To buttress their thesis, the scholars organize their book into autonomous chapters under three major sections. Part 1, on film history as a scholarly discipline, is mainly Allen's responsibility. Of the three chapters, two are his. He begins with "Film History as History, " reviewing the nature of historical inquiry, critiquing the empirical and conventionalist approaches to history, and arguing that a new philosophy of science, "Realism," may provide important, fresh insights into the complexities of film history. While Allen acknowledges that the term creates numerous problems for film scholars, who traditionally associate it with theoretical issues relating to artistic phenomena, he nevertheless argues that the new philosophy may be beneficial to film history because of its approach to film's systematic nature. The focus is on a theoretical methodology that produces tentative historical models for evaluating complex interactive elements. That is, we test historical explanations "by reference both to historical evidence and to other competing explanations." The assumption is that a world exists independent of the investigator. By explaining that "world," the investigator refers to it. Where this approach differs from empiricist approaches is that "realism" thinks of reality as one-dimensional and the realist historian makes no attempt to explain the regularity of the real world. The realist historian acknowledges the complexity of reality and understands that explanations about it are only partial answers to complex problems. Thus the realist approach focuses not only on "the observable layer of reality but also [on] the workings of the GENERATIVE MECHANISMS that produce the observable event." Realism goes beyond questions of HOW and WHAT to questions of WHY. It takes "as its object of study the structures or mechanisms that cause observable phenomena--mechanisms that are rarely observable directly." In short, realism provides descriptive models for studying these mechanisms.

Gomery begins the middle chapter, "Researching Film History," with a critical but respectful overview of film scholarship and proceeds to identify the reasons for the embryonic status of our scholarly discipline. He then turns to the specific evidentiary problems of film scholars, concentrating on issues of film preservation and textual variation. From there he focuses on defining the object of film study, pointing out the variety of perspectives possible.

Allen's concluding chapter in Part 1, "Reading Film History," picks up his earlier theme that film historians need to confront their material, not accept it passively. After critiquing the "narrative" approach to general film histories, he suggests a number of ways readers can question what they read. He then offers a superb case study on how his methodology relates to film's first two major historical surveys: Robert Grau's THE THEATRE OF SCIENCE (1914), and Terry Ramsaye's A MILLION AND ONE NIGHTS (1926). In addition to listing the basic ideas shared by the two authors, he also explains persuasively how the age's general fascination with technology significantly influenced Grau and Ramsaye's writing and interpretation of film history. Each of the three chapters drums home the idea that we need to challenge the assumptions and interpretations made by film historians.

Part 2, on the traditional approaches to film history, contains four chapters, two by each author, that examine the techniques, difficulties, and advantages connected with aesthetic, technological, economic, and social film history, respectively. Allen's "Aesthetic Film History" begins by examining the masterpiece approach through the 1960s and pointing out the changes that have occurred as a result of developments in film theory and criticism. For example, he argues that up until the 1960s, film theory ("general propositions about the nature and functions of cinema") was divided into two major categories: FORMATIVISM and REALISM. While giving short shrift to Realism (the Bazinian variety), Allen describes how formative theorists (e.g., Hugo Munsterberg, Sergei Eisenstein, and Rudolf Arnheim) affected the film histories written by Lewis Jacobs, Terry Ramsaye, and Arthur Knight. He then discusses how the AUTEUR theory evolved out of the French film frustrations of the 1950s, its impact on Andrew Sarris, and the fact that since the mid-1960s most general film surveys "either take an explicitly auteurist position or show its influence." After summing up the important assumptions of the masterpiece approach, he proceeds to describe its limitations and then indicates the opportunities that semiotics offers for a new approach to aesthetic film history. Allen's case study on the background of SUNRISE (1927) demonstrates the many benefits that result from examining a film in its historical and institutional contexts, but tells us almost nothing about the aesthetics of the film itself.

Gomery authors the next two chapters on technological and economic film history. In the first, "Technological Film History," he succinctly summarizes two major theories--the "Great Man" approach and technological determination and the economics of technological change--that have been applied to film history. The former limits the investigator, according to the author, to four basic tasks: (1) distinguishing between important and insignificant technological breakthroughs, (2) establishing who gets the credit for the technological development, (3) explaining how the breakthrough developed, and (4) placing the breakthrough in its appropriate historical context. The economics of technological change, on the other hand, examines the issues in a larger context, focusing on how companies pursue maximum profits. Using a framework of invention, innovation, and diffusion, Gomery provides a detailed methodology for the examination of technological changes in the film industry. In his next chapter, "Economic Film History," he draws an important distinction between business and economic approaches, pointing out that the former concentrates on providing and delivering services and products while the latter is interested in the processes that are used to produce and deliver services and products. He cites the Marxist approach as an illustration of how some film historians evaluate how the film industry evolved. Industrial analysis is a second approach. Unlike Marxists, Gomery explains, economic historians examine only economic variables--e.g., structure, conduct, and performance--and avoid issues of ideology and sociology. As always, the evaluations gloss over aesthetic questions, reinforcing the book's major strengths and weaknesses.

Allen's "Social Film History" concludes Part 2. His focus is divided between questions posed by Ian Jarvie in MOVIES AND SOCIETY (1970)--(1) Who makes movies and why? (2) Who sees films, how and why? (3) What is seen, how and why? (4) How do films get evaluated, by whom and why?--and Richard Dyer's approach to categorizing the star system in STARS (1979)--(1) promotion, (2) publicity, (3) films, and (4) criticism and commentary. The Jarvie framework provides Allen with an opportunity to suggest the scope of a truly comprehensive social history of Hollywood and explain why it has yet to be written. The most significant contribution of this section is the author's overview of the Frankfurt school and its attempt to blend the works of Marx and Freud into social analysis. To illustrate how Dyer's categories might apply to social film history, Allen offers a flawed overview of Joan Crawford's career. The problem with this section, as Mary Beth Haralovich points out, is that Allen is too narrow in his focus. While praising the author's grasp of the generative mechanisms within the film industry that influenced audience-star relationships, Haralovich notes the value of extending the analysis of Crawford's image "with the historical specificity of women's clothing design and with the working class women who might have constituted her audience."[47]

Part 3, on doing film history, consists of two chapters by Gomery and one by Allen. Not only is the material skillfully presented but it also generates enthusiasm for writing film history. The three chapters should be required reading for all introductory film history courses. Gomery leads off with "Writing Film History," a discussion about how local film historians can examine how movies functioned in their communities, who owned the movie theaters, what technology was employed, and whether films were ever censored in the area. To demonstrate various methodologies for novices, the enterprising author provides three local film history projects. Project 1 is a straightforward account of how using a local newspaper as a resource provides a clear-cut analysis of the way technological change occurred at a local level, in this instance the switch from silent to sound film in Milwaukee, Wisconsin. Project 2 is a more complicated but practical exercise in examining the economics of local exhibition, using readily available data (urban histories, government reports, trade papers, journal articles, and interviews) to chart the rise of Chicago's powerful Balaban and Katz theater chain. Project 3, based upon Allen's unpublished research on Durham, North Carolina, demonstrates the different patterns in moviegoing between a large city (New York) and small city (Durham) from 1905 to 1910. Gomery then concludes his excellent discussion with a list of available data for doing similar projects: e.g., directories, fire insurance maps, local histories, film trade papers, public records, and trade papers.

---

[47]   "The Social History of Film," p.10.

Allen's "Reintegrating Film History" reasserts the core aspects of the Realist approach to film history--i.e, movies are a complex phenomenon that contain many interactive elements. Where the main body of the book examines four separate branches of film history, this chapter, using the rise of Cinema Verite as a case study, stresses the four-step model extrapolated from the fundamental tenets of realism: (1) describe the event being investigated to highlight the generative mechanisms allegedly responsible for it; (2) investigate these mechanisms; (3) discuss the interrelationships among the generative mechanisms; and (4) evaluate the relative impact of these mechanisms. In the intriguing analysis that follows, Allen masterfully identifies many of the generative mechanisms that gave birth to Cinema Verite in America: (1) aesthetic mechanisms: e.g., an AVANT-GARDE film movement using sync-sound location shooting of uncontrolled situations as an alternative to classical Hollywood filmmaking in the early 1960s; (2) technological mechanisms: e.g., development of lightweight mobile cameras and recorders; (3) economic mechanisms: e.g., the low cost of advertising on ABC television in the late 1950s and the strategy designed by the Bell and Howell Company to sponsor "Close-Up," a public affairs series using Cinema Verite; and (4) political mechanisms: e.g., the effect of World War II on the use of 16mm films and camera equipment. Particularly interesting is the author's analysis of the interrelationships among generative mechanisms, pointing out that Cinema Verite filmmakers like Robert Drew, Richard Leacock, and Don Pennebaker drew criticism from many people because they insisted on showing a situation rather than describing it. While no definitive explanations are given for the emergence of Cinema Verite, Allen makes it clear how the desire to offer an alternative to classical Hollywood filmmaking resulted from a number of complex factors, many being accelerated by World War II and the neo-realist movement of the postwar period.

Gomery's "A Selective Guide to Reading" completes the scholarly analysis of resources available for studying film history. Organized to coincide with the topics covered in the previous nine chapters, the brief descriptions of significant material on film study concentrate primarily on American books. The author makes a point of dismissing contemporary film biographies, film buff studies, and work on the movies since 1960. Regrettably, a number of mistakes in spelling and citations mar this otherwise valuable annotated bibliography. A useful index concludes the work. Recommended for special collections.

Slide, Anthony. FILMS ON FILM HISTORY. Metuchen: The Scarecrow Press, 1979. 242pp.

This splendid resource book contains data on more than 500 films--features, shorts, documentaries, compilations--dealing with the development of the movies. The major omissions relate to documentaries on the making of movies and productions made for television. The major complaints relate to the fact that the filmography is more about film personalities than about film history. In almost every other respect, Slide provides an invaluable guide to films about particular studios, personalities, or genres. The films are arranged alphabetically by title, and there is a subject index for readers interested in an alternative route. Each annotation includes information about length, gauge (in which the compilation or documentary was originally made and not the film's excerpts included), cast and crew credits, summary of the subject matter, and occasional critical comments. As always, the author's scholarly intuition provides more than does the average reference material. In this case, he lists many films not currently available in America, on the valid assumption that these films might someday be in distribution. In addition, he profiles two of the most important archivists in film history: Paul Killiam and Robert Youngston. The book concludes with a directory of film companies and distributors. A must for any film reference library.

*Slide, Anthony, ed. THE PICTURE DANCING ON THE SCREEN: POETRY OF THE CINEMA. Vestal: The Vestal Press, 1988. Illustrated. 180pp.

A unique and very entertaining piece of scholarship, this attractive collection of poems includes pieces from film magazines of the early 1900s as well as contributions from serious writers and screen personalities. Particularly interesting are the poems about celebrities like Lillian Gish, Mae Marsh, Humphrey Bogart, and Marilyn Monroe. There are also poems authored by James Cagney, Gene Lockhart, Frank Morgan, and and James Mason. Once again, Slide demonstrates his superb contribution to the study of film history. A bibliography, author index, and subject index are included. Well worth browsing and a charming gift for film lovers.

FILM HISTORIES

GENERAL

Bardeche, Maurice, and Robert Brasillach. THE HISTORY OF MOTION PICTURES. Trans. and ed. Iris Barry. New York: W. W. Norton, 1938. Illustrated. 412pp. New York: Arno Press, 1970.

Written by two politicized French authors, this controversial book mainly recounts a film history of five national cinemas (France, Russia, Germany, Italy, and America) from 1895 to 1935 (with Barry providing an overview of the years from 1936 to 1938).[48] The authors divide their subject into six major sections. Part One covers the birth of film from the mid-1890s to 1908, focusing on the pioneering experiments, the contributions of the Lumiere brothers and Georges Melies, the significance of the Musee Grevin, the styles of early comedies and animated cartoons, the rise of narrative films, and the appearance of talking films at the 1900 Paris Exposition. Part Two discusses the pre-World War I period (1908-1914), highlighting FILM D' ART, the Italian costume films, European national cinemas, the rise of film comedy, the appeal of serials, and the development of the American film industry. Part Three continues the surveys of the national cinemas during World War I, drawing attention to Italy's loss and Scandinavia's gain in status with producers in the United States and paying appropriate homage to the famous names of the day. Part Four discusses how each of the national cinemas (including Scandinavia) contributed to the art of the film between 1919 and 1923, again citing the major artists and trends. Part Five sentimentalizes why the mid- to late-1920s are considered the classic era of silent movies. Attention is also given to the authors' reasons for believing that the art of the film died with the coming of sound. Part Six examines the talkies between 1929 and 1935, touching on a number of predictable topics and events in each of the national cinemas (including Scandinavia). A final section reflecting forty years of film history harps on the fact that film to date has "been primarily an industry, and often the basest of them." Barry does a fine job of noting the authors' errors and biases, particularly their anti-American tone. The book's commentary ends with films in 1938. A film titles index and a general index are included. Recommended for special collections.

*Beaver, Frank E. ON FILM: A HISTORY OF THE MOTION PICTURE. New York: McGraw-Hill Book Company, 1983. Illustrated. 530pp.

"The intention of ON FILM," Beaver writes, "is to trace the development and progress of an art form that was born of technological innovation, nurtured by commercial enterprise, and brought to full stature by a host of international visionaries: directors, producers, studio chieftains, cinematographers, editors,

---

[48]   For a critical commentary on the authors, see *Alice Yaeger Kaplan, REPRODUCTIONS OF BANALITY: FASCISM, LITERATURE, AND FRENCH INTELLECTUAL LIFE (Minneapolis: University of Minnesota Press, 1986), pp.142-92.

performers, and writers." Emphasizing primarily artistic and stylistic accomplishments, this conventional chronology clearly favors the silent era over the sound decades (235 pages for the former; 275, the latter). The illustrations are attractively reproduced, and almost all of the major AUTEURS are dutifully included. The bland and predictable concise statements about film notables lack critical insight. Moreover, the book's comprehensive ambitions periodically result in the downplaying or ignoring of a number of important movies. A glossary and general index are included. Worth browsing.

*Bohn, Thomas W., and Richard L. Stromgren. LIGHT AND SHADOWS: A HISTORY OF MOTION PICTURES. 3rd ed. Palo Alto: Mayfield Publishing Company, 1987. Illustrated.

One of the most richly designed and imaginative film histories, this highly entertaining and enjoyable textbook offers a broad coverage of the social, economic, aesthetic, political, and technological influences on the evolution of moving pictures. Bohn and Stromgren state in their preface that "Balance remains the byword of our text. As in previous editions, no lengthy side tours are taken to tangential topics. Although we've considerably expanded our coverage of film's evolution as an art, we have also, for the most part, deliberately avoided extended analyses of individual films and directors, which would be intrusive and break up the flow of our narrative." Moreover, they have "refrained from subjecting students to an encyclopedic barrage of birth and death dates, film titles, and footnotes. In short, we've not let data overwhelm and obscure what we think is an exciting story." To the book's credit, its strictly chronological approach incorporates valuable excerpts from primary documents, as well as providing useful chapter overviews and summaries, brief bibliographies, numerous photographs, an annotated outline of film history, and intriguing charts and statistical summaries. Anyone interested in a quick review of traditional scholarship neatly packaged will appreciate the skill with which the authors have synthesized a wealth of details. On the negative side, the attempt to make film history "an exciting story" oversimplifies many crucial events and developments. Particularly disturbing is the decision to ignore sources for a number of questionable assertions about the history of film. Thus we never learn what original thinking the authors brought to their efforts and whether their assertions mask crucial controversies and oversimplify complex issues. For example, they still claim that the movies operated as "chasers" at the turn-of-the-century, oversimplify what brought about changes in exhibition during the early days of films, and gloss over the influence that Italian epics had on Griffith's feature films. Almost every chapter opts for the storytelling approach rather than for the critical analyses.

On balance, readers interested in a general and attractive text on film history will enjoy this visually attractive book. Teachers trying to get film students off to a serious introduction to film study, however, are better off with a host of other texts. Well worth browsing.

*Casty, Alan. DEVELOPMENT OF THE FILM: AN INTERPRETIVE HISTORY. New York: Harcourt Brace Jovanovich, 1973. Illustrated. 426pp.

Following the familiar path of film chronologies, this work takes an AUTEURIST approach and tries to blend sophisticated observations with fast-moving prose. Casty sees the history of film as "not only the process of advancing or expanding into a state of the art that effectuates more and more complex combinations of its possiblities, but also the nature of the process. That nature is to grow out and extend, rather than replace, to reassemble basic constituents, although with the obvious discovery and introduction of new elements along the way." His strategy is to highlight a three-stage dialectic to film history: e.g., interaction among various periods, between different cultures and business settings, and between various stages of growth and an AUTEUR's career. What he concludes is that the key stages occurred during the expressionist movement in silent films, the shift to realism during the 1930s and 1940s, and the diffusion of styles that characterized the post-WWII period. The study's value is limited by the matter-of-fact observations, the absence of references, the highly subjective evaluations, and the uncaptioned, lackluster illustrations. An index is included. Worth browsing.

*Cook, David A. A HISTORY OF NARRATIVE FILM. New York: W. W. Norton and Company, 1981. Illustrated. 721pp.
   The best of the current crop of film history texts, this imaginative and scholarly book offers a highly literate and valuable chronolgy of the evolution of films from the nineteenth century to the late 1970s. Cook emphasizes the development of narrative form, arguing that "Many of the greatest films ever made were created by artists seeking to break the constraints of this form as it defined itself at different points in time, and there is much evidence to suggest that since the 1950s the cinema has been moving in a non-narrative direction." One of the more enjoyable features of this detailed textbook is that you do not have to share Cook's controversial theory. Although he downplays the role of documentary films, animated movies, and the experimental AVANT-GARDE cinema, the gifted author provides more reliable information on these genres and the narrative film than his competitors. Particularly impressive is his handling of technological and industrial data as he discusses the evolution of film aesthetics.
   Taking an international perspective, the seventeen heavily illustrated chapters incorporate the basic information on films, major figures, important studios, significant national cinemas, and crucial events in film history. Well-captioned illustrations support assertions in the text, footnotes regularly indicate sources for his conclusions, and comprehensive bibliographies suggest further areas for study. Best of all, Cook's appreciative and informed approach to his material underscores the book's sympathetic and compassionate tone.
   This is the book to use if one seriously wants to begin to understand film history. Cook is to this generation, what Jacobs and Knight were to theirs. Highly recommended for all collections.

Cowie, Peter. EIGHTY YEARS OF CINEMA. New York: A. S. Barnes and Company, 1977. Illustrated. 323pp.
   An expanded and valuable revision of the error-ridden 1969 edition, this intriguing chronology of film history from the early days of movies to the mid-1970s is a pleasure to peruse. The idea of a year-by-year chronology of important dates, names, and films is an invaluable scheme, and Cowie regales his readers with tidbits not readily collected elsewhere. The entry for each year includes important information on films, including the country of origin, director, and a brief critical commentary. The most enjoyable section, however, is titled, "Facts of Interest." For example, the 1915 entry reminds us that Carl Laemmle opened Universal City (and produced 250 movies in his first year of operation), the Technicolor Corporation was founded, Triangle Pictures Corporation was established, Gloria Swanson got her first star billing, and Orson Welles was born. In addition, several black-and-white illustrations make the painless history lesson visually interesting. A film index is included. Well worth browsing.

*Cowie, Peter, ed. A CONCISE HISTORY OF THE CINEMA--VOLUME I: BEFORE 1940. New York: A. S. Barnes & Company, 1971. Illustrated. 212pp.
   In a skeleton narrative, a number of well-known film historians list the key films and personalities in America, Britain, France, Italy, Germany, Austria, Scandinavia, and Eastern Europe; in addition they indicate trends in documentaries, animation, economics, and technology. A selected bibliography and film title index are included. Well worth browsing.

*Cowie, Peter, ed. A CONCISE HISTORY OF THE CINEMA--VOLUME II: SINCE 1940. New York: A. S. Barnes and Company, 1971. Illustrated. 261pp.

This valuable companion volume continues the chronological overview, adding information on Japan, India, Brazil, Spain, Canada, Cuba, Switzerland, and Greece. Special attention is also called to the work of Luis Bunuel and Torre Nilsson. No bibliography is included. A film title index is provided. Well worth browsing.

Cowie, Peter, ed. HOLLYWOOD 1920-1970. New York: A. S. Barnes and Company, 1977. Illustrated. 286pp.

Originally a series of five separate paperback books on the history of America's film capital, this publication unites the works in one coffee-table edition. David Robinson covers the 1920s, stressing the social, economic, and political context that nurtured the Hollywood ethos. John Baxter reviews the 1930s, paying particular attention to film genres and the nature of the studio system. Charles Higham and Joel Greenberg discuss the 1940s, highlighting Hollywood's range of interests and its loyal audiences. Gordon Gow tackles the 1950s, pointing out the factors that led to the breakup of the studio system and the methods filmmakers used to survive. Finally, John Baxter chronicles the 1960s, revealing how the film industry rebounded as a result of new talent and a greater freedom of expression. An index is included. Well worth browsing.

*Ellis, Jack C. A HISTORY OF FILM. 2nd ed. Englewood Cliffs: Prentice-Hall, 1985. Illustrated. 447pp.

Written by a scholar who understands the classroom as well as the film industry, this useful textbook not only tells a good story, but also gives valuable insights into crucial film controversies about theory, personalities, and events. Ellis is one of the very few film historians who provides a sympathetic commentary on the problems of minorities in the film industry. For example, in discussing Griffith, the author explains that "Some critics--unable to allow for what is essentially a style, a set of conventions, a way of thinking about people and events--have tended to deplore the content while praising the form. Though other artists are infrequently subjected to this sort of dichotomy (such a separation is generally regarded as an asthetic impossibility), perhaps a similar situation existed with the dramatists immediately preceding Shakespeare, those who fashioned the framework on which the great Elizabethan plays would be created."

The chronologically developed narrative takes us from the dawn of history, through eighteenth-century experiments, to the rise of the film industry and the present makeup of international filmmaking. Ellis makes good use of illustrations, offering the best perspective on the relationship between the history of photography and film narratives. Particularly impressive are his thumbnail summaries and filmographies at the end of each of the book's twenty-three detailed and literate chapters. If Ellis's review has one problem, it is in the area of dates. A more careful editing job should correct the problems.

For instructors searching for an inexpensive and intelligent account of the evolution of film aesthetics, this a good book to consider. Recommended for special collections.

Fell, John L. A HISTORY OF FILMS. New York: Holt, Rinehart and Winston, 1979. Illustrated. 588pp.

A cleverly conceived and executed teaching resource, this general overview of film history offers a highly enjoyable introduction to the evolution and development of film narratives. Fell's AUTEURIST approach may create problems for modern scholars, who demand more theoretical and sweeping discussions of the film continuum. But instructors who want a global analysis of film history for non-film majors studying the art of the cinema as an elected course will find the author's capsule summaries, carefully identified events and issues that influenced film history,

and intelligent observations a good book to consider. It compares favorably with the
Bohn and Stromgren textbook. The problem for undergraduates seriously examining
the basics of film scholarship is not that Fell doesn't provide source information and
valuable bibliographies (he does) but that there isn't enough information given the
existence of the Cook volume. Well worth browsing.

*Kardish, Lawrence. REEL PLASTIC MAGIC: A HISTORY OF FILMS AND FILMMAKING
IN AMERICA. Boston: Little, Brown and Company, 1972. Illustrated. 297pp.
    A cleverly designed and fast-moving account of movie history, this book takes
few risks and offers no new insights. The brief, sweeping story of the rise from
technical ingenuity to worldwide film power to the alleged decline and fall of Hollywood
to a recovering giant with a bright future is told in seven chapters. The best parts
of the tale are the charming selective illustrations. The four-page annotated and
"highly selective" bibliography is an embarrassment to an undertaking of this type.
A title and general index are included. Worth browsing.

*Knight, Arthur. THE LIVELIEST ART: A PANORAMIC HISTORY OF THE MOVIES.
Rev. ed.. New York: The Macmillan Company, 1978. Illustrated. 304pp.
    Written by one of the most informed and under-rated film teachers of the present
day, this updating of the 1957 classic is an ambitious attempt to place film in the
context of historical and artistic conditions and remains one of the most influential
books in establishing movies as a subject worthy of academic study. Seven sweeping
chapters condense a lifetime of research and first-hand experiences into a valuable
perspective on films as an art form, an industry, and a social force in society.
Knight's concern with key films and personalities naturally overlooks some masters
and overemphasizes others. Moreover, the decision in this edition to drop his
stimulating annotated bibliography of the 100 best books on film is disappointing, as
is the absence of any reference material to support his penetrating accounts of
specific national film movements. Nevertheless, Knight's taste is far superior to that
of many other historians schooled in contemporary scholarly methodologies. An index
is provided. Recommended for special collections.

Lindgren, Ernest. A PICTURE HISTORY OF THE CINEMA. London: Vista Books,
1960. Illustrated. 160pp.
    Despite Lindgren's bias toward Russian films and his distaste for American
movies, this useful book makes available to readers stills from many significant motion
pictures. For the most part, Lindgren's text is accurate, informative, and helpful.
Worth browsing.

The Marshall Cavendish Learning System. THE MOVIES. London: Marshall Cavendish
Books, 1970. Illustrated. 64pp.
    Strictly for children, this beautifully illustrated volume gives a quick overview
of movies, touching on production techniques, important personalities, and major
trends. Particularly interesting is the last chapter and its treatment of IF . . .
from the film's inception till its completion. Worth browsing.

*Mast, Gerald. A SHORT HISTORY OF THE MOVIES. 4th ed. New York:
Bobbs-Merrill, 1971. Illustrated. 562pp.
    In one of the best studies of the art of the film, Mast emphasizes the techniques
and themes of major motion pictures that are available for 16mm rental. In his preface,
the author explains that "The past decade of film theory has been committed to
examining the ways that film art and entertainment are embedded in the economic
constraints and ideological constructs of our culture. The fourth edition . . .

[of this book] has not deserted its primary commitment to the major styles, periods, genres, and works of film art--and to the auteurs and artisans who created that art. On the other hand, even the most expressive and distinctive examples of film art reveal clear signs of the way our culture defines social, sexual, and personal relationships, of the ways that artistic texts (filmic or otherwise) REPRESENT certain emotional and social relationships, so that highly artifical conventions of fictional construction come to seem 'natural,' 'inevitable,' and 'simply true' to the spectator." Mast's decision, begun in the book's third edition, to increase his emphasis on social and economic factors is continued here, but the focus remains primarily on film masterpieces.   The judgments are challenging, the writing perceptive, and the films selected representational and conservative. A good bibliography and a valuable set of filmographies are included. Recommended for special collections.

*Neale, Stephen. CINEMA AND TECHNOLOGY: IMAGE, SOUND, COLOUR. Bloomington: Indiana University Press, 1985. Illustrated. 171pp.

*Reader, Keith. THE CINEMA. New York: David McKay, 1979. Illustrated.   200pp.

Rhode, Eric. A HISTORY OF THE CINEMA: FROM ITS ORIGINS TO 1970. New York: Hill and Wang, 1976. Illustrated. 674pp.
     Once you get over the author's anti-American bias, this reflective history book offers a fascinating and engrossing discussion of the evolution of motion pictures from the invention of photography in the eighteenth century to social, economic, aesthetic, and political issues that shaped international cinema at the end of the 1960s. What makes Rhode's sweeping overview of film genres, studios, national cinemas, AUTEURS, and technological breakthroughs unique is his unique perspective. Where other film historians skillfully blend traditional accounts with current research, Rhode prides himself on fresh interpretations and personal recollections. He seems to step back from the vast documentation accumulated over the past sixty years and comments on the events and personalities as if they were complex issues requiring a balance judgment on the strengths and weaknesses of each period, reminding us that we are reading about human beings instead of demi-gods. Dividing his material into five major periods--Before 1920, the 1920s, the 1930s, 1940-1956, and 1956-1970--he weaves into his comprehensive view of international cinema a very personal and a highly informed set of judgments that force the reader to pause and reflect on the issues, rather than focus on dates, names, films, and places.   Rarely in works of this sort does one find such original comments and literate assertions. Although not suitable for introductory courses on film history, this study is ideal for graduate students reevaluating several years of course work and reductionist perspectives. No one in this selected category of film historians appears as sure of himself or his approach as does Rhode. The result is that the book has an appeal that goes far beyond classroom requirements and emerges as an important commentary on film history valuable to serious scholars. Endnotes, a bibliography, and an index are included. Recommended for special collections.

Robinson, David. THE HISTORY OF WORLD CINEMA, Rev. and expanded. New York: Stein and Day, 1981. Illustrated. 494pp.
     An intelligent and concise account of film history, this book offers a thumbnail overview of general issues from the eighteenth-century interest in moving pictures, to the end of the 1970s and the status of the international film industry. As Robinson points out in his preface, "What I hope to achieve is, indeed, an outline of film history--a skeleton chart, with a few landmarks dotted in, on which the reader can plot his [sic] own experiences of cinema." The illustrations are adequate, the observations traditional, and the format acceptable. Ten chapters identify the major developments, comment on the standard topics, and summarize the important films and

personalities. The trouble is that it is too truncated for serious students and not appealing enough for introductory courses. Its greatest value may be in offering undergraduates an out-of-class review of material covered in more detail in separate courses. Its greatest weaknesses are the absence of footonotes and a bibliography. A good set of filmographies and an index are included. Well worth browsing.

Rotha, Paul, in collaboration with Richard Griffith. THE FILM TILL NOW: A SURVEY OF WORLD CINEMA. New York: Twayne Publishers, 1960. Illustrated. 820pp.
      This highly personal account of Rotha's opinions about the silent era is invaluable for its observations on artistic developments and the inclusion of worthwhile appendexes, while Griffith's commentary on sound films and their relationship to filmgoers is entertaining and stimulating reading. The book is one of the best and most accurate sources on film history in general. Recommmended for special collections.

Schickel, Richard. MOVIES: THE HISTORY OF AN ART AND AN INSTITUTION. New York: Basic Books, 1964. Illustrated. 208pp.
      This short and respectful account of film history, written by LIFE's film critic, has a heavy emphasis on American movies. Schickel's observations are provocative and entertaining. Ten fast-moving chapters call attention to the standard works and pioneers who nurtured the early flickers into a great motion picture industry. Unfortunately, this affectionate study is marred by glaring bloopers--e.g., MOANA (1926) was co-directed by Robert Flaherty and F. W. Murnau--and outrageous judgments--e.g., THE ROAD/LA STRADA (1954) is a "wretched" film. An index is included. Worth browsing.

Sultanik, Aaron. FILM: A MODERN ART. New York: Cornwall Books, 1986. 503pp.

Taylor, Deems, Bryant Hale, and Marcelene Peterson. A PICTORIAL HISTORY OF THE MOVIES. Rev. and enlarged. New York: Simon and Schuster, 1949. Illustrated. 376pp.
      Unfortunately, this well-conceived book is poorly designed. Many valuable stills on films up to 1941 are badly reproduced, the chronology is muddled, and the commentary inaccurate. Approach with caution.

*Tyler, Parker. CLASSICS OF THE FOREIGN FILM: A PICTORIAL TREASURY. New York: Bonanza Books, 1962. Illustrated. 253pp.
      One of the best picture commentaries yet available on foreign films. The text is well-written, informative, and accurate. Tyler is particularly good on choosing excellent stills and then putting down precise, useful annotations. Recommended for special collections.

Wiseman, Thomas. CINEMA. New York: A. S. Barnes and Company, 1965. Illustrated. 181pp.
      This terse, general history of movies makes up in its subjective commentary what it lacks in illustrative excellence. The author claims that he is providing "people seriously interested in the cinema, but not as yet very informed about it, with a concise introduction to the subject." Like Sgt. Friday of DRAGNET fame, Wiseman gives us just the "facts." Typical of the sweeping and highly subjective interpretations is his assertion that "Comedians like Harold Lloyd and Buster Keaton, though not in the same class as Chaplin, were often brilliantly inventive." Unfortunately, the book's twelve chapters do not go deeply enough into their topics

to be considered serious history, nor are there enough pictures to make the book valuable as a pictorial guide. A bibliography and index are included. Worth browsing.

Wright, Basil. THE LONG VIEW. New York: Alfred A. Knopf, 1974. Illustrated. 730pp.

Along with Rotha's comprehensive view of film history, this valuable study presents the perspective of a noted filmmaker on the events and personalities that shaped the art and manufacturing of motion pictures. Unlike almost every other film historian, content to describe and to record specific events and issues instrumental in creating an international film continuum, Wright offers intriguing insights into the personal problems of the filmmakers themselves. This is both the book's strength and weakness. Nowhere else can one find an insider's approach to film history that reveals so candid an assessment of personal likes and dislikes over ninety years of film history. On the other hand, Wright's subjective reactions distort not only his interpretations of films and personalities, but also undercut his credibility. The book contains so many factual errors that it is best read as an autobiographical journey through the film world rather than an objective history of film. Worth browsing.

BRITAIN

Armes, Roy. A CRITICAL HISTORY OF BRITISH CINEMA. New York: Oxford University Press, 1978. Illustrated. 374pp.

Most British film histories struggle with explanations of why the nation's record is so spotty and sporadic. The pattern is to brag about the first decade of pioneering films, explain away the remainder of the silent era, carp about the debilitating influence of American studios on British film production, throw some bones to government aid and documentary filmmakers, praise the wartime propaganda efforts, despair over the literary pretentiousness of the postwar period, praise the rise of exciting new filmmakers in the late fifties and early sixties, and then lament over the disillusionment of the seventies. Armes's account is no exception. His critical perspective on eighty years of British filmmaking is divided into four major sections. Part One analyzes how the British participated in the invention of the cinema, the development of an indigenous industry, and the birth of narrative film. The author asserts that film evolved as it did not because of any "readily perceivable determining factors contained in its beginnings," but because the middle-class businessmen, seeking fame and profits, felt that their interests would be achieved by mastering "technical perfection in the complete reproduction of life." The result was a film industry that stood silently by as other nations developed the art of the cinema.

Part Two traces the end of the silent era (marked by the release of the 1929 film BLACKMAIL), through the 1930s with the emergence of two distinct British theatrical film traditions: "prestige productions with literary pretensions and international casts which (apart from those made by Korda) usually failed to break into the American market and so lost money, and the commercially very successful but generally despised comedies aimed primarily at the home market . . . ." An entire chapter is devoted to the styles of Alfred Hitchcock (a director who trifled with international uncertainties) and Anthony Asquith (a director obsessed with Edwardian nostalgia), using both men as illustrations of British filmakers devoid of any theorical awareness of what movies were capable of doing. For the most part, the British are seen as content with making conventional film narratives based on nineteenth-century literary models and as being dominated by Hollywood products. The one British producer comparable to the American movie moguls is the Hungarian-born Alexander Korda, whose London Films are depicted as episodic formulas with "parallel plots and epigrammatic dialogue." Most important, Armes insists that Korda's "imperial rhetoric" reveals "the dominant myths of the age," showing an establishment based upon status and power that bears little relation to the democracy it professes to admire and to encourage. The section closes with a positive analysis of why John Grierson and the documentary movement shaped British attitudes toward films through the bleak days of World War II.

Part Three continues the author's social and cultural perspective with a discussion of the documentary World War II films, especially those made by Humphrey Jennings. Pointing out the essential unity between the war years and the post-WWII period, Armes explores the difficulties of the British film industry and the major roles played by J. Arthur Rank, Michael Balcon, David Lean, Carol Reed, and Anthony Asquith. Two men singled out for special attention are Michael Powell and Thorold Dickinson. Although they made different types of films, each director, in Armes's judgment, rejected the conventions of realism developed during the war and remained remote from the literary traditions of his peers.

Part Four presents an overview of why films declined as a mass entertainment medium for working-class audiences in the 1950s, and how filmmakers experimented with new approaches to comedies, action films, and screen adaptations in an effort to draw young people back into movie theaters. The emphasis is on a number of popular directors and commercially successful movies like the horror remakes at Hammer Films. Pointing out that the late 1950s witnessed a rise of new talent in dramatic and literary circles, Armes reviews how documentary films, under the umbrella of Free Cinema and the Woodfall Company, responded to these developments. The 1960s continued the British film renaissance, with the irony being that many of the most prestiguous filmakers working in England were foreigners: e.g., Michelangelo Antonioni, Francois Truffaut, Stanley Kubrick, Joseph Losey, and Roman Polanski. The author then turns his attention to the growing influence of television in the training of British filmmakers like Ken Russell, Kenneth Loach, and Peter Watkins. The concluding chapter on alternative cinemas strikes a bleak note, observing how dependent the British film industry had once more become as a result of relying on American financing, and how that funding had rapidly disappeared.

In his epilogue, Armes argue that his eighty-year history demonstrates that "the British cinema has been characterized by a greater degree of conservatism than any other medium of expression." This is evident not only in theatrical films, but also in documentaries. The result is that there is little imagination left in contemporary British films or filmmakers. The one hope that the author holds out is that TV will free the movie "from its traditional role of providing entertainment for an undifferentiated mass audience."

Since Armes is a formidable critic, his prosaic writing style in this overly ambitious and flawed survey should not discourage anyone from perusing his many terse plot synopses and thumbnail evaluations of personalities and events. What is missing in this straightforward account is a sense of enthusiasm for the subject. It's almost as if the author felt he had the thankless task of finding something positive to say about British film history. Endnotes, a bibliography, and an index are provided. Well worth browsing.

*Barr, Charles, ed. ALL OUR YESTERDAYS: 90 YEARS OF BRITISH CINEMA. London: British Film Institute, 1986. Illustrated. 446pp.

A provocative collection of essays, this anthology is linked to the ambitious retrospective on British films co-sponsored by the Museum of Modern Art and the British Film Institute in New York between 1984 and 1987. As Barr states, this work "brings together a number of DIACHRONIC studies of particular 'traditions' and other aspects and strands of British national cinema, tracing them through the decades." Barr is determined to offset two especially caustic opinions about British film history: Satyajit Ray's 1963 comment, "I do not think the British are temperamentally equipped to make the best use of the movie camera";[49] and Francois Truffaut's 1967 quip "that

---

[49]   Satyajit Ray, OUR FILMS (Bombay: Orient Longman, 1976), p.144.

there's something about England that's anticinematic."[50] Because this attitude is "so prevalent and deep-rooted," Barr begins the collection with an incisive review of "what it is that switches so many people off the subject. . . ." Particular attention is paid to the evolution of indigenous journals from CLOSE-UP (1927) to SCREEN (1971) that have set the tone for the derisive evaluation of British filmmakers in comparison with Hollywood and European art house directors. The author takes careful aim at the paradox of significant British artists like Charlie Chaplin and Alfred Hitchcock, who are universally recognized, and the argument that the British are "temperamentally unsuited" for filmmaking.

Five of the twenty-one essays discuss the complex relationship between film and other media and form the nucleus of this revisionist approach to nearly a century of British film history. Also included are essays on film and its ties to government, the realist and non-realist approaches to filmmaking, a look at independent filmmaking from 1929 to 1984, an overview of British animation, British films and the underworld, Scotland as an illustration of how disparate communities are united under one umbrella, the impact of Hollywood on British filmmakers, and a series of case studies on three films--MANDY (1952), THE SHIP THAT DIED OF SHAME (1955), and FRENZY (1972); three stars--Paul Robeson, Diana Dors, and Dirk Bogarde; two directors--Lewin Fitzhamon and Humphrey Jennings; and one organization--The Film Society from 1925 to 1939. What emerges is a delightful introduction and long overdue re-evaluation of Britain's film contributions to the cinema. An appendix listing key British films over the past ninety years, a selected bibliography, and a general index are included. Recommended for special collections.

Betts, Ernest. THE FILM BUSINESS: A HISTORY OF BRITISH CINEMA, 1896-1972. London: George Allen and Unwin, 1973. Illustrated. 349pp.

Written by an author who first began writing about films in the late 1920s for CLOSE UP, this book "considers not only the films themselves but their financial and political background, British films being preeminently a concern of the state." Betts takes the by-now predictable attitude that his native films are by the 1960s "as much American as British, if not more so." He divides his superficial history into seven major parts. The first section, subdivided into six terse chapters, traces the beginnings of British movies with appropriate kudos to William Friese-Greene and Birt Acres; moves on to the works of Cecil Hepworth, Robert W. Paul, and others; lists the early intervention of the government in industry matters; describes the patriotic efforts of men like George Pearson and G. B. ("Bertie") Samuelson during World War I; and touches on how the Quota Act of 1927 led to an "abuse of quickies" in the late 1920s. The section concludes with an outdated attack on America's role in British film affairs and repeats a number of discredited myths about the transition to sound films.

Part 2--"Development"--is subdivided into five uneven chapters and insists that the slow creative progress of British films was not due to the lack of interest by "the Wardour Street tradesmen," but to "the peculiar structure of the industry and the external pressures [read Parliament and Hollywood] applied to it." Following a chapter on the rise of principal British film companies, Betts surveys the influence of J. Arthur Rank, John Maxwell, and Lady Yule during the 1930s, the crises that occurred as World War II approached, and the conditions of filmmaking in Britain during this hectic decade.

Part 3--"The Film Matures"--is subdivided into six entertaining chapters, focusing primarily on important directors and producers like Alfred Hitchcock, Anthony Asquith, Victor Saville, Herbert Wilcox, Alexander Korda, Filippo del Giudice, and Gabriel Pascal. In addition to touching on their films and showing the political and social context in which they were made, Betts stresses the problems of censorship during the 1930s. Typical of his style is the observation that "The

---

[50]   Francois Truffaut, with Helen G. Scott, HITCHCOCK (New York: Simon and Schuster, 1967), p.89.

conditions of film-making when Korda entered the field were not encouraging. Films, it is true, were being produced but their directors too often share an unhappy relationship with the distributors and an absurdly complicated ritual of borrowing and lending is required to get a film off the ground."

Part 4--"Documents and War Films"--is subdivided into four chapters and is an upbeat account of how the documentary movement provided a superb contrast to crass and lackluster entertainment films. Particular attention is devoted to the effect that World War II had on documentary and theatrical filmmakers, with an emphasis on the use of propaganda to bolster the war effort. The most enjoyable sections describe the shift in popular taste that started in 1943 and the filmmakers who led the way. Most of the commentary reads like a list of film titles, followed by a brief annotation.

Part 5--"End of the Great Days"--is subdivided into five intriguing chapters surveying the changes brought about by the war, the 1944 report of an inquiry detailing the monopolistic structure of the pre-WWII industry (TENDENCIES TO MONOPOLY IN THE CINEMATOGRAPH FILM INDUSTRY), the impact of that report in the post-WWII period, how TV affected the downtrodden filmmakers in the 1950s, and the importance of Ealing Studios to British film history. The writing is straightforward, and the thumbnail information provides a succinct guide to the standard observations reported elsewhere.

Part 6--"Transition Stage"--contains two short chapters on the fate of British Lion Films and how the late fifties saw the end of the "old tradition of great starry productions in luxury settings . . . [and] film now . . . [which became] part of the great debate of the mid-century and is absorbed in the cultural revolution." Although we're given a brief synopsis of which films worked and which failed, the material is too brief and subjective to be of much value.

Part 7--"Into the 1970s"--is subdivided into three simplistic chapters zeroing in on a number of new faces and personalities that characterize an industry that in 1971 is at a "standstill" and where "a good 50 percent of the technicians in the industry are out of work, and at a time, too, when both commercially and artistically British films are at their highest level." Betts reiterates his opposition to government interference and to the continued influence of American films. Ending on a note of pessimism, he decries the business nature of filmmaking and the obstacles it places in the way of creative filmmakers.

Although the book suffers from a rushed narrative and from an unscholarly foundation, it does provide the reactions of an informed critic, screenwriter, and publicist who worked inside the British film industry for many years. His highly subjective observations give one a feel for the traditional antibusiness charges hurled against the British system for over eighty years. An appendix containing John Grierson's views on the status of the documentary in the post-WWII period, a selective bibliography, endnotes, and a general index are included. Well worth browsing.

Butler, Ivan. CINEMA IN BRITAIN: AN ILLUSTRATED SURVEY. South Brunswick: A. S. Barnes and Company, 1973. Illustrated. 307pp.

Curran, James, and Vincent Porter, eds. BRITISH CINEMA HISTORY. Totowa: Barnes and Noble Books, 1983. 320pp.

A revisionist anthology primarily concerned with social and economic perspectives, this intriguing work includes provocative essays (some of which are surveys and some of which are case studies) by nineteen scholars. The book, divided into four uneven parts, begins with two general overviews of film history. Raymond Williams argues that film history cannot be separated from other aspects of life, while Philip Corrigan attacks conventional film historians for their failure to analyze how films influenced the day-to-day lives and values of British audiences over an eighty-year period.

Part 2 focuses on the development of the British cinema from its roots in the 1890s, through its emergence as a significant entertainment force in the 1930s and 1940s, to its decline during the post-World War II era. Michael Chanan's opening essay describes how British films evolved from a cottage industry in the 1890s, to a worldwide industry in the 1920s, in large measure because the government agreed (i.e., the Cinematograph Film Act of 1927) to protect British producers from being ruined by Hollywood distributors. Simon Hartog bridges the years from 1927 to the end of the 1930s, showing how the state's involvement in British films played a crucial role in shaping business practices and production policies. Margaret Dickinson then discusses the problems that led British films between the forties and the sixties to shift from an extremely important mass medium and business, to a minor form of entertainment and a secondary part of the leisure industry.

Part 3 investigates the structures and practice of filmmaking, starting with Stuart Hood's assessment of John Grierson, the documentary movement, and the contradictory forces that influenced the rise of the movement in the late twenties to its demise in the fifties. Trevor Ryan follows up with a review of the British Labour movement's unsuccessful cinematic battle against mainstream Hollywood and British feature films. Rosaleen Smyth's essay on how the Colonial Office propagandized British values in movies distributed in Africa reveals one more unsuccessful attempt to produce alternatives to mainstream films. On the other hand, Nicholas Pronay and Jeremy Croft use the production and distribution of THE LIFE AND DEATH OF COLONEL BLIMP (1943) as a prime example of how the Ministry of Information did a first-rate propaganda job during World War II. Robert Murphy follows with a reworking of familiar arguments on why the Rank Organization failed to gain a foothold in the American market between 1944 and 1949. Vincent Porter offers his perspectives on two different but powerful British film producers--Michael Balcon (Ealing Studios) and James Carreras (Hammer Films)--and the influences each had on post-WWII British film production. Janet Woollacott takes a feminist position on the production of James Bond movies, arguing that 007's relationship with women ever since the early sixties reflects shifts in ideology synthesized in THE SPY WHO LOVED ME (1977). Simon Blanchard and Sylvia Harvey conclude the section on structures and practice with a superficial critique of the post-WWII independent cinema, concentrating on the years from 1966 to 1981.

Part 4 deals with the cultural and ideological significance of selected film genres. Jeffrey Richards begins with an analysis of imperial films of the 1930s: e.g., films emphasizing British culture, like the trilogies produced by Alexander Korda--SANDERS OF THE RIVER (1935), THE DRUM (1938), and THE FOUR FEATHERS (1939)--and Michael Balcon--RHODES OF AFRICA (1936), THE GREAT BARRIER (1936), and KING SOLOMON'S MINES (1937). Sue Ansinall looks back on the way in which "women's" movies from 1943 to 1953 (films with heterosexual emphases that appealed to women) registered changes in gender roles that reinforced the transition in society from relatively independent jobs, to ones of subordinate status. Ian Green takes a similar route in his essay on the Ealing Studio comedies from PASSPORT TO PIMLICO (1949) to THE MAN IN THE WHITE SUIT (1955), insisting that these comic social fantasies imperceptibly conditioned audiences to accept the STATUS QUO. John Hill examines the "socially-realistic" films of the late 1950s and early 1960s--e.g., ROOM AT THE TOP (1958), LOOK BACK IN ANGER (1959), SATURDAY NIGHT AND SUNDAY MORNING (1961), and THIS SPORTING LIFE (1963)--and attacks their alleged "progressive" attitudes toward class structure and heterosexual relationships. Marion Jordon's concluding review of the CARRY ON film series from 1958 to 1980 makes a futile case for the movies' being a reflection of vanishing masculine blue-collar values.

Given the range of topics and the stimulating accumulation of details, the overall benefits of the anthology are considerable. The one major regret is that the films themselves don't have a greater share of the history. In that way, it would be more useful as a historical survey rather than as a hit-or-miss potpourri of interesting observations. Fifty helpful pages of endnotes, an appendix statistically summarizing historical changes in British films, and a selective bibliography (almost exclusively of British publications) are included. Recommended for special collections.

*Gifford, Denis. BRITISH CINEMA: AN ILLUSTRATED GUIDE. New York: A. S. Barnes and Company, 1968. Illustrated. 176pp.

"This book," Gifford immodestly explains, "is a first attempt to put between handy covers at a handy price the complete story of British films in factual form. It is a kind of All Time Who's Who of stars and directors, 546 of them, selected for their contribution to the overall seventy year scene." Gifford may not deliver all that he promises, but what is there was useful for its day. The main body of the work is an alphabetically arranged dictionary from Birt Acres to Mai Zetterling, containing information about name, year of birth and year of death (when appropriate), profession within the industry, birthplace, name at birth, profession prior to entering the film industry, year begun in films and specific job, pertinent family data, terse commentary on work done in films, and a chronological filmography with dates. At the back of the book is an alphabetically arranged film title index of theatrical movies, including the director's name in parentheses when that individual is not listed in the major section. Well worth browsing.

Gifford, Denis. THE ILLUSTRATED WHO'S WHO IN BRITISH FILMS. London: B. T. Batsford, 1978. Illustrated. 334pp.

A no-frills approach to a thousand British film personalities who worked during eighty years of film history, this book is a follow-up to Gifford's 1968 effort. The alphabetically arranged entries include not only stars but also character actors and directors. Occasionally, a few writers and producers sneak in when their careers overlap with performing or directing. Fourteen separate bits of statistics appear in most of the entries, ranging from professional name to titles and honors, birth date, and date of entry into the profession, and extensive filmography. Regrettably, less than a third of the people profiled get their pictures in the book. On the other hand, there is an invaluable biographical bibliography listed by personalities, including those whose film contributions extend beyond the scope of the book itself. Well worth browsing.

Perry, George. THE GREAT BRITISH PICTURE SHOW. Foreword David Puttnam. Boston: Little, Brown and Company, 1985. Illustrated. 368pp.

Slightly revised and updated from a 1974 edition, this lucid and entertaining study is written by the film critic of the ILLUSTRATED LONDON NEWS. His twenty-six chatty chapters explore British film history from its pre-cinematic days in the early 1880s, through the silent era, the Depression and World War II, up to the present boom with Oscars for GANDHI (1983) and CHARIOTS OF FIRE (1985). What is most refreshing about Perry's approach is the balance between national pride and objectivity. For example, he writes that "Any examination in detail of the British contribution to the motion picture reveals a disappointing diminution in its importance since the remarkable pioneering period which lasted from the last decade of the nineteenth century to around 1906." He then adds, "The number of world-reknowned figures produced by Britain is few, and most are actors and actresses fortunate enough in voice or physique to claim attention on either side of the Atlantic." Perry also admits that his country lags behind in the number of "internationally regarded 'pantheon' directors," acknowledging that giants like Hitchcock and Chaplin are identified more with America than with Britain. Part of the reason given for the nation's failure is that it shares a common language with America, leading to a dichotomy of British filmmaking. The story of how that split occurred and evolved allows Perry to critique movie moguls, government regulations and support, famous personalities, and important studios. A fifty-nine page annotated biographical guide to personalities, a slight bibliography, and a useful index are included. Recommended for special collections.

Warren, Patricia. THE BRITISH FILM COLLECTION 1896-1984: A HISTORY OF THE BRITISH CINEMA IN PICTURES. Foreword Sir Richard Attenborough. Salem: Salem House, 1984. Illustrated. 248pp.

A splendid illustrated guide to British films in the grand tradition of the Griffith-Mayer book, THE MOVIES, this study offers something for everyone. Six beautifully illustrated chapters, each beginning with a brief introduction, review the evolution of British movies from the earliest attempts that ran for less than a minute and were restricted to daylight filmmaking, through the decade of the teens when the British Board of Film Censors (established in 1912) helped shape the industry's direction, to the rise of new film companies in the twenties, and into the booming thirties with imaginative production heads like Michael Balcon, John Maxwell, J. Arthur Rank, Herbert Wilcox, and Alexander Korda. Additional chapters with high-quality reproductions chart how the stars and personalities, operating under government control, responded to the propaganda challenges of World War II and the effect the postwar period had on British studios, followed by a description of the changes taking place in the British film industry during the fifties, to the social and political upheavals that ushered in a wave of realistic films in the sixties, to the economic perils faced by every major British studio in the seventies, and concluding with an upbeat summary of how a "fragmented and frustrated" British industry responded to challenges in the eighties.

Crisp writing, entertaining information, and striking illustrations characterize this effort. A bibliography and index of films are included. Recommended for special collections.

FRANCE

*Armes, Roy. FRENCH CINEMA. New York: Oxford University Press, 1985. Illustrated. 310pp.

The best one-volume English-language history of French film, this well-researched and thoughtfully written study is a comprehensive and invaluable guide to events, personalities, and films. The focus is on the "successive styles of film production adopted by groups of film makers in response to changing theoretical conceptions of cinema and differing economic, social and cultural circumstances." Armes is not concerned with denigrating artists who failed to keep step with evolving patterns, but with calling attention to filmmakers who were unique in their own work. He, therefore, dwells on "discontinuities and similarities over time," on a "cluster of attitudes and approaches and assumptions" that he designates a filmmaker's style. Relying heavily on the principles outlined by Thomas Kuhn in his book, THE STRUCTURE OF SCIENTIFIC REVOLUTIONS, Armes offers an intriguing study that examines "developments as they occur without clouding the issue by bringing in concepts appropriate only for a later period." Thus, the periods covered in the book's highly informative thirteen chapters are related to "internal economic developments of production, distribution, and control in the cinema [i.e., the outbreak of World War I and the Nazi occupation]." Most enjoyable is the author's refusal to see film history as a progressive story. An extensive bibliography and useful index are included. Highly recommended for special collections.

Armes, Roy. FRENCH FILM. New York: E. P. Dutton and Company, 1970. Illustrated. 160pp.

A brief survey in words and pictures of forty directors from Louis Lumiere to Claude Lelouch, this handy analysis does a good job of reviewing recurrent images and diverse styles in the French cinema. The stills are well-chosen and nicely reproduced. Five concise chapters cover the heritage of the silent era (e.g., Georges Melies, Max Linder, Louis Feuillade, Abel Gance, Jacques Feyder, and Rene Clair), the AVANT-GARDE period to the days of the German occupation (e.g., Jean Cocteau, Jean Renoir, Jean Vigo, Max Ophuls, and Marcel Carne), the postwar era (e.g., Claude Autant-Lara, Henri-Georges Clouzot, Jacques Tati, and Robert Bresson), the new cinema of 1959 (e.g., Roger Vadim, Louis Malle, Claude Chabrol, Francois Truffaut, and Alain Resnais), and Jean-Luc Godard's impact on the sixties (e.g., Jacques Demy, Alain Robbe-Grillet, and Pierre Etaix). A bibliography and film index are included. The major drawback is the extremely fragile binding. Well worth browsing.

Buss, Robin. THE FRENCH THROUGH THEIR FILMS. New York: Ungar Publishing Company, 1988. Illustrated. 165pp.
An ambitious cultural study of French filmmaking from the turn of the century to the present, this highly entertaining and enjoyable study offers a novel approach to French film history. It can be read as history or used as a reference guide. Buss divides his material into two major parts. In the first section, he provides five chapters discussing not only the evolution of French films, but also how they grew out of their times and how they treated social and geographical differences, major historical events, and everyday family life. In reflecting on his overview, Buss concludes the intriguing section with a reminder that it may be more important for sociologists and historians to examine the people who saw the films, than the films themselves. Having admitted that his approach has produced a diverse picture filled with contradictions, he writes, "What I have tried to do is . . . to show, not the French, but the French as they appear in their films." In the second half of the book, Buss provides annotated filmographies on twelve topics: culture, history, war and empire, politics and religion, the middle class, working class and industry, provincial and rural life, Paris, crime and the law, women and the family, childhood and youth, and fantasies. Access to information on the more than 200 films listed is facilitated by a film title index and a general index. Well worth browsing.

*Martin, Marcel. FRANCE. New York: A. S. Barnes and Company, 1971. Illustrated. 191pp.
This illustrated guide to 400 major personalities in French film history provides thumbnail information on key films from the silent era to 1971. The alphabetically arranged entries give birth dates, place of birth (and death date when appropriate), brief career facts, and a filmography. A valuable film index provides the dates. Well worth browsing.

Sadoul, Georges. FRENCH FILM. London: The Falcon Press, 1953. Illustrated. 131pp. New York: Arno Press, 1972. 130pp.
Part of the National Cinema series under the general editorship of Roger Manvell, this valuable evaluation and pioneering record of French film history examines how that nation contributed to the development of film as an art and as a form of social expression. Ten concise chapters provide data not only on the major AUTEURS but also on the conditions that influenced their work. The one noticeable omission is Jean Cocteau's ORPHEUS/ORPHEE (1950). An index is included. Recommended for special collections.

*Slide, Anthony. FIFTY CLASSIC FRENCH FILMS, 1912-1982: A PICTORIAL RECORD. New York: Dover Publications, 1987. Illustrated. 152pp.

GERMANY

*Bucher, Felix, with Leonhard H. Gmur. GERMANY: AN ILLUSTRATED GUIDE. New York: A. S. Barnes and Company, 1970. Illustrated. 298pp.

A worthwhile dictionary covering the work of over 400 directors, performers, technicians, and other essential personnel, this handy guide also provides an index to 6,000 films from the end of World War I to 1969. The alphabetically arranged entries include information on year of birth (and death when appropriate), a thumbnail comment on the individual's role in film industry (e.g., actor or director) and where he/she began, concluding with a filmography (all in German and without dates). Especially useful are the wallet-size illustrations that periodically appear throughout the book. Worth browsing.

Manvell, Roger, and Heinrich Fraenkel. THE GERMAN CINEMA. New York: Praeger Publishers, 1971. Illustrated. 159pp.

In a brief but valuable study of the German film from 1895 to the late sixties, Manvell and Fraenkel provide a good overview of the main phases of German films as they move through pioneering days to moments of great beauty and periods of infamy, concluding with a renaissance in the 1960s. Of the eight chapters, two explore the silent era, touching on the significant contributions of Reinhardt, Pabst, and Murnau; one covers the sound film before Hitler; two detail filmmaking in Nazi Germany; and three chronicle the post-war period to the resurgence in German film artistry. The authors make clear that in their view "there has been a tendency to over-interpret the silent film before Hitler, especially in the case of the so-called expressionist films. We do not want to under-estimate the dedicated work of Siegfried Kracauer, who was known personally to both of us, but we believe his book FROM CALIGARI TO HITLER greatly exaggerates the significance of many of the films about which he writes, and so distorts through overemphasis what is no doubt a partial truth in his arguments. Lotte Eisner, we believe, in her book L'ECRAN DEMONIAQUE, offers a more balanced approach to the macabre and expressionist German cinema . .   .   These films, though often impressive and beautiful, are, we think, less 'significant', both socially and psychologically, than they have been made to seem." Endnotes, a bibliography, and two indexes on names and films are included. Well worth browsing.

Wollenberg, H. H. FIFTY YEARS OF GERMAN FILM. London: The Falcon Press, 1948. Illustrated. 48pp. New York: Arno Press, 1972.

A simpler account of the development of the German film industry than Kracauer's, the emphasis is still sociological, but Wollenberg's comments add to Kracauer's thoughts. The book also contains some useful illustrations. Well worth browsing.

ITALY

Jarratt, Vernon. THE ITALIAN CINEMA. London: The Falcon Press, 1951. Rpt. New York: Arno Press, 1972. 115pp.

A major source on Italian film history from 1907 to the late 1940s, this pioneering study provides a good balance between the early days and the important post-WWII neo-realism period. The nine brief but informative chapters focus on the contributions of producers like Gustavo Lombardo, Ernesto Pacelli, Alberto Fassini, Alberto Blanc, Alberto del Gallo di Roccagiovane, Enrico di S. Martino, and Rodolfo Kanzler, as well as directors like Enrico Guazzoni, Giovanni Pastrone, Alessandro Blasetti, Mario Camerini, Renato Castellani, Mario Costa, Francesca De Robertis, Vittorio De Sica, Luisa Ferida, Alberto Lattuada, Roberto Rossellini, Mario Soldati, Luchino Visconti, and Luigi Zampa. The comments are both descriptive and evaluative. The many black-and-white illustrations add considerably to the book's appeal and function as a postive reinforcement of the author's critical observations. Three drawbacks are Jarratt's confusing treatment of financial issues (e.g., mixing Italian lire with English pounds), the absence of documentation, and the terseness of the material. A selective filmography of leading directors' films from 1930 to 1938, a cast and credits listing of post-WWII films, an index of film titles, and an index of names are included. Recommended for special collections.

Malerba, Luigi, and Carmine Siniscalo, eds. FIFTY YEARS OF ITALIAN CINEMA. Trans. Herman G. Weinberg. Foreword Richard Griffith. Rome: Carlo Bestetti, Edizioni d'Artre, 1954. Illustrated. 208pp.

 This beautifully illustrated overview exposed American readers to a wealth of information that had been unknown about Italian films since the early days of fascism. In three very general chapters, the editors do a good job of tying the neo-realistic movement of the mid-1940s, to the pioneering years from 1904 to 1930. What is particularly enjoyable is the emphasis on reminding us just how much world cinema owes to silent Italian productions and later Italian masterpieces. Regrettably, there is no bibliography, filmography, or index. Well worth browsing.

Leprohon, Pierre. THE ITALIAN CINEMA. Trans. Roger Greaves and Oliver Stallybrass. New York: Praeger Publishers, 1972. Illustrated. 256pp.

 Written by a prominent French critic, this first detailed English-language study of Italian film history (first published in French in Paris in 1966) examines its subject from its industrial roots in the late 1890s to the end of the sixties. Leprohon's critical acumen compensates for the names, dates, and titles approach that characterizes this sweeping study. Seven fact-filled chapters discuss the early years (1895-1908), the golden age (1909-1916), the period of decline (1917-1929), the Fascist years (1930-1943), the neo-realism period (1943-1950), the AUTEURS of the "difficult" decade (1951-1959), and the Italian cinema up to the modern period (1960-1969). Especially valuable is a biographical dictionary of 150 Italian filmmakers. A selective bibliography and index are included. Well worth browsing.

JAPAN

*Anderson, Joseph, and Donald Richie. THE JAPANESE FILM: ART AND INDUSTRY. Foreword Akira Kurosawa. Rutland: Charles E. Tuttle Company, 1959. Illustrated. 456pp.

 In one of the best books on the subject, invaluable for studying the films of Kon Ichikawa and Akira Kurosawa, Anderson and Richie present important insights into the Japanese directors' attempts to revere or to revolt against tradition. The first history of the Japanese cinema chronicles the years from 1896 to 1959, with Anderson responsible for the basic historical research, and Richie for the final drafts. In addition to analyses of industrial development, personalities, and political effects, the resourceful authors explore the relationship between the filmmakers and the traditional arts, and provide separate chapters critiquing the aesthetic qualities of the important artists in each major period. Many fascinating observations, coupled with striking stills and gossipy comments, contribute to the enduring quality of this pioneering work. As a bonus, there are two worthwhile appendexes, outlining the memorable directors as pupils and teachers, and tracing the development of the major companies. An index is included. Highly recommended for special collections.

Richie, Donald. JAPANESE MOVIES. Tokyo: Japanese Travel Bureau, 1961. Illustrated. 203pp.

 A condensed version of THE JAPANESE FILM. Worth browsing.

*Richie, Donald. JAPANESE CINEMA: FILM STYLE AND NATIONAL CHARACTER. New York: Doubleday and Company, 1971. Illustrated. 261pp.

This text, an extensively revised, expanded, and updated version of JAPANESE MOVIES, offers readers capsule views of the history of Japan's film industry from 1896 to 1971. Richie also provides an appendix on Japanese films then available in the United States in 16mm with addresses of the distributors. Especially noteworthy about this popular history is the author's skill in presenting difficult concepts about Japanese filmmakers and their unique talents in an easy-to-understand narrative. An index is included. Well worth browsing.

Richie, Donald. THE JAPANESE MOVIE. Rev. ed.. Tokyo: Kodansha International, 1982. Illustrated. 212pp.
An updated and informative account of the important stages of Japanese film history, this charming coffee-table study starts with the 1894 motion picture presentation to the royal family and takes us to the early 1980s. Richie focuses as much on aesthetics as he does on names, dates, and events. The highlight of this work, as compared to his other significant studies, is the splendid collection of handsomely reproduced illustrations. An index is included. Recommended.

Sato, Tadao. CURRENTS IN JAPANESE CINEMA. Trans. Gregory Barrett. Tokyo: Kodansha International, 1982. Illustrated. 288pp.
Written by one of Japan's most influential film critics, this important anthology of Sato's writings offers us a basic introduction to what the Japanese think about their cinematic history. Twelve highly insightful essays discuss Japanese stars, the influence of foreign films on the developing film industry, the evolution of period dramas in film, film heroines, Japanese war films, the meaning of "life" in Kurosawa's works, the importance of the family in Japanese movies, the types of movie villains, cinematic techniques, American-Japanese relations in Japanese films, and the growth of the Japanese cinema in the 1960s. An index is included. Recommended for special collections.

*Svensson, Arne. JAPAN. New York: A. S. Barnes and Company, 1971. Illustrated. 190pp.
This valuable dictionary provides us with the only available English guide to career filmographies of the major Japanese directors, players, and technicians, together with accurate credits and useful plot synopses for the most significant films of Japan. In addition, there is a welcome index and over 100 well-produced illustrations. Well worth browsing.

Tucker, Richard N. JAPAN: FILM IMAGE. London: Studio Vista, 1973. Illustrated. 144pp.
A fast-moving overview of Japanese cinema, heavily influenced by the writings of Anderson and Richie, this entertaining account frequently challenges standard interpretations of historical events and key works by major directors. Early sections pay homage to the factors contributing to the evolution of the Japanese cinema, but only for the purposes of establishing a context for Tucker's discussions on the post-WWII era and major filmmakers. The bulk of the writing deals with the social values and experiences of key filmmakers between 1945 and 1970. In addition to profuse illustrations and capsule summaries of cultural changes affecting the film industry, Tucker's book provides a useful perspective on Western attitudes to Japanese cinema. A bibliography is included, but no index. Well worth browsing.

UNITED STATES

*Crowther, Bosley. THE GREAT FILMS: FIFTY GOLDEN YEARS OF MOTION PICTURES. New York: G. P. Putnam's Sons, 1967. Illustrated. 258pp.

This well-illustrated and informative book represents Crowther's arbitrary selection of movies he has enjoyed and considers to have opened new ground, and whose content has set the precedent for thousands of other films. Among the obvious are THE BIRTH OF A NATION (1915), INTOLERANCE (1916), THE CABINET OF DR. CALIGARI/DAS KABINETT DES DR. CALIGARI) (1919), NANOOK OF THE NORTH (1922), GREED (1923), BATTLESHIP POTEMKIN (1925), THE GENERAL (1926), THE CROWD (1928), THE BLUE ANGEL (1930), ALL QUIET ON THE WESTERN FRONT(1930), LA GRANDE ILLUSION (1938), BICYCLE THIEVES (1949), RASHOMON (1950), and BLOW-UP (1966). The controversial selections include THE PUBLIC ENEMY (1931), KING KONG (1933), and CAMILLE (1936). A supplemental list of 100 distinguished films, a bibliography, and a film index are included. Well worth browsing.

Everson, William K. THE AMERICAN MOVIE. New York: Atheneum, 1963. Illustrated. 149pp.
This short, well-written introduction to movies is a good beginning for young people who want a fast, knowledgeable overview. The printing is good, the illustrations intelligently chosen, and the content credible. Special praise goes to Everett Aison for his superb design of the book. Regrettably, no index is provided. Well worth browsing.

Fahey, David, and Linda Rich. MASTERS OF STARLIGHT: PHOTOGRAPHERS IN HOLLYWOOD. New York: Ballantine Books, 1987. Illustrated. 287pp.

Griffith, Richard, and Arthur Mayer. THE MOVIES: THE SIXTY-YEAR STORY OF THE WORLD OF HOLLYWOOD AND ITS EFFECT ON AMERICA FROM PRE-NICKELODEON DAYS TO THE PRESENT. New York: Simon and Schuster, 1957. New York: Bonanza Books, 1970. Illustrated. 495pp.
One of the best of the illustrated history film books; Griffith and Mayer almost always provide valuable information, rare stills, and delightful commentary. The writing is crisp and affectionate as we revisit topically, rather than chronologically, the birth and growth of movies seen mainly from an American perspective. Once you recognize that the authors are interested more in nostalgia than in critical analyses, the popular coffee-table book becomes a treasured experience. A general index is included. Recommended for special collections.

*Jacobs, Lewis. THE RISE OF THE AMERICAN FILM: A CRITICAL HISTORY. With an essay "Experimental Cinema in America 1921-1947." New York: Teachers College Press, 1968. Illustrated. 632pp.
This reissue of the 1939 text is one of the best historical accounts of the period from 1890 to 1939. Jacobs presents a meaningful narrative about American films from the time they appeared as insignificant toys, to the emergence of artists and the advent of great sound movies. In clear, instructive, and enjoyable prose, he provides helpful plot synopses as well as useful introductions and summaries of the trends, conditions, and attitudes of the significant periods. It remains one of the most important sources for the sociological study of motion pictures. For the new edition, Jacobs wrote a helpful commentary on the American experimental film from 1921 to 1947. Highly recommended for special collections.

*Karr, Kathleen, ed. THE AMERICAN FILM HERITAGE: IMPRESSIONS FROM THE AMERICAN FILM INSTITUTE ARCHIVES. Washington, D.C.: Acropolis Books, 1972. Illustrated. 184pp.

An enjoyable collection of critical-sociological reflections of film history, this useful American Film Institute (AFI) publication also operates as an effective bit of propaganda for the AFI's archival programs. Karr points out in her introduction that the Library of Congress was one of the few places in the world that preserved evidence of film history since 1894. Nearly three-quarters of a century later, when the AFI was established in June, 1967, it "recognized" the need for historic preservation. Karr's assertions ring both true and hollow. That is, a number of AFI executives clearly lobbied and worked hard for such priorities, but over the years their efforts met with less than enthusiastic support from higher administrative quarters. What is non-debatable is that this anthology offers intriguing examples of what an extensive historical preservation program can net in terms of social and historical documentation. Among the many notable authors included are Kevin Brownlow, William K. Everson, Sam Kula, Leonard Maltin, Tom Shales, David Shepard, Paul C. Spehr, and Stephen F. Zito. Among the many entertaining and helpful essays are those dealing with films like MISS LULU BETT (1921), THE VANISHING AMERICAN (1925), THE EMPEROR JONES (1933), ONLY ANGELS HAVE WINGS (1939), HIGH SIERRA, and CITIZEN KANE (both in 1941), and MISSION TO MOSCOW (1943). Particularly noteworthy among the historical essays are Shephard's "Thomas Ince" and Zito's "The Black Film Experience." There is also information on the early use of color, the birth of film animation, and the rise of the narrative film. More than 200 illustrations, beautifully reproduced, add considerably to the book's appeal. An index is provided for the anthology of thirty-four short articles. Well worth browsing.

*MacGowan, Kenneth. BEHIND THE SCREEN: THE HISTORY AND TECHNIQUES OF THE MOTION PICTURE. New York: Delacorte Press, 1965. Illustrated. 528pp.

This general outline of film history really ends at the coming of sound, at which point MacGowan surveys the division of labor connected with film production. Very little serious commentary is given about European and Asian contributions. It makes for very enjoyable reading, mainly because of the author's delightful quoted materials and interesting statistics.[51] What separates it from more traditional works is the author's emphasis on the technology and economics of the film continuum. Well worth browsing.

Zinman, David. 50 CLASSIC MOTION PICTURES: THE STUFF THAT DREAMS ARE MADE OF. New York: Crown Publishers, 1970. Illustrated. 311pp.

Although not so well written as Crowther's book, this work is a respectable examination of Hollywood's fabulous period in the 1930s and 1940s. Zinman provides cast listings, production details, a fine selection of production stills, and general comments on many standard film favorites, including KING KONG (1933), MUTINY ON THE BOUNTY (1935), GONE WITH THE WIND (1939), and CASABLANCA (1942). A bibliography and index are included. Worth browsing.

FILMS

HISTORY OF THE MOTION PICTURES SERIES

Originally designed for a half-hour television series entitled, "Silents Please," this uneven and controversial collection traces the history of the movies from their infancy through the late 1920s.

---

[51]   Robert C. Dickson, "Kenneth MacGowan," FILMS IN REVIEW 14:8 (October, 1963):475-92.

Paul Killiam, the mastermind behind the series, has done a fine job of editing significant movies, adding new musical scores to enhance the viewing, and providing a nostalgic narration that points out the key facts about the individual film and its significant personalities.

Certain segments of the series are devoted, not to a single silent film, but to covering trends or careers. The running time for each segment is approximately twenty-five minutes, and all are in black-and-white.[52]

SEGMENTS

FILM FIRSTS I. First example of now familiar techniques and stories.

FILM FIRSTS II. Edwin S. Porter, Georges Melies, Thomas Ince, and D. W. Griffith.

AMERICA. Griffith's American Revolution shot on actual location with documentary realism.

FALL OF BABYLON. From INTOLERANCE, using full-scale sets of old Babylon.

ORPHANS OF THE STORM I & II. The French Revolution with Lillian and Dorothy Gish.

THE CLOWN PRINCES. Chaplin, Harold Lloyd, Larry Semon, Charlie Chase, Laurel and Hardy, Ben Turpin, and Billy West.

FUN FACTORY. Some of the best slapstick from Mack Sennett's studio.

SLAPSTICK. The era of visual comedy featuring death-defying stunts.

WILL ROGERS. His career from rodeo to radio.

DR. JEKYLL AND MR. HYDE. The first great American horror film, with John Barrymore.

DRACULA. The first screen version, directed by F. W. Murnau (1922).

THE AMERICANO. Douglas Fairbanks quelling a revolution.

GIRLS IN DANGER. Ladies in distress from Mae Marsh to Gloria Swanson.

---

[52] For a thorough discussion of the series, see Richard Schickel, "The Silents Weren't Just Voiceless Talkies," THE NEW TIMES MAGAZINE (November 28, 1971):32-3, 54-64.

THE THIEF OF BAGDAD. Douglas Fairbanks, directed by Raoul Walsh.

SON OF THE SHEIK. Rudolph Valentino's last film.

YANKEE CLIPPER. William Boyd, typhoons, and mutiny.

THE BLACK PIRATE. Douglas Fairbanks's duels, sea battles, and acrobatics, including his famous slide-down-the-sail.

BLOOD AND SAND. Life of a matador, featuring Rudolph Valentino.

GARDEN OF EDEN. Glamorous adult fairytale (1928).

THE GENERAL. The last and best classic silent comedy, directed by and starring Buster Keaton.

SAD CLOWNS. Charlie Chaplin, Buster Keaton, and Harry Langdon.

THE EAGLE. Rudolph Valentino as a Russian Robin Hood, directed by Clarence Brown.

THE HUNCHBACK OF NOTRE DAME. Lon Chaney (1923).

ROAD TO YESTERDAY. Cecil B. DeMille's spectacular mix of feudal oppression and modern (1920s) hedonism.

TEMPEST. John Barrymore in one of the last stylish silent classics.

WILLIAM S. HART. Film highlights climaxed by Hart's farewell to the screen.

VARIETY. The best film of its star, Emil Jannings, and its director, E. A. Dupont; technically innovative.

FILM ORIGINS

As Eisenstein observed, the origins of film do not involve "some incredible virgin-birth" in the nineteenth century. The answer to why countless scholars, monks, philosophers, inventors, and entertainers became preoccupied with recording and projecting the illusion of movement is buried in the annals of history. Whether in the 20,000-year-old Lascaux cave drawings of animals in suspended motion, the crude magnifying glasses of the ancient Egyptians and Babylonians, or the strange optical illusions of the ancient Chinese shadow plays, the evidence suggests that throughout recorded time many cultures experimented with the art of approximating "motion." One group was interested in the scientific possibilities of "capturing" movement and analyzing it. Another group was excited about the commercial possibilities associated with the illusion of motion. Both groups worked hard at solving the problem of how to simulate reality.

Many people contributed to the solution. H. Mark Gosser points out that

> In this long evolution of art and science, we see the beginning of sequential storytelling; of the optical principles which would eventually give life to the cinema; of the machine technology that set it all in motion and of the origins of audio-visual effects that today, in much more sophisticated forms, we quickly refer to as the techniques of filmmaking.[53]

Historians of antiquity identify a number of optical studies, magic shadow shows, and scientific theories related to the problems of reproducing physical reality. However, the case can sometimes be overstated. For example, Martin Quigley, Jr., argues that

> Aristotle developed the theoretical basis of the science of optics. Archimedes made the first systematic use of lenses and mirrors. Alhazen, the Arab, pioneered in the study of the human eye, a prerequisite for developing machines to duplicate requisite functions of the human eye.[54]

Such claims, particularly those related to Archimedes and his "burning-mirror" tales, can become, as Gosser observes, "intellectually silly."[55] Nevertheless, there is a sizeable list of ancient and medieval devices and theories that experimented with the illusion of motion. Some experimenters even got their names into the "official" record. For example, Roger Bacon in the mid-1200s toyed with scientific devices for creating magic shadow shows and is sometimes credited with demonstrating the scientific value of recording motion. In the early 1500s, Leonardo da Vinci advanced Aristotle's notions on light and optical phenomena, developing and describing the fundamental tenets of a CAMERA OBSCURA, or "dark room" effect.[56] Near the end of the sixteenth century, a Neapolitan "entertainer" named Giovanni Battista Della Porta, applied da Vinci's theory to professional "magic shows." In the seventeenth century, Athanasius Kircher, a mathematician and German Jesuit priest, popularized his new invention, "the Magic Lantern," in his 1646 book, ARS MAGNA LUCIS ET UMBRAE (THE GREAT ART OF LIGHT AND SHADOW).[57] By the time he came out with a second edition in 1671, he was already comparing the advantages of his magic lantern to those

---

[53]   Mark Gosser, "Introduction," QUARTERLY REVIEW OF FILM STUDIES 9:1 (Winter 1984):1.

[54]   Martin Quigley, Jr., MAGIC SHADOWS: THE STORY OF THE ORIGIN OF MOTION PICTURES (New York: Quigley Publishing Company, 1960), p.13.

[55]   Mark Gosser, "The Literature of the Archeology of Cinema," QUARTERLY REVIEW OF FILM STUDIES 9:1 (Winter 1984):4.

[56]   For a good overview of the CAMERA OBSCURA, see John H. Hammond, "Movement, Color and Sound in a 'Darke Roome'," QUARTERLY REVIEW OF FILM STUDIES 9:1 (Winter 1984):32-9.

[57]   Barbara Hunwitz, "Translations of Passages from the Two Editions of Athanasius Kircher's ARS MAGNA LUCIS ET UMBRAE," QUARTERLY REVIEW OF FILM STUDIES 9:1 (Winter 1984):70-3.

of his nearest competitors, Christiaen Huygens and Thomas Walgensten.[58] These are but a few of the people, theories, and inventions prior to the burst of cinematic experimentation that took place in the nineteenth century.[59]

What is clear is that throughout the centuries, entertainers, intellectuals, and propagandists studied, experimented, and researched the fundamental principles of the moving picture.[60] What is not clear are the direct causal links between the magic shadow shows over the ages, and the ingenious developments that occurred in the nineteenth century. For example, Eadweard Muybridge wrote in his preface to ANIMAL LOCOMOTION (1877) that

> The importance of a correct knowledge of the various functions of the limbs in locomotion was recognized in the early ages of Greece. Aristotle devoted much attention to the subject, and Xenophon, Pliny, Vegetius, and many other writers of ancient times tell us of the great interest manifested by their respective contemporaries in the training and employments of the horse.
>
> None of these distinguished authors, however, have left us any information as to the manner in which the various movements they write about were executed.
>
> No investigation--worthy of the name--is known to have been made until the middle of the seventeenth century.[61]

On the other hand, Kurt W. Marek (whose pseudonym is C. W. Ceram) claims that

> cinematography, the product of sciences become dynamic, began in the nineteenth century; the suggestions advanced by Heron of Alexandria remained dormant, for the spirit of his age was static. So, too, nothing came of the insights of Ptolemy or of Ibn al Haitam. All the speculation about a few obscure lines on the "moving pictures" in Lucretius is absurd. Even more ridiculous is the attempt to connect the cave paintings of Altamira, the Egyptian series reliefs, the friezes on mausoleums and the Panthenon, with [the] nineteenth century's "living pictures." All such efforts stem from a fondness for mechanistic theories of evolution, from a tendency to see the history of civilized man as a continuously progressive process going on for five thousand years. In fact, there is no more connection between the early concepts of images in series and the cinema than there is between the landings of the Vikings in Vineland with Columbus's discovery of Central America in 1492.[62]

From Marek's perspective (and those of most general film historians), the 1800s marked a shift from the mechanical and static attempts to depict the past, to a technical and dynamic revolution based upon scientific curiosity. It was as if the nineteenth-century scientific community put the issue of reproducing reality on its list of major priorities.

---

[58]   Charles Musser, "Towards a History of Screen Practice," QUARTERLY REVIEW OF FILM STUDIES 9:1 (Winter 1984):63-4.

[59]   Quigley in his book (pp.163-76) provides a useful descriptive chronology of the notable dates, inventions, and personalities from ancient times to 1896.

[60]   For a good overview of books on ancient film history, see "The Literature," pp.3-10.

[61]   Eadweard Muybridge, "Introduction," ANIMALS IN MOTION, ed. Lewis S. Brown (New York: Dover Publications, 1975), p.19.

[62]   C. W. Ceram, ARCHAEOLOGY OF THE CINEMA (New York: Harcourt, Brace and World, 1965), pp.15-6.

Clearly, no single theory has emerged to clarify how and where movies began. One promising approach, however, is suggested by Charles Musser. Rather than accepting a shotgun approach to the invention of the movies, he suggests that we place the medium within the broad context of "screen history." That is, he suggests that we study films "as a continuation and transformation on magic lantern traditions in which showmen displayed images on a screen, accompanying them with voice, music and sound effects."[63] The watershed event occurs in the seventeenth century, when Kircher and his contemporaries demystified the magical arts and emphasized instead technological innovations. Prior to Kircher's era, illusionists and clergy emphasized the "magical" nature of their demonstrations. They used numerous cultural events and objects to amaze their audiences. As Musser observes, investigating the history of those shadow plays, magic shows, and crude optical effects takes us into familiar historical terrain, only with a different focus: the continuity of screen practice. Once we get to the mid-1600s, we concentrate on how screen practice was transformed from an emphasis on the unknown to an emphasis on how images were projected, how "the show was a catoptric not a magical art."[64] The shift in focus also helps explain how the demystifiers were unintentionally laying the foundations for the complex relationships among producers, products, and the public that characterize the history of film. Studying film history from this perspective keeps our attention on "practice (methods of production, modes of representation)" rather than on "isolated cultural objects (films, lantern slides)."[65]

Whichever methodology is chosen, it is axiomatic that the nineteenth century provides the synthesis for all the inventions, patents, and claims to the birth of the motion picture. Henry V. Hopwood lists more than 160 related patents involved with film between 1851 and the end of 1898, while C. Francis Jenkins adds up close to 240 U. S. patents in a forty-seven-year period beginning in 1860.[66] Nevertheless, to this day, the disagreement continues as to which were the most important patents and who were the founders.

There is, however, surprising agreement as to what the essential factors were: (1) the concept of persistence of vision, (2) a flexible and transparent material for photographing and projecting, (3) perforations on this photographic material, (4) a suitable camera and projector, (5) a shutter for this equipment, (6) storage for the photographic material before, during, and after its progression in the camera and projector, and (7) appropriate lens and lighting conditions for the use of the equipment.

Each of these factors progressed in different stages. For example, the first half of the 1800s witnessed a highly competitive race to solve the basic problems of cinematography and put it to profitable uses. One of the earliest steps was the Czech inventor J. E. Purkye's work on the properties of the eye in 1818. In less than six years, two English scholars and physicians, John Ayrton Paris and Peter Mark Roget, had reaffirmed Da Vinci's experiments on the persistence of vision. Having established the mistaken notion[67] that the eye retains an image on the retina for close to a tenth

---

[63]   "Towards a History of Screen Practice," p.59.

[64]   "Towards a History of Screen Practice," p.61.

[65]   "Towards a History of Screen Practice," p.64.

[66]   Walter H. Stainton, "Movie Pre-History," FILMS IN REVIEW 16:6 (June-July 1965):333.

[67]   Michael Chanan explains that "Film depends on the interaction between the perceptual threshold of duration and the statistical periodicity of projection. Experiment has shown that a second signal following the first at an interval smaller than the threshold has the effect of MASKING the first one, as if the

of a second AFTER the image itself changes or disappears, Paris manufactured his optical toy, the THAUMOTROPE, in 1826. It was an intriguing situation, as John Frazer cleverly observes, in that "'while theories can be wrong, the invention based on the theory can still work.'"[68] Following the enormous popularity of the THAUMOTROPE, the public was inundated with optical entertainments that featured a variety of moving images. The inventors represented many Western nations, while their inventions paid homage to ancient times. For example, Dr. Joseph Plateau of Brussels produced the PHENAKISTISCOPE, and Simon Ritter von Stampfer of Vienna created the STROBOSCOPE, both in 1832.[69] Two years later, William George Horner of England distributed the ZOETROPE. By the mid-1870s, these types of spinning discs and drums were replaced by animated drawings on Emile Reynauld's PRAXINOSCOPE.[70]

The more one studies film history, the more one realizes that the dramatic shifts from animated sequences in the mid-1800s, to actualities and sketches at the turn of the century, to narrative and comic films in the early 1900s, did not evolve in a linear fashion. While many film historians point to certain events as watershed moments in the birth and growth of the medium, no one has uncovered the generative mechanisms that led to the appearance of motion pictures. As Ted Perry points out,

Many external influences are crucial, such as the social, political, artistic and popular entertainment forms of the period. The early evolution of the cinema was deeply affected by such diverse things as nineteenth-century naturalism, twentieth-century futurism, still photography, the dime novel and stage melodrama. Several early film-makers were influenced by cartoon and comic strip artists,[71] as in the case of Porter's almost literal adaptation of Winsor McKay's

---

system compensates for the likelihood of change during the period of minimal perceptual delay by allowing incoming signals within this period to CORRECT earlier ones. In other words, information about changes is incorporated at a PRIMARY level, while the process of observation at more complex levels continues uninterrupted. That is precisely why, beyond the perceptual threshold of duration, periodicity in the incoming signal is read automatically and unconsciously (and inevitably) as part of the structure which determines how the message is to be analyzed and coded in the first place, and not as part of the symbolic meaning which is drawn out of the message at a higher level." Chanan then goes on to add, "This finally scotches the myth of persistence of vision as it was understood in the nineteenth century." See Michael Chanan, THE DREAM THAT KICKS: THE PREHISTORY AND EARLY YEARS OF CINEMA IN BRITAIN (London: Routledge & Kegan Paul, 1980), pp.67-8. See also Joseph Anderson and Barbara Fisher, "The Myth of Persistence of Vision," JOURNAL OF THE UNIVERSITY FILM ASSOCIATION 30:4 (Fall 1978):3-8; and "Cinevideo and Psychology," ibid., 32:1-2 (Winter-Spring 1980).

[68]   John Frazer, "The Pre-History and Early Years of the Cinema," QUARTERLY REVIEW OF FILM STUDIES 8:1 (Winter 1983):51.

[69]   For concise, clear explanations of these devices, see David A. Cook, pp.2-3.

[70]   For a good overview of the evolution of animation at the dawn of film, see Conrad Smith, "The Early History of Animation: Saturday Morning TV Discovers 1915," JOURNAL OF THE UNIVERSITY FILM ASSOCIATION 29:3 (Summer 1977):23-30.

[71]   For more information on how cartoons influenced the rise of films, see Francis Lacassin, "The Comic Strip and Film Language," trans. David Kinzle, FILM QUARTERLY 26:1 (Fall 1972):11-23; John L. Fell, "Cellulose Nitrate Roots: Popular Entertainments and the Birth of Film Narrative," BEFORE HOLLYWOOD: TURN-OF-THE-CENTURY AMERICAN FILM, ed. Paul Anbinder (New York: Hudson Hills Press, 1987), pp.39-44; and Tom W. Hoffer, "From Comic Strips to Animation: Some

DREAMS OF A RAREBIT FIEND . . . [Filmmakers also] borrowed from one another (less politely said, they stole and copied . . .).

It will still be some time before the whole truth is known about the degree of influence among the Italian, American, Danish and British film-makers during this early period. And when discussing influences, no one should discount the enormous influence imposed upon the early cinema by the rise of industry in the nineteenth century. The fact that film companies often called themselves film manufacturers tells us not only about the organizational image upon which such companies were structured but also how this image and means of production affected the final form of the film.[72]

Implicit in Perry's argument is the value of studying history from the perspective of evolving visual forms--e.g., different plot lines, spatial composition, and camera angles and positions--as well as from the perspectives of masterpieces, AUTEURS, sociology, and economics.

An examination of technological history reveals that another reason for the change in nineteenth-century optical entertainments was the breakthrough in the development of photography.[73] Ever since the early 1600s, scientists had understood how silver nitrate reacted to light to produce "pictures." What hadn't been resolved, Jack C. Ellis explains, was a means of stopping the darkening process and of maintaining the tonality of the image reversal.[74] Contributing to the solution were the experiments of Joseph Nicephore Niepce (from 1813 to 1833), Louis Jacques Mande Daguerre (from 1825 through the 1830s), William Henry Fox Talbot (in the 1830s), and John Herschel (in the 1840s). During these years these men had reduced the amount of exposure time required to take and fix an image on paper or plate. By 1849, as Frank E. Beaver observes, the Langenheim brothers of Philadelphia had purchased Talbot's process for making glass plates and were manufacturing glass plate transparencies, thereby making "the projection of photographs possible."[75] This nineteenth-century preoccupation with the effects of light coincided, as Olive Cook notes, with centuries of fascination with the laws of perspective. "It was the fascination of transforming light shining or suddenly obscured behind translucent pictures painted on glass," she writes, "that led to the metamorphosis of the peepshow into the great popular entertainments, the Panorama and the Diorama."[76] Mark Gosser, on the other hand, argues that Charles Wheatstone's 1838 invention of the "stereoscope" (an optical instrument to unite dissimilar images) inspired fellow film pioneers to solve the problems of recording and reproducing motion. According to Gosser,

---

Perspective on Winsor McCay," JOURNAL OF THE UNIVERSITY FILM ASSOCIATION 28:2 (Spring 1976):23-32.

[72] Ted Perry, "Formal Strategies as an Index to the Evolution of Film History," CINEMA JOURNAL 14:2 (Winter 1974-75):25-6.

[73] John L. Fell, "Dissolves by Gaslight: Antecedents to the Motion Picture in Nineteenth-Century Melodrama," FILM QUARTERLY 23:3 (Spring 1970):22-34.

[74] *Jack C. Ellis, A HISTORY OF FILM, 2nd ed. (Englewood Cliffs: Prentice-Hall, 1985), p.15.

[75] Beaver, p.9.

[76] Olive Cook, MOVEMENT IN TWO DIMENSIONS: A STUDY OF THE ANIMATED AND PROJECTED PICTURES WHICH PRECEDED THE INVENTION OF CINEMATOGRAPHY (London: Hutchinson Publishing Company, 1963), p.28.

The first step in this direction was taken by Jules Duboscq in 1852. Duboscq's work began a period during which stereoscopic inventions played the most important role in the emerging technology of the motion picture. Specifically, from 1852 to 1868 stereoscopy was the key contributing technology to the evolution of the motion picture system. Years later, between 1890 and 1893, the stereo devices of [Frederick Henry] Valery and [William] Friese-Greene were also advances in the technology of the cinema.[77]

While Gosser acknowledges that stereoscopy did not not have much of an impact on film technology after 1870, he identifies four principles and two components that directly contributed to the evolution of film technology.[78] What was also needed was a more practical substance to record and project lifelike images. At the approximate time that Reynauld was signaling the shift in optical entertainments, Coleman Sellers and Henry Renno Heyle were pioneering a wet-plate, stop-action method that significantly advanced one's ability to reproduce the illusion of movement.

As nineteeth-century inventors and scholars experimented with the problems of vision, photographic processes, animation, motion, sound,[79] and color,[80] others worked on technical apparatus such as cameras and projectors.[81] Among the more famous of the early pioneers concerned with the camera were Eadweard Muybridge (England)[82] and Etienne-Jules Marey (France). In addition to Muybridge, the pioneers most often credited with resolving the problems of projection prior to 1887 are Baron Franz von Uchatius (Austria), Jules Duboscq (France), Charles Wheatstone (England), and Henry Heyle (America). The pioneers most often credited with creating celluloid film are Hannibal Goodman and George Eastman.

Between 1887 and 1896, the breakthroughs in solving the problems of recording and projecting the illusion of movement narrowed to the contributions of little more than a dozen inventors: in England, Birt Acres, William Friese-Greene,[83] and Robert W. Paul; in France, Georges Demeny, Auguste and Louis Lumiere, Jean Aime

---

[77]   H. Mark Gosser, SELECTED ATTEMPTS AT STEREOSCOPIC MOVING PICTURES AND THEIR RELATIONSHIP TO THE DEVELOPMENT OF MOTION PICTURE TECHNOLOGY (New York: Arno Press, 1977), p.2.

[78]   SELECTED ATTEMPTS, pp.292-300.

[79]   For a useful example of what the early experiments were like, see Rosalind Rogoff, "Edison's Dream: A Brief History of the Kinetophone," CINEMA JOURNAL 15:2 (Spring 1976):58-68.

[80]   For a good example of how stereoscopic inventions merged with color experimentation, see Walter Stainton, "The Prophet Louis Ducos Du Hauron," CINEMA JOURNAL 6: (1966-67):47-51.

[81]   Helen Gibson as told to Mike Kornick, "In Very Early Days," FILMS IN REVIEW 19:1 (January 1968):28-34.

[82]   Harlan Hamilton, "LES ALLURES DU CHEVAL, Eadweard James Muybridge's Contribution to the Motion Picture," FILM COMMENT 5:3 (Fall 1969):16-35. Among the more interesting revisionist assertions being debated today is that Leland Stanford hired Muybridge to record a horse's hoofs leaving the ground to improve the rich man's breeding and training interests rather than to win a bet.

[83]   Terry Ramsaye, "Friese-Greene Is a Legend," FILMS IN REVIEW 11:7 (August-September 1951):15-18. For more information on the various competing patents, see Stainton, "Movies Pre-History," pp.333-42.

[84]   Leroy was born in America, but worked in France.

Leroy,[84] and Louis Aime Augustin Le Prince;[85] in Germany, Oskar Messter and the brothers Emile and Max Skladanowsky; and in the United States, Thomas Armat,[86] Herman Casler, William Kennedy Laurie Dickson, Thomas Alva Edison, C. Francis Jenkins, and Woodville Latham. Clearly, the popularity of peep shows accelerated interest in screen projection. Or, as Musser observes, "The commercialization of the motion pictures represented not simply the beginning of a new industry but also the continuation and transformation of established practices."[87] The two most important dates appear to be December 28, 1895, when the Lumiere brothers demonstrated their portable, clawlike projector, the Cinematographe, in Paris; and April 23, 1896, when Edison unveiled "his" Kinetoscope in New York City.

The reason for qualifying Edison's conceptual accomplishments relates to the important and questionable dealings that the Wizard of Menlo Park had with his employee Dickson, the Latham family, Cassler, Armat, and Jenkins. In simplified terms, Dickson, late in 1887, started his film work for Edison. Over the next seven years, the Edison-Dickson union experimented with a variety of inventions relating to sound films, intermittent movement, camera equipment, new film bases, and film projectors. What is readily apparent is that technological challenges rather than aesthetic desires dominated the birth of film. The emphasis was clearly on solving mechanical problems rather than on creating artistic or realistic reproductions of physical reality. In 1894, Dickson had a falling-out with Edison and left the company a year later to enter partnership with Elias B. Koopman, Henry N. Marvin, and Herman Cassler to form the K. M. C. D. syndicate (later the American Mutoscope and Biograph Company). By 1895, the seeds of the great patent wars had been planted as Edison sought recognition and control of the major film developments over less known inventors. What seems non-debatable, however, is Bohn and Stromgren's assertion that "Edison contributed more as a promoter of the technology and as one of the first American motion picture executives than as a pure inventor."[88]

[85]   Walter H. Stainton, "A Neglected Pioneer," FILMS IN REVIEW 14:3 (March 1963):160-66.

[86]   For a discussion of projected motion pictures before December 1895, see Gene G. Kelkres, "A Forgotten First: The Armat-Jenkins Partnership and the Atlanta Projection," QUARTERLY REVIEW OF FILM STUDIES 9:1 (Winter 1984):45-58; and H. Mark Gosser, "The Armat-Jenkins Dispute and the Museums," FILM HISTORY: AN INTERNATIONAL JOURNAL 2:1 (Winter 1988):1-12.

[87]   *Charles Musser, ed., THOMAS A. EDISON PAPERS--A GUIDE TO MOTION PICTURE CATALOGS BY AMERICAN PRODUCERS AND DISTRIBUTORS, 1894-1908. (Frederick: University Publications of America, 1985), Microfilm, p.4.

[88]   Bohn, p.8. For a good overview of Edison's work, see Robert Conot, A STREAK OF LUCK: THE LIFE AND LEGEND OF THOMAS ALVA EDISON (New York: Seaview Books, 1979), pp.320-33.

BOOKS

GENERAL

Anbinder, Paul, ed. BEFORE HOLLYWOOD: TURN-OF-THE-CENTURY AMERICAN FILM. New York: Hudson Hills Press, 1987. Illustrated. 169pp.

A classy survey of the first two decades of American cinema, this welcome study is based on research involving sixty-nine rare surviving silent films. The idea originates with the impressive film exhibition entitled BEFORE HOLLYWOOD: TURN-OF-THE-CENTURY FILM FROM AMERICAN ARCHIVES, mounted by the American Federation of Arts and under the dual leadership of Jay Leyda and Charles Musser. Both men reviewed the holdings of five major collections: the American Film Institute, the International Museum of Photography at George Eastman House, the Library of Congress, the Museum of Modern Art, and the UCLA Film Archive. Among the criteria used to determine what films would be included in the exhibition were the abilities of the films to reproduce the visual experience of the original audiences, to present a mix of directorial styles, and to offer insights into the range of film material beyond mainstream productions.

Another vital part of the project was a special 1983 conference held at the Library of Congress, during which a number of specialists not only presented intriguing papers, but also spent twenty-five hours viewing unique movies. What emerged was a set of provocative essays on specific aspects of film history. For example, Richard Koszarski's "OffScreen Spaces: Images of Early Cinema Production and Exhibition" illustrates through a number of beautifully reproduced photographs a novel context for studying turn-of-the-century films. John L. Fell's "Cellulose Nitrate Roots: Popular Entertainments and the Birth of Film Narrative" explores the debt that early films owe to the comic strip and stage melodrama. Neil Harris's "A Subversive Form" discusses how early film challenged accepted protocols for authorship and thus undermined traditional patterns for establishing professional reputations. Brooks McNamara's "Scene Design and Early Film" explores how pioneering filmmakers perfected a kind of seamless realism in their set designs that became the standard for American movies. Charles Musser's "The Changing Status of the Actor" traces the steps that transformed the role of the actor from an inconsequential aspect of film and an embarrassing assignment, to one that not only advanced the performer's public recognition and financial rewards, but also provided significant artistic challenges. Judith Mayne's "Uncovering the Female Body" considers both the familiar and the strange in early film images of women. Russell Merritt's "Dream Visions in Pre-Hollywood Film" analyzes how fledgling filmmakers used hallucinations, visions, and nightmares to extend the narrative powers of film. The set of essays concludes with Alan Trachtenberg's "Photography/Cinematography," exposing how pioneering filmmakers applied photographic techniques to the world of moving images.

The remainder of this attractive publication includes six programs dividing the unusual films according to theme: e.g., "An Age of Entertainments," "Pleasures and Pitfalls," and "America in Transition." A bibliography and index are included. Recommended for special collections.

Balshofer, Fred J., and Arthur C. Miller. ONE REEL A WEEK. Berkeley: University of California Press, 1967. Illustrated. 218pp.

Balshofer, one of the early film producers and founders of the New York Motion Picture Company, studied under Sigmund Lubin beginning in 1905. Within a few years, he was on his own and employing Miller as one of his cameramen. The fourteen-year-old Miller eventually went on to photograph HOW GREEN WAS MY VALLEY (1941), THE SONG OF BERNADETTE, THE OX-BOW INCIDENT (both in 1943), and THE RAZOR'S EDGE (1946). Thus, their reflections on an emerging industry are not only interesting but first-hand recollections. They comment on personalities, techniques, and incidents. Their narrative plus well-chosen illustrations produces a valuable and delightful book. Recommended for special collections.

Barnouw, Erik. THE MAGICIAN AND THE CINEMA. New York: Oxford University Press, 1981. Illustrated. 128pp.

"This book," Barnouw writes, "seeks to recapture the brief period when the history of magic and the history of cinema intersected, to the swift and worldwide benefit of cinema, and the discomfiture of the world of magic." Eight succinct and lucid chapters survey the role that magicians like Jean Eugene Robert-Houdin, John Nevil Maskelyne, and Etienne Gaspard Robert (Robertson) played in pioneering film animation and trick photography. The early chapters explain the importance of optics and magic lanterns in nineteenth-century magic performances, particularly Robertson's sensational FANTASMAGORIE that ran from 1794 to 1800 in Paris, and that ignited a rash of imitations throughout Europe and the United States well into the 1860s. A turning point in magic lantern shows, Barnouw explains, occurred during the early 1820s when limelight replaced oil as a source of illumination. The more powerful light increased the range of illusions available to magicians, spiritualists, and lecturers. The middle chapters discuss the sophistication of magic lanterns, including the use of "dissolves" in which one machine could show either simultaneous slides or superimpositions. In addition to describing the uses made by Georges Melies, who became owner and manager of the Theatre Robert-Houdin in 1888, Barnouw reminds us that other future filmmakers--e.g., Cecil Hepworth, G. Wilhem Bitzer, Albert E. Smith, and J. Stuart Blackton--had roots in magic shows using optical trickery. The final chapters describe the effect that the projection of moving pictures had on the world of magic. The author tells us that following the successful Lumiere projection in December, 1895, Louis Lumiere entrusted the British premiere of his novelty to Felicien Trewey, a friend and the era's great shadowgraphist. We're also told about the significance of the relationship among Robert W. Paul, David Devant (a celebrated British shadowgraphist), and Carl Hertz (a noted magician). Other celebrities reviewed include Emile and Vincent Isola, Leopoldo Fregoli, Walter R. Booth, Alexander Victor, and Harry Houdini. A brief description of their individual contributions makes it clear why so many technical devices--e.g., dissolves, fades, masking, and superimpositions--grew out of nineteenth-century magic traditions.

Barnouw's fast-paced prose, plus beautifully reproduced and rare illustrations, makes this publication a pleasure to read. The book's brevity limits its scholarly insights, but does not detract from its use as an introduction to a neglected area of early film history. Endnotes, a bibliography, and an index conclude the work. Well worth browsing.

*Bowers, David Q. NICKELODEON THEATRES AND THEIR MUSIC. Vestal: The Vestal Press, 1986. Illustrated. 212pp.

The major work on the subject, this excellent survey presents a valuable study on the architecture of the early five-cent theaters and the ingenious musical instruments that gave sound to the silent films. The book covers the years from 1905 to 1915, coupled with intriguing captions and important archival leads. Many of the illustrations are rare; all are handsomely reproduced. So long as Bowerr stays with nickelodeon history, he is credible and persuasive. Regrettably, his opinions on other aspects of film history follow discredited routes, and the ground-breaking book appears periodically not only dated, but also poorly researched. Overall, the two major sections--on the theaters and their music--provide enough exciting material to satisfy even the most critical reader. Three appendexes, dealing with recent developments of organ building, Wurlitzer Theatre instruments, and Fanny Wurlitzer reminiscences, plus a bibliography and index add to the book's value to film scholarship. Recommended for special collections.

Ceram, C. W.. ARCHAEOLOGY OF THE CINEMA. New York: Harcourt Brace & World, 1965. Illustrated. 264pp.

One of the most ambitious books on the pre-history of film, this account is balanced, usually accurate, and highly entertaining. "What I am really concerned with," writes Kurt W. Marek (using the pen name of Ceram), "is the genesis of the cinema as technique, and my book ends at 1897, the year which saw the birth of the cinema INDUSTRY." Along the way, the resourceful author provides thumbnail sketches of the key personalities whose lives were affected by film history. For example, we're told that Baron Uchatius, the Austrian general and chemist who allegedly projected the first films, killed himself; George Eastman committed suicide; Le Prince mysteriously vanished with all his equipment on a journey through France; and Reynauld spent the last years of his life in a mental institution. Marek steadfastly rejects the notion that the invention of the cinema was a progressive process dating back to the ancient Greeks. "What matters in history," he insists, "is not whether certain chance discoveries take place, but whether they take effect." In his judgment, the only discoveries that significantly affected cinematography are those occurring during the period from 1792 and 1888. Moreover, he pinpoints the end of the prehistory of cinematography at precisely 1832, "with Plateau's Phenakisticope and Stampfer's Stroboscope."

Even more entertaining and enlightening than Marek's critical observations are the plentiful and well-chosen stills. Not only are the 293 handsome reproductions a treat to examine, but they also supplement the author's many informative observations. A useful bibliography and index conclude the book. Recommended for special collections.

Coe, Brian. THE HISTORY OF MOVIE PHOTOGRAPHY. London: Ash & Grant, 1981. Illustrated. 176pp.

"This book," Coe writes in his introduction, "sets out to try to put the story [of the practical developments that made movies possible] into perspective and to show how the main streams of development which produced the motion picture came together at the end of the last century." The eight charmingly illustrated chapters that follow take us from the shadow plays of ancient India and Java, to the experiments using optical devices to enhance the illusions of reality, through the birth of photography and the rise of the men who made the cinematic machines, to the first moving pictures and the experiments with sound and color films, and concludes with an overview of the various attempts to reduce the realism of moving pictures to a standardized screen format. The writing is clear, informative, and accessible. A bibliography and index are available. Well worth browsing.

Cook, Olive. MOVEMENT IN TWO DIMENSIONS: A STUDY OF THE ANIMATED AND PROJECTED PICTURES London: Hutchinson Publishing Company, 1963. Illustrated. 143pp.

Beginning with an emphasis on film history's "magical" roots, Cook sets out to draw a line between the astonishing productions of ancient sorcerers-priests, and the nineteenth-century inventors who gave birth to cinematography. "The aerial images projected by magicians with the aid of concave mirrors, and the phantoms flung upon the screen by the lantern," she writes, "were the distant ancestors of the fantastic, irrational, magic aspects of the film." The first of her eight anecdotal chapters traces the story through the standard medieval and Renaissance pioneers, pointing out that Kircher's 1946 publication was the watershed, and ends with a brief commentary on the importance of the Phantasmagoria. Chapter 2, "Peepshows and Panoramas," suggests the similarities between the forerunners of the contemporary travelogues and newsreels and the CAMERA OBSCURA. Chapter 3, "Far Eastern Shadows," explores the history of shadow shows in India, Java, and China. Chapter 4, "Karagoz," points out the similarities between the Oriental shadow plays and their counterparts in Europe's famous shadow puppet shows during the Middle Ages. Chapter 5, "The Chinese Shades," continues the history of the shadow plays in the seventeenth and eighteenth centuries. Chapter 6, "Dissolving Views," describes the impact of the magic lantern on shadow plays, stressing the importance and variety of slide shows.   Chapter 7, "Living Models," surveys the history of photographic slides illustrating fiction and song, making the point that "These remarkable slides immediately preceded the cinema as a form of popular entertainment, and employed many of the devices which we are inclined to regard as peculiar to film, particularly the flash-back and the convincing presentation of the fantastic." Chapter 8, "The Persistence of Vision," concludes the pre-film history with a general overview of the steps related to the commercial application of moving pictures.

Cook's focus throughout is on the unusual rather than on the relevant, and the chronology suffers from an overemphasis on the insignificant instead of the important figures in film history. Yet there are some interesting discussions of the early mirror shows, panorama and peep show performances, shadow plays, and magic lanterns. A bibliography and index are provided. Worth browsing.

*Fell, John, L., ed. FILM BEFORE GRIFFITH. Berkeley: University of California Press, 1983. Illustrated. 395pp.

Dismissing many of the pre-cinematic accounts found in film histories as combinations of "romance and avoidance behavior," Fell justifies his revisionist history as a result of several new forces in film scholarship (e.g., film historians are now being taught historical methodology). What Fell offers, therefore, is examples of the current methodologies. "When we learn to ask the right questions," he quips, "we may view these formative years in such a way as to excavate the foundations of today's popular film culture." To help formulate that perspective, Fell divides his anthology into three sections. Part I, "Places and Productions," focuses on several early film companies as well as a number of heretofore esoteric prefilm areas (e.g., Peter Morris's "Images of Canada" and Eric Reade's "Australian Silent Films, 1904-1907: The Features Begin"). Fell's plan is to emphasize good scholarship rather than landmark events. The result is that we discover new sources of information and find fresh controversies about the links between ideology and film inventions. Particularly valuable is Charles Musser's "American Vitagraph: 1897-1901." Part II, "Exhibition and Distribution," concentrates on movie audiences and how films were affected by copyright laws and evolving distribution patterns.   Among those contributing important essays are Jeanne Thomas Allen, Robert Allen, Raymond Fielding, and Garth Jowett. Part III, "The Films," provides a retrospective analysis decades after the movies first appeared. Intriguing perspectives are presented by Katherine Singer Kovacs's "George Melies and the FEERIE," Marshall Deutelbaum's "Structural Patterning in the Lumiere Films," Andre Gaudreault's "Temporality and Narrativity in Early Cinema," Lucy Fischer's "The Lady Vanishes: Women, Magic, and the Movies," and Tom Gunning's "An Unseen Energy Swallows Space: The Space in Early Films and Its Relation to American Avant-Garde." Actually, this is one of those rare books in which I did not find a single essay without something meaningful to say. A bibliography, a film index, and a general index are included.   Recommended for special collections.

Fielding, Raymond, ed. A TECHNOLOGICAL HISTORY OF MOTION PICTURES AND TELEVISION. AN ANTHOLOGY FROM THE PAGES OF THE JOURNAL OF THE SOCIETY OF MOTION PICTURE AND TELEVISION ENGINEERS. Berkeley: University of California Press, 1967. Illustrated. 255pp.

Here is an intelligent and useful anthology of articles selected from close to 475 issues of the society's journals. Fielding provides us with marvelous material from the recollections of Jenkins, Dickson, Armat, Paul, Louis Lumiere, Gaumont, and Laute. In addition, there are significant essays on Oskar Messter and Max Skladanowsky.   Unfortunately, no attempt is made to verify or correct conflicting claims, and the book suffers from the lack of an index. Recommended for special collections.

*Gernsheim, Helmut, and Alison Gernsheim. L. J. M. DAGUERRE: THE HISTORY OF THE DIORAMA AND THE DAGUERREOTYPE. 2nd rev. ed. New York: Dover Publications, 1968. Illustrated. 226pp.

This revised edition comes twelve years after the original 1955 publication and includes valuable information both on Daguerre's contributions to the diorama, and insightful illustrations about the large screen picture show that became the rage in nineteenth-century Europe. The authors take full advantage of their impressive collection of pictures at the University of Texas to give a good overview of the famous painter's life. Born at Cormeilles-en-Parisis on November 18, 1787, the man credited with "fixing" the images of the CAMERA OBSCURA had his early life disrupted by the French Revolution. His limited formal education was overshadowed by his natural intelligence, and he quickly demonstrated his gifts for drawing and landscape sketches. Following a variety of apprenticeships, the ambitious youth made a name for himself as a Paris acrobat and dancer. His interest in the arts led him eventually to a job with Pierre Prevost, the noted painter of panoramas, that lasted about eight years (1807-1815). From this vantage point, Louis Jacques Mande Daguerre moved on to stage designing at such impressive places as the Theatre Ambigu-Comique and the Paris Opera. By 1823, he was involved in exhibitions of diorama pictures. A year later the versatile artist was experimenting with photography. This was not as unusual as one might expect, because painters often used the CAMERA OBSCURA to aid their art. Within three years he had begun his important relationship with Nicephore Niepce, the inventor of heliography (a unique photographic process using silver salts), first through letters and then as partners in photographic experiments. After Niepce's death on July 5, 1833, Daguerre continued the partnership with the late inventor's son, Isidore Niepce. Over a handful of years, the two men perfected the daguerreotype process and gained international fame. Daguerre lived another decade, dying on July 10, 1851.

This splendid biography recounts the main elements of the painter-inventor's life, pointing out how he was drawn to discovering the sensitive "proces-positif" on a metal plate, and then upgrading the concept. Moreover, the ample visual material documenting the painter's enthusiasm for the diorama adds another dimension to his engrossing experiments with the daguerreotype. The story is told in seven fact-filled chapters, and includes nine valuable appendexes, a bibliography, endnotes, and an index. Recommended for special collections.

H. Mark Gosser. SELECTED ATTEMPTS AT STEREOSCOPIC MOVING PICTURES AND THEIR RELATIONSHIP TO THE DEVELOPMENT OF MOTION PICTURE TECHNOLOGY, 1852-1903. New York: Arno Press, 1977. Illustrated. 344pp.

Originally a 1975 master's thesis for Temple University, this worthwhile study "chronicles the development of stereoscopic technology and interprets and evaluates its importance in the evolution of motion pictures." The plan is to examine claims that stereoscopy was the catalyst for the birth of the movies. The evidence reviewed suggests that it was not. Gosser's major contributions are in showing how stereoscopic investigation relates to the development of film technology. His methodology forces him to consider the relationship that stereoscopy had to other cinematic technological developments--e.g., a camera or projection system, the rise of movie peep shows, and the evolution of flexible film. Among the conclusions he reaches are that stereoscopic inventors like Coleman Sellers, Charles Wheatstone, Henry DuMont, and Pierre Hubert Desvignes laid the foundation for the concept of intermittent motion (the transport mechanism used to move film through cameras and projectors). In addition, Gosser makes a good case for the movie peep shows being outgrowths of the stereo moving picture peep shows of the 1860s, and for the endless perforated band originating in the stereoscopic inventions of Desvignes, Pierre Czugajewicz, Sellers, DuMont, Louis Ducos, and Wheatstone. Gosser points out, however, that except for the patents of Valery (1890) and Friese-Greene (1893) "stereoscopy did NOT materially influence the evolution of film technology." Particularly informative are the many diagrams and illustrations that help explain the work of the various inventors. Several appendexes, a bibliography, and a postscript are also provided. Recommended for special collections.

Hendricks, Gordon. BEGINNINGS OF THE BIOGRAPH: THE STORY OF THE INVENTION OF THE MUTOSCOPE AND THE BIOGRAPH AND THEIR SUPPLYING CAMERA. New York: The Beginnings of the American Film, 1964. Illustrated. 78pp.
     On September 14, 1896, at the Alvin Theater in Pittsburgh, the finest cameras and projector yet known made their debut. This equipment effected the start of the most important company of the first decade of motion pictures: Biograph. Hendricks, in clear and interesting prose, makes a very important contribution to film history by presenting an accurate and documented study of the company's key personalities: Henry Marvin, Elias B. Koopman, Herman Cassler, and W. L. K. Dickson. This book is the major work on the subject and corrects the errors of all previous history books. Recommended for special collections.

Hogben, Lancelot. FROM CAVE PAINTING TO COMIC STRIP. London: Max Parrish and Company, 1949. 288pp.

Hopwood, Henry V. LIVING PICTURES: THEIR HISTORY, PHOTO-PRODUCTION AND PRACTICAL WORKING. New York: Arno Press, 1970. Illustrated. 377pp.

Hopwood, Henry V. LIVING PICTURES. London: The Hatton Press, 1915. Illustrated. 377pp.

*Lennig, Arthur, ed. CLASSICS OF THE FILM. Madison: Wisconsin Film Society Press, 1965. Illustrated. 250pp.
     This collection, concerned with significant and enduring movies, is a provocative and entertaining book. "The films in this volume," Lennig explains, "like the analyses, are of varying quality. Some of the writers are just beginning the thankless chore of writing about pictures; others, more experienced, continue this sisyphean task." The anthology's first four sections, on American, German, French, and Scandinavian films, leave something to be desired, but the essays on Bunuel movies and horror films are delightful. Well worth browsing.

*Lennig, Arthur, ed. FILM NOTES. Madison: Wisconsin Film Society Press, 1960. Illustrated. 160pp.
     This book presents some original, uneven, and controversial comments about the silent films of Germany, Russia, Scandinavia, and America. There is also a brief section on the great comedians of the 1920s. Not for film buffs, the book will be valuable for serious students who might be interested in the discussion of relatively unknown movies like THE GHOST THAT NEVER RETURNS, FRAGMENT OF AN EMPIRE (both in 1929), and WARNING SHADOWS/SCHATTEN (1923). Well worth browsing.

*McBride, Joseph, ed. PERSISTENCE OF VISION: A COLLECTION OF FILM CRITICISM. Madison: The Wisconsin Film Society Press, 1968. 222pp.
     Third in this active film society's publications, this volume is more valuable and better written than its predecessors. In particular, students should enjoy McBride's comments on Welles and Lennig's observations on Flaherty, as well as his treatment of Lugosi and Karloff, Sarris on the 1940s, and the CASABLANCA dossiers. The first

section, on the silent film, has some useful essays on Keaton, Gance, and Dreyer. Well worth browsing.

Niver, Kemp R. BIOGRAPH BULLETINS: 1896-1908. Ed. Bebe Bergsten. Los Angeles: Historical Films, 1971. Illustrated. 464pp.

An invaluable publication, this reference work offers a superb record of the first twelve years in the development of the pioneer film company eventually known as the Biograph. Throughout the 400 pages of the book are facsimile press opinions of the company's films, sales letters, film catalogs, and 200 handbills. The latter are great sources of information since they contain plot synopses and highlight the special features of the film described. In addition, each film entry is accompanied by a still, and the entire book is indexed with an alphabetical list of film titles, cameramen's names, date photographed, and copyright dates. Recommended for special collections.

Niver, Kemp R. THE FIRST TWENTY YEARS: A SEGMENT OF FILM HISTORY. Ed. Bebe Bergsten. Los Angeles: Locale Research Group, 1968. Illustrated. 176pp.

Like Hendricks, Niver is a dedicated and competent historian involved in correcting the errors of film records. In this fine illustrated edition, the author presents important information about more than 100 of the films released between 1894 and 1913. The comments, stills, and statistics provide an intriguing account of these crucial years. Among the filmmakers included are Edwin S. Porter, Georges Melies, and D. W. Griffith. Well worth browsing.

*Niver, Kemp R. IN THE BEGINNING: PROGRAM NOTES TO ACCOMPANY ONE HUNDRED EARLY MOTION PICTURES. New York: Brandon Books, 1967. Illustrated. 60pp.

This invaluable monograph is a handy reference guide to the many programs that Brandon Films (now associated with Films Incorporated) has prepared for film courses. It is an abridged version of THE FIRST TWENTY YEARS. Well worth browsing.

Niver, Kemp R. MOTION PICTURES FROM THE LIBRARY OF CONGRESS PAPER PRINT COLLECTION 1894-1915. Ed. Bebe Bergsten. Introduction Erik Barnouw. Washington: Library of Congress, 1985. Illustrated. 509pp.

A splendid revision of the original 1967 edition, this remarkable catalog is an indispensable guide to over 3,000 motion pictures produced before the start of film copyrighting. Niver provides titles, copyright dates, producers' names, film lengths (on 16mm), subject matter, and sometimes credits for the film, including cast and directors. Among its many unique contributions are information on 300 Griffith films, three dozen Melies listings, and nearly thirty Keystone Company titles. An alphabetically arranged sequence, followed by a credit list and index, is included. Recommended for special collections.

North, Joseph H. THE EARLY DEVELOPMENT OF THE MOTION PICTURE 1887-1909. New York: Arno Press, 1973. 313pp.

Originally presented as a 1949 Ph.D. dissertation at Cornell University, this interesting study outlines the contributions of early inventors like Thomas Alva Edison, William Kennedy Laurie Dickson, the Latham family, Enoch Rector, the Lumieres, Thomas Armat, C. Francis Jenkins, Elias B. Koopman, Henry N. Marvin, and Herman Cassler, from 1887 to 1909. The stages of the motion picture's development are covered in thirteen chapters dealing with the principal inventors, the first public exhibitions of movies in metropolitan cities, the first public exhibitions of the movies on the road, the problems of exhibitors, the variety of film productions from 1895 to 1900, the lawsuits, the transition period from episodic movies to story films (1900-1903), the development of film exchanges, the establishment of screen theaters, the rise of film producers for mass appeal movies, and the advent of David Wark Griffith. While much of the material now appears dated, North's study highlights the basic areas of research and offers useful primary source references. A bibliography is included. Worth browsing.

*Pratt, George C., ed. SPELLBOUND IN DARKNESS: READINGS IN THE HISTORY AND CRITICISM OF THE SILENT FILM. Greenwich: New York Graphic Society, 1973. Illustrated. 576pp.

Conceived and executed by one of our best living film historians, this valuable anthology has material collected from such diverse publications as THE NEW YORK DRAMATIC MIRROR, THE NEW YORK TIMES, PHOTOPLAY, THE MOVING PICTURE WORLD, and the MOTION PICTURE ALMANAC. Volume One covers the early films up to Griffith's INTOLERANCE, and Volume Two emphasizes individual directors--DeMille, Griffith, Chaplin, von Stroheim, Flaherty, and Dreyer--as well as the influence of foreign cinemas on Hollywood. It is a fine assortment of essays, unique material, and shooting scripts. Recommended for special collections.

Quigley, Martin, Jr. MAGIC SHADOWS: THE STORY OF THE ORIGIN OF MOTION PICTURES. Washington, D.C., Georgetown University Press, 1948. New York: Quigley Publishing House, 1960. Illustrated. 191pp.

In academic prose, Quigley presents a sketchy outline of the arguments against movies' having originated with nineteenth-century inventors. His introductory remarks stress that Athanasius Kircher, a German Jesuit priest known as the "Doctor of a Hundred Arts," gave birth to the idea of moving pictures at the Collegio Romano in Rome in about 1845. Others who came after him perfected his ideas relating to "the magic lantern," and developed the required materials necessary to reproduce the "animation of life in light and shadow plays." The sixteen unfootnoted chapters that follow hyperbolically highlight the contributions of such people as Aristotle, Roger Bacon, Leonardo da Vinci, Giovanni Battista della Porta, Gaspar Schott, Pieter van Musschenbroek, John Ayrton Paris, Joseph Antoine Ferdinand Plateau, Franz von Uchatius, William and Frederick Langenheim, Etienne-Jules Marey, Thomas Alva Edison, and Louis and Auguste Lumiere. Although Quigley makes unconvincing if very interesting statements about several periods in ancient history, his choice of illustrations and intriguing speculations make the book enjoyable reading. A useful chronology and a helpful index add to the work's value. Well worth browsing.

Reade, Eric. AUSTRALIAN SILENT FILMS: A PICTORIAL HISTORY, 1896-1929. Melbourne: Lansdowne Press, 1970. Illustrated. 192pp.

This unique and concise volume covers the following significant periods: beginnning films (1896-99), the Salvation Army successes (1900-03), the rise of feature films (1904-07), exciting showmen (1908-10), the golden age (1911-13, when two feature films were being made every month), the silent revolution (1914-19, when industrial problems arose), the tough years (1920-23), and the end of the silent era (1924-29). The book also has a valuable appendix on silent films and an index. Recommended for special collections.

*Rudisill, Richard. MIRROR IMAGE: THE INFLUENCE OF THE DAGUERREOTYPE ON AMERICAN SOCIETY. Alburquerque: University of New Mexico Press, 1971. Illustrated. Unpaginated.

In this handsomely produced and scholarly written book on the early days of pre-photography, Rudisill offers a superb look at the cultural, commercial, and social aspects of the new science. Worth browsing.

*Slide, Anthony, with the assistance of Paul O'Dell. EARLY AMERICAN CINEMA. Cranbury: A. S. Barnes and Company, 1970. Illustrated. 192pp.

A valuable introduction to the first decade of American filmmaking, this pioneering study provides information on important studios like Biograph, the Essanay Film Manufacturing Company, Kalem, Keystone, and Vitagraph. The nine chapters also review the contributions of Griffith, Chaplin, Sennett, and Pearl White, who were responsible for making movies a legitimate form of entertainment. Useful illustrations, a bibliography, and an index are included. Well worth browsing.

*Spehr, Paul C. THE MOVIES BEGIN: MAKING MOVIES IN NEW JERSEY, 1887-1920. Newark: Newark Museum and Morgan Press, 1977. Illustrated. 191pp.

From 1887 to 1920, New Jersey was considered by a number of people to be America's moving picture capital. Among the famous film personalities working in the area were Thomas Alva Edison, Pearl White, Mary Pickford, Anita Loos, Mack Sennett, Edwin S. Porter, Fred Balshofer, Rudolph Valentino, Hannibal Goodman, Lionel Barrymore, Theda Bara, and D. W. Griffith. Thanks to the imaginative research done by the Library of Congress film specialist Spehr, this slim but reflective analysis provides intriguing information on why the New Jersey dynasty finally lost out to Hollywood. What is exemplary about the historical treatment of technological, commercial, and artistic developments is the author's restraint in presenting presumed causal relationships. Consider the case of David Horsley. Spehr writes, "Is it possible that Hollywood was born at 900 Broadway in Bayonne, New Jersey? In a sense it is. In November of 1911, David Horsley brought his company of cowboys and Indians, Mutt and Jeff, and a comic villain named Desperate Desmond from Bayonne to a Los Angeles suburb and established the first studio in the village of Hollywood." Rather than dwell on this intriguing supposition, Spehr moves quickly to dispel any doubts by pointing out that the movie migration away from the big urban centers began in 1908, not 1911, and that California and New Jersey were both beneficiaries of producers' desires for more flexible facilities located near lovely countrysides. Except for some occasional inaccuracies regarding screen credits[89] and a generally prosaic chronology, the handsomely illustrated book (published as part of the Newark museum's bicentennial celebration) is a pleasant work and very informative. A bibliography and index are included. Well worth browsing.

Tarbox, Charles H. LOST FILMS, 1895-1917. Los Angeles: Film Classic Exchange, 1983. Illustrated. 280pp.

"Almost all of the thirty thousand and more films made between 1895 and 1917," explains Tarbox, "are 'lost' films. They no longer exist." The author's "notes" and profuse illustrations are therefore valuable not only because they deal with personalities who appeared in the movies or functioned as directors, technicians, and producers, but also because they represent the opinions of someone who had a deep interest in the early period of film. Six fact-filled chapters, profusely illustrated with very rare visual material, tell an intriguing story of why, where, when, and how the film industry progressed over two decades. A general index, followed by two short indexes of geographical locations and film titles, adds to the book's value to scholars. Recommended for special collections.

Wood, Leslie. THE MIRACLE OF THE MOVIES. London: Burke Publishing Company, 1947. Illustrated. 352pp.

---

[89]   See George Wead, ""The Birth of Hollywood," AMERICAN FILM 2:10 (September 1977):78-9.

This talkative account of film history is a romantic story of the development of the motion picture industry, useful only in a marginal manner for those interested in learning about the problems, personalities, and products in those incredible early years. The emphasis is on British and American film history. Worth browsing.

EADWEARD MUYBRIDGE

Haas, Robert Bartlett. MUYBRIDGE: MAN IN MOTION. Berkeley: University of California Press, 1975. Illustrated. 300pp.

This outstanding biography does a fine job of evaluating the British experimenter's contributions to prefilm history. Haas states in his preface that Muybridge "was a one-man show. He carried instantaneous, sequential photography to its peak in his time. He developed a machine for projecting sequential photographs in apparent motion. These he showed before audiences over the western world between 1879 and 1895. Making his living by this means until his retirement, which coincided with the rise of the film industry, he was his own underwriter, producer, scriptwriter, cameraman, director, processor, editor, exhibitor, narrator, advertising man, and distributor. In addition, he showed motion pictures, for a time, in the first theater specifically built for that purpose." The eight informative chapters that follow have a crisp, factual style. In addition to offering fresh insights into Muybridge's florid career, the tasteful art historian provides a number of excellent illustrations, beautifully reproduced in this handsome edition. An index is included. Recommended for special collections.

Hendricks, Gordon. EADWEARD MUYBRIDGE: THE FATHER OF THE MOTION PICTURE. New York: Grossman Publishers, 1975. Illustrated. 271pp.

Pointing out that the author's previous books all testify to the importance of Muybridge's stature in the history of motion pictures, Hendricks insists that "craftsmen and inventors had been inspired by his pioneer work, and that after they had improved his methods--chiefly by devising apparatus to take motion pictures from a single point of view instead of multiple points of view--the only remaining obstacle was the lack of a continuous, flexible film." The book's ten chapters detail the significant aspects of Muybridge's life: the early years, celebrity status in San Francisco, success and marriage, the murder trial, Central America, the photographing of Stanford's horse Occident, success and scandal in Europe, the Philadelphia years, photography and painting, and the final years. What is refreshing is Hendricks's argumentative style; he refuses to let issues remain hanging. For example, he rejects the notion that Muybridge came to America in search of gold (a commercial career is the real reason). He points out that, contrary to earlier reports, Muybridge exhibited his first motion pictures projected by the Zoopraxiscope in the fall of 1879. In short, the details provided in this rich biography challenge the claims of all earlier works. Adding to the book's considerable value is an extensive collection of stills, illustrating many aspects of Muybridge's career. Even if one resists Hendricks's sweeping claim that Muybridge is the "father of the motion picture," one can appreciate the care with which the author has made his case. Valuable endnotes, interesting appendexes, a chronology, a bibliography, and an index are included. Recommended for special collections.

MacDonnell, Kevin. EADWEARD MUYBRIDGE: THE MAN WHO INVENTED THE MOVING PICTURE. Boston: Little, Brown and Company, 1972. Illustrated. 159pp.

A reflective but factually flawed overview of the distinguished photographer's successes and pictures, this coffee-table book is easy reading and enjoyable viewing. In Part One, MacDonnell's introductory essay offers a debatable interpretation of the major highlights in Muybridge's life. Born Edward James Muggeridge on April 9, 1830, the ambitious youngster changed his first name when he was twenty years of age, presumably because of "sheer romanticism." (The author fails to mention that the surname was changed in 1865.) In 1852, Muybridge left his native Kingston, England, and went to America in search of riches. By 1867, he not only had learned photography, but was making a name for himself as a talented recorder of the Yosemite Valley. In 1868, the U. S. government hired him as director of photographic surveys, providing him with the opportunity to photograph much of the uncharted areas of the American West Coast, Wyoming, and Montana. As the author reports these standard facts, he takes care to comment on shutter speeds, and the size of glass plates and cameras, plus the incredible difficulties Muybridge overcame to produce striking pictures. Mention is also made of fees Muybridge received as well as the various honors bestowed on the famous inventor, writer, and lecturer. Interestingly, MacDonnell repeats much of the discredited account of the photographer's services to ex-governor Leland Stanford and the action-pictures of a horse galloping, while making it clear that the pictures had nothing to do with a bet since Stanford was not a gambling man. The author is much more interested, however, in discussing film and shutter speeds and disputing Muybridge's assertions about his photographic technique. Moreover, MacDonnell calls attention to the importance of the great photographer's private life in the development of his career. Married at the age of forty-two (Hendricks claims Muybridge was forty; his bride, nineteen) to a divorcee named Flora Shallcross Stone, he soon found his work competing with his marriage. The Modoc Indian War in 1873 plus numerous professional assignments kept Muybridge away from home for much of the year. Only after the birth of a son in April, 1874, did the wandering photographer discover that his wife had a lover and that the child was not his. In less than twenty-four hours after hearing the news, Muybridge dispatched the father. On February 5, 1875, he was acquitted of murder. Flora tried to divorce him, but failed. She twice tried unsuccessfully to receive alimony. Before she could try a third time, she died in 1875. Muybridge meanwhile had taken off for Central America. By the end of the year, he was back in San Francisco, bringing with him an incredible number of pictures dealing with life in Mexico, Guatemala, and Panama. Within a year, he renewed his former business relationship with Stanford. This move led to the most controversial of all Muybridge's contributions to cinematography, the alleged invention of the motion picture. According to MacDonnell, until "Muybridge gave a lecture on the evening of 4 May 1880 at the San Francisco Art Association Rooms, during which he showed moving pictures of animals[,] no one had ever before projected moving photographs on a screen to an audience." He then adds, "To Muybridge belongs the honor of inventing the movies." (Hendricks also acknowledges Muybridge as "the father of the motion picture," but claims that the May 4 date is a press preview and that the first projections were done in the fall of 1879.) The remainer of the extended essay covers Muybridge's photographic studies, publications, and experiments. Particular attention is paid to his celebrated studies on animal and human locomotion funded by the University of Pennsylvania. In 1900, the distinguished innovator returned to his Kingston roots, where he died four years later on May 8. Part Two provides ample evidence of Muybridge's photographic skills. Part Three contains several interesting appendexes, including information on Muybridge's murder trial, his photographic technique, and the author's reflections on the research for the book. A bibliography concludes the work. Well worth browsing.

Muybridge, Eadweard. ANIMALS IN MOTION, ed. Lewis S. Brown. New York: Dover Publications, 1975. Illustrated. 414pp.
    A wonderful source book for artists, animators, and art directors, this superb collection of Muybridge's 4,000 high-speed shots of thirty-four different animals and birds presents 123 different types of animal action--e.g., walking, running, leaping, and flying. The impressive shots, allegedly taken at speeds up to 1/2000th of a second, include as many as fifty shots per action. The famous photographer, working with a three-year grant from the University of Pennsylvania, provides three different

angles--e.g., 90-degree, 60-degree, and rear--for each of the typical animal actions. Almost every illustration in this abridged edition of the original 1877 eleven-volume edition, ANIMAL LOCOMOTION, is reproduced the same size as in the original work. Out of a total of 781 initial plates, 219 dealt with animal motion. Nearly all are contained in the present volume. Collectively, they demonstrate Muybridge's unique contributions to photography and the birth of moving pictures. Worth browsing.

Muybridge, Eadweard. THE HUMAN FIGURE IN MOTION, ed. Robert Taft. New York: Dover Publications, 1975. Illustrated. 400pp.

The largest selection of Muybridge's high speed photographs of humans in action contains 4,789 pictures, illustrating nearly 165 different types of motion. Taken from the author's 1,887 plates, eleven-volume book, ANIMAL LOCOMOTION, this abridged version contains 195 plates, splendidly reproduced, which allegedly were shot originally at up to 1/6000th of a second. The numerous pictures on each plate show the action from three angles: front, rear, and three-quarter view. The images of the mostly undraped subjects present in considerable detail the great photographer's fascination with the human body. Taft makes it clear in his introduction why the University of Pennsylvania invested in more than 100,000 negatives at a cost of $50,000, and what the value of the finished work is for artists, students, animators, and art directors. Worth browsing.

FILMS

GENERAL

ANIMATED CARTOONS: THE TOY THAT GREW UP (16mm: n.d., 17 mins., b/w, sound, R-RAD/S-RAD)

A wordy but worthwhile visual study of the early, primitive movie equipment and the growth of the art and technique of animated drawings. Among the topics presented are Plateau, Reynauld, and their machines: Phenakistiscope and Praxinoscope. One gets a chance to see how color-tinted images were used with slotted disks to create successive stages of action that gave the illusion of moving pictures.

BIOGRAPHY OF THE MOTION PICTURE CAMERA (16mm: n.d., 21 mins., b/w, sound, R-RAD/S-RAD)

A chatty but intriguing visual study of Marey, this one emphasizes the early inventor's investigations into recording motion, as well as the first films of the Lumieres and Edison. Unfortunately, Dickson's work is omitted. One does get a sense, however, of the manner in which the experiments on capturing motion evolved.

DAGUERRE: THE BIRTH OF PHOTOGRAPHY (16mm: n.d., 29 mins., b/w, sound, R-RAD/S-RAD)

This interesting film depicts the contributions of Daguerre, Niepce, and Talbot to the birth of photography. It illustrates how Niepce produced the Heliographic process, Daguerre the first permanent photography, and Talbot the Calotype process.

IN THE BEGINNING. UNIT I (16mm: 1893-1903, 22 1/2 mins., b/w, R-FNC)[90]

---

[90]   Kemp Niver has created twenty-three units, consisting of ninety-nine films in all, to use in studying the history of film in the United States, Britain,

These thirteen films produced and copyrighted by Edison and photographed by Porter between 1898 and 1903 are superb for seeing the growth of film from its Kinetoscope days to the early days of matte shots and dissolves.

ORIGINS OF THE MOTION PICTURE (16mm: n.d., 21 mins., b/w, sound, D-MMA) Based upon Quigley's book, MAGIC SHADOWS, this worthwhile film provides some excellent visual material on Plateau, Stampfer, Marey, Edison, and the Lumieres.[91] The movie also includes some valuable footage on a prototype of Dickson's "Black Maria," and offers some insights into the films produced there.

THE PIONEER YEARS (1896-1914)

Once technology proved the feasibility of recording and projecting moving pictures, the business and artistic communities began staking their claims to the new popular entertainment.[92] While some promoters doubted that films had a long future, few entrepreneurs doubted the novelty's profit-making potential. Among the most powerful film leaders in the late 1890s were the Lumieres, Charles Pathe, Leon Graumont (France); R. W. Paul (England); and the Vitagraph Company, The American Mutoscope and Biograph Company (formerly the K. M. C. D.), and Edison (United States).

As discussed in Chapters 2, 3, 5, and 6, a number of factors--e.g., industrialization, immigration, increased leisure time, a rapidly growing middle class, the public's insatiable appetite for novelty, the popularity of nineteenth-century melodramas, dioramas, and magic shows--all played a part in making movies a craze at the turn of the century. Not even problems with the brief duration of the fifty-foot films or the imperfect projectors could seriously affect the public's interest in movies.

Contributing to the popularity of movies and the attention paid to industry problems was the appearance of clever entrepreneurs who began edging out the film pioneers who had invented and patented the technology. Relatively quickly, the less-than-a-minute films moved out of penny arcades, store-front theaters, blacktop tents, and vaudeville houses[93] into fixed theaters like Thomas L. Tally's Electric

France, and Denmark up to 1912. I recommend them very highly and suggest getting a copy of Film's Incorprated's catalog for a complete listing of all units.

[91]   For some useful information of the filmmakers made by the two brothers from Lyons, see Andy Grundberg, "The Earliest Images: The Lumiere Brothers' Films," NEW YORK TIMES C (March 14, 1989):17.

[92]   For a look at one of the early attempts to establish a film center, see Richard Alan Nelson, "Florida: The Forgotten Film Capital," UNIVERSITY FILM ASSOCIATION 29:3 (Summer 1977):9-21.

[93]   For an interesting study of intermedia competition, see Jeanne Thomas Allen, "Copyright and Early Theater, Vaudeville and Film Competition," JOURNAL OF THE UNIVERSITY FILM ASSOCIATION 31:2 (Spring 1979):5-11. For a valuable explanation of how traveling movie shows made fixed movie theaters possible and preferable, see Calvin Pryluck, "The Itinerant Movie Show and the Development of the Film Industry," JOURNAL OF THE UNIVERSITY FILM AND VIDEO ASSOCIATION 36:4 (Fall 1983):11-22. See also Mark E. Swartz, "An Overview of Cinema on the Fairgrounds," JOURNAL OF POPULAR FILM AND TELEVISION 15:3 (Fall 1987):102-8; Edward Lowry, "Edwin J. Hadley: Travelling Film Exhibitor," JOURNAL OF THE UNIVERSITY FILM ASSOCIATION 28:3 (Summer 1976):5-12; and Burnes St. Patrick Hollyman, "The First Picture Shows: Austin, Texas (1894-1913)," ibid., 29:3 (Summer 1977):3-8.

Theatre (1902), George C. Hale's "Hale Tours" (1904),[94] and Harry and John Harris's "nickelodeons" (1905).[95] By 1906, the nickelodeons had taken over film exhibition. They had started with bi-weekly program changes, but very quickly had moved to showing new attractions daily. Many people benefited by the proliferation of movie theaters, especially the producers of projectors and the general public. On the other hand, as Musser points out, there were casualties, particularly among traveling showmen, semi-professional exhibitors, and their suppliers.[96] According to Charlotte Herzog, the shift from seeing a film in a peep show to watching it with an audience in a movie theater tells "a story about where the movies came from and where they were going."[97] Moreover, the shift signaled the transition away from the inventors and magicians who dominated the prefilm history, to the showmen and entrepreneurs who populated the early decades of the movies.

The content of the first films was extremely varied.[98] "Not only did they produce topical and scenic motion pictures," explains Joseph H. North, "similar in an abbreviated form to those which can be seen in any newsreel theatre today, but they also from the very beginning, it seems, produced, on a limited scale, motion pictures of little dramatic incidents, comedies, trick films, and vaudeville turns."[99] For example, the Lumiere brothers produced films called "actualities" (realistic pictures). These documentaries, shot outdoors, focused on everyday occurrences: a train arriving at a station, a father feeding his child, and a gardener watering his lawn. Edison's cameramen not only took advantage of the public's curiosity about scenic reality, but also used the medium as an ingenious way of "photographing" dramatic events like a trolley-car ride and firefighters in action.

---

[94]   In addition to Fielding's article on Hale's Tours, see Tom Gunning, "An Unseen Energy Swallows Space: The Space in Early Films and Its Relation to American Avant-Garde," FILM BEFORE GRIFFITH, pp.355-66. Charles H. Tarbox points out (p.33) that "the important thing about the Hale films were [sic] not the films themselves, but the manner in which they were shown. The Hale Tours were a combination of an amusement park ride with a motion picture film and they were installed in many cities."

[95]   As Q. David Bowers explains, "The term NICKELODEON is derived from NICKEL, the price of admission, and ODEON, the French word for theatre. In modern times, nickelodeon has also referred to coin-operated musical instruments of various sorts, but in the early part of the present century a nickelodeon was a five-cent theatre and nothing else." See *Q. David Bowers, NICKELODEON THEATRES AND THEIR MUSIC (Vestal: The Vestal Press, 1986), p.vii. Also particularly useful is a collection of essays on the nickelodeon from 1907 to 1913 in *Gerald Mast, ed., THE MOVIES IN OUR MIDST: DOCUMENTS IN THE CULTURAL HISTORY OF FILM IN AMERICA (Chicago: The University of Chicago Press, 1982), pp.41-99.

[96]   THOMAS A EDISON PAPERS, pp.13-4.

[97]   Charlotte Herzog, "The Archeology of Cinema Architecture: The Origins of the Movie Theater," QUARTERLY REVIEW OF FILM STUDIES 9:1 (Winter 1984):11. For another interesting perspective on how one theater was affected by the shift to movie houses, see John W. Frick, NEW YORK'S FIRST THEATRICAL CENTER: THE RIALTO AT UNION SQUARE (Ann Arbor: UMI Research Press, 1985).

[98]   Richard Sanderson, A HISTORICAL STUDY OF THE DEVELOPMENT OF AMERICAN MOTION PICTURE CONTENT AND TECHNIQUES PRIOR TO 1904 (Unpublished Ph.D. dissertation, University of Southern California, 1961). New York: Arno Press, 1977.

[99]   Joseph H. North, THE EARLY DEVELOPMENT OF THE MOTION PICTURE 1887-1909 (New York: Arno Press, 1973), p.99.

Starting with the single-shot films of the late 1890s, filmmakers like the Lumieres and Edison went on to cultivate the public's fascination with "seeing" celebrities and famous landmarks.[100] There were also ACTUALITIES RECONSTITUEES ("reconstructed newsreels") that recreated significant events of the day, similar to the MARCH OF TIME films of the 1930s and 1940s. The illusion of reality engendered by these "moving pictures" was enhanced by pictures taken around the world. Even when the films were "faked" (taken in a studio but made to appear to be "authentic" shots of Africa, Europe, and the Orient), audiences enjoyed the the visual illustrations of the world.

What is being hotly debated today is whether the emphasis on actualities and topical films precluded the medium's artistic development. Conventional wisdom argues that the early filmmakers emphasized the element of motion, TABLEAUX-VIVANTES, giving no attention to temporal organization. Movies were perceived as a photographer's work in motion, thereby focusing the producer's attention solely on spatial composition. The various plot lines that appeared did so in linear fashion. That is, there was a beginning, middle, and end, with virtually no editing or imaginative camera angles involved. In short, traditional scholarship argues that in the first years of the twentieth century it was the predictability of the by-now cliche-ridden films that necessitated a shift away from actualities, and toward dramatic stories.

However, a new generation of scholars insists that early films and editing concepts were anything but "primitive."[101] For example, Musser points out that the first films were constantly being edited by exhibitors and projectionists as well as by producers. As early as 1896, theater owners took an active role in determining a film's length, what particular sections of a film should be shown, and in what order. At times, the early exhibitors actually inserted offscreen supplementary material (e.g., sound effects and spoken commentary) they had purchased for optional use. While it is true that producers eventually assumed primary responsibility for the editorial and narrative features of a film, editing at the outset was considered not only an exhibitor's option, but also his responsibility.[102] Moreover, it was not unusual for these showmen to provide a narration for a selection of short films. "In many instances," Musser explains, "spectators were expected to bring a level of

---

[100] Traditional scholars generally argue that film history progressed along two lines (documentary and fiction), symbolized by the works of the Lumieres and Georges Melies. Noel Burch offers an alternative perspective. In essence, he argues that the real contrast was between the works of Edison and the Lumieres. The former sought to reproduce "perceptual reality as a whole, of 'life.'" The latter, perceived as "the direct heirs of Muybridge and Marey, . . . [were] motivated by an essentially scientific aspiration to analyze movement." The struggle between these two pioneering influences--e.g., an image of reality versus an examination of motion--illustrates not only basic ideological differences, but also trends in contemporary filmmakers and national cinemas. See *Noel Burch, TO THE DISTANT OBSERVER: FORM AND MEANING IN THE JAPANESE CINEMA, trans. and ed. Annette Michelson (Berkeley: University of California Press, 1979), pp.62-3.

[101] See Burns Hollyman, "Alexander Black's Picture Plays: 1893-1894," CINEMA JOURNAL 16:2 (Spring 1977):26-33.

[102] Charles Musser, commenting as a respondent to a May 22, 1987, panel, "Early Cinema: Issues in Research and Theory," at the Society for Cinema Studies Convention in Montreal. Elsewhere, Musser notes that post-production editing was common on the lecture circuit as well as in traditional movie settings. Moreover, it was done by musicians, special effects specialists, lecturers, etc. See "Towards A History of Screen Practice," p.65.

familiarity to their appreciation of screen narrative that later would be provided by intertitles."[103] By the end of 1897, exhibitors had introduced a novel approach to screen projection: a stereopticon to accompany moving picture projection. According to Musser, the simultaneous slide-film show allowed the film operator a "whole range of editorial possibilities . . . [and] heightened concern for the succession of images and with narrative in general."[104]

Tom Gunning reminds us that from the medium's first days, moviemakers appealed to the interests of the audience, rather than being held hostage to film technology. And what appealed to audiences at the turn of the century was the excitement of movies themselves and what possibilities the new medium possessed. Gunning believes "that the relation to the spectator set up by the films of Lumiere and Melies (and many other filmmakers before 1906) had a common basis, and one that differs from the primary spectator relations set up by narrative film after 1906."[105] Labeling his concept, "the cinema of attractions," he stresses the notion of movies' being able to SHOW something and to SOLICIT the audience's attention. What traditional historians dismiss as "monolithic shots" devoid of editing, Gunning claims is trick photography in which stop-motion filming allowed for skillful editing techniques in order to benefit from the public's fascination with the new invention. Moreover, rather than appealing to the interests of a passive viewer, Gunning asserts that filmmakers addressed directly the audience's desires for spectacular showmanship.[106] The thrust of his argument is that "Every change in film history implies a change in its address to the spectator, and each period constructs its spectator in a new way."[107]

Gunning's speculations about the "cinema of attractions" reflect a growing scholarly interest in the popularity of optical illusions during the nineteenth century, and their effect on the birth of movies. Owing much to the remarkable FANTASMAGORIE shows performed by Etienne Gaspard Robert (called Robertson) from 1794 to 1800 in Paris, magic shows became a sensation throughout the Western world.[108] In the decades that followed, the magicians kept close watch on the film inventors, seeing each new development as a means for improving stage illusions. Once moving pictures became a reality, as Erik Barnouw explains, magicians made their presence felt in two ways. The first approach was behind-the-scenes in animating, editing, and staging the "tricks" for the movies. The second stage was when the magicians themselves--e.g., David Devant, John Nevil Maskelyne, Charles

[103]   Charles Musser, "American Vitagraph: 1897-1901," CINEMA JOURNAL 22:3 (Spring 1983):4-5.

[104]   "American Vitagraph," pp.10-1. For a useful introduction to the links between inventions and industrial patterns in the film industry, see Robert C. Allen, "Vitascope/Cinematographe: Initial Patterns of American Film Industrial Practice," JOURNAL OF THE UNIVERSITY FILM ASSOCIATION 31:2 (Spring 1979):13-8.

[105]   Tom Gunning, "The Cinema of Attraction: Early Film, Its Spectator and the Avant-Garde," WIDE ANGLE 8:3-4 (1986):64.

[106]   Tom Gunning, "Primitive Cinema: The Trick's on Us." Paper presented at the Society for Cinema Studies Conference, Montreal, Canada, May 1987. Tom Gunning, "'Primitive' Cinema--A Frame-up? or The Trick's on Us," CINEMA JOURNAL 28:2 (Winter 1989):3-12.

[107]   "Cinema of Attraction," p.70.

[108]   For a useful introduction to the author of the first American book on magic and its effect on magic lanterns, see Erik Barnouw, "The Fantasms of Andrew Oehler," QUARTERLY REVIEW OF FILM STUDIES 9:1 (Winter 1984):41-4.

Betram, and Leopoldo Fregoli--performed their "magic" acts on screen. The former approach was more important than the latter. In Barnouw's words,

It was in the trick film that magicians made a contribution to film--not by appearing in film--though some still might--but by adapting to film their particular heritage of technical hanky-panky and finding new opportunities for it. They became important as film creators rather than as performers. The trick film vogue was short-lived, but sufficiently intense to spur wide imitation. Magicians and non-magicians participated in its moment of glory.[109]

Ironically, the more magicians appeared on screen, the more they lost their hold on audiences. Before they faded out, however, they presented the public with a spectacular summation of a century-long tradition of ghosts, phantoms, skeletons, vanishing tricks, metamorphoses, and delightful mayhem.

Neither Musser nor Gunning deny that by the turn of the century, scenic and topical pictures began to lose their luster. As discussed in Chapters 3 and 5, the movie pioneers soon began to capitalize on the mass audience's interest in nineteenth-century melodramas. But as the scholars point out, the transition away from actualities and topical subjects to story films was gradual. At first, the changes were noticeable in the form of chase films, comedies, and "trick" movies. Then, as the film lengths grew from fifty feet to six hundred feet between 1902 and 1903, story films captured the audiences' attention.

What is also being debated today is the nature of the pioneering American film audiences.[110] (As discussed in Chapters 3 and 6, we need to remember that the concept of "film audiences" itself is a nebulous term.) The consensus is that people who made up film audiences were of four types: middle-class people who rebelled against traditional religious inhibitions, middle- and working-class people infatuated with melodramas and magic shows, urban working-class people who used movies as an educational experience, and immigrants who saw in movies a means of learning about the "American way." Closely linked to the presumed effect that pioneering movies had on their multi-natured audiences was the emotional appeal of melodramas. Theorists assert that film melodramas gave the impression of an ordered universe in which standards of right and wrong were delineated. Whether consciously or not, audiences (then and now) went to films to learn about their culture and/or to satisfy their needs and desires. This unproven theory further asserts that the popular genre hammered home the idea that resocialization depended on individual behavior rather than on group dynamics. Moreover, it was assumed that nineteenth-century secularization had replaced the traditional notion of absolute rights and wrongs. What the new melodramatic movies were doing was reinstituting cosmic values of the past. Thus the pioneering audiences were finding in the new medium not only modern role models, but also a key to the dominant values of the modern world. Those who worried about the effects of these modern movies saw a counterproductive value system that nurtured fear, prejudice, and anti-intellectualism. Neil Harris points out that

It was the concentration on the accidental, arbitrary, and absurd postures human beings assumed that provided much of the really subversive quality of these first films. Moralists were worried about other things. Filmmakers, many

---

[109] Erik Barnouw, THE MAGICIAN AND THE CINEMA (New York: Oxford University Press, 1981), pp.87-8. The point is also made by Musser, who argues that the various magic lantern shows continued centuries of screen conventions related to storytelling traditions. See "Towards a History of Screen Practice," pp.65-8.

[110] For an idea of how filmmakers responded to the need for films aimed at a better class of people, see Roberta Pearson, "Cultivated Folks and the Better Classes: Class Conflict and Representation in Early American Film," JOURNAL OF POPULAR FILM AND TELEVISION 15:3 (Fall 1987):120-8.

of whom came from the working class, were eager to strike a chord in audiences of their peers. Their films often took the side of the victims of misfortune rather than that of representatives of the establishment. Crime was sometimes presented sympathetically. Ridicule punctured authority and loaded the very wealthy with satire. The early urban audiences were streetwise. While inclined to be sentimental about personal attachments--romance, children, animals--they were more skeptical of abstract generalizations."[111]

The battle continues to this day between the cultural traditionalists, who insist that movies undermine social responsibility and rigid codes of conduct, and the exponents of popular culture, who argue that a democratic society requires pluralistic values.

Georges Melies was one magician-turned-film director whose emphasis and techniques went beyond the problems of simply showing motion and exploiting "trick photography."[112] Grounded in the nineteenth-century melodramatic theater known as FEERIES--spectacle shows "in which acrobatics, music, and mime were the main ingredients"[113]--his film work with theatrical tricks involving machines and double exposures laid the groundwork not only for animated films, but also for many of the techniques connected with stop-motion photography. John Frazer explains that Melies was an artist very much rooted in his generation and quite responsive to the traditions of popular variety shows--e.g., circuses, cafe-concerts, and music halls--and to British and French pantomimes. The latter, particularly the neorealistic pantomimes in the late 1880s and 1890s, focused on special effects that resulted in an astonishing number of transformations. "The similarity between this presentation style and the vocabulary of transformations created by Melies for the curtainless cinema," Frazer points out, "suggests the influence that the pantomime spectacle had on early films."[114] But Melies was far from being a mere translator of theatrical tricks into screen illusions. "From him," Paul Hammond argues, "we can learn to consider the cinema as a medium animated by marvelous moments owing little allegiance to the banal narrative structures that held them prisoner. From Melies, we can elucidate a structure of the cinema that consists of revelatory and cathartic images liberated from their obligations to good sense."[115] Equally important, Melies's aesthetics led him into exploring a novel approach to cinematic narratives. As Andre Gaudreault points out, "Melies demonstrates an alternative attitude toward story-telling, one less focused on the story QUA story."[116]

As interest in developing narrative styles in film progressed,[117] Edwin S. Porter, in 1901, began his famous experiments. He emphasized cinematic rather than

---

[111]   Neil Harris, "A Subversive Form," BEFORE HOLLYWOOD, p.48.

[112]   Katherine Singer Kovacs, "Georges Melies and the FEERIE," CINEMA JOURNAL 16:1 (Fall 1976):1-13;

[113]   Kovacks, p.1.

[114]   John Frazer, ARTIFICIALLY ARRANGED SCENES: THE FILMS OF GEORGES MELIES (Boston: G. K. Hall and Company, 1979), p.4.

[115]   Paul Hammond, MARVELLOUS MELIES (New York: St. Martin's Press, 1975), p.9.

[116]   Andre Gaudreault, "Theatricality, Narrativity, and Trickality: Reevaluating the Cinema of Georges Melies," JOURNAL OF POPULAR FILM AND TELEVISION 15:3 (Fall 1987):112.

[117]   Barry Salt, "Film Form, 1900-1906," SIGHT AND SOUND 47:3 (Summer 1978):148-53. For an example of Melies's influence in America, examine the work of his brother, Gaston, who not only managed Melies's Star Film Company in the United States,

stage techniques to show movement. That is, he used parallel editing (alternating two simultaneous actions) and cross-cutting (interweaving fragments of two separate scenes) instead of merely having the action take place in front of a fixed camera as on the stage.[118] In films like THE LIFE OF AN AMERICAN FIREMAN and THE GREAT TRAIN ROBBERY (both in 1903), Porter was doing for film editing what Melies had done for film narrative. His unique storytelling skills demonstrated that the medium, utilizing cinematic time and logic, could act as an emotional magnet for the emotions of countless viewers around the globe.   Consequently, Porter's experiments fueled the growing tendency in the early part of the 1900s for filmmakers to move away from fantasy, to the portrayal of reality.[119]

By 1907, the "pure competition" days of the early period, with its limited patterns of production, distribution, and exhibition, also dramatically changed, shifting away from short films about everyday occurrences, to longer story movies, the rise of film exchanges, improved production facilities, and a growing need for a division of labor--e.g., screenwriters, producers, directors, camera crews, and performers. Motivated not only by profits, but also by personal ambitions, the new class of filmmakers tied their fortunes to patent ownership and social respectability. At the same time, the early years witnessed the growing hostility to "moving pictures." As discussed in Chapter 3, organized religion and social reformers saw in this new form of mass communication a threat not only to traditional values, but also an ideological threat to traditional social institutions. By 1907, the forces of censorship were on the move in the form of political and social measures to curb the freedom of filmmakers.

In the meantime, other filmmakers were contributing to the art of the film. In France, for example, Ferdinand Zecca incorporated into his productions many of the exciting techniques being developed in England and America. Not surprisingly, the noted director tried his hand at all sorts of films, from socially conscious movies to outrageous comedies. What was unique about Zecca was the way in which he applied by-now standard concepts like the chase to comic situations, thereby not only expanding cinematic language, but also refining editing techniques.

Zecca was only one of many innovative artists who worked for Charles Pathe, the genius who presided over the most powerful international film organization prior to World War I.[120] By 1908, according to Cook, Pathe Freres, with extraordinary production facilities at Vincennes, accounted for twice as many films on American screens as all the major American film companies collectively.[121] Among Pathe's illustrious performers was Max Linder (nee Gabriel Levielle), the dapper comedian hailed by a number of scholars as the first important film comedian.

Pathe Freres's principal competition was Gaumont Pictures. And Gaumont's primary asset was Louis Feuillade, a screenwriter-turned-director, whose claim to fame was his imaginative serial detective movies like FANTOMAS (1913-14), LES VAMPIRES (1915-16), and JUDEX (1916). in addition to the serials' stunning location

---

but also was very active in the film business between 1903 and 1913. See Patrick McInroy, "The American Melies," SIGHT AND SOUND 48:4 (Autumn 1979):250-4.

[118]   Noel Burch, "Porter or Ambivalence," SCREEN 19:4 (Winter 1978-79):91-105; Charles Musser, "The Early Cinema of Edwin Porter," CINEMA JOURNAL 19:1 (Fall 1979):1-35; Andre Gaudreault et al., "Detours in Film Narrative: The Development of Cross-Cutting," ibid., pp.39-59; and Jack Spears, "Edwin S. Porter," FILMS IN REVIEW 21:6 (June-July 1970):327-54.

[119]   In this connection, see Raymond Fielding, "Hale's Tours: Ultrarealism in the Pre-1910 Motion Picture," CINEMA JOURNAL 10:1 (Fall 1970):34-47, Rpt. FILM BEFORE GRIFFITH, pp.116-30.

[120]   Georges Sadoul, "Napoleon of the Cinema," SIGHT AND SOUND 27:4 (Spring 1958):183.

[121]   Cook, p.47.

photography, they pioneered the concept of MISE EN SCENE (the aesthetics of the scene as opposed to the art of the shot). Unlike the artists who dominated film history up to the end of World War II, Feuillade stressed the imaginative use of action and composition within the shot, leaving the manipulation of one shot to another to American and Russian artists.   Roy Armes observes that in many respects the innovative director "provides a synthesis of [Louis] Lumiere's realism and Melies's fantasy. . . ."[122] Gaumont also benefited from the services of Jean Durand (a forerunner of the frantic comedies popularized by Mack Sennett and Rene Clair), Alice Guy-Blache (the first female director), and Emile Cohl (the pioneer of many aspects of modern-day animation). Given the talent and economic influence of companies like Pathe Freres and Gaumont Pictures, it is not surprising that France dominated global film production, distribution, and exhibition until World War I forced the French industry into a steep decline.

In Britain, the industry had moved quickly to establish itself after Friese-Greene's 1889 cinematographic patents and the rivalry among the various inventors in the mid-1890s. Foremost among the British pioneers was R. W. Paul, who not only took full advantage of Edison's unguarded patents, but also became the chief British manufacturer of projectors and cameras during the early days of film. Meanwhile, the art of the film was being advanced by "The School of Brighton,"[123] consisting primarily of three remarkable filmmakers--George Albert Smith, James A. Williamson,[124] and Esme Collings. Although Collings quickly left the fold, the other two photographers-turned-filmmakers contributed to the development of film narrative in the areas of editing and composition. Operating during the last few years of the nineteenth century, the Brighton group, more than any of their peers, recognized the necessity for cinematic pacing in creating an effective story film. This intuitive concept led to various experiments in moving the narrative from a beginning to a middle and an end. For example, David Robinson credits Smith with patenting the double exposure in films in 1897.[125] Robinson then goes on to say that

> Fascinated by the trick techniques exploited by Melies, but lacking his extravagant notions and possibilities for MISE EN SCENE they [British producers] had tended to stage tricks in natural locations: their own front gardens, the countryside near Brighton, side streets in provincial suburbia. English film-makers had also developed one of the cinema's most potent dramatic motifs: the chase.[126]

As Georges Sadoul points out, "The lesson of the Brighton School--that a character must evolve in depth--is almost lost today. The lesson of montage, the alternating close-ups and long shots, was learned more slowly but more securely."[127] While acknowledging the school's many significant contributions to narrative form, Cook

---

[122]   *Roy Armes, FRENCH FILM (New York: E. P. Dutton and Company, 1970), p.26.

[123]   Georges Sadoul, "Early Film Production in England: The Origin of Montage, Close-ups, and Chase Sequence," trans. Yvonne Templin, HOLLYWOOD QUARTERLY 1:3 (April 1946):249-59.

[124]   Martin Sopocy, "A Narrated Cinema: The Pioneer Story Films of James A. Williamson," CINEMA JOURNAL 18:1 (Fall 1978):1-28.

[125]   Robinson, p.32.

[126]   Robinson, p.46.

[127]   Sadoul, p.258.

cautions that it "is difficult to substantiate [the claims of scholars like Sadoul] since few of the films in question have come down to us. . . ."[128]

Another notable pioneer in British films was an ex-arc lamp designer named Cecil M. Hepworth, a producer-director specializing in action movies using animals. According to Rachel Low and Roger Manvell,

> Hepworth's films increased in length, scope, and complexity side by side with those of other producers, but their more thoughtful approach and originality gave him a pre-eminence which increased through the years. Even in these first ten years of British films, he shared with R. W. Paul the honour of being one of the two most important British producers."[129]

A case in point was RESCUED BY ROVER (1905), a film featuring the producer's wife, infant, and dog, which demonstrated a skill with continuity and camerawork remarkable for its time.

Despite England's important technical breakthroughs, its filmmakers seemed unable to provide quality moving pictures. As Donald Spoto points out, the early British filmmakers "could not combine technical expertise with an aesthetic sense or even the ability to sustain anything other than a grade-school kind of narrative.[130] As a result, Hollywood found a ready market for its films, and by the start of World War I the Americans were becoming the dominant force in the British film industry.

Italian film production prior to World War I also played a key role in the development of cinematic art.[131] Preoccupied with historical dramas, Italian filmmakers like Enrico Guazzoni (the 1912 QUO VADIS?) and Giovanni Pastrone (the 1914 CABIRIA) not only epitomized the epic grandeur of spectacular filmmaking, but also helped provide the impetus for feature film production. Their work inspired some of the most popular filmmakers of the silent era: e.g., David Wark Griffith, Cecil B. DeMille, and Ernst Lubitsch. As Vernon Jarrett observes,

> It must be admitted that many histories of the cinema, in paying to D. W. Griffith their well-deserved tributes, have sometimes been a little less than generous to his predecessors, Guazzoni and Pastrone. Griffith himself, who had seen both films shortly before he began to plan BIRTH OF A NATION and

---

[128] Cook, p.19.

[129] Rachel Low and Roger Manvell, THE HISTORY OF THE BRITISH FILM: 1896-1906 (London: George Allen and Unwin, 1948), p.22.

[130] *Donald Spoto, THE DARK SIDE OF GENIUS: THE LIFE OF ALFRED HITCHCOCK (Boston: Little, Brown and Company, 1983), p.51.

[131] For some interesting overviews, see Robert Kass, "50 Years of Italian Cinema," FILMS IN REVIEW 6:7 (August-September 1955):313-7; ___, "The Italian Film Renaissance," ibid., 4:7 (August-September 1953):336-48; Vinicio Marinucci, "Fact, Fiction and History were in the Beginning: First Part of a History of Italian Cinema," FILMS AND FILMING 7:4 (January 1961):15-6, 43; ___, "History--Before and After Mussolini: Second Part of a History of Italian Cinema," ibid., 7:5 (February 1961):37-8, 40; ___, "The Theatre Supplies the Funny Men: Third Part of a History of Italian Cinema," ibid., 7:7 (April 1961):33-5; ___, "Eroticism and the Good Italian Earth: Fourth Part of a History of Italian Cinema," ibid., 7:8 (May 1961):33-4; ___, "The Development of Realism with a Sense of Humour: Fifth Part of a History of Italian Cinema," ibid., 7:9 (June 1961):31-2; ___, "The Search for a New Style in Musicals: Sixth Part of a History of Italian Cinema," ibid., 7:10 (July 1961):33-4; and ___, " A Crisis that Led to Better Things: Final Part of a History of Italian Cinema," ibid., 7:11 (August 1961):41.

INTOLERANCE, in fact while he was still at work on JUDITH OF BETHULIA, made no secret of the impression that they had made on him.[132]

Moreover, as Pierre Leprohon points out, the genius of Italian filmmakers went beyond popular historical films and "created a kind of symbiosis between the audience and the artistic illusion and was responsible . . . [not only] for the immediate success of the cinema in Italy . . . [but also] for introducing dramatic fiction into a framework of reality . . . peculiar to the cinema."[133]

The next major milestone can be seen in the SOCIETE FILM D'ART movement, that began in France in 1908. Over the next seven years, serious literary works were adapted for the screen to try to bring a new social, economic, and artistic dignity to the new medium which had, so far, been developed as mere entertainment. Some famous writers whose works appeared on the screen were Shakespeare, Tolstoy, Balzac, and Maupassant. The stage's greatest actors and actresses were engaged to play in these films, the most famous probably being Sarah Bernhardt. The acting, however, was not designed for films; the emphasis was theatrical and not cinematic. That is to say, the camera remained fixed while the actors and actresses performed in front of it rather than allowing the director to use techniques such as parallel editing and cross-cutting to tell the story.[134] Despite their numerous cinematic limitations, the FILM D'ART movies proved popular at the box office. Their success in France inspired other European nations as well as the United States to imitate both the concept and the approach. By the time of their demise in the mid-teens, these staid cinematic narratives had demonstrated the feasibility of adapting major literary works into commercially successful moving pictures.

It is important to understand that many European films presented values contrary to British and American Victorian values. Women were more reckless in their behavior; men more passionate in satisfying their desires. The notions of patience, propriety, and restraint were noticeably absent. Therefore, a paradox developed. At the same time that French and Italian productions were inspiring American filmmakers to increase film lengths from one and two reels to six reels, their salacious content was also producing a shift on the part of American exhibitors away from screening foreign films and toward showing domestic movies with more Victorian values. The main reason, as discussed in Chapter 3, was that the American film industry was intent on gaining greater respectability. The shift toward American films had less to do with taste than with profits. To underwrite the increasing costs associated with feature films, theater acquisitions, the star system, and better production facilities, the filmmakers needed the help of the financial community. That help would come only when the film industry seemed more respectable to the conservative bankers and industrialists.

As the new medium grew into an international industry, techniques particularly suitable for film emerged.[135] By 1908, filmmakers had in their cinematic repertoire such skills as tracking movements, photographic tricks, close-ups, cross-cutting, and parallel editing. They had learned that movies were more than mere moving photography.

---

[132]   Vernon Jarratt, THE ITALIAN CINEMA (New York: Falcon Press, 1951), p.19.

[133]   Pierre Leprohon, THE ITALIAN CINEMA (New York: Praeger Publishers, 1972), p.19.

[134]   For more information, see Jon Gartenberg, "Camera Movement in Edison and Biograph Films, 1900-1906," CINEMA JOURNAL 19:2 (Spring 1980):1-16.

[135]   For interesting reactions to the changes taking place in American film at this time, see *Stanley Kauffmann, with Bruce Henstell, eds., AMERICAN FILM CRITICISM: FROM THE BEGINNINGS TO "CITIZEN KANE" (New York: Liveright, 1972), pp.3-54.

Although France, Italy, and England collectively contributed more to film aesthetics than did the United States during the first decade of film history, the second decade saw a different trend. As discussed in Chapters 2, 3, 5, and 6, 1909 marked a watershed period in American film history. Ten film companies (Edison, Biograph, Vitagraph, Essanay, Selig, Lubin, Kleine,[136] and Kalem, as well as the American branches of Melies and Pathe), formed the Motion Picture Patents Company (MPPC). Over the next eight years, the monopolistic and conservative MPPC sought unsuccessfully to control the production, distribution, and exhibition of films on the world market. Its major shortcomings related to its refusal to change. Opposed both to the star system and to feature-length films, the MPPC eventually was overwhelmed as much by an inability to keep in touch with the audiences, as by the ingenuity of the independent filmmakers. Despite its many failings, the MPPC deserves credit not only for dramatically improving the quality of cinematic equipment, but also for significantly shaping the future business focus of the film industry.

The year 1909 also saw the emergence of the first great American film director, David Wark Griffith, and a noticeable drift of movie companies from the East Coast to the West Coast, particularly Hollywood. Over the next five years, as discussed in chapters 3, 5, and 6, significant aspects of the film underwent profound changes: e.g., the content of its films (thanks mainly to Griffith's Biograph productions), the rise of a star system, the advent of feature films, and the emergence of picture palaces. By the end of 1914, Hollywood not only had become the focus of American movies, but also, because of World War I, the film capital of the world.

BOOKS

GENERAL SILENT FILM HISTORIES

*Brownlow, Kevin. THE PARADE'S GONE BY. New York: Alfred A. Knopf, 1968. Illustrated. 595pp.

In this splendid recreation of the atmosphere and successes of the silent era as remembered by the artists of the age, Brownlow gives us a fascinating record of these movies. He interviewed silent film stars, supporting players, directors, cameramen, editors, and producers; and the results provide new insights for film historians. Although there are over 300 stills, the pictures are of less value than the narrative, since some stills are not identified.[137] An index is provided. Recommended for special collections.

Butler, Ivan. SILENT MAGIC: REDISCOVERING THE SILENT FILM ERA. Foreword Kevin Brownlow. New York: Ungar Publishing Company, 1988. Illustrated. 208pp.

*Franklin, Joe. CLASSICS OF THE SILENT SCREEN: A PICTORIAL TREASURY. New York: Bramhall House, 1959. Illustrated. 255pp.

Written by a man who really enjoys movies, this nostalgic and interesting collection of film illustrations is a tender reminder of a marvelous era. The first of two major sections briefly reviews fifty American movies, as well as offering several stills from the films. The second section profiles seventy-five movie stars. A number of appendexes deal with questions most often asked of the author, and the cast and

---

[136]   George Kleine was the only non-producer. His role was as a distributor.

[137]   Serious students should also read Brownlow's letter to FILMS IN REVIEW 20:4 (April 1969):257-8, in which he lists corrections to the text. The 1975 paperback edition includes the corrections at the end of the book.

reproduction credits of the fifty reviewed films. Regrettably, there is no general index. Well worth browsing.

*Lennig, Arthur. THE SILENT VOICE--A TEXT, THE GOLDEN AGE OF THE CINEMA. Troy: Lennig, 1969. 158pp.

This enterprising book, written by a teacher, at the State University of New York, has some intriguing material on Lumiere, Melies, Porter, Griffith, the Fairbankses, Flaherty, and von Stroheim. Also enjoyable are Lenning's worthwhile comments on the early masterpieces. Worth browsing.

*O'Leary, Liam. THE SILENT CINEMA. New York: E. P. Dutton and Company, 1965. Illustrated. 160pp.

A handy, quick run-through of the history of the silent age with a generous and beautifully reproduced collection of 140 stills, the narrative reveals nothing new but nevertheless serves as a pleasant and useful guide to pictures of famous personalities and important national cinemas. This is one of the few good pictorial histories available in paperback. Well worth browsing.

BRITISH SILENT FILM HISTORIES

Allister, Ray. FRIESE-GREENE: CLOSE-UP OF AN INVENTOR. London: Marsland Publications, 1949. Illustrated. 192pp. New York: Arno Press, 1972.

An English inventor's contributions to film development are discussed, with biographical information providing an insight into one of the most tragic of the early pioneers. Here was a man who did more to further British motion pictures through mechanical and scientific invention than any other pioneer, yet who served three jail terms for debt and violation of bankruptcy laws. Unrecognized during his lifetime, he has since become known as a great inventor. Unfortunately, few significant studies about his achievements have yet been done. An index is included. Worth browsing.

Barnes, John. THE BEGINNINGS OF CINEMA IN ENGLAND. New York: Barnes and Noble, 1976. Illustrated. 240pp.

Covering the same period marked by Hendricks's Edison studies, this book focuses primarily on events unfolding in England. Barnes traces the evolution of British film history from October 17, 1894 (the day the first Kinetoscope parlor opened in London) through the end of 1896 (when films had become a fixture in British Music Halls). Thirteen fact-filled and highly specialized chapters describe, in detail, how Robert W. Paul dominated the early years, his debts to Edison's "accomplishments," and the help provided by Birt Acres, beginning in March, 1895. Attention is also paid to the impact of the Cinematographe-Lumiere, brought to London in Spring of 1895, and the role played by Felicien Trewey by the exploitation of the French invention on British production and manufacturing. The many diagrams and illustrations liberally sprinkled throughout the study add considerably to our understanding of the various patents and inventions. Two appendexes (dealing with British Films from 1895 to 1896 and a chronology of the major events), extensive endnotes, and a film index are included. Recommended for special collections.

British National Film Archive. CATALOGUE: SILENT FILMS. London: The British Film Institute, 1960. Three volumes.

Each of the three volumes provides a carefully indexed and comprehensive listing of films preserved in the British National Film Archives. Volume 1 lists silent news films, 1895-1933; Volume 2, silent nonfiction films, 1895-1934; and Volume 3, silent fiction films, 1895-1930. Recommended for special collections.

Chanan, Michael. THE DREAM THAT KICKS: THE PREHISTORY AND EARLY YEARS OF CINEMA IN BRITAIN. London: Routledge and Kegan Paul, 1980. 353pp.

"Film," Chanan tells us in his opening chapter, "has taught us to see the world anew, but it seems that the one thing it could not properly picture was its own birth." To discover how that birth occurred, the author examines how the institutions of film--the industry, the stars, the idioms, genres, styles, etc.--were influenced by technological and economic factors in the earliest days of the new medium. He argues that film from its inception is not so much "a window onto reality," but instead "a world apart, which produces its own meanings" and formulas. Taking into account the importance of ideology in conditioning the world on and in film, he points out that inventors like Janssen, Muybridge, and Marey were not so much interested in motion picture projection, as they were in solving problems related to astronomy and animal locomotion. Chanan goes beyond the general issues about the process of discovery and invention and the investigative relationship between them to examine how specific subjects--e.g., war--were treated in terms of everyday lives. He seeks to explain what made the magic lantern unique to entertainment and mass communication, as well as how it cut across class lines and reshaped existing institutions to affect the modern day myth of the "average man." His six thought-provoking and academic chapters present challenging new ideas on the prehistory of film, the dialectics of invention, music hall and popular culture, and middle-class culture and its impact on British society, as well as how the industry developed its own cinematic language, and how films took on a direction that their founders never dreamed possible. A bibliography and index are included. Well worth browsing.

Gifford, Denis. THE BRITISH FILM CATALOGUE 1895-1985: A REFERENCE GUIDE. New York: Facts on File, 1986. No pagination.

A chronological guide, this valuable book on British entertainment films, whether short or feature, silent or sound, does a good job of satisfying researchers' needs. The main entries from 1895 to 1985 are catalogued by numbers running from 00001 to 15289, with the upper left hand corner of each page listing the numbers included on that page. To examine a particular year's theatrical releases, one locates the particular year, follows the chronological breakdown by months to find information about the main title for each film (followed by any alternative title if appropriate), the running time (silent films reported in terms of actual footage; sound films in minutes), censor's certificate (A, AA, H, U, and X), silent or sound, color systems, screen ratio, stereoscopy, production company, distributor company, reissue, producer, director, story source, screenplay, narrator (when appropriate), cast and characters, subject (films are classified in twenty-three different categories such as adventure, comedy, and sport), synopsis, awards, and special information (e.g., the first noticed close ups). There is also an extensive index that lists film titles alphabetically, including alternative titles, title changes for reissue, title changes for American release, and serial episode titles and series. The catalog number precedes each entry. Recommended for special collections.

Hepworth, Cecil M. CAME THE DAWN: MEMORIES OF A FILM PIONEER. New York: Phoenix House, 1951. Illustrated. 207pp.

This useful and entertaining biography by a pioneer English film producer and inventor explains his work with arc lights and printing machines, the beginning of a British producing studio, and his fascination for movies about England. It also shows why he failed in commercial ventures. Although the facts are sometimes stretched, Hepworth is worth reading for his interesting tales and recollections. Well worth browsing.

Low, Rachel and Roger Manvell. THE HISTORY OF THE BRITISH FILM: 1896-1906. London: George Allen and Unwin, 1948. Illustrated. 136pp.

This invaluable book is divided into two major sections: Part One deals with production, distribution, and exhibition; Part Two, with the films themselves. The two distinguished authors provide important information about the pioneer British producers--R. W. Paul, William Barker, Charles Urban, James Williamson, G. A. Smith, and Cecil Hepworth--and their early studios, financial situations, and ingenious exhibition procedures. Also valuable are the authors' insights into the trick photography of the "Brighton School," particularly the efforts of Williamson and Smith. Unfortunately, for some unexplained reason, the book neglects the early inventors, particularly Friese-Greene. Five scholarly appendexes plus two indexes are included. Recommended for special collections.

Low, Rachel. THE HISTORY OF THE BRITISH FILM: 1906-1914. London: George Allen and Unwin, 1949. Illustrated. 309pp.

The second volume in this distinguished series is also divided into two main sections. Part 1 examines the nature of the audience, the rise of picture palaces and theater chains, early labor unions, censorship, the educational use of movies, special legislation, and other interesting sociological factors. Part 2 discusses the documentary, dramatic, and comic movies of the period. Special attention is paid to three films: RICHARD III (1911), EAST LYNNE (1913), and DAVID COPPERFIELD (1913). A bibliography, an appendix listing 283 films released between January 1906 and August 1914, and a general index are included. Recommended for special collections.

Low, Rachel. THE HISTORY OF THE BRITISH FILM: 1914-1918. London: Allen and Unwin, 1950. Illustrated. 332pp.

In this third volume, the author again divides her study into two sections. Part 1 examines the audience size, distribution and exhibition, the growth of theaters, trade organizations, and censorship and wartime restrictions. Part 2 discusses the subject matter of the movies made during the period; in this volume there is a fascinating chapter on film technique plus a variety of excellent appendexes--one lists the credits for more than 500 films made during these four years. Special attention is paid to two films: JANE SHORE (1915) and THE VICAR OF WAKEFIELD (1916). A general index is included. Recommended for special collections.

Low, Rachel. THE HISTORY OF THE BRITISH FILM: 1918-1929. London: George Allen and Unwin, 1971. Illustrated. 544pp.

The most impressive volume of this extraordinary series, it breaks with the standard two-section approach of the earlier books. Low here gives an eight chapter chronology that includes information on artistic and critical theory in the twenties, a discussion on exhibition and the public (e.g., relations with the public, the major exhibitors, censorship, and the educational use of film), the film trade in terms of renting companies, the significant producers of the decade, the social and economic impact of sound movies, the techniques of film production, and the quality of British theatrical films throughout the twenties. In addition to the familiar scholarly sources and statistical documentation, the author provides quotes from her interviews with prominent figures of the period. Particularly valuable is a filmography that runs nearly three hundred pages and covers the release of theatrical films from November 1918 to the middle of 1929. Endnotes, a bibliography, and a general index are included. Highly recommended for special collections.

Oakley, Charles. WHERE WE CAME IN: SEVENTY YEARS OF THE BRITISH FILM INDUSTRY. London: George Allen and Unwin, 1964. Illustrated. 245pp.

After reading the Low histories, you might want to glance at this general guide to British film development from the early fairground days up to 1960. The one exceptional feature is an introductory fourteen-page chronology listing major events, beginning in 1895 with Birt Acres photographing a handful of "topical" items and concluding with the retirement of J. Arthur Rank in 1962. The twenty-two chapters that follow chart the dramatic shifts between impressive achievements and dismal results, stressing, along the way, the names of the important producers, directors, performers, and studios. Oakley's two major weaknesses are unreliability and periodic inconsistencies. A general index is included. Well worth browsing.

UNITED STATES SILENT FILM HISTORIES

Blum, Daniel. A PICTORIAL HISTORY OF THE SILENT SCREEN. New York: Grosset and Dunlap, 1953. Illustrated. 334pp. New York: G. P. Putnam's Sons, 1982.

This profusely illustrated text is fine for rare stills, but weak on textual comments. The chronological overview serves as a good excuse for a collection of 3,000 illustrations portraying the art of the silent film. Worth browsing.

*Everson, William K. AMERICAN SILENT FILM. New York: Oxford University Press, 1978. Illustrated. 387pp.

Written by one of the most dedicated and perceptive historians and educators in the short annals of film scholarship, this controversial book relies on respect more than on evidence. Everson ignores standard historiographical approaches to his general study, mixing a host of factual and subjective claims regarding the rise and development of the film industry. His passion for events and films overshadows the glaring absence of evidence to support his assertions. Nineteen stimulating chapters reassess the conventional accounts of how silent movies remain subservient to the talkies that followed, and Everson gives his unique and respectful interpretations of genres, personalities, and events that molded the glory of silent movies. His grasp of the problems, the breakthroughs, and the achievements not only mirrors his enthusiasm for the subject, but also illustrates why he is considered one of the world's authorities on American film history. As an impressionistic guide through the early decades, this book remains a model of clarity and taste. As a historical document for studying film history, it remains an anachronism of scholarship gone with the wind. An appendix on film scholarship and a chronology of silent film highlights, and an index are included. Recommended for special collections.

Fulton, A. R. MOTION PICTURES: THE DEVELOPMENT OF AN ART FROM SILENT FILMS TO THE AGE OF TELEVISION. Norman: University of Oklahoma Press, 1960. Illustrated. 320pp.

"Although, for the most part, the films chosen for this study are discussed chronologicallly," Fulton explains, "this book is a history only in that these films represent the origin of the motion pictures as a machine and the emergence of the art dependent upon it." Fulton's sixteen affectionate chapters tracing the growth of the movies from the technological breakthroughs in the eighteenth century to the late 1950s provides a good overview of the influence of technology on film aesthetics. The material has long since been overshadowed by the work of modern historians. This pioneering study, however, reveals the major emphases early film scholars placed on a causal relationship between aesthetics and industrial developments. Endnotes, a glossary, and an index are included. Worth browsing.

Grau, Robert. THE THEATRE OF SCIENCE. New York: Broadway Publishing Company, 1944. Illustrated. 378pp. New York: Benjamin Blom, 1969. Illustrated. 465pp.

One of the most useful records of the early 1900s is this valuable study of the key figures of the American film industry. Whatever Grau's stylistic limitations and entreprenurial schemes, the study itself offers insights into the "great man" theory of film history, as well as useful profiles of producers, performers, and directors. The author's gossipy writing style and fawning rhetoric toward specific individuals, only add to the book's value as a historical record of the times. Especially noteworthy are the dozens of pages of portrait shots. Regrettably, there are no indexes to aid cross-referencing. Recommended for special collections.

Hammond, John H. THE CAMERA OBSCURA: A CHRONICLE. Bristol: Adam Hilger, 1981. 182pp.

A major drawback is the book's ahistorical approach to aesthetics and optical ideology. Otherwise, this is a beautifully illustrated work and an impressively researched document. Well worth browsing.

Jenkins, Reese V. IMAGES AND ENTERPRISE: TECHNOLOGY AND THE AMERICAN PHOTOGRAPHIC INDUSTRY 1839 TO 1925. Baltimore: Johns Hopkins University Press, 1975. Illustrated. 371pp.

"Despite its relatively peripheral position in the economy," Jenkins explains, "the [photographic] industry reflected in its changes during the nineteenth and early twentieth centuries many important features of the growth of American business. Specifically, because of the technical character of its products, the historical study of the industry permits an examination of the changing relationship of technology and science to business during the period in which the United States moved from a predominantly rural and agrarian society to a predominantly urban and industrial society. Moreover, it permits an exploration, at least within the American context, of the emergence of America into a position of world leadership in industry that European firms had previously dominated and that was linked closely to the internationally German optical and fine chemicals cartels." What Jenkins does in his five chapters is identify a number of the significant forces affecting the industry's evolution over an eighty-six-year period, focusing mainly on the role performed by technology "in the formulation of business strategy, the organization of enterprise, and the structure of the industry." Particularly useful is an invaluable chronology of George Eastman's career in film and the reasons why he became such a powerful figure in the photographic world. An appendix dealing with technological diffusion, bibliographic information, and an index is included. Recommended for special collections.

Manchel, Frank. WHEN PICTURES BEGAN TO MOVE. Englewood Cliffs: Prentice-Hall, 1969. Illustrated. 76pp.

"In his intriguing history of the industry Frank Manchel pictures the inventors, the giants among the early directors and glamorous stars; he also describes the tricks of distribution, the hi-jacking of films, and the incorporation of artistic and ethical concepts in silent films. Candid and informative, the book has a note of nostalgia that is echoed in the photographs of the great people and the great pictures. Ages 12-15."[138]

---

[138]   Zena Sutherland, "Book Review: WHEN PICTURES BEGAN TO MOVE," SATURDAY REVIEW 52:33 (August 16, 1969):59.

*Ramsaye, Terry. A MILLION AND ONE NIGHTS: A HISTORY OF THE MOTION PICTURE THROUGH 1925. New York: Touchstone, 1986. Illustrated. 868pp.

Here is a reissue of the 1926 edition of the most lively, the most enjoyable, and the least accurate history of the silent era. Ramsaye, a journalist with a fine imagination and a great love for movies, puts spice, gossip, and rumor into his charming version of the early days. His discussions of early film history champion the contributions of Edison and Armat, while minimizing those of Muybridge and Marey. Don't read it for facts, just for pleasant and fascinating fiction that passes even today in many places for fact. Recommended for special collections.

THOMAS ALVA EDISON

Conot, Robert. A STREAK OF LUCK: THE LIFE AND LEGEND OF THOMAS ALVA EDISON. New York: Seaview Books, 1979. Illustrated. 500pp.

*Hendricks, Gordon. THE EDISON MOTION PICTURE MYTH. Berkeley: University of California Press, 1961. Illustrated. 216pp.

Up to 1961, Edison was considered the father of the film and the Kinetoscope (the grandfather of all subsequent film projectors), and Dickson was a runaway son. No more. With a wealth of details gleaned from patents, notes, financial records, memoirs, diaries, and first-hand reports, Hendricks presents a strong defense of the young Englishman. Although the text stops at 1892, Dickson emerges as one of the most important men in the history of motion pictures. If the book has one major weakness, it is the unrelenting attacks on Edison's contributions to film history. As Gosser notes in his review, "Edison did, after all, develop several projectors after Dickson left the firm, and founded a motion picture production company which lasted until 1918."[139] That criticism aside, this seminal study redirected the scholarly approach to early film history. Recommended for special collections.

Hendricks, Gordon. THE KINETOSCOPE: AMERICA'S FIRST COMMERCIALLY SUCCESSFUL MOTION PICTURE EXHIBITOR. New York: The Beginnings of the American Film, 1966. Illustrated. 182pp.

This is Hendrick's third book on reconstructing, rewriting, and reinterpreting the fuzzy historical records of the early, clumsy days of film experimentation. As a result of his wonderful and painstaking research, we learn more than ever before about the fantastic Kinetoscope, its films, and how it came to be. This invaluable document also comes with sixty interesting illustrations. Recommended for special collections.

*Musser, Charles, ed. THOMAS A. EDISON PAPERS--A GUIDE TO MOTION PICTURE CATALOGS BY AMERICAN PRODUCERS AND DISTRIBUTORS, 1894-1908. Frederick: University Publications of America, 1985), Microfim. 50pp.

A terse introduction to the six-reel microfilm edition of important film catalogs, this useful guide calls attention to the earliest documents published by Edison's sales agents in 1894, and takes us up to the end of 1908, when the Motion Picture Patents Company was formed. The catalogs that were distributed during this significant period of film history offer plot synopses, reviews, and advertisements. Today, only

---

[139] "The Literature," p.5.

a limited number of those once profuse publications exist. "This edition," Musser explains, "presents a portrait of the films and the equipment generally available to exhibitors and audiences in the United States. It includes substantial runs of catalogs published by seven of the ten producer/distributors that eventually joined the Motion Picture Patents Company." Regrettably, no publications were discovered for the Essanay Company, and only a smattering for the American Vitagraph Company and the Kalem Company. The process involved research visits to numerous museums, libraries, federal archives and records centers, historical societies, and private collections in America and abroad. This booklet is divided into five key sections, including three that summarize the highlights of this valuable resource collection. Scholars, therefore, owe Musser and his colleagues a debt of gratitude for this undertaking. Recommended for special collections.

GEORGES MELIES

Frazer, John. ARTIFICIALLY ARRANGED SCENES: THE FILMS OF GEORGES MELIES. Boston: G. K. Hall and Company, 1979. Illustrated. 269pp.

"My intention," explains Frazer, "was to write a book that would provide the closest equivalent experience to the actual viewing of the films of Georges Melies and to make the reader want to see these films." The result is a splendid three-part study of the French fantasy filmmaker. Part One--"The Artist's World, 1900"--describes the aggressive, optimistic milieu of the BELLE EPOQUE that saw the synthesis of the nineteenth century's interest in sciences and aesthetics. Frazer points out how Melies's open-mindedness to new ideas in science, coupled with his theatrical background in magic, made him the ideal figure in shifting theatrical illusions to the cinema. Care is taken to relate Melies's achievements to the developments taking place in the traditional and popular arts and to the influences that shaped the innovative Parisian's movies. Part Two--"The Career of Georges Melies"--provides a biographical account of the filmmaker's life and career from 1861 to 1938. In addition to emphasizing the importance of Melies's background with shop machinery and clockmaking, to his future in magic and illusions, Frazer points out the similarities between Melies and other notable magicians like Jean-Eugene Robert-Houdin, John Nevil Maskelyne, and David Devant. In addition to learning how the painter experimented with film and started the Star Film Company, we learn about Melies's work habits, the transformation of the Theatre Robert-Houdin into an evening cinema, the role of Melies's brother Gaston in running the Melies Manufacturing Company in America, the factors (primarily economic) leading to Melies's pre-WWI decline, the hardships he faced in the 1920s, and his death from cancer on January 21, 1938. Part Three--"The Films of Georges Melies"--provides a chronological account of the movies themselves, with helpful film notes and critical commentary. Particularly useful are the plot synopses, the production details, and the significant technical and artistic breakthroughs in relation to Melies's film career at the time.

This thoughtful and careful study offers the best of two worlds. On the one hand, it is succinct enough to satisfy immediate needs without burdening the general reader with esoteric information. On the other hand, the material is intelligently organized and detailed enough to appeal to serious students. The book ends with an Envoi, notes, a bibliography, a general filmography, two appendexes (a Melies filmography and a filmography of Gaston Melies's films), and an index. Recommended for special collections.

Hammond, Paul. MARVELLOUS MELIES. New York: St. Martin's Press, 1975. Illustrated. 159pp.

"The 500 films that Georges Melies made between 1896 and 1912," explains Hammond in this thoughtful study, "include conjuring turns, burlesques, reconstructed newsreels, melodramas, fantastic voyages, stag films, fairy stories, satires, costume dramas, literary adaptations and advertising films." Hammond insists that his subject is anything but an "engaging primitive." To prove the point, he divides this first book on Melies into two major sections: the filmmaker's life and work (from 1861 to 1938) and a critique of the Star Films (of which fewer than ninety survive). Particular attention is paid to Melies's many different careers as a conjurer, set-designer, painter, satirist, lyricist, and filmmaker. The principal drawback of this otherwise important examination is the reproduction quality of the miniaturized illustrations. Two brief chapters introduce the main sections, in addition to three appendexes--Georges Melies Trickography, Georges Melies Filmography, and Gaston Melies Filmography--and an index. Well worth browsing.

FILMS

THE BRIGHTON SCHOOL

THE BEGINNINGS OF BRITISH FILMS (16mm: 1901-1911, 29 mins., b/w, silent, R-MMA)

"This reel," explains the catalog, "includes a dramatic news event, the funeral procession of a famous queen; a cleverly made trick film that shows the contemporary fascination with flying machines; and two melodramas." The filmmakers included are R. W. Paul, Cecil Hepworth, and Charles Urban. Particularly interesting is the range of early British cinematic imagination from the turn-of-the-century to the beginnings of the teens when highly stylized acting and painted backdrops revealed how much British filmmakers had fallen out of step with the burgeoning international film industry.

RESCUED BY ROVER (16mm: 1905, 8 mins., b/w, silent, R-KIT)

Directed by Cecil Hepworth, this unusual film (also available in the MMA program just listed) demonstrates how the British were advancing narrative form and rhythm at the same time as Porter was experimenting with story construction. The story involves a family dog saving his owner's infant. Particularly impressive are the director's development of the plot without the use of intertitles, and the effective way in which suspense is maintained throughout the action.

THOMAS ALVA EDISON

AN EDISON ALBUM (16mm--1896-1907, 12 mins., b/w, silent, R-KIT)

This package contains a variety of interesting examples of early film history: e.g., THE KISS (1896), A ROMANCE OF THE RAILS (1902), and RESCUED FROM AN EAGLE'S NEST (1907). The first film was shot in Edison's famous West Orange studio, "The Black Maria." The simple two-room structure, mounted on a revolving turntable base, had a skylight roof that was used to catch the sunlight as the structure rotated at different periods of the day. The second film allegedly set the stage for Porter's decision to make THE GREAT TRAIN ROBBERY (1903). The third film stars Griffith in his first film role, directed by Porter. For additional films, see EMG's EDISON COLLECTION 1, 2 (1895-1903).

LOUIS FEUILLADE

FANTOMAS. Episode 2: JUVE VS. FANTOMAS/JUVE CONTRE FANTOMAS (16mm: 1913, 64 mins., b/w, silent, R-MMA)

The common perception is that FANTOMAS is a continuous serial. In fact, it is a series of five separate one-hour films adapted from popular novels by Pierre Souvestre and Marcel Allain. Rene Navarre stars as the master criminal who triumphs against the corrupt and hypocritical establishment. Sadoul points out that "a strange kind of poetry" results from the director's juxtaposing of "meticulous realism on the one hand and impossible exploits on the other. . . ."[140] Roy Armes believes that episode 2 "contains some of the most celebrated sequences in Feuillade's work--the gun battle among the barrels on the quai de Bercy, and the scene of inspector Juve donning a spiked belt over his pyjamas as he settles down to await the boa constrictor which he expects Fantomas to send against him."[141]

FILM D'ART MOVEMENT

QUEEN ELIZABETH/LES AMOURS DE LA REINE ELISABETH (16mm: 1912, 43 mins., b/w, silent, English titles, R-MMA)
Directed by Louis Mercanton, the story concerns the British queen's romance with Essex and her being tricked into executing him for being unfaithful. Besides showing the great Sarah Bernhardt performing with absurd stage gestures (illustrating how the film acting of the period was theatrical, not cinematic), this motion picture exemplifies how the public felt when movies became prestigious and elaborate entertainment. It also served as a justification for producing feature films rather than the then standard five-to twelve-minute movie.

THE GREAT ACTRESSES OF THE PAST PROGRAM (16mm: 1911-16, 76 mins., b/w, silent, R-MMA)
This anthology includes performances by theatrical stars such as Gabrielle Rejane, Sarah Bernhardt, Minnie Maddern Fiske, and Eleanora Duse. The four films excerpted are two French films--MADAME SANS-GENE (1911) and LA DAME AUX CAMELIAS (1912), one American film--VANITY FAIR (1913), and one Italian film--CENERE (1916). Especially noteworthy about this anthology is the ability to contrast different styles of international film acting.

DAVID WARK GRIFFITH

THE LONELY VILLA (16mm: 1909, 11 mins., b/w, silent, R-MMA)
Although Griffith's films are discussed at length in Chapter 6, I want to point out here a movie that can quickly illustrate the great director's talents in this early period of filmmaking. The story of an aborted robbery gives Griffith the chance to use cross-cutting and parallel editing to create the tension for a last-minute rescue, a technique that he was to use over and over again. Mack Sennett wrote the script, and G. W. "Billy" Bitzer photographed the action.

MAX LINDER

MAX LINDER PROGRAM (16mm: 1906-1912, 23 mins., b/w, silent, R-MMA)
One of the most inventive and talented of all silent film comedians, Linder led the way in early slapstick routines. The three films included exhibit his versatility. MAX LEARNS TO SKATE/LES DEBUTS D'UN PATINEUR (1906) exploits the problems

---

[140]   Georges Sadoul, FRENCH FILM (London: The Falcon Press, 1953), p.14.

[141]   *Roy Armes, FRENCH CINEMA (New York: Oxford University Press, 1985), p.28.

of a novice ice skater. TROUBLES OF A GRASS WIDOWER (1908) illustrates how marital problems turn the comic into a disastrous housekeeper. MAX AND HIS DOG/MAX ET SON CHIEN DICK (1912) makes clever use of special effects in helping Max solve his courting problems.

A SELECTION OF LINDER FILMS (16mm: 1905-1921, b/w, silent, R-EMG)
     A series of seven films starting in 1905 (the films can be rented individually for five dollars), this collection shows Linder in his favorite role as a dandy, demonstrating considerable acrobatic skills. He was not only the first famous screen comedian, but also the acknowledged inspiration of many later comics like Mack Sennett and Charles Chaplin. Among the films available are MAX LEARNS TO SKATE (1905), MAX AND THE STATUE (1912), and SEVEN YEARS BAD LUCK (1921).

THE LUMIERES

THE FIRST PROGRAMS (16mm: 1895-1900, 19 mins., b/w, silent, R-EMG, KIT)
     A fine example of what appealed to the general public in the initial days of moving pictures, these first films also reveal the Lumieres's background in still photography. Among the films included are WORKERS LEAVING THE LUMIERE FACTORY/LA SORTIE DES USINES and ARRIVAL OF EXPRESS AT LYONS/L'ARRIVEE D'UN TRAIN (both in 1895). For additional films, see FNC's LUMIERE PROGRAM 1, 2 (1895-1908).

GEORGES MELIES

THE FILMS OF GEORGES MELIES (16mm: n.d., 60 mins., b/w, sound, kinescope, R-IND)
     This film shows the development of the famous French pioneer filmmaker with extracts from his films as well as useful comments by his granddaughter.[142] One comes away with a good sense of his storytelling powers and his experimental genius.

MAGIC OF MELIES (16mm: nof.,[143] R-FNC)
     This film "anthology" of Melies's early works includes JUPITER'S THUNDERBOLTS, THE MAGIC LANTERN (both in 1903), and THE MERMAID (1904). All three show the techniques employed by Melies in developing trick photography. Although the quality is poor, we get a sense of the reflective aspect of the famous film magician's work.

MELIES COLOR FILMS (16mm: nof., R-FNC)
     A series that illustrate the early work by Melies on color motion pictures, these films provide information about a technique involving the hand-painting of frames.

THE PALACE OF THE ARABIAN NIGHTS/LE PALAIS DES MILLE ET UNE NUITS (16mm: 1905, 19 mins., b/w and/or color, silent, R-BUD, MMA)

---

[142] For a useful listing of films about Melies, see ARTIFICIALLY ARRANGED SCENES, p.239.

[143] No other information given.

Another example of trick photography and fantasy, the film serves as the inspiration for much of Alexander Korda's 1940 version of THE THIEF OF BAGDAD. "The similarity," as John Frazer points out, "extends beyond the merely technical. Korda's film has the same direct uninhibited appeal to childhood imagination as Melies's work. The film is filled with the same fantasy, fakery, and lack of concern for everyday logic."[144]

THE DOCTOR'S SECRET/HYDROTHERAPIE FANTASTIQUE (16mm: 1910, 9 mins., b/w, silent, R-MMA)
While others were moving away from fantasy and absurdist comedies, Melies continued in the same direction begun at the turn of the century, as evidenced by this film about charlatans and bogus remedies for obesity.

THE CONQUEST OF THE POLE/LA CONQUETE DU POLE (16mm: 1912, 20; mins., b/w, silent, R-MMA, ROM)
By 1912, Melies had declined considerably in importance and production. This film, however, represents for many scholars an example of the delightful and skillful techniques that the pioneering filmmaker had achieved by this point in his career. Among the many conventions perfected is the pantomime of the stereotyped Old Father Pole, who ate people who wandered into his domain. Moreover, Melies makes impressive use of alternative camera shots, resulting in the shifting audience perspectives.

A TRIP TO THE MOON/LE VOYAGE DANS LA LUNE (16mm: 1902, 14 mins., b/w, silent, R-BUD, MMA)
Probably the best of Melies's surviving works, this film is an example of how he defied both the technical difficulties and fashions of filmmaking at the turn of the century. The storyline owes a debt to H. G. Wells's THE FIRST MEN ON THE MOON (1901) and Jules Verne's FROM EARTH TO THE MOON (1865).[145] The result is a charming, highly imaginative, and amusing story that shows how Melies went beyond merely adapting magic to the movies.

EDWIN S. PORTER

THE GREAT TRAIN ROBBERY (16mm: 1903, 11 mins., b/w, silent, R-MMA)
Often called the first story film made in the United States, this movie was one of the most influential of the early attempts at screen narratives. It is the best example of innovative filmmaking prior to the emergence of Griffith in 1908.

THE LIFE OF AN AMERICAN FIREMAN (16mm: 1903, 6 mins., b/w, silent, R-MMA)
Another film that may seem rather crude to today's audience but that was highly acclaimed in its day. Here is one of the first attempts at developing the last-minute rescue of a woman and her children from what seems to be an inevitable doom. It was this type of formula that Griffith was to develop in later years.

---

[144] ARTIFICIALLY ARRANGED SCENES, p.158.

[145] See ARTIFICIALLY ARRANGED SCENES, pp.95-9.

FERDINAND ZECCA

FERDINAND ZECCA PROGRAM (16mm: 1900-1906, 28 mins., b/w, silent, R-KIT)
This intriguing collection includes one early trick film--WHENCE DOES HE COME?/D'OU VIENT-IL? (1905)--illustrating the French film pioneer's penchant for humor as well as fantastic effects. The other films--e.g., A FATHER'S HONOR/L'HONNEUR D'UN PERE (1905), REVOLUTION IN ODESSA/REVOLUTION EN RUSSIE (1905)--demonstrate Zecca's approach to action filmmaking, where one shot equals one scene and chases play a major role in the story development. For more visual examples, see the MMA catalog.

THE AMERICAN FILM (1914-1918)

The twenty years from the appearance of the first Kinetoscope parlors in 1894, to the outbreak of World War I in 1914, witnessed rapid changes in the history of film. Movies moved from being mainly actualities and vaudeville turns, to feature films utilizing a basic cinematic language. It was a time when movies moved from infancy to adolescence.

It was also a period in which many small-time business people made movies. As Kathleen Karr points out,

Chicago, Philadelphia, and Fort Lee, New Jersey, were all early contenders for the center of the movie business with Essanay, Selig, Lubin, Pathe, Solax and other movie studios in residence, but so were Providence, Rhode Island; Wilkes-Barre, Pennsylvania; and Saranac Lake, New York; among other locales.[146]

Instead of running small nickelodeons, the new generation of aggressive exhibitors determined to move into production and distribution, built attractive movie houses. The demise of the MPPC ushered in a new era for independent filmmakers whose roots were in Europe, not America. These first- and second-generation Americans prided themselves on their ability to satisfy audience desires, particularly those dreams of being assimilated into the "American way" of life. This group of independents--e.g., Samuel Goldwyn, William Fox, Adolph Zukor, Carl Laemmle, Jesse Lasky, Marcus Loew, and Lewis J. Selznick--became more powerful in film circles than the MPPC thought possible.

Moreover, World War I, fought primarily in Europe, devastated the European film market. Not only did munitions manufacturers in England, France, Italy, and Germany confiscate the essential ingredients required for raw film, but also the war itself destroyed distribution channels and production facilities for European filmmakers. Thus, beginning in 1914, America moved to the center of the film world. It is a position American films maintain to this day.

As discussed in Chapters 2, 3, 5, and 6, there were many important developments between 1914 and 1919. First, Griffith left Biograph, became an independent producer, and revolutionized the art of the cinema with his feature films. Second, several of Griffith's associates--e.g., Mack Sennett and Mary Pickford--dramatically altered the course of film history. Sennett's Keystone films epitomize the art of slapstick silent film comedy and showcase some of film's great film clowns--Charles Chaplin, Mabel Normand, Ben Turpin, and Ford Sterling. Pickford's

---

[146]   Kathleen Karr, "Hooray for Providence, Wilkes-Barre, Saranac Lake--and Hollywood," THE AMERICAN FILM HERITAGE: IMPRESSIONS FROM THE AMERICAN FILM INSTITUTE ARCHIVES (Washington, D.C.: Acropolis Books, 1972), p.104.

screen popularity plus her business genius, along with the athletic showmanship of her second husband, Douglas Fairbanks, Sr., significantly shaped the evolution of the film industry, as well as the nature of the star system. Helping to structure the future of Hollywood's global power was Thomas H. Ince, who solidified the way in which movies could be mass produced. Collectively, these individuals laid the foundation for an oligopolistic American film industry.[147]

In the aftermath of World War I, the pattern for Hollywood's golden years took shape. An international distribution network that channeled feature films and short subjects was in place. First-run theaters served as the lynchpins for massive profits, while producer-distributors like Zukor, Fox, and Laemmle amassed large theater chains and built awesome vertical power bases.

That same interwoven foundation also provided the basis for a powerful self-censorship. It began as a reaction to external threats. As early as 1907, city councils had installed control mechanisms for monitoring film content. Starting in 1911, state censorship boards began to spring up. A year later, Congress barred interstate commerce of objectionable fight films. And in 1915, the U.S. Supreme Court ruled in the Mutual Film case that prior restraint of film exhibition was justified, thereby excluding the film industry from protection under the First Amendment. By 1916, the film producers were more than willing to set in place a self-censorship that would insure some form of protection from idiosyncratic state and municipal censorship codes and commissions.

As Hollywood poised itself for the post-WWI period, its prospects were phenomenal. Not only was there a coterie of great talent working steadily to elevate the art of the film in production facilities unparalleled around the world and buffered by a seemingly invincible distribution-exhibition system, but also the public had made clear the types of film formulas that it enjoyed. All that was needed was a hands-off policy by the federal government to allow the aggressive movie entrepreneurs to solidify their real estate holdings and fine-tune Hollywood's mass production of film comedies, Victorian melodramas, westerns, and popular literary works.

BOOKS

Lyons, Timothy James. THE SILENT PARTNER: THE HISTORY OF THE AMERICAN FILM MANUFACTURING COMPANY 1910-1921. New York: Arno Press, 1974. Illustrated. 256pp.

Originally presented as a 1972 Ph.D. dissertation at the University of Iowa, this intriguing study draws useful historical parallels between the decline of the major studios in the 1960s, and the decline of the Motion Picture Patents Company (MPPC) in the early teens. "Today's [1972] industrial scene in Hollywood," Lyons writes, "can be viewed as not totally unlike the business picture of 1908: today, however, the roles are reversed--the 'new independents' are challenging the 'old independents.'" The thrust of his argument is that small companies are always trying to merge with bigger companies, while the latter are always wary of the former. Using the producing firm of the American Film Manufacturing Company (1910-1921) as an illustration of the process, the author demonstrates how independents challenged the MPPC, how the amalgamation operated, and what happened to those companies unable to keep pace with the times. Various aspects of the company--e.g., business structure, employees, and the product--are investigated, thereby making the film industry and business the major focus of the study. As a result, we learn how real estate men like John R. Freuler and Harry E. Aitken tried to use film exhibition as a means to maximize their land holdings. Their shift from exhibition to distribution to production represented the pattern followed by the independents from 1908 to 1920. As

[147]   Janet Staiger, "Dividing Labor for Production Control: Thomas Ince and the Rise of the Studio System," CINEMA JOURNAL 18:2 (Spring 1979):16-25.

competition increased, especially after World War I, the American Film Manufacturing Company floundered. Located in Santa Barbara, California, rather than in Hollywood, it lacked the creative personnel available to production companies in the film capital. Without a theater chain or a powerful film exchange, it soon went out of business. In effect, as Lyons points out, "By 1921, it was apparent that American had served well its role as 'silent partner' to distributing chains, but the company was unable to prosper on its own. American had been dominated by its 'partner' interests for so long that the company had failed to recognize either the innovations in narrative and cinematic techniques being developed throughout the industry, or the business integration which was occurring." A bibliography, filmography, excerpts from PHOTOPLAY ART, II (August 1916), and a list of the company's personnel are included. Recommended for special collections.

Crafton, Donald. BEFORE MICKEY: THE ANIMATED FILM 1898-1928. Foreword Otto Messmer. Cambrdige: The MIT Press, 1982. Illustrated. 413pp.

Heraldson, Donald. CREATORS OF LIFE: A HISTORY OF ANIMATION. New York: Drake Publishers, 1975. Illustrated. 298pp.

Maltin, Leonard. OF MICE AND MAGIC: A HISTORY OF AMERICAN ANIMATED CARTOONS. New York: McGraw-Hill Book Company, 1980. Illustrated. 470pp.

FILMS

THOMAS H. INCE

CIVILIZATION (1916) (16mm: 1916, 100 mins., b/w, silent, R-BUD, EMG, KIT, MMA)
     Produced by Thomas H. Ince and co-directed by Raymond B. West and Reginald Barker, this epic drama makes a bizarre plea for pacifism and rebukes the World War I hysteria in America in the mid-teens. Howard Hickman stars as a German count who invents a new torpedo that can wreak havoc on its enemies. C. Gardner Sullivan's script has the count die and Jesus enter his body in order to demonstrate to the world the misery that wars create. The film is considered to be Ince's most popular work.

THE SCANDINAVIAN TRADITION (1906-1927)

     Of all the European countries making films during World War I, the Scandinavian countries, Sweden and Denmark were not only the most productive, but also among the few to develop cinematic traditions that challenged American artistry. Their appeal, however, was to a much narrower audience. In particular, Swedish and Danish artists experimented with visual qualities of landscapes, the nature of humanity's struggle against the unknown, and an acting style related more to the film than to the stage.[148] According to Roger Manvell, "Sweden and and Denmark . . . made a contribution to world cinema all out of proportion to their size. No other country with a population of four, or even seven, million . . . made so many films or

---

[148]   Evaluating early Danish film, as Ron Mottram points out (p.346), is simplified considerably by the fact that "only 5 percent of the films made in Denmark in this period [the mid- to end of the first decade of the 1900s] have survived. . . ."

. . . . influenced film-making elsewhere to the same extent."[149] On the other hand, Cook characterizes the Scandinavian cinema as "stately, solemn, and static. . . ."[150]

Both nations began their involvement early in film history. Sweden's roots were tied mainly to the efforts of two men, Charles Magnusson and Julius Jaenzon. Both started as cameramen in the mid-1890s. Of the two, Magnusson was the one most responsible for shaping the destiny of the Swedish cinema. He began filming as a hobby, Eric Rhode points out, making "newsreel-type films in the manner of the Lumieres."[151] Soon he went into exhibition. By 1909, Magnusson was managing the fledgling AB Svenska Biografteatern Company (in 1919 it became the AB Svensk FilmIndustri). That same year, Jaenzon, who had earned a reputation as an expert cameraman, joined him. Overnight, they revolutionized Swedish films. Years later Cowie would assert that Jaenzon was "the finest lighting cameraman of his generation."[152] Magnusson's forte lay in locating and developing artistic talent. He was also interested in duplicating the patterns set by FILM D'ART productions in other countries. A key year was 1912, when he not only moved the company from Kristianstad to Stockholm, but also produced twenty-five films, nine of which were directed by two young and remarkable directors, Mauritz Stiller and Victor Sjostrom.[153] As Forsyth Hardy concludes, Magnusson's handling of these two men transformed "a small struggling unit into a mature and vigorous school of cinema."[154]

The careers of Sjostrom and Stiller share several prominent similarities. Each man began first as a stage actor and then became a noted film director of screen adaptations from the works of the Nobel Laureate novelist Selma Langerlof. Each owed a great deal of his success to his cinematic contacts with Janezon. Moreover, as Hardy comments, "Both were conscious of the contribution which national legend and national character could make to the screen."[155] In addition, each man had a relatively brief and unhappy experience in Hollywood during the mid-1920s.

Of the two, Stiller is considered the lesser artist.[156] Preoccupied with style rather than with profound film content, he nonetheless gained an early reputation

---

[149] Roger Manvell, "Author's Preface," SCANDINAVIAN FILM, by Forsyth Hardy (London: Falcon Press, 1952), p.ix.

[150] Cook, p.109.

[151] Rhode, p.206.

[152] SWEDEN 1, p.67.

[153] *Peter Cowie, SWEDISH CINEMA (New York: A. S. Barnes and Company, 1966), p.12.

[154] Hardy, p.6.

[155] Hardy, p.7.

[156] Aleksander Kwiatkowski sums up the differences between the two men in talking about their screen adaptations: "Mauritz Stiller also used literary texts as a basis for his films, giving preference to lighter subjects--comedy and suspense. Whereas Sjostrom's adaptations remained completely faithful to the original works as well as to the environments he was restructuring, Stiller made free use of literary material in order to achieve his own impressive visions, frequently associated with a very personal, emotional approach to the subject he was handling. Sjostrom--to quote the director Benjamin Christensen--was imitating 'the very rhythm of life.' Stiller, an immigrant from Finland lacking permanent roots to some extent and differing from Sjostrom in character, mood and the aims of his art, elaborated the surface texture of life." See *Aleksander Kwiatkowski,

for pleasant comedies like LOVE AND JOURNALISM/KARLEK OCH JOURNALISTIK (1916), THOMAS GRAAL'S BEST FILM (1917), and EROTIKON (1920). He earned a permanent place in film history, however, through his screen adaptations of Langerlof's supernatural and dreamlike works. The best known versions are SIR ARNE'S TREASURE/HERR ARNES PENGAR (1919), GUNNAR HEDE'S SAGA (1922), and GOSTA BERLING'S SAGA (1924). Beaver sums up the general reaction to these epic screen narratives by saying that "collectively [they] contained those filmic elements which established Stiller's directorial prominence: expressive use of landscapes, vivid action sequences, and a keen sense for authentic historical recreations."[157] The BERLING film not only was Stiller's final Swedish film, but also featured the young Greta Garbo in her starring film debut. The director and his protege moved on to Berlin, where their work caught the attention of MGM executives who then brought them to Hollywood in 1925. Three years later a discouraged and disillusioned Stiller, having completed no films for MGM and only two for Paramount--HOTEL IMPERIAL (1927) and WOMAN ON TRIAL (1927)--returned to Sweden where at forty-nine years of age he died on November 8, 1928.

Sjostrom, on the other hand, had a much longer career in films as an actor and director. Humanistic in outlook and psychologically probing in technique, he constantly experimented with film form and content. In directing films like INGEBORG HOLM (1913), TERJE VIGEN (1917), and THE PHANTOM CHARIOT/KORKARLEN (1920), he revealed his impressive poetic qualities and pantheistic approach to depicting human feelings and emotions. In 1923, MGM lured him to Hollywood (where he worked under the name of Seastrom), and over the next seven years he directed nine films, including THE SCARLET LETTER (1926) and THE WIND (1928). These films demonstrate Sjostrom's visual powers in depicting profound moral and religious conflicts.[158] He returned to Sweden in 1928, directed several more films, and then went into semi-retirement. Among the many artists he inspired was Ingmar Bergman, who, in 1957, gave his mentor the memorable screen role of Isak Borg in WILD STRAWBERRIES/SMULTRONSTALLET.[159] Sjostrom died three years later.

When Stiller and Sjostrom left Sweden, they took with them the best of that nation's creative talent, thereby forcing the Swedish film industry into an eclipse that did not pass until the post-World War II period. But during the apogee of the Swedish film, as Maurice Bardeche and Robert Brasillach conclude, "the classical standards of the silent film were, slowly and painfully, to be formulated, and it would be impossible to exaggerate the radical importance of the part which Sweden played in formulating the aesthetic."[160]

Denmark was another country that tried to fill the European film vacuum from 1914 to 1918. In fact, it achieved considerable notoriety in the early days because of the controversial nature of risque films made by Ole Olesen's Nordisk Film Company, founded in 1906 and still operating today. Over the next eighteen years, the remarkable Danish film pioneer made hundreds of films. According to his

---

SWEDISH FILM CLASSICS: A PICTORIAL SURVEY OF 25 FILMS FROM 1913 TO 1957 (New York: Dover Publications, 1983), p.vi.

[157]   Beaver, p.158.

[158]   One critic who goes against the consensus is Paul Rotha. In discussing Sjostrom's Hollywood period, Rotha finds most of his films--except for THE SCARLET LETTER--"uneven." Moreover, Rotha feels that Sjostrom remained "stationary in his outlook, thinking in terms of his early Swedish imagery; [and] . . . made little use of the cinema itself." In Sjostrom's defense, the critic points out that "The lyricism of Sjostrom, of the Swedish film itself, . . . cannot flourish in the American factory."

[159]   Rotha, pp.186-7

[160]   Bardeche and Brasillach, pp.139-40.

biographer, Bebe Bergsten, the ex-carnival barker and peep show owner felt
compelled to educate audiences around the world to the ways of the Danish wealthy
and privileged classes. "Olesen quickly learned," she writes, "that if he spent money
to make pictures of exceptional quality, he could expect profits on a grand scale."
She then adds that the existing sixteen Danish films he produced "are far superior
to those that still remain elsewhere in the world of the same vintage."[161] Olesen's
skill in treating such taboo subjects as prostitution and abortion rested primarily on
his judicious cinematic imagery and his concern with realistic performances given by
Valdemar Psilander and Asta Neilsen.[162]

Following in the steps taken by early American filmmakers, the Danes (primarily
through the efforts of Nordisk) capitalized on the natural beauty of their countryside.
Where the two industries differed, Ellis points out, was in the use of location
shooting. While the Americans romanticized their national culture in naturalistic
melodramas, the Danes dwelt on "the darker and more mystical tradition of
Scandinavian folklore and literature."[163]

The first noted Danish film director was Benjamin Christensen, who specialized
in mysterious and supernatural stories like WITCHCRAFT THROUGH THE AGES
(1922). He provided a cinematic foundation for the emerging Danish film industry.

But Denmark's foremost director was Carl Theodor Dreyer, who began working
as a screenwriter and editor in the early teens. He directed his first film in 1918,
THE PRESIDENT/PRAESIDENTEN. His second film, LEAVES FROM SATAN'S
BOOK/BLADE AF SATANS BOG (1919), exemplified the fusing of Griffith's influence
with Scandanavian traditions, as well as underscoring the importance that Dreyer gave
to "invisible" camera movement. In the years to come, Dreyer, as we shall see, moved
from one country to another, pursuing his unique cinematic style. But his total
commitment to exploring through film, the complex relationship between organized
religion and the individual spirit, had its origins in the silent Danish film industry.

The Scandinavian tradition left a legacy carried on by many filmmakers, not the
least of whom were Ingmar Bergman, Woody Allen, Luis Bunuel, and Robert Bresson.
Its psychological probing of the human spirit encouraged artists like Stiller, Sjostrom,
and Dreyer to experiment with thought-provoking themes and reflective techniques
that built on the advances made by filmmakers in Europe and America.

BOOKS

GENERAL

Bergsten, Bebe. THE GREAT DANE AND THE GREAT NORTHERN FILM COMPANY.
Los Angeles: Historical Films, 1973. Illustrated. 116pp.

A valuable biography of Ole Oleson, this affectionate study offers the best
existing material on the Danish film pioneer who at forty years of age began to make
films in Copenhagen, Denmark. Bergsten traces Oleson's career from sailor to film
exhibitor to movie producer, while, at the same time, describing the evolution of the
Danish film industry. Among the many interesting facts we learn about Oleson's firm,
the Nordisk Film Company ("the oldest continuously operating motion picture studio

---

[161]   Bebe Bergsten, THE GREAT DANE AND THE GREAT NORTHERN FILM COMPANY (Los Angeles:
        Historical Films, 1973), p.29. See also Ron Mottram, "The Great Northern Film
        Company: Nordisk Film in the American Motion Picture Market," FILM HISTORY: AN
        INTERNATIONAL JOURNAL 2:1 (Winter 1988):71-86.

[162]   Robinson, pp.83-4.

[163]   Ellis, p.78.

in the world") is that it turned out over 100 movies in its 1906 debut, the Danish press in the early years paid more attention to films than did the press corps in most other places on the globe, and Oleson employed nearly 500 people in comparison to the standard American firms, which rarely hired more than 100 individuals. In fast-moving, clear prose, Bergsten recounts how Nordisk branched out to European and American markets, as well as contributed to the birth and growth of the feature film. To support such claims, she includes a full-length article, "Growth of the Feature Film," by Nordisk's general manager, Ingvald C. Oes, from the November 23, 1912, issue of THE MOVING PICTURE WORLD. In addition to the excellent quality of the many rare and stimulating illustrations, the book contains brief critiques and production credits for sixteen existing films from 1911 and 1912. A general index and a cast index are included. Recommended for special collections.

Cowie, Peter. FINNISH CINEMA. Cranbury: A. S. Barnes and Company, 1975. Illustrated. 128pp.

Acknowledging that many readers might question the need for a book on Finland's cinematic history, Cowie states that he wants to improve the nation's fuzzy image with film students. He begins by describing the differences between Finland and other Scandinavian countries and by noting that its directors have to target their domestic releases mainly for rural audiences. Labeling the making of Finnish films essentially a "cottage industry," Cowie points out that from its inception, the Finnish film industry "has been largely self-sustaining, free of outside influences both artistic and commercial." The story of the several hundred movies made in Finland since 1907 (the majority of which were made between 1935 and 1955) relies on Cowie's having analyzed approximately sixty existing copies, with a special focus on Nyrki Tapiovaara (a legendary director who revolted against Finland's cliche-ridden cinema in the 1930s and 1940s and became a hero to the Finnish directors of the 1960s and 1970s). The reason given for the current decline in Finnish films is the popularity of television. The material is interesting, informative, and useful. Along with many helpful illustrations, there are a filmography, bibliography, and index. Well worth browsing.

*Cowie, Peter, with Arne Svensson. SWEDEN 1: AN ILLUSTRATED GUIDE.   New York: A. S. Barnes and Company, 1970. Illustrated. 224pp.

This alphabetically arranged filmography of 250 directors, actors, screenwriters, producers, and technicians is valuable and informative.   With some exceptions, the entries rely heavily on material collected and published in Sweden by Sven G. Winquist. The most notable difference among the annotations is that the performers, whose film careers are closely intertwined with their stage careers, are cited primarily for their Swedish work, while the directors have more complete listings.   All the film titles are in English, but there is no information provided on whether the film was ever released in an English-speaking country. For more information on the films themselves, the reader is directed to SWEDEN 2. Almost twenty-five percent of the profusely illustrated guide is devoted to a film title index, which also provides the Swedish title of the film. Well worth browsing.

*Cowie, Peter. SWEDEN 2: A COMPREHENSIVE ASSESSMENT OF THE THEMES, TRENDS, AND DIRECTORS IN SWEDISH CINEMA. New York: A. S. Barnes and Company, 1970. Illustrated. 256pp.

An update of the author's SWEDISH CINEMA, this thoughtful and valuable book is not only an admirable supplement to SWEDEN 1, but also a major source of information about Swedish film history. The major portions of the study are devoted to the country's two important periods of achievement: 1914 to 1921, when Stiller and Sjostrom were in residence; and 1955 to 1970, when Ingmar Bergman was at his artistic height. Some interesting illustrations and a strong bibliography complete the work. No index is included. Recommended for special collections.

*Cowie, Peter. SWEDISH CINEMA. Cranbury: A. S. Barnes and Company, 1966. Illustrated. 224pp.
   This pioneering study has since been updated by SWEDEN II, but it serves to illustrate how resourceful Cowie was in his initial work. In addition to focusing on Sweden's three reigning princes of film, it calls attention to other noted directors of the past (e.g., Gustaf Molander, Anders Henrikson, Hampe Faustman, Hasse Ekman, Arne Mattson, and Peter Weiss) as well as leaders of the new Swedish cinema (e.g., Bo Widerberg, Jorn Donner, Vilgot Sjoman, and Mai Zetterling). Filmographies, a bibliography, and a general index are included. Well worth browsing.

Lauritzen, Einar. SWEDISH FILMS. Introduction Richard Griffith. New York: Museum of Modern Art, 1962. Illustrated. 32pp.
   Written in conjunction with a film exhibition of Swedish films from 1905 to 1957 at the Museum of Modern Art, this interesting booklet highlights what the collaborators feel about Swedish cinematic history. Griffith, then the MOMA's film library curator, stresses how the early Swedish pictures of the teens and twenties drew their inspiration from national origins, how the industry went into "a strange eclipse and amazing comeback symbolized by Ingmar Bergman." The major portion of the survey presents terse, descriptive, and evaluative annotations of movies from 1909 to 1957, along with lovely illustrations. Thumbnail biographies of the directors are included at the end of the booklet. Unfortunately, there is no index. Well worth browsing.

Hardy, Forsyth. SCANDINAVIAN FILM. London: The Falcon Press, 1952. Illustrated. 62pp.
   Focusing on the film industries of Denmark, Sweden, and Norway, this trim volume is packed with subjective judgments and intriguing observations. Regrettably, there is neither a bibliography nor footnotes to support the highly respected author's wide-ranging assertions about art and industry. Historical overviews include a rich sampling of film titles (with very little description or credits) set against an evolving national tradition. The six stimulating chapters serve as an excellent outline for a much-needed detailed chronology. An index is included. Well worth browsing.

*Kwiatkowski, Aleksander. SWEDISH FILM CLASSICS: A PICTORIAL SURVEY OF 25 FILMS FROM 1913 TO 1957. New York: Dover Publications, 1983. Illustrated. 103pp.
   A compact and useful filmography, this entertaining picture book has over 150 well-produced pictures from early movies like INGEBORG HOLM (1913), LOVE AND JOURNALISM/ KARLEK OCH JOURNALISTIK (1916), and SIR ARNE'S TREASURE/HERR ARNES PENGAR (1919) to famous Bergman films like SMILES OF A SUMMER NIGHT/SOMMARNATTENS LEENDE, THE SEVENTH SEAL/DET SJUNDE INSEGLET (both in 1955), and WILD STRAWBERRIES/SMULTRONSTALLET (1957). The introductory comments on the history of Swedish film are straightforward and informative. Although the sections on the films are too brief to satisfy serious students, they do contain information about date of release, name of production company, minimal cast and credit data, a synopsis, and a commentary. Additional profiles on the directors are provided at the back of the book. Regrettably, there is no index or bibliography. Well worth browsing.

CARL THEODOR DREYER

*Bordwell, David. THE FILMS OF CARL-THEODOR DREYER. Berkeley: University of California Press, 1981. Illustrated. 251pp.

A formalist approach to the great Danish director's work, this erudite study concentrates on the issue of cinema as art and pursues questions like "How may we analyze Dreyer's films as narrative and stylistic systems? How do the films relate to the dominant conceptions of what cinema is and does? What implications do the films have for contemporary filmmakers?" The five opening and elegantly written chapters explore important concepts related to Dreyer's work, the man and his legend, and the narrative form of his early films as well as the construction of space and problematic unities. The next five profusely illustrated and stimulating chapters analyze his major films: THE PASSION OF JOAN OF ARC/LA PASSION DE JEANNE D'ARC (1927), VAMPYR/THE DREAM OF ALLAN GRAY (1932), DAY OF WRATH/VREDENS DAG (1944), THE WORD/ORDET (1954), and GERTRUD (1964). The concluding chapter discusses how Dreyer's career and major films explain and expand our understanding of social formations internal and external to the phenomenon of film. A valuable biographical filmography, endnotes, a bibliography, and an index conclude this splendid study. Recommended for special collections.

*Skoller, Donald, ed. DREYER IN DOUBLE REFLECTION: TRANSLATION OF CARL TH. DREYER'S WRITINGS ABOUT THE FILM (OM FILMEN). New York: E. P. Dutton and Company, 1973. Illustrated. 205pp.

The essays included in this anthology extend from 1920 to 1960 and are presented chronologically in order to provide insights into the artist and his work. "The individual pieces," Skoller writes, "are like entries in a public diary, an artist's log covering four decades of dynamic interaction with the growing film culture of the twentieth century." What is intriguing about Skoller's scholarship (he did not translate the writings; instead, he edited the translations and provides introductory notes for each of the entries) is the succinct but effective way in which he brings us closer to Dreyer's art and thought processes. Particularly helpful are the visuals obtained from the Danish Film Museum and the effective groupings that collectively illustrate the filmmaker's style. Particularly interesting are the discussions of anti-Semitism and Renee (Maria) Falconetti's method of relaxing after a day's shooting on THE PASSION OF JOAN OF ARC/LA PASSION DE JEANNE D'ARC (1928). Regrettably, there is no index or bibliography. Well worth browsing.

*Milne, Tom. THE CINEMA OF CARL DREYER. New York: A. S. Barnes and Company, 1971. Illustrated. 192pp.

An intelligent and sensitive study of a man who over a fifty-year period made only fourteen films, but who emerged as one of the most impressive filmmakers in the history of cinema. "Not only was Dreyer a perpetual wanderer," explains Milne, "making films in Norway, Sweden, France and Germany in the intervals of finding employment in Denmark; he remained in a constant state of conflict with the world around him: artist against businessman; master of the silent film trying to prove that he was also master of sound; great MODERN film-maker demonstrating by example that the cinema's past remains vividly alive." Seven fast-moving chapters demonstrate why historians consider films like LA PASSION DE JEANNE D'ARC and DAY OF WRATH masterpieces. A handful of adequate illustrations, a good filmography, and an ordinary bibliography complete the book. Regrettably, no index is provided. Well worth browsing.

VICTOR SJOSTROM

Forslund, Bengt. VICTOR SJOSTROM: HIS LIFE AND HIS WORK. Trans. Peter Cowie et al. New York: New York Zoetrope, 1988. Illustrated. 295pp.

FILMS

SWEDEN

VICTOR SJOSTROM

THE PHANTOM CHARIOT/KORKARLEN (Sweden--16mm: 1920, 92 mins., b/w, silent, R-BUD, EMG, FNC, KIT, MMA; S-REE)
     One of Sweden's most acclaimed silent films, this unusual special effects adaptation of a Lagerlof novel was written and directed by Sjostrom and beautifully photographed by Jaenzon. Sjostrom plays the lead character, who is an alcoholic and ex-convict trying to regain not only his soul, but also the love of his wife and children. What made the film so popular was the imaginative camerawork and the effective use of flashbacks. "The double exposures in the graveyard scene and in the scenes with the phantom chariot are beautifully executed," writes Einar Lauritzen, "and, as always, in Julius Jaenzon's photography, the interplay of light and shadow is superb."[164]

MAURITZ STILLER

THE STORY OF GOSTA BERLING/GOSTA BERLING'S SAGA (Sweden--16mm: 1924, 105 mins., b/w, musical score only, R-BUD, KIT; S-REE)
     Although this film was made in Scandinavia, it brought the director Mauritz Stiller and his great discovery, Greta Garbo, to Hollywood, and gave the world one of its most enduring legends. The story of love is secondary to the extraordinary characterizations, photographic excellence, and lyrical rhythm.[165]

DENMARK

BENJAMIN CHRISTENSEN

WITCHCRAFT THROUGH THE AGES/HAXAN (Denmark--16mm: 1922, 75 mins., b/w, musical score only, R-BUD, EMG, JAN, KIT; S-REE)
     Filmed in Sweden and considered by many historians to be Christensen's best film, this film recounts in documentary fashion, a history of witchcraft and the measures taken to combat it. The treatment of medieval diabolism not only created a controversy over the depiction of nudity and sexual perversion, but also, as Ellis points out, makes the film "a disturbing, even curiously 'modern' work with a singular tension among diverse elements. . . ."[166]

THE GREAT GERMAN SILENTS (1919-1927)

b

     The pioneering contributions made by Messter and the Skladanowsky brothers in the 1890s put Germany in the vanguard of nations witnessing the emergence of moving pictures. In the twenty years that followed, however, German filmmakers

---

[164]   *Einar Lauritzen, SWEDISH FILMS (New York: Museum of Modern Art, 1962), p.12.

[165]   Bosley Crowther, "The Story of Gosta Berling," THE GREAT FILMS, pp.31-34.

rarely attracted a mass following. Cook attributes this failure to the presence of many disreputable individuals throughout the industry. The first notable change came in 1912, with the AUTORENFILM (Germany's response to FILM D'ART), and in 1913, with Stellan Rye's THE STUDENT OF PRAGUE/DER STUDENT VON PRAG.[167] Robinson suggests that the increase in stature, beginning in the early teens,[168] resulted from the involvement in German films of Max Reinhardt and Asta Nielsen.

By the start of World War I, German movies were becoming a significant part of the international system of production, distribution, and exhibition. The war, however, left the Germans isolated. The one notable cinematic gain of the period was that it fostered a close artistic relationship between Germany and its neutral Scandinavian neighbors. Eventually, a number of Swedish and Danish artists like Stiller, Garbo, and Dreyer would migrate to the German film industry. On the other hand, the kaiser's enemies waged a propaganda campaign through movies that seriously damaged Germany's reputation as well as its morale. To counteract that public relations problem, discussed in Chapter 2, the German high command, in December 1917, solidified the various elements of the country's film industry into a giant monopoly, Universum Film Aktiengesellschaft (later known as UFA). Housed at Neubabelsberg, near Berlin, the UFA began its own propaganda response by attracting the best creative talent possible. But the end of the war in 1918, the UFA's goals were directed toward art, and away from propaganda.[169]

No longer controlled by the military, the giant filmmaking conglomerate became responsive to the nation's intellectual and creative renaissance that was taking place in medicine, drama, music, architecture, and painting. Equally important, intellectuals and artists now saw film as a marvelous medium to communicate the mood and tenor of the times. The fact that ninety-seven percent of Germany's over 5,000 movie houses could book any films they chose added to the cultural excitement. Still further, the end of the war reopened Germany's valuable contacts with the international film community. Thus facilities, artists, freedom, and ideology coalesced to produce one of the most extraordinary periods in film history. That is, at a time when the nation was disillusioned and economically chaotic, its filmmakers were enjoying one of the richest eras of creative expression.

Guided by the powerful producer Erich Pommer, and influenced principally by the stage innovations of Max Reinhardt and the psychological theories of Freud, the UFA channeled its production policies toward complete studio control. Location shooting was eliminated. Notions of naturalism and sentimentality were abandoned. The new theme was Expressionism. Art would demonstrate the internal realities of the external world. The emphasis would be on subjective rather than objective feelings. Filmmakers would share in the exciting experimentation taking place in the arts.

To that end, the artists focused on three specific types of films. First were films related to historical and mythological fantasies: e.g., Ernst Lubitsch's PASSION/MADAME DUBARRY (1919), DECEPTION/ANNA BOLEYN (1920), Fritz Lang's DESTINY/DER MUDE TOD (1921), and DIE NIBELUNGEN (1924).[170] The Lubitsch films specialized in spectacular crowd scenes, superbly lit by artificial lights and ingeniously edited, while the Lang films employed similar stunning effects in dramatizing Germany's traditional haunting tales of love and death. Second were the

---

[166]   A HISTORY OF FILM, p.78.

[167]   Cook, p.107.

[168]   Robinson, pp.86-7.

[169]   For a good overview of UFA's management arrangements, see Paul Monaco, CINEMA & SOCIETY: FRANCE AND GERMANY DURING THE TWENTIES (New York: Elsevier, 1976), pp.26-31.

[170]   DIE NIBELUNGEN was released in two parts: SIEGFRIED and KRIEMHILD'S REVENGE.

SCHAUER films (fantasy films dealing with the supernatural and the bizarre): e.g., Robert Wiene's THE CABINET OF DR. CALIGARI/DAS KABINETT DES DR. CALIGARI (1919),[171] Paul Wegener-Henrik Galeen's THE GOLEM (1920), Frederich Wilhelm Murnau's NOSFERATU (1922), and Lang's METROPOLIS (1926). These macabre films explored the psychological terror of monsters, fiends, and madmen. Third were the KAMMERSPIELFILM ("chamber play films") that focused on the present despair in Germany: e.g. Murnau's THE LAST LAUGH/DER LETZE MANN (1924), E. A. Dupont's VARIETY, and Georg Wilhelm Pabst's THE JOYLESS STREET/DIE FREUDLOSE GASSE (both in 1925). Unlike the previous two types, these films placed the emphasis on the pathetic lives of ordinary working-class people.

What all three classifications shared was a concern for composition and mood both within a shot and from shot to shot. No matter what the film, screenwriters, set designers, cinematographers, performers, lighting technicians, and directors orchestrated every aspect of the visual image to reinforce a probing of the character's private feelings. Among the most memorable developments of this period was the ability of the camera to project a subjective point of view.[172] In films like THE LAST LAUGH and VARIETY, one sees what a drunken doorman saw as he reeled around the room, or what a trapeze artist viewed as he swung through the air. As a result of the encouragement given to filmmakers, Germany earned an international reputation in categories other than directing--e.g., Emil Jannings, Pola Negri,[173] Conrad Veidt, Werner Krauss, Lil Dagover, and Asta Nielsen; set designing--e.g., Hermann Warm, Walther Rohrig, Walter Reimann, Robert Herlth, Albin Grau, and Erno Metzner; cinematography--e.g., Fritz Arno Wagner and Karl Freund; and screenwriting--e.g., Karl Mayer and Hans Janowitz.

The debate today is about what caused the end of Germany's golden age. One hypothesis states that the rise of the Nazi party and Hitler's appointment as Chancellor not only drove many artists out of Germany, but also redirected the goals and orientation of the German film industry. That view is discussed in Chapter 2. A second hypothesis claims that the claustrophobic nature of the expressionistic studio-made film eventually drained the filmmakers themselves. Not only they, but also their audiences, lost interest in the direction German films had taken. In short, the movement fizzled.[174] A third hypothesis, and the one most favored by general

---

[171]   At the time that the film was made, Pommer was head of Decla-Bioscop, an independent film company that merged with the UFA in 1920. See Herbert G. Luft, "Erich Pommer: Part I," FILMS IN REVIEW 10:8 (October 1959):457-469; and ___, "Erich Pommer: Part II, ibid., 10:9 (November 1959):518-33.

[172]   For more information, see Lutz Bacher, THE MOBILE MISE-EN-SCENE: A CRITICAL ANALYSIS OF THE THEORY AND PRACTICE OF LONG-TAKE CAMERA MOVEMENT (New York: Arno Press, 1978); and FILM READER 4, ed. Blaine Allan (Evanston: Northwestern University, 1979).

[173]   It's worth noting that many of these personalities were emigres who had left their homelands to join the avant-garde movement in Germany. For example, Negri, who was Polish, began her acting career in her early teens in Warsaw, and had become a film star before she was twenty. She migrated to Germany during World War I, where she worked primarily with Reinhardt and Lubitsch. In 1922, she left Germany for Hollywood. For a brief overview of the star's career from its beginnings until her death on August 1, 1987, see Ted Thackery, Jr. and Gerald Faris, "Pola Negri, 'Vamp' of Silent Films, Dies," LOS ANGELES TIMES 1 (August 3, 1987):3, 13.

[174]   For a useful overview of this perspective, see Ellis, pp. 104-5; and Anthony Asquith, "The Tenth Muse Climbs Parnassus," THE PENGUIN FILM REVIEW 1 (August 1946):10-26.

film historians, is that Paramount and MGM took advantage of the UFA's financial plight in 1925 and forced the off-balance filming unit into a pact (the Parafamet Agreement) that forestalled bankruptcy,but literally drained the company of its major assets. Within two years, many of the most creative talents in the German industry--e.g., Murnau, Freund, Jannings, Pommer, and Mayer--were in Hollywood, with others soon to follow.[175]

BOOKS

GENERAL

Collier, Jo Leslie. FROM WAGNER TO MURNAU: THE TRANSPOSITION OF ROMANTICISM FROM STAGE TO SCREEN. Ann Arbor: UMI Research Press, 1988. 174pp.

*Eisner, Lotte H.. THE HAUNTED SCREEN: EXPRESSIONISM IN THE GERMAN CINEMA AND THE INFLUENCE OF MAX REINHARDT. Berkeley: University of California, 1969. Illustrated. 360pp.
This work was first published as the French L'ECRAN DEMONIAQUE, then as the expanded German DAMONISCHE LEINWAND, followed by the further revised and expanded French edition of 1965. Now this important study of the German silent film (sound films are discussed briefly) is available in English. Written with warmth and insight, it is an impressive analysis by a young German journalist who saw the close connection between the state's policy toward film distribution, exhibition, and production and the artistic trends of the time. The emphasis is on German Romanticism in literary works and theatrical productions and the influence of those works and productions on filmmakers like Lang, Murnau, Wiene, Pabst, Mayer, Wagner, and Freund. In addition, there are 300 well-chosen illustrations, and an appendix on the DREIGROSCHENOPER Lawsuit (brought by Bertolt Brecht and Kurt Weill against Nero films for using their songs in Pabst's film, THE THREEPENNY OPERA/DIE DREIGROSCHENOPER), a selective filmography, and an index. Recommended for special collections.

Huaco, George A. THE SOCIOLOGY OF FILM ART. New York: Basic Books, 1965. 229pp.
"This book," Huaco explains, "is an investigation of the emergence, duration, and decline of stylistically unified waves of film art in terms of possible sociohistorical conditions." He identifies three kinds of phenomenon that over sixty years of film history have resulted in three great periods of film art. First is the presence of isolated filmmakers; second, the "stylistically homogenous clusters" of the filmmakers' works; and third, "waves of film-art style." Huaco insists that his sociological approach allows homogenity of style to go beyond a mere compilation of common themes, motifs, and styles to an analysis of the larger cultural context and the ability to link the cluster "to specific social structures and configurations in the larger social system." The three great periods reviewed are the German expressionist film (1920-1931), Soviet expressive realism (1925-1930), and Italian neo-realism (1945-1955).
Although marred by a number of aesthetic and methodological problems, this intriguing approach is stimulating and inventive. Best of all, it is presented clearly and effectively. A bibliography and index are included. Well worth browsing.

---

[175] For an extended list of UFA personnel who migrated to Hollywood, see Cook, pp.126-7.

*Kobal, John, ed. GREAT FILM STILLS OF THE GERMAN SILENT ERA: 125 STILLS
FROM THE STIFTUNG DEUTSCHE KINEMATHEK. Introduction Lotte H. Eisner. New
York: Dover Publications, 1981. Illustrated. 111pp.
    In her stimulating introduction, Eisner speaks of the power of stills to evoke a
desire to see the films themselves. "The chiaroscuro in these stills," she writes, "is
meaningfully applied; the poses of the actors and the space in which they move become
tangible. In a word, these images exude STIMMUNG, a word that is practically
untranslatable; 'mood' might be an English equivalent." Whether because of the
conditions imposed by World War I or because of Reinhardt's theatrical experiments
in stage lighting, German set designers and lighting technicians became a fixture in
the nation's silent films. Thus the chance to study the effects that these artists
achieved in dozens of memorable films is exciting. There are also some lovely candid
shots of the people on the various sets. Moreover, this fine collection of stills
illustrates the work of important directors like Robert Wiene, Fritz Lang, G. W.
Pabst, Ernst Lubitsch, F. W. Murnau, Joe May, and E. A. Dupont. At the same time,
it provides a stunning gallery of pictures of the era's great stars like Greta Garbo,
Pola Negri, Emil Jannings, and Conrad Veidt. Each picture comes with a caption
giving production credits and the name(s) of the performer(s) in the shot.
Alphabetical listings of directors, films, and performers are included. Well worth
browsing.

*Kracauer, Siegfried. FROM CALIGARI TO HITLER: A PSYCHOLOGICAL HISTORY
OF THE GERMAN FILM. Princeton: Princeton University, 1969. Illustrated.   361pp.
    Originally published in 1947, this classic study is concerned with understanding
how films in the twenties laid the groundwork for Hitler's Germany. "It is my
contention," explains Kracauer, "that through an analysis of the German films deep
psychological dispositions predominant in Germany from 1918 to 1933 can be
exposed--dispositions which influenced the course of events during that time and
which will have to be reckoned with in the post-Hitler period." The introduction to
the book's four major sections describes the specific traits of a German cinema rooted
firmly in a middle-class mentality that remained constant although various themes and
characterizations incorporating them changed frequently. Part One--"The Archaic
Period (1895-1918)"--explores the steps leading up to the rise of Germany's film
masterpieces, pointing out the important conditions in the industry's growth that
accounted for its extraordinary skills after 1918. Part Two--"The Postwar Period
(1918-1924)"--analyzes the types of films in vogue following World War I, speculating
on their relationship to audience needs and desires. For example, Kracauer asserts
that "The sex films testified to primitive needs arising in all belligerent countries after
the war. Nature itself urged that people who had, for an eternity, faced death and
destruction, reconfirm their violated life instincts by means of excess. It was an all
but automatic process; equilibrium could not be reached at once." In discussing
Lubitsch's historical spectacles, Kracauer asserts that "The only tenable explanation
is that, whether consciously or not, the majority of people lived in fear of social
changes and therefore welcomed films which defamed not only bad rulers but also good
revolutionary causes. These films outrightly encouraged the existing resistance to
any emotional shift that might have enlivened the German Republic." Part Three--"The
Stabilized Period (1924-1929)"--charts the decline in the German film industry,
stressing how economic exigencies became a paramount concern for the filmmakers and
affected not only aesthetic standards but also film content. In Kracauer's view, "The
decline of the German screen is nothing but the reflection of a widespread inner
paralysis." Thus the films in this period are grouped into three categories showing
the existence of the paralysis, how that paralysis affected people individually, and
how it affected the nation collectively. Part Four--"The Pre-Hitler Period
(1930-1933)"--explores the contradictory impulses in Germany to give Hitler power
but to reject him personally. The films, from Kracauer's perspective, reveal how after

1930 the "paralysis had subsided" and a struggle emerged between the forces of authoritarianism and antiauthoritarianism. In the end, Hitler wins out: "Personified daydreams of minds to whom freedom meant a fatal shock, and adolescence a permanent temptation, these figures filled the arena of Nazi Germany." The 1969 edition concludes with a supplement dealing with propaganda and the Nazi war films.

Clearly, this study suffers from a Freudian bias that sometimes forces Kracauer to label films arbitrarily. It also suffers from too heavy a sociological emphasis in trying to relate German film to the national state of mind. Nevertheless, the discussions, credits, and plot synopses make it one of the best available sources on the German silent period. Moreover, no work on psychoanalytical film criticism has yet approached Kracauer's sweep or insights. A bibliography and index are included. Recommended for special collections.

*MASTERWORKS OF THE GERMAN CINEMA: THE GOLEM, NOSFERATU, M, THE THREEPENNY OPERA. Introduction Roger Manvell. New York: Harper and Row, 1973. Illustrated. 300pp.

This useful anthology of film scripts begins with a good introduction to the German silent cinema. Manvell not only reviews the economic and political conditions that underlined the nation's instability in the post-WWI era, but also points out the "theatrical" characteristics of the German film studios that resulted in a number of film classics. Each of the four films is discussed briefly, with an emphasis on its unique qualities. For example, Manvell explains that the director Paul Wegener's THE GOLEM (1920) was his third version of the medieval legend in six years (the other two had been in 1914 and 1917), that the film underscored Wegener's fascination with period pieces and fantasy, that he had played the Golem (a clay giant originally brought to life to help the Jewish people who eventually turns into a monster) in the last two versions of the legend, and that the concept was "a clear case of wishful thinking which oversteps itself because of its dependence upon 'unlawful' black magic." A critical appendix includes excerpts from well-known books that critique the films. Well worth browsing.

Wellwarth, George E., and Alfred G. Brooks, eds. MAX REINHARDT 1873-1973: A CENTENNIAL FESTSCHRIFT OF MEMORIAL ESSAYS AND INTERVIEWS ON THE ONE HUNDRETH ANNIVERSARY OF HIS BIRTH. Binghamton: Max Reinhardt Archive, 1973. Illustrated. 132pp.

"When Max Reinhardt died in New York City on October 31, 1943," explains Alfred G. Brooks, "his passing was noted and mourned, but it was overshadowed by the daily horrors of World War II. His creative career had spanned the birth and demise, the rejection and acceptance, of the host of forms and movements which sought to provide new perspectives in the visual and performing arts during the first half of the Twentieth Century. Reinhardt influenced playwrights, critics, painters, designers, architects, composers, dancers, actors, directors, and managers. His basically eclectic nature led him to develop an enormous stylistic range which ranged from the studio to the circus, to palaces, vast outdoor arenas, garden theaters, opera houses, small baroque theaters, and cathedral squares; all the world was for him a receptive home for theater." This book serves as a reminder of how he affected the world of art. Following a commentary by Reinhardt on actors, there are essays and memorial interviews from a number of prominent personalities: e.g., Stella Adler, William Dieterle, Otto Klemperer, Gregory Peck, Otto Preminger, Robert Ryan, and Jack Warner. Worth browsing.

*Wiene, Robert, et al. THE CABINET OF DR. CALIGARI. Trans. R. V. Adkinson. New York: Simon and Schuster, 1972. Illustrated. 104pp.

This version of the film script is based a shot-by-shot examination of the National Film Archive print and contains a limited discussion of technical matters. In addition to some lovely stills, the anthology includes excerpts from Kracauer's FROM

CALIGARI TO HITLER, a brief observation on Carl Mayer's debut by Erich Pommer, and a short essay on Mayer by Paul Rotha. Well worth browsing.

HENRY KOSTER

Atkins, Irene Kahn. HENRY KOSTER. Methuen: The Scarecrow Press, 1987. Illustrated. 178pp.

FRITZ LANG

*Armour, Robert A. FRITZ LANG. Boston: Twayne Publishers, 1977. Illustrated. 199pp.

An AUTEURIST approach, this book starts off with an overview of Lang's life and career, from his birth in Vienna, Austria, on December 5, 1890, to his turning away from his studies in architecture and engineering to a passion for painting, through his military experiences in World War I, to the scriptwriting jobs that led to a contract with Decla in 1918, his elevation to director, and the great German silent and sound films he made with his second wife (Thea von Harbou), the climactic meeting with Goebbels that led to his flight from Germany (and eventual separation from Harbou), the brief stay in France before he signed a contract with MGM and came to America, his directorial experiences in Hollywood before and during World War II, Lang's fondness for detective and criminal thrillers in the 1950s, his eventual return to Germany in 1960 to make his last film (THE THOUSAND EYES OF DR. MABUSE/DIE TAUSEND AUGEN DES DR MABUSE), and his final years back in Hollywood, where he died on August 2, 1976.

Armour argues that the "central theme" of Lang's films "reflects the struggle within his people as they respond to the pushes and shoves from the dual sides of their character." This Jekyll and Hyde approach is demonstrated both internally and externally. "The personal, inner struggles in Lang's films," the author explains, "are the elements that give psychological realism to his characters, but the external struggles between the central characters and the forces that try to dominate them are the elements that motivate and give meaning to the inner struggles." Lang is particularly intrigued by the struggle between man and his fate. Other plot devices that Lang uses in depicting the struggle are violence, hallucination, mistaken identity, and Christian symbols. The book's remaining eight chapters review examples of Armour's thesis in Lang's career in Germany and America.

What Armour lacks in analytical skills, he makes up in his broad sweep of the director's general characteristics. Each of Lang's major films and his personal dilemmas are discussed in enough detail to stimulate further research. Two annoying features are a number of poorly reproduced illustrations and incomplete bibliographic information. A filmography, endnotes, bibliography, and index are included. Well worth browsing.

*Bogdanovich, Peter, FRITZ LANG IN AMERICA. New York: Praeger, 1969. Illustrated. 144pp.

Through an awkward use of the interview-article, Bogdanovich attempts to present a portrait of this unique artist. Over a period of six days in 1965, the two artists talked about Lang's experiences from FURY (1936) to THE THOUSAND EYES OF DR. MABUSE/DIE TAUSEND AUGEN DES DR MABUSE (1961). The focus is on Lang as an AUTEUR, with the central unifying theme of all the director's work being a concern with an individual's "struggle against fate." Unfortunately, we learn little that is critical about Lang's films, and much of what passes for facts is more than questionable. The one notable contribution is Lang's extensive commentary on his own work in the United States.[176] A filmography is included. Well worth browsing.

Eisner, Lotte. FRITZ LANG. Trans. Gertrud Mander and ed. David Robinson. New York: Oxford University Press, 1977. Illustrated. 416pp.

This extraordinary book, written in collaboration with Lang, is yet another example of Eisner's invaluable insights into German film history. She writes not only from personal contacts, but also from an art historian's perspective. Thus one major theme of the book is to show how each of Lang's films took "its specific style from the subject matter." Another major focus of the book is to allow Lang to have his last say on what others had said and written about him. "This book," she writes, "is . . . the first attempt to do justice to a creative artist who always strove for perfection, and who meditated deeply about himself and about others, without pursuing false illusions; and a fighter who was interested in the battle rather than the victory."

Eisner divides her efforts into three major sections. Part One covers Lang's German films before Hitler and LILOM (1933). Particularly noticeable is the author's attempt to honor the director's request that he not be associated with expressionism. Consequently, Eisner points out repeatedly how Lang parodies expressionism in his films and takes his cue from German romanticism rather than from the tenor of the times. Part Two examines the American period from FURY (1936), through films like THE RETURN OF FRANK JAMES (1940), MAN HUNT (1941), HANGMEN ALSO DIE (1943), THE WOMAN IN THE WINDOW (1944), SCARLET STREET (1945), and concludes with BEYOND A REASONABLE DOUBT (1956). Interestingly, Eisner has more difficulty analyzing the American films than the German ones. What is splendid about this section, however, is the amount of information she gleans from her conversations with Lang. As E. Ann Kaplan notes, the information is of three types: practical details about the making of the films themselves, the differences between what Lang intended in each film and how they actually appeared, and insights into Lang's actual scripts that have not been generally available to scholars.[177] Part Three deals with Lang's second German period from 1959 to 1960. In addition to the short but interesting commentary on THE THOUSAND EYES OF DR. MABUSE/DIE TAUSEND AUGEN DES DR. MABUSE (1960), there is an intriguing collection of statements by Lang himself on "how often his remarks have been misunderstood and misinterpreted."

The obvious weaknesses in this otherwise superb study relate to Lang's influence on the publication itself. Not only did Eisner submit the manuscript to him as it evolved for editing and approval, but she also often acceded to his wishes about using tact in dealing with thorny issues. For example, Thea von Harbou gets a more gentle treatment than Eisner wanted, primarily because Lang wished that part of his past downplayed. Moreover, as Jeremy Kingston points out, ". . . in chapters on individual films curious omissions and shifts of approach can be detected."[178]

---

[176] For useful articles on Lang in America, see Scott Eyman, "Fritz Lang Remembered," TAKE ONE 5 (March 1977):15-6; Gavin Lambert, "Fritz Lang's America: Part One," SIGHT AND SOUND 25:1 (Summer 1955):15-21, 55-6; ___, "Fritz Lang's America: Part Two," ibid., 25:2 (Autumn 1955):92-7; Fritz Lang, "Fritz Lang Talks About the Problems of Life Today," FILMS AND FILMING 8:9 (June 1962):20-1; and Alfred Appel, Jr., "FILM NOIR: The Director--Fritz Lang's American Nightmare," FILM COMMENT 10:6 (November-December 1974):12-7.

[177] Kaplan, E. Ann, FRITZ LANG: A GUIDE TO REFERENCES AND RESOURCES (Boston: G. K. Hall and Company, 1981), pp.364-5.

[178] Jeremy Kingston, "A Prey to Catastrophe," FILMS AND FILMING 23:10 (July 1977):44.

Those reservations aside, this is the best book available on Lang and his work. A bibliography and filmography are included, but no index. Recommended for special collections.

*Jensen, Paul M. THE CINEMA OF FRITZ LANG. New York: A. S. Barnes and Company, 1969. Illustrated. 223pp.

The first English-language book on Lang, this handy, brief, and AUTEURIST study takes the position that "The pessimistic fatality in Fritz Lang's films never completely obscures the romanticism, because the director balances voluntary actions of individuals against the confining strictures of environment and heredity. This cinematic situation has certain corollaries in Lang's real life: he rejected the career planned for him, and left the security of his home to travel in exotic lands. But eventually his freedom was cut off when he was compelled, by outside forces climaxing in the First World War, to give up his bohemian artist's life and conform to that most regimented of environments, the army." The outcome, according to Jensen, is that although Lang's films "occasionally involve fantasy and abstractions such as Death, Lang's determinism has never been of a supernatural or religious sort. Instead, he is concerned with the earthly forces which affect the actions of individuals; society, psychology, and environment are depicted with the objective and scientific eye of a naturalist." The analyses that follow demonstrate a clear bias in favor of the German films as compared to the American ones, with Jensen offering safe and traditional interpretations of Lang's career. Since many of the critical judgments have been disputed by the great director in his collaboration with Eisner, the Jensen book now exists as a peripheral source of information. A filmography and bibliography are included, but no index. Worth browsing.

Kaplan, E. Ann. FRITZ LANG: A GUIDE TO REFERENCES AND RESOURCES. Boston: G. K. Hall and Company, 1981. 488pp.

"This book," the researcher explains, "is intended not only as a definitive annotated bibliography of Fritz Lang, but also a means of providing scholars with detailed information about Lang's works, including distribution of the films and resources in film study centers." In almost every respect, Kaplan does an outstanding job of meeting her goals. Two introductory chapters give an overview of the critical writings on Lang and summarize the traditional AUTEURIST approaches to the director's career. What is particularly valuable in these opening essays is the way in which the author uses the overview as a means of commenting on the major shifts that have taken place in film criticism since the early 1970s. For example, to date, no other work on Lang exposes us to the fresh perspectives that semiologists, Marxists, and psychoanalytic critics bring to his long and distinguished career. The biggest contribution is in the area of French scholarship. Another intriguing contribution is Kaplan's assertion that recent film scholarship has discredited "the individual importance of the director and of the relevance of his or her life to the work."

The major portion of the reference guide is divided into three separate sections. The first part includes original synopses of Lang's surviving films, emphasizing the visual as well as the narrative features. Credits, notes, and reviews are listed in the forty-three chronologically arranged entries. The second part is a splendid year-by-year annotated bibliography, beginning with 1921, and continuing through 1980, and covering material mainly in English, French, and German. The comments are crisp, intelligent, and stimulating. The third part presents material on Lang's writings (many unpublished), performances, and other film-related activity. In addition, there is information on archival sources, film distributors, three appendexes (film sources, translations of foreign titles, and German films about Fritz Lang), and three indexes (proper names, film titles, subjects). My one minor reservation is that I found it difficult to locate annotations about the two Simon and Schuster film scripts dealing with M and METROPOLIS. Recommended for special collections.

*Lang, Fritz. M. English translation and description of action Nicholas Garnham. New York: Simon and Schuster, 1968. Illustrated. 112pp.

Containing only a brief introduction by the translator, this beautifully illustrated transcription of the screenplay does not tell us the source for the particular version that he translated. Garnham sets the stage by arguing that "Perhaps the key sequence in M is the one in which Lang cuts back and forth between a meeting of underworld leaders and a meeting of police chiefs. He uses every means at his command to equate these two groups, inter-cutting, camera angles and groupings, the same smoke-filled light, overlapping gestures and speech. The equation of what are traditionally seen in gangster pictures as good and evil is central to Lang's universe. The world he portrays is a Manichean one in which the forces of good and evil, equally matched, constantly fight for man's soul as the police and the underworld both relentlessly pursue M the murderer." Well worth browsing.

*Lang, Fritz. METROPOLIS: A FILM BY FRITZ LANG. New York: Simon and Schuster, 1973. Illustrated. 131pp.

Based upon a shot-by-shot viewing of a print available both in Britain and the United States, this useful publication includes in the transcription excerpts from Thea von Harbou's original novel, METROPOLIS. Two introductory essays by Paul M. Jensen and Siegfried Kracauer are reprints from their respective books, THE CINEMA OF FRITZ LANG and FROM CALIGARI TO HITLER: A PSYCHOLOGICAL HISTORY OF THE GERMAN FILM. Regrettably, the illustrations fall far below the standards set in the publisher's other script translations and no credit is given to the translator. Worth browsing.

*Ott, Frederick W. THE FILMS OF FRITZ LANG. Secaucus: The Citadel Press, 1979. Illustrated. 287pp.

ERNST LUBITSCH

Carringer, Robert, and Barry Sabath. ERNST LUBITSCH: A GUIDE TO REFERENCES AND RESOURCES. Boston: G. K. Hall and Company, 1980. 262pp.

Another fine addition to film scholarship from the Reference Publication in Film Series, this book provides an indispensable record of the essential critical, historical, and biographical data on a great director. The introductory essays covering Lubitsch's life and a critical survey of the scholarship on his work are followed by sections on Lubitsch's films, writings about him, other related activities, archival sources, film distributors, and author and film title indexes. Recommended for special collections.

*Weinberg, Herman G. THE LUBITSCH TOUCH: A CRITICAL STUDY OF THE GREAT FILM DIRECTOR. New York: E. P. Dutton and Company, 1968. Illustrated. 344pp.

Not only is this the first full-length study of Lubitsch, but it is also an indispensable source of rare information. Weinberg, as only he can, presents a sensitive, affectionate biography of the witty, brilliant, and creative king of satire. The one major drawback is the author's lack of traditional historiography, resulting in many uncited sources, as well as unsubstantiated claims. The major assets are interviews, reminiscences, anecdotes, and tributes from Lubitsch's colleagues, excerpts from NINOTCHKA and TROUBLE IN PARADISE, an excellent filmography, and a valuable bibliography. Regrettably, there is no index. Recommended for special collections.

FRIEDRICH WILHELM MURNAU

*Eisner, Lotte. MURNAU. Berkeley: University of California Press, 1973. Illustrated. 287pp.
   "Unlike Fritz Lang and G. W. Pabst, the two other great directors of the German cinema," Eisner observes, "F. W. Murnau has been mostly loved and admired by a specialist minority. His films are not widely known to the larger cinema public. In Germany, indeed, he is practically unknown, even though he is one of the rare directors of German origin (Lang and Pabst are both Austrian by birth). In France, mainly on the strength of NOSFERATU and TABU, he has always had his admirers; and when he died in a car accident in California, in 1931, when talking pictures were just getting into their stride and he, at forty two, was in his prime, it was particularly in French journals that his work was recalled with enthusiasm. In the United States, on the other hand, his death was virtually ignored and he was quickly forgotten." Thanks in large part to this book and to Eisner's other writings, and in spite of the fact that nearly half of Murnau's twenty-one films are lost while others remain in poor condition, the brilliant director is now considered one of the giants in film history.
   Originally published in French in 1964, this expanded and enlarged translation traces the filmmaker's life and career from his birth (ne Friedrich Wilhelm Plumpe) in Bielefeld, Germany, on December 28, 1888, through his formal schooling at the University of Berlin and the University of Heidelberg, the young man's early contacts with Max Reinhardt's revolutionary ideas on lighting, to service in the military during World War I, the eventual collaboration with other Reinhardt enthusiasts in a film company called MURNAU VEIDT FILMGESELLSCHAFT in 1919, culminating in his emigration to Hollywood in 1926 and his tragic death five years later. Thirteen of the book's fourteen chapters, however, are devoted to observations by others on Murnau's screenwriting abilities, insights into cinematography, and discussions of his twenty-one films. Murnau's annotated copy of NOSFERATU (1922), a filmography, a bibliography, and an index are included. Recommended for special collections.

CONRAD VEIDT

*Allen, J. C. CONRAD VEIDT: FROM "CALIGARI" TO "CASABLANCA." Pacific Grove: The Boxwood Press, 1987. Illustrated. 253pp.

FILMS

E. A. DUPONT

VARIETY/VARIETE (16mm: 1925, 90 mins., b/w, silent, R-CFS, EMG, MMA, RAD/S-MOV)
   Produced by Erich Pommer and co-scripted by E. A. Dupont and Leo Birinski, the director Dupont's film is an example of Germany's KAMMERSPIELFILM and is the story of a pardoned criminal who is unable to escape from his crime. Emil Jannings stars as a trapeze artist insanely jealous of his wife's love affair with a fellow artist. This film shows the growth in the art of the cinema by use of varied camera angles, multiple exposures, and fluid transitions, all in addition to creating a successful suspense story. Particularly noteworthy is the camera work of Karl Freund.[179]

---

[179]   Herbert Luft, "Karl Freund," FILMS IN REVIEW 14:2 (February 1963):93-108.

FRITZ LANG

DESTINY/DER MUDE TOD (Germany--16mm: 1921, 80 mins., b/w, silent, R-EMG, MMA/S-ESS)
Expanding the concepts of historical films developed by the Americans and Italians, Germany focused not only on mood and settings, but also on expressing the romanticism of Germany's past. Fritz Lang's film (co-scripted with his wife, Thea von Harbou) is part fairy tale and part legend. Two lovers are joined by a stranger, the Angel of Death, who eventually succeeds in bringing about their deaths but not in destroying their love. The film is preoccupied with fantasy, symbolism, and rhythm.[180] Particular praise went to the designers Walther Rohrig, Hermann Warm, and Robert Herlth; to actress Lil Dagover; and to the cinematographers Fritz Arno Wagner, Erich Neitzschmann, and Hermann Salfrank.

M (Germany--16mm: 1931, 103 mins., b/w, English subtitles, sound, R-JAN)
Sometimes titled as M, THE MURDERER AMONG US, the script was co-authored by Lang and Harbou and is considered by many of the director's critics to be his best work. The story centers around a manhunt for a child murderer (Peter Lorre) and has some excellent examples of lighting, cutting, and camera angles. Most of all, the film is acclaimed for its brilliant counterpointing of sound with image. As Lotte Eisner points out, "The sound occasionally precedes an image, or laps over into the following image, thus binding it even closer to the previous one. Overlapping allusions of sound and associations of ideas accelerate the rhythm of the action and give it density."[181] Although this is Lang's first sound film, it was his last key German work and really ends the major period in Germany's film history.[182]

METROPOLIS (16mm: 1926, 96 mins., b/w, silent, R-BUD, FES, EMG, FNC, IMA, IVY, JAN, KIT, ROA, SWA, WES, WHO, WIL)
Directed by Lang (and co-scripted with von Harbou) this ambitious science-fiction spectacle represents one of the best examples of UFA's great studio work and the technical virtuosity of its highly skilled staff. The heavy-handed story of love overwhelming the divided forces of organized labor and big business is secondary to the impressive sets, the mass movement of extras, and the intriguing special effects. "It is of primary importance," writes Eisner, "to recognise the positive aspects of this film, for instance its grand prelude. In this silent film, sound has been VISUALIZED with such intensity that we seem to hear the pistons' throb and the shrill sound of the factory siren with radiating trumpet-like rays of light. There is movement up and down, backwards, forwards; the pistons are placed in three-dimensional space, and are substantial in spite of the misty flood of light, in

---

[180] For a useful article on Lang's use of symbolism, see Nicholas Bartlett, "The Dark Struggle," FILM 32 (Summer 1962):11-3.

[181] *Lotte Eisner, THE HAUNTED SCREEN: EXPRESSIONISM IN THE GERMAN CINEMA AND THE INFLUENCE OF MAX REINHARDT (Berkeley: University of California Press, 1969), p.321. For some useful insights into the film, see *Marsha Kinder and Beverle Houston, CLOSE-UP: A CRITICAL PERSPECTIVE ON FILM (New York: Harcourt Brace Jovanovich, 1972), pp.58-66; and Joseph M. J. Chang, "M: A Reconsideration," LITERATURE/FILM QUARTERLY 7:4 (1979):300-8.

[182] M was also the end of Lang's collaboration with von Harbou. Half Jewish and opposed to Hitler, he fled Germany and eventually came to the United States. Harbou remained behind, worked for the Nazis, and died in 1954.

spite of the superimposition to indicate them as monumental symbols of labour."[183] Particular credit for many of the effects goes to the technical genius of Eugen Schufftan (who later in America changed his name to Eugene Schuftan) and to the cinematographers Karl Freund and Gunther Rittau.[184]

ERNST LUBITSCH

MADAME DUBARRY/PASSION (16mm: 1919, 124 mins., b/w, silent, R-BUD, EMG, KIT, MMA; S-EMG, REE)

This highly romanticized tale of a royal courtesan (Pola Negri) to Louis XV (Emil Jannings) and the tragic emotions that preceded her death during the French Revolution is considerd by many critics to be the most memorable of the director Lubitsch's historical spectacles. Inspired by the dramatic works of Max Reinhardt, who was Lubitsch's mentor, the film demonstrates the superb mixing of fabulous sets and extraordinary crowd scenes.

FRIEDRICH W. MURNAU

THE LAST LAUGH/DER LETZE MANN (16mm: 1924, 81 mins., b/w, silent, R-EMG, MMA, RAD)

Scripted by Mayer, designed by Rohrig and Herlth, and starring Emil Jannings, this brilliant film suggests the greatest achievements of Germany's Golden era. The superb visual story of an aging doorman's decline meticulously avoids inter-titles and exemplifies the concepts of subjective camerawork perfected by cinematographer Freund.

NOSFERATU (16mm: 1922, 63 mins., b/w, silent, R-MMA)

This unauthorized adaptation of Bram Stoker's DRACULA is fine, so long as it stays in the streets and the countryside. Indoors, the awkward studio sets and limited budget only magnify the brilliance of Fritz Arno Wagner's location photography.

---

[183] Lotte Eisner, FRITZ LANG, trans. Gertrud Mander and ed.   David Robinson (New York: Oxford University Press, 1977), p.83. Dennis F. Mahoney makes an interesting case that the character of Rotwang is conceived in anti-Semitic terms, portrayed "as a 'Jewish scientist' and foreign element who is the root cause of all the problems besetting society." See Dennis F. Mahoney, "Searching For a Scapegoat: The Portrait of Rotwang as a 'Jewish Scientist' in Fritz Lang's METROPLIS," Paper delivered at the 1988 NEMLA Conference, Providence, Rhode Island, March 24, 1988.

[184] Alan Williams, "Structures of Narrativity in Fritz Lang's METROPOLIS," FILM QUARTERLY 27:4 (Summer 1974):17-24; Don Willis, "Fritz Lang: Only Melodrama," ibid., 33:2 (Winter 1979-80):2-11; Lane Roth, "METROPOLIS: The Lights Fantastic--Semiotic Analysis of Lighting Codes in Relation to Character and Theme," LITERATURE/FILM QUARTERLY 6:4 (Fall 1978):342-6; Paul Jensen, "METROPOLIS," FILM HERITAGE 3:2 (Winter 1968):22-8; Andreas Huyssen, "The Vamp and the Machine: Technology and Sexuality in Fritz Lang's METROPOLIS," NEW GERMAN CRITIQUE 24-25 (1981-82):221-37; and John Tulloch, "Genetic Structuralism and the Cinema: A Look at Fritz Lang's METROPOLIS," THE AUSTRALIAN JOURNAL OF SCREEN THEORY 1 (1976):3-50.

GEORG WILHELM PABST

THE JOYLESS STREET/DIE FREUDLOSE GASSE (16mm: 1925, 89 mins., b/w, silent, R-MMA)

Directed by the Austrian-born Pabst and featuring such stars as Asta Nielsen, Greta Garbo, and Werner Krauss, this realistic and cynical film points the way to most of Pabst's future work. Through the story of young lovers trapped by economic and moral decay in postwar Vienna, the director develops the ability of the camera to depict psychological crises.[185] Particularly noteworthy is Pabst's technique in shifting the action within a shot by cutting imperceptibly to another shot.

ROBERT WIENE

THE CABINET OF DR. CALIGARI/DAS KABINETT DES DR. CALIGARI (16mm: 1919, 55 mins., b/w, silent, R-JAN, RAD)

Under Wiene's direction, this film shows the influence of the expressionist and the cubist schools of art, and is particularly useful for illustrating the Germans' subjective skill in handling lighting and set design in film. Much of the credit goes to the screenwriters Karl Mayer and Hans Janowitz and to the designers Hermann Warm, Walther Rohrig, and Walter Reimann. The psychological tale is told by an inmate of a mental institution. By the use of camera angles integrated with horizontal and vertical sets, the idea of the narrator's distorted point of view is successfully communicated to the audience. Initially, the film had the doctor, not the patient, as the insane villain. A framing device switched the relationship, and historians are still debating who--the producer, Pommer, or the original director, Lang--was responsible. The impressive cast includes Conrad Veidt, Werner Krauss, and Lil Dagover.

THE SOVIET FILMS (1896-1929)

Of all the European cinemas prior to World War I, the Russian film industry may have been the most unusual. The Lumieres introduced the nation to filmgoing in 1896, with other countries gradually entering the Russian market over the next decade. This market was maintained and dominated primarily by foreigners from France, Denmark, and Germany. The Russians themselves did not begin producing their own films until 1908, but even then, they relied almost exclusively on France and Germany for the essential raw film stock and film equipment. The pre-WWI Russian films also derived much of their technique and style from popular Italian epics and American westerns. Notable exceptions, discussed in Chapter 3, were the stories about Jewish pogroms, which had a major influence on the development of the Yiddish cinema in Europe and America.

One of the principal debates in film history books dealing with the period before the Bolshevik Revolution in 1917 centers on the popularity of filmgoing in czarist Russia. Yon Barna points out that

Even before the First World War the Russian cinema already enjoyed an international reputation. By the end of the war there were over two thousand cinemas in Russia, and of the total footage of film that passed through the hands of the distributing houses--about twelve million metres--only 30 per cent

---

[185]   Herbert G. Luft, "G. W. Pabst," FILMS IN REVIEW 15:2 (February 1964):93-116; ___, "G. W. Pabst," FILMS AND FILMING 13:7 (April 1967):18-23.

came from abroad. Quantitatively speaking, therefore, national production was important.[186]

Richard Taylor reports that "The cinema had grown rapidly after its introduction into the Russian Empire until by 1917 it was the most popular form of entertainment for the urban masses."[187] On the other hand, historians like Ellis argue that attendance was limited primarily to the middle class, who had the leisure time, money, and mobility to see the mostly foreign films in the few movie houses available to the public.[188] Cook goes further, claiming that films lacked a popular base because viewing them cost too much for the working classes and because their inferior quality discouraged attendance by the ruling classes.[189] Nevertheless, Robinson agrees with Taylor, insisting that films, no matter how pedestrian, enjoyed an incredible popularity throughout the Czar's vast realm.[190] It's hard to believe that, since there were few cinemas outside urban areas, there were few urban areas in Russia, and film in Russia was primarily an urban amusement.[191]

A second debate centers on the significance of the pre-revolutionary period to the golden age of Russian films in the 1920s. Most general historians move rapidly to the end of the late teens, ignoring the work of key theorists like Vsevolod E. Meyerhold, Vladimir Mayakovsky, and Lev V. Kuleshov during the period from 1913 to 1917. A few generalists like Cook stress the importance of the theorists' AVANT-GARDE manifestos, key screen adaptations of literary works, and the growing concern for film as film.[192] And David Bordwell is almost alone in arguing that the work of futurist poets and theorists like Meyerhold and Mayakovsky provided the basic conceptualization for the revolutionary Soviet theories about editing.

In the years immediately following the 1917 Revolution, the Soviets revised every aspect of their society, including its artistic values. The cinema presented a unique problem. The czarist regime never considered the film industry a tool for propaganda. "It remained," as Taylor points out, "a form of entertainment, rather than a weapon for education, enlightenment or mobilization."[193] The Revolution, however, had turned the cinema into a political tool. Although Lenin had declared film indispensable for educating the country to its new future, the pre-revolutionary filmmakers hated and feared the Soviets. Not only did these filmmakers flee Russia, but they also destroyed or took with them almost every piece of material and equipment necessary to run a film industry. The new government, lacking film equipment, raw stock, technicians, and cinemas, decided to compensate in part by creating new film aesthetics related to socialist standards. The focus was on showing life as it ought to be under Soviet rule. The emphasis was on using film as a major propaganda arm of the state. Schools were started, and people from all aspects of the culture drifted

---

[186]   Yon Barna, EISENSTEIN, Foreword Jay Leyda, trans. Lise Hunter (Bloomington: Indiana University Press, 1973), p.75.

[187]   Richard Taylor, THE POLITICS OF THE SOVIET CINEMA 1917-1929 (New York: Cambridge University Press, 1979), p.152.

[188]   Ellis, p.106.

[189]   Cook, p.133.

[190]   Robinson, p.124.

[191]   Interview with Dr. Denis J. Youngblood, University of Vermont, January 28, 1988.

[192]   Cook, p.133.

[193]   Taylor, p.152.

toward film production. From these ranks came such brilliant theorists and directors as Sergei M. Eisenstein,[194] Vsevolod I. Pudovkin,[195] Alexander P. Dovzhenko,[196] Dziga Vertov,[197] Lev Kuleshov,[198] and Esther Shub.[199]

With few exceptions, these individuals responded to Lenin's insistence that a film industry be responsive to the needs of a Soviet society. It would take almost seven years (1918-1924) before the filmmakers had adequate raw film stock, a stabilized distribution network, and access to international filmmaking to mature their personal work. Consequently, they were forced to experiment with the limited footage and scarce film material that existed in the by-now isolated and nationalized Soviet film industry. At the VSESOYUZN GOSUDARSTVENYI INSTITUT KINEMATOGRAFIA (V.G.I.K.), the Moscow state school founded in 1919, two brilliant film

---

[194] Some useful articles by and about Eisenstein are the following: David Bordwell, "Eisenstein's Epistemological Shift," SCREEN 15:4 (Winter 1974-75):32-46; Sergei Eisenstein, "One Path to Colour: An Autobiographical Fragment," SIGHT AND SOUND 30:2 (Spring 1961):84-6, 102; Jay Leyda, "Eisenstein's Bezhin Meadow," ibid., 28:2 (Spring 1959):74-6, 105; Paul Seydor, "Eisenstein's Aesthetics: A Dissenting View," ibid., 43:1 (Winter 1973-74):38-43; Ronald Levaco, "The Eisenstein-Prokofiev Correspondence," CINEMA JOURNAL 13:1 (Fall 1973):1-16; Herbert Marshall, "A Note on Eisenstein's Shot Montage of a Monologue from Pushkin's Drama BORIS GODUNOV," QUARTERLY REVIEW OF FILM STUDIES 3:2 (Spring 1978):137-68; James Goodwin, "Eisenstein: Ideology and Intellectual Cinema," ibid., pp.169-92; Evelyn Gerstein, "Ivan The Terrible: A Peak In Darien," FILM COMMENT 5:1 (Fall 1968):52-57; Eric Rhode, "Sergei Eisenstein," TOWER OF BABEL: SPECULATIONS ON THE CINEMA (New York: Chilton Books, 1967), pp.51-66; Robert Siegler, "Masque: An Extrapolation of Eisenstein's Theory of Montage-as-Conflict to the Multi-Image Film," FILM QUARTERLY 21:3 (Spring 1968):15-21; and Brian Henderson, "Two Types of Film Theory," ibid., 24:3 (Spring 1971):33-42.

[195] Herman G. Weinberg, "Vsevolod Pudovkin," FILMS IN REVIEW 4:7 (August-September 1953):325-37; and Paul E. Burns, "Linkage: Pudovkin's Classics Revisited," JOURNAL OF POPULAR FILM AND TELEVISION 9:2 (Summer 1981):70-7.

[196] The most complete information is in Marco Carynnyk, A DOVZHENKO BIBLIOGRAPHY (Cambridge: the MIT Press, 1973). In addition, see Paul Burns, "Cultural Revolution, Collectivization, and Soviet Cinema: Eisenstein's OLD AND NEW and Dovzhenko's EARTH," FILM AND HISTORY 2:4 (1981):84-96; Ivor Montagu, "Dovzhenko: Poet of Life Eternal," SIGHT AND SOUND 27:1 (1957):44-8; and David Robinson, "Dovzhenko: Notes on the Director's Work Before ZVENIGORA," THE SILENT PICTURE 8 (1970):11-4.

[197] David Bordwell, "Dziga Vertov: An Introduction," FILM COMMENT 8:1 (Spring 1972):38-45; "The Vertov Papers," trans. Marco Carynnyk, ibid., pp.46-51; Vlada Petric, "Dziga Vertov as Theorist," CINEMA JOURNAL 18:1 (Fall 1978): 29-44; "The Writings of Dziga Vertov," trans. Val Telberg and S. Brody, FILM CULTURE 25 (Summer 1962):50-65; Seth Feldman, "Cinema Weekly and Cinema Truth: Dziga Vertov and the Leninist Proportion," SIGHT AND SOUND 43:1 (Winter 1973-74):34-7; and Lucy Fischer, "ENTHUSIASM: From Kino-Eye to Radio-Ear," FILM QUARTERLY 31:2 (Winter 1977-78):25-34.

[198] Ronald Levaco, "Kuleshov," SIGHT AND SOUND 40:2 (Spring 1971): 86-91, 109; and Stephen P. Hill, "Kuleshov: Prophet Without Honor?" FILM CULTURE 44 (Spring 1967):1-37.

[199] For more information on Shub, see Chapter 2.

theorists--Kuleshov and Vertov[200]--developed revolutionary film concepts.[201] Kuleshov explored how a shot's film content could be manipulated by juxtaposing it with other shots, while Vertov applied these editing "truths" to specific documentary material.[202] Both persuaded their followers that editing was the key to using the "reality" of film to "educate" the public to the public's social, political, and economic responsibilities in shaping a new nation. These theories were particularly effective because the government centralized film production through the People's Commissariat of Propaganda and Education at the same time that it established the V.G.I.K. Moreover, Vertov and Kuleshov not only inspired many of the Soviet's great directors, but also influenced their outstanding cinematographers (e.g., Eduard K. Tisse, Eisenstein's cinematographer, and Anatoli N. Golovnya, Pudovkin's cinematographer).[203]

Both Eisenstein and Pudovkin advanced the Soviet concept of editing, but from different perspectives. It was Eisenstein, leaning heavily on his interest in the circus, the theater, and the Japanese language, as well as on his background in engineering, who perfected the concept of montage, a method of editing that emphasized the importance of shots, selectively joined together, to create a new impression on the audience.[204] Intrigued with Pavlov's work, the young artist saw in montage the means by which to provide a stimulus that would evoke a desired response from his audience. Each spectator, Eisenstein theorized, is attracted by a variety of elements that grip the viewer's attention and affect his or her experience. These "attractions" can be predetermined and mathematically calculated. Thus a filmmaker constructing a film based upon "attraction" principles is able to move from a static reflection of an event "to a new level of action based on a "FREE MONTAGE OF ARBITRARILY SELECTED, INDEPENDENT . . . ATTRACTIONS. . . ."[205] The theory is known as the "Montage of Attractions." At the same time, the brilliant theorist, influenced by the Italian COMMEDIA DELL'ARTE, advocated the theory of "Typage," a plan whereby professional actors were replaced by everyday people who, as Seton explains, "manifested the physio-psychological characteristics of the

---

[200] In fact, Kuleshov's youth and enthusiasm (he was in his late teens) so annoyed the older faculty that he got permission to develop his ideas in a workshop setting rather than through more formal channels. The Kuleshov workshop functioned from 1919 to 1925, when the outspoken theorist was told to stop his teaching activities. For the next nineteen years, he made no films. Then, in 1944, back in the good graces of the government, he was appointed head of V.G.I.K., where he worked until he died in 1970. Cf. Cook, pp.139-41.

[201] The primary mission of VKIG was to produce pro-Soviet propaganda (Agitki) in the form of newsreels. The principal "textbook" was Griffith's INTOLERANCE (1916). For more information, see Vance Kepley, Jr. and Betty Kepley, "Foreign Films on Soviet Screens, 1921-1931," QUARTERLY REVIEW OF FILM STUDIES 4:4 (Fall 1979):429-42; and Vance Kepley, Jr., "INTOLERANCE and the Soviets: An Historical Investigation" WIDE ANGLE 3:1 (January 1979):22-7.

[202] Vertov was born Denis Arkadyevich Kaufman and had two equally famous brothers (Boris and Mikhail) who distinguished themselves in film.

[203] Levaco, p.88.

[204] David Bordwell, "The Idea of Montage in Soviet Art and Cinema," CINEMA JOURNAL, 11:2 (Spring 1972):9-17; and Dana B. Polan, "Eisenstein as Theorist," ibid., 17:1 (Fall 1977):14-29.

[205] Sergei M. Eisenstein, "Montage of Attractions," LEF 3 (1923). Quoted in *Marie Seton, SERGEI M. EISENSTEIN: A BIOGRAPHY (London: Denis Dobson, 1978), p.70.

personages, and/or crowds, necessary to interpret the action."[206] As Eisenstein progressed in his thinking, he stressed other forms of montage, such as "intellectual montage," whereby two distinctly different shots were joined to produce a visual metaphor that could not exist without purposeful editing. As always, the plan was to "shock" and to "upset" spectators. These types of shot combinations emphasized a "collision of images" approach ignored by filmmakers outside the immediate Soviet sphere. The purpose, as in all of Soviet art during the silent era, was not only to attract a viewer's interest but also to galvanize the emotions.

On the other hand, Pudovkin concentrated on "linking shots" to produce his emotional narrative effects. That is, shots built from one to the next, with editing piecing them together according to a specific theme: e.g., the parent and son in MOTHER/MAT (1926) acting as the focal point for the construction of the various shots and scenes throughout the entire film. Although Eisenstein half-facetiously described the differences between Pudovkin and himself as "Linkage--P, and Collision--E,"[207] the fact remains that both men frequently used both approaches in their development of montage.[208]

Dovzhenko, together with his superb cameraman, Daniel Demutski, took a different tack from either Eisenstein or Pudovkin. Taking advantage of their editing principles, he focused on a more personal and lyrical approach to the goals of Soviet filmmaking. Simple events like working the land in EARTH/ZEMLYA (1930) function as inspiring events of great significance for the future of the Soviet people. More important for him than individual shots linked or forcibly juxtaposed was the relationship between and among sequences. Whereas artists like Eisenstein and Pudovkin paid attention to the story and the drama respectively, Dovzhenko aimed for visual poetry.

The period from 1919 to 1929 also saw the emergence of a number of other important Soviet filmmakers, including Abram Room, Friedrich Ermler, Grigori Kozintsev, Victor Turin, and Leonid Trauberg. Collectively, these unique artists experimented with new ways to bring the conventional film genres into the socio-political framework of the Soviet film industry.

Most general film histories call attention to the many similarities and contrasts among the three principal film industries in the post-WWI period: Germany, the Soviet Union, and the United States. Each had centralized the production, distribution, and exhibition of films by the early 1920s: Germany through a major trust (UFA), the Soviet Union through complete government control, and the United States through an oligopoly. Each worked under major constraints: Germany, dire economic problems; the Soviets, government censorship; and Hollywood, industry self-censorship. In addition, each actively experimented with the structure of film narratives, particularly in the relationship between film and reality: Germany with lighting, design, and camera movement; the Soviets with montage; and the Americans with formula filmmaking. Although the three nations produced very different types of films, priorities, and artists, they each had a profound effect on the history of film.

---

[206]   Seton, p.79.

[207]   FILM FORM, p.38.

[208]   Seton claims (pp.92-3) that Eisenstein and Pudovkin had a "natural animosity and rivalry." Their feud grew over the years, with Eisenstein calling Pudovkin "a fool," and Pudovkin describing Eisenstein as a man "over-intellectual . . . whom he pitied because he was incapable of human feelings."

BOOKS

GENERAL

Babitsky, Paul, and John Rimberg. THE SOVIET FILM INDUSTRY. New York: Frederick A. Praeger, 1955. 377pp.

Authored by an expatriate Soviet screenwriter (Babitsky) and by an American graduate student in sociology and Soviet affairs (Rimberg), this useful book concentrates on the day-to-day production aspects of the Soviet cinema. Babitsky draws on nearly fifteen years of filmmaking experience for studios in Kiev and Moscow to describe the propagandistic nature of Soviet films. The emphasis is on showing how Soviet filmmakers are terrorized, the frequent arrests and purges, and the shift after WWII to portraying America as a nation to be feared. Rimberg uses his training in organizational studies to depict the nature of the Soviet film industry and the lives of its famous directors. "This book," the authors point out, "depicts the principal steps by which the Communist party consolidated its power over the Soviet motion-picture industry."

Divided into six chapters, the analysis begins with a discussion of the Central Administration of the Soviet film industry from 1917 to 1953. "Political exploitation of motion pictures," Rimberg explains, "requires control over the decisions of administrative officals within the film industry. Shortly after the Bolshevik COUP D'ETAT of 1917 the Communist party initiated indirect regulation, aiming ultimately at complete domination of the administrative apparatus. Through continual reorganization, enlargement, and centralization of the administrative structure of the motion-picture industry, complete operational responsibility was finally vested in the government of the U.S.S.R. to ensure political control by the Party." Chapters 2 and 3, written by Babitsky, describe screenwriting and working inside Soviet studios. The focus is on showing how every artistic work is measured almost exclusively "in terms of its ideological content." Chapter 4, written by Rimberg, provides a quantitative content analysis of heroes and villains in Soviet films from 1923 to 1950. The remaining two chapters, also written by Rimberg, deal with the economic struture of the Soviet cinema industry, as well as the process of exporting and importing films.

Although clearly antagonistic to the Soviet film system, this book provides the first significant English-language perspective on the structure of the filmmaking process in the Soviet Union. Particularly useful are the authors' discussions of politics, people, and pictures.[209] Three appendexes on Soviet decrees and directors, plus three indexes on films, persons, and subjects, are included. Well worth browsing.

Black, Lendley C. MIKHAIL CHEKHOV AS ACTOR, DIRECTOR, AND TEACHER. Ann Arbor: UMI Research Press, 1987. 116pp.

Originally written as a 1984 University of Kansas doctoral diddertation, this intriguing analysis is divided into two parts. The first section chronicles Chekhov's life from his birth in 1891 to his death in 1955. Among the topics highlighted are the influence of religion in his early years, his studies in acting in St. Petersburg, and his becoming the head of the Second Moscow Art Theatre in 1924. Because of

---

[209] For useful articles on the history of Soviet films, see Dwight Macdonald, "Part Four: The Russian Cinema," DWIGHT MACDONALD ON MOVIES (Englewood Cliffs: Prentice-Hall, 1969), pp.181-90, 249-67; Stephen P. Hill, "A Quantitative View of Soviet Cinema," CINEMA JOURNAL 11:2 (Spring 1972):18-25; Harvey Denkin, "Linguistic Models in Early Soviet Cinema," ibid., 17:1 (Fall 1977):1-13; and R. Yourenev, "A Short History of the Soviet Cinema," FILMS AND FILMING 7:6 (March 1961):15-16, 39.

Chekhov's work with Constantin Stanislavsky, together with a penchant for Shakespearian roles, he established himself as one of the great artists of his era. Black also explains what happened after the nephew of the great playwright emigrated from the Soviet Union in 1928, stressing how Chekhov acted and directed in Germany, France, England, and the United States. By 1943, he began working in Hollywood. Besides tutoring actors and delivering lectures on performing, Chekhov acted in nine films including SONG OF RUSSIA (1944), SPECTER OF THE ROSE (1946), and RHAPSODY (1954). His role as a wise and kindly analyst in SPELLBOUND (1945) won him an Oscar nomination for Best Supporting Actor. The writing is crisp and informative, although at times the slant seems more like cheerleading than analysis. The second section, the most valuable part of the study, describes Chekhov's system of acting. If you can't make it to New York, where the actor's theories are taught, this useful book introduces his ideas. Endnotes, a bibliography, and an index are included. Well worth browsing.

Birkos, Alexander S. SOVIET CINEMA: DIRECTORS AND FILMS. Hamden: Archon Books, 1976. Illustrated. 344pp.
     The first major guide to the films and careers of Soviet filmmakers, this reference guide offers two alphabetically arranged directories. The first provides a list of directors, together with brief profiles and filmographies. The second lists films, supplying information on content, critical reactions, and political biases. Particularly interesting is an introduction describing succinctly, the history of Soviet films, with an emphasis on party politics and sociopolitical influences. In addition, Birkos provides a description of the major Soviet studios. Well worth browsing.

Carter, Huntley. THE NEW THEATRE AND CINEMA OF SOVIET RUSSIA. New York: Arno Press, 1970. Illustrated. 277pp.
     Originally published in 1924, the book's aim "is to analyze and synthesise [sic] the theatre which has been established in Soviet Russia since the Russian Revolution of 1917, and which is the direct outcome of that world-influencing event." Carter's preface makes clear the ignorance abroad surrounding the development of a New Russian theater during the twenties and speculates on the reasons for it. He then divides his material into five main sections. Part One deals with the origins of the new theater, its historical limitations, the role played by the Soviet government in the new theater's conception and organization, the eventual classification of all Soviet theaters into three categories--left, centre, and right, and their three representative personalities--Vsevo;od E. Meyerhold (left), Anatoli V. Lunacharsky (centre), and Constantin Stanislavsky (right). Part Two examines the left group: i.e., revolutionary, proletkult, political satire theaters, and club theaters of workers, peasants, and students; improvisational theaters; and outdoor, mass, and street theaters. Part Three focuses on the center group: i.e., state theaters, Moscow and Petrograd; children's theaters; progressive theaters subsidized by the state; old and new Jewish theaters; and the Center Kamerny theater. Part Four evaluates the right group: i.e., the Moscow Art theatre; studio theaters; small cafes and little theaters that cater to the middle class created by the New Economic Policy (NEP). Part Five surveys the four principal cinematic categories: the Gos-Kino, the Prolet-Kino, the Revolutionary Kino, and the Bourgeois or Commercial Kino. In his summary chapter, Carter points out that the new theater "is not a theater made up of a number of separate and unrelated bits . . . It forms an organism, every part of which has a function, whilst all parts function as one." Six interesting appendexes are included but no index. Well worth browsing.

Cohen, Louis Harris. THE CULTURAL-POLITICAL TRADITIONS AND DEVELOPMENTS OF THE SOVIET CINEMA 1917-1972. New York: Arno Press, 1974. Illustrations. 724pp.

Originally presented as a 1973 Ph.D. dissertation for USC, this study analyzes the most important developments during a fifty-five-year period; surveys the "artistic and creative trends and political principles manifested in Socialist Realism and with respect to the Soviet cinema specifically as expressed by party functionaries and by the masters of the film art"; evaluates how effective Soviet film ideology has been with Soviet audiences; discusses the Soviet filmmaking process in educational and research institutes, production facilities, and funding sources; and determines "the benefits derived from cultural relations, exchanges, festivals and archival activities." In short, Cohen wants to show what Soviet filmmakers are trying to do in their films. Among the conclusions reached are that (1) Soviet film history reveals that cinema is concerned with "serving the political and economic goals of the Soviet people, their government and the Communist party since the 'Great October Socialist Revolution' a little over fifty-five years ago"; (2) the 1971 Twenty-Forth Party Congress "stressed the further promotion of all forms of ideological work, literary and art criticism, the increased role of cinema and the other arts in the formation of the 'new man,' the political education of the masses and the raising of the cultural level of the people;" and (3) "The primary guarantees for creative success in the Soviet cinema remain a truthful depiction of the leading trends of Socialist realism, clearcut conceptual positions, a clear awareness of the tremendous educational role of the cinema and other forms of artistic creativity, mastery of the Marxist-Leninist theory and the continuous strengthening of the relations with the people and finally upgrading one's own mastery or skills." Nine appendexes and a bibliography are included. Well worth browsing.

Constantine, Mildred, and Alan Fern. REVOLUTIONARY SOVIET POSTERS. Baltimore: Johns Hopkins University Press, 1974. Illustrated. 112pp.
"Kept from view once their immediate utility had passed," Constantine and Fern explain, "the brilliant Soviet movie posters of the 1920s were victims of shifting ideas about the nature of art and the place of the AVANT-GARDE in a new society. This book brings together a substantial number of these startling and prophetic graphic designs, the work of a group of artists whose names are virtually unknown but who were centers of controversy and creativity in their time." What is most impressive about this beautifully reproduced collection of fifty-six posters in black and white, and sixteen in full color is the way in which they capture the exciting new developments taking place in Soviet films: e.g., montage, unique camera angles, and dramatic perspectives. Endnotes, a bibliography, and an index are included. Well worth browsing.

Dickinson, Thorold, and Catherine De La Roche. SOVIET CINEMA. London: The Falcon Press, 1948. New York: Arno Press, 1972. Illustrated. 136pp.
Dickinson is helpful for his comments on the pre-sound days of Russian films and on the techniques of many of the later moviemakers, while De La Roche's capsuled approach to the post-sound period suffers from the quality of the subject matter discussed. Worth browsing.

Lary, N. M. DOSTOEVSKY AND SOVIET FILM: VISIONS OF DEMONIC REALISM. Ithaca: Cornell University Press, 1986. Illustrated. 278pp.

*Leyda, Jay. KINO: A HISTORY OF THE RUSSIAN AND SOVIET FILM. New York: The Macmillan Company, 1960. Illustrated. 1,025pp.
In one of the best available books on the subject, Leyda describes the development of Russian cinema as an art form, relating Soviet films to their responsibility for implementing and maintaining the philosophy of the state. "My chief aim," Leyda states, "has been to write a documented account of the artistic

development of the Soviet cinema, and to trace the growth of its artists." He spent three years working in Soviet film schools and uses this background to his advantage in his seventeen chapters which are divided into significant periods to provide a perspective lacking in more traditional film histories.[210] Beginning with the czarist days, he explains the efforts of the revolutionary artists to glorify their political successes. Rarely in English does one even find mention of the significant filmmaker Leonid Andreyev; Leyda has excellent material on him and on other important figures of the first forty years of Soviet film production. One drawback is that two-thirds of the history deals with Soviet films up to the end of the twenties. A postscript, five appendexes, a bibliography, and an index are included in this detailed and invaluable study.[211] Recommended for special collections.

Marshall, Herbert. MASTERS OF THE SOVIET CINEMA: CRIPPLED CREATIVE BIOGRAPHIES. London: Routledge and Kegan Paul, 1983. Illustrated. 252pp.

"The material in this book," Marshall writes passionately, "is a montage of memorabilia, culled from my own personal recollections, diaries, notes, unpublished autobiography, as well as letters, documents, press cuttings, articles and books in various languages, but mainly from soviet sources." Each of the four famous Soviet directors--Vsevolod I. Pudovkin, Dziga Vertov, Alexander P. Dovzhenko, and Sergei M. Eisenstein--was a friend of Marshall's, the latter who spent nearly twelve years of his life during the 1930s working closely with members of the Soviet Film Agency both inside and outside of the Soviet Union. The book's title is derived from a speech made by Sergei I. Yutkevich, a man who once befriended Eisenstein and later turned on him. In talking about the dark days of Stalin, Yutkevich despaired over "How many crippled creative biographies rise up in one's memories." Marshall focuses on four personalities and movingly contrasts the differences between their public honors and their private torments. Reading this book is an engrossing experience. Endnotes and an index are included. Well worth browsing.

Polan, Dana B. THE POLITICAL LANGUAGE OF FILM AND THE AVANT-GARDE. Ann Arbor: UMI Research Press, 1985. 141pp.

Originally written as a 1981 Standford University Ph.D. dissertation, this in-depth study explores various approaches to what Eisenstein called an "ideational cinema, a cinema which deals in conceptualizations of the world." Polan argues that "As soon as cinema theory and practice move beyond an understanding of cinema as documentary reproduction and representation, the ideological position[ing] of political cinema becomes ambiguous, difficult, problematic. Unable to envison or accept the complexities of aesthetic mediation, a tradition of sociologically oriented aesthetics kept art in the realm of the representational. The formula is simple: to change consciousness, SHOW a political situation." Polan thus proceeds to illustrate in her four key chapters how major filmmakers went about changing audience consciousness. Among the filmmakers she discusses are Sergei M. Eisenstein, Bertolt Brecht, and Nagisa Oshima. "In these quests for a cinema that would truly be a practice of cinema and a cinema of practice, we are in contact with a new role for understanding, now given a critical, intervening, practical function. Such an art, in going beyond poesis, beyond signification, indeed beyond art, might well realize the function Marx assigned to a new mode of being and acting in the world." She then adds, "As Marx says, '[in past revolutions] form went beyond content, here content goes beyond form.'"

---

[210] For more information on Leyda's career, see Andrew L. Yarrow, "Jay Leyda, Film Historian, Writer and a Student of Sergei Eisenstein," NEW YORK TIMES B (February 18, 1988):10.

[211] For updating purposes, read Jay Leyda, "Between Explosions," FILM QUARTERLY 22:4 (Summer 1970):33-8.

This in-depth and very readable study includes valuable endnotes, an extensive bibliography, and a brief index. Well worth browsing.

Rimberg, John. THE MOTION PICTURE IN THE SOVIET UNION, 1918-1925: A SOCIOLOGICAL ANALYSIS. New York: Arno Press, 1973. 238pp.

Reiterating Rimberg's position about the power struggle among the government, the filmmakers, and the audience, this 1959 Columbia University Ph.D. dissertation analyzes the relationship among the three groups at the same time that it gives an overview of the Soviet film industry. A bibliography and appendix are included. Well worth browsing.

*Schnitzer, Luda and Jean, and Marcel Martin, eds. CINEMA IN REVOLUTION: THE HEROIC ERA OF THE SOVIET FILM. Trans. and with additional material David Robinson. New York: Hill and Wang, 1973. Illustrated. 208pp.

This unique collection captures the enthusiasm and excitement of the silent Soviet cinema. "They were astonishing and wonderful days," exclaims Sergei I. Yutkevitch in the introductory essay, "the beginnings of a revolutionary art. When we talk about the years when we started artistic work, people are always surprised by the birth-dates of almost all the directors and the major artists of those times. We were incredibly young!" What the editors have done is assemble the recollections and reactions of twelve major figures--e.g., Sergei M. Eisenstein, Grigori Vsevolod Alexandrov, Lev V. Kuleshov, Dziga Vertov, Vsevolod I. Pudovkin, Alexander P. Dovzhenko, and Mikhail I. Romm--and provide us with a stimulating and nostalgic opportunity to experience vicariously the mood and excitement of the times. As Robinson astutely points out, these "essays do not add up to an exact and total history of the times perhaps--indeed partialities and prejudices are very evident from time to time--but they do present a vivid picture of . . . a unique epoch. . . ." A terse glossary of persons and an index are included. Well worth browsing.

Stoil, Michael Jon. CINEMA BEYOND THE DANUBE: THE CAMERA AND POLITICS. Metuchen: The Scarecrow Press, 1974. Illustrated. 208pp.

A mundane mixture of film criticism with political and social analyses, this book "is written primarily for those with little or no knowledge of the history of film-making in Eastern Europe so that it can be used successfully as an introductory text on the subject." One positive feature is that Stoil examines the film history of the Soviet Union separately from those of Poland, Czechoslovakia, Hungary, Yugoslavia, Bulgaria, Romania, and Albania. The first of the book's nine terse chapters provides a general overview of socialist film history from 1908 to 1973, arguing, to cite one issue, that the unique collaborative nature of filmmaking results in "American film-makers trying to make a profit and Soviet film-makers trying to make a point . . . [using] identical methods to solve the identical problem." Stoil goes on to add, "The only divergences from 'Western' film-making that technology will permit are in the censorship of scenarios and the administration of the studio. In these two areas, however, the Soviet methods are not as unique as they might have been. Soviet film studio organization, for example, was revised in 1936 to consciously imitate the more efficient organization of Hollywood studios." Other chapters review Eastern European filmmaking, with two chapters devoted to "Cinema of the Fantastic and Utopian" and "Cinema and Ideology." While the author offers no imaginative analyses of film or history, he does suggest the framework for a more detailed and thought-provoking study. A bibliography, film title index, and general index are included. Worth browsing.

Taylor, Richard. THE POLITICS OF THE SOVIET CINEMA 1917-1929. New York: Cambridge University Press, 1979. 214pp.

Concerned with political organization and propaganda, this book examines "the Soviet cinema in the 1920s from the perspective of its political function in the development of the new Soviet society . . . the attitude of the Soviet authorities toward the cinema, and the actual uses to which the cinema was put." Taylor begins his eight-chapter study with a pre-history of the Russian cinema up to 1917, trying to set the stage for the events that followed the October Revolution. Chapter 2 examines the historical role of propaganda in Russian labor movements and how the Bolshevicks used films to mobilize public opinion during the early years of Soviet rule. Chapters 3 through 5 describe how the chaotic state of the film industry in the immediate aftermath of the October Revolution forced the new government to abandon plans precipitously to nationalize the film industry and instead to move more slowly to gain complete control. The first attempt at centralization in Goskino in 1922 failed badly, but three years later Sovkino achieved the goals that the Soviets had wanted ever since the first days of the Revolution. Chapter 6 identifies what happened once the government took control of the film industry, pointing out how Sovkino became the scapegoat for the ever-changing cultural policies of the state. Chapter 7 discusses how Sovkino underwent changes in 1930, the increased importance of newsreels and documentaries for propaganda purposes, and the problems faced by administrators who realized that Soviet audiences still preferred Hollywood movies to Soviet feature films. Chapter 8 concludes the remarkable study with Taylor's conclusions about how the Soviet cinema was finally brought under the complete authority of the Communist party by the end of the 1920s. "In the 1920s," he writes, "Soviet filmmakers had been able to portray reality as the Party saw it. Reality as it really was yielded to reality as it ought to be, and that new reality was called 'socialist realism.'" Extensive endnotes, a valuable bibliography, and a general index are included. Recommended for special collections.

Taylor, Richard, and Ian Christie, eds. THE FILM FACTORY: RUSSIAN AND SOVIET CINEMA IN DOCUMENTS. Cambridge: Harvard University Press, 1988. Illustrated. 457pp.

Voronstov, Yuri, and Igor Rachuk. THE PHENOMENON OF THE SOVIET CINEMA. Trans. Doris Bradbury. Chicago: Imported Publications, 1981. Illustrated. 423pp.

Written from inside the Soviet Union, this stimulating publication begins by telling us that "The history of the Soviet cinema is rich in vivid and talented films, heated disagreements and discussions, struggles against mistakes, and the overcoming of false norms with bold searches for new ones." The eleven chapters that follow offer interpretations of films and filmmakers generally disputed in Western publications. For example, Voronstov and Rachuk comment that "critics warned Kuleshov that his enthusiasm for the specifics of cinema was somewhat onesided and detracts attention from the most important point--ideological purposiveness--and brings him too close for comfort to formalism." They then add that in the director's film THE DEATH RAY/LUCH SMERTI (1925), "These warning were justified . . . [and] he was justifiably reproached for having allowed his enthusiasm for montage and interesting camera angles, all the formal methods he loved, to make THE DEATH RAY a grab-bag of acrobatic tricks, fights, and dynamic chases, while relegating content to second place." One irritating feature is that the book's binding is very fragile. A filmography is included, but no index. Approach with caution.

Youngblood, Denis J. SOVIET CINEMA IN THE SILENT ERA, 1918-1935. Ann Arbor: UMI Research Press, 1985. Illustrated. 336pp.

"The history of the Soviet film industry in the twenties may be described," Youngblood explains, "as the inexorable move from organizational chaos to total centralization and from aesthetic radicalism to socialist realism. How these twin objectives were achieved in little more than a decade, and why these ends seemed desirable, is the subject of this study." The nine fact-filled chapters of this revised

1980 Stanford University Ph.D. dissertation describe in detail the early stages of the revolutionary shift (1918-23), the turning point (1924), the new focus stated in the Sovkino policy and the industry's reaction (1925-26), the filmmaking conditions and the films themselves (1925-26), the attacks on Sovkino (1927-28), the crisis in production that ensued (1927-28), the Party Conference and the restructuring attempts (1928-29), the purge years and the attacks on Formalism (1929-34), the coming of sound, and the triumph of realism (1935). What Youngblood concludes is that "the aesthetics of Soviet silent cinema were in general more conservative than those of Dziga Vertov and its films less brilliant than POTEMKIN. . . ." At the same time, she argues effectively that the Soviet cinema produced an extraordinary number of artists and critics. What is especially intriguing is her assertion that what contributed to the revolutionary nature of Soviet cinema was its threat to the status of literature and drama as the mainstay of popular entertainment. Moreover, her treatment of socialist realism reveals the oversimplifications of previous authors in dealing with the relationship between the state and the artist. Two appendexes (film production by studio and by year from 1918 to 1935, and the various genres in the same years), extensive endnotes, an impressive bibliography, and an index are included. Recommended for special collections.

ALEXANDER P. DOVZHENKO

*Carynnyk, Marco, ed. and trans. ALEXANDER DOVZHENKO: THE POET AS FILMMAKER--SELECTED WRITINGS. Cambridge: The MIT Press, 1973. 323pp.
   "Translating Alexander Dovzhenko's poetic prose," Carynnyk tells us, "has posed special problems. His writing gains much of its force from the easy, colloquial, but very sensitive movement of his Ukrainian sentences. But by the standards of modern written English, the relationship among their parts is often ambiguous, illogical, or awkward . . .   To find the meaning often involves taking the original sentence apart and reasoning about the meaningful relation of its constituents." Scholars are, therefore, indebted to Carynnyk not only for his thoughtful editing, but also for providing the first English-language collection of Dovzhenko's writings.
   Divided into three main sections, the book begins with a forty-six page introductory essay outlining the filmmaker's life and career. (A fine chronology of Dovzhenko's life from his birth on September 12, 1894, to his death on November 26, 1956, appears as an appendix.) Carynnyk emphasizes how much the artist's love for native folksongs, myths, and legends permeated every aspect of his personality and art. Events before the 1917 Revolution (e.g., Russia and Poland tearing apart his Ukrainian homeland and trying to obliterate its customs and society) only intensified his allegiance to the national culture. In the early days of the new Soviet state, Dovzhenko blended his revolutionary zeal for an independent Ukrainian state with a zeal for painting. While the Soviets were resolving their political problems with Ukrainian nationalists, the young painter and intellectual immersed himself in literary and artistic causes. But by the summer of 1926, he became discouraged with his lack of success and abandoned his artwork to become a filmmaker. Within three years, he had gained an international reputation as the forerunner of a remarkable Ukrainian cinema. Carynnyk devotes most of the introduction to describing his reactions to Dovzhenko's eight completed films, the political problems the innovative director faced throughout his controversial career, the nature of the charges leveled against him, the reasons he turned to writing during World War II and the re-emergence of attacks on him for his nationalistic commitments, and the bleak postwar years that eventually led to a fatal heart attack in 1954. "Taking the whole of Alexander Dovzhenko's output, writings as well as films," explains the editor, "one realizes quickly that he was a stubbornly singleminded man."
   The remaining three sections deal with Dovzhenko's autobiography, Notebooks, and an annotated filmography. The autobiography went through at least six versions between February 14, 1928, and August 28, 1954. The version Carynnyk uses is based on a draft written at the end of 1939 and published eighteen years later in a

Ukrainian journal, DNIPRO. Although Dovzhenko kept notebooks and diaries throughout most of his career, the excerpts published here draw heavily on the artist's known and available publications between 1941 and 1956. The filmography lists all of Dovzhenko's films (released and censored) and provides full cast and technical credits, plus minor comments about production and additional information. Extensive endnotes and a general index are included. Recommended for special collections.

Kepley, Vance, Jr. IN THE SERVICE OF THE STATE: THE CINEMA OF ALEXANDER DOVZHENKO. Madison: University of Wisconsin, 1986. Illustrated. 190pp.
   This invaluable study of nine of Dovzhenko's films focuses on the two conflicting views of the artist: "the lyrical poet and the modern polemicist, the spokesman for tradition and the advocate of revolutionary change." What makes Kepley's efforts so significant is the paucity of English-language information on the Ukrainian filmmaker who was never formally associated with the Moscow-based film movement that fathered Eisenstein, Vertov, and Pudovkin and that relied considerably on the American and Western European films for technical inspirations. The author believes these factors, plus Dovzhenko's use of native folklore for his film inspirations, are responsible for the problems of studying the artist's cinematic career. Kepley, on the other hand, argues that there is more to Dovzhenko's work than the traditional image of him as a "romantic artist with somewhat mystical assumptions about his own work." In eleven reflective and insightful chapters, the author explores how the artist conceived and shaped his work in response to a social matrix. "I am principally interested," Kepley writes, "in how Dovzhenko seized on topical political and social issues and fashioned narratives that spoke to the timely interests of his Soviet audience." The discussions of ARSENAL (1929), EARTH/ZEMLYA (1930), IVAN (1932), AEROGRAD/AIR CITY/FRONTIER (1935), SHORS (1939), and MICHURIN (1948) demonstrate how an analysis of films in their historical context illuminates the specific issues that dramatically influence Dovzhenko's feelings both for traditional folklore and for Soviet objectives. The writing is crisp, entertaining, and informative. A terse filmography, brief chronology, good bibliography, and adequate index are included. Recommended for special collections.

SERGEI M. EISENSTEIN

*Aitken, Gillon R., trans. POTEMKIN: A FILM BY SERGEI EISENSTEIN. New York: Simon and Schuster, 1968. Illustrated. 104pp. New York: Frederick Unger Publishing Company, 1984.
   A bare bones approach to Eisenstein's famous film script, this brief book begins with Andrew Sinclair's succinct summary of the failed 1905 Revolution against the Russian csar and the mutiny aboard the battleship Potemkin. We are then given an uncredited excerpt from Eisenstein's FILM FORM, in which he discusses how his film, BATTLESHIP POTEMKIN/BRONENOSETS POTEMKIN was constructed. Cast and production credits follow, with the major portion of the book devoted to a simplistic presentation of the script. The best parts of the publication are its visuals.   No bibliography or index is provided. Approach with caution.

*Aumont, Jacques. MONTAGE EISENSTEIN. Trans. Lee Hildreth et al.   Bloomington: Indiana University Press, 1987. Illustrated. 243pp.

Barna, Yon. EISENSTEIN. Foreword Jay Leyda. Trans. Lise Hunter.   Bloomington: Indiana University Press, 1973. Illustrated. 287pp.
   Originally published in Bucharest in 1966, then revised and translated for this edition, this reflective and anecdotal biography offers important perspectives not found in other studies. As Leyda points out, "Yon Barna has given more attention than any other commentator or critic of Eisenstein to the large number of UNREALIZED

ideas in a career that gave us only seven finished films." The author divides his
material into fifteen analytical and informative chapters that investigate the great
director's work from "its emotional sources, the circumstances in which it was born,
that special concurrence of sensory and social events that determines the conditions
for the appearance of a work." In the process, Barna makes little effort to analyze
the artistic nature of Eisenstein's work.

The early chapters cover more quickly much of the same ground covered in
Seton's memorable portrait, while at the same time offering fresh insights and new
information. For example, Barna talks more about Eisenstein's generosity in terms of
money and ideas than does Seton. He also takes issue with her assessment of the
director's social attitudes, explains the role that films played in Eisenstein's childhood
and future work, speculates about the apparent paradox between the artist's love of
mathematics and his inductive approach to filmmaking, and directly questions many
of Seton's claims about Eisenstein's personal reflections. In Barna's judgment, "Even
the most dependable of his biographers have sometimes been led astray by unverified
information." Particularly interesting are Barna's assertions that Eisenstein had very
few ideas on the theater prior to his working for Meyerhold, that Esther Shub and
Lev Kuleshov played key roles in Eisenstein's cinematic apprenticeship, and that the
incident of the tarpaulin raises a number of unanswered questions about the depiction
of historical events in BATTLESHIP POTEMKIN (1925).

Once we get to Eisenstein's travels abroad, the book steps up its criticism of
earlier works and demonstrates the need for more information about the controversial
years that followed. For example, Seton makes little mention of Eisenstein's meetings
in New York with Griffith, while Barna asserts they were the most important contacts
the Soviet director made in America. Although Barna lauds the work done by
Gottesman and Geduld on QUE VIVA MEXICO!, he fails to answer questions about
what exactly the relationship between Stalin and Sinclair was, and how that impacted
on the latter's behavior toward Eisenstein. Where Barna is superb is in describing
the reception that Eisenstein received upon his return to the Soviet Union, the chaotic
years of the 1930s, and the fate of Eisenstein's last four films.

Among the issues ignored are the questions of Eisenstein's alleged homosexuality,
the curious behavior of Douglas Fairbanks, Sr., and the way in which the Soviet
intellectual handled Eisenstein's Jewish heritage.   Overall, EISENSTEIN should be
read as a companion volume to Seton's biography. It concludes with a useful
bibliographical essay and a general index. Recommended for special collections.

*Eisenstein, Sergei M. FILM ESSAYS AND A LECTURE, trans. and ed. Jay Leyda.
Introduction Grigori Kozintsev. New York: Praeger Publications, 1970. Illustrated.
220pp.

"Eisenstein's first essays," Kozintsev points out, "had an individuality peculiar
to him. One was struck by the oddness of juxtaposition: the wildest artistic ideas
with an academically impassive tone, and scientific phraseology. . . ." In the fourteen
essays and sundry material that follow, we are given glimpses into how the "art of
Eisenstein was inseparable from his temperament and his taste." Many of the almost
verbatim notes suggest the master's classroom technique and offer important
observations about cinematic art.   Particularly interesting are essays like "The New
Language of the Cinema," "The Dynamic Square," and "Lessons from Literature."
Recommended for special collections.

Eisenstein, Sergei M. IMMORAL MEMORIES: AN AUTOBIOGRAPHY. Trans. Herbert
Marshall. Boston: Houghton Mifflin Company, 1983. Illustrated. 292pp.

On February 2, 1946, Sergei M. Eisenstein suffered a serious heart attack.
Confined to the Kremlin Hospital, he began writing his autobiography, which he did
not expect to be published either in his lifetime or Stalin's. Now those very private
thoughts are available to the public for the first time. In reminiscing in the preface
about this extraordinary individual, Marshall writes, "Outside he was a Soviet

Russian; inside, according to some, he was a Christian. According to others, he was a Jew; to yet others, a homosexual; to a few, a cynical critic . . . and what else? It was difficult to know what he was fundamentally. He never expressed it verbally. Still, there was one medium through which he expressed his innermost feelings--his drawings and caricatures." And thus Marshall sets the stage for what the book jacket proudly proclaims to be "the first major addition to the Eisenstein canon in English in more than thirty years."

The translator's preface not only sets the tone for reading this invaluable autobiography, but also raises a number of controversial issues surrounding the brilliant author's life and career. For example, Marshall asserts that Eisenstein was inspired by THE BIRTH OF A NATION (1915) and WAY DOWN EAST (1920) as well as by INTOLERANCE (1916), pointing out that "What remains realistic and convincing in Griffith's films is exaggerated and unconvincing in Eisenstein's." In discussing the events following the banning of BEZHIN MEADOW/BEZHIN LUG (1935), he talks about the witchhunt atmosphere surrounding the special Conference of Cinema Workers in January 1935 and claims that Eisenstein's "intellectual brilliance and erudition" were offset by Sergei Dynamov, "A brilliant intellectual . . . [who] led the attack on Eisenstein's theory of intellectual cinema as 'bourgeoisie-influence formalism.'" Marshall is also much more critical of the director's friends and associates than are Eisenstein's other biographers. A case in point is Grisha Alexandrov. While other sources brush over the split between the two men following their return from Mexico, Marshall attacks Alexandrov for being an ingrate and a Stalinist toad who finally got his just deserts after Stalin's death. In fact, the translator offers the most hard-hitting comments about Stalin's role in many of Eisenstein's lifelong career problems in and out of the Soviet Union. What is particularly surprising, given Marshall's conspicuous political perspectives, is Eisenstein's apparent lack of interest in commenting on his political difficulties with Soviet officials over a thirty-year period. To aid in appreciating Eisenstein's highly emotional and associative writing style, Marshall appends a splendid listing of events to show what the author was doing at the time specific entries are discussed. A second appendix on Eisenstein's "Hope of the Future" and a general index are included. Recommended for special collections.

*Eisenstein, Sergei. FILM FORM: ESSAYS IN FILM THEORY and THE FILM SENSE, trans. and ed. Jay Leyda. New York: Meridian Books, 1957. Illustrated.   561pp. Reissued separately New York: Harcourt, Brace in 1969.

Eisenstein's theories on film, presented in summary form, offer valuable insights into his films and his influence. Although difficult for beginners, they are a treasure-house for serious students of film. This book contains the director's ideas on the relationship between theater and cinema and the theories of montage as conflict, as well as his celebrated article, "Dickens, Griffith, and the Film Today." THE FILM SENSE presents his ideas on words and images, synchronization of the senses, and color and meaning. Although both books contain useful appendexes, THE FILM SENSE is especially valuable because of the appendexes on Eisenstein's work in North America. Recommended for special collections.

Eisenstein, Sergei. NONINDIFFERENT NATURE. Trans. Herbert Marshall. Cambridge: Cambridge University Press, 1987. Illustrated. 428pp.

*Eisenstein, Sergei. NOTES OF A FILM DIRECTOR, trans. X. Danko. London: Lawrence and Wishart, 1959. Illustrated. 238pp. New York: Dover Publications, 1970.

"In selecting articles for this volume," explains Eisenstein, "articles that I have written over many years and on various occasions, I am moved by just one desire: to help film-makers to master all the potentialities of the cinema." To achieve that desire, the essays are grouped into three categories: "About Myself and My Films," "Problems of Film Direction," and "Portraits of Artists." In a concluding essay, "Always Forward (By Way of an Epilogue)," Eisenstein praises the vast potential of

film, "an art born to spread the greatest ideas of our era among the millions." Once
one gets away from the excessively flowery language, this book provides useful
background information about the great director's methods and theories, plus an
excellent collection of drawings he designed for ALEXANDER NEVSKY (1938) and
IVAN THE TERRIBLE (1944-45). Well worth browsing.

*Eisenstein, Sergei M. ON THE COMPOSITION OF THE SHORT FICTION SCENARIO.
Trans. Alan Y. Upchurch, introduction Jay Leyda. New York: Frederick Ungar
Publishing Company, 1985. Illustrated. 61pp.
     A significant discussion on adapting a short story into a screenplay, this
publication grew out of lectures the author delivered at the V.G.I.K. shortly after
the Nazis invaded Russia in 1941, when the government required morale-building
material quickly. According to Leyda, Eisenstein proposed that all Soviet filmmakers
and filmmaking elements be adapted "to the production of short, well-aimed film stories
in all effective forms, that could be grouped together for national distribution." To
demonstrate his point, the great director compares two parallel scripts to show why
one is better than the other. Well worth browsing.

*Hetherington, John, trans. THE COMPLETE FILMS OF EISENSTEIN: TOGETHER
WITH AN UNPUBLISHED ESSAY BY EISENSTEIN. New York: E. P. Dutton, 1974.
Illustrated. 156pp.
     Beginning with a rare essay by Eisenstein on the use of the close-up, this
worthwhile publication offers a succinct but useful introduction to the director's
career. An annotated biography highlights the major events starting with the birth
of Sergei Mikhailovitch Eisenstein in Riga on January 23, 1898, to a Jewish father
who was an engineer-architect and a mother who was Slavic, to the young man's
architectural studies at the Petrograd School of Public Works from 1914 to 1917,
followed by his 1918 enlistment in the Red Army where he worked in Agit-propaganda,
to his being mustered out in 1920 and his fateful meeting with Maxim Straukh when
both men decided to devote themselves to work in the theater, and then to the
experiences over the next four years that eventually led him into filmmaking. What
is enjoyable about Hetherington's analysis over the next twenty-four years, until
Eisenstein's death on February 9, 1948, is the deft way in which the author pinpoints
the traumas in the director's life. The major portion of the book is devoted to a visual
filmography, using key frame reproductions to illustrate Eisenstein's work from
STRIKE/STACHKA (1925) to IVAN THE TERRIBLE PART II/IVAN GROZNY II (1946).
Regrettably, the uneven quality of reproductions detracts from the usefulness of the
exercise. Well worth browsing.

*Leyda, Jay, ed. EISENSTEIN 2: A PREMATURE CELEBRATION OF EISENSTEIN'S
CENTENARY. Trans. Alan Y. Upchurch et al. New York: Frederick Ungar Publishing
Company, 1985. Illustrated. 59pp.
     Part of a series to translate specific aspects of the director's correspondence
and interviews, this thin book includes a 1925 interview that Eisenstein gave at the
time of his departure from the Proletkult, a letter by Valeri Pletnyov defending the
policies of the Proletkult theater, and a fruitless letter by Eisenstein to the editor
of KINO-NEDELYA (2) trying to stop the pointless debate. Particularly enjoyable are
more than a dozen letters between Eisenstein and Esther Shub from 1929 to 1946.
Well worth browsing.

*Leyda, Jay, ed. EISENSTEIN: THREE FILMS--BATTLESHIP POTEMKIN, OCTOBER,
ALEXANDER NEVSKY. Trans. Diana Matias. New York: Harper & Row, 1974.
Illustrated. 189pp.

Leyda reminds us, in the book's introduction, that Eisenstein's claim to sole authorship of the three films is very debatable. "In each of these scenarios," explains the distinguished scholar, "Eisenstein had a writer-collaborator. For BATTLESHIP POTEMKIN it was Nina Agadzhanova, co-author of the anniversary scenario 1905, where the mutiny on the POTEMKIN was one of many episodes it was thought necessary to reconstruct for such a film; to the end of his life Eisenstein never ceased to show his gratitude to 'Nuna's' contribution to BATTLESHIP POTEMKIN. In preparing the anniversary film of OCTOBER there is no doubt that Eisenstein and Alexandrov collaborated on the scenario (published herein), though no one was in any doubt who contributed its boldest invention and imagery. The initiative for ALEXANDER NEVSKY came from its co-author, Pyotr Pavlenko, without whose dramatic experience and political reliability Eisenstein could not even have started its production; and who will say that Prokofiev's score could have been replaced by another composer's with the same powerful effect?" What Leyda is arguing is that Eisenstein dominated the films, but that others provided the dramatic framework. He also makes a distinction among the three "scenarios" in the anthology: the first is an "emergency" script embodying material that had been shot and had yet to be shot; the second is a "shooting script" outlining material yet to be shot; and the third is the familiar "screenplay" or "treatment." Because of Leyda's scholarly emphasis, this approach to Eisenstein's film scripts has a unique appeal. Well worth browsing.

*Marshall, Herbert, ed. THE BATTLESHIP POTEMKIN. New York: Avon Books, 1978. Illustrated. 385pp.
An invaluable anthology of essays and reviews on a film acknowledged by many film historians to be one of the ten best movies ever made, this splendid book provides information on how Eisenstein felt about his film, how the project originated, the shooting of the film, the reactions in Western Europe and America to the film, and the influence of the movie on other works of art. Particularly interesting is Marshall's introduction to the collection, which surveys in hard-hitting prose, every aspect of the 1925 masterpiece from pre-production ideas, to post-production censorship. Regrettably, there is neither a bibliography nor an index. Recommended for special collections.

*Mayer, David. SERGEI EISENSTEIN'S "POTEMKIN": A SHOT-BY-SHOT PRESENTATION. New York: Grossman Publishers, 1972. Illustrated. 252pp.
"This shot-by-shot analysis does not attempt," Mayer explains, "to recreate POTEMKIN's filmic effects through the use of stylistic literary equivalents. Its approach has been to present an exact description of what is seen on the screen. It meticulously avoids personal interpretation of Eisenstein's intentions or the character's motivation. The goal has been to distill each shot description to its clearest, most precise form, projecting those elements that best transmit the film's story." The charm of Mayer's approach is that we can examine the film either for its entertainment value or for its artistic structure. The book's introduction summarizes how Eisenstein conceived of the film as a "newsreel" of the 1905 mutiny of Russian sailors against their csarist officers on the battleship POTEMKIN, divided the action into five tragic acts, and orchestrated different moods and content for each of the film's five acts while making certain that each act contained "an almost identical feature: toward the middle of each, mood and tone jump from one extreme to another." Particularly noteworthy in Mayer's methodology is the use of frame reproductions from the Museum of Modern Art print of BATTLESHIP POTEMKIN. Over 200 examples, representing "every major camera setup, plot situation, and characterization have been placed adjacent to the shots they illustrate." Recommended for special collections.

*Moussinac, Leon. SERGEI EISENSTEIN: AN INVESTIGATION INTO HIS FILMS AND PHILOSOPHY. Trans. D. Sandy Petrey. New York: Crown Publishers, 1970. Illustrated. 226pp.

Originally published in 1964 in the highly praised CINEMA D'AUJOURD'HUI series of Editions Seghers in Paris, this first-rate study of Eisenstein, by the pioneer French critic and close friend of the Russian director, is a must for all students of Soviet cinema. It contains original essays, reviews, comments by critics and peers, letters, and an excellent bio-filmography. An index is included.   Recommended for special collections.

*Nizhny, Vladimir. LESSONS WITH EISENSTEIN, trans. and ed. Ivor Montagu and Jay Leyda. New York: Hill and Wang, 1962. Illustrated. 182pp.
Montagu points out in the foreword that because of Eisenstein's theoretical style, Russians consider him a "scientist." He then explains that "It is not a misnomer, since his approach to aesthetics made it a distinctly materialistic branch of psychology. He set himself, by analysis of cause and effect, to discover and establish general laws of construction of works of art, to establish the special methods peculiar to cinema." What was unique about the famous director was that he not only saw theory and production as inexorably intertwined, but he also felt as passionately about teaching as he did about filmmaking. Nizhny was an ex-student of Eisenstein and later a lecturer at the same school. Before his death in the mid-1950s, he meticulously went through the legacy of Eisenstein's unfinished notes and files to recreate, on paper, what the famous director tried to teach in his lectures and training sessions. As another student noted, using an unusual baseball metaphor, "Sergei Mikhailovich was not so much directly, in the usual sense of the word, an instructor; what he did was to make himself available and open to those who studied with him and, depending on their abilities, energies and tremendous efforts off their bat, each could get from him whatever corresponded to his own ability."   Based upon selected records kept of Eisenstein's classes at the V.G.I.K. in 1928-29, Nizhny has written an outstanding source book about film direction. An appendix by Eisenstein about how to teach the theory and practice of film direction, endnotes, and a general index are included. Recommended for special collections.

*Seton, Marie. SERGEI M. EISENSTEIN: A BIOGRAPHY. Rev. ed.   London: Denis Dobson, 1978. Illustrated. 533pp.
One of the most intriguing film biographies ever published, this highly subjective and very personal portrait originally appeared in 1952. Seton, a close companion and confidant of Eisenstein during the 1930s, offers intimate assessments of the great artist's innermost thoughts and unique conflicts as well as his reactions to the public dilemmas that he faced throughout his stormy career. What emerges is a story of a man with an extraordinary range of interests and a profoundly complex personality.
The basic facts are set against Seton's controversial, psychological interpretations. For example, starting with Eisenstein's birth in Riga, Latvia, the author speculates on who and which of the child's relatives (e.g., father or paternal grandparents) renounced their Jewish heritage and the reasons for it. Seton concludes that the boy grew up with no "allegiance to the traditions of his father's people or the Jewish creed." Nevertheless, we learn later on of the attacks on Eisenstein related to his birthright and the reactions that anti-Semitism engendered in him during Hitler's control of Nazi Germany. Seton also explores the effect that Eisenstein's parents had on him, the importance of the circus (especially the clowns) in his growing up, the loneliness he experienced and how it shaped his future relationships, and his strong personal identification with Leonardo da Vinci and Sigmund Freud.
Once Seton takes us into the early days of the 1917 Revolution, the image of a lonely, insecure, introspective, and rebellious youth is firmly established. By the time he becomes involved in the Proletkult Theater and nurtures an animosity toward traditional stage conventions, Eisenstein's reasons for his theories on collective heroes and a montage of "attractions" are readily understandable. In fact, she provides a splendid introduction to his silent films, their documentary look, the importance of

"typage" in casting the films, the techniques carried over from the Proletkult Theater days (particularly his attitude toward classical tragedies), and the enthusiasm that the artist brought with him to the making of Soviet films. Although the author does a fine job of explaining the roles that people like Vsevolod E. Meyerhold, Maxim Shtraukh, Pera Attasheva, Edmund Meisel, and Grigori Alexandrov played in Eisenstein's life and thinking, she does a poor job of discussing the influences of key figures like Eduard K. Tisse, Dziga Vertov, Esther Shub, and Lev Kuleshov. Moreover, her Freudian interpretations of Eisenstein's presumed behavior detract from the more persuasive sections of the profile. One also detects a surprising unwillingness to discuss certain political issues. For example, her analysis of Eisenstein's relationship with Stalin lacks the candor of other commentators like Herbert Marshall and Yon Barna. There is also little said about the "true' nature of the agricultural "revolution" that Stalin produced and Eisenstein treated in THE GENERAL LINE/OLD AND NEW/STAROIE I NOVOIE (1929), namely, the annihilation of millions of kulaks. On the other hand, Seton provides valuable insights into the director's work habits, his theoretical principles, the personal competition between Eisenstein and Pudovkin, the nature of the conversations he held in Moscow with Theodore Dreiser, the contrasts between what Eisenstein thought about the revolutionary nature of Soviet art and what office holders like Anatoli V. Lunacharsky (the commissar of education) and Boris Shumyatsky (head of the Soviet film industry) believed, and the complicated negotiations that finally brought Eisenstein to Hollywood.

The most disappointing sections of the biography are those related to the making of the sound films. While it is obvious that Seton did not have access to classified documents during the book's initial release, she did have the opportunity to check the Geduld-Gottesman, Montagu, and Barna publications before this revised edition appeared. Nevertheless, she makes few changes in her original assessments of what occurred between Upton Sinclair and Eisenstein or of the role that Stalin played in the disastrous QUE VIVA MEXICO! (1931), as well as the productions of BEZHIN MEADOW/BEZHIN LUG (1935), ALEXANDER NEVSKY/ALEXNDR NEVSKII (1939), and THE THREE PARTS OF IVAN THE TERRIBLE/IVAN GROZNY (1944-1946). What is particularly unsatisfactory is the author's explanation of Eisenstein's problems both as a Jew and an artist with the Nazi-Soviet Pact of 1939,#Gand how he resolved those difficulties (e.g., his willingness to tolerate anti-Semitic remarks by close personal friends). Where Seton is splendid is in delineating Eisenstein's loyalty to Soviet long-range goals and his attempts to adjust to changing political and aesthetic directives. Whatever reservations one has about her Freudian speculations on his public behavior and the effects that people like Stalin and Sinclair had on his creative life, you still come away impressed by the amount of inside information Seton provides.

This biography rightly holds a special place in the literature on Eisenstein. Although one must be cautious in taking at face value many of the personal reflections, it remains the best source of information on his life. Seven valuable appendexes and a general index are included. Recommended for special collections.

*Swallow, Norman. EISENSTEIN: A DOCUMENTARY PORTRAIT. New York: E. P. Dutton and Company, 1977. Illustrated. 155pp.

Based upon a two-part television film produced for the BBC's OMNIBUS series that was shown originally in Britain at the end of 1970, this book records what twenty-five of Eisenstein's close friends and colleagues felt about him. The book is also a written record of the commentary used in the film, which features four main topics: "the life of Eisenstein as reflected by the places he knew, by contemporary photographs, and by quotations from his writings; selected sequences from each of his films; his own drawings and designs, whether created for a particular film or theater production or merely done for personal pleasure; and the recollections of those who knew him." Although no mention is made either on the front cover or in the opening of the book, the blurb on the back of the cover indicates that many of the recollections used in the film and presumably in the book resulted from the author's close collaboration with Eisenstein's former co-author and co-director G. V. Alexandrov. Slight endnotes, bibliography, filmography, and index are included. Well worth browsing.

Taylor, Richard, ed. S. M. EISENSTEIN: SELECTED WORKS. VOLUME I: WRITINGS, 1922-34. Bloomington: Indiana University Press, 1988. Illustrated. 334pp.

LEV V. KULESHOV

*Levaco, Ronald, ed. and trans. KULESHOV ON FILM: WRITINGS OF LEV KULESHOV. Berkeley: University of California Press, 1975. 226pp.
   "The distinguished and enduring fifty-year career of Lev Kuleshov," states Levaco, "virtually spans the history of Russian and Soviet film. Landmark theoretician, director, professor at VGIK, . . . the successes and failures of Kuleshov's life reflect the very ethos of the Soviet cinema." He was born on January 14, 1899, published his first noteworthy ideas on film in 1918, began making AGITKI films the following year, formed his influential Workshop at the beginning of the 1920s, ran into trouble with state policies during the 1930s; became head of the State Institute of Cinematography in the mid-1940s, found himself a major international figure in the 1960s, and died on March 29, 1970. Except for this important collection of twelve of his essays and a brief work entitled, "Art of the Cinema," almost nothing by and about him is available in the English language. A bibliography, filmography, and index are included. Recommended for special collections.

VSEVOLOD I. PUDOVKIN

Dart, Peter. PUDOVKIN'S FILMS AND FILM THEORY. New York: Arno Press, 1974. Illustrated. 237pp.
   Originally written as a 1965 University of Kansas Ph.D. dissertation, this book is offered more as an introduction to readers beginning a serious study of Pudovkin, than as an in-depth examination of his work. Dart divides his information into two main parts. Section One, "Pudovkin's Films," quickly summarizes his early life and passes on to the reasons why INTOLERANCE (1916) allegedly persuaded the once anti-film student suddenly to enroll in the V.G.I.K. and become skilled in making propaganda movies. Particular attention is given to the influence of people like Vladimir Gardin, Lev Kuleshov, and Anna Nicolaevna Zemtsova in Pudovkin's career. Brief discussions of the artist's films are interlaced with comments on production problems and techniques. In addition, Dart includes a rare interview that the filmmaker had with I. Rostovtsev on Pudovkin's early films and a useful Pudovkin filmography. Section Two, "Pudovkin's Film Theory," reviews the director's theories on montage and the implications of those theories, as well as two articles that Pudovkin wrote: "On Montage" and "Stanislavsky's System in the Cinema." A smattering of illustrations and an index are included. Well worth browsing.

*Pudovkin, Vsevolod I. FILM TECHNIQUE AND FILM ACTING. Trans. and ed. Ivor Montagu. London: Vision Press, 1958. Illustrated. 387pp.
   According to Montagu, "The ideas set out in FILM TECHNIQUE remain basic to any idea of the film, to appreciation of the relation of real material to film appearance, to any understanding of exactly what we are doing when we create an effect upon the screen, and they will so remain as long as cinema continues." In this compact edition of Pudovkin's two classic works, we get an understanding not only of the artist's theories on film scenarios and the use of actors in films, but also on the relationship between the stage and the screen. A critical filmography is included. Recommended for special collections.

*TWO RUSSIAN FILM CLASSICS: "MOTHER," A FILM BY V. I. PUDOVKIN; "EARTH,"
A FILM BY ALEXANDER DOVZHENKO. New York: Simon and Schuster, 1973.
Illustrated. 102pp.
A no-frills scenario approach to the famous films, the versions printed "are taken
from the scenarios originally published in Russia and [are] intended in each case as
a literary rendering of the film. Any significant divergences between the scenario
and the version of the film now available to English or American viewers are indicated
by footnotes in the text." Gillon R. Aitken's translation of MOTHER is based on a
1935 Russian publication. Diana Matias's version of EARTH is from a 1966 Russian
volume, entitled ZEMLYA: KNYIGA-FILM. Well worth browsing.

DZIGA VERTOV

Feldman, Seth R. DZIGA VERTOV: A GUIDE TO REFERENCES AND RESOURCES.
Boston: G. K. Hall, 1979. 232pp.
This valuable reference book offers a comprehensive introduction to the
English-language and Soviet material on Vertov available to film scholars. Because a
number of resources were still off limits when he wrote this book, Feldman includes
"incomplete references and material whose content (and, in the case of some films,
whose existence) cannot be verified at this time." What emerges in the eight fact-filled
chapters is not only a splendid overview of the artist's life and work, but also an
in-depth list of writings about him as well as important archival and distribution
information.
The opening section on Vertov's biographical background provides the essential
details of his career. Born Denis Arkadievich Kaufman on January 2, 1896, he was
the first of the family's three children. His early schooling was in musical theory and
performance. The Vertovs fled their Byalistock home in 1915 when the Germans
invaded Poland. The flight took them to Russia, where the adventuresome Vertov
enrolled in the Psychoneurological Institute in Petrograd. It was there that he became
enamoured of the AVANT-GARDE movement in art, poetry, films, and theater. Typical
of Feldman's concern with detail and objectivity, he points out that Kaufman then
changed his name to Dziga Vertov to illustrates his topsy-turvey life ("Dziga" both
refers to "a child's toy top" and is the Ukranian word meaning "gyspsy"). He also
includes Jay Leyda's claim that in the mid-1930s Vertov told him that "Dziga"
represented the noise a film made during the editing process, while "Vertov"
"described the rewinding of the film itself." Although Vertov insisted that it was an
epiphany experienced in a railway station in 1918 that led to his becoming a filmmaker,
Feldman suggests that a more logical reason was the AVANT-GARDE artist's 1918 cafe
meetings with Aleksandr Lemberg, a newsreel cameraman, which led to Vertov's initial
entry into films as Mikhail Kol'tsov's secretary with the Moscow Cinema Committee.
The "education" that Kulesov received in film editing and distribution, his first
exposure to film aesthetics, his own compilation experiments, and Vertov's initial
collaboration with Elizaveta Ignat'evna Svilova (the woman who not only became his
wife in 1923, but also his life-long editor) explain the direction in which the film
theorist was heading and why. Feldman then sketches in Vertov's work in organizing
mobile filming and screening units, the importance after the Revolution of the
KINOPRAVDA newsreel series from 1922 to 1925, the relationship between Vertov and
his brother, Mikhail Kaufman, the recognition and criticism given to Vertov by the
Soviet film industry, the mixed reactions to his European trip in the early 1930s and
its consequences for him within the Soviet Union, the impact of World War II on
reviving his career, and the years of obscurity before his death on February 12,
1954. Feldman presents the details in a clear and effective manner.
The other seven sections are also succinct summaries of important information,
analyses, and references. Feldman's work reinforces the already high regard that film
scholars have for this remarkable resource series published by G. K. Hall. An author
and film index are included. Recommended for special collections.

Feldman, Seth R. EVOLUTION OF STYLE IN THE EARLY WORK OF DZIGA VERTOV. New York: Arno Press, 1977. 233pp.

Originally written as a 1975 SUNY/Buffalo doctoral dissertation, this useful study begins with the proviso that "the name Dziga Vertov will be taken to mean not only the linguistic connotations of the phrase [discussed in the review aforementioned] but also, where applicable, the presence of those of Vertov's colleagues--especially Mikhail Kaufman--whose contributions have not been clearly credited." The dissertation itself examines the influences on Vertov from his early days to the development of his theories on KINOGLAZ ("Film-Eye") and the completion of KINOPRAVDA, stressing "the nature of his work and the contribution his work has made to our understanding of cinema." Feldman places the artist's aesthetic and political values in the historical context of the October Revolution of 1917, calling attention to Vertov's AVANT-GARDE theories and their relationship to the non-fiction film. By focusing on the years from 1917 to 1925, the author manages to discuss not only the evolution of the Soviet film industry, but also the nature of cubo-futurism and the birth of formalism. Chapter One discusses Vertov's personal growth as an artist, the Italian and Russian AVANT-GARDE, the birth of newsreel and documentary traditions, and the role of cinema during the early days of Soviet politics. Chapter Two reviews the influence of KINOPRAVDA on Soviet aesthetics during the 1920s, on Soviet films, and on Vertov's emerging screen values. Chapter Three not only analyzes the filmmaker's projects between 1923 and 1925, but also critiques the films that resulted as by-products of the major film productions.

Given the limited amount of information available and Feldman's thoughtful presentation, this slim volume serves as a good introduction to Vertov's fledgling years. An appendix describing sixteen issues of KINONEDELIA (forty-two newsreels devoted to emphasizing Bolshevik influence throughout the Soviet Union), a filmography, and a bibliography are included. Well worth browsing.

Petric, Vlada. CONSTRUCTIVISM IN FILM: THE MAN WITH A MOVIE CAMERA--A CINEMATIC ANALYSIS. Cambridge: Cambridge University Press, 1987. Illustrated. 325pp.

Taking a close, critical look at one of the most extraordinary works to emerge from the AVANT-GARDE movement in the Soviet Union during the 1920s, Petric places Vertov's influential film within its cultural context. The analysis is divided into three major parts. Chapter 1 describes the filmmaker's relationship to the popular theories of his times: i.e., constructivism, futurism, formalism, and suprematism. The emphasis is on showing the importance of Vladimir Mayakovsky's radical publication, LEF in developing Vertov's revolutionary poetic filmmaking style. Petric carefully examines not only what drew the various AVANT-GARDE artists together, but also what differences arose between Vertov and his contemporaries like Aleksei Gan and Sergei M. Eisenstein. The turning points, as the author explains, came as a result of the government's espousal of socialist realism and the failure of the New Economic Policy (NEP) to liberate the artists from the demands of popular filmmaking. The reason for Vertov's eventual removal from public view beginning in the early 1930s, Petric observes, is because "Vertov's cinematic experimentation was proclaimed 'unsuitable' and considered undeserving of support from the Ministry of Cinematography."

Chapter 2 provides a formal analysis of key sequences from THE MAN WITH A CAMERA that demonstrate the director's style and illustrate his theoretical principles. Although Petric's plan is to offer a vast number of frame enlargements to illustrate how Vertov's ideas actually operated in the film, the idea is somewhat blunted because the 450 frame enlargements are printed in the back of the book and not in the chapter itself. Thus, Petric's extensive annotations explaining Vertov's theories on "Productive Art" (the notion that the art of creation is analogous to industrial production) appear more dry and academic than necessary. Nonetheless, the author more than proves his point that close structural analysis works much better on paper than it does while watching the film projected at regular speed on the screen.

Chapter 3 offers an examination of the three fundamental visual patterns (vertical, horizontal, and circular) used in the majority of shot compositions in the movie. "Integrated by montage," Petric notes, "these patterns attain an optical 'pulsation' that--on the screen--transforms recorded 'life-facts' into representationally ambiguous imagery, thus defying the spectator's customary perception of reality and its interpretation." The thrust of the chapter is to emphasize the unconventional nature of the film and why it makes a strong case for film as "an autonomous means of expression."

For anyone interested in an extensive and challenging discussion of a major AVANT-GARDE filmmaker, this book is must reading. Several appendexes, a selective bibliography, and a general index are included. Recommended for special collections.

FILMS

ALEXANDER P. DOVZHENKO

ARSENAL (16mm: 1928, 80 mins., b/w, silent, R-BUD, EMG, KIT, MMA; S-COR, REE)

While most of Dovzhenko's stories are concerned with a simple plot line (in this film, the revolt of the workers), he is one of the most poetic of silent directors. His major contributions to the film were in the form of a new realism coupled with a continuity of storytelling and lyrical beauty.[212]

EARTH/ZEMLYA (16mm: 1930, 54 mins., b/w, silent, R-BUD, COR, EMG, KIT; S-KIT)

This film is considered by many historians to be Dovzhenko's greatest film. Georges Sadoul states that the filmmaker had the following objectives in making it: "I wanted to show the state of a Ukrainian village in 1929, that is to say, at the time it was going through an economic transformation and a mental change in the masses. My principles are: 1. Stories in themselves do not interest me; I chose them in order to get the greatest expression of essential social forms. 2. I work with typical material and apply synthetic methods; my heroes and their behavior are representative of their classes. 3. The material of my film is extremely concentrated temporally and, at the same time, I make it pass through the prism of emotions, which gives it life and eloquence. I never remain indifferent in the face of this material. It is necessary to both love and hate deeply and in great measure if one's art is not to be dogmatic and dry."[213] The basic plot focuses on the kulaks refusing to accept Ukrainian collectivization. As Marco Carynnyk points out, "The film's topical allusions quickly pass from the spectator's mind--Dovzhenko is more concerned with the continuity of history than with the struggle between rich and poor peasants--and the spectator is left with inarticulate sentiments of death's proper place in the cycle of life."[214]

SERGEI EISENSTEIN

BATTLESHIP POTEMKIN/BRONENOSETS POTEMKIN (16mm: 1925, 70 mins., b/w, music and sound effects only, R-IMA, IVY, JAN, KIT, TWY, WES, WHO; S-BLA;

---

[212]   Marco Carynnyk, "The Dovzhenko Papers," FILM COMMENT 7:3 (Fall 1971):34-41.

[213]   DICTIONARY OF FILMS, pp.248-9.

[214]   *Marco Carynnyk, ed. and trans., ALEXANDER DOVZHENKO: THE POET AS A FILMMAKER--SELECTED WRITINGS (Cambridge: the MIT Press, 1973), p.xx.

L-MMA. Silent version is also available; R-BUD, EMG, FNC, IMA, KIT, MMA, WHO, WIL; S-BLA)

Conceived by Eisenstein and Nina Agadzhanova, the film was commissioned by the central committee and had its premier on December 21, 1925, at the Bolshoi Theater. Leon Moussinac's initial reaction after the French screening in 1926 captured the essence of what has been written about the film since then: "The irresistible dynamism, the maximum use of the most direct forms of expression, the return to elemental nature, the conscious and deliberate abandonment of individual stars, the powerful presentation of groups, the movements of crowds, the desire to use film to make palpable a collective soul, all decisions which represent an overwhelming new contribution. . . ."[215] One way in which the twenty-seven year old Eisenstein accomplished his art was through the multiple use of film montage. As David Mayer points out, "Eisenstein's exploration of the possible varieties of montage expression led him to RHYTHMIC MONTAGE. In this development, the content of the action within the frame was felt to have as much weight as the actual physical length of each chosen shot. Thus it was possible to increase tension not only by shortening each succeeding strip of film in accordance with a plan, but also in violation of the plan."[216] This film about the 1905 rebellion of the Battleship POTEMKIN'S crew also illustrates how Eisenstein utilized his training in the Proletkult Theater to incorporate a documentary look into film.[217] Moreover, one can detect the influence of INTOLERANCE (1916) in Eisenstein's use of parallel editing and cross-cutting for creating tension. Eduard K. Tisse is the cinematographer.

STRIKE/STACHKA (16mm: 1925, 97 mins., b/w, silent, R-BUD, COR, EMG, IMA, KIT; S-REE)

Originally conceived by Eisenstein and Valery Pletniev, the film, as John Hetherington points out, "was the fifth episode of a seven-part epic entitled TOWARDS DICTATORSHIP (of the proletariat). This series of didactic films was to show the different aspects and methods of revolutionary struggle before 1917--demonstrations, strikes, clandestine publishing, prison escapes, etc."[218] This was Eisenstein's first feature film, and he portrays a group of workers who are

---

[215]   *Leon Moussinac, SERGEI EISENSTEIN: AN INVESTIGATION INTO HIS FILMS AND PHILOSOPHY, trans. D. Sandy Petrey (New York: Crown Publishers, 1970), p.13.

[216]   *David Mayer, SERGEI M. EISENSTEIN'S "POTEMKIN": A SHOT-BY-SHOT PRESENTATION (New York: Grossman Publishers, 1972), p.9.

[217]   Teachers might find it helpful in explaining Eisenstein's techniques to show the famous "Odessa Steps" sequence from POTEMKIN (16mm: 1925, 20 mins., b/w, R-MMA) to illustrate how the great director manipulates time and space in film. That is to say, by the use of montage Eisenstein makes physical time and the actual event take longer and appear more dramatic and symbolic in the narrative film. The excerpt is also useful for showing the advantages of type casting (choosing individuals for their physical characteristics rather than for their acting ability) in creating a film metaphor. In this connection, see two articles on casting: Lola G. Yoaken, "Casting," FILM QUARTERLY 12:2 (Winter 1958):36-42; and Charles Winick, "The Face Was Familiar," FILMS AND FILMING 11:4 January (1965):12-17. See also Norman Fruchter, "Film Critique No. 5: BATTLESHIP POTEMKIN," SCREEN EDUCATION 30 (July-August 1965):37-52; and Sergei M. Eisenstein, "Organic Unity and Pathos in the Composition of POTEMKIN," CAHIERS DU CINEMA IN ENGLISH 3 CdC no. 82 (April 1958):36-43.

[218]   *John Hetherington, trans. THE COMPLETE FILMS OF EISENSTEIN: TOGETHER WITH AN UNPUBLISHED ESSAY BY EISENSTEIN (New York: E. P. Dutton and Company, 1974), p.19.

ruthlessly suppressed as a result of their demonstrations. The film also marks the beginning of the remarkable relationship between the director and his great cinematographer, Eduard K. Tisse. A final portion of the film script is reproduced in FILM SENSE, and there is an interesting examination of several possible endings that were considered.[219] A decade after making the film, Eisenstein considered it an example of "'the infantile malady of leftism.'"[220]

TEN DAYS THAT SHOOK THE WORLD/OCTOBER/OKTIABR (16mm: 1928, 67 mins., b/w, silent, R-FNC)

Inspired in part by John Reed's book on the October Revolution, this project was conceived by Eisenstein and Grigori Alexandrov, commissioned by the central committee, and photographed by Eduard Tisse. The action covers the events of the Russian Revolution from February to October 1917. It contains many famous episodes, an example of which is the raising of the bridge, considered one of the most praised sequences in film history. Here, as in the other Eisenstein films, the director demonstrates that one can change the meaning of a film by changing the position of the shots. His plan was to make TEN DAYS THAT SHOOK THE WORLD even more realistic than BATTLESHIP POTEMKIN by using "association montage." In simplified terms, Eisenstein edited various combinations of shots to produce not only a new meaning, but also a specific psychological effect. The experiment never really succeeded in unifying the film. Moreover, it raised a number of questions about Eisenstein's theories related to "intellectual cinema," where he consciously tried to merge emotions, documentary effects, and film narrative into a coherent film. "Taken as a whole," explains Norman Swallow, "OCTOBER is less disciplined than BATTLESHIP POTEMKIN and suffers from some of the defects of STRIKE, mixing satire with realism and naturalism with fantasy. Many of its most brilliant passages are more splendid in isolation than as integral parts of a complete film."[221]

SERGEI EISENSTEIN (16mm: 1958, 50 mins., b/w, English narration, sound, (R-FNC)
This is a film biography of the Russian director, which not only treats his life, but also shows extracts from his plays and major films.

VSEVOLOD I. PUDOVKIN

MOTHER/MAT (16mm: 1926, 100 mins., b/w, silent, R-BUD, COR, KIT, MMA)
In Pudovkin's best films, as Paul E. Burns explains, "His narratives begin as narrow family dramas of the struggle for survival under the Old Regime and evolve into great political and social epics which culminate in the broadening of the family of man. This process of development combines themes of the oppression, the alienation, and the liberation of mankind."[222] This film, adapted from Gorky's novel of the same name, concerns a working-class mother, the struggles she endured, the mistakes she unwittingly commits, and her triumphant death while leading a May Day demonstration. One can readily see in the film, Pudovkin's complex cutting methods combined with an emphasis on pictorial composition.

---

[219]   Ivor Montagu, "Rediscovery: STRIKE," SIGHT AND SOUND 26:2 (Autumn 1956):105-8.

[220]   Seton, p.70.

[221]   *Norman Swallow, EISENSTEIN: A DOCUMENTARY PORTRAIT (New York: E. P. Dutton and Company, 1977), p.60.

[222]   "Linkage: Pudovkin's Classics Revisited," pp.70-1.

THE END OF ST. PETERSBURG/KONYETS SANKT-PETERBURGA (16mm: 1927, 80 mins., b/w, silent, R-BUD, COR, EMG, KIT, MMA, TWY, WES; S-BLA)
    This story of human misery recounts the political awakening of a peasant youth who, like the heroine in MOTHER, becomes a revolutionary as the result of an unwitting mistake. Commissioned for the tenth anniversary of the 1917 Russian Revolution, it covers the same historical period as that in OCTOBER, but uses the individual to represent the masses. "The film is significant," Rob Edelman explains, "in that it is one of the first to satisfactorily blend a fictional scenario into a factual setting; the graphic, carefully realized battle scenes here are reminiscent of those in THE BIRTH OF A NATION (1915). And, typically, Pudovkin cast real pre-Revolution stockbrokers and executives as stockbrokers and executives."[223]

STORM OVER ASIA/THE HEIR OF GENGHIS-KAHN/POTOMOK CHINGIS-KAHN (16mm: 1928, 98 mins., b/w, silent, R-BUD, Music and sound effects version available from BUD, FES, IMA)
    Pudovkin's treatment of the exploitation of the Mongolians by foreigners offers a new perspective on the filmmaker's theme of oppression. As Burns points out, "The poverty of the tradition-bound society of the nomadic hunter-trapper is a poverty of pride."[224] Consequently, the film is more interested in maintaining traditional values than in participating in a global Soviet struggle. Set in Mongolia in 1918, the film illustrates Pudovkin's effective use of naturalistic treatment; the camera often lingers over the faces of the people with their strange costumes and their mannerisms in the marketplace, as well as the sweeping scope of the landscape. Also evident is the director's experimentation, which involves trying to show emotions in visual terms while at the same time telling the stereotyped story of the bad guys versus the good ones and using non-professional actors.

PUDOVKIN (16mm: 1960, 60 mins., b/w, English narration, sound, R-FNC)
    This film biography shows the great director at work and includes excerpts from his motion pictures.

DZIGA VERTOV

KINOPRAVDA (16mm: 1922-3, 77 mins., b/w, English subtitles, silent, R-FNC)
    A series of innovative, monthly newsfilms that appeared between 1922 and 1925, these early examples demonstrate Vertov's ideas of "film truth" (KINOPRAVDA). The plan, as Petric explains, "was not concerned with the truthful recording of reality for its own sake. He insisted that authentic film material ('life facts') be reorganized into cinematic structures ('film things'), a new unity with a particular ideological meaning [and] that the 'deciphering' of life through the cinema 'must be done according to the Communist view of the world.' Consequently, the 'Film-Eye' method combined an aesthetic concept of documentary (unstaged) film with an ideological attitude toward art in general."[225]

---

[223] Rob Edelman, "Vsevolod Pudovkin," THE INTERNATIONAL DICTIONARY OF FILMS AND FILMMAKERS: VOLUME II--DIRECTORS/FILMMAKERS, p.431.

[224] "Linkage: Pudovkin's Classics Revisited," pp.70-7.

[225] Petric, p.30.

THE MAN WITH THE MOVIE CAMERA/CHELOVEK'S KINOAPPARATOM (16mm: 1929, 93 mins., b/w, silent, R-BUD, EMG, KIT, MMA)

As the film itself explains, Vertov created the film as "an experiment in the cinematic communication of visible events, executed without the aid of intertitles, without a script, without theater, without sets and actors." In addition, as Vlada Petric points out, "It introduces numerous innovative stylistic features through its genuine montage structure, which challenges conventional narrative movies as well as traditional documentary filmmaking."[226] Often credited with inspiring the NOUVELLE VAGUE in the 1950s, this film shows Vertov's evolution from a documentary filmmaker to a cine-poet. Together with his brother, Mikhail Kaufman, as cinematographer, and his wife, Elizaveta Svilova, as editor, the screen pioneer investigates the relationship between film and reality. A matter-of-fact visual tour of Moscow becomes the basis for showing how editing and photography operate as moving pictures. The audience first sees a scene and then is shown how the filmmakers create the scene.[227]

HOLLYWOOD IN THE TWENTIES (1920-1927)

The ferment in film art created by the Scandinavian, German, and Soviet cinemas understandably attracted the attention of serious film artists in the West. But nowhere were there more dramatic changes in the combined art and industry of the movies than in Hollywood, the acknowledged motion picture capital of the world. There, as Giannetti and Eyman point out, "the population had grown from 5,000 [in 1910] to 36,000 in ten years, by 1930, it would be 157,000. Twenty Hollywood studios were churning out features and shorts for a weekly attendance of forty million people."[228] As discussed in Chapters 3, 5, and 6, producers, distributors, and exhibitors sensed the need to merge forces and reap great profits. Why not? Investments paid big dividends as the dawn of new advertising strategies ushered in an age of consumerism that gave America a sense of unparalleled prosperity. Self-confidence was every person's middle name. The independents who had once railed against the monopolistic ambitions of the conservative MPPA now sought to create an oligopoly of their own. The difference in strategy was that the MPPA had put its trust in production, while the new band of entrepreneurs put their trust in a "vertical" system of production, distribution, and exhibition.

At first, the changes were most evident in the 21,000 new theaters constructed by the mid-teens, the longer films, and the exorbitant salaries paid to the growing number of stars. Not surprisingly, most Americans assumed that a film company's success was linked inexorably to the company's star personalities. There were even performers who bought into that movie myth and invested in their own production companies, the most famous being United Artists with D. W. Griffith, Mary Pickford, Douglas Fairbanks, Sr., and Charlie Chaplin. How they discovered their mistake and what they did about it are discussed in Chapter 6. But clearly stars were not synonymous with corporate success. That is not to say that stars were not important commodities. They were, and their enormous salaries testify to that fact. But industry insiders knew that the real bosses were the money men who held sway in New York,

---

[226] CONSTRUCTIVISM IN FILM: THE MAN WITH A MOVIE CAMERA--A CINEMATIC ANALYSIS, p.viii.

[227] For more information, see Stephen Crofts and Olivia Rose, "An Essay Towards MAN WITH A MOVIE CAMERA," SCREEN 18:1 (Spring 1977):9-58; Dai Vaughan, "Great Films of the Century: The Man with the Movie Camera," FILMS AND FILMING 7:2 (November 1960):18-20, 43; and Herman G. Weinberg, "The Man With the Movie Camera," FILM COMMENT 4:1 (Fall 1966):40-2.

[228] Giannetti and Eyman, p.52.

not Hollywood. Moreover, Wall Street now began to invest heavily in the movie industry. As Robinson explains, "This was the period of the first of America's perennial 'Red Scares'; and it appears that Big Business saw the cinema not only as a potentially good investment, but also as an effective way to combat Bolshevism, through the sort of films which would unquestionably celebrate the American way of life."[229] To protect their investments and the "American way," the true heads of the film industry put their money into first-run movie houses, price discrimination schemes, zoning practices, a pattern of play dates, theater circuits, overseas distribution, and production facilities that mass-produced films according to formulas, rather than the unpredictable visions of artists.

Beginning in the post-WWI era, the rush for movie supremacy through the control of real estate and preferential treatment became the paramount features of the movies. For example, in 1920, the Cohns (Jack and Harry) and Joe Brandt established the C. B. C. Film Sales Company (the forerunner of Columbia Pictures, formed two years later),[230] while Adolph Zukor merged his considerable production and distribution holdings (Famous Players-Lasky, later Paramount) with the Balaban and Katz theater chain in Chicago to become by the mid-1920s the biggest film company in America. In 1924, Marcus Loew bought control of Metro Pictures to form MGM and thus guarantee films for his vast theater chain. The way these movie moguls functioned and the dream worlds they created have been described in pejorative novels by writers like F. Scott Fitzgerald, Budd Schulberg, and Nathanael West, and in films like MERTON OF THE MOVIES (1924, 1932, 1947), SHOW PEOPLE (1928), and SINGIN' IN THE RAIN (1952).

These were also the years that gave rise to the Film Booking Office of America (later to become Radio-Keith-Orpheum Corporation)[231] and to incredible revolutions with "talkies" through the efforts of Lee De Forest, Western Electric, the Radio Corporation of America, William Fox, and Warner Bros. This was the era in which Technicolor made dramatic advances in color processes.[232] This was also the decade during which Zukor's block-booking practices were declared illegal, and the Academy of Motion Picture Arts and Sciences was formed.

As a result of this industrial metamorphosis, the studio system was born and flourished until the mid-1950s. In simplified terms, movies now were mass-produced on an "assembly-like" basis. Executive producers like Irving Thalberg[233] (first at Universal and then at MGM) took control of filmmaking, so that by the mid-1920s directors, screenwriters, art designers, cinematographers, make-up artists, editors, and performers were relegated to standardized roles in front of and behind the camera. Artistic decisions were dictated less by issues of composition and acting and more by carefully planned shooting schedules and budgets designed to take advantage

---

[229]   THE HISTORY OF WORLD CINEMA, p.104.

[230]   For most of the background information on this period, see Chapters 3, 5, and 6. Three helpful articles for a brief overview are Christopher North, "Industry Highlights," FILMS IN REVIEW 19:10 (December 1968); 613-17; ___, "Film History for Exhibitors," ibid., 21:8 (October 1970):473-77; and Douglas Gomery, "Toward a History of Film Exhibition: The Case of the Picture Palace," CINEMA JOURNAL 14:2 (Winter 1974-75):17-26).

[231]   For a fine summary of RKO, see the 1987 BBC TV series, RKO: THE HOLLYWOOD YEARS.

[232]   For a good introduction to the conditions that led to the adaptation of color processes, see Gorham A. Kindem, "Hollywood's Conversion to Color: The Technological, Economic, and Aesthetic Factors," JOURNAL OF THE UNIVERSITY FILM ASSOCIATION 31:2 (Spring 1979):29-36.

[233]   For information on Thalberg, see Chapters 5 and 6.

of seasonal fluctuations at the box office. Lest anyone doubt the wisdom of this products-approach to moviemaking, it is worth remembering that Hollywood films of this era began their world dominance of more than seventy-five percent of all the theater screens around the globe.

By the mid-1920s, each of the major companies was turning out "A" feature films, "B" pictures, short subjects, animated cartoons, and newsreels, all geared to the needs of the organization's massive exhibition demands and the presumed desires of the mass audience. Although each studio had its own corporate image, they all relied on formula films to maximize profits and minimize risks. That is, the studios reduced film content to a set of simplified conventions that operated primarily through stereotypes. As discussed in Chapters 2 and 5, the secret of success was not only in satisfying audience expectations in regard to a particular formula's characters, plot, and values, but also in imbuing each stereotype with a certain inventiveness. Often that inventiveness was linked to a social consciousness related to issues like capital punishment, child abuse, mental illness, and poverty. "The extent to which a film seriously reflected social thought and examined specific social issues," explain Bohn and Stromgren, "depended on which of three kinds of social commentary it contained: incidental, gratuitous, or conscious."[234] As discussed in Chapter 2, these formulas included gangster films, westerns, "women's" films, problem pictures, sports movies, comedies, horror films, science fiction movies, war films, murder mysteries, and historical dramas. In fact, one of the few formulas not in vogue by the 1920s was the musical. The coming of sound would add that formula to the industrial film environment.

In many respects, the growth of the large studios and their insistence on tightly controlled film production led to the widespread assertion that film quality declined in Hollywood in the twenties. The reactions of the public in general and of screenwriters in particular are discussed in Chapters 3 and 5. While it is true that artists like D. W. Griffith, Robert Flaherty,[235] Freidrich W. Murnau, Victor Sjostrom, Mauritz Stiller, and Erich von Stroheim found it nearly impossible to exist as contract directors, it is also true that other artists like Allan Dwan, Henry King, Ernst Lubitsch, King Vidor,[236] and Raoul Walsh[237] succeeded. Moreover, the

---

[234] Bohn and Stromgren, p.107.

[235] For more information, see Hugh Gray, "Robert Flaherty and the Naturalist Documentary," HOLLYWOOD QUARTERLY 5:1 (Fall 1950):41-8; David Flaherty, "A Few Reminiscences," FILM CULTURE 20 (1959):14-6; F. W. Murnau and Robert J. Flaherty, "Turia, An Original Story," ibid., pp.17-26; ___, "TABU (TABOO), A Story of the South Seas," ibid., pp.27-38; Eric Barnouw, "Robert Flaherty (Barnouw's File)," ibid., 53-5 (Spring 1972):161-90; Frances Flaherty, "Flaherty's Quest for Life," FILMS AND FILMING 5:4 (January 1959):8; Helen Van Dongen, "Robert Flaherty, 1884-1951," FILM QUARTERLY 18:4 (Summer 1965):3-14; and Richard Corliss, "Robert Flaherty: The Man In the Iron Myth," FILM COMMENT 9:6 (November-December 1973):38-42.

[236] For more information, see George J. Mitchell, "King Vidor," FILMS IN REVIEW 15:3 March 1964):179-81; Charles Higham, "King Vidor," FILM HERITAGE 1:4 (Summer 1966):15-25; H. G. Luft, "A Career that Spans Half a Century," FILM JOURNAL 1:2 (Summer 1971):27-46; Joel Greenberg, "War, Wheat and Steel: King Vidor Interviewed," SIGHT AND SOUND 37:4 (Autumn 1968):192-7; "King Vidor at NYU," CINEASTE 1:4 (Spring 1968):2-8;; Raymond Durgnat, "King Vidor: Part 1," FILM COMMENT 9:4 (July-August 1973):10-49; ___, "King Vidor: Part 2," ibid., 9:5 (September-October 1973):16-51; Peter B. Flint, "Trailblazer and Rebel," NEW YORK TIMES B (November 2, 1982):8; and Andrew Sarris, "The Remembered Vitality of King Vidor," VILLAGE VOICE (December 7, 1982):51.

[237] For more information, see Harris Dienstfrey, "Hitch Your Genre to a Star," FILM

argument can be made that the stabilization of the industry made possible the money and the network that provided the audiences for the classic comedies of Charlie Chaplin, Buster Keaton,[238] Harold Lloyd,[239] and Harry Langdon.[238]

Other trends also crept ominously onto the scene in the early 1920s. The cynicism and disillusionment of the post-WWI era had created a backlash against Victorian values. American society funneled its bitterness into a mood of sensationalism and sexual freedom that became known as the "Jazz Age." Movie personalities were among the most visible exponents of ths "new morality." A number of Hollywood scandals related to sex, dope, rape, and murder drew widespread attention to the licentious and free-wheeling habits of the film colony. Reformers, politicians, and self-styled do-gooders began to attack the immorality and

---

CULTURE 34 (Fall 1964):35-7; Walter Conley, "Raoul Walsh--His Silent Films," THE SILENT PICTURE 9 (Winter 1970-71):2-18; Julian Fox, "Action All the Way," FILMS AND FILMING 19:9 (June 1973):32-40; ___, "Going Hollywood," ibid., 19:10 (July 1973):32-40; ___, "Hollow Victories," ibid., 19:11 (August 1973):32-40; Manny Farber, "Raoul Walsh: He Used to Be a Big Shot," SIGHT AND SOUND 44:1 (Winter 1974-75):42-4; "A Tribute to Raoul Walsh," THE UNIVERSITY OF CONNECTICUT FILM SOCIETY (Summer 1974):3-31; Roger McNiven, "The Western Landscape of Raoul Walsh," VELVET LIGHT TRAP 15 (Fall 1975):50-5; ___, "Raoul Walsh: 1887-1981," FILM COMMENT 17:4 (July-August 1981):77-9; and "Director Raoul Walsh to Be Buried in Simi Valley," THE HOLLYWOOD REPORTER (January 5, 1981):3.

[238]   For more information, see Christopher Bishop, "The Great Stone Face," FILM QUARTERLY 12:1 (Fall 1958):10-15; ___, "An Interview With Buster Keaton," ibid., pp.15-22; Arthur B. Friedman, "Buster Keaton: An Interview," ibid., 19:4 (Summer 1966):2-11; David Robinson, "Rediscovery: Buster," SIGHT AND SOUND 29:1 (Winter 1959):41-3; John Gillett and James Blue, "Keaton at Venice," ibid., 35:1 (Winter 1965/66):26-30; Penelope Houston, "The Great Blank Page," ibid., 37:2 (Spring 1968):63-7; Joseph McBride, "Running, Jumping and Standing Still," ibid., 42:2 (Spring 1973):79; Elliott Rubenstein, "Observations on Keaton's STEAMBOAT BILL," ibid., 44:4 (Autumn 1975):244-7; George Wead, "The Great Locomotive Chase," AMERICAN FILM 2:9 (July-August 1977):18-24; Jeremy Cott, "The Limits of Silent Comedy," LITERATURE/FILM QUARTERLY 3:2 (Spring 1975):99-107; William Everson, "Rediscovery: TOO HOT TO HANDLE," FILMS IN REVIEW 26:3 (March 1975):163-6, 178; Sylvain Du Pasquier, "Buster Keaton on Gags," ed. and trans. Norman Silverstein, JOURNAL OF MODERN LITERATURE 3:2 (April 1973):269-91; and Donald McCaffrey, "The Mutual Approval of Keaton and Lloyd," CINEMA JOURNAL 6 (1967):8-15.

[239]   Harold Lloyd, "The Funny Side of Life," FILMS AND FILMING 10:4 (January 1964):19-21; Arthur B. Friedman, "Interview With Harold Lloyd," FILM QUARTERLY 15:4 (Summer 1962):6-13; Bosley Crowther, "The Freshman," THE GREAT FILMS, pp.44-48; *Donald W. McCaffrey, 4 GREAT COMEDIANS: CHAPLIN, LLOYD, KEATON, LANGDON (New York: A. S. Barnes and Company, 1968), pp.60-83; Newson E. Garringer, "Harold Lloyd Made a Fortune by Combining Comedy and Thrills," FILMS IN REVIEW 13:7 (August-September 1962):407-22; Anthony Slide, "Harold Lloyd," THE SILENT PICTURE 11/12 (Summer-Autumn 1971):4-8; and Stuart Kaminsky, "Harold Lloyd: A Reassessment of His Comedy," ibid., 16 (Autumn 1972):21-9.

[240]   For more information, see Vernon L. Schonert, "Harry Langdon," FILMS IN REVIEW 18:8 (October 1967):470-85; George Geltzer, "Letters," ibid., 18:9 (November 1967):583; Dennis Gifford, "Letters," ibid., 18:10 (December 1967):656; Herman G. Weinberg, "The Weinberg Touch: Harry Langdon," ibid., 32:7 (August-September 1981):441; Richard Leary, "Capra and Langdon," FILM COMMENT 8:4 (November-December 1972):15-7; Penelope Gilliatt, "The Current Cinema: Langdon," THE NEW YORKER 47 (April 24, 1971):130-4; and Harold Truscott, "Harry Langdon," SILENT PICTURE 13 (Winter-Spring 1972):2-17.

unconventional life-style of the modern Sodom and Gomorrah. By 1921, no fewer than thirty-six censorship bills were pending in state legislatures and the Congress. Faced by growing public resentment and political interference, the predominantly Jewish movie tycoons hired the Gentile William Harrison Hays in January 1922 to act as their official spokesman through the newly created film self-regulation agency known as the Motion Picture Producers and Distributors Association of America (MPPDA).[241] His charge was to bring dignity to a film industry run by Jews and functioning in a society that detested "outsiders" who challenged traditional values and beliefs. For the next six years, the ex-Postmaster General of the U. S. worked to create a self-censorship system within the industry. The best result came in 1927 with the "Don'ts and Be Careful" Code.[242] Although the coming of sound and the Great Depression wrecked Hays's first efforts, he continued the battle throughout his remaining eighteen years in office. In the meantime, the MPPDA and eight key studios (MGM, Paramount, First National, Fox Film Corporation, Producers Distributing Corporation, Film Booking Office, Universal Pictures, and Warner Bros.) brought a measure of stability to the film industry.

But most important for motion picture audiences and critics, the 1920s were the greatest age of silent films. These were the brilliant years of stars and directors like Frank Borzage, Lon Chaney, Sr., Charles Chaplin,[243] Cecil B. DeMille, Douglas Fairbanks, Sr., Robert Flaherty, John Ford,[244] Greta Garbo, Lillian Gish, D. W.

---

[241] It is a striking coincidence that in a Jewish-dominated industry, every head of the MPPDA has been non-Jewish.

[242] See Appendices III and IV.

[243] For information on the films, articles, and books dealing with Chaplin, Gish, Griffith, and Fairbanks, see Chapter 6.

[244] For more information see "Legendary John Ford, 78, Dies; Personally Honored by U. S.," VARIETY (September 5, 1973):4, 20, 47; Roger Greenspun, "John Ford 1895-1973," NEW YORK TIMES D (September 9, 1973):15; David Sterritt, "John Ford: An Epic Half-Century of American Filmmaking," THE CHRISTIAN SCIENCE MONITOR (September 13, 1973):16; Peter Bogdanovich, "The Cowboy Hero and the American West . . . as Directed by John Ford," ESQUIRE (December 1983):417-25; Kirk Ellis, "On the Warpath: John Ford and the Indians," JOURNAL OF POPULAR FILM AND TELEVISION 8:2 (Summer 1980):34-41; Pierre Greenfield, "Print the Fact: For and Against the Films of John Ford," TAKE ONE 12:5 (November 1977):15-9; Michael Barkin, "Notes on the Art of John Ford," FILM CULTURE 25 (Summer 1962):9-12; Joseph McBride and Michael Wilmington, "The Civil War," FILM COMMENT 7:3 (Fall 1971):21-3; Martin Rubin, "Mr. Ford and Mr. Rogers: The Will Rogers Trilogy," ibid., 10:1 (January-February 1974):54-7; Tag Gallagher, "John Ford: Midway--The War Documentaries," ibid., 11:5 (September-October 1975):40-6; Michael Budd, "A Home in the Wilderness: Visual Imagery in John Ford's Westerns," CINEMA JOURNAL 16:1 (Fall 1976):62-75; William K. Everson, "Forgotten Ford," FOCUS ON FILM 6 (Spring 1971):13-9; Jeffrey Richards, "Ford's Lost World," ibid., pp.20-30; Mark Haggard, "Ford in Person," ibid., pp.31-7; Allen Eyles, "Ford in Print," ibid., pp.38-9; Rebecca Pulliam, "The Grapes of Wrath," VELVET LIGHT TRAP 2 (August 1971):3-7; Russell Campbell, "FORT APACHE," ibid., pp.8-12; Joseph McBride and Michael Wilmington, "The Wings of Eagles," ibid., pp.13-5; ___, "Sergeant Rutledge," pp.16-8; Richard Thompson, "Two Rode Together," ibid., pp.18-21; Nancy Schwartz, "The Role of Women in SEVEN WOMEN," ibid., pp.22-4; Ellen R. Belton, "Ceremonies of Innocence: Two Films by John Ford," ibid., 14 (Winter 1975):21-4; Michael Dempsey, "John Ford: A Reassessment," FILM QUARTERLY 28:4 (Summer 1975):2-15; David Coursen, "John Ford: Assessing the Reassessment," ibid., 29:3 (Spring 1976):58-60; Joseph McBride, "Drums Along the Mekong: I Love America, I am Apolitical," SIGHT AND SOUND 41:4 (Autumn 1972):213-6; ___,

Griffith, Buster Keaton, Harry Langdon, Harold Lloyd, Ernst Lubitsch, Tom Mix, Friedrich W. Murnau, Pola Negri, Victor Sjostrom, Mauritz Stiller, Gloria Swanson, Rudolph Valentino,[245] King Vidor, Josef von Sternberg,[246] Erich von Stroheim,[247] Raoul Walsh, and William Wellman.[248]

"Bringing in the Sheaves," ibid., 43:1 (Winter (1973-74):9-11; George Mitchell, "Ford on Ford," FILMS IN REVIEW 14:3 (March 1963):129-45; Kingsley Canham, "Old Master Re-Visited," FILMS AND FILMING 16:10 (July 1970):75-6; Douglas McVay, "The Five Worlds of John Ford," ibid., 8:9 (June 1962):14-7, 53; Fred Kaplan, "Vietnam! Vietnam!--An Exclusive Report on John Ford's Propaganda Documentary for the USIA," CINEASTE 7:3 (Fall 1976):20-3; H. Peter Stowell, "John Ford's Literary Sources: From Realism to Romance," LITERATURE/FILM QUARTERLY 5:2 (Spring 1977):164-73; Charles Silver, "The Apprenticeship of John Ford," AMERICAN FILM 1:7 (May 1976):62-7; Todd McCarthy, "John Ford and Monument Valley," ibid., 3:7 (May 1978):10-6; Jean Mitry, "The Birth of a Style," trans. William T. Conroy, Jr., WIDE ANGLE 2:4 (1978):4-7; William C. Siska, "Realism and Romance In the Films of John Ford," ibid., pp.8-13; Peter Lehman, "An Absence Which Becomes a Legendary Presence: John Ford's Structured Use of Off-Screen Space," ibid., pp.36-42; Marilyn Campbell, "The Quiet Man," ibid., pp.44-51; and Michael Budd, "Genre, Director and Stars in John Ford's Westerns: Fonda, Wayne, Stewart, and Widmark," ibid., 52-61. See also Peter Bogdanovich's 1972 documentary film DIRECTED BY JOHN FORD, available for rental from Films Incorporated and Texture Film and for sale from Texture Film; and Rita TheBerge, "Program Notes: DIRECTED BY JOHN FORD," CINEMATEXAS PROGRAM NOTES 12:2 (March 31, 1977):31-9.

[245] For more information, see Theodore Huff, "The Career of Rudolph Valentino," FILMS IN REVIEW 3:4 (April 1952):145-63; and H. L. Mencken, "On Hollywood--and Valentino," CINEMA JOURNAL 9:2 (Spring 1970):13-23.

[246] For more information, see Herman G. Weinberg, "The Legion of Lost Films, Part I," SIGHT AND SOUND 31:4 (Autumn 1962):173-4; ___, "Correspondence: Sternberg and Stroheim," ibid., 35:1 (Winter 1965-66):50-1; ___, "Josef Von Sternberg," FILM HERITAGE 1:2 (Winter 1965-66):13-7; F. A. Macklin, "Interview With Josef Von Sternberg," ibid., pp.3-11; Andrew Sarris, "Pantheon Directors," FILM CULTURE 28 (Spring 1963):9-10; Peter Bogdanovich, "Josef Von Sernberg," MOVIE 13 (Summer 1965):17-23; ___, "Encounters With Josef Von Sternberg," ibid., pp.24-5; O. O. Green, "Six Films of Josef Von Sternberg," ibid., pp.26-31; Don Willis, "Sternberg: The Context of Passion," SIGHT AND SOUND 47:2 (Spring 1978):104-9; Carole Zucker, "Some Observations on Sternberg and Dietrich," CINEMA JOURNAL 19:2 (Spring 1980):17-24; and Herbert G. Luft, "Josef Von Sternberg," FILMS IN REVIEW 32:1 (January 1981):1-16.

[247] Herman Weinberg has an important filmography on von Stroheim in the British Film Institute Index Series. See also William K. Everson, "The Career of Erich Von Stroheim 1885-1957," FILM IN REVIEW 8:7 (August/September 1957):305-14; Special Issue of FILM CULTURE devoted to Von Stroheim, 4:3 (18) (April 1958); Herman G. Weinberg, "The Legion of Lost Films: Part I," p.174; Dennis Marion, "Stroheim: The Legend and the Fact," ibid., 31:1 (Winter 1961-62):22-3, 51; and Jonathan Rosenbaum, "Second Thoughts on Stroheim," FILM COMMENT 10:3 (May-June 1974):6-13.

[248] For more information, see Andrew Sarris, "Fallen Idols," FILM CULTURE 28 (Spring 1963):33; Louise Brooks, "On Location With Billy Wellman," ibid., 53-5 (Spring 1972):145-61; Julian Fox, "A Man's World: An Analysis of the Films of William Wellman," FILMS AND FILMING 19:6 (March 1973):32-40; ___, "A Man's World: Concluding an Analysis of The Films of William Wellman," ibid., pp. 32-40; and S.

BOOKS

GENERAL

Barry, Iris. LET'S GO TO THE MOVIES. New York: Payson and Clarke, 1926. Illustrated. 293pp. New York: Arno Press, 1972.

A clever and amusing commentator on the silent films, Barry is particularly good at presenting useful comments on the feature films of the period. Well worth browsing.

Baxter, John. THE HOLLYWOOD EXILES. New York: Taplinger Publishing Company, 1976. Illustrated. 242pp.

An intriguing account of the European expatriates in Hollywood from the twenties to the fifties, this fast-moving chronicle describes how they were recruited, how they reacted to their new surroundings, and how they felt about the search for fame and fortune in America. Baxter first explains what Hollywood was in the early days and the reasons people home and abroad flocked to an area that contained a "fabulous machine . . . [that held] a secret that could change the world." He also does a first-rate job of setting the stage for the attitudes of the movie moguls that dominated the film industry for thirty years. For example, in talking about the early pioneers, Baxter points out the attitudes of the era: "'You know what I call a good invention?' said Thomas Alva Edison. 'Something so practical that even a little Polish Jew would buy it.' Notwithstanding this highly suspect claim to the invention of the motion picture, Edison, anti-Semitic like his friend Henry Ford, would not have appreciated the irony of a booming American film industry controlled by the kind of people he regarded as fit only to be its audience." The author then goes on to explain how a small group of European Jews did take over the movies and brought with them many relatives, friends, and personalities who shaped the image of American films. Among the many people discussed in the book's delightful twelve chapters are Charles Boyer, Bertolt Brecht, Marlene Dietrich, Greta Garbo, Emil Jannings, Stan Laurel, Ernst Lubitsch, Pola Negri, Max Reinhardt, and Karl Zuckmayer. Many lovely illustrations and a useful index are included. Recommended for special collections.

*Brownlow, Kevin, and John Kobal. HOLLYWOOD: THE PIONEERS. New York: Alfred A. Knopf, 1979. Illustrated. 272pp.

A companion piece to the wonderful thirteen-part Thames Television series HOLLYWOOD, this beautifully illustrated history contains 300 unique photographs that include stills, on-the-set shots, and portraits. Kobal has done a first-rate job in discovering pictures that are shown here for the first time in print. Brownlow's lucid and informative narrative and annotations effectively blend into this history of American silent films the recollections of performers, directors, technicians, producers, gossip columnists, and stunt men who participated in the development of the industry from the pioneering days at Fort Lee, New Jersey, through the Griffith years and the move westward, to the coming of sound. It's a pleasure from start to

---

Eyman and Allen Eyles, "'Wild Bill' William A. Wellman," FOCUS ON FILM 29 (March 1978):8-30; Russell Campbell, "Wild Bill's Wild Boys," THE VELVET LIGHT TRAP 15 (Fall 1975):1; Gillian Klein, "Wellman's WILD BOYS OF THE ROAD: The Rhetoric of a Depression Movie," ibid., pp.2-6; Greg Beal, "Program Notes: WILD BOYS OF THE ROAD," CINEMATEXAS PROGRAM NOTES 11:1 (September 8, 1976):31-9; ___, "Program Notes: BATLEGROUND," ibid., 11:2 (October 11, 1976):51-4; Jimmie L. Reeves, "Program Notes: A STAR IS BORN (1937)," ibid., 23:2 (October 12, 1982):1-6; Dan Ackerman, "Program Notes: THE STORY OF G. I. JOE," ibid., 10:3 (March 30, 1976):39-45; and A. Murphy, "Program Notes: BATTLEGROUND," ibid., 26:4 (April 12, 1984):53-64.

finish. An index is included. Recommended for special collections and for gifts to good friends.

Castle, Charles. OLIVER MESSEL: A BIOGRAPHY. Foreword Sir John Gielgud. London: Thames and Hudson, 1986. Illustrated. 264pp.

Mayer, Arthur. MERELY COLOSSAL: THE STORY OF THE MOVIES FROM THE LONG CHASE TO THE CHAISE LOUNGE. New York: Simon and Schuster, 1953. Illustrated. 264pp.
    This marvelous man began his film career as a salesman for Samuel Goldwyn, produced copy for Mae West's publicity campaigns, wrote material to advertise Marlene Dietrich, operated a second-hand film theater on Broadway, and became one of the best film teachers. This book, often unreliable on factual matters, is a delightful source of anecdotes on the greats of Hollywood and has some wonderful material on the 1920s. Well worth browsing.

Petrie, Graham. HOLLYWOOD DESTINIES: EUROPEAN DIRECTORS IN AMERICA, 1922-1931. London: Routledge & Kegan Paul, 1985. Illustrated. 257pp.

*Prevots, Naima. DANCING IN THE SUN: HOLLYWOOD CHOREOGRAPHERS, 1915-1937. Ann Arbor: UMI Press, 1987. Illustrated. 281pp.

*Robinson, David. HOLLYWOOD IN THE TWENTIES. New York: A. S. Barnes and Company, 1968. Illustrated. 176pp.
    This tightly written and highly useful account of the 1920s is a good introduction to film production, distribution, and exhibition at the end of the silent era. In nine fact-packed chapters, Robinson presents a provocative, entertaining, and nostalgic overview of the important stars and the memorable films, lacing his narrative with perceptive and stimulating observations. Major objections are the poor quality of the stills and their almost negligible use. An index is included. Well worth browsing.

*Seldes, Gilbert. THE SEVEN LIVELY ARTS. New York: A. S. Barnes and Company, 1957. 306pp.
    This entertaining book, first published in 1924, was brought up to date in the 1957 edition. Its major chapters on film deal with Keystone, Chaplin, and the film tycoons. Readers should also look at Seldes's related comments on comic strips, musical comedy, vaudeville, radio, popular music, and the dance. Well worth browsing.

Walker, Joseph, and Juanita Walker. THE LIGHT ON HER FACE. Hollywood: The ASC Press, 1984. Illustrated. 290pp.

FILM COMEDY

*Durgnat, Raymond. THE CRAZY MIRROR: HOLLYWOOD COMEDY AND THE AMERICAN IMAGE. New York: Horizon Press, 1970. Illustrated. 280pp.
    Stressing that movies present an illuminating, although distorted, picture of the age in which they are made, Durgnat offers an unconventional and thought-provoking analysis of the great American comics. Five major sections collectively containing forty-two chapters offer a chronological exploration of film nostalgia, social history,

and movie criticism. What makes Durgnat's discussions so entertaining is his ability to draw on a vast number of films with widely differing forms of comic invention. Endnotes, a bibliography, and an index of comedy films are included. Recommended for special collections.

Halliwell, Leslie. DOUBLE TAKE AND FADE AWAY: HALLIWELL ON COMEDIANS. London: Grafton Books, 1987. Illustrated. 322pp.

*Kerr, Walter. THE SILENT CLOWNS. New York: Alfred A. Knopf, 1975. Illustrated. 373pp.

A beautifully illustrated and provocative study by someone who loves the stage more than he admires films, this intriguing analysis relies heavily on previously published works and maintains a somewhat patronizing tone in its discussions about the course of film history. For example, Kerr writes, "Though I shifted my own allegiance to the legitimate theater when I was in my early twenties--ironically, the coming of sound may have had something to do with that shift, leading me from words to more and better words--I did for a long time have a nostalgic pull toward certain quivering memories of my youth."

On the positive side, the author presents an important reminder of the growth of film comedy from the early Arbuckle, Linder, and Sennett days, to the age of the immortals like Chaplin, Keaton, Lloyd, Langdon, and Laurel and Hardy. Kerr's intelligent reflections not only stir memories but also ruffle standard interpretations of what these artists meant to the history of film. Kerr's greatest contributions are his astute observations showing the crucial role that stage traditions played in the evolution of great film comedy and comedians.

On the negative side, there is the author's irritating smugness as he condescendingly discusses film artists and their gropings in the new medium. In talking about Lloyd's brand of comedy, for example, Kerr writes, "Sympathy by default, or refraction, is rather primitive gamesmanship; but it does its own small share of the film's emotional work and, surprisingly, seems an inoffensive tactic--belonging to the period--when the films are looked at again today." More significantly, as Andrew Sarris observes, authors--e.g., James Agee, Rudi Blesh, Kevin Brownlow, William K. Everson, and Andrew Sarris--are cited in anecdotal terms rather than as scholarly sources.[249] And even overlooking the lack of suitable citations, there is the question of Kerr's grasp of what he professes to review in the films themselves.[250]

Given the wit and wisdom of the author, this book merits a close reading and serious consideration in the study of silent film comedy. An index is included, but no bibliography. Well worth browsing.

Lahue, Kalton C., and Sam Gill. CLOWN PRINCES AND COURT JESTERS: SOME GREAT COMICS OF THE SILENT SCREEN. South Brunswick: A. S. Barnes and Company, 1970. Illustrated. 406pp.

A brief summary of the lives and careers of fifty comics and comediennes, this botched undertaking suffers from its sentimental prose and its questionable judgments. A case in point is the authors' uncharitable evaluation of Arbuckle's troubles in the 1920s: "To be sure, Arbuckle's situation was of his own making. Not

---

[249] Andrew Sarris, "Why THE SILENT CLOWNS Isn't All That Original," VILLAGE VOICE (March 8, 1976):98.

[250] For negative reactions to Kerr's comments on Keaton, see *Daniel Moews, KEATON: THE SILENT FILMS CLOSE UP (Berkeley: University of California Press, 1977), pp.319-21.

one who matured early and took life in its stride, Fatty's success had clashed with his immaturity. His was a life of excess--too much food, too much drink and too many women. Four years before, one of his parties in Boston had cost the studio well over $100,000 to hush up. It was almost a dress rehearsal for the San Francisco event in 1921." The best parts of the book are the numerous illustrations. No bibliography or index are included. Approach with caution.

*Mast, Gerald. THE COMIC MIND: COMEDY AND THE MOVIES. Indianapolis: The Bobbs-Merrill Company, 1973. Illustrated. 353pp.
    "It is a cliche," Mast explains at the start of this valuable analysis of film comedy, "that clowns cry; it has rarely been admitted that they might also think. This book examines a specific breed of clown--the one who translated comedy into cinematic terms--and tries both to establish that he did think and to indicate how." The author divides his material into five main sections: (1) "Assumptions, Definitions, and Categories;" (2) "Primitives"; (3) "Chaplin and Keaton"; (4) "Other Silent Clowns"; and (5) "Sound Comedy."Although the talkies get short shrift in the evolution of screen comedy, Mast does a first-rate job in broadening our understanding of what the silent era contributed to modern film comedy. The writing is clear, entertaining, and informative. A bibliography and index are included. Recommended for special collections.

*McCaffrey, Donald W. 4 GREAT COMEDIANS: CHAPLIN, LLOYD, KEATON, AND LANGDON. New York: A. S. Barnes and Company, 1968. Illustrated. 175pp.
    This is one of the most refreshing and original studies in modern film scholarship. In his re-evaluation of the great silent clowns, McCaffrey focuses on the shorts and great features of the early days of comedy. His close reading of the films introduces new insights into the comedians' techniques and styles, showing how they developed their art over a period of years. A useful bibliography is included, but no index. Recommended for special collections.

Manchel, Frank. YESTERDAY'S CLOWNS: THE RISE OF FILM COMEDY. New York: Franklin Watts, 1973. Illustrated. 154pp.
    "This, as the author explains in his prefatory note, is not a complete history of film comedy but a survey of its beginnings and the great stars and directors. The text includes biographical information, discussion of techniques and of individual films, and critical comments on comedians' and comediennes' styles. The writing style is casual and smooth, the photographs delectable. A list of selected readings and a relative index are included."[251]

*Robinson, David. THE GREAT FUNNIES: A HISTORY OF FILM COMEDY. New York: E. P. Dutton and Company, 1969. Illustrated. 160pp.
    This is a very brief pictorial history of the great movie comics, with a lovely selection of stills. Robinson does a good job of reviewing seventy years of film laughter, while highlighting, through pictures, the best of the screen personalities. The writing is crisp, descriptive, and evaluative. An index is included, but no bibliography. Well worth browsing.

---

[251] Book Review: YESTERDAY'S CLOWNS: THE RISE OF FILM COMEDY," BULLETIN OF THE CENTER FOR CHILDREN'S BOOKS (December 1973):68.

MARY ASTOR

*Astor, Mary. A LIFE ON FILM. New York: Dell, 1972. Illustrated. 245pp.

*Astor, Mary. MY STORY: AN AUTOBIOGRAPHY. Garden City: Doubleday and Company, 1959. Illustrated. 332pp.

CLARA BOW

Morella, Joe, and Edward Z. Epstein. THE "IT" GIRL: THE INCREDIBLE STORY OF CLARA BOW. New York: Delacorte Press, 1976. Illustrated. 284pp.

Stenn, David. CLARA BOW: RUNNIN' WILD. New York: Doubleday, 1988. Illustrated. 338pp.

LON CHANEY

Anderson, Robert G. FACES, FORMS, FILMS: THE ARTISTRY OF LON CHANEY. New York: A. S. Barnes and Company, 1971. Illustrated. 216pp.

Riley, Philip J. LONDON AFTER MIDNIGHT: A RECONSTRUCTION. New York: Cornwall Books, 1985. Illustrated. 178pp.

RONALD COLMAN

Colman, Juliet Benita. RONALD COLMAN: A VERY PRIVATE PERSON. New York: William Morrow and Company, 1975. Illustrated. 294pp.

*Quirk, Lawrence J. THE FILMS OF RONALD COLMAN. Secaucus: The Citadel Press, 1977. Illustrated. 255pp.

JACKIE COOPER

*Cooper, Jackie, and Dick Kleiner. PLEASE DON'T SHOOT MY DOG: THE AUTOBIOGRAPHY OF JACKIE COOPER. New York: William Morrow and Company, 1981. Illustrated. 351pp.

CECIL B. DEMILLE

DeMille, Cecil B.. THE AUTOBIOGRAPHY OF CECIL B. DEMILLE. Ed. Donald Hayne. Englewood Cliffs: Prentice-Hall, 1959. Illustrated. 465pp.
     This posthumously published account is a nostalgic, enjoyable, and discursive reminder of one of the most controversial men in film history. Despite consistent charges by many film historians that the supreme showman's movies were "superficial," "meretricious," and "pretentious," there are few critics who would deny that DeMille's style and content in his seventy films made over a forty-six-year career became synonymous with Hollywood's sumptuous production values. No one ever knew better than DeMille how to craft a popular historical and spectacular movie. Moreover,

he was, bar none, the most influential producer-director in the film industry during the twenties.

Although he sometimes takes undeserved credit in this book for several firsts in film technique--e.g., "Rembrandt lighting," which Griffith and Bitzer had developed before him--DeMille presents a candid description of his commercial commitment to box-office popularity. Clearly, his meticulous attention to fashion details in his films influenced not only the craftmanship of his peers, but also affected the world of fashion design and interior decorators. The book also includes some excellent stills.[252] A filmography and index are included. Well worth browsing.

DeMille, William C. HOLLYWOOD SAGA. New York: E. P. Dutton, 1939. Illustrated. 319pp.

Cecil's older brother gives a reflective and witty account of the film wars from the days of the Triangle Film Corporation, to the end of the 1930s. He also has some insightful comments on his brother's production methods and temperament. Well worth browsing.

Essoe, Gabe and Raymond Lee. DEMILLE: THE MAN AND HIS PICTURES. New York: A. S. Barnes and Company, 1970. Illustrated. 319pp.

This poorly produced pictorial survey combined with a brief and choppy biographical narrative is a weak addition to the growing body of information on the most popular director of the 1920s. What emerges is a fuzzy sense of DeMille's visual gifts and his flair for capturing the morality of the twenties. The most important part is by Charles Bickford, Charlton Heston, and Henry Wilcox on their reactions to DeMille. A filmography is included but no bibliography or index. Approach with caution.

*Higham, Charles. CECIL B. DEMILLE. New York: Charles Scribner's Sons, 1973. Illustrated. 335pp.

Benefiting considerably from the full cooperation of DeMille's daughter Cecilia (Mrs. Joseph Harper), the author utilizes the vast amount of information made available to him to provide additional insights into the famous producer-director's films. At the same time, Higham offers wonderful summary observations about the man's strengths and weaknesses: "Life, for him, was an immense test of Christian patience and endurance, which he sustained with true heroism. The public saw him as a consistently successful, entertainingly egotistical film tycoon; the critics as a shrewd and arrogant vulgarian." What Higham offers us is a valuable portrait of an artist far more complex than anyone acknowledged. Regrettably, the author ignores citing his sources or providing bibliographical material to verify the numerous new anecdotes about DeMille, his movies, and the events that surrounded them. A filmography and an index are included. Well worth browsing.

*Ringgold, Gene, and DeWitt Bodeen. THE FILMS OF CECIL B. DEMILLE. New York: The Citadel Press, 1969. Illustrated. 377pp.

---

[252] For other perspectives, see Joseph and Harry Feldman, "Cecil B. DeMille's Virtues," FILMS IN REVIEW 1:9 (December 1950):106; Cecil B. DeMille, "After 70 Pictures," ibid., 7:3 (March 1956):97-102; Art Arthur, "C. B. DeMille's Human Side," ibid., 23:4 (April 1967):221-25; and DeWitt Bodeen, "Cecil B. DeMille: August 12, 1881-January 21, 1959," ibid., 32:7 (August/September 1981):385-97.

This is one of the outstanding picture collections about screen personalities and their movies. The valuable analysis does a fine job of highlighting DeMille's gift for Biblical spectacles and exotic domestic comedies. Not only do Ringgold and Bodeen skillfully illustrate the wide range of cinematic interests that the filmmaker pursued from his first film, THE SQUAW MAN (1913), to his last movie, THE BUCCANEER (1959), but they also provide a flavor of the times by including several contemporary reviews. The stills are well-chosen, many are new to publication, the comments and credits are accurate, and the narrative is helpful in moving from film to film. A concluding chapter summarizes DeMille's nearly twenty-year role (June 1, 1936-January 22, 1945) as the host of the "Lux Radio Theatre." Regrettably, no bibliography or index is provided. Recommended for special collections.

ROBERT J. FLAHERTY

*Barsam. Richard. THE VISION OF ROBERT FLAHERTY: THE ARTIST AS MYTH AND FILMMAKER. Bloomington: Indiana University Press, 1988. Illustrated. 144pp.

Calder-Marshall, Arthur. THE INNOCENT EYE: THE LIFE OF ROBERT J. FLAHERTY. New York: Harcourt, Brace and World, 1963. Illustrated. 304pp.
This book is a descriptive approach to Flaherty's life, undertaken with the support of the famous director's widow. Calder-Marshall's early chapters present a sober, detailed, and objective account of Flaherty's experiences as an explorer in the Canadian arctic. Later chapters provide a good understanding of the irregular work habits of the father of the documentary film, his extravagance, and his marvelous talent. Much of the research in the biography was originally done by Paul Rotha and Basil Wright as a tribute to Flaherty, but his unexpected death in 1951 cut short their research and resulted in an unedited manuscript available either at the Museum of Modern Art or Columbia University's Butler Library. Calder-Marshall took only what he wanted from that version of the Rotha-Wright material and specifically omitted the critical reactions to Flaherty's films. The acts of omission are most conspicuous in the film discussions and in the highly selective bibliography. Five appendexes offer synopses of Flaherty's major works: NANOOK OF THE NORTH (1920), MOANA (1926), MAN OF ARAN (1934), THE LAND (1941), and LOUISIANA STORY (1948). A filmography is also included. Well worth browsing.,

Flaherty, Frances Hubbard. THE ODYSSEY OF A FILM-MAKER: ROBERT FLAHERTY'S STORY. Urbana: Beta Phi Mu, 1960. New York: Arno Press, 1972. Illustrated. 45pp.
This lovingly told biography by Flaherty's wife is a brief, very readable, and beautifully produced book. Although it is not very informative, the illustrations and the narrative are a tender reminder of a great artist. Worth browsing.

Griffith, Richard. THE WORLD OF ROBERT FLAHERTY. New York: Duell, Sloan and Pearce, 1953. Illustrated. 165pp.
One of the best sources of material on the great pioneer documentary filmmaker, many of the excerpts are taken from his letters, journals, and diaries. Griffith, a close friend of the Flahertys, makes certain to emphasize the positive rather than the negative and thus slants the book more toward an affectionate anthology than an in-depth study. Nonetheless, there are many useful items provided, including some informative remarks by Flaherty's wife, Frances, and friend Pat Mullen. It is important, however, to stress that this book is more a potpourri of assorted data than a scholarly examination. No index is included. Well worth browsing.

Murphy, William T. ROBERT FLAHERTY: A GUIDE TO REFERENCES AND RESOURCES. Boston: G. K. Hall and Company, 1978. 171pp.

This invaluable review of Flaherty's films, career, and critical reception maintains the high standards demonstrated by other works in this important reference series. "The biographical narrative," Murphy explains, "describes the major events in Flaherty's life as they influenced the production and content of his films. To judge the films alone on face value and not understand the circumstances in which they were made is to ignore a great deal about the continuity of Flaherty's creative processes." In describing the nature of the critical section, Murphy points out, "It is in criticism rather than in biography that the foreign language material was able to enrich the discussion. Above all, the criticism section focuses on Flaherty's relationship to the documentary and especially to John Grierson whose writings have formed the foundations of documentary film as it is known today." Along with nearly 300 annotated citations written by critics of Flaherty, there are more than fifty citations describing the writings by the filmmaker himself. The film synopses reflect Murphy's enthusiasm for the project. A list of archival sources and film distributors is included, as well as an author index and a film title index. Recommended for special collections.

Rotha, Paul. ROBERT J. FLAHERTY: A BIOGRAPHY. Ed. Jay Ruby. Philadelphia: University of Pennsylvania Press, 1983. Illustrated. 359pp.
    Ruby has done a wonderful job in bringing the 1959 Rotha-Wright manuscript to publication. "I have prepared this edition of the biography," the editor explains, "by comparing the edited manuscript that Rotha deposited in the John Grierson Archive, University of Sterling, Scotland, with the unedited draft from the Flaherty Papers [housed in Columbia University's Butler Library]. I have tried to adhere as closely as possible to what I believe Rotha intended. I have not updated the study in any significant way even though it was written more than twenty years ago. The value of this book is the chance it gives readers to understand the life and work of an American film pioneer from the viewpoint of a leader of the British documentary film movement who knew Flaherty for a major part of his professional life. The work has an integrity of opinion which would be disturbed by footnoting the text with recent material." For those who want a more current perspective, Ruby strongly recommends consulting Murphy's valuable 1978 reference work. He also points out that his book should be seen in two historical contexts: "First, it is about a figure who has attracted attention both for the films he made and for the life he led. Second, the book was authored more than twenty years ago by a prime mover in the British film world." Copious endnotes by John Goldman, a bibliography, and an index are included. Recommended for special collections.

JOHN FORD

*Anderson, Lindsay. ABOUT JOHN FORD. New York: McGraw-Hill Company, 1981. Illustrated. 256pp.
    "Sean Aloysius O'Feeney [John Ford, who was] born in Portland, Maine, on February 1st, 1895, died in Palm Desert, California, on August 31st, 1973," the author he observes; "was always a most contrary character." Anderson describes Ford as "Aggressive and defensive in about equal measure," and adds that "he was gentle and irascible, bloody-minded and generous, courageous, uncompromising and endlessly evasive. He could be kind and he could be cruel. He was an artist, strictly professional, obstinately personal, with a profound sense of family, community and nation. He was fiercely anarchic. Very often he drank too much, but it rarely interfered with his work. He was probably the greatest director working in the world's richest film making tradition, and at one time he was the most successful." What follows is an enthusiastic record of Anderson's many meetings with Ford, beginning in 1951 when Anderson was a young artist, and concluding with their last get-together in 1973, shortly before Ford's death. In addition, there is a valuable section dealing with letters about Ford, written by actors (e.g., Harry Carey, Jr.,

John Carradine, Henry Fonda, and Mary Astor) and screenwriters (e.g., Dudley Nichols, Frank S. Nugent, and Nunnally Johnson). Throughout the highly entertaining and informative book, one also gets a good overview of Ford's films and the critical reactions they received. A filmography and index are included. Recommended for special collections.

*Baxter, John. THE CINEMA OF JOHN FORD. New York: A. S. Barnes and Company, 1971. Illustrated. 176pp.

In this unusual study, Baxter points out that Ford's "films, in their force, popular appeal and exploitation of the medium's resources are outstanding popular art, while their intricate moral structure and insight into the relationship of man and environment make them central to any understanding of American ideals." The author offers a highly debatable interpretation of how Ford broke the standard rules applied to formula films, yet united all of his 112 feature films with his unique personality. Moreover, Baxter argues that Ford's brand of "realism" bears little resemblance to what is generally described as realism--"historical accuracy, fidelity to agreed rules of human behavior, rejection of irrelevant theatrical devices." Interestingly, he tells us more about who Ford was and what he represented through negative than through positive statements. That is, "Ford is not primarily sentimental, simple, an action director, nor especially American; his interest in character and morality dictates his choice of plots and locales more than any nationalistic beliefs . . . He is not an uncomplicated story-teller; suppression of narrative is part of his style, since it accentuates the flow of daily events and emphasizes history at the expense of the individual life." Thirteen reflective and analytical chapters present fresh and imaginative approaches to Ford's films from the early silents beginning in 1917, to his last movie, SEVEN WOMEN, in 1966. Among the topics discussed are the importance of Ford's Catholicism and his Irish heritage, the role of natural settings in symbolizing themes, the role of the family as a basic Ford metaphor, and the function of aging heroes in later Ford movies. A terse filmography and bibliography are provided, but no index. Well worth browsing.

*Bogdanovich, Peter. JOHN FORD. Berkeley: University of California Press, 1968. Illustrated. 144pp.

Mixing a taped interview format with a historical overview, this affectionate and laudatory book offers a good introduction to the mood and thoughts of Ford in the mid-1960s as he reflected on his career and life. Bogdanovich begins with a decription of the atmosphere on the set of CHEYENNE AUTUMN (1964), pointing out the importance of music in Ford's directorial style and the reverential treatment of the cast toward their extraordinary director. The author frequently interweaves his observations on a particular scene with comments about Ford's methods or behavior as interpreted by a screenwriter, cameraman, or actor. Most of the book concerns Ford's own observations on his films. The remaining sections set the stage for the perceptive analysis. A fine filmography is included, but no bibliography or index. Well worth browsing.

Ford, Dan. PAPPY: THE LIFE OF JOHN FORD. Englewood Cliffs: Prentice-Hall, 1979. Illustrated. 324pp.

Written by the director's grandson, this intelligent biography makes excellent use of Ford's professional and personal papers, as well as the author's own close ties with relatives and friends who knew his complex, crusty, and brilliant grandfather. The focus of the twenty-two anecdotal chapters is on intimate recollections of the remarkable man over his seventy-eight-year life. While there are many references to Ford's major films, the discussions center on the director's strengths and weaknesses, his treatment of various personalities, and his legendary escapades. The writing is clear, entertaining, and very informative.   "Scholarly assessments of my grandfather's career," Ford comments, "I leave to more qualified students of film history. From the outset, it was my intention to concentrate on the personal, family, and professional aspects of the life of John Ford." An index is included. Well worth browsing.

*French, Warren. FILMGUIDE TO "THE GRAPES OF WRATH." Bloomington: Indiana University Press, 1973. 87pp.

Pointing out that THE GRAPES OF WRATH (1940) was an exploitation film made to capitalize quickly on the popularity of the book, French offers a detailed discussion of the film, its contributors, and the critical reaction the Darryl Zanuck-John Ford production received. The writing is crisp, analytical, and perceptive. Worth noting is that this was the first in the valuable FILMGUIDE series and set the format--i.e., credits, outline, critique of the director and the production, analysis, and summary critique--for the guides that followed. As in later editions, there is a filmography, bibliography, list of rental sources, and an appendix comparing the novel, screenplay, and film. Regrettably, there is no index. Well worth browsing.

*McBride, Joseph, and Michael Wilmington. JOHN FORD. New York: Da Capo Press, 1975. Illustrated. 234pp.

A recasting of the authors' insights from earlier articles, this noteworthy publication begins with a description of McBride's emotions and reactions to Ford's death and burial during the summer of 1973. A surprising amount of time is devoted to discussing the director's gratitude for President Nixon's appearance at the 1973 American Film Institute's Lifetime Achievement ceremonies honoring Ford and to presenting the subsequent phone conversations with the president. In addition to an interview with Ford, the remaining eight chapters analyze thematically fourteen of the director's major films: e.g., "The Noble Outlaw"--STRAIGHT SHOOTING (1917), STAGECOACH (1939), WAGON MASTER (1950), "Men at War"--THEY WERE EXPENDABLE (1945), MY DARLING CLEMENTINE (1946), FORT APACHE (1948); "Ireland"--THE QUIET MAN (1952), THE RISING OF THE MOON (1957); and "What Really Happened"--SERGEANT RUTLEDGE (1960), THE MAN WHO SHOT LIBERTY VALANCE (1962), THE CIVIL WAR (episode in HOW THE WEST WAS WON) (1962). Especially valuable are the authors' comments on what Ford owed to other directors' work.   A filmography and bibliography are included, but no index. Recommended for special collections.[253]

*Place, J. A. THE WESTERN FILMS OF JOHN FORD. Secaucus: Citadel Press, 1974. Illustrated. 247pp.

An uneven theoretical discussion of Ford's westerns, presumably adapted from PLace's 1973 master's thesis at UCLA, this profusely illustrated book would be much more enjoyable if the comments were as plentiful as the pictures. The author claims that the book's purpose "is to examine the emotions Ford creates in his Westerns." Instead of developing that intriguing perspective in thought-provoking analyses, the author tantalizes us with insightful assertions but then relies primarily on the feelings stirred by the pictures to do the work of the narrative. There is also a problem with picture selections, in that they seem a potpourri of what's available, rather than what is appropriate to Place's interpretations. Regrettably, no index or bibliography is included. Worth browsing.

---

[253]   For a valuable review of this book, as well as of the Place and Sarris works on Ford, see Roger Greenspun, "Books," FILM COMMENT 12:6 (November-December 1976):58-61.

*Place, J. A. THE NON-WESTERN FILMS OF JOHN FORD. Secaucus: The Citadel Press, 1979. Illustrated. 287pp.

Stronger than Place's study on Ford's Westerns, this interesting publication strikes a good balance between commentary and visuals. The study itself, originally done as Place's doctoral dissertation at the University of California-Santa Cruz, is filled with stimulating perspectives about five film categories in which Ford excelled: e.g., Americana films, war films, Irish films, action films, and "foreign" films. The last category refers to movies like ARROWSMITH (1931), MARY OF SCOTLAND (1936), THE LONG VOYAGE HOME (1940), and MOGAMBO (1953). Each of the thirty-nine film analyses includes complete cast and technical credits, a plot synopsis, and critical commentaries. Regrettably, no index or bibliography is included. Well worth browsing.

Sarris, Andrew. THE JOHN FORD MOVIE MYSTERY. Bloomington: Indiana University Press, 1975. Illustrated. 192pp.

A controversial examination of Ford's films from SHOOTING STRAIGHT (1917) to SEVEN WOMEN (1966), this analytic study is divided into four major sections: "Early Days," "1930-1939: The Storyteller," "1940-1947: The Poet-Laureate," and "1948-1966: The Poet and Rememberer of Things Past." The opening section on Ford's beginnings offers a good commentary on previous scholarship, pointing out why the director has remained an enigma for so long. "Ford was a man of images rather than a man of Letters," Sarris observes, "and it was thus unlikely that he would explain himself adequately in literary-psychological terms." The critic then proceeds in methodical fashion to discuss Ford's film career, noting along the way what various commentators have said about specific films and where they were on target or missed the mark. Comparisons are also made between the director's films, the performances of numerous Ford stock players, and the different stages in Ford's career. Except for the poor selection of stills, this is the best overview of Ford's work and a must for anyone interested in the director's art. A filmography and bibliography are included, but no index. Recommended for special collections.[254]

*Sinclair, Andrew. JOHN FORD: A BIOGRAPHY. New York: Frederick Ungar Publishing Company, 1984. Illustrated. 305pp.

A curious account of Ford's personal and professional life, this tribute, written by a filmmaker who admired the legendary director, is filled with private accounts of a man who was a spy in World War I, a naval intelligence officer in World War II, and a noted despot on his film sets. The emphasis is on showing how Ford epitomized traditional values and used the movies to champion the "American way." While one admires the author's respect for Ford's patriotism, it is somewhat disconcerting to see the director's artistic style and recurring conventions glossed over in order to hammer home Ford's perennial comments: "I come from a family of peasants. They came here and got an education. They served this country well. I love America. I am not political." Twenty-one anecdotal chapters review the familiar pattern of Ford's life while adding very few fresh insights into his films or thoughts. An excellent filmography and extensive index are included. Worth browsing.

*Stowell, Peter. JOHN FORD. Boston: Twayne Publishers, 1986. Illustrated. 168pp.

---

[254] For another perspective, see William C. Siska, "Book Review: THE JOHN FORD MOVIE MYSTERY," JOURNAL OF THE UNIVERSITY FILM ASSOCIATION 30:1 (Winter 1978):37-8.

[255] For other perspectives, see Philip French, "Book Review: JOHN FORD," SIGHT AND SOUND 49:1 (Winter 1979-1980):59-60; and Todd McCarthy, "Dark Aspects of John Ford Go Unlighted In Sinclair's Biog," VARIETY (May 3, 1979):24.

Rather than taking a broad look at Ford's legendary career, Stowell focuses on fourteen of the director's talking films released between 1933 and 1962. The purpose is to discuss Ford's role in shaping and influencing five American myths connected with the overall mythology of the American frontier: the American Adam--Will Rogers, the American frontier--STAGECOACH, YOUNG MR. LINCOLN, and DRUMS ALONG THE MOHAWK (all in 1939), American agrarianism--THE GRAPES OF WRATH (1940) and TOBACCO ROAD (1941), American individualism--FORT APACHE (1948), SHE WORE A YELLOW RIBBON (1949), and RIO GRANDE (1950), and American civilization--MY DARLING CLEMENTINE (1946) and THE MAN WHO SHOT LIBERTY VALANCE (1962). Two concluding chapters discuss narrative structure in STAGECOACH and THE SEARCHERS (1956) and the relationship among the American Dream, the myths, and Jeffersonian democracy. The author concludes that "Ford's films express a deep ambivalence with respect to change and stability, past and future, freedom and restriction, individualism and community, wilderness and civilization. These tensions cannot be resolved. Only mediation was acceptable, a mediation that was an uneasy alliance held together by the mythic hero. This ambivalence extended to Ford's liberal and conservative ideology. However, on some issues he had no such qualms. He always favored agrarianism over industrialism, equality over class, the West over the East, empiricism over legalism, and experience over knowledge. To this extent we may describe Ford's ideology as falling within the broad parameters of liberal Jeffersonian democracy." Endnotes, bibliography, filmography, and index are included. Well worth browsing.

GRETA GARBO

Bainbridge, John. GARBO. Garden City: Doubleday, 1955. Illustrated.   256pp.

*Conway, Michael, et. al. THE FILMS OF GRETA GARBO. New York: Bonanza Books, 1963. Illustrated. 155pp.

Sands, Frederick, and Sven Broman. THE DIVINE GARBO. New York: Grosset, 1979. Illustrated. 243pp.

Walker, Alexander. GARBO: A PORTRAIT. New York: Macmillan Company, 1980. Illustrated. 191pp.

Zierold, Norman. GARBO. New York: Stein and Day, 1969. Illustrated.   196pp.

JOHN GILBERT

*Fountain, Leatrice Gilbert, and John R. Maxim. DARK STAR. Introduction Garsin Kanin. New York: St. Martin's Press, 1985. Illustrated. 287pp.

WILLIAM S. HART

Hart, William S. MY LIFE EAST AND WEST. New York: Benjamin Blom, 1968. Illustrated. 346pp.
    Originally published in 1929, this flowery autobiography provides a sense of how Hart spoke and pontificated about his work and his life. Nearly two-thirds of the book deals with his early years on the prairie and his life in the theater before the great star teamed up with Ince to make memorable silent films about the West as he

knew it. The book's value rests with Hart's idealized version of the past, rather than his understanding of films. An index is provided. Well worth browsing.

REX INGRAM

O'Leary, Liam. REX INGRAM: MASTER OF THE SILENT CINEMA. New York: Barnes and Noble, 1980. Illustrated. 224pp.

BUSTER KEATON

*Anobile, Richard. BUSTER KEATON'S "THE GENERAL." New York: Darien House, 1975. Illustrated. 256pp.

A flawed attempt at visually reproducing, in print, Keaton's masterpiece by means of 2,100 frame enlargements, this book misses the point of cinematic editing and pacing. The pictures may be interesting independent of the film, but they cannot recapture either in spirit or in mood the comic effects that the artist achieved in the projected movie. On the other hand, one gets a good feel for the story line and the difference between an idea and its execution. An essay by Raymond Rohauer and an interview with Marion Mack (the female lead in the film) are included.[256] Well worth browsing.

*Blesh, Rudi. KEATON. New York: Macmillan, 1966. Illustrated. 409pp.

There are few film historians who do not view Keaton as Chaplin's only serious rival in performance and possible superior in filmmaking. In this fine biography, Blesh explains how Keaton's brief decade of film activity (1919 to 1929) resulted in twelve feature films and nineteen short subjects that earned the comedian film immortality. Where Blesh shines is in the retelling of Keaton's childhood adventures, the crucial lessons learned from Fatty Arbuckle, and the behind-the-scenes stories about the Keaton films. Where the author falters is in relying too much on the information supplied by a close-mouthed Keaton. Moreover, Blesh's material lacks the freshness of the period in which it was published, having been written a decade earlier but not available until 1966. Nevertheless, it remains one of the most charming and entertaining of the growing number of Keaton biographies. A filmography and an index are included. Recommended for special collections.

*Dardis, Tom. KEATON: THE MAN WHO WOULDN'T LIE DOWN. New York: Charles Scribner's Sons, 1979. Illustrated. 340pp.

"Unlike Chaplin," Dardis points out, "Keaton always refused to identify himself as an artist, preferring to be regarded as a technician of laughter, a master of pratfalls. To Keaton, who attended school for only one day in his entire life, artists were people with an education." Dardis then goes on to write, "Buster possessed all the wrong character traits for a successful comedian. He was pathologically shy, he detested what he called low comedy, and he had a terror of crowds. He was totally uninterested in money; although he made an immense amount of it, he lost every penny. His first two wives were absolutely unsuitable, and he was very much his own worst enemy. He exhibited a curious mixture of extreme shyness and testy arrogance in his dealings with the world. Buster was a truly private person, and none of his close friends ever claimed to know what he really felt about his work." For those who wish to begin to unravel the enigma of the "Great Stone Face," this is the book to read. Not only has Dardis obtained the support of Keaton's sister and

---

[256] For more information, see "Marion Mack Is Dead; Silent-Film Actress, 87," NEW YORK TIMES D (May 15, 1989):10.

associates, gained access to the comedian's files at MGM and 20th Century-Fox as well as Keaton's own production papers, but he has also written a highly enjoyable and entertaining work. Even more, he has taken the Keaton story beyond the end of the twenties and brought the great artist's life into perspective through the several decades leading to his death on February 1, 1966. A filmography, bibliography, and index are included. Recommended for special collections.

Keaton, Buster, and Charles Samuels. MY WONDERFUL WORLD OF SLAPSTICK. Garden City: Doubleday and Company, 1960. Illustrated. 282pp.

In this candid and intimate biography, one of the most beloved of all film comedians modestly recounts the events in his personal and professional life. Typical of Keaton's style is his opening statement, in which he comments that "Down through the years my face has been called a sour puss, a dead pan, a frozen face, the Great Stone Face, and, believe it or not, 'a tragic mask.' On the other hand that kindly critic, the late James Agee, described my face as ranking 'almost with Lincoln's as an early American archetype, it was haunting, handsome, almost beautiful.' I can't imagine what the great rail splitter's reaction would have been to this, though I sure was pleased." And that's the way it goes as Keaton talks about his sixty years in show business, downplaying the eloquence of his art and stressing instead the basic steps that were used to stage his immortal sketches. The major omissions relate mainly to his traumatic marriage to Natalie Talmadge. Unfortunately, the stills add little to the autobiography and there is no index. Recommended for special collections.

*Lebel, Jean-Patrick. BUSTER KEATON. Trans. P. D. Stovin. New York: A. S. Barnes and Company, 1967. Illustrated. 179pp.

Aiming for loftier heights than Lebel can reach, this book discusses Keaton's artistry in grandiose language and in sweeping strokes rather than by analyzing individual films. Consider this passage near the end of a loosely constructed series of discussions on the comedian's complete works: "Now that we have witnessed Keaton's higher form of adjustment, how vain seem the interpretations of those who only see in his work the manifestation of a radical strangeness or an impotence in the face of the world. Having ascertained that not merely objects but whole human mechanical entities as well (the cinema included) are Keaton's favourite territory for confronting the world, none will ever find in him that pseudo-obsession with the mechanized world we live in (incarnation of man's fear of life and the future) that has constantly been drummed into our ears." Seven chapters of such explication becomes tedious because the intriguing ideas never get firmly anchored in a coherent perspective. The book has a filmography, but no index or bibliography. Worth browsing.

*Moews, Daniel. KEATON: THE SILENT FILMS CLOSE UP. Berkeley: University of California Press, 1977. 337pp.

Working on the assumption that Keaton's nine independent films made before he joined MGM are nearly flawless, Moews considers them first as a group and then in individual chapters. The specific films analyzed are OUR HOSPITALITY (1923), SHERLOCK, JR. and THE NAVIGATOR (both in 1924), SEVEN CHANCES and GO WEST (both in 1925), BATTLING BUTLER and THE GENERAL (both in 1926), COLLEGE (1927), and STEAMBOAT BILL, JR. (1928). According to Moews, "Keaton's customary formulas are dramatic adaptations of adolescent experience, though the aspects of adolescence stressed in the films are always farcically exploited for what is funny in them rather than being realistically or uncritically presented. The Keaton hero and his adventures are intended to be taken seriously, but never too seriously and never entirely seriously." Except for the absence of stills that could have enlivened the structural discussions, the author does a fine job of blending Keaton's art into its historical context and the growth of film comedy. An excellent bibliographical chapter reviews the strengths and weaknesses of previous scholars, as well as highlighting the problems with then-existing prints of the nine Keaton films. An index is included. Recommended for special collections.

*Robinson, David. BUSTER KEATON. Bloomington: Indiana University Press, 1969. Illustrated. 199pp.

Another useful contribution by the CINEMA ONE series, this study of Keaton builds on the scholarship done by others while adding fresh and stimulating insights on the artist's work. What Robinson says of the comedian might also apply to him: "[Keaton] never really repeated himself or imitated himself through all . . . [his] three dozen films. If he played a gag more than once it was generally in order to do it better or to build upon it, never because he needed to be parsimonious with his resources." Almost all of the book's seventeen reflective chapters are devoted to descriptions and examinations of the star's silent films, one by one. A filmography but no bibliography or index is included. Well worth browsing.

*Rubenstein, Elliot. FILMGUIDE TO "THE GENERAL." Bloomington: Indiana University Press, 1973. 83pp.

Beginning with the standard elements in this useful series edited by Harry Geduld and Ron Gottesman, Rubenstein provides complete cast and technical credits, an outline of the film, comments on the production process, an analysis, and a summary critique. Moreover, there is the by-now obligatory comparison of Keaton and Chaplin. In this instance, Rubenstein cites the difference between the two artists' performances in LIMELIGHT (1952): "Chaplin, as always, gets caught up in himself--in the mysterious spaces of his own pants, in the beauty of the music only he knows how to make, ultimately in his very passion for his own performance; Keaton, his eyes as devastating as ever behind inch-thick prop spectacles, doggedly struggles to make it through an operation in which almost every object in sight slyly turns on him." To Rubenstein's credit, the comparison as well as the study is sympathetic and insightful. On the other hand, this speculative interpretation focuses too narrowly on the star's persona and not enough on the film itself. Particular attention is paid to the importance of inanimate objects in Keaton's comic world. While Rubenstein is content to describe what occurs in the film, he shows little interest in examining the film text or the narrative patterns that were used to develop the comic effects. A good annotated bibliography is included, but no index. Well worth browsing.

Wead, George. BUSTER KEATON AND THE DYNAMICS OF VISUAL WIT. New York: Arno Press, 1976. 370pp.

Originally written as a 1973 Northwestern University doctoral dissertation, this communications-oriented examination takes a very narrow approach to Keaton's work. Wead begins by asserting that "silent film comedy is art because it 'plays upon,' or stylizes, communication." He then argues that studying "American comedy at the syntactic level . . . ignore[s] neither details nor meaning." The model stylization that he chooses for his consideration of silent film comedy involves the nature of redundancy and entropy. "Behind this present study," he explains, "is the belief that silent film comedy was popular because it was simply an elaboration of a mechanical sense implicit in the culture that developed cinema." To demonstrate his assumptions, Wead divides his project into two main sections. Part 1 explores what Keaton inherited from the early days of film comedy. Part 2 discusses how the great comic applied his values to silent film comedy. Although dry reading, the approach offers interesting insights. A bibliography is included. Worth browsing.

*Wead, George, and George Lellis. THE FILM CAREER OF BUSTER KEATON. Pleasantville: Redgrave Publishing Company, 1977. 174pp.

A valuable reference guide for scholars interested in French, Italian, and English sources on Keaton, this annotated bibliography is the one to use in beginning an exhaustive study of the comedian. The authors make little effort to evaluate their sources, although there are few instances in which one comes away in doubt about their attitudes. The book follows the by-now familiar format in this important series edited by Ron Gottesman. Following a good biographical overview, the material is divided into a section critically surveying Keaton's work, a section on his films (e.g., synopsis, credit, and notes), a section on the writings about Keaton, a section dealing with his other performances, and a section on archival sources. Information is also provided on film distributors, along with film title and author indexes. Well worth browsing.

LAUREL AND HARDY

*Anobile, Richard J. A FINE MESS: VERBAL AND VISUAL GEMS FROM THE CRAZY WORLD OF LAUREL AND HARDY. New York: Crown Publishers, 1975. Illustrated. 256pp.

The sixth volume in this unusual series focuses on more than 1,000 frame enlargements from a compilation film, THE CRAZY WORLD OF LAUREL AND HARDY (1965). The stills, presented in sequences, are from the comedians' sound movies: TOWED IN A HOLE, THE MUSIC BOX (both in 1932), BUSYBODIES (1933), GOING BYE-BYE (1934), and SWISS MISS (1938). For those who know the films, the exercise brings back many fond memories. On the other hand, the uninitiated may lose much of the fun created by expert timing and execution. It's also annoying not to have a table of contents to locate the specific films, which are presented haphazardly. Worth browsing.

*Barr, Charles. LAUREL AND HARDY. Berkeley: University of California Press, 1968. Illustrated. 144pp.

In a well-thought-out interpretation, Barr analyzes the skill and art of the great comedy team. Asserting that the men are "the most universal of comics, in range as in appeal," he points out in his introduction to the book's seventeen chapters that Laurel and Hardy "are supreme liberators from bourgeois inhibitions, yet essentially they are, or aspire to be, respectable bourgeois citizens." Barr begins the study of their films with a short chapter on their first official movie together, PUTTING ON PANTS (1927). He then moves on to a discussion of techniques, the structure of their films, and the nature of their gags. Other chapters examine their types of films, which Barr divides into five categories: their silent comedies before they became a team, their silent comedies as a team (1927-1929), their sound shorts (1929-1935), their feature films up to 1940 (1931-1940), and their feature films after 1940. As the author makes clear, the highpoint in the comedians' careers was during the transition from shorts to feature films in the years from 1931 to 1935. His presentation is helped considerably by numerous illustrations. An index, filmography, bibliography, and source for rentals are provided. Well worth browsing.

*Everson, William K. THE FILMS OF LAUREL AND HARDY. New York: The Citadel Press, 1967. Illustrated. 223pp.

Except for the scant biographical commentary, Everson presents a handy list of synopses and critical judgments together with many well-selected stills. No index is provided. Well worth browsing.

Guiles, Fred Lawrence. STAN: THE LIFE OF STAN LAUREL. New York: Stein and Day, 1980. Illustrated. 240pp.

Taking the position that Stan Laurel ranks with Chaplin and Keaton, Guiles builds an interesting biography out of scores of interviews with the performer's family and friends (especially the personal diaries of the artist's three-time wife, Virginia Ruth Laurel). The journalistic narrative is often hyperbolic (e.g., "It is no exaggeration to say that, universally, Laurel and Hardy have provoked more decibles of laughter than anyone else in films") and relies very heavily on personal memories rather than on footnoted sources. Most of the new material relates to Laurel's private life and his problems with money, alcohol, and human relationships. A sparse filmography, thin bibliography, and an adequate index are included. Worth browsing.

*Maltin, Leonard, ed. THE LAUREL AND HARDY BOOK. New York: Curtis Books, 1973. Illustrated. 301pp.

A potpourri of material, this delightful book provides a little bit of everything that appeals to Laurel and Hardy fans. In one chapter, McCabe offers a succinct commentary on the relationship between Chaplin and Laurel; in another chapter, Maltin describes how the team's scripts were translated to film, the types of films they made, the importance of language in building their international audiences, and what it was like working with Laurel and Hardy. Other chapters include comments on their theatrical tours, what the critics thought of their work, the team's TV appearances, Laurel in his later years, the Sons of the Desert society, the members of the Laurel and Hardy stock company, and indexes to their films individually and collectively. Well worth browsing.

McCabe, John. THE COMEDY WORLD OF STAN LAUREL. Garden City: Doubleday and Company, 1974. Illustrated. 221pp.

An informal look at the genius behind the famous comedy team, this sympathetic portrait covers terrain not developed in the author's more extensive MR. LAUREL AND MR. HARDY. Basically a summary of the men's partnership and how it developed, the book is essentially a miscellany. "Fittingly," McCabe explains, "because that was Stan's approach to comedy. His comedic concepts were never tidily arranged in his own mind, as he was often to remark. He disliked generalizations on comedy in the main, and one looks with difficulty for prime themes or essential strands of idea in his notes, scripts, or story discussions with the gag men and directors he worked with through the years." An index is provided. Worth browsing.

*McCabe, John. MR. LAUREL AND MR. HARDY. Foreword Dick Van Dyke. New York: Grosset and Dunlap, 1966. Illustrated. 262pp.

In one of the best studies yet on the two marvelous comedians, McCabe gives a tender account of the sensitive Stan and the mirthful Oliver, their years together, and the importance of Laurel as the guiding genius. Nine loosely constructed chapters describe the influence of Hal Roach on their comedies, the years at MGM, and the sad days at 20th Century-Fox. The author manages to balance personal anecdotes with stimulating analyses of the films. Periodically, he becomes reflective: "Laurel and Hardy lasted twenty-nine years (1926-55) as an active working team, and yet in all that time their basic gags were not many and they remained the same." What kept them in the public's eyes all those years, McCabe concludes, is their quality of "innocence." A filmography and index are included. Well worth browsing.

McCabe, John, Al Kilgore, and Richard W. Bann. LAUREL AND HARDY. New York: E. P. Dutton, 1975. Illustrated. 400pp.

The best pictorial survey of the comedians' films, this profusely illustrated chronology contains almost 1,500 photographs (many for the first time in print) with fine captions about 105 Stan and Ollie movies. The authors' love for their subject is evident throughout the book. Regrettably, there is no index or bibliography. Recommended for special collections.

Nollen, Scott Allen. THE BOYS: THE CINEMATIC WORLD OF LAUREL AND HARDY. Jefferson: McFarland, 1989. Illustrated. 160pp.

*Skretvedt, Randy. LAUREL AND HARDY: THE MAGIC BEHIND THE MOVIES. Foreword Steve Allen. Beverly Hills: Moonstone Press, 1987. Illustrated. 462pp.

This is the best book to-date on the mechanics of the Laurel and Hardy films, aided by first-hand observations of those who worked on them.   Skretvedt first introduces the team individually, then moves quickly into their relationship with Hal Roach, and follows with a description of how the team was developed. Having established the basic biographical information, Skretvedt delves seriously into the team's methods of filmmaking, their silent and sound films with Roach, and their later films at 20th Century-Fox, and concludes with an affectionate epilogue and thumbnail portraits of the team's supporting players. Each of the film discussions includes an abbreviated list of cast and technical credits, a brief plot synopsis, an extended analysis of the production process, and its results. An index is provided. Recommended for special collections.

HARRY LANGDON

Rheuban, Joyce. HARRY LANGDON: THE COMEDIAN AS METTEUR-EN-SCENE. Rutherford: Associate University Presses, 1983. Illustrated. 244pp.

In acknowledging the difficulty of establishing authorship in Hollywood films, Rheuban observes that the problem is more complicated than usual when studying the films of Harry Langdon. Too much misinformation and misperception have become part of the historical record. "Langdon's influence on the mise-en-scene of the films in which he appeared as a performer," explains Rheuban, "has been overlooked, and the originality that is evident in the films he directed has been ignored. Even Langdon's origination of the comic impersonation and performance style exhibited in his films has been denied. Frank Capra and Mack Sennett are probably, directly and indirectly, the original sources of most of these misconceptions." Thus the first of the book's nine intriguing chapters highlights the claims put forth by Capra and Sennett, and the reasons why Rheuban feels that Langdon originated his own comic persona and style of performance. The author's case, focusing less on narrative elements (e.g., gag and story structure, characterization, and amoral values) and more on the star's "understanding of the nature of filmic space and time," rests mainly on various trade reviews and reports in theatrical periodicals ranging from the artist's vaudeville background beginning in 1906, to the early film comedies starting in 1924, and concluding with the comic's last films in the early- to mid-1940s. The arguments are stimulating; the writing, reflective and descriptive. A filmography, bibliography, and index are included. Recommended for special collections.

HAROLD LLOYD

Cahn, William. HAROLD LLOYD'S WORLD OF COMEDY. New York: Duell, Sloan and Pearce, 1964. Illustrated. 208pp.

A mediocre biography of the marvelous comic, this wordy and meandering publication will disappoint all but the most tolerant of film buffs. No real insights are provided into Lloyd's ingenious satirization of the healthy, All-American hero--the glass character.   Cahn tells us very little about the comedian's production practices or his relationship with directors, fellow performers, and scriptwriters.   Almost nothing is done with the films themselves or with the similarities and dissimilarities between Lloyd and his competitors. And finally, a book like this should have included appendexes and credit lists. An index is included. Approach with caution.

Dardis, Tom. HAROLD LLOYD: THE MAN ON THE CLOCK. New York: The Viking ress, 1983. Illustrated. 357pp.

Equal in many respects to the author's outstanding study of Keaton, this valuable comprehensive study of Lloyd is a good place to begin one's understanding of who the comedian was, and what he meant to film and to American cultural history. Dardis begins by reminding us of the reasons why the comedian's reputation has not fared as well as those of his two foremost rivals: e.g., the unavailability of Lloyd's films, the mistaken impression that he was little more than a daredevil comedian, and his presumed boring persona. The twelve anecdotal and informative chapters that follow explain why James Agee observed that in creating laughter, "few people have equalled him, and nobody has ever beaten him." Dardis's treatment is sympathetic, intelligent, and entertaining. A filmography, endnotes, bibliography, and index are included. Recommended for special collections.

*Lloyd, Harold, and Wesley W. Stout. AN AMERICAN COMEDY. New York: Dover, 1971. Illustrated. 138pp.

Originally written in 1928, this autobiographical book is a chatty, rambling account of Lloyd's major years in film. Unfortunately, it offers little on technique, personalities, or even a few good anecdotes. What is important about this new edition, however, is the inclusion of sixty-seven illustrations, an essay in which Lloyd talks about his comedy, Richard Griffith's brief introductory comments, and an index. Well worth browsing.

McCaffrey, Donald W. THREE CLASSIC SILENT SCREEN COMEDIES STARRING HAROLD LLOYD. Cranbury: Associated University Presses, 1976. Illustrated. 264pp.

"The focus of the examination," McCaffrey writes, "is on three of . . . [Lloyd's] silent-screen features, GRANDMA'S BOY (1922), SAFETY LAST (1923), and THE FRESHMAN (1925)." McCaffrey originally finished the study in 1962, but then revised and updated it for this valuable publication. His examination of the structure, characters, and comic techniques of the three films is buttressed by references to contemporary reviews of the films and by an application of various comic theories. Following a useful chapter on historical background, the author provides seven chapters on Lloyd's comic patterns as evidenced in the comic idea, the plot motivation, the main crisis, and the climax in each of the three films. Three specific techniques--(1) Lloyd's "use of the success story, (2) his blend of slapstick and genteel traditions of comedy, and (3) his use of stock comic material"--serve as the basis for a number of McCaffery's detailed discussions. A filmography, a summary of the author's June 1965 interviews with Lloyd, a bibliography, and an index are included. Well worth browsing.

Schickel, Richard. HAROLD LLOYD: THE SHAPE OF HIS LAUGHTER. Greenwich: New York Graphic Society, 1974. Illustrated. 218pp.

A lovely coffee-table review of Lloyd's life and career, this intelligent biography sets out to offset the traditional views of the comedian as a performer whose films lacked "soul" and whose private life was devoid of "emotional resonance." Schickel's reflective approach does not insist "that received opinion about him [Lloyd] is completely wrong." Nor does he argue "that there was some hidden psychological wound or some previously unsuspected depth of vision or feeling that only now, at some distance in time, we can perceive, and thereby find new values in his films." What the author does assert, however, is that it is "self-evident that any performer who achieved and sustained over a period of years the enormous popularity that Lloyd enjoyed must have had virtues that his more recent critics have ignored." Schickel's examination encompasses the years from Lloyd's birth (April 30, 1893) to his death (March 8, 1971). It charts how the youngster from Burchard, Nebraska, epitomized the American Dream of fame and fortune, discusses the artist's comic techniques, comments on the sociological value of Lloyd's films in interpreting American society in the 1920s, and speculates on why the man became disillusioned in his declining years. Given the book's format and audience constraints, it is a delightful combination of critical commentary and pictorial beauty. A filmography by Eileen Bowser is included, but no index or bibliography. Well worth browsing.

ERNST LUBITSCH

Poague, Leland A. THE CINEMA OF ERNST LUBITSCH. South Brunswick: A. S. Barnes and Company, 1978. Illustrated. 183pp.

A close reading of Lubitsch's Hollywood years, this representative study examines many of the twenty-eight American films from an AUTEURIST perspective.[257] In particular, Poague attempts to go beyond the standard looks at the "Lubitsch touch" to the director's concern "with the emotional realities beneath the facades of frivolity." The author argues that Lubitsch was interested primarily in stripping away the human facade and exploring the human condition. "In other words," Poague writes, "Lubitsch shifted his focus from the edges of the frame, those artifical boundaries which allowed him to leave things out, to the centre of the frame, that privileged area where the human comedy is enacted. The logic of development in Lubitsch's American films is thus consistent in its broad outlines, from men's manners to men's hearts, from the edges to the centre, from the surface to the substance."

The study itself is divided into five thematic categories of films. Chapter 1--"Time and Man: THE MARRIAGE CIRCLE (1924) and THE SHOP AROUND THE CORNER (1940)"--develops the author's thesis that Lubitsch was more interested in humanistic values than in visual gimmicks. Chapter 2--"Frivolity and Responsibility: LADY WINDERMERE'S FAN (1925), THE STUDENT PRINCE (1927), and THE MERRY WIDOW (1934)"--focuses on the director's use of satire and romance, pointing out Lubitsch's interest in showing the dilemmas posed by social decorum in conflict with personal integrity. Chapter 3--"Self-Aware Illusions: ONE HOUR WITH YOU (1932), TROUBLE IN PARADISE (1932), and TO BE OR NOT TO BE (1942)"--analyzes the relationship between reality and illusion, reminding us that every Lubitsch film is preoccupied in one way or another with the distinctions between fact and fantasy. Chapter 4--"Love's Parade (Uncertain Feelings): SO THIS IS PARIS (1926), THE LOVE PARADE (1929), and NINOTCHKA (1939)"--charts Lubitsch's changing attitudes toward love, marriage, and sexual relationships. The focus is on the deterioration of marriage among the rich and how to improve their lot. Chapter 5--"Age Shall Not Wither: HEAVEN CAN WAIT (1943) and CLUNY BROWN (1946)"--reveals the last stages of Lubitsch's career and his preoccupation with behaving responsibly in the face of uncontrollable events.

Putting aside the author's somber approach to his subject and a tendency toward dullness, this interesting study suggests many provocative insights into Lubitsch's Hollywood career. A filmography and index are included. Well worth browsing.

---

[257]   Andrew Sarris, "Lubitsch in the Thirties: Part One," FILM COMMENT 7:4 (Winter 1971-72):54-57; and ___, "All Talking! All Singing! All Lubitsch!: Ernst Lubitsch in the Thirties--Part Two," ibid., 8:2 (Summer 1972):20-1.

PATSY RUTH MILLER

Miller, Patsy Ruth. MY HOLLYWOOD--WHEN BOTH OF US WERE YOUNG: THE MEMORIES OF PATSY RUTH MILLER. Introduction Douglas Fairbanks, Jr. West Hanover: Arcata/Halliday, 1988. Illustrated. 208pp.

COLLEEN MOORE

Moore, Colleen. SILENT STAR: COLLEEN MOORE TALKS ABOUT HER HOLLYWOOD. Garden City: Doubleday and Company, 1968. Illustrated. 262pp.
In this informal and chatty autobiography, the author (born Kathleen Morrison) focuses on her great successes in such memorable silent films as FLAMING YOUTH (1923) and LILAC TIME (1928). What is admirable about her discussions of the 1920s is the low-key approach to the famous personalities and the events taking place in the film industry. As a result, we gain some useful insights into the famous Hollywood scandals involving Fatty Arbuckle and William Desmond Taylor. No index is provided. Worth browsing.[258]

POLA NEGRI

Negri, Pola. MEMOIRS OF A STAR. Garden City: Doubleday and Company, 1970. Illustrated. 453pp.

HAL ROACH

*Everson, William K. THE FILMS OF HAL ROACH. New York: The Museum of Modern Art, 1971. Illustrated. 96pp.
In a brief but valuable overview, Everson comments on Roach's style, memorable pictures, and his great stars. One gets a sense of how a twenty-year-old drifter wandered into films as a cowboy extra in 1912, began producing his own movies two years later, became successful first with Harold Lloyd and the OUR GANG series, and then struck pay-dirt with the teaming of Laurel and Hardy. Among his other noteworthy achievements touched on in this slim tribute are productions like the TOPPER series and OF MICE AND MEN (1940). Everson also includes a 1969 interview with Roach plus a bibliography, filmography, and forty worthwhile stills.[259] Well worth browsing.

RUDOLPH VALENTINO

Arnold, Alan, VALENTINO: A BIOGRAPHY. Foreword John Paddy Carsairs. New York: Library Publishers, 1954. Illustrated. 165pp.

Shulman, Irving. VALENTINO. New York: Trident Press, 1967. Illustrated. 499pp.

---

[258] For a succinct and useful overview, see Jack Spears, "Colleen Moore," FILMS IN REVIEW 13:7 (August-September 1963):403-24; and Glenn Fowler, "Colleen Moore, Ultimate Flapper of the Silent Screen, Is Dead at 87," NEW YORK TIMES D (January 27, 1988):23.

[259] Anthony Slide, "Hal Roach on Film Comedy," THE SILENT PICTURE 6 (Spring 1970):2-7.

KING VIDOR

*Baxter, John. KING VIDOR. New York: Simon and Schuster, 1976. Illustrated. 94pp.
    "Based upon conversations recorded in London late in 1974, and on interviews not previously published in English," Baxter explains, "this book is offered with respect to a man who, by any reasonable criterion, is among the greatest filmmakers of modern times." Baxter divides his problematic interpretations and analyses into six concise and stimulating chapters. His chronological survey begins with the birth of King Wallis Vidor in Galveston, Texas, in 1894; skips lightly over the steps leading to Vidor's first feature, THE TURN IN THE ROAD (1918); and then picks up momentum as he discusses Vidor's illustrious film career that ends late in the fifties with SOLOMON AND SHEBA (1959). The fast-moving history is supported by a set of beautifully reproduced illustrations. A filmography and bibliography are included, but no index. Well worth browsing.

*Denton, Clive. THE HOLLYWOOD PROFESSIONALS (Volume 5): KING VIDOR, JOHN CROMWELL, MERVYN LEROY. New York: A. S. Barnes and Company, 1976. Illustrated. 192pp.

Durgnat, Raymond, and Scott Simmon. KING VIDOR, AMERICAN. Berkeley: University of California Press, 1988. Illustrated. 382pp.

Vidor, King. A TREE IS A TREE. New York: Harcourt, Brace, and Company, 1952. Illustrated. 315pp.
    The exceptional director of THE BIG PARADE (1925), THE CROWD (1928), and HALLELUJAH! (1929) presents us with a modest, well-written, and enjoyable account of film production and studio life. Although he fails to teach us anything about his directing methods, Vidor relates some fascinating accounts of Hearst, John Gilbert, and the shameful events that took place at Mabel Normand's funeral. A filmography and index are included. Well worth browsing.

Vidor, King. KING VIDOR ON FILM MAKING. New York: David McKay Company, 1972. Illustrated. 239pp.
    This has to be one of the most fascinating books on filmmaking in the last decade. It weaves autobiography, history, and technique into an educational experience available nowhere else. An index is included. Well worth browsing.

JOSEF VON STERNBERG

*Baxter, John. THE CINEMA OF JOSEF VON STERNBERG. New York: A. S. Barnes and Company, 1971. Illustrated. 192pp.
    "Who was he," Baxter asks, "this small--five feet five inches--stooped Viennese Jew with the disconcerting pale eyes and quiet, metallic voice? A poet, 'a hard boiled egg,' a pornographer, charlatan, martinet, genius, fraud; he was called all these, and by people normally given neither to rhapsodies nor outbursts of rage." Baxter argues that the answer to the question lies in Sternberg's early years and in his finding a niche in American society and culture. Thus, the first of this book's eighteen chapters reviews the events from Jonas Sternberg's birth on May 29, 1894, to a poor Orthodox Jewish couple, to the boy's lack of a proper education and his migration at fourteen to America, to his vagabond life and the changing of his name to Josef at seventeen (the "von" was added in 1924 to give him a more aristocratic

air), and the importance of museums and galleries in providing the impressionable young man with not only a sense of escape from the harsh world around him, but also a source of entertainment and education. Sternberg's fascination with cinematic artistry is then discussed in the following seventeen chapters, beginning with THE SALVATION HUNTERS in 1925, and ending with his last film, THE SAGA OF ANATAHAN in 1952. In the process of describing the artist's unique contributions to film history, Baxter also comments on the important people who influenced Sternberg's career: e.g., Marlene Dietrich, Erich von Stroheim, Irving Thalberg, Emil Jannings, Alexander Korda, and Howard Hughes. When von Sternberg died on December 22, 1969, according to Baxter, the world still did not understand the director's complex personality or his extraordinary talent. As the author comments, "To destroy a career for ideals as obscure as those that racked his heroes, to travel the world searching for a phantom of reality of his own devising, to build around his lover a fantasy of sexual perfection that in its total impossibility of attainment could only bring him pain and despair; these are the sacrifices of logic which are alone apparent to the supreme artist who has seen and accepted his destiny." A filmography and a select bibliography are included, but no index. Well worth browsing.

*Baxter, Peter, ed. STERNBERG. London: British Film Institute, 1980. Illustrated. 144pp.
    This valuable anthology offers novel and important insights into von Sternberg's career over a fifty-year period. Baxter points out in his perceptive introduction to the book's sixteen essays how often our interpretations of art are orchestrated by "the apparatus maintaining the social formation and   . . .   the specificity of its operation   . . .   determined by the historical moment of its functioning." As an example, Baxter reminds us that when THE BLUE ANGEL/DER BLAUE ENGEL (1929) opened in London and New York, attention focused on the star-performer (Jannings) and not on the director-creator (von Sternberg). "In order to grasp the reality of the director's presence in dominant cinema," the editor asserts, "it is necessary to grasp the reality of commodity production, a reality that began to set the terms of cultural production long before the cinema was invented." Among the contributing authors reprinted in this AUTEUR anthology are Louis Chavance, Siegfried Kracauer, Marcel Oms, Barry Salt, and Josef von Sternberg. A filmography and bibliography are included, but no index. Well worth browsing.

Zucker, Carole. THE IDEA OF THE IMAGE: JOSEF VON STERNBERG'S DIETRICH FILMS. Rutherford: Fairleigh Dickinson University Press, 1988. Illustrated. 159pp.

Sarris, Andrew. THE FILMS OF JOSEF VON STERNBERG. New York: Museum of Modern Art, 1966. Illustrated. 56pp.
    This short, handy, and informative survey of von Sternberg's eighteen films beginning in 1925 provides good notes to particular movies and a valuable introduction to the great director's fascination with artificial settings, contrived lighting, and special effects. Sarris's discussion of the director's fascination with blending social realism and pictorial splendor does an effective job of explaining why von Sternberg is so admired for his visual style and atmospheric films. The book has many fine illustrations and important screen credits. No bibliography or index is provided. Well worth browsing.

Studlar, Gaylyn. REALM OF PLEASURE: VON STERNBERG, DIETRICH, AND THE MASOCHISTIC AESTHETIC. Urbana: University of Illinois Press, 1988. Illustrated. 247pp.

Von Sternberg, Josef. FUN IN A CHINESE LAUNDRY. New York: The Macmillan Company, 1965. Illustrated. 348pp. San Francisco: Mercury House, 1988.

Von Sternberg's autobiography is an intriguing discussion of directing, personalities, and a bygone age. The usual chatty and meandering anecdotal approach to a famous man's career is replaced by an intelligent, provocative, and meaningful discussion of theory and practice. This is a must for his students. An index is included. Recommended for special collections.

*Weinberg, Herman G. JOSEF VON STERNBERG: A CRITICAL STUDY OF THE GREAT DIRECTOR. New York: E. P. Dutton and Company, 1967. Illustrated. 254pp.

No book is more valuable for information on von Sternberg's style, subjects, and interests. Weinberg, in a loving tribute, presents chapters on the director's career, a personal interview with him, a collection of critical reviews, extracts from the scenario of SHANGHAI EXPRESS (1932), the entire narration of THE SAGA OF ANATAHAN (1952), the best available filmography and bibliography, and fifty significant illustrations. Recommended for special collections.

ERICH VON STROHEIM

Curtiss, Thomas Quinn. VON STROHEIM. New York: Farrar, Straus and Giroux, 1971. Illustrated. 357pp.

In an address delivered at a retrospective screening of von Stroheim's films and presented as a foreword to this biography, Rene Clair says of the director's art, "It is among the most authentic work of our profession. The passage of time may have lessened its shock; the physical changes all around us may have disfigured it; the films that it influenced and the imitations it inspired have tended to blur its originality. But this work of Erich von Stroheim, even though mutilated by others, shines with a power and newness that a quarter of a century cannot diminish." The author of this book, working closely with its subject, sets out to show us why. The general terrain he covers may be familiar to those who have read the earlier Finler and Noble biographies; a number of the conclusions are not. Except for some errors dealing with Griffith, Curtiss presents a useful study not only of a great director, but also of a valuable era in film history. Although von Stroheim completed only eight films and was often cited as the classic example of artistic arrogance and profligacy, he also is cited as a major reason for the weakness of Hollywood's studio system. That is, assembly-line production policies do not tolerate maverick directors who create excessively long, very expensive, and extremely time-consuming and complex productions. Curtis's biography functions as a major summary of why a number of the director's films--e.g., FOOLISH WIVES (1922), GREED (1924), THE MERRY WIDOW (1925), and THE WEDDING MARCH (1928) are considered some of the most innovative and socially realistic movies in cinematic history. At the same time, the author acknowledges the artist's fascination with decadence, depravity, and eroticism both in his screen roles and in his directing. But he also makes it clear that the artist's sense of mood and wit is what transposed ordinary melodramas into inspired filmmaking. Moreover, Quinn was a close friend of von Stroheim and thus provides insights into the artist's life and career not found elsewhere. Particularly impressive are the many handsomely produced illustrations. An appendix on the nine-hour screening of GREED and a filmography are included, but no index. Recommended for special collections.

*Finler, Joel W. STROHEIM. Berkeley: University of California Press, 1968. Illustrated. 144pp.

No figure in film history is more mysterious, more controversial, or more magnificent than the Viennese Jew who terrorized the studios and the stars of Hollywood; he was often labeled "the man you love to hate." The sixteen compact chapters that makeup this AUTEUR study concentrate on analyzing five films: FOOLISH WIVES (1922), GREED (1924), THE MERRY WIDOW (1925), THE WEDDING MARCH (1926-28), and QUEEN KELLY (1928), with almost forty percent of those chapters present a lengthy and stimulating discussion of GREED. Other von Stroheim films are discussed in a routine fashion. A sparse filmography and bibliography are included, but no index. Well worth browsing.

*Finler, Joel W., ed. GREED: A FILM BY ERICH VON STROHEIM. New York: Simon and Schuster, 1972. Illustrated. 352pp.

One of the best in the Classic Film Script series, this work contains von Stroheim's original ten hour shooting script for GREED. Finler compares the actual script, initially published by the Belgian Cinematheque in 1958, with the most complete print of the film, and then indicates the crucial discrepancies between the two: e.g., (1) scenes indicated in the script but missing from the print are identified by brackets; (2) new title cards substituting for edited sequences are identified in footnotes; and (3) other notable omissions in the move from script to screen are identified either with brackets or footnotes. In addition, a series of introductory articles by von Stroheim, Finler, Herman G. Weinberg, and Jean Hersholt reviews the problems and difficulties that the director had with his employers and distributors. Except for Finler's useful overview, the articles are reprints from other publications. Recommended for special collections.

*Koszarski, Richard. THE MAN YOU LOVE TO HATE: ERICH VON STROHEIM AND HOLLYWOOD. New York: Oxford University Press, 1983. Illustrated. 343pp.

The best book yet on von Stroheim's life and career, this thoughtful and analytical study strips away much of the confusion and misinformation about the volatile artist. Koszarski begins immediately in his preface to dismiss timeworn claims--e.g., that the director's movies about imperial decay provide biographical information about his noble lineage (in fact, Von Stroheim, the first-born son of a Jewish hatter, had limited service in the military and may actually have been a deserter). Koszarski also makes the point that the ENFANT TERRIBLE rejected formulas and film theories: "He knew he was an artist, and that chance had made the cinema his canvas. His problem was how to get his ideas up onto the screen, and his only conscious solution was to be direct, avoid fancy stylistic tricks, and maintain complete honesty in the face of his material." Oblivious to standardized Hollywood procedures and sane business management, he failed to gain the artistic freedom and security granted his one soul-mate, Charlie Chaplin. In the end, what fascinates the author and permeates his highly enjoyable biography is how it was possible for "this wandering soldier of fortune . . . to accomplish so much with such limited training and education, and why was he forced to stop?"

In the prologue to the book's ten chapters, the author outlines how and why Erich Oswald Stroheim, beginning with his emigration to America in 1924, enobled himself with a "von" and then, until his death on May 12, 1957, maintained a fictionalized posture toward his past behavior. The chapters themselves are devoted to examining individual films. An epilogue reminds us that, in the end, the man who fabricated so many honors did indeed receive the Legion of Honor shortly before he died. As Koszarski notes, von Stroheim "must have enjoyed the irony." Extensive endnotes, a filmography, and an index are included. Recommended for special collections.

Noble, Peter. HOLLYWOOD SCAPEGOAT: THE BIOGRAPHY OF ERICH VON STROHEIM. London: The Fortune Press, 1950. New York: Arno Press, 1972. Illustrated. 246pp.

This first biography in English of von Stroheim is a general, loosely organized account of the great director's fascination with sex on the screen and with his problems with the Hollywood censors and stars like the Gish sisters, Gloria Swanson, Douglas Fairbanks, and John Gilbert. For the most part, the facts are there along with many useful stills and a good list of cast credits and reference material. Although von Stroheim at first cooperated with the author, he later became dissatisfied with the results and withdrew all support of the book. Thirteen appendexes and an index are included. Well worth browsing.

*Weinberg, Herman G. STROHEIM: A PICTORIAL RECORD OF HIS NINE FILMS. New York: Dover Publications, 1975. Illustrations. 259pp.

After a chatty, meandering, and almost incoherent introduction that calls attention more to Weinberg's cultural interests than to the subject of the book, this beautifully illustrated survey becomes a delightful guide to von Stroheim's films. The introduction to each of the chronologically presented films--BLIND HUSBANDS (1919), THE DEVIL'S PASSKEY (1920), FOOLISH WIVES (1922), MERRY GO ROUND (1923), GREED (1924), THE MERRY WIDOW (1925), THE WEDDING MARCH (1928), QUEEN KELLY (1928-unfinished), and WALKING DOWN BROADWAY (1932-33-never released)--consists of a list of cast and technical credits, then a brief synopsis of the plot, and finally a splendid assortment of frame enlargements with melodramatic annotations explaining the shot. The book concludes with a terse chapter describing von Stroheim's uncompleted projects. Well worth browsing.

Weinberg, Herman, G., ed. THE COMPLETE "GREED" OF ERICH VON STROHEIM: A RECONSTRUCTION OF THE FILM IN 348 STILL PHOTOS FOLLOWING THE ORIGINAL SCREENPLAY PLUS 52 PRODUCTION STILLS. New York: Arno Press, 1971. Illustrated. Unpaginated.

In providing us with a superb reconstruction of von Stroheim's brilliant film, Weinberg has made a major contribution to film scholarship. The extraordinary stills, together with the foreword and epilogue in this handsome and expensive book, provide the reader with the story of one of the most horrendous filmmaking experiences ever in movie history. Recommended for special collections.

Weinberg, Herman G. THE COMPLETE "WEDDING MARCH" OF ERICH VON STROHEIM: A RECONSTRUCTION OF THE FILM, PART ONE, "THE WEDDING MARCH," PART TWO, "THE HONEYMOON," IN 255 STILL PHOTOS FOLLOWING THE ORIGINAL SCREENPLAY, PLUS 13 PRODUCTION STILLS. Boston: Little, Brown and Company, 1974. Illustrated. 330pp.

Another superb research job by Weinberg, this extraordinary reconstruction comes complete with charming anecdotes, valuable information, and beautiful pictures. The expository opening essay is worth borrowing the book for; the chance to leaf through this visual record is worth buying the book for. Surprisingly, no bibliography is provided. Recommended for special collections.

RAOUL WALSH

Walsh, Raoul. EACH MAN IN HIS TIME: THE LIFE STORY OF A DIRECTOR. New York: Farrar, Straus and Giroux, 1974. Illustrated. 385pp.

Written by a man in his mid-eighties, this is a macho account of what it was like from the very early days of film history, through the heyday of the studio era, and into the rise of television. The action-oriented director of hits like THE THIEF OF BAGDAD (1924), WHAT PRICE GLORY? (1926), THE ROARING TWENTIES (1929), HIGH SIERRA, THEY DIED WITH THEIR BOOTS ON (both in 1941), GENTLEMAN JIM (1943), WHITE HEAT (1949), and BATTLE CRY (1955) is a delightful storyteller but a weak historian. Dates are omitted, incidents presented out of context, and details ignored or obscured. If you're interested in sexual exploits and zany adventures, then this colorful autobiography is fun reading. On the other hand, this free-wheeling book is a disappointment when it comes to providing insights into filmmaking and film history. A nice collection of stills and an index are included, but no bibliography or filmography is provided. Worth browsing.

WILLIAM A. WELLMAN

Wellman, William A. A SHORT TIME FOR INSANITY: AN AUTOBIOGRAPHY. Foreword Richard Schickel. New York: Hawthorn Books, 1974. Illustrated. 276pp.

"For me," writes Schickel, "Bill Wellman is a significant historical figure, as are most of his colleagues . . . For the films they made during our formative years had as much to do with the creation of a generation's sensibility--moral as well as aesthetic--as anything the politicians of their time did, and far more than any writers or painters or social scientists." Schickel goes on to say, "I'm not going to spoil his story by rehearsing the tale of how a nice middle-class youth from New England managed to become, in about a decade, a high school dropout, a World War One flying hero with the French air force, a screen actor (briefly), and, finally, a director--in the process winning, for his first major production, WINGS, the first Academy Award ever given for best picture of the year." Schickel's tributes don't, however, prepare us for this rambling autobiography written from a hospital bed, where the sixty-five-year-old author was recovering under sedation from a serious illness. The ten highly personal chapters operate as a stream of consciousness experience, with Wellman spurting out amusing and entertaining anecdotes that tell us more about his relationships with people than about the action-packed films--e.g., WINGS (1927), THE PUBLIC ENEMY (1931), WILD BOYS OF THE ROAD (1933), THE CALL OF THE WILD (1935), A STAR IS BORN (1937), BEAU GESTE (1939), THE OX-BOW INCIDENT (1943), THE STORY OF G. I. JOE (1945), and THE HIGH AND THE MIGHTY (1954)--he created over a forty-year career. A filmography and index are included. Worth browsing.

FILMS

GENERAL

THE GOLDEN AGE OF COMEDY (Youngson--16mm: 1957, 85 mins., b/w, sound, R-SWA, TWY, WHO)

This superb comedy anthology has scenes and sequences from some of the best of the Mack Sennett and Hal Roach comedies made between 1923 and 1928. Among the famous personalities shown are Will Rogers, Jean Harlow, Carole Lombard, Ben Turpin, Harry Langdon, The Keystone Cops, the Sennett Bathing Beauties, and Laurel and Hardy.

FRANK BORZAGE

SEVENTH HEAVEN (Fox--16mm: 1927, 123 mins., b/w, music and sound effects only, R-FNC, KIL, MMA; S-BLA)

Director Frank Borzage deserves much of the credit for translating Austin Strong's play about two lovers whose lives become tragically affected by World War I into an immensely popular film. As John Belton points out, "What distinguished Borzage's melodramas from Griffith's is their spirituality. Where Griffith concerns himself primarily, like Dickens, with the restitution of the family unit or the creation of a new family-like unit, Borzage's interests lie chiefly in the salvation of the characters--his concern is not with external but internal order. Where Griffith's characters contain irrepressible physical vitality--a vitality that make the films immediate and direct--Borzage's characters, though also physical beings, radiate from within a unique, spiritual energy that makes then appear luminescently unreal."[260] Particularly noteworthy is the unusual climax of the film. Praise also goes to the movie's stars: Janet Gaynor and Charles Farrell.

LON CHANEY

THE HUNCHBACK OF NOTRE DAME (Universal--16mm: 1923, 90 mins., b/w, silent, R-EMG, FNC, IVY, KIT, ROA, SWA, TWY, WE, WES, WHO; S-BLA)
        This classic Victor Hugo novel has been filmed several times, but no one ever topped Lon Chaney's incredible acting in this touching and unforgettable version of the tormented bellringer who was more pitied than feared. Wallace Worsley directed.[261] A tinted print with a musical score is available from the Killiam Collection.

THE PHANTOM OF THE OPERA (Universal--16mm: 1925, 79 mins., b/w, silent, R-BUD, FNC, IVY, KIT, ROA, SWA, TWY, WES, WHO; S-BLA)
        One of the best films of the 1920s, this marvelous story about a warped musician with a disfigured face who terrorizes the Paris Opera not only offers great moments of horror, but also superb production designs and photography. Rupert Julian directed. A tinted version is available from the Killiam Collection.

JAMES CRUZE

THE COVERED WAGON (Paramount-16mm: 1923, 71 mins., b/w, musical score only, R-FNC, KIT)
        Directed by James Cruze, this film became recognized as the first successful western epic to depict, cinematically, the westward movement of the pioneers. It works best when the melodramatic story is ignored and you concentrate on Cruze's ability to infuse a sense of American history on a visual record of stunning Nevada locations.[262]

CECIL B. DEMILLE

KING OF KINGS (Paramount--16mm: 1927, 115 mins., b/w, music and sound effects only, R-BUD, CIN, EMG, FNC, IVY, KIT,[263] TWY)

---

[260]   *John Belton, THE HOLLYWOOD PROFESSIONALS (Volume 3): HOWARD HAWKS, FRANK BORZAGE, EDGAR G. ULMER (New York: A. S. Barnes and Company, 1974), p.78.

[261]   Richard E. Braff, "A New Lon Chaney Index," FILMS IN REVIEW 21:4 (April 1970): 217-28.

[262]   George Geltzer, "James Cruze," FILMS IN REVIEW 5:6 (June-July 1954):283-91; Alan Stanbrook, "Great Films of the Century: THE COVERED WAGON," FILMS AND FILMING 6:8 (May 1960):12-14, 35; and Bosley Crowther, "The Covered Wagon," THE GREAT FILMS, pp.26-30.

[263]   Kit Parker rents a version partially in color.

Produced and directed by DeMille, the screenplay by Jeanie Macpherson plays fast and loose with Biblical accounts of Jesus of Nazareth. The focus is on the conversion of Mary Magdalene (Jacqueline Logan), with attention also paid to the traditional episodes in the life and death of Jesus (H. B. Warner). DeMille risked the future of his production company on this multi-million-dollar spectacle, and the public adored it and turned the film into one of DeMille's all-time hits. Many religious groups protested the film's perspective. Nevertheless, the great showman always defended his efforts.   According to one source, DeMille claimed that "One of the greatest rewards of my career . . . was realized when . . . [a] pastor told me, 'If it were not for THE KING OF KINGS, I would not be a Lutheran pastor, and three hundred and fifty Jewish children would have died in the ditches.'"[264]

MALE AND FEMALE (Paramount--16mm: 1919, 97 mins., b/w, silent, R-MMA)
Another DeMille-Macpherson collaboration, this visual guide to life among the wealthy is a stagey adaptation of James Barrie's THE ADMIRABLE CRICHTON. The emphasis on showing contrasting life-styles, sexual mores, and class differences overshadowed the simplistic production and put DeMille in the forefront of post-World War I Hollywood producers and directors. For years after, this glitzy style suggested to many people that he was the best spokesperson in depicting the Jazz Age on the screen. The film featured Gloria Swanson, Thomas Beighan, and Bebe Daniels.[265]

THE TEN COMMANDMENTS (Paramount--16mm: 1923, 146 mins., b/w, silent, R-FNC)
Credited by some historians as being the film that brought DeMille his recognition as an important artist, the story gave him the opportunity to blend historical spectacle with topical issues. The genius of the undertaking was the director's ability to pose as a defender of traditional morality while, at the same time, taking full advantage of the audience's voyeuristic and erotic desires. As Eric Rhode points out, "Theatricality is on the grandest scale, with masterly lighting and art direction sustaining large gestures; a succession of sharply etched and seemingly three-dimesional compositions suspend disbelief; while some of the miracles, such as the parting of the Red Sea, remain among the most impressive ever filmed."[266]

ROBERT J. FLAHERTY

NANOOK OF THE NORTH (Revillon Freres--16mm: 1922, 100 mins., b/w, sound version, R-BUD, FNC, IMA, IVY, KIT, WIL; S-BLA)
This Robert Flaherty masterpiece records the struggle of the Eskimos against the forces of nature and their short-lived victory over hunger.   Originally, the director was hired by the Revillon Freres Fur Company to explore the Canadian arctic, but Flaherty's two grueling years of research led him to make the first major documentary film.[267] In considering the merits of the film, it is worth remembering his wife Frances Flaherty's argument that "a Flaherty film must not be confused with the documentary movement that has spread all over the world, for the reason that

---

[264]   Gabe Essoe and Raymond Lee, DEMILLE: THE MAN AND HIS PICTURES (Cranbury: A. S. Barnes and Company, 1970), p.124.

[265]   DeWitt Bodeen, "Bebe Daniels," FILMS IN REVIEW 15:7 (August- September 1964): 412-40.

[266]   Rhode, p.224.

[267]   In addition to the previously cited material, see Bosley Crowther, "Nanook of the North," THE GREAT FILMS, pp.24-26.

the documentary movement (fathered not by Robert Flaherty but by a Scotsman, John Grierson) was from its beginning all preconceived for social and educational purposes, just as many of our most famous films have been preconceived for political purposes, for propaganda, and, as Hollywood preconceives, for the box office. These films are timely, and they serve, often powerfully and with distinction, the timely purposes for which they are made. But there are other films, and the Flaherty films are among these, that are timeless. They are timeless in the sense that they do not argue, they celebrate. And what they celebrate, free and spontaneously, simply and purely, is the thing itself for its own sake."[268]

JOHN FORD

THE IRON HORSE (Fox--16mm: 1924, 110 mins., b/w, silent, R-MMA)[269]
Although he began directing movies in 1917 and gained attention as the director of Harry Carey, Sr., westerns, Ford established his reputation as a master of epic westerns with this story about the building of the first transcontinental railroad. "While not a masterpiece," explains Jean Mitry, "THE IRON HORSE is at least the most 'solid ' Western from the end of the silent era. In the best moments, Ford achieves a simple and stark beauty, still schematic in its development but powerful, airy and vigorous. He goes beyond the story line to exalt man's gesture; he begins to develop a mode of expression that condenses the essential fact or the pure act, rendering transparent the character of the individuals."[270]

WILLIAM S. HART

THE TOLL GATE (Paramount--16mm: 1920, 55 mins., b/w, silent, R-BUD, EMG, IVY, KIT, MMA, WES; S-BLA)
Here is one of the best surviving films starring William S. Hart, the greatest cowboy star of the silent era, in his famous role as the "good-badman" who shuns his freedom to save a young child's life.[271] A tinted print with a musical score only is available from the Killiam Collection.

BUSTER KEATON

THE GENERAL (Metro-16mm: 1927, 90 mins., b/w, silent, R-BUD, EMG, FNC, IVY, KIT, MMA, SWA, TWY, WEL, WES, WHO; S-BLA)
Buster Keaton directed, wrote, and starred in this memorable film about a hero during the Civil War who decides to rescue a stolen train. Probably the best film the dry, sardonic, and cerebral comedian ever made for showing his brilliant timing and superb visual gags.[272] Worth noting is the fact that Keaton prided himself on the film's historical accuracy. The major emphasis, however, is on presenting a

---

[268]   Frances Hubbard Flaherty, THE ODYESSEY OF A FILM-MAKER: ROBERT FLAHERTY'S STORY (Urbana: Beta Phi Mu, 1960), p.11.   For a more detailed discussion of the documentary movement, see Chapter 2.

[269]   Killiam rents a 16mm version with sound effects and music.

[270]   "The Birth of a Style," p.5.

[271]   See Chapter 2 for information about W. S. Hart and Westerns.

[272]   Philip Strick, "Great Films of the Century: THE GENERAL," FILMS AND FILMING 7:12

positive image of the Confederacy. In his words, "You can always make villains out of the Northerners, but you cannot make a villain out of the South."[273] A tinted print with musical score only is available from the Killiam Collection.

THE NAVIGATOR (Metro--16mm: 1924, 62 mins., b/w, musical score only, R-FNC)
      Co-directed with Donald Crisp and scripted by Clyde Bruckman, Joseph Mitchell, and Jean Havez, this brilliant comedy is an example of Keaton's fascination with the struggle of man versus the machine. "His is no romance," explains Rudi Blesh, "impeded but not deterred by machinery; it is, rather, a precarious wooing that hinges on a duel with a mechanical enemy."[274] The ingenious comedy deals with a rich playboy (Keaton) and his helpless girlfriend (Kathryn McGuire) who are stranded alone at sea aboard a mammoth ocean liner. Once more it is Keaton's timing and superb sight gags that make the film so enduring.

HENRY KING

TOL'ABLE DAVID (First National--16mm: 1921, 109 mins., tinted version, silent, R-FES, TWY, WIL; S-BLA)
      Henry King directed this highly acclaimed story of David (Richard Barthelmess), the youngest son of simple mountain people, who grows to maturity in the rugged outdoor world. Particularly outstanding are King's sensitive direction, his striking location shots, and his lucid continuity.[275]

HARRY LANGDON

THE STRONG MAN (First National--16mm: 1926, 78 mins., b/w, silent, R-TWY)
      Directed by Frank Capra, who was also an unacknowledged co-author with Arthur Ripley, this delightful story about a baby-faced World War I hero who eventually winds up in America as an assistant to a German performer is a good example of the debate raging over the creation of Langdon's comedy. Capra's influence is evident in the camera work and story line, while Langdon's virtuoso gags demonstrate his theatrical training and skill.

HAROLD LLOYD

      The only authentic 16mm Lloyd films available at this time are 14 one- and two-reelers, which can be rented on an individual basis from Em Gee Film Library. His other films have been so horribly re-edited as to make them a mockery of Lloyd's brilliant "All-American boy" characterizations. The supporting casts included Bebe Daniels and Snub Pollard.

(September 1961):14-16, 40; and Bosley Crowther, "The General," THE GREAT FILMS, pp.60-65.

[273]   Cited in Dardis, p.138.

[274]   Rudi Blesh, KEATON (New York: Macmillan, 1966), p.251.

[275]   Jack Jacobs, "Richard Barthelmess," FILMS IN REVIEW 9:1 (January 1958):12-21; and Roy Pickard, "The Tough Race," FILMS AND FILMING 17:12 (September 1971):38-44.

ERNST LUBITSCH

LADY WINDERMERE'S FAN (Warners--16mm: 1925, 85 mins., b/w, silent, R-BUD, EMG, IMG, KIT, MMA, TWY)

A splendid contrast with the films that Lubitsch made in Europe, this Julien Josephson screen adaptation of Oscar Wilde's play highlights Lubitsch's move away from historical melodramas and into the world of romantic comedies. As Poague notes, the film "is concerned with social reality and social illusion: the reality in this case being a strong set of social rules, and the illusion being that one can break those rules with impunity."[276] Irene Rich plays the sophisticated mother of the naive Lady Windermere (May McAvoy), who foolishly seeks to end her marriage. The sophisticated charm of the decor, clothes, and individual performances illustrates the director's impatience with prepared scripts and his willingness to impose visual flourishes whenever he felt a pictorial innuendo was appropriate.

FRIEDRICH W. MURNAU

SUNRISE (Fox-16mm: 1927, 95 mins., b/w, musical and sound effects only, R-KIL, MMA; S-BLA)

After THE LAST LAUGH, Murnau came to Hollywood and made this moving parable about good and evil, starring Janet Gaynor and George O'Brien. Very evident in this love story of two country "greenhorns" who get confused in the big city are the masterly techniques first developed at UFA.[277]

VICTOR SJOSTROM

THE SCARLET LETTER (MGM--16mm: 1926, 98 mins., b/w, silent, R-MGM)

Frances Marion's sensitive screen adaption of the classic Hawthorne novel allowed ample opportunities for Sjostrom to develop excellent characterizations and to create riveting psychological effects. Lillian Gish gives a fine performance as the woman destroyed by unremitting religious persecution.

MAURITZ STILLER

HOTEL IMPERIAL (Paramount--16mm: 1927, 78 mins., b/w, silent, R-FNC, MMA)

After being fired from MGM, Stiller moved over to Paramount to make the first of his two Hollywood films. Working with Jules Furthman's imaginative script and guided by the producer Erich Pommer, Stiller obtained a wonderful performance from

---

[276]   Leland A. Poague, THE CINEMA OF ERNST LUBITSCH (South Brunswick: A. S. Barnes and Company, 1978), p.41.

[277]   David Martin, "George O'Brien," FILMS IN REVIEW 13:9 (November 1962):541-60; Dorothy B. Jones, "SUNRISE: A Murnau Masterpiece," INTRODUCTION TO THE ART OF THE FILM, pp.102-29; Mary Ann Doane, "Desire in SUNRISE," FILM READER 2 (1978):71-7; J. Dudley Andrew, "The Gravity of SUNRISE," QUARTERLY REVIEW OF FILM STUDIES 2:3 (August 1977):356-87; Robert C. Allen, "William Fox Presents SUNRISE," ibid., pp.327-38; Steve Lipkin, "SUNRISE: A Film Meets Its Public," ibid., pp.339-55; Molly Haskell, "SUNRISE," FILM COMMENT 7:2 (Summer 1971):16-9; Robin Wood, "Murnau's Midnight and Sunrise," ibid., 12:3 (May-June 1976):4-19; Dudley Andrew, FILM IN THE AURA OF ART (Princeton: Princeton University Press, 1984), pp.28-58; and Allen and Gomery, pp.91-105.

Pola Negri as a patriotic chambermaid whose hotel is commandeered by the Russians during World War I. Particularly controversial in this atmospheric melodrama is the sexist treatment of Negri, who chooses to sacrifice her honor to save a friend's life.

RUDOLPH VALENTINO

BLOOD AND SAND (Paramount--16mm: 1922, 113 mins., b/w, silent, R-BUD, EMG, IVY, KIT, MMA, SWA, WEL, WIL; S-BLA)
   Fred Niblo directed this classic screen version of Vincent Blasco Ibanez's romantic book about the tragic life of a Spanish bullfighter who is torn between his love for two women and his love for the bullring. Rouben Mamoulian's 1941 remake, starring Tyrone Power, Linda Darnell, and Rita Hayworth, was a beautiful and spectacular version that focused more on the visual beauty of the action than on the dramatic love triangle. A tinted version with musical score and narration is available from the Killiam Collection.

THE FOUR HORSEMEN OF THE APOCALYPSE (MGM--16mm: 1921, 120 mins., b/w, silent, R-FNC)
   The director Rex Ingram[278] brought Rudolph Valentino to stardom in June Mathis's unusual screen adaptation of the Ibanez novel depicting the fortunes of war, love, and fate. One gets a sense of the exotic and erotic nature of the roles that appealed to Valentino's legion of fans. In addition to the star's extraordinary performance, credit goes to the director for his skill in developing lovely visual moods and settings. As Liam O'Leary aptly comments, "Ingram infused the film with great visual beauty, a sensitivity to light and shade, and an unusual feeling for composition."[279] Vincente Minnelli's 1962 remake, starring Glenn Ford, helped further no one's career.

KING VIDOR

THE CROWD (MGM--16mm: 1928, 93 mins., b/w, musical score only, R-MGM)
   Director King Vidor also helped write the scenario for this socially conscious film about the dismal existence of an office worker in a large city. Heavily influenced by the German Expressionist film movement and fatalistic to the point of mocking the values of the American Dream, it nonetheless proved popular with American audiences near the end of the decade. The picture gave James Murray's career a short boost in popularity and led to widespread recognition once more for Vidor's talent.[280]

JOSEF VON STERNBERG

UNDERWORLD (Paramount--16mm: 1927, 83 mins., b/w, musical score only, R-MMA)

---

[278] For more information, see George Geltzer, "Hollywood's Handsomest Director," FILMS IN REVIEW 3:5 (May 1952):213-19; DeWitt Bodeen, "Rex Ingram and Alice Terry: Part One," ibid., 26:2 (February 1975):73-89; and ___, "Rex Ingram and Alice Terry: Part Two--The Studio at Nice and the End of a Career," ibid., 23:3 (March 1975):129-42.

[279] Liam O'Leary, "THE FOUR HORSEMEN OF THE APOCALYPSE," THE INTERNATIONAL DICTIONARY OF FILMS AND FILMMAKERS Volume I: FILMS, p.160.

[280] Vernon L. Schonert, "James Murray," FILMS IN REVIEW 19:10 (December 1968):618-23; and Bosley Crowther, "The Crowd," THE GREAT FILMS, pp.66-70.

A Robert N. Lee screenplay based upon a Ben Hecht story, this prototype of the gangster film demonstrates von Sternberg's marvelous ability to use artificial reality in a creative and fascinating style. The imaginative and innovating film may seem dated in light of the gangster films that followed it in the 1930s, but the conventions it employs were unique for the times. A valuable exercise is to compare it with Hecht's screenplay for SCARFACE (1932) and also to compare the stylistic differences between Howard Hawks, who directed the later film, and the young von Sternberg. Also worth examining are the stylized 1927 performances by George Bancroft, Clive Brook, and Evelyn Brent.

ERICH VON STROHEIM

BLIND HUSBANDS (Universal--16mm: 1919, 66 mins., b/w, silent, R-BUD, EMG, FNC, IMG, IVY, KIT, MMA, SWA)
    Written and directed by, and also starring von Stroheim, this film about a beautiful wife neglected by her rich husband and the compromising situation she finds herself in marks one of the most brilliant film debuts in cinematic history. Von Stroheim's earlier work as a film extra and minor technician gave no indication that he possessed the talent to win critical fame simultaneously in three categories. Particularly impressive in this romantic melodrama set in Vienna are von Stroheim's attention to detail, the film's realistic atmosphere, and his masterly impersonation of an erotic and cruel seducer. Equally staggering was the cost of the film, which, according to Carl Laemmle, was ten times the amount budgeted.

FOOLISH WIVES (Universal--16mm: 1922, 88 mins., b/w, silent, R-BUD, EMG, FES, FNC, IMA, IVY, MMA, SWA, WEL, WIL; S-REE, TFF)
    Despite the cost of von Stroheim's lavish production techniques, the conservative studio head Laemmle suggested this intriguing story about a phony Russian nobleman (von Stroheim) who preys on the frailities of wealthy women visiting the Riviera. The theme was similar to that of BLIND HUSBANDS, but the new production was far more lavish. Koszarski suggests that it be seen against the spectacles being made by von Stroheim's peers--e.g., THE FOUR HORSEMEN OF THE APOCALYPSE (1921) and WAY DOWN EAST (1920)--and points out that spectacular movies were the rage of the picture palaces.[281] What is also significant about von Stroheim's third film is the fact that he had already established a coterie of key personnel who would stay with him throughout most of the decade: e.g., Richard Day (art designer), Ben Reynolds, and William Daniels (both cinematographers). Furthermore, this is the film that first pitted Thalberg against von Stroheim, setting in motion the perennial and simplistic debate over art versus commerce. In this instance, commerce won the immediate victory. Thalberg decided FOOLISH WIVES was too long, and the film was reedited twice, first by Arthur Ripley and then by Julius Stern. It failed at the box office and marked the beginning of von Stroheim's historic struggles with studio management.

RAOUL WALSH

WHAT PRICE GLORY? (Fox--16mm: 1926, 122 mins., tinted, musical score only, R-KIL)

---

[281]   *Richard Koszarski, THE MAN YOU LOVE TO HATE: ERICH VON STROHEIM AND HOLLYWOOD (New York: Oxford University Press, 1983), p.72.

Director Walsh presented a rollicking screen adaptation of the play about Flagg and Quirt, the officer and the soldier whose constant bickering underscores the stupidity and human waste that occurs in war. Fine acting by Edmund Lowe, Victor McLaglen, and Dolores Del Rio.[282]

EXPERIMENTATION IN FRANCE (1921-1930)

By the end of World War I, the European cinema was in the throes of an artistic revolution. Almost everyone was reacting to the exciting ideas generated by the breakthroughs in the sciences. It had become quite fashionable among certain artistic vanguards to minimize sentimentality in favor of objectivity, to replace teary-eyed expositions with the detached and objective language of physics and mathematics. In these literary and intellectual circles, the heroes of the day were natural and social scientists like Einstein, Freud, and Heisenberg. At the same time, as discussed earlier, young and imaginative filmmakers in Germany, the Soviet Union, and the Scandinavian countries disregarded the traditional screen emphases on stage and literary adaptations, and, instead, channeled their energies into producing expressionist films of original screenplays, using montage and MISE EN SCENE to transform reality into something personal and/or political. The European filmmakers were all reacting in different ways to the staginess of the FILM D'ART movement and to developments taking place in Hollywood feature films made by artists like DeMille, Chaplin, Griffith, von Stroheim, and Ince. Whatever the Europeans liked, they adapted to fit the nationalistic spirit of their work. Thus German films became distinct from French films, which were distinct from Soviet films.

But there was yet another aesthetic movement affecting Europe's post-WWI radical filmmaking styles. For the first time since the birth of moving pictures, influential people were claiming that film was the equal of the traditional arts. A major impetus for film's new status, as Richard Abel points out, was a group of friends who made up the pre-WWI generation of Paris's AVANT-GARDE poets and intellectuals: Guillaume Apollinaire, Max Jacob, Riccioto Canudo, Blaise Cendrars, Maurice de Waleffe, Fernand Leger, Robert Delaunay, and Marc Chagall. "Among the ideas they came to share," Abel explains, "were two of particular importance: simultaneity and speed characterized the new experience of modern life, and the creation of a simultaneous style should be the goal of modern art."[283] In a series of manifestos published between 1912 and 1914, the group popularized the unique qualities that they felt the cinema possessed for depicting modern life. Abel Gance, later one of the great filmmakers but in 1912 a struggling young ex-actor turned film producer, was one significant observer who shared the group's feelings that contemporary films should disorient modern audiences, making them aware not only of the beauty of heretofore ignored objects but also of the absurdity of a rational society. Influenced primarily by Apollinaire, the poets, artists, and intellectuals adored American westerns, comedies, and serials. Their idols became William S. Hart, Charlie Chaplin, and Pearl White. Not only were these stars entertaining and optimistic, but their films also captured the speed and excitement that symbolized the modern age. The French equivalents are found in the works of Georges Melies, Emile Cohl, Max Linder, Louis Feuillade, and Ferdinand Zecca.

Ironically, the advent of World War I only intensified the group's love of American movies. The French knew firsthand the ravages of battle and rejected almost immediately the vast number of European films dwelling on pessimistic and dreary themes that reinforced Europe's despair. Moreover, French filmmaking had to be abandoned during crucial periods of the conflict, so that American movies monopolized nearly all of the nation's screens. Thus, as Abel observes, ". . . through a unique set of historical circumstances, the chief source of entertainment and artistic stimulus

[282] DeWitt Bodeen, "Dolores Del Rio," FILMS IN REVIEW 18:5 (May 1967):266-83.

[283] Richard Abel, "The Contribution of the French Literary Avant-Garde to Film Theory and Criticism (1907-1924)," CINEMA JOURNAL 14:3 (Spring 1975):20.

in Paris during World War I was American films."[284] By the end of the conflict, the pioneering film enthusiasts had been joined by the emerging dadaists/surrealists--e.g., Louis Aragon, Andre Breton, Jean Cocteau, Louis Delluc, Paul Eluard, Marcel L'Herbier, Pierre Reverdy, and Philippe Soupault--who in the years that followed incorporated their moviegoing excitement into personal films of their own. The state of the French film industry was ideal for the CINEMA D'ART movement. Although economically unstable, it was enjoying considerable popularity at the end of World War I. The fragmented, independent producers who characterized the industry aggressively competed for bookings in the predominantly independent movie houses. The immediate reaction of the AVANT-GARDE in the post-WWI era was to put its experiences into print and on celluloid. "Film and poetry," explains Abel, "were engaged in the same task--the transformation of reality."[285]

Of primary interest to these enthusiasts intent on visually reproducing thoughts and feelings was the ability of film close-ups to isolate objects in unique spatial relationships and to force a new perspective on the objects. What intrigued the artists was the way photography could render an apparently meaningless object mysterious and foreboding. For example, Chaplin's films frequently created enigmatic "image-objects" from guns, lamps, and gazes, while utilizing every aspect of the film frame to provide a sinister environment for the ensuing action. The various theorists, writing in a plethora of specialized film journals, focused attention on the ability of the camera to approximate the vision of the human eye. Their emphasis on visualizing everyday objects shifted attention away from plots and characterizations to mental states. Typical of the enthusiasm in 1920 was the rhetoric of the art historian Elie Faure, who saw in postwar film the opportunity to rejuvenate the plastic arts:

> That the starting point of the art of the moving picture is in plastics seems to be beyond all doubt. To whatever form of expression, as yet scarcely suspected, it may lead us, it is by volumes, arabesques, gestures, attitudes, relationships, associations, contrasts and passages of tones--the whole animated and insensibly modified from one fraction of a second to another--that it will impress our sensibility and act on our intelligence by the intermediation of our eyes.[286]

Filmmakers were encouraged to experiment with quick cutting, moving cameras, montage effects, and impressionistic shots, but with the understanding that the camera should approximate the psychological reactions resulting from a human eye.[287] The emphasis was on transforming reality to fit the impressions and values of the artist.

The ideas generated by the Parisian AVANT-GARDE spread throughout the film world. While artists in Scandinavia, Germany, the Soviet Union, and the United States had different motives in their work, each--e.g., Stiller, Murnau, Eisenstein, and Chaplin--intuitively sensed the desire of mass audiences to be entertained by "the element of surprise," by "the unexpected, the incongruous, the enigmatic--the new world of surreality."[288] Many new artists also simulated the twentieth century's early fascination with a subjective representation of human consciousness. The symbolic film

---

[284]   Abel, p.23.

[285]   Abel, p.26.

[286]   Elie Faure, "The Art of Cineplastics," FILM: AN ANTHOLOGY, ed. Daniel Talbot (New York: Simon and Schuster, 1959), p.7.

[287]   Abel, p.35.

[288]   Abel, pp.30, 36.

experiments themselves were minor compared to the number of traditional films being made by the giant national film industries. They were not, however, insignificant or ignored by intellectuals. As Stuart Liebman succinctly explains,

> Kandinsky and Schoenberg whose stylistic commitments to expressionism are well known, wanted to combine film with other theatrical effects to create magic color "symphonies." The dadaists Man Ray and Rene Clair (ENTR'ACTE) chose image deforming processes to structure their dazzling "irrational" paratactic picaresques. Richter, Eggeling, Survage and Ruttmann saw in graphic animation techniques the means to evolve flat geometric shapes in a continuously flowing time unavailable in painting.[3570]

But of all the European countries, France proved to be the most resilient when it came to revolution and art.[3571]

By 1919, the French AVANT-GARDE was dominated by a group who admired the principles of the late nineteenth-century French painters and who were therefore referred to as the "Impressionists." Their intellectual leader was Louis Delluc,[3572] and a primary source of ideas was his influential but short-lived magazine CINEMA. Hence the group was called CINEASTES. Although Delluc was a journalist, novelist, drama critic, and filmmaker, his greatest contributions were as a film critic from 1917 to 1922. What made him unique, as Eugene C. McCreary points out, was that

> Delluc loved more than he hated, admired more eloquently than he scorned--qualities of the prophet, rare in the critic. He possessed an extraordinary capacity for picking out the superb detail or the noteworthy sequence submerged for most in the mass of idiocies that comprised so many feature films of the period. What he selected for discussion was almost never the story and even less frequently the "meaning" of the film. He picked out and expounded upon a significant moment of the experience of viewing a film--a gesture, an attitude, a setting, the film's rhythm or form--never simply for its own sake but for the role it played (or could play) in the total effect of the film.[3573]

Delluc's strength derived from his ability not only to concentrate on details but also to make comprehensive judgments on what films should be and could be. He saw the future of films as an important part of society's political and social existence. "I have known for a long time now," he wrote in 1920, "that the cinema is destined to provide us with the impressions of fleeting and eternal beauty that only the spectacle of nature and sometimes of human activity can produce--impressions of grandeur,

---

[3570] Stuart Liebman, "Books: THE CUBIST CINEMA," FILM COMMENT 12:5 (September-October 1976):66.

[3571] The following articles are useful: Louis Marcorelles, "French Cinema . . . The Old and the New," SIGHT AND SOUND 27:4 (Spring 1958):190-95; Penelope Houston, "The Rewards of Quality," ibid., 31:2 (Spring 1964):71-72; Peter John Dyer, "Journey into the Night," FILMS AND FILMING 5:10 (July 1959):12-14, 32-33; and Peter John Dyer, "Some Personal Visions," ibid., 5:2 (November 1958):13-15, 30-31; and Ronald H. Blumer, "The Camera as Snowball: France 1918-1927," CINEMA JOURNAL 9:2 (Spring 1970):31-39.

[3572] For more information, see Roy Armes, THE INTERNATIONAL DICTIONARY OF FILMS AND FILMMAKERS, VOLUME II, pp.124-5; and Eugene C. McCreary, "Louis Delluc, Film Theorist, Critic, and Prophet," CINEMA JOURNAL 16:1 (Fall 1976):14-35.

[3573] McCreary, p.15.

simplicity, distinctness that suddenly render art useless."[293] Among the films he created to illustrate his impressionistic values are the atmospheric FEVER/FIEVRE (1921) and THE WOMAN FROM NOWHERE/LA FEMME DE NULLE PART(1922).

Those artists--e.g., Germaine Dulac, Abel Gance, Jean Epstein, and Marcel L'Herbier--who shared Delluc's vision and enthusiasm for film also perceived it as more than a mechanical distraction and escapist entertainment. Excited by the possibilities demonstrated in their World War I moviegoing experiences, they explored the medium's responsiveness to melancholy and symbolic literary adaptations related to the modern age.[294] While national cinemas like those of Germany, Britain, and the Soviet Union depended heavily on government support, French filmmakers prided themselves on their independence and on their individuality. Dozens of small studios readily rented their facilities on a pay-as-you-go basis. As a result of the loosely structured French film industry, the impressionists took advantage of the accessibility of relatively inexpensive film equipment and the support of novelty-seeking audiences to explore in their symbolic screen treatments the complicated relationships among the physical sciences, the social sciences, and the creative handling of space and time. Each artist strove to produce movies that not only were distinctly French films, but also primarily cinematic.

What grouped many AVANT-GARDE artists together at the end of World War I was a desire to experiment with the form and content of full-length commercial films. For example, L'Herbier's EL DORADO (1921) probes the tragic life of a barroom dancer through a variety of expressionist techniques; Gance's I ACCUSE/J'ACCUSE (1919) focuses on the irrational impulses in French society that propelled the nation into the beastiality of World War I and shows the war dead rising from their unmarked graves to haunt the living; Epstein's FAITHFUL HEART/COEUR FIDELE (1923) has the story of a blue-collar love triangle in Brittany serve as the excuse for extraordinary imagery; and Dulac's THE SMILING MADAME BEUDET/LA SOURIANTE MADAME BEUDET (1922) uses the conventions of a traditional French murder mystery as an opportunity to examine stream of consciousness ideas on screen. These four symbolic film representations of French society and their cinematic emphases on psychological and abstract techniques epitomized the characteristics of France's first AVANT-GARDE film movement.

AVANT-GARDE cinema in France was not limited, however, to Delluc's ideas. For example, Gance, one of the most enduring artists in a decade of cinematic discoveries, fits into no one group exclusively. That may be the reason why his films have been ignored throughout much of film history. "It is a mystery to us," write Steven Philip Kramer and James Michael Welsh, ". . . why the work of Abel Gance, who has been recognized as one of the founders of the French cinema and whose contributions in his native country match those of Griffith in the United States and Eisenstein in the Soviet Union, should have gone unnoticed for so many years in America."[295] They observe that his six major films--I ACCUSE/J'ACCUSE (two versions, 1919 and 1938), THE WHEEL/LA ROUE (1921), NAPOLEON VU PAR ABEL GANCE (1927), BEETHOVEN (1936), and CYRANO ET D'ARTAGNAN (1963)--are among the works of the screen, that as Gance himself was fond of saying, were made

---

[293]   McCreary, p.34.

[294]   Rhode, p.121.

[295]   *Steven Philip Kramer and James Michael Welsh, ABEL GANCE (Boston: Twayne Publishers, 1978), p.10. For more information, see William M. Drew, "Abel Gance: Prometheus Bound," TAKE ONE 6:8 (July 1978):30-2, 45; Kevin Brownlow, "Bonaparte et la Revolution," SIGHT AND SOUND 41:1 (Winter 1971-72):18-9; and James M. Welsh and Steven Philip Kramer, "Abel Gance's Accusation Against War," CINEMA JOURNAL 14:3 (Spring 1975):55-67.

"not to live . . .   but in order not to die."[296] Each of these remarkable films demonstrates the filmmaker's insistence on blending innovative techniques with spectacular stories about historical personalities and events.

After Delluc's tragic death from tuberculosis in 1924, a second AVANT-GARDE film movement, developing parallel to Delluc's efforts, dominated Parisian film circles from the mid- to late-1920s. Gathering its inspiration from the tenets of dadaism, cubism, futurism, and surrealism, the new focus moved away from commercial feature-length films, and toward short, personal movies that approximated visual poems and individual dreams. Andre Breton was the group's spiritual leader; his surrealistic perspective focused on the relationship between dreams and reality in literature and aesthetics.[297] What Breton wanted to study was the gray area between sleep and waking, the multiple layers of imagery that occupy the conflicting states of mind that characterize "surreality." His interest was not merely art for the sake of art. Breton was a moralist who objected to the "shackles" placed upon the public by traditional social, educational, and political institutions. Thus, his clarion call for surrealistic films that attacked conventional film aesthetics was also very much a revolutionary cry for attacking society's sacred cows: religion, sex, morality, and politics. Moreover, he believed that the best way to effect his revolutionary goals was by shocking and scandalizing middle-class attitudes and behavior.

This manifesto of a "crisis in consciousness" became the stuff that surrealist films were made of. Reality and dreams were presented as indistinguishable on screen. For example, Clair's ENTR'ACTE (1924) incorporated the insane qualities of a dream along with the zaniness of pioneering French film comedy in its ridicule of traditional funeral rituals; Leger's MECHANICAL BALLET/BALLET MECANIQUE (1924) abandoned plot altogether to concentrate on abstract images of ballerinas in motion; and Luis Bunuel's remarkable AN ANDALUSIAN DOG/UN CHIEN ANDALOU (1928) became the premier surrealist statement with depictions of shocking images of the unconscious. In addition, Dulac experimented with sexual fantasies and thought processes in THE SEASHELL AND THE CLERGYMAN/LA COQUILLE ET LE CLERGYMAN (1928); L'Herbier presented the group's greatest intellectual realization of dadaist's notions in films like THE BIG MAN/L'HOMMAGE DU LARGE (1921) and THE INHUMAN/L'INHUMAINE (1923); and Man Ray's RETURN TO REASON/RETOUR A RAISON (1923), LEAVE ME ALONE/EMAK BAKIA (1927), and THE STARFISH/L'ETOILE DE MER (1928) demonstrated not only his intriguing cubist imagery but also how an American in Paris could safely invest his time in films and not be hurt financially or artistically.[298]

Many of the AVANT-GARDE filmmakers of the 1920s also shared an interest, as Raymond Durgnat observes, in "'populism,' not in the usual political sense, but in the film one, as being about the PETITS GENS, the lower middle classes and lower."[299] The interest lasted from the mid-1920s to the mid-1930s, during a period, as Durgnat explains, "when a mixture of economic stagnation and preparation for war shifted the emphasis different ways in different countries."[300] For example, America had Allan Dwan's MANHANDLED (1924) and King Vidor's THE CROWD (1928), while Germany had Leopold Jessner and Paul Leni's BACKSTAIRS/HINTERTREPPE (1921) and F. W. Murnau's THE LAST LAUGH/DER LETZE MANN (1924). However, as

---

[296] Kramer and Welsh, p.11.

[297] Andre Breton, MANIFESTES DU SURREALISME (Paris: Jean Jacques Pauvert, 1962).

[298] For more information, see Steven Kovacks, "Man Ray as Film Maker: Part I," ARTFORM 11:3 (November 1972):77-82; and ___, "Man Ray as Film Maker: Part II," ibid., 11:4 (December 1972):62-6.

[299] "King Vidor: Part 1,"p.15.

[300] "King Vidor: Part 1," p.15.

Durgant insists, "French populism remains the best remembered--with [Jean] Vigo's L'ATALANTE, Clair's SOUS LES TOITS DE PARIS and LE QUARTORZE JUILLET, [Jean] Renoir's TONI and THE CRIME OF MONSIEUR LANGE/LE CRIME DE MONSIEUR LANGE, and [Marcel] Carne's HOTEL DU NORD and LE JOUR SE LEVE."[301]

In addition to experimenting with temporal-spatial relationships, our irrational psyches, and reality's illogical nature, the second AVANT-GARDE movement became interested in the abstract representation of cities. For example, Alberto Cavalcanti's RIEN QUE LES HEURES (1926), with its bizarre images of Parisian slums during a twenty-four hour period, stimulated similar interpretations of cities in Germany--e.g., Walther Ruttman's BERLIN: THE SYMPHONY OF A CITY (1927)--and in Holland--e.g., Joris Ivens's RAIN (1928). As Jack Ellis explains, "Though the concern of these films is more with visual and rhythmical patterns than with social content, they served as a transition from the avant-garde of the twenties to the documentaries of the thirties."[302]

France also became the haven for film refugees like Fritz Lang, Erich Pommer, Victor Tourjansky, Alexander Kamenaka, Dmitri Kirsanov, Jacques Feyder, Luis Bunuel,[303] Salvador Dali, Man Ray, Alberto Cavalcanti, and Carl Dreyer. In spite of the staggering blow that the expensive and prohibitive transition to sound dealt the French industry, many of these amazing artists continued their experimentations with new forms of story-telling, AVANT-GARDE projects, psychological characterizations, and popul99arist themes.

If the AVANT-GARDE films had one major failing it was their obsession with technique. The majority of French film audiences failed to understand, let alone appreciate, what the surrealists were trying to say about bourgeoise society and culture. Thus the films themselves had limited circulation and even less impact on the general public. A decade later, as we will see, a more experienced and socially conscious group of artists would aim their experimental ideas directly at mass audiences and become very successful.

The debate today about the innovative French cinema of the 1920s centers on how good the films were and what impact they had on their times and on future filmmakers. Many authors like Ellis, Bohn, Stromgren, Cook, and Robinson gloss over the pretentiousness of the film styles and focus instead on the unique innovations connected with reproducing thoughts and feelings on the screen that characterized the experimental movements. Few critics even allude to the fact that many filmmakers of the period were repulsed by AVANT-GARDE works and diassociated themselves from the techniques of men like Gance and L'Herbier. Rhode, however, is an exception, an author who offers an extensive analysis (thirty-eight pages) that is critical of most of the French experimental films between 1919 and 1929. While he acknowledges the value of the movements to raise global consciousness about the status of the new art, he stresses the filmmakers' obsessive symbolic aesthetics that blinded them to rational filmmaking. He describes the value of working without

---

[301]   "King Vidor: Part 1," p.15.

[302]   A HISTORY OF FILM, 2nd ed., p.129.

[303]   Some useful articles are Tony Richardson, "The Films of Luis Bunuel," SIGHT AND SOUND 23:3 (January-March 1954):125-30; Derek Prouse, "Interviewing Bunuel," ibid., 29:3 (Summer 1960):118-19; Robert M. Hammond, "Luis Alcoriza and the Films of Luis Bunuel," FILM HERITAGE 1:1 (Fall 1965):24-34; Peter Harcourt, "Luis Bunuel: Spanish and Surrealist," FILM QUARTERLY 20:3 (Spring 1967):2-19; J. F. Aranda, "Surrealist and Spanish Giant: First Part of An Analysis of Bunuel's Work for the Cinema," FILMS AND FILMING 8:1 (October 1961):17-18; J. F. Aranda, " . . . Second Part," ibid., 8:2 (November 1961):29-30, 45; and Alf Maclochlainn, "Pointed Horror: The Films of Luis Bunuel and Georges Franju," THE FILM JOURNAL 1:2 (Summer 1971):16-21.

detailed shooting schedules and scripts and applauds the ideas of improvisational art imbued with free-flowing associations, while reminding us that these experimentalists were as much interested in pandering to the jaded tastes of the newly formed film societies and CINE clubs, as they were in expanding the range of film expression. Rhode also takes the AVANT-GARDE to task for its selfconscious techniques, complaining that "Too much the product of theory, of a WILLED idea about the nature of film, they bear all the marks of faded fashion and mechanical trickery." He goes on to say that "The avant-garde tended to confuse originality with novelty, and indeed was most bold when least consciously experimental; when its output was indistinguishable in kind, if not quality, from anyone else's."[304]

BOOKS

THE AVANT-GARDE CINEMA

*Armes, Roy. FILM AND REALITY: AN HISTORICAL SURVEY. Baltimore: Penguin Books, 1974. Illustrated. 253pp.

"The following pages," Armes tells us, "trace three strands of development through the eighty or so years of the cinema's history. The aim is to put the study of film history into some kind of perspective and to allow the general reader to find his bearings more easily amid the voluminous and increasingly fragmentary mass of critical writings currently available about the cinema. Rather than take a single aesthetic standpoint, from which the whole of the cinema's output is to be assessed, this volume adopts a triple perspective." The three perspectives that highlight Armes's broad view of film history deal with "the uncovering of the real, the imitating of the real, and the questioning of the real." Thus, the first section of the book discusses the evolution of film realism from Lumiere and Melies, to the rise of CINEMA-VERITE and realism on contemporary television. Arguing that the purpose of this tradition is "to show the world as it is," the author points out how the artists try to eliminate, as much as possible, any interference between the event and the audience. The second section of the book analyzes how filmmakers from Edison and the early founders of the Hollywood studio system to those of the post-World War II era discarded the traditions of the film realist and turned instead to an "imitation of life" perspective. This tradition, he explains, "is used not as an end in itself but as means of creating satisfying fictions. It is the cinema's role as the universal storyteller that gave rise to Hollywood and prompted the growth of a world-wide entertainment industry." The third section of the book traces what Armes considers the least developed of the cinema's perspectives on reality, "Film Modernism." Referring to a desire to examine "the dreamlike aspects of the film experience . . . in a way which reduces objects and people to mere ciphers," he describes how experimentalists from Bunuel and Eisenstein to Resnais and Godard have merged the real and the unreal to create exciting and novel approaches to construct "a multiple perspective in the manner of a cubist painting." Throughout this highly stimulating investigation, the author presents a lucid and absorbing look at film history. A bibliography and index are included. Recommended for special collections.

Curtis, David. EXPERIMENTAL CINEMA. New York: Universe Books, 1971. Illustrated. 168pp.

Working from the thesis that the experimental film is vital to the art and development of motion picture history, Curtis presents a short but critical history of the crucial stages and of the personalities who discovered and expanded film technique. The material is divided into four main sections: "The European

---

[304]   Rhode, p.127.

Avant-Garde," France (1919-1930), Germany (1919-1930), Russian experimenters, and transitional Animators; "America Between the wars," AVANT-GARDE filmmakers (1921-1934), popularization of filmmaking, and Hollywood--innovation and experiment; "America Since the War," East Coast (Cinema 16 and the Gryphon Group), West Coast (Art in Cinema Series), and the new film poets; and "The Co-Operative movement--Internationalism--New Directions," short film craftsmen, optical (film as film and found footage), the informal vision, minimal movies and anti-aesthetic sex, and structural cinema. In addition, there is an excellent collection of stills. A bibliography and index are included. Well worth browsing.

Gould, Michael. SURREALISM AND THE CINEMA (OPEN-EYED SCREENING). South Brunswick: A. S. Barnes and Company, 1976. Illustrated. 171pp.

"Although the book contains much material on the films of Luis Bunuel," Gould tells us at the outset, "there is little space given to the work of other such historically important surrealist film-makers as Jean Cocteau and Rene Clair. Surrealism can be an endless topic, and this is not meant to be a comprehensive study of 'known' surrealist film-makers (a 'Ten Most Wanted' List), nor a review of a movement in cinema. This is just a selective book about films; a book about art; about perception; revelation; and appreciation." In short, this is a book that offers challenging ideas about important subjects in a down-to-earth manner. Following a quick overview of the roots of the surrealist movement--e.g., Breton, Duchamp, Dali, Ernst, and Chirico--and the pioneering films, Gould provides six entertaining chapters on Bunuel, von Sternberg, Hitchcock, Fuller, animated filmmakers, and experimental films. A bibliography and index are included. Well worth browsing.

Hedges, Inez. LANGUAGES OF REVOLT: DADA AND SURREALIST LITERATURE AND FILM. Durham: Duke University Press, 1983. Illustrated. 166pp.

"In the second and third decades of the century," Hedges observes in her introduction to five stimulating chapters, "many of the most fundamental conditions of human life had changed so rapidly that some artists and writers decided that literature and the arts should become a central mechanism for the adaptation of human attitudes, values, and perceptions to the actual situation. In the face of radical social, economic, political and ideological disruptions of the existing order--intensified by the trauma of world war--these artists and writers discovered that the existing traditions of their various arts were inadequate to express the new awareness they had found. Collectively, they turned their energies into transforming their instruments and techniques for producing meaning--the symbol systems or 'languages' of their arts--into languages of revolt." Hedges pinpoints the small group of dissidents--Hans Arp, Tristan Tzara, Marcel Janco, Hugo Bell, and Richard Huelsenbeck--who congregated in Zurich, Switzerland, in 1916, and formed the nucleus of the dada group. In describing not only the achievements but also the influence of the movement on many artistic conventions, she adds considerably to our understanding of the radical visual and narrative techniques found in the cinematic works of Andre Breton, Luis Bunuel, Rene Clair, Germaine Dulac, and Marcel Duchamp. The highly theoretical analyses offer stimulating observations on how we learn from the unfamiliar and how language functions in bringing about new perceptions. Endnotes and an index are provided. Well worth browsing.

Kovacks, Steven. FROM ENCHANTMENT TO RAGE: THE STORY OF SURREALIST CINEMA. Rutherford: Fairleigh Dickinson University Press, 1980. Illustrated. 297pp.

Curious about the relationship between surrealism and movies, the author of this study examines two key questions: "First, what was the nature of the surrealists' interest in movies? Second, how did their movies reflect the aims and concerns of the movement?" Kovacks focuses his investigation on the significant years of the movement in Paris between 1923 and 1930. The crucial figure is Andre Breton and his two important Surrealist Manifestos (1924 and 1929). Chapter 1 discusses the role that American serials had on the development of themes--e.g., vampirism and eroticism--for surrealist movies; the impact of Guillaume Apollinaire, Jacques Vache, and Louis Delluc; and the early attempts at translating surrealism to the screen. The remaining five chapters offer case studies showing how artists like Louis Aragon, Robert Desnos, Rene Clair, Francis Picabia, Man Ray, Salvador Dali, and Luis Bunuel applied the tenets of surrealism --e.g., the unconscious activities of the human mind, the nature of the dream state, and the duplication of the thought--process to their bizarre and haunting films. Kovacs concludes that despite the fame of many surrealist films, the filmmakers were disappointed with the cinema as a medium for exploring their radical ideas. A bibliography and index are included. Recommended for special collections.

*Lawder, Standish D. THE CUBIST CINEMA. New York: New York University Press, 1975. Illustrated. 265pp.
    "I should like to explain at the outset," Lawder writes, "what this book is, and what it is not. It is not, strictly speaking, a history of cinema, nor is it an orthodox art-historical study. Its principal concern lies in between, for it focuses on the interrelationships between film and modern art, predominantly painting, from 1895 to about 1925; that is to say, from the inception of film to that moment when Cubism and its derivative styles began to lose supremacy within the tradition of European modernism. I have sought to examine these arts of film and painting to discover and document similarities of expression, common sources, and the mutual interchange of talent and ideas." Among the artists that Lawder discusses in his nine stimulating chapters are Blaise Cendrars, Germaine Deluc, Viking Eggeling, Abel Gance, Vassily Kandinsky, Fernand Leger, Pablo Picasso, Francis Picabia, Hans Richter, La Rove, Walter Ruttman, Guido Seeber, Arnold Schoenberg, and Leopold Survage. For some unexplained reason, important individuals like Man Ray and Moholy-Nagy are omitted from the valuable discussions about how modern artists perceived the first commercial movies and how those perceptions affected the nature of modern art during the cubist period. If there is one basic problem with this otherwise outstanding book, it is the author's insistence on forcing many of the major filmmakers of the era into a catch-all genre labeled "Cubist cinema." As Stuart Liebman points out in his excellent review of THE CUBIST CINEMA, ".   .   . with a single important exception [Leger's MECHANICAL BALLET/BALLET MECANIQUE] all the works Lawder discusses   .   . . cannot be comfortably accomodated with 'orthodox' cubist strategies and aims which were, finally, epistemological as much as pictorial. However much the films' geometricized idioms of non-representational elements owe to cubist innovations, to whatever extent these works reflectively allude to the conditions of their fracture or appearance, their styles remain more intimately related to such epigone movements as international DeStijl and Orphism than to the formal intentions of the cubist masters."[305] An appendix dealing with a shot analysis of MECHANICAL BALLET/BALLET MECANIQUE, useful endnotes, and an index are included. Well worth browsing.

LeGrice, Malcolm. ABSTRACT FILM AND BEYOND. Cambridge: The MIT Press, 1977. Illustrated. 160pp.
    Focusing on a chronological overview of the preoccupations of abstract filmmakers (individuals concerned not only with non-representation forms but also with the cinematic manipulation of time), this straightforward account offers a sensible and useful introduction to the evolution of abstraction in art from Paul Cezanne to Andy Warhol. The terse comments, aided by a fine selection of visual illustrations, make

---

[305]   Liebman, p.66.

difficult works more accessible to the general public. Endnotes, a bibliography, and an index are included. Well worth browsing.

Manvell, Roger, ed. EXPERIMENT IN THE FILM. London: Grey Walls, 1949. Illustrated. 285pp. New York: Arno Press, 1972.

A collection of essays by eight important critics who have difficulty in agreeing on an interpretation of "experimentation," the book leaves each essayist "free to choose between making a more general study of film-making in his country from an experimental point of view, or, where the consistent production of unusual films had taken place, making a specific study of that form of cinema which has come to be termed the avant-garde in compliment to France where the most notable school of advanced experiment in film took place between 1925 and 1932." Manvell has a useful introductory article suggesting the range that the experiments take and commenting on the influences of early pioneers like Griffith, Porter, Melies, Eisenstein, Pudovkin, and Dreyer. Especially useful are essays by Hans Richter, Jacques B. Brunius, and Lewis Jacobs. Well worth browsing.

*Matthews, J. H. SURREALISM AND FILM. Ann Arbor: University of Michigan Press, 1971. Illustrated. 191pp.

Jacques B. Brunius, one of the leading surrealist theorists, wrote that the cinema is "the least realistic art." Using that perspective as a starting point, the author of this analytical study begins by trying to understand "why surrealists look to the movies to question the fundamental conventions of realism, and why they are persuaded that films lend themselves to discrediting these conventions." Matthews opens his five-part study with an examination of the principles of surrealism, the problems that commercial films presented for charter members, and the in-roads made by artists like Philippe Soupault, Louis Aragon, and Robert Desnos. The focus is on explaining how theorists like Brunius, who criticized the popular cinema, were rebutted by arguments that aesthetic and technical issues were not primary concerns of surrealists. "The ideal film," explains the author, "serves the surrealist as a storehouse for visual images upon which, he anticipates, his imagination will satisfy its hunger for the marvelous. Exactly how these images are to be assembled, and with what display of technical finesse, is therefore less important to him than that their presence be felt, providing his imagination with something it can digest and transform surrealistically. So far as surrealists interest themselves in methods, they do so by asking how the film-maker can best engineer the 'irruption of poetry.'" The three major sections dealing with surrealist film scripts and filmmakers investigate what priorities the surrealists established for their films, how they undermined the tenets of the commercial cinema, and how they evaluated their own works. "The central concern, throughout," Gould insists, "is to clarify these demands, so as to shed light on their consequences for the cinema." Reactions to Gould's scholarly work will depend on one's background in the subject. The more one brings to the book, the more enjoyable it is. Novices should therefore take note that this is not an introductory work. Endnotes and an index are included. Well worth browsing.

Monaco, Paul. CINEMA & SOCIETY: FRANCE AND GERMANY DURING THE TWENTIES. New York: Elsevier, 1976. 194pp.

Eschewing aesthetics, this imaginative and well-written study tries "to interpret comparatively the mass, public meaning of the most popular French and German films of the decade following World War I." Monaco begins with the debatable assumption that "national products" successful at the box office reveal significant information of the national "group mind." For example, he concludes that "The popular French films of the 1920s portrayed the major themes of the orphan, the individual abandoned in the world, the hero, the presence of children, the amount of blood seen, and were disposed to landscape and seascape photography." This profile contrasts directly to

German films of the same period that "produced popular movies presenting the themes of betrayal, the foreigner as evildoer, the street and the city as ugly and dangerous, the outcast as hero, suicide, and the imagery of clocks and unseen blood."

That the two national cinemas produced distinctly different products is nondebatable. What is controversial, however, is Monaco's assertions that the differences were linked directly to the aftermath of World War I and that his interpretations of what those themes mean are justified. Consider the case of the French "orphans." The author argues that "The orphan films represent a recurrent, dreamlike working off of the French national trauma of having experienced in short order the disintegration of those very alliances [with the British and Americans] that had meant victory instead of defeat in the First World War and that were assumed to be the necessary guarantee of French security in the future." Consider, as well, Monaco's claim that German villains were never what they appeared to be, because "The characterization of the trickster, the man of many disguises, or a sneaky creature who conceals his true identity coincides with the stock anti-Semitic description of the Jew." In neither case does the author insist that these are the only possible interpretations or even the key aspect of the relationship between the spectator and the film in question. But he does argue that these "major themes" taken from the nation's most popular movies "reflect, respectively, a differentiated collective obsession with particular historical events and their aftermath."

Working in Monaco's favor are his considerable scholarly insights, formidable writing skills, and fertile imagination. Whether one agrees with his bold declarations is secondary to the fresh documentation that he uses throughout the book's five fast-moving chapters. Facts about film attendance, business arrangements, official censorship, and historical events blend superbly with lively theories about why film trends developed as they did. Excellent endnotes add further to the originality of his ideas, particularly in his critical discussions of the standard works written by Kracauer and Huaco. One often gets the feeling that there are several agendas operating in the text: a strong defense of Freudian and sociological methodologies as they apply to historical interpretations, a hard-hitting attack on past approaches to analyzing the social function of popular cinema, and a novel look at a significant period in film history.

Working against Monaco is a very weak introductory chapter that misleads the reader into believing this is a simplistic and superficial exercise. After making trite remarks about movies being a business and a powerful weapon for propaganda, he focuses on why it is impossible to demonstrate what effect film has on its audience. No serious documentation is offered and what little there is is dubious. For example, he makes the misleading claim that after a brief excursion into political filmmaking in 1933 and 1934, Goebbels's Ministry of Propaganda "yielded to market conditions." What does that mean in terms of the Jews who were driven out of the industry, the films that never got made, the Nazi film programs orchestrated around the country, the films produced for foreign consumption as compared to those for domestic use, the control of film criticism, etc.? And what is one to make of the silly, empty statement that "The real art of the cinema historically is the artistry of the entrepreneur"? The weakest section, however, is an explanation of how films relate to Freud's dream theories. The comparison between Monaco's comments here and his remarkable breadth in the main body of the book is staggering. In the early material, he appears naive and staid; in the later sections, wise and daring.

Once one gets past the misleading introduction, the book becomes a delightful experience. Two appendexes on the films discussed, a bibliography, and an index are included. Well worth browsing.

LUIS BUNUEL

*Aranda, J. Francisco. LUIS BUNUEL: A CRITICAL BIOGRAPHY. Trans. and ed. David Robinson. New York: Da Capo Press, 1976. Illustrated. 327pp.

The first major English-language examination of Bunuel's life and films, this study is also one of the most stimulating accounts. Reading about the director's forty-five tumultuous years making surrealistic films--from AN ANDALUSIAN DOG/UN CHIEN ANDALOU (1928) to THE PHANTOM OF LIBERTY/LE FATOME DE LA LIBERTE (1974)--and seeing many of his essays and film critiques in print again are only half the enjoyment. The other half is reacting to Robinson's numerous corrections, additions, and disagreements with the extended biographical essay by the Spanish author, who is also a well-known film critic. For example, Aranda tells a story of Bunuel's childhood that allegedly shows the director's early sadistic interests. Robinson then adds a footnote in which he points out that Bunuel denies that the story is true. Elsewhere, Aranda claims, as do others, that Dali was a member of Bunuel's RESIDENCIA DES ESTUDIANTES at the Museum of Natural History of Madrid; Robinson points out that isn't true, although Dali was a frequent visitor there. Aranda asserts that "Surrealism in Spain was contemporary with the French movement"; Robinson argues that Bunuel denies this, insisting that he personally inducted Dali into the ideas of surrealism in Paris, four months after the release of UN CHIEN ANDALOU. Regrettably, no editor points out that the film was released in 1928, not 1929. Inaccuracies like that appear throughout fifteen entertaining and informative chapters. Particularly valuable are the sections highlighting Bunuel's fascination with American comedies and his intriguing years in Mexico. A second but much smaller section of the book is divided into three parts: surrealist and other literary texts between 1922 and 1933, the film criticism of Bunuel, and two unrealized scenarios. Especially noteworthy are the insights we gain from reading Bunuel's film criticism about Hollywood narratives and genres. A filmography, bibliography, and index are included. Well worth browsing.

*Buache, Freddy. THE WORLD OF LUIS BUNUEL. Trans. Peter Graham. New York: A. S. Barnes and Company, 1973. Illustrated. 207pp.
    A detailed discussion of Bunuel's major films from UN CHIEN ANDALOU (1928) to TRISTANA (1970), this interesting monologue plunges into its subject with a heavy-handed analysis of Bunuel's first film. After recovering from Buache's mistaken claim that UN CHIEN ANDALOU was made in 1929, you become curious about just how much interpretation he will offer of a film that was supposed to defy analysis. Bauche begins with the explanation that "This film, which is a kind of openly re-enacted dream, derives from a method known as 'paranoia-criticism,' which Dali saw as being 'based on the critical and systematic objectivisation of delirious associations and interpretations' and Andre Breton defined as 'the ultra-confusional activity that arises from an obsessive idea.' But the sole aim of the film is not merely to shock, but to have an incendiary effect on people who think they have a clear conscience." Bauche then proceeds to comment on the centrality of the eye imagery in Bunuel's films and to locate countless film allusions suggesting "that carnal passion is endowed with magical powers." Taken collectively, the sixteen chapters represent a good cross-section of reactions to Bunuel's films and life, thereby providing a basic introduction to the subject. Brief endnotes, a useful filmography, and an index are included. Worth browsing.

Bunuel, Luis. MY LAST SIGHT. Trans. Abigail Israel. New York: Alfred A. Knopf, 1983. 256pp.
    Reflecting on his fifty-year career in film, the master of surrealist cinema shares his memories about a middle-class childhood in Spain, his days as an engineering student in Madrid, his pilgrimage to Paris in search of AVANT-GARDE ideas, the artists and intellectuals who influenced UN CHIEN ANDALOU (1928), the inevitable journey to Hollywood where friendships with stars like Chaplin and Garbo compensated for the lack of film work, the flight to Mexico and the thirty-year sojourn that resulted in memorable Spanish films (often done with blacklisted American screenwriters), and the triumphant return to Europe in 1960 that produced screen

classics like VIRIDIANA (1961), THE EXTERMINATING ANGEL/EL ANGEL EXTERMINADOR (1962), BELLE DE JOUR (1966), and TRISTANA (1970). "In this semiautobiography," he writes, "where I often wander from the subject like the wayfarer in a picaresque novel seduced by the charm of the unexpected intrusion, the unforeseen story, certain false memories have undoubtedly remained, despite my vigilance . . . I am the sum of my errors and doubts as well as my certainties. " The portraits Bunuel draws of his contacts with personalities like Garcia Lorca, Fritz Lang, William Wyler, Nicholas Ray, Alfred Hitchcock, Jeanne Moreau, and Catherine Deneuve add to our appreciation of his work. Regrettably, no index is included. Well worth browsing.

*Durgnat, Raymond. LUIS BUNUEL. Berkeley: University of California Press, 1967. Illustrated. 152pp.
     This very impressionistic and highly informative critic does a wonderful job in his early chapters on the great Spanish film exile, and no one has yet offered any analysis nearly so detailed as Durgnat's study of UN CHIEN ANDALOU (1928). Even though the treatment of Bunuel's other twenty-six films suffers by comparison, this is a good sourcebook for information on the director's evolving career over a thirty-six-year period. According to the author, Bunuel's work "has progressed as an unfolding rather than a repetition. For all its flaws, his work is an organic whole, containing innumerable echoes, assonances, cross-references, which generate further tensions. Each film, fascinating in itself, sets Bunuel's old loyalties a new problem. " The book's focus is on the director as a moralist and the influence of surrealism on his career. In addition to a good set of stills, there are a filmography and bibliography, but no index. Well worth browsing. [306]

*Higginbotham, Virginia. LUIS BUNUEL. Boston: Twayne Publishers, 1979. Illustrated. 222pp.
     A useful introduction to the one artist whose career output has been almost exclusively devoted to surrealistic values, this study "seeks to discuss the director's major themes and cinematic techniques . . . [and] analyzes the visual style of the films and the preoccupations which lie beneath their narrative surface." Each of the book's six chapters offers a succinct, interesting, and provocative overview of what led the Spanish-born Bunuel on a search for independence and support to France, America, Mexico, and then back to France. For those who wondered why he disappeared from popular view after his three short films--AN ANDALUSIAN DOG/UN CHIEN ANDALOU (1928), THE GOLDEN AGE/L' AGE D'OR (1930), LAND WITHOUT BREAD/LES HURDES (1932)--and reappeared in Mexico after World War II, where he then made seventeen controversial works between 1947 and 1960, this book sketches in the basic details.
     Typical of Higginbotham's provocative analysis is her discussion in Chapter One of the artist's formative years in Spain and his first years in France. She points out that his forty-seven-year-old father's marriage to a seventeen-year-old teenager[307] provides some explanation of why Bunuel appears preoccupied in many of his films with the sexual relationship between older men and younger women. We're never told if the marriage was as distasteful as her allusions to Bunuel's films makes it seem. Nor does she make it clear that Luis was the first of the couple's seven children,

[306]   For a fuller review, see Frank Manchel, "Books: LUIS BUNUEL," FILM SOCIETY REVIEW 4:6 (1969):41-3.

[307]   Aranda (p.11) claims that Leonardo Bunuel was twenty years older than his twenty-three old bride Maria Portoles. He gives her birthdate as 1883; Leonardo's birthdate is omitted. Bauche claims (p.37) that Leonardo was born in 1852; Maria, 1882; thus their marriage represented a thirty-year difference.

what life at home was like, or that Luis was his mother's favorite child. The author then touches on the importance of the boy's Jesuit education in understanding the artist's anti-clericism, his rebellious spirit, and his rejection of traditional values. The two most important elements from his Spanish heritage, she finds, are Bunuel's "profound eroticism" and his obsession with death. Higginbotham next moves quickly to the years in Madrid (1917-1925), where the college-age Bunuel fell under the influence of Spanish intellectuals enamoured with the language of geometry and physics. She notes how his friendships with people like Rafael Alberti, Garcia Lorca, and Salvador Dali not only resulted in lifetime ties, but also shaped his commitment to the principles of surrealism. What's useful in her approach is a willingness to pause periodically and summarize how and what those principles were. In the case of surrealism, Higginbotham points out how Breton's 1924 Surrealistic Manifesto emerged from the ashes of dadaism, where the Spanish vanguard rejected certain of his values, and how Dali directly influenced Bunuel's production of UN CHIEN ANDALOU. Having outlined the basis for the director's poetic vocabulary and his perspectives on art, she concludes with a swift look at his film apprenticeship in Paris from 1925 to 1930. In addition to reiterating the familiar assertion that Lang's DESTINY/DER MUDE TOD (1921) inspired Bunuel to become a filmmaker, the author traces the steps from the young Spaniard's training with Jean Epstein on films like MAUPRAT (1926) and THE FALL OF THE HOUSE OF USHER/LA CHUTE DE LA MAISON USHER (1928) to his objections connected with the techniques of Abel Gance and other AVANT-GARDE filmmakers of the period. Higginbotham also identifies the commercial filmmakers who directly influenced the new director's cinematic style and focus. By the end of the thirty-two page analysis, the author has done a competent job of outlining many of the elements that will recur throughout Bunuel's career. Whether she has been persuasive in her assertions is another matter.

Even if one disagrees with this study's quick judgments on causal relationships, the book's tone and balanced presentation will recommend it as a stimulating biography. Good endnotes, a useful filmography, and a brief index are included. Well worth browsing.

*AGE D'OR, L'/UN CHIEN ANDALOU: FILMS BY LUIS BUNUEL. Trans. Marianne Alexandre. New York: Simon and Schuster, 1968. Illustrated. 124pp.

For some unexplained reason, THE GOLDEN AGE/L'AGE D'OR (1930) precedes UN CHIEN ANDALOU (1928) in this volume. Bunuel's second film, divided into six discontinuous segments and commenting on a host of film formulas and techniques, is introduced by an excerpt from Ado Kyrou's LE SURREALISME AU CINEMA describing the aims of the reigning surrealists of the day. Another excerpt from the same book comments on the battles over the film's content. Following some brief notes from Bunuel himself and an explanation that this publication is based on the director's own shooting script, the complete scenario is presented. Two critical reactions (one by Jean Vigo; the other by Cyril Connolly) introduce UN CHIEN ANDALOU. A filmography is also included. Well worth browsing.

*Mellen, Joan, ed. THE WORLD OF LUIS BUNUEL: ESSAYS IN CRITICISM. New York: Oxford University Press, 1987. Illustrated. 428pp.

This welcome anthology offers a valuable cross-section of critical reactions to the director's films, from UN CHIEN ANDALOU (1928) to THAT OBSCURE OBJECT OF DESIRE (1977). What distinguishes it from previous publications is the heavy emphasis upon French and Spanish essays originally appearing in journals like POSITIF, JEUNE CINEMA, and CINE CUBANO that have heretofore not been translated into English. The translations allow us to contrast the traditional French perspective on Bunuel as a surrealist filmmaker with the Hispanic view of Bunuel "as a satirist and critic of the angst-ridden decadence of Spanish culture, with its anachronistic hidalgos (played most convincingly by Fernado Rey) living in genteel poverty in remembrance of glories past." Mellen divides her anthology into five main sections: an introduction covering Bunuel's career; biographical glimpses by informed authors like J. Francisco Aranda and Carlos Fuentes; observations on the director as a filmmaker not only by Bunuel himself, but also by Donald Richie and Raymond Durgnat; comments on the films by Bunuel, Ado Kyrou, Henry Miller, Victor Casus, Andre Bazin, Juan Bunuel (the director's son), Emilio G. Rierra, and Louis Seguin; and a concluding debate on THE DISCREET CHARM OF THE BOURGEOISIE/LE CHARME DISCRET DE LA BOURGEOISIE (1972), involving critics like John Simon, Charles T. Samuels, and Irving Louis Horowitz. My favorite contribution is Mellen's insightful overview of Bunuel's career, in which she masterfully summarizes his many conflicting characteristics as a Surrealist, Marxist, Freudian, post-Freudian, anarchist, and rebel. A filmography and index are included. Recommended for special collections.

Morris, C. B. THIS LOVING DARKNESS: THE CINEMA AND SPANISH WRITERS 1920-1936. New York: Oxford University Press, 1980. 196pp.

*Sandro, Paul. DIVERSIONS OF PLEASURE: LUIS BUNUEL AND THE CRISES OF DESIRE. Columbus: Ohio State University Press, 1987. Illustrated. 172pp.
     An outstanding analysis employing contemporary critical theory to ten Bunuel films, this lucid study explores "the ways Bunuel disrupts and transforms the pleasures that narrative films promise." The interpretations are linked to Sandro's definitions of "desire" and "narrative form." The former he defines "as a lack or want, the absence of something." The latter relates to classical Hollywood narratives that function "as a temporal sequence of events" representing "time IN TERMS of causality." Moreover, Sandro makes a distinction between desire as found in the director's films and desire resulting from them. The three contexts in which the concept is used in the analyses relate to "desire as theme; . . . as an organizing force within the fictional universe of each film; and . . . as a structural effect of each film on spectators." To the author's credit, he takes his analyses beyond the stage of mere thematic recitations to insightful discussions that reveal the ties between textual and spectator desires: "frustrating deferrals of pleasure, disorienting displacements, seductive dissonances, and conflicts of tone and effect."
     While that correlation forms the main body of the book, a secondary goal is to place Bunuel's career within a historical context. Sandro's succinct explanations about predominant modes of film practice and various theoretical problems offer an excellent introduction to current cinematic discourse. Particularly impressive is his overview of Bunuel's three specific working contexts: the independent, AVANT-GARDE period in France during the mid-twenties through the 1930s, the post-WWII feature-length film period in Mexico and France that lasted through the mid-sixties, and his superstar status from the mid-sixties to mid-seventies working in Europe's "art cinema." The films that the author discusses--i.e., AN ANDALUSIAN DOG/UN CHIEN ANDALOU (1928), THE GOLDEN AGE/L'AGE D'OR (1930), THE EXTERMINATING ANGEL/EL ANGEL EXTERMINADOR (1962), THE DISCREET CHARM OF THE BOURGEOISIE/LE CHARME DISCRET DE LA BOURGEOISIE (1972), MEXICAN BUS RIDE/SUBIDA AL CIELO (1952), ILLUSION TRAVELS BY STREETCAR/LA ILLUSION VIAJA EN TRANVIA (1953), THE PHANTOM OF LIBERTY/LE FANTOME DE LA LIBERTE (1974), BELLE DE JOUR (1966), and THAT OBSCURE OBJECT OF DESIRE/CET OBSCUR OBJECT DU DESIRE (1977)--contrast and compare his early and mature periods. Underlying the explanations is Sandro's perceptive argument that Bunuel was reacting in each of his films to the classical Hollywood narrative that seamlessly stitched its conventions and values in such a way as to co-opt the viewer's feelings and attitudes. Throughout the seven scholarly chapters, the author raises useful reservations about film's so-called abilities to approximate the realm of the unconscious and charts the strategies that the director used as he moved in various historical contexts to challenge classical Hollywood narrative style.

Given the difficulty of the films and the lack of balanced critical studies on the director's compelling achievements, this work is a delight to read. Endnotes and an index are included. Recommended for special collections.

RENE CLAIR

Clair, Rene. REFLECTIONS ON THE CINEMA. London: William Kimber, 1953. 160pp.
"Most of the passages that follow," Clair comments, "were written between 1922 and 1935, that is during the last years of the silent film and the first years of sound. My aim in publishing them now is to throw into fresh relief some of the problems which arose in the cinema at a critical stage of development and which, in spite of that development, have lost none of their importance to-day." Clair divides his material into three major sections. Part One, "The Silent Days," contains seven speculative essays on the hope and ambitions of the early filmmakers. The exercise provides some additional insights on such artists as Griffith, Eisenstein, von Stroheim, Chaplin, and Douglas Fairbanks, Sr.[308] Part Two, "Cutting Our Losses," includes five essays ranging from the effects of Jesse Lasky's visit to Europe in 1928 to problems with adapting stageplays to the film. Part Three offers seven essays, mainly contrasting the Hollywood of the silent era with that of the following three decades. The last section briefly discusses how films are made. An index is included. Worth browsing.

*Clair, Rene. CINEMA YESTERDAY AND TODAY. Trans. Stanley Applebaum. New York: Dover, 1972. Illustrated. 260pp.
This revised edition of REFLECTIONS ON THE CINEMA brings Clair's comparisons between the silent and sound eras up to the end of the 1960s. Well worth browsing.

*A NOUS LA LIBERTE/ENTR'ACTE: FILMS BY RENE CLAIR. Trans. Richard Jacques and Nicola Hayden. New York: Simon and Schuster, 1970. Illustrated. 140pp.
"Rene Clair has stated," the publisher tells us, "that at the time of a film such as A NOUS LA LIBERTE he did not write a literary script and the film was based on brief terse notes which would be tedious to read. It should be pointed out also that the dialogue was not written, but more or less improvised." The script used in this edition, therefore, is transcribed from a shot-by-shot analysis by the editors. As for ENTR'ACTE, the publisher explains that no script exists, "except for a letter written by Francis Picabia, at Maxims, on the restaurant's notepaper, to supply Rene Clair with some ideas for future production." That note is included in this publication, along with a shot-by-shot description of the film. Well worth browsing.

Dale, R. C. THE FILMS OF RENE CLAIR. Volume 1: EXPOSITION AND ANALYSIS; Volume 2: DOCUMENTATION. Metuchen: Scarecrow Press, 1986. Illustrated. 1,074pp.
In this important study of the quintessential French film director from the mid-1920s to the early 1950s, Dale documents why critics and audiences around the globe admired Clair's "nimble wit, vivacity, lightness, calligraphic style, and love of motion." Dale reminds us that "Throughout his career, Clair saw himself as a cinematic author, by which he meant a creator who guides his film from its original conception through its writing, directing and, finally, editing. Because he insisted on working that way, rather than as a writer or a director or an editor, his films

---

[308] R. C. Dale, "Rene Clair in Hollywood," FILM QUARTERLY 24:2 (Winter 1970-71):34-40.

are the product of a single creative psyche; they are the work of a real AUTEUR DE FILMS in the fullest and most genuine sense of the term." The one "informing principle" that Dale discovers in Clair's works is a "value system based upon motion." In Volume 1, the author offers a chronological account of Clair's development as an artist, while, at the same time, discussing each of the director's twenty-six films and and pointing out their sources, as well as the reactions to them. The volume concludes with a bibliography and index. Volume 2 provides extensive descriptions of the movies, including invaluable commentaries on the significant differences between the original release prints and those now in circulation. Dale also includes in the second volume a number of Clair's own thoughts on his work and critical observations on the director's style, themes, and techniques as they relate to the films at the time of their release. What adds to the unique value of this welcome study is the inclusion of material that Dale gleaned from his numerous conversations and correspondence with Clair over an extended period. The volume ends with an index. Recommended for special collections.

Greene, Naomi. RENE CLAIR: A GUIDE TO REFERENCES AND RESOURCES.   Boston: G. K. Hall and Company, 1985. 168pp.

McGerr, Cecilia. RENE CLAIR. Boston: Twayne Publishers, 1980. Illustrated. 239pp.
     Warren French, the editor of this valuable performing arts series, observes in his foreword that "Rene Clair has shared the curious fate of some of the other giants of cinema--D. W. Griffith, Abel Gance, Orson Welles--of scoring his great successes early and then fading into relative obscurity, even though he remained active in French filmmaking until 1965." Whatever familiarity his name has to general American audiences is associated with just three sound films: UNDER THE ROOFS OF PARIS/SOUS LES TOITS DE PARIS (1930), LE MILLION, and GIVE US FREEDOM/A NOUS LA LIBERTE (both in 1931). The films' continuous popularity during the heyday of the Depression, French aptly explains, is due both to their indisputable entertainment value and to Clair's skill in depicting cinematic motion at a time when sound had made much of the cinema static. Few people are aware, however, that Clair was also the director of such significant silent short films as THE CRAZY RAY/PARIS QUI DORT (1923) and ENTR'ACTE (1924); interesting American films like I MARRIED A WITCH (1942) and AND THEN THERE WERE NONE (1945); and memorable later French films like MAN ABOUT TOWN/LE SILENCE EST D'OR (1947), THE BEAUTY OF THE DEVIL/LA BEAUTE DU DIABLE (1950), THE BEAUTIES OF THE NIGHT/LES BELLES-DE-NUIT (1952), and THE GRAND MANEUVER/LES GRANDES MANOEUVRES (1955). The major value of this publication is in providing an informative and comprehensive discussion of the noted French director's career and thereby putting both his work and his contributions in proper perspective. The author's eleven lucid and stimulating chapters take us from Clair's birth (born Rene Chomette) in Paris on November 11, 1898, through his early years as an actor in Gaumont films, to the direction of his first film, THE CRAZY RAY/PARIS QUI DORT (1923), to his first sound movies and his emigration to London in the mid-1930s to work for Alexander Korda, then to his emigration to America in 1940 and the films he made in Hollywood until 1946, to his return to Paris after the end of World War II, and conclude with discussions of his film career over the next eleven years and his eventual retirement to writing in 1967. A filmography, bibliography, and index are included. Well worth browsing.

CARL THEODOR DREYER

*Bordwell, David. FILMGUIDE TO "LA PASSION DE JEANNE D'ARC."   Bloomington: Indiana University Press, 1973. 83pp.

One of the original volumes in this useful series, this book begins with cast and technical credits, followed by an outline of the film and a discussion of the director. The distinguished author, then a young graduate assistant in the Department of Speech and Dramatic Art at the University of Iowa, points out that LA PASSION DE JEANNE D'ARC, Dreyer's ninth film, was very much influenced by Benjamin Christensen's work. Overall, Bordwell concludes that "As a result of Dreyer's intense will, his rigorous control of every artistic element, and his unique forms, styles, and themes, his films have a contemplative density--their own 'holy seriousness'--which makes few concessions to what Hollywood vacuously calls 'entertainment values.'" The remainder of the volume reviews the production of the film, Bordwell's detailed analysis, a summary critique, a filmography, a bibliography, and endnotes. Well worth browsing.

*CARL THEODOR DREYER: FOUR SCREENPLAYS--PASSION OF JOAN OF ARC/VAMPYR/ DAY OF WRATH/ORDET. Trans. Oliver Stallybrass. Introduction Ole Storm. Bloomington: University of Indiana Press, 1970. Illustrated. 312pp.
"The editor of this volume," Dreyer comments, "has, to my delight, selected the scripts of precisely those four of my films which I myself like best and rate highest--partly because they were difficult to make, partly because they gave me unusual opportunities for stylistic experiment. Each of the four posed new and very different theoretical and practical problems, which I had first to investigate and then to surmount." Storm's reflective introduction explores the artist's observations by drawing useful comparisons among the films as well as setting their production within a historical context. Well worth browsing.

ABEL GANCE

*Brownlow, Kevin. NAPOLEON: ABEL GANCE'S CLASSIC FILM. New York: Alfred Knopf, 1983. Illustrated. 310pp.
The distinguished author begins his critical study by reminding us that when NAPOLEON VU PAR ABEL GANCE opened at the Paris Opera in April 1927, the audience saw an abbreviated version; a month later, the complete version was screened to a cheering audience; and then the film mysteriously disappeared, not to be seen in its entirety again until Brownlow's splendid reconstruction in 1981. This riveting account of how the film was made and the process that was involved in reconstructing it is told in a straightforward manner and with extraordinary skill. Endnotes and an index are included. Recommended for special collections.[309]

*Kramer, Steven Philip, and James Michael Welsh. ABEL GANCE. Boston: Twayne Publishers, 1978. Illustrated. 200pp.
An artist who worked in film for over sixty years, Abel Gance is considered by many critics to be one of the exemplary AUTEURS of the cinema. That is not to say that he did not make his share of pedestrian films. But as French points out in his foreword to this important book, "Gance regards the greater number of his pictures that he has directed as assignments that he was compelled to accept for financial reasons and as ventures that failed to give him an opportunity to bring his personal vision to life on the screen. Although Gance recognized that filmmaking was a business and complied with the demands of the producers insensitive to the artistic potential of the medium, he has steadfastly maintained that the motion picture was primarily an art form and that only those that were inspired by an artist's vision

---

[309] See also Max Alexander, "NAPOLEON Campaigns in the Battle for Preservation," NEW
         YORK TIMES H (June 18, 1989):20.

were worth remembering and preserving." Until the publication of this book, there has been no satisfactory English-language introduction to the career of a man who, in the authors' words, epitomizes "what the cinema might have become but never did." Beginning with Gance's birth on October 25, 1889, in Paris and going to the 1973 Brownlow reconstruction of NAPOLEON VU PAR ABEL GANCE, Kramer and Welsh trace the artist's life in films, moving from acting to directing and producing films, making forays into the theater, and then returning to a life of cinematic experimentations (e.g., "Polyvision" triptych techniques) in NAPOLEON VU PAR ABEL GANCE (1927). The book's nine informative, lucid, and entertaining chapters include not only valuable insights into Gance's films and techniques, but also opportunities to study many of his theoretical writings and speculations about films previously unavailable to English-speaking students. Endnotes, a filmography, a bibliography, and an index are included. Recommended for special collections.

MAN RAY

Baldwin, Neil. MAN RAY: AMERICAN ARTIST. New York: Clarkson N. Potter, 1988). Illustrated. 449pp.

*Ray, Man. SELF PORTRAIT. Boston: Little, Brown and Company, 1963. Illustrated. 398pp.

Schwarz, Arturo. MAN RAY: THE RIGOUR OF IMAGINATION. New York: Rizzoli International Publications, 1977. Illustrated. 384pp.
    Painter, creator of poetic objects, photographer, writer, and filmmaker, Man Ray throughout his life (1890-1977) was a media pioneer. "Today, more than any other period in the past," Schwarz observes, "the artist is drawn to an interdisciplinary approach to the arts. Dada and surrealism have been instrumental in liberating him from established artistic and technical categories. For Man Ray this freedom did not have to be conquered, it was part of his nature, as natural as breathing. Whenever he felt the urge to materialize an idea he chose the medium most suitable to express it with the same ease with which a carpenter picks up from his bench the tool most suitable for his purpose." To illustrate his point, Schwarz divides his material into three major sections: "The Two-Dimensional Medium" (focusing on Ray's New York cubist paintings from 1915-1916, his friendships with Francis Picabia and Marcel Duchamp, his work in Paris from 1921 to 1940, the Hollywood stint from 1940 to 1951, and the return to Paris from 1951 to 1976); "The Three-Dimensional Medium" (focusing on examples of Ray's dadaist and surrealistic objects and paintings); and "Light: The One-Dimensional Medium" (focusing on Ray's dadaist and surrealistic photography and filmmaking). In addition to excellent visual reproductions, the book includes an extensive bibliography and index. Recommended for special collections.

FILMS

LUIS BUNUEL

THE ANDALUSIAN DOG/UN CHIEN ANDALOU (Mexico--16mm: 1928, 17 mins., b/w, silent with music, R-FNC, KIT, MMA)
    Luis Bunuel and Salvador Dali, two young Spaniards newly settled in Paris, combined their talents to make the most famous surrealistic film in movie history. It defies "logic," as the artists not only present their insights and interpretation of Freudian psychology, but also react to narrative traditions of the classic Hollywood film. Interestingly, Durgnat argues that the film is based upon the "Surrealist's

misunderstanding of Freudian theory, according to which the unconscious has its patterns of experiences, i.e., its stories, its connections, its reasons, its opinions about religion, politics, etiquette, and so on. Hence the film tells a story, possesses a structure, and has a polemical impact."[310]

ALBERTO CAVALCANTI

RIEN QUE LES HEURES (France--16mm: 1926, 37 mins., b/w, silent, R-KIT, MMA)
   A dawn-to-dusk chronicle of the Parisian slums by the Brazilian ex-architect Alberto Cavalcanti, who, influenced by the dadaist movement, offers a symbolic commentary on the modern city.

RENE CLAIR

ENTR'ACTE (France--16mm: 1924, 15 mins., b/w, silent, R-KIT, MMA)
   Prepared especially as an intermission piece between the two acts of Francis Picabia's dadaist ballet RELACHE, this highly acclaimed film, with a score by Erik Satie, relies almost exclusively on a series of disconnected and hilarious images. Clair points out that Picabia, the screenwriter for this memorable film, "defined his work as a whole, as well as the film itself: 'ENTR'ACTE does not believe in very much, in the pleasure of life perhaps; it believes in the pleasure of inventing, it respects nothing except the desire to burst out laughing, thinking and working are of equal value and are indispensible to each other.'"[311]

THE ITALIAN STRAW HAT/UN CHAPEAU DE PAILLE D'ITALIE (France--16mm: 1927, 76 mins., b/w, musical score only R-BUD, EMG, FES, FNC, IMA, MMA; S-REE)
   Set in 1895, this magnificent comedy deals with a befuddled bridegroom (Albert Prejean) who finds himself obligated to save a woman's honor by replacing her unique straw hat. The fanciful attack on middle-class values is done with a barrage of slapstick routines and farcical chases reminiscent of Melies at his best.

LOUIS DELLUC

FEVER/FIEVRE (France--16mm: 1921, 40 mins., b/w, silent, R-KIT, MMA)
   An impressionistic portrayal of life on the French waterfront, the imagery reflected Delluc's admiration for KAMMERSPIEL films. This sad tale of a sailor's wife who yearns for a life she will never live illustrates Delluc's fatalistic attitude in the aftermath of WWI.

---

[310]   *Raymond Durgnat, LUIS BUNUEL (Berkeley: University of California Press, 1968), p.22. See also Erdmute Wenzel White, "Dream as Reality: Bunuel/Dali's UN CHIEN ANDALOU," THE KINGDOM OF DREAMS IN LITERATURE AND FILM: SELECTED PAPERS FROM THE TENTH ANNUAL FLORIDA STATE UNIVERSITY CONFERENCE ON LITERATURE AND FILM, ed. Douglas Fowler (Tallahassee: Florida State University Press, 1986), pp.104-13.

[311]   *A NOUS LA LIBERTE/ENTR'ACTE: FILMS BY RENE CLAIR: Trans. and description of the action Richard Jacques and Nicola Hayden (New York: Simon and Schuster, 1970), p.112.

CARL THEODOR DREYER

THE PASSION OF JOAN OF ARC/LA PASSION DE JEANNE D'ARC (France--16mm: 1928, 119 mins., b/w, music and sound effects only, R-EMG, FES, FNC, IMA, KIT, MMA; S-REE, TFF)

Dreyer's masterpiece, done mainly in close-ups, re-creates the last days of the martyred peasant girl (Renee Falconetti) and her execution. Co-scripted by Dreyer and Joseph Delteil, the film relies heavily on historical details and remains today one of the great treasures of the cinema. As Bordwell aptly observes, "The film's unprecedented stylistic rigor, the elevation of its subject, the impeccable credentials of its cast, and its refusal to cater to popular conceptions of entertainment constituted a daring bid for consideration as a full-fledged art work."[312] A great deal of credit also goes to the Polish cameraman, Rudolph Mate, and to the German art designer, Hermann Warm.

GERMAINE DULAC

THE SEA SHELL AND THE CLERGYMAN/LA COQUILLE ET LE CLERGYMAN (France--16mm: 1928, 28 mins., b/w, silent, R-KIT, MMA)

This surrealistic film by one of the pioneering female artists deals with an impotent priest who, in his dream-world, pursues his ideal woman. It exemplifies the filmmaker's self-conscious camera movements that announced her anti-establishment values. Not surprisingly, many censors failed to understand that the illogical images in the cryptic movie were mainly Freudian phallic and castration symbols. Scripted by Antonin Artaud, the story can be seen as a woman's search for self-knowledge. The filmmakers themselves quarreled over the interpretation. Nevertheless, the screenwriter stated that the movie "is the first film ever written which makes use of subjective images untainted by humor. There were others films before it which introduced a similar break in logical thought patterns, but humor always provided the clearest explanation for breaking the LINKS between patterns."[313] Interestingly, it is also the film that almost all of the surrealists generally disliked.[314]

---

[312] *David Bordwell, FILMGUIDE TO LA PASSION DE JEANNE D'ARC (Bloomington: Indiana University Press, 1973), p.61. For more information, see Raymond Durgnat, FILMS AND FEELING (Cambridge: The M.I.T Press, 1967), pp.25, 47-8, 51; Herman G. Weinberg, SAINT CINEMA: SELECTED WRITING, 1929-1970 (New York: Drama Books Specialists, 1970), pp.27-9, 243; Alan Stanbrook, "Great Films of the Century: THE PASSION OF JOAN OF ARC," FILMS AND FILMING 7:10 (June 1961):11-3, 40-1; Herbert G. Luft, "An Interview with Dreyer," ibid., p.4; Peter Cowie, "Dreyer at 65," ibid., 10:6 (March 1964):45-6; Boerge Trolle, "The World of Carl Dreyer," SIGHT AND SOUND 25:1 (Winter 1955-56):122-7; Carl Dreyer, "Thoughts on My Craft," ibid., pp.128-9; Tom Milne, "Darkness and Light: Carl Dreyer," ibid., 34:4 (Autumn 1965):167-72; Roger Manvell, "The Passion of Joan of Arc," ibid., 19:8 (December 1950):337; Frank Ward, "The Passion of Joan of Arc," FILMS IN REVIEW 3:1 (January 1952):42; and Kirk Bond, "The World of Carl Dreyer," FILM QUARTERLY 19:1 (Fall 1965):26-38.

[313] Cited in Steven Kovacks, FROM ENCHANTMENT TO RAGE: THE STORY OF SURREALIST CINEMA (Rutherford: Fairleigh Dickinson University Press, 1980), p.168.

[314] Higginbotham, p.32.

JEAN EPSTEIN

FALL OF THE HOUSE OF USHER, THE/LA CHUTE DE LA MAISON USHER (France--16mm: 1928, 62 mins, b/w, silent, R-EMG, MMA, TFF, TWY; S-REE, TFF)
     One of the most admired films by the AVANT-GARDE in the 1920s, this highly symbolic interpretation of Edgar Allan Poe's novel specializes in surrealistic visual effects on death and horror. The dreamlike atmosphere created by Epstein's multiple exposures and eerie sets later inspired a number of scenes in Jean Cocteau's classic BEAUTY AND THE BEAST/LA BELLE ET LA BETE (1946).

FERNAND LEGER

BALLET MECANIQUE (France--16mm: 1924, 13 mins., b/w, silent, R-EMG, KIT, MMA)
     A cubist masterpiece growing out of Leger's artistic interests in mechanical movements of objects in motion interacting with different colors and shapes, this short film illustrates the capricious nature of the cubists' attack on western representational art. Standish D. Lawder sums up what is widely felt about Leger's pulsating film dealing with modern urban life: "His film is a spectacle in constant movement, infused with presence of modern machinery in motion, rushing pell-mell from and to nowhere, full of fragmented images and aggressive signals of advertising--a hard, intense, and vitally alive man-made environment, like the city, like his painting THE CITY."[315]

ABEL GANCE

NAPOLEON VU PAR ABEL GANCE (France--35mm: 1927, 5 hours and 13 mins., b/w, music, R-IMA)
     Considered by many film historians to be one of the towering achievements of the silent era, this extraordinary work ignores Napoleon's flaws and concentrates instead on his heroic and inspiring qualities. The focus is on Bonaparte's childhood and the events leading to his Italian campaign. What has attracted recent attention is not Gance's romanticized narrative, but his remarkable visual effects. As Kramer and Welsh remind us, the film is notable "for its pyrotechnical accomplishment--for its dynamic editing, its innovative camera movement, its daring use of superimposed images (many more in some instances than any single viewer would be capable of separating), and finally, for that experiment which Gance called 'Polyvision,' the precursor of Cinerama, which Gance patented in 1926. Almost equally important, however, is his unique visualization of metaphor. The 'DOUBLE TEMPETE' with its parallel editing of the storm at sea and the storm at the convention is a remarkable achievement."[316]

MAN RAY

LEAVE ME ALONE/EMAK BAKIA (France--16mm: 1927, 15 mins., b/w, silent, R-KIT, MMA)
     This extraordinary film marked Ray's debut in the cinema and is considered by knowledgable critics to be a blending of the tenets of dadaism and surrealism. Asked what he said about the work at the premiere, the artist recalled his comment: ". .

---

[315]   Standish D. Lawder, THE CUBIST CINEMA (New York: New York University Press, 1975), p.167.

[316]   Kramer and Welsh, p.101.

. my film was purely optical, made to appeal only to the eyes--there was no story, not even a scenario. Then somewhat more truculently; this was not an experimental film--I never showed my experiments--what I offered to the public was final, the result of a way of thinking as well as of seeing . . . I concluded in a more conciliatory tone: how many films had they sat through for hours and been bored? My film had one outstanding merit, it lasted no more than fifteen minutes. . . ."[317]

JAPAN IN THE SILENT ERA (1896-1930)

In many ways, the history of Japanese cinema is different from development of film history elsewhere.[318] Although Japan's initial contact, beginning in 1896, with the basics of the moving picture phenomenon came from the first films, cameras, and projectors manufactured by the Lumieres, Edison, and Armat, the Japanese did not produce their own films until the final years of the nineteenth century. Until then, the projectors, raw film, cameras, and movies themselves were imported, mainly from the French and the Americans. In fact, the Japanese did not build their own studios until 1909 and relied on foreign equipment for their products until the start of World War I. Moreover, movies in Japan initially were not shown in makeshift theaters or targeted for working class people, nor was there widespread concern about the actual or psychological dangers that nitrate films posed for the audience. Just the opposite was true. "In Japan," Donald Richie asserts, ". . . from the first, the movies were completely respectable. They were plainly upper-class entertainment, and this was known because it cost quite a bit to get in to see them."[319] Moving pictures gained instant respectability not only because of the intellectual climate in the country, but also because of the endorsement of the royal family.

To understand why, as well as the direction that Japanese film history took over the next eighty years, we first need to recognize the importance of the year 1868. Prior to that date, and going back three centuries to the time when Japan first had contact with Western nations, the Japanese developed a strong aversion to foreign influences. The ruling powers constantly feared that Europeans would not only invade the country, but also that they would disrupt commercial, religious, and political stability in the Oriental world. Consequently, as Richard N. Tucker explains, "The Shogun, a sort of generalissimo who really ruled Japan in the name of the Emperor, countered the foreign threat by closing down the country completely, by issuing in 1624 the 'Edict of Isolation.' For nearly two hundred and thirty years Japan was hermetically sealed from the rest of the world."[320]

---

[317]   Cited in Arturo Schwarz, MAN RAY: THE RIGOUR OF IMAGINATION (New York: Rizzoli International Publications, 1977), p.295.

[318]   This section and those that follow on Japan are distillations of the important research done by Joseph L. Anderson, Noel Burch, David Desser, Joan Mellen, Donald Richie, Tadao Sato, and Richard N. Tucker. My purpose here is to provide, for serious students, an overview of reference material, concepts, personalities, and films. The latter is a particular problem since few of the nearly 300 existing films (out of the thousands produced between World War I and the end of World War II) are in release in the United States. In citing Japanese films in the American style, given name first and last name last, I mean no disrespect to the Japnanese. This is, however, an English-language reference guide and follows the pattern used by English-language scholars.

[319]   Donald Richie, THE JAPANESE MOVIE, rev. ed. (Tokyo: Kodansha International, 1982), p.10.

[320]   Richard N. Tucker, JAPAN: FILM IMAGE (London: Studio Vista, 1973), p.9. Joan Mellen comments in 1975 that "Because of the disruptive role played by foreign

Known as the Tokugawa period (after the famous military leader Ieyasu Tokugawa),[321] the years from 1624 to 1867 were a time of stability and repression, when urban societies flourished, samurai gained prominence, and merchants were despised. As David Desser observes, the peaceful nature of the era made the samurai obsolete as warriors. Their real value in the growing Tokugawa bureaucracy was as administrators and government functionaries. "They became not only the most likely," Desser points out, "but literally the only candidates for bureaucratic posts."[322] (The different types of samurai--e.g., retainers, unemployed professional soldiers, gamblers, gangsters--during this time were to play a significant role in the conventions of the Samurai film.) A major characteristic of the Tokugawa period, Noel Burch tells us, was the striking similarity between European and Japanese feudalism that stressed the concepts of decentralization and a property-based society. The emphasis was on subordinating personal freedom to the will of the family, the provincial lords (BAKAFU), the shogun, and the emperor. This period of isolation, Burch observes, unified the Japanese people more than in any other society known to history: "Even the Japan of the 1970s, after a hundred years of capitalism and a thirty-year inoculation of American individualist ideology, still bears the unmistakable stamp of three centuries of standardization. . . ."[323] By the middle of the nineteenth century, however, the once-despised merchants had become an extremely powerful middle class, supporting many of the debt-ridden warlords and masterless samurai.

In oversimplied terms, the arrival of U. S. Commodore Matthew Perry's mercantile expedition in 1853 crystalized the growing opposition to Japan's 300 years of Tokugawa rule and the nation's isolation.[324] "While the Tokugawa regime spent two-and-a-half centuries degenerating into a stagnant but self-perpetuating bureaucracy," Alain Silver explains, "attempting to preserve its hegemony by bringing progress of social time to a standstill, it was unable to eradicate the need for upward mobility even in a country with more than a millenium of feudal tradition."[325] Perry's reports of the scientific and cultural advances made in the West intrigued the Japanese merchant classes. By 1868, when the sixteen-year-old Meiji became emperor of Japan, the business interests had convinced the nation's leaders that Japan needed to become a "modern" country. A series of sweeping social, political, and cultural changes was inaugurated, not the least of which were international trade with the West and the centralization of government power. The important point, as Burch emphasizes, is that "The Meiji Restoration of 1867 [sic] in no sense constituted a sudden shift of power from the feudal classes to the bourgeoisie

---

nations in Japanese history and because of the ambivalence and trauma this engendered in the national psyche, a certain xenophobia remains part of the Japanese way." See *Joan Mellen, VOICES FROM THE JAPANESE CINEMA (New York: Liveright, 1975), pp.4-5.

[321] Personal names are used in the Western style, i.e., with the surname last.

[322] *David Desser, THE SAMURAI FILMS OF AKIRA KUROSAWA (Ann Arbor: UMI Research Press, 1983), p.22.

[323] Burch, p.26.

[324] Perry's successful gunboat diplomacy not only intimidated the Japanese government into signing a treaty with America in 1854, but also encouraged other Western countries to use the same tactics. The unrest created by the capitulation of the ruling shogunate to foreigners was a significant factor in his downfall in 1867 and led to the Meiji Restoration the following year.

[325] *Alain Silver, THE SAMURAI FILM (South Brunswick: A. S. Barnes and Company, 1977), p.17.

. . . [it] was simply the linchpin of Japan's uniquely concatenated transition to capitalism."[326]

The dramatic reforms of the Meiji government (1868-1912)[327] had such a lasting effect on Japanese society that storytellers, dramatists, and filmmakers still use 1868 as a dividing point to contrast the values and ideas of modern and ancient times. Eventually, the Japanese cinema would rely almost exclusively on two genres: JIDAI-GEKI (period-dramas) and GENDAI-GEKI (contemporary films). As Joseph L. Anderson points out, the JIDAI-GEKI stories are set almost exclusively "in the latter part of the Tokugawa era, from the early 1600s to 1867 . . . [and end] with the beginning of the Meiji Restoration in 1868."[328] Mellen notes that eventually these historical films used "the past as a means of exposing the injustices of the present, and at . . . [their] best evoke[d] a new interpretation of history by challenging accepted values, particularly those of the BUSHIDO [the samurai code]."[329] In addition, as Ellis observes,

> Each category . . . [would have] its own conventions, not only in regard to sets and costumes, but also production style and even acting. Studios, directors, and actors . . . [would tend] to specialize in one or the other of the two modes. The JIDAI-GEKI (historical) . . . [would account] for forty percent of Japanese production, but . . . [enjoy] constant popularity with the domestic audience and . . . [achieve] the first success abroad.[330]

The GENDAI-GEKI, on the other hand, appeared as a response to reactionary film forces emphasizing that feudal values were superior to modern concerns and interests. As the Japanese film industry evolved, the realism in contemporary stories would gain prominence over the romanticized and exaggerated tales of noble samurai.

The crucial point here, as Tadao Sato states, was that the start of the Japanese film industry at the turn of the century occurred only thirty years after the Meiji era began:

> Although a modern, Westernized nation was already in the making, the feelings of the population were slower to change, and both literature and drama were steeped in traditionalism . . . Since film had its origins as an entertainment form for the masses, it drew heavily on traditional drama and literature for material, especially from KABUKI and KODAN ("historical tales"). The former usually concerned a samurai giving up his life out of loyalty for his lord, and the latter a samurai avenging the death of a parent. Thus early film contained a paradox: it was a new means of expression but what it expressed was old.[331]

---

[326]   Burch, p.29.

[327]   By 1890, Japan had become a constitutional monarchy, with a bicameral legislature known as the Diet. In the years that followed, a struggle was waged by the the heirs of the old feudal classes and by the new constitutional forces that eventually returned Japan to a military state during the 1930s and 1940s.

[328]   Joseph L. Anderson, "Japanese Swordfighters and American Gunfighters," CINEMA JOURNAL 12:2 (Spring 1973):1.

[329]   Mellen, p.10.

[330]   Ellis, p.250.

[331]   Tadao Sato, CURRENTS IN JAPANESE CINEMA, trans. Gregory Barrett (Tokyo: Kodansha International, 1982), p.7.

The close ties between the Japanese and their traditional arts set the tone not only for what types of films would prove popular for the initial decades of Japanese cinema, but also why many Western critics would misunderstand the development of the medium in Japan.

Of the three central dramatic traditions--KABUKI (period dramas), BUNRAKU (doll-dramas), and SHIMPA (romantic contemporary tales), the most important was KABUKI. As James R. Brandon explains, "Kabuki is a popular Japanese theater form in which stylized acting is combined with lyrical singing, dancing, and spectacular staging. The characters with which the word KABUKI is written in fact mean song, dance, and acting."[332] Since these elements were present in early Japanese film presentations, Japanese cinema was never really a silent film presentation. There might not have been sound tracks, but there were almost always music, dialogue, sound effects, and declamatory narratives performed along with the films.

At first glance, many Westerners notice that there is a striking resemblance between KABUKI plays and American film genres. Both rely heavily on conventions to maintain cultural links to the past, to symbolize society's shared values, and to attract audiences. In addition, a number of Japanese filmmakers use "inventions" that not only are unique to them but are also able to update society's values, to take advantage of contemporary cultural conflicts, and to apply recent technological developments. But there the important similarities end. Far more fruitful is an examination of the differences between the two approaches to film formulas, particularly in the areas of taxonomy and subject matter.[333] Moreover, Japanese film genres offer such a unique perspective and their AUTEURS possess such a unique ideology vis-a-vis Western filmmakers, that simplistic comparisons often create more confusion than insights.

The paradox of early Japanese films using modern technology to impart centuries-old values was intensified by the close ties of films with the KABUKI, NOH, BUNRAKU, and SHIMPA plays. That is not to say that the Japanese theater universally embraced film. It did not. Shortly after the turn of the century, movies had become mass entertainment, capitalizing in Japan, as they did worldwide, on the public's fascination for spectacle, exotic locations, and popular performers. This appeal to "low-brow" tastes did not sit well with either the middle- and upper-class families or stage artists and troupes. But unlike Western societies, where the stage maintained a strong boycott against the fledgling form of entertainment, many of Japan's dramatists found a variety of ways to make cinema functionally useful to the theater, where movies were usually housed until 1910.[334] Films were used to advertise

---

[332]   James R. Brandon, "KABUKI," ACADEMIC AMERICAN ENCYCLOPEDIA, Volume 12, p.4. See also Sato, pp.15-30.

[333]   For a valuable discussion of Japanese genres, see Sato, p.16; Burch, pp.151-3; and THE SAMURAI FILMS OF AKIRA KUROSAWA, pp.13-25. Sato makes an important distinction between two major male types: the TATEYAKU (the ideal image of the samurai) and the NIMAIME (the kind, handsome, and gentle male who was neither clever nor strong). The former would become the mainstay of period dramas; the latter, of contemporary dramas. Burch makes the point (p.259) that the Japanese have "a need for confirmation" that is so strong that it functions as a "sufficent basis for communal spectacle. . . ." Desser offers specific comparisons between Hollywood Westerns and Japanese samurai films, stressing (p.13) the fact that both genres "function as 'myth-makers.'"

[334]   Historians disagree about the degree of support that the early films received from the theater. For example, Anderson and Richie point out that a large body of theater owners and famous actors resented the arrival of film because of snobbery and the potential box-office dangers from actors appearing in the new toy. See Joseph L. Anderson and Donald Richie, THE JAPANESE FILM: ART AND

plays, to provide employment for stage actors, and to enliven actual productions themselves.[335] Above all, the new form of entertainment preserved historical traditions by making the KABUKI, NOH, BUNRAKU, plays,[336] and SHIMPA [337] the basic source of the early Japanese films.

Throughout the silent era, the period dramas maintained an adolescent attitude toward the past, glorifying feudal values and focusing on the lives of the rich and the powerful. This theatrical heritage, in turn, as Tucker explains, imposed two important conditions on the nascent Japanese cinema:

> Having grown out of a theatrical background the film accepted one of the precepts of the theatre--all players must be male. Such playing is far from being a display of transvestite behavior, but rather a subtle and refined portrayal of the essence of the female characteristics in the KABUKI plays. Thus the cinema accepted without question that all parts should be played by men, and it was twenty years before women appeared in films. The second condition imposed by the theatrical background was the use of the BENSHI.[338]

INDUSTRY (Rutland: Charles E. Tuttle Company, 1959), p.29. Sato points out (pp.15-6) that the caste system in KABUKI made the movies very attractive for all but leading players. Since stars were either the natural or adopted sons of famous actors, other actors found the more democratic film world a good place for advancement and wealth.

[335] Anderson and Richie describe (pp.27-8) a practice known as RENSA-GEKI ("chain-drama"), where films of outdoor locations were used in plays.

[336] The oldest of Japan's dramatic art forms, the one-act dance and declamatory presentations were started as a unique entertainment for the upper classes in the twelfth century. Over time, however, the general public came to know and cherish the set of masks, gestures, and religious symbols associated with the strong chracterizations and subtle dramas.

[337] THE JAPANESE MOVIE, p.16. It should be pointed out that SHIMPA plays began in the late 1880s and for a brief time challenged the popularity of KABUKI plays. Eventually, SHIMPA became as stylized as KABUKI, incorporating many of the older form's traditions. The standard plot featured lovestruck heroes whose lives ended tragically. For more information, see Burch, p.59; and Sato, p.20.

[338] Tucker, p.11. The female impersonators were known as ONNAGATA or OYAMA. As Sato explains (p.21), they first appeared in the seventeenth century as the result of a government ban declaring that actresses (who were mainly prostitutes) could not appear on stage. It eventually became a standard part of KABUKI. Anderson and Richie disagree (pp.28-9) with Tucker's claim that no women appeared in Japanese cinema until the end of World War I, pointing out that an all-woman KABUKI group existed in the early 1900s and that the group made a film in 1909, entitled DAWN AT THE SOGA BROTHERS' HUNTING GROUNDS/SOGA KYODAI KARIBA NO AKEBONO. Worth noting is Akira Kurosawa's observation that during the Meiji era, "Japan's age of swift modernization, . . . women were still expected to make extreme sacrifices so that their fathers, husbands, brothers or sons could advance." See *Akira Kurosawa, SOMETHING LIKE AN AUTOBIOGRAPHY, trans. Audie E. Bock (New York: Alfred A. Knopf, 1982), p.21. For a more detailed explanation of the ties between KABUKI and Japanese cinema, see Burch, pp.75-86. For a useful contrast between Western and Eastern female impersonators, see THE SAMURAI FILMS OF AKIRA KUROSAWA, p.29.

These two fixtures, plus an element of self-glorification for the past, characterized Japanese films for the first three decades of their existence.[339]

Joseph L. Anderson offers an excellent insight into how the process worked. "The katsuben," he writes, "was the person who stood or sat to the left of the movie screen . . . [and was called] a BENSHI which is a vague term meaning speaker or orator."[340] What was extraordinary about the BENSHI's role, Anderson explains, was that he made films "(1) AN EXTENSION OF AN INDIGENOUS NARRATIVE PRACTICE . . . and (2) AN ADDITION TO THE TRADITIONAL VOCAL STORYTELLING VENUES. The katsuben was also a product of the marginality of the Japanese movie business."[341] He not only had a popular following of his own, but also took charge of the pace of the film as well as its meaning. It was the BENSHI, therefore, who educated, often erroneously, the public to the ways of the West through film. It was the BENSHI who enabled Japanese filmmakers to ignore problems of screen language and technical breakthroughs developed in the West, because he could fill in whatever narrative elements were missing or confusing to the audience. Most important, it was the BENSHI the public came to see, not the films per se. "At first," Tucker points out, "this meant the industry boomed because it could put across, to a wide public, exciting plays in a form that they knew and accepted. Eventually it was to be an enormous handicap to the film-makers."[342]

Once Japanese production began in 1898, it moved at a modest but steady pace. The nation committed itself to learning as much as possible about this new Western "toy." Within a decade, four companies had not only taken control of the developing industry, but also formed a combine, the Greater Japan Film Machinery Manufacturing Company, Limited., known as Nikkatsu,[343] which rivaled the output of any major foreign filmmaking operation. Out of this combine, with its two large studios (one in Tokyo, the other in Kyoto) came the first Japanese movie star, Matsunosuke Onoe, a minor KABUKI actor, who was developed by the first significant Japanese producer-director, Shozo Makino. Together, in their costumed, self-glorifying depictions of the past, they played on the nation's desire to blend tradition with contemporary values.[344] Between 1909 and 1926, Onoe and Makino dominated the period drama formula,[345] while at the same time providing opportunities for other BENSHI to develop a following in films. The appearance of a prominent KABUKI actor in a film, Richie explains, was an event tantamount to Sarah Bernhardt's appearing

---

[339]   Richie points out that the links between the Japanese theatrical traditions and film resulted in tragedy being the most common theme in silent Japanese films. For the reasons why, see THE JAPANESE MOVIE, rev. ed., pp.42-6.

[340]   Joseph L. Anderson, "Spoken Silents in the Japanese Cinema, Essay on the Necessity of Katsuben," JOURNAL OF FILM AND VIDEO 40:1 (Winter 1988):13.

[341]   "Spoken Silents," p.13.

[342]   Tucker, p.11.

[343]   Anderson and Richie, p.30. In 1912, the trust was renamed the NIPPON KATSUDO SHASHIN (Japan Cinematograph Company) and is known as Nikkatsu.

[344]   For a good overview of the two film pioneers, see THE JAPANESE MOVIE, pp.13-6; and Anderson and Richie, pp.31-3.

[345]   Sato estimates (p.18) that Onoe starred as a powerful samurai warrior in over a thousand period dramas between 1909 and 1926.

n FILM D'ART and thus affecting how the film was made and interpreted to audiences.[346]

Nikkatsu's major competition in the silent era was the Shochiku Cinema Company, a theatrical organization that turned to filmmaking in 1920 and was committed to bringing Japanese cinema into the modern era. Loosely modeled on Hollywood's vertical system of production, distribution, and exhibition, it encouraged the development of new talent and an "international reconciliation" between Japanese and foreign cinematic tastes.[347]

While it is true that Western audiences did not discover the novelty or art of Japanese films until 1951,[348] when Akira Kurosawa's RASHOMON (1950) won top honors at the Venice Film Festival, the Japanese always had a tremendous fascination with American movie techniques and innovations. In the pre-WWI period, for example, the Japanese filmmakers kept pace with the increasing film lengths, experimented with color, and dabbled in changing camera positions. (The standard procedure in Japanese films was to shoot the action from the viewpoint of a spectator sitting in the third row of the orchestra.) Such experimentation met with mixed results, primarily because of the public's unwillingness to abandon traditional tastes and the power of the BENSHI to maintain the STATUS QUO.

With the coming of World War I and wartime shortages, experimentation came to an abrupt halt. Fascination with American movies, however, remained high throughout the war years. What appealed to the Japanese was the freedom evident in the optimistic love stories of ordinary people. "The inevitable happy ending," Sato comments, "was both a source of hope and envy, and a refreshing contrast to Japanese films with their tragic endings, since romantic love was regarded as immoral and frowned on."[349] Of particular interest to the Japanese were Hollywood westerns, especially the works of William S. Hart. As Anderson observes, "Hart's ruthless skill with a weapon and his fits of violence crossed with anger were closer to the behavior of traditional Japanese heroes than [Tom] Mix's horsemanship, fist fights, stunts, and Sunday-school morality."[350]

The problem for Japanese filmmakers, however, was that they viewed the medium as being at odds with realistic depictions of the past. As Richie points out, the ability of the motion picture camera to represent events realistically "did not suit the Japanese eye . . . [where the public] usually dismissed . . . surface . . . as superficial, and [perceived] reality . . . [as] . . . not real unless it has been rearranged."[351] An illustration of the problem is the way that key Soviet and Japanese filmmakers approached two basic editing concepts: additive and reductive. In the additive process, Richie explains,

> the montage is built. Eisenstein, for example, shot scenes which would be later used to add to the montage, to create it. The other kind of editing is a

---

[346]   THE JAPANESE MOVIE, p.15.

[347]   Anderson and Richie, p.41. For a commentary on fifty years at the prolific Shochiku film studios, see Renee Tajima, "Shochiku and Violence Too," VILLAGE VOICE (November 1, 1988):73.

[348]   It is worth noting, however, that Western audiences did enjoy the acting of Sessue Hayakawa, and he became a famous star in America, beginning in the early 1900s.

[349]   Sato, p.33.

[350]   "Japanese Swordfighters," p.2.

[351]   THE JAPANESE MOVIE, p.17.

reductive process: editing as elimination. Kurosawa, for example, cuts--taking out one detail after another.

The assumptions behind these two methods are different. Eisenstein believes that he is CREATING the essence of his subject; Kurosawa believes that he is REVEALING the essence of his.[352]

Such assumptions also breed other assumptions concerning how reality exists and is depicted.

Attempts by Western critics to explain the nature of Eastern assumptions have frequently led to a gross misunderstanding about the essence of Japanese cinema.[353] In fact, they have led to the false assumption that the Japanese cinema is imitative. That is, it merely assimilates other techniques and ideas from more established cinemas. That is certainly not the case. As Burch argues, ". . . the Japanese do not copy, they ADAPT; whatever has been borrowed has been profoundly and CREATIVELY transformed, and besides, many aspects of Japanese culture are entirely indigenous. . . ."[354]

A more fitting term for discussing "Japanese" reality, therefore, is MONO NO AWARE, which Richie defines as "that awareness of the transience of all earthly things, the knowledge that it is, perhaps fortunately, impossible to do anything about it: that celebration of resignation in the face of things as they are."[355] The feeling that life operates in cycles and that the best that one can do is accept indifferently and gracefully the transient nature of physical being permeates not only Japanese films, but also Japanese society. As late as the mid-1970s, Mellen found that "At best, people are encouraged, stoically, to respond to failure and disappointment with an attitude of MONO NO AWARE, sad resignation before the unalterable injustices of human life."[356]

Given the nature of MONO NO AWARE, film theorists speculate over why Japanese films appear to present greater problems to American audiences than do other foreign films. For example, Ellis makes the assumption that "The differences [between Japanese and American films] appeared to be more cultural, or in any case stylistic, than grammatical or syntactical."[357] That is, the Japanese base their universal themes on unique conventions and personal assumptions that emphasize slow pacing, sentimentality, and didacticism. "If American film makers most frequently concerned themselves with action and Europeans with the psychology of character, as was sometimes said," Ellis explains, "the Japanese seemed to more interested in overall mood."[358] Anderson makes a similar point, asserting that

---

[352]   Donald Richie, "Viewing Japanese Film: Some Considerations," EAST-WEST 1:1 (December 1986):27-8.

[353]   For a useful overview, see Joseph L. Anderson and Loren Hoekzem, "The Spaces Between: American Criticism of Japanese Film," WIDE ANGLE 1:4 (1977):2-6.

[354]   Burch, p.31.

[355]   *Donald Richie, JAPANESE CINEMA: FILM STYLE AND NATIONAL CHARACTER (Garden City: Doubleday and Company, 1977), p.77. For another perspective on the differences between MONO NO AWARE and cinematic drama, see SOMETHING LIKE AN AUTOBIOGRAPHY, pp.105-6.

[356]   Mellen, p.13.

[357]   Ellis, p.250.

[358]   Ellis, pp.250-1.

The American film maker will often ignore tone and mood to maintain plot consistency. The Japanese does just the opposite. For him, plot functions as a subordinate to other narrative values. Japanese realism and referents to reality are based upon a minimum of formal plot elements such as motivation, causal relationships, plausibility. This a-logical structure tends to give a documentary or reality flavor even to the most presentational style or "unrealistic" content. The tempo, the mood, and the structure that is hard to parse flow as in life itself. Thus situations and even acting need not conform to conventional "life-like" dramatic criteria.[359]

In short, the emphasis is on the elements that contribute to the story's mood, rather than to actual events. Burch goes even further, insisting that the basic contrast between Japanese and Western filmmakers relates to the issue of AUTEURISM. Unlike the West, where an individual is perceived as the originator of unique works, "The Japanese social system denies the very concept of originality, acknowledges and indeed deliberately emphasizes the material reality of the circulation of signs."[360] In other words, tradition rather than innovation is the key to understanding the art of Japanese cinema.

By the end of World War I, the silent Japanese cinema had begun a short-lived struggle to shake off aspects of its theatrical STATUS QUO.[361] It had developed closer ties with the West, and progressive forces in Japan intensified their demands for an anti-BENSHI cinema. Spearheading the reform movement was the increasing popularity of foreign movies.[362] The progressive forces, therefore, decided to push for the adoption of more Western techniques in Japanese films. For example, the director Norimasa Kaeriyama led the way in films like THE GLOW OF LIFE/SEI NO KAGAYAKI and MAID OF THE DEEP MOUNTAINS/MIYAMA NO OTOME (both in 1918), where women replaced the OYAMA (female impersonators), linear narratives replaced the fixed frontal images of the traditional KABUKI films, and naturalistic movies replaced many of the romantic SHIMPA films.[363] Although Kaeriyama's works were not the first to suggest such cinematic ideas, his films ignited a desire among post-WWI filmmakers, who had grown up with movies, to throw off the BENSHI traditions.[364] As Sato explains, these young people--e.g., Kenji Mizoguchi,[365]

---

[359]   "Japanese Swordfighters," p.21.

[360]   Burch, pp.31-2.

[361]   A major debate exists over whether Japanese cinema remained in a "primitive" state for an extended period of time because its filmmakers "lagged" behind developments in Western cinema. Burch offers (p.66) the novel perspective that whatever the merits of the case, the Japanese cinema remains an excellent resource for studying just what were primitive techniques in the silent era because its films preserved those traits well into the 1930s.

[362]   For a good impression of the types of foreign films that appeared in Japan between 1919 and 1929, see SOMETHING LIKE AN AUTOBIOGRAPHY, pp.73-4.

[363]   For a good overview of Kaeriyama's style, see Anderson and Richie, pp.36-7.

[364]   THE INTERNATIONAL ENCYCLOPEDIA OF FILM, p.303.

[365]   For more information, see Tadao Sato, "On Kenji Mizoguchi," Trans. by Paul Andrew, FILM CRITICISM 4:3 (Spring 1980):2-16; Donald Richie and Joseph L. Anderson, "Kenji Mizoguchi," SIGHT AND SOUND 25:2 (Autumn 1955):76-81; Robert Cohen, "Mizoguchi and Modernism: Structure, Culture, Point of View," ibid., 47:2 (Spring 1978):110-8; "Mizoguchi's Spectrum," Trans. Leonard Schrader and Haruji Nakamura, Introduction Donald Richie, CINEMA 6:3 (Spring 1971):12-9; and Robin

Teinosuke Kinugasa,[366] Hiroshi Inagaki, Eizo Tanaka, Heinosuke Gosho,[367] Mikio
Naruse--were not only obsessed with Western movies, but also with liberal ideas.[368]
The films they wanted to make stressed social responsibilities and the problems of
ordinary people.[369] In addition, other young filmmakers like Yutaka Abe, Henry
Kotani, Frank Tokunaga, and Thomas Kurihara, who had studied moviemaking abroad,
came back to Japan to incorporate, into their native productions, many of the Western
techniques.[370] Some of the era's more noteworthy films were Tanaka's THE LIVING
CORPSE/IKERU SHIKABNE (1917), Kurihara's AMATEUR CLUB/AMACHUA KURABU
(1920), Kotani's ISLAND WOMAN/SHIMA NO ONNA (1920), Mizoguchi's TURKEYS IN
A ROW/SHICHIMENCHO NO YUKUE (1924), Abe's THE WOMAN WHO TOUCHED THE
LEGS/ASHI NI SAWATTA ONNA (1926), and Gosho's TRICKY GIRL/KARAKURI
MUSUME (1927).

One of the most revolutionary directors of the era was Minoru Murata, whose
watershed film, SOULS ON THE ROAD/ROJO NO REIKON (1921) is viewed by most
historians of the Japanese cinema as comparable in effect to THE BIRTH OF A NATION
(1915). Inspired in part by INTOLERANCE (1916), linked by a common mood, and
involving complex cutting techniques, SOULS ON THE ROAD/ROJO NO REIKON
consists of two interwoven stories--one dealing with a couple of ex-convicts searching
for a new life, the other about a poor man who finds happiness with his family. "In
this concern for the emotional tone of situations," explains Anderson, "can be seen
the origins of the mood film--a most significant Japanese genre in which emphasis is
on the projection of an overall mood or atmosphere rather than direct narrative."[371]
In addition, SOULS ON THE ROAD/ROJO NO REIKON broke completely with the
traditional films about the wealthy and the past. As Tucker explains, "Murata had
made the film almost entirely on location, he had used women and, perhaps most
important of all, he had blended these elements with a camera and acting style that
was naturalistic, restrained and evocative of mood, displaying a maturity not seen
before in Japanese films."[372]

While such attempts were attractive to progressive film distributors (who, like
their Western counterparts, valued any new ideas that might increase profits), the
twenties gave rise to a fierce nationalism that was to dominate Japan for the next three
decades. Moreover, the power of the BENSHI on the silent film industry was almost
impenetrable. In fact, as Anderson and Richie explain, Kaeriyama had to deceive his
bosses into thinking his films were made for foreign rather than Japanese audiences
in order to get the films produced:

Wood, "Mizoguchi: The Ghost Princess and the Seaweed Gatherer," FILM COMMENT 9:2
(March/April 1973):32-40.

[366]   For more information, see Burch, pp.123-39.

[367]   For more information, see Joseph L. Anderson and Donald Richie, "The Films of
Heinosuke Gosho," SIGHT AND SOUND 26:2 (Autumn 1956):76-81; and John Gillet,
"Coca Cola and the Golden Pavilion," ibid., (Summer 1970):153-6, 166.

[368]   Sato, p.8.

[369]   Burch, p.100.

[370]   THE JAPANESE MOVIE, p.18. See also Anderson and Richie, pp.38-46.

[371]   Joseph L. Anderson, "Seven from the Past: Aspects of the Pre-War Japanese
Cinema," SIGHT AND SOUND 27:2 (Autumn 1957):83.

[372]   Tucker, p.14. Other historians credit Osanai Kaoru with co-directing the film.

The majority opinion in those days was that short-length shots, editing, dramatic lighting, and close-ups were for foreigners, and this rather arbitrary division of the film vocabulary along national lines was much encouraged by the BENSHI, who knew that anything foreign, whether titles or actresses, was a definite threat.[373]

As a result, the BENSHI played a significant role in narrating SOULS ON THE ROAD/ROJO NO REIKON. Moreover, as Burch asserts, the progressive movement failed because the linear narrative of the West "was antithetical to Japanese art, literature and language."[374]

Contributing greatly to the power struggle in Japanese films was the catastrophic Kanto earthquake of 1923. Not only did it destroy Japan's industrial centers of Tokyo and Yokohama, but it also wiped out the nation's key film studios that were located there. Here the major film historians disagree on the direction Japanese films took during the remainder of the decade. While a handful of commentators insist that a new wave took over the film industry, the majority of critics argue that the rebuilding process strengthened the power of the BENSHI forces in the film industry. The theory is that the political, economic, and social unrest produced by the earthquake (e.g., inflation, strikes, and the shift from an agrarian society to an industrial society) created a strong desire for traditional values and escapist entertainment. In fact, Burch asserts that the class struggle that emerged from these conditions produced an anti-Western attitude, evident in the rise of a number of patriotic societies committed to restoring not only ancient values, but also respect for a Japanese rather than a Western culture.[375] The same patriotic spirit was manifested in the period dramas that glorified the age of BUSHIDO, "the way of the samurai," and the adolescent fantasies of the contemporary dramas.

To solidify the popularity and authority of the traditional elements, a new film combine (ZAIBATSU) was inaugurated in 1925, instituting a studio system somewhat similar to the Hollywood model and dedicated to supplying mass-produced movies for the general public.[376] A key difference between the two systems was that the Japanese model was predicated on a master teacher-student concept, whereby aspiring filmmakers apprenticed themselves to mature craftspeople and had to demonstrate their ability to write scripts and function successfully as assistant directors before being allowed to work independently in the system. Anderson and Richie, however, argue that the modern filmmakers gained control not only because an influx of foreign films sensitized Japanese audiences to Western techniques, but also because the public began clamoring for Western techniques in Japanese films.[377]

Whatever the case, it is clear that Japanese cinema in the silent era began to challenge the KABUKI traditions. Coming to the forefront were the two genres that would dominate the industry for the next seventy years: JIDAI-GEKI and GENDAI-GEKI. The most popular historical films were a subgenre called CHAMBARA (sword-fighting films), which took particular interest in the lives of samurai during

---

[373]   Anderson and Richie, p.37.

[374]   Burch, p.98.

[375]   Burch, pp.141-2.

[376]   Anderson and Richie provide (pp.39-44) valuable insights into the struggle between Nikkatsu and rival film companies that led to the new trust. They also explain how the new filmmakers brought about the demise of the OYAMA in the mid-1920s.

[377]   Anderson and Richie, pp.47-62.

the Tokugawa period. The genre's most famous practitioners were Ito Daisuke[378] and Masahiro Makino.[379] The emphasis was on a violent and heroic interpretation of a golden age of warriors.

The contemporary films took an increasing interest in location shooting, the use of women in modern roles,[380] and the plight of ordinary people. Among the subgenres that appeared were the SHOMIN-GEKI (lighthearted comedies about ordinary people), specializing in films about the flapper craze in Japan as seen from the perspective of youth; and YAKUZA-EIGA (gangster films), dealing with urban crimes. Among the important directors who made SHOMIN-GEKI hits were Yasujiro Ozu[381] and Yasujiro Shimazu. A number of films also experimented with subjective camerawork, experimental narratives, and psychological moods. These films, especially Murata's SEISAKU'S WIFE/SEISAKU NO TSUMA (1924) and THE STREET JUGGLER/MACHI NO TEJINASHI (1925), Kinugasa's A PAGE OUT OF ORDER/A CRAZY PAGE/KURUTTA IPPEIJI (1926) and CROSSWAYS/SHADOWS OF THE YOSHIWARA/JUJIRO (1928), shared a coincidental interest to the work being done by the German expressionists and French impressionists.[382]

As the twenties moved to a close, the Japanese film industry was still dominated by two major combines--Nikkatsu and Shochiku--that controlled the production, distribution, and exhibition of films, although Independents still found it possible to exist. Moreover, the BENSHI and SHIMPA films were still popular, JIDAI-GEKI and GENDAI-GEKI were becoming entrenched as the nation's two distinctive film genres, and Japan had become one of the largest film producing nations in the world. But outside of the Orient, almost no Westerner saw Japanese films, nor did foreign nations appreciate the ramifications emerging from Japan's growing economic and social problems. In addition, the death of Emperor Toshio in 1926 brought an end to the liberal spirit that characterized his reign and ushered in a more right-wing era. In the two decades that followed, the new age of Japanese militarism would not only drastically alter her position in the world, but also her significant film industry.

---

[378] For more details, see Burch, pp.110-6; and Anderson and Richie, pp.64-6.

[379] For more information, see Anderson and Richie, p.64.

[380] The concept of "modern roles" is somewhat misleading, since Sato tells us (p.73) that "Since the beginning of Japanese cinema the leading female role was either an entertainer, a geisha, or a prostitute, and several films with such heroines--such as Mizoguchi's works--were masterpieces."

[381] For more information, see Chishu Ryu, "Yasujiro Ozu," SIGHT AND SOUND 33:2 (Spring 1964):92; "Ozu Spectrum" trans. Haruiji Nakamura and Leonard Schrader, CINEMA 6:1 (Summer 1970):2-8; Jonathan Rosenbaum, "Ozu," FILM COMMENT 8:2 (Summer 1972):4, 6; Kristin Thompson, "Notes on the Spatial System of Ozu's Early Films," WIDE ANGLE 1:4 (1977):8-17; and Tadao Sato, "The Art of Yasujiro Ozu," trans. Goro Iiri, ibid., pp.44-6.

[382] While most film historians claim that Kinugasa's films resembled the KAMMERSPIEL school of filmmaking (chamber films that emphasized the depair of modern times), Anderson and Richie insist (pp.54-5) that the Japanese were more concerned with "reproducing the impression made by an object" (Impressionism) rather than with presenting "the inner life of humanity" (Expressionism).

BOOKS

Barrett, Gregory. ARCHETYPES IN JAPANESE FILMS: THE SOCIOPOLITICAL AND RELIGIOUS SIGNIFICANCE OF THE PRINCIPAL HEROES AND HEROINES. Selinsgrove: Susquehanna University Press, 1989. Illustrated. 252pp.

*Burch, Noel. TO THE DISTANT OBSERVER: FORM AND MEANING IN THE JAPANESE CINEMA. Rev. and ed. Annette Michelson. Berkeley: University of California Press, 1979. Illustrated. 387pp.

Building upon the fact that until the end of World War II, the Japanese film industry was the only national cinema emerging from an almost exclusively non-European heritage, Burch analyzes Japanese films historically within the cultural, social, and political context of the twentieth century. It is not, however, your standard film history reader. Although the major portions of the work concentrate on the films made between 1917 and 1945, Burch's primary interest is in contrasting the differences between "the dominant modes of Japanese and Western cinema. . . ." A secondary interest is a "critical analysis of the ideologically and culturally determined system of representation from which the film industries of Hollywood and elsewhere derive their power and profit." Burch's Marxist approach to art in general and film in particular makes for a stimulating interpretation of key Japanese filmmakers like Teinosuke Kinugasa, Yasujiro Ozu, Mikio Naruse, Tamizo Ishida, Kenji Mizoguchi, and Hiroshi Shimizu. What emerges from the innovative and challenging analyses are revealing observations about Japanese filmmaking: i.e., "the essentially 'irreligious' character of the Japanese, their rejection of anthropocentrism and all the 'centrisms' that derive from the West (the role which, in this respect, their architecture has played in their films is absolutely crucial, as Barthes indirectly suggests) and, of course, the all-important 'irrevocable dismissal of content', i.e., of the form-content hierarchies which are ours." Despite the scholarly background required for appreciating Burch's six chapters, the wealth of material presented makes the effort well worth while. A rich array of illustrations, a good bibliography, an adequate set of director filmographies, a useful list of archive holdings, and two indexes (title and name) conclude this impressive study. Recommended for special collections.

*Silver, Alain. THE SAMURAI FILM. South Brunswick: A. S. Barnes and Company, 1977. Illustrated. 242pp.

This informative study provides not only historical data, but also critical commentary on the semimythical heroes of Japanese society. The author makes clear that the term SAMURAI encompasess more than just the idea of a noble warrior loyal to his provincial lords (DAIMYOS). It also includes anachronistic men of action who were bandits, mercenaries, and opportunists. The story of their rise to power, the problems it created for them as they became a recognized group but had no status, and and their eventual elimination as a force in society is presented clearly and concisely. So too is the nature of BUSHIDO and its lingering heritage in Japanese culture and politics. In addition, Silver points out to his Western audience that the famous filmmakers of this intriguing sword-fighting genre include more than just Akira Kurosawa, Kenji Mizoguchi, and Daisuke Ito. Among the other artists reviewed are Masaki Kobayashi, Heinosuke Gosho, Hiroshi Inagaki, and Masahiro Shinoda.

The significant research is divided into two sections. The first and the longest part, "The Samurai Film," consists of seven chapters, including a general introduction to the samurai in history, the samurai in fiction, the works of Kurosawa, the different subgenres, the nature of this alien hero, the contributions of Gosha, and the reactions of the 1960s to the period drama. Profusely illustrated, the scholarly narrative touches on all the key themes and characters in the genre's literary and cinematic development. The section concludes with a useful glossary of Japanese terms. Part two, "Bibliography/Filmography," coauthored with James Ursini, offers an extensive listing of books and periodicals, breakdowns by directors and series, and an index.

Not knowing Japanese and seeing only films available on the West Coast are handicaps that periodically mar the author's analyses and conclusions. The language problem, as Sybil Thornton points out, causes him to make "little mistakes like Sanadu for Sanada, UJIGAMA for UJIGAMI, and ASHINAGA (long-legged) for ASHIGARU (foot-soldier). . . ."[383], while his almost exclusive exposure to samurai films from the 1960s on sometimes results in overlooking important early films or in misleading descriptions and interpretations. "As a result," Thornton concludes in her valuable review, "he fails to realize that there is a set of dramatic conventions related to time and place--or to clan--and that the samurai film, especially, like the Japanese film in general, is one of the only political forms of film in the world."[384]

Whatever limitations are imposed by these scholarly gaps, the book's dry tone and the poor reproduction of stills are more than overcome by the author's attention to important samurai films and an analysis of their conventions. Until a more comprehensive and in-depth study appears, this work is a valuable resource. Recommended for special collections.

FILMS

TEINOSUKE KINUGASA

PAGE OF MADNESS/A PAGE OUT OF ORDER/KURUTTA IPPEIJI (16mm: 1926, 60 mins., b/w, sound, R-NLC)

Directed by Teinosuke Kinugasa, this AVANT-GARDE film is a fine example of the influence that Western filmmaking had on the Japanese cinema during the mid-1920s. The events take place within an insane asylum and reveal the director's talent for cinematic technique and mood. At the same time, the film itself illustrates the important differences between European and Japanese style.[385]

SOUND COMES TO AMERICA (1927-1941)

In the silent days, the art of the film had achieved significant action and movement; the length of the motion pictures had increased sufficiently to tell an effective story; editing and the close-up had elevated the once despised mechanical toy to the status of an important art form; and the shift of film production to the West Coast had resulted in the rise of a formula filmmaking that allowed the film

---

[383] Sybil Thornton, "Book Review: THE SAMURAI FILM," FILM QUARTERLY 31:2 (Winter 1977-78):59.

[384] Thornton, p.59.

[385] For more information, see Burch, pp.127-39.

business to become a major international industry.[386] With the advent of sound, it was as if the film had begun all over again.[387]

In America of the mid- to late-1920s, the conversion from silent movies to sound films would go through three stages: (1) a restructuring of the industry that included not only a change of production, exhibition, and management techniques, but also a period of novelty and anti-authoritarian movies; (2) a realignment of film content along traditional values, with the reconstructed industry imposing stringent regulations on its employees and production policies; and (3) a preparation for the nation's inevitable involvement in a global war, along with the film industry's refinement of its aesthetic capabilities. It was at this point that studios became identified not only with particular "styles," but also with specific genres. As discussed in Chapters 2, 3, and 5, the introduction of sound also revolutionized the lives of Hollywood personalities and planted the seeds of political battles between employers and employees, the federal government and Hollywood, and socially minded reformers and the film industry.

As a result, the years between 1926 and 1930 provided some of the most rash controversial events in film history. On the one hand, as Rachel Low observes, it would be a mistake to emphasize that sound had played a significant role during the silent era:

To say that the film had never really been silent but had always had musical accompaniment is to miss the point of the transformation. Cinema music, even when the cue sheets or special scores had been provided by the film makers, was not under their control and the film as they put it in the can carried only the image. It therefore had to tell its story by visual means. What producers now had was direct control of sound during the performance and, moreover, this sound included the human voice. The new films were not just sound films, they were talkies. Dialogue was to change the narrative structure of the film profoundly."[388]

On the other hand, as discussed in Chapter 3, the switch to sound was a process that had been evolving since the birth of moving pictures. The complicated sound patents developed by Eugen Augustin Laute, Josef Engl, Josef Massolle, Hans Vogt, Theodore W. Case, Earl I. Sponable, and Lee De Forest (resulting in two major sound-on-film options) led William Fox to the mistaken and disastrous assumption that he singlehandidly could control world film exhibition. At the same time, Warner Bros. took advantage of the film industry's refusal to capitalize on the revolutionary sound

---

[386] Burch (p.145) asserts that the novelty of "talking pictures" seriously affected the ability of independent Western artists to express non-conformist ideas. By making production, distribution, and exhibition so expensive to operate, the sound revolution left filmmaking a tool of dominant ideologies between the early 1930s and the end of the fifties.

[387] The following articles are useful: Leslie Halliwell, "Merely Stupendous: Part One," FILMS AND FILMING 13:5 (February 1967): 4-12; ___, ". . .Part Two," ibid., 13:6 (March 1967):48-56; ___, ". . .Part Three," ibid., 13:7 (April 1967):44-52; ___, ". . .Part Four," ibid., 14:4 (January 1968):10-15; ___, ". . .Part Five," ibid., 14:5 (February 1968:38-44; ___, ". . .Part Six," ibid., 14:6 (March 1968):42-7; ___, ". . .Part Seven," ibid., 14:7 (April 1968):49-53; Duncan Crow, "The First Golden Age," SIGHT AND SOUND 23:3 (January-March 1954):148-51, 168; Barry Salt, "Film Style and Technology in the Thirties," FILM QUARTERLY 30:1 (Fall 1976):19-32; and William Thomaier, "Early Sound Comedy," FILMS IN REVIEW 9:5 (May 1958):254-62.

[388] Rachel Low, THE HISTORY OF THE BRITISH FILM 1929-1939: FILM MAKING IN 1930s BRITAIN (London: George Allen and Unwin, 1985), p.73.

breakthroughs and staked its future on Vitaphone's sound-on-disc patents. (In 1931, the industry would decide in favor on the sound-on-film approach, but by then Warner Bros. would have gained a major foothold in the industry.)

Rather than capitulate to rapidly moving technological events, a declining box office, and the threat posed by the growing popularity of radio, the reigning film corporations--MGM, Famous Players-Lasky (later Paramount), First National, Universal, and Producers Distributing Corporation--signed an agreement not to enter into the "sound" battle being waged by the two financial giants, Rockefeller (RCA) and Morgan (AT&T). But with the success of feature films like DON JUAN (1926) and THE JAZZ SINGER (1927),[389] as well as the popularity of Fox Movietone newsreels, the majors capitulated in 1928, and by the end of the decade, "talkies" took over every phase of the film industry. Well, not exactly! It is more accurate to say that by the start of the thirties most silent films had sound and musical soundtracks.[390] Talking films as we know them did not begin to take hold until 1930. Nevertheless, many historians claim the film industry would never have survived the Depression if not for the incredible popularity of the new sound films.

Meanwhile, the transition period brought about dramatic changes, one of the most obvious being in the structure of the majors themselves. After the takeovers, receiverships, and bankruptcies were finalized, the new giants in order of importance were MGM, Paramount, Warner Bros., Fox Film Corporation (later 20th Century-Fox), RKO, Universal Pictures, Columbia Pictures, and United Artists. At the same time, a small group of independent producers like Samuel Goldwyn, David O. Selznick, Walt Disney, and Alexander Korda (more later) found a way to survive the stranglehold that the "Big Eight" had on the industry, as did smaller companies like Eagle-Lion, Grand National, Monogram (later Allied Artists), and Republic Pictures. By the end of the thirties, the struggle between the independents and the majors for economic freedom would set in motion the demise of the studio system.

The changes were no less dramatic in the production of films. As discussed in Chapters 3 and 5, filmmakers at first made sound king and put all their resources into a technology that had no interest or ability to capitalize on moving cameras, clever editing, or striking close-ups.   The "frozen cameras," the "insensitive" omnidirectional microphones, and the emphasis on spoken dialogue not only destroyed the careers of many prominent performers (one estimate is that ninety percent of silent screen actors failed to make the move from silent to sound films), but also catapulted American and British stage and radio stars into the limelight. Even more unsettling for the industry was the sudden importance of sound engineers, voice coaches, and musicians. Many of these people had no interest in the art of films, and their presence and influence in the industry was deeply resented by almost every creative person on the studio lots.

The technical emphasis during the last two years of the 1920s was on "natural" and "synchronous" sounds and dialogue in productions that harkened back to the "stagey" films of the FILM D'ART era. Not until sound engineers discovered means to "dub" (switch voices in the editing process) and to "post synchronize" sound effects, dialogue, and music (add these sounds after the film was shot) did the screen once more exhibit its skill in creating the illusion of "realistic moving pictures." Only then did the industry realize that the art of film was not limited to one type of sound--e.g., synchronous, asynchronous, and contrapuntal--or to the dominance of

[389]   Johnathan D. Tankel, "The Impact of THE JAZZ SINGER on the Conversion to Sound," JOURNAL OF THE UNIVERSITY FILM ASSOCIATION 30:1 (Winter 1978):21-5.

[390]   For an interesting perspective on the role of industrial films in the coming of the sound revolution, see Robert Finehout, "Pioneering the Talkies," AMERICAN CINEMATOGRAPHER 69:1 (January 1988):36-40.

sound over image.[391] What became evident, however, was the crucial importance of dialogue in the sound film. Nowhere was that more evident than in the increasing number of screenwriters employed on a single film. Whether the practice itself was good for screenwriters is discussed in Chapter 5. The fact is that screenwriting became a major collaborative venture, just as it had always been in the slapstick comedies of the silent era. Equally controversial is the issue of whether the best films of the period were the result of successful writing-directing teams (e.g., John Ford-Dudley Nichols and Frank Capra-Robert Riskin) or studios' management of performers, directors, and technicians.

Experimentation with sound also brought new attempts at revolutionizing screen sizes, the use of color, the nature of sound, acting methods, and production policies. But in the midst of this upheaval, certain directors came forward who effectively combined the revolutionary age with the art of the silent film and then furthered the development of the cinema: Dorothy Arzner, Busby Berkeley, Tod Browning, Frank Capra, George Cukor, Michael Curtiz, Walt Disney, John Ford, Howard Hawks,[392]

---

[391] For an excellent succinct overview, see Cook, pp.235-57.

[392] For some worthwhile articles, see the following: Peter John Dyer, "Sling The Lamps Low," SIGHT AND SOUND 31:3 (Summer 1962):134-39, 155; Jacques Rivette and Francois Truffaut, "Howard Hawks," trans. Anne and Thornton K. Brown, FILMS IN REVIEW 7:9 (November 1956):443-52; Andrew Sarris, "The World of Howard Hawks: Part One," FILMS AND FILMING 8:10 (July 1962):21-12, 48-49; ". . . Part Two," ibid., 8:11 (August 1962):44-48; Joseph McBride and Michael Wilmington, "Do I Get to Play the Drunk This Time: An Encounter With Howard Hawks," SIGHT AND SOUND 40:2 (Spring 1971):97-100; Leigh Brackett, "A Comment on the Hawksian Woman," TAKE ONE 3:6 (July-August 1971):19-20; Michael Goodwin and Naomi Wise, "Howard Hawks: An Interview," ibid., 3:8 (November-December 1971):19-25; Robin Wood, "To Have (Written) and Have Not (Directed): Reflections on Authorship," FILM COMMENT 9:3 (May-June 1973):30-5; Molly Haskell, "Howard Hawks: Masculine Feminine," ibid., 10:2 (March-April 1974):34-9; William Paul, Hawks vs. Durgnat," ibid., 14:1 (January-February 1978):68-71; Raymond Durgnat, "Hawks Isn't Good Enough," ibid., 13:4 (July-August 1977):8-19; ___, "Durgnat vs. Paul: Last Round in the Great Hawks Debate," ibid., 14:2 (March-April 1978):64-8; Joseph McBride, "Hawks," ibid., 14:2 (March-April 1978):36-41, 70-1; Alexandre Astruc, "SHERIFF: Alexandre Astruc Does Justice to Howard Hawks," trans. Dorothea Hoekzema, WIDE ANGLE 1:2 (Summer 1976):5-6; ___, "RIO LOBO By Howard Hawks," ibid., pp.7-9; William Luhr, "Howard Hawks: Hawks Thief--Patterns of Continuity in RIO BRAVO, EL DORADO, and RIO LOBO," ibid., pp.10-20; Marilyn Campbell, "HIS GIRL FRIDAY: Production for Use," ibid., 22-5, 27; Peter Lehman et al., "Howard Hawks: A Private Interview," ibid., pp.28-57; Robin Brantley, "What makes a Star?--Howard Hawks Knew Best of All," NEW YORK TIMES H (January 22, 1978):11, 19; Louis Black, "Program Notes: TWENTIETH CENTURY," CINEMATEXAS PROGRAM NOTES 13:2 (October 18, 1977):47-53; Lauren Rabinowitz, "Program Notes: HIS GIRL FRIDAY,' ibid., 13:2 (November 21, 1977):79-84; Nina Nichols, "Program Notes: HIS GIRL FRIDAY," ibid., 17:1 (October 1, 1979):75-9; Michael A. Selig, "Program Notes: SCARFACE: THE SHAME OF A NATION," ibid., 18:1 (January 16, 1980):29-34; Gwen Rowling, "Program Notes: THE BIG SLEEP," ibid., 20:1 (February 16, 1981):67-77; ___, "Program Notes: RED RIVER," ibid., 20:1 (February 25, 1981):89-98; Jimmie L. Reeves, "Program Notes: THE BIG SLEEP," ibid., 21:1 (October 14, 1981):63-72; Olive Graham, "Program Notes: HIS GIRL FRIDAY," ibid., 22:2 (March 9, 1982):11-5; and Steve Blackburn, "Program Notes: TO HAVE AND HAVE NOT," ibid., 24:1 (February 10, 1983):37-42.

Mervyn LeRoy,[393] Ernst Lubitsch, Rouben Mamoulian,[394] Lewis Milestone, King Vidor, Josef von Sternberg, Raoul Walsh, William A. Wellman, James Whale, and William Wyler.[395] Whether they functioned as contract directors (talented individuals with long-term studio contracts who were assigned films rather than people who became involved in pre-production plans) or as individuals who exercised greater control over the films they made, they collectively restored movement, imagination, and beauty to moving pictures.

As discussed in Chapters 2, 3 and 5, the coming of sound not only involved technological experimentation, but also resulted in a dramatic alteration of film content. The obvious change was in the elimination of intertitles to explain the actions and the feelings of the characters.[396] On another level, minor silent film genres about gangsters, backstage entertainers, murderers, and monsters suddenly became the rage as the public clamored for "realistic" stories about fast-talking bootleggers, smart-stepping chorus lines, haunted houses with creaky doors, and terrifying creatures in foreign lands. More than ever before, movies took their themes, plots, and characters from the nation's headlines, speakeasies, theaters, and literary circles. The onslaught of a predominantly Eastern establishment corps of directors, performers, choreographers, set designers, producers, and screenwriters not only resulted in a reinterpretation of past movie myths about the family, the Puritan ethic, and historical figures, but also in an attack on the staid and hypocritical positions that Hollywood had taken on the role of women in society, the sexual relationships between men and women, and America's sense of justice. Whether in LITTLE CAESAR (1930), SUSAN LENNOX: HER FALL AND RISE (1931), I AM A FUGITIVE FROM A CHAIN GANG (1932), KING KONG, WILD BOYS OF THE ROAD, DUCK SOUP, or 42nd STREET (all in 1933), the filmmakers were reaching out to Depression audiences with a message of understanding, reassurance, optimism, and social protest. Their

---

[393]   Peter B. Flint, "Mervyn LeRoy, 86, Dies; Producer," NEW YORK TIMES B (September 14, 1987):16.

[394]   Peter B. Flint, "Rouben Mamoulian, Stage and Film Director, Dies," NEW YORK TIMES D (December 7, 1987):11.

[395]   For more information, see Charles Afron, "Wyler, William," THE INTERNATIONAL DICTIONARY OF FILMS AND FILMMAKERS: VOLUME II--DIRECTORS/FILMMAKERS, pp.599-601; Kevin Brownlow, "The Early Days of William Wyler," FILM 37 (Autumn 1963):11-3; Gary Carey, "The Lady and the Director: Bette Davis and William Wyler," FILM COMMENT 6:3 (Fall 1970):18-24; Alan Cartnal, "Wyler on Wyler," INTERVIEW 4 (March 1974):10-11; Richard Griffith, "Wyler, Wellman, and Huston: Three Directors With a Past and a Future," FILMS IN REVIEW 1:1 (February 1950):1-5, 48; Ken Doeckel, "William Wyler: A Great Director Has Been Reduced to Exploiting His Virtuosity," ibid., 22:8 (October 1971):468-84; Curtis Lee Hanson, "William Wyler," CINEMA (Cal) 3:5 (Summer 1967):22-35; Charlton Heston, "The Questions No One Asks about Willy," FILMS AND FILMING 4:11 (August 1958):9, 32; John Howard Reid, "A Little Larger Than Life: First Part of an Analysis of Wyler's Work for the Cinema," ibid., 6:5 (February 1960):9-10, 32-3; ___, "Second Part--A Comparison of Size," ibid., 6:6 (March 1960):12, 31-2, 35; George Stevens, Jr., "The Test of Time: William Wyler," AMERICAN FILM 1:6 (April 1976):4-5; Larry Swindell, "William Wyler: A Life in Film," ibid., pp.6-27; Charlton Heston, "The BEN HUR Journal," ibid., 28-36; ___, "Dialogue on Film: William Wyler," ibid., 37-52; Stanley Kauffmann, "Take Two: ROMAN HOLIDAY," ibid., 3:6 (April 1978):66-9, 78-9; Gene D. Phillips, "William Wyler: An Interview," FOCUS ON FILM 24 (Spring 1976):5-12; and Karel Reisz, "The Later Films of William Wyler," SEQUENCE 13 (1951):19-30.

[396]   William F. Van Wert, "Intertitles," SIGHT AND SOUND 49:2 (Spring 1980):98-105.

anti-authoritarian perspective was reinforced even more in the myriad of series films, short subjects, animated cartoons, and newsreels that became an integral part of the thirties film program.[397] Everywhere you looked on screen, movies tried hard to offset everyday anxieties. The plan was straightforward: keep the audience preoccupied with the novelty of talking pictures and escapist entertainment. Whether through obfuscation or direct examples, the underlying role of the motion picture was to protect the American Dream by focusing attention on irresponsible leaders, changing values, and unresponsive institutions. In that way, the system survives; only the scapegoats change.[398]

The second stage of the sound revolution occurred near the end of 1933, when dwindling box-office receipts resulted in the closing of 2,500 movie theaters, the inauguration of the double-feature movie bill, and giveaway programs. Moreover, the emergence of the Legion of Decency compelled the film industry to rethink its social and financial relationship with the general public, organized religion, and Wall Street. Ever since the movies became a force in society at the turn of the century, politicians and reformers had been troubled by the values propagated by an industry run by "outsiders." Now with the nation battered by a crippling Depression, the fears about "cinematic immorality" reached monumental proportions as the Payne Fund studies allegedly found evidence to support the worst fears about the negative effects of movies on society. As discussed in Chapter 3, the Catholic church, strongly supported by Protestant and Jewish groups, decided to move against the film industry, and by June of 1934 it had coerced Hays and the film moguls into strictly enforcing the Production Code drafted in 1929 by the Catholic publisher Martin Quigley and the Jesuit priest Father Daniel A. Lord. The new Production Code Office, under the firm hand of the Catholic layman Joseph I. Breen, maintained a stranglehold over film content for the next two decades. During this period, new myths about the American Dream were created: e.g., the guilty always get punished, love conquers all, the poor are happier than the rich, and everything turns out for the best. Most indicative of the Breen Office's values was the dramatic transformation from the anti-authoritarian comedies of W. C. Fields, the Marx Brothers,[399] and Mae West[400] to the screwball comedies of Frank Capra and Howard Hawks. The change was also apparent in the shift from gangster movies to G-Man films, from topical stories about fallen women to uplifting screen adaptations like OF HUMAN BONDAGE (1934), DAVID COPPERFIELD, BECKY SHARP, and A TALE OF TWO CITIES (all in 1935).

Hollywood's emphasis on respectability was based on more than social, religious, and economic pressures. A nationalistic spirit propelling many European and Asian nations to a state of war had also politicized the United States. As discussed in Chapters 2, 3, 5, and 6, the use of propaganda in commercial feature films became a major issue among legislators, the clergy, performers, screenwriters, directors, and moguls. Whether it was the rise of fascist leaders like Hitler and Mussolini, the war in China, Stalin's policies in the Soviet Union, MGM's blatant misuse of power

---

[397]   For a good overview on nonfeature film activities, see Bohn and Stromgren, pp.215-8.

[398]   For a good illustration of the debate over the film as a social document in the early 1930s, see H. A. Potemkin, "Dog Days in the Movie," CLOSE-UP 9:4 (December 1932):268-72; and Clifford Howard, "American Tendencies," ibid., pp.285-6.

[399]   Robert Altman et al., "Portrait of the Artist as an Old Man: Groucho Marx," TAKE ONE 3:1 (September-October 1971):10-16; Joe Adamson, "Duck Soup For The Rest Of Your Life," ibid., pp.18-21.

[400]   Eric Braun, "Doing What Comes Naturally: Part I," FILMS AND FILMING 17:1 (October 1970):27-28, 30-32; "Part II," ibid., 17:2 (November 1970):38-42; and Steven V. Roberts, "76--And Still Diamond Lil," THE NEW YORK TIMES MAGAZINE Sunday, November 2, 1969, pp.64-65, 67, 70-82.

in its attack on Upton Sinclair's 1934 California gubernatorial bid, the divisiveness of the Spanish Civil War, the Republican-controlled Hollywood's distrust of the New Deal, or the film colony's sympathy for Popular Front causes, the studios were in political turmoil and remained so until America entered the war in late 1941. (Once the war was decided, the battles emerged again.) Movies of the middle period, therefore, reflected Hollywood's attempt to put the best possible face on its loyalties to American traditions, its respect for authority, and its willingness not to transmit "immoral" messages to its allegedly impressionable audiences. The fact that the studio heads frequently ignored or misinterpreted society's problems and who was responsible for them, or used any means possible to control their employees' behavior off screen as well as on screen resulted in gross misunderstandings about personal and public alternatives to the STATUS QUO, acrimonious fights between the Screenwriters Guild and the Screen Playwrights, and the 1937 strike of the International Alliance of Theatrical Stage Employees against the major studios.[401] All these factors underscored the horrendous political and economic wars among Hollywood's creative personnel and craft unions that continued over the next two decades.

By the end of 1937, Hollywood found its optimistic messages waning at the box office. The public, troubled both by the Depression and the international war clouds, once more became receptive to socially conscious films about the world it inhabited. For every spectator who applauded child stars like Mickey Rooney, Judy Garland, Shirley Temple, and Deanna Durbin, as well as the series films starring Hopalong Cassidy and Roy Rogers, there were others who warmed to the consciousness-raising works of Charlie Chaplin, Michael Curtiz, William Dieterle, John Ford, Fritz Lang, Walter Wanger, Orson Welles,[402] and William Wyler. The difficulty lay in how far to go in raising social-consciousness and how to film it without offending the Breen Office or influential political figures.

The same problems also beset liberal and left-wing filmmakers like James Cagney, Melvyn Douglas, Dashiell Hammett, Lillian Hellman, John Howard Lawson, Dudley Nichols, Edward G. Robinson, Budd Schulberg, and Donald Ogden Stewart. As discussed in Chapter 5, Hollywood had its political battles so tangled up with its economic struggles, that it became difficult to know whether the moguls hated these artists more for their "Popular Front" views, or for their claims of unfair labor practices. What was clear was that as America moved closer to the brink of war, its film industry was torn apart by those who demanded that the Production Code be damned; that foreign nations who violated human rights, regardless of our isolationist stance or promise to represent all countries fairly, be condemned verbally and visually. On the other hand, there were people like Louis B. Mayer who insisted that more was accomplished with subtlety and finesse than with indignant outbursts and precipitous behavior. The output of films in the final years before Pearl Harbor, as discussed in Chapter 2, reflects the struggle between the left and the right in Hollywood in dealing with America's anxieties, responsibilities, and confusion.

With all of Hollywood's monumental problems, one filmmaker formented an additional crisis: Orson Welles. An undisputed genius, who came to film from work on the stage and in radio, he was given unparalleled freedom by RKO Pictures to

---

[401] For details on the consequences of the April 30, 1937, strike of Hollywood painters, draftsmen, make-up artists, hairdressers, and scenic artists, see Ida Jeter, "The Collapse of the Federated Motion Picture Crafts: A Case Study of Class Collaboration in the Motion Picture Industry," JOURNAL OF THE UNIVERSITY FILM ASSOCIATION 31:2 (Spring 1979):37-45.

[402] Mike Prokosch, "Orson Welles: An Introduction," FILM COMMENT 7:2 (Summer 1971):18-32; and David Bordwell, "Citizen Kane," ibid., pp.38-47.

make six feature films, the first being his feature film debut with CITIZEN KANE (1941).[403] The story surrounding the controversial production is readily available in books annotated later. Suffice it to say that his remarkable contributions to screenwriting,[404] cinematography, film acting, narrative development, sound editing, and AUTEURISM place him among the giants of filmmaking.[405] At the time, however, his influence was minimal because his cinematic ideas were not only revolutionary, but also controversial. In particular, the film's subject matter raised the wrath of William Randolph Hearst, whose organization led a vicious and powerful campaign against both the film and the entire Welles Mercury Theater team. As a result, CITIZEN KANE became a box-office flop, along with Welles's next two films, the memorable THE MAGNIFICENT AMBERSONS (1942) and the intriguing JOURNEY INTO FEAR (1943). RKO Pictures then gave up on its film genius, and Welles abandoned Hollywood to work to travel throughout the country until the end of World War II.

If any period of American film is ripe for debate, it is the golden age of film. Did the coming of sound destroy or expand the art of the film? Did the Breen Office effectively "silence" the screen's social conscience and make movies empty-headed and oppressively reactionary, or did it provide an outlet for the global anxieties of the times? Were the movie moguls irresponsible in their refusal to raise the public's consciousness about fascism in the world? Did left-wing and liberal filmmakers have any influence in propagandizing film content? Did the studio system prevent serious writers from functioning in the film industry? Were movies corrupting America's youth or did they provide a temporary safety value for the difficulties of a confused and frustrated generation of young people who saw all their traditional safeguards ruptured by the Depression and world conflict? Could the movies have survived without the heavy dependence on Wall Street? And were the movie moguls themselves astute businessmen or crude philistines? Those are only a few of the issues being debated today.

BOOKS

GENERAL

Affron, Charles. CINEMA AND SENTIMENT. Chicago: The University of Chicago Press, 1982. Illustrated. 202pp.

Bandler, Bernard II, et al., eds. HOUND AND HORN: ESSAYS ON CINEMA. New York: Arno Press, 1972.

---

[403] For a good overview of Welles's earlier forays into filmmaking, see Frank Brady, "The Lost Films of Orson Welles," AMERICAN FILM 4:2 (November 1978):63-9; and "Special Issue on Orson Welles," PERSISTENCE OF VISION 7 (1989).

[404] The controversy over Welles's role in developing the screenplay for CITIZEN KANE is covered in all of the major works on Welles and in the film itself. In addition, readers should also consult Chapter 5 and the annotated works on John Housman, Howard Koch, and Herman J. Mankiewicz.

[405] Orson Welles died on October 10, 1985. For valuable observations on his extraordinary career, see "Orson Welles is Dead at 70; Innovator of Film and Stage," NEW YORK TIMES A (October 11, 1985):1, B6; Vincent Canby, "Orson Welles Began An Ongoing Revolution," ibid., 2 (October 20, 1985):1, 17; and Andrew Sarris, "Was Welles a Wizard or a Whirling Dervish?" VILLAGE VOICE 30:19 (May 7, 1985):47.

From 1929 to 1933, this unique little periodical provided fascinating comments about the trends and developments in the cinema. Among the contributors were Allen Tate, Ezra Pound, Kenneth Burke, Francis Fergusson, and Herbert Read. Well worth browsing.

*Baxter, John. HOLLYWOOD IN THE THIRTIES. New York: A. S. Barnes and Company, 1968. Illustrated. 160pp.
    This is a useful, comprehensive, and fascinating account of the fabulous 1930s, with an emphasis on the major studios: Metro-Goldwyn-Mayer, Paramount, Warner Bros., and Universal. Baxter is particularly good at recalling important personalities and pictures and should help in setting the scene for further study in the period. Unfortunately, the book has no bibliography, which is necessary for this type of study. Well worth browsing.

*Blum, Daniel. A NEW PICTORIAL HISTORY OF THE TALKIES. Rev.   John Kobal. New York: G. P. Putnam's Sons, 1973. Illustrated. 392pp.
    Originally issued in 1958, this visual survey of the sound era is hampered by its weak narrative and poor production design. Approach with caution.

Byrge, Duane, and Robert Milton Miller. A CRITICAL STUDY OF THE SCREWBALL COMEDY. Ann Arbor: UMI Research Press, 1989. Illustrated. 200pp.

Cameron, Ian, ed. MOVIE READER. New York: Praeger Publishers, 1977. Illustrated. 120pp.
    An imaginative and stimulating publication, this anthology of thirty-three essays and reviews from the magazine MOVIE opens with a chart summarizing the editorial board's taste in directors at the time of the first issue of MOVIE in May 1962. Five categories are listed: "Great" (only Howard Hawks and Alfred Hitchcock), "Brilliant" (twelve names listed, including Joseph Losey, Leo McCarey, and Jacques Tourneur), "Very Talented" (twenty-seven names listed, including Seth Holt, Jerry Lewis, and Gerd Oswald), "Competent or Ambitious" (eighty names are listed, including Don Chaffey, Robert Day, and Jack Webb), and "The Rest" (sixty names are listed, including Julian Amyes, Muriel Box, and Russell Rouse). These types of judgments not only reflect the editor's quirky preferences but also their commitment to the AUTEUR theory. The book is divided into eight sections: "General Articles," "Alfred Hitchcock," "Otto Preminger," "Howard Hawks," "Nicholas Ray," "Joseph Losey," "Director Studies," and "Film Reviews." Among the distinguished writers commenting on the importance of genre directors and trends are Victor F. Perkins, Ian Cameron, Paul Mayersberg, Robin Wood, Charles Barr, and Raymond Durgnat. Despite the absence of an index and the poor quality of the visuals, this collection offers an excellent guide to the movement begun in the 1960s to reevaluate the art of film. Recommended for special collections.

Dimmitt, Richard B. A TITLE GUIDE TO THE TALKIES. 2 Volumes.   Metuchen: The Scarecrow Press, 1965, 1967. 2,133pp.
    Covering the period from October 1927 until December 1963, Dimimitt provides a massive list of information on 16,000 American feature-length film titles, copyright dates, producers, studios, screenwriters, and original sources. Each entry has its

---

[406]   For a fuller review, see Frank Manchel, "Books: HOLLYWOOD IN THE THIRTIES," FILM SOCIETY REVIEW 4:5 (January 1969):40-1.

own citation number, which is referred to in the name index. Interestingly, no mention is made of director, general release date, and distribution company. Recommended for special collections.

Michael, Paul, et al., eds. THE AMERICAN MOVIES REFERENCE BOOK: THE SOUND ERA. Englewood Cliffs: Prentice-Hall, 1969. Illustrated. 629pp.

Upon publication everyone's favorite whipping boy for weak scholarship, omissions, and general presentation, time and encouragement has not produced a revised and expanded edition. It is divided into six sections on history, performers, films, directors, producers, and awards. A bibliography and index are included. Approach with extreme caution.[407]

Davy, Charles, ed. FOOTNOTES TO THE FILM. London: Lovat Dickson, Ltd., 1938. New York: Arno Press, 1970. Illustrated. 334pp.

Intended as a practical discussion of studio filmmaking, this book is a valuable guide to the techniques, artists, and movie-going public of the 1930s. The contributors are often key figures like Alfred Hitchcock, Robert Donat, Basil Wright, Graham Greene, Alberto Cavalcanti, John Grierson, Alexander Korda, Alistair Cooke, and Forsyth Hardy. Their brief essays are worthwhile, and the book contains more than twenty interesting illustrations. Well worth browsing.

*Geduld, Harry. THE BIRTH OF THE TALKIES: FROM EDISON TO JOLSON. Bloomington: Indiana University Press, 1975. Illustrated. 337pp.

Designed to commemorate the fiftieth anniversary of the sound revolution in American films, this pioneering analysis of the early days of the talkies is the first major attempt to put into perspective the events of the transitional period. Six detailed chapters boldly examine the steps taken by the major studios to deal with the technological revolution. At the time of publication, the book was attacked for its factual errors and pedantic prose. Whatever its faults, the scholarly effort deserves recognition for not only inspiring more accurate studies but also for refocusing film studies toward more serious examinations of film history. Five excellent appendexes offer invaluable information on conflicting opinions on the state of the film industry in the late 1920s, the types of films released in 1929, and the various sound patents of the period. This is one book that deserves serious reevaluation. Endnotes and an index are provided. Well worth browsing.

Gregg, Eugene S. THE SHADOW OF SOUND. New York: Vantage Press, 1968. 174pp.

Written by a man who was head of the export department of Electrical Research Products Inc.--the new company formed by Western Electric to handle their new sound inventions--this book deals with the turbulent years of the early talkies. Not only is this readable, brief narrative informative on Hollywood and its stars, but it is also very useful on the world scene, and on the business war that followed the exporting of sound devices to foreign countries. Well worth browsing.

Higham, Charles, and Joel Greenberg. THE CELLULOID MUSE: HOLLYWOOD DIRECTORS SPEAK. London: Angus and Robertson, 1969. Illustrated. 268pp.

This informative and interesting book provides some helpful information on Hitchcock, Lang, Cukor, Minnelli, Vidor, Wilder, and Milestone. The writing is clear, brief, and enjoyable. Worth browsing.

---

[407]   If you do decide to get a copy, read Earl Anderson, "Sophomoric Scholarship," FILMS IN REVIEW 20:8 (October 1969): 496-501.

Jenkins, Bruce, and Susan Krane. HOLLIS FRAMPTON: RECOLLECTIONS, RECREATIONS. Cambridge: The M. I. T. Press, 1984. Illustrated. 128pp.

Keyser, Les, and Barbara. HOLLYWOOD AND THE CATHOLIC CHURCH: THE IMAGE OF ROMAN CATHOLICISM IN AMERICAN MOVIES. Chicago: Loyola University Press, 1984. Illustrated. 295pp.

Kiesling, Barrett C. TALKING PICTURES: HOW THEY ARE MADE, HOW TO APPRECIATE THEM. Richmond: Johnson Publishing Co., 1937. Illustrated. 332pp.
    This is an interesting but outdated breakdown of the division of labor that went into making the sound motion picture in the early days of the Talkie revolution in films. Throughout the twenty-eight short chapters, the author, a former publicity man with the old Famous Players-Lasky, presents the various roles of technicians, screenwriters, and directors. Worth browsing.

Kirsten, Lincoln, et al., eds. FILMS: A QUARTERLY OF DISCUSSION AND ANALYSIS. Nos. I-IV New York: Arno Press, 1972.
    This unique magazine, with its international flavor, had some of the best contributors on the period 1938-1940--the time covered here--and the editors have taken extracts from the period to show the periodical's worth. Sample writers include Alberto Cavalcanti, Richard Griffith, John Grierson, and Rudolf Arnheim. There is also some good information on film criticism, production, and historical development. Well worth browsing.

MacPherson, Kenneth, and Winifred Bryher, eds. CLOSE-UP: 1927-1932.   Foreword Herman Weinberg. Ten volumes. New York: Arno Press, 1972.
    With the aid of a new cumulative index, consisting of three separate parts--author, film title, and subject--prepared especially for this reprint edition, this valuable magazine dealing primarily with aesthetics, theory, and criticism provides a valuable addition to film scholarship. It also contains a rare collection of stills. Recommended for special collections.

*Mandelbaum, Howard, and Eric Myers. SCREEN DECO: A CELEBRATION OF HIGH STYLE IN HOLLYWOOD. New York: St. Martin's Press, 1985. Illustrated. 211pp.

Maltin, Leonard. THE GREAT MOVIE SHORTS: THOSE WONDERFUL ONE- AND TWO-REELERS OF THE THIRTIES AND FORTIES. New York: Crown, 1971. Illustrated. 236pp.
    This is the major source of information for those who want plot synopses and helpful commentaries about the important film personalities and significant shorts of the first two decades of the sound era. Recommended for special collections.

*Maltin, Leonard. MOVIE COMEDY TEAMS. Introduction Billy Gilbert. New York: Signet, 1970. Illustrated. 352pp.
    A brief but handy reference tool, this book summarizes many of the familiar stories about the famous comic teams of American films. Well worth browsing.

Manchel, Frank. THE TALKING CLOWNS: FROM LAUREL AND HARDY TO THE MARX BROTHERS. New York: Franklin Watts, 1976. Illustrated. 120pp.

"The approach of Frank Manchel in THE TALKING CLOWNS . . . is excellent because it concentrates on four film institutions, Laurel and Hardy, W. C. Fields, Mae West, and the Marx Brothers. The stars are obviously favorites of the author and one becomes acquainted with them as individuals and learns a great deal about their working techniques . . . Careful analysis of what makes things funny along with filmdom facts plus an outstanding bibliography proclaim THE TALKING CLOWNS a winner."[408]

Manchel, Frank. WHEN MOVIES BEGAN TO SPEAK. Englewood Cliffs: Prentice-Hall, 1969. Illustrated. 76pp.

"In a sequel to WHEN PICTURES BEGAN TO MOVE . . . the history of the motion picture industry is covered up to the present [1969], the most interesting aspect of the book being the efforts of the sound-film pioneers to develop and perfect the techniques made possible by De Forest's invention of the audio amplifier . . . . Frank Manchel discusses the outstanding directors, the landmark films, the end of the star era, and the unionization of the industry, formula films, wartime movies, the McCarthy influence, foreign cinema, and the effect of television on the industry. Not comprehensive, but a balanced picture given in crisp, informal writing. Ages 12-15."[409]

Nash, Jay Robert, et. al. THE MOTION PICTURE GUIDE 1927-1983. 12 volumes. Evanston: Cinebooks, 1985.

An ambitious attempt to cover every movie made in English and many important foreign films as well, the first nine volumes offer information on the sound era. Volume ten focuses on silent movies, while volumes ten and eleven categorize major film awards, title changes, film series, and a proper name index. Collectively, over 35,000 movies are presented in alphabetically arranged entries, with details about production and cast credits, critical ratings (ranging from zero--not worth watching--to masterpieces), year of release, foreign country production (when appropriate), running time (at the time of release), producing and distributing companies, color or b/w, synopses, information about remakes and sequels, genre/subject classifications, and MPAA ratings (including Parental Recommendation warnings). The two volumes I spotchecked (Volumes 3 and 8) were impressive in accuracy and critical commentaries.[410] Well worth browsing.

Naumberg, Nancy, ed. WE MAKE THE MOVIES. New York: W. W. Norton and Company, 1937. Illustrated. 284pp.

---

[408]   Jerome Cashman, "Children's Shelf: When Movies Were Young," LOS ANGELES TIMES (May 15, 1977):11.

[409]   Zena Sutherland, "Book Review: WHEN MOVIES BEGAN TO SPEAK," SATURDAY REVIEW 52:45 (November 8, 1969):71.

[410]   While many other reviewers also find the work useful, it is important to note that Dan Greenberg, in his scathing review of the series, concludes that "THE MOTION PICTURE GUIDE represents not only a failure of research achievement, but an equal failure of the evaluative machinery by which our society supposedly judges major publication projects." See Dan Greenberg, "Books: THE MOTION PICTURE GUIDE," FILM QUARTERLY 41:2 (Winter 1987-88):63.

Designed to introduce readers to the fundamentals of film production, this book begins with Jesse Lasky's essay on what it means to be a film producer and follows with articles on story ideas, treatments, designing sets, casting, acting (written by Bette Davis and Paul Muni), sound recording, shooting, cutting, and a concluding chapter on exhibition by Walt Disney. All in all, an interesting and enjoyable study. Well worth browsing.

Quigley, Martin, Jr., and Richard Gertner. FILMS IN AMERICA, 1929-1969: A PANORAMIC VIEW OF FOUR DECADES OF SOUND. New York: Golden Press, 1970. Illustrated. 319pp.

This book furnishes concise, comprehensive information about 400 significant movies, but fails to make any useful critical analyses. One still, at least, accompanies each film review. Worth browsing.

Parish, James Robert. THE SLAPSTICK QUEENS. South Brunswick: A. S. Barnes and Company, 1973. Illustrated. 298pp.

Salem, James M. A GUIDE TO CRITICAL REVIEWS: PART IV--THE SCREENPLAY FROM "THE JAZZ SINGER" TO "DR. STRANGELOVE." Two volumes. Metuchen: The Scarecrow Press, 1971. 1420pp.

This is a valuable research tool for anyone interested in locating popular reviews of over 12,000 American and foreign feature films released between October, 1927, and December, 1963. The one misleading note is that the term "screenplay" refers to released films, rather than film scripts. The entries, alphabetically arranged, provide information on periodical, volume, issue, date, and page. An appendix indicates the names of winners in the major Oscar and New York Film Critics' awards. The work's one serious flaw is its commitment to include reviews instead of scholarly and critical evaluations. Regrettably, no indexes are provided for access to directors and stars. Recommended for special collections.[411]

*Sarris, Andrew. THE AMERICAN CINEMA: DIRECTORS AND DIRECTIONS, 1929-1968. New York: E. P. Dutton and Company, 1968. 383pp.

In a limited amount of space, Sarris manages to squeeze a lot of useful information about 200 directors. The original material was published in the Spring 1963 issue of FILM CULTURE and is expanded and updated for this extremely stimulating volume. His iconoclastic analyses group the filmmakers into highly subjective categories: e.g., "Pantheon Directors" (Charles Chaplin, Robert Flaherty, John Ford, D. W. Griffith, Howard Hawks, Alfred Hitchcock, Buster Keaton, Fritz Lang, Ernst Lubitsch, F. W. Murneau, Max Ophuls, Jean Renoir, Josef von Sternberg, and Orson Welles). Other categories include "The Far Side of Paradise," "Expressive Esoterica," "Fringe Benefits," "Less Than Meets the Eye," "Lightly Likable," "Strained Seriousness," and "Subjects for Further Research." Each alphabetically arranged entry in each category gives the director's name, year of birth (and death when appropriate), followed by a chronological filmography of feature films. Sarris then offers a brief critical commentary evaluating the director's work and contributions to film history. Debates are still raging over the critic's assertions that the director of the 1954 film, TAZA, THE SON OF COCHISE (Douglas

---

[411] For additional information incorporated into books about the theater, see James M. Salem, A GUIDE TO CRITICAL REVIEWS: PART II--THE MUSICAL, 1909-1974, 2nd ed. (Metuchen: The Scarecrow Press, 1976); and ---, A GUIDE TO CRITICAL REVIEWS: PART III--FOREIGN DRAMA, 1909-1977, 2nd ed. (Metuchen: The Scarecrow Press, 1979).

Sirk) is a greater artist than the director of the 1951 film THE AFRICAN QUEEN (John Huston). The fun is in picking out your favorite directors and matching your opinions with Sarris's AUTEURIST approach. A directorial chronology from 1915 to 1967 and a directorial index are included. The latter is a misnomer since it really is an alphabetical listing of film titles. Recommended for special collections.

Scherman, David E., ed. LIFE GOES TO THE MOVIES. New York: Time-Life Books, 1975. Illustrated. 304pp.

Scotland, John. THE TALKIES. Foreword Cecil M. Hepworth. New York: The Industrial Book Company, 1931. Illustrated. 194pp.
    Useful for its discussion of the effects of sound development upon production, distribution, and exhibition of motion pictures, this poorly written account by an unknown author (Scotland is a pseudonym) has over thirty valuable illustrations on equipment and studio conditions. Worth browsing.

Seldes, Gilbert. AN HOUR WITH THE MOVIES AND THE TALKIES. Philadelphia: J. B. Lippincott, 1929. 156pp.
    Here is a provocative and insightful commentary on the significant changes that occurred as the result of sound movies. Seldes is primarily concerned with the industry's inability to produce another Chaplin and the film world's failure to reach its artistic destiny. The author offers some valuable suggestions for today's filmmakers as well. Worth browsing.

Seldes, Gilbert. THE MOVIES COME FROM AMERICA. Preface Charles Chaplin. New York: Charles Scribner's Sons, 1937. Illustrated. 120pp.
    A general and informal history of the motion picture and the changes that took place in the industry when sound took over. Seldes, a wonderful commentator on an extraordinary era, discusses with authority and ease, the social, economic, and political forces that shaped the film world up to 1936. Worth browsing.

*Sitney, P. Adams. VISIONARY FILM: THE AMERICAN AVANT-GARDE. New York: Oxford University Press, 1974. Illustrated. 452pp.

*Slide, Anthony. GREAT RADIO PERSONALITIES IN HISTORIC PHOTOGRAPHS. Vestal: The Vestal Press, 1988. Illustrated. 117pp.
    A charming photo album containing 239 pictures of familiar and unfamiliar personalities from the golden age of broadcasting, this nostalgic book is not only fun to leaf through, but also useful since it recalls the early careers of film stars like Bob Hope, Lucille Ball,[412] Bing Crosby, Bud Abbott and Lou Costello, Roy Rogers, and Jimmy Durante. Each glossy picture comes with an accurate and interesting thumbnail sketch. Regrettably, there is no index. Well worth browsing.

---

[412] For more information, see Peter B. Flint, "Lucille Ball, Spirited Doyenne of TV Comedies, Dies at 77," NEW YORK TIMES A (April 27, 1989):1, B17; "Lucille Ball Dies; Leaves Legacy of Laughter," BURLINGTON FREE PRESS A (April 27, 1989):1, 14; and Charles Champlin, "In Appreciation: Lucy's Enduring Comedy Captured Our Hearts," ibid., pp.D10-11.

Slide, Anthony, ed. THE BEST OF ROB WAGNER'S SCRIPT. Metuchen: The Scarecrow Press, 1985. 173pp.

Springer, John. FORGOTTEN FILMS TO REMEMBER: AND A BRIEF HISTORY OF FIFTY YEARS OF THE AMERICAN TALKING FILM. Secaucus: Citadel Press, 1980. Illustrated. 256pp.

Stern, Seymour, and Lewis Jacobs, eds. EXPERIMENTAL CINEMA, 1930-1934. With a New Cumulative Index. New York: Arno Press, 1972.
    Aimed at a leftist audience, this controversial and militant magazine specialized in film aesthetics and Soviet techniques of montage. Among its many worthwhile contributors were V. I. Pudovkin, Sergei M. Eisenstein, and Alexander P. Dovzhenko. Well worth browsing.

Thrasher, Frederick. OKAY FOR SOUND. New York: Duell, Sloan, and Pearce, 1946. Illustrated. 303pp.

Tuska, Jon, et al., eds. CLOSE-UP: THE CONTRACT DIRECTOR. Metuchen: The Scarecrow Press, 1976. Illustrated. 457pp.
    The first book in a series with essays on important film directors since the early days of sound to the present, this volume focuses on ten personalities under long-term contracts with the major Hollywood studios. Each of the men here, and in the volumes to follow, provides his interpretation of what the industry was and is, what it is like to work in the studio system, and how he struggled to achieve his individual goals. What is unique about the series is that the content is derived from personal interviews commissioned for this project. The ten subjects in this volume are Walter Lang, H. Bruce Humberstone, William Dieterle, Joseph Kane, William Witney, Lesley Selander, Yakima Canutt, Lewis Milestone, Edward Dmytryk, and Howard Hawks. Although the interviews are conducted by a handful of different people, they remain uniformly interesting and entertaining. Each is concluded with a brief filmography. A general index is included. Well worth browsing.

Tuska, Jon, et al., eds. CLOSE-UP: THE HOLLYWOOD DIRECTOR. Metuchen: The Scarecrow Press, 1978. Illustrated. 444pp.
    The second volume in the trilogy on film directors, this work is the least original in that most of the subjects have been studied in much greater detail in valuable autobiographies and biographies. The nine directors in question are Billy Wilder, Henry King, Frank Capra, Spencer Gordon Bennet, William Wyler, William Wellman, John Huston, Douglas Sirk, and Alfred Hitchcock. The filmographies at the end of each essay only reaffirm the paucity of information contained here and available in greater detail elsewhere. A general index is included. Worth browsing.

Tuska, Jon, et al., eds. CLOSE-UP: THE CONTEMPORARY DIRECTOR. Metuchen: The Scarecrow Press, 1981. Illustrated. 431pp.
    The final volume in this trilogy, this broad spectrum of career studies focuses on ten controversial directors: Sydney Pollack, Sam Fuller, Sam Peckinpah, George Roy Hill, Robert Altman, Dick Richards, Hal Ashby, Peter Bogdanovich, Martin Scorsese, and Roman Polanski. Each extended essay contains a critical discussion of the director's work plus a modest filmography. Because the essays are based on personal interviews, they tend to be rambling and anecdotal, rather than incisive and factual analyses. A general index is included. Well worth browsing.

Walker, Alexander. THE SHATTERED SILENTS: HOW THE TALKIES CAME TO STAY.
New York: William Morrow and Company, 1979. Illustrated. 218pp.
    An important chronicle of the years from mid-1926 to the end of 1929, this study
discusses the amazing revolution that "passed with such breakneck speed, at such
inflationary cost, with such ruthless self-interest, that a whole art form was sundered
and consigned to history almost before anyone could count the cost in economic terms
or guess the consequences in human ones--and certainly before anyone could keep
an adequate record of it." Walker provides an in-depth analysis of the confusion that
took place in the studios, the mistakes and accidents that shaped the direction talking
pictures would take in the decades to follow, and the unremitting greed and ambition
of the filmmakers who scrambled to take advantage of the sound revolution.
Throughout, the author manages to capture the panic of the times and the human
tragedies caused by the coming of sound. What helps is Walker's splendid research
that became possible because the important trade journals--e.g., FILM WEEKLY,
MOTION PICTURE, MOVING PICTURE WORLD, NEW YORK WORLD, PHOTOPLAY,
THEATRE MAGAZINE, and VARIETY--only recently were made available on microfilm.
Twelve fact-filled chapters explain in detail how the "fun" went out of moviemaking
and a "management" philosophy took over. A selected filmography, bibliography, and
index are provided. Recommended for special collections.

JUNE ALLYSON

*Allyson, June, and Frances Spatz Leighton. JUNE ALLYSON. New York: G. P.
Putnam's Sons, 1982. Illustrated. 262pp.

GEORGE ARLISS

Arliss, George. MY TEN YEARS IN THE STUDIOS. Boston: Little, Brown and
Company, 1940. Illustrated. 349pp.

FRED ASTAIRE

*Astaire, Fred. STEPS IN TIME: AN AUTOBIOGRAPHY. New York: Harper and
Brothers, 1959. Illustrated. 338pp.; New York: Harper & Row, 1987. Foreword
Ginger Rogers. Illustrated. 338pp.

*Croce, Arlene. THE FRED ASTAIRE/GINGER ROGERS MOVIE BOOK. New York:
Outerbridge and Lazard, 1972. Illustrated. 192pp.

*Freedland, Michael. FRED ASTAIRE. New York: Grosset and Dunlap, 1976.
Illustrated. 277pp.

Green, Stanley, and Burt Goldblatt. STARRING FRED ASTAIRE. New York: Dodd,
Mead, 1973. Illustrated. 436pp.

*Harvey, Stephen. FRED ASTAIRE. New York: Pyramid Books, 1975. Illustrated.
158pp.

Thompson, H. FRED ASTAIRE: A PICTORIAL TREASURY OF HIS FILMS. New York: Crescent Books, 1970. Illustrated. 160pp.

TALLULAH BANKHEAD

Bankhead, Tallulah. TALLULAH: MY AUTOBIOGRAPHY. London: Victor Gollancz, 1952. Illustrated. 355pp.

*Brian, Denis. TALLULAH, DARLING. New York: Pyramid Publications, 1972. Illustrated. 285pp. New York: Pyramid Publications, 1980.

Gill, Brendan. TALLULAH. New York: Holt, Rinehart and Winston, 1972. Illustrated. 287pp.

Israel, Lee. MISS TALLULAH BANKHEAD. New York: G. P. Putnam's Sons, 1972. Illustrated. 384pp.

*Tunney, Kieran. TALLULAH: DARLING OF THE GODS. New York: Manor Books, 1974. Illustrated. 228pp.

THE BARRYMORES

Alpert, Hollis. THE BARRYMORES. New York: Dial Press, 1964. Illustrated. 397pp.

Barrymore, John. CONFESSIONS OF AN ACTOR. New York: Blom, 1971. Illustrated. 134pp.

Barrymore, Lionel, and Shipp Cameron. WE BARRYMORES. New York: Appleton-Century-Crofts, 1951. Illustrated. 311pp.

Fowler, Gene. GOOD NIGHT SWEET PRINCE: THE LIFE AND TIMES OF JOHN BARRYMORE. New York: Viking Press, 1944. Illustrated. 477pp.

Kobler, John. DAMNED IN PARADISE: THE LIFE OF JOHN BARRYMORE. New York: Atheneum, 1977. Illustrated. 401pp.

Kotsilibas-Davis, James. THE BARRYMORES: THE ROYAL FAMILY IN HOLLYWOOD. New York: Crown, 1981. Illustrated. 384pp.

CECIL BEATON

Beaton, Cecil. CECIL BEATON: MEMOIRS OF THE 40s. New York: McGraw-Hill, 1972. Illustrated. 310pp.

Spencer, Charles. CECIL BEATON: STAGE AND FILM DESIGNS. New York: St. Martin's Press, 1975. Illustrated. 115pp.

*Vickers, Hugo. CECIL BEATON: A BIOGRAPHY. New York: Primus, 1985. Illustrated. 656pp.

RALPH BELLAMY

Bellamy, Ralph. WHEN THE SMOKE HIT THE FAN. New York: Doubleday and Company, 1979. Illustrated. 318pp.

INGRID BERGMAN

Bergman, Ingrid, and Alan Burgess. INGRID BERGMAN: MY STORY. New York: Delacorte Press, 1980. Illustrated. 494pp.

*Brown, Curtis F. INGRID BERGMAN. New York: Pyramid Books, 1973. Illustrated. 157pp.

*Steele, Joseph Henry. INGRID BERGMAN: AN INTIMATE PORTRAIT. New York: Popular Library, 1959. Illustrated. 332pp.

*Quirk, Lawrence J. THE FILMS OF INGRID BERGMAN. New York: The Citadel Press, 1970. Illustrated. 224pp.

HUMPHREY BOGART

*Barbour, Alan. HUMPHREY BOGART. New York: Pyramid Books, 1973. Illustrated. 191pp.

Benchley, Nathan. HUMPHREY BOGART. Boston: Little, Brown and Company, 1975. Illustrated. 242pp.

Eyles, Allen. BOGART. Garden City: Doubleday and Company, 1975. Illustrated. 128pp.

*Gehman, Richard. BOGART. Greenwich: Gold Medal Books, 1965. Illustrated. 159pp.

Goodman, Ezra. BOGEY: THE GOOD-BAD GUY. New York: Lyle Stuart, 1965. Illustrated. 223pp.

*Hanna, David. BOGART. New York: Leisure Books, 1976. Illustrated. 201pp.

*Hyams, Joe. BOGIE: THE BIOGRAPHY OF HUMPHREY BOGART. New York: New American Library, 1966. Illustrated. 211pp.

*Hyams, Joe. BOGART AND BACALL: A LOVE STORY. New York: David McKay, 1975. Illustrated. 245pp.

*McCarty, Clifford. BOGEY: THE FILMS OF HUMPHREY BOGART. New York: Bonanza Books, 1965. Illustrated. 190pp.

Michael, Paul. HUMPHREY BOGART: THE MAN AND HIS FILMS. Indianapolis: Bobbs-Merrill, 1965. Illustrated. 191pp.

TOD BROWNING

*Rosenthal, Stuart, and Judith Kass. THE HOLLYWOOD PROFESSIONALS (Volume 4): TOD BROWNING, DON SIEGEL. New York: A. S. Barnes and Company, 1975. Illustrated. 207pp.

JAMES CAGNEY

*Bergman, Andrew. JAMES CAGNEY. New York: Pyramid Books, 1973. Illustrated. 156pp.

*Cagney, James. CAGNEY BY CAGNEY. New York: Pocket Books, 1976. Illustrated. 216pp.

*Dickens, Homer. THE FILMS OF JAMES CAGNEY. Secaucus: The Citadel Press, 1972. Illustrated. 249pp.

Freedland, Michael. CAGNEY. New York: Stein and Day, 1975. Illustrated. 255pp.

*McGilligan, Patrick. CAGNEY: THE ACTOR AS AUTEUR. New York: A. S. Barnes and Company, 1975. Illustrated. 240pp.

Offen, Ron. CAGNEY. Chicago: Henry Regnery, 1972. Illustrated. 217pp.

FRANK CAPRA

*Capra, Frank. FRANK CAPRA: THE NAME ABOVE THE TITLE. New York: Macmillan Company, 1971. Illustrated. 513pp.
    One of the great film autobiographies, this superb memoir details Capra's life and career with splendid anecdotes and valuable insights into film history. Born May 18, 1897, in the village of Bisqaquino, Sicily, Capra (the sixth of seven children) immigrated with his parents and three of their other children to America in 1903. He was the only member of the family to attend public school and graduate from college (1918). Following a hitch in the Coast Artillery in World War I, he eventually entered the film industry in late 1921, and within two years was working as gag writer for Hal Roach on the "Our Gang" series. He then moved over to Sennett's studio, where he became a key figure in the rise of Harry Langdon. When the difficult but talented

comedian broke with Sennett in 1926, he took Capra along as his director. Trouble between the two men soon developed and the following year Capra was out of a job and ready to abandon films for good. Harry Cohn, however, convinced Capra to join him in directing poverty row productions and, as the cliche goes, the rest is film history. Within a decade, not only was Columbia Pictures a big studio, but also Capra was acknowledged as one of the great Hollywood directors. His film IT HAPPENED ON NIGHT (1934) earned Capra his first Oscar, as well as the other four top Oscars for the first time in film history. Over the next twenty years, Capra helped set the standards for the motion picture industry and became one of its most honored personalities.

The story of what happened to Capra as he rose from the ghetto to become a Hollywood legend, the personal problems success created for him, and the contributions he made to the evolution of film as a respectable art form are told with candor and wit. Thomas M. Pryor's review of Capra's autobiography sums up the reactions of most film commentators: "This is the finest, most entertaining book yet written about Hollywood, embracing the whole intricate, complex and generally stormy fusion of art and commerce."[413] An index is included. Highly recommended for all collections.

Carney, Raymond. AMERICAN VISION: THE FILMS OF FRANK CAPRA. Cambridge: Cambridge University Press, 1986. Illustrated. 510pp.

An affectionate and informed biography, this is the book to read after Capra's autobiography. It offers fresh insights into Capra's career and the characters he created for the screen. Particularly impressive is Carney's ability to tie the filmmaker's work to elements in the traditional arts and to Capra's peers in the film industry. "To talk about Capra's life and work as in some way representative of a general American expressive predicament," Carey explains, "requires locating the films within a larger tradition of Post-Romantic expression, particularly with respect to specific works of ninteenth- and twentieth-century American literature, drama, art, philosophy, and history." The skill with which the author develops his thesis provides a model for future studies of this type. A filmography, bibliography, and index are included. Recommended for special collections.

*Glatzer, Richard, and John Raeburn, eds. FRANK CAPRA: THE MAN AND HIS FILMS. Ann Arbor: University of Michigan Press, 1975. Illustrated. 190pp.

Focusing their attention on Hollywood's "golden age" from the birth of the talkies to the rise of television, Glatzer and Raeburn point out that "Six times   .   .   . [between 1932 and 1939] his movies were nominated for the Academy Award as the best picture of the year; almost all of his films were extraordinarily successful at the box office; and beginning in 1936 with MR. DEEDS GOES TO TOWN, his signature was always featured in the credits ABOVE the title of each film, a tribute to the cash value of his name." Moreover, they explain, his World War II series WHY WE FIGHT was cited by Winston Churchill "as the most powerful 'statement of our cause' he had ever encounted." The immediate postwar period witnessed what many people believe was Capra's greatest film, IT'S A WONDERFUL LIFE (1946), nominated for an Oscar for Best Film but overshadowed by William Wyler's THE BEST YEARS OF OUR LIVES. To illuminate Capra's genius and personality, the editors divide their first-rate anthology into two major sections: the man and the films. The collection itself offers a liberal selection of reprints, original essays, and an interview with Capra. The material is stimulating and significant. A filmography and bibliography are included, but no index is provided. Recommended for special collections.

---

[413] Thomas M. Pryor, "Frank Capra: NAME ABOVE THE TITLE One of the Best Books on H'wood That Was," VARIETY (June 2, 171):20.

*Estrin, Allen. THE HOLLYWOOD PROFESSIONALS: FRANK CAPRA, GEORGE CUKOR, CLARENCE BROWN. New York: A. S. Barnes and Company, 1978. Illustrated. 192pp.

A useful introduction to the Italian immigrant who became the spokesperson for the average American on screen, this terse collection of film biographies gives a brief overview of Capra's career along with those of Cukor and Brown. The thumbnail filmographies, illustrations, and bibliographies are adequate. An index is included. Worth browsing.

*Griffith, Richard. FRANK CAPRA. London: British Film Institute, 1950. Illustrated. 38pp.

Maland, Charles J. FRANK CAPRA. Boston: Twayne Publishers, 1980. Illustrated. 218pp.

Scherle, Victor, and William Turner Levy, eds. THE FILMS OF FRANK CAPRA. Introduction William O. Douglas. Secaucus: The Citadel Press. Illustrated. 278pp.

Released at the time of Capra's eightieth birthday, this profusely illustrated study offers a useful review of the films and the personalities who made them. Following a series of interesting observations by people who know Capra and worked with him, Scherle and Levy offer a film-by-film history of his work, starting with his first silent film, FULTAH FISHER'S BOARDING HOUSE (1922), and concluding with his final feature film, POCKETFUL OF MIRACLES (1961). For added measure, there is a summary of his twenty-minute documentary, RENDEVOUS IN SPACE (1964). An index is included. Well worth browsing.

*Silke, James R. ed. FRANK CAPRA: ONE MAN--ONE FILM. Washington, D. C.: American Film Institute, 1971. Illustrated. 27pp.

*Willis, Donald C. THE FILMS OF FRANK CAPRA. Methuen: The Scarecrow Press, 1974. Illustrated. 214pp.

When originally published, this pioneering study provided the best introduction to Capra's seventeen important films. Today, its greatest value lies in the author's thoughtful comments on how Capra adapted books and plays to the screen. Endnotes, a filmography, a review of Capra's autobiography, and an index are included. Well worth browsing.

Wolfe, Charles. FRANK CAPRA: A GUIDE TO REFERENCES AND RESOURCES. Boston: G. K. Hall and Company, 1987. 464pp.

The best source for a quick, reliable, and valuable overview of the man and his films. The publication features not only biographical and critical comments on the films, but also excellent annotations of the key writings on and by Capra. An author and a film-title index are included. Recommended for special collections.

MAURICE CHEVALIER

Chevalier, Maurice. BRAVO MAURICE! London: Allen and Unwin, 1973. Illustrated. 240pp.

Chevalier, Maurice. THE MAN IN THE STRAW HAT: MY STORY. Trans. Caroline Clerk. New York: Thomas Crowell, 1949. Illustrated. 245pp.

Ringgold, Gene, and DeWitt Bodeen. CHEVALIER: THE FILMS AND CAREER OF MAURICE CHEVALIER. Secaucus: The Citadel Press, 1973. Illustrated. 245pp.

CLAUDETTE COLBERT

*Everson, William K. CLAUDETTE COLBERT. New York: Pyramid Books, 1976. Illustrated. 159pp.

GARY COOPER

*Arce, Hector. GARY COOPER. New York: Bantam Books, 1980. Illustrated. 260pp.

Carpozi, George, Jr. THE GARY COOPER STORY. New Rochelle: Arlington House, 1970. Illustrated. 263pp.

*Dickens, Homer. THE FILMS OF GARY COOPER. New York: The Citadel Press, 1970. Illustrated. 280pp.

*Jordan, Rene. GARY COOPER. New York: Pyramid Books, 1974. Illustrated. 160pp.

Kaminsky, Stuart. COOP: THE LIFE AND LEGEND OF GARY COOPER. New York: St. Martin's Press, 1980. Illustrated. 295pp.

JOSEPH COTTON

*Cotton, Joseph. VANITY WILL GET YOU SOMEWHERE. San Francisco: Mercury House, 1987. Illustrated. 235pp.

JOAN CRAWFORD

Castle, Charles. JOAN CRAWFORD: THE RAGING STAR. London: New English Library, 1977. Illustrated. 207pp.

*Crawford, Christina. MOMMIE DEAREST. New York: William Morrow, 1978. Illustrated. 286pp.

*Harvey, Stephen. JOAN CRAWFORD. New York: Pyramid Books, 1974. Illustrated. 159pp.

*Johnes, Carl. CRAWFORD: THE LAST YEARS. New York: Dell, 1979. 172pp.

*Kobal, John. ed. JOAN CRAWFORD. Introduction Anna Raeburn. Boston: Little, Brown and Company, 1986. Illustrated. 117pp.

Newquist, Roy. CONVERSATIONS WITH JOAN CRAWFORD. Secaucus: The Citadel Press, 1980. Illustrated. 175pp.

*Thomas, Robert. JOAN CRAWFORD. New York: Bantam Books, 1979. Illustrated. 382pp.

*Quirk, Lawrence J. THE FILMS OF JOAN CRAWFORD. New York: Citadel Press, 1968. Illustrated. 222pp.

MICHAEL CURTIZ

*Canham, Kingsley. THE HOLLYWOOD PROFESSIONALS (Volume 1). New York: A. S. Barnes and Company, 1973. Illustrated. 200pp.

BETTE DAVIS

Davis, Bette. THE LONELY LIFE: AN AUTOBIOGRAPHY. New York: G. P. Putnam's Sons, 1962. Illustrated. 254pp.

*Davis, Bette, with Michael Herskowitz. THIS 'N THAT. New York: G. P. Putnam's Sons, 1987. Illustrated. 207pp.

Higham, Charles. BETTE: THE LIFE OF BETTE DAVIS. New York: Macmillan Publishing, 1981. Illustrated. 316pp.

Hyman, B. D., and Jeremy Hyman. NARROW IS THE WAY. New York: William Morrow and Company, 1987. 285pp.

Noble, Peter. BETTE DAVIS: A BIOGRAPHY. London: Skelton Robinson, 1948. Illustrated. 231pp.

*Stine, Whitney. MOTHER GODDAM: THE STORY OF THE CAREER OF BETTE DAVIS. New York: Hawthorn Books, 1974. Illustrated. 374pp.

*Vermilye, Jerry. BETTE DAVIS. New York: Pyramid Books, 1973. Illustrated. 159pp.

Walker, Alexander. BETTE DAVIS: A CELEBRATION. Boston: Little, Brown and Company, 1986. Illustrated. 192pp.

OLIVIA DE HAVILLAND

*Kass, Judith. OLIVIA DE HAVILLAND. New York: Pyramid Books, 1976. Illustrated. 160pp.

MARLENE DIETRICH

*Dickens, Homer. THE FILMS OF MARLENE DIETRICH. New York: The Citadel Press, 1968. Illustrated. 223pp.

Dietrich, Marlene. MARLENE. Trans. Salvator Attasio. New York: Grove Press, 1989. Illustrated. 273pp.

Frewin, Leslie. DIETRICH: THE STORY A STAR. New York: Stein and Day, 1967. Illustrated. 192pp.

*Higham, Charles. MARLENE. New York: W. W. Norton, 1977. Illustrated. 319pp.

*Kobal, John. MARLENE DIETRICH. New York: E. P. Dutton, 1968. Illustrated. 160pp.

*Silver, Charles. MARLENE DIETRICH. New York: Pyramid Books, 1974. Illustrated. 160pp.

WALT DISNEY

Bailey, Adrian. WALT DISNEY'S WORLD OF FANTASY. Compiled and Designed Julie and Steve Ridgeway. New York: Everest House, 1982. Illustrated. 253pp.
    Published with the backing of the Disney organization, this beautifully illustrated biography is just what you might expect from a highly successful and promotionally minded business. The story of a contractor's son from the American Mid-west who rose to power and prominence is a modern telling of the American Dream. On the positive side, the visuals and layout provide readers with an excellent overview of what the studio and Disney's heirs want you to know and remember about the brilliant showman. An index is included. Well worth browsing.

Bowles, Jerry. FOREVER HOLD YOUR BANNERS HIGH! THE STORY OF THE MICKEY MOUSE CLUB & WHAT HAPPENED TO THE MOUSEKETEERS. Garden City: Doubleday and Company, 1976. Illustrated. 151pp.
    On October 3, 1955, the Mickey Mouse Club had its TV debut and for the next four years it became one of the decade's most popular children's shows. This useful and nostalgic study provides behind-the-scenes anecdotes about the productions, the personalities, and the impact the popular show had on its generation. The author, a Mouseketeer First-Class, works hard at showing why the show is an important part of cultural history. In addition to providing cast and technical credits for the TV series, this book offers enjoyable illustrations. No index is provided. Worth browsing.

Bron, Elizabeth Lee, and Lynn Gartley. WALT DISNEY: A GUIDE TO REFERENCES AND RESOURCES. Boston: G. K. Hall, 1979. 226pp.

A valuable resource on the artist who created a fantasy world out of cartoon characters and established an entertainment empire that is still going strong thirty years after his death in 1966, this reference book provides a good starting point for information on Disney's films, writings, comments about him, and archival resources. As Bron and Gartley explain, "Disney's career as a filmmaker spanned a period of more than forty years and was not confined to the production of feature films. Throughout his life, he pursued very different aspects of the entertainment industry, moving from animation to live-action filming, then combining animation and live-action, adapting what his artists knew about movement of the human body to create auto-animatronics. These life-like robots, used at Disneyland and Disney World, were attempts by Disney to control the environment of an audience, not in a film theatre, but in a fantasy community. Walt Disney was never to confine his efforts to one pursuit. He saw interconnections among drawing, film, television, and advances in technology, using each to extend the abilities of the other." In presenting their respectful and evenhanded account of his work and his achievements, the authors minimize the filmmaker's flaws, choosing instead to let their useful annotated bibliography indicate areas of controversy. Except for a disappointing section critiquing Disney's career, this resource guide maintains the high standards of this significant series. An author and a film index are provided. Recommended for special collections.

*Carvainis, Maria, ed. THE DISNEY POSTER BOOK. New York: Harmony Books, 1977. Illustrated. 47pp.

*Feild, Robert D. THE ART OF WALT DISNEY. New York: Macmillan, 1942. Illustrated. 290pp.

Finch, Christopher. THE ART OF WALT DISNEY: FROM MICKEY MOUSE TO THE MAGIC KINGDOM. New York: Harry N. Abrams, 1973. Illustrated. 458pp.
    A magnificently illustrated review of the Disney studios and the men who created a slew of box-office hits, this highly entertaining pictorial guide suffers from a weak narrative and from a lack of critical candor. Disney himself won over thirty Oscars, but the credit for those movies belongs not to the great filmmaker alone, and this account does not significantly acknowledge the work of Disney's fabulous animators. Nevertheless, the visuals more than justify examining the book. Well worth browsing.

*Maltin, Leonard. THE DISNEY FILMS. New York: Crown Publishers, 1973. Illustrated. 312pp.

Miller, Diane Disney, and Pete Martin. THE STORY OF WALT DISNEY. New York: Henry Holt and Company, 1956. Illustrated. 247pp.
    Originally published as a series of articles for THE SATURDAY EVENING POST in 1956, this affectionate biography by Disney's daughter offers the standard biography of the fabulous showman. Born on December 5, 1901, Walter Elias Disney, the fourth son of Elias and Flora Disney, grew up with his brother and only sister in Marceline, Missouri. The tale of how he turned a small-garage filmmaking operation into a multi-million-dollar entertainment empire is romantically and affectionately told in this pedestrian narrative, with surprisingly weak visuals. No index is provided. Worth browsing.

Mosley, Leonard. DISNEY'S WORLD: A BIOGRAPHY. New York: Stein and Day, 1985. Illustrated. 330pp.

A valuable and highly readable account of Disney's career and personal life, this entertaining and informative book offers an even balance between Schickel's hard-hitting biography, and the standard commentaries on the filmmaker's rise to fame and fortune. Particularly impressive is the care that Mosley takes in debunking false information about Disney, his contributions to film history, and the problems he faced in revolutionizing sound, color, and animated films. This is an excellent companion piece to Schickel's work. A good annotated chronology also of Disney's film history and an index are included. Recommended for special collections.

*Schickel, Richard. THE DISNEY VERSION: THE LIFE, TIMES, ART AND COMMERCE OF WALT DISNEY. New York: Simon and Schuster, 1968. 384pp.

An important and hard-hitting biography, this unauthorized account takes the public to task for uncritically accepting many of Disney's controversial and misleading works.[414] Nine penetrating chapters point out the bold and aggressive steps that led Disney to success, stressing not only his achievements, but also the tremendous debts he owes to other filmmakers and studios. A biographical essay and index are included. Recommended for special collections.

*Thomas, Frank, and Ollie Johnston. DISNEY ANIMATION: THE ILLUSION OF LIFE. New York: Abbeville Press, 1984. Illustrated. 382pp.

A splendid account of the animation techniques of the Disney Studio, this popular edition of the original 1981 book is ideal for examining how Disney's great animated films were conceived and executed. The visuals are superb, the comments insightful, and the overview fascinating. Even if the entire behind-the-scenes politics are minimized, the detailed explanations about animation technology are "must" reading for anyone serious about understanding the history and art of Disney's works. An index is included. Highly recommended for special collections.

*Thomas, Robert. WALT DISNEY: AN AMERICAN ORIGINAL. New York: Simon and Schuster, 1976. Illustrated. 379pp.

Thomas, Robert. WALT DISNEY: MAGICIAN OF THE MOVIES. New York: Grosset and Dunlap, 1966. Illustrated. 176pp.

*Walt Disney Productions. WALT DISNEY'S "SNOW WHITE AND THE SEVEN DWARFS." New York: The Viking Press, 1979. Illustrated. 228pp.

Published for the first time in book form and filled with more than 400 magnificent paintings, drawings, sketches, and storyboards, this handsome book offers the most complete and absorbing details on the making of this inspired 1938 masterpiece. Not only do we get excellent reproductions from the film, but also we get commentaries about the challenges faced by the animators who from 1934 to 1937 struggled to create a new art form. Highly recommended for special collections.

MELVYN DOUGLAS

*Douglas, Melvyn, and Tom Arthur. SEE YOU AT THE MOVIES: THE AUTOBIOGRAPHY OF MELVYN DOUGLAS. Lanham: University Press of America, 1986. Illustrated. 258pp.

---

[414]   For a fuller review, see Frank Manchel, "Books: THE DISNEY VERSION," FILM SOCIETY REVIEW 4:1 (1968):44-5.

W. C. FIELDS

*Anobile, Richard J., ed. DRAT! BEING THE ENCAPSULATED VIEW OF LIFE OF W. C. FIELDS IN HIS OWN WORDS. Introduction Ed McMahon. New York: Signet Books, 1969. Illustrated. 149pp.

*Anobile, Richard J., ed. A FLASK OF FIELDS: VERBAL AND VISUAL GEMS FROM THE FILMS OF W. C. FIELDS. Introduction Judith Crist. New York: Darien House, 1972. Illustrated. 272pp.

Anobile, Richard J. ed. "GODFREY DANIELS!" VERBAL AND VISUAL GEMS FROM THE SHORT FILMS OF W. C. FIELD. Introduction Raymond Rohauer. New York: Darien House, 1975. Illustrated. 224pp.

*Deschner, Donald. THE FILMS OF W. C. FIELDS. Introduction Arthur Knight. New York: The Citadel Press, 1966. Illustrated. 192pp.

Everson, William K. THE ART OF W. C. FIELDS. New York: Bonanza Books, 1967. Illustrated. 232pp.

Gehring, Wes D. W. C. FIELDS: A BIO-BIBLIOGRAPHY. Westport: Greenwood Press, 1984. 233pp.

Fields, Ronald J. W. C. FIELDS BY HIMSELF: HIS INTENDED AUTOBIOGRAPHY. Englewood Cilffs: Prentice-Hall, 1973. Illustrated. 510pp.

Fields, W. C. FIELDS FOR PRESIDENT. York: Dodd, Mead and Company, 1940. Illustrated. New York: Dodd, Mead and Company, 1971. Ed. Michael M.   Taylor. Illustrated. 163pp.

Fowler, Gene. MINUTES OF THE LAST MEETING. New York: The Viking Press, 1954. 277pp.

*Jeeves, Mahatma Kane (W. C. Fields). W. C . FIELDS IN "THE BANK DICK." New York : Simon and Schuster, 1973. Illustrated. 124pp.

Monti, Carlotta, with Cy Rice. W.   C. FIELDS AND ME. Englewood Cliffs: Prentice-Hall, 1971. Illustrated. 227pp.

*Niville, John T. et al. W. C. FIELDS IN "NEVER GIVE A SUCKER AND EVEN BREAK" AND "TILLIE AND GUS." New York: Simon and Schuster, 1973. Illustrated. 124pp.

*Taylor, Robert Lewis. W. C. FIELDS: HIS FOLLIES AND FORTUNES. Garden City: Doubleday and Company, 1949. Illustrated. New York: Signet Books, 1967. Illustrated. 286pp.

*Yanni, Nicholas. W. C. FIELDS. New York: Pyramid, 1974. Illustrated. 157pp.

ROBERT FLOREY

Taves, Brian. ROBERT FLOREY, THE FRENCH EXPRESSIONIST. Foreword Lloyd Nolan. Methuen: The Scarecrow Press, 1987. Illustrated. 418pp.

ERROL FLYNN

Conrad, Earl. ERROL FLYNN: A MEMOIR. New York: Dodd, Mead, and Company, 1978. Illustrated. 222pp.

*Flynn, Errol. MY WICKED, WICKED WAYS. New York: Dell, 1959. 512pp.

*Freedland, Michael. THE TWO LIVES OF ERROL FLYNN. New York: Bantam Books, 1978. Illustrated. 257pp.

*Haymes, Nora Eddington Flynn. ERROL AND ME. New York: Signet Books, 1960. Illustrated. 176pp.

*Higham, Charles. ERROL FLYNN: THE UNTOLD STORY. New York: Doubleday and Company, 1980. Illustrated. 585pp.

*Morris, George. ERROL FLYNN. New York: Pyramid Books, 1975. Illustrated. 160pp.

*Parish, James Robert, ed. ERROL FLYNN. Kew Gardens: Cinefax, 1969. Illustrated.

*Thomas, Tony, et al. THE FILMS OF ERROL FLYNN. New York: The Citadel Press, 1969. Illustrated. 224pp.

HENRY FONDA

*Kerbel, Michael. FONDA. New York: Pyramid Publications, 1975. Illustrated. 160pp.

Springer, John. THE FONDAS: THE FILMS AND CAREERS OF HENRY, JANE, AND PETER FONDA. New York: The Citadel Press, 1970. Illustrated. 279pp.

*Stewart, Jack. HENRY, JANE AND PETER: THE FABULOUS FONDAS. New York: Tower, 1976. 208pp.

Teichman, Howard. FONDA: MY LIFE. New York: New American Library, 1981. Illustrated. 372pp.

JOHN FORD

*Anobile, Richard J. JOHN FORD'S "STAGECOACH" STARRING JOHN WAYNE. New York: Avon Books, 1975. Illustrated. 256pp.

Another imaginative and flawed attempt at examining important films through the use of frame enlargements, this version uses 1,200 blow-ups to simulate the movie that "revolutionized" the making of Hollywood westerns. Anobile asserts in his introduction that "the script, more than the setting, is what makes STAGECOACH such a film classic." For those who accept that premise, this is a valuable publication because the dialogue is placed at the bottom of the appropriate frame enlargement. Those who believe that the greatness of the film lies in its editing and moving visuals will be disappointed not only by the fuzzy quality of a number of visuals, but also by the static quality of the idea. Also included are John Ford's comments on the film, reprinted from the October, 1971, issue of ACTION. Worth browsing.

*Ford, John, and Dudley Nichols. "STAGECOACH": A FILM BY JOHN FORD AND DUDLEY NICHOLS. New York: Simon and Schuster, 1971. Illustrated. 152pp.

Based upon Dudley Nichols's original screenplay, the useful edition also includes Ernest Haycox's April, 1937, COLLIER'S MAGAZINE short story, "Stage to Lordsburg," which served as the source for the historic film. The stills in this CLASSIC FILM SCRIPT publication match the quality of the selections in other books in the series. Worth browsing.

CLARK GABLE

*Carpozi, George, Jr. CLARK GABLE. New York: Pyramid Books, 1961. Illustrated. 160pp.

*Essoe, Gabe. THE FILMS OF CLARK GABLE. New York: Citadel Press, 1970. Illustrated. 255pp.

Gable, Kathleen. CLARK GABLE: A PERSONAL PORTRAIT. Englewood Cliffs: Prentice-Hall, 1961. Illustrated. 153pp.

*Harris, Warren G. GABLE AND LOMBARD. New York: Simon and Schuster, 1974. Illustrated. 189pp.

*Jordan, Rene. CLARK GABLE. New York: Pyramid Books, 1973. Illustrated. 159pp.

*Kobal, John, ed. CLARK GABLE. Introduction James Card. Boston: Little, Brown and Company, 1986. Illustrated. 104pp.

*Morella, Joe, and Edward Z. Epstein. GABLE AND LOMBARD AND POWELL AND HARLOW. New York: Dell, 1975. Illustrated. 272pp.

*Samuels, Charles. THE KING: A BIOGRAPHY OF CLARK GABLE. New York: Popular Library, 1963. Illustrated. 262pp.

*Tornabene, Lyn. LONG LIVE THE KING: A BIOGRAPHY OF CLARK GABLE. New York: G. P. Putnam's Sons, 1976. Illustrated. 396pp.

Wayne, Jane Ellen. GABLE'S WOMEN. Englewood: Prentice-Hall Press, 1987. Illustrated. 304pp.

Williams, Chester. GABLE. New York: Fleet Press Corp., 1968. Illustrated. 154pp.

JUDY GARLAND

Dahl, David, and Barry Kehoe. YOUNG JUDY. New York: Mason/Charter, 1975. Illustrated. 250pp.

Deans, Mickey, and Ann Pinchot. WEEP NO MORE MY LADY. New York: Hawthorne Books, 1972. Illustrated. 247pp.
    Written by the tragic star's fifth and last husband, this sad and sensitive biography traces Garland's career from the days at M-G-M, where she was mercilessly exploited, to the closing days of her life when Judy Garland appeared to many as a pathetic victim of the star system. Worth browsing.

DiOrio, Al, Jr. LITTLE GIRL LOST: THE LIFE AND HARD TIMES OF JUDY GARLAND. New Rochelle: Arlington House, 1973. Illustrated. 298pp.

Edwards, Anne. JUDY GARLAND. New York: Simon and Schuster, 1974. Illustrated. 349pp.

*Finch, Christopher. RAINBOW: THE STORMY LIFE OF JUDY GARLAND. New York: Grosset and Dunlap, 1975. Illustrated. 255pp.

*Juneau, James. JUDY GARLAND. New York: Pyramid, 1974. Illustrated. 157pp.

Melton, David. JUDY: A REMEMBRANCE. Hollywood: Stanyan Books, 1972. Illustrated.

*Morella, Joe, and Edward Epstein. JUDY: THE FILMS AND CAREER OF JUDY GARLAND. New York: Citadel Press, 1969. Illustrated. 217pp.

*Steiger, Brad. JUDY GARLAND. With a Special Introduction by Joe Cohen. New York: Ace Publishing Corporation, 1969. Illustrated. 190pp.
    This is a breezy and lightweight biography that does not do justice to its subject. Its one redeeming feature is its complete filmography with brief excerpts from the film reviews that appeared when the movies were released. Approach with caution.

Torme, Mel. THE OTHER SIDE OF THE RAINBOW: WITH JUDY GARLAND ON THE DAWN PATROL. New York: William Morrow and Company, 1970. Illustrated. 241pp.
    Although not the best book on the subject, this is the most moving because it deals in depth with the warm and wonderful star's television venture, which ended in frustration. Worth browsing.

CARY GRANT

*Deschner, Donald. THE FILMS OF CARY GRANT. Secaucus: Citadel, 1973. Illustrated. 276pp.

Donaldson, Maureen. AN AFFAIR TO REMEMBER. New York: Putnam, 1989. Illustrated.

Godfrey, Lionel. CARY GRANT: THE LIGHT TOUCH. New York: St. Martin's Press, 1981. Illustrated.

Harris, Warren G. CARY GRANT: A TOUCH OF ELEGANCE. New York: Doubleday, 1987. Illustrated. 296pp.

Higham, Charles, and Roy Moseley. CARY GRANT: THE LONELY HEART. New York: Harcourt Brace Jovanovich, 1989. Illustrated. 416pp.

*Vermilye, Jerry. CARY GRANT. New York: Pyramid Books, 1973. Illustrated. 160pp.

JEAN HARLOW

*Brown, Curtis F. JEAN HARLOW. New York: Pyramid Books, 1977. Illustrated. 160pp.

*Conway, Michael, and Mark Ricci, eds. THE FILMS OF JEAN HARLOW. New York: Bonanza Books, 1965. Illustrated. 159pp.
    The best source for Harlow's filmography, including synopses, credits, and stills. Worth browsing.

Shulman, Irving. HARLOW: AN INTIMATE BIOGRAPHY. New York: Bernard Geis Associates, 1964. Illustrated. 409pp.
    Based upon the memoirs of Harlow's press agent and friend, Arthur Landau, this sensational and behind-the-scenes biography only touches the surface of the lovely and tragic movie queen who died mysteriously at twenty-six. Approach with caution.

HOWARD HAWKS

*Belton, John. THE HOLLYWOOD PROFESSIONALS (Volume 3): HOWARD HAWKS, FRANK BORZAGE, EDGAR G. ULMAR. New York: A. S. Barnes and Company, 1974. Illustrated. 182pp.

Born on May 30, 1896, in Goshen, Indiana, to Frank and Helen Hawks, Howard Winchester Hawks had two brothers and three sisters. His mother's poor health eventually forced the family to relocate, and in 1906 they settled in Pasedena, California. Since the Hawkses were wealthy, Howard had the best of everything, including his early education at Phillips Exeter. After graduating from Pasadena High School, he received a degree in engineering from Cornell University, and then served in the U.S. Army Air Force during World War I. At the same time Hawks was pursuing his love of flying, he was pursuing his love of moving pictures. He began working in films in 1916 as a property man at Famous Players-Lasky, but his real ambition was to become a director. Marshall Neilan encouraged Hawks by allowing him to assist in the direction of several scenes in the Mary Pickford film, THE LITTLE PRINCESS in 1917. After the war, Hawks developed his talents as a screenwriter, thanks in part to his friendship with Thalberg, who recommended to Lasky that Hawks take over Paramount Pictures's story department in 1924. Unable to get any directing assignments, Hawks left Paramount two years later to become a director at the Fox Company in 1926, where his first major directing assignment was THE ROAD TO GLORY (1926), based on a story idea he developed. After making eight films for Fox (1926-1929), he decided to become a free-lance director, refusing to tie himself down to one studio. The history of what Hawks achieved between THE DAWN PATROL (1930) and RIO LOBO (1970) is filled with marvelous anecdotes and insights not only into the career of a great director, but also into the development of American films. Hawks died at eighty-one on December 26, 1977.

The outline of Hawks's career is adequately covered in this pioneering extended essay in this critical anthology. Belton's useful analysis of Hawks's films from THE ROAD TO GLORY to RIO LOBO emphasizes the comic nature of the director's films, as well as touching on his fascination with male camaraderie and action-packed themes. A filmography and index are included, but no footnotes or bibliography. Well worth browsing.

*Bogdanovich, Peter. THE CINEMA OF HOWARD HAWKS. New York: Museum of Modern Art, 1962. Illustrated. 38pp.

*Branson, Clark. HOWARD HAWKS: A JUNGIAN STUDY. Foreword Judith Harte. Santa Barbara: Capra Press, 1987. Illustrated. 335pp.

"Filmmaker Howard Hawks," explains Harte, "unlike Jung, the psychologist, did not produce his myriad collection of cinematic renderings with the intended purpose of making conscious psychological discoveries. Hawks was an entertainer, not a psychologist; although he had the ability to express, however unintentionally, profound psychological insights. He produced his artful series of cinematic renderings much as the psyche produces a series of dreams." Branson's imaginative and absorbing study explores how Hawks's work exemplifies Jung's theories about father-son relationships in films. The author divides his research into two major sections: Hawks and Jung, and Hawks's films from FIG LEAVES (1926) to RIO LOBO (1970). After reviewing the director-producer's thirty-nine films, Branson provides an excellent appendix classifying Hawks's recurring motifs and patterns. The author's dry style and psychological interpretations limit the book's appeal to film buffs but make for stimulating speculations for serious students. A filmography, bibliography, glossary of cinematic terms, and an index are included. Well worth browsing.

Mast, Gerald. HOWARD HAWKS: STORYTELLER. New York: Oxford University Press, 1982. Illustrated. 406pp.

A well-written and engrossing analysis of Hawks's life and career, this informative book examines how the filmmaker used a host of film genres to satisfy his values and artistic concerns. Mast stresses the controversies that surround Hawks's career. "On the one hand," the author writes, "Hawks's reputation with the industry was enormous; no other director--not Ford, not Capra, not Hitchcock, not

Lubitsch (the directors whom Hawks liked to be compared)--enjoyed greater freedom from the power of an individual Fox, Paramount, or MGM than Hawks, who worked for every major studio." Moreover, Mast argues, Hawks shaped the conventions of American film genres that we associate with the Hollywood era. "On the other hand," the author explains, "although the industry honored Hawks with favorable contracts on his own terms, it never honored him with its artistic awards." Ten insightful chapters reveal not only the unique emphasis that the filmmaker placed on using stars as major icons in his films, but also the fact that Hawks remained remarkably consistent in shaping his works to his personal codes. Endnotes, a bibliography, a filmography, and an index are included. Recommended for special collections.

*McBride, Joseph. HAWKS ON HAWKS. Berkeley: University of California Press, 1982. Illustrated. 190pp.
    A collection of outstanding observations taken from a series of interviews with Hawks between 1970 and 1977, this valuable resource captures better than any other publication the thoughts and goals of the unique filmmaker. "The most versatile of all great American directors," McBride points out, "He worked with equal ease in screwball comedies, westerns, gangster movies, musicals, private-eye melodramas, and adventure films. He made some of the best movies of such male stars as John Wayne, Humphrey Bogart, Cary Grant, and Gary Cooper, and his portrayals of tough, sexy, sophisticated women such as Lauren Bacall, Carole Lombard, Rosalind Russell, and Angie Dickinson were far ahead of their time. He collaborated with a remarkable array of first-rate writers, including Ernest Hemingway and William Faulkner." Thirty-seven brief chapters offers Hawks's reactions and evaluations of these people and the films they made together. If you want to know how Hawks felt about his six decades in the film industry, this is the book to read. A filmography, bibliography, and index are included. Recommended for special collections.

*McBride, Joseph, ed. FOCUS ON HOWARD HAWKS. Englewood Cliffs: Prentice-Hall, 1972. Illustrated. 178pp.
    At the time of publication, McBride observed, "The reason Howard Hawks has been so underrated for so many years is that he has always been more concerned with the tangible elements of film-making--actors, mood, action, audience enjoyment--than in courting prestige by making self-consciously important 'statements.'" To correct this critical oversight, this valuable anthology contains more than a dozen important essays, including two new articles by Henri Langlois and Peter Bogdanovich, plus a superb analysis by Andrew Sarris. In addition, there is a filmography and bibliography. Recommended for special collections.

Willis, Donald C. THE FILMS OF HOWARD HAWKS. Metuchen: The Scarecrow Press, 1975. Illustrated. 235pp.
    A succinct but useful study of thirty-five of Hawks's forty-two films, this informative book focuses on the contributions of stars like Bogart, Grant, and Wayne to the filmmaker's career. Although Willis refuses to classify Hawks as the greatest director Hollywood ever produced, he ranks him among the best. And, as Willis comments, ". . . if Hawks has no single, unquestionable great movie to his credit, I think he has more near misses than any other American director." Willis divides his study into five sections on the director's work with film genres: comedies, westerns, action dramas, other genres, and war dramas. Each brief essay comes with stills and endnotes. An interview with Hawks, a filmography, and an index are included. Well worth browsing.

*Wood, Robin. HOWARD HAWKS. New York: Doubleday and Company, 1968. Illustrated. 200pp.

This well-written and intelligent study of Hawks is primarily a thematic analysis of the great director's work. This persuasive and controversial study offers good discussions of such films as ONLY ANGELS HAVE WINGS (1939), TO HAVE AND HAVE NOT (1944), RIO BRAVO (1959), SCARFACE (1932), THE THING FROM ANOTHER WORLD (1951), RED RIVER (1948), and EL DORADO (1967). Wood also provides a fine filmography and some excellent illustrations.   Recommended for special collections.

SUSAN HAYWARD

*Linet, Beverly. SUSAN HAYWARD: PORTRAIT OF A SURVIVOR. New York: Atheneum, 1980. Illustrated. 338pp.

*McClelland, Doug. SUSAN HAYWARD: THE DIVINE BITCH. New York: Pinnacle Books, 1973. Illustrated. 221pp.

*Moreno, Eduardo. THE FILMS OF SUSAN HAYWARD. Secaucus: The Citadel Press, 1979. Illustrated. 286pp.

EDITH HEAD

Head, Edith, and Paddy Calistro. EDITH HEAD'S HOLLYWOOD. Foreword Bette Davis. New York: E. P. Dutton, 1983. Illustrated. 240pp.

KATHARINE HEPBURN

*Carey, Gary. KATHARINE HEPBURN. New York: Pocket Books, 1975.   Illustrated. 238pp.

*Dickens, Homer. THE FILMS OF KATHARINE HEPBURN. New York: The Citadel Press, 1970. Illustrated. 244pp.
    In one of the best introductions in this series, Dickens provides the star's many fans with a useful biography plus a lavish amount of stills, plot synopses, and credits. Well worth browsing.

*Higham, Charles. KATE: THE LIFE OF KATHARINE HEPBURN. New York: W. W. Norton, 1975. Illustrated. 244pp.

*Kanin, Garson. TRACY AND HEPBURN: AN INTIMATE MEMOIR. New York: The Viking Press, 1971. 307pp.
    For more than twenty-five years, two of Hollywood's greatest superstars maintained an open but unpublished secret life of their own, while they made nine good movies for M-G-M, 20th Century-Fox, and Stanley Kramer. Then following Tracy's death on June 20, 1967, reports filtered into the press about his private life with Ms. Hepburn. So it became only a matter of time before one of their personal friends, in this case Kanin, decided to publish what were the behind-the-scenes events. What emerges in this book are two personalities neither personally attractive nor likable. Hopefully, more will be done with the couple than the weak attempt so far. Worth browsing.

Newquist, Roy. A SPECIAL KIND OF MAGIC. Chicago: Rand McNally and Company, 1967. Illustrated. 156pp.

For those who want to know more about GUESS WHO'S COMING TO DINNER, you will find some valuable and delightful comments about Tracy, Hepburn, Poitier, and Kramer in this unusually candid book. Worth browsing.

*Marill, Alvin H. KATHARINE HEPBURN. New York: Pyramid Books, 1973. Illustrated. 160pp.

WILLIAM HOLDEN

*Holtzman, Will. WILLIAM HOLDEN. New York: Pyramid Publications, 1976. Illustrated. 160pp.

*Quirk, Lawrence J. THE FILMS OF WILLIAM HOLDEN. Secaucus: The Citadel Press, 1973. Illustrated. 255pp.

LESLIE HOWARD

Howard, Leslie Ruth. A QUITE REMARKABLE FATHER. New York: Harcourt, Brace and Company, 1959. Illustrated. 307pp.

AL JOLSON

Freedland, Michael. JOLSON. New York: Stein and Day, 1972. Illustrated. 256pp.

Goldman, Herbert G. JOLSON: THE LEGEND COMES TO LIFE. New York: Oxford University Press, 1988. Illustrated. 411pp.

*Oberfirst, Robert. AL JOLSON: YOU AIN'T HEARD NOTHIN' YET. New York: A. S. Barnes and Company, 1980. Illustrated. 341pp.

Sieben, Pearl. THE IMMORTAL JOLSON: HIS LIFE AND TIMES. New York: Fell, 1962. Illustrated. 231pp.

BORIS KARLOFF

*Barbour, Alan, et al. KARLOFF. Kew Gardens: Cinefax, 1969. Illustrated. 64pp.

Bojarski, Richard, and Kenneth Deals. THE FILMS OF BORIS KARLOFF. Secaucus: The Citadel Press, 1974. Illustrated. 287pp.

*Gifford, Denis. KARLOFF, THE MAN, THE MONSTER, THE MOVIES. New York: Curtis Books, 1973. Illustrated. 352pp.

Jensen, Paul M. BORIS KARLOFF AND HIS FILMS. New York: A. S. Barnes and Company, 1974. Illustrated. 194pp.

Lindsay, Cynthia. DEAR BORIS. New York: Alfred A. Knopf, 1975. Illustrated. 273pp.

Underwood, Peter. KARLOFF. New York: Drake Publishing, 1972. Illustrated. 238pp.

HENRY KING

Coppedge, Walter. HENRY KING'S AMERICA. Methuen: The Scarecrow Press, 1986. Illustrated. 164pp.

Born on January 24, 1886,[415] in Montgomery County, Virginia, Henry King was the middle son of Isaac Green and Martha Ellen King. After his father's death in 1898, Henry took a number of jobs to help the family, while he also went to schools, ultimately graduating from Roanoke College. It was during this period that he developed a love for technology, particularly the dynamics of the combustion engine in railroading. Rather than complete his formal education, King first tried his hand in the railroad offices of the Northern and Western Railroad and then explored a life in the theater. After five years on the road (1906-1911), King decided to get a job in moving pictures. He worked in a number of westerns for the Lubin Company in the early teens before moving to the Balboa Amusement Company in 1914, where he not only acted in films but also began directing films in late 1915. "Because Henry King's career as a director was so long--lasting from 1915 through 1962--and because the type and subject of the films on which he worked was [sic] long," explains Anthony Slide, the general editor of this series, "it might be argued that it would be hard to uncover any basic theme or outlook to his work." Fortunately, Coppedge demonstrates that King's film career offers a particular view of American life and society. Although the author deals quickly with the filmmaker's background and entrance into films, he does provide a detailed analysis of five King films--TOL'ABLE DAVID (1921), STELLA DALLAS (1925), STATE FAIR (1933), JESSE JAMES (1939), and THE GUNFIGHTER (1950). The writing is informative, the analyses perceptive, and the stills adequate. Until a more comprehensive work appears, this is not only the only full-length study of King but also the best place to begin a study of him. Endnotes, a chronology of King's life and career, and a bibliography are included, but no index is provided. Well worth browsing.

*Denton, Clive, et al. THE HOLLYWOOD PROFESSIONALS (Volume 2): HENRY KING, LEWIS MILESTONE, SAM WOOD. New York: A. S. Barnes and Company, 1974. Illustrated. 192pp.

This collection of extended essays has Denton covering King, Kingsley Canham discussing Milestone, and Tony Thomas on Sam Wood. The King material presents a quick overview of the director's life and career, with thumbnail observations about specific films. "Perhaps King's greatest strength as a director," suggests Denton, "is that constant ability to make us really believe that two people are in love." Although the authors rarely cite sources, they do use numerous quotations and offer useful filmographies. No index or bibliography is included. Worth browsing.

---

[415]   Some sources list the date as 1888.

HEDY LAMARR

*Lamarr, Hedy. ECSTASY AND ME: MY LIFE AS A WOMAN. New York: Macfadden-Bartell, 1966. Illustrated. 256pp.

WALTER LANTZ

Adamson, Joe. THE WALTER LANTZ STORY: WITH WOODY WOODPECKER AND FRIENDS. New York: G. P. Putnam's Sons, 1985. Illustrated. 254pp.

PETER LAWFORD

Lawford, Patricia Seaton, with Ted Schwarz. THE PETER LAWFORD STORY: LIFE WITH THE KENNEDYS, MONROE, AND THE RAT PACK. New York: Carroll and Graf Publishers, 1988. Illustrated. 271pp.

MERVYN LEROY

LeRoy, Mervyn, and Alyce Canfield. IT TAKES MORE THAN TALENT. New York: Alfred A. Knopf, 1953. 300pp.
   One of the most enduring and entertaining of Hollywood's famous directors reveals the ins and outs of the movie business with some pleasant anecdotes peppered along the way. Born on October 15, 1900, in San Francisco, Mervyn LeRoy was related to Jesse Lasky, who finally gave his relative an opportunity to work in films at the end of World War I. The first few years in Hollywood proved unproductive, and the ambitious LeRoy returned to his career as a stage actor in the early 1920s. By 1924, he had decided that he might have a brighter future in films as a screenwriter and director than as a performer. Four years later, he made his directorial debut at First National with NO PLACE TO GO. Over the next thirty-seven years, he made a number of memorable movies, including LITTLE CAESAR (1930), I AM A FUGITIVE FROM A CHAIN GANG (1932), TUGBOAT ANNIE, GOLDDIGGERS OF 1933 (both in 1933), RANDOM HARVEST (1942), MADAM CURIE (1943), THIRTY SECONDS OVER TOKYO (1944), and MISTER ROBERTS (1955). His last film was MOMENT TO MOMENT. LeRoy died on September 13, 1987. Although this book covers his life up to the early fifties, it is useful for personal history, rather than for film information. Well worth browsing.

LeRoy, Mervyn, and Dick Kleiner. MERVYN LEROY: TAKE ONE. New York: Hawthorn Books, 1974. Illustrated. 244pp.
   LeRoy gives a more complete but not particularly modest account of his life in films in his second autobiography. The comments on his childhood are more short quips than reflective comments. For example, one paragraph reads, "When I was about five years old, I went to bed one night to the cozy pleasure of my mother's goodnight kiss. When I woke up the next morning she was gone." He never discovered why his parents separated. Occasionally, he provides some tidbits on his friendship with Pearl White, his relationship with his cousins, Jesse and Blanche Lasky, and his early years in films. In describing the coming of sound and his role in making talkies, he writes, "As a veteran of stage and vaudeville, I knew the value of the spoken word. I understood dialogue, because I had been an actor. I welcomed the coming of sound and couldn't wait until I had a chance to direct a talking picture." And then there is his comment about Gretchen Young, a beautiful actress who came to him for a job, and how he decided she needed a name more befitting her appearance and personality: "light and airy, flowerlike and dainty." And so he gave her one: "Thus Loretta Young

was born, that day in my office." If you don't mind LeRoy's writing style and are willing to overlook the sloppiness of his "facts," this autobiography offers an entertaining version of a popular's director's views on Hollywood. A filmography and index are included. Worth browsing.

CAROLE LOMBARD

*Maltin, Leonard. CAROLE LOMBARD. New York: Pyramid Books, 1976. Illustrated. 160pp.

Swindell, Larry. SCREWBALL: THE LIFE OF CAROLE LOMBARD. New York: William Morrow and Company, 1975. Illustrated. 324pp.

MYRNA LOY

*Karyn, Kay. MYRNA LOY. New York: Pyramid Books, 1977. Illustrated. 160pp.

*Kotsilibas-Davis, James, and Myrna Loy. MYRNA LOY: BEING AND BECOMING. New York: Alfred A. Knopf, 1987. Illustrated. 372pp.

*Quirk, Lawrence J. THE FILMS OF MYRNA LOY. Secaucus: The Citadel Press, 1980. Illustrated. 256pp.

ERNST LUBITSCH

*Anobile, Richard J., ed. ERNST LUBITSCH'S "NINOTCHKA" STARRING GRETA GARBO AND MELVYN DOUGLAS. New York: Darien House, 1975. Illustrated. 256pp.
    In the book's introduction, Anobile writes that "NINOTHCKA typifies the style of film audiences craved in the '30s. One must suspend reality to completely enter the film's world. Despite all the maneuverings of the characters and their 'grave' problems, it is readily apparent that neither of them really have a care in the world. They never work, yet they constantly sip champagne and frequent nightclubs. All this might have finally run the film into boredom but for one very intangible element: Garbo." Whether one accepts Anobile's judgment on what makes the film so popular or chooses to credit Lubitsch and/or his trio of writers is secondary to the appeal of this visual reconstruction of the film. The more than 1,500 frame blow-up pictures presented sequentially coupled with the dialogue from the original soundtrack offer a nostalgic and entertaining experience. Although no substitute for the film, it is a useful study tool. Well worth browsing.

Paul, William. ERNST LUBITSCH'S AMERICAN COMEDY. New York: Columbia University Press, 1983. Illustrated. 367pp.
    One of the best AUTEUR studies in this decade, Paul's valuable examination skips lightly over the silent films and focuses almost exclusively on the films of the 1930s and 1940s. What emerges is a complex picture of an artist who on the one hand had enormous power and prestige denied to many of his peers, and who on the other hand followed very closely Hollywood trends and patterns. "As the mass audience itself became in effect a condition of creation," Paul explains, "film more than any other art fostered an acute awareness of the contexts that surrounded an individual work, the role of genres and conventions in shaping the final film to fit audience expectations. Hollywood movies are not less art for all that, and even in the heyday of the Hollywood studios it was possible for a number of directors like Lubitsch to

fashion careers of artistic integrity." For a basic introduction to how an apolitical and ahistorical artist like Lubitsch performed so marvelously in a competitive marketplace, this is the book to read. A filmography, bibliography, and index are provided. Recommended for special collections.

BELA LUGOSI

*Bojarski, Richard. THE FILMS OF BELA LUGOSI. Secaucus: The Citadel Press, 1980. Illustrated. 256pp.

Cremer, Robert. LUGOSI: THE MAN BEHIND THE CAPE. Chicago: Henry Regnery, 1976. Illustrated. 307pp.

Lennig, Arthur. THE COUNT: THE LIFE AND FILMS OF BELA "DRACULA" LUGOSI. New York: G. P. Putnam's Sons, 1974. Illustrated. 347pp.

THE LUNTS

*Brown, Jared. THE FABULOUS LUNTS: A BIOGRAPHY OF ALFRED LUNT AND LYNN FONTANNE. Foreword Helen Hayes. New York: Atheneum, 1986. Illustrated. 523pp.

IDA LUPINO

Stewart, Lucy Ann Ligett. IDA LUPINO AS FILM DIRECTOR, 1949-1953: AN AUTEUR APPROACH. New York: Arno Press, 1980. 199pp.

*Vermilye, Jerry. IDA LUPINO. New York: Pyramid Books, 1977. Illustrated. 160pp.

ROUBEN MAMOULIAN

*Milne, Tom. ROUBEN MAMOULIAN. Bloomington: Indiana University Press, 1969. Illustrated. 176pp.
    In this cautious, tender examination of an ignored filmmaker, Milne opens up a new area of study for those interested in an underrated craftsman. The films made by the former Armenian stage director were some of the best of the early sound period: APPLAUSE (1939), DR. JEKYLL AND MR. HYDE (1932), QUEEN CHRISTINA (1933), and BECKY SHARP (1935). After those pictures, his reputation declined, unjustly. By reviewing Mamoulian's collaboration with Tyrone Power--the remakes of THE MARK OF ZORRO (1940) and BLOOD AND SAND (1941)--students should discover a valuable source of screen entertainment.[416] Well worth browsing.

FREDRIC MARCH

*Quirk, Lawrence J. THE FILMS OF FREDRIC MARCH. New York: The Citadel Press, 1971. Illustrated. 255pp.

---

[416]   An interesting interview is available by James R. Silke, ed., ROUBEN MAMOULIAN: STYLE IS THE MAN (Washington D. C.: The American Film Institute, 1971).

THE MARX BROTHERS

*Adamson, Joe. GROUCHO, CHICO, HARPO AND SOMETIMES ZEPPO. New York: Simon and Schuster, 1973. Illustrated. 512pp.

*Anobile, Richard, J., ed. HOORAY FOR CAPTAIN SPAULDING! New York: Darien House, 1974. Illustrated. 224pp.

Anobile, Richard J., ed. WHY A DUCK? VISUAL AND VERBAL GEMS FROM THE MARX BROTHERS MOVIES. Introduction Groucho Marx. Preface Richard F. Shepard. New York: Darien House, 1971. Illustrated. 288pp.
     This book is a delightful recreation of the Marx Brothers' films, with over 600 frame blow-ups and captions. Well worth browsing.

Arce, Hector. GROUCHO. New York: G. P. Putnam's Sons 1979. Illustrated. 541pp.

*Barson, Michael, ed. FLYWHEEL, SHYSTER, AND FLYWHEEL: THE MARX BROTHERS' LOST RADIO SHOW. New York: Pantheon Books, 1988. Illustrated. 331pp.

*Crichton, Kyle. THE MARX BROTHERS. Abridged edition. New York: Popular Library Edition, 1952. Illustrated. 310pp.
     Once five sons--Leonard (Chico), Adolph (Harpo), Julius (Groucho), Milton (Gummo), and Herbert (Zeppo)--lived in a house lorded over by their father, whom they nicknamed Frenchy, and wisely administered by their clever mother, Minnie. Unfortunately, this pleasant, easy-going analysis oversimplifies the art and development of Minnie's boys while totally ignoring the importance of such people as S. J. Perelman and Margaret Dumont in the Marx Brothers's films. Well worth browsing.

*Eyles, Allen. THE MARX BROTHERS: THEIR WORLD OF COMEDY. New York: A. S. Barnes and Company, 1966. Illustrated. 175pp.
     This invaluable book devotes most of its pages to a discussion of their films, providing fine synopses, good screen credits, some remarkable dialogue, and excellent filmographies. Begin your study with this book. Recommended for special collections.

Marx, Arthur. LIFE WITH GROUCHO. New York: Simon and Schuster, 1954. 310pp.
     This affectionate and interesting biography is by Groucho's son. It unfortunately reveals very little about the great comic's techniques. Approach with caution.

*Marx, Groucho. GROUCHO AND ME. New York: Bernard Geis Associates, 1959. 256pp.
     This is an entertaining but nontechnical account of Groucho's view of himself and his career. Well worth browsing.

*Marx, Groucho. THE GROUCHO LETTERS: LETTERS FROM AND TO. New York: Simon and Schuster, 1967. 319pp.

Surely one of the most unusual collection of letters ever published by a show biz personality, this book offers a variety of laughs connected with men of letters, friends, family, and strangers. Well worth browsing.

Marx, Groucho. THE GROUCHOPHILE. New York: The Bobbs-Merrill Company, 1976. Illustrated. 384pp.

Marx, Groucho, and Richard Anobile. THE MARX BROTHERS SCRAPBOOK. New York: Darien House, 1973. Illustrated. 256pp.

*Marx, Harpo, with Rowland Barber. HARPO SPEAKS! New York: Bernard Geis Associates, 1961. Illustrated. 384pp.
    In the most wonderful of books on the Marx Brothers, the ingenious Harpo tells of his personal and professional lives in critical and entertaining words. Highly recommended for special collections.

*Marx, Maxine. GROWING UP WITH CHICO. Englewood Cliffs: Prentice-Hall, 1980. Illustrated. 200pp.

*Wolf, William. THE MARX BROTHERS. New York: Pyramid, 1975. Illustrated. 157pp.

Zimmerman, Paul D., and Burt Goldblatt. THE MARX BROTHERS AND THE MOVIES. New York: G. P. Putnam's Sons, 1968. Illustrated. 224pp.
    This book covers the same ground as the Eyles text with the same emphasis and scholarship. It lacks the important bibliography, but surpasses its competitors with more than 200 well-chosen photographs and a much higher price. Worth browsing.

VINCENTE MINNELLI

Casper, Joseph Andrew. VINCENTE MINNELLI AND THE FILM MUSICAL. South Brunswick: A. S. Barnes and Company, 1977. Illustrated. 192pp.
    This scholarly examination of a major film director's career looks briefly at the melodramas and comedies that spanned twenty-five years, but stresses Minnelli's popular musicals like CABIN IN THE SKY (1942), MEET ME IN ST. LOUIS (1944), THE ZIEGFELD FOLLIES (1945), THE PIRATE (1948), AN AMERICAN IN PARIS (1951), THE BAND WAGON (1953), BRIGADOON (1954), KISMET (1955), GIGI (1958), and ON A CLEAR DAY YOU CAN SEE FOREVER (1970). Six chapters united by two specific themes--i.e., the Hollywood musical and Minnelli's career--reveal how the man and the medium met during the film musical's formative years. Casper is particularly effective in discussing the director's preoccupation with fantasy and dramatic conventions. The numerous visuals do a good job of complementing the intelligent narrative. A bibliography and index are provided. Recommended for special collections.

Minnelli, Vincente, and Hector Arce. I REMEMBER IT WELL. New York: Doubleday and Company, 1974. Illustrated. 391pp.

PAUL MUNI

Druxman, Michael B. PAUL MUNI: HIS LIFE AND HIS FILMS. New York: A. S. Barnes and Company, 1974. Illustrated. 227pp.

Lawrence, Jerome. ACTOR: THE LIFE AND TIMES OF PAUL MUNI. New York: G. P. Putnam's Sons, 1974. Illustrated. 380pp.

TYRONE POWER

*Arce, Hector. THE SECRET LIFE OF TYRONE POWER. New York: Bantam Books, 1979. Illustrated. 291pp.

*Belafonte, Dennis, and Alvin H. Marill. THE FILMS OF TYRONE POWER. Secaucus: The Citadel Press, 1979. Illustrated. 224pp.

*Lawrence, Fred. TYRONE POWER: THE LAST IDOL. New York: Doubleday and Company, 1979. Illustrated. 471pp.

GEORGE RAFT

Parish, James Robert, and Steven Whitney. THE GEORGE RAFT FILE: THE UNAUTHORIZED BIOGRAPHY. New York: Drake Publishers, 1973. Illustrated. 288pp.

Yablonsky, Lewis. GEORGE RAFT. New York: McGraw-Hill Book Company, 1974. Illustrated. 289pp.

RONALD REAGAN

Reagan, Ronald, and Richard G. Hubler. WHERE'S THE REST OF ME? THE RONALD REAGAN STORY. New York: Duell, Sloan and Pearce, 1965. Illustrated. 316pp.

*Rogin, Michael Paul. RONALD REAGAN, THE MOVIE AND OTHER EPISODES IN POLITICAL DEMONOLOGY. Berkeley: University of California Press, 1987. Illustrated. 366pp.

*Thomas, Tony. THE FILMS OF RONALD REAGAN. Secaucus: The Citadel Press, 1980. Illustrated. 224pp.

EDWARD G. ROBINSON

*Hirsch, Foster. EDWARD G. ROBINSON. New York: Pyramid Books, 1975. Illustrated. 160pp.

*Parish, James Robert, and Alvin H. Marill. THE CINEMA OF EDWARD G. ROBINSON. New York: A. S. Barnes and Company, 1972. Illustrated. 270pp.

Robinson, Edward G., and Leonard Spigelgass. ALL MY YESTERDAYS: AN AUTOBIOGRAPHY. New York: Hawthorn Books, 1973. Illustrated. 344pp.

GINGER ROGERS

Eels, George. GINGER, LORETTA, AND IRENE WHO? New York: G. P. Putnam's Sons, 1976. Illustrated. 393pp.

*Dickens, Homer. THE FILMS OF GINGER ROGERS. Secaucus: The Citadel Press, 1975. Illustrated. 256pp.

*McGilligan, Patrick. GINGER ROGERS. New York: Pyramid Books, 1975. Illustrated. 159pp.

Richards, Dick. GINGER: TRIBUTE TO A STAR. Brighton: Clifton Books, 1969. Illustrated. 192pp.

MICKEY ROONEY

Rooney, Mickey. I. E. AN AUTOBIOGRAPHY. New York: G. P. Putnam's Sons, 1965. Illustrated. 249pp.
    This is a disappointing book about a very talented man whose career started at fifteen months of age and ran for the next fifty years on a stormy and exciting course. Readers may find some pleasure in the many candid anecdotes. Worth browsing.

NORMA SHEARER

*Jacobs, Jack, and Myron Braum. THE FILMS OF NORMA SHEARER. New York: A. S. Barnes and Company, 1976. Illustrated. 250pp.

Quirk, Lawrence J. NORMA: THE STORY OF NORMA SHEARER. New York: St. Martin's Press, 1988. Illustrated. 278pp.

BARBARA STANWYCK

*Lane, Jeffrey, and Diane Kolyer. BARBARA STANWYCK. Washington, D.C.: American Film Institute, 1986. Illustrated. 84pp.

Smith, Ella. STARRING MISS BARBARA STANWYCK. New York: Crown Publishers, 1973. Illustrated. 340pp.

*Vermilye, Jerry. BARBARA STANWYCK. New York: Pyramid Books, 1975. Illustrated. 159pp.

JAMES STEWART

*Jones, Ken D., et al. THE FILMS OF JAMES STEWART. New York: A. S. Barnes and Company, 1970. Illustrated. 256pp.

*Thomas, Tony. A WONDERFUL LIFE: THE FILMS AND CAREER OF JAMES STEWART. Secaucus: The Citadel Press, 1987. Illustrated. 256pp.

*Thompson, Howard. JAMES STEWART. New York: Pyramid Books, 1974. Illustrated. 160pp.

GEORGE STEVENS

Petri, Bruce. A THEORY OF AMERICAN FILM: THE FILMS AND TECHNIQUES OF GEORGE STEVENS. New York: Garland Publishing, 1987. Illustrated. 420pp.

One of the great American directors, George Steven was born on December 18, 1904, in Oakland, California. He broke into the movies as an assistant cameraman in 1924, was the chief cinematographer for the Hal Roach Studios two years later (where he filmed most of the Laurel and Hardy shorts, the "Our Gang" series, and the films of Harry Langdon), and by 1932 was directing films at Universal Studio. Over the next thirty-seven years, he directed some of the most memorable movies Hollywood ever produced: ALICE ADAMS (1935), SWING TIME (1936), GUNGA DIN (1939), WOMAN OF THE YEAR (1941), A PLACE IN THE SUN (1951), SHANE (1952), GIANT (1956), and THE DIARY OF ANNE FRANK (1959). His last film was THE ONLY GAME IN TOWN (1969). Stevens died on March 8, 1975. It's hard to believe that Petri's book, originally written as his 1974 Ph.D. dissertation for Harvard University, is the only full-length study on the versatile filmmaker. Although the film-by-film analysis, beginning with ALICE ADAMS and ending with THE ONLY GAME IN TOWN, offers valuable insights into the movies themselves, it lacks the scope and insights presented in the documentary on the father, GEORGE STEVENS: A FILMMAKER'S JOURNEY, by his son, George Stevens, Jr. Until a better work appears in print, Petri's study remains the best source of information on Stevens. The author offers a complete filmography, a wonderful appendix cataloguing the personnel in Stevens's films, and endnotes. No index is included. Well worth browsing.

SHIRLEY TEMPLE

*Basinger, Jeanine. SHIRLEY TEMPLE. New York: Pyramid Books, 1975. Illustrated. 158pp.

Black, Shirley Temple. CHILD STAR: AN AUTOBIOGRAPHY. New York: McGraw-Hill Company, 1988. Illustrated. 548pp.

Edwards, Anne. SHIRLEY TEMPLE: AMERICAN PRINCESS. New York: William Morrow and Company, 1988. Illustrated. 444pp.

*Windler, Robert. THE FILMS OF SHIRLEY TEMPLE. Secaucus: The Citadel Press, 1978. Illustrated. 256pp.

SPENCER TRACY

Davidson, Bill. SPENCER TRACY: TRAGIC IDOL. New York: E. P. Dutton, 1987. Illustrated. 232pp.

*Deschner, Donald. THE FILMS OF SPENCER TRACY. New York: The Citadel Press, 1968. Illustrated. 255pp.

*Swindell, Larry. SPENCER TRACY: A BIOGRAPHY. New York: The World Publishing Company, 1969. Illustrated. 319pp.

*Tozzi, Romano. SPENCER TRACY. New York: Pyramid Books, 1973. Illustrated. 159pp.

WILLARD VAN DYKE

Cannom, Robert. VAN DYKE AND THE MYTHICAL CITY OF HOLLYWOOD. Culver City: Murray and Gee, 1948. Illustrated. 424pp.

JOSEF VON STERNBERG

*Von Sternberg, Josef. MOROCCO AND SHANGHAI EXPRESS: TWO FILMS BY JOSEF VON STERNBERG. New York: Simon and Schuster, 1973. Illustrated. 136pp.
    Based upon dialogue continuities provided by Universal City Studios, this valuable record of von Sternberg's films includes comments by Andrew Sarris reprinted from his book THE FILMS OF JOSEF VON STERNBERG. The visuals are lovely, but uncaptioned. Well worth browsing.

JOHN WAYNE

*Barbour, Alan G. JOHN WAYNE. New York: Pyramid Books, 1974. Illustrated. 160pp.

Bishop, George. JOHN WAYNE: THE ACTOR, THE MAN. Thornwood: Caroline House, 1979. Illustrated. 254pp.

*Boswell, John, and Jay David. DUKE: THE JOHN WAYNE ALBUM--THE LEGEND OF OUR TIME. New York: Ballantine Books, 1979. Illustrated. 160pp.

*Eyles, Allen. JOHN WAYNE AND THE MOVIES. New York: A. S. Barnes and Company, 1976. Illustrated. 320pp.

Levy, Emanuel. JOHN WAYNE: PROPHET OF THE AMERICAN WAY OF LIFE. Methuen: The Scarecrow Press, 1988. Illustrated. 379pp.

*Ricci, Mark, et. al. THE FILMS OF JOHN WAYNE. New York: The Citadel Press, 1970. Illustrated. 288pp.

Tomkies, Mike. DUKE: THE STORY OF JOHN WAYNE. Chicago: H. Regnery, 1971. Illustrated. 149pp.

ORSON WELLES

*Bazin, Andre. ORSON WELLES: A CRITICAL VIEW. New York: Harper & Row, 1978. Foreword Francois truffaut. Profile Jean Cocteau. Trans. Jonathan Rosenbaum. Illustrated. 138pp.

At the time Bazin first saw CITIZEN KANE (1941) during its Paris preview in 1946, the twenty-eight-year old critic had been reviewing films for only two years. Welles's film so inspired Bazin that the brilliant critic devoted his first full-length study (1950) to the American filmmaker. "For all film-lovers who had reached the age of cinematic reason by 1946," Bazin writes in his preface, "the name of Orson Welles is identified with the enthusiasm of rediscovering the American cinema; still more, he epitomizes the conviction, shared by every young critic of the time, of being present at a rebirth and a revolution in the art of Hollywood." Eight years later, Bazin amplified and expaned his perceptive study. The book was republished in French in 1972. This edition, containing Cocteau's original profile, plus Truffaut's intriguing foreword, is the first time the work appeared in English.

Bazin's overview of Welles contains basic information on the filmmaker, who was born on May 6, 1915, in Kenosha, Wisconsin, to Richard Head and Beatrice Ives Welles. Acknowledgng the debt that Welles owed his father (a love of travel) and his mother (a love of music and the spoken word), the critic describes the child prodigy's incredible achievements as well as the key role that Dr. Maurice Bernstein played in Welles's formative years. The opening chapter comments on how Welles chose to travel in Ireland rather than attend Harvard University, how he bluffed his way into Dublin's highly acclaimed Gate Theatre and began his professional acting career (the sixteen-year-old Welles had no professional acting background), how he eventually became a Broadway performer through the good graces of Thornton Wilder and Katharine Cornell, how Welles's production of a black MACBETH for the Federal Theatre's Negro Theatre of Harlem earned him not only fame, but also the friendship of John Houseman (the head of the Negro Theatre), how these two men jointly started the influential Mercury Theatre in 1938 and created a sensation with their modern-dress production of JULIUS CAESAR, how their productions required the Mercury Theatre players to do radio shows (the Mercury Theatre of the Air at CBS) that included the memorable October 30, 1938, radio presentation of H. G. Wells's THE WAR OF THE WORLDS, how the Mercury Theatre collapsed in 1939, and how Welles took his performers from the Mercury Theatre to work for RKO and its new studio head, George J. Schaefer. Chapter 2, "Hollywood 1939-1941: The Great Diptych," describes Welles's incredible film contract (the twenty-four-year old Welles was given complete artistic control over a three-year period to make one film a year and receive not only a basic salary of $150,000, but also twenty-five percent of each film's gross income), the reception Welles received in Hollywood from the time he arrive in June 1939, through his problems with the making of CITIZEN KANE and THE MAGNIFICENT AMBERSONS (1942). Chapter 3, "The Great Diptych: Geology and Relief," reflects on the critical significance of Welles's career and his cinematic techniques. Chapter 4, "Hollywood 1941-1944: A Costly Genius," offers a flawed discussion on Welles's third film, JOURNEY INTO FEAR (1943), edited and released by the new reconstituted forces at RKO (Schaefer, Welles, and his Mercury Theatre friends had been run out of RKO in 1942); comments on Welles's documentary fiascos in South America (a series of wartime propaganda films initiated by Nelson Rockerfeller to improve America's relations south of the border--the films never reached the screen), reviews his war efforts for President Roosevelt (e.g., speeches and radio broadcasts), and provides observations on Welles's acting in films like JANE

EYRE (1943) and TOMORROW IS FOREVER (1944). Bazin also reacts to Welles's
Hollywood directorial failure, THE STRANGER (1946), the filmmaker's marriage to
Virginia Nicholson (1934-1940) and her marriage to screenwriter Charles Lederer,
William Randolph Hearst's nephew, in 1940, Welles's marriage to Rita Hayworth
(1943-1947), and the making of THE LADY FROM SHANGHAI (1948). The one glaring
error is that Bazin perpetuates the erroneous image of Welles as a spendthrift who
wasted time and money. More recent accounts demonstrate conclusively that in
comparison with other famous directors of the day, Welles did no worse than most in
handling budgets and in many cases did far better with the resources given him.
The problem may be that none of his films did well at the box office and his flamboyant
personality made him an anathema to everyone but his cast and crew. Chapter 5,
"Around Europe: Obstinacy and Uncertainty," discusses Welles's idiosyncratic
attempts at making a Broadway comeback and his controversial film work on MACBETH
(1948),   THE   THIRD   MAN   (1949),   OTHELLO   (1952),   and   MR.
ARKADIN/CONFIDENTIAL REPORT (1955). The last chapter, "Return to Hollywood:
'Using Up My Energy,'" provides a brief summary of Welles's work back in the film
capital and mostly laments what had become of "its prodigal son." Mention is made
of Paola Mori, Welles's third and last wife (1955-1985), Welles's unreleased film version
of DON QUIXOTE and the filmmaker's love of Shakespeare. Bazin does, however,
spend time on the special qualities of Welles's TOUCH OF EVIL (1958). In concluding
his "provisional biography," the great critic wrote, "Nearly ten years ago, I
described Orson Welles as 'a Renaissance man in twentieth-century America.' I confess
that I didn't know at the time how right I was, and that the comparison is even more
appropriate today."
    Bazin's important study is more than an appreciative overview and a nostalgic
reminder of how Welles impressed one of film's most influential critics. It is a valuable
introduction to the controversial career of an extraordinary film personality. An index
is included. Recommended for special collections.

*Bessy, Maurice. ORSON WELLES. Trans. Ciba Vaughan. New York: Crown
Publishers, 1971. Illustrated. 192pp.
    In this invaluable and well-researched book, Bessy offers a good evaluation of
the director and his works, plus useful quotations from Welles himself. Originally
published in 1963 in Paris, this text opens with Bessy's observation that Welles's
childhood, life, and work are all intertwined. The critical-biographical commentary
that follows explores the major controversies surrounding Welles's quixotic career and
provides valuable opinions about the filmmaker's acting and directorial skills. For
example, in evaluating the central characters Welles created and played, Bessy
concludes that "The weakness at the core of Macbeth, Charles Foster Kane, Mr.
Arkadin, as well as Othello and Inspector Quinlan in TOUCH OF EVIL is the weakness
of excess, the weakness of the barbarian and of the parvenu who knows only how
to abuse the powers and facilities that a civilization, whose rules they do not
understand, has placed for a moment in their hands." In addition to Bessy's thoughts,
the publication contains several interviews with Welles, the unpublished screenplay
of SALOME, a section of critical commentaries on CITIZEN KANE (1941), and film
evaluations by a host of French (e.g., Cocteau, Astruc, Bazin, and Chalais) and
American (e.g., Kael, Kauffmann, and MacDonald) critics. A bibliography,
filmography, and index are included. Recommended for special collections.

Brady, Frank. CITIZEN WELLES: A BIOGRAPHY OF ORSON WELLES. New York:
Charles Scribners Sons, 1989. Illustrated. 655pp.

Carringer, Robert L. THE MAKING OF "CITIZEN KANE." Berkeley: University of
California Press, 1985. Illustrated. 180pp.

Considered by many film critics one of the greatest works in film history, CITIZEN KANE is not only one of the most discussed and analyzed motion pictures in the pages of cinema literature, but also one of the most controversial. The debate centers on who created the film, what are its sources, what does the film mean, how should it be judged, and what occurred throughout the film continuum. Carringer's valuable study "attempts to show that the collaborative process provides the best framework for understanding the remarkable achievement this film represents." Six detailed chapters chronologically tracing the film continuum identify the key contributors, their relationship to Welles, and describes the role they played in the film process. Although not the definitive word on the subject, the analyses offers an important document in the ongoing debate. It should be read alongside Kael's controversial book. Endnotes, a bibliography, and an index are included. Recommended for special collections.

*Cowie, Peter. THE CINEMA OF ORSON WELLES. New York: A. S. Barnes and Company, 1965. Illustrated. 207pp.

A brief overview of Welles's life precedes this useful publication dealing with films directed by the controversial filmmaker up to the mid-1960s. Cowie is good at making perceptive comments and enhancing our understanding of the director's film universe. For example, in the introductory chapter, the author observes, "The heroes of Welles's world are human in several respects . . . but one of the principles that seems to underlie all the films is that material ambition will always override human relationships." The eight succeeding chapters illustrate that perception in films like CITIZEN KANE (1941), THE MAGNIFICENT AMBERSONS (1942), THE STRANGER (1946), THE LADY FROM SHANGHAI (1948), MACBETH (1948), OTHELLO (1952), MR. ARKADIN/CONFIDENTIAL REPORT (1955), TOUCH OF EVIL (1958), and THE TRIAL/LE PROCES (1962). In the book's final chapter, Cowie concludes that "Welles's work--his themes, his style--has an organic unity, despite its terrible birth pangs, with the long periods of creative inactivity, the patently harmful interventions by his sponsors and the subsequent mishandling of the montage." A handful of appendexes, a bibliography, and a filmography are included, but no index is provided. Worth browsing.

Cowie, Peter. A RIBBON OF DREAMS. New York: A. S. Barnes and Company, 1973. Illustrated. 262pp.

"On viewing Welles's work yet again for the purpose of revising and expanding the little paperback that I wrote seven years ago," explains Cowie, "I am more than ever convinced of his place among the immortals. Here is an artist whose humanism and ideas have triumphed over the flashy, meretricious image that critics from Kerr to Kael have imposed on him. It is the mature passion of Welles's cinema that counts; a cinema in which romance and dreams still hold sway at a time when bitter realism is the arbiter of taste." In addition to amplifying his views on the films covered in the 1965 edition, Cowie includes chapters on CHIMES AT MIDNIGHT/FALSTAFF/CAMPANADAS A MEDIANOCHE (1966) and THE IMMORTAL STORY (1968), expands the number of bibliographical entries, and provides a much-needed index. The major drawback between this edition and the earlier one is the decline in the quality of the visual material. Well worth browsing.

*Gottesman, Ronald, ed. FOCUS ON "CITIZEN KANE." Englewood Cliffs: Prentice-Hall, 1971. Illustrated. 178pp.

"Though CITIZEN KANE was widely acclaimed from the beginning and has never suffered from neglect or obscurity," Gottesman explains, "much of the early praise was offered for the wrong reasons and the film has suffered more than most at the hands of parochial, ill-informed, and shallow reviewers and commentators." To demonstrate how the film's many mysteries might best be approached, Gottesman divides his material into five major sections, beginning with three essays on the history of the film (Gottesman), an interview with Welles (Juan Cobos et al.), and an evaluation of Welles himself (William Johnson). The second section provides five reviews of the film, written by commentators like John O'Hara, Bosley Crowther, and Otis Ferguson. The third section offers reactions by people who created CITIZEN KANE--e.g., Welles, Bernard Herrmann, Greg Toland--and critics who have studied it--e.g., Roy A. Fowler, Andrew Sarris, Peter Cowie, and Arthur Knight. The fourth section provides useful commentaries by Jorge Luis Borges, Andre Bazin, Francois Truffaut, Michael Stephanick, and Charles Higham. As a bonus, Gottesman includes a letter of clearance from the Breen Office, a plot synopsis, a content outline, a script excerpt, a filmography, a bibliography, and an index. This book has become a standard text on the film. Highly recommended for special collections.

*Gottesman, Ronald, ed. FOCUS ON ORSON WELLES. Englewood Cliffs: Prentice-Hall, 1975. Illustrated. 218pp.

A careful and valuable collection of essays on the filmmaker, this anthology contains articles by Kenneth Tynan, Peter Bogdonavich, Charlton Heston, Richard T. Jameson, Phyllis Goldfarb, Joseph McBride, Peter Cowie, John Russell Taylor, and Charles Champlin. A filmography, bibliography, and an index. Highly recommended for special collections.

*Higham, Charles. THE FILMS OF ORSON WELLES. Berkeley: University of California Press, 1970. Illustrated. 210pp.

A well-intentioned book, but with poorly researched materials and a light-weight perspective,[417] this survey of the filmmaker's career spends most of its time summarizing film plots and making controversial assertions about the films and their meanings. One of the book's weakest aspects is the failure to caption the lovely and profuse selection of stills.[418] Several appendexes, a selected filmography, a bibliography, and an index are included. Worth browsing.

Higham, Charles. ORSON WELLES: THE RISE AND FALL OF AN AMERICAN GENIUS. New York: St. Martin's Press, 1985. Illustrated. 373pp.

A vast improvement over the author's earlier work, this unauthorized biography offers a maverick interpretation of Welles's achievements. Indicative of the book's tone is Higham's opening comment that "Even at a time when we in America are seeing in the Reagan era a resurgence of the up-and-at-'em values of the Eisenhower society, which he [Welles] hates, even though though the quests for money and power and beauty are again the obsessive concerns of millions, Welles still has a special place in American hearts. In a sense, he represents the rebel as Establishment figure, enshrined in the pantheon, puffing away at giant cigars, relishing the wine of life. It is no accident that his favorite part is that of Falstaff." Higham presents the life of Welles as a saga, one that is filled with marvelous anecdotes of a child prodigy spoiled by unique parents and reared in his teenage years by the kindly family physician, who bluffed his way into the show business world and then broke all the rules, and who finally wandered through the ends of the earth in search of money and freedom to create his idiosyncratic productions. The curious aspect of this entertaining and provocative biography is that it is based on hordes of documents

---

[417] In connection with the book, see Richard Wilson, "It's Not Quite All True," SIGHT AND SOUND 39:4 (Autumn 1970):188-93.

[418] In fairness to Higham, the reader might consult his response to the book's many bad reviews: Charles Higham, " Movie Mailbag: And Now--The War of the Welles," NEW YORK TIMES D (September 13, 1970):17, 31.

(many housed in the archives of Indiana University) and dozens of interviews, yet the author provides few footnotes and little documentation. Several appendexes offer a discography, a filmography, and a bibliography. An index is provided. Well worth browsing.

*Kael, Pauline. THE CITIZEN KANE BOOK: RAISING KANE, THE SHOOTING SCRIPT, BY HERMAN J. MANKIEWICZ AND ORSON WELLES. Boston: Little, Brown and Company, 1971.

In one of the most widely discussed publications of the past decade, Kael in her original two-part NEW YORKER profile challenged Welles's contributions to the making of CITIZEN KANE. Now we have the material reprinted along with the actual script, more than eighty stills from the film, plus some helpful commentary by Gary Carey on RKO's cutting continuity of the film. Don't miss reading this one, but at the same time take a look at the reactions of people connected with the film itself.[419] A Mankiewicz filmography and index are included. Recommended for special collections.

*Leaming, Barbara. ORSON WELLES: A BIOGRAPHY. New York: The Viking Press, 1985. Illustrated. 562pp.

The authorized biography on Welles, this remarkable study is a pleasure to read and a gold mine of information. The author not only has a witty and thought-provoking talent for dealing with complex and challenging ideas, but also a healthy respect for scholarship and research. Written over a four-year period during which Leaming assimilated thousands of documents and worked closely with Welles on his reactions to his turbulent life and career, the biography offers fresh insights into the artist's experience with the Federal Theatre, the Mercury Theatre, Hollywood, President Roosevelt, and countless film and political personalities. Wherever one turns in the book, the reader encounters valuable information on Welles's personal life, stormy battles with producers and financiers, and the making of Welles's controversial productions. Adding to the book's appeal is a series of "interchapters" that provide Welles's comments on the details Leaming is presenting. As Welles himself states in the opening pages of the book, ". . . I am friends with the biographer. [The book thus] . . . becomes a dialogue of a certain kind, a drama between two people." This is the work to read if one wants to begin examining the man's life and career with. Endnotes and an index are included. Highly recommended for special collections.

*McBride, Joesph. ORSON WELLES. New York: The Viking Press, 1972. Illustrated. 192pp.

A stimulating overview of Welles's career, this rambling and subjective study was written with the aid of Peter Bogdonavich. The material covers the filmmaker's first work (a four-minute "home movie" entitled THE HEARTS OF THE AGE in 1934), shot at the Todd School in Woodstock, Illinois, and the brief prologues that Welles filmed for two stage productions at the end of the 1930s), continues through the Hollywood years and the vagabond exploits in Europe, and concludes with a discussion of THE IMMORTAL STORY (1968). What hurts the book's appeal to serious students are the absence of any documentation, the poorly produced visuals, the absence of an index, and the chatty nature of the narrative. On the positive side, McBride offers some intriguing responses to Kael's assertions about the authorship of CITIZEN KANE

---

[419] For another perspective, see George Coulouris and Bernard Herrmann with Ted Gilling, "The Citizen Kane Book," SIGHT AND SOUND 41:2 (Spring 1972):71-73; and Mordecai Richler, "Book Review: THE CITIZEN KANE BOOK," NEW YORK TIMES BOOK REVIEW (October 31, 1971):3, 20.

and a smattering of quotations gleaned from interviews with people who worked with Welles. Worth browsing.

*McBride, Joseph. ORSON WELLES. New York: Harcourt, Brace, Jovanovich, 1977. Illustrated. 159pp.

Better organized than McBride's earlier work on Welles and liberally sprinkled with nostalgic visuals of the films, this thumbnail biography is fast-reading and entertaining. McBride not only provides basic information, but also manages to insert numerous instances of Welles's unpredictable and flamboyant personality. For example, the opening chapter gleefully recounts how the filmmaker bamboozled the Motion Picture Academy of Arts and Sciences into thinking he couldn't accept his 1971 honorary Oscar in person because he was on location overseas (he was nearby watching the event on TV), and describes why four years later he was more than willing to appear for his Life Achievement Award from the American Film Institute (Welles thought he could turn the event into a fund-raising affair for his next production). McBride's considerable critical faculties are evident throughout book's nine lively chapters, providing readers with a valuable quick summary of Welles's abilities as an actor and as a filmmaker. A bibliography, a filmography, and an index are included. Well worth browsing.

Naremore, James. THE MAGIC WORLD OF ORSON WELLES. New York: Oxford University Press, 1978. Illustrated. 339pp.

"With all the critical literature and publicity surrounding Orson Welles," Naremore points out, "surprisingly little has been written about the historical context in which he has worked, or about the political and psychological implications of his films. His active involvement in politics during the thirties and forties, for example, is usually mentioned only in passing. He is, of course, a humanist and an intellectual who for nearly all his life has been involved in the public arts; to discuss his work at the social level is therefore to understand one of its basic functions, and to learn something about the contradictory role of the artist in the movies." Naremore views Welles as a "cultural paradox." That is, Welles's romantic and "almost modernist sensibilities" seem out of place in a commercial environment. "Nearly everything about his public persona contributes to the image of a rebel, a man disillusioned and driven into exile by technology." To demonstrate Welles's social and psychological vision, Naremove provides detailed analyses of the artist's major films from CITIZEN KANE (1941) to F FOR FAKE (1973), stressing the idiosyncratic nature of Welles's art and showing why he is anything but what he claimed for himself, "a poor slob trying to make movies." The writing is stimulating, the observations fresh, and the book a valuable contribution to film scholarship. Endnotes, a filmography, and an index are included. Recommended for special collections.

Noble, Peter. THE FABULOUS ORSON WELLES. London: Hutchinson, 1956. Illustrated. 276pp.

This early journalistic account of Welles provides some useful information on his fights with the Federal Theater, THE WAR OF THE WORLDS fiasco, and the butchering of THE MAGNIFICENT AMBERSONS. A pioneering work that came out when Welles was still in midstream, this affectionate and thoughtful biography still holds up in comparison with later and fuller accounts of Welles's caeer. The one major drawback is Noble's failure to document his assertions about film productions, radio shows, and stageplays. Nevertheless, the author's judgments about what Welles did and why up, to the time he was forty, still remain fairly accurate. Valuable visuals and index are included. Well worth browsing.

Taylor, John Russell. ORSON WELLES: A CELEBRATION. Little, Brown and Company, 1986. Illustrated. 176pp.
    Taylor begins his appreciative and affectionate look at Welles with the oft-told story in MR. ARKADIN/CONFIDENTIAL REPORT (1955): "A scorpion asked a frog to give him a ride on his back. The frog was dubious. 'But what if you sting me?' he said. 'Why should I sting you?' said the scorpion; 'I couldn't do that without destroying myself as well.' Persuaded, the frog set out across the river with the scorpion on back; and halfway across, the scorpion stung him anyhow. As they both sank, the frog protested, 'There is no logic in this.' To which the drowning scorpion replied, 'I know . . . it's my character.'" Taylor uses this anecdote as the key to reviewing Welles's life and asking whether the artist was more like the frog or the scorpion. Although the answer is up for grabs, the more than 200 beautiful black-and-white illustrations, skillfully captioned, offer a wonderful summary of Welles the actor, filmmaker, politician, and creative genius. A bibliography and filmography are included, but no index is provided. Recommended for special collections and as a gift for those who want to remember the best of Orson Welles.

MAE WEST

*Bavar, Michael. MAE WEST. New York: Pyramid Books, 1975. Illustrated. 159pp.

*Tuska, Jon. THE FILMS OF MAE WEST. Secaucus: The Citadel Press, 1973. Illustrated. 191pp.

Weintraub, Joseph, ed. THE WIT AND WISDOM OF MAE WEST. New York: G. P. Putnam's Sons, 1967. Illustrated. 94pp.

*West, Mae. GOODNESS HAD NOTHING TO DO WITH IT. 2nd ed. Enlarged and revised. New York: Macfadden-Bartell, 1970. Illustrated. 223pp.

FAY WRAY

Wray, Fay. ON THE OTHER HAND: A LIFE STORY. New York: St. Martin's Press, 1989. Illustrated. 270pp.

WILLIAM WYLER

Anderson, Michael. WILLIAM WYLER. Boston: Twayne Publishers, 1979. Illustrated. 272pp.
    One of the most honored Hollywood artists, William Wyler won three Oscars for Best Director--MRS. MINIVER (1942), THE BEST YEARS OF OUR LIVES (1946), and BEN HUR (1959)--and was highly acclaimed for his directing films like COUNSELLOR AT LAW (1933), DEAD END (1937), JEZEBEL (1938), WUTHERING HEIGHTS (1939), THE LETTER (1940), THE LITTLE FOXES (1941), THE HEIRESS (1949), ROMAN HOLIDAY (1953), THE DESPERATE HOURS (1955), FRIENDLY PERSUASION (1956), THE CHILDREN'S HOUR (1961), THE COLLECTOR (1965), and FUNNY GIRL (1968). Born on July 1, 1902, in Mulhausen, Alsace-Lorraine, William (Willy) Wyler was the middle son of his Jewish, French-German parents. Although he was at best an average student, the rambunctious youngster developed a love for literature at an early age and during his career as a filmmaker was famous for his screen adaptations of literary works by contemporary English and American authors. A chance meeting with Carl Laemmle, his mother's cousin, in 1920, secured him a job as an office boy at Universal Studios in Hollywood the following year. Over the next three years, he worked himself

up to assistant director. By 1925, Wyler was directing westerns and then moving on to more versatile assignments when the talkies arrived. COUNSELLOR AT LAW was his first important film, and its success certified Wyler's powers as a prominent director. With the apparent collapse of Universal in the mid-1930s, he joined Sam Goldwyn and directed many of the films that made both men famous. During World War II, Wyler served as lieutenant colonel, making a number of important documentaries, including MEMPHIS BELLE (1944). After the war, he resumed his career with the Oscar-winning film, THE BEST YEARS OF OUR LIVES, the movie Wyler is most proud of. His last released film is THE LIBERATION OF L. B. JONES. In 1972, during the production of FORTY CARATS, he decided to retire from filmmaking. Four years later, at the time he received the American Film Institute's Lifetime Achievement Award, Wyler had won almost every honor the film industry presents. Nevertheless, his reputation was clouded by the films he made after 1950. The contemporary generation found his later work superficial and geared more toward profits than toward art. He died at seventy-nine on July 28, 1981.

"What Wyler brought to the movies," explains the author of this revisionist study, "was a European sophistication and temperament, an outlook which undoubtedly included as a primary ingredient a fascination with America and things American. Wyler's best films feature American characters in American settings, but the detachment and concern with form so evident in his style very much suggest the point of a view of an interested, sympathetic outsider." Anderegg's AUTEUR analysis does a fine job of reminding us that we should concentrate on Wyler's work prior to the coming of TV and the breakdown of the studio system, arguing that Wyler's work reveals that he was a master of MIS EN SCENE. Nine stimulating chapters amplify that view. A chronology, endnotes, a bibliography, a filmography, and an index are included. Recommended for special collections.

Madsen, Axel. WILLIAM WYLER: THE AUTHORIZED BIOGRAPHY. New York: Thomas Y. Crowell, 1973. Illustrated. 456pp.

The most complete study of Wyler's life and career, this entertaining and informative work benefits considerably from the filmmaker's willingness to share his thoughts and memories with the author. The six chatty and anecdotal chapters provide useful insights into Wyler's relationships with stars, screenwriters, dramatists, and producers. Although large parts of the book consists of reconstructed dialogue and take pleasure in rekindling movie myths about the making of specific films and the course of Hollywood history, it's valuable to have Wyler's version in print. In fact, one of the book's drawbacks is that we don't get enough information. For example, Wyler played a major role in forming the Committe for the First Amendment and supporting blacklisted performers and writers. Madsen writes that "Wyler was appalled [at the Hollywood witchhunts], especially at the foreign-borns like himself--Jack Warner, Goldwyn, and even Capra--wrapping themselves in the rightous mantle of superpatriotism. The grand fight within the Directors' Guild was over DeMille and his group of right wingers trying to get control." One needs only compare this paltry comment with Elia Kazan's superb recounting of the DeMille fight at the Directors' Guild to see how much more could be said. Wyler seems either to be modest or else he wants to forget his personal heroics, a theory supported by Lillian Hellman's recollection of her attempts to thank Wyler for his many kindnesses to her during this period.[420] Endnotes, a filmography, a bibliography, and an index are included. Well worth browsing.

---

[420]   Cited in Janet Maslin, "Wyler Is Dead at 79; Director Had Won 3 Academy Awards," NEW YORK TIMES A (July 29, 1981):19.

LORETTA YOUNG

Morella, Joe, and Edward Z. Epstein. LORETTA YOUNG: AN EXTRAORDINARY LIFE. New York: Delacorte Press, 1986. Illustrated. 302pp.

FILMS

GENERAL

MUSICALS OF THE THIRTIES ANTHOLOGY. (16mm: n.d., 78 mins., b/w, sound, R-MMA)

Some useful excerpts are available from the following films: RIO RITA (1929), floorshow sequence; 42ND STREET (1933), "Shuffle off to Buffalo" and "Young and Healthy" sequences; GOLD DIGGERS OF 1933, Busby Berkeley[421] sequence; GOLD DIGGERS OF 1935, Busby Berkeley sequence; FLYING DOWN TO RIO (1933), "Carioca" sequence; MUSIC IN THE AIR (1934), excerpt with Gloria Swanson; and IN CALIENTE (1935), "The Lady in Red" sequence.

SOUND FILM ANTHOLOGY (16mm: n.d., 75 mins., b/w, sound, R-MMA)

Some examples of camera technique, which once again became inflexible because of the limited knowledge of how to make the microphone mobile and how to use sound effectively in coordination with motion, can be seen in this film "anthology." It includes excerpts from THE JAZZ SINGER (1927), which was billed as a "talkie" but was essentially silent. One can see in the various scenes where sound is used, how the actors had to stand close to a hidden microphone in order to be heard and filmed at the same time. A second selection is LIGHTS OF NEW YORK (1927), the first all-talking picture, which reveals the early and naive preoccupations with sound. The players say anything as long as they keep talking, and the film demonstrates the artistic inferiority of the first sound motion pictures. In addition, this anthology includes SHAW TALKS FOR MOVIETONE (1927), a whimsical monologue by the eminent dramatist that exemplifies the sound film's reaching out for new material, in this case getting famous people to speak for the movies; THE SEX LIFE OF THE POLYP (1928), a funny monologue by Robert Benchley, which illustrates one of the first attempts at sustained dialogue; and STEAMBOAT WILLIE (1928), not only the first Mickey Mouse cartoon to be shown publicly, but also an inventive approach to some of the mechanical problems involved in recording sound with motion.

DOROTHY ARZNER

CHRISTOPHER STRONG (RKO--16mm: 1933, 77 mins., b/w, sound, R-FNC)

Typical of Arzner's work, this intriguing story of Cynthia Darrington (Katharine Hepburn) focuses on a female aviator determined to achieve her goals by breaking the rules of a male-oriented society. Zoe Aikins's screenplay, based on a novel by Gilbert Frankau, may appear dated to many contemporary viewers, but careful attention should be paid to the early feminist perspective. As Clair Johnston

---

[421] William Murray, "The Return of Busby Berkeley," THE NEW YORK TIMES MAGAZINE (March 2, 1969), pp.26-27, 46, 48, 51, 58-54, 56, 58; Patrick Brion and Rene Gilson, "A Style of Spectacle: Interview With Busby Berkeley," CAHIERS DU CINEMA IN ENGLISH 2, Cdc 174 (January 1966):26-37; Ralph Crandall, "Filmography," ibid., pp.38-41; and Jean-Louis Comolli, "Dancing Images: Busby Berkeley's Kaleidoscope," ibid., pp.22-25.

observes, "Cynthia achieves her project through role reversal: by an over-identification with the male universe, flying planes, breaking records, and living and competing in a male world."[422]

FRED ASTAIRE

SWING TIME (RKO--16mm: 1936, 103 mins., b/w, sound, R-FES, FNC, RKO)
    Produced by Padro Berman, directed by George Stevens, and choreographed by Hermes Pan, this imaginary romance about a gambling hoofer (Fred Astaire) engaged to a woman back home but in love with his dancing partner (Ginger Rogers) was scripted by Howard Lindsay and Allan Scott (based on Erwin Gelsey's short story, "Portrait of John Garnett") and features the music of Jerome Kern and the lyrics of Dorothy Fields. The plot may creak but the many memorable dance routines and the marvelous tunes ("A Fine Romance" and "The Way You Look Tonight") make this one of the best of the Astaire-Rogers's collaborations. A joy to watch and a splendid example of the magic of the musical film in the thirties.

JOHN BARRYMORE

SVENGALI (Warner Bros.--16mm: 1931, 76 mins., b/w, sound, R-BUD, EMG, FES, KIT, MGM, WHO, WIL)
    Archie Mayo directed this third version of George du Maurier's romantic novel about the evil genius Svengali (Barrymore), who hypnotized the beautiful Trilby (Marian Marsh). Don't miss Barrymore in this one.[423]

TOD BROWNING

DRACULA (Universal--16mm: 1931, 75 mins., b/w, sound, R-SWA)
    Based upon the Hamilton Deane-John L. Balderston stageplay adapted from Bram Stoker's novel, this classic depiction of the vampire (Bela Lugosi) who can only be killed by a woman willing to sacrifice herself for someone she loves was strikingly photographed by Karl Freund. The film not only launched Universal's famous cyle of horror films in the 1930s, but made Lugosi one of the legends in Hollywood films. The makeup is by Jack Pierce.

FREAKS (MGM--16mm: 1932, 69 mins., b/w, sound, R-MGM)
    Based on a story by Tod Robbins, the Leon Gordon-Willis Goldbeck screenplay told the touching story of a circus family that included a woman who tried to murder her husband, a dwarf, and the revenge that his friends took on her. It remains one of the most controversial horror films of the decade, mainly because critics are divided over whether the director Browning was exploiting the physical appearances of his authentic circus cast, or sensitizing Depression audiences to the humanity of less fortunate people in society.

---

[422]   Claire Johnston, "Dorothy Arzner: Critical Strategies," THE WORKS OF DOROTHY ARZNER: TOWARDS A FEMINIST CINEMA, ed. Claire Johnston (London: British Film Institute, 1975), p.4.

[423]   Spencer M. Berger, "The Film Career of John Barrymore," FILMS IN REVIEW 3:10 (December 1952):481-99.

FRANK CAPRA

IT HAPPENED ONE NIGHT (Columbia--16mm: 1934, 105 mins., b/w, sound, R-BUD, IMA, KIT, MOD, SWA, WEL, WHO, WIL)
One of the great screwball comedies of the thirties, this excellent film presented Clark Gable as the tough, wisecracking newspaperman who catches up with Claudette Colbert, a runaway spoiled brat. The movie remains today the most honored film by the Academy, receiving all four of the top Oscars (actor, actress, director, and film), plus an Oscar for screenwriting (Robert Riskin).

LOST HORIZON (Columbia--16mm: 1937, 120 mins., b/w, sound, R-BUD, FNC, IMA, IVY, KIT, MOD, ROA, SWA, TWY, WES, WEL, WHO)
Capra was at his best in directing Robert Riskin's screenplay based on James Hilton's imaginative novel about a hijacked plane that carries its passengers to a unique adventure. Ronald Colman plays the kidnapped English diplomat who finds Utopia in the mysterious Shangri-la, hidden away in the Tibetan mountains. Sam Jaffe is outstanding as the aged high lama. Nominated for seven Oscars, including Best Picture, Best Supporting Actor (H. B. Warner), Best Sound Recording (John P. Livadary), Best Assistant Director (C. C. Coleman, Jr.), and Best Score (Dimitri Tiomkin), it won for Best Interior Design (Stephen Goosson) and Best Film Editing (Gene Havlick and Gene Milford).[424]

MR. SMITH GOES TO WASHINGTON (Columbia--16mm: 1939, 95 mins., b/w, sound, R-BUD, FNC, IMA, KIT, MOD, ROA, SWA, TWY, WEL, WHO, WIL)
Produced and directed by Capra, the Sidney Buchman screenplay (based on a Lewis R. Foster story) told the story of an idealist (James Stewart) who is appointed to the Senate and who then seeks to reform not only the corrupt politicans in his home state, but also to challenge the ethics of Congress. One of the most touching scenes in all of Capra's films is the battle by the dedicated Stewart to prove that "the only causes worth fighting for are the lost causes." Nominated for ten Oscars, including Best Film, Best Actor, Best Supporting Actor (Harry Carey), Best Director, Best Screenplay, Best Interior Decoration (Lionel Banks), Best Sound Recording (C. L. Lootens), Best Original Score (Dimitri Tiomkin), and Best Film Editing (Gene Havlick and Al Cark), it won for Best Original Story.[425]

MERIAN C. COOPER AND ERNEST SCHOEDSACK

KING KONG (RKO--16mm: 1933, 111 mins., b/w, sound, R-FES, FNC, JAN; S-BLA)

---

[424] In 1986, the American Film Institute released a restored version of the original film. Thanks to the skill of Robert Gitt, the material that had been edited out of the film is now available to contemporary audiences. For more information, see Stephen Farber, "Cuts in Film LOST HORIZON Restored," NEW YORK TIMES C (September 3, 1986):19; and Andrew Sarris, "Footage Fetish: Recovering LOST HORIZON," VILLAGE VOICE (September 23, 1986):55.

[425] In addition to the Capra books, see Nick Browne, "The Politics of Narration: Capra's MR. SMITH GOES TO WASHINGTON," WIDE ANGLE 3:3 (1979):4-11; and Marie Mahoney, "Program Notes: MR. SMITH GOES TO WASHINGTON," CINEMATEXAS PROGRAM NOTES 24:1 (February 9, 1983):29-36.

Directed and conceived by Merian C. Cooper and Ernest Schoedsack, this all-time fantasy classic recounts the story of a giant ape whose love for a beautiful woman (Fay Wray) destroys him. Willis H. O'Brien's special effects are still regarded today as some of the best ever made.[426]

WILLIAM DIETERLE

THE STORY OF LOUIS PASTEUR (Warners--16mm: 1936, 87 mins., b/w, sound, R-MGM)
In this first of three outstanding biographies[427] for Warner Bros., Dieterle told of the struggle and prejudice that the great chemist (Paul Muni) had to overcome in his fight against disease and jealous colleagues. Nominated for four Oscars, including Best Film, it won for Best Actor, Best Original Story (Pierre Collings and Sheridan Gibney), and Best Screenplay (Collings and Gibney).

W. C. FIELDS

THE BANK DICK (Universal--16mm: 1940, 73 mins., sound, R-FES, SWA)
Directed by Edward Cline and scripted by Fields under the pseudonym Mahatma Kane Jeeves, this nonsensical story offers a devastating attack on middle-class morality in rural America. Fields plays Egbert Souse, the town of Lompoc's major drunk, who, having won some money in a contest years back, works as little as possible. At one point, he cons a visiting producer into letting him direct a film of a story Souse has written. During the shooting, he accidentally foils a bank robbery and winds up with a job as the bank guard. In the meantime, he is hoodwinked into buying some stock with money he embezzles from the bank. Souse's salvation occurs when he is kidnapped during a bank robbery, eventually is responsible for the thief's capture, given a $4,000 reward, and sells his story to a movie studio for $10,000. As Nicholas Yanni points out, the film "may have been one of Fields's most perfectly realized film scripts, and was certainly the apex of his career in movies."[428]

MILLION DOLLAR LEGS (Paramount--16mm: 1932, 66 mins., b/w, sound, R-MMA, SWA)
The director Edward F. Cline handled W. C. Fields in his first talking role as the president of Klopstokia. In a picture filled with knock-about comedy, wild chase scenes, and hilarious gags, Jack Oakie and Ben Turpin assist with the laughs.

VICTOR FLEMING

GONE WITH THE WIND (Selznick--16mm: 1939, 222 mins., color, sound, R-MGM)

---

[426]   In addition to Gottesman's book, see Bosley Crowther, "King Kong," THE GREAT FILMS, pp.92-97; and Aljean Harmetz, "Fay Wray Writes the Story of Her Life," NEW YORK TIMES C (February 20, 1989):13, 18. See also Chapter 2 for further information on this horror film.

[427]   The other two film biographies are THE LIFE OF EMILE ZOLA (1937) and JUAREZ (1939).

[428]   *Nicholas Yanni, W. C. FIELDS (New York: Pyramid, 1974), p.109.

Initially directed by George Cukor but taken over by Fleming, this screen adaptation of Margaret Mitchell's best-selling novel was scripted by Sidney Howard (with uncredited help from an assortment of writers including Ben Hecht and F. Scott Fitzgerald), photographed by Ernest Haller, John R. Cosgrove, and Lee Zavitz, and designed by William Cameron Menzies. The credit for the film's success belongs mainly to David O. Selznick, who, as discussed in Chapter 5, dared to take on the project no one believed possible in the mid-1930s. It remains today the epitome not only of the great days of MGM and the studio system, but also a treasury of pre-WWII film stereotypes and melodramatic conventions. Nominated for twelve Oscars, including Best Actor (Clark Gable), Best Supporting Actress (Olivia de Havilland), Best Sound Recording (Thomas T. Moulton), Best Original Score (Max Steiner), and Best Special Effects (Photographic: John R. Cosgrove, Sound: Fred Albin and Arthur Johns), it won for Best Film, Best Actress (Vivien Leigh), Best Supporting Actress (Hattie McDaniel), Best Director, Best Screenplay, Best Color Photography (Ernest Haller and Ray Rennahan), Best Interior Decoration (Lyle Wheeler), and Best Film Editing (Hal C. Kern and James E. Newman). Menzies received a special Oscar for his color photography of melodramatic mood in a feature film.[429]

THE WIZARD OF OZ (MGM--16mm: 1939, 100 mins., color, R-FES, MGM)

Produced by Mervyn LeRoy, assisted by Arthur Freed, with costumes by Adrian, editing by Blanche Sewall, and scripted by Noel Langley, Edgar Alan Woolf, and Florence Ryerson, this brilliant production remains the best screen adaptation of the L. Frank Baum classic of Dorothy and her fantastic trip to the magical land of Oz. Among the film's many virtues, commented on in Chapter 2, are its revolutionary approach to film musicals, the magnificent use of technicolor and special effects, and the remarkable screen characterizations that expanded on Baum's original work. Best of all, there are the great performances of Judy Garland (Dorothy), Frank Morgan (the wizard/Professor Marvel), Ray Bolger (the scarecrow/Hunk), Bert Lahr (the cowardly lion/Zeke), Jack Haley (the tin man/Hickory), and Margaret Hamilton (the wicked witch/Miss Gulch). Particularly interesting is the contrast between the framing device of having Dorothy's adventure appear as a dream (directed by King Vidor who filled in for Fleming, who left the unfinished film to take over the direction of GONE WITH THE WIND) and the color photography of the Oz story. Nominated for six Oscars, including Best Film, Best Color Photography (Harold Rossen), Best Interior Decoration (Cedric Gibbons and William A. Horning), and Best Special Effects (Photographic: A. Arnold Gillespie, Sound: Douglas Shearer), it won for Best Musical Song ("Over the Rainbow"; music by Harold Arlen, lyrics by E. Y. Harburg) and Best Original Score (Herbert Stothart). Garland was awarded a special Oscar for her outstanding performance as a screen juvenile.[430]

JOHN FORD

STAGECOACH (United Artists--16mm: 1939, 96 mins., b/w, sound, R-BUD, EMG, FES, FNC, IMA, IVY, KIT, MOD, ROA, TWY, WEL, WES, WIL)

---

[429] For an excellent visual analysis of the film, see the 1988 Peabody award-winning TV documentary THE MAKING OF A LEGEND: "GONE WITH THE WIND," available on videotape.

[430] For an excellent visual and oral analysis of the film, see Ronald Haver's outstanding work on the Criterion Collect Lasardisc. In addition to an excellent overview, the disc contains clips from the 1925 silent version of the film, outakes from the 1939 production, and a variety of publicity material.

John Wayne became a star in this classic film about a stagecoach ride across the Arizona plains in the 1870s. Dudley Nichols's screenplay, adapted from a story by Ernest Haycox, became the prototype for many of the Hollywood westerns in the 1940s and early 1950s, while the director-producer Ford's use of Monument Valley and straightforward narrative skills elevated the genre to a major art form. The reasons for the film's immediate commercial and critical success were summed up by Andre Bazin, who pointed out that the film "is the ideal example of a style brought to classic perfection. John Ford struck the ideal balance between social myth, historical reconstruction, psychological truth, and the traditional theme of the Western MISE EN SCENE."[431] Nominated for seven Oscars, including Best Picture, Best Director, Best Black-and-White Photography (Bert Glennon), Best Interior Direction (Alexander Toluboff), and Best Film Editing (Otho Lovering and Dorothy Spencer), it won two for Best Supporting Actor (Thomas Mitchell) and Best Musical Score (Richard Hageman, Frank Harling, John Leipold, and Leo Shukin).[432]

GRETA GARBO

CAMILLE (MGM-16mm: 1937, 108 mins., b/w, sound, R-MGM)
Director George Cukor did a masterly job in using the screenplay by Zoe Atkins, Frances Marion, and James Hilton (based on Alexander Dumas's famous work, LA DAME AUX CAMELLIAS) to guide Garbo in one of her greatest roles. The enthralling actress gave new insights into the affairs of the tragic, beautiful courtesan in nineteenth-century Paris, who was capable of a great, unselfish love. As Richard Corliss aptly writes, "Some of . . . [the] effects can be credited to cinematographer Karl Freund, . . . [but] It's a technically audacious performance, one that weds an encyclopedic knowledge of the craft with an innate, acute sense of the character's behavior. . . ."[433] Garbo lost the Oscar to Luise Rainer in THE GOOD EARTH.

GRAND HOTEL (MGM--16mm: 1932, 113 mins., b/w, sound, R-MGM)
Directed by Edmund Goulding, scripted by William A. Drake and Frances Marion, and based on Vicki Baum's book and play, the credit for this remarkable film about the variety of people who populate a ritzy hotel, rightly belongs to the producer Irving Thalberg. It is the granddaddy of the star-studded Hollywood spectaculars featuring famous peronalities in a series of stories set in a single location. Among

---

431   *Andre Bazin, "The Evolution of the Western," WHAT IS CINEMA? II, ed. Hugh Gray, Forword Francois Truffaut (Berkeley: University Of California Press, 1971), p.149.

432   For more information, see Mike Sullivan, "Program Notes: STAGECOACH (1939)," CINEMATEXAS PROGRAM NOTES 5:8 (September 17, 1973):1-5; Ed Lowry, "Program Notes: STAGECOACH (1939)," ibid., 11:2 (October 14, 1976):67-78; Lindsay Anderson, "John Ford," CINEMA 6:3 (Spring 1971):21-36; Joseph McBride and Michael Wilmington, "Prisoner of the Desert," SIGHT AND SOUND 40:4 (Autumn 1971):210-14; and Nick Browne, "The Spectator-in-the-Text: The Rhetoric in STAGECOACH," FILM QUARTERLY 24:2 (Winter 1975-76):26-38, Rpt. *NARRATIVE, APPARATUS, IDEOLOGY, ed. Philip Rosen (New York: Columbia University Press, 1986), pp.102-19.

433   *Richard Corliss, GRETA GARBO (New York: Pyramid, 1974), p.124.

the stars are Greta Garbo, John Barrymore, Joan Crawford,[434] Wallace Beery, Lionel Barrymore,[435] Jean Hersholt, and Lewis Stone. Although it won for the Best Picture, it received no other nominations.

NINOTCHKA (MGM--16mm: 1939, 110 mins., b/w, sound, R-FES, MGM)
    Lubitsch directed this hilarious, cynical comedy about a priggish Russian trade official (Garbo) who finds herself in love with a devil-may-care capitalist (Melvyn Douglas). Scripted by three of the best screenwriters in Hollywood history (Charles Brackett, Billy Wilder, and Walter Reisch), it is considered a fine example of film escapism in the late 1930s and of Lubitsch's directorial touches in film comedy. Nominated for four Oscars, including Best Film, Best Actress, Best Original Story (Melchior Lengyel), and Best Screenplay, it failed to win any of the film capital's gold statuettes, but remains the director's most commercially successful film.

QUEEN CHRISTINA (MGM--16mm: 1933, 100 mins., b/w, sound, R-MGM)
    Rouben Mamoulian directed Garbo and John Gilbert in this romanticized story of a young girl, reared as a boy, who became a seventeenth-century queen of Sweden.[436] One of the film's most appealing aspects is the performance of Gilbert as the macho lover. His career allegedly had been destroyed by the coming of sound and the fact that early sound recording devices made his voice sound effeminate. Other sources claim it was his bitter feud with L. B. Mayer that destroyed the actor's career. At the time this film was made, the Garbo-Gilbert romance was over, but she insisted he be her star in the film, hoping it would restore his career. It didn't, but critics still debate the reasons why today.

HOWARD HAWKS

BRINGING UP BABY (MGM-16mm: 1938, 102 mins., b/w, sound, R-FNC)
    Filled with Hawks's marvelous ability to give new life to time-worn film conventions, this madcap adventure involves an inhibited professor (Cary Grant) and a zany millionairess (Katharine Hepburn) who become involved with a runaway leopard and a hunt for a missing dinosaur bone.[437] Scripted by Dudley Nichols and Hagar Wilde, most film historians praise the film's comic inventiveness, the producer-director's gift for surprising, fast-paced comedic sight gags, and his marvelous insights into human relationships.[438]

---

[434]   Lawrence J. Quirk, "Joan Crawford," FILMS IN REVIEW 7:10 (December 1956):481-501; Ronald L. Bowers, "Joan Crawford's Latest Decade," FILMS IN REVIEW 17:6 (June-July 1966):366-68; and Eric Braun, "Forty Years a Queen: The Joan Crawford Story," FILMS AND FILMING 11:8 (May 1965):7-14.

[435]   Bert Gray, "A Lionel Barrymore Index," FILMS IN REVIEW 13:4 (April 1962):220-29.

[436]   David Robinson, "Painting the Leaves Black: Rouben Mamoulian Interviewed," SIGHT AND SOUND 30:3 (Summer 1961):123-27.

[437]   Critics disagree over which Hawks film is his best. In the interest of space, I have chosen this work as an example of the director's genius. Other examples are included throughout this book.

[438]   In addition to consulting the books on Hawks, see Gwen Rolling, "Program Notes: BRINGING UP BABY," CINEMATEXAS PROGRAM NOTES 20:2 (April 2, 1981):69-75.

MERVYN LEROY

I AM A FUGITIVE FROM A CHAIN GANG (Warner Bros.--16mm: 1932, 90 mins., b/w, sound, R-MGM)
Rarely in screen history has there been a more powerful attack on prison injustices than in this haunting and stirring story, scripted by Sheridan Gibney, Howard J. Green, and Brown Holmes (based upon Robert Elliott Burns's semi-autobiographical novel), dealing with the misery and suffering of an ex-soldier (Paul Muni) unjustly placed on a Georgia chain gang.[439] It was nominated for three Oscars: Best Film, Best Actor, and Best Sound Recording (Nathan Levinson). Interestingly, the film's final scene and the one most often praised in the film was the result of an accident, when the kleig lights on the set suddenly blew out.[440]

LITTLE CAESAR (Warners--16mm: 1930, 80 mins., b/w, sound. R-FES, MGM)
Another example of the artistic achievements in the early talkies is Mervyn LeRoy's film about the petty gangster (Edward G. Robinson) who rises to power in the rackets. The film illustrates how sound played a subordinate role to the picture and to filmic technique. Its straightforward, economical cutting, with each sequence growing out of a particular detail, provided an organizational unity that only a first-rate craftsman could achieve. Excellent in its feeling for pace (dialogue was kept terse, images were cut to the essential) and sharp in characterization, the movie still remains as one of the classic examples of the gangster genre.[441] The film's only Oscar nomination was for Best Writing Adaptation (Francis Faragoh and Robert N. Lee).

ERNST LUBITSCH

THE MAN I KILLED (Paramount--16mm: 1931, 3 mins., b/w, sound, R-MMA)
This short extract from Ernst Lubitsch's film deals with a sequence on Armistice Day in 1919 in France, suggesting the irony of the occasion. The original title of the film is BROKEN LULLABY.

TROUBLE IN PARADISE (Paramount--16mm: 1932, 86 mins., b/w, sound, R-WIL)
Scripted by Samson Raphaelson, and based on Laslo Aladar's play, Ernst Lubitsch directed this zany comedy of daring jewel thieves starring Herbert Marshall, Miriam Hopkins, and Kay Francis. Lubitsch considered it his best film.

THE MARX BROTHERS

A DAY AT THE RACES (MGM--16mm: 1937, 109 mins., b/w, sound, R-FES, MGM)

---

[439]   Mervyn LeRoy, "The Making of Mervyn LeRoy," FILMS IN REVIEW 4:5 (May 1953):220-25.

[440]   For details, see Mervyn LeRoy and Dick Kleiner, MERVYN LEROY: TAKE ONE (New York: Hawthorn Books, 1974), p.110.

[441]   Robert C. Roman, "Edward G. Robinson," FILMS IN REVIEW 17:7 (August-September 1966):419-34); and Allen Eyles, "Edward G. Robinson," FILMS AND FILMING 10:4 (January 1964):13-17.

Scripted by George Oppenheimer, Robert Pirosh, and George Seaton, Sam Wood directed this wild and zany story, in which the Marx Brothers are involved with running a sanatorium, which depends, for its future, on the good spirits of Margaret Dumont and a horse's fast reaction to a vicious man's picture.[442]

DUCK SOUP (Paramount--16mm: 1933, 70 mins., b/w, sound, R-FES, MMA, SWA)
Director Leo McCarey teamed up with the screenwriters Bert Kalmar and Harry Ruby to give the zany Marx Brothers the opportunity to wreak havoc on the sensible logic of the mythical kingdom of Fredonia. The tiny bankrupt nation is ordered by its wealthy benefactress (Margaret Dumont) to appoint as head of state, Rufus T. Firefly (Groucho Marx), and no one has ever been the same since.[443]

A NIGHT AT THE OPERA (MGM--16mm: 1935, 90 mins., b/w, sound, R-FES, MGM)
Wood directed this film, which is considered to be the greatest of the Marx Brothers films, which involved the boys and Dumont arranging a debut for friends at the New York Opera. Scripted by George S. Kaufman and Morrie Ryskind, it is an excellent example of the distinction between the comics' work at Paramount, and the films they made at MGM.

ROUBEN MAMOULIAM

APPLAUSE (Paramount--16mm: 1929. 80 mins., b/w, sound, R-MMA, SWA)
Scripted by Garrett Fort, this remarkable early sound film was the first work directed by the Russian emigre Mamoulian. The backstage story about a burlesque star (Helen Morgan) who sacrifices everything for her daughter is famous for its technical innovations involving two microphones to permit the camera greater movement than previously thought possible in sound movies.

LEWIS MILESTONE

ALL QUIET ON THE WESTERN FRONT (Universal--16mm: 1930, 103 mins., b/w, sound, R-FES, SWA)
Scripted by George Abbott, Maxwell Anderson, and Del Andrews, Lewis Milestone's film version of the Erich Remarque novel about the First World War and the disillusioned German youth caused an uproar when it first appeared, mainly because of its sensational (for the times) camera mobility and cutting complexity. Thanks to Lew Ayres's brilliant performance and Milestone's humane insights, it remains one of the greatest anti-war films ever made. Nominated for four Oscars, including Best Writing Achievement and Best Cinematography (Arthur Edeson), it won for Best Film and Best Director.

W. S. VAN DYKE

SAN FRANCISCO (MGM--16mm: 1936, 115 mins., b/w, sound, R-MGM)
One of the best-loved films of the thirties, scripted by Anita Loos, this far-fetched story, involving a saloon keeper (Clark Gable), an opera singer (Jeanette MacDonald), and a tough priest (Spencer Tracy), dealt with the fall of the Barbary

---

[442]   Jerome S. Simon, "George Seaton," FILMS IN REVIEW 22:9 (November 1971):521-40.

[443]   Serge Davey and Jean-Louis Noames, "Taking Chances, Interview With Leo McCarey," CAHIERS DU CINEMA IN ENGLISH 7, Cdc 163 (February 1965):42-54.

Coast. Nominated for six Oscars, including Best Film, Best Actor (Tracy), Best Director, Best Original Story (Robert Hopkins), and Best Assistant Director (Joseph Newman), it won for Best Sound Recording (Douglas Shearer).

THE THIN MAN (MGM--16mm: 1934, 100 mins., b/w, sound, R-MGM)
    Myrna Loy and William Powell starred magnificently in this first screen presentation of Dashiell Hammett's funny and clever detective family, who offer you both wit and suspense. Scripted by Frances Goodrich and Albert Hackett, the delightful film evolved into one of the studio's most popular series. It was nominated for four Oscars: Best Film, Best Actor, Best Director, and Best Writing Adaptation.

GEORGE STEVENS

GUNGA DIN (RKO--16mm: 1939, 129 mins., b/w, sound, R-FES, FNC)
    One of the most popular and entertaining films of the 1930s, this action-packed version of Rudyard Kipling's famous poem starred Cary Grant, Douglas Fairbanks, Jr., and Victor McLaglen as the rugged British officers who save their regiment and learn the worth of an Indian water carrier (Sam Jaffe). Scripted by Fred Guiol, Ben Hecht, Charlie MacArthur, and Joel Sayre, it contains a number of racist images that vividly illustrate the thinking of Hollywood in the pre-WWII era. The film's only Oscar nomination was for Best Black-and-White Cinematography (Joseph H. August).

KING VIDOR

HALLELUJAH! (MGM--16mm: 1929, 107 mn., b/w, sound, R-MGM)
    Scripted by Wanda Tuchock, King Vidor's film is an example of how the creative director effectively handled the problem of using sound with motion rather than relying on each as a separate entity. This motion picture is not only the first all-black sound film, but it is also one of the most important art films of the early thirties. Strangely enough, it's in the singing sequences that Vidor's cinematic skill is weakest.[444] The film's only Oscar nomination was for Best Director.

JOSEF VON STERNBERG

MOROCCO (Paramount--16mm: 1930, 97 mins., b/w, sound, R-WIL)
    Director Josef von Sternberg, after his great success the year before with Marlene Dietrich in THE BLUE ANGEL, now introduced his brilliant discovery to Hollywood and co-starred her with Gary Cooper and Adolphe Menjou in Jules Furthman's sexy screenplay of one woman's sacrifice for the French Foreign Legion. Even today one is amazed at von Sternberg's ability to retain the best of his silent techniques at a time when sound so dominated production techniques. It was nominated for four Oscars: Best Actress, Best Director, Best Cinematography (Lee Garmes), and Best Interior Decoration (Hans Dreier).

----

[444]   Curtis Harrington, "The Later Years: King Vidor's Hollywood Progress," SIGHT AND SOUND 22:4 (April-June 1953):179-82, 203; Herbert G. Luft, "King Vidor: A Career That Spans Half A Century," THE FILM JOURNAL 1:2 (Summer 1971):26-46, 64-71; and Louis Black, "Program Notes: HALLELUJAH!" CINEMATEXAS PROGRAM NOTES 13:2 (October 11, 1977):27-34.

ORSON WELLES

CITIZEN KANE (RKO--16mm: 1941, 119 mins., b/w, sound R-FES, FNC, JAN)
Widely regarded as one of the best films ever made, this movie traces the life of a prominent publisher and millionaire who became a major force in the period in which he lived. It is outstanding in every category.[445] Nominated for nine Oscars, including Best Film, Best Actor (Orson Welles), Best Director, Best Black-and-White Cinematography (Gregg Toland), Best Black-and-White Interior Decoration (Perry Ferguson, Van Nest Polglase, Al Fields, and Darrell Silvera), Best Sound Recording (John Aalberg), Best Scoring of a Dramatic Film (Bernard Herrmann), and Best Film Editing (Robert Wise), it won for Best Original Screenplay (Herman J. Manckiewicz and Orson Welles).

WILLIAM A. WELLMAN

THE PUBLIC ENEMY (Warners--16mm: 1931, 84 mins., b/w, sound, R-MGM)
Scripted by Harvey Thew, this film about the rise and fall of a Chicago hoodlum (James Cagney) remains one of the archetypal formulas of the gangster genre. Not only does it have Cagney's riveting performance as the youngster from the slums who takes the now-cliche-ridden short cut to fortune and power, but the film also contains many famous scenes, including Cagney's pushing a grapefruit in his moll's face (Mae Clarke), and the shocking conclusion in which the machine-gunned body of the protaganist is left at his mother's front door. Despite Wellman's extraordinary pacing and masterly use of sound effects, the film received only one Oscar nomination: Best Original Story (John Bright and Kubeck Glasmon). This is the film that made Cagney a star.

MAE WEST

I'M NO ANGEL (Paramount--16mm: 1933, 88 mins., b/w, sound, R-UNI)
Scripted by Harlan Thompson and Mae West, the film directed by Wesley Ruggles featured West as the honky-tonk dancer who has a flaming romance with a rich playboy (Cary Grant). In this film she issues her famous line, "Beulah, peel me a grape."

SHE DONE HIM WRONG (Paramount--16mm: 1933, 68 mins., b/w, sound, R-MMA)

---

[445] Almost every book in film history discusses this film. In addition to *Pauline Kael, THE CITIZEN KANE BOOK: RAISING KANE, THE SHOOTING SCRIPT, BY HERMAN J. MANKIEWICZ AND ORSON WELLES (Boston: Little, Brown and Company, 1971), see DIALOGUE WITH THE WORLD, pp.25-7; Marion Sheridan et al., THE MOTION PICTURE AND THE TEACHING OF ENGLISH, pp.93-102; Boleslaw Sulik, "Film Critique No. 3: CITIZEN KANE," SCREEN EDUCATION 29 (May-June 1965):30-40; John Cutts, "Great Films of the Century: CITIZEN KANE," FILMS AND FILMING 10:3 (December 1963):15-9; Andrew Sarris, "CITIZEN KANE: The American Baroque," FILM CULTURE 2 (May 1962):14-6; Joseph McBride, "Welles before Kane," FILM QUARTERLY 23:3 (Spring 1970):19-22; Joseph McBride, "Citizen Kane," FILM HERITAGE 4:1 (Fall 1968):7-18; Patrick Ogle, "Technological and Aesthetic Influences Upon the Development of Deep Focus Cinematography in the United States," SCREEN 13:1 (Spring 1972):45-72; *Andre Bazin, "The Evolution of the Language of Cinema," WHAT IS CINEMA?, pp.23-40; and Glenn Collins, "George Coulouris, 85 is Dead; Actor Relished Villainous Roles," NEW YORK TIMES B (April 27, 1989):16.

Lowell Sherman directed West in her most famous role as the Bowery bombshell in the 1890s who captivated even the Salvation Army's legal eagle (Cary Grant). Scripted by John Bright and Harvey Thew, the film drove the censors wild, particularly when West delivers the famous line, "Come up 'n see me some time," and sings the suggestive songs, "Easy Rider," and "A Guy What Takes His Time." Although the picture received no Oscars, it reportedly kept Paramount afloat during the worst days of the Depression.

JAMES WHALE

FRANKENSTEIN (Universal--16mm: 1931, 71 mins., b/w, sound, R-FES, SWA, TWY)
Scripted by Francis Faragoh and Garnett Fort, James Whale directed this early sound masterpiece of Mary Shelley's novel about a monster who was more sinned against than sinning. Bela Lugosi always regretted that he had turned down the key role because the make-up would have disguised his suave appearance. But it made Boris Karloff a famous star.[446]

WILLIAM WYLER

DEAD END (United Artists--16mm: 1937, 92 mins., b/w, sound, R-FNC, WHO)
Scripted by Lillian Hellman, and based on Sidney Kingsley's play, this film represents the types of projects that the director William Wyler and the producer Sam Goldwyn produced in the late 1930s. This tale of the New York slums and how they affected a variety of individuals offered choice roles for many significant performers: e.g. Humphrey Bogart, Joel McCrea, Marjorie Main, Sylvia Sidney, and Claire Trevor. It is also the film that launched the career of the "Dead End Kids": Billy Halop, Huntz Hall, Bobby Jordan, and Leo Gorcey. Much of the movie's visual impact belongs to the camerawork of Gregg Toland. The film received four Oscar nominations: Best Film, Best Supporting Actress (Trevor), Best Cinematography, and Best Interior Direction (Richard Day).

THE FRENCH, GERMAN, BRITISH, AND SOVIET FEATURE FILM (1929-1940)

FRANCE

The transition from silent to sound films, coupled with the political, social, and economic problems generated by the Depression, only added to the plight of the already beleaguered international film industry. Stylized acting, creative editing, and expressionistic lighting techniques differentiated the various national cinemas. After years of struggle, artists had developed not only a familiarity with the equipment and the film process, but also a sense of confidence in their abilities to make meaningful moving pictures. Moreover, many different types of exhibition circuits had adjusted their programs and theaters to meet the needs of pre-conditioned audiences willing to pay nominal sums at the box office. The cost of again remodeling movie houses (a big building boom had gripped the entire film industry following World War I) was second to the issues of what system to install, sound-on-film or

---

[446] William Thomaier, "James Whale," FILMS IN REVIEW 13:5 (May 1962):278-90; Lillian Gerard, "Boris Karloff: The Man Behind The Myth," FILM COMMENT 6:1 (Spring 1970):46-48; Gordon Hitchens, "Historical Notes on Dr. Frankenstein and His Monster," ibid., pp.49-51; and Paul Jensen, "James Whale," ibid., 7:1 (Spring 1971):52-57.

films-with-discs, whether there would be enough product to provide weekly program changes, and whether talking films were a fad. Still further, as discussed in Chapter 2, most European governments, profoundly disturbed by the propagandistic nature of films, had long since established strong censorship regulations designed to safeguard the STATUS QUO. The addition of dialogue only increased challenges to authoritaries. In short, the coming of sound produced chaos.

Nowhere were the problems more evident than in France. Ever since World War I, the French film industry had been in the economic doldrums. Poorly organized, badly managed, and financially undernourished, the isolated studios operating on a pay-as-you-produce basis were not only overwhelmed by the staggering costs of installing new equipment and producing talking films, but also of paying copyright fees for foreign sound patents. As Basil Wright explains, "The real problem for France in those first days of the talkies was that there was no indigenous sound system. The Americans and the Germans, both with systems of their own (Western Electric and R.C.A. in the one case, and Tobias-Klangfilm in the other), were able to move in and make a killing."[447] In fact, the Paris Agreement of 1930, establishing the sound-on-film process as the standard form of talking films, made it possible for all European film industries to finally commit themselves to a complete overhaul of their production and exhibition facilities to accommodate sound films.

The filmmakers in France hardest hit by the coming of sound were the experimentalists. Their easy access to inexpensive facilities and relatively simple equipment disappeared almost immediately. With few exceptions, most of the silent film AVANT-GARDE, shocked and outraged by the debilitating technological and economic course of events in the film world, returned to their original METTIERS.

The mainstream filmmmakers who remained found the unstable industry falling into the hands of foreigners. By 1930, the American and German sound monopolies negotiated a lucrative arrangement with the French that divided the distribution of talking films made in France into foreign and domestic markets, much the same as the Hollywood moguls divided markets in the United States. The French dependency on external funding and patents forced the French film industry into a massive reorganization of its structure.

One approach was a short-lived attempt by foreign companies to set up production outlets in and around Paris to handle multilingual clones of English-language productions.[448] For example, Paramount Pictures tried to make several versions of the same film at the same time, using the same sets and story but with different performers and directors. In cases where the studio wanted duplicates of its American films, sets were recreated at the Joinville location. These foreign-language versions did nothing to advance the reputation of moving pictures or increase the bankrolls of the Hollywood companies. By 1932, the plan was abandoned in favor of using the French studios to "dub" English-language films for foreign consumption.

Although the efforts of the German film company, Tobias, to overcome the problems created by sound also met with limited success, the organization did give a number of directors a rare opportunity to experiment with sound technology. For

---

[447] Wright, p.140.

[448] One of the interesting side effects was that Paramount hired Alexander Korda, a Hungarian-born director and producer who had migrated to Hollywood in 1927, worked a few years in America before moving on to Berlin and then Paris in 1930, to direct several films in France, the most significant being a screen adaptation of Marcel Pagnol's hit play MARIUS (1931). By 1932, Paramount assigned Korda to work in London and thereby unintentionally, as we shall see later, initiated a major new direction for British films. Pagnol then went to direct his own films, including the highly acclaimed THE BAKER'S WIFE/LA FEMME DU BOULANGER (1938). For a current reassessment of Pagnol, see Stephen Harvey, "Pagnol, From the Source," NEW YORK TIMES H (February 21, 1988):23, 30.

example, Clair, who shared his generation's disgust over the fate of silent film art, worked at Tobias adapting his sense of cinematic fantasy to the modern film. In many respects, he combined his knowledge of silent films with a minimal use of sound to get the best of both eras. Starting with UNDER THE ROOFS OF PARIS/SOUS LES TOITS DE PARIS (1930), LE MILLION, GIVE US FREEDOM/A NOUS LA LIBERTE (both in 1931), and THE FOURTEENTH OF JULY/LE QUATORZE JUILLET (1932), Clair demonstrated how one could subvert "the illusion of realistic sound in order to liberate the medium and restore to it its poetic powers."[449] The major focus in Clair's extraordinary musical comedies was on vision, shots, and editing. Just as the Soviets had perfected the concept of montage, Clair refined the relationship between a shot and sound, using both synchronous and asynchronous sound. While his films were much more popular with mass audiences than were his silent works, he nevertheless loathed the idea of working in a commercial system. By the mid-1930s, political and social conditions in Germany and France had curtailed considerably Tobias's ability to experiment with film art. As a result, Clair left France in 1935 to work first in England and then in Hollywood, where except for one brief return to Paris in 1939, he stayed until the end of World War II.

Audience enthusiasm for talking films prompted French financiers to reassess their long-standing reluctance to invest in movie companies. This, in turn, led to a second approach to reorganizing the French film industry, that of merging existing film resources into two principal firms: Gaumont and Pathe. Like the film monopolies in America, the key to French film control was in distribution and exhibition. Both Gaumont (under new management in 1929) and Pathe expanded their already sizable theater circuits and maximized the effectiveness of their first-run theaters. Unlike the American monopolies, however, the French giants targeted their products at working-class, rather than middle-class audiences. Nonetheless, the production goals of both nations were the same: accommodate the weekly needs of the theaters. French films quickly adapted the Hollywood approach to filmmaking: formula films with escapist themes, popular performers, and familiar plots, all designed to distract audiences from their everyday problems. Individualism was discouraged in favor of specialization. That is, films were made like products on an assembly line, with each contributor (e.g., director, screenwriter, and editor) performing a specific assignment rather than being part of a collaborative effort. Unfortunately for the French filmmakers, imitation of American products inevitably resulted in audiences' preferring the original to the copy. The predictable outcome was that nearly three-quarters of the movies on French screens during the 1930s were American films.

In addition to the standard problems artists faced when working in a studio system run with a big business approach to profits, there was the issue of official censorship. In the summer of 1919, the French government, after years of flirting with a variety of approaches, established a form of national control designed primarily to influence the moral content of the arts. Simply put, a thirty-member board was empowered to decide censorship battles. The one major restriction was that the board's decision could not infringe on the prerogatives of local police officials. The lasting effect of this legislation was that official censorship remained inextricably linked to government officeholders. Those who shaped the nation's political life also determined the place of art in society.

The art suffering most from this national policy was the moving picture. Not only was the industry excluded from the decision-making process, but also the lines of authority between the state and local municipalities remained unclear. As a result, far more censorship than anyone expected occurred. In February 1928, after nearly a decade of battling the censors in costly court fights, the film industry orchestrated a new piece of national legislation giving the film industry representation on a commission of censors. While such a commission had more liberal credentials than its

---

[449]   Lucy Fischer, "Rene Clair, LE MILLION, and the Coming of Sound," CINEMA JOURNAL 16:2 (Spring 1977):38.

predecessor, it still functioned as an arm of elected politicians who now expanded, their responsibilities to the censoring of objectionable political material. The impetus for political film censorship had begun right after the 1918 Armistice with a ban on German films and accelerated in 1926, when a sitting government hostile to the Soviet Union became alarmed over the new Soviet films commemorating the October 1917 Revolution and making the rounds of the French cine-clubs and film societies.

Sensitive to the potential of films to challenge the STATUS QUO, influential political factions took aim at the AVANT-GARDE movements sponsoring such films, and by 1930, film censorship was rampant. For example, Bunuel, who quickly saw the advantages of sound in advancing his revolutionary ideas, made THE GOLDEN AGE/L'AGE D'OR (1930), an unrelenting attack on religious and social mores. Under the restructured French film industry and revised censorship legislation, Bunuel's satiric work surprisingly passed the censor's scrutiny at the national level but ran afoul of the local authorities who feared that it would create disorder in the theaters.[450] It was a favorite justification used by local authorities in banning films by Feyder, Eisenstein, Pudovkin, and Vertov. The great danger to film was not in the banning or re-editing of specific films, but rather, as Strebel explains,

> The elaborately laid out censorship decrees, the extensive bureaucracy of commissions and subcommissions which was built up surrounding censorship control, the auspicious sounding title of Conseil Superieur de Cinema, the activities of the local police as secondary censors, the power of certain pressure groups to effect bans and the relative impotence of other groups to effect the removal of bans, all contributed toward a climate in which producers and distributers were reluctant to take a chance.[451]

This repressive atmosphere contributed to the growing crisis in the French film industry.

In the years between 1930 and 1934, the stifling and inflexible atmosphere that was choking the imaginative life out of French films was masked periodically by the rare work of a few artists. In addition to Clair's aforementioned films, there were Dreyer's VAMPYR (1932), Duvivier's POIL DE CAROTTE (1932 version), Cocteau's BLOOD OF THE POET/LE SANG D'UN POETE (1932), and Jean Benoit-Levy's LA MATERNELLE (1933). The most memorable films, however, were the works of Vigo. Although his tragic death at twenty-nine robbed French cinema of a great artist, the few films he created--e.g., A PROPOS DE NICE (1930), ZERO FOR CONDUCT/ZERO DE CONDUITE (1933), and L'ATALANTE (1934)--remain superb examples of his stunning imagery, the lyricism of his editing techniques, and his fertile imagination. It should be pointed out that working outside the studio system only increased Vigo's considerable problems with censors, distributors, and exhibitors. He was after all a revolutionary, who as, Kracauer points out, "used the camera as a weapon, not as an anesthetic."[452]

As the Depression-racked French film industry moved into the mid-1930s, it suffered further setbacks. The departure of Clair, the death of Vigo, and the demise of the two major film companies, all in 1934, made industry observers certain that France could no longer aspire to a national cinema. Financial investment came to a standstill, making many French filmmakers unemployed. On a much more terrifying note, political unrest throughout France brought the nation to the brink of civil war.

---

[450] For a good overview of the censorship problems besetting L'AGE D'OR, see Elizabeth Grottle Strebel, FRENCH SOCIAL CINEMA OF THE NINETEEN THIRTIES: A CINEMATOGRAPHIC EXPRESSION OF POPULAR FRONT CONSCIOUSNESS (New York: Arno Press, 1980), pp.36-9.

[451] FRENCH SOCIAL CINEMA, p.49.

[452] Siegfried Kracauer, "Jean Vigo," HOLLYWOOD QUARTERLY 2:3 (April 1947):261.

Only a "Popular Front" alliance by the left-wing groups in 1935 prevented a Fascist takeover during the remainder of the decade. Because the fortunes of the film industry were so closely linked to the nation's political climate, events in the industry operated as a microcosm of the nation's problems. Studio employees went on strike, producers and directors fought constantly over political issues, and everyone in the industry debated the role of the cinema in society.

Imagine everyone's surprise, therefore, when this tumultuous period resulted in some of France's greatest films. Over the next five years, creative filmmakers like Jacques Feyder, Charles Spaak, Julien Duvivier, Marcel Carne, Jacques Prevert, and Jean Renoir took advantage of the change in political control to amass a series of film classics that were inspired by what many film historians call "poetic realism," a movement derived from the French literary, theatrical, and artistic traditions of naturalism and realism responsive to the strengths and weaknesses of the Populist Front movement in France from 1935 to 1937.[453]

While agreeing with much of that standard historical assessment, Elizabeth Grottle Strebel argues that in the years from 1935 to 1939, a small group of films (no more than five to ten percent of the commercial feature film production) developed into a new movement that she labels "social cinema."[454] She sees filmmakers like Renoir, Carne, Feyder, Duvivier, Prevert, and Spaak as responding to the changing social, economic, and political conditions in France and beginning "to document and analyze contemporary social issues like class divisions, unemployment, societal frustrations, the plight of the aged, anti-Semitism and pacifism. Their focus was upon the lower middle and working classes, long-neglected subjects of cinematographic interest."[455] Rather than concentrating on poetic realism, she considers it important to examine first the roots of social cinema and how it evolved from the work of independent filmmakers between 1929 and 1934, thereby calling attention to how such filmmakers later offered alternatives to the restructured French film industry. Such changes became possible because the Popular Front government conceived of film as an instrument of the state. Their social and political ideology found an outlet with the poetic realists who argued for class solidarity, documented the end of an aristocratic order, and made the tragedy of the human condition a central part of their work. Moreover, the new administration, fiercely opposed to the Nazi movement, developed a conciliatory attitude toward the Soviet Union, resulting in a lessening of political censorship. This, in turn, made attacks on social injustice not only possible, but also commercially viable. Still further, the failure of the film monopolies to survive beyond the early 1930s reestablished the role of small, independent studios in French filmmaking. In essence, technology once more became accessible and comprehensible to visionary artists who now were in tune with mass audiences. Thus encouraged by the government and spurred on by personal commitment, the filmmakers got in step with the political activism of the times. What Strebel also finds significant about the social cinema movement was its collaborative nature. Unlike the studio system, the new approach functioned primarily like a repertory company, with a filmmaking team working on a series of films, rather than being assigned on a film-by-film basis.

Typical of the film renaissance was the collaborative writer-director team of Spaak and Feyder in films like THE GRAND GAME/LE GRAND JEU (1934), CARNIVAL IN FLANDERS/LA KERMESSE HEROIQUE, and PENSION MIMOSAS (both in 1935). Feyder, a writer-director who had started in films in 1911 as an actor in Melies's movies, had been making films since the mid-teens. When his controversial film, THE NEW GENTLEMEN/LES NOUVEAUX MESSIEURS (1928) was banned, he left France and

---

[453]   Cook, pp.333-4.

[454]   FRENCH SOCIAL CINEMA, p.3.

[455]   FRENCH SOCIAL CINEMA, p.3.

spent four years in Hollywood before returning to Paris in 1934 to resume his work in the French cinema. His ability to depict the squalor of life equally well in a story about the French Foreign Legion and in a tale of racketeering at home helped launch the era of poetic-realistic films in France.

Spaak, Belgium-born like Feyder, had not begun his screenwriting career until the end of the 1920s. Over the next forty years, he would work with many important directors (e.g., Julien Duvivier, Jean Renoir, Robert Siodmak, Marcel Carne, and Phillipe De Broca), but nothing he wrote surpassed the naturalistic films made during the poetic-realistic period. In addition to the recognition gained from the bittersweet fatalism of the Feyder films, he also gained fame for his work on Duvivier's ESCAPE FROM YESTERDAY/LA BANDERA (1935) and THEY WERE FIVE/LE BELLE EQUIPE (1936), and Renoir's THE LOWER DEPTHS/LES BAS-FONDS (1937) and GRAND ILLUSION/LA GRANDE ILLUSION (1938).

Another brilliant writing-directing team in the poetic-realistic era was that of Marcel Carne and Jacques Prevert. The former, who first began studying filmmaking in 1928, gained his experience working for Clair and Feyder. In 1935, at twenty-six, he made his directorial debut and within four years had created three of the period's most important films: PORT OF SHADOWS/QUAI DES BRUMES,[456] HOTEL DU NORD, (both in 1938), and DAYBREAK/LE JOUR SE LEVE (1939). Having learned much from Clair and Feyder about technique and details, Carne created powerful images of ill-fated people caught in a web of circumstances that they could neither fathom nor escape. Although the contribution of Prevert was crucial to the success of these great films, his optimistic temperament was often at odds with Carne's brooding pessimism. He just refused to believe that love or art could not overcome despair. Furthermore, his identification with the poor and the helpless bred in him an ironic and sardonic wit that became a trademark in his unrelenting attacks on authority. What made the screenwriter one of the nation's most influential artists between 1935 and 1945, as Philip Kemp points out, was his ability to translate "ordinary, banal speech into a lyrical street poetry, reinvesting cliches with their original emotional truth."[457] Interestingly, neither Carne nor Prevert was able to make successful films independent of the other.

The greatest genius of the age, however, was Jean Renoir.[458] Although a filmmaker since the 1920s and the creator of critically acclaimed films like NANA and

---

[456] For a good examination of the film, see Raymond W. Whitaker, THE CONTENT ANALYSIS OF FILM: A SURVEY OF THE FIELD, AN EXHAUSTIVE STUDY OF "QUAI DES BRUMES," AND A FUNCTIONAL DESCRIPTION OF THE FILM LANGUAGE (Unpublished Ph.D. dissertation, Northwestern University, 1966).

[457] Philip Kemp, "Prevert, Jacques," THE INTERNATIONAL DICTIONARY OF FILMS AND FILMMAKERS IV: WRITERS AND PRODUCTION ARTISTS, p.347.

[458] For more information, see Elizabeth Grottle Strebel, "Jean Renoir and the Popular Front," SIGHT AND SOUND 49:1 (Winter 1979-80):36-41. For a useful discussion of how Renoir collaborated with other artists during the mid- to late-1930s, see FRENCH SOCIAL CINEMA, pp.170-6. Also, in addition to Christopher Faulkner's indispensable resource guide, the following articles are helpful: Jacques Rivette and Francois Truffaut, "Renoir in America," SIGHT AND SOUND 24:1 (July-September 1954):12-7; ___, "Renoir in America," FILMS IN REVIEW 5:9 (November 1954):449-56; Jean Renoir, "I Know Where I'm Going," Trans. David A. Mage, ibid., 3:3 (March 1952):97-101; John Peter Dyer, "Renoir and Realism," SIGHT AND SOUND 29:3 (Summer 1960):130-5, 154; Louis Marcorelles, "Conversation With Jean Renoir," ibid., 31:2 (Spring 1962):78-83, 103; Rui Nogueira and Francois Truchaud, "Interview With Jean Renoir," ibid., 37:2 (Spring 1968):56-62; Daniel Millar, "The Autumn of Jean Renoir," ibid., 37:3 (Summer 1968):136-41, 161; Jean Beranger, "The Illustrious Career of Jean Renoir," YALE FRENCH STUDIES 17 (Summer 1965):27-37; Peter Svatel et al., "Questions and

THE LITTLE MATCH GIRL/LA PETITE MARCHANDE D'ALLUMETTES (both in 1927), most of his early works suffered at the box office because of their experimental narratives. Like the work of von Stroheim, whom Renoir admired, the French filmmaker also found it very difficult to make his "realistic" impressions of everyday life commercially acceptable to his studio bosses.

Although the coming of sound initially added to Renoir's economic and artistic problems, it soon provided him with a means for refining his talent for visual metaphors on human relationships in a specific MILIEU. His forte was in anchoring a character's behavior and values to the person's upbringing, social status, and environment. What makes his characters so unforgettable, as Strebel points out, is that he refuses to pass judgment on them because they are "rooted in their social backgrounds and environments. . . ."[459] Starting with THE BITCH/LA CHIENNE (1931) and moving through films like TONI (1935) and THE CRIME OF MONSIEUR LANGE/LE CRIME DE MONSIEUR LANGE (1935), the second son of the great French Impressionist painter exhibited his brilliant camera work in creating bittersweet moods and extraordinary characterizations.[460] His collaboration with Prevert on THE CRIME OF MONSEIUR LANGE/LE CRIME DE MONSEIUR LANGE, with Spaak on GRAND ILLUSION/LA GRANDE ILLUSION (1938), and with Karl Koch on THE RULES OF THE GAME/LA REGLE DU JEU (1939) marks the highpoints of his career during the 1930s. Following an ill-fated attempt to placate the Fascist regime in Italy in 1939, he fled to Hollywood where, like many of his compatriots, he remained until the end of World War II.

In addition to outstanding directors and screenwriters, the era of poetic realism gave rise to a number of great performers. Among the most famous are Jean Gabin, Michel Simon, Arletty, Jean-Louis Barrault, Harry Baur, Pierre Blachar, Marcel Dalio, Louis Jouvet, Raimu, Francoise Rosay, and Michele Morgan. Their presentation of the class struggle both in historical and contemporary settings epitomized the social cinema of the mid- to late-1930s, capturing not only the passing of an aristocratic

---

Answers With Jean Renoir," TAKE ONE 1:7 (1967):4-6; Todd McCarthy, "Jean Renoir: A Colossus Among Cinema Directors, Dies at 84," VARIETY (February 21, 1979): 34; Don Safran, "Jean Renoir's Death Breaks the Line of French Masters," HOLLYWOOD REPORTER (February 14, 1979):22; Arthur Knight, "Memories of a Past Master," ibid., (February 16, 1979):12; Vincent Canby, "The Riches of Jean Renoir," NEW YORK TIMES D (May 12, 1974):1, 11; Valentin Almendarez, "Program Notes: BODU SAVED FROM DROWNING," CINEMATEXAS PROGRAM NOTES 7:9 (October 22, 1974):1-5; ___, "Program Notes: LE CRIME DE MONSIEUR LANGE," ibid., 8:36 (March 13, 1975):1-6; Ann Rowe Seaman, "Program Notes: TONI," ibid., 9:3 (November 1975):63-8; Kristin Laskas, "Program Notes: THE LOWER DEPTHS," ibid., 10:2 (March 10, 1976):95-101; ___, "Program Notes: THE SOUTHERNER," ibid., 10:3 (March 23, 1976):9-13; Marjorie Baumgarten, "Program Notes: BODU SAVED FROM DROWNING," ibid., 13:2 (October 25, 1977):79-84; Nina Nichols, "Program Notes: FRENCH CAN CAN," ibid., 17:2 (October 17, 1979):23-7; and Rod Buxton, "Program Notes: LE CRIME DE MONSIEUR LANGE," ibid., 23:2 ()ctober 19, 1982):27-33.

[459] FRENCH SOCIAL CINEMA, p.237.

[460] Cook (pp.340-1) summarizes the ground-breaking work done by Renoir in freeing the camera from the problems created by panchromatic stock and incandescent lighting and thus restoring the ability of the filmmaker to use "depth-of-field" photography. For more detailed information, see Charles Henry Harpole, GRADIENTS OF DEPTH IN THE CINEMA IMAGE (New York: Arno Press, 1978); ___, "Ideological and Technological Determinism in Deep-Space Cinema Images," FILM QUARTERLY 33:3 (Spring 1980):11-21; and *Andre Bazin, WHAT IS CINEMA?, ed. Hugh Gray (Berkeley: University Of California Press, 1967), pp.23-40.

order and the rise of a more egalitarian society, but also the fears and anxieties of age engulfed by economic, political, and social chaos.[461]

BOOKS

GENERAL

*THE ART OF THE CINEMA, Yale French Studies 17 (Summer 1956).
   For those in search of critical material on pre-World War II French directors, this valuable monograph offers information on Ophuls, Cocteau, Clouzot, and Renoir, plus some worthwhile commentary on THE ROAD/LA STRADA and neo-realism.

Strebel, Elizabeth Grottle. FRENCH SOCIAL CINEMA OF THE NINETEEN THIRTIES: A CINEMATOGRAPHIC EXPRESSION OF POPULAR FRONT CONSCIOUSNESS.   New York: Arno Press, 1980. 292pp.
   Originally written as a 1973 Princeton University Ph.D. dissertation, this highly original study has three major objectives: "(1) to explain why social cinema arose when it did, by examining those economic, social and political factors which facilitated its development, (2) to establish the nature and contours of this new movement by identifying its proponents and by analyzing the dominant thematic concerns and general cinematographic orientation of its films, and (3) to examine the dynamic interaction between film and society at this time." Strebel's basic sources are film periodicals, yearbooks, and brochures of the era, as well as the movies themselves. In looking closely at the film process from pre- to post-production, she touches on vital issues like film financing, censorship, the filmmakers' social backgrounds, the role of government in filmmaking, and the influence of the press. "The major questions asked of each film," the author explains, "are what kinds of social strata are represented, how do these different social strata interact, what social milieus do the films focus upon, what are the fundamental social problems of each social milieu, and what are the attitudes of the various social groups towards society."
   The body of the study is divided into three main sections. Part 1, dealing with the restraints on a socially critical cinema, covers the period of relative stability between 1929 and 1934, with several chapters on censorship control, film production, and the early proponents of social cinema. Part 2, covering the genesis of social cinema, concentrates on the transition period between 1934 and 1937, offers three chapters on the social, political, and economic changes that impacted on the film industry, the creators of social cinema, and the new approaches to filmmaking. Part 3, focusing on French social cinema, discusses the political history of the French left and social awareness in commercial cinema. An epilogue summarizes Strebel's ideas on the roots of social cinema, the political struggles to liberate film from economic and social pressures, the importance of the leftist coalition Popular Front, and the relationship of the movement to social cinema. A bibliography is included. Recommended for special collections.

---

[461] One specific event that contributed to the fate and fortunes of French filmmakers before and after the advent of World War II was the infamous L'AFFAIR NATAN. Simply put, Bernard Natan, who ran Pathe-Cinema, defrauded not only many of the company's stockholders, but also many of its creditors in the mid-1930s. Moreover, he did it with the help of government officials. His trial and conviction in 1938 intensified anti-Semitic feeling in France and led to a widespread feeling that Jews were responsible both for corruption in the film industry, and for the general morass in French society.

MARCEL CARNE

*LE JOUR SE LEVE: A FILM BY MARCEL CARNE AND JACQUES PREVERT. Trans. Dinah Brooke and Nicola Hayden. New York: Simon and Schuster, 1970. Illustrated. 128pp.

Based upon the French version of Jacques Prevert's own shooting script published in L'AVANT-SCENE DU CINEMA, this useful translation contains fine visuals and Andre Bazin's commentary on the relationship of the film to "poetic realism." The famous critic concludes the essay with the observation that "In spite of its structure and realist appearance, LE JOUR SE LEVE is nothing less than a 'psychological' or even 'social' drama. As in tragedy, the essential quality of this story and its characters is purely metaphysical." Worth browsing.

JEAN COCTEAU

Anderson, Alexandra, and Carol Saltus. JEAN COCTEAU AND THE FRENCH SCENE. New York: Abbeville Press, 1984. Illustrated. 240pp.

Born in Paris, on July 5, 1889, Jean Cocteau was one of the most versatile artists ever to work in films. Although born into an upper-class family, he grew up heavily influenced by the bohemiam life that appealed to his maternal grandfather, the person Cocteau was most attached to in his formative years. The future filmmaker was an excellent student but unwilling to conform to the rigid discipline of academic life. It didn't help when Cocteau discovered early in life that he was a homosexual. The need to be accepted on his terms played a key role in the emerging artist's lonely and isolated formative years. By the time he was in his teens, he turned his obvious creative talents to poetry and the ballet. Prevented from serving in World War I, because of his ill-health, Cocteau not only gained recognition for his attempts to aid the troops at the front, but also fame as an author for Diaghilev's BALLETS RUSSES, headquartered in Paris. In the 1920s, his fame increased as he became a noted painter, an admired musical commentator, and a gifted writer. His most significant relationship in the early postwar period was Raymond Radiguet, a homosexual writer who died tragically at twenty-three. In the years to come, the memories of that relationship would surface in Cocteau's work. When talkies arrived, Cocteau began adapting his poetic insights into films, starting with THE BLOOD OF A POET/LE SANG D'UN POETE (1930-1932). Over the next thirty years, he continued his love for the arts by working in music, literature, film, and painting. He died on October 11, 1963.

This anthology, released to celebrate the centenary of Cocteau's birth, contains eight essays on the artist's work by some of the most respected writers: Dore Ashton, Steve Harvey, Neal Oxenhandler, Arthur Peters, Ned Rorem, Roger Shattuck, and Frances Steegmuller. "Far more than grand opera and concert halls," Arthur King Peters states in the book's preface, "Cocteau's taste ran to the milieu of popular entertainment, the music hall, the circus, and the theater, and these cultural arenas figure in many of his works." The collection of early photographs, artwork, and film stills that illustrate the noteworthy essays in this volume provide clear examples of how Cocteau interpreted his life in Paris. A Jean Cocteau Chronology and index are included. Well worth browsing.

Cocteau, Jean. THE JOURNALS OF JEAN COCTEAU. Trans. Wallace Fowlie. Bloomington: Indiana University Press, 1964. Illustrated. 250pp.

This is an invaluable collection of the great filmmaker's thoughts about a host of topics. A bibliography is included. Recommended for special collections.

*Cocteau, Jean. TWO SCREENPLAYS: THE BLOOD OF A POET/ THE TESTAMENT OF ORPHEUS. Trans. Carol Martin-Sperry. Baltimore: Penguin Books, 1969. Illustrated. 147pp.

The scripts of Cocteau's first film, THE BLOOD OF A POET/LE SANG D'UN POETE (1930-1932), and his last film, THE TESTAMENT OF ORPHEUS (1959) are supplemented by over fifty stills from the productions. In the preface (written in 1946), Cocteau takes issue with critics who label his first movie a "surrealistic film." Instead, he insists he was one of the few people working in the cinema who was more interested in images produced by "a kind of half-sleep" than in "the deliberate manifestations of the unconscious." As he explains, "I applied myself only to the relief and to the details of the images that came forth from the great darkness of the human body. I adopted them then and there as the documentary scenes of another kingdom." In describing his intentions in his last film, the unique filmmaker tells us that he was only interested in pleasing himself. A Cocteau filmography is included. Well worth browsing.

Cocteau, Jean. MY JOURNEY ROUND THE WORLD. Trans. W. J. Strachan. London: Peter Owen, 1958. 175pp.

In the mid-1930s, Marcel Khill, inspired by Cocteau's memoirs, PORTRAIT-SOUVENIR (1935-1936), suggested that the two men recreate the adventures of Phileas Fogg and Passepartout. This impressionist report is the result of Khill and Cocteau's travels around the world in eighty days. An index is included. Worth browsing.

Cocteau, Jean. THE HAND OF A STRANGER. Trans. Alec Brown. London: Elek Books, 1956. 187pp.

Originally published as JOURNAL D'UN INCONNU in 1953, this translation appeared at the time Cocteau was elected to the ACADEMIE FRANCAISE. The series of essays reveals the author's feelings about friendship, invisibility, the pain of death, and the birth of a poem. Worth browsing.

Cocteau, Jean. THE DIFFICULTY OF BEING. Trans. from LA DIFFICULTE D'ETRE (1947) Elizabeth Sprigge. London: Peter Owen, 1966. 160pp.

An intriguing analysis of why he felt as he did and how myths influenced his character and work, this valuable collection of essays touches on a range of topics: his childhood, his writing style, his relationship with Raymond Radiguet, his thoughts on the theater, and his feeling about Diaghilev and Nijinsky. In a March 1947 foreword to the book, the author concludes, "So there it is. This is how it strikes me in the peace of this countryside . . . In the end, everything is resolved, except the difficulty of being, which is never resolved." Regrettably, no index is provided. Recommended for special collections.

Cocteau, Jean. COCTEAU ON THE FILM. Recorded Andre Fraigneau and trans. Vera Travaill. New York: Roy Publications, 1954. Illustrated. 140pp.

"Jean Cocteau," Farigneau explains, "occupies a unique place in the cinematograph of our day. He was the first among the major poets to become interested in film as a means of artistic expression. He learned the technique of film-making, or, more exactly, he re-invented it for his own personal use. Thus he created CINEMATIC POETRY, an exciting addition to the poetry of the theatre and of the novel, of graphic art and choreography, with which he had previously enriched French art." This book on the relationship between the film and the audience is in the form of an extempore conversation and thus may offer some difficulty to the reader. Serious students may appreciate the artist's ability to be objective about his art and his work. A Cocteau filmography is included, but no index is provided. Well worth browsing.

Crowson, Lydia Lallas. THE AESTHETIC OF JEAN COCTEAU. Hanover: University
Press of New England, 1978. 200pp.

Evans, Arthur B. JEAN COCTEAU AND HIS FILMS OF ORPHIC IDENTITY.
Philadelphia: The Art Alliance Press, 1977. Illustrated. 174pp.
    An absorbing study of Cocteau's preoccupation and self-identification with the
Greek god Orpheus, this analysis was first written Evan's 1972 master's thesis in
Humanities at Goddard College. Three intelligent chapters discuss useful ideas on
narrative versus poetic film, thematic guideposts for a comprehension of Cocteau, and
the interpretation of Cocteau's three films on Orpheus. A bibliography and index are
included. Recommended for special collections.

*Gilson, Rene, ed. JEAN COCTEAU: AN INVESTIGATION INTO HIS FILMS AND
PHILOSOPHY. Trans. Ciba Vaughan. New York: Crown Publishers, 1964. Illustrated.
192pp.
    Originally published in the CINEMA D'AUJOURD'HUI SERIES in 1964, this
invaluable translation sheds enormous light on one of the foremost Renaissance
filmmakers in motion picture history. Gilson, an important French critic and editor
of the magazine, CINEMA '68, offers a first-rate analysis of the basic characteristics
of Cocteau's work. The remainder of the anthology contains excerpts from Cocteau's
writings and screenplays, along with a good selection of critical and subjective
evaluations by people like Andre Bazin, Chris Marker, and Jean Marais. A
filmography, bibliography, discography, phonography, chronology of references, and
index are included. Recommended for special collections.

Keller, Majorie. THE UNTUTORED EYE: CHILDHOOD IN THE FILMS OF COCTEAU,
CORNELL, AND BRAKHAGE. Cranbury: Fairleigh Dickinson University Press, 1986.
Illustrated. 268pp.
    An unusual study focusing on three AVANT-GARDE filmmakers, this stimulating
project stresses the importance of thematic content in the history of AVANT-GARDE
cinema. As Keller explains, "Childhood is a particularly central theme in a tradition
where artists have used the film medium to reflect on their own uniqueness." In
describing why Cocteau is included, Keller points out that "In all his creative
endeavors, he considered himself a poet: of the theater, the novel, journalism, and
film. Moreover, his work in film remains vitally close to literary sources. He relied
a great deal on the Romantic tradition, especially in THE BLOOD OF A POET (1930).
BEAUTY AND THE BEAST (1945) was generated from a fairy tale. And he was
indebted to his own theatrical Orphism in the making of the film version." Endnotes,
a bibliography, and an index are included. Recommended for special collections.

Peters, Arthur King. JEAN COCTEAU AND ANDRE GIDE: AN ABRASIVE
FRIENDSHIP. New Brunswick: Rutgers University Press, 1973. Illustrated. 426pp.

Phelps, Robert, ed. PROFESSIONAL SECRETS: AN AUTOBIOGRAPHY OF JEAN
COCTEAU--DRAWN FROM HIS LIFETIME WRITINGS. Trans. Richard Howard. New
York: Farrar, Straus and Giroux, 1970. Illustrated. 331pp.
    Drawing from more than thirty books and memoirs on the great French artist,
Phelps has put together a stimulating and valuable record of the man and his
thoughts. "All his life," the author writes, "he was a WUNDERKIND, an eager,
trusting, enchanted (and enchanting) child. He believed in fairy tales, in secret
signs, in 'MONSTRES SACRES,' and in emblematic destinies like those of Oedipus,

Orpheus, Antigone, and his own 'ENFANTS TERRIBLES.' At the same time, he was the sort of child who urgently needs to please, to hold the attention of the grown-ups, to feel himself noticed, cherished, forgiven, remembered, and loved. In a sense, everything he wrote was an effort to delight or seduce." Phelps arranges his biography of Cocteau's fifty years as a master BRICOLEUR in the traditional arts into four major parts: LE PRINCE FRIVOLE--the years from 1889 to 1914; LE RAPPEL A L'ORDRE--the years from 1914 to 1929; LE SANG D'UN POETE--the years from 1929 to 1946; and LA DIFFICULTE D'ETRE--the years from 1946 to 1963. Most of the observations are drawn from thirty works by Cocteau himself. Regrettably, there is no index. Well worth browsing.

*Steegmuller, Francis. COCTEAU: A BIOGRAPHY. Boston: Little, Brown and Company, 1970. Illustrated. 583pp.
        Winner of the National Book Award, this outstanding biography separates the fact from fiction of the fifty-year history of Cocteau's fights, failures, and triumphs. Steegmuller, in lively, interesting, and scholarly writing, presents a revealing history of Paris as well as an in-depth study of Cocteau's homosexual world. This is the book to read for those interested in a serious study of Cocteau with. Appendices, endnotes, a bibliography, and an index are included. Highly recommended for special collections.

JEAN RENOIR

*Bazin, Andre. JEAN RENOIR. Ed. and Introduction Francois Truffaut. Trans. W. W. Halsey II and William H. Simon. New York: Simon and Schuster, 1971. Illustrated. 320pp.
        A highly respected book on film aesthetics, this reconstructed biography taken from the great critic's reviews, essays, and commentaries on Renoir offers an original and feisty assessment not only of the impressive filmmaker, but also of AUTEUR theory. According to Truffaut's introduction, "JEAN RENOIR is the BEST book on the cinema, written by the BEST critic, about the BEST director." And Andrew Sarris comments that "The effect of this collective enterprise is to shed new light on the source of modern anti-montage aesthetics in the appreciation of Renoir by Bazin."[462] Divided into two major sections, a history of Renoir's life and career and analyses of three key films in the 1930s, the superb study stresses both Renoir's techniques and humanistic values. An index is included. Highly recommended for all collections.

Braudy, Leo. JEAN RENOIR: THE WORLD OF HIS FILMS. New York: Doubleday and Company, 1972. Illustrated. 286pp.
        More than a film-by-film analysis, this significant study explores Renoir's cinematic genius in lucid, detailed, and absorbing prose. The author's approach to thirty-six of Renoir's more than forty films, made in four countries over four-five years, includes references to the artist's other work in drama, literature, and biography, "in terms first of the two great motifs nature and theater, then in terms of the definition of society, to which they must be related, and finally in terms of Renoir's emphasis on actors and the emergent theme of the artist, who must make the coherence and resolve the conflicts between art and nature, individuality and society, instinct and civilization, into a larger and more comprehensive vision of the world--the contingent dialectic of Renoir's films." Of particular interest in the book's thoughtful six chapters is Braudy's treatment of the basic relationships in the filmmaker's art;

---

[462]   Andrew Sarris, "Bazin & Renoir: An Uncanny Rapport," VILLAGE VOICE (June 28, 1973):70. For another perspective, see Paul Thomas, "The Sorcerer's Apprentice: Bazin and Truffaut on Renoir," SIGHT AND SOUND 44:1 (Winter 1974/75):16-8.

the stage contrasted with realism, the magical versus the mechanical, the flexible versus the inflexible, and the social commitment contrasted with an aesthetic distance. Stills, a filmography, and an index are provided. Recommended for special collections.

*Durgnat, Raymond. JEAN RENOIR. Berkeley: University of California Press, 1974. Illustrated. 429pp.

A massive collection of material presented in pedantic fashion, this detailed biography offers an admiring look at Renoir's films while downplaying the filmmaker's weaknesses and failures. Sixty-four uneven chapters take us through the artist's life and work, suggesting many original and intriguing observations, often supplemented by numerous quotations and allusions to other material. The major drawback is that Durgnat not only avoids footnoting his material but also those references that appear in the bibliography often lack complete and accurate information. A bibliography and index are included. Well worth browsing.

Faulkner, Christopher. JEAN RENOIR: A GUIDE TO REFERENCES AND RESOURCES. Boston: G. K. Hall and Company, 1979. 356pp.

The basic book on Renoir, this resource guide does a fine job not only of collecting important data, but also of evaluating the material. The biographical chronicle lists the essential details on Renoir's life, beginning with his ancestry, family, and birth on September 15, 1894, in Paris. Brief annotations comment on the boy's being the subject of his father's impressionistic paintings; Renoir's experiences (twice wounded) in the World War I cavalry and the air force; the young man's postwar work in pottery and ceramics and its later effect on the films; his first marriage at twenty-five to Andree Heuschling and her influence on his becoming a filmmaker (stage-named Catherine Hessling, she appeared in his silent films of 1924-1929, till they separated in 1930); the problems he faced with the advent of sound, succeeding only when his second sound film, THE BITCH/LA CHIENNE in 1931, established his international reputation; his involvement with "The October Group" and his shift in 1932 to left-wing politics. Then follows entires on the filmmaker's golden age from 1935 to 1939, the difficulties he experienced because of the political unrest in France, his arrival in Hollywood, and his contract with 20th Century-Fox in 1941; his life in the film capital the next five years doing films for Universal and RKO; his marriage in 1944 to Dido Freire and his sole Oscar nomination the following year for directing THE SOUTHERNER (he won an honorary Oscar in 1975), his becoming an American citizen in 1946 while also retaining his French citizenship. Then in later years his trip to India to make THE RIVER/LE FLEUVE/IL FIUME in 1949, his return to France in 1951, the films he made until retiring in 1969, and the books he worked on till his death at eighty-four in February, 1979. In the section critiquing Renoir's career, Faulkner points out the flaws in the various a-historical approaches to the filmmaker's work and argues that Renoir's career should be divided into two parts: the one before 1939, the year he left France, and the one from 1940 on, when he arrived in America. Included as well in this outstanding study are a Renoir filmography, an annotated listing of primary sources for a study of Renoir, a splendid critical bibliography of secondary sources, a listing of archives and libraries containing useful Renoir material, a list of distributors, a film index, and an author index. Highly recommended for special collections.

Faulkner, Christopher. THE SOCIAL CINEMA OF JEAN RENOIR. Princeton: Princeton University Press, 1986. 210pp.

Conceived when Faulkner was preparing his laudable JEAN RENOIR: A GUIDE TO REFERENCES AND RESOURCES, this book seeks to fill the scholarly gap concerning Renoir's political activity in France during the 1930s, and to reinforce Faulkner's belief that the filmmaker's career changes significantly in the 1950s. The reason for the shift in Renoir's work, according to the author, is his association with the French left and his thematic use of Popular Front values between 1935 and 1939. As in his earlier book, Faulkner takes issue with orthodox AUTEUR studies that insist that Renoir made essentially one film throughout his entire career and points out that "persistent, unspoken assumptions underlying studies of individual authorship have produced a massive repression of Renoir's political allegiances and the immediate social intelligibility of the films he directed." Following a stimulating introduction discussing the relationship between aesthetics and ethnography, Faulkner uses two chapters to analyze seven films Renoir made in the 1930s, one chapter to discuss two of Renoir's films made in America during the 1940s, and one chapter to discuss three films Renoir made in India and France during the 1950s. Among the conclusions the author reaches is that the later films abandoned the artist's socialist ideology and concentrated instead on the notion of aesthetic harmony as the means to achieving his pre-WWII goals. The writing is impressive, the revisionist content exciting, and the effect persuasive. Footnotes, a bibliography, and an index are included. Recommended for special collections.

*Gilliatt, Penelope. JEAN RENOIR: ESSAYS, CONVERSATIONS, REVIEWS. New York: McGraw-Hill Book Company, 1975. Illustrated. 136pp.
     Originally published as articles, interviews, and critiques in THE NEW YORK TIMES and THE NEW YORKER, this affectionate collection records the feelings of the respected critic not only for a friend, but also for a much admired artist. "This book," Gilliatt explains, "is by no means a comprehensive book about his films, although I have seen them many times. Nor is it distinctly analytic: his work forbids distance, since it invites you into his company, like great music or Chekhov. His work is eloquent enough to talk for itself, and so is he. I hoped more to transcribe some of the taste and purity of his conversation, and the mood and technique of the movies that I particularly love." Gilliatt's observations were recorded over a five-year period (1969-1974) and are organized into three major sections: "LE GRAND MONSIEUR DE DEUX GUERRES, LIBERE PAR LUI-MEME," "LE MENEUR DE JEU," and "Concerning 11 Films." A filmography and an index are included. Well worth browsing.

*Leprohon, Pierre, ed. JEAN RENOIR. Trans. Brigid Elson. New York: Crown Publishers, 1971. Illustrated. 256pp.
     Originally published by CINEMA D'AUJOURD HUI in 1967, this worthwhile study serves as a good companion piece to the Braudy book, not only because of Leprohon's helpful biographical and critical essay, but also because it contains original, textual material on Renoir. The first of the anthology's five major sections contains the editor's critical commentary on Renoir's life and his films from THE WATER GIRL/THE WHIRLPOOL OF FATE/LA FILLE DE L'EAU (1924) to THE ELUSIVE CORPORAL/THE VANISHING CORPORAL/LA CAPORAL EPINGLE (1962). Following Leprohon's AUTEUR analysis, there are Renoir's personal observations, excerpts from his works, a range of critical reactions to his work, and comments by people like Jean Cocteau, Jacques Becker, Gaston Modot, and Andre-G. Brunelin. A filmography, bibliography, and index are also included. Well worth browsing.

*Mast, Gerald. FILMGUIDE TO "THE RULES OF THE GAME." Bloomington: Indiana University Press, 1973. 85pp.
     "Jean Renoir," Mast tells us, "is one of the few film directors to be acknowledged an artistic master by all schools of film criticism--literary, auteurist, humanist, scholarly, popularist, sociological, and technical. Renoir's films seem to satisfy everyone's notions of what a great work of film art should be: interesting story, vital characters, brilliant acting, social criticism, poetic symbolism, philosophical observations, structural complexity, and stunning visual compositions. In an astonishingly long career (1924-69) no other director of films (with the obvious exception of Chaplin) has created so many works of consistent high quality and so

few works that require apology or rationalization from admirers." After providing the credits to THE RULES OF THE GAME/LA REGLE DU JEU (1939) and an outline of the film, Mast offers a useful overview of the director's career, arguing the by-now orthodox AUTEUR position that Renoir's humanistic concerns are what unite this masterpiece to all of Renoir's other films. The most valuable section of this "review" book are Mast's extended analysis of the film and a summary critique. Because his AUTEURIST approach emphasizes the literary and aesthetic qualities of Renoir's approach, contemporary schools of film criticism will find the analysis limited. It does, however, provide one valuable perspective on a gifted filmmaker. A filmography and bibliography are included, but no index is provided. Worth browsing.

*Renoir, Jean. "RULES OF THE GAME": A FILM BY JEAN RENOIR. Trans. John McGrath and Maureen Teitelbaum. New York: Simon and Schuster, 1970. Illustrated. 172pp.
     One of the few books in this series with a significant collection of essays in addition to the text of the film itself, this publication opens with a valuable quotation by Renoir: "When I made THE RULES OF THE GAME I knew what I was doing. I knew the malady which was afflicting my contemporaries. This does not mean that I knew how to give a clear idea of this in my film. But instinct guided me. My awareness of the danger we were in, enabled me to find the right situations, gave me the right words, and my friends thought the same way I did. How worried we were! I think the film is good. But it is not very difficult to work well when your anxiety acts as a compass, pointing you in the right direction." The interviews with Renoir on "The Birth of RULES OF THE GAME," "The Era of the Auteur," and the search for the film's locations provide useful perpectives on examining the film. The latter also contains observation's by Marcel Dalio, the film's star. Other bonuses are a short analysis by Joel W. Finler and a brief historical note on the problems connected with the film's production. Well worth browsing.

*Renoir, Jean. "GRAND ILLUSION": A FILM BY JEAN RENOIR. Trans. Marianne Alexandre and Andrew Sinclair. New York: Simon and Schuster, 1968. Illustrated. 108pp.
     Except for Renoir's personal assurances that the story on which the film is based and a brief commentary by Erich von Stroheim on his intital meeting with the director, this publication deals exclusively with the text of the film. Well worth browsing.

Renoir, Jean. MY LIFE AND MY FILMS. New York: Atheneum, 1974. Illustrated. 287pp.
     Renoir begins his third book, and the first about himself, in a somewhat misleading way: "The history of the cinema, above all, of the French cinema, during the past half-century may be summarized as the war of the film-maker against the industry. I am proud to have had a share in that triumphant struggle." Yet the story he unfolds in this lightweight autobiography is one of a man's friendships and acquaintances rather than of an artist's challenges in creating film masterpieces. Renoir believes not only that Bazin has brilliantly analyzed his films, but also that we are largely the product of our times. Thus he hopes to shed light on his life and career by telling us about the people and the events that brought him to his eightieth birthday. Anyone vaguely familiar with Renoir's work should find something of interest in these gentle reminiscences about growing up the second son of a famous painter, fighting in World War I, implementing a desire to make films, learning to collaborate with the people involved in the film productions, and why it is necessary to find new friends to suit the times. Particularly enjoyable are his anecdotes about Dedee (Catherine Hessling, his first wife), and the reasons why he was forced to choose between his marriage and his commitment to film; his reminder of how popular

Hitler was at the start of World War II, because "so many decent people .   .   .
[counted] on Hitler to rid them of things which irritated them, such as unpunctual
trains and strikes in the public services"; his thumbnail comments on famous
personalities he worked with in Paris and Hollywood; his opinion that the greatest
danger we face is progress, "not because it doesn't work but precisely because it
does"; and his views on art in general. Some readers, like Roger Greenspun, may
object strongly to Renoir's repeated attacks on American filmmaking. In Greenspun's
words, "Generalities about the individualism of French cinema vs. the manufactured
'perfection' of Hollywood .   .   .   are predictable enough (and untrue enough) to
tax any reader's patience."[463] An index is included. Well worth browsing.

*Sesonske, Alexander. JEAN RENOIR: THE FRENCH FILMS, 1924-1939.   Cambridge:
Harvard University Press, 1980. Illustrated. 463pp.
    A highly regarded study by a scholar who knew Renoir for more than a decade,
this detailed analysis of the filmmaker's work during the 1930s is the most complete
examination to-date. Except for the first of the book's twenty-one chapters--which
discusses CATHERINE and THE WATER GIRL/THE WHIRLPOOL OF FATE/LA FILLE
DE L'EAU (1924), each chapter deals individually with a single film, providing
production information and technical descriptions of specific scenes. "I have not often
offered overall evaluations of any film," Sesonske explains, "although it should be
obvious that I believe all of them interesting and several of them masterpieces." He
also points out that "For most of the films I have tried to show how the cinematic forms
that constitute Renoir's style in this period work to enhance, strengthen, sometimes
even create the dramatic substance of the film or to convey a comment or point of
view on the characters, their situation, or the world they inhabit."   Sesonske's
approach is aided considerably by numerous frame enlargements from the films. The
book's major drawbacks, neatly summarized by Paul Thomas, include the absence of
an overiding theme resulting in the book's chapters' reading like individual
monologues, a number of editorial errors, and the author's failure to broaden his
conclusions from specific comments to general observations. Having made these
criticisms, Paul, like most readers of this invaluable publication, concludes that the
book deserves to be studied by experienced readers who love Renoir's films.[464]
Endnotes, a bibliography, and an index are included. Recommended for special
collections.

JEAN VIGO

*Gomes, P. E. Salles, JEAN VIGO. Trans.   Allan Francovich. Berkeley: University
of California Press, 1972. Illustrated.   256pp.
    In this useful and well-written biographical and critical study, Gomes offers an
unusual portrait of a superb artist who made sharp and powerful social comments in
his four important films before he died at twenty-nine of rheumatic septicaemia.   Born
on April 26, 1905, in Paris, Jean Vigo was the son of Eugene Bonaventure de Vigo,
a militant anarchist who was murdered twelve years later in prison. The harsh
treatment afforded his father haunted Vigo throughout his life, and he waged a
constant war against authority wherever he found it. Frail and sickly, his troubled
childhood turned him into a political libertarian and social misfit. He did, however,
develop a love for photography by the time he was in his teens and proved to be a
good student at his second boarding school at Chartres. Upon his graduation in 1925,

---

[463]   Roger Greenspun, "Possibly the Greatest: MY LIFE AND MY FILMS," NEW YORK TIMES
BOOK REVIEW (November 17, 1974):7.

[464]   Paul Thomas, "Book Review: JEAN RENOIR: THE FRENCH FILMS, 1924-1935 [sic]," FILM
QUARTERLY 34:1 (Summer 1981):25-7.

the twenty-year-old Vigo decided to devote his life to filmmaking and to repairing his father's reputation. Over the next nine years, until his death on October 5, 1934, Vigo, who had contracted tuberculosis, worked with his father's friends in a number of social causes, while making only four films, two of which were experimental shorts, A PROPOS DE NICE (1929) and TARIS (1931). Nevertheless, the two features--ZERO FOR CONDUCT/ZERO DE CONDUITE (1933) and L'ATALANTE (1934)--are considered among France's most treasured films of the decade.

Originally published in French in 1957, this biography was authorized by Vigo's family. Chapter one, dealing with Vigo's father, who took the name Miguel Almereyda because it "sounded Spanish and anarchist," describes the influence that the revolutionary had on his son. Chapter 2, detailing Vigo's life and career up to his second experimental film TARIS, provides valuable information on his schooling, his health problems, how he developed a love for film, and the roots of his revolutionary faith. Chapters 3 and 4, analyzing his two feature films, offer valuable information on his cinematic technique and the inspirations for the films. Chapter 5, describing Vigo's final days and his death, summarize his political and artistic values at the end of his life. The author provides a helpful appendix, commenting on "The Critical Success and Impact of Vigo's Works." Overall, the material is fascinating, the information significant, and the tone appreciative. Endnotes, a filmography, and an index are included. Recommended for special collections.

Simon, William G. THE FILMS OF JEAN VIGO. Ann Arbor: UMI Research Press, 1981. 130pp.

Originally written as Simon's 1974 Ph.D. dissertation for New York University, this revised edition focuses on Vigo's cinematic output. "Although he only made four films," the author writes, "totalling approximately 165 minutes, something under three hours, this limited output earned him his present reputation as a pre-eminent master of film, one of the great directors." Simon stresses the differences in mode and structure of the four films, arguing that "the diversity in their conception and structural principles is almost unprecedented in film history, even for directors with vastly larger OEUVRES." The author documents the reasons for the different tasks that Vigo set out to accomplish in each of his films and how each film is unique for the genre it represents. While other studies concentrate on the filmmaker's originality and thematic concerns, Simon provides the best detailed analysis of what made the films so unconventional and original. Endnotes, a bibliography, and an index are included. Recommended for special collections.

*Smith, John M. JEAN VIGO. New York: Praeger Publishers, 1972.   Illustrated. 144pp.

In this account of Vigo's four films, Smith focuses on the resources for Vigo's films and their thematic concerns. "Every major work of art, or group of such works," the author asserts, "can be seen as standing at the end of a long development. The outstanding early works of the cinema--Melies, Sennett, Chaplin, Griffith--could not have sprung solely from the infant medium itself; it also draws on long developments in the theatre (including vaudeville and the music-hall) and literature. The films of Jean Vigo concentrated in the years from 1930 [sic] to 1934, have an analogous position, when the cinema had completed its first great cycle, that of the silent film; Vigo is able to draw fully on the achieved fullness of the medium--a stage has been completed, and is there for him to use. In addition, he draws on three main national traditions, the French, the American, and the Russian." Smith offers his useful thematic interpretations of Vigo's works in four chapters, one film per chapter. While a number of the observations appear forced and debatable, the overall perspective of the study is intriguing and stimulating. A chronology of Vigo's life and career, a filmography, and a bibliography are included, but no index is provided. Well worth browsing.

FILMS

JEAN BENOIT-LEVY

LA MATERNELLE (France--16mm: 1932, 86 mins., b/w, English subtitles, sound, R-MMA)
 Jean Benoit-Levy and Marie Epstein's case study of an unwanted child is not only an example of the period's concern with psychological insight and concentrated characterization, but is also one of the early uses of the documentary approaches in a film.

MARCEL CARNE

DAYBREAK/LE JOUR SE LEVE (France--16mm: 1940, 85 mins., b/w, English subtitles, sound, R-BUD, EMG, FES, IMA, IOW, KIT, TFF, WES; S-IMA, REE, TFF)
 Scripted by Jacques Viot, adapted by Jacques Prevert, and directed by Marcel Carne, this tragic story deals with the fate of a man (Jean Gabin) who kills the person who raped his sweetheart (Arletty) and spends his last night fending off the police before he kills himself at dawn. For many critics, this film represents the high point of France's period of "poetic realism."[465]

RENE CLAIR

THE MILLION/LE MILLION (France--16mm: 1930, 90 mins., b/w, no English titles, sound, R-IMA, MMA, TFF; S-KIT, REE, TFF)
 An innovative musical comedy illustrates Clair's experimental genius in treating motion with sound and tells the story of a penniless bohemian whose fortune rests on a lottery ticket. One of the film's strengths is its remarkable use of counterpoint, and it demonstrates the broad appeal of the director's screen technique. Moreover, as Lucy Fischer points out, "Clair not only elaborates the poetic possibilities of the musical sound film but situates within the work itself a literal reference to the formal model upon which it is based."[466]

GIVE US FREEDOM/A NOUS LA LIBERTE (France--16mm: 1931, 97 mins., b/w, sound, English subtitles, R-BUD, FES, FNC, IMA, IOW, KIT, TFF; S-REE)
 Clair's brilliant film indictment of industrialization demonstrates his unique ability to mesh traditional conventions with innovating sound techniques. The story concerns an escaped convict (Raymond Cordy) who becomes an industrial giant and who then rejects the world of business for the life of a vagabond. In addition to many praiseworthy editing methods, the film also indicates the somber direction that AVANT-GARDE filmmakers were taking by the early 1930s.[467]

UNDER THE ROOFS OF PARIS/SOUS LES TOITS DE PARIS (France--16mm: 1930, 96 mins., b/w, sound, English subtitles, R-BUD, EMG, FES, FNC, IMA, KIT, TFF, WES; S-KIT, REE)

---

[465] For more information, see Philip Kemp, "LE JOUR SE LEVE," THE INTERNATIONAL DICTIONARY OF FILMS AND FILMMAKERS: VOLUME I, pp.229-30.

[466] Fischer, p.50

[467] Bosley Crowther, "A Nous La Liberte," THE GREAT FILMS, pp.88-91.

A brisk musical comedy about young love in the Paris garrets, this early sound film exemplifies the great writer-director's theories on contrapuntal sound. "In this film," explains R. C. Dale, "the plot does indeed matter about as much as the plot of a symphony."[468]

JEAN COCTEAU

THE BLOOD OF A POET/LE SANG D'UN POETE (France-16mm: 1932, 51 mins., b/w, English subtitles, sound, R-BUD, EMG, FES, FNC, IOW, IVY, KIT, TFF; S-FES, FNC, REE, TFF)
    Cocteau began his first of many intriguing and puzzling film poems with this complex screenplay about a poet who has "to die" in order to be reborn as a true artist.[469]

MARCEL PAGNOL

THE BAKER'S WIFE/LA FEMME DU BOULANGER (France--(16mm: 1938, 120 mins., b/w, English subtitles, sound, R-REE; R-REE)
    Based on Jean Giono's novel, JEAN LE BLUE, the film, scripted and directed by Pagnol, shows what happens to a French village when its baker (Raimu) has marital problems. According to Armes, the work "can stand as a summation of Marcel Pagnol's work in the cinema and of a certain style of 1930s cinema."[470]

JEAN RENOIR

GRAND ILLUSION/LA GRANDE ILLUSION (France--16mm: 1938, 111 mins., b/w, English subtitles, sound, R-BUD, COR, FNC, IMA, IVY, JAN, TFF, WES, WHO; S-IVY, REE, TFF)
    Renoir directed and co-scripted with Charles Spaak, this brilliant anti-war film about a German prisoner-of-war camp for Allied soldiers. Jean Gabin and Pierre Fresnay play the two Frenchmen shot down by the Germans and interned by Erich von Stroheim. The relationship between Fresnay and von Stroheim, both officers and aristocrats separated only by national allegiances, underscores one aspect of the film's pacifist message as the men struggle to resolve not only their differences, but also the fact that World War I signalled an end to the life and values of Europe's LA BELLE EPOQUE. At the same time, Fresnay's relationship with Gabin and Marcel Dalio (who plays the Jewish prisoner Rosenthal) identifies both the film's attack on anti-Semitism and the class system, as well as the stupidity of war. Particularly interesting is the film's ability to illustrate the many "grand illusions" that its characters have about race, class, creed, and nationalism. Another extraordinary feature is Renoir's ability to preach against war without showing the battle conventions of war films and without

---

[468]   R. C. Dale, THE FILMS OF RENE CLAIR, Volume 1: EXPOSITION AND ANALYSIS (Methuen: The Scarecrow Press, 1986), p.140.

[469]   For more information, see Roy Armes, "LE SANG D'UN POETE," THE INTERNATIONAL DICTIONARY OF FILMS AND FILMMAKERS: VOLUME I, pp.409-10.

[470]   Roy Armes, "LA FEMME DU BOULANGER," THE INTERNATIONAL DICTIONARY OF FILMS AND FILMMAKERS: VOLUME I, pp.154-5.

resorting to sentimentality.[471] Although nominated for Best Picture, it lost the Oscar to YOU CAN'T TAKE IT WITH YOU.

THE RULES OF THE GAME/LA REGLE DU JEU (France--16mm: 1939, 110 mins., b/w, English subtitles, sound, R-BUD, COR, EMG, FES, FNC, IVY, JAN, KIT, TFF, WES; S-IMA, REE, TFF)

Renoir directed and co-scripted with Karl Koch and Camille Francois, this satirical and disturbing story about love, evil, and death in the pre-WWII society of the French upper class. The complicated plot involves the gathering of a group of people at the estate of the Marquis, Robert de la Chesnaye (Marcel Dalio) and his wife, Christine (Nora Gregor). During the course of the weekend, the guests and family servants rekindle old love affairs, hunt, party, discuss the changing values in the world, and comment on French culture. Near the end of the film, Andre Jurieu (Roland Toutain), a noted pilot and lover of Christine, brought to the Chateau by Octave (Renoir), Christine's true love, is killed accidentally and the Marquis dismisses it as "regrettable." In depicting the jaded morality and class-consciousness of the guests and their hosts, Renoir explores the sordid and crass life-styles of the French elite through a series of brilliant cinematic techniques stressing the contrasts between nature and the theater, the ironies of life, and the conflicts that emerge from contrasting life-styles. The film is considered by many critics to be Renoir's greatest work.[472]

JEAN VIGO

L'ATALANTE (France--16mm: 1934, 82 mins., b/w, English subtitles, sound, R-BUD, EMG, KIT, TFF; S-KIT, REE, TFF)

---

[471]   For a summary of the film's origins and current history, see Christopher Faulkner, JEAN RENOIR: A GUIDE TO REFERENCES AND RESOURCES, pp.103-6. In addition to the many commentaries on the film, also listed in Faulkner, see James Kearns, "Classics Revisited: LA GRANDE ILLUSION," FILM QUARTERLY 14:2 (Winter 1960):10-17; Eugene Lourie, "Grand Illusions," AMERICAN FILM 10:4 (January-February 1985):29-32, 34; Anthony Cagle, "Program Notes: LA GRANDE ILLUSION," CINEMATEXAS PROGRAM NOTES 11:3 (October 26, 1976):19-23; Rita TheBerge, "Program Notes: LA GRANDE ILLUSION," ibid., 11:3 (October 26, 1976):19-23; John Gibson, "Program Notes: LA GRANDE ILLUSION," ibid., 26:3 (March 20, 1984):15-8; and Robin Wood, "LA GRANDE ILLUSION," THE INTERNATIONAL DICTIONARY OF FILMS AND FILMMAKERS: VOLUME I, pp.182-4.

[472]   The best summary of the origins and fate of the film, as well as an annotated bibliography for material on the film is in Faulkner's reference guide. For more information, see Suzanne Budgen, "Some Notes on the Source of LA REGLE DU JEU," TAKE ONE 1:12 (July-August 1968):8-10; Charles Raimirez-Berg, "Program Notes: LA REGLE DU JEU," CINEMATEXAS PROGRAM NOTES 7: 26 (October 16, 1974):1-7; George A. Wood, Jr., "Game Theory and THE RULES OF THE GAME," CINEMA JOURNAL 13:1 (Fall 1973):25-34; Michael Litle, "Sound Track: RULES OF THE GAME," ibid., pp.35-44; Julia Lesage, "S/Z and RULES OF THE GAME," JUMP CUT 12/13 (Winter 1976-77:45-51; Philippe R. Perebinossoff, "Theatricals in Jean Renoir's THE RULES OF THE GAME and GRAND ILLUSION," LITERATURE/FILM QUARTERLY 5:1 (Winter 1977):50-6; Robin Wood, "REGLE DU JEU," THE INTERNATIONAL DICTIONARY OF FILMS AND FILMMAKERS: VOLUME I, pp.389-91; Jacques Joly, "Between Theater and Life: Jean Renoir and RULES OF THE GAME," trans. Randall Conrad, FILM QUARTERLY 21:2 (Winter 1967-68):2-9; and Richard Whitehall, "Great Films of the Century: LE REGLE DU JEU," FILMS AND FILMING 9:2 (November 1962):21-5.

Co-scripted by Vigo and Albert Riera, based on a scenario by Jean Guinee (R. de Guichen), Vigo's last feature film is a lyrical look at newlyweds (Jean Daste and Dita Parlo) and their problems aboard a barge as it moves through France's internal canals. Boris Kaufman's memorable photography and Maurice Jaubert's lyrical music enhance considerably Vigo's marvelous ability to create scenes of exquisite charm and profound emotions. Although the film lacks a tight narrative structure, the combined scenes and sequences provide one of the most enchanting experiences in film history. As William G. Simon points out, "Vigo expresses the power and value of the imagery. The very practice of Vigo's art is characterized by a freedom from convention and by a constant inventiveness and originality of form and style."[473] Michel Simon gives a brilliant performance as Pere Jules, as the old sailor who works on the barge and helps the couple adjust to life and marriage.

ZERO FOR CONDUCT/ZERO DE CONDUITE (France--16mm: 1933, 44 mins., b/w, sound, English subtitles, R-BUD, EMG, FES, FNC, IMA, KIT, TFF; S-IMA, KIT, REE)
        This is the first feature-length movie made by Jean Vigo and concerns life in a French boarding school. Scripted, directed, and edited by the great filmmaker, its marvelous irony, satire, and sensitivity to the oppressiveness of incompetent schoolteachers makes the film a useful reminder to educators as to what teaching is all about. Boris Kaufman's cinematography and Maurice Jaubert's music add considerably to the film's effective attack on the injustices perpetuated in the name of a basic education.[474]

GERMANY

Although the German film industry was experiencing considerable financial difficulties during the mid-1920s, it had one major advantage over other film-producing nations making the transition from silent to talking films. German scientists Gunther Vogt, Erich Engl, and Josef Massolle had developed recording patents for Tri-Ergon that were then perfected at Tobias-Klangfilm after World War I. Thus, an interesting situation occurred. On the one hand, the stabilization of the mark at the start of the 1920s forced many German film companies into bankruptcy. Taking advantage of the monetary crisis, American firms like Paramount and MGM inundated the German market with Hollywood products. To defend its national industry, the Weimer Republic, like the British Parliament, established a quota system, stipulating that for every American film distributed, a German movie had to be made. Although many of these "quota quickies" never reached the screen, Hollywood filmmakers were sufficiently worried so that they negotiated the "Parufamet Agreement" of 1925, making UFA, Germany's major producing and exhibiting organization, dependent on American money. That is, in exchange for a substantial loan, UFA gave Paramount and MGM almost CARTE BLANCHE in the nation's

---

[473]   William G. Simon, THE FILMS OF JEAN VIGO (Ann Arbor: UMI Research Press, 1981), p.120. For more information, see Eric Rhode, "Jean Vigo," TOWER OF BABEL, pp.17-34; Bart Teush, "The Playground of Jean Vigo," FILM HERITAGE 9:1 (Fall 1973):11-22; Robin Wood, "L'ATALANTE," THE INTERNATIONAL DICTIONARY OF FILMS AND FILMMAKERS: VOLUME I, pp.40-1; John Grierson, "L'ATALANTE: A Review," CINEMA QUARTERLY 3 (Autumn 1934):46-9; Charles Raimirez-Berg, "Program Notes: L'ATALANTE," CINEMATEXAS PROGRAM NOTES 7:22 (October 9, 1974):1-6; and Nick Barbaro, "Program Notes: L'ATALANTE," ibid., 10:2 (February 26, 1976):39-45.

[474]   For more information, see M. B. White, "ZERO DE CONDUITE," THE INTERNATIONAL DICTIONARY OF FILMS AND FILMMAKERS: VOLUME I, pp.535-6.

production and exhibition policies.[475] This, in turn, made German filmmakers very receptive to Hollywood's early sound experiments, especially in the area of musicals. The most prominent example was von Sternberg's THE BLUE ANGEL/DER BLAUE ENGEL (1929), with its haunting mixture of sound and beautifully composed MISE EN SCENE.

On the other hand, the sound patents owned by Tobias-Klangfilm allowed the German film companies to move quickly into talking films and sound experimentation. Thus, early German filmmakers contributed significantly to the development of sound film theory. For example, G. W. Pabst's WESTFRONT 1918 (1930) and COMRADESHIP/KAMERADSCHAFT (1931) illustrated the compatibility of silent film camerawork with modern sound principles in pacifist war films and demonstrated how sound could enhance cinematic naturalism in his important adaption of Brecht's THE THREEPENNY OPERA/DIE DREIGROSCHENOPER (1931). Leontine Sagan's GIRLS IN UNIFORM/MAEDCHEN IN UNIFORM (1931) used dialogue and striking sound effects to undermine senseless discipline in a woman's school. Also worthy of note was a series of "mountain films" like THE BLUE LIGHT (1931), depicting brave rescues of helpless people trapped on the German Alps.

The most memorable German contributions to sound film theory, however, were found in Fritz Lang's M (1931) and THE LAST WILL OF DR. MABUSE/DAS TESTAMENT DES DR. MABUSE (1932). The former work, regarded by many historians as the director's crowning achievement, not only captures the cynicism and despair of the pre-Hitler period, but also masterfully crafts the use of expressionism in sight and sound imagery. The later film, in which the arch criminal Dr. Mabuse is presumably modeled after Hitler, reveals Lang's expressionistic skills in relating popular films to political protests. In this case, the Fascists recognized many of the obvious parallels and eventually had the film banned.

By the mid-1930s, the Nazi regime, working closely with the powerful Alfred Hugenberg, head of UFA, had taken over the German film industry and turned it into an escapist hate-machine for Josef Goebbels's calculated film propaganda. In response, many prominent filmmakers--e.g., Fritz Lang, Erich Pommer, E. A. Dupont, Robert Wiene, Robert Siodmak, Billy Wilder, Max Ophuls, and Douglas Sirk, Fred Zinnemann--fled Germany and made their way to Hollywood. As discussed in Chapter 2, the Nazis orchestrated the mass media to suit their political, economic, and social objectives. Political censorship was strictly enforced at every level of the film process; racial policies drove Jewish performers, producers, distributors, screenwriters, critics, and exhibitors out of the industry; and importation of foreign films was carefully regulated to insure that only escapist films compatible with Nazi values were acceptable. Whether one accepts the argument that Goebbels did not nationalize the German film industry until 1942 and thereby left the commercial cinema alone until then is secondary to what was done in the industry and how Nazi ideology controlled the film experience from 1933 to 1945. It is also important to understand that by the mid-1930s, the state was financing specific types of films, the most controversial being blatant anti-Semitic works like THE ETERNAL JEW/DER EWIGE JUDE (1940) and the Leni Riefenstahl documentaries. Some historians, discussed in Chapter 2, point to the artistic quality of certain historical, documentary, and biographical films and argue that despite the ruthless nature of the Nazi regime, the fundamental skill of German filmmakers remained relatively high. Most historians, however, feel that the quality of the German film industry deteriorated considerably as a result of state control and censorship.

---

[475] For more information, see FROM CALIGARI TO HITLER, pp.132-4; and Rhode, pp.170-1.

BOOKS

FRITZ LANG

*Von Harbou, Thea. M/FRITZ LANG. Trans. Nicholas Garnham.   London: Lorrimer Publishing, 1968. Illustrated. 112pp.

A useful publication based on the original German screenplay for the 1931 film, this edition includes cast and technical credits, along with a brief introduction to the screenplay. According to Garnham, Lang views the world from the perspective of a Greek deity, "imposing a pattern on a warring universe." That is, the filmmaker's style, "His awareness of the forces of evil and chaos, always on the prowl, makes him fasten like a vice round his world and his characters." Well worth browsing.

JOSEF VON STERNBERG

*Mann, Heinrich, and Josef von Sternberg. THE BLUE ANGEL: THE NOVEL AND THE FILM. New York: Frederich Unger Publishing Company, 1979. Illustrated. 340pp.

To commemorate the fiftieth anniversary of von Sternberg's classic film, this publication offers a valuable opportunity to compare the screen adaption of Mann's 1905 novel, PROFESSOR UNRATH with the continuity script of the 1930 film. As Stanley Hochman notes in the book's foreword: "In Mann's novel we tend to celebrate when Professor Rath is brought low by the fury of the townspeople; in Sternberg's film we are horror-stricken by the vision of an essentially honorable man destroyed by desire." Well worth browsing.

*Von Sternberg, Josef. THE BLUE ANGEL: A FILM BY JOSEF VON STERNBERG. New York: Simon and Schuster, 1968. Illustrated. 111pp.

Published before von Sternberg's death, this "authorized translation of the German continuity" carries his endorsement. The director writes in the Introduction that "No comprehensive scenario was ever made. Most of the film was improvised on the stage. Its creation, including all difficulties, are mentioned in my book . . . Very little of the dialogue was in English, and consisted mostly of Berlin slang. Dietrich and Jannings spoke English with each other, in the English version. Both the German and the English version were photographed, one after the other. Less stress was placed on the dialogue, though it is best when understood." Recommended for special collections.

FILMS

FRITZ LANG

M (Germany--16mm: 1931, 103 mins., b/w, sound, R-BUD, COR, FES, FNC, IMA, IVY, JAN, KIT, TWY)

Directed by Lang, with a script by his first wife, Thea von Harbou, this classic tale of a child murderer (Peter Lorre) was originally entitled MURDERER AMONG US. It deals not only with the psychological problems of a killer who cannot help himself, but also with how the police and the underworld work to rid society of a problem affecting everyone's lives. At the time the picture was being filmed, a number of prominent people drew links between the film's initial title and Adolf Hitler. More important than the superficial cops-and-robbers plot are Lang's brilliant camera and sound techniques that illustrate the problems of mental illness and society's inability to understand the criminal mind.   Particularly impressive are the cross-cutting techniques comparing the tactics of the police and the underworld, the use of mirrors to highlight the difficulties the murderer experiences, and the use of music, silence, and dialogue to heighten the film's tension.[476]

JOSEF VON STERNBERG

THE BLUE ANGEL (Germany--16mm: 1929, 114 mins., b/w, sound, R-BUD, EMG, FES, FNC, IMA, IVY, JAN, KIT, ROA, SWA, TWY, WEL, WHO; S-FES, KIT, REE, TFF)

Scripted by von Sternberg, Robert Liebmann, and Karl Vollmoeller, with dialogue by Carl Zuckmayer (based on Heinrich Mann's novel, PROFESSOR UNRATH, this classic film about a staid schoolteacher (Emil Jannings) and his tragic love affair with a two-bit cabaret singer (Marlene Dietrich) brought Dietrich to Hollywood and started a memorable relationship in films between the fabulous star and her great director. Sternberg's brilliant use of MISE EN SCENE and sound brought a depth to the early talkies that not only helped set new directions for sound films, but also foreshadowed his exquisite use of composition and lighting in future work.[477]

BRITAIN

The fate of British films is inextricably linked to Hollywood's industrial structure and artistic practices. Like the Americans, the British had more than their share of economic problems in the wake of the transition from silent to talking films. There were the obvious difficulties of converting equipment, studios, and theaters to sound. There were also heated labor battles over salaries, responsibilities, and recognition. Like the Americans, British film workers became unionized in the 1930s and helped reshape the structure of the industry. But unlike the Americans, Britain's commercial cinema struggled in vain to find a big enough market to match its ambitions and its talents. Not only had the reorganization of the American film industry, discussed in Chapter 3, sealed off distribution and exhibition outlets for independents and foreign filmmakers in America, but Hollywood had also taken control of foreign screens in key European countries. England was a prime example. Filmmakers had a much better chance of getting their products seen in a British movie house if they were American, than if they were British. In addition, as Rachel Low observes, "Despite a persistent drain to Hollywood there has never been a shortage of film-making talent in Britain. It has been production finance that has been hard to find."[478] Low's point is not that large production budgets automatically result in quality feature films, but rather that the almost mandatory shoestring British products invariably paled in comparison with Hollywood films.

In an effort to extricate the British film industry from American domination, Parliament enacted the Cinematograph Film Act (1927), which limited the number of foreign movies that could be shown on British screens. The issue hinged on British

---

[476] For more information, see Joseph S. M. J. Chang, "M: A Reconsideration," LITERATURE/FILM QUARTERLY 7:4 (1979):300-8; and Catherine Henry, "M," THE INTERNATIONAL DICTIONARY OF FILMS AND FILMMAKERS: VOLUME I, pp.270-2.

[477] For more information, see Richard Arthur Firda, "Literary Origins: Sternberg's THE BLUE ANGEL," LITERATURE/FILM QUARTERLY 7:2 (1979):126-36; Richard Whitehall, "THE BLUE ANGEL," FILMS AND FILMING 9:1 (October 1962):19-23; Peter Baxter, "On the Naked Thighs of Miss Dietrich," WIDE ANGLE 2:2 (1978):18-25; and John Baxter, "DER BLAUE ENGEL," THE INTERNATIONAL DICTIONARY OF FILMS AND FILMMAKERS: VOLUME I, pp.60-1.

[478] Rachel Low, THE HISTORY OF THE BRITISH FILM 1929-1939: FILM MAKING IN 1930s BRITAIN (London: George Allen and Unwin, 1985), p.52. p.xiv.

film booking practices. Prior to 1927, Hollywood's power was so great, that Brit
exhibitors agreed to block and blind book American products. Consequently,
interest in British films was almost non-existent. By the mid-1920s, the industry w
at a standstill, with no incentive to change. (Interestingly, the British symbol
the film business was "Wardour Street," the London center for distribution, rat
than various production facilities; in contrast, Americans used "Hollywood," not "W
Street.") The 1927 act stipulated that exhibitors now had to have a five percent qu
of screen time devoted to "British film footage." The emphasis on "footag
sidestepped the question of quality. Thus, the worst fears of the exhibitors c
true.[479] Fly-by-night British producers, often bankrolled by Hollywood, made "qu
quickies" to comply with the law. The one advantage, however, came in restrict
the block and blind booking arrangements. The new legislation, as Roger Manv
points out, encouraged the further development of cinema circuits, or chains
theatres under single ownerships, in order to increase the power of the circuit-own
exhibitors to bargain with the distributors.[480]

Without question, this quota system contributed to the revival of public inter
in, and rapid expansion of, the British film industry during the Depression and
transition to sound. It also accounted for the bad name that British films had in
film world. Within a decade, the law was changed due to the Cinematograph Film A
1938 to differentiate between good and bad films, with a larger quota provided
quality films. But the dilemma of how to support a quality British film industry s
remained. That is, Hollywood still reigned supreme at the British box office. "Brit
producers still had no American market, and," as Low explains, "without this, th
films would continue to be made on budgets which could not rival Hollywood product
standards."[481]

Another important comparison is the attitude of the British toward films
general. Like the Americans, they had long since recognized the importance of f
in affecting social and political values. By the time talkies arrived, the British Bo
of Film Censors, founded in 1912, was classifying films either as "U," acceptable
universal audiences, or "A," acceptable for adults and adolescents under sixteen a
accompanied by adults. The reasons why films ran into trouble followed the fami
patterns: e.g., being anti-authoritarian, offending traditional religious views, be
too sexually suggestive, and insulting nations friendly to Britain. Unlike Americ
censorship, however, the British equivalent was more concerned with foreign impo
than with domestic products. Like most European nations, British political censors
was a highly visible and contentious issue, as evidenced by the role that British f
societies played in the process.[482] One notable outcome of the debates over fil

---

[479] Often overlooked in the discussions about European countries "protecting" the
national cinemas from American exploitation is the fact that not every fore
businessperson profited from the protectionist policies. What Monaco (p.
states about German and French attitudes during the 1920s applies as well to
British situation: "Film rental agents and distributors who imported the fore
films were naturally opposed to such limitations [e.g., taxes, tariffs,
quotas].   To this relatively small group was added the large number
independent movie-theater owners who also took a stand against the restrict
of foreign-film imports."

[480] Roger Manvell et al., THE INTERNATIONAL ENCYCLOPEDIA OF FILM (New York: Cr
Publishers, 1972), p.241.

[481] Low, p.52.

[482] For a good overview, see *Bert Hogenkamp, DEADLY PARALLELS: FILM AND THE L
IN BRITAIN 1929-1939 (London: Lawrence and Wisehart, 1986), pp.13-104; and L
pp.54-72.

controversial status was the formation of the British Film Institute in 1933, and the National Film Archives two years later.

Also like the Americans, the British had their indigenous star talent-e.g., George Arliss, Laurence Olivier, Vivien Leigh, Jessie Matthews, Charles Laughton, Elsa Lanchester, Anna Neagle, Leslie Howard, Gracie Fields, Will Hay, Merle Oberon, George Formby, Jack Hulbert, Tom Walls, and Robert Donat--commingled with foreign performers--e.g., Paul Robeson, Marlene Dietrich, Douglas Fairbanks, Sr. and Jr., Richard Dix, Robert Young, Raymond Massey, Conrad Veidt, and Tyrone Power--in number of important international productions. Where the British went wrong, in addition to making badly acted and poorly produced quota quickies, was in believing that their stage-bound traditions in silent films gave them the edge in the talking movie era.

The fact that an overemphasis on literal adaptations of popular stage plays and classic books had left the British film industry impoverished and isolated in the 1920s failed to make an impression on the filmmakers dealing with the coming of talkies. Thus, for the first half of the 1930s, many British films repeated the same mistakes found in the FILM D'ART movement. The one exception was the shoestring comedy starring music hall comedians and singers like Fields, Formby, and Hay. As a result, most English films were not even welcome in Britain's 4,000 movie houses, let alone in American theaters. Although a number of people--e.g., Basil Dean, John Maxwell, George Pearson, Marcel Varnel, Victor Saville, Ivor Montagu, Walter Forde, Michael Powell,[483] Graham Cutts, Anthony Asquith, Carol Reed, Thorold Dickinson, Edgar Wallace, Herbert Wilcox--played a special role in upgrading the British film industry of the 1930s, four men were especially influential: Alexander Korda, Michael Balcon, J. Arthur Rank, and Alfred Hitchcock.

After coming to England at Paramount's behest in 1931, the enterprising Korda created his own production company, London Film Productions, in 1932. For the next decade, he worked with his two brothers--Zoltan and Vincent--on establishing British films as the equal of Hollywood productions.[484] Among their most notable achievements were THE PRIVATE LIFE OF HENRY VIII (1933), THE SCARLET PIMPERNEL (1934), THE GHOST GOES WEST, SANDERS OF THE RIVER (both in 1935), REMBRANDT (1936), ELEPHANT BOY (1937), DRUMS (1938), FOUR FEATHERS (1939), THE THIEF OF BAGDAD (1940), and THE JUNGLE BOOK (1942). Many of Korda's films, as Jeffrey Richards points out, created a genre called "The Cinema of Empire." That is, films that are not merely set in territories under British rule, "but films which detail the attitudes, ideals and myths of British Imperialism."[485] Among the myths that these imperial films developed were the importance of the public school code, the nature of the white man's burden, the function of class structure, the role of the military, the heroes of the empire, and the different categories of natives. Korda's Imperial film cycle not only lasted until 1940 and spawned Hollywood clones like LIVES OF A BENGAL LANCER (1935), WEE WILLIE WINKIE (1937), and GUNGA DIN (1939), but also planted the seeds for a second Imperial film cycle starting in the 1950s and extending through the 1980s (discussed in Chapter 3).

---

[83] For an update on the reception of Powell's films in America, see "Powell Retropsective Reflects a Happy Life in Film," NEW YORK TIMES C (July 8, 1988): 12.

[84] One of the major objections to Korda's productions was their heavy reliance of foreign rather than British direction. Among the many imported directors were Rene Clair, Jacques Feyder, Josef von Sternberg, Erich Pommer, William Cameron Menzies, and Paul Czinner.

[85] Jeffrey Richards, VISIONS OF YESTERDAY (London: Routledge & Kegan Paul, 1937), p.1.

Korda's greatest weakness was also his greatest strength. He refused to compromise on budgets or projects. Driven by the desire to have his films rival Hollywood's best movies, he surrounded himself with the best talent available, regardless of the cost. For performers like Oberon, Olivier, Howard, Leigh, Laughton, and Donat, the benefits were considerable. But for Korda's investors, his extravagant projects resulted in a rollercoaster existence. Early films like THE PRIVATE LIFE OF HENRY VIII, THE SCARLET PIMPERNEL, and REMBRANDT brought fame and profits, but they were the exception rather than the norm. Public acclaim often masked the fact that Korda's extravagant productions at his opulent Denham studios cost more than they made at the box office. Before Korda retired from filmmaking in the mid-1950s, his film empire experienced three bankruptcies. The first one, in 1937, often is credited with contributing to a temporary crisis in British filmmaking prior to World War II. At that time, he migrated to Hollywood, where he worked until the mid-1940s.

Balcon's production credits extended beyond one company. Having founded Gainsborough Pictures in 1924, he was in large part responsible for giving Hitchcock his first big break. Moreover, Balcon's skill as a business manager and producer made him sensitive to the inherent weakness in British films that relied heavily on screen adaptations of novels and stage plays. His first attempts at Gainsborough Pictures met with little success, and he later moved on to Gaumont-British (where he also produced Hitchcock's films), Ealing Studios, and the Rank Organization. Having gotten his start in silent films, the imaginative producer reacted cautiously to the coming of talkies. Only after spending some time in Hollywood did he grasp what needed to be done to make British films commercially competitive with American products. By 1929, he was back in England reassembling a creative team of directors that included Victor Saville and James Whale. At Gainsborough's Islington studios he produced a few important works, including JOURNEY'S END (1930). After a fire temporarily destroyed Islington, he set up operations at several studios (all owned by Gaumont-British or Gainsborough), and over the next six years, working primarily with Hitchcock and a skilled staff, Balcon adapted Hollywood's filmmaking strategies to such significant films as THE MAN WHO KNEW TOO MUCH, MAN OF ARAN (both in 1934), THE 39 STEPS (1935), THE SECRET AGENT, and SABOTAGE (both in 1936), as well as a string of successful British comedies featuring popular English performers like Matthews and Hulbert. The inability of these films to justify their costs eventually forced Balcon to leave Gaumont-British in December 1936 and sign a contract with MGM. By 1938, however, he was put in charge of Ealing Studios where he remained for the next two decades. In the years to follow, as discussed in Chapter 2, he contributed significantly to the British war films, and, as will be treated later, played a major role in the British film industry during the postwar period.

Joseph Arthur Rank came to British films by an entirely different route quite different from Korda's and Balcon's. A devout Methodist and wealthy businessman he became concerned in the early 1930s about the lack of suitable films to show in religious schools. Through a series of explorations and investments, he eventually became a major figure in British filmmaking. By the mid-1930s, however, he was just getting established and gaining control of important theater chains and film studios. His major production contributions would come during World War II and the postwar period.

To appreciate the changes occurring in films during the 1930s, it is instructive to study the evolution of one director: Alfred Hitchcock.[486] As Marshall Deutelbaum observes,

[486] For more information, see Russell Maloney, "Alfred Joseph Hitchcock," NEW YORKER (September 10, 1938):28-32; Patricia Ferrara, "The Discontented Bourgeois: Bourgeois Morality and the Interplay of Light and Dark Strains in Hitchcock' Films," NEW ORLEANS REVIEW 14:1 (Winter 1987):13-6; Raymond Bellour, "Hitchcock

To speak of Alfred Hitchcock is to evoke a remarkable set of histories: the history of cinema generally, in which Hitchcock plays an exemplary role as a technical and stylistic innovator; a history of Hitchcock's films themselves, seen alternately as a matter of decline (for those who prefer his British films) or

The Enunciator," CAMERA OBSCURA 2 (1977):69-94; Robert E. Kapsis, "Hitchcock: Auteur or Hack--How the Filmmaker Reshaped His Reputation Among Critics," CINEASTE 14:3 (1986):30-5; ___, "Hollywood Filmmaking and Reputation Building : Hitchcock's THE BIRDS," JOURNAL OF POPULAR FILM AND TELEVISION 15:1 (Spring 1987):4-15; ___, "The Historical Reception of Hitchcock's MARNIE," CINEMA JOURNAL 40:3 (Summer 1980):46-63; Philip Dynia, "Alfred Hitchcock and the Ghost of Thomas Hobbes," ibid., 15:2 (Spring 1976):27-41; Royal S. Brown, "Herrmann, Hitchcock, and the Music of the Irrational," ibid., 21:2 (Spring 1982):14-49, rev. and rpt. FILM THEORY AND CRITICISM: INTRODUCTORY READINGS, Third Edition, eds. Gerald Mast and Marshall Cohen (New York: Oxford University Press, 1985), pp.618-649; Charles Thomas Samuels, "Hitchcock," MASTERING THE FILM AND OTHER ESSAYS by Charles Thomas Samuels, ed. Lawrence Graver (Knoxville: The University of Tennessee Press, 1977), pp.69-84; John Belton, "Reply to Samuels' Article on Hitchcock," AMERICAN SCHOLAR 39 (1970):728-31; ___, "Dexterity in a Void: The Formal Aesthetics of Alfred Hitchcock," CINEASTE 10:3 (Summer 1980):9-13; Gerald Pratley, "Alfred Hitchcock's Working Credo," FILMS IN REVIEW 3:10 (December 1952):500-3; Jerry Vermilye, "An Alfred Hitchcock Index," ibid., 17:4 (April 1966):231-48; Charles Higham, "Hitchcock's World," FILM QUARTERLY 16:2 (Winter 1962-63):3-16; Mary Ann Doane, "CAUGHT and REBECCA: The Inscription of Femininity as Absence," ENCLITIC 5-6:1-2 (Fall 1981-Spring 1982); Fredric Jameson, "Reading Hitchcock," OCTOBER 23 (Winter 1982):15-42; Catherine De La Roche, "Conversation with Hitchcock," SIGHT AND SOUND 25:3 (Winter 1955-56):157-8; Peter John Dyer, "Young and Innocent," ibid., 30:2 (Spring 1961):80-3; Penelope Houston, "The Figure in the Red Carpet," ibid., 32:4 (Autumn 1963):158-64; Axel Madsen, "Who's Afraid of Alfred Hitchcock," ibid., 37:1 (Winter 1967-68):26-7; Alfred Hitchcock, "Alfred Hitchcock Talking, . . ." FILMS AND FILMING 5:10 (July 1959):7, 33; Raymond Durgnat, "To Catch a Hitch," QUARTERLY REVIEW OF FILM STUDIES 8:1 (Winter 1983):43-8; ___, "The Strange Case of Alfred Hitchcock--Part One," ibid., 16:5 (February 1970):58-62; ___, ". . . Part Two," ibid., 16:6 (March 1970):58-62; ___, ". . . Part Three," ibid., 16:7 (April 1970):58-60; ___, ". . . Part Four," ibid., 16:8 (May 1970):58-61; ___, ". . . Part Five," ibid., 16:9 (June 1970):114-8; ___, ". . . Part Six," ibid., 16:10 (July 1970):52-8; ___, ". . . Part Seven," ibid., 16:11 (August 1970):57-61; ___, ". . . Part Eight," ibid., 16:12 (September 1970):84-8; ___, ". . . Part Nine," ibid., 17:1 (October 1970):60-4; ___, ". . . Part Ten," ibid., 17:2 (November 1970):35-7; Ian Cameron, and V. F. Perkins, "Hitchcock," MOVIE 6 (January 1963):4-6; V. F. Perkins, "ROPE," ibid., 7 (February 1963):11-3; Ian Cameron and Richard Jeffrey, ibid., "The Universal Hitchcock," ibid., 12 (Spring 1965):21-4; Michael Walker, "The Old Age of Alfred Hitchcock," ibid., 18 (Winter 1970-71):10-3; Budge Crawley et al., "Hitchcock," TAKE ONE 1:1 (1966):14-7; Lee Russell [Peter Wollen], "Alfred Hitchcock," NEW LEFT REVIEW 35 (January-February 1966):89-93; David Lubin, "Buts & Rebuts--Hitchcock: A Defense and Update," FILM COMMENT 15:3 (May-June 1979):66-8; Elisabeth Weis, "The Sound of One Wing Flapping," ibid., 14:5 (September-October 1978):42-8; Alain J. Silver, "Fragments of a Mirror: Uses of Landscape in Hitchcock," WIDE ANGLE 3:1 (1976):52-61; Daniel Sallitt, "Point of View and 'Intrarealism' in Hitchcock," ibid., 4:1 (1980):20-9; Deborah Linderman, "The Screen in Hitchcock's BLACKMAIL," ibid., 4:1 (1980):20-9; James B. McLaughlin, "All In the Family: Alfred Hitchcock's SHADOW OF A DOUBT," ibid., pp.12-9; Michael Renov, "From Identification to Ideology: The Male System of Hitchcock's NOTORIOUS," ibid., pp.30-7; Tania Modleski, "Never to Be Thirty-Six Years Old: REBECCA as Female Oedipal Drama," ibid., 5:1 (1982):34-41; Leland Poague, "The Detective in Hitchcock's FRENZY: His Ancestors and Significance," JOURNAL OF POPULAR FILM 2:1

development (for those who champion his later American movies); a history of
film criticism, especially given Hitchcock's status as a primary test case for the
auteur theory which held that commercial films ("classical films" in the more
current usage) can and should be discussed in the same terms as were
previously reserved for "art" films; a history of contemporary film theory,
understood at least in part as involving a return to more sociological concerns
after the excesses of auteurism; ETC.[487]

Although most historians and biographers acknowledge the close link between
Hitchcock's films and his personal life, a debate rages over how much the private
Hitchcock matches the public figure and the screen genius.
        Born Alfred Joseph Hitchcock in Leytonstone, London, on August 13, 1899, the
master of suspense films[488] was second to none in terms of the filmmakers he
influenced. During his childood, the lower middle-class youngster, a devout Catholic,
developed a number of lifelong fears about authority figures and punishment, deriving
in large measure from his demanding parents and the stern Jesuit education he
received at St. Ignatius College. These fears later became an integral part of his
sinister plots, superb montage effects, and startling camera techniques.[489] A loner
most of his life, Hitchcock compensated for his shyness and Puritanical sense of guilt

---

(Winter 1973):47-58; ___, "Hitchcock and the Ethics of Vision," FILM CRITICISM:
A COUNTER THEORY, by William Cadbury and Leland Poague (Ames: Iowa State
University Press, 1982), pp.91-155; Gabriel Miller, "Hitchcock's Wasteland
Vision: An Examination of FRENZY," FILM HERITAGE 11:3 (Spring 1976):1-10; "It's
the Manner of Telling: Interview With Alfred Hitchcock," ibid., pp.11-22; Richard
Schickel, "We're Living In a Hitchcock World, All Right," NEW YORK TIMES MAGAZINE
(October 29, 1972), pp.22-3, 40, 42, 46, 48, 50, 52, 54; Ernest Lehman, "He Who
Gets Hitched," AMERICAN FILM 3:7 (May 1978):8-9, 64; ___, "Hitch," ibid., 5:9
(July-August 1980):18; and Robin Wood, "Fear of Spying," ibid., 9:2 (November
1983):28-35.

[487]   *Marshall Deutelbaum and Leland Poague, eds., A HITCHCOCK READER (Ames: Iowa
State University Press, 1986), p.xi.

[488]   For more information, see Noel Carroll, "Toward a Theory of Film Suspense,"
PERSISTENCE OF VISION 1 (1984):65-89; O. B. Hardison, "The Rhetoric of Hitchcock
Thrillers," MAN AND THE MOVIES, ed. W. R. Robinson (Baton Rouge: Louisiana State
University Press, 1967), pp.137-52; John B. Turner, "On Suspense and Other Film
Matters: An Interview With Alfred Hitchcock," FILMS IN REVIEW 1:3 (April
1950):21-2, 47; John Pett, "A Master of Suspense: An Analysis of Hitchcock's Work
for the Cinema," FILMS AND FILMING 6:2 (November 1959):9-10, 33; ___, ". . .
Part Two," ibid., 6:3 (December 1959):9-10, 32; Ian Cameron, "Hitchcock and the
Mechanisms of Suspense," MOVIE 3 (October 1962):4-7; ___, "Hitchcock: Suspense
and Meaning," ibid., 6 (January 1963):8-12; Gavin Lambert, "Hitchcock and the
Art of Suspense: The Paranoia of Fear," AMERICAN FILM 1:4 (January-February
1976):16-23; and ___, "Hitchcock and the Art of Suspense: Part II," ibid., 1:5
(March 1976):60-7.

[489]   For more information, see David Corey, FEARFUL SYMMETRIES: THE CONTEST OF
AUTHORITY IN HITCHCOCK NARRATIVE (Unpublished Ph.D. dissertation, New York
University, 1980); David Bombyk, "Bookkeeping on an Analyst's Coach: A French
Critic's Approach to Hitchcock," TAKE ONE 5:1 (1976):45-6; James Monaco, "The
Cinema and Its Double: Alfred Hitchcock," ibid., 5:2 (May 1976):6-8; Andre Bazin,
"Hitchcock Versus Hitchcock," CAHIERS DU CINEMA IN ENGLISH 2, CdC 39 (1966):51-9;
Claude Chabrol, "Hitchcock Confronts Evil," ibid., pp.67-71; Kirk Bond, "The
Other Hitchcock," FILM CULTURE 41 (Summer 1966):30-5; Warren Sonbert, "Alfred
Hitchcock: Master of Morality," ibid., pp.35-8; and George Kaplan [Robin Wood],

by developing a love for ritual, practical jokes,[490] movies, railway timetables, the theater, detective fiction, and the works of Charles Dickens.[491] The latter, in particular, taught him not only to be cynical about authority figures but also to appreciate the commercial value of self-promotion, both of which the director used to great advantage throughout his career. After completing his formal schooling in 1913, the fifteen-year-old Hitchcock found a job in advertising. Over the next five years he supplemented his daily schedule with evening art courses and frequent visits to the movies and theater.[492] Clearly, the films that had the greatest impact on him were those made in America and in Western Europe.

In 1920, the ambitious draftsman landed a part-time job as a designer of title cards with the London office of Zukor's Famous Players-Lasky. Within months, he proved so skillful at a variety of assignments, that the firm hired him full-time and gave him the opportunity to learn the filmmaking process from screenwriting and art direction, to assistant directing. Most importantly, Hitchcock came under the influence of the director George Fitzmaurice, who taught him the value of carefully prepared storyboards and the importance of running an orderly and well-disciplined set. These were lessons that the impressionable Hitchcock never forgot. Once he began directing, he quickly gained a controversial reputation for meticulous pre-production planning and for running an extremely business-like set. His biographers and collaborators disagree, however, on just how reserved the famous director was in his day-to-day behavior, pointing especially to his lifelong penchant for practical jokes, his abuse of performers, and his alleged infatuations with blond actresses.

Hitchcock's next big break came in 1923. The British fortunes of Famous Players-Lasky had dropped precipitously, forcing the company to abandon its production schedule and to rent its facilities to independent filmmakers like the team of Michael Balcon, Victor Saville, and John Freedman. Working with the director Graham Cutts, the Balcon-Saville-Freedman team's first film at Famous Players-Lasky's Islington Studios was WOMAN TO WOMAN (1923), a project that relied heavily on Hitchcock's talents and gave him his first screen credit (art director). After the Balcon-Saville-Freedman team, now known as Gainsborough Pictures, bought the studios the following year, Hitchcock became a fixture in their productions. Cutts's jealousy of his young assistant forced Balcon to let the valuable Hitchcock become a director. To insure the success of the twenty-six-year old's directorial debut, Balcon sent him to Germany to make two films--THE PLEASURE GARDEN and THE MOUNTAIN EAGLE (both in 1925). Not only had he worked there under Cutts's direction, but also it seemed less risky having an unknown director get his start out of the country. Although the finished films displeased C. M. Woolf, the distributor,[493] who shelved them until the early part of 1927, the German experience contributed significantly to Hitchcock's cinematic style and film content, particularly in creating psychological

---

"Alfred Hitchcock: Lost in the Wood," FILM COMMENT 8:4 (November-December 1972):46-53.

[490]   For an interesting perspective, see Andrew Sarris, "Alfred Hitchcock, Prankster of Paradox," FILM COMMENT 10:2 (March-April 1974):8-9.

[491]   For more information, see Edward Buscombe, "Dickens and Hitchcock," SCREEN 11:4-5 (1970):97-114. For another literary influence, see Deloy Simper, "Poe, Hitchcock, and the Well-Wrought Effect," LITERATURE/FILM QUARTERLY 3:3 (Summer 1975):226-31.

[492]   To get a sense of Hitchcock's dramatic interests in his pre-directorial days, see his essay, "Gas," written in 1919, and reprinted in SIGHT AND SOUND 39:4 (Fall 1970):186-7.

[493]   Woolf proved to be a constant nemesis for Hitchcock. In addition to the Gainsborough period, the distributor also made life uncomfortable for Hitchcock at Gaumont-British during the production of THE MAN WHO KNEW TOO MUCH (1934).

moods and terrifying suspense. During the same period, Hitchcock came under the influence of Soviet filmmaking, which taught him about audience manipulation and led eventually to his reliance on montage for his basic screen effects.[494] It was Hitchcock's third film, THE LODGER (1926), that not only brought him his first fame, but also began his controversial relationship with Ivor Montagu.[495] Released after THE PLEASURE GARDEN but before THE MOUNTAIN EAGLE (all in 1927), THE LODGER also included his first cameo role (soon to be his cinematic signature). Another major event in 1926 was Hitchcock's marriage to Alma Reville, a noted British film editor and co-worker. To this day, biographers and collaborators disagree about the extent of her influence on his films, even though she received screen credits as a writer on nearly a third of his fifty-three feature works.

Disturbed by the treatment he was getting at Gainsborough, Hitchcock, in 1927, took a job with British International Pictures (BIP). Two years would pass before he could complete his work for Gainsborough, but his debut for BIP was not only his first talkie, BLACKMAIL (1929), but also Britain's first successful sound film. It established Hitchcock as one of England's foremost directors. Although the years at BIP gave him the opportunity to display his cinematic imagination in a wide range of film genres, he particularly disliked the restrictive nature of being a contract director forced to follow company directives on uninspired projects.

In 1933, Hitchcock moved over to Gaumont-British (and a reunion with Balcon) where he soon gained considerable recognition for a series of action-packed spy thrillers--e.g., THE MAN WHO KNEW TOO MUCH (1934), THE 39 STEPS (1935),[496] THE SECRET AGENT, and SABOTAGE (both in 1936)[497]--and caught the attention of Hollywood producers. It was during this period, feminist and psychological critics would argue later, that he began manipulating screen actresses and using them as outlets for his alleged repressed sexuality.[498] When Gaumont-British suddenly stopped production in the mid-1930s, Hitchcock returned briefly to Gainsborough, where he made YOUNG AND INNOCENT (1937) and THE LADY VANISHES (1938). His final British film, JAMAICA INN (1939), was an independent work for Mayflower Productions, owned by Eric Pommer and Charles Laughton.

In 1938, Hitchcock, nervous about the declining fortunes of the British film industry, irritated by the condescending attitudes of British critics toward the types of films he made, and envious of the technical facilities in Hollywood, signed what turned out to be an important but controversial contract with David O. Selznick,

---

[494] For information on another major influence on Hitchcock, see Robert Stam, "Hitchcock and Bunuel: Desire and the Law," STUDIES IN THE LITERARY IMAGINATION 16:1 (1983):7-27.

[495] For Montagu's perspective, see Ivor Montagu, "Working with Hitch," SIGHT AND SOUND 49:3 (Summer 1980):189-93.

[496] John Buchan's novel was published as THE THIRTY-NINE STEPS, but Hitchcock titled his film, THE 39 STEPS. In this book, Hitchcock's title remains in the narrative as he printed it, but the limitations of the computerized index require the Buchan form.

[497] For more information, see Michael A. Anderegg, "Conrad and Hitchcock: THE SECRET AGENT Inspires SABOTAGE," LITERATURE/FILM QUARTERLY 3:3 (Summer 1975):215-25.

[498] For more information, see Susan Jhiard, "Hitchcock's Women," CINEASTE, 13:4 (Winter 1984):30-3; Jeanne Thomas Allen, "The Representation of Violence to Women: Hitchcock's FRENZY," FILM QUARTERLY 38:3 (Spring 1985):30-8; Alfred Appel, Jr., "The Eye of Knowledge: Voyeuristic Games in Film and Literature," FILM COMMENT 9:3 (May-June 1973):20-6; and Vittorio Giacci, "Alfred Hitchcock: Allegory of Ambiguous Sexuality," WIDE ANGLE 4:1 (1980):4-11.

binding the British director to the American producer for a period of five years or five films.[499] The twenty-three British films he had made over a thirteen-year period would become a source of debate over the wisdom of his moving to Hollywood.

As Britain headed into World War II, her film industry ranked second only to Hollywood in terms of national output. Few historians agree, however, about the price the English paid for that distinction. On the one hand, the quota system now was resulting in quality productions. In addition, as Basil Wright points out,

> It was not until right at the end of the thirties that the real Britain, the Britain of the slump, of appeasement mentalities, of mass unemployment, malnutrition and other social injustices came to be discussed, however tentatively, on the screen. And this could hardly have happened had not MGM arrived in Britain with certain ambitions and lots of dollars.[500]

On the other hand, Britain still found itself under the thumb of Hollywood companies like MGM. Large sums of money were being poured into British productions made by Americans in order for the joint ventures to qualify for the new quotas: e.g., MGM's A YANK AT OXFORD, THE CITADEL (both in 1938), and GOODBYE, MR. CHIPS (1939). The more British film personnel came off the unemployment line, the more they secured American control in the British film industry.

BOOKS

GENERAL

*Barr, Charles. EALING STUDIOS. Woodstock: Overlook Press, 1980. 198pp.

"In 1929," Barr explains, "shortly after sound came to the cinema, the theatre director Basil Dean formed a company to produce films; he called it Associated Talking Pictures. The company's start was promising; and Dean raised the money to build a studio for it. The site chosen was Ealing Green, in the London borough of Ealing. Construction began and finished the same year, 1931." Over the next twenty-five years, Ealing Studios developed a well-deserved reputation for making distinctive, quality films. While Dean's company made most of the pictures during the 1930s, the studio also leased its facilities to other companies. The financial crisis in the British film industry during the late 1930s persuaded Dean to return to the theater and Michael Balcon took over as production head of the restructured Ealing Studios. Over the next two decades, Ealing became famous for its unique brand of comedies and realistic dramas. An agreement between the Rank Organization and Ealing in 1944 helped both companies surmount distribution problems created by the war and by the influence of Hollywood in the postwar period. But by the early 1950s, Ealing could no longer afford to operate as an independent producer and sold its facilities to the BBC. In 1955, the company went out of business.

Twelve valuable and informative chapters analyze Ealing's growth, problems, and unique filmmaking style. The one drawback is the author's failure to document his sources. Otherwise, the smooth-flowing narrative provides a fine overview of the films, personalities, and accomplishments of this highly regarded studio. A filmography and index are provided, but no bibliography. Well worth browsing.

---

[499] For more information, see Philip French, "Alfred Hitchcock: The Film-maker as Englishman and Exile," SIGHT AND SOUND 54:2 (Spring 1985):116-22.

[500] Wright, p.106.

*Hogenkamp, Bert. DEADLY PARALLELS: FILM AND THE LEFT IN BRITAIN 1929-1939. London: Lawrence and Wishart, 1986. Illustrated. 240pp.

"In the following study," Hogenkamp explains, "I have reconstructed the history of the workers' and left film movement in Great Britain in the 1930s from the various sources which I have examined: notices and articles in newspapers and other contemporary periodicals, records in archives, interviews with participants, and films which have survived the Blitz, wear, internal combustion or simple neglect." Hogenkamp's strategy is to allow the movement to speak for itself by relying heavily on quoted material. What defines the movement is any epithet--e.g., "workers," "socialist," "left," or "progressive"--except "independent," because he insists that the groups "defined themselves not so much by their independence from commercial film production, distribution and exhibition, as rather by their dependence--voluntary, self-imposed--on the labor movement."

The material is divided into seven detailed and intriguing chapters concerning the crucial role of film in the early days of British cinema, the rise of workers' film societies, the battle over the distribution and exhibition of the BATTLESHIP POTEMKIN, the establishment of the Socialist Film Council, the initiation of workers' films through Kino and the Workers' Film and Photo League, the Popular Front movements as they impacted on Great Britain, and the connections between filmmakers like Ivor Montagu, John Grierson, Ralph Bond, Helen Biggar, and Paul Rotha and the established socialist theatrical traditions. Although the focus is clearly on British films, the book spends considerable time discussing the importance of Soviet films not only in stimulating labor films, but also in fighting covert and overt British film censorship.

Given the scarcity of information about the topic and the considerable research provided by this decade-long investigation, this work deserves widespread distribution and examination. Its polemical style may make some readers wary of its conclusions, but not of its serious purpose. Valuable endnotes, a good filmography, a terse bibliography, and a useful index are included. American readers can obtain the book from Humanities Press International. Well worth browsing.

Low, Rachel. THE HISTORY OF THE BRITISH FILM 1929-1939: FILM MAKING IN 1930s BRITAIN. London: George Allen and Unwin, 1985. Illustrated. 452pp.

A detailed and revealing study on the development of the British film industry from the arrival of talking pictures in 1929, to the outbreak of World War II in 1939, this seventh and final book in Low's acclaimed series offers a fresh perspective on the confusing speculative boom in production that followed the enactment of the 1927 quota legislation and the eventual crisis that occurred in the mid-1930s. The standard position has been that Alexander Korda's extravagant production policies caused his principal backer, the Prudential Insurance Company, to abandon him in 1937, and thereby create a panic in the investment community that led to a crisis in British filmmaking. Low's important historical perspective forces a reassessment, shifting the blame away from Korda's excesses, and toward the role played by the Aldgate Trustees, a film company set up in 1935 by Max Schach (an ex-film critic and producer from Germany who fled to England in 1934). Her thesis is that the Aldgate shenanigans that scandalized the industry forced the city of London to cut off investments in the British film industry. How all this occurred and why are only one facet of Low's sterling study of the industry.

The book is divided into nine chapters, covering such topics as Hollywood's exploitation of the British film market, the organization of labor, the quota system, film censorship, the arrival of the talkies, language problems, the experimentation with color films, and the production policies throughout the decade. Low painstakingly explains why British films unfairly got a bad name, and how producers like the Korda brothers and Michael Balcon maneuvered to put British films on an equal footing with the Americans. Particularly interesting are the financial machinations associated with the rise of the famous Denham and Ealing Studios. Although focusing primarily on business considerations, she does offer informative and capsule observations on what the feature films were like, and how the public reacted to specific personalities like Jessie Matthews, Anna Neagle, Merle Oberon, Leslie Howard, Robert Donat, Gracie Fields, George Formby, and Will Hay. Attention is also paid to the work of directors like Victor Saville and Alfred Hitchcock.

Except for the periodic and detailed technical data, the story reads well and moves along at a good clip. Not only are there a number of good case studies and valuable illustrations, but Low also provides a filmography of 1,600 feature films complete with cast and technical credits. An index is provided. Recommended for special collections.

Murphy, Robert. REALISM AND TINSEL: CINEMA AND SOCIETY IN BRITAIN 1939-48. New York: Routledge, 1989. Illustrated. 278pp.

Perry, George. FOREVER EALING: A CELEBRATION OF THE GREAT BRITISH FILM STUDIO. Foreword Peter Ustinov. London: Michael Joseph, 1981. Illustrated. 200pp.

An intelligent and well-written history of the famous studio, this profusely illustrated study offers good analyses, provocative observations, and entertaining anecdotes. The one major drawback to this popular account skillfully condensed in six fast-moving chapters is the absence of any documentation. A filmography, a bibliography, and an index are included. Well worth browsing.

Wilson, David, ed. PROJECTING BRITAIN: EALING STUDIOS FILM POSTERS. Introduction Bevis Hillier. London: British Film Institute, 1982. Illustrated. 67pp.

ANTHONY ASQUITH

Minney, R. J. THE FILMS OF ANTHONY ASQUITH. New York: A. S. Barnes and Company, 1976. Illustrated. 284pp.

Born on November 9, 1902, in London, to Herbert Asquith (the Prime Minister of England from 1908 to 1915), Anthony Asquith had a distinguished career in films. He received his basic cinematic training during a six-month visit to Hollywood in the mid-1920s and began directing thrillers in England in 1926. Among his most noted films are PYGMALION (1938), FRENCH WITHOUT TEARS (1939), WE DIVE AT DAWN (1943), THE WAY TO THE STARS (1945), THE WINSLOW BOY (1948), THE BROWNING VERSION (1951), THE IMPORTANCE OF BEING EARNEST (1952), and THE DOCTOR'S DILEMMA (1958). His last film was THE YELLOW ROLLS ROYCE (1964). Asquith died on February 21, 1968.

Regrettably, this lightweight biography does not do justice to this important British filmmaker. The narrative is chatty, the film analyses are weak, and the documentation is poor. A filmography and index are included, but no bibliography or endnotes are provided. Worth browsing.

MICHAEL BALCON

Balcon, Michael. MICHAEL BALCON PRESENTS A LIFETIME OF FILMS. London: Hutchinson, 1969. Illustrated. 239pp.

From this entertaining autobiography, we learn not only about the inner workings of Ealing Studios and its famous comedy series featuring Alec Guinness, but also about such outstanding films as THE OVERLANDERS (1946), MAN OF ARAN (1934), and THE CRUEL SEA (1952). The man whose distinguished career runs parallel to the emergence of British films as a major force in world cinema was responsible for over 350 movies. "I was born," he explains, "when the film (or motion picture) was new and novel. In my early twenties I chose film-making as my career. I did so very much as a young man in the last decade might have chosen television.

The medium was in an early and formative state; it was exciting, its potential was great. Virtually everything that has happened in the industry for nearly half a century affected me personally: the struggle to create an industry at all, the coming of sound; the recognition (by legislation) of the industry as one worthy of government interest, economically and culturally, the dynamic effects of the Second World War on the very nature of British films, the commercial and political events which have shaped the industry--sometimes for better, sometimes worse--the social changes which revolutionized production, the efforts to find a place in the world film scene--all these things were integral to my daily working life." Baldwin recounts his forty-six years in film (1922-1968) with modesty and tact. Except for the predictable attacks on Hollywood, the book offers a good perspective on film history. An index is included. Well worth browsing.

Danischewsky, M., ed. MICHAEL BALCON'S 25 YEARS IN FILM. London: World Film Publications, 1947. Illustrated. 112pp.
    "Sir Michael Balcon," writes David Puttnam in the preface, "was the central and outstanding figure in the creation of what is commonly termed the 'British film industry.' He wasn't the most gifted: David Lean, Alexander Korda, Carol Reed, Michael Powell, and any number of others must scrap over that distinction. 'Mick' Balcon was simply the most 'British'; wherever he worked, there lay the HEART of British films." A valuable commemorative publication to celebrate Balcon's career up to 1947, this handsomely produced book accompanied the Museum of Modern Art's retrospective screening of the producer's works. It contains an excellent annotated chronology by Catherine A. Surowiec, a useful filmography by Geoff Brown and Rachel Low, and a first-rate bibliography by Gillian Hartnoll et al. An index is included. Well worth browsing.

BASIL DEAN

Dean, Basil. MIND'S EYE. London: Hutchinson, 1973. Illustrated.

ROBERT DONAT

Trewin, J. C. ROBERT DONAT: A BIOGRAPHY. London: Heinemann, 1968. Illustrated. 252pp.

JOHN GIELGUD

*Gielgud, John, et al. GIELGUD: AN ACTOR AND HIS TIME. New York: Clarkson N. Potter, 1979. Illustrated. 255pp.

Harwood, Ronald, ed. THE AGES OF GIELGUD: AN ACTOR AT EIGHTY. New York: Limelight Editions, 1984. Illustrated. 182pp.

REX HARRISON

Harrison, Rex. REX: AN AUTOBIOGRAPHY. New York: William Morrow and Company, 1975. Illustrated. 256pp.

ALFRED HITCHCOCK

*Bogdanovich, Peter. THE CINEMA OF ALFRED HITCHCOCK. New York: Museum of Modern Art, 1963. Illustrated. 48pp.

Based upon the museum's 1963 retrospective, this extended interview conducted over a three-day period in mid-March was the first significant publication in America on Hitchcock's work. The comments deal with the older director's films from THE PLEASURE GARDEN (1925) to THE BIRDS (1963). The fun comes in comparing Bogdanovich's style with Truffaut's, done roughly at the same time. No index is included. Well worth browsing.

Brill, Lesley. THE HITCHCOCK ROMANCE: LOVE AND IRONY IN HITCHCOCK'S FILMS. Princeton: Princeton University Press, 1988. Illustrated. 296pp.

*Deutelbaum, Marshall, and Leland Poague. A HITCHCOCK READER. Ames: Iowa State University, 1986. Illustrated. 355pp.

The authors of this splendid anthology aim their scholarly work at two audiences: "For Hitchcock scholars . . . [it] is a summary of some aspects of their field, and it continues or renews debate over various aspects of the subject. For students, our primary audience, . . . [it] is an introduction to the field, a map of what may be for individual students a quite foreign territory." In both cases, Deutelbaum and Poague get high marks for selection, organization, and information. Part 1, "Taking Hitchcock Seriously," reopens the question Robin Wood asked in his important 1965 study and offers affirmative opinions by Wood, Jean Douchet, Maurice Yacowar, and Leonard J. Leff. Part 2, "Hitchcock in Britain," provides six essays on six films--THE LODGER (1926), BLACKMAIL (1929), MURDER! (1930), THE MAN WHO KNEW TOO MUCH (1934), THE 39 STEPS (1935), and THE LADY VANISHES (1938)--by Hitchcock scholars Leslie W. Brill, Leland Poague, William Rothman, Elisabeth Weis, Charles L. P. Silet, and Patrice Petro. Part 3, "Hitchcock in Hollywood," examines four films---SHADOW OF A DOUBT (1943), SPELLBOUND (1945), NOTORIOUS (1946), and STRANGERS ON A TRAIN (1951)--analyzed by James McLaughlin, Thomas Hyde, Richard Abel, and Robin Wood. Part 4, "The Later Films," blends commentaries by Robin Wood, Ian Cameron, and Richard Jeffrey on Hitchcock's cinematic style with film analyses by Robert Stam, Roberta Pearson, Marshall Deutelbaum, Marian E. Keane, Stanley Cavell, Margaret M. Horowitz, and Michelle Piso on REAR WINDOW (1954), THE WRONG MAN (1956), VERTIGO (1958), NORTH BY NORTHWEST (1959), THE BIRDS (1963), and MARNIE (1964). Part 5, "Hitchcock and Film Theory: A "PSYCHO" Dossier," concludes this provocative and intriguing collection with three challenging essays: Raymond Bellour's "Psychosis, Neurosis, Perversion"; Barbara Klinger's "PSYCHO: The Institutionalization of Female Sexuality"; and Leland Poague's "Links in a Chain: PSYCHO and Film Classicism." Each of the five sections begins with useful introductory comments by one of the editors, pointing out how critical reactions to Hitchcock have evolved from the AUTEUR theories of the 1950s, to current Marxist, psychological, and feminist perspectives. In addition to the helpful endnotes in the twenty-five essays, (eighteen of which are reprints), the anthology includes a filmography and an index. Highly recommended for classroom use and special collections.

Durgnat, Raymond. THE STRANGE CASE OF ALFRED HITCHCOCK, OR, THE PLAIN MAN'S HITCHCOCK. Cambridge: MIT Press, 1975. Illustrated. 419pp.

Taking the maverick's point of view, Durgnat sets out to present a unique (and very controversial) perspective on Hitchcock's career by asserting that the famed producer-director has been misinterpreted and misunderstood by his fans and critics alike. For example, Durgnat accurately claims there were three British periods--Gainsborough, British International, and Gaumont-Gainsborough--rather

than just one period from 1925 to 1938. The critic is on shakier grounds when h
credits Selznick for keeping Hitchcock away from FILM NOIR projects, argues tha
the Warner Bros. period shows the producer-director with "no clear direction," an
insists that following THE BIRDS (1963), "Hitchcock appears as a Hollywoo
'conservative', making a magisterial use of its traditional elements, without using ne
stylistic and thematic freedoms."

Expanded and revised from a series of articles written for FILMS AND FILMIN'
in 1970, the highly original material is divided into two major sections: "The Record
and "The Evidence." Both sections tax your patience and test your preconceptions
Durgnat's bias is that Hitchcock is first and last an entertainer, not a visionar
artist. In developing that tack, the author's chronological discussion focuses c
identifying common entertainment patterns that Hitchcock shared with other films an
directors. Although he finds value in categorizing Hitchcock's works into themes an
genres, Durgnat takes issue with almost every previous commentator who ha
categorized the director's films as thrillers, picaresque pursuits, and morality plays
If one school downplays the importance of REAR WINDOW (1954), Durgnat defend
it; if another school extols STRANGERS ON A TRAIN (1951), he downgrades it
Durgnat also singles out CAHIERS DU CINEMA critics like Claude Chabrol and Eri
Rohmer for being too closley attuned to Hitchcock's "moral preoccupations," assertin
that "they were, perhaps, sensitised by sharing with him a Roman Catholi
background or sympathies." Although he grudgingly acknowledges the value of th'
AUTEURIST approach in the 1950s, he rejects its long-term value for moder
scholars. The force of Durgnat's combative narrative is so upsetting to Hitchcock'
defenders, that one reviewer of the book writes that "Durgnat makes dubious an
pretentious judgments, goes off on tangents, free-associates, drops names and--no
for the first time--gets carried away by his own mercurial arguments, which leav
Hitchcock himself, Durgnat's ostensible subject, high and dry, as unruffled an
imperturbable as ever."[501]

If you enjoy radical interpretations and sophisticated allusions, this is
challenging book to examine. On the other hand, if you prefer strong, logica
arguments clearly presented, this uneven critique is very annoying. A bibliography
filmography, and index are included. Well worth browsing.

*Freeman, David. THE LAST DAYS OF ALFRED HITCHCOCK: A MEMOIR FEATURIN'
THE SCREENPLAY OF ALFRED HITCHCOCK'S "THE SHORT NIGHT." Woodstock: Th
Overlook Press, 1984. Illustrated. 281pp.

The weakest book on Hitchcock, this superficial account originated as an articl
for ESQUIRE[502] and then got blown up into a book. It presents the opinions of th
last screenwriter to work with the master of supsense before he died. Freeman ha
gotten the assignment to rewrite the script for THE SHORT NIGHT, after Hitchcoc
had "fired" Ernest Lehman.[503] The six months Freeman spent with Hitchcock, betwee
December 1978 and May 1979, serve as the excuse for this rambling publication
Divided into two parts, the first section describing the screenwriter's experience
borders on sensationalism and crudity. It tells us little that is new and an awful lc

---

[501] Paul Thomas, "Book Review: THE STRANGE CASE OF ALFRED HITCHCOCK and THE ART O
ALFRED HITCHCOCK," FILM QUARTERLY 30:3 (Spring 1977):58.

[502] David Freeman, "The Last Days of Alfred Hitchcock," ESQUIRE 97:4 (Apri
1982):81-105.

[503] Lehman denies that his old friend had "fired" him, but offers no explanation o
why Freeman was given the rewriting assignment. For more information, see Ernes
Lehman, "Working with Hitchcock," NEW YORK TIMES BOOK REVIEW (February 3, 1985)
p.35.

that is old hat. "When I was working with him," Freeman writes, "he was seventy-nine years old and sometimes lost in the solitude of great physical pain, mostly from arthritis. He moved in and out of senility, and yet for all that, he seemed in no hurry to finish his work, even though his life was clearly limited." In a breezy section, heavily padded with comments about past films, Freeman tells us that Hitchcock liked playing with the director's pacemaker, admonished the youthful screenwriter for not putting more nudity into the script, constantly got drunk, kept repeating old stories, and claimed that Ingrid Bergman had been in love with him for over thirty years. The problem with Freeman's lifeless anecdotes is his lack of intellectual curiosity. Hitchcock literature is replete with tales of his bouts with obesity, alcoholic stupors, and infatuations with beautiful stars. In writing his book, the author tries to impress the reader with the research that he did on earlier films and on Hitchcock himself. To suggest, therefore, that the producer-director's behavior was radically different at this stage in his life (except for the feeble state of his health) is either sloppy research or bad reporting. The second and larger section offers a comparison between the Lehman and the Freeman scripts. The impression left is that neither script advanced anyone's reputation. A filmography is included, but no bibliography or index is provided. Worth browsing.

*Haley, Michael. THE ALFRED HITCHCOCK ALBUM. Englewood Cliffs: Prentice-Hall, 1981. Illustrated. 192pp.
     A visually attractive book with a glib narrative, this disappointing publication adds little to material available either in other picture albums or introductory studies. Haley, an actor and free-lance writer, clearly admires his subject but presents Hitchcock's career and work in a diffident manner, revealing little that is interesting or fresh about the private Hitchcock or the public figure. Although the more than 150 illustrations are nicely captioned and handsomely reproduced, they are not enough to overcome the triteness of the historical overview. A filmography, bibliography, and index are included. Approach with caution.

*Harris, Robert A., and Michael S. Lasky. THE FILMS OF ALFRED HITCHCOCK. Secaucus: The Citadel Press, 1976. Illustrated. 256pp.

*LaValley, Albert J., ed. FOCUS ON HITCHCOCK. Englewood Cliffs: Prentice-Hall, 1972. Illustrated. 186pp.
     One of the best collections in this series, LaValley begins his anthology with a useful overview of the critical responses to Hitchcock as an artist. "To many serious film critics," the editor writes, "Hitchcock has been a disappointing figure, a great visual artist with a penchant for 'pure' cinema, a master of montage and narrative technique, who wasted his gifts on melodramatic genres." On the other hand, the CAHIERS DU CINEMA critics of the 1950s, particularly Chabrol, Rohmer, and Truffaut, idolized Hitchcock. They insisted, LaValley reminds us, that Hitchcock's British thrillers in the 1930s perfected "his limited art and the American movies   .   .   . [diluted] his skills." And if British film critics despaired over the decline in Hitchcock's tight editing style resulting from the unwelcomed influence of Selznick and the star system, "the French celebrated the way the films opened out into the murkier psychological areas, their subjective quality, and the long, mysterious, and troubling tracking shots that were added to the methods of the Eisensteinian montage and quick cutting."
     The debate over the merits of Hitchcock's art are amplified in the book's three major sections. Part 1, "Hitchcock on Hitchcock," includes two interviews with the director and two essays by him. Part 2 "Hitchcock Controversy," offers five stimulating essays by Lindsay Anderson, Andre Bazin, Robin Wood, Andrew Sarris, and Raymond Durgnat, collectively evaluating and chronicling the director's progress from THE PLEASURE GARDEN (1925) to PSYCHO (1960). Part 3, "The Films," contains nine essays dealing with his Hollywood period, ranging from James Agee's

review of NOTORIOUS (1946) and Raymond Chandler's comments on STRANGERS ON A TRAIN (1951), to Leo Braudy's analysis of Hitchcock's techniques and Jack Edmund Nolan's evaluation of Hitchcock's TV films. In addition, LaValley provides an added bonus, analyzing "the Plane and Cornfield Chase" in NORTH BY NORTHWEST (1959). A filmography and bibliography are included. Recommended for special collections.

*Leff, Leonard J. HITCHCOCK AND SELZNICK: THE RICH AND STRANGE COLLABORATION OF ALFRED HITCHCOCK AND DAVID O. SELZNICK IN HOLLYWOOD. New York: Weidenfeld and Nicolson, 1987. Illustrated. 385pp.
    Leff's study on one of the most important and controversial partnerships in Hollywood history is filled with delightful anecdotes and fresh perspectives. In discussing the years from 1938 to 1948, the resourceful Oklahoma State University professor sidesteps many of the biases of previous Hitchcock and Selznick biographies to construct a iconoclastic look at why the two men shared an extraordinary association. "Their personalities and their aesthetics clashed," the author tells us at the outset. "Their mutual exploitation, their conflicting managerial styles, their long periods apart, their increasingly tense periods together, and their negotiation and near continual renegotiation of employment agreements also buffeted their relationship." Whether one agrees with Leff's conclusion that the producer needed the director of "little British thrillers" more than Hitchcock needed Selznick, the account of their decade-long association adds considerably to our understanding not only of the two strong-willed personalities, but also of Hollywood filmmaking.
    Leff's opening chapter, "Transatlantic Overtures," is the weakest section in the book's eight chapters. Most of its breezy prose deals with sketchy biographical portraits of the Hollywood mogul and the droll British director, quickly establishing Leff's position on several controversial topics. For example, the author dismisses the notion that Hitchcock's British films were exceptional, asserting instead that the early 1930s saw Hitchcock burdened with "Dull stories, capricious producers, and tyrannical distributors." Few insights are provided on the reasons why Hitchcock wanted to work in Hollywood, or why Selznick moved cautiously in signing the director that none of the other American studios felt could succeed in the American film system.
    Chapter 2, "Signing Hitchcock," begins to suggest the range of Leff's research of heretofore unpublished documents and his uneasiness with recent interpretations of Hitchcock's "dark side." In addition to offering persuasive reasons why MGM backed away from hiring Hitchcock in 1937, the author establishes the major problems that the director presented to Hollywood: e.g., a slow and expensive filmmaker preoccupied with experimentation and indifferent to the star system. Particularly useful is the section on the March 1939 contract that tied Hitchcock to Selznick for the next decade and the testy business relationship that followed.
    Chapter 3, "Rebecca," provides the first full opportunity to appreciate Leff's scholarship and reactions to current theories on Hitchcock. An overriding concern is to show what contributions both the director and the producer made on Hitchcock's first American movie, REBECCA (1940), a work that received eleven Oscar nominations and won two awards for Best Film and Best Cinematography (George Barnes). Without mentioning the fact that Hitchcock never won an Oscar for Best Director (he was nominated five times--1940, 1943, 1945, 1954, and 1960--and received the 1967 Irving G. Thalberg Memorial Award from the Motion Picture Academy), Leff makes it clear that REBECCA owes more to Selznick than it does to Hitchcock. Another interesting perspective concerns Hitchcock's treatment of Joan Fontaine. While many scholars focus on the director's controversial treatment of the inexperienced actress, Leff stresses Selznick's attentiveness to her needs and abilities, arguing that it was the producer, not the director, who fought for special handling of Fontaine. Elsewhere in the book, Leff cites both Fontaine and Teresa Wright as examples of actresses who praised the director for his commitment to family values and for his ability to instil confidence. A third valuable perspective concerns the reasons why Hitchcock enjoyed working with Walter Wanger and how that relationship affected not only his dealings with Selznick, but also the director's emerging problems in Hollywood.

Chapter 4, "Between Engagements," reveals the strengths and weaknesses of the author's approach to his subject. On the positive side, Leff deftly attacks claims that Hitchcock mistreated his actresses, pointing out that his treatment of Fontaine in REBECCA resulted in other actresses and some producers clamoring to work with the director. In analyzing the Wanger-RKO loanout productions--e.g., FOREIGN CORRESPONDENT (1940), MR. AND MRS. SMITH (1941), SUSPICION (1942), SABOTEUR (1942), and SHADOW OF A DOUBT (1943); Leff highlights the negative image that Hitchcock developed for being "an exceedingly slow director," but emphasizes that Hitchcock may not have been the real culprit. Particularly interesting are the periodic contrasts between the freedom accorded Hitchcock in Hollywood, and that given to his peers like Frank Capra, Howard Hawks, John Ford, and Lewis Milestone. In the process, we get constant reminders of how producers used marketing research to test the viability of titles, stars, and publicity strategies for future film releases; studio politics affected contracts and assignments; and the importance of Hitchcock's public image to his future. Leff's discussion of the Darryl F. Zanuck-Hitchcock collaboration, LIFEBOAT (1943), epitomizes the weakness of the author's emphasis on the Selznick-Hitchcock collaboration. It not only forces him to quickly skip over the production problems, but also to ignore the controversies that the film generated about Hitchcock's approach to Nazi ideology and the alleged effect that it had on the war effort. Although the material on Sidney Bernstein, then head of the British Ministry of Information, and the two British shorts he had Hitchcock make for the British government add to our understanding of the director's behavior during World War II, Leff adds little to the debate between Hitchcock and Michael Balcon over the latter's accusation of the director's "desertion" of England during wartime. Important information is also missing on Alma Reville's contributions to her husband's work during this crucial period. Because Leff does such a fine job describing the intricacies of the Selznick-Hitchcock productions, one feels cheated at not having his detailed analyses on the loanout films.

Chapter 5, "Suspicion," is Leff at his best. Beginning with a reminder that the six films that Hitchcock made away from Selznick proved Hitchcock's strengths as a producer-director and increased his dissatisfaction with his employer, the author proceeds to a valuable analysis of SUSPICION (1946) that also includes a superb discussion of filmmaking within the context of the Hollywood studio system. Careful attention is paid to the process of collaborative screenwriting, marketing research, satisfying censoring bodies within and without the American film industry, the different roles of a producer and a director, the nature of the casting process, the impact of other films on current productions, the relationship between national mood and film content, the importance of sneak previews, and the influence of non-industry people on the film continuum. Particularly interesting are Leff's comments on how May Romm (Selznick's personal psychiatrist) functioned as a technical advisor to the film, how Hitchcock treated Ingrid Bergman and Gregory Peck, and what role Ben Hecht played in the production process. The chapter also contains one of the book's funniest quips. In commenting on the innocence and plainness of the newly arrived Bergman in Hollywood, the actress Joan Bennett cracked, "We have enough trouble getting jobs as it is. Do they have to import kitchen maids?"

Chapter 6, "Notorious," fuels the continuing debate over which of the two men benefited most from their contentious relationship. At the outset, Leff teases us with pithy comments about Hitchcock and Selznick that touch on critical issues but are never developed. For example, the author makes a sudden shift in his approach to the "dark side" of Hitchcock, asserting that the director's insistence on "negative acting" and his attitude that "it's only a moo-vie" drew him naturally "to the story of a woman made over, a woman as sex object." Later in the chapter, Leff, in an apparent turnabout, cites Hitchcock biographer Donald Spoto directly, appearing to accept the biographer's theory that the director's treatment of the male leads was motivated by "sexual feelings he neither understood, nor desired. . . ." As for Selznick, the author asserts that the now-embattled producer (e.g., marital problems, cost overruns on DUEL IN THE SUN, and an affair with Jennifer Jones) was "Short on confidence and long on tricks. . . ." The crucial observation, however, pertains to the producer's awkward distribution arrangements with United Artists, where

Selznick had been perceived as a major source of revenue and instead had become a major liability. Building on these types of assertions, Leff then crafts his analysis of NOTORIOUS (1946) around Selznick's problems with Charlie Chaplin (an enraged director of United Artists), Hitchcock (an ambitious employee eager to form his own independent company), Ben Hecht (a high-priced, Jewish screenwriter, who insists on incorporating his hatred of the Nazis into the characterizations of the film's villains), and RKO (the company that operates as a "cover" for Selznick's deception of United Artists). In addition to the intriguing details of the various scripts, the casting of the film, the problems with the major censors (e.g., the Production Code Administration, the Federal Bureau of Investigation, and the Office of War Information), and Hitchcock's not-so-private dealings with Sidney Bernstein over the formation of their independent company, Transatlantic Pictures (announced in the Spring of 1946), Leff spices his narrative with useful insights into filmmaking during the war years. The author's detailed presentation of the distraught producer and the evasive director emerges not only as a solid piece of research, but also as a good melodrama. The one highly questionable judgment is Leff's argument that Hitchcock "lived to make pictures, not money." That sounds more like the director's public pronouncements than the enormously successful businessman who used his name and image to create a financial empire that he scrupulously monitored.

Chapter 7, "The Paradine Case," investigates the last film that Hitchcock made under his contract to Selznick. Acknowledging from the start that the 1947 film represents the "nadir of Hitchcock in the 1940s," Leff charts what went wrong and why. He also makes it a point to blame almost everyone connected with THE PARADINE CASE (1947) for its failure. Hitchcock's mistakes include scriptwriting weaknesses, a preoccupation with getting Transatlantic Pictures established, a lack of concern with the tastes of American audiences, and the slowest production pace of any Hitchcock film. The most interesting claim, however, is that the headstrong director was frightened about his future. While other biographers claim the director was going through "male menopause" (John Russell Taylor) or demonstrating his dissatisfaction with the Selznick empire (Donald Spoto), Leff argues that Hitchcock was distracted by the possibility that the break with Selznick would not give the Englishman (Hitchcock waited fifteen years before becoming an American citizen) a better situation or even a comparable "safety net." Curiously, Hitchcock's notorious habit of dozing during the shooting is rationalized as "conserving energy" or prtending "to doze to gain control." Among the charges leveled at Selznick, who had the reputation of being a "woman's producer," are his mishandling of Ingrid Bergman (and thus her refusal to star in THE PARADINE CASE), the undercapitalization of his new distribution company, Selznick Releasing Organization, and his distractions resulting from his wife's successful new career as a Broadway producer (e.g., A STREETCAR NAMED DESIRE), and the horrendous reception of DUEL IN THE SUN. A particularly ironic touch is Leff's observation that Selznick received harsher treatment from the media than did Hitchcock although they both shared in the blame, and that the producer's valiant efforts to get the director an Oscar nomination resulted in Ethel Barrymore's getting a nomination for supporting actress, a performance that Selznick shredded in the editing process.

The concluding chapter, "Transatlantic Postlude," serves as both a summation of the Selznick-Hitchcock collaboration and a commentary on the two men's progress after they separated. Except for the analysis of why Transatlantic Pictures failed and how Hitchcock landed at Warner Bros., Leff presents little new information. The discussions on Hitchcock's first two post-Selznick productions--e.g., ROPE (1948) and UNDER CAPRICORN (1949)--do little more than review material found elsewhere. Moreover, the author leaves us with a number of very debatable judgments. For example, the claim that Hitchcock was "a generous man" does not square with his proclivity for downplaying the work of his collaborators or exploiting subordinates. The few lines describing Hitchcock's uneven career at Warner Bros.--e.g., STAGE FRIGHT (1950), STRANGERS ON A TRAIN (1951), I CONFESS (1952), and DIAL M FOR MURDER (1954)--vastly oversimplify Hitchcock's progress in the early 1950s. The same is true for his enormous success at Paramount--e.g., REAR WINDOW (1954),

TO CATCH A THIEF (1955), THE TROUBLE WITH HARRY (1955), THE MAN WHO KNEW TOO MUCH (1956), VERTIGO (1958), and PSYCHO (1960). Hitchcock's MGM production NORTH BY NORTHWEST (1959) is cited as an example of how difficult negotiating with Hitchcock had become. No mention is made of THE WRONG MAN (1957) or of the importance of Lew Wasserman in Hitchcock's career. Furthermore, Hitchcock's limited role in his TV series ALFRED HITCHCOCK PRESENTS (1955-1962) and THE ALFRED HITCHCOCK HOUR (1962-1965) presents Leff with the problem of reconciling his earlier claim that the producer-director lived for his work and not money and is never addressed. The final years at Universal-International--e.g., THE BIRDS (1963), MARNIE (1964), TORN CURTAIN (1966), TOPAZ (1969), FRENZY (1972), and FAMILY PLOT (1976)--are dismissed as examples of Hitchcock's "eclipse" without any indication why. Talking about him as a "Hollywood legend" who "could point to the masterpieces of his British and American period as justification for his vanity" hardly does justice to the facts. The treatment accorded Selznick is equally disappointing. In the end, Leff might have done better to conclude his compelling study with the producer's astute observations about Hollywood's golden years: "When I think of what we were   .   .   .   I commence to regain some perspective and some objectivity."

The limitations of the final chapter aside, this outstanding study is absorbing and stimulating research presented in a fast-moving and entertaining narrative. As Stephen Harvey observes, "Mr. Leff focuses   .   .   .   on this team's thorny symbiosis, and comes up with a conclusion as persuasive as it is heretical."[504] The beautifully reproduced illustrations and the witty anecdotes add considerably to the important information packed into each of the book's eight chapters. Filmographies of the two legendary figures, endnotes, a bibliography, and an index also add to Leff's considerable achievement. Recommended for special collections.

*McCartey, John, and Brian Kelleher. ALFRED HITCHCOCK PRESENTS: AN ILLUSTRATED GUIDE TO THE TEN-YEAR CAREER OF THE MASTER OF SUSPENSE. New York: St. Martin's Press, 1985. Illustrated.

*Modleski, Tania. THE WOMEN WHO KNEW TOO MUCH: HITCHCOCK AND FEMINIST THEORY. New York: Methuen, 1988. Illustrated. 149pp.

A highly original and challenging approach to Hitchcock's treatment of women, this intelligent study begins by re-examining the popular theories on how the master of suspense manipulated and abused females for the purposes of satisfying his and our voyeuristic pleasures. One of the book's primary theses, Modleski tells us, "is that time and time again in Hitchcock films, the strong fascination and identification with femininity revealed in them subverts the claims to mastery and authority not only of the male characters but of the director himself." Rather than become embroiled in the ongoing debate about Hitchcock's understanding of women's roles in a patriachy versus his misogynistic imagery, Modleski argues that the director's films are "characterized by a thoroughgoing ambivalence about femininity--which explains why it has been possible for critics to argue with some plausibility on either side of the issue." Using a psycholanalytic approach, she makes a plausible case for women's refusing to succumb to "patriarchial assimilation." In fact, Modleski insists that Hitchcock's stories--e.g., BLACKMAIL (1929) and NOTORIOUS (1946)--showing women oppressed result in female spectators' becoming angry and thereby produce emotions contrary to those of many male spectators. She eventually concludes that Hitchcock is both sympathetic and misogynistic to women. An interesting feature of this feisty analysis is Modleski's concept of the nature of the female and male spectator. By focusing on the problems of identity and identification, she examines

---

[504]   Stephen Harvey, "Contentious but Catalytic," NEW YORK TIMES BOOK REVIEW (January 17, 1988):13.

the bisexuality of women, the importance of mother-daughter relationships to women's experiences, the "'compulsory heterosexuality' of mainstream film," the victimization of women, and the "dialectic of identification and dread in the male's spectator's response to femininity." After analyzing seven films, from BLACKMAIL to FRENZY (1972), the author concludes that "putting the blame for crimes against women where it belongs . . . is available in the Hitchcock text if one cares to look; it has been the task of my study simply to put this knowledge more securely than ever in the possession of women."

Clearly, this is not your standard study of Hitchcock's world. Little time is spent on repeating general information, readers are expected to be familiar not only with psycholanalytic literature but also feminist positions spelled out in key works, and one has to be very conversant with Hitchcock's works to enter the debate. For anyone interested in the cutting edge of feminist criticism in the eighties, this is the book to read. Endnotes, well-selected illustrations, a good bibliography, and an index are included. Regrettably, there is no filmography. Recommended for special collections.

*Perry, George. THE FILMS OF ALFRED HITCHCOCK. New York: E. P. Dutton and Company, 1965. Illustrated. 160pp.
"This is a small book," Perry explains, "about a great talent. Not critical analysis. nor definitive biography, this is instead a handbook and guide to the forty-nine films of four decades and the man who created them." Perry's style is straightforward, his comments brief and useful, and the illustrations are splendid. A filmography and index are included, but no bibliography is provided. Worth browsing.

Perry, George. HITCHCOCK. New York: Doubleday and Company, 1975. Illustrated. 126pp.
This author's second, concise survey of Hitchcock's work and themes offers a good summary of the generalizations and opinions regarding the director's progress from THE PLEASURE GARDEN (1925) to FRENZY (1972), for example, the comments on VERTIGO (1958). "It has been regarded as a structural weakness of the film," Perry tells us, "that Hitchcock revealed the secret to the audience only two-thirds of the way through, but left James Stewart guessing. It is certainly true that his main interest in the story, which is that of a neurotic detective recreating the image of a girl from his past, would have preserved its mystery more effectively if the murder plot had not been shown. It is as if we, the audience, had been led up a para-psychological gumtree." More than eighty illustrations, many in color, underscore Perry's reactions to fifty Hitchcock films. Except for the limited information in the captions, this book is a handy guide to the standard Hitchcock image. A filmography and index are included, but no bibliography is provided. Worth browsing.

*Rohmer, Eric, and Claude Chabrol. HITCHCOCK: THE FIRST FORTY-FIVE FILMS. Trans. Stanley Hochman. New York: Frederick Ungar Publishing Company, 1979. Illustrated. 178pp.
The pioneering study that elevated Hitchcock's reputation in critical circles, this publication of the original 1957 first full-length book on the director operates as the touchstone of most debates on Hitchcock's artistry. Rohmer and Chabrol, then CAHIERS DU CINEMA critics and soon to become important directors in France's NOUVELLE VAGUE, explain in their foreword the options they considered in analyzing Hitchcock's works. "Our first idea," Rohmer and Chabrol write, "was to follow a logical rather than a chronological order and to isolate both the themes ordinarily found in our director and the general characteristics of his style." Rejecting that notion because it forced an unnatural separation between form and content, they stated their now-classical thesis that "The idea of 'exchange,' which we find

everywhere in his work, may be given either a moral expression (the transfer of guilt), a psychological expression (suspicion), a dramatic expression (blackmail--or even 'suspense'), or a concrete expression (a to-and-fro movement)." Their second notion was to concentrate on the important films and ignore the lesser ones, but they rejected it because they didn't know how to make the selections. Moreover, they found a number of the earlier films comparable in skill to Hitchcock's later works. In the end, they took the chronological approach, dividing the first forty-four films into three main sections: the English period, the American period associated with Selznick, and the American period from ROPE (1948) to the remake of THE MAN WHO KNEW TOO MUCH (1956). At the end of their seminal study, the authors conclude that "In Hitchcock's work form does not embellish content, it creates it. All of Hitchcock can be summed up in this formula." A filmography and an index are included. Recommended for special collections.

*Rothman, William. HITCHCOCK--THE MURDEROUS GAZE. Cambridge: Harvard University Press, 1982. Illustrated. 371pp.

"This book," the Harvard Professor of visual and environmental studies explains, "follows five Hitchcock films from beginning to end. Using frame enlargements as illustration and evidence, I attempt to put in words the thinking inscribed in their succession of frames. (In transcribing dialogue and describing gestures, expressions, and movements of the camera, I relied on no scripts and checked my language only by direct observation of the films themselves.) My aim was to demonstrate something fundamental about Hitchcock and about the making and viewing of films, and to reflect on the implications of this demonstration for our understanding of the conditions and history of the art of film." The precise shot-by-shot analyses of THE LODGER (1926), MURDER! (1929), THE 39 STEPS (1935), SHADOW OF A DOUBT (1943), and PSYCHO (1960) reveal Rothman's considerable self-confidence about the validity of his chronologically arranged, close readings of the films, as well as the strengths and weaknesses of the methodology. On the positive side, the approach clearly demonstrates how much Hitchcock employed montage to achieve his superb effects, especially in the famous shower scene in PSYCHO. Rothman's technique also affords him many opportunities to speculate philosophically on the reasons why Hitchcock did what he did, why audiences react to the action and reaction shots as they do, and what ties PSYCHO has to THE LODGER. Best of all, the process adds fresh insights into Hitchcock's earlier and less appreciated films. On the negative side, the arrogance of assuming that one can detect from the image alone "the range of Hitchcock's ambitions" is, at times, pretentious and pedantic. Among other things, it ignores the contributions of collaborators, the commercial demands of the moment, and the limitations of the technology of the era.

Those readers sympathetic to Rothman's style and methodology will value his scholarship and unique insights. Even his detractors should applaud his use of 600 frame enlargements to add new perspectives to Hitchcock's entertainment values. Endnotes and an index are included. Well worth browsing.

Ryall, Tom. ALFRED HITCHCOCK AND THE BRITISH CINEMA. Urbana: University of Illinois Press, 1986. Illustrated. 193pp.

Simone, Sam P. HITCHCOCK AS ACTIVIST: POLITICS AND THE WAR FILMS. Ann Arbor: UMI Research Press, 1985. 203pp.

Originally written as a 1982 Ph.D. dissertation for Brigham Young University, this uneven study often reads like a publicity release for Hitchcock Productions, Incorporated. For example, Simone tells us at the outset, that he will show Hitchcock "to be a staunch activist in his support of freedom and liberty. His films champion the United States, whose government personifies and extends national and international democracy as the basic political form of the free-world ethic." Specious anecdotes--e.g., Hitchcock's being "jailed" by his father, and the FBI's keeping the

director under surveillance for several months--are reported as fact rather than
questioned; complex situations--e.g., the relationship between Hitchcock and his
wife, Alma Reville--are reduced to fan magazine rhetoric: "Their life together was
to be one of mutual love and respect as they faced the challenges and problems of
the cinema world--it was a perfect match." Anyone even vaguely familiar with Leonard
J. Leff's HITCHCOCK AND SELZNICK will recognize three flaws: Simone's naivete in
accepting Hitchcock's assertions at face value, his failure to credit collaborators with
script contributions, attributing almost every idea instead to the director himself,
and his lack of sophistication in seeing topical issues inserted in films as indications
of artistic insights rather than as commercial ploys and wartime propaganda.

Simone's limitations as a film critic and historian are all the more disappointing
because of the intriguing thesis of the book. Paralleling four Hitchcock films--e.g.,
FOREIGN CORRESPONDENT (1940), SABOTEUR (1942), LIFEBOAT (1944), and
NOTORIOUS (1946)--with political history, the author explores the director's political
ideology concerning World War II. Simone's basic questions examine "how World War
II espionage and sabotage are made evident in Hitchcock's films of that period; what
political ideology is advocated in selected Hitchcock films of World War II; and how
Alfred Hitchcock creates and resolves suspense in his political films. Following a
useful overview of Hitchcock's career, the author analyzes each of the films. In each
instance, Simone does a better job of reviewing political history than he does in
analyzing film history. The concluding chapter provides the "answers" to the author's
original questions. The quality of the examination is reflected in the author's umbrella
observation that "During the course of World War II, the Axis and Allies carried out
acts of espionage and sabotage which Hitchcock represented in specific films.
Hitchcock's interest and knowledge in such affairs, together with his desire as activist
to aid the Allies' war effort through his creative film talent, led him in the 1940s to
make the four films we have examined." What led Hitchcock to make these films had
more to do with studio politics, a desire for artistic freedom, and an understanding
of clever commercial filmmaking than with the director's political conscience or his
independent choices. Good endnotes, a strong bibliography, and an index complete
this weak publication. Approach with caution.

*Spoto, Donald. THE ART OF ALFRED HITCHCOCK: FIFTY YEARS OF HIS MOTION
PICTURES. New York: Hopkinson and Blake, 1976. Illustrated. 525pp.

A useful introductory and comprehensive study, Spoto relies heavily on
interviews with Hitchcock collaborators--e.g., Peggy Ashcroft, Ingrid Bergman, Hume
Cronyn, Joan Fontaine, Grace Kelly, Tippi Hedren, Tom Helmore, Ernest Lehman,
Simon Oakland, Jessica Tandy, Samuel Taylor, and Teresa Wright--as well as
Hitchcock himself on the set of FAMILY PLOT (1976) to fill in the details about the
style and content of Hitchcock's films. No serious attempt is made to present an
in-depth, comprehensive perspective on the producer-director's private life or
business machinations. Instead, the resourceful author regales us with a useful,
subjective   portrait   of   an   intriguing   personality   and   offers   fascinating
behind-the-scenes anecdotes about Hitchcock's films and techniques, the reactions
of his cast and crews to specific incidents, and entertaining glimpses of his prankish
behavior and personal life-style. Except for the first chapter, which covers the period
from 1925 to 1934, each of the remaining thirty-six chapters is devoted to examining
individual films through plot synopses, characterizations, and critical commentaries.
Given his concern with personal reactions, it is not surprising that the author moves
more rapidly through the British period than he does in the chapters after Hitchcock
comes to America in 1939. As long as Spoto sticks to factual details, he provides a
lively and informative review of the films and of Hitchcock's concern with entertaining
his audiences.   Among the best sections are those that deal with films like
SPELLBOUND (1945), VERTIGO (1958), NORTH BY NORTHWEST (1959), PSYCHO
(1960), and THE BIRDS (1963). Spoto runs into trouble, however, when he speculates
about the psychological and sociological motivations for Hitchcock's menacing themes
and sinister characterizations, often making critical judgments that lack credibility

and theoretical support--e.g., comparisons between Hitchcock and literary authors, interpretations of what exists beneath the surface in and between various films, the symbolic meaning of particular episodes and characters, and an emotional defense of Hitchcock's moral cynicism. In addition to a much appreciated filmography and an index, Spoto provides valuable storyboards from FAMILY PLOT. An index is included. Well worth browsing.

*Spoto, Donald. THE DARK SIDE OF GENIUS: THE LIFE OF ALFRED HITCHCOCK. Boston: Little, Brown and Company, 1983. Illustrated. 594pp.

Offering an absorbing portrait of Hitchcock both as a man and as an artist, this book emerges as the most comprehensive and controversial examination of Hitchcock to-date.[505] Unlike Spoto's earlier work, the new study goes into greater detail about events, personalities, and cinematic allusions and thus presents sociological and psychological theories that deserve serious consideration. The skill with which Spoto builds his case that Hitchcock was "living with inner demons of lust and possessiveness, dark fantasies about killing, and of unfulfilled sexual daydreams" is impressive, if not necessarily persuasive. Although much of the basic Hitchcock material is covered in Taylor's authorized biography, Spoto's approach opens up considerably more possibilities and provides many more bold interpretations.

Arranged chronologically, the book's first seven of sixteen chapters set the stage for the author's shocking assertions about Hitchcock's character and intentions in most of his fifty-three films, works that Spoto insists are more biographical than anyone previously understood. For example, we're told that Hitchcock's infatuation with Madeleine Carroll during the production of THE 39 STEPS (1935) was symptomatic of his repressed sexuality and of his poor self-image (reinforced constantly by weight problems and a class-conscious British society that denigrated the artistic achievements of anyone working in a low-brow medium like film). The stories the ungenerous director circulated about his role in developing the screenplay of THE LADY VANISHES (1938) are dismissed as lies, indicative of Hitchcock's obsession with taking full credit for work done by others and refusing to reward and to praise his collaborators.

Spoto's three chapters on the Selznick-Hitchcock era (1939-1949) not only challenge many previous assumptions about the relationship between the two powerful and creative personalities, but also provide dozens of interesting and colorful anecdotes. For example, Hitchcock's crude habit of dozing at story conferences is attributed more to his obesity and gastronomical orgies than to his not being the center of attention or to his boredom with subordinates. The sections describing Michael Balcon's attacks on Hitchcock as a "traitor" during World War II reopen the debate on what role artists play during periods of national crises. The analysis of REBECCA (1940) uses Hitchcock's alleged infatuations with the inexperienced Joan Fontaine and his long-term associate Joan Harrison to underscore the forty-year-old Hitchcock's chaste relationship with his wife, Alma Reville, and the sexual problems it created for him for the next forty years. The analysis of SHADOW OF A DOUBT (1943) functions as an opportunity to show why the film is Hitchcock's "first spiritually autobiographical work" and "a handbook of all the literary and cultural influences on his life." Hitchcock's two films with Ben Hecht and Ingrid Bergman--e.g., SPELLBOUND (1945) and NOTORIOUS (1946)--illustrate, for Spoto, the director's inner feelings of "repressed passion, desire and danger, and the conflicts of duty." Particularly interesting are Spoto's speculations on why Hitchcock continually agreed to renew his contract with Selznick, gladly took assignments with

---

[505] A major academic concern relates to the relationship between a filmmaker and the works he or she produces and how this relationship is analyzed. For an example of the controversy, see Howard Davis, "Books: Hitchcock's Dark Side," ON FILM 12 (Spring 1984):50-3.

Walter Wanger, and eventually signed with the British exhibitor Sidney Bernstein to form the short-lived Transatlantic Pictures.

Although Spoto only devotes one chapter to Hitchcock's Warner Bros. period (1950-1954), he packs it with useful information as well as a few callous anecdotes. A case in point is Raymond Chandler's cutting comment on watching Hitchcock emerge from his limousine when the disgruntled screenwriter of STRANGERS ON A TRAIN loudly said, "Look at that fat bastard trying to get out of his car!" On the other hand, Spoto can be extremely insightful in his commentaries, particularly in pointing out the importance of the double motif in STRANGERS ON A TRAIN, how Grace Kelly personified Hitchcock's dream heroine, and the crucial role that Lew Wasserman played in the director's career and financial security.

Spoto's chapter on Hitchcock's Paramount years (1954-1962) focuses primarily on two topics: (1) the producer-director's astute business acumen in making a fortune through the TV series ALFRED HITCHCOCK PRESENTS and THE ALFRED HITCHCOCK HOUR (both managed by Joan Harrison) and a Hitchcock mystery magazine that exploited his name, and (2) the difficulties that Hitchcock had with the screenwriter John Michael Hayes and the performers Vera Miles and Kim Novak. The author hammers away at Hitchcock's mercurial emotional state, arguing that after the remake of THE MAN WHO KNEW TOO MUCH (1954) the director became preoccupied with "an obsessive fear of lost identity," evident in films like THE WRONG MAN (1957), VERTIGO (1958), NORTH BY NORTHWEST (1959), PSYCHO (1960), THE BIRDS (1963), and MARNIE (1964).

In Chapter 13, dealing with the move to Universal-International in 1962, Spoto reminds us that from the time Hitchcock arrived in America in 1939 to the end of the 1950s, he had experienced the most prolific period in his life ("24 feature films, 2 short films, and 15 television shows"). The final twenty years of his life (1960-1980), however, resulted in only "6 features and 5 television shows." The reasons for this sharp decline, Spoto insists, have more to do with Hitchcock's "sad and ultimately destructive passion," than with his age and financial security. To balance his harsh criticism of the producer-director's ugly and disgraceful behavior toward actresses and collaborators, Spoto continually reminds us that the scripts owed an enormous debt to Hitchcock's ideas and cinematic genius.

The book's final three chapters, covering the period from 1964 to Hitchcock's death in 1980, detail how awards and critical respectability compensated for the disastrous box-office failures of MARNIE (1964), TORN CURTAIN (1966), and TOPAZ (1969). Anecdotes about Hitchcock's falling-out with Herrmann, his success with FRENZY (1972), and his treatment of Lehman on the production of the director's last film, FAMILY PLOT (1976), are blended with stimulating behind-the-scenes stories about Hitchcock's feelings upon receiving a honorary Oscar in 1967, being given the American Film Institute's seventh Lifetime Achievement Award and being knighted by Queen Elizabeth II (both in 1979). Interestingly, Spoto's observations about the screenwriter David Freeman's relationship with Hitchcock on the uncompleted THE SHORT NIGHT present a far more complimentary portrait of the screenwriter than does Freeman in his book. The author concludes his study with Hitchcock's death on April 29, 1980. [506]

---

[506] For more information, see Bob Thomas, "Suspense Master Alfred Hitchcock Dead at 80," BURLINGTON FREE PRESS A (April 30, 1980):1, 16; Todd McCarthy, "Alfred Hitchcock, 80, Dies in Hollywood; Master of Suspense," VARIETY (May 7, 1980):350, 354; "Services on Friday
Master of Suspense for Sir Alfred, Master of Suspense," HOLLYWOOD REPORTER (April 30, 1980):1, 16; Arthur Knight, "The Passing of a Master," ibid., (May 9, 1980):10; Peter B. Flint, "Alfred Hitchcock Dies; A Master of Suspense," NEW YORK TIMES A (April 30, 1980):1, D23; and Vincent Canby, "Alfred Hitchcock Was the Poet of Civilized Suspense," NEW YORK TIMES 2 (May 11, 1980):1, 19.

Few books on film personalities demonstrate Spoto's considerable thoroughness in interviewing the subject's childhood associates, examining records, and recording conversations. Regrettably, the author's psychological musings on Hitchcock's state of mind seriously undermine the book's enormous value to the academic community. A case in point is Spoto's assertion that "Isolated as a child and as an adolescent, virtually closeted with his mother until his marriage at the age of twenty-seven, taught as a student and as an apprentice to cultivate the good opinions of others, Hitchcock harbored a lifelong terror of breaking the law and thus being thought a 'bad boy.' . . . His quiet, observant personality and his retreat behind a mass of restricting obesity made him at once safe from the (mostly imagined) blandishments of women and from competition with other men." Other examples include the author's speculations about Hitchcock's fetishes with toilets, the strained comparison between Hitchcock and the sixteenth-century Flemish painter Hieronymus Bosch, and his labored analyses of Hitchcock's alleged infatuations with Ingrid Bergman, Grace Kelly, Audrey Hepburn, Kim Novak, Vera Miles, and Tippi Hedren. The "dark side" of Hitchcock--e.g., alcoholism, marital strains, repressed sexuality--omitted or downplayed in Taylor's authorized biography becomes in this book the stuff that great motion pictures are made of. Those who share Spoto's view of Hitchcock's genius and feel that screenwriters like Charles Bennett, Brian Moore, Samuel Taylor, Ernest Lehman, and John Michael Hayes have not been given their proper due will find this book an outstanding critical work. Other critics like Paul Thomas will conclude that "For all the value of the information it provides, THE DARK SIDE OF GENIUS is finally a kind of self-consuming artefact."[507] Endnotes, a bibliography, a filmography, and an index are included. Recommended for special collections.

Taylor, John Russell. HITCH: THE LIFE AND TIMES OF ALFRED HITCHCOCK. New York: Pantheon, 1978. Illustrated. 321pp.

"Two facts are obvious: everybody knows Alfred Hitchcock, and nobody knows him," the author states at the outset of his reflective biography. The difficult task that Taylor sets for himself is to tell us something new and important about the scrupulously enigmatic film producer-director that has not been revealed in countless articles, books, and interviews over a highly visible fifty-three year career. The groundwork for this ambitious project is considerable: e.g., interviews with Hitchcock, his family, friends, and co-workers; visits to libraries and archives; and a screening of the films themselves. Although Taylor makes it clear that the "real Alfred Hitchcock must in some sense exist outside his films," he quickly comes to the conclusion that "Hitchcock is not so much in his films: he IS his films."

Having stated the problem, the author divides his informative research into two major sections: "England" and "America." The former includes eight concise chapters on Hitchcock's childhood and film career up to 1938 and adds to our understanding of Hitchcock's relationship with his stern father and his doting mother, the young clerk's life at the W. T. Henley Telegraph Company from 1913 to 1920, his debt to the Balcon-Saville-Freedman team, the difficult relationship he had with the director Graham Cutts, and the important role that Alma Reville played in his development as a director. Filled with many entertaining anecdotes (only a few of which are new), the chapters synthesize the by now familiar portrait of the shy and troubled Hitchcock transferring his private life to the public screen. The section on America provides the best behind-the-scenes stories, especially about films like VERTIGO (1958), PSYCHO (1960), THE BIRDS (1963), FRENZY (1972), and FAMILY PLOT (1976).

---

[507] Paul Thomas, "Book Review: THE DARK SIDE OF GENIUS," FILM QUARTERLY 37:1 (Fall 1983):37. For additional perspectives, see Richard Grenier, "Book Review: THE DARK SIDE OF GENIUS," NEW YORK TIMES BOOK REVIEW (March 6, 1983):1, 32-3; and Hume Cronyn, "Letters: Hitchcock," ibid., (April 10, 1983):45.

In matters related to Hitchcock's true personality, as compared to the public figure or the well-publicized character, Taylor is far less successful. "As an examination of the man's mind," writes Michael Armstrong, "it is perhaps less successful, tending to fall back on the customary scholastic delights of Catholicism, fear of the police, subconscious guilt transference and suppressed sexual desires, all reputedly lurking in every frame of his work."[508] At the end, we're left with an affectionate retelling of the basic biographical facts, bolstered by many amusing anecdotes, and a nagging feeling that the "real" Hitchcock, determined to manipulate his fans and friends for his own self-interest, was concerned only with entertaining his audiences and lacked intellectual depth or curiosity. As Kenneth Turan observes in his review of the book, ". . . it is Taylor's willingness to be a bit too tolerant of Hitchcock that is the book's central flaw. Obviously, he would not have got the director's cooperation were they not relatively close personal friends, but when that friendship leads to a generally uncritical point of view, even spilling over into worshipfulness, it is unclear whether the bargain was worth the price."[509] An index is included, but no bibliography or filmography is provided. Well worth browsing.

*Truffaut, Francois, with the collaboration of Helen G. Scott. HITCHCOCK. New York: Simon and Schuster, 1967. Illustrated. 256pp. New York: Simon and Schuster, 1980. 367pp.

A seminal document delving into the art and mind of Hitchcock, this book illustrates the strengths and weaknesses of the interview format. The measuring rod is the quality of the interviewer. While some reviewers dismiss Truffaut's ability to understand Hitchcock's mind or to appreciate the work of the producer-director's collaborators,[510] others applaud his rapport and approach to the study of the older man's work and technique. The earlier edition takes us from Hitchcock's childhood through TORN CURTAIN (1966), mixing biographical data with cinematic analyses. Using a chronological approach to uncover the strengths and weaknesses of the "complete film-maker," Truffaut, in a series of edited coversations between 1962 and 1966 (totaling more than fifty hours), demonstrates AUTEUR criticism at its best. In this instance, over 500 questions were used to examine "(a) the circumstances attending the inception of each film; (b) the preparation and structure of the screenplays; (c) specific directorial problems on each film; (d) Hitchcock's own assessment of the commercial and artistic results in relation to his initial expectations for each picture." Central to Hitchcock's work are his views on suspense, which the master explains as a "stretching out of the imagination" and insists is different from mysteries that are "seldom suspenseful" because the emphasis is on "a sort of intellectual puzzle." The mutual respect between Truffaut and Hitchcock is evident in the candid exchanges on the merits of individual films, the difficulties in perfecting screenplays, the handling of performers, and the cavalier disregard for plausibility in creating suspense. One comes away with an awareness not only of Hitchcock's love affair with technique and cinematic challenges, but also his unusual attitudes on characterizations. Moreover, the material is always lively, informative, and

---

[508]   Michael Armstrong, "Glimpses of Hitch," FILMS AND FILMING 25:7 (April 1979):46.

[509]   Kenneth Turan, "Nothing Too Personal," AMERICAN FILM 4:3 (December-January 1979):74.

[510]   Spoto argues in THE DARK SIDE OF GENIUS (p.495) that "the interviews reduced the writers, the designers, the photographers, the composers, and the actors to little other than elves in the master carpenter's workshop." Although crediting both men with providing important information of Hitchcock's superb film technique, Spoto insists that the book "is also a masterpiece of Hitchcockian self-promotion."

entertaining, helped enormously by over 470 excellent illustrations. Although Truffaut's obvious admiration for Hitchcock occasionally proves counterproductive in achieving the book's goals, the revised edition offers a reflective and penetrating summary of Hitchcock's work that elevates the book to a special place in the literature on film. A filmogaphy, bibliography, and index are included. Highly recommended for special collections.[511]

Yacowar, Maurice. HITCHCOCK'S BRITISH FILMS. Hamden: Archon Books, 1977. Illustrated. 314pp.

"Our objective," Yacowar writes, "is to provide a detailed description and analysis of each of Hitchcock's first twenty-three features, covering his first fifteen years of filmmaking." Yacowar's formalistic approach avoids any consideration of social and political contexts and emphasizes instead "the way each film works within itself as a drama of themes and devices." His basic premise is that the director uses his films to test the audience's moral values. That is, a character on screen acts foolishly and thus operates as a measuring rod of our ability to recognize poor judgments and bad behavior. The self-contained analyses, therefore, offer fascinating interpretations on a controversial period in Hitchcock's career. Stressing the producer-director's obsession with irony both in his technique and in his content, the study points out the range of genres--e.g., thrillers, dramas, romantic comedies, musicals--that occupied Hitchcock in his formative years and in the development of his characteristic themes--e.g., "the conflict between love and duty, or selfish interest and public responsibility, or freedom and morality; and his vision of man's quavering illusion of order over a basic and indomitable chaos." In addition, recognition is given to a number of Hitchcock's collaborators: e.g., the screenwriters Eliot Ventigmilia, Hal Young, Charles Bennett, and Jack Cox; as well as the important contributions of Ivor Montagu and Ian Hay.

The drawback in this otherwise imaginative book is the author's perspective on irony. As William Rothman comments, "Yacowar's picture of Hitchcock's authorship as 'ironic'--the exact antithesis of [John Russell] Taylor's picture [in HITCH: THE LIFE AND TIMES OF ALFRED HITCHCOCK]--is tempting, but must be rejected . . . [because it imagines] Hitchcock as cheerfully assuming an authorship which hides his true nature only by failing to recognize the profound darkness in Hitchcock's art."[512] Those readers who side with Rothman in thinking that Hitchcock consciously used the medium of film to express his feeling and values will have difficulty with Yacowar's critical conclusions. In addition, as Robin Wood observes, the author makes a handful of factual errors dealing with aspects of Hitchcock's work in Hollywood.[513]

Those reservations aside, Yacowar's research does a good job of adding fresh ammunition to the defenders of Hitchcock's British films as being indispensible to his status as an artist and not as a "mere entertainer." Endnotes and an index are included. Well worth browsing.

Weis, Elisabeth. THE SILENT SCREAM: ALFRED HITCHCOCK'S SOUND TRACK. Rutherford: Fairleigh Dickinson University Press, 1982. Illustrated. 188pp.

---

[511]   For other perspectives, see Gavin Millar, "Hitchcock Versus Truffaut: If I Lose My Leg I Lose Rosie," SIGHT AND SOUND 38:2 (Spring 1969):82-8; and Leo Braudy, "Hitchcock, Truffaut, and the Irresponsible Audience," FILM QUARTERLY 21:4 (Summer 1968):21-7.

[512]   William Rothman, "How Much Did Hitchcock Know?" QUARTERLY REVIEW OF FILM STUDIES 5:3 (Summer 1980):391.

[513]   Robin Wood, "Book Review: HITCHCOCK'S BRITISH FILMS," TAKE ONE 6:6 (May 1978):54.

"This study," the author inform us, ".   .   . is a first step toward defining one director's style descriptively rather than prescriptively--by what I have found instead of what theoretically ought to be." Its dual purpose, she explains, is "To enrich our understanding of Hitchcock, and to set up a few terms by which the aesthetics of the sound track can be discussed." Although Weis readily admits that it wasn't until Hitchcock developed an understanding of the relationship between sight and sound that his work matured, she stresses the importance of examining his silent films to establish the limitations he faced in terms of sound equipment and theory. The book's title, based upon the opening close-up of a woman screaming in the silent film THE LODGER (1926), underscores the notion of Hitchcock's progress from the mid-1920 to the early 1970s. The author's nine detailed chapters cover the main points about expressionistic sound, interior monologues, subliminal sounds, and general aural motifs; although, as John Russell Taylor observes, Weis "does skirt around   .   .   . [Hitchcock's] surprising casualness about choosing the composers of his scores, though of course instinct rather than conscious knowledge can here also have been operative."[514] The technical discussions limit the audience for this scholarly work. Endnotes, a filmography, a bibliography, and an index are included. Well worth browsing.

*Wood, Robin. HITCHCOCK'S FILMS. 3rd. Rev. and enlarged ed. South Brunswick: A. S. Barnes and Company, 1977. Illustrated. 174pp.

This updated version of the Wood's highly original and invaluable 1965 analyses of STRANGERS ON A TRAIN (1951), REAR WINDOW 1954), VERTIGO (1958), NORTH BY NORTHWEST (1959), PSYCHO (1960), THE BIRDS (1963), MARNIE 1964), and TORN CURTAIN (1966) includes a new chapter giving Wood's current appraisal of Hitchcock. Ten years later and more objective about AUTEURISM, Wood candidly points out problems--e.g., "excesses, imbalances, and distortions"--that he found in his initial approach to Hitchcock. This time round he strikes a balance between the director's strengths and weaknesses, rather than maintaining his advocacy role of the 1960s. In addition to worthwhile discussions about the influence of German expressionism and Soviet cinema on Hitchcock's works, the erudite author offers important observations on the director's attitude toward actors, his pre-production planning, his voyeuristic tendencies, the lingering psychological effects of Hitchcock's Jesuit education, and his relationship with audiences. The analyses of the films remain the same as in the original edition, since Wood believes they represent his critical development and serve as a useful reminder of critical attitudes in the 1960s. He does comment, however, that the review of THE BIRDS is his weakest commentary. Regrettably, Wood does not upgrade the quality of photographs. A bibliography and index are included. Recommended for special collections.

LESLIE HOWARD

Howard, Leslie Ruth. A QUITE REMARKABLE FATHER. New York: Harcourt, Brace and Company, 1959. Illustrated. 307pp.

ALEXANDER KORDA

Kulik, Karol. ALEXANDER KORDA: THE MAN WHO COULD WORK MIRACLES. New Rochelle: Arlington House, 1975. Illustrated. 409pp.

---

[514]   John Russell Taylor, "Hitchcock," SIGHT AND SOUND 52:1 (Winter 1982-83):72.

Born Sandor-Laszlo Kellner on September 16, 1893, in Puszta Turpaszto, Hungary, Alexander Korda grew up loving films and became a director by the time he was twenty-one. During World War I, he gained prominence as Hungary's premier filmmaker. But life for a Jewish filmmaker in postwar Hungary was harried; and in 1919, he took his first wife, Antonia Farkas (film name, Maria Corda), and began a decade-long odyssey of making movies in Europe and America. In 1931, he took up permanent residence in England and established London Film Productions. Over the next eight years, Korda produced many notable films at his impressive Denham Studios. The coming of World War II and bad financial management not only lost him his production facilities, but also landed him in Hollywood between 1939 and 1942. Upon returning to England, through a mixture of cunning and charm, Korda resurrected his film company and purchased Shepperton Studios. He remained a major force in film until the mid-1950s, when his extravagant management again forced him to sell his film holdings. He died on January 13, 1956.

Originally written as a 1971 thesis at the Slade Film Unit, University College, London, this expanded study remains the most thorough biography of Korda. Well researched and fully documented, the book's twenty valuable chapters offer the basic information on the unique filmmaker's life and career. Particularly interesting are the sections dealing with Korda's second wife, Merle Oberon, his brief merger with MGM-British (1943-45), his propaganda efforts during World War II and his bold maneuvers in the early 1950s. "Alexander Korda," the author concludes, "was the only film producer in Britain who consistently tried to match swords with Hollywood. It was his very foreignness which allowed him to fight a losing battle for so long." Endnotes, an excellent filmography, an extensive bibliography, and an index are included. Recommended for special collections.

Korda, Michael. CHARMED LIVES: A FAMILY ROMANCE. New York: Random House, 1979. Illustrated. 498pp.

The most entertaining book on the fabulous Korda brothers and their glamorous careers, this absorbing biography by Sir Alex's nephew provides fascinating anecdotes and valuable insights on the behind-the-scenes history of the British and American film industries during the 1930s and 1940s. The author divides his witty and personal observations into three major sections, focusing primarily on Alexander Korda, but with lots of lively stories about Zoltan and Vincent. Although the films (Alexander directed over forty pictures and produced more than twice that number) are given short shrift, the author gives us perceptive comments on the studios the family created, nurtured, and lost, as well as the effect the brothers had on the careers of Merle Oberon, Laurence Olivier, Charles Laughton, and Vivien Leigh. Typical of the author's wit is his account of the encounter between the English actress Ann Todd and Sir Alex. Discovering that the producer had reneged on his promise to give her a choice role, ". . . she stormed into his office in a rage and told him what a wicked thing it was to do. 'Ah,' he said, 'I KNOW it was, but I wouldn't have done it to anyone else." When she asked Korda to explain, he took her by the arm and gently replied, "Because you and I are such good friends that I knew you would forgive me." Regrettably, the author does not document his sources and offers no bibliography or filmographies. An index is included. Recommended for special collections.

Tabori, Paul. ALEXANDER KORDA. New York: Living Books, 1966. Illustrated. 324pp.

Written by a fellow Hungarian and an ex-employee of Korda, this light-weight biography uses some dramatic license to tell the story of a farm bailiff's son who rose to become one of the most influential filmmakers on two continents. It is a pleasant but unreliable introduction to the man responsible for such spectaculars as THE PRIVATE LIFE OF HENRY VIII (1933), THE SCARLET PIMPERNEL (1934), THINGS TO COME, REMBRANDT (both in 1936), ELEPHANT BOY (1937), THE FOUR FEATHERS (1939), THE THIEF OF BAGDAD (1940), THE JUNGLE BOOK (1942), THE

WINSLOW BOY, THE FALLEN IDOL (both in 1948), THE THIRD MAN (1949), THE TALES OF HOFFMANN (1951), CRY, THE BELOVED COUNTRY (1952), and RICHARD III (1956). Minor documentation, a weak filmography, and an index are included. Worth browsing.

ELSA LANCHESTER

Lanchester, Elsa. CHARLES LAUGHTON AND I. London: Faber and Faber, 1968. Illustrated. 269pp.

Lanchester, Elsa. ELSA LANCHESTER HERSELF. New York: St. Martin's Press, 1983. Illustrated. 327pp.

CHARLES LAUGHTON

Brown, William. CHARLES LAUGHTON: A PICTORIAL TREASURY OF HIS FILMS. New York: Falcon Enterprises, 1970. Illustrated. 162pp.

Callow, Simon. CHARLES LAUGHTON: A DIFFICULT ACTOR. New York: Grove Press, 1988. Illustrated. 318pp.

Higham, Charles. CHARLES LAUGHTON: AN INTIMATE BIOGRAPHY. New York: Doubleday, 1976. Illustrated. 277pp.

Singer, Kurt. THE LAUGHTON STORY: AN INTIMATE STORY OF CHARLES LAUGHTON. Philadelphia: The John C. Winston Company, 1954. Illustrated. 308pp.

DAVID LEAN

Pratley, Gerald. THE CINEMA OF DAVID LEAN. New York: A. S. Barnes and Company, 1974. Illustrated. 256pp.
    Born on March 25, 1908, in Croydon, London, David Lean grew up in a Quaker family that forbad him to watch films. By the time he reached adolescence, Lean had found numerous ways to overcome these objections and developed a passion for movies that led him to forsake a career as an accountant (his father's profession) and to turn instead to film as his life's work. At twenty, he began as a tea boy at Gaumont-British studios and worked up his way to editing. From 1930 to 1941, he gained a reputation as one of Britain's finest cutters and contributed significantly to pictures like PYGMALION (1938), MAJOR BARBARA (1941), and ONE OF OUR AIRCRAFT IS MISSING (1942). The latter film earned him a chance at co-directing with Noel Coward the memorable World War II film, IN WHICH WE SERVE (1942). Lean continued his relionship with Coward by setting up Cineguild, an independent film company (disbanded in the early 1950s), that resulted in Lean's directing three more Coward screenplays: THIS HAPPY BREED (1944), BLITHE SPIRIT (1945), and BRIEF ENCOUNTER (1946). Another important collaborator of Lean's was Ronald Neame, who not only was a partner in Cineguild, but also an excellent cinematographer who had worked on all of Lean's previous films except BRIEF ENCOUNTER. In the mid-1940s, Lean, using Neame as his screenwriter, made GREAT EXPECTATIONS (1947). After completing OLIVER TWIST (1948), screenplay by Lean and Stanley Haynes, the now well-established director began a series of films starring his first wife, Ann Todd: THE PASSIONATE FRIEND/ONE WOMAN'S STORY (1949), MADELEINE (1950), and

BREAKING THE SOUND BARRIER (1952). With the completion of HOBSON'S CHOICE (1954), Lean turned his back on films geared primarily for an English audience and focused his attention on international subjects. Among the most significant are SUMMERTIME/SUMMER MADNESS (1955), THE BRIDGE ON THE RIVER KWAI (1957), LAWRENCE OF ARABIA (1962), DOCTOR ZHIVAGO (1965), and A PASSAGE TO INDIA (1984).

Pratley's appreciative look at Lean's films ignores the filmmaker's childhood and his days as one of England's foremost editors. Fifteen uneven chapters concentrate on the screenwriter-director's fifteen films from IN WHICH WE SERVE (1942) to RYAN'S DAUGHTER (1970). Each chapter includes cast and technical credits, a brief synopsis of the film, a comment by Lean on the production, and a terse critical reaction by the author. Only the profuse illustrations accompanying each chapter are noteworthy. No bibliography or endnotes are provided, but an index is included. Well worth browsing.

Silver, Alain, and James Ursini. DAVID LEAN AND HIS FILMS. London: Leslie Frewin, 1974. Illustrated. 255pp.

VIVIEN LEIGH

Barker, Felix. THE OLIVIERS. Philadelphia: J. B. Lippincott, 1953. Illustrated. 371pp.

*Edwards, Anne. VIVIEN LEIGH: A BIOGRAPHY. New York: Simon and Schuster, 1977. Illustrated. 319pp.

Lasky, Jesse L., Jr., and Pat Silver. LOVE SCENE: THE STORY OF LAURENCE OLIVIER AND VIVIEN LEIGH. New York: Thomas Y. Crowell Company, 1978. Illustrated. 256pp.

Robyns, Gwen. LIGHT OF A STAR. New York: A. S. Barnes and Company, 1971. Illustrated. 256pp.

Vickers, Hugo. VIVIEN LEIGH: A BIOGRAPHY. Boston: Little, Brown and Company, 1989. Illustrated. 384pp.

Walker, Alexander. VIVIEN: THE LIFE OF VIVIEN LEIGH. New York: Weidenfeld and Nicolson, 1987. Illustrated. 342pp.

RAYMOND MASSEY

Massey, Raymond. A HUNDRED DIFFERENT LIVES: AN AUTOBIOGRAPHY. Boston: Little, Brown and Company, 1979. Illustrated. 447pp.

Massey, Raymond. WHEN I WAS YOUNG. Boston: Little, Brown and Company, 1976. Illustrated. 271pp.

JESSIE MATTHEWS

*Matthews, Jesse, and Muriel Burgess. OVER MY SHOULDER: AN AUTOBIOGRAPHY. New Rochelle: Arlington House, 1974. Illustrated. 240pp.

RODDY MCDOWALL

*Castell, David. THE FILMS OF RODDY MCDOWALL. London: Barnden Castell Williams, 1975. Illustrated. Unpaginated.

ANNA NEAGLE

Neagle, Anna. ANNA NEAGLE SAYS "THERE'S ALWAYS A TOMORROW": AN AUTOBIOGRAPHY. London: W. H. Allen, 1974. Illustrated. 236pp.

LAURENCE OLIVIER

Cottrell, John. LAURENCE OLIVIER. Englewood Cliffs: Prentice-Hall, 1975. Illustrated. 416pp.[515]

Gourlay, Logan, ed. OLIVIER. New York: Stein and Day, 1974. Illustrated. 208pp.

Holden, Anthony. LAURENCE OLIVIER. New York: Atheneum, 1988. Illustrated. 504pp.

Morley, Margaret. THE FILMS OF LAURENCE OLIVIER. Secaucus: The Citadel Press, 1978. Illustrated. 160pp.

Tanitch, Robert. OLIVIER: THE COMPLETE CAREER. New York: Abbeville Press, 1985. Illustrated. 191pp.

J. ARTHUR RANK

Wood, Alan. MR. RANK: A STUDY OF J. ARTHUR RANK AND BRITISH FILMS. London: Hodder and Stoughton, 1952. 288pp.
  This rather chatty and informal history of the Yorkshire flour-miller who entered the fabulous world of movies and high finance is the major source available on the Rank Organization. Wood also provides some useful discussion of American involvement in British production, government interference, and filmmaking problems in Britain up to 1951.   An index is included, but endnotes or bibliograpy is provided. Worth browsing.

---

[515]   For a good overview, see Mel Gussow, "Laurence Olivier, 82, Classical Actor Is Dead," NEW YORK TIMES A (July 12, 1989):1, B6; and Peter Hall, "Olivier: Exit the Emperor," ibid., H (July 23, 1989):1, 26.

BASIL RATHBONE

Druxman, Michael B. BASIL RATHBONE: HIS LIFE AND HIS FILMS. New York: A. S. Barnes and Company, 1975. Illustrated. 357pp.

MICHAEL REDGRAVE

Findlater, Richard. MICHAEL REDGRAVE, ACTOR. London: William Heinemann, 1956. Illustrated. 170pp.

Redgrave, Michael. IN MY MIND'S I: AN ACTOR'S AUTOBIOGRAPHY. New YORK: The Viking Press, 1983. Illustrated. 256pp.

RALPH RICHARDSON

*O'Connor, Garry. RALPH RICHARDSON: AN ACTOR'S LIFE. New York: Atheneum, 1982. Illustrated. 261pp.

ANN TODD

Todd, Ann. THE EIGHTH VEIL--ANN TODD. London: Kimber, 1980. Illustrated. 173pp.

HERBERT WILCOX

Wilcox, Herbert. TWENTY FIVE THOUSAND SUNSETS: THE AUTOBIOGRAPHY OF HERBERT WILCOX. London: Bodley Head, 1967. Illustrated. 233pp.

FILMS

ANTHONY ASQUITH

PYGMALION (Britain--16mm: 1938, 85 mins., b/w, sound, R-FNC, JAN, WHO)
  Scripted by George Bernard Shaw, W. P. Liscomb, and Cecil Lewis, this second screen version of Shaw's play (the first was a 1935 German film adaptation) actively involved the famous playwright in production plans initiated at the end of 1935. The producer Gabriel Pascal then signed Leslie Howard to star as Professor Higgins and Anthony Asquith to direct. Together the three men worked on Shaw to "open up" the film to the requirements of the screen and not to insist on a faithful stage adaptation. The major changes involved toning down the author's pedantic exortations and increasing the humor in Higgins's experiment. Adding to the film's warm reception was the fine cast, including Wendy Hiller (Eliza Doolittle) and Wilfred Lawson (Alfred Doolittle). Nominated for four Oscars, including Best Film, Best Actor (Howard), and Best Actress, it won for Best Screenplay.

ALFRED HITCHCOCK

BLACKMAIL (Britain--16mm: 1929, 86 mins., b/w, sound, R-BUD, EMG, FNC, IVY, JAN, KIT, MMA, IMG)

Hitchcock's first sound film was intended "as an exercise on the traditional conflict between love and duty." The original plan was to capture the routine duties of a detective "arresting, fingerprinting, booking, and jailing a criminal."[516] Based upon Charles Bennett's popular 1928 stageplay, the screenplay (co-authored by Hitchcock, Bennett, and Benn W. Levy) focuses on a woman (Anny Ondra)[517] accidentally killing a stranger (Cyril Ritchard) who was sexually assaulting her and then being blackmailed by a man (Donald Calthrop). The irony occurs when the detective (Frank Webber) assigned to the murder case is also the woman's beau. In the original plan, the blackmailer dies in a police chase and, as Hitchcock explains "the girl would have been arrested and the young man would have had to do the same things to her that we saw at the beginning: handcuffs, booking at the police station and so on. Then he would meet his older partner in the men's room, and the other man would have said, 'Are you going out with your girl tonight?' and he would have answered, 'No, I'm going straight home.'"[518] Hitchcock's producers, however insisted on an upbeat ending, whereby the detective persuades the woman to conceal her part in the murder. The film's importance rests not only on Hitchcock's technical achievements in the expressionistic use of sound, but also on his production problems during his formative years.[519]

THE 39 STEPS (Britain--16mm: 1935, 80 mins., b/w, sound, R-BUD, EMG, FNC, IMA IVY, JAN, KIT, ROA, WHO)

Regarded by many film historians as one of the classic films of the 1930s, the screenplay by Alma Reville and Charles Bennett fleshed out the weak characterizations in the original John Buchan novel, while exploiting the European political turmoil of the mid-1930s. Robert Donat and Madeleine Carroll, as a pair of innocent people mysteriously caught in a web of international intrigue, personify Hitchcock's technique of showing ordinary people resourcefully outwitting highly placed and influential villains. Superb camerawork, excellent editing, brilliant use of sound, and remarkable humor combine to make the illogically developed adventure story into an exciting thriller that distracts the audience's attention from the plot's structural flaws and enhances its entertaining action chases. Here Hitchcock's "MacGuffin"--a gimmick to get the story started and to stimulate the viewer's interest--is a secret formula that once introduced becomes secondary to watching Donat and Carroll escape from one danger after another.[520]

---

[516]   Maurice Yacowar, HITCHCOCK'S BRITISH FILMS (Hamden: Archon Books, 1977), p.99.

[517]   Because the Polish-actress Anny Ondra's accent presented too many problems for the early days of sound, her dialogue was post-dubbed by Joan Barry. Ondra retired from films shortly after the film was released.

[518]   Cited in *Francois Truffaut, with the collaboration of Helen G. Scott, HITCHCOCK (New York: Simon and Schuster, 1967), p.45.

[519]   For more information, see Leland Poague, "Criticism and/as History: Rereading BLACKMAIL," A HITCHCOCK READER, eds. Marshall Deutelbaum and Leland Poague (Ames Iowa State University, 1986), pp.78-89; and Harry Ringel, "BLACKMAIL: The Opening of Hitchcock's Surrealistic Eye," FILM HERITAGE 9:2 (Winter 1973-74):17-23.

[520]   In addition to the Hitchcock books, see Stuart Y. McDougal, "Mirth, Sexuality and Suspense: Alfred Hitchcock's Adaptation of THE THIRTY-NINE STEPS," LITERATURE/FILM QUARTERLY 3:3 (Summer 1975):232-9. For Hitchcock's explanation of the "MacGuffin," see Truffaut and Scott, pp.98-9.

ALEXANDER KORDA

HE PRIVATE LIFE OF HENRY VIII (Britain--16mm: 1933, 97 mins., b/w, sound, -BUD, EMG, FNC, IVY, KIT, ROA, TWY, WHO)

   A clever and witty spectacle starring Charles Laughton, Merle Oberon, Robert onat, and Elsa Lanchester, this film, scripted by Lajos Biro and Arthur Wimperis, as directed by Korda. The depiction of how the lecherous king treated his six wives enefited from Robert Armstrong's impressive sets and from Georges Perinal's amerawork. The production is often cited as the first British film to capture aternational audiences and compete successfully with Hollywood movies in American eaters. Nominated for two Oscars, including Best Film, it won for Best Actor Laughton).[521]

SOVIET UNION

   Given the limited resources of the Soviet filmmakers, their relative isolation from ne international film community, and the government's vivid memory of what preigners did to the industry during the first years of the October Revolution, it understandable that the Soviets decided to perfect their own sound system (the ager sound-on-film process) rather than become dependent on foreign patents or ontrol again. Moreover, the nature of the Soviet film industry freed the filmmakers om being closely tied to the audience's demand for novelty and gratification. As a esult, artists like Eisenstein, Vertov, Pudovkin, Dovzhenko, and Alexandrov could xplore at greater leisure the strengths and weaknesses of the new technology. By ne end of the 1920s, most of them had developed position papers on how sound might ffectively mesh with silent film montage theories.

   But Soviet experimentation in sound was overshadowed at first by a significant end away from cinematic realism and toward Socialist Construction. As Seton xplains,

> The immediate result of this new ideological interpretation was that scenarists and directors began to seek a new humanism in which personal character should find a greater expression. Events could no longer be portrayed through mass action but must be seen as the action of typical individuals.[522]

hus, the film intellectuals of the revolutionary years were denigrated for their bstract and formalistic perspectives. What was needed now, the new leadership roclaimed, was an emphasis on acessibility, on making the movies meaningful to the verage individual.

   Among the personalities finding extreme difficulties with the new approach was isenstein. His trip to Hollywood in 1930 and the events that followed in Mexico led o his returning to the Soviet Union unprepared to deal with the change in Stalin's rtistic policies.[523] Discouraged over his battles with Sinclair, he found working with oris Shumyatsky, the commissar of information, even worse. His first sound film,

---

[21]   For more information, see Sidney Gilliat et al., "Sir Alexander Korda," SIGHT AND SOUND 25:4 (Spring 1956):214-5; and Anthony Slide, "THE PRIVATE LIFE OF HENRY VIII," THE INTERNATIONAL DICTIONARY OF FILMS AND FILMMAKERS: VOLUME I, pp.372-3.

[22]   Seton, p.247.

[23]   For some useful articles on the subject, see Clifford Howard, "Eisenstein in Hollywood," CLOSE-UP 6:1 (August 30, 1930):139-42; Sergei M. Eisenstein, "AN AMERICAN TRAGEDY," trans. W. Ray, ibid., 10:2 (June 1933):109-24; ___,

BEZHIN MEADOW/BEZHIN LUG (1935), never was allowed to be completed. If not fc
the impending German invasion later in the decade, it is unlikely that his brilliam
historical spectacle, ALEXANDER NEVSKY/ALEXANDR NEVSKII (1938) would hav
been made and positively received. The success, however, led eventually to th
creation of his proposed trilogy on Csar Ivan IV, the man who first united the Russia
people. Despite the critical and social acceptance of the first part, IVAN TH
TERRIBLE/IVAN GROZNY (1945), the second film, IVAN THE TERRIBLE: PAR
II/IVAN GROZNY II (1946), angered Stalin and never was shown during Eisenstein
life, nor did he ever get to film much of IVAN THE TERRIBLE: PART III/IVA
GROZNY III. A debilitating heart attack in 1946 led to a long period of inactivity an
then to eventual death at forty-eight on February 11, 1948.

BOOKS

SERGEI M. EISENSTEIN

*Ellis, A. E., trans. IVAN THE TERRIBLE: A FILM BY SERGEI EISENSTEIN. Ne
York: Simon and Schuster, 1970. Illustrated. 264pp.
    According to the note to this edition, "The script of IVAN THE TERRIBLE wei
through three different stages: first the scenario, that is Eisenstein's original concep
of the film, which has already been published in English in a translation by Ive
Montagu and Herbert Marshall; secondly the shooting script, which contains sever
important divergences from the scenario, notably in the placing of the scenes fro
Ivan's childhood (which in the scenario comes right at the beginning) and the firs
scene at the Polish court (which came between Anastasia's poisoning and the scen
beside her coffin in the cathedral); and thirdly a transcript of the actual fil
prepared from the final edited version)." This publication bases much of its versic
on prints that American and/or British viewers saw on their screens in the earl
1970s. It does have, however, a number of shots not actually in the film an
periodically fails to mention shots that are in the film. The book begins with a Sovie
film scholar capsulizing the history of the film, including excerpts ranging fro
Eisenstein's writings about the project, to his difficulties in conceptualizing th
complexities of Ivan's character. In addition, there are two eyewitness accounts c
the paradoxical reactions to IVAN THE TERRIBLE PART II. On the one hand, Mikha
Romm (a member of the ruling body that evaluated the film) attacks it as a
"accumulation of errors," while Nikolai Cherkasov (who starred as Ivan) praises
as a masterpiece. Although Part III--"Ivan's Struggles"--was never filmed, we ar
given the shooting script along with some sketches. Well worth browsing.

Geduld, Harry M., and Ronald Gottesman, eds. SERGEI EISENSTEIN AND UPTO
SINCLAIR: THE MAKING & UNMAKING OF "QUE VIVA MEXICO!."   Bloomington
Indiana University Press, 1970. Illustrated. 449pp.
    After finishing THE GENERAL LINE/OLD AND NEW/STAROIE I NOVOIE (1929)
Eisenstein traveled throughout Western Europe and America to interact with prominer
filmmakers in order to better understand new developments in film technology. Hi
traumatic experiences in Hollywood with abortive Paramount Pictures productions lik
AN AMERICAN TRAGEDY (1930) led him to an extraordinary project with Upto
Sinclair. Between November 1930 and June 1932, the two men conceived and develope
a plan to make a film about the revolutionary spirit in Mexican culture, QUE VIV
MEXICO! (1931). Sinclair agreed to finance the film, then for a variety of reason
withdrew his support, and the project was halted. "The episode of QUE VIV

"Cinematography With Tears!" ibid., 10:1 (March 1933):3-17; ___, "Detective Wor
At GIK," ibid., 9:4 (December 1932):287-94.

MEXICO!," explain the authors, "remains the cinema's greatest artistic misfortune and its most celebrated scandal."

What Geduld and Gottesman offer in their detailed study is the best attempt to date on what pressures were brought to bear on the Mexican government, Eisenstein, and Sinclair to prevent the movie from being made. While a number of issues still remain obscure, this valiant study, divided into two major sections and relying heavily on the Eisenstein-Sinclair correspondence, is a good place to begin orienting oneself to the problems. An annotated bibliography and index are included. Recommended for special collections.[524]

*Montagu, Ivor. WITH EISENSTEIN IN HOLLYWOOD: A CHAPTER OF AUTOBIOGRAPHY, INCLUDING THE SCENARIOS OF SUTTER'S GOLD AND AN AMERICAN TRAGEDY. New York: International Publishers, 1967. Illustrated. 358pp.

In 1930, Eisenstein, Alexandrov, and Tisse came to America, signed a contract with Paramount, wrote unsuccessful scenarios, worked on an abortive Mexican film project, and returned in disgrace to the Soviet Union. In answering the question as to why the group failed in Hollywood, Montagu writes, "The only thing that is certain is that all these factors operated: mistrust of 'intellectuals' (especially 'foreigners'), tribal rivalry within the company, our own tactical mistakes, and political fears. It cannot be known which defeated us, which --if any--would not have been decisive without the others." This excellent, entertaining book is a gold mine of information about the quartet (Montagu is included). It also includes the two Hollywood scenarios and an index. Recommended for special collections.

*Thompson, Kristin. EISENSTEIN'S "IVAN THE TERRIBLE": A NEOFORMALIST ANALYSIS. Princeton: Princeton University Press, 1981. Illustrated. 356pp.

Between 1940 and 1943, Eisenstein worked on a proposed film trilogy of Russia's first csar, who unified the nation in the sixteenth century. Part 1, labeled IVAN THE TERRIBLE, deals with Ivan's being crowned, the opposition he faces from the nobility (Boyars), their poisoning of his wife, and Ivan's being forced to abdicate. Part 2, labeled THE BOYARS' PLOT, recounts how the populace returned Ivan to the throne, the attempt by his Aunt to assassinate him and place her demented son in power, and Ivan's successful violent purge of his opposition. Part 3, labeled IVAN'S STRUGGLES, was to recount the csar's battles in the Baltic provinces. Regrettably, the director died before he could complete shooting on the last third of the trilogy. Thompson's neoformalistic approach teaches us new ways to critique not only Eisenstein's film, but also film in general. The emphasis is on narrative and stylistic analyses, with the author examining how specific structures within the film relate to the entire film. Her purpose, she explains, is to analyze "IVAN's strangeness, not to reduce, explain, categorize, or tame it." Although the author makes considerable demands on the reader's familiarity with IVAN, the experience of reading highly original and insightful prose is worth the difficult task. An appendix summarizing IVAN THE TERRIBLE Part 3, a valuable bibliography, an index, and a host of stills are included. Recommended for special collections.

---

[524] For more information, see Jay Leyda, "Eisenstein's Mexican Tragedy," SIGHT AND SOUND 27:6 (Autumn 1958):305-8, 329; and Marie Seton, "Eisenstein's Images and Mexican Art," ibid., 23:1 (July-September 1953):8-13.

FILMS

SERGEI M. EISENSTEIN

ALEXANDER NEVSKY/ALEXANDR NEVSKII (Russia--16mm: 1938, 107 mins., b/w,
English subtitles, sound, R-BUD, COR, EMG, FES, FNC, IMA, IVY, JAN, KIT, MMA,
WES; S-IMA, REE, TFF)
    Helped by Sergei Prokofiev's brilliant musical score and Eduard K. Tisse's
superb photography, the project conceived by Eisenstein and Pyotr Pavlenko presents
one of the screen's outstanding historical recreations. Intended as a patriotic effort
to rally the nation around Stalin in the face of an impending invasion from Nazi
Germany, the film tells the heroic story of Prince Alexander Nevsky's peasant army
and their defeat of the thirteenth-century invading German nobles. Nikolai Cherkasov
plays the Russian prince who plans the great battle on the ice of Lake Peipus.
Particularly noteworthy is Eisenstein's magnificent use of music and image to compare
and contrast emotions and movements.[525]

IVAN THE TERRIBLE Part 1/IVAN GROZNY (Russia--16mm: 1945, 96 mins., b/w,
English subtitles, sound, S-IMA, REE, TFF)
    According to Kristin Thompson, "Eisenstein made IVAN during World War II,
when it served largely as patriotic propaganda. Its central concern with the
maintenance of Russian unity against encroaching Europeans made it an obvious
parallel for the contemporary wartime situation." She then goes on to point out that
the film is much more than a historical document, insisting that "anyone who has seen
the film has necessarily been struck by its profusion of visual and sonic elements:
there are so many stylistic structures that even several viewings will not allow us
to sort them all out."[526] Particularly impressive is the director's collaboration with
Prokofiev and Tisse to create a film masterpiece. Not everyone, however, shares this
opinion. Pauline Kael speaks for many people when she writes, "Eisenstein's two-part
extravaganza on the evils of tyranny is obviously a magnificent work and it imposes
its style on the viewer, yet it's so lacking in human dimensions that you may stare
at it in a kind of outrage."[527]

IVAN THE TERRIBLE Part 2/IVAN GROZNY II (Russia--16mm: 1946, 90 mins., b/w,
English subtitles, sound, R-BUD, COR, EMG, FES, FNC, IMA, IOW, JAN, KIT, WES;
S-IMA, REE, TFF)
    Eisenstein's treatment here in showing how the csar squelched a Boyar's plot
to overthrow him caused the film director great problems with Soviet censors. The
film was not released until 1958, eight years after it was finished. Of particular
interest is Eisenstein's experiment with color and his attempt to orchestrate it as he

---

[525]   See Israel Nestyev, SERGEI PROKOFIEV, HIS MUSICAL LIFE (New York: Alfred A.
Knopf, 1946).

[526]   *Kristin Thompson, EISENSTEIN'S IVAN THE TERRIBLE: A NEOFORMALIST ANALYSIS
(Princeton: Princeton University Press, 1981), p.3.

[527]   Pauline Kael, 5001 NIGHTS AT THE MOVIES: A GUIDE FROM A TO Z (New York: Holt,
Rinehart and Winston, 1982), p.287.

did with images and sounds.

THE DOCUMENTARY FILM IN BRITAIN AND AMERICA (1929-1940)

Ever since the dawn of motion pictures, "actualities," factual films, and documentaries had developed alongside the more popular commercial feature films. Every country had its share of travelogues, newsreels, educational films, and short subjects on local subjects. World War I had stimulated the growth of speciality units producing non-fiction films for propagandistic purposes, and, by the early 1920s, governments as well as private organizations were paying production costs to publicize specific points of view. For example, the Soviets had agit-films; Britain's British Instructional produced WWI-compilation films; and America's Revillon Fur Company sponsored Robert Flaherty's NANOOK OF THE NORTH (1922). As the silent era drew to an end, many prominent filmmakers--e.g., Miriam C. Cooper, Ernest B. Schoedsack, Fredrich W. Murnau, Dziga Vertov, Joris Ivens, Jean Vigo, Walter Ruttman, Alberto Cavalcanti, Marc Allegret, and Jean Epstein--gained international fame for their extraordinary contributions to the art of the factual film.

The coming of sound brought the documentary film into even greater prominence. Although Flaherty generally is credited with "fathering" the genre, it was John Grierson, a Scotsman, who provided the form with a label and a new direction. As discussed in Chapter 2, Grierson and his progressive left-wing peers (Basil Wright, Paul Rotha, Stuart Legg, Harry Watt, John Taylor, Edgar Anstey, Donald Taylor, Humphrey Jennings, and Arthur Elton) shifted the emphasis away from the Hollywood narrative films, and toward a realistic depiction of the problems of everyday people living in a complex, industrial environment. Moreover, as Robinson explains,

> From the artistic point of view what was most important in this organisation of the documentary movement was the tendency of documentary film-makers to form themselves into regular units. This meant not only that artists were working together in teams and in steady employment (never a common feature of British film making) but that there was a possibility of regular training for recruits such as had never existed before in the British cinema. This organisational aspect of the British documentary movement was to be of especial importance when the documentary came to be geared to the needs of war.[528]

These filmmakers saw in the filmed documentary a unique opportunity to influence the ideas, emotions, and attitudes of a complacent public.[529]

The debate today centers on how "realistic" the British documentary movement was, the nature of Grierson's influence on his peers, and the role of propaganda in films. Of all the contemporary film historians, Rhode appears the most critical of Grierson's methods, accusing him not only of misunderstanding what the Soviets were doing with montage and how to apply it appropriately to British documentaries, but also of being too caustic and narrow in his pronouncements "about the role of imagination and intuition in filmmaking."[530]

Britain was not alone in advancing the use of the documentary film. As discussed in Chapter 2, the Soviet Union and Nazi Germany spent considerable time and resources on mastering the art of film propaganda. Americans also pursued the range of factual films in magazine series like THE MARCH OF TIME and protest films

---

[528]   Robinson, p.216.

[529]   Some useful articles are David Robinson, "Looking for Documentary I: The Background to Production," SIGHT AND SOUND 27:1 (Summer 1957):6-11; and ___, ". . . Part II," ibid., 27:2 (Autumn 1957):70-5.

[530]   Rhode, pp.288-9.

like THE SPANISH EARTH (1937). A much more controversial approach was developed by the Roosevelt Administration first in its Department of Agriculture films like THE PLOW THAT BROKE THE PLAINS (1936) and THE RIVER (1937), and then in its U.S. Film Service (initiated in 1938). Spearheaded by Pare Lorentz and his commitment to "films of merit," the concept of government-sponsored films advocating a specific solution to a national problem ran into congressional opposition because of its alleged partisan propaganda. Nevertheless, the quality of the films themselves and the effects they generated set the stage for massive government film projects during and after World War II.

BOOKS

GENERAL

Baechlin, Peter, and Maurice Muller-Strauss. NEWSREELS ACROSS THE WORLD. New York: UNESCO, 1952. Illustrated. 100pp.
    A short but useful coverage of the history of newsreels, and their production-distribution difficulties. Worth browsing.

Hopkinson, Peter. SPLIT FOCUS. London: Hart-Davis, 1969. Illustrated. 119pp.
    Written by a British filmmaker who went through World War II, this excellent book provides invaluable information about the stock footage that is used in so many movies and television programs. Hopkinson recounts what it was like making the original films, but more important, he writes about the political philosophy of the times, the people, and the filmmakers. It is one of the most worthwhile books to come out of the 1960s. Recommended for special collections.

*Levin, G. Roy. DOCUMENTARY EXPLORATIONS: 15 INTERVIEWS WITH FILMMAKERS. New York: Doubleday and Company, 1971. Illustrated. 420pp.
    This uneven anthology provides exhaustive filmographies and interesting interviews with Wright, Anderson, Franju, Van Dyke, Leacock, Maysles Brothers, and Wiseman. In addition, there is a weak overview of the origins of the documentary tradition. Well worth browsing.

*Stott, William. DOCUMENTARY EXPRESSION AND THIRTIES AMERICA. New York: Oxford University Press, 1973. Illustrated. 361pp.
    Focusing on life during the Great Depression, this book combines literary analysis with cultural history. "As a literary analysis," Stott explains, "this book seeks to prove that documentary--whether in film, photograph, writing, broadcast, or art--is a genre as distinct as tragedy, epic, or satire, but a genre unlike these traditional ones in that its content is, or is assumed to be, actually true." He then adds, "As cultural history, this book surveys the documentary expression of the 1930s and early 1940s, and suggests not only that a documentary movement existed then but that recognition of it is essential to an understanding of American life at the time." Stott divides his literate study into four major sections: "Documentary," "The Documentary Motive and the Thirties," "The Documentary Nonfiction of the Thirties," and "LET US NOW PRAISE FAMOUS MEN." Endnotes, a bibliography, and an index are included. Well worth browsing.

BRITAIN

Balcon, Michael, et al., eds. TWENTY YEARS OF BRITISH FILMS 1925-1945. London: Falcon Press, 1947. New York: Arno Press, 1972. Illustrated. 116pp.

A general introduction by periods to the history of British films, with comments by Forsyth Hardy on the documentary movement, this short book also includes many illustrations. Unfortunately, it has no index, bibliography, or screen credits. Worth browsing.

Wright, Basil. THE USE OF THE FILM. London: The Bodley Head, 1948. New York: Arno Press, 1972. 72pp.

This valuable and concise book is a theoretical commentary on the documentary and its value to the public. It offers an interesting discussion of the film as a medium of information exchange, opinion-forming, and public service. Well worth browsing.

FILMS

JOHN GRIERSON

aRANTON TRAWLER (Britain--16mm: 1934, 11 mins., b/w, sound R-MMA)

A filmic essay on dragnet fishing, but more important for its lesson for filmmakers on the preeminence of form to content, this film contains a masterful technique of counterpoint in movement and sound.

NIGHT MAIL (Britain--16mm, 24 mins., b/w, sound, R-MMA)

This film is an artistically exciting portrayal of a train trip on the postal special from London to Glasgow, with an excellent poem by W. H. Auden matched by superb cutting and visual images.

SONG OF CEYLON (Britain--16mm: 1934, 40 mins., b/w, sound, R-MMA)

Praised as one of the masterpieces of documentary films, this motion picture tells the story of Singhalese people in the 1930s. Grierson produced the movie and Basil Wright directed.

ROBERT FLAHERTY

MAN OF ARAN (Britain--16mm: 1934, 77 mins., b/w, sound, R-BUD, EMG, FNC, KIT; S-FNC)

Robert Flaherty spent three years on the Aran Island making this poignant and marvelous documentary of Irish fishermen living with, and against, their natural environment. Historians have cited it as one of the films that greatly influenced rising British documentary directors.

UNITED STATES

Snyder, Robert L. PARE LORENTZ AND THE DOCUMENTARY FILM. Norman: University of Oklahoma Press, 1968. Illustrated. 232pp.

During the hard days of the Depression, the U. S. government decided to produce a series of motion pictures about the various crises facing the country. An unknown and untried filmmaker, working with dedicated artists and with a meager budget of $6000, began to make film history with his first movie, THE PLOW THAT

BROKE THE PLAINS. Before Congress and the war destroyed their organization, Lorentz had made two more memorable films--THE RIVER and THE FIGHT FOR LIFE. Snyder puts it all into print in a useful, intelligent, and important document. Several appendexes, a filmography, and an index are included. Recommended for special collections.[531]

FILMS

PARE LORENTZ

THE PLOW THAT BROKE THE PLAINS (U. S.--16mm: 1936, 21 mins., b/w, sound, R-MMA)

Lorentz wrote and directed this very important film about the social and economic situations in the Great Plains over a long period of time, suggesting at the same time the need for government intervention. The film was photographed beautifully by Paul Strand, Ralph Steiner, and Leo Hurwitz. Virgil Thomson contributed the marvelous music.

THE RIVER (U. S.--16mm: 1937, 30 mins., b/w, sound, R-MMA)

Again Lorentz is the writer/director. Helped by the brilliant photography of Willard Van Dyke and the superb musical anthology created by Virgil Thomson, this may well be one of the finest documentaries ever made. It shows the need for flood control on the Mississippi River and for the creation of the Tennessee Valley Authority.

THE ITALIAN FASCIST CINEMA (1929-1944)

The influence of theatrical traditions (e.g., FILM D'ART, the circus, melodramas, opera, and variety shows) on pre-WWI Italian cinema carried over into the 1920s. While national film industries like France, Germany, and the Soviet Union were purging themselves of these "non-cinematic" elements or incorporating them into the style of modern film techniques, the Italian cinema appeared to stagnate. Once the Fascist government took over Italy in 1922, the widely accepted perception by foreigners was that the Italian film functioned merely as a puppet of Benito Mussolini. Moreover, a series of financial crises drove many people out of the industry. Those who remained barely made a living. By the end of the 1920s, when Italian filmmakers began working with sound, the industry was in disarray. Consequently, many film historians conclude that not much of interest occurred in the Italian film industry between the two world wars. Indicative of the reactions is Elaine Mancini's observations that

The twenties were the most pathetic decade in Italian film history: the industry lacked imagination, energy, and contact with its public; it became overcrowded with speculative companies, that closed one after the other, often without producing anything; and it insisted on making films in the same style and usually with the same techniques of the earlier decade.[532]

---

[531] For a more extended review, see Frank Manchel, "Books: PARE LORENTZ AND THE DOCUMENTARY FILM," FILM SOCIETY REVIEW 4:2 (October 1968):45-6.

[532] Elaine Mancini, STRUGGLES OF THE ITALIAN FILM INDUSTRY DURING FASCISM, 1930-1935 (Ann Arbor: UMI Research Press, 1985), p.24.

Pierre Leprohon concurs, stating that "From 1916-17 to 1932-3, Italian films produced nothing of original value . . . That is to say that for fifteen years or so, for the whole duration of a crucial period in the art of the film, Italy was absent, and played no part in the developments from which, when the time came, as in 1908, it would merely draw the benefits."[533]

On the surface, their judgments appear reasonable. The post-WWI years saw the Italian cinema reeling under the weight of the DIVE (an extravagant and badly conceived star system), the narrow focus of Italian filmmakers on trite comedies and static musicals, and the industry's misperception of audience expectations. An example of the industry's instability was the feeble attempt, beginning in 1919, by eleven notable producers to merge their tenuous assets into a film monopoly, the UNIONE CINEMATOGRAFICA ITALIANA (UCI). Even with many of the nation's best directors working for it, the overall quality of the UCI films was dismal; the subjects and styles of the films, retrogressive.[534] What little hope for success disappeared in 1922, when the industry's financial support collapsed and credit became nonexistent for many film projects. Production dropped from sixty feature films in 1921, to a third that number in 1923.[535] By 1930, the year that Italian talkies first appeared, and three years after the demise of the UCI, the industry turned out little more than twenty-five films a year.

It is important, however, to understand that the Fascists used the 1920s as a germinating period for their ideas on film propaganda. While it is true that censorship codes held virtually no force from the mid-1920s on (with so few films being released, the focus was on getting more films made than on enforcing specific regulations), Mussolini's regime found ways to promote Fascist ideas through film. For example, in 1924, a state film agency, the INSTITUTO LUCE (L'UNION CINEMATGRAFICA EDUCATIVA), was established for the purpose of producing and distributing newsreels and documentaries. LUCE lasted through World War II, playing a major role in politicizing the nation to the Fascist point of view. Another key cinema program in the 1920s was run through the OPERA NAZIONALE DOPOLAVORO (OND). Given the responsibility for supervising "constructive" leisure time activities of regional groups, this semi-independent state agency eventually became, in the mid-1920s, a tool of the Fascists in garnering support for its totalitarian policies. By the late 1930s, the OND not only had more than 760 movie houses under its control, but also had a "a fleet of travelling 'cinema wagons' that in 1937 numbered 42 and claimed to have reached approximately 9,900,000 spectators in 28,641 showings."[536] In short, the Fascists were keenly aware of the cinema's propagandistic purposes before 1930.

Most film historians acknowledge that an Italian "film renaissance" occurred as a result of the sound revolution. Recognizing the need for a complete overhaul not only in structure but also in content, the Italian film industry underwent a metamorphosis. Leading the resurgence were film theorists like Sebastiano Arturo Lucianni and Eugenio Giovannetti. They cajoled Italian filmmakers into reevaluating the relationship between theater and film, emphasizing that the strength of the latter lay in its function as a major art form serving the public.[537] That is not to say that theatrical influences disappeared in Italian talkies. Important artists like Luigi Pirandello and Alessandro Blasetti still made significant contributions to film content.

---

[533]   Leprohon, p.60.

[534]   Mancini, p.25.

[535]   Mancini, p.26.

[536]   James Hay, POPULAR FILM CULTURE IN FASCIST ITALY: THE PASSING OF THE REX (Bloomington: Indiana University Press, 1987), p.15.

[537]   Mancini, p.35.

What was different, however, was the focus in Italian talkies on native music and the problems of everyday people. As Ted Perry explains,

> The best of these films provide the audience with an innocent escape from the world outside the movie house. This notion of escape pervades the themes of the period's films. Characters often try to escape from themselves, or to escape from their own social class into another, higher one.[538]

There was also a lobbying effort by theorists who advocated a greater role for films to play in shaping a a modern society. The problem was how, and revisionist historians like Hay insist that the true significance of the Italian Fascist films is that they prepared an entire generation for the cinematic revolution that followed the fall of Fascism in 1944.[539] It should also be recognized that these revolutionary spirits created an environment that encouraged an anti-democratic society and strengthened the aims and goals of Mussolini's infamous regime.

It was during the transition to sound that Italy nurtured a new generation of performers, many of whom grew out of cinematic traditions rather than theatrical experiences. Among the film artists developing their craft in the 1930s were Geoffredo Alessandrini, Michelangelo Antonioni,[540] Umberto Barbaro, Alessandro Blasetti, Mario Camerini, Renato Castellani, Luigi Chiarini, Giuseppe De Santis, Carmine Gallone, Augusto Genina, Pietro Germi, Alberto Lattuada, Raffaello Matarazzo, Mario Mattoli, Roberto Rossellini, Luchino Visconti,[541] and Luigi Zampa. Among the noted performers were Vittorio De Sica, Fosco Giachetti, and Germana Paolieri. This committed generation thus led the attack on past practices and argued for a new

---

[538]   Ted Perry, "The Road to Neorealism," FILM COMMENT 14:6 (November-December 1978):9-10.

[539]   Among the notable films dealing with the period are AMARCORD/I REMEMBER (1974), THE GARDEN OF THE FINZI-CONTINIS/GIARDINO DEI FINZI-CONTINI (1970), and 1900 (1977). For a more complete listing, see Hay, p.xv.

[540]   The following articles are helpful: Michele Manceaux, "An Interview With Antonioni," SIGHT AND SOUND 30:1 (Winter 1960-61):4-8; Richard Roud, "Five Films," ibid., pp.8-11; Geoffrey Nowell-Smith, "The Event And The Image: Michelangelo Antonioni," ibid., 33:1 (Winter 1964-65):14-20; Penelope Houston, "Keeping Up With The Antonionis," ibid., 33:4 (Autumn 1964):163-8; ___, "The Landscape of the Desert," ibid., 34: (Spring 1965):80-1, 103; Marsha Kinder, "Antonioni In Transit," ibid., 36:3 (Summer 1967):132-7; Jean-Luc Godard, "Night, Eclipse, Dawn: An Interview With Michelangelo Antonioni," CAHIERS DU CINEMA IN ENGLISH 1 Cdc 160 (January 1966):19-29; Gordon Gow, "Antonioni Men," FILMS AND FILMING 16:9 (June 1970):40-4, 46; Stephen Handzo, "Michelangelo in Disneyland: ZABRISKIE POINT," FILM HERITAGE 6:1 (Fall 1970):7-24; Thomas Hernacki, "Michelangelo Antonioni and the Imagery of Disintegration," ibid., 5:3 (Spring 1970):12-21; and Kimball Lockhart, "Antonioni, Michelangelo," THE INTERNATIONAL DICTIONARY OF FILMS AND FILMMAKERS: VOLUME II, pp.23-6.

[541]   Some useful articles are Giulio Cesare Castello, "Luchino Visconti," SIGHT AND SOUND 25:4 (Spring 1956):184-90, 220; Luchino Visconti, "Drama of Non-Existence," CAHIERS DU CINEMA IN ENGLISH 2, Cdc 174 (January 1966):12-18; Jean Collet, "The Absences of Sandra," ibid., pp.18-21; Gianfranco Poggi, "Luchino Visconti and the Italian Cinema," FILM QUARTERLY 13:3 (Spring 1960):11-22; and Walter F. Korte, Jr., "Marxism and Formalism in the Films of Luchino Visconti," CINEMA JOURNAL 11:1 (Fall 1971):2-12. See also Walter F. Kotre, Jr., MARXISM AND THE SCENOGRAPHIC BAROQUE IN THE FILMS OF LUCHINO VISCONTI (Unpublished Ph.D. Dissertation, Northwestern University, 1970).

approach to filmmaking, one based on the aesthetics of the film rather than on those of the stage.

These theoretical debates, although lagging behind those in countries like France, Germany, and the Soviet Union, produced similar film periodicals in which critics and filmmakers argued about the need for new directions in a nationalistic film industry rather than in a cinema dominated by foreign values (i.e., Hollywood movies). The major concerns of Italian film critics and artists during the formative years from 1930 to 1935 were on aesthetics, cinematic techniques, and audience involvement. Of special interest was the alleged negative role that foreign films (notably Hollywood movies) played in the cultural life of the nation. Thus it became quite fashionable to ridicule democratic values, capitalistic ideology, and a bourgeois society. Fascism became the popular alternative to a materialistic America. Following the lead set by other European countries, Italy set quotas to protect its national film industry and defend its cultural values. As a result, production climbed significantly from 1930 to 1939.

Much of the credit for the increased production of the initial period goes to the managerial talents of Stefano Pittaluga and his methods of running CINES, the major film company in the late 1920s and early 1930s. Not only did Pittaluga's firm dominate the transition era by having the most elaborate production facilities, the best organizational structure, and the largest stable of talent, but it also had the most intelligent production policies. His unexpected death in 1931, however, put the studio adrift. Although the appointment of the scholarly Emilio Cecchi as artistic director in 1932 led to an infusion of new talent and exciting changes (e.g., the creation of a nonfiction program), the studio continued its downhill slide when Cecchi left the following year. In 1935, a fire destroyed much of the studio's valuable property and what remained was used sparingly over the next six years by a variety of filmmakers.

Revisionist film histories also point to the contributions of Luigi Freddi and his handling of the LUCE-CINECITTA complex during the mid-1930s as an example of how the Italian film industry gained international recognition. Adriano Apra and Patrizia Pistagnesi claim that

> Apart from the fact, of more than secondary importance, that practically everyone involved in the neo-realist movement was formed within the Fascist orbit, that the film industry, apart from damages from the war, remained (built up by Luigi Freddi and the General Cinema Direction since 1934) and that neo-realism owes a large debt to the professionalism that developed in these industrial structures, it must be noted that some of the themes around which the poetics of neo-realism developed had precedents in the 30s.[542]

The issue of neo-realism's roots will be addressed later. Here it is worth noting that histories of the Italian Fascist cinema sometimes stress the seeds of inspiration germinating in Italian films more than calling attention to the industry's takeover by the Fascists and the mediocre quality of the product between 1935 and 1944. The point needs to made that the neo-realists were rebelling, in part, to the vapid romantic dramas (often called "white telephone films") and the propaganda movies of the Fascist period.

By the late 1930s, the Italian film industry had cultivated a stable of performers and directors, and a number of original screenplays emerged. Important new screenwriters were Aldo De Benedetti and Alberto De Stafani. Although the Fascist Italian cinema still relied heavily on proven formulas, these formulas were reshaped and redirected through competition with Hollywood films. Among the films foreshadowing the future neo-realistic movement were Rossellini's THE WHITE SHIP/LA NAVE BIANCA (1941), Blasetti's FOUR STEPS IN THE CLOUDS/QUATTRO PASSI FRA LE NUVOLE, and De Sica's THE CHILDREN ARE WATCHING US/I BAMBINI CI

---

[542] *Adriano Apra and Patrizia Pistagnesi, THE FABULOUS THIRTIES: ITALIAN CINEMA 1929-1944 (New York: Rizzoli International Publications, 1979), p.31.

GUARDANO (both in 1942). Of particular importance, as Cook points out, was that the Blasetti and De Sica films were both scripted by Cesare Zavattini, the Marxist screenwriter "who was shortly to become to neo-realism what Carl Meyer had been to the KAMMERSPIELFILM--its chief ideological spokesman and its major scenarist."[543]

That being said, it is still important to reiterate that after 1935, the Fascist government gained control over the nation's film industry. In addition to the establishment of the CENTRO SPERIMENTALE DI CINEMATOGRAFIA (a state-subsidized film school with incredible resources and facilities for training filmmakers), the tightening of political censorship, and the increased importance of LUCE in the cultural life of the nation, Mussolini's regime moved to make the cinema an arm of the state. A constant refrain one reads in today's revisionist histories is that the Italian filmmakers isolated themselves from Fascist policies. That interpretation is challenged by Gian Piero Brunetta, an Italian film historian who has analyzed movies in Italy in the 1930s. In commenting on recent accounts, he points out that

> During the entire postwar period, efforts were made, from the historical point of view, to regard the phenomenon of fascist cinema as marginal and episodic and to identify as genuinely fascist only films dealing directly with fascism and fascists. The part of the film industry that collaborated with fascism, accepted all its directives, or attempted to conform to the climate created by the regime was not taken into consideration. The prevailing condition that only a dozen propagandistic films were made is only partly true. The truth is that the film industry did not miss any of the regime's identification with great moments of history, that it followed and registered all the ideological changes at the top as well as the basic choices of the regime's cultural policy, thus reflecting, even in films that were seemingly not directly propagandistic, the fundamentally fascist directives.[544]

The issue of collaboration, discussed later, also plagues interpretations of the French film industry during World War II, and, to some degree, Hollywood during the post-WWII era. Suffice it to say that the film process involves more than a released movie, the alleged intentions of filmmakers, and the known acts of commission.

The cinematic output of the Italian Fascist cinema, in artistic terms, is still being debated. The focus is on whether the films from 1929 to 1944 were merely escapist movies or propagandistic; or whether there is an "unknown Italian cinema" unjustly ignored. On the one hand, historians like Robinson insist that the period was replete with "grandoise costume and operatic spectacles" and "vapid social dramas and comedies which earned the categorisation of 'telefono bianco', from the style of their decors. . . ."[545] Moreover, Gian Luigi Rondi argues that

> The Second World War, with its destruction, deaths, and foreign occupations, had jolted the Italians out of the soporific illusions of the rosy, optimistic cinema which for twenty years they had been subjected to by the dictatorship. For twenty years they had been fed on evasions, and the awakening after that, face to face with reality, had been absolutely frightful.[546]

---

[543]   Cook, p.380.

[544]   Cited in *Mira Liehm, PASSION AND DEFIANCE: FILM IN ITALY FROM 1942 TO THE PRESENT (Berkeley: University of California Press, 1984), p.322.

[545]   Robinson, p.231.

[546]   Rondi, p.11.

On the other hand, Perry points out that

> If the Italian cinema of the Fascist period had provided no more than a conduit
> for the passage from naturalism to Neorealism, it would be worth cursory study.
> But the fifteen years from the coming of sound to the end of Mussolini's reign
> provided much more: an entertainment industry that rivalled Hollywood in the
> charm and sophistication of its narratives, its acting and direction.[547]

In addition, there is now a revived interest on the part of filmmakers and film
historians in the nature and role of Italian Fascist cinema. This interest in fascism,
according to James Hay, is "bound up with cultural as well as with stylistic changes
that enabled Italian filmmakers to reassess and redefine its place in modern Italian
culture and political consciousness."[548] At the same time, De Sica reminds us that
in thinking about the dark days of Mussolini and the systematic murder of thousands
of Jews, we should recognize "That period was the blackest page in the history of
mankind. Yet, today in Italy there are many fascists--young people who do not believe
what it was like then. And unfortunately, there are many old people who have
forgotten. That is why I felt I must make THE GARDEN OF THE FINZI-CONTINIS--as
an act of atonement and as a warning."[549]

BOOKS

GENERAL

*Hay, James. POPULAR FILM CULTURE IN FASCIST ITALY: THE PASSING OF THE
REX. Bloomington: Indiana University Press, 1987. Illustrated. 280pp.
      A comprehensive examination of Italian cinema during the Fascist era, this
formalistic study relies heavily on current cultural theory for its complex examination
of the relationship among the state, the industry, and the public during the 1920s
and 1930s. Central to the analysis is an awareness of how modernization destabilized
Italy and made its citizens uncertain about their past and future. Cinema emerges
for Hay as the "cultural form which at that moment most vividly highlighted these
tensions and enabled those in Italy most affected by modernization to cope with the
highly unstable nature of their cultural foundation." To develop his thesis, Hay
applies Raymond Williams's intricate "process approach" methodology to examine a
variety of cultural codes and techniques that symbolize the collaborative, competitive,
and multi-discursive nature of Italian Fascist cinema. The plan is to discredit
simplistic descriptions of the era that glibly dismiss approximately 700 released films
as "overtly propagandistic." What Hay intriguingly argues is that film, like any other
culture force, is a heterogenous medium best understood as helping mediate reality,
thereby rendering the notion of a cultural consensus developed through propaganda
highly debatable. For the author, the most meaningful questions are those that probe
the movies' central role in providing audiences of the 1920s and 1930s with satisfying
images and models that deal with the effects of modernization on them and on their
communities. In that way, one can discern how the rejuvenated Fascist film industry
influenced the movie public's attitudes on changing social relationships and values.

---

[547]   Perry, p.13.

[548]   Hay, p.xvii.

[549]   Guy Flatley, "The Victory of Vittorio De Sica," NEW YORK TIMES 2 (January 16,
       1972):1, 9.

Italian movie formulas and popular stars become artifacts for analyzing the nation's alleged collective values during this destabilizing period. Particular attenion is directed to the role of the audience in the process. For example, Hay points to the rise of "new" middle and working classes that not only formed a major portion of the audience for the Italian Fascist cinema, but that also shared much of the nation's fears about its uncertain past and future. Thus the more the films described a "new order" based upon rural traditions but targeted at resolving the dilemmas of an urban industrialized society, the more the audiences felt at home both in the cinema and in society. Hay sees the Italian Fascist cinema emerging as an ongoing dialogue between the filmmakers and their peers about the social and political function of cultural forms.

At the same time, the author wants to explain the types of "paradoxes and ambivalences that are inscribed in the narrative structures" of the Italian Fascist movies. Hay takes for granted that the tensions within society produce a "profound cultural ambivalence" that is reflected in the films of the times. He, therefore, finds it constructive to compare Hollywood films and conventions (which often accounted for ninety percent of the films being screened in Italian movie theaters) with those of the Italian Fascist cinema, while also contrasting Italy's early film history with its later neo-realistic styles. One major conclusion is that the Italian Fascist government did not establish or maintain social conformity through the film industry. A second and more debatable conclusion relates to the propagandistic nature of the Italian Fascist film industry. While Hay argues that no message is ever uniformally accepted by a mass audience, he fails to draw a credible distinction between Fascist films made before and after 1935. Few revisionist scholars deny the independence of commercial filmmakers prior to the state's taking over the film industry. Some even make a good case that had the commercial filmmakers been as supportive of the Fascist ideology after 1935, they would have been unable to move so effortlessly into the post-WWII film world. What Hay does not adequately explain is the role played by mass audiences after the 1935 takeover.

If there is one drawback to this otherwise stimulating and profusely illustrated study, it is Hay's tendency to include many astute observations that become blurred by an overdose of theoretical qualifications. Helpful appendexes, valuable endnotes, a good bibliography, and a useful index are included. Well worth browsing.

*Apra, Adriano, and Patrizia Pistagnesi. THE FABULOUS THIRTIES: ITALIAN CINEMA 1929-1944. Introduction Alberto Arbasino. New York: Rizzoli International Publications, 1979. Illustrated. 116pp.

In 1978, the Museum of Modern Art presented a collection of forty-four films from the Italian Fascist cinema, many of which had not been seen in this country since 1941. No significant attempt is made to discuss how the intellectual climate in Italy or the Italian cinema contributed to the growth and development of Fascist ideology. Instead, Apra and Pistagnesi put a positive image on the films themselves, deploring the way in which this shameful period of history has resulted in downplaying the significance of the films of people like Goeffredo Alessandrini, Alessandro Blasetti, Mario Camerini, Renato Castellani, Luigi Chiarini, Vittorio De Sica, Carmine Gallone, Augusto Genina, Raffaello Matarazzo, Mario Mattoli, Amleto Palermi, Ferinando Maria Poggioli, Roberto Rossellini, Mario Soldati, and Luchino Visconti. Following an entertaining "morphological lexicon of the Italian 1930s," the authors offer articles on the history of the "Unknown Cinema," a look back in time by Blasetti, comments by Visconti, and two interviews with Camerini. The illustrations are excellent; the comments, superficial and self-serving. Useful biographies are provided on each of the aforementioned filmmakers. Well worth browsing.

Mancini, Elaine. STRUGGLES OF THE ITALIAN FILM INDUSTRY DURING FASCISM, 1930-1935. Ann Arbor: UMI Research Press, 1985. Illustrated. 298pp.

Originally written as a 1981 NYU Ph.D. dissertation, this detailed, fast-moving, and intelligent study examines a five year period during which the Italian cinema struggled for its freedom. "The major issues connected with these five years," Mancini writes, "include the cinema's artistic evolution, the attempts to construct a viable industry with a stable base, the delineation of the cultural framework in Italy that the cinema reflected and to which it contributed, and the extent to which the industry's policies mirrored governmental policies." Rather than accept the standard interpretations of the film industry's being a puppet of the Fascists, Mancini argues that Mussolini's government took little note of the commercial industry for almost a decade. And when that policy changed in the early 1930s, it did so mainly as an attempt to solve the industry's economic troubles. Moreover, she explains how the film industry worked to insulate itself from government control and depended on box-office results to shape its content and stories. That is, she describes the existence of directives and state agencies calling for film quotas and censorship regulations, but makes it clear that close ties with the Fascist government (e.g., a banking credit system for subsidizing film production, the creation of a state-sponsored school--CENTRO SPERIMENTALE DI CINEMATOGRAFIA--in Rome, the establishment of government agency--the DIREZIONE GENERALE PER LA CINEMATOGRAFIA--to insure compliance with Fascist regulations, and the formation of a specific government program--Imperialism--that the Fascists wanted supported in commercial feature film content) did not occur until the mid-1930s.

Mancini divides her material into six fact-filled chapters. The first chapter provides a good summary of the silent period, highlighting the important developments and ideas that had a direct bearing on Italian film in the early 1930s. For example, she discusses the era of the DIVE, the unique contributions of Gabriele D'Annunzio's emphasis on heroism, patriotism, and machismo in his epic films, and the bombastic exhortations of the futurists for an abstract cinema. In the process, Mancini points out how Italian futurism vanished in the sound period, while D'Annunzio's inspirational ideas gained a foothold in talkies. Also valuable are her descriptions of the significant changes that took place in Luigi Pirandello's twenty-year association with the film industry, the economic status of Italian filmmaking when sound arrived, the evolution of Stefano Pittaluga, and the reactions of Italian filmmakers to the challenges of the sound revolution.

Chapter 2 analyzes the transition to sound, focusing on the strong incentives the technological revolution brought to the Italian film industry and the two-year planning process that led to the conversion of all commercial feature films to talkies. Particular attention is given to the crucial factors in rejuvenating the commercial cinema: e.g., the theoretical writings of Sebastiano Arturo Lucianni and Anton Giulio Bragaglia, Pirandello's sole completed scenario (written with Adolf Lantz) for SIX CHARACTERS IN SEARCH OF AN AUTHOR (1930), and the contributions of Mario Camerini. Mancini also clarifies the problems that leaders faced in trying to resuscitate the Italian film industry, pointing out that demand for product far exceeded existing resources.

Chapter 3 chronicles the years from 1931 to 1935, discussing in detail the history of CINES, Italy's most important studio of the period, and the key roles played by Pittaluga and Emilio Cecchi in shaping the industry's destiny during the 1930s. Because CINES's influence was so pervasive, the author divides her history into four areas: the silent period, the initial stages of the sound revolution until 1935, the role of Luigi Freddi up to and through World War II, and the postwar era from 1949 to 1956. Production policies are described along with political and economic issues (i.e., the effect of the collapse of the BANCA ITALIANO DI SCONTO in 1921, how Pittaluga got his start in films, his move to CINES in the mid-1920s and the steps he took to acquire theaters, the inauguration of the new CINES-PITTALUGA studio in January 1930, the nature of government subsidy for the new studio, the unexpected death of Pittaluga in 1931 and the appointment of Emilio Cecchi the following year to the position of artistic director, the establishment of a documentary division at CINES, the debates over the studio's being a national rather than a European film company, the departure of Cecchi in 1933, the confusion that followed, and the disastrous fire of September, 1935). Especially interesting are Mancini's observations on the work done by foreign directors (e.g., Pierre Chenal, Gustav Machaty, Walter Ruttmann, Jean Epstein, and Max Ophuls) and the contrasting production policies of CINES and LUCE.

Chapter 4 is devoted exclusively to Alessandro Blasetti, the critic, theoretician, and filmmaker whose Fascist beliefs and nationalistic pride had a major impact on Italian film. For example, his writings in the influential periodical CINEMATOGRAFO from 1927 to 1931 provide an important overview of the strengths and weaknesses of the Italian film during the transition to sound films. His nineteen films from 1928 to 1941 not only initiated a new style for depicting the conflict between urban and rural life as well as for creating meaningful characterizations, but also in establishing the legitimacy and commercial value of Italian themes. Among the topics most appealing to the filmmaker were those concerning employment, nationalism, economic stability, and educational enrichment. What is most appealing to the author is the filmmaker's "unerring cinematic eye, his sense of rhythm, his strong character portrayals" in his films of the late 1930s and early 1940s. In addition to useful plot summaries and critical commentaries, Mancini points out how many directors who were anti-Fascist--e.g., Emilio Cecchi, Aldo Vergano, Alfredo Guarini, Ivo Perilli, Mario Camerini--ran into few problems with the censors, while Blasetti, who was pro-Fascist, had considerable difficulties.

Chapter 5 offers a direct contrast between commercial and state-sponsored filmmaking in Fascist Italy. Breaking with the pattern established by the previous chapters, the author examines documentaries, newsreels, and educational material produced by LUCE, placing them in a historical and political context. The advantages of this approach to the study are twofold. First, Mancini demonstrates the relative independence of the commercial film industry from Fascist control. Second, she reviews the evolution of LUCE from the early twenties to 1945. In the process, we learn why Mussolini founded LUCE in 1924 ("to provide instruction in cultural, foreign, and national affairs through film"), its method of organization, how people were recruited and what roles they played in the film process, the relationship between LUCE and Freddi's state film office, the various administrations that ran LUCE, and the ongoing debate over state versus private control of the film agency. Some of the most informative sections describe the content of the films themselves, with particular emphasis on how the on-again, off-again friendship between Hitler and Mussolini affected what was shown in LUCE's newsreels. The state-run company disappeared with the fall of the Fascists at the end of World War II. As Mancini comments, LUCE "had followed the regime's slogan: 'Believe, obey, fight.' It had believed, obeyed and lost."

In her concluding chapter, the author stresses the ambivalent status of the commercial film industry from 1935 to the end of WWII. Reiterating the argument that almost none of the films during the period under review "contained overt political content" and only a few "contained covert Fascist ideology," Mancini insists on the commercial industry's artistic freedom from 1930 to 1935. At the same time, she concedes that filmmakers did not operate in a vaccum. The steps taken by the Fascists to protect and regulate the production, distribution, and exhibition of films in Italy clearly strengthened the relationship between the industry and the state. "I am not suggesting," Mancini writes, "that propaganda films and films bearing a kinship with Fascist ideology did not exist. The regime supplied too many encouragements and too much assistance for that kind of filmmaking to be ignored." What she is saying is that the commercial film industry did not function as a puppet of the state, that ways were found to circumvent Fascist policies and agencies, and that few filmmakers joined the Fascist party. Moreover, Mancini concludes that up to the fall of the Fascist regime, the government remained uncertain about its relationship to film and the advantages of the cinema being made a political organ of the state.

What makes this revisionist history invaluable to serious film study is the author's willingness not only to reexamine approximately 120 films from a controversial period of film history, but also to challenge long standing value judgments and offer fresh perspectives. Several appendexes containing scenarios and a filmography, endnotes, a bibliography, and an index are included. Recommended for special collections.

MICHELANGELO ANTONIONI

*Antonioni, Michelangelo. THAT BOWLING ALLEY ON THE TIBER: TALES OF A DIRECTOR. Trans. William Arrowsmith. New York: Oxford University Press, 1986. 208pp.

Born in Ferrara, Italy, in 1912, Michelangelo Antonioni first studied business and economics before pursuing his love for films in the late 1930s. His initial forays were in film criticism, which led to screenwriting and assistant directing assigments with Roberto Rossellini, Enrico Fulchignoni, and Marcel Carne in 1942. He made his directorial debut with GENTE DEL PO (1943). A year later, Antonioni formally began studying directing at the CENTRO SPERIMENTALE DI CINEMATOGRAFIA. Over the next six years, he made a series of short films and established a close working relationship with the composer Giovanni Fusco, an important collaborator on Antonioni's later and most significant films. During the 1950s, the socially conscious director used his films to attack conditions in Italy. Among his most famous films are THE OUTCRY/IL GRIDO (1956-7), THE ADVENTURE/L' AVVENTURA (1959), THE NIGHT/LA NOTTE (1960), THE ECLIPSE/L'ECLISSE (1962), RED DESERT/IL DESERTO ROSSO (1964), BLOW-UP (1966), and THE PASSENGER/IL GRIDO (1975).

This valuable publication presents Antonioni's ideas for film projects in the form of thirty-three "narrative nuclei," short pieces ranging from a paragraph to several pages. Particularly useful is Arrowsmith's preface, discussing the filmmaker's thoughts on his profession. Endnotes are included, but no filmography or index is provided. Well worth browsing.

*Cameron, Ian, and Robin Wood. ANTONIONI. Rev. ed.. New York: Praeger Publishers, 1971. Illustrated. 152pp.

Basically, this is Cameron's useful monograph, printed in FILM QUARTERLY, with additional comments by Wood on BLOW-UP (1966), RED DESERT/IL DESERTO ROSSO) (1964), and ZABRISKIE POINT (1969). A filmography and bibliography are included, but no index is provided. Well worth browsing.

*Cameron, Ian. "Special Issue: Antonioni," FILM QUARTERLY 16:1 (Fall 1962).

This is a carefully written and perceptive analysis of Antonioni's basic camera work. Well worth browsing.

*Chatman, Seymour. ANTONIONI OR, THE SURFACE OF THE WORLD. Berkeley: University of California Press, 1985. Illustrated. 290pp.

"What is impressive about Antonioni's film," Chatman writes, "is not only that they are good but that they have been made at all. Films depend directly on mass public support in the form of ticket purchases. Antonion's films do not appeal to large audiences, and like many another artist he has to be more tenacious, tough-minded, and resilient to pursue his exacting goals through many difficult years." Chatman then goes on to describe what makes the filmmaker's work so difficult for the average filmgoer: "Perhaps because his subtleties of form make the content seem more abstruse than it really is. The slow editing pace, the careful, subtle, measured camera movements, and the long hold on faces and details of location violate their expectations and elicit the question that producers most dread--What's this movie about anyway?" If any current study can do something to increase Antonioni's accesssbility to large audiences or rekindle academia's neglect of this important filmmaker, Chatman's superb analysis is it. Relying heavily on the director's own words and a wide range of published criticism on the films themselves, the author presents an outstanding thematic review of Antonioni's work from his early days in filmmaking up to the present. Ten detailed chapters liberally illustrated with frame enlargements thoughtfully examine plots, themes, and techniques that constitute Antonioni's original and creative stylistic "language." Endnotes, a filmography, an excellent bibliography, and an index are included. This is the book to read if you want an introductory look at Antonioni's films. Recommended for special collections.

*Cowie, Peter. ANTONIONI, BERGMAN, RESNAIS. New York: A. S. Barnes and Company, 1963. Illustrated. 160pp.

*Leprohon, Pierre, ed. MICHELANGELO ANTONIONI: AN INTRODUCTION. New York: Simon and Schuster, 1963. Illustrated. 207pp.
      A translation from the CINEMA D'AUJOURD'HUI SERIES, the book is valuable mainly for its numerous Antonioni quotations and its appendix. Divided into four sections, it contains a number of critical and personal comments by people who have seen his films and worked with the unusual director. Well worth browsing.

Rifkin, Ned. ANTONIONI'S VISUAL LANGUAGE. Ann Arbor: UMI Research Press, 1982. 199pp.
      Originally written as the author's 1977 Ph.D. dissertation for the University of Michigan, this revised study "begins with an introduction structured to orient the reader to the historical moment of Antonioni's point of entry into the world of international filmmaking." Rifkin explains that the filmmaker's "early style shared many elements with the neo-realists, particularly his mise-en-scene--the way in which a filmmaker arranges the actors in a setting to bring a drama to life. However, Antonioni broke away from this in 1950 when he ceased making short documentaries and began feature-length fiction films. His mise-en-scene increasingly and deliberately assumed a less illusionistic and decidedly more abstracted relation to reality. The main part of the study examines the elements of Antonioni's mise-en-scene to show how he renders his unique world view using the concepts and visual impact of place, placement, movement and color to convey dramatic information." Six thoughtful chapters examine that unique view, offering fresh insights and stimulating interpretations on Antonioni's objectives and films. Endnotes, a bibliography, and an index are included. Well worth browsing.

*Strick, Phillip. ANTONIONI: A MONOGRAPH. London: Motion Publications, 1965. Illustrated. 58pp.
      A brief sketch of the author's life with an uneven discussion of his major films, Strick concludes with a series of critical quotations on Antonioni's film by reviewers. Worth browsing.

ROBERTO ROSSELLINI

*Brunette, Peter. ROBERTO ROSSELLINI. New York: Oxford University Press, 1987. Illustrated. 425pp.
      Born in Rome on May 8, 1906, Roberto Rossellini was the oldest of four sons in a family that traced its origins back to Renaissance Italy. Rossellini's father, a prominent architect who helped construct modern Rome, occupied a prominent place in contemporary society and exposed his family to intellectual movements and the arts. In fact, his work in building two important movie theaters allowed his sons to develop a love for motion pictures. Rossellini's fascination for moving pictures added considerably to his interest in mechanical inventions. Except for a serious bout with influenza during World War I, he enjoyed an ideal childhood and was able to do much as he pleased up to the 1930s. After his father's death, however, money became

scarce and Rossellini was forced to look for a job. He found filmmaking more interesting than his other options and took advantage of the family's contacts in the film industry to get a job editing and dubbing films, as well as writing screenplays. By 1934, using his own money, Rossellini began making documentary shorts. Like many emerging filmmakers, he became involved with the CENTRO SPERIMENTALE DI CINEMATOGRAFIA. In fact, his friendship with Vittorio Mussolini, the Fascist dictator's son, and their involvement on the film LUCIANO SERRA, PILOTA (1938) created political problems for Rossellini in the postwar period. More important in the formative stages of his screen career was the influence of the director Francesco De Robertis, a famous navy officer, who experimented with documentary techniques during the late 1930s and early 1940s. His involvement with De Robertis led to Rossellini's debut as a feature-film director with his films, THE WHITE SHIP/LA NAVE BIANCA (1941). In addition to establishing Rossellini as a major force in Italian films, it also cemented a close working relationship with the filmmaker's brother, Renzo Rossellini (the composer on many of Rossellini's films) and Eraldo Da Roma (one of the foremost editors of neo-realistic films). Four years later, Rossellini gained worldwide attention with ROME, OPEN CITY/ROMA, CITTA APERTA (1945). Following the success of this important neo-realistic film, the director made a number of significant films, including PAISAN/PAISA (1946), GERMANY, YEAR ZERO/GERMANIA, ANNO ZERO (1947), GENERAL DELLA ROVERE/IL GENERALE DELLA ROVERE (1959), and THE RISE OF LOUIS XIV/LA PRISE DU POUVOIR PAR LOUIS XIV (1966). During the 1950s, following a scandalous affair and marriage to Ingrid Bergman (following her Mexican divorce, the couple was married in 1950; eight years later an Italian court ruled the marriage invalid), Rossellini's film career went into a sharp decline. By the late 1950s, he turned most of his attention to stage productions and television work, with only occasional forays into film. In fact, his most noted film of the 1960s is the TV production, THE RISE OF LOUIS XIV/LA PRISE DU POUVOIR PAR LOUIS XIV. In 1969, the great director's reputation was reestablished and he was elected president of CENTRO SPERIMENTALE DI CINEMATOGRAFIA. After serving for a year, he left to pursue his TV and stage interests. Rossellini died on June 3, 1977.

Brunette's detailed and scholarly study, the first full-length examination of Rossellini, clearly and impressively analyzes the career of the man many people consider to be Italy's greatest director. As the author points out, "Certainly, the sheer variety of Rossellini's achievement is astounding. Such films as OPEN CITY and PAISAN make him a central, founding figure of neorealism, the startling return to reality in postwar Italian filmmaking that has drastically influenced all subsequent cinema practice. In his imaginative, purposeful use of what might be called 'antinarrative' devices such as dead time and dedramatization, he is also an obvious forerunner of Antonionni and other filmmakers who began to be noticed in the early sixties." Although Brunette downplays biographical information and focuses instead on the artist's films and his ideas on cinema, the book's five major sections--"Before OPEN CITY," "The War Trilogy and After," "The Bergman Era," "INDIA and the 'Commercial' Period," and "The Grand Historical Project"--include insights into the reltaionships between Rossellini's personal and professional challenges. Endnotes, a filmography, and an index are included. Recommended for special collections.

*Guarner, Jose Luis. ROBERTO ROSSELLINI. Berkeley: University of California Press, 1970. Illustrated. 144pp.

A useful overview of Rossellini's career from his early Fascist films to his TV work on SOCRATE (1970), this book provides helpful critical and biographical observations plus many stills, a filmography, and bibliography. Unfortunately, no index is provided. Well worth browsing.

Rossi, Patrizio. ROBERTO ROSSELLINI: A GUIDE TO REFERENCES AND RESOURCES. Boston: G. K. Hall, 1988. 281pp.

LUCHINO VISCONTI

*Nowell-Smith, Geoffrey. LUCHINO VISCONTI. New York: Doubleday and Company, 1968. Illustrated. 189pp.

Another Renaissance filmmaker who also has deep roots in the Italian opera and theater, Visconti had a long cinema career but made few movies. Nowell-Smith does his best to help illuminate the man, his work, and his virtues. The book contains the best use of illustrations in the Cinema One series. Well worth browsing.

Servadio, Gaia. LUCHINO VISCONTI: A BIOGRAPHY. New York: Franklin Watts, 1983. Illustrated. 262pp.

Born on November 2, 1960, in Milan, Italy, Luchino Visconti was the third son of wealthy parents who traced their ancestry back to the time of Charlemagne. The young aristocrat grew up with a love for music, stage design, and horse-racing, but decided on a career in film after spending time with Jean Renoir during the production of A DAY IN THE COUNTRY/UNE PARTIE DE CAMPAGNE (1936). After making his directorial debut with OBSESSION/OSSESSIONE (1942), Visconti, now an avowed Marxist, pursued his interest in theater and did not make another film until DAYS OF GLORY/GIORNI DI GLORIA (1945). This documentary film, co-directed with Marcello Pagliero, was followed by Visconti's second feature film, THE EARTH TREMBLES/LA TERRA TREMA (1947). For the remainder of his life, the socially conscious director alternated his work between films and stage plays. Among his more famous films are FEELING/SENSO (1954), WHITE NIGHTS/LE NOTTI BIANCHE (1957), ROCCO AND HIS BROTHERS/ROCCO E I SUOI FRATELLI (1960), THE LEOPARD/IL GATTOPARDO (1963), THE DAMNED/LACADUTA DELGI DEI (1970), and DEATH IN VENICE/MORTE A VENEZIA (1971). Visconti died on March 17, 1976, while editing his last film, THE INNOCENT/L'INNOCENTE (1976).

This affectionate and informative biography captures the turmoil in the life of Luchino Viscont, Duke of Modrone, providing many entertaining anecdotes about the famous people he met and worked with, his love affairs, and his political beliefs. Its major benefit is that it relates the filmmaker's personal life to his work. Endnotes, a bibliography, a listing of Visconti's professional output, and an index add to the human side of the director portrayed in fourteen informative chapters. Well worth browsing.

Stirling, Monica. A SCREEN OF TIME: A STUDY OF LUCHINO VISCONTI. New York: Harcourt Brace Jovanovich, 1979. Illustrated. 295pp.

A valuable examination of the man who began as a wealthy playboy and became one of the world's most respected artists, this well-written and entertaining biography reads more like a fascinating novel than a scholarly document. Although Stirling aims her analysis at a popular audience and foregoes documentation, her insightful comments on Visconti's problems with Fascist censors during World War II, his fabulous triumphs in opera, theater, and film, and his monumental struggles to express his unique view of society are based on extensive research and personal contact with Visconti during the making of his last film. A bibliography and an index are included. Well worth browsing.

CESARE ZAVATTINI

Zavattini, Cesare. ZAVATTINI: SEQUENCES FROM A CINEMATIC LIFE. Englewood Cliffs: Prentice-Hall, 1970. Illustrated. 297pp.

Zavattini is regarded by many as one of the most important theorists in Italian film history. This is a valuable self-portrait that traces his career from the birth of neo-realism, while at the same time presenting interesting insights into many famous film personalities. Regrettably, no index is provided. Well worth browsing.

FILMS

ALESSANDRO BLASETTI

1860 (Italy--16mm: 1933, 73 mins., b&w, sound with subtitles, R-MMA)

A sweeping and impressive film based on a story by Gino Mazzucchi, the film focuses on the effects that Garibaldi's invasion of Sicily had on a young married couple. It is considered to be Blasetti's greatest work. Peter Bondanella points out that the director's "use of non-professional, Sicilian-speaking characters   .   .   . [foreshadowed] an attention to linguistic detail that will be continued in a number of postwar neorealist works. In addition, the complex battle scenes he organizes demonstrates his great technical skill in handling large numbers of actors."[550]

JAPAN AND THE TALKIES (1931-1945)

Although Japan's conversion to talkies paralleled developments in the West, there were some striking differences. One major difference was that Japan moved much more slowly than did Western nations. In fact, she didn't genuinely begin to convert to talkies until the mid-1930s. Until then, her audiences contented themselves with a mixture of traditional fare and technological novelties. The idea of talking films, however, had interested Japan since the turn of the century. As Anderson and Richie point out, Japan, like other nations, had experimented with sound movies early in her cinematic history and found them to be commercially unacceptable, especially since the public felt comfortable with BENSHI presentations.[551] A second major difference, therefore, was that what was novel to foreign audiences in the late 1920s was not so for Japanese audiences, who were quite accustomed to sound effects, narration, dialogue, and music with their movies. Moreover, American talkies, which led the way in getting Western nations to convert to sound, initially proved to be a disaster in Japan because audiences found the dialogue dubbed by foreigners annoying and out-of-touch with contemporary Japanese speech. It was not until 1931, with the exhibition of a subtitled version of MOROCCO (1930), that the Japanese discovered that the best approach to the problem of foreign sound films was subtitling rather than dubbing.[552] In addition, film giants like Nikkatsu and Shochiku were reluctant to invest large sums of capital into converting studios and theaters to talkies when no one was certain of what was the best approach--sound-on-film or discs--to talking films.

When the conversion to sound finally became a necessity in the early thirties, it started a competitive war in the Japanese film industry reminiscent of the fierce battles between the Motion Picture Patents Company (MPPC) and the Independents. Intense competition among the Japanese companies became ruthless and unprincipled. Thugs were hired to sabotage studio productions, to intimidate key personnel, and

---

[550]   *Peter Bondanella, ITALIAN CINEMA: FROM NEOREALISM TO THE PRESENT. New York: Frederick Ungar Publishing Company, 1983. p.15.

[551]   For an excellent summary of Japan's transition to sound films, see Anderson and Richie, pp.72-89.

[552]   Anderson and Richie, p.76.

to disrupt distribution. While Nikkatsu and Shochiku raided each other's key personnel and sought to increase theater holdings, Photo Chemical Laboratories (P. C. L.), a minor company started at the end of the twenties, grew more powerful. It took advantage of the big companies' mistakes, capitalized on technological breakthroughs, and recruited the disillusioned cadre of Nikkatsu AND Shochiku. By 1937, P. C. L. had become the Toho Motion Picture Company, Japan's largest film producer and distributor. The BENSHI was gone,[553] and the Hollywood model of filmmaking was entrenched.

A major difference, however, between the American and Japanese film factory orientation is that while both callously exploit their employees to maximize profits, the Japanese companies give the impression that they function as a family. The area where that paternalism is most evident, Richie comments, is in the Japanese film unit:

> Director, writer, photographer, composer, and art director form a very unusual association, in which approaches are understood and agreed upon before a foot of film is exposed. The strength of the association depends, of course, upon the director . . . Almost equally important is the strong personal loyalty which the grips, the carpenters, the ordinary unit people show toward the director.[554]

The value of such loyalty in the film continuum is evident from pre-production planning to the exhibition of the films themselves.[555]

Before considering the Japanese film industry's aesthetic direction from the early thirties until the end of World War II, it is important to understand how the political scene and the move to "Westernize" Japan were interwoven. By the end of the 1920s, a massive backlash against industrialization was affecting the nation, with many right-wing elements asserting that the modernization process had undermined traditional Japanese values, cheapened the cultural life of the country, and corrupted the political system. At the same time, a short-lived Marxist movement was capturing the imagination of young people, who warmed to the ideals of individualism, an anti-class system, and a new approach to how society should be run. The existence of a Marxist movement and the obsessive consumerism that pervaded Japan was cited as further proof of the deterioration of the nation's social structure. Whatever the justification for such assertions, it became clear that by 1930, there was a dramatic shift away from the liberal ideas of the West and a return toward the conservative values of Japan's feudal era. Throughout the 1930s, patriotism became the rallying cry whereby a once-deposed military establishment regained power and systematically attacked any vestiges of Western influence in the nation.

The films of the period, especially the short-lived left-wing genre called KEIKO EIGA ("tendency films"),[556] reflected the political climate and contributed to the

---

[553] For an intriguing account of what happened to one prominent BENSHI, see SOMETHING LIKE AN AUTOBIOGRAPHY, pp.82-5.

[554] Donald Richie, "Preface," JAPANESE FILM DIRECTORS, p.10.

[555] For some valuable insights into how the film units operated, see Kurosawa's description of his experiences as an assistant director with Kajiro Yamamoto's "group" in SOMETHING LIKE AN AUTOBIOGRAPHY, pp.90-108.

[556] Basically a reaction to the jingoistic climate, KEIKO EIGA ("tendency films") challenged the establishment's paternalistic values and its solutions to social problems. Social realism gained a foothold in the industry, while veiled attacks on domestic policies occurred in both JIDAI-GEKI and GENDAI-GEKI. It is also worth noting that "tendency films" reflected the interest in Soviet films that had been imported into Japan and the nation's early flirtation with Communism.

formation of a uniquely Japanese film aesthetic. That is, the films put human characters center stage, meticulously depicted the MILIEU, and offered the barest of plots.[557] According to Bock, "The first 'golden age' of Japanese film occurred in the 1930s, when the Great Depression widened the gulf between the rich and the rest, and the Japanese as an audience began to display their preference for films about 'people like you and me.'"[558] Equally important, as Burch observes, "Japanese cinema in the 1930s is predominantly characterized by latent and overt conflict between the dominant representational modes of the West and emerging Japanese modes."[559] On the technical side, Japanese filmmakers favored long and medium shots rather than close-ups, concentrated on mood rather than on plot development, and relied on cut-away shots for transitions rather than on fades or dissolves. On the content side, filmmakers debated on screen the virtues of a paternalistic society, the subservient role of women, and the concept of "We" versus "I" ideology.[560] Types rather than individual characterizations became the order of the day, while the emphasis in the memorable films was on attacking the way that right-wing forces stressed sacrificing one's family responsibilities in favor of nationalistic duty to strengthen their militaristic goals.

Of the major filmmakers, some of the most important were Heinosuke Gosho, Tamizo Ishida, Mansaku Itami, Daisuke Ito, Teinosuke Kinugasa, Kenji Mizoguchi, Mikio Naruse, Yasujiro Ozu, Yasujiro Shimazu, Hiroshi Shimizu, and Sadao Yamanaka. Each director displayed a concern with the problems of ordinary people, while crafting works that were not only, as Burch points out, "uniquely Japanese," but also equal in quality "to the finest achievements of the traditional arts of previous centuries."[561] In addition, most of these artists were in no rush to make sound films. Their primary interest was in maintaining a national aesthetic that made films commensurate with the traditional arts. If they could find a way to incorporate talkies into the system, they adapted the new technology. If not, the BENSHI and silent screen techniques would do until the technology was perfected. What's more, the Japanese public encouraged that position.

The trend toward social-realism that had developed after World War I intensified as sound films emerged in the West. For example, Daisuke Ito was a screenwriter-turned-director[562] who was interested in period dramas with social statements. Cited by Sato as the "first director to raise this genre to an avant-garde art form," the action-driven Ito "combined adept storytelling with a rapid succession of images brimming with beauty and pathos, and the impassioned performance of his favorite lead, Denjiro Okochi."[563] In works like his three-part drama entitled A DIARY OF CHUJI'S TRAVELS/CHUJI TABI NIKKI (1927), Ito's love for blood thirsty

---

[557]   THE JAPANESE MOVIE, p.60.

[558]   Audie Bock, JAPANESE FILM DIRECTORS (Tokyo: Kodansha International, 1978), p.13.

[559]   Burch, p.186.

[560]   THE JAPANESE MOVIE, p.49. Tucker also offers (pp.23-4) some useful observations on the concept of "We" versus "I" in a popular literary genre called SHISHOSETSU. In talking about the shallowness of these "confessional" novels, he provides insights into Japanese film adaptations.

[561]   Burch, p.143.

[562]   Because of the apprentice-type training in the Japanese film industry prior to World War II, almost every director first had to go through an period of learning everything about filmmaking, from being a grip and an assistant director, to being a screenwriter and an editor.

[563]   Sato, p.39.

stories about outlaw warriors fighting violently for an ancient code of honor, often veiled his attacks on modern Japanese society. Over the next three decades, the director kept his "nihilistic" and "frustrated" heroes in constant revolt against feudal values. "The social critique," Mellen explains, "was implicit in his choice of such a hero, and the development of the social criticism in his films was a result of his maturing as an artist."[564]

Given the thirties' growing fascination with contemporary dramas, it was not surprising that Japan's first successful talkie was Heinosuke Gosho's THE NEIGHBOUR'S WIFE AND MINE/MADAMU TO NYOBO (1931), a SHOMIN-GEKI comedy that cleverly integrated sound with silent screen images. "Because every sound had to be synchronized," Kyoko Hirano points out, "Gosho explored many technical devices, and also used multiple cameras, different lenses, and frequent cuts to produce a truly 'filmic' result."[565] Not only did THE NEIGHBOUR'S WIFE AND MINE/MADAMU TO NYOBO signal the rise of comedy films in Japan, but it also started the trend that made domestic dramas the most representative genre of the pre-WWII era. In film after film by Gosho, Naruse, Ozu, and Shimazu, the emphasis, Sato explains, would be on "the family in a tense confrontation with society. . . ."[566] As for Gosho himself, he would become renowned, Arne Svensson observes, for blending "pathos and humor, realism and lyrical symbolism" and for exploring "with great feeling . . . the ordinary man and his problems, often with a certain amount of sentimentality."[567] Over the next thirty-seven years, Gosho would pursue his poetic fascination with the lives of everyday people, working in a variety of genres but always "with a basic belief in humanistic values."[568]

The coming of Japanese talkies infused the industry with a new competitive spirit, a penchant for comedy, and a desire for realism. No longer was it commercially viable to present self-glorifying costumed dramas or unrealistic stories of contemporary life. Audiences began demanding human tales of ordinary people whether in feudal times or in the present. Such popular tastes worried the right-wing forces rapidly gaining control of the nation's destiny. They feared that an overemphasis on individualism in melodramatic love stories and urban dramas would undermine the public's acceptance of subordinating one's personal fortunes to the welfare of the family, the community, and the emperor. As a result, film censorship of anti-feudal values increased significantly. Thus comedy and satire became weapons that filmmakers used to mask their attacks on the governing reactionary forces.

As the decade progressed, Japanese film content underwent a metamorphosis. The early years saw a left-wing emphasis, especially in the period dramas. Stories about the Tokugawa era concentrated on RONIN (wandering, unemployed samurai with strong personalities).[569] Rather than stress superhuman men fighting heroic battles, a filmmaker like Mansaku Itami in his movie KAKITA AKANISHI/AKANISHI KAKITA (1936) focused on a simpleminded warrior who suffered from the greed, intolerance, and caste system of a repressive society. Itami's lyrical character study, with good

---

[564]   Mellen, p.23.

[565]   Kyoko Hirano, "Gosho, Heinosuke," THE INTERNATIONAL DICTIONARY OF FILMS AND FILMMAKERS: VOLUME II DIRECTORS/FILMMAKERS, p.226.

[566]   Sato, p.139.

[567]   *Arne Svensson, JAPAN (New York: A. S. Barnes and Company, 1971), p.20.

[568]   Hirano, p.226.

[569]   For a good overview of the nature of masterless samurai in period dramas, see THE SAMURAI FILMS OF AKIRA KUROSAWA, pp.33-4.

humor and witty situations, is one example of the 1930s' alternatives to the make-believe costume dramas of the silent era.

No one summarizes the shift in the Japanese cinema from the early to the late 1930s better than Sadao Yamanaka. According to Alan Stanbrook, Yamanaka was the "finest director in the years following the golden age of jidai-geki . . . [and although his] interests were less social than Itami's . . . [they were] more human."[570] Like Itami, however, Yamanaka's best period dramas--e.g., THE LIFE OF BANGOKU/BANGOKU NO ISSHO (1932), THE ELEGANT SWORDSMAN/FURYU KATSUJINKEN (1934), THE VILLAGE TATTOOED MAN/MACHI NO IREZUMI MONO (1935), and HUMANITY AND PAPER BALLOONS/NINJO KAMIFUSEN (1937)--dealt with homeless, wandering RONIN and the lives of ordinary people. His unemployed samurai epitomized the inhumanity of the Tokugawa era. "The contribution of both Yamanaka and Itami," explain Anderson and Richie, "was that they approached Japanese history as though it was contemporary, looking for values in it that they looked for in their own lives."[571] But by the mid-1930s, the Japanese establishment had become increasing hostile to pessimistic films about unheroic samurai. As the state began to resemble more and more a quasi-Fascist society, the censors became more ruthless in their attacks on liberal filmmakers. Following the screening of HUMANITY AND BALLOONS, a memorable story about a down-and-out RONIN who commits suicide by hanging (he pawned his sword for rice), Yamanaka was punished for his left-wing political positions, drafted into the army, and sent to the Chinese front in 1938, where he was killed in action. The tragic death of the thirty-one-year-old artist moved a number of film historians to refer to him as the "Japanese Vigo."

Kenji Mizoguchi was a more complex figure than most of his contemporaries. Although deeply influenced by the literary and cinematic achievements of the West, he remained genuinely committed to the artistic sensibilities of the East. Although many of his period dramas and contemporary stories would flirt with left-wing values--e.g., the plight of the poor, the oppression of women, and the cruelty of a class system--he constantly put his aesthetic interests above political concerns. Consequently, many Western commentators are baffled by the fact that the man who could make "tendency films" in the late 1920s could also turn out war propaganda films in the early 1940s. Japanese critics, on the other hand, accept the director's oscillation as part of the price one pays to work in the Japanese film industry.

A painter at heart, Mizoguchi had tried to make a living in commercial art, failed, and eventually drifted into film as an actor at the start of the 1920s. By the end of the decade, he had become a director with forty-one films to his credit. Almost all of them revealed Mizoguchi's obsession with the cinematic innovations being developed in the West. He was particularly intrigued with any techniques that strengthened the narrative, heightened pathos, and intensified the conflict among the characters. His period dramas emphasized tragic situations and reflected his fascination with the cultural values and psychological insights of the Tokugawa era. But with the 1930s' emphasis on a Japanese aesthetic, Mizoguchi abandoned his silent film style and began developing an anti-Western orientation. He, more than any other Japanese filmmaker, symbolized the battle between East and West taking shape in the Japanese cinema. As Burch points out, the director's style now became preoccupied with "a kind of rhetorical reversal of Western film codes of shot size, i.e., the further the camera is from the characters, the more 'intimate' is the message, the more intense the emotion to be conveyed."[572] Retaining his love for dramatic narratives and intense psychological conflicts, Mizoguchi nevertheless became a master of Japanese filmmaking. "The director's love for painting," explain Schrader and Nakamura, "his

---

[570] Alan Stanbrook, "Break with the Past: Part One," FILMS AND FILMING 6:6 (March 1960):10.

[571] Anderson and Richie, p.95.

[572] Burch, p.236.

concern for the composed scene, his reliance upon the aesthetically pleasing,
continues the aesthetic of the traditional Japanese artist which is that of the 'climate
of beauty.'"573
    The director also evidenced a lifelong concern with the problems of women and
their redemptive powers. In film after film, he would show the psychological, social,
and economic abuse that Japanese women faced in a paternalistic society, while
remaining constant in their love for those who mistreated them. Mizoguchi's unflagging
concern with the problems of women, as Bock observes, was a curious obsession:

> Mizoguchi falls within the strong tradition of "feminists" in Japanese film,
> literature, and drama. However, this English loan word has nuances in Japanese
> that differ considerably from its western usage.   Aside from its predictable
> meaning, "proponent of women's rights, equality or liberation," it has a second,
> more popular usage: "a man who is indulgent toward women; a worshipper of
> women."574

In many of Mizoguchi's films, women suffered, sacrificed, and died so that the men
they loved would prosper. His redemptive heroines appear to condemn societies that
make them subservient to men, yet, as Bock points out,

> Mizoguchi's ideal woman is the one who can love. This love consists,
> however, of a selfless devotion to a man in the traditional Japanese sense. She
> becomes the spiritual guide, the moral and often financial support for husband,
> lover, brother or son.575

It is for that reason that critics like Tucker argue that the basic theme in all of
Mizoguchi's films is that "man is nothing without the love of a woman, that woman's
love redeems an often harsh and cruel world."576 Whatever one's feelings about
Mizoguchi's reaction to the status of women, it is clear that through his depiction of
their state, he attacked the notion that profit, position, and power are more important
than human relationships and compassion.
    By the mid-1930s, with his two acclaimed films OSAKA ELEGY/NANIWA EREJI
and SISTERS OF THE GION/GION NO SHIMAI (both in 1936), his famous cinematic
style was set. His thematic concerns focused on the problems of the poor, often
unfortunate women; his film techniques stressed "exceptionally long takes, systematic
rejection of editing in general, and of the reverse-field figure in particular, and of
the close-up."577 Both the themes and the "one-scene, one-shot" methodology
emphasized a total commitment to mood rather than to storytelling, to stirring an
audience's emotions rather than appealing to their intellect. In the years that followed
and until his death in 1956, Mizoguchi's work earned him a reputation, in Bock's
words, as "A lover of novelty, worshipper and hater of women, inventor of authentic
period films and fully played emotion in a distanced, lyrical long take, [and] whimsical
in politics and love. . . ."578

573   "Mizoguchi Spectrum," p.12.

574   Bock, p.40.

575   Bock, p.41.

576   Tucker, p.59.

577   Burch, p.225.

578   Bock, p.52.

Like Mizoguchi, Mikio Naruse was a formidable filmmaker symbolizing the ongoing debate between Western and Japanese filmmaking. He too set out to incorporate Western film techniques into realistic Japanese films depicting the plight of poor people and eventually developed an anti-Western bias in his cinematic style. But unlike the volatile, fatalistic Mizoguchi, the docile, sullen Naruse had no interest either in period dramas or in fighting his studio bosses. He took what jobs were offered and kept to the assigned shooting schedules and production budgets. What he did maintain in almost all of his nearly ninety SHOMIN-GEKI films was a pessimistic view of life. Unlike other directors who supplied their innocent characters with spiritual or temporal options to misfortune and disillusionment, Naruse insisted on his characters' confronting their inevitable tragedies. Although his career as a writer-director spanned nearly fifty years (1920-1967) and lacks a specific focus, Naruse remains one of Japan's best artists but least appreciated directors.

What is especially noteworthy in Naruse's SHOMIN-GEKI achievements, as Bock points out, are his noble heroines who retain "A stubborn dedication to their own self-respect in the face of overwhelming crassness, vulgarity and exploitation from even those who should be most sensitive and protective toward the individual. . . ."[579] Naruse's bare-boned cinematic style is also noteworthy for his ability to create unforgettable images of poor people trapped by circumstances and yet determined to honor their family responsibilities,[580] no matter what the human cost. In some of his greatest successes--e.g., WIFE! BE LIKE A ROSE!/TSUMA YO BARA NO YO NI (1935) and THE WHOLE FAMILY WORKS/HATARAKU IKKU (1939)--the pessimistic melodramas, modeled on American cliches, clearly demonstrate a Japanese aesthetic and sensitivity to the human condition, heightened by Naruse's studio lighting and austere camera placement. As Kurosawa explains,

> Naruse's method consists of building one very brief shot on top of another, but when you look at them all spliced together in the final film, they give the impression of a single long take. The flow is so magnificent that the splices are invisible. This flow of short shots that looks calm and ordinary at first glance then reveals itself to be like a deep river with a quiet surface disguising a fast-raging current underneath.[581]

In Kurosawa's judgment, he was a remarkable artist. "Despite his compliance with studio demands, "Bock reminds us, "[Naruse] never compromised on the lies of life and movies. There are no happy endings,   . . .   but there are incredibly enlightened defeats."[582]

Hiroshi Shimizu's films are the exact opposite of Naruse's pessimistic SHOMIN-GEKI. His world, as Stanbrook comments, "is a sunny one, where the sadness of things rarely intrudes."[583] For that reason alone, Shimizu is more popular in the West than in Japan. The problem for modern scholars is that only a sixth of the director's 150 films made between 1924 and 1950 are available for analysis.[584]

If one goes by traditional accounts, Shimizu is described by critics like Burch

---

[579] Bock, p.101.

[580] For a good discussion of the role of the family in Japanese films, see CURRENTS IN JAPANESE CINEMA, pp.124-44.

[581] SOMETHING LIKE AN AUTOBIOGRAPHY, p.113.

[582] Bock, p.118.

[583] Alan Stanbrook, "On the Track of Hiroshi Shimizu," SIGHT AND SOUND 57:2 (Spring 1988):122.

[584] "On the Track," p.122.

as being the "most spontaneously Japanese director of his generation. . . ."[585] Seen
as more commercial and less sophisticated than other directors of SHOMIN-GEKI,
Shimizu's popularity with Japanese audiences was based, allegedly, on two key
elements: his traditional film style (a minimum of editing techniques and camera
placements) and his obsession with stories about children.[586] In his most famous
films--A STAR ATHLETE/HANAGATA SENSHU and CHILDREN IN THE WIND/KAZE
NO NAKA NO KODOMO (both in 1937)--Shimizu gets considerable praise for his lyrical
images of young people in unguarded moments.

But thanks to a recent retrospective of Shimizu's films at Britain's National Film
Theatre, the neglected artist is undergoing a re-evaluation. Stanbrook summarizes
Shimizu's new standing by first denying the improvisational nature of his work and
arguing that Shimizu's films were "the most consciously planned Japanese works of
the 1930s and 1940s."[587] In each of his episodic comedies, according to Stanbrook,
one can see the director's love of life and human behavior, locate a multitude of
recurring motifs and themes, and appreciate his use of moving camera shots.[588] Why
Japanese audiences appear reluctant to honor his memory remains a mystery, no doubt
related to his occidental orientation.

National identity also plays a controversial role in another of the era's great
filmmakers. Considered by many of his countrymen "to be the most Japanese of all
their directors,"[589] Yasujiro Ozu nevertheless poses considerable problems for
Western audiences, who often find his reactionary message of acceptance intolerable
and his film technique tedious. Nakamura and Schrader point out that he "is the only
foreign filmmaker who had had virtually no impact on American films or criticism."[590]
The reason, the critics speculate, is due to his rigid, austere cinematic style:

> There are no pans, no dissolves, almost no tracking shots. The camera is
> always at one height, three feet above the ground. The cutting technique is
> predictable, repetitive, and circular. Ozu's style is, in fact, "revolutionary,"
> in its resolution to eschew any "effects."[591]

Regrettably, not enough people have taken the time to appreciate the beauty of Ozu's
approach to filmmaking.

His career, as Richie comments, followed the traditional Japanese pattern: "a
period of early exploration among things Western followed by a slow and gradual
return to things purely Japanese."[592] Starting as a screenwriter and as an assistant
director at Sochiku in the early 1920s, he began directing in 1927. At first, Ozu
demonstrated a distaste for fantasy and a fondness for silly farces. Although he would
soon abandon nonsense films for serious social comedies about the lives of poor people,

---

[585]   Burch, p.247.

[586]   Anderson and Richie discuss (pp.124-5) the importance of novels about children,
        JUNBUNGAKU, being made into films during the 1930s.

[587]   "On the Track," p.123.

[588]   "On the Track," pp.123-5.

[589]   Donald Richie, OZU (Berkeley: University of California Press, 1974), p.xi.

[590]   Nakamura and Schrader, p.2.

[591]   Nakamura and Schrader, p.2.

[592]   OZU, p.xi. For a good introduction to the influence of American films on Ozu's
        work, see Sato, pp.33-4.

the young Ozu experimented constantly with film technique, almost always with the intention of reducing camera movement to maximize the composition of the action and setting, but most of all the characterizations. In Richie's judgment,

> All of Ozu's technique has only one object--the revelation of character. His waiting, listening camera records, not the heights of emotion but those moments, those sighs, which both precede and come after such moments--those little tropisms through which true emotion is to be apprehended.[593]

Over the next thirty years, the director would become famous for his remarkable "portraits" of parent-child relationships where both come to terms with the transience of earthly things and accept the cyclical nature of the natural order.

By the early 1930s, Ozu's fascination with GENDAI-GEKI had resulted in a specific type of eventless story, centering on family life, with its everyday tensions and humorous incidents, but emphasizing objects and gestures rather than plot development. At the heart of Ozu's films is an undying respect not only for Japan's traditional arts, but also for her ceremonial customs. He more than any other Japanese filmmaker is able to capture the extraordinary elements of life in the most commonplace of actions and behavior. Furthermore, as Richie observes, "Ozu was not simply bored by plot. He actively disliked it."[594]

Unlike Western narratives, filled with subplots and motivation, Ozu's narratives, as Bock explains, contain universal insights into our everyday challenges: "the struggles of self-definition, of individual freedom, of disappointed expectations, of the impossibility of communication, of separation and loss brought about by the inevitable passages of marriage and death."[595] For example, In his lighthearted, silent SHOMIN-GEKI creations like I WAS BORN BUT . . ./UMARETE WA MITA KEREDO (1932), he uses children as an excuse to ridicule adult social values. But in the end, as Paul Schrader comments, "The greatest conflict (and the greatest resulting disillusionment) in Ozu's films is not political, psychological, or domestic, but is, for want of a better term, 'environmental.'" That is, Schrader goes on to say, "That the aged cannot communicate with the young, that the parents cannot communicate with their children, that the craftsman cannot communicate with the office workers--these are all dimensions of the problem that the modern Japanese cannot communicate with his environment."[596] Among the things that separate Ozu from his peers, as Richie discovered, are "the autononomy of the single scene in Ozu's films, and the enormous importance assigned to character-revealing dialogue,"[597] as well as his traditional message that we should accept our fate rather than rebel against it.

Ozu's poetical approach reached its peak with THE ONLY SON/HITORI MUSUKO (1936)--not only his first sound film but, as Burch argues, his most "radical experiment . . . with . . . division between the verbal and spatio-temporal parameters. . . ."[598] In telling the story of a mother's sacrifices for her son and the disillusionment that follows, the director insists that the best way to deal with

---

[593]   Donald Richie, "Yasujiro Ozu: The Syntax of His Films," FILM QUARTERLY 17:2 (Winter 1963-64):13.

[594]   OZU, p.25.

[595]   Bock, p.71.

[596]   Paul Schrader, TRANSCENDENTAL STYLE IN FILM: OZU, BRESSON, DREYER (Berkeley: University of California Press, 1972), p.35.

[597]   OZU, p.22.

[598]   Burch, p.175.

disappointment is to accept the fact that children will not only fail to live up to our expectations but also go off on their own. "Ozu's method," Richie points out, "like all poetic methods, is oblique. He does not confront emotion, he surprises it. . . ."[599] As Bock summarizes Ozu's films, "In avoiding virtuoso technique as well as dramatic structure he went straight into the irrationality of character and that terrible truth: life is disappointing, isn't it?"[600]

Yasujiro Shimazu took a different approach from Ozu. He loved contemporary melodramas and is sometimes credited with being the originator of neo-realistic Japanese films.[601] In SHOMIN-GEKI works like MAIDEN IN THE STORM/ARASHI NO NAKA NO SHOJO (1933) and THE WOMAN THAT NIGHT/SONO YORU NO ONNA, OUR NEIGHBOUR MISS YAE/TONARI NO YAE-CHAN (both in 1934), he made films devoted to the problems of the middle class. Shimazu's most famous film, A BROTHER AND HIS YOUNGER SISTER/ANI TO SONO IMOTO (1939), epitomized his skills in family dramas, while demonstrating his commitment to Western film techniques in plot development and characterization.

By 1937, Japan, in her determination to become the most powerful nation in Asia and building on her annexation of Manchuria in 1931, took up arms against China, and began her role in what would eventually become World War II, or as the Japanese called it, "The Pacific War."[602] According to Anderson, the military campaigns caught the Japanese film industry by surprise:

Japan had never developed a war film genre. The country's minor participation in the First World War and the earlier conflicts with Russia and China apparently failed to interest audiences or provide strong inspiration for scenarists. But the presence of actual war was something the film industry could not ignore.[603]

The problem was that the filmmakers didn't know what to do. For almost a decade, period dramas were on the decline, and the public seemed preoccupied with SHOMIN-GEKI and urban love stories of everyday people. How was the film industry supposed to survive if it changed its commercial successes into acceptable propaganda films for the government? But the military leaders had no intention of debating the matter or of ignoring the propaganda value of moving pictures. Laws were passed and tight government regulations imposed on all filmmakers. "From 1936 to 1945," Sato

---

[599]   "The Syntax of His Films," p.16.

[600]   Bock, p.88.

[601]   Anderson and Richie point out (p.96) that while it is clear that the Japanese were working on "neo-realistic" films in the 1930s, such films epitomize the weaknesses of Japan's approach to realism: "a tendency to overstatement, which creates crude melodrama; over-sentimentality; and a presentation of social problems without the slightest hint as to how they may be solved."

[602]   For more information, see Peter B. High, "The War Cinema of Imperial Japan," WIDE ANGLE 1:4 (1977):19-21; ___, "An Interview With Kihachi Okamoto," ibid., pp.25-7; Tadao Sato, "War as a Spiritual Exercise: Japan's 'National Policy Films,'" trans. Peter B. High, ibid., 22-4; and *Ruth Benedict, THE CHRYSANTHEMUM AND THE SWORD, PATTERNS OF JAPANESE CULTURE (London: Routledge, 1967). For a discussion of the role of Japanese documentaries during the war period, see Anderson and Richie, pp.102-3.

[603]   "Seven from the Past," p.86.

explains, "Japanese film was in complete bondage to the Home Ministry and the Media Section of the Army."[604]

Unlike many Western nations, as discussed in Chapter 2, who used their film industries to rally their citizens against a "racial" enemy, the Japanese government took a unique approach.[605] It created a "National Policy Film" (SEN'I KOYO EIGA) aimed at inspiring the public. As Peter B. High describes the strategy,

> This was a genre of combat films portraying war as an opportunity to train and elevate the spirit. Certainly, as war propaganda, these films lacked almost all of the features we would respond to in the West. Almost gentle in tone, they rarely stressed hatred of the enemy or even the ultimate rightness of Imperial Japan. Rather, they taught reverence for the nation's BUSHI-warrior heritage--utter self-sacrifice is noble and necessary, the core of one's life.[606]

According to Sato, these "national policy films" had three distinct characteristics. The first, the abstract nature of the enemy, has already been mentioned. The second was a focus on the humanity of the Japanese soldiers. The third was to treat "war as a kind of spiritual training. . . ."[607]

Films between 1937 and 1945 thus became the means for reeducating the public to traditional "Japanese" values. The emphasis, Anderson and Richie point out, was to eliminate "insincere thoughts and words from the screen; deepen respect toward fathers and elder brothers."[608] Lest anyone misunderstand what was required, the Home Ministry issued specific instructions in 1940:

(1) ONLY HEALTHY ENTERTAINMENT FILMS WITH POSITIVE VALUES WILL BE PASSED FOR VIEWING BY THE PUBLIC. (2) WHILE NOT SPECIFICALLY BANNED AT PRESENT, FURTHER PROLIFERATION OF COMEDIANS AND SATIRISTS ON SCREEN WILL BE RESTRICTED BY LAW. (3) PETTY-BOURGEOIS FILMS, FILMS EXTOLLING PRIVATE HAPPINESS, FILMS DEALING WITH THE SUPER-RICH, FILMS WITH SCENES OF WOMEN SMOKING OR CABARET LIFE, DIALOGUES HEAVILY PEPPERED WITH FOREIGN WORDS AND SCENES WITH POINTLESS COMEDY ROUTINES ARE HEREBY PROHIBITED. (4) FILMS DEPICTING THE PRODUCTIVE SECTORS OF NATIONAL LIFE, ESPECIALLY AGRICULTURE, ARE TO BE ENCOURAGED. (5) PREPRODUCTION INSPECTION OF ALL SCENARIOS SHALL BE RIGOROUSLY ENFORCED. IF SAID INSPECTION REVEALS PASSAGES IN VIOLATION OF THE ABOVE

---

[604] "War as a Spiritual Exercise," p.22. For examples of the way that the censors operated, see SOMETHING LIKE AN AUTOBIOGRAPHY, pp.119-32. By the beginning of the 1940s, ten major companies comprised the film industry. To coordinate efforts to bolster morale, the government demanded that the companies merge into two organizations. The producer Masaichi Nagata, however, insisted on a third company, Dai-Nihon Eiga (The Greater Japan Motion Picture Company). Formed in 1942, it specialized in period dramas and was the home of experienced directors like Kenji Mizoguchi, as well as newcomers like Akira Kurosawa and Kon Ichikawa. Each of the three companies, however, was limited to releasing just two films a month to the two newly reorganized theater circuits. For more information, see Anderson and Richie, pp.142-5.

[605] For a valuable comparison between Western and Japanese propaganda films, see Anderson and Richie, pp.132-40.

[606] "The War Cinema of Imperial Japan," p.19.

[607] CURRENTS IN JAPANESE CINEMA, pp.101-3.

[608] Anderson and Richie, p.129.

INSTRUCTIONS, REWRITING SHALL BE ORDERED UNTIL THE VIOLATIONS HAVE BEEN CORRECTED.[609]

The force of these stern directives and the total power granted to the state made resistance to the Home Ministry's rules virtually impossible. Nevertheless, it is clear, especially after December 7, 1941, that many people in the film industry not only complied willingly, but enthusiastically. That is not to say that every film made during the war years was a propaganda film. A number of notable works by newcomers like Akira Kurosawa as well as veteran directors like Gosho, Itami, Ito, Mizoguchi, Ozu, and Yamamoto demonstrated a humanism rare in wartime movies. It is to say, however, that most of these men and their colleagues also contributed significantly to the propaganda war.[610]

Thus we come to the issue of culpability and what responsiblity the Japanese filmmakers bear for the tragedies of World War II. It is a question we will face not only here but also in other sections on Nazi cinema in Germany, French films under Nazi Occupation, and Fascist films in Italy. Obviously, the problem goes beyond film and relates to basic issues of the relationship between art and moral behavior. In that regard, Will Crutchfield outlines many of the essential questions we need to ask:

What precisely is the responsibility of the artist as citizen of a tyrannical or evil state? To keep art going for art's and his fellow citizens' sake, whatever the compromises? To set art in opposition to the regime, whatever the risks? To leave? And then: What right have others to evaluate the artist's decisions in the face of evil, or his failures to perceive it? Is it to be asserted that the inner life and the outer life may not be compared, that the artist and the citizen cannot be made answerable for one another? Or if the artist must bear the citizen's guilt, what suffices for its expiation?

Crutchfield offers no simple answers to his thorny questions, but he does point out that no nation fails to find itself confronted with them.

In considering the culpability of Japanese filmmakers,[612] it is worth remembering, as Burch reminds us, that, unlike other nationals who could emigrate to democratic countries during WWII, Japanese filmmakers had no such options.[613] At the same time, he points out that ". . . if one were to examine the political records of most of the major film-makers of the 1930s, it seems fairly clear . . . that the fusion of traditional values and militarist ideology was a major factor in the

---

[609]   "War as a Spiritual Exercise," p.22. Anderson and Richie comment (p.129) that the Home Ministry eventually patterned its policies after those of Goebbels.

[610]   Although space does not permit discussing the role of documentaries during this period, almost all of the film histories on Japanese cinema point out the growing importance and maturity of Japanese documentary films during this period, especially in works like Tomu Uchida's EARTH/TSUCHI (1939) and Kajiro Yamamoto's HORSE/UMA (1941).

[611]   Will Crutchfield, "Beautiful Music from a Twisted Time, NEW YORK TIMES B (August 28, 1988):27.

[612]   For a detailed discussion of what individual filmmakers did during the war years, see Anderson and Richie, pp.121-2, 132-58.

[613]   Burch, p.143.

development of a specifically Japanese cinema, [and that it] holds true at the level of the individual as well."[614] In concurring with that judgment, Richie points out that

> The record of any Japanese director (including that of Mizoguchi) shows him satisfying the authorities and then, if possible, also making films which are close to nature, which capture the episodic nature of life, which insist upon atmosphere and mood--which, indeed, combine the strengths and the individuality of the Japanese cinema. Most artists attempt this in war. They have little other choice.[615]

From the vantage point of history, it is easy to minimize the passions that motivated patriots to participate fully in a propaganda war against the enemy and focus instead on the positive contributions that were made in spite of the difficult times. The point here is not to open old wounds. It is rather to remember what the war was about and the choices people made during a period when such choices had tragic consequences for the world.

The point should also be made that race hatred permeated the thinking of both the Japanese and the Americans during the period between the two world wars. John W. Dower, in his impressive comparative historical study of the two cultures, examined not only propaganda films but also cartoons, songs, slogans, confidential reports, and official documents. The evidence he presents makes it clear that World War II was, in part, a race war on both sides. Within the United States, it reinforced obnoxious stereotypes about an inferior nation of myopic, pint-size Orientals who were incompetent warriors ready to perform ritual deaths. The Japanese, for their part, pictured us as a degenerate and monstrous race of spineless beings easily defeated in battle. Whether one looks at America's or Japan's propaganda tools, Dower points out,

> Each of these exercises in ideology and propaganda can be seen as a tapestry of truths, half-truths, and empty spaces. When the American and Japanese examples are set side by side, the points each neglected to cover become clearer; and it becomes plain that both sides reveal more about themselves than about the enemy they are portraying. Certainly, no one views a documentary film such as KNOW YOUR ENEMY--JAPAN decades later to learn about the Japanese in war; they do so primarily to learn about the Americans. Similarly, READ THIS AND THE WAR IS WON and THE WAY OF THE SUBJECT are of retrospective interest not for what they tell us of Japan's enemies, but for what they tell us about the mind-set of the Japanese at war.[616]

By the time World War II ended, the state and the industry was using the mass media to wage a propaganda campaign on a grand scale. A major effect of their increased proficency was to allow nations and individuals to distance themselves psychologically from the awesome technological destruction that advanced technology made possible. Here is not the place to detail the death and destruction wrought by the Axis and Allied powers. We need only note that more than 55 million people died because of crimes committed against humanity by a handful of nations who were able to convince their citizens, in large part through the use of mass media, that war was necessary and justified.

Those historians who, like Ruth Benedict, seek to minimize the guilt of Japanese

---

[614]   Burch, p.243.

[615]   THE JAPANESE MOVIE, p.72.

[616]   John W. Dower, WAR WITHOUT MERCY: RACE AND POWER IN THE PACIFIC WAR (New York: Pantheon Books, 1986), p.27.

filmmakers, argue that the Japanese were anti-militaristic in their propaganda films.[617] Those historians who, like Tadao Sato, take a sterner point of view, insist that an absence of "hysterical wartime propaganda" does not mask the fact that the films "succeeded in creating a specifically Japanese form of cinematic persuasion."[618]

By 1945, the Japanese film industry was in a state of flux. Many of its filmmakers had stagnated intellectually during the conflict, but had become more technically proficient and less parochial in attitude. In part this was the result of a policy that encouraged international productions with the Axis powers and the countries that Japan occupied in Asia: e.g., Korea, China, and Indonesia. Defeat in combat had left the nation not only bewildered and ashamed, but also surprisingly receptive to the wishes of the American victors. The issue for filmmakers was to explore what could be done to bolster morale and still conform to the requirements of an occidental occupation.

BOOKS

GENERAL

*Bock, Audie. JAPANESE FILM DIRECTORS. Preface Donald Richie.   Tokyo: Kodansha International, 1978. Illustrated. 370pp.

In addition to offering analyses of ten Japanese directors, this valuable reference book also focuses on three signficant periods in Japanese film history. The first period, the 1930s, witnessed the maturity of Kenji Mizoguchi, Yasujiro Ozu, and Mikio Naruse. Bock's discussions include insights into Mizoguchi's tragic themes and his fascination with noble heroines, as well as clues to why Ozu and Naruse strongly influenced the evolution of the SHOMIN-GEKI. The second period, the 1950s, describes the humanistic concerns of the postwar generation as evidenced in the films of Akira Kurosawa, Kon Ichikawa, Keisuke Kinoshita, and Masaki Kobayashi. Following commentaries illustrated with handsomely reproduced stills, the author concentrates on the ethical values and social forces that influenced these directors and the veterans from Japan's first "golden era" in the 1930s. The third period, the 1960s, highlights the dramatic shift in mood that gripped the nation and found new directors like Nagisa Oshima, Masahiro Shinoda, and Shohei Imamura rejecting the "naive universal humanism of the past," and turning instead to a new "search for the essence of Japaneseness." In the works of these modern filmmakers, Bock explores Oshima's political pessimism, Shinoda's "aesthetic sado-masochism," and Imamura's fascination with "irrational mythic consciousness." Although each of the three periods is subsumed in individual chapters on the directors themselves, the cumulative effect is to critique the growth of the Japanese film from a period of concern with a "We" versus "I" ideology, through a commitment to ethical values, and eventually to an era where "sex, violence, anti-narrativity, and self-referentialism" gained center stage in the film industry.

The importance of the study is related to the interviews that Bock had with each of the directors, thereby providing first-hand reactions to the three historical periods. The chronologically arranged chapters include footnotes and annotated filmographies. A concluding bibliography and index complete this important reference book. Recommended for special collections.

---

[617]   Benedict, p.193-4.

[618]   "War as a Spirtual Exercise," p.23. In a revised version of this article in CURRENTS IN JAPANESE CINEMA, Sato offers (pp.104-5) an explanation of why Occupation Forces did not treat Japanese film directors as badly as they did film industry executives.

AKIRA KUROSAWA

*Kurosawa, Akira. SOMETHING LIKE AN AUTOBIOGRAPHY. Trans. Audie E. Bock.
New York: Alfred A. Knopf, 1982. Illustrated. 210pp.

The most famous of all Japanese directors, Kurosawa is credited with
popularizing his nation's films all over the world. At seventy-one, he decided to write
his autobiography, but refused to go beyond the success of RASHOMON (1950). The
editor speculates that Kurosawa works on the maxim that "If you can't say anything
nice. . . ." Kurosawa claims his inspiration for the book came from two directors:
Jean Renoir and John Ford, both men he admires and hopes he has emulated in films.

Told in anecdotal form, the autobiography recounts how from birth (March 23,
1910) Kurosawa led a troubled life in Taisho Japan (1912-1926), often being considered
a weakling and a coward. The youngest of seven children (four boys, three girls),
he showed little interest in formal education. That is, until he met Seiji Tachikawa,
a primary schoolteacher who inspired Kurosawa to study the fine arts. Another early
influence on the difficult child was Keinosuke Uekusa, a schoolboy friend and later
a screenwriter on some of Kurosawa's important postwar films--e.g., ONE WONDERFUL
SUNDAY/SUBARASHIKI NICHIYOBI (1947) and DRUNKEN ANGEL/YOIDORE TENSHI
(1948). Kurosawa's childhood stories about living in the country, working in the city,
and assimilating both traditional and modern values from his parents help explain not
only how his character was shaped and influenced his films, but also how Japan
fluctuated between becoming an industrialized nation and yet remaining committed to
feudal values. The source for the feudal values was the boy's father, a graduate of
a military academy and a strong advocate of physical fitness. Growing up in a
"samurai household," Kurosawa developed a love for the BUSHIDO and an imperial
manner in dealing with subordinates and studio executives. At the same time, we
discover the author's strong love for painting and how it became a major part of his
formal education in high school and led eventually to his interest in Marxist ideas in
the late 1920s. We also learn about his great love for Russian literature and how it
relates to his efforts to reshape the direction of postwar Japanese films. Among the
best sections of the autobiography are those outlining why he demands artistic control
over his work, the reasons why he abandoned painting, why he worked for the
underground Communist movement in Japan, the influence that his older brother Heigo
had on the young man's aspiring film career, the way that a 1936 P. C. L.
advertisement for apprentices brought him into the film industry, the importance of
the emerging film company in teaching him his craft, and the debt that he owes to
his mentor Kajiro Yamamoto. As the autobiography unfolds, we also glean some
understanding of why he always scripted his own films, developed his own repertory
group, became a heavy drinker, developed a temper, and hated the Japanese film
bureaucracy. Particularly fascinating for cinema students are his accounts of life at
Toho, the director's insights into screenwriting, the problems of wartime censorship,
and the creation of his postwar films.   The writing is straightforward and
entertaining.

What is most disappointing about the book is the author's failure to deal candidly
with the war years from 1937 to 1945. Rather than reveal his motives and experiences
during the Pacific War, Kurosawa focuses exclusively on his battles with censors and
thus deprives us of any insights into the wartime propaganda he produced. In fact,
he is effusive about how much he appreciated the liberal behavior of the occupation
forces and how they contributed to his immediate postwar films. It is also frustrating
not to know more about the events that led to his emotional problems in the 1960s,
why he attempted suicide in 1971, and his current contemptuous attitude toward
society in general.

On balance, this highly personal and limited introspective account offers a
pleasant introduction to Kurosawa's life and career. An appendix containing random
thoughts on filmmaking and an index are included. Well worth browsing.

KENJI MIZOGUCHI

Andrew, James Dudley, and Paul Andrew. KENJI MIZOGUCHI: A GUIDE TO REFERENCES AND RESOURCES. Boston: G. K. Hall, 1981. 333pp.

Born on May 16, 1898, in Tokoyo, Kenji Mizoguchi was born to working class parents who fell on hard times. His unhappy childhood, exerting a major influence on the content of his films, consisted not only of his being shifted from one relative to another, but also of his developing an inferiority complex that strongly affected his personality. He entered films as an actor and graduated to directing in the early 1920s. Of the more than seventy-five films he directed between 1923 and 1956, the best deal with the lives of women and the healing power of their love. Mizoguchi died on August 24, 1956.

The brothers who authored this valuable resource guide benefited from their individual talents. Dudley Andrew, noted film scholar, drew on Paul's ability to read Japanese and his interest in Japanese culture. Consequently, the useful biographical sketch of the filmmaker is based almost entirely on Japanese sources. Dudley understandably gets the credit for the perceptive critical evaluation of Mizoguchi's films. The bulk of the annotations on material by and about the director is from French, English, and Japanese periodicals and journals. Interestingly, the authors acknowledge that most of the printed material attributed to Mizoguchi was the work of ghostwriters, but they insists that the filmmaker did not "entirely dissociate . . . [himself] from the ideas expressed in these articles." Other informative sections in this appreciated publication include a filmography, archival sources, film distributors, appendexes on Japanese characters for reference material, an author index, and an article index. Recommended for special collections.

McDonald, Keiko. MIZOGUCHI. Boston: Twayne Publishers, 1984. Illustrated. 187pp.

YASUJIRO OZU

Richie, Donald. OZU. Berkeley: University of California Press, 1974. Illustrated. 276pp.

The major work on Ozu to date, this extremely lucid analysis does a masterly job of interpreting the director's cinematic style, working habits, and theoretical principles. The preface explains what makes Ozu an essentially Japanese director and why he puts such great emphasis on character in his films. The book explores the artist's thematic concerns, pointing out recurring motifs in a career that spanned nearly forty years. Richie then offers insightful information on the construction of Ozu's scripts, the evolution of his shooting style, his editing techniques, and the unique qualities of the director's works. A superb biographical-filmography chapter concludes the major sections of the book. In addition, this outstanding scholarly work includes a bibliography, endnotes, and an index. One comes away not only with an in-depth appreciation of Ozu as an artist, but also with a good overview of the cultural and philosophical contexts in which he worked. Highly recommended for general collections.

FILMS

KENJI MIZOGUCHI

FORTY-SEVENTH RONIN: Part II/GENROKU CHUSHINGURA (Japan--16mm: 1942, 111 mins., b/w, sound with English subtitles; R-FNC)

Known in Japan as A TALE OF ROYAL RETAINERS IN THE GENROKU ERA (Part II), this romanticized tale of undying loyalty and self-sacrifice in the name of honor was made under pressure from the military government. The story focuses on what happens when the noble Lord Asano commits a breach of etiquette at the Shogun's palace and is forced to commit HARI-KARI. As further punishment, his vassals are dispersed and his property confiscated. The bulk of the narrative deals with the responsibilities and obligations the samurai have to their dead DAIYMO and how their actions will appear both to the public and to the shogun. The film is a good example not only of Mizoguchi's political naivete, but also of his commitment to strong narratives and emotional intensity.[619]

SISTERS OF THE GION/GION NO SHIMAI (Japan--16mm: 1936, 95 mins., b/w, sound, R-FNC)
A dramatic and moving story of two prostitutes, both sisters, one traditional, the other modern, the film demonstates Mizoguchi's cinematic style and thematic concerns. Based upon an idea by Michoguchi, Yoshikata Yoda tries to build sympathy for the older woman, who clings to traditional values, but is forced at the end to show that only the younger sister will survive, since she is able to adapt to contemporary times. What is visually striking about the film is the director's "painterly style," in which he stresses visual perspective within each carefully composed shot as opposed to editing shots together to create intense emotions. Isuzu Yamada and Yoko Umemura give outstanding performances as the two sisters believing in different values.

THE STORY OF THE LAST CHRYSANTHEMUM/ZANGIKU MONOGATARI (16mm: 1939, 148 mins., b/w, sound with English subtitles, R-FNC)
Known in Japan as TALE OF LATE CHRYSANTHEMUMS, the slight plot concerns the fortunes of a KABUKI actor who challenges the traditions of the past, leaves his father's troupe, becomes a famous performer, and returns in triumph to his family. The woman who encouraged him throughout his career is abandoned in favor of his new status. While there are those who attack the film because of the way women are oppressed, other critics defend Mizoguchi by arguing that his women are brighter and braver than the men they encounter. Yoda's controversial screenplay was photographed superbly by Shigeto Miki and Yozo Fuji.

YASUJIRO OZU

I WAS BORN BUT . . ./UMARETE WA MITA KEREDO (Japan--16mm: 1932, 89 mins., silent; R-NCE, NYF; S-NYF
Emphasizing the problems that children have with adult behavior yet maintaining a realistic attitude toward Japanese class structure, this deceptively simple story deals with the unsuccessful attempt by the sons of an office employee to make him more independent of his boss. By the end of the film, the two sons have not only understood their father's role in life, but have also prepared themselves to follow in his footsteps. To Ozu's credit, he presents no villains and offers no excuses for life's cruelties.

THE ONLY SON/HITORI MUSUKO (Japan--16mm: 1936, 82 mins., b/w, sound with English subtitles, R-FNC, MMA)

---

[619] For a good summary of the importance of this national legend and its place in Japanese film history, see Burch, pp.236-8.

A moving tale of a widowed lower-class woman who sacrifices everything for her son's education only to discover in later years that her efforts were in vain, the film illustrates Ozu's fascination with sound and silent techniques. As he explains, "In spite of my understanding perfectly well that everything is different in a talkie, this movie had the style of a silent."[620] Also worth noting is Tucker's observation that "The tension in THE ONLY SON operates on a number of levels all of which have a greater impact if one remembers the strength of the concept of family and duty."[621] That is, a balance is maintained between the disillusionment of both the mother and the son, as well as the conflict between modern and feudal ideology. Tadao Ikeda wrote the screenplay, based upon an original idea by Ozu.

PASSING FANCY/DEKIGOKORO (Japan--16mm: 1933, 103 mins., b/w, silent; R-FNC)
    A preoccupation in Japanese films in general, and Ozu films in particular, is the pathos associated with the rearing of children by single parents. In this film, scripted by Tadao Ikeda, a widowed father's embarrassing infatuation with a younger woman causes a strain between the man and his son. The eventual reconciliation between the parent and the child illustrates how Japanese filmmakers used realistic stories about children as a way of avoiding film censors, who were opposed to negative images of Japanese society.   Particularly impressive is Ozu's use of the MILIEU to personify the themes of loneliness and jealousy.

THERE IS A FATHER/CHICHI ARIKI (Japan--16mm; 1942, 87 mins., b/w, sound with English subtitles, R-FNC)
    Employing an unparalleled predominance of long shots and considered by Burch to be Ozu's last masterpiece,[622] the story concerns a widowed schoolteacher who abandons his career after learning about a fatal accident for which he assumes responsibility. It is an example of Ozu's preoccupation with the concept of "shame" in his films. Chishu Ryu, as the toubled parent, gives one of the great performances of the pre-WWII years and was one of the director's most popular and important stars.

WORLD WAR II AND FILM (1939-1945)

    The world conflict destabilized the economic, social, and political foundations that supported the international film community. Not only were production facilities and movie houses ruined or destroyed by bombing raids, political reorganizations, and hand-to-hand warfare, but many distribution outlets also disappeared and remained closed for the duration of the war, raw materials for filmmaking were rationed, financing was extremely limited, and censorship problems became more severe. Not until the late 1940s would there again be a functioning worldwide film market, and then the changes in structure from the past were dramatic.
    The most obvious change in film content was the shift away from escapist movies and toward semi-documentary dramas. The seeds for this realistic trend had been planted during the rise of the Soviet cinema, the second French AVANT-GARDE, and the documentary movements in Britain and America. Global conflict made it nearly impossible for film industries to avoid depicting what was taking place in the real world.

---

[620]   "Ozu Spectrum," p.3.

[621]   Tucker, p.50.

[622]   Burch, p.180.

The effects that World War II had on Hollywood and the international film industry have been described in Chapters 2, 3, and 5. Here we need only touch on a few reminders to explain how some national film industries were transformed by war's destabilizing powers.

FRANCE

One of the most controversial film programs during World War II was that of the French film industry from 1939 to 1944.[623] The story has been covered in detail by others. Here we need only offer a capsule overview. Following a declaration of war between France and Germany in September 1939, the French film industry almost disappeared. Many of her artists became totally involved in the war effort or fled the country. The nation's defeat in June of 1940 only intensified the industry's problems. Demoralized and divided, France saw its artists in flight or lacking adequate resources or facilities to work. Thus began a climate of recrimination and rationalization over who was to blame for the nation's defeat and the industry's plight.

High on the accusation list were Jews, particularly Leon Blum (the first Jewish prime minister of France in 1936 and head of the Popular Front) and Bernard Natan (the convicted film embezzler). Anti-Semitism was not unique to Vichy France or to the French film industry. The film historian Robert Brasillach was complaining in the 1930s that the Jews were dominating the mass media: "The movie business practically closed its doors to aryans. The radio had a Yiddish accent. The most peaceful people began to look askance at the kinky hair, the curved noses, which were extraordinarily abundant. All that is not polemic; it is history."[624] The historians Michael R. Marrus and Robert O. Paxton describe the consequences of 1930s' racism on a larger scale: "France's international weaknesses, its economic decline, its parliamentary disorder, its diminished sense of national purpose, its declining birthrate, its flagging bourgeois culture--all could be attributed to Jews, so notoriously not French yet so vividly evident in so many spheres of French activity."[625] That is not to paraphrase the old adage, "Scratch a Frenchmen and find an anti-Semite." There were many French citizens who not only spoke out against this racism, but also gave their lives in defense of Jewish freedom and rights. It is to say, however, that a large portion of French society found it politically, socially, and economically beneficial to persecute Jews. Finding such anti-Semitism effective as it participated in the "cleansing" of the French film industry, Vichy France turned its back when Jewish filmmakers were expunged from the movies and focused instead on using the cinema as a key means

---

[623] In addition to Evelyn Ehrlich, CINEMA OF PARADOX: FRENCH FILMMAKING UNDER THE GERMAN OCCUPATION (New York: Columbia University Press, 1985); and *Roy Fowler, THE FILM IN FRANCE (London: Pendulum Publications, 1946), the following are also useful to consult: Hazel Hackett, "The French Cinema During the Occupation," SIGHT AND SOUND 15 (Spring 1946):1-3; Lincoln Kristein, "French Films During the Occupation," MUSEUM OF MODERN ART BULLETIN (January 1945):16-20, Elizabeth Grottle Strebel, "French Cinema, 1940-1944, and Its Socio-Psychological Significance: A Preliminary Probe," HISTORICAL JOURNAL OF FILM, RADIO AND TELEVISION 1 (1981):33-46; William Novik, "Four Years in a Bottle: A Critical Study of French Film Production Under the Occupation," PENGUIN FILM REVIEW 2 (1947):45-53; Francois Garcon, "Nazi Film Propaganda In Occupied France," NAZI PROPAGANDA: THE POWER AND THE LIMITATIONS, ed. David Welch (Totawa: Barnes and Noble Books, 1983), pp.161-79; and Olwen Vaughn, "The French Cinema Under the German Occupation," THEATRE 2 (Winter 1945-46):28-31.

[624] Cited in *Michael R. Marrus and Robert O. Paxton, VICHY FRANCE AND THE JEWS (New York: Basic Books, 1981), p.38.

[625] Marrus and Paxton, p.41.

for rebuilding the nation's self-image and helping France find a stronghold in the presumed "New Europe" envisioned by Nazi Germany.

Goebbels's original plan was to have German films replace both French and American productions, thereby not only increasing revenue for his Nazi propaganda programs, but also influencing the leisure activities of the French public. But a nation accustomed to quality films found little of interest in the mediocre and banal films of the era. Very quickly, Goebbels sensed his mistake and ordered support for a rejuvenated French film industry, subject, of course, to Nazi and Vichy censorship. By June of 1942, the Nazis had centralized production in Paris and many French film personnel were back making movies. While most of the more than 220 movies made during the occupation remained indistinguishable from those popular films of the 1930s, nearly thirty percent created a new look for the French cinema. Attacked in the 1950s by the emerging young critics of the CAHIERS DU CINEMA as being too detached, ornate, and pretentious, the films--e.g., Marcel L'Herbier's THE FANTASTIC NIGHT/LA NUIT FANTASTIQUE (1941), Marcel Carne's THE DEVIL'S OWN ENVOYS/LES VISITEURS DU SOIR, Jean Gremillon's SUMMER LIGHT/LUMIERE D'ETE (both in 1942), Henri-Georges Clouzot's THE RAVEN/LE CORBEAU, Robert Bresson's ANGELS OF THE STREETS/LES ANGES DU PECHE, Jean Dellannoy's THE ETERNAL RETURN/L'ETERNAL RETOUR, Claude Autant-Lara's LOVE STORY/DOUCE (all in 1943), and Marcel Carne's CHILDREN OF PARADISE/LES ENFANTS DU PARADIS (1944)--also have gained praise for their remarkable beauty.

What makes the period so controversial is the issue of collaboration versus resistance. In forming an answer, it is useful to consider Zeev Sternhill's observation that

> the growth of the fascist idea [in France] can ultimately be attributed to the presence of a favorable environment. The pure fascists were always small in number and their energies were scattered. However, the existence of quasi-fascist channels of transmission--people, movements, journals, study circles--devoted to attacking materialism and its by-products--liberalism, capitalism, Marxism, and democracy--created a certain intellectual climate which was to undermine the moral legitimacy of an entire civilization. This ideology of revolt advocated a revolution of the spirit and the will, of manners and morals. It offered not only new political and social structures but also new types of relationships between man and society, between man and nature. In periods of economic growth and abundance, peace, and stability such an ideology has only a limited hold on society, but in times of severe crisis the revolutionary potential of such a system of thought becomes clearly evident, and it can fuel mass movements of an exceptional destructive force. [626]

Applying that observation to the French film industry during the Nazi occupation, it appears that the filmmakers found a moral climate that made the ends justify the means. And the question to consider, simply stated, is "Does the commitment to one's art take precedence over one's responsiblities to one's country and to one's fellow human beings?" The French filmmakers who contributed to the French film industry's remarkable resilience under Nazi occupation insist that they did what they did for the benefit and well-being of the French people. Historians like Evelyn Ehrlich certify that these were indeed their intentions, but point out that these artists often forsook their Jewish colleagues, benefited financially from their work, and, consciously or not, supported Nazi policy in occupied France. John Gross comments that

---

[626]   Zeev Sternhill, NEITHER RIGHT NOR LEFT: FASCIST IDEOLOGY IN FRANCE, trans. David Maisel (Berkeley: University of California Press, 1986), p.302.

It could of course be argued that the very act of making films under the Nazi dispensation was morally offensive; however much you tried to ignore the fact, you were giving comfort to the devil. But at least it can be claimed on the other side that none of the films made during the Occupation offered the Germans the explicit support, and that only one full-length feature--an attack on Freemasonry called FORCES OCCULTES--was made at their direct behest.[627]

There are those who insist we cannot judge the actions of the filmmakers because we do not know what we would have done had we been in their place. What any of us would have done had we been there is not the question. What is at issue is an ideal of justice that society holds out to its citizens and by which acts of commission and omission are held accountable throughout history. A question here is "Are artists excluded from such an ideal?"

BOOKS

FRANCE

GENERAL

Bazin, Andre. FRENCH CINEMA OF THE OCCUPATION AND RESISTANCE: THE BIRTH OF A CRITICAL AESTHETIC. Foreword Francois Truffaut. Trans. Stanley Hochman. New York: Frederick Ungar Publishing Company, 1981. Illustrated. 166pp.

A collection of thirty essays Bazin wrote for student publications (that were published irregularly) from 1943 to 1946, this interesting book offers a unique perspective on the work of French filmmakers during this period, as well as the thinking of one of France's greatest film critics. The interesting point, made by Truffaut in his valuable introduction, is that the Bazin essays don't comment directly on the occupation (only after the liberation of France was it possible to begin to speak openly about conditions during the Nazi occupation), but deal more directly with Bazin's developing aesthetic standards. To help explain key points about the critic's attitude toward films, Truffaut frequently provides footnotes to the reprinted articles. An index is included. Well worth browsing.

Ehrlich, Evelyn. CINEMA OF PARADOX: FRENCH FILMMAKING UNDER THE GERMAN OCCUPATION. New York: Columbia University Press, 1985. Illustrated. 255 pp.

Thought-provoking from beginning to end, this intriguing analysis takes us from the fall of France in June, 1940, to the aftermath of the liberation in 1945, charting the issues that led many people inside and outside France to debate the question of cinematic artistry versus collaboration with the Nazis. Ehrlich begins her revisionist study with an overview of what the nation faced in the chaotic days after its defeat, and why the cinema occupied a unique role with the French people. A basic argument she presents throughout the book is that those who made the movies did so for more than just financial gain: ". . . they believed they had a responsibility to entertain and lift the spirits of the public, and to sustain what they could of French cultural life." Over the four years that the Nazis occupied France, filmmakers like Pierre Billon, Robert Bresson, Marcel Carne, Henri-Georges Clouzot, Jean Cocteau, Jean Giraudoux, and Marcel Pagnol, as well as actors like Arletty, Jean-Louis Barrault, Jean Marais, and Roger Duchesne contributed to the more than 220 movies that kept

---

[627]   John Gross, "Books of the Times: CINEMA OF PARADOX," NEW YORK TIMES C (July 26, 1985):25.

French film theaters packed during the occupation. Ehrlich takes the position that none of these films "provided any direct support for the Germans," that the majority of them "maintained the French standards of craftsmanship that had given the industry its international reputation," and that "some of these films would mark a beginning of a new style in French filmmaking, one that would be the standard until the 1960s." What is paradoxical, she points out, is how technically excellent films flourished in a time of subjugation. The central question is "How was it possible for a relatively independent, aesthetically important cinema to survive the destruction of a nation?" In fairness to Ehrlich, she makes no attempt to evaluate the films or downplay the gravity of the charges levied against the filmmakers themselves. Instead, she insists that one of her major concerns is to put the debate in a historical context and explain why things happened as they did. A second major concern is to examine the motives of the people involved in order to better determine questions about French collaboration and resistance. In her words, ". . . before one can ask whether the choices made were justifiable, one must first ask why they were made."

In the first of the book's eight chapters, the author details the condition of the French cinema from the start of the war on September 3, 1939, to the nation's defeat on June 25, 1940. Attention is drawn to the importance that the Third Republic attached to film production, the stringent censorship policies it imposed to insure the industry's help in maintaining morale, and the failed attempts to solidify good relationships between French and Italian filmmakers. Ehrlich does a first-rate job of blending political events with the fortunes of the filmmakers themselves, telling us about their wartime assignments, the plight of major Jewish emigree filmmakers and performers (e.g., Gregor Rabinovitch, Jacques Haik, the Hakim brothers, Robert Siodmak, Leonide Moguy, Max Ophuls, Boris Kaufman, Marcel Dalio, and Jean-Pierre Aumont), and the steps the Nazis took to exploit their own films. Particularly significant are Ehrlich's reminders that many artists fled France rather than work for the victors (e.g., Jean Renoir, Francois Rosay, and Michele Morgan), that the Nazis moved quickly to expunge any Jews from the film industry, and that the infamous anti-Semitic German film JEW SUSS/JUD SUSS (1940) was shown to French audiences, who made it "one of the biggest hits of the season, breaking box office records in Lyon, Toulouse, and Vichy. . . ." Curiously, and without citing evidence, the author defends the French public on its reactions to JEW SUSS/JUD SUSS, asserting that they "were probably less interested in the film's ideological message than its lavish production." The chapter concludes with the image of the Nazi films doing well in French theaters and that there was no need or desire by the Nazis for a resumption of French filmmaking.

Chapter 2 reviews what steps Vichy France took to salvage the dispirited and disordered French film industry between 1940 and 1942. Ehrlich makes the fascinating point that the incentive for such a move came from the Petain government's desire to retain control of its communication services rather than let them come under Nazi domination. The author then describes the reorganization of the SERVICE DU CINEMA under the management of Guy de Carmoy (later arrested by the Nazis) and Louis-Emile Galey, how it fitted into Vichy France's corporationist philosophy, and the formation of the COMITE D'ORGANIZATION DE L'INDUSTRIE CINEMATOGRAPHIQUE (COIC), one of the first of the 234 COMITES D'ORGANIZATION (CO) to deal with resource allocations. Ehrlich's discussion on the structure and operation of the COIC makes a major contribution to understanding how this quasi-offical organization fueled the post-war debate over collaboration versus resistance. Among the issues she addresses are the struggle by both Vichy France and the film industry to maintain control of filmmaking, the removal of Jews in the film industry as a prerequisite to resuming film production, and the substantial benefits that accrued to producers in the unoccupied zone because the Nazis refused to support French filmmaking in the occupied territories. Nowhere else in film literature is there a better overview of the facilities used by the French filmmakers, the means of financing, the political issues associated with film production, the types of censorship problems and the absurdities that resulted, and the content of the approximately three dozen films made between

1940 and 1942. Moreover, one gets a good sense of why the filmmakers themselves appreciated the Nazis' finally centralizing French film production in Paris in May, 1942. Whatever reservations one has about Ehrlich's overall conclusions over the credit due Vichy France for its insuring the survival of French filmmaking, she deserves praise for periodically reminding her readers that "The credit for the COIC's successes must be balanced by a recognition of its responsibility in perpetuating the most obnoxious aspects of that regime."

Chapter 3 covers the the Nazi initiatives between 1940 and 1941 to make the French film industry a subsidiary of the German film industry. Starting with the various attempts by the victors to supervise French filmmaking, the author unintentionally focuses on her semantic dilemma: e.g., her constant references to the "German" rather than the "Nazi" occupation. She states that cinematic activities in France were administered directly by the Wehrmacht in France (hence the notion of German occupation), "but in fact controlled by Goebbels' Ministry of Propaganda in Berlin" (thus my argument for "Nazi" occupation). That issue aside, there is no doubt that the principal agency controlling French filmmaking was the PROPAGANDA ABTEILUNG (the Propaganda Department). At first, the plan was to have German films substitute for French films in France's theaters. When that failed, the Nazis decided to resume French production. What delayed that decision, however, was the personal ambition of Alfred Greven, the head of CONTINENTAL FILM SOCIETE A RESPONSABILITE LIMITEE. Although he took his orders directly from Max Winkler (director of Nazi film activities) and Goebbels, Greven managed to make their needs subordinate to his fortunes. The author's insightful discussions on how Continental obtained a strong financial base and extraordinary film resources with which to lure distinguished French filmmakers into its fold is a model of scholarly analysis. Despite her introductory remarks, she makes it quite clear that the French filmmakers who signed on were as much motivated by financial rewards as was Greven. At the same time, Ehrlich argues that Greven assured his artists that they would not have to make propaganda movies for the Nazis. This leads to another key issue that the author skillfully enunciates: the Nazi motivation for its "liberal" treatment of French filmmakers. Conceived as a pacification scheme for the period of occupation, the Nazis hoped that well-made French films would accomplish three objectives: (1) maintain France's cinematic reputation as a plus for the Nazis in pushing for their notion of a "New Europe," (2) keep moviegoing a habit and thereby gain future audiences for German films, and (3) reduce unrest in the occupied areas and thus minimize the need for troops so that they could be used elsewhere. Ehrlich never lets us forget that we are considering the question of collaboration versus resistance. For example, she insists that "the ultimate paradox of Continental Films" is that by a German company's becoming a powerful force in French cinema Germans helped save French filmmaking. The problem Ehrlich creates for herself is how to present the facts without operating as an apologist for the filmmakers themselves.

Chapter 4, on the relationship between the film industry and the Jews, provides a sketchy overview of how both the Nazis and Vichy used anti-Semitism to further their different agendas. Ehrlich's descriptions of the initial legal and economic measures used to "cleanse" the film profession (ASSAINISSEMENT) offer little that is new and lack the force of her research elsewhere. The most interesting material concerns the fate of the popular 1930s actor Harry Baur and the director Sacha Guitry. Moreover, her assertion that in comparison with the fate of other European Jews as a group, French Jews in the film business "were relatively privileged" seems strained and hollow.

Chapter 5 deals with the middle years of the occupation (1941-1942), describing in detail how the French film industry was reborn. Noting the fact that the French were "becoming Germanized and the film industry reflected the change," Ehrlich discusses the five-stage censorship policy established by the COIC in October 1941 and the enormous increase in film production from June 1941 to September 1942. She superbly explodes the myth that many producers refused to back French films during this sixteen-month period on the grounds that they weren't profitable. Not only does she explain that the films WERE profitable, but she also lists the factors why this was true. As Ehrlich states, "For producers, at least, the occupation was indeed the golden age of the French cinema." Another significant contribution this chapter makes to film scholarship is the author's comparison between the "average" French productions of the 1930s and those of the occupation. Among her conclusions are that (1) there was almost no difference, (2) there was considerable continuity of style, (3) and there was little discontinuity among film personnel. In the process, she once again affirms the thesis that money was the primary motivation for film production. Moreover, she stresses how much the films gave the impression of business going on as usual.

Chapter 6 provides a valuable look at the "new aesthetic" developed under Nazi occupation. Unlike the "average" films, a select group of about thirty movies appeared which, on the one hand, the CAHIERS DU CINEMA critics in the 1950s cynically called "the cinema of quality," and, on the other hand, many critics have described as the CINEMA D'EVASION. Ehrlich's position is that the nature of the times caused the birth of a new style, and before we rush to form judgment on the movement, we first should understand how the films differed from those of the past, and why the changes were made. Accordingly, she explains why the prestige films of the 1930s were characterized by their "humanistic and despairing" values and the belief that nothing anyone could do would alter French society. In contrast to the individual vision of the filmmakers of the 1930s, she stresses the constraints imposed on the artists working under Nazi occupation. Her analysis results in a new terminology for the films' sense of detachment and highly stylized compositions: "the cinema of isolation." A lengthy and stimulating discussion of how the style originated is followed by a controversial rationale that again suggests that Ehrlich is less objective than she intends to be. Simply put, she claims that artists like Jean Anouilh, Jean Aurenche, Claude Autant-Lara, Pierre Bost, Marcel Carne, Henri-Georges Clouzot, Jean Cocteau, Jean Giraudoux, Jean Gremillon, Sacha Guitry, and Jaques Prevert made films during the occupation for the express purpose of offering "renewal and hope" to the French people. She describes how the artists drew on theatrical traditions and historical events and makes it clear that the postwar political and stylistic attacks on the films result, in part, because AUTEUR critics resented screenwriters' being given more recognition than directors for the quality of the films. Throughout, Ehrlich remains entranced by the paradox of a "political configuration" that led Germans to save French art. However, it is difficult to evaluate the intentions of those artists from the present perspective, and it is difficult to ignore who paid for these films and the benefits that accrued to the Nazis as a result of these works.

Chapter 7 takes an inconclusive look at Goebbels's policy toward French filmmaking. To Ehrlich's credit, she opens with a superb quotation by Andre Weil-Curiel that concludes with Cocteau's words, "Long live shameful peace. . . ." Continually reminding us of the debate on collaboration versus resistance, she takes us once more through the intentions of the filmmakers and the policies of the Nazis, this time delving into the reasons why the Nazis worked to make the French film industry survive. The major areas of interest are her shaky interpretations of Goebbels's diaries, the concept of a "New Europe," Goebbels's jealousy of Hollywood's influence, and Nazi censorship. The key point, she concludes, is that the debate must be "recast" in terms of how much the filmmakers contributed to WHAT the Nazis wanted done. That is, assuming that the French filmmakers really did what they claimed they did, they would have been disowned by the Nazis had they won the war. "Because Germany lost the war," she explains, "the French were free to recriminate among themselves from an entirely different perspective."

Chapter 8 chronicles the growing awareness that Nazi Germany was losing the war, the steps taken by the occupation forces to defend its position, and the consequences those actions had on the French film industry. One of the more interesting observations is that as the war wreaked havoc both on production and box-office receipts, the cost of the remaining films made under Nazi control increased considerably. The author then begins to document the involvement of French filmmakers in the resistance movement, pointing out that not until the summer of 1944 did any of the resistance movement in the film industry join "active combat." Particularly disappointing is Ehrlich's discussion on the "purification" of the collaborators. A mere three pages provide a capsule summary of individuals charged, those persons convicted, and the films denounced. Nowhere is there the thoughtful, challenging analysis of the previous chapters where the author aggressively challenged "myths" about alleged collaboration and built a strong case for rethinking the events between 1940 and 1944. Instead, more time is given to an examination of whether Clouzot's THE RAVEN/LE CORBEAU (1943) was an "anti-French" film. In the end, she insists that there were more shades of gray in the moral issues than the resistance preferred. Although admitting that money as well as patriotism was a key factor in the four-year history of French films, and that many filmmakers willingly turned their backs on what happened to their Jewish associates and what motivated the liberal Nazi policy toward the French film industry, Ehrlich nevertheless insists that the filmmakers cannot be faulted, because they "believed that by making films they were helping France."

In a brief concluding chapter, the author bemoans what happened to the French film industry in the immediate aftermath of World War II. This sad situation only serves to reinforce her admiration for the achievements of the industry during the Nazi occupation. Refusing to pass judgment on the filmmakers' conscious decision to follow their artistic commitments more than their political or moral responsibilities, she states, "That the French cinema survived at all is an accomplishment--unless one considers that the cinema survived because two of the most odious regimes in history wanted it and aided it to survive."

Few books in film history offer as much provocative and useful information as this original and bold study. Whether one agrees with the author's specific conclusions is secondary to the gratitude serious students owe her for raising important issues in such a lucid and scholarly work. Two appendexes listing the films made between June 1940 and August 1944 and box-office figures, important endnotes, a good bibliography, and an index are included. Recommended for special collections.

*Fowler, Roy. THE FILM IN FRANCE. London: Pendulum Publications, 1946. Illustrated. 56pp.

JEAN-PIERRE AUMONT

Aumont, Jean-Pierre. SUN AND SHADOW: AN AUTOBIOGRAPHY. Foreword Francois Truffaut. Trans. Bruce Benderson. New York: W. W. Norton and Company, 1977. Illustrated. 315pp.

JEAN-LOUIS BARRAULT

Barrault, Jean-Louis. MEMORIES FOR TOMORROW: THE MEMOIRS OF JEAN-LOUIS BARRAULT. Trans. Jonathan Griffin. New York: E. P. Dutton and Company, 1974. Illustrated. 336pp.

MARCEL CARNE

*Carne, Marcel. CHILDREN OF PARADISE: A FILM BY MARCEL CARNE. Trans. Dinah Brooke. New York: Simon and Schuster, 1968. Illustrated. 218pp.

Turk, Edward Baron. CHILD OF PARADISE: MARCEL CARNE AND THE GOLDEN AGE OF FRENCH CINEMA. Cambridge: Harvard University Press, 1989. Illustrated. 495pp.

SIMONE SIGNORET

Signoret, Simone. NOSTALGIA ISN'T WHAT IT USED TO BE. New York: Harper & Row, 1978. Illustrated. 416pp.

FRENCH WAR FILMS

MARCEL CARNE

CHILDREN OF PARADISE/LES ENFANTS DU PARADIS (France--16mm: 1946, 188 mins., b/w, English subtitles, sound, R-FNC)

In one of the most controversial films in screen history, [628] Carne and his screenwriter Jacques Prevert intertwined the lives of the Shakespearean actor Frederick Lemaitre (Pierre Braseur), the mime Debureau (Jean-Louis Barrault), the cynical villain Lacenaire (Marcel Herrand), and the woman who enchanted them all, Garance (Arletty).[629] Technically brilliant, the film was chosen by the French Academy of Cinema Arts and Techniques as the greatest French sound film in movie history. Like THE BIRTH OF A NATION (1915) and TRIUMPH OF THE WILL (1935), this film raises the issue of ideology versus art, and whether one should judge a film on its merits as a film, or on its historical and social context. That is, should acts of omission and social responsibility be subservient to questions of aesthetics?

JEAN DELANNOY

THE ETERNAL RETURN/L'ETERNAL RETOUR (France--16mm:1943, 100 mins., b/w, sound, R-FNC)

Scripted by Jean Cocteau, this allegorical story stars Jean Marais and Madeleine Sologne as a modern day Tristan and Iseult who die because of love rather than as a result of contemporary dangers. On the one hand, Roy Armes makes the point that "The Nordic overtones to which so many British critics took exception when it was shown in London in 1945--Richard Winnington, for example, called it 'a pleasure for the Nazis'--seem not to have troubled French historians, but Delannoy is here far from any hint of the presumed Resistance stance of PONTCARRAL."[630] On the other hand, Georges Sadoul insists that "To the French public, this illustrious theme is a cultural treasure, with no taint of collaborationist tendencies; in addition, the patriotism of the beloved director of PONTCARRAL was never in doubt."[631]

---

[628] Although many film historians attack the film as a "collaborationist" work, its defenders point out that the production violated a number of Nazi regulations. For specific examples, see Stanley Feingold, "Marcel Carne and the Nazis," THE NEW YORK TIMES BOOK REVIEW (June 18, 1989):36.

[629] For more information, see *Nancy Warfield, "Notes on LES ENFANTS DU PARADIS," THE LITTLE FILM GAZETTE OF N. D. W. 2:1 (March 1967); and Edward Baron Turk, "The Birth of CHILDREN OF PARADISE," AMERICAN FILM 4:9 (July-August 1979):42-9.

[630] FRENCH CINEMA, p.115.

[631] FRENCH FILM, p.100.

UNITED STATES

Hollywood experienced monumental difficulties at home and abroad in altering mass audiences to the nation's stake in the international struggle. Throughout most of the thirties, the film capital had maintained an isolationist policy, insisting, in its hundreds of annually produced escapist films, that Americans lived in the best of all possible worlds where problems were minimal and opportunities unlimited. Moreover, as discussed in Chapter 5, the movies made it clear that the gathering war clouds abroad posed no threat to our safety and had little relationship to our society. By 1940, however, the nation's mood began to change and filmmakers not only began producing pro-war movies--e.g., THE FIGHTING 69th (1940), SERGEANT YORK (1941)--but also films in support of our friends in trouble--FOREIGN CORRESPONDENT, THE GREAT DICTATOR (both in 1940), A YANK IN THE RAF, PIMPERNEL SMITH, MAN HUNT, and SOMEWHERE IN FRANCE (all in 1941).

When war finally came in December 1941, Hollywood reworked its popular film genres to depict our armed forces in combat abroad and the domestic front mobilized in the nation's defense. As discussed in Chapter 2, the issue of how best to serve the nation's propaganda needs was debated between Washington's Office of War Information, and Hollywood's War Activities Committee. The debate still continues today over the decisions on how Hollywood and Washington simplified the issues and depicted the contributions of Allies and Americans to winning the war. No one argues, however, that the film capital failed in its patriotic service. Many of the film industry's key personnel served in military units, produced propaganda films for training purposes, and entertained the troops.

Given the wartime rationing of crucial goods, the restrictions on travel, the separation of families, the extended working hours, and the level of anxieties, moviegoing reached its highest levels in film history. At first, the films focused on various aspects of the war effort, but by 1943, both Washington and Hollywood realized that escapist entertainment did more for morale than unrealistic combat and action-packed films. As discussed in Chapter 2, nearly two-thirds of the film capital's releases during the war years were concerned with combat. The emphasis was on keeping the home front happy with traditional genres stressing the values that America and her allies were fighting to preserve. In fact, as Ellis points out, the highest grossing films of the period were MRS MINIVER, YANKEE DOODLE DANDY (both in 1942), THE SONG OF BERNADETTE (1943), GOING MY WAY, MEET ME IN ST. LOUIS, THIRTY SECONDS OVER TOKYO (all in 1944), THE BELLS OF ST. MARY'S, THE LOST WEEKEND, and SPELLBOUND (all in 1945). Of these films, only two--MRS. MINIVER and THIRTY SECONDS OVER TOKYO--were directly tied to World War II.[632] Adding to the disenchantment with Hollywood's chauvinistic wartime melodramas was the growing appreciation of the combat footage and documentary films made by directors like Capra, Ford, Huston, and Wyler, who were serving in various branches of the military and having their films processed through the Office of War Information. As discussed in Chapter 2, these extraordinary films, with the exception of Huston's LET THERE BE LIGHT (1946) which was not released until 1980, received wide distribution both in America and abroad. As a result, audiences became much more sophisticated about film content and forced Hollywood to take a more realistic approach in depicting the war. While movies like HANGMEN ALSO DIE (1943), LIFEBOAT (1944), and A WALK IN THE SUN (1945) reflected a more gritty approach to the war than did the earlier films like ACROSS THE PACIFIC and WAKE ISLAND (both in 1942), they proved to be less popular than standard Hollywood escapist movies. On a more practical level, the studio bosses had no intention of finding themselves stuck with a batch of war movies after the conflict was over, as had happened after World War I. By 1944, it was clear that the Allies were approaching total victory; only WHEN was in question. Consequently, the filmmakers focused more

---

[632] A HISTORY OF FILM, p.218.

on sentimental stories, affectionate musicals, and adventure films during the final years of World War II.

One of the most important artists of the Hollywood war years was Preston Sturges. "Without hesitation," explains Dale Johnson, "one can view the vision of American society in Sturges's films as being very much his own. That personal vision is responsible for bringing the screwball comedy into the contemporary American home front during World War II. Sturges makes this comedic form relevant to wartime life by establishing the conflict between civilians and the new 'class'--soldiers."[633] Although he had been working in the film industry as a screenwriter since 1930, the ex-playwright made his mark as the writer-director of such hits as THE GREAT MCGINTY (1940), THE LADY EVE, SULLIVAN'S TRAVELS (both in 1941), THE PALM BEACH STORY (1942), THE MIRACLE OF MORGAN'S CREEK, and HAIL THE CONQUERING HERO (both in 1944). Each of these witty and sophisticated satires, created at Paramount, attacked many of the nation's misperceptions about status and money and reworked several aspects of the classical Hollywood narrative.[634] His decision to leave Paramount in 1944 and work with Howard Hughes resulted in a number of undistinguished films (the one exception being the 1948 UNFAITHFULLY YOURS). By 1949, the relationship was severed and Sturges moved to Paris.[635]

Basil Wright makes the perceptive observation that many of Hollywood's "non-war" films set the stage for a unique reevaluation of American society. From the perspective of an outsider, he saw horror films like CAT PEOPLE (1942), I WALKED WITH A ZOMBIE, THE SEVENTH VICTIM (both in 1943), and ISLE OF THE DEAD (1945) as offering criticisms of "American society as a whole; not merely the American Dream or the One Nation Myth, but some sort of an analysis of those differences despite what the Federal structure managed to cohere." In effect, we no longer appeared to ourselves or to foreigners as sharing a common culture, but rather as pockets of people with different cultures and habits.[636]

---

[633]   Dale Johnson, "HAIL THE CONQUERING HERO," CINEMATEXAS PROGRAM NOTES 28:1 (March 4, 1985):36.

[634]   For more information, see Siegfried Kracauer, "Preston Sturges or Laughter Betrayed," FILMS IN REVIEW 11:1 (February 1950):11-3; Phyllis Zucker, "Filmography of Preston Sturges," ibid., 22:3 (March 1971):184; Nel King and G. W. Stonier, "Preston Sturges," SIGHT AND SOUND 28:3-4 (Summer-Autumn 1959):185-6; Penelope Houston, "Preston Sturges," ibid., (Summer 1965):130-4; Eric Jonsson (pseudonym for Andrew Sarris), "Preston Sturges and the Theory of Decline," FILM CULTURE 26 (Fall 1962):17-21, Rpt., Andrew Sarris, ed., INTERVIEWS WITH FILM DIRECTORS (New York: Bobbs-Merrill, 1967), pp.511-20; Manny Farber and W. S. Poster, "Preston Sturges: Success In the Movies," ibid., pp.9-16, Rpt., *Manny Farber, NEGATIVE SPACE (New York: Praeger, 1971), pp.89-104; Michael Budd, "Notes on Preston Sturges and America," FILM SOCIETY REVIEW (January 1968):22-6; Andrew Sarris, "Preston Sturges in the 30s," FILM COMMENT 6:4 (Winter 1970-71):80-5; Richard Corliss, "Preston Sturges," CINEMA 7:2 (Spring 1972):24-36, Rpt., *Richard Corliss, TALKING PICTURES: SCREENWRITERS IN THE AMERICAN CINEMA 1927-1973 (New York: Penguin Books, 1975), pp.41-4; Vincent Canby, "A Fresh Assay of the Comic Gold of Preston Sturges," NEW YORK TIMES II (January 16, 1983):1, 23; and Leslie Bennetts, "A Fond Son Is Reviving Preston Sturges's Fame," ibid., C (March 24, 1988):34.

[635]   Not everyone shares my admiration for Sturges. Wright, for example, claims (pp.179-80) that was a "falsity" to Sturges's work: "It was perhaps the sincerity of someone who was capable of seeing life in the round but not as a whole."

[636]   Wright, pp.181-2.

Despite the considerable contributions to the war effort and the enormous advances made in the art of film as a result of unique filmmaking opportunities, some of Hollywood's patriotic decisions were to haunt the industry for the next three decades. Two unfortunate side effects resulted from Hollywood's enthusiasm in supporting our Russian Allies and in overstating our military exploits. Thus movies like MISSION TO MOSCOW, SONG OF RUSSIA, NORTH STAR (all in 1943) refueled doubts about individual loyalties to America, while films like SAHARA (1943) and OBJECTIVE BURMA! (1945) angered our Allies, who felt too much credit was going to the Yanks instead of to the courageous British forces in Africa and Asia. Another lamentable legacy, discussed in Chapter 2, was the atrocious racial stereotyping of the Axis powers that later became the cultural baggage of unthinking filmmakers who failed to distinguish between images made for wartime propaganda and conventions used in war films. Each of these wartime gestures was to have major consequences for the future of American film and for its status in the postwar world.

The years from 1940 to 1945 offer real challenges to contemporary film scholars. For example, were the era's films, as Ellis asserts, primarily "an extension of those of the thirties--appropriately trimmed with references to the war--[rather] than a prelude to those of the second half of the forties"?[637] Did FILM NOIR originate during the war years, what were its antecedents, and who were its major exponents? Scholars are also taking considerable interest in the work done in those years by key directors like Curtiz--e.g., YANKEE DOODLE DANDY, CASABLANCA (both in 1942), MILDRED PIERCE (1945), Hitchcock--e.g., SUSPICION (1941), SHADOW OF A DOUBT (1943), LIFEBOAT (1942), SPELLBOUND (1945), Wellman--THE OX-BOW INCIDENT (1943), THE STORY OF G. I. JOE (1945), and Wyler--THE LITTLE FOXES (1941). Among the issues they are concerned with in the aforementioned works are stylistic changes, thematic patterns, and studio influences.

BOOKS

GENERAL

*Champlin, Charles. THE MOVIES GROW UP 1940-1980, Rev. and enlarged edition. Foreword Alfred Hitchcock. Chicago: Swallow Press, 1981. Illustrated. 284pp.

Originating as a series of ten lectures entitled, "Whatever Happened to Andy Hardy" delivered in the early 1970s, this thoughtful, broad overview hits the major aspects of mainstream filmmaking in America from the post-WWII period to the start of the 1980s. Champlin's breezy journalistic style quickly retraces the impact of TV on Hollywood, the steps people took to recapture dwindling audiences, and the major events and movies that reshaped the American film industry. Hardnosed readers will object to many oversimplifications, a handful of notable omissions, and embarrassing sexist language, while less demanding readers will appreciate the skill with which the inventive author succinctly summarizes important trends and key works. Lovely illustrations, a bibliography, and an index are included. Well worth browsing.

*Higham, Charles, and Joel Greenberg. HOLLYWOOD IN THE FORTIES. New York: A. S. Barnes and Company, 1968. Illustrated. 192pp.

In this compendium of brief critical comments neatly tied together by a nostalgic narrative, Higham and Greenberg present a useful, accurate, and informative guide to hundreds of personalities, pictures, and trends. The emphasis is on genre analysis with the book's eleven chapters devoted to topics like "Black Cinema," "Melodrama," "Fantasy and Horror," "Problem and Sociological Films," "War Propaganda," "Prestige Pictures: Biographies and Literary Adaptations," "Women's

---

[637] A HISTORY OF FILM, p.217.

Pictures," "Comedies," and Musicals." Regrettably, the authors provide no bibliography or endnotes. An index is included. Wellworth browsing.

Luhr, William, ed. WORLD CINEMA SINCE 1945. New York: Frederick Ungar Publishing Company, 1987. Illustrated. 708pp.

The best and most complete source of information on world cinema since the end of World War II, this impressive anthology boldly examines the film continuum and the growing influence of television in thirty different countries from Africa, Argentina, and Australia to the Soviet Union and the United States. The extended survey contributions by noted scholars like Dudley Andrew (France), Elaine Mancini (Belgium, the Netherlands, and Switzerland), Andrew Sinclair (Great Britain), Peter Bondanella (Italy), Bruce Kawin (United States), and Andrew Horton (Yugoslavia) point out the role governments play in film production, the rise of new technologies and their influence on directors (more than 1,400 directors are discussed) and films (over 3,300 films are covered). Each chapter includes illustrations, endnotes, and a bibliography. While errors occasionally arise and debatable judgments appear, this impressive volume makes the first major breakthrough in identifying the scope and depth of world filmmaking. An index of directors and an index of film titles are included. Highly recommended for general collections.

*Viertel, Salka. THE KINDNESS OF STRANGERS. New York: Holt, Rinehart and Winston, 1969. 338pp.

*Wilson, Ivy Crane, ed. HOLLYWOOD IN THE 1940s: THE STARS' OWN STORIES. Foreword Liz Smith. New York: Frederick Ungar Publishing Company, 1980. Illustrated. 168pp.

JOAN FONTAINE

*Fontaine, Joan. NO BED OF ROSES: AN AUTOBIOGRAPHY. New York: Berkeley, 1979. Illustrated. 326pp.

RITA HAYWORTH

Kobal, John. RITA HAYWORTH. New York: W. W. Norton, 1978. Illustrated. 328pp.

*Morella, Joe, and Edward Z. Epstein. THE LIFE OF RITA HAYWORTH. New York: Delacorte Press, 1983. Illustrated. 261pp.

*Peary, Gerald. RITA HAYWORTH. New York: Pyramid Publications, 1976. Illustrated. 160pp.

Ringgold, Gene. THE FILMS OF RITA HAYWORTH. Secaucus: The Citadel Press, 1975. Illustrated. 256pp.

JOHN HUSTON

*Anobile, Richard J., ed. THE MALTESE FALCON. New York : Darien House, 1974. Illustrated. 256pp.

A nostalgic attempt to reconstruct visually and in printed dialogue what many critics consider the greatest detective film ever made, this book uses over 1400 blown-up photos to present the third version of Dashiell Hammett's popular novel. It's fun to look at the pictures and read the exchanges between Bogie and his famous adversaries. Well worth browsing.

Hepburn, Katharine. THE MAKING OF "THE AFRICAN QUEEN" OR HOW I WENT TO AFRICA WITH BOGART, BACALL AND HUSTON AND ALMOST LOST MY MIND. New York: Alfred A. Knopf, 1987. Illustrated. 134pp.
A coffee-table approach with general comments about three months of frantic filmmaking, this entertaining book offers pleasant anecdotes and handsome illustrations. Worth browsing.

*Huston, John. AN OPEN BOOK. New York: Alfred A. Knopf, 1980. Illustrated. 391pp.
Born in Nevada, Missouri, on August 5, 1906, John Marcellus Huston was the only son of Walter Huston and Reah Gore.[638] After his parents divorced six years later, Huston found himself being shuttled between them. Often he went on the road with his father, a vaudevillian, or watched horse races with his mother, a reporter. His health suffered and when he was twelve, Huston was hospitalized for a heart condition and kidney problems. (He was to have serious medical problems throughout his life.) These experiences profoundly influenced his life and career as the sickly boy set out to prove he was a man's man. He not only studied boxing (eventually becoming a prominent California boxer), but also became one of the world's best drinkers and reknowned womanizers (e.g., Huston was married and divorced five times and had celebrated affairs with a number of his leading ladies, including Bette Davis and Olivia de Havilland). Dropping out of high school during his junior year, Huston pursued a variety of careers (acting, painting, the military, and journalism) before his father (now a famous actor working in films) got him a job as a screenwriter for Samuel Goldwyn in the early 1930s. In 1933, with several script credits to his name and a legendary reputation for dissolute behavior, Huston accidentally killed a woman in a driving accident. Although exonerated by the coroner's jury, Huston felt terribly guilty and spent the next five years drifting from one job to the next. By 1937, he was determined to set his life right and returned to Hollywood as a screenwriter for Warner Bros., scripting such impressive films as JEZEBEL (1938), JUAREZ (1939), HIGH SIERRA, and SERGEANT YORK (both in 1941). His first writing-directing assignment was THE MALTESE FALCON (1941), the third screen adaptation of Dashiell Hammett's novel. After making two more films for Warner Bros., Huston joined the Army Signals Corps in 1942, and made three of the most famous documentary films of World War II: REPORT FROM THE ALEUTIANS (1943), BATTLE OF SAN PIETRO (1944), and LET THERE BE LIGHT (1945). The latter film, dealing with mental illness among servicemen, was considered so radical for its time that the military suppressed its release until 1980. Back from the service and beginning in 1947, the highly decorated Huston made of number of films that were among the best of the postwar period: THE TREASURE OF THE SIERRA MADRE, KEY LARGO (both in 1948), and THE ASPHALT JUNGLE. Outspoken and furious at the film industry's blacklisting tactics, he often took great risks in challenging anti-Communist elements in Hollywood. Among the best of his more than forty films, many of which he both

---

[638] For useful information, see Peter B. Flint, "John Huston, Film Director, Writer, and Actor, Dies at 81," NEW YORK TIMES A (August 29, 1987):1, 33; and Andrew Sarris, "John Huston 1906-1987," VILLAGE VOICE (September 15, 1987):99. See also the 1966 NET TV documentary, THE LIFE AND TIMES OF JOHN HUSTON, ESQUIRE, available from the Indiana AV Center; and Joni Lorin and Frank Marvin's 1989 documentary film, JOHN HUSTON: THE MAN, THE MOVIES, THE MAVERICK.

scripted and directed, are THE RED BADGE OF COURAGE (1951), THE AFRICAN QUEEN (1952), MOULIN ROUGE (1953), THE MISFITS (1961), FAT CITY, THE LIFE AND TIMES OF JUDGE ROY BEAN (both in 1972), THE MAN WHO WOULD BE KING (1975), PRIZZI'S HONOR (1985), and THE DEAD (1987). He not only received almost every honor his profession offered, but also had the distinction of directing both his father and his daughter, Anjelica, in their Oscar-winning performances--Walter Huston in THE TREASURE OF THE SIERRA MADRE, and Anjelica Huston in PRIZZI'S HONOR. Huston died at eighty-one, August 28, 1987.

His autobiography, published when he was seventy-four and had completed thirty-six films, is filled with marvelous anecdotes about the man, his films, and his adventures.   "My life," he writes, "is composed of random, tangential, disparate episodes. Five wives; many liasons, some more memorable than the marriages. The hunting. The betting. The thoroughbreds. Painting, collecting, boxing. Writing, directing, and acting in more than sixty pictures. I fail to see any continuity in my work from picture to picture--what's remarkable is how different the pictures are, one from another." Although the author prefers to discuss his robust activities and womanizing more than his films, he does keep the reader highly entertained. An index is included. Well worth browsing.

Kaminsky, Stuart. JOHN HUSTON: MAKER OF MAGIC. Boston: Houghton Mifflin Company, 1978. Illustrated. 237pp.

Not one of the author's better efforts, this affectionate biography recounts familiar material about one of Kaminsky's favorite filmmakers. Twenty-three chapters lacking much-needed documentation gloss over the general characteristics of Huston's thirty-year career in film. Clearly, the author's two interviews with the writer-director and those with Don Siegel, William Wyler, and Eli Wallach produced few new insights. A filmography, bibliography, and index are included. Worth browsing.

Madsen, Axel. JOHN HUSTON: A BIOGRAPHY. Garden City: Doubleday and Company, 1978. Illustrated. 280pp.

Another breezy chronological treatment of Huston's life, this lackluster biography relies on legendary stories and ribald anecdotes to mask the superficial analysis of the writer-director's films. One searches in vain for insights into Huston's cinematic techniques, patterns in films up to the mid-1970s, why the NOUVELLE VAGUE critics found it necessary to denigrate the great filmmaker's work, and the crucial behind-the-scenes information on his projects. A filmography and an index are included, but no endnotes or bibliography are provided. Worth browsing.

*McCarty, John. THE FILMS OF JOHN HUSTON. Secaucus: Citadel Press, 1987. Illustrated. 256pp.

With the exception of information on Huston's final film, THE DEAD (1987), this book contains the most complete filmography of the writer-actor-director's career in films. The comments are adequate, the pictures above average, and the credits first-rate. "Huston remains what he has always been," McCarty writes, "a globe-trotting maverick who prefers to live and work away from Hollywood." McCarthy's entertaining anecdotes and spicy stories would have been more welcome if documented and expanded. A filmography of Huston's roles as an actor and a slim bibliography are included, but no index is provided. Well worth browsing.

Nolan, William F. JOHN HUSTON: KING REBEL. Los Angeles: Sherbourne Press, 1965. Illustrated. 247pp.

A surprisingly good pioneering examination of Huston's life and films up to the mid-1960s, this biography remains competitive with the later reviews of the writer-director-actor's career, mainly because of the many quotations provided by Huston's friends and co-workers. The writing is chatty, the analyses good, and the anecdotes highly amusing. The major problem is reliability. Although a bibliography is included, the narrative offers no documentation to support many debatable claims. A list of Huston's projects is provided, but no index exists to help locate important dates and events. Well worth browsing.

Pratley, Gerald. THE CINEMA OF JOHN HUSTON. South Brunswick: A. S. Barnes and Company, 1977. Illustrated. 224pp.
      The result of fourteen hours of interviews with Huston, this appreciative study relies heavily on the writer-director-actor's interpretations of his work and its merits. Pratley mainly takes a backseat as he lets Huston do the work for him. Given the subsequent publication of Huston's autobiography, this book offers a good opportunity to see how Huston rethought his attitudes about Hollywood, his projects, and the people he worked with. A filmography is included, but no bibliography or index. Well worth browsing.

ALAN LADD

Linet, Beverly. LADD: THE LIFE, THE LEGEND, THE LEGACY OF ALAN LADD. New York: Arbor House, 1979. Illustrated. 294pp.

*Marily, Henry, and Ron DeSourdis. THE FILMS OF ALAN LADD. Secaucus: The Citadel Press, 1981. Illustrated. 256pp.

ANGELA LANSBURY

Bonanno, Margaret Wander. ANGELA LANSBURY: A BIOGRAPHY. New York: St. Martin's Press, 1987. Illustrated. 225pp.

GREGORY PECK

Freedland, Michael. GREGORY PECK: THE MAN BEHIND THE LEGEND. New York: William Morrow and Company, 1980. Illustrated. 250pp.

*Thomas, Tony. GREGORY PECK. New York: Pyramid Publications, 1977. Illustrated. 160pp.

JANE RUSSELL

Russell, Jane. MY PATHS AND DETOURS: AN AUTOBIOGRAPHY. New York: Franklin Watts, 1985. Illustrated. 341pp.

FRANK SINATRA

*Howlett, John. FRANK SINATRA. New York: Simon and Schuster, 1979. Illustrated. 174pp.

Jewell, Derek, and George Perry. FRANK SINATRA: CELEBRATION. Boston: Little, Brown and Company, 1985. Illustrated. 192pp.

*Kelley, Kitty. HIS WAY: THE UNAUTHORIZED BIOGRAPHY OF FRANK SINATRA. New York: Bantam Books, 1986. Illustrated. 575pp.

Ringgold, Gene, and Clifford McCarty. THE FILMS OF FRANK SINATRA. Secaucus: The Citadel Press, 1971. Illustrated. 249pp.

Rockwell, John. SINATRA: AN AMERICAN CLASSIC. New York: Random House, 1984. Illustrated. 255pp.

*Sciacca, Tony. SINATRA. New York: Pinnacle Books, 1976. Illustrated. 248pp.

Shaw, Arnold. SINATRA: TWENTIETH-CENTURY ROMANTIC. New York: Holt, Rinehart and Winston, 1968. Illustrated. 371pp.

*Sinatra, Nancy. FRANK SINATRA, MY FATHER. Garden City: Doubleday and Company, 1985. Illustrated. 340pp.

*Wilson, Earl. SINATRA: AN UNAUTHORIZED BIOGRAPHY. New York: Signet, 1976. Illustrated. 361pp.

PRESTON STURGES

*Curtis, James. BETWEEN FLOPS: A BIOGRAPHY OF PRESTON STURGES. New York: Harcourt, Brace, Jovanovich, 1982. Illustrated. 339pp.

Cywinski, Ray. PRESTON STURGES: A GUIDE TO REFERENCES AND RESOURCES. Boston: G. K. Hall and Company. 1984. 134pp.

Dickos, Andrew. INTREPID LAUGHTER: PRESTON STURGES AT THE MOVIES. Metuchen: The Scarecrow Press, 1985. Illustrated. 170pp.
     Born in Chicago, on August 29, 1898, Preston Biden's parents separated a year after his birth. He spent most of his formative years with his mother (Mary Estelle Dempsy) in Europe. During their first visit in 1901, she divorced his father and married Solomon Sturges, who adopted the boy in 1902. The Sturgeses were divorced seven years later, and the cosmopolitan mother married a Turkish businessman marketing cosmetics. In 1914, Sturges returned to the United States and managed the family cosmetics company. Three years later, he enlisted in the Army Air Force. After the war, he resumed his duties at the cosmetics company, and when the firm went under in 1920, he devoted himself to working on a series of inventions. In 1923, he married Estelle de Wolfe Mudge, the first of his four wives. The start of the Great Depression saw the end of the marriage and the beginning of Sturges's brief career as a playwright. In 1929, he tried his hand at screenwriting for Paramount Pictures. A year later, Sturges not only decided to pursue a screen career but also to try his luck at marriage again, this time with Eleanor Post Hutton (they were divorced in 1932). Over the next eight years, he scripted a number of popular films, including

THE INVISIBLE MAN, THE POWER AND THE GLORY (both in 1932), DIAMOND JIM (1935), EASY LIVING (1937), and IF I WERE A KING (1938). In 1938, he has tried marriage again, this time with Louise Sargent Tevis (they were divorced in 1946). Sturges made his writer-directorial debut with THE GREAT MCGINTY, followed by CHRISTMAS IN JULY (both in 1940). During the war years, his credits included THE LADY EVE, SULLIVAN'S TRAVELS (both in 1941), I MARRIED A WITCH, THE PALM BEACH STORY (both in 1942), THE MIRACLE OF MORGAN'S CREEK, and HAIL THE CONQUERING HERO (both in 1944). In 1944, he went into partnership with Howard Hughes and formed the short-lived California Production Company (he quit the firm two year later). During the postwar period, his only noteworthy films were UNFAITHFULLY YOURS (1948) and THE BEAUTIFUL BLONDE FROM BASHFUL BEND (1949). By 1950, Sturges found it difficult to get anyone to produce his plays or films. He married his fourth wife, Anne Nagle, in 1951, completed his last film, THE FRENCH THEY ARE A FUNNY RACE/LES CARNETS DU MAJOR THOMPSON (released in 1957), and died of a heart attack on August 6, 1959.

"The fact is," Dickos writes, "Preston Sturges is so much more than the sum of his parts--screenwriter, slapstick artist, cynic, wit, satirist, sentimentalist--that explicating his style offers insight into his sensibility, but cannot deliver that total, full-bodied, savor of Sturges' universe that watching his film does." In the first section of this useful study, Dickos offers a good biographical sketch, stressing not only the importance of Sturges's mother on his life and career, but also the types of people, places, and events that shaped his films. A second section provides analyses of Sturges's screenwriting styles, with particular emphasis on the structure of his comedies. The final section deals with the twelve films that Sturges wrote and directed. An annotated chronology, endnotes, bibliography, filmography, and index are included. Recommended for special collections.

*Henderson, Brian, ed. FIVE SCREENPLAYS BY PRESTON STURGES.   Berkeley: University of California Press, 1985. Illustrated. 848pp.

Between 1939 and 1944, Sturges wrote and directed five classic comedies: THE GREAT MCGINTY, CHRISTMAS IN JULY, THE LADY EVE, SULLIVAN'S TRAVELS, and HAIL THE CONQUERING HERO. The beauty of this publication is that it allows us to study the first four of eight films that the writer-director made for Paramount, and the last one he did for the studio. A splendid introduction not only explains the style of the screenplays and how they relate to the production process, but also provides a good biographical sketch of Sturges's life and career. Recommended for special collections.

*Ursini, James. THE FABULOUS LIFE AND TIMES OF PRESTON STURGES: AN AMERICAN DREAMER. New York: Curtin Books, 1973. Illustrated. 240pp.

"Preston Sturges," Ursini explains, "was and remains to this day a baffling phenomenon. The apparent contradiction he encompassed as a man and an artist, the extraordinary life he led, and the frenetic quality of his films indicate, at least partially, the uniqueness of this perplexing career. For a decade, from 1940 (the year he became a director as well as a writer) until 1950, Sturges was on top of what he lovingly called 'this cockeyed caravan.'" The story of what happened to him and the reasons for his bitter, satirical creative style are pieced together through interviews, reviews, and public documents in this fast-moving and informative biography. Seven entertaining chapters offer useful insights and amusing anecdotes that help in interpreting Sturges's films.   Endnotes, a bibliography, and a filmography are provided, but no index is included. Recommended for special collections.

ROBERT TAYLOR

*Quirk, Lawrence J. THE FILMS OF ROBERT TAYLOR. Secaucus: The Citadel Press, 1975. Illustrated. 223pp.

*Wayne, Jane Ellen. THE LIFE OF ROBERT TAYLOR. New York: Warner Books, 1973. Illustrated. 349pp.

FILMS

ALFRED HITCHCOCK

SHADOW OF A DOUBT (Universal--16mm: 1943, 108 mins., b/w, sound, R-SWA, WIL)
The Thornton Wilder-Sally Benson-Alma Reville screenplay based upon Gordon McDonnell's original short story is a superb example of Hitchcock's use of the "double" motif. The plot concerns Charley Oakley (Joseph Cotton), a murderer who hides from the police by visiting his relatives in California. Although his niece Charlie (Teresa Wright) at first feels extremely close to her uncle, she gradually comes to recognize his homicidal nature and becomes a threat to him. In attempting to kill her aboard a train, he accidentally falls to his death. The duality in the film goes beyond the names of the two main characters and the emphasis on their similar natures to other characterizations, events, and sequences. Often cited by Hitchcock as his favorite American film, it is also one of the director's most spiritually autobiographical films.[639]

PRESTON STURGES

THE GREAT MCGINTY (Paramount--16mm: 1940, 83 mins., b/w, sound, R-SWA)
Originally written in 1933 as THE BIOGRAPHY OF A BUM, Sturges had to wait nearly six years before he persuaded the Paramount brass to let him make the film. In fact, he sold the screenplay for ten dollars in exchange for the opportunity to direct it. The Oscar-winning script gave Sturges the confidence and recognition that propelled him through the forties. The story of "Old-time, big-city-boss politics represents," as Andrew Dickos observes, "the spirit of modern America best. Through Sturges's depiction of the way such government operates, we understand the historical implications of a land conceived in the byplay of democracy and acquisitiveness, of a country existing in a framework of freedom that, ironically, nurtures oppression."[640]

THE LADY EVE (Paramount--16mm: 1941, 97 mins., b/w, sound, R-WIL)
One of the last of Hollywood's great screwball comedies, the film tells the story of an innocent and wealthy academic (Henry Fonda) on sabbatical who meets a gold-digging woman (Barbara Stanwyck) aboard an ocean liner and falls madly in love

---

[639] For more information, see Simon Harcourt-Smith, "STAGE FRIGHT and Hitchcock," SIGHT AND SOUND 19 (July 1950):207-8; and Francois Truffaut, "Skeleton Keys," CAHIERS DU CINEMA IN ENGLISH 2, CDC 39 (1966):60-6.

[640] Andrew Dickos, INTREPID LAUGHTER: PRESTON STURGES AT THE MOVIES (Metuchen: The Scarecrow Press, 1985), p.83.

with her. Richard Corliss classifies the film as a "screwball romance" and insists that not only is it the "richest" Sturges created, but "It is also the most perfectly realized of all his films, as smooth, hard and cutting as the diamonds in Barbara Stanwyck's jewel-digging eyes."[641] Monckton Hoffe recived an Oscar nomination for Best Original Story.

THE MIRACLE OF MORGAN'S CREEK (Paramount--16mm: 1944, 99 mins., b/w, sound, R-FNC)

An inspired attack on small-town American values, this superb comedy stars Betty Hutton as the ideal girl-next-door gone haywire. The writer-director Sturges presents us with a heroine whose reputation is threatened by a unwanted pregnancy that parodies the nativity. Moreover, as Jeanine Basinger observes, the film "makes a shambles of the world 'our boys' were supposed to be fighting to preserve. It is a purely American film--self-critical, loaded with energy, packed with dialogue and event, perfectly timed, and literally reeling with comedy."[642] Sturges received an Oscar Nomination for Best Original Screenplay for both this film and HAIL THE CONQUERING HERO.

SULLIVAN'S TRAVELS (Paramount--16mm: 1941, 90 mins., b/w, sound, R-WIL)

The most ambitious of all writer-director Sturges's films, this satiric tale of a Hollywood director named John L. Sullivan (Joel McCrea) who takes to the open road to learn about the entertainment desires of needy people balances slapstick comedy and superb dialogue with sensitive imagery and socially conscious issues. As Ann Laemmle explains, "Sturges was one of the greatest social satirists of his time and SULLIVAN'S TRAVELS reveals the almost systematic irony of America in general and, specifically, life as lived in Hollywood and in the movies and by the rich and the middleclass. In this atmosphere of social satire endemic to all Sturges films, two particularly Sturgeon (?) themes are obviated . . . the rich versus the poor and what Andrew Sarris calls 'the modesty of heroes who dread being little fish in the big pond.'"[643]

THE NEW REALISM IN ITALIAN FILMS (1945-1954)

The tragic experiences of World War II and the realistic techniques of the documentary movement became evident in many countries in the postwar period, particularly in Italy.[644] Filmmakers quickly turned away from standard escapist productions and replaced them with humanistic movies that examined the despair and

---

[641]   Corliss, p.29. See also Mark Alvey, "THE LADY EVE," CINEMATEXAS PROGRAM NOTES 24:2 (March 7, 1983):1-6; and Stanley Cavell, "Pursuits of Happiness: A Reading of THE LADY EVE," NEW LITERARY HISTORY 10 (1979):581-601.

[642]   Jeanine Basinger, "THE MIRACLE OF MORGAN'S CREEK," THE INTERNATIONAL DICTIONARY OF FILMS AND FILMMAKERS, Volume 1--FILMS, p.300. See also Nina Nichols, "THE MIRACLE OF MORGAN'S CREEK," CINEMATEXAS PROGRAM NOTES 19:2 (November 4, 1980):55-62.

[643]   Ann Laemmle, "SULLIVAN'S TRAVELS," CINEMATEXAS PROGRAM NOTES 23:1 (September 30, 1982):52. See also Elliot Rubenstein, "Hollywood Travels: Sturges and Sullivan," SIGHT AND SOUND 47:1 (Winter 1977-78):50-2.

[644]   Some useful articles on Italian films: Mario Cannella, "Ideology and Aesthetic Hypotheses In the Criticism of Neo-Realism," SCREEN 14 (1973-74):5-60; Ted Perry, "Roots of Neorealism," FILM CRITICISM 3:2 (Winter 1979):3-7; Ben Lawton, "Italian

suffering of ordinary individuals. Taking their cues from their personal experiences, artists documented how people felt, what they faced in the postwar world, and the internal conflicts over what had happened during the war.

The approach in Italy was called "neo-realism," a unique new left film movement that arose to depict the social and political effects of the war upon working class people.[645] The stories were rooted in real events rather than fictionalized accounts. Their mood exuded a sense of immediacy and urgency. The approach utilized both amateurs and actors in deliberately nonprofessionally photographed film that emphasized the political, social, and economic conditions emerging from the ashes of a Fascist society. At first, audiences accepted this ragged style of pseudodocumentary filmmaking because they could identify with the misery and hardships of the

---

Neorealism: A Mirror Construction of Reality," ibid., pp.8-23; Peter Brunette, "Just How Brechtian is Rossellini?" ibid., pp.30-42; Cesare Zavattini, "Some Ideas on the Cinema," SIGHT AND SOUND 22:3 (October-December 1953):64-9; Gavin Lambert, "The Signs of the Predicament: Italian Notes," ibid., 24:3 (January-March 1955):147-51, 166; Eric Rhode, "Why Neo-Realism Failed," ibid., 30:1 (Winter 1960-1961):26-32; *Andre Bazin, "An Aesthetic of Reality: Cinematic Realism and the Italian School of Liberation," WHAT IS CINEMA? II., pp.16-40; Vernon Young, "Italy: The Moral Cinema," FILM QUARTERLY 15:1 (Fall 1961):14-21; Kevin Gough-Yates, "The Destruction of Neo-Realism," FILMS AND FILMING 16:12 (September 1970):14-20, 22; Peter John Dyer, "The Realists--A Return to Life," ibid., 6:2 (November 1959):12-4, 32; and John Francis Lane, "A Style Is Born," ibid., 5:7 (April 1959):13-5, 32.

[645] There are several conflicting claims about how the term "neo-realism" was coined. Some commentators, like Eric Rhode, identify Umberto Barbaro, a professor at the CENTRO SPERIMENTALE, as the author, and point to his 1943 essay published in FILM, in which he lists four crucial aspects of the need for a new film movement: (1) stop using "the naive and mannered cliches which formed the larger part of Italian films"; (2) get rid of "those fantastic and grotesque fabrications which exclude human problems and the human point of view"; (3) ignore historical dramas and screen adaptations unless a clear political necessity is demonstrated; and (4) get rid of the bombastic dialogue that has Italian characters "inflamed by the same noble sentiments . . . all of them equally aware of the problems of life." Quoted in "Why Neo-Realism Failed," p.27. Other commentators, like Gaia Servadio, accept Visconti's version that after sending Mario Serandrei, his film editor, the first rushes of OBSESSION/OSSESSIONE, the editor waited a couple of days and then wrote to Visconti, praising the work and then adding, "I don't know how to define this kind of cinema other than as 'neo-realistic'." Quoted in Gaia Servadio, LUCHINO VISCONTI: A BIOGRAPHY (New York: Franklin Watts, 1983), p.78. Bazin observes that "Some components of the new Italian school existed before the Liberation: personnel, techniques, aesthetic trends. But it was their historical, social, and economic combination that suddenly created a synthesis in which elements also made themselves manifest." See WHAT IS CINEMA? Volume II, p.19. Tag Gallagher notes that Don Ranvaud located three earlier versions of the term in 1931 and 1932, and that Mussolini's son Vittorio edited a magazine called CINEMA, which in 1941 argued for a "revolutionary art inspired by the sufferings and hopes of humanity." The problem, Gallagher argues, is that "CINEMA did not use the word at all, while Barbaro and Serandrei employed it not to signal a new ITALIAN cinema but to describe certain old FRENCH films made by Renoir, Carne, and Duvivier. More important, after using the word (just twice) in 1943, they did not use it again until late 1948." See Tag Gallagher, "NR=MC2: Rossellini, 'Neo-Realism,' and Croce," FILM HISTORY: AN INTERNATIONAL JOURNAL 2:1 (Winter 1988):95, 87.

characters and appreciate the films' ideological messages.[646] Later on, the New Left's Marxist imagery would prove embarrassing to the nation's domestic goals and international relations.

It is important to remember that the roots of Italian neo-realism were embedded in the cinematic traditions of the past. Resentment against the static studio look of escapist feature films had been brewing among Italians ever since the early 1930s. For example, Italian filmmaker Leo Longanesi had argued in 1933 that

> We must make films as simple and bare as possible in their direction, films without artifice, shot without scripts, and as far as possible taken from life . . . It would be enough to go out into the street, to stop at any point and observe what is happening for half an hour, and with attentive eyes and without a preconceived style, to make a film which would be both an Italian film and a true one.[647]

Paul Monaco goes further, pointing out that "several traditions which spawned Neo-Realism could be found in Italian culture, going back to a populist melodrama that had thrived in the previous century."[648]

What was needed, however, for Italian neo-realism to emerge as a movement were four historical conditions, identified by George Huaco, that had given rise to other important film movements: "(1) a cadre of directors, cameramen, editors, actors, and other technicians; (2) the industrial plant required for film production; (3) a mode of organization of the film industry which is either in harmony with or at least permissive of the ideology of the wave; (4) a political climate which is either in harmony with or at least permissive of the ideology and style of the wave."[649] Each of these conditions was in place by 1945.

The chief theoretician for neo-realism was Zavattini. Although he never formalized the principles for the film movement, the superb screenwriter proved the catalyst for the undercurrents in the Italian film industry. From the hindsight of 1953, he commented that

> The most important characteristic, and the most important innovation, of what is called neo-realism, it seems to me, is to have realised that the necessity of the "story" was only an unconscious way of disguising a human defeat, and

---

[646] Rhode offers (pp.439-40) this provocative thesis: a major change taking place in film content throughout Western society was that movies about children had taken on a harsher tone. In place of young, precocious children, typical of the characterizations found in movies of the 1930s, we saw victimized children. Neo-realism, in particular, thrived on presenting children who "exposed the vanities of adults." The problem with this approach, Rhode points out, was that it "was a form of moral blackmail" and eventually became highly suspect and unpopular. Wright provides (pp.230-45) a wider range of film examples on the same subject, dealing with Rossellini's GERMANY, YEAR ZERO/GERMANIA ANNO ZERO (1947), Jean Benoit-Levy and Jean Epstein's LA MATERNELLE (1933), Leontine Sagan's GIRLS IN UNIFORM/MACHEN IN UNIFORM (1932), Sidney Meyer's THE QUIET ONE (1949), Luis Bunuel's THE YOUNG AND THE DAMNED/LOS OLVIDADOS (1950), Rene Clement's FORBIDDEN GAMES/JEUX INTERDITS (1952), and Lindsay Anderson's IF . . . (1969).

[647] Cited in "The Destruction of Neo-Realism," pp.20, 22.

[648] *Paul Monaco, RIBBONS IN TIME: MOVIES AND SOCIETY SINCE 1945 (Bloomington: Indiana University Press, 1987), p.4.

[649] George Huaco, THE SOCIOLOGY OF FILM ART (New York: Basic Basic Books, 1965), p.19. Other film movements cited in Huaco's study are German expressionism and Soviet expressive realism.

that the kind of imagination it involved was simply a technique of superimposing dead formulas over living facts. Now it has been perceived that reality is hugely rich, that to be able to look directly at it is enough; and that the artist's task is not to make people moved or indignant at metaphorical situations, but to make them reflect (and, if you like, to be moved and indignant too) on what they and others are doing, on the real things, exactly as they are.[650]

Early in the 1940s, Zavattini had extracted from the Fascist production practices of the past essential features that could be valuable in portraying the pathos of Italian society glossed over by Fascist filmmakers. For example, he argued that some Italians were "content with the illusion that one day they will say: 'from the very beginning, perhaps twenty individuals understood that the right way wasn't Hollywood's, that the spectacle which began on the boulevards with the Lumiere brothers was the beginning of the sickness.'" He theorized that "A return to man, to the creature who in himself is 'all spectacle': this would liberate   .   .   .   [filmmakers]. Set up the camera in the street, in a room, see with insatiable patience, train ourselves in the contemplation of our fellow-man in his elementary actions." In short, he urged filmmakers to avoid trick photography inherited from the first days of film and instead realize that "The wonder must be in us, expressing itself without wonder: the best dreams are those outside the mist, which can be seen like the veins of leaves."[651]

In arguing his case for a "realistic" cinema, Zavattini pointed to the breakthroughs achieved by Soviet filmmakers and French "poetic realism."[652] The emphasis was not only on depicting life as it existed among the working class, but also on maintaining a moral perspective on the social and economic pressures that ordinary people experience. A foreshadowing of what was to come occurred just months before the Allies landed in Sicily, when Visconti released his film, OBSESSION/OSSESSIONE (1942), a realistic love story based on James M. Cain's novel, THE POSTMAN ALWAYS RINGS TWICE. This unauthorized screen adaptation caused a stir with its naturalistic portrait of human frailties. By 1944, with the Fascists and Nazis in turmoil, Zavattini's cinematic theories had gained widespread support among Italian filmmakers and intellectuals, mainly because they bridged long-standing disagreements between Catholics and Marxists. Now everyone had an opportunity to share in presenting testimony to their common problems. Moreover, conditions in the country plus wartime experiences created the right historical context for the birth of neo-realism. The following year, Rossellini's ROME, OPEN CITY/ROMA, CITTA APERTA inaugurated the new Italian cinema.[653] Building on

---

[650]   "Some Ideas on the Cinema," p.64.

[651]   Cesare Zavattini, ZAVATTINI: SEQUENCES FROM A CINEMATIC LIFE, trans. William Weaver (Englewood Cliffs: Prentice-Hall, 1970), p.2.

[652]   Both Bazin (pp.38-40) and Gough-Yates points out (p.15) that American authors like Cain, Faulkner, Steinbeck, Hemingway, Dos Passos, and Caldwell influenced the birth of neo-realism. Wright claims (p.221) that the path to neo-realism had first been established by Renoir's GRAND ILLUSION/LA GRANDE ILLUSION (1937) and Ford's THE GRAPES OF WRATH (1940).

[653]   Monaco argues (p.5) that one important feature of the new movement, evident in ROME, OPEN CITY, was the focus "on the dramatic confrontation and the temporary symbiosis of Catholicism and Marxism." Moreover, he points to the analysis by Huaco that divides the key neo-realist filmmakers into two major categories--Catholic liberals and Marxists. Rhode claims (p.458) that another important feature of the film was its editing techniques, giving the impression that this was a highly personal essay combining fiction and fact. The approach had a profound effect on the French New Wave in the late 1950s.

incidents witnessed between 1943 and 1945 (the period during which the film was made), the director recorded the struggle of the partisans against the Nazis and the police in the final stages of World War II. Rossellini's handling of the material and his commitment to capturing the mood of the times had a profound effect on a significant handful of his contemporaries.

From 1945 to 1955, the documentary-like emphasis on using non-professional actors, location shooting, humanistic interests, and detailed insights into contemporary society resulted in a number of memorable films. "Affectionately . . . luridly . . . energetically," Penelope Houston observes, ". . . they built a national cinema out of their own recent history."[654] The themes of these films, according to Huaco, were directly related to the background of the neo-realist directors:

> In summary, the neorealist film directors were a well-educated group of predominantly bourgeois origin. Their political orientation was polarized into Catholic or Marxist, with a clear predominance of the latter. Despite this predominance, these two political groups contributed approximately equal numbers of neorealist films. The previous occupations of the directors were predominantly those of writer or journalist. It is suggested that these occupations and the political orientation of most of the directors are among the causal antecedents of the thematic focus on social problems and social criticism which characterized neorealism.[655]

The fact that these men eventually had to compromise their ideals with the social and economic realities of the film industry is not surprising. What is unusual is how well they did, considering the forces that opposed them.

Each of their best socially conscious movies was noted for its psychological intensity, post-synchronized sound (with the emphasis on natural sounds rather than dialogue and music), and generally pessimistic tone in dealing with issues like unemployment, social injustice, and poverty. For example, Rossellini's PAISAN/PAISA (1946) details the hardships faced by Italians in the closing days of World War II. Six different episodes trace the impact on everyday people of the Allied landing in Sicily in 1943 to the defeat of Italy in 1944. "The word 'paisa' means 'Countryman,'" explains Ian Johnson, "and each sequence represents a personal, local, reaction between Italian and invader."[656] De Sica's SHOESHINE/SCIUSCIA (1946) depicts the sordid life of children trying unsuccessfully to survive in a traumatized and chaotic country. Interestingly, winning the Oscar for the Best Foreign Film of 1946 only accented the different feelings toward the film inside and outside of Italy. As Guy Flatley points out,

> SHOESHINE--and Rossellini's OPEN CITY, which also dealt compassionately with the doomed and the dispossessed of a shattered Italy--changed the face and the soul of Italian cinema. But neither film did much to change the sad financial state of its director, since the Italian public was more in the mood to laugh at Hollywood comedies than weep over the grubbiness of their own lives.[657]

Visconti's THE EARTH TREMBLES/LA TERRA TREMA (1948), the initial film in an unfinished trilogy, documented the inability of Sicilian fishermen to withstand the

---

[654]   *Penelope Houston, THE CONTEMPORARY CINEMA Baltimore: Penguin Books, 1963), p.23.

[655]   Huaco, p.206.

[656]   Ian Johnson, "PAISA," FILMS AND FILMING 12:5 (February 1966):36.

[657]   Flatley, p.9.

power and oppression of a greedy bureaucracy or the fortunes of a hostile universe. That same year, De Sica's BICYCLE THIEVES/LADRI DI BICICLETTE recorded the fortunes of a desperate parent who loses face with his son in an unsuccessful effort to earn a living in wartorn Italy.[658] A timeless story, it is, as Wright observes, "a kind of archetypal example of the world's cruelty and indifference to children. . . ."[659]The last great neo-realistic film was De Sica's UMBERTO D (1952), a thoroughly depressing tale about a retired bureaucrat who finds himself alone and abandoned. Significantly, it was also the last collaboration between De Sica and Zavattini.

In many respects, UMBERTO D epitomized the problems that neo-realism created for its artists. First, its images not only of working-class miseries, but also of Italian society were considered to be an embarrassment to the government because of the negative cinematic impression that was being exported. The official line was that things were getting better and that these types of films were deemed counter-productive. In fact, the neo-realists found themselves in serious political trouble when an influx of Hollywood movies in the late 1940s destabilized the Italian film industry.[660] To protect the industry, the government passed legislation, sponsored by Giulio Andreotti, that not only put a heavy tax on American films and required Italian exhibitors to show indigenous films for at least eighty days a year, but also "reintroduced strict precensorship, putting the state in control of the movie industry."[661] The effect of the "Andreotti Law" was to discourage investors from funding neo-realistic films, since the government censors generally frowned on productions undermining national interests. Secondly, like most neo-realistic films, UMBERTO D did poorly at the domestic box office and underscored the disdain that Italians in the early 1950s had for negative scenarios about their problems. Moreover, such films now rarely left the country and thus lost a major source of their income. Third, critics like Andrew Sarris felt that directors like De Sica had drained neo-realism of its profundity: "If Visconti and Rossellini invented neorealism in OSSESSIONE and OPEN CITY and then invested it with the ultimate profundity of LA TERRA TREMA and PAISAN, De Sica milked it dry with SHOESHINE and THE BICYCLE THIEF." He went on to add that, "Lacking an insight into the real world, De Sica relied instead on tricks of pathos that he had learned too well as an actor."[662] Other critics attacked the Neo-Realists for their technical lapses, sentimentality, and stereotypical plots. Fourth, the Marxist ideology that functioned

---

[658] Joel E. Kanoff makes the important point that the oft-used English-language title [THE BICYCLE THIEF] is "misleading and injurious to the film" because the Italian-language title means "BICYCLE THIEVES." According to Kanoff, the director intentionally made an allegory that "suggests a universe interrelated inextricably by perverse economic ties--the bicycle one man needs to work and support his family, another man steals to support his, and still another sells. See Joel E. Karnoff, "LADRI DI BICICLETTE," THE INTERNATIONAL DICTIONARY OF FILMS AND FILMMAKERS VOLUME I, p.249.

[659] Wright, p.228.

[660] Many European film industries experienced similar problems in the late 1940s when Washington used its overseas influence to aid Hollywood in regaining its foreign markets. Needing financial aid from America, countries like France, Italy, Germany, and France were forced to enter into unfavorable film agreements that allowed Hollywood to saturate European theaters with American films. For a useful summary, see Wright, pp.246-7.

[661] Liehm, pp.90-1.

[662] *Andrew Sarris, CONFESSIONS OF A CULTIST: ON THE CINEMA, 1955/1969 (New York: Simon and Schuster, 1971), p.30.

as the underlying theme of neo-realism served as an irritant to the Italian government as it developed stronger ties with Western nations. Thus by the early 1950s, social, economic, and political conditions all contributed to the demise of the radical film movement.

Although neo-realism lasted only a decade in post-war Italy, its cinematic influence was felt throughout the film world up to the present. More pointedly, almost every Italian filmmaker of note, from Fellini[663] and Antonioni to Bernardo Bertolucci and Lina Wertmuller, have reacted to the ideas and approaches that grew out of the postwar Italian film industry. Not only did intellectuals and filmmakers see filmmaking in a new light, but also personal cinematic statements made in novel and non-traditional ways gained commercial respectability. The postwar movement set the stage for a revisionist look at history that not only emphasized a realistic and naturalistic perspective, but also focused attention on the importance of silent film techniques. Together with the prominence of postwar-French existentialism, as Rhode points out, neo-realism popularized a number of exciting concepts for contemporary filmmakers: "a concern with immediacy, states of being and questions of bad faith, a hostility to dogma and institutional authority, and an openness to misrepresentation."[664] Clearly, the neo-realist period from 1945 to 1955 rivals in its achievements those found in any of film history's extraordinary movements.

BOOKS

GENERAL

Armes, Roy. PATTERNS OF REALISM: A STUDY OF ITALIAN NEO-REALIST CINEMA. New York: A. S. Barnes and Company, 1971. Illustrated. 226pp.

---

[663] The following articles are useful: Gideon Bachmann, "An Interview With Federico Fellini," SIGHT AND SOUND 30:2 (Spring 1963):82-7; Eric Rhode, "Federico Fellini," TOWER OF BABEL, pp.121-36; Pierre Kast, "Guiletta and Federico: Visits With Fellini," CAHIERS DU CINEMA IN ENGLISH 5, CdC #164 (March 1965):24-33; Irving R. Levine, "I Was Born for The Cinema," FILM COMMENT 4:1 (Fall 1966):77-84; Peter Harcourt "The Secret Life of Federico Fellini," FILM QUARTERLY 19:3 (Spring 1966):4-19; Forrest Williams, "Fellini's Voices," ibid., 21:3 (Spring 1968):21-5; Enzo Peri, "Fellini: An Interview," ibid., 15:1 (Fall 1961):30-3; Eugene Walter, "The Wizardry of Fellini," FILMS AND FILMING 12:9 (June 1966):18-26; James R. Silke, ed., FEDERICO FELLINI (Washington, D.C.: The American Film Institute, 1970); Franke M. Burke, "Reason and Unreason In Federico Fellini's I VITELLONI," LITERATURE/FILM QUARTERLY 8:2 (1980): 116-24; Mary Cantwell, "Fellini on Men, Women, Love, Life, Art and His New Movie," NEW YORK TIMES H (April 5, 1981):1, 24; Margaret Croyden, "The Maesto on Fantasy, Finance and the Art of Film," ibid., H (June 22, 1984):1, 22; Leslie Bennetts, "Film Society Pays Tribute to 'Il Maestro,'" ibid., C (June 11, 1985):11; Vincent Canby, "Fellini: Master of Ageless Comedy," ibid., H (June 9, 1985):1, 21; Clyde Haberman, "Fellini Builds Reggiolo, The Town of His Dreams," ibid., H (June 18, 1989):15, 24; Rita TheBerge, "Program Notes: FELLINI SATYRICON," CINEMATEXAS PROGRAM NOTES 12:3 (April 27, 1977):5-9; ___, "Program Notes: 8 1/2," ibid., 17:3 (November 20, 1979):35-44; John Henley, "Program Notes: I VITELLONI," ibid., 14:3 (April 11, 1978):67-73; and Eddie De Leon, "Program Notes: 8 1/2," ibid., 22:3 (April 27, 1982):1-6.

[664] Rhode, p.472.

One the best early books on Italian neo-realism, Armes examines the films themselves, the people who made them, and the effect they have not only on the audience, but also on other filmmakers and movements in the cinema. A filmography, bibliography, and index are included. Well worth browsing.

*Bondanella, Peter. ITALIAN CINEMA: FROM NEOREALISM TO THE PRESENT. New York: Frederick Ungar Publishing Company, 1983. Illustrated. 440pp.

"This book," Bondanella explains, "the first comprehensive English treatment of the contemporary Italian cinema in many years, is the fruit of some ten years of teaching and research in the area. One of the major goals of the work has been to rescue the study of Italian cinema from the monolingual bias of most American and English critics, who rarely possess an adequate knowledge of the language these films speak or the culture they reflect." Ten well-researched and analytical chapters examine the major films and directors, the important trends, and the close links between society and Italian filmmaking. Endnotes, a bibliography, a listing of rental information, and an index are included. Recommended for special collections.

*Liehm, Mira. PASSION AND DEFIANCE: FILM IN ITALY FROM 1942 TO THE PRESENT. Berkeley: University of California Press, 1984. Illustrated. 396pp.

Liehm's third and best book on Italian cinema, this valuable study examines the major influences in the traditional arts, philosophy, and society on Italian filmmaking. Twelve reflective and challenging chapters, starting with a splendid discussion or the importance of the Fascist cinema in the 1930s to the Italian film industry after 1942, chart the major trends and ideas that characterize modern filmmaking in Italy. The author builds on her contacts with many key filmmakers to create a compelling survey on what led to the current crisis in the Italian film industry. Extensive endnotes, a strong bibliography, a film index, and a name index are included. Recommended for special collections.

Overbey, David, ed. SPRINGTIME IN ITALY: A READER ON NEO-REALISM. Hamden: The Shoe String Press, 1978. 242pp.

MICHELANGELO ANTONIONI

Lyons, Robert J. MICHELANGELO ANTONIONI'S NEO-REALISM: A WORLD VIEW. New York: Arno Press, 1976. 207pp.

Originally written as Lyons's 1973 Ph.D. dissertation for Bowling Green State University, this study "deals in the extremes of the real world which Antonioni defines in terms that seem to focus on absurdity versus an ideal, that interestingly enough, yields a conventionality not customary to revolutionary thought." The author emphasizes the importance of the ideal in the filmmaker's world. Dividing the analysis into three main periods: the early films and the director's ties to the social concerns of neo-realism, Antonioni's middle period (1956-1964) and his focus on psychological studies of individuals, and the director's two English films--BLOW-UP (1946) and ZABRISKIE POINT (1970)--that offer cultural criticisms broader in scope than in the earlier periods. A bibliography is included. Well worth browsing.

VITTORIO DE SICA

*De Sica, Vittorio. THE BICYCLE THIEF: A FILM BY VITTORIO DE SICA. Trans. Simon Hartog. New York: Simon and Schuster, 1968. Illustrated. 100pp.

De Sica, Vittorio. MIRACLE IN MILAN. Baltimore: Penguin Books, 1968. Illustrated. 21pp.

FEDERICO FELLINI

Alpert, Hollis. FELLINI: A LIFE. New York: Atheneum, 1986. Illustrated. 338pp.

Born in Rimini, Italy, on January 20, 1920, Federico Fellini grew up in the Adriatic Sea resort town and was deeply influenced not only by the values of his middle-class family, but also by his contacts with the Catholic church, the Facist party, and traveling circus performers. Each of these four groups, along with many individuals from Rimini, appear frequently as key elements in Fellini's screenplays and films. His formal education in a series of religious schools produced the writer-director's anti-clerical attitudes generally associated with his most famous screen characters, while his childhood encounters with local prostitutes shaped many of his movie scenes of sexual fantasies. By the time Fellini was nineteen, he had abandoned the idea of becoming a lawyer, forsaken a career in journalism, and had started his training as a screenwriter. Between 1939 and 1943, when the Allied forces landed in Italy, Fellini did his best to stay out of the army and to make a living as a screenwriter. In 1943, he not only married the actress Giulietta Masina (who starred in seven of Fellini's films), but also became deeply involved in the neo-realistic movement. Over the next eight years, the now prominent screenwriter worked on a number of important projects, including ROME, OPEN CITY/ROMA, CITTA APERTA (1945), PAISAN/PAISA (1946), THE MIRACLE/IL MIRACOLO, and WAYS OF LOVE/L'AMORE (both in 1948). At the same time, he often worked as an assistant director on many of his assignments. In 1950, Fellini made his directorial debut with VARIETY LIGHTS/LUCI DEL VARIETA. Drawing mostly on his personal experiences and idiosyncratic filmmaking style, the controversial writer-director played a major role in establishing the rebirth of Italian filmmaking with pictures like THE WHITE SHEIK/LO SCEICCO BIANCO (1952), THE YOUNG AND THE PASSIONATE /I VITELLONI (1953), THE ROAD/LA STRADA (1954), THE NIGHTS OF THE CABIRIA/LE NOTTI DI CABIRIA (1957), THE SWEET LIFE/LA DOLCE VITA (1960), 8 1/2/OTTO E MEZZO (1963), JULIET OF THE SPIRITS/GIULIETTA DELGI SPIRITI (1965), FELLINI SATYRICON (1969), and I REMEMBER/AMARCORD (1973). His most recent film is GINGER AND FRED (1986).

Alpert's full-length biography offers a chatty, anecdotal portrait of the controversial filmmaker, choosing to focus on reconstructed dialogue and popular stories, rather than on a scholarly analysis of the films and their influence in world cinema. The author, a good reporter and an entertaining storyteller, provides us with a current, highly readable overview of Fellini's career. The absence of much-needed documentation makes the work far less authoritative than the dust cover claims. A bibliography, a filmography, and an index are included. Well worth browsing.

Bondanella, Peter, ed. FEDERICO FELLINI: ESSAYS IN CRITICISM. New York: Oxford University Press, 1978. Illustrated. 314pp.

A representative collection of essays that have appeared in English, French, and Italian journals since 1950, this valuable anthology emphasizes three Fellini films: THE ROAD/LA STRADA (1954), 8 1/2/OTTO E MEZZO (1963), and FELLINI SATYRICON (1969). Discussions of other films are included, however, in the book's three major sections. "The emphasis," Bondanella explains, "reflects not only the objective fact that many of the best critical studies devoted to Fellini analyze these three films but also my subjective and personal belief that critical debate on Fellini's place in film history should concentrate on these three works." The anthology also attempts to be representative not only of significant national tastes as they relate to the filmmaker's work, but also of various methodologies and approaches to analyzing the films: e.g., "Marxist, religious, historical, philosophical, psychological, literary, and semiological points of view." In addition, there are five commentaries by Fellini, reflecting his views on neo-realism, the differences between film and television, and contemporary society. A bibliography and filmography are included, but no index i provided. Recommended for special collections.

*Budgen, Suzanne, FELLINI. London: The British Film Institute, 1966. Illustrated 124pp.
     "On a pedestrian level," J. Peter Harcourt writes in the preface, Fellini's film derive from Neo-Realism . . . But on another level, Fellini seems more to belong to that great family of artists whose work transcends its social origins." Budgen' short, useful, and readable reference work on Fellini takes the cultural approach emphasizing the filmmaker's personal relationship to his films up to THE SWEET LIFE/LA DOLCE VITA (1960). The book also contains extracts from a Belgian television interview with the director on THE ROAD/LA STRADA (1954). chronology of Fellini's cinematic career (compiled by John Russell Taylor), endnotes and an index are included. Well worth browsing.

*Costello, Donald P., FELLINI'S ROAD. Notre Dame: University of Notre Dame Press 1983. Illustrated. 214pp.
     "Federico Fellini," Costello observes, "ought to be the hero of the 'me generation.' Pop psychology has taken up his obsessive theme--the search for sel . . . 'The only thing I want to know,' Fellini has said, is 'WHY AM I HERE? WHAT IS MY LIFE?'" Costello takes this metaphorical search as the theme of his analyse on four of the filmmaker's works: THE ROAD/LA STRADA (1954), THE SWEET LIFE/LA DOLCE VITA (1960), 8 1/2/OTTO E MEZZO (1963), and JULIET OF THE SPIRITS/GIULIETTA DELGI SPIRITI (1965). The analyses are provocative, the writing elegant, and the information valuable. Endnotes are provided, but no index is included. Recommended for special collections.

*Grazzini, Giovanni, ed. FEDERICO FELLINI: COMMENTS ON FILM. Trans. Joseph Henry. Fresno: The Press at California State University, Fresno, 1988. Illustrated 231pp.
     "Like the images he creates," Henry observes, "the simplest statements of Federico Fellini have their own complexity. For as he explains to us throughout thi book, life for him is a constant interplay between reality and fantasy, between surfac and the mystery that lies beneath." The Italian film critic Grazzini's extensive interview with the artist offers a wonderful opportunity to examine Fellini's views on his childhood, career, and the goals in his films. Recommended for special collections

*Ketchum, Charles B. FEDERICO FELLINI: THE SEARCH FOR A NEW MYTHOLOGY New York: Paulist Press, 1976. 94pp.
     Relying heavily on Fellini's own words, this reflective and impressive brief study discusses how the artist is creating new symbols to deal with modern society and it secular values. The author focuses primarily on "the cinematographer's contribution to the contemporary religious critique" and "is interested in Fellini the mature creative artist whose expressive genius has commanded the attention of the Western world. Ketchum divides his book into two sections: the artist and the films. Part One explores Fellini's views on the inability of traditional symbols to explain our current life-styles. Part Two focuses on THE ROAD/LA STRADA (1954), THE SWEET LIFE/LA DOLCE VITA (1960), and 8 1/2/OTTO E MEZZO (1963). A bibliography and endnote are included, but no bibliography is provided. Recommmended for special collections

*Murray, Edward. FELLINI THE ARTIST, Second, Enlarged edition. New York Frederick Ungar Publishing Company, 1986. Illustrated. 282pp.

A valuable but highly readable study of Fellini's films from THE WHITE SHEIK/LO SCEICCO BIANCO (1952) to the mid-1980s, this new edition includes information of four films not covered in the 1976 edition: FELLINI'S CASANOVA (1976), ORCHESTRA REHEARSAL (1979), CITY OF WOMEN (1981), and AND THE SHIP SAILS ON (1984). Murray divides his material into four major sections: a biographical and historical perspective, Fellini's attitude toward his work, ten major films from 1952 to 1976, and Fellini's works from 1976 to 1984. The analyses are aimed at a popular audience, but the many useful collection of excerpts from Fellini interviews and comments make the book useful to serious students. "Most of Fellini's later pictures," Murray concludes, "seem thin in content; indeed, they suggest he is trying to conceal the emptiness within through recourse to spectacle. Oddly enough, in spite of Fellini's increasing reliance on fantastic display, his recent more surrealistic films are much less memorable visually than the earlier masterpieces--derived, for the most part, from neorealism--that originally earned him his reputation. Generally speaking, Fellini's films are most impressive when reality and fantasy (or poetry and surreal expressionism--call it what you will) co-exist." A revised filmography and bibilography are included, along with an index . Well worth browsing.

Price, Barbara Anne, and Theodore Price. FEDERICO FELLINI: AN ANNOTATED INTERNATIONAL BIBLIOGRAPHY. Metuchen: The Scarecrow Press, 1978. 282pp.
    An intelligent and useful resource, this book offers valuable descriptive and informative comments on primary and secondary sources, along with helpful appendexes on where to rent the films (now outdated), adaptations made from Fellini's films, and translations for the films in six languages. An index is included. Well worth browsing.

Rosenthal, Stuart. THE CINEMA OF FEDERICO FELLINI. South Brunswick: A. S. Barnes and Company, 1976. Illustrated. 190pp.
    An original study of Fellini's career up to I REMEMBER/AMARCORD (1974), this refreshing book takes a thematic rather than a film-by-film approach. Rosenthal divides his material into three sections. "Chapter One," he explains, "examines the link between Fellini and his characters AND between the characters and the audience, stressing the shift from objectivity to personalism that has gradually taken place in his movies since the Forties. Once the close ties among Fellini's characters, and his viewers are understood, it is possible to appreciate the formal side of Fellini's work as something more than just brauvura effects. Chapters Two and Three are concerned with how Fellini's style of expression reflects his intense personal interest in his characters. The remainder of the book provides more extensive discussions of individual films." Particularly interesting are the author's analysis of I REMEMBER/AMARCORD and how it reflects the filmmaker's bitter re-evaluation of his childhood in Rimini and the negative influences of the Fascist party on the town. Wonderful illustrations, a bibliography, a filmography, and an index are included. Recommended for special collections.

*Salachas, Gilbert, ed. FEDERICO FELLINI. Trans. Rosalie Siegel. New York: Crown Publishers, 1969. Illustrated. 224pp.
    Originally published in the CINEMA D'AUJOURD'HUI SERIES in 1963, this useful book begins with an extensive and meandering essay by Salachas on Fellini's life and career up the mid-1960s. Salachas does provide, however, some entertaining anecdotes and interesting quotations. More valuable are the book's collection of Fellini comments, excerpts from seven of his screenplays, and a spectrum of critical reviews. A filmography, bibliography, and index are included. Well worth browsing.

Solmi, Angelo. FELLINI. Trans. Elizabeth Greenwood. New York: Humanities Press, 1968. Illustrated. 183pp.

Divided into two major sections, the book first charts the familiar themes in Fellini's movies by discussing their relationship to his life and shows in detail how the director's life is incorporated into the films. Solmi is particularly good when it comes to presenting the economic and artistic difficulties Fellini has encountered. The absence of documentation makes the narrative suspect, but the husband-wife authors of FEDERICO FELLINI: AN ANNOTATED INTERNATIONAL BIBLIOGRAPHY insist that ".   .   . he has made use of many sources, secondary and primary, many in Italian publications not easily available to American critics, or at least not used by them."[665] A bibliography and filmography are included, but no index is provided. Recommended for special collections.

Stubbs, John C., et al. FEDERICO FELLINI: A GUIDE TO REFERENCES AND RESOURCES. Boston: G. K. Hall and Company, 1978. 346pp.
A fine reference work on Fellini, this extensive resource guide contains the standard sections of the series: a biographical background, a critical survey of the works, the films: synopsis, credits, and notes, writings about Fellini, his writings and other related activities, archival sources, film distributors, a film title index, and an author index. Its one drawback is that many of the annotations lack the depth and detail found in the Price bibliography. Recommended for special collections.

LUCHINO VISCONTI

*Visconti, Luchino. TWO SCREENPLAYS: LA TERRA TREMA/SENSO. Trans. Judith Green. New York: The Orion Press, 1970. Illustrated. 186pp.

FILMS

GENERAL

NEO-REALISM (Texture Films/RAI--16mm: 1971, 30 mins., b/w, sound, R-TEX; S-TEX)
This is a helpful and interesting overview of Italian neo-realism because it shows not only selected scenes from ROME, OPEN CITY, PAISAN, and UMBERTO D, but also has recent comments from various filmmakers about the impact of the movement years ago. Among the people shown and interviewed are Roberto Rossellini, Vittorio De Sica, Cesare Zavattini, Pier Paolo Pasolini, Bernardo Bertolucci, and Michelangelo Antonioni.

VITTORIO DE SICA

BICYCLE THIEVES/LADRI DI BICICLETTE (Italy--16mm: 1949, 87 mins., English subtitles, sound, R-COR, FNC)
Scripted by Zavattini, the director De Sica's film deals with the heartbreaking story of a man's search for the bicycle he needs to earn a living and is interwoven with a father-son relationship that concerns the moral collapse of an individual because of economic deprivation.[666] Andre Bazin speaks for many critics, when he

---

[665]   Barbara Anne Price, and Theodore Price. FEDERICO FELLINI: AN ANNOTATED INTERNATIONAL BIBLIOGRAPHY (Metuchen: The Scarecrow Press, 1978), p.106.

[666]   For useful analyses, see Peter Harcourt, "Film Critique No. 6: BICYCLE THIEF,"

writes, "De Sica and Zavattini have transferred neorealism from the Resistance to the Revolution."[667]

UMBERTO D (Italy--16mm: 1952, 89 mins., b/w, English subtitles, sound, R-BUD, FNC, JAN)

Directed by De Sica, Zavattini's scenario about the pitiful conditions of old people and their loneliness is a brilliant illustration of the Neo-Realistic movement in Italian filmmaking.[668] "Exemplary in its humanity," explains Leprohon, "UMBERTO D is exemplary also in its neo-realistic approach. It comes closer than any other film to Zavattini's ideal: the portrayal of life as it is lived from day to day, with no concessions made to abstract composition or conventional effects."[669]

FEDERICO FELLINI

THE ROAD/LA STRADA (Italy--16mm: 1954, 107 mins., b/w, English subtitles, sound, R-FES, JAN)

This is the story of three people whose loneliness on the roads of Italy commmunicates such emotional appeals to the audience that the film is one of the most acclaimed pictures in film history. Scripted by Fellini, Tullio Pinelli, and Ennio Flaiano, the neo-realistic film epitomizes the social realism of Fellini's work in the 1950s. Magnificent performances are given by Anthony Quinn, Giulietta Masina, and Richard Basehart.

ROBERTO ROSSELLINI

ROME, OPEN CITY/ROMA, CITTA APERTA (Italy--16mm: 1945, 103 mins., b/w, English subtitles, sound, R-FNC)

Rossellini's film about Italy's final days of Nazi occupation is one of the most artistic and significant movies ever made. Its documentary qualities--e.g., on-location action, use of non-professional performers, contemporary relevance, and post-sychronized sound--more than compensate for its technical weaknesses. Anna Magnani gives a superb performance as the pregnant fiancee shot down in the streets.[670] Federico Fellini worked on the script.

SCREEN EDUCATION 30 (July-August 1965):53-61; and Charles Berg, "Program Notes: THE BICYCLE THIEF," CINEMATEXAS PROGRAM NOTES 4:36 (March 20, 1973):1-6.

[667] *Andre Bazin, "Bicycle Thief," WHAT IS CINEMA? Volume II, p.53.

[668] See Douglas McVay, "Poet of Poverty: Part One--The Great Years," FILMS AND FILMING 11:1 (October 1964):12-6; ___," . . . Part Two," ibid., 11:2 (November 1964):51-4; and Nick Barbaro, "Program Notes: UMBERTO D," CINEMATEXAS PROGRAM NOTES 12:1 (January 26, 1977):15-20.

[669] Leprohon, p.131.

[670] Victoria Schultz, "Interview With Roberto Rossellini, February 22-25, 1971, In Houston, Texas," FILM CULTURE (Spring 1971):1-43; Richard Whitehall, "Gallery of Great Artists: Anna Magnani," FILMS AND FILMING 7:10 (July 1961):15-6, 43; and Bosley Crowther, "Open City," THE GREAT FILMS, pp.193-7.

LUCHINO VISCONTI

THE EARTH TREMBLES/LA TERRA TREMA (Italy--16mm: 1948, 162 mins., b/w, English subtitles, sound, R-FNC)

A moving story about Sicilian fishermen waging an unsuccessful fight against a marketing monopoly, this classic neo-realist film used only nonprofessional actors. The on-location shooting and the stylized camerawork suggest Eisenstein's influence.

BRITAIN IN THE POSTWAR PERIOD (1945-1955)

Of all the national cinemas emerging from World War II, none had a stronger documentary tradition than the British film industry. As discussed in Chapter 2, the movement inspired by John Grierson had spilled over into semi-documentary films made during WWII--e.g., ONE OF OUR AIRCRAFT IS MISSING (1942), FIRES WERE STARTED (1943), THE WAY AHEAD (1944), THE WAY TO THE STARS (1945)--and had given first the British people, and then the world, an appetite for realistic stories shot on location and using nonprofessional actors. Often overlooked in discussions about the influence of the documentary movement on feature films is the converse effect: how feature films contributed to the art of the documentary. The British film industry during World War II is an ideal example of the reciprocal relationship between the two cinematic forms. According to Wright, it was difficult to distinguish between war films and non-war films, "not only because of the proximity of the action but also because the crisis of the war was forcing British people as a whole to re-examine some of their national characteristics and, indeed, to question the social and economic structure of the nation."[671] It was not unusual, therefore, to find many films populated by a cast of characters representing a cross-section of British society, with each person personifying the problems of building a united front against a common enemy. "Following the example of the down-to-earth British documentaries," Andrew Sinclair observes, "war pictures and thrillers, comedies and even romantic pictures seemed to work best when they evoked the atmosphere of the street rather than the studio."[672]

Like Hollywood, Wardour Street entered the postwar period with a great deal of confidence. Not only had it managed to produce some extraordinary films during the dark days of battle, but it also had developed and retained a number of gifted directors: e.g., Anthony Asquith, John and Ray Boulting, Thorold Dickinson, Charles Frend, Guy Hamilton, Frank Launder, David Lean, Roy Neame, Laurence Olivier, Michael Powell, Emeric Pressburger, and Carol Reed--and extraordinary performers--e.g., Richard Attenborough, Dirk Bogarde, Robert Donat, Cedric Hardwicke, Rex Harrison, Stanley Holloway, Trevor Howard, Celia Johnson, Vivien Leigh, Margaret Lockwood, James Mason, John Mills, Robert Morley, Robert Newton, Michael Redgrave, Ralph Richardson, Margaret Rutherford, Alistair Sim, Ann Todd, and Peter Ustinov. Moreover, box-office receipts were at an all-time high, production was rapidly increasing, and the government maintained a strong quota system to protect domestic films.[673]

---

[671]   Wright, p.193.

[672]   Andrew Sinclair, "Great Britain," WORLD CINEMA SINCE 1945, ed. William Luhr (New York: Frederick Ungar Publishing Compnay, 1987), p.252.

[673]   Immediately after the war, Parliament mandated that forty percent of the films shown in British theaters had to British-made films.

Very soon, however, Wardour Street and Hollywood found themselves embroiled in a commercial war on British soil. The problems grew out of J. Arthur Rank's ambitions to break into the American market. By the end of World War II, as Robert Murphy explains, Rank "controlled two-thirds of the available studio space, two cinema circuits, each of approximately 300 halls, the largest British distribution company and total assets of over $200 million."[674] Convinced that his big-budget productions would compete favorably with Hollywood products, Rank orchestrated a deal with Universal Pictures in late 1945, and together they set up the distributing firm of United World Pictures. The idea was to block book sixteen films a year (eight by Rank, eight by Universal) in American and British theaters.[675] But before the plan could be implemented, block booking was declared illegal in America as a result of the PARAMOUNT antitrust case (discussed in Chapter 3).

Rank then switched the deal to a distribution company he had created in 1944, Eagle-Lion Films Ltd., and announced that it would handle twenty films (ten by Universal, ten by Rank).[676] In this way, Rank tried to insure the American distribution and exhibition of his films--e.g., HENRY V, THE SEVENTH VEIL (both in 1945), CAESAR AND CLEOPATRA (1946).[677] At first, the scheme worked. But in 1947, Parliament, as it had done in the 1930s, took exception to Hollywood's influence in the British film industry and passed legislation that imposed a seventy-five percent film tax on imported foreign film profits. The government hoped that its new law would stimulate more British production, reduce the industry's dependence on Hollywood films, and help solve the nation's trade deficits. Once again, Parliament confused numbers with quality and the results were less than satisfactory. Moreover, Hollywood retaliated with a boycott of the British market that drove the British film industry into a financial crisis. The fact was that American films enjoyed a greater popularity with the restricted British public (operating on rationing economy until 1951) than did the majority of poorly produced theatrical and problem-centered British films.

There were, however, encouraging signs by the end of the decade. Hollywood withdrew its boycott in 1948 (the same year that Parliament passed a law dispensing with exhibitors' quotas) and a new era of cooperation was initiated between the Americans and the British. For example, as Ernest Betts explains, the Board of Trade established the National Film Finance Corporation in the fall of 1948,

with the authority to grant loans to independent producers. The Corporation was given a provisional life of five years, by which time it was hoped that the

---

[674] Robert Murphy, "Under the Shadow of Hollywood," ALL OUR YESTERDAYS: 90 YEARS OF BRITISH CINEMA, ed. Charles Barr (London: British Film Institute, 1986), p.60. A number of historians claim that Rank caused most of the British film industry's problems in the postwar period because he tried to imitate Korda's Hollywood's successes in the 1930s. Rhode, however, insists (p.382) that the accusation is based on the false assumption that Rank controlled the British film market. His only monopoly was in the London area.

[675] For more details, see Robert Murphy, "Rank's Attempt at the American Market," BRITISH CINEMA HISTORY, eds. James Curran and Vincent Porter (Totawa: Barnes and Noble Books, 1983), pp.164-78.

[676] "Rank's Attempt on the American Market," p.169. See also Don Miller, "Eagle-Lion: The Violent Years," FOCUS ON FILM 31 (November 1978):27-39.

[677] It is also worth noting that Rank distributed the products of other companies: e.g., The Archers, which produced THE RED SHOES (1948) and TALES OF HOFFMAN (1951); The Associated British Picture Corporation, which produced MINE OWN EXECUTIONER and WHILE THE SUN SHINES (both in 1947); and Two Cities, which produced BLITHE SPIRIT (1945) and ODD MAN OUT (1947).

production industry would be sufficiently strengthened to stand on its own feet. The Government contributed . . . 5 million [pounds] to the enterprise, for which a special bill was passed.[678]

One of the largest beneficiaries of the new corporation was Alexander Korda, who had returned to Britain after the war. Among the films he made with the borrowed money were THE THIRD MAN (1949), THE WOODEN HORSE, and SEVEN DAYS TO NOON (both in 1950). Another positive sign, starting in 1950, was the reduction of the import levy and the use of "frozen" American revenues to finance filmmaking in Britain. Murphy sees the latter as extremely important:

In fact, as the Hollywood studio system crumbled under the impact of the divorcement decrees and the rapid spread of television, "runaway production" became widespread, in France, Spain and Italy as well as in Britain. Encouraged by lower costs and by the subsidy for British film instituted as the Eady Levy from 1950, American involvement in British film production rose through the 50s. By 1956 one-third of all British films had American backing.[679]

As Sinclair observes, among the more impressive "American or mid-Atlantic" ventures were those films made by John Huston: THE AFRICAN QUEEN (1951), MOULIN ROUGE (1953), BEAT THE DEVIL (1953), and MOBY DICK (1956).[680] In short, Wardour Street, like Hollywood, found the postwar period to be a confusing and tumultuous time.

Despite all the financial instability and the problems it created during the postwar years--e.g., massive unemployment, declining production, and an overabundance of mediocre films--the British film industry produced a number of remarkable films, mainly adapted from literary and theatrical sources and focusing on personal problems: e.g., BRIEF ENCOUNTER (1946), GREAT EXPECTATIONS, ODD MAN OUT (both in 1947), OLIVER TWIST, THE RED SHOES, HAMLET, THE FALLEN IDOL (all in 1948), THE QUEEN OF SPADES, THE THIRD MAN (both in 1949), THE WINSLOW BOY (1950), THE BROWNING VERSION, THE TALES OF HOFFMAN (both in 1951), THE IMPORTANCE OF BEING EARNEST, and BREAKING THE SOUND

---

[678] Ernest Betts, THE FILM BUSINESS: A HISTORY OF BRITISH CINEMA 1896-1972 (New York: Pitman Publishing Company, 1973), p.220.

[679] "Under the Shadow of Hollywood," p.62. The "Eady Levy" was a plan established by Parliament to aid British filmmakers directly. As George Perry explains, "The plan was named after the Second Secretary of the Treasury, Sir Wilfrid Eady, who was its principal author. The Eady Plan was calculated to cause a tax reduction of . . . 300,000 [pounds], but would make available . . . 3 million [pounds] annually for the industry, half of which would go direct to the producers. The contribution of the other half by the exhibitors, into a production pool, was voluntary . . . Although the Eady Plan ameliorated the producers' problems to a certain extent, it failed to halt losses. So in 1951 it was strengthened and exhibitors were required to pay rather more into the Fund. . . ." See George Perry, THE GREAT BRITISH PICTURE SHOW (Boston: Little, Brown and Company, 1985), p.142.

[680] Sinclair, p.255. Rhode points out (p.438) that the Eady Levy did little to help British films over the long term, and, in effect, had disastrous effects when Hollywood pulled out of the British market in the late 1960s. Moreover, Wright finds (p.379) many of Huston's runaway productions "expensive" travesties and "crashing" disappointments.

BARRIER (both in 1952).[681] Each of these splendid movies revealed the influence of World War II on filmmaking techniques, characterizations, and film content.

The leading example of the influence of the semi-documentary style on British film comedies was Ealing Studios under the helm of Sir Michael Balcon (knighted in 1945). Although many viewers didn't begin to appreciate the studio's comic genius fully until 1949, the structure for the comedies had been evolving ever since Balcon had taken control of company in the mid-1930s. Balcon's methods of production and distribution were in sharp contrast to those of J. Arthur Rank and Alexander Korda. Unlike the latter, as Wright explains, Balcon believed "that British production would remain economically viable only if costs were kept low enough to be recovered from the home market alone."[682] By the end of the war years, as George Perry points out, "Ealing was basically a middle-class institution of a mildly radical disposition, as well as a determinedly small-scale operation. Balcon cast its members, for all their idiosyncrasies, in his own mold."[683] Running throughout the small string of comedies (only a third of the studio's postwar output), as Perry observes, was "the theme of the small group pitted against and eventually triumphing over the superior odds of a more powerful opponent." Equally important, he adds, was "the Ealing-type notion to portray the maverick not as a lone rebel but as someone who finds himself when he becomes part of the team. . . ."[684]

To achieve his ends, Balcon had assembled a mix of young directors--e.g., Henry Cornelius, Robert Hamer, and Alexander Mackendrick--with a crew of skilled World War II documentary directors--e.g., Alberto Cavalcanti, Charles Crichton, Charles Frend, and Harry Watt. Balcon then added accomplished screenwriters--e.g., T. E. B. "Tibby" Clarke,[685] Monja Danischewsky, Roger MacDougall, and William Rose. To populate the forthcoming parodies of national life, Balcon selected a group of character actors rather than star personalities: e.g., Guinness, Holloway, and Sim.[686] Abhorring bureaucracy and government interference, he fostered a healthy exchange of ideas and then encouraged his staff, within limits, to train their "far out" imaginations on some "realistic" approaches to the nation's postwar social, political, and economic problems. The result was a string of exceptional comedies that delighted audiences at home and abroad: e.g., WHISKEY GALORE,[687] THE TITFIELD THUNDERBOLT, PASSPORT TO PIMLICO, KIND HEARTS AND CORONETS (all in 1949), THE LAVENDER HILL MOB, THE MAN IN THE WHITE SUIT (both in 1951), and THE LADYKILLERS (1955). The irony of Balcon's austere methods of production

---

[681]   For a helpful overview, see Alan Lovell, "The Unknown Cinema of Britain," CINEMA JOURNAL 11:2 (Spring 1972):1-8.

[682]   Wright, p.308.

[683]   George Perry, FOREVER EALING: A CELEBRATION OF THE GREAT BRITISH FILM STUDIO (London: Pavilion Books, 1981), p.111.

[684]   FOREVER EALING, p.111.

[685]   For more information, see "T. E. B. Clarke, Writer, Dies at 81," NEW YORK TIMES A (February 15, 1989):24.

[686]   Perry makes the insightful observation that one of Balcon's major weaknesses during the peak of his art was the producer's failure to discover and develop the talents of actresses. A case in point was the casting of Audrey Hepburn in a minor role in THE LAVENDER HILL MOB (1951). See FOREVER EALING, p.126.

[687]   An amusing example of Hollywood censorship is that WHISKEY GALORE was retitled TIGHT LITTLE ISLAND in America, because alcholic beverages could not appear in movie advertisements or on theater marquees.

and distribution, as Wright points out, was that they, rather than those of Rank or Korda, made the most money in the overseas market.[688]

Nevertheless, the British film industry's perennial distribution and exhibition woes caught up with Ealing Studios in the early 1950s. The restrictive mood that nourished the realistic-type Ealing comedies disappeared after 1951 and the remarkable unit began to disintegrate. At the same time, film attendance throughout the nation started to fall rapidly, not only because of the growing appeal of television, but also because of the shrinking number of movie theaters in Britain. In 1955, Ealing Studios was taken over by the BBC-TV and eventually disbanded.

In the decade that had passed since the end of the war, Britain could boast not only about its contributions to a new film style, but also about the production of a corps of film classics that gained a permanent place in film history.

BOOKS

GENERAL

Aldgate, Anthony, and Jeffrey Richards. BRITAIN CAN TAKE IT: THE BRITISH CINEMA IN THE SECOND WORLD WAR. New York: Basil Blackwell, 1986. Illustrated. 312pp.

Following the outbreak of war, Britain's cinemas closed down because of the fear that mass deaths might occur in crowded places as a result of enemy air raids. The theaters soon reopened but exhibitors, producers, and distributors faced problems from wartime government restrictions, bomb damage, an embargo on theater construction, and shortage of equipment, films, and staff. Nevertheless, as Aldgate points out in his superb opening chapters, the British film industry flourished during World War II. There were several reasons why. "There were approximately 4,800 cinemas in existence at the outbreak of the war and although a number of them were forced to close over the next six years, it has been estimated that 'the maximum number closed at any one stage of the war was probably never more than 10 per cent of the total.' To combat the shortfall in the supply of films (there was undoubtedly a considerable decline in the number of long films being registered, with 638 registered in the year immediately before the war but only 480 on average for each of the war years), the distributors suggested that the amount of programme changes could be reduced, and more use made of such simple expedients as the re-issuing of old films and giving some of the new films an extended run." The care with which the authors document their impressive narrative of this six-year period is maintained throughout the book's twelve chapters (each author is responsible for six chapters). Eleven key films--LET GEORGE DO IT (1940), 49TH PARALLEL, PIMPERNEL SMITH (both in 1941), NEXT OF KIN, THE YOUNG MR. PITT, WENT THE DAY WELL?, IN WHICH WE SERVE, THUNDER ROCK (all in 1942), FIRES WERE STARTED (1943), WESTERN APPROACHES/THE RAIDER (1944), and THE WAY TO THE STARS (1945)--are discussed in historical context and illustrate many of the issues on the mind of the British during the period. Endnotes, beautiful illustrations, a filmography of the eleven films, and an index are included. Recommended for special collections.

Chanan, Michael. LABOUR POWER IN THE BRITISH FILM INDUSTRY. New York: Zoetrope, 1976. 57pp.

---

[688]   Wright, p.309.

*DeFelice, James. FILMGUIDE TO "ODD MAN OUT." Bloomington: Indiana University Press, 1975. 85pp.

Durgnat, Raymond. A MIRROR FOR ENGLAND: BRITISH MOVIES FROM AUSTERITY TO INFLUENCE. New York: Praeger Publishers, 1971. Illustrated. 336pp.
    In this very interesting history of British films since 1945, Durgnat points out the significant contributions the English have made to the world cinema, starting with Lean's GREAT EXPECTATIONS (1947), and including the angry young men cycle--ROOM AT THE TOP (1958), LOOK BACK IN ANGER (1959) of the late 1950s up to the Hammer movies of the late 1960s. The author's twenty-five years of British history effectively covered in six chapters illustrate many of the major recurring themes that are "a mixture of cynical realism about society, working class references (the 'kitchen sink'), the 'New Morality,' 'Swinging London,' and stronger cosmopolitan influences, particularly via a renewed influx of American finance. Durgnat's dry writing style limits the book's popular appeal, but not its value to serious students. A bibliographical section, a filmography, a film artists index, foreign film artists and films index, and a other-name index are included. Well worth browsing.

*Kelly, Terence, with Graham Norton and George Perry. A COMPETITIVE CINEMA. London: The Institute of Economic Affairs, 1967. Illustrated. 204pp.
    Arguing that the economic woes of the British film industry are tied to business dealings of the nation's two major distributors (Rank and Associated British Cinemas (ABC), Kelly, Norton, and Perry also show the role played by American companies (e.g., Columbia, Disney, Twentieth Century-Fox, and United Artists are aligned with Rank; Warner Bros., Seven Arts, M-G-M and Paramount with ABC). The arguments are original, the recommendations intriguing, particularly the proposals for a film school.[689] Well worth browsing.

*Manvell, Roger. NEW CINEMA IN BRITAIN. New York: E. P. Dutton and Company, 1969. Illustrated. 160pp.
    This concise, readable, and well-illustrated guide to English film covers the period from 1946 to the end of the sixties. Manvell emphasizes the work of serious directors like Tony Richardson, Lindsay Anderson, and Karel Reisz. No bibliography or endnotes is provided, but a director's index is included. Worth browsing.

*Manvell, Roger, ed. THE CINEMA (1950, 1951, 1952). London: Penguin Books, 1950, 1951, 1952.
    These three paperback books provide a series of philosophical essays on motion pictures as an art form. The collection includes writings by Robert Flaherty, Basil Wright, Karel Reisz, Herbert Read, Carol Reed, David Lean, Sergei Eisenstein, and John Gillett. Well worth browsing.

Manvell, Roger, ed. THREE BRITISH SCREEN PLAYS: BRIEF ENCOUNTER, ODD MAN OUT, SCOTT OF THE ANTARCTIC, Foreword Frank Lauder. London: Methuen and Company, 1950. Illustrated. 299pp.

----

[689] For more information on the economic situation, read Bernard Hsura, "Patterns of Power," FILMS AND FILMING 10:7 (April 1964):49-56; Raymond Durgnat, "TV's Young Turks: Part One," ibid., 15:6 (March 1969):4-8, 10; and ___, ". . . Part Two," ibid., 15:7 (April 1969):26-30.

Perry, George. MOVIES FROM THE MANSION: A HISTORY OF PINEWOOD STUDIOS. London: Elm Tree Books, 1976. Illustrated. 191pp.

Pirie, David. HAMMER: A CINEMA CASE STUDY. London: British Film Institute, 1980.

*Taylor, John Russell, ed. MASTERWORKS OF THE BRITISH CINEMA: BRIEF ENCOUNTER, THE THIRD MAN, KIND HEARTS AND CORONETS, SATURDAY NIGHT AND SUNDAY MORNING. New York: Harper & Row, 1974. Illustrated. 352pp.
    "The two great legends about the British cinema," Taylor points out, "are that it has no auteurs and that its finest works are the products of the team spirit." A good introductory essay examines the issues of whether those legends are accurate, and if they are, what are the consequences for appreciating the art of British films. Cast and technical credits precede each film scripts. Well worth browsing.

*Vermilye, Jerry. THE GREAT BRITISH FILMS. Foreword Deborah Kerr. Secaucus: The Citadel Press, 1978. Illustrated. 255pp.
    Vermilye offers a thin review of Britain's "golden age" (1933-1971) by providing terse summaries of seventy-five films from THE PRIVATE LIFE OF HENRY VIII (1933), to THE GO-BETWEEN (1970). Cast and technical credits, handsome reproductions, and a superficial synopsis-critical essay make up this mainly picture-book history. No bibliography or index is included. Worth browsing.

Walker, Alexander. HOLLYWOOD, UK: THE BRITISH FILM INDUSTRY IN THE SIXTIES. New York: Stein and Day, 1974. Illustrated. 493pp.
    This highly informative study "is an attempt to illustrate the diversity of talents and motives, economic changes, historical accidents and occasional artistic achievements making up what was called the British film industry during a brief, turbulent part of its existence--the sixties." Walker draws upon his personal experiences, interviews with filmmakers, and published reports to offer a witty and entertaining social history of the decade's trends and iconography. Walker, an ex-film critic for the London EVENING STANDARD, divides his material into three major sections: "Look at Life," "Playtime," and "Sheer Fantasy." Footnotes, an industry chronology (1959-1970), and an index are included. Recommended for special collections.

Walker, Alexander. NATIONAL HEROES: BRITISH CINEMA IN THE SEVENTIES AND EIGHTIES. London: Joseph, 1985. Illustrated.

RICHARD BURTON

Alpert, Hollis. BURTON. New York: G. P. Putnam's Sons, 1986. Illustrated. 270pp.

Bragg, Melvyn. RICHARD BURTON: A LIFE. Boston: Little, Brown and Company, 1988. Illustrated. 533pp.

Cottrell, John, and Fergus Cashin. RICHARD BURTON: VERY CLOSE UP. Englewood Cliffs: Prentice-Hall, 1971. Illustrated. 385pp.

PETER FINCH

Faulkner, Trader. PETER FINCH: A BIOGRAPHY. Foreward Liv Ullmann. New York: Taplinger Publishing Company, 1979. Illustrated. 312pp.

STEWART GRANGER

*Granger, Stewart. SPARKS FLY UPWARD. New York: G. P. Putnam's Sons, 1981. Illustrated. 416pp.

ALEC GUINNESS

Tynan, Kenneth. ALEC GUINNESS. New York: The Macmillan Company, 1954. Illustrated. 108pp.

TREVOR HOWARD

Knight, Vivienne. TREVOR HOWARD: A GENTLEMAN AND A PLAYER. New York: Beaufort Books, 1986. Illustrated. 279pp.

JOHN MILLS

Bell, Mary Hayley. WHAT SHALL WE DO TOMORROW? Philadelphia: Lippincott, 1969. Illustrated. 235pp.

Mills, John. UP IN THE CLOUDS, GENTLEMEN PLEASE. New Haven: Ticknor and Fields, 1981. Illustrated. 290pp.

CAROL REED

Moss, Robert F. THE FILMS OF CAROL REED. New York: Columbia University Press, 1987. Illustrated. 312pp.

PETER SELLERS

Evans, Peter. PETER SELLERS: THE MASK BEHIND THE FACE. Englewood Cliffs: Prentice-Hall, 1968. Illustrated. 249pp.

Sellers, Michael, et al. P. S. I LOVE YOU: AN INTIMATE PORTRAIT OF PETER SELLERS. New York: E. P. Dutton, 1982. Illustrated. 239pp.

*Sylvester, Derek. PETER SELLERS. New York: Proteus, 1981. Illustrated. 128pp.

PETER USTINOV

*Thomas, Tony. USTINOV IN FOCUS. New York: A. S. Barnes and Company, 1971. Illustrated. 192pp.

FILMS

ANTHONY ASQUITH

THE BROWNING VERSION (Britain--16mm: 1951, 90 mins., b/w, sound, R-BUD, IMG, JAN, KIT, TWY)
Directed by Asquith, Terence Rattigan's screenplay (adapted from his play) focuses on a bitter classics teacher whose bad health forces him to retire from teaching and finally deal with his spiteful wife. In many respects the scenes of anger and duplicity foreshadow the picture of academia presented in WHO'S AFRAID OF VIRGINIA WOOLF? (1968). A great performance by Michael Redgrave keeps this film from being dated.

ALEC GUINNESS

KIND HEARTS AND CORONETS (Britain--16mm: 1949, 106 mins., b/w, sound, R-FES, FNC)
Roger Hammer directed and wrote the screenplay (with John Dighton) of this brilliant TOUR DE FORCE for Alec Guinness. The plot deals with the social outcast of a wealthy family who decides to murder every relative standing between him and the family fortune. Guinness plays eight parts. The biting and satiric farce is considered one of Ealing Studio's finest comedies.

THE LAVENDER HILL MOB (Britain--16mm: 1951, 80 mins., b/w, sound, R-BUD, FNC, IMA, KIT, ROA, TWY, WES, WHO)
Another brilliant example of Ealing comedies in the postwar period, T. E. B. Clarke's screenplay, directed by Charles Crichton, illustrates the effect of the realistic movement on British films. The story is about a gang's attempt to dispose of 100 million pounds in gold bars. Guinness gives a superb performance as the meek bankteller who masterminds the robbery.[690]

THE MAN IN THE WHITE SUIT (16mm: 1951, 85 mins., b/w, sound, R-CCC, CON, ROA, TWF, TWY/L-TWY)
Another classic Guinness film, this time it's about a chemist's discovery of a presumably indestructible material that threatens the existence of the garment industry. Alexander Mackendrick directed[691] and co-authored the screenplay with John Dighton and Roger MacDougall (based upon MacDougall's play).

DAVID LEAN

BREAKING THE SOUND BARRIER (Britain--16mm: 1952, 109 mins., b/w, sound, R-FNC)

---

[690] Douglas McVay, "Gallery of Great Artists: Alec Guinness," FILMS AND FILMING 7:8 (May 1961):12-13, 36; and Aljean Harmetz, "For Film Director, 78, a Second Wind of Success,' NEW YORK TIMES C (MARCH 20, 1989):13, 18.

[691] J. B. Hoare, "The Man In the White Suit," SCREEN EDUCATION YEARBOOK (1960-1961), pp.21-3.

Scripted by Terrence Rattigan, this David Lean film explores the human conflicts of people interested in conquering the difficulties in flying faster than the speed of sound. The thoughtful movie makes a powerful argument for continuing to search for answers about the unknown, even though lives may be lost. Strong performances are given by Ralph Richardson[692] and Ann Todd.

BRIEF ENCOUNTER (Britain--16mm: 1946, 99 mins., b/w, sound, R-BUD, FES, KIT, TWY)

Scripted by Noel Coward and based on his stage play, this remarkably restrained romance between two middle-aged people who remain married to other spouses not only points up how much morality has changed since the end of World War II, but also remains one of the most sensitive films about the conflicts between love and guilt. It is superbly acted by Trevor Howard[693] and Celia Johnson.[694]

EMERIC PRESSBURGER AND MICHAEL POWELL

THE RED SHOES (Britain--16mm: 1948, 139 mins., color or b/w, sound, R-ARC, BUD, FNC, IMA, TWY, WES, WEL, WHO)

The producer Emeric Pressburger and the director Michael Powell's adaptation of a Hans Christian Anderson tale is another example of England's postwar interest literary or dramatic translations. Together with Keith Winter, the famous producer and director fashioned a heart rendering screenplay that was photographed memorably by Jack Cardiff, edited by Reginald Mills, and choreographed by Robert Helpmann. It is one of the most beautifully photographed color films ever made, and the ballet scenes have yet to be surpassed.[695] Outstanding performances are given by Anton Walbrook, Moira Shearer, Robert Helpmann, Ludmilla Tcherina, and Leonide Massine.

CAROL REED

ODD MAN OUT (Britain--16mm: 1947, 117 mins., b/w, sound, R-BUD, FNC, IMA, JAN, KIT, TWY)

Scripted by F. L. Green and R. C. Sherriff, the plot deals with the fatal wounding of an Irish revolutionary (James Mason) during a bank robbery, the dying man's last hours, and the manner in which it affects the lives of others. It is considered to be one of the best films in the postwar period and is a fine example of how English films tried to relate the characters on the screen to real-life situations. Carol Reed's direction not only uses Belfast to excellent dramatic advantage in depicting the search for the protagonist, but also gets a remarkable performance from his cast.

---

[692] Alan A. Coulson, "Ralph Richardson," FILMS IN REVIEW 20:8 (October 1959):457-72.

[693] Richard Whitehall, "Gallery of Great Artists: Trevor Howard," FILMS AND FILMING 7:5 (February 1961):12-13, 36; and A. R. Fulton, MOTION PICTURES: THE DEVELOPMENT OF AN ART FROM SILENT FILMS TO THE AGE OF TELEVISION (Norman: University of Oklahoma Press, 1970), pp.214-26.

[694] Douglas McVay, "Lean--Lover of Life," FILMS AND FILMING 5:11 (August 1959):9-10, 34.

[695] Marian Eames, "Gray Thoughts on RED SHOES," FILMS IN REVIEW 1:9 (December 1950):20-24.

HOLLYWOOD IN THE POSTWAR YEARS (1945-1955)

The cultural, political, and economic forces shaping a new world dramatically and drastically revolutionized the American film industry.[696] At first, no one in Hollywood realized that the resurgence of national cinemas in Europe, the labor strikes in Hollywood, the red-baiting activities in Congress, and America's changing attitudes toward leisure-time pursuits would have any significant effect on the wealthiest and most powerful film industry in the world. As discussed in Chapters 3 and 5, Hollywood's ability to survive the financial problems caused by the Depression and World War II made its filmmakers arrogant about their achievements and overly confident about their future. After all, Hollywood films had scored their biggest box-office success in 1946,[697] and the major companies were making big money distributing their backlog of movies to the newly reopened European and Asian markets.

To paraphrase Charles Dickens, Hollywood's best of times was also its worst of times.[698] In June of 1946, the government finally punctured the film industry's oligopolistic balloon. The five major companies--Loew's, Inc., Paramount, Warner Bros., 20th Century-Fox, and RKO--and the three minors--Columbia, Universal, and United Artists--were enjoined by the federal courts in nine areas, including special arrangements for minimum price fixing, formula deals, clearances, block booking, and pooling agreements. As discussed in Chapter 3, the government's victory in the PARAMOUNT antitrust case destroyed Hollywood's vertical system and made the film business more competitive in production, distribution, and exhibition.

The immediate impact of the PARAMOUNT antitrust case was felt at every level of the industry. Not only was there a massive increase in unemployment and a sharp decline in production, but also expensive film formulas (e.g., musicals, war films,

---

[696] Two useful articles on Hollywood in the Forties are John Russell Taylor, "The High 40's," SIGHT AND SOUND 30:4 (Autumn 1961):988-91; and Barry Salt, "Film Style and Technology In the Forties," FILM QUARTERLY 31:1 (Fall 1977):46-57. Some useful articles on Hollywood in the 1950s are the following: Penelope Houston, "Hollywood In the Age of Television," SIGHT AND SOUND 26:4 (Spring 1957):175-9; John Gillett, "The Survivors," ibid., 28:3-4 (Summer-Autumn 1959):150-5; Theodore Huff, "Hollywood on Hollywood," FILMS IN REVIEW 4:4 (April 1953):171-83; Colin Young, "The Hollywood War of Independence," FILM QUARTERLY 12:3 (Spring 1959):4-15; and ___, "The Old Dependables," ibid., 13:1 (Fall 1959):2-17.

[697] Charles Champlin points out that "Estimates vary widely, but a reasonable calculation is that in 1946 the movies in the United States drew an average of 90 million customers each week. The Department of Commerce figure on the total box-office receipts for that year is a shade under $1.7 billion. The number of films produced in Hollywood had dropped from 546 in 1942 to 425 in 1946, but the film rentals received by Hollywood, so FORTUNE magazine figured, had increased from $300 million to $400 million in the same years." See *Charles Champlin, THE MOVIES GROW UP 1940-1980 (Chicago: Swallow Press, 1981), p.18.

[698] Champlin makes a similar observation, pointing out (p.23) that "Production shrank from 425 films in 1946 to 405 in 1948, slipped further to 354 in 1953, and to fewer than 300 in 1954. Those 90 million admissions a week in 1946 had dropped to 46 million in 1954, on their way to a low of around 17 million tickets a week at the start of the 1970s." He goes on to say (p.31) that "By one estimate, movie-theater attendance dropped by more than half in the decade between 1946 and 1956. By another estimate, one-fourth of the 19,000 theaters in the United States closed between 1946 and 1953."

and historical epics) got shelved and low-budget dramas became stylish.[699] In addition, many people in the industry took twenty-five percent pay cuts, and studios began to disband their stable of stars, producers, directors, and screenwriters.[700] This austerity shift immediately put a number of the "B"-production companies out of business, with more to follow in the 1950s.

Every major company felt its fortunes dwindling, save one: United Artists. Not having a stable of high-paid personnel, lacking a large theater circuit, and being devoid of studio facilities finally paid off for the maverick corporation. While other companies tried to reduce their mammoth overheads, the unencumbered United Artists continued its film-by-film operations. It warmed quickly to the modern "package deals," and by the 1950s became the prototype of the new Hollywood.[701]

The government also moved against Hollywood in other ways. The Justice Department went after Technicolor and Eastman Kodak for price fixing and monopolizing the market for color raw stock and processing. In 1947, the House Un-American Activities Committee (HUAC) reopened its deliberations on communists in the film industry.[702] One year later, the United States Supreme Court ruled that the lower court had not gone far enough in its attempt to destroy the oligopolistic nature of the film industry and insisted that theaters must not be owned by film producers. In 1949, Paramount Pictures, Inc. separated into two companies: one for production, one for distribution. Over the next decade, as more divestitures took place, new theater circuits emerged and star working with independent filmmakers and the once all-powerful production companies. By 1958, all of the defendants of the PARAMOUNT antitrust case (with the exception of Warner Bros.) had undergone major changes in management. The key to the future success of the big film companies was now in distribution rather than in production.

---

[699] A major exception was Arthur Freed's production, THE PIRATE (1948). The success of this big-budget MGM musical gave rise to a series of lavish spectaculars in the 1950s that mark the high point of this important Hollywood genre.

[700] An important contributing factor to the disbanding of the studio system's stable of performers was Olivia de Havilland's court case against Jack Warner. In simplified terms, the star had completed her seven-year contract with Warner Bros. in 1943. But because of her refusal to do certain roles, she had undergone several suspensions, thereby "extending" the duration of her contract by two years. In effect, Warner was still trying to loan her out to RKO and Columbia in 1945. "The issue, as Rudy Behlmer explains, "was whether or not seven years meant calendar years or years of work." The parties in question filed competing suits. Warner accused the star of failing to live up to her contract; she countered by claiming Warner was in violation of a California law that limited contracts to seven years. In early 1945, the Supreme Court of California made a landmark decision, ruling in favor of De Havilland. It was this decision that opened the door to the exodus of key personnel from the studios. In Behlmer's words, "The seven-year law was called the Anti-Peonage law and the calendar year ruling is referred to as the 'de Havilland decision in the law books." See *Rudy Behlmer, ed., INSIDE WARNER BROS. (1935-1951) (New York: Viking Penguin, 1985), pp.234-5.

[701] A major reason for the success of United Artists in the 1950s was the company's new management team of Arthur Krim and Robert Benjamin. These young and aggressive lawyers, who remained in office until 1978, put their emphasis on film financing and left the creative decisions to the filmmakers. For more information, see Chapters 3 and 6.

[702] For important information on blacklisting, see Chapter 5. See also Kim Yost, "Scarlet Women: The Depiction of Female Communists In Hollywood Film," FILAMENT 4 (1984):19-21.

The restructuring of the American film industry also occurred in the area of film content.[703] Longtime fans of genre movies like westerns and science-fiction films saw the formulas becoming more complex and responsive to the effects of the postwar period. As discussed elsewhere, the conventions of the western in movies like DUEL IN THE SUN, MY DARLING CLEMENTINE (both in 1946), FORT APACHE, RED RIVER (both in 1948), SHE WORE A YELLOW RIBBON (1949), RIO GRANDE, THE GUNFIGHTER, BROKEN ARROW, WINCHESTER '73, (all in 1950), HIGH NOON, BEND OF THE RIVER (both in 1952), and SHANE (1953) took on "adult" themes of racism, moral ambiguity, and the questioning of authority.[704] Similar revolutions were taking place in science-fiction films like DESTINATION MOON (1950), FIVE, THE THING, THE DAY THE EARTH STOOD STILL (all in 1951), THE BEAST FROM TWENTY THOUSAND FATHOMS, IT CAME FROM OUTER SPACE, THE WAR OF THE WORLDS, INVADER FROM MARS (all in 1953), and THEM (1954).[705]

Spurred on by economic, social, and political considerations, as well as from the growing popularity of neo-realism and the influx of foreign films on American screens[706], Hollywood in the mid- to late-1940s responded most positively to directors who applied the principles of documentary filmmaking to the commercial feature film. The order of the day became smaller casts, location shooting, and socially conscious themes. In addition, a number of "new" directors--e.g., Jules Dassin, Edward Dmytryk, Elia Kazan, Joseph Losey, Robert Rossen, Don Siegel, and Fred Zinnemann--(the last corps of directors to be trained in the studio system) imbued their "problem" films with a psychological twist that altered the traditional acting styles of Hollywood performers. As discussed in Chapter 3, two of the most prominent "problem" film topics of the post-war period were anti-Semitism--e.g., TILL THE END OF TIME (1946), CROSSFIRE, GENTLEMAN'S AGREEMENT (both in 1947)--and race relations--PINKY, HOME OF THE BRAVE, LOST BOUNDARIES, INTRUDER IN THE DUST (all in 1949), and NO WAY OUT (1950). Other areas of sociological and psychological dealt with the problems of returning veterans--e.g., THE BEST YEARS OF OUR LIVES (1946), THE MEN (1950), BRIGHT VICTORY (1951); mental illness--THE LOST WEEKEND (1945), SMASH-UP (1947), THE SNAKE PIT (1948); and corruption in the boxing world--BODY AND SOUL (1947), THE SET-UP, and CHAMPION (both in 1949).[707] "The difference between the Thirties and the post-war period in respect of films about American social problems," as Wright observes, "was, in broad terms, the difference between concentration and diffusion."[708] No longer

---

[703]   Rhode makes the intriguing point (p.436) that Hollywood reshaped much of its film content because it wanted "to reconcile the need to report accurately on the condition of society with the need to describe the more mature post-war conception of human personality." In hindsight, Rhode views the film capital's attempts as basically weak and concludes (p.437) that most of the films of the period were "on the level of sophisticated prattle. . . ."

[704]   Frank Manchel, CAMERAS WEST (Englewood Cliffs: Prentice-Hall, 1971), pp.108-16.

[705]   For more information, see Frank Manchel, AN ALBUM OF GREAT SCIENCE FICTION FILMS, Rev. ed. (New York: Franklin Watts, 1982), pp.31-7.

[706]   Worth remembering is that a number of prominent foreign directors working in Hollywood but soon to return to Europe did their their best work between 1945 and 1950: e.g., Jean Renoir's THE SOUTHERNER (1945), Max Ophuls's LETTER FROM AN UNKNOWN WOMAN (1948), and CAUGHT (1949).

[707]   For further elaboration, see Frank Manchel, GREAT SPORTS MOVIES (New York: Franklin Watts, 1980), pp.34-41.

[708]   Wright, p.364.

did the filmmakers limit their cinematic examinations to a specific place or particular period. The post-war films extended their attacks to American society and to institutional weaknesses. These modern sociological and psychological dramas, with their on-location shooting schedules and probing characterizations, stimulated the development of new and lighter camera and sound equipment, novel recording techniques, and new panchromatic film stock that produced more dramatic black-and-white contrasts.

Nowhere was the influence of the documentary more noticeable than in gangster films and spy stories. As discussed elsewhere,[709] the emphasis was on a more complex characterization of heroes and villains. A case in point is the contrast between THE MALTESE FALCON (1941) and THE BIG SLEEP (1946). The pre-WWII film had an amoral and sentimental Sam Spade worried about his reputation and fighting cultured crooks and effeminate hoodlums. The post-WWII film had a tough but compassionate Philip Marlowe concerned more about survival, than about money, and up against fashionable gamblers and ruthless blackmailers.[710] The issues were less clear-cut and the relationships among people blurred the boundaries of good and evil. In a sense, it was becoming harder to recognize the heroes. Everyone seemed corrupt. Morality became a relative notion, not easily defined, and tied to circumstances. Families, friends, and sweethearts no longer could be trusted. Trapped by fate and terrified by events they seemed unable to control, the big-city protagonists struggled to find a solution to their inexplicable dilemmas. Existentialism had taken hold of· screen values, and movies explored heretofore forbidden film territory.

At the heart of the "new realism" that also linked THE MALTESE FALCON with THE BIG SLEEP was a film style labeled FILM NOIR.[711] Although there are many opinions on what the label signifies, Jon Tuska's explanation of the style's intentions

---

[709]   Frank Manchel, GANGSTERS ON THE SCREEN (New York: Franklin Watts, 1978), pp.61-78.

[710]   For a useful overview, see Julian Symons, "Philip Marlows: Which Is Chandler's Ideal Detective? The Case of Raymond Chandler," NEW YORK TIMES MAGAZINE (December 23, 1973):12-3, 22, 25, 27.

[711]   For useful information, see *Bruce Crowther, FILM NOIR: REFLECTIONS IN A DARK MIRROR (London: Columbus Books, 1988; *Foster Hirsch, THE DARK SIDE OF THE SCREEN: FILM NOIR (San Diego: A. S. Barnes and Company, 1981); *E. Ann Kaplan, ed., WOMEN IN FILM NOIR (London: British Film Institute, 1978); Amir Massoud Karimi, TOWARD A DEFINITION OF THE AMERICAN FILM NOIR (1941-1949) (New York: Arno Press, 1976); Robert Ottoson, A REFERENCE GUIDE TO THE AMERICAN FILM NOIR: 1940-1958 (Metuchen: The Scarecrow Press, 1981); Jon Tuska, DARK CINEMA: AMERICAN FILM NOIR IN CULTURAL PERSPECTIVE (Westport: Greenwood Press, 1984); *Alain Silver and Elizabeth Ward, FILM NOIR: AN ENCYCLOPEDIC REFERENCE TO THE AMERICAN FILM STYLE (Woodstock: Overlook Press, 1979); James Damico, "FILM NOIR: A Modest Proposal," FILM READER 3, ed. Bruce Jenkins et al. (Evanston: Northwestern University, 1978), pp.48-57; Raymond Borde and Etienne Chaumeton, "The Sources of FILM NOIR," ibid., pp.58-66; Jonathan Buchsbaum, "Tame Wolves and Phony Claims: Paranoia and FILM NOIR," PERSISTENCE OF VISION 3/4 (Summer 1986):35-47; R. Barton Palmer, "FILM NOIR and the Genre Continuum," ibid., pp.51-60; Richard Maltby, "FILM NOIR: The Politics of the Maladjusted Text," JOURNAL OF AMERICAN STUDIES 18 (1984):49-71; Raymond Durgnat, "Paint It Black: The Family Tree of FILM NOIR," CINEMA (August 1970):49-56; Tom Flinn, "Three Faces of FILM NOIR," THE VELVET LIGHT TRAP 5 (Summer 1972):11-6; Robert G. Porfiro, "No Way Out: Existential Motifs in the FILM NOIR," SIGHT AND SOUND 45:4 (Autumn 1976):212-7; John S. Whitney, "A Filmography of FILM NOIR," JOURNAL OF POPULAR FILM 5:3-4 (1976):321-71; Dale E. Ewing, Jr., "FILM NOIR: Style and Content," ibid., 16:2 (Summer 1988):60-9; Paul Kerr, "Out Of What Past? Notes on the 'B' Film Noir," SCREEN EDUCATION 32-33 (Autumn/Winter 1979/80):45-65; Paul Schrader, "Notes on

offers a good starting point: "FILM NOIR is . . . a darkling vision of the world, a view from the underside, born of fundamental disillusionment perhaps, but also invariably the result, no matter how timid, of a confrontation with nihilism."[712] Clearly, FILM NOIR's ancestry can be traced back to literary sources, the pessimism that grew out of two world wars, and the emergence of a hard-boiled detective fiction during the 1930s. Moreover, good arguments can be made that indicated that American FILM NOIR movies surfaced before the end of World War II: e.g., STRANGER ON THE THIRD FLOOR (1940), CITIZEN KANE, HIGH SIERRA, THE MALTESE FALCON (all in 1941), THE GLASS KEY, THIS GUN FOR HIRE (both in 1942), THE FALLEN SPARROW (1943), DOUBLE INDEMNITY, GASLIGHT, MURDER, MY SWEET (all in 1944), CORNERED, JOHNNY ANGEL, and MILDRED PIERCE (all in 1945).

Wherever one places FILM NOIR's origins, the style itself flourished in the post-WWII era. In crime melodramas from THE BIG SLEEP, THE DARK MIRROR, THE POSTMAN ALWAYS RINGS TWICE, and GILDA, (all in 1946) to BORN TO KILL, CROSSFIRE, THEY WON'T BELIEVE ME (all in 1947), THE NAKED CITY, THE LADY FROM SHANGHAI, THE NIGHT HAS A THOUSAND EYES, SORRY, WRONG NUMBER (all in 1948), D.O.A., THEY LIVE BY NIGHT, WHITE HEAT (all in 1949), and THE ASPHALT JUNGLE (1950), ordinary people, living in a moral vacuum and moving about in a hostile world symbolized by dark and lonely streets, cheated, lied, lusted after and murdered family and friends. Many of these monuments to human corruption were directed by European exiles--e.g., Dieterle, Lang, Preminger, Siodmak, Wilder--who first broke into movies during the German expressionist era and then fled their homelands when Hitler rose to power. The combination of their personal cynicism and the low-key lighting used on location shooting intensified the impression that FILM NOIR captured the mood of city life in the postwar period. In addition, as discussed in Chapter 3, feminist critics argue that the consistent images of dark women, spider women, and evil seductresses who pervade FILM NOIR in films like THE MALTESE FALCON, DOUBLE INDEMNITY, MILDRED PIERCE, and GILDA epitomize male fantasies of women terrified by the age in which they are first cut off from their men and forced into non-traditional roles as a result of World War II and then forcibly displaced from their new responsibilities when the war was over and perceived as un-American if they didn't resume their domestic roles.

The destabilization of the film industry, the restructuring of the filmmaking process, the widespread cynicism evident in FILM NOIR, the fear of an atomic apocalypse, the industry paranoia that the government would regulate American films, and the cold war, all contributed to renewed interest in film censorship. Hays resigned as the film czar in 1945 and was succeeded by the virulent anti-Communist Eric Johnston, who renamed the industry's self-censorship office, the Motion Picture Association of America (MPAA). Over the next decade, the MPAA's code faced challenges from liberals and independent producers who felt that many of its religious, political, and sexual taboos were outdated. What made these challenges so threatening was that the PARAMOUNT case had undermined the authority of the MPAA. So long as the studios owned the theater circuits, they not only made films that kept the theater owners happy, but also controlled, through the MPPA, what the theaters exhibited. The breakup of the vertical system, therefore, altered production policies and undermined the MPAA's authority over theaters.

At first, however, it looked as if economic problems and political threats would keep the STATUS QUO in operation throughout the late 1940s and 1950s. A major contributing factor was the blacklisting that took place in the industry, beginning in 1949 and carrying through into the 1960s. As discussed in Chapter 5, many screen personalities--e.g., Charles Chaplin, Jules Dassin, Carl Foreman, John Garfield,

---

FILM NOIR," FILM COMMENT 8:1 (Spring 1972):8-13; and Janey A. Place and L. S. Peterson, "Some Visual Motifs of FILM NOIR," ibid., 10: 1 (January-February 1974):30-2.

[712] Tuska, p.xvi.

Lillian Hellman, Joseph Losey, Larry Parks, Dalton Trumbo, and Michael Wilson--either were forced out of the Hollywood system or, in the case of the screenwriters, used a "front" to get their work produced. Thus it became easier to intimidate creative people into following the "rules." Some producers even tried releasing anti-Red movies--e.g., GUILTY OF TREASON, THE RED MENACE, I MARRIED A COMMUNIST,[713] THE RED DANUBE (all in 1949), I WAS A COMMUNIST FOR THE FBI (1951), WALK EAST ON BEACON, THE STEEL FIST, RED SNOW, BIG JIM MCLAIN, THE HOAXERS, and MY SON JOHN (all in 1952). Although the Motion Picture Academy of Arts and Sciences indicated the influence of such films--e.g., Oscar nominations went to THE RED DANUBE for Best Art Direction-Set Direction; I WAS A COMMUNIST FOR THE FBI, Best Feature Documentary; MY SON JOHN, Best Writing; THE HOAXSERS, Best Feature Documentary, these types of films proved unpopular at the box office and the formula slowly disappeared.[714]

The turning point came in the 1950s, as the courts and the public became disenchanted with Hollywood's policies. In 1952, the United States Supreme Court's decision on the exhibition of THE MIRACLE (1948) set in motion sweeping and profound reforms. An Italian import, THE MIRACLE had opened in New York and Joseph Burstyn, its American distributor, found himself embroiled in a battle with the New York Board of Regents. The local censoring body objected to the film's "religious" values and banned the picture. As discussed in Chapter 3, the United States Supreme Court not only ruled in Burstyn's favor, but also appeared to overturn a 1915 decision that excluded movies from the protection of the First and Fourteenth amendments. Although the decision dealt only with the issue of religion not being sufficient to censor a film, the Court's behavior encouraged more censorship fights. Over the next six years, other cases struck at the heart of state and municipal censorship policies. By the mid-1950s, external censorship against the film industry was declining rapidly.

At the same time, Hollywood insiders took on the industry's self-regulating mechanisms. For example, Otto Preminger and United Artists embarrassed the MPAA when they fought the censor's decision not to award a Seal of Approval to THE MOON IS BLUE (1953). Arguing that their film had nothing harmful in its treatment of adultery, Preminger and United Artists released the film (the first major movie to be distributed without the MPAA's approval since the establishment of the Breen Office in 1934) and won support from the public. Three years later, the filmmaker and United Artists again refused to accept the MPAA's decision not to give THE MAN WITH A GOLDEN ARM (1956) a Seal of Approval. Once more, Preminger and United Artists took their case to the public, and the MPAA's credibility continued to erode as the movie made big money to the box office.[715] Incidents like these eventually led to the demise of the code by the mid-1960s. Moreover, the power of the witch-hunters began to ebb by the end of the decade and a number of people on the blacklist began getting jobs again in the industry. (Regrettably, elements of blacklisting continue to the present, as Judy Chaiken made clear in her 1987 TV documentary, LEGACY OF THE BLACKLIST.)

But the greatest threat of the period came from television. By 1952, the new medium began coast-to-coast operations, thereby increasing the pressure on the city of dreams, which was facing tremendous economic problems. Declining audiences, the

---

[713]   Harry Wasserman, "Ideological Gunfight at the RKO Corral: Notes on Howard Hughes' I MARRIED A COMMUNIST," THE VELVET LIGHT TRAP 11 (Winter 1974):7-11.

[714]   For an interesting commentary on how Soviet filmmakers found themselves making anti-American films during the postwar period, see THE LONG VIEW, p.421.

[715]   Ellis correctly points out (p.284) that although United Artist was quite self-righteous about its motives (going so far as to resign from the MPPA during the years it exhibited the two films), the company "rejoined after it had collected all of its profits from the two offending films."

re-emergence of national cinemas, overseas tariffs and quotas, government anti-Communist investigations, antitrust litigation, increasing production costs, and shrinking profits had the once mighty Hollywood on the verge of a complete breakdown. Added to all these problems was the rapidly increasing number of TV sets in American homes. Within two years, the new medium would become the number one form of popular entertainment in America. In the meantime, the moguls refused to deal with the phenomenon. Not only did most of the moguls refuse to invest in TV, but they also strongly discouraged their employees from working in the new medium. Jack Warner allegedly forbid his people to own TV sets in the late 1940s.

As discussed in Chapter 3, film producers searched for a novelty so as to get back their customers. The new attraction was widescreens featuring blockbuster productions in glowing color, with hi-fidelity sound and a greater sense of visual depth. In 1952, Cinerama and 3-D movies reappeared. One year later, 20th Century-Fox brought out CinemaScope. Paramount retaliated with VistaVision in 1954, the same year that exhibitors began to organize once more against a new common enemy: television. The war of anamorphic lenses (i.e., compressing an image in shooting a film and then "expanding it" during projection) and wider screens with greater depth illusion was expanded in 1955, when Mike Todd, an independent producer, unveiled his Todd-AO, a 70mm non-anamorphic aperture, in Zinnemann's blockbuster adaptation of OKLAHOMA.

While each of these technological innovations had its own strengths and weaknesses,[716] the strategy of making big films with stunning color, hi-fidelity sound, and greater depth illusion paid off at the box office. The top moneymaking films of the period were SAMSON AND DELILAH (1950), DAVID AND BATHSHEBA (1951), THE GREATEST SHOW ON EARTH (1952), THE ROBE (1953), WHITE CHRISTMAS (1954), and CINERAMA HOLIDAY (1954).[717] With the exception of WHITE CHRISTMAS (a film made in the United States), what made these "runaway" films (co-national movies produced with multinational personnel outside the United States) especially attractive to American filmmakers is that they not only did well (commercially and aesthetically) at home, but also helped solve the problem of how to spend foreign revenues derived from overseas distribution but "frozen" in the European countries. In fact, as discussed in Chapter 3, the success of these productions led to an American "invasion" of overseas cinemas, resulting in the establishment of multinational film corporations and a Hollywood stranglehold on the international financing of films.

One major content change resulting from the blockbuster films and from the technological revolutions was a rethinking of what constituted the art of the moving picture. The formal theories of the silent era had been replaced by the realism of the postwar period, or as Cook states, a "new film aesthetic based upon composition in width and depth, or MISE EN SCENE, rather than upon montage."[718] In simplified terms, the new approach focused on "long takes" or on extended sequences, rather than on assembling the film in the editing room. The emphasis was now on authenticity rather than on cutting techniques. While it is clear that realism had always been

---

[716]   Cook points out (pp.421-2) that wide-film systems cost exhibitors too much money for the limited number of films made for the process and thus the various systems--e.g., Todd-AO and Cinerama--are used for "roadshow" productions (exclusive screenings at special prices in specific cities). Of particular significance, however, is that the experimentation in the 1950s resulted "in a nearly total conversion from optical to magnetic sound recording (though sound was still played back optically in exhibition)."

[717]   *Patrick Robinson, MOVIE FACTS AND FEATS: A GUINNESS RECORD BOOK (New York: Sterling Publishing Company, 1980), p.45.

[718]   Cook, p.423.

present in films, what was novel about the widescreen aesthetic was that it elevated deep-focus photography and long-takes to the forefront of the film world.

But by 1955, Hollywood knew its days as the king of entertainment were over. One by one, the film studios began unloading their old movies on television and buying into the new medium. For the first time in decades, AVANT-GARDE artists, new performers, and independent filmmakers in America appeared to gain the upper hand in the film industry.[719] Not only did individuals make personal films, but the New York "underground" searched for new areas of technique and subject matter. Financially, appearances were deceiving. As discussed in Chapter 3, the real power was still held by the major companies who not only controlled distribution, but also the money flowing from the banks. Few investors were (or are) willing to put money into a film project that didn't have the backing of a major company.[720] Aesthetically, however, fresh faces and approaches to filmmaking appeared everywhere in the commercial cinema, and filmmakers like James Broughton, Stan Brakhage, James Davis, Maya Deren, Elia Kazan, Joseph Losey, Delbert Mann, Burt Lancaster, Anthony Mann, Jonas Mekas, Nicholas Ray, Robert Rossen, Don Siegel, Douglas Sirk, John Sturges, Robert Wise, and Fred Zinnemann; as well as stars like Marlon Brando, Ernest Borgnine, Montgomery Clift, Doris Day, James Dean, Kirk Douglas, Audrey Hepburn, Judy Holliday, Angela Lansbury, Janet Leigh, Jerry Lewis, Dean Martin, Robert Mitchum, Marilyn Monroe, Sidney Poitier, Anthony Quinn, and Elizabeth Taylor offered new challenges to the older, more recognized Hollywood personalities.

In fairness to the veteran directors,[721] they not only adjusted to the times, but also did some of their finest work: e.g. George Cukor--A DOUBLE LIFE (1947), ADAM'S RIB (1949), BORN YESTERDAY (1951), PAT AND MIKE (1952), A STAR IS BORN (1954); Jules Dassin--BRUTE FORCE (1948), THE NAKED CITY (1949);[722] Walt Disney--TREASURE ISLAND (1950), THE ADVENTURES OF ROBIN HOOD (1952),

---

[719] Leonard J. Leff points out that the changing nature of the Hollywood labor force contributed to the rise of the independent movement. "In 1945," he explains, fewer than one quarter of the working members of the screen Actors Guild and the Screen Directors Guild were under contract to one of the major companies." See *Leonard J. Leff, HITCHCOCK AND SELZNICK: THE RICH AND STRANGE COLLABORATION OF ALFRED HITCHCOCK AND DAVID O. SELZNICK IN HOLLYWOOD (New York: Weidenfeld and Nicolson, 1987), p.268. Another contributing factor was the deal that MCA agent Lew Wasserman negotiated for his client Jimmy Stewart in the making of WINCHESTER '73 (1950). According to Allen Eyles, Universal didn't believe that Stewart had the right image to play a tough cowboy. Wasserman countered by proposing a unique Hollywood deal. For the first time, Eyles points out, "an actor participated in the profits [of a film] instead of being paid a regular salary or flat fee." Universal accepted the offer, thinking it could save a bundle of money, and in the end lost hundreds of thousands of dollars on the deal. The arrangement helped transform the packaging of Hollywood movies. See Allen Eyles, JAMES STEWART (New York: Stein and Day, 1984), p.99. For other interpretations, see HOLLYWOOD IN TRANSITION, p.53; and Michael Pye, MOGULS: INSIDE THE BUSINESS OF SHOW BUSINESS (New York: Holt, Rinehart and Winston, 1980), pp.45-7.

[720] For examples of how the need for financial "security" changed the relationship among film, Broadway, and television, see Robert McLaughlin, BROADWAY AND HOLLYWOOD: A HISTORY OF ECONOMIC INTERACTION (New York: Arno Press, 1974); and Andrew Dowdy, "MOVIES ARE BETTER THAN EVER": WIDE-SCREEN MEMORIES OF THE FIFTIES (New York: William Morrow and Company, 1973), pp.206-12.

[721] Famous foreign directors who did not fare well in the post-WWII era included Fritz Lang, Ernst Lubitsch, and Jean Renoir. For more information, see Champlin, pp.34-5.

[722] As a result of the Hollywood witch-hunts, Dassin left America at the end of the

THE LIVING DESERT, PETER PAN (both in 1953), 20,000 LEAGUES UNDER THE SEA (1954); John Ford--MY DARLING CLEMENTINE (1946), FORT APACHE (1948), SHE WORE A YELLOW RIBBON (1949), THE QUIET MAN (1952); Henry Hathaway--THE HOUSE ON 92nd STREET (1945); KISS OF DEATH (1947), CALL NORTHSIDE 777 (1948), THE DESERT FOX (1951); Howard Hawks--THE BIG SLEEP (1946), RED RIVER (1948), I WAS A MALE WAR BRIDE (1949), THE THING (1951), GENTLEMEN PREFER BLONDES; Alfred Hitchcock--STRANGERS ON A TRAIN (1951), REAR WINDOW (1954), TO CATCH A THIEF (1955); John Huston--THE TREASURE OF THE SIERRA MADRE (1948), THE ASPHALT JUNGLE (1950), THE RED BADGE OF COURAGE, THE AFRICAN QUEEN (both in 1951); Henry King--TWELVE O'CLOCK HIGH, THE GUNFIGHTER (both in 1950), THE SNOWS OF KILIMANJARO (1952), LOVE IS A MANY-SPLENDORED THING; Fritz Lang--RANCHO NOTORIOUS (1952), THE BIG HEAT (1953); Joseph L. Mankiewicz--A LETTER TO THREE WIVES (1949), ALL ABOUT EVE (1950), FIVE FINGERS (1952); Vincente Minelli--THE PIRATE (1948), FATHER OF THE BRIDE (1950), AN AMERICAN IN PARIS (1951), THE BAD AND THE BEAUTIFUL (1952), THE BAND WAGON (1953); George Stevens--A PLACE IN THE SUN (1952), SHANE (1953); Billy Wilder--THE LOST WEEKEND (1945), SUNSET BOULEVARD (1950), STALAG 17 (1953); and William Wyler--THE BEST YEARS OF OUR LIVES (1946), WASHINGTON SQUARE (1949), CARRIE (1952), ROMAN HOLIDAY (1953). Many of these memorable films starred veteran actors doing some of their best work: e.g., Fred Astaire, Humphrey Bogart, Gary Cooper, Bette Davis, Judy Garland, Olivia De Havilland, Katharine Hepburn, William Holden, Gene Kelly, Alan Ladd, Gregory Peck, Otto Preminger, James Stewart, and John Wayne.

Thus, as the fifties hit their mid-point, the Hollywood of old was confronting the new challenges of television, divestiture, and foreign threats with a healthy reliance on dependable formulas revitalized with new stars and approaches, but with considerable trust in the ability of traditional directors and personalities to weather the storm.   Among the issues scholars are debating today are whether the realistic thrust of the forties disappeared in the 1960s, whether the rise of multinational corporations was a positive influence on national cinemas, what effect the anti-Communist scare had on the FILM NOIR movement, what role television played in the late forties in changing film content, whether the anti-censorship victories of the 1950s matured movies, whether MISE EN SCENE or montage is the true art of the film, and what lasting effects the PARAMOUNT antitrust case had on the American and foreign film industries.

BOOKS

GENERAL

*Biskind, Peter. SEEING IS BELIEVING: HOW HOLLYWOOD TAUGHT US TO STOP WORRYING AND LOVE THE FIFTIES. New York: Pantheon Books, 1983. Illustrated. 371pp.

According to Biskind, "It has never been a secret . .   that movies influence manners, attitudes, and behavior. In the fifties, they told us how to dress for a rumble or a board meeting, how far to go on the first date, what to think about Martians or, closer to home, Jews, blacks, and homosexuals. They taught girls [sic] whether they should have husbands or careers, boys whether to pursue work or pleasure. They told us what was right and what was wrong, what was good and what was bad; they defined our problems and suggested solutions. And they still do." In case there are sceptics who refuse to accept that one-on-one simplification, Biskind sets out to demonstrate how Hollywood ideology, with its "hidden and not-so hidden

---

forties to make films in Europe. His first American film after the blacklisting period was UP TIGHT (1968).

messages," functioned in the years between 1948 and 1960. He divides his entertaining and provocative excavation of Hollywood's "world-view" into three major parts, using a handful of films in each section to identify how specific movies reveal not only a core of common conventions and themes but also a common concern with the pressing issues of the day: i.e., "conformity, dissent, minorities, delinquency, and sex roles." Part 1, "Consensus and Its Discontents," contains two chapters--"Who's In Charge Here?" and "The Organization Man Goes to War"--and, like each of the major sections, is more concerned with the outcome of the film continuum than with filmmmakers' intentions or the pressures of the marketplace. Part 2, "Us and Them," has two chapters--"Pods and Blobs" and "The Enemy Within"--and focuses on a wide range of films from THE THING (1951) to THE SEARCHERS (1956). Part 3, "Male and Female," is limited to just one chapter--"All in the Family"--and examines what home life was like in movies like RED RIVER (1948), GIANT (1956), MILDRED PIERCE (1945), EXECUTIVE SUITE (1954), THE FOUNTAINHEAD (1949), and ALL THAT HEAVEN ALLOWS (1956).

Although the analyses prove more speculative than definitive, Biskind's wit and judgment make the experience intellectually exciting and emotionally enjoyable. Adding to the book's considerable value are illustrations, endnotes, and an index. Well worth browsing.

*Brode, Douglas. THE FILMS OF THE FIFTIES: "SUNSET BOULEVARD" TO "ON THE BEACH." Secaucus: The Citadel Press, 1976. Illustrated. 288pp.

A lightweight pictorial survey of the decade, this missed opportunity begins with an intelligent introduction and then deteriorates into a simplistic potpourri of 101 movies that highlight the trends of the decade. The publisher's standard quality of pictorial reproductions is maintained, but the author's level of discussion is below par for the series. Except for the screen credits and visuals, there is no compelling reason to consult this book. No footnotes, bibliography, or index are provided. Approach with caution.

Dowdy, Andrew. MOVIES ARE BETTER THAN EVER: WIDE-SCREEN MEMORIES OF THE FIFTIES. New York: William Morrow and Company, 1973. Illustrated. 242pp.

A superficial and annoying survey of Hollywood in the 1950s, this simplistic history races through the decade without making any significant comments on the films, the filmmakers, or the industry. A good example of the frivolous nature of the enterprise is evident in the titles of the book's thirteen ill-conceived chapters: e.g., "Gone With the Tube," "I Married a Communist & Other Disasters of the Blacklist," "There's an Ecdysiast in My Popcorn," and "Midnite Follies--the Kinky Flicks." Except for a good selective bibliography and an index to the author's thumbnail observations, there is no reason to consult this publication. Approach with caution.

*Gow, Gordon. HOLLYWOOD IN THE FIFTIES. New York: A. S. Barnes and Company, 1971. Illustrated. 208pp.

One of the best of the narrative histories presented in this series, Gow offers more than the usual critical commentaries on important personalities, pictures, and studios. In the author's terse introduction to the book's eight intelligent and insightful chapters, he explains how Hollywood's profit-oriented mentality became more prominent in the 1950s than at any other time in its stormy history. Gow's theme is that the film industry's commercial state of mind went through a transformation during the decade. The reasons were twofold: the need to prove that films were better entertainment than TV and the need to adjust to the fact that independent producers were replacing the studio production policies of the past. From this base, Gow argues, "sprang the new spirit of Hollywood, slow to develop but steadily bringing a more individual quality to specific films and delving into areas of sociology which Hollywood had touched upon only with caution in the financial heyday." Except for the stills, which are below par for this series, and the absence of any footnotes and bibliographic material, this book remains an important resource on the period. Well worth browsing.

Manchel, Frank. THE BOX-OFFICE CLOWNS: BOB HOPE, JERRY LEWIS, MEL BROOKS, WOODY ALLEN. New York: Franklin Watts, 1979. Illustrated. 120pp.

"Manchel presents a comparison of four comedians' changing popularity in the course of their careers as society's attitudes, values, and tastes changed. The anecdotes, quotes, photos, and fast-moving, incisive biographical sketches which concentrate on careers rather than personal events will appeal mainly to film buffs who are familiar with the films cited. The author offers opinions of the actors' talents, criticism of their movies, and judgments on the relative importance of each comedian in the context of American film comedy that readers will find interesting whether or not they agree."[723]

*Manvell, Roger. NEW CINEMA IN THE USA: THE FEATURE FILM SINCE 1946. New York: E. P. Dutton and Company, 1968. Illustrated. 160pp.

This beautifully illustrated paperback guide to American feature films since 1946 is a useful introduction to beginners who want a quick survey on Kazan, Sturges, Wyler, Stevens, Donen, Huston, Welles, and Wilder. Manvell's topical rather than chronological style offers a novel approach to an overview of traditionalists and innovators experimenting with film formulas in order to face the post-WWII challenges in the movie world. As long as one accepts the book's obvious limitations, it becomes a charming experience. An index is included. Well worth browsing.

*Mayer, Michael F. FOREIGN FILMS ON AMERICAN SCREENS. Introduction Arthur Knight. New York: Arco Publishing Company, 1965. Illustrated. 119pp.

At the time of publication, this pioneering work was one of the most useful collections of film stills, list of awards, and general comments on foreign film distribution. It remains today a valuable resource for studying the post-WWII period in Hollywood. Well worth browsing.

Zinman, David. 50 FROM THE 50's: VINTAGE FILMS FROM AMERICA'S MID-CENTURY. New Rochelle: Arlington House, 1979. Illustrated. 418pp.

An ecclectic approach to the transitional decade, Zimmer's highly subjective list ranges from outstanding films like ALL ABOUT EVE (1950), THE ASPHALT JUNGLE (1950), THE BRIDGE ON THE RIVER KWAI (1957), and A PLACE IN THE SUN (1951) to questionable works like THE BRAVE BULLS (1951), PEYTON PLACE (1957), PICNIC (1956), and THAT'S MY BOY (1951). The title is also somewhat misleading, since the collection also includes a number of foreign films like GENERAL DELLA ROVERE/IL GENERALE DELLA ROVERE (1959), THE ROAD/LA STRADA (1956), RASHOMON (1950), and DIABOLIQUE/LES DIABOLIQUES (1955). Each film comes with a detailed precis, a provocative analysis, and a set of well-produced stills. Whether one agrees with Zinman's selections or interpretations is secondary to the nostalgia and pleasure the book generates. A limited bibliography and adequate index are provided. Well worth browsing.

---

[723] Daniel Josslin, "Book Review: THE BOX-OFFICE CLOWNS," SCHOOL LIBRARY JOURNAL (February 1980):68.

AVANT-GARDE

*Deren, Maya. AN ANAGRAM OF IDEAS ON ART, FORM AND FILM. FILM CULTURE 39 (Winter 1965).

This book, originally published in 1946, is republished along with other comments about and by Deren, one of the most unusual filmmakers in the last twenty years. It is an interesting and valuable commentary for those interested in the AVANT-GARDE movement. Well worth browsing.

*Battcock, Gregory, ed. THE NEW AMERICAN CINEMA: A CRITICAL ANTHOLOGY. New York: E. P. Dutton and Company, 1967. Illustrated. 256pp.

In this compendium of twenty-nine essays mainly concerned with the New York underground, Battcock tries, not always successfully, to shed some light on the techniques and theories of the avant-garde filmmakers. Among the contributors are Jonas Mekas, Andrew Sarris, Rudolf Arnheim, Parker Tyler, Amos Vogel, Stan Vanderbeek, Carl Linder, Gregory Markopoulous, Dwight MacDonald, Susan Sontag, and Stan Brakhage. An index is included. Well worth browsing.

*Mekas, Jonas. MOVIE JOURNAL: THE RISE OF THE NEW AMERICAN CINEMA, 1959-1971. New York: The Macmillan Company, 1971. 434pp.

Taken from many of his writings in THE VILLAGE VOICE, this book gives an excellent example of Mekas's attacks on traditional films and intellectual critics. It is difficult to read if you're used to rational, objective prose, but for those who prefer impressionistic and emotional outbursts, this text is not to be missed. Well worth browsing.

*Renan, Sheldon. AN INTRODUCTION TO THE AMERICAN UNDERGROUND FILM. New York: E. P. Dutton and Company, 1967. Illustrated. 318pp.

Six biased and brief chapters serve as a useful guide to the low-budget, mainly non-profit world of the unique AUTEURS of the American cinema. Recommended for special collections.

*Sitney, P. Adams, ed. FILM CULTURE READER. New York: Praeger Publishers, 1970. Illustrated. 438pp.

This is by far the best available introductory text on American AVANT-GARDE films. In five valuable sections, we have some of the best material published from FILM CULTURE'S indispensable and unique press. Among the contributors are Hans Richter, Jonas Mekas, Carl Dreyer, Andrew Sarris, Parker Tyler, Rudolf Arnheim, Herman G. Weinberg, Erich von Stroheim, Maya Deren, and Stan Brakhage. Recommended for special collections.

Stauffacher, Frank, ed. ART IN CINEMA: A SYMPOSIUM ON THE AVANT-GARDE FILM. San Francisco: Museum of Modern Art, 1947. Illustrated. 104pp.

Written as a companion piece to accompany the experimental film program at the museum, this handy, brief guide is an informative, entertaining, and useful publication. A bibliograhy and index are included. Recommended for special collections.

Turim, Maureen Cheryn. ABSTRACTION IN AVANT-GARDE FILMS. Ann Arbor: UMI Press, 1985. Illustrated. 165pp.

"My purpose in undertaking a theoretical investigation of the cinematic avant-grade," Turim explains in her complex study, "stems from my own fascination with an attraction to these films. My goal was to develop theories which help to explain their functioning. But equally, I choose them as an object of investigation because, by the very radicality of their functioning, they suggest the necessity for revising and expanding film theory, and the implications extend to theories of figuration, representation and the processes of signification in general." The author draws upon the writings of deconstructionists and semiologists to analyze the works of modern AVANT-GARDE filmmakers like Michael Snow, Dore O., Peter Kubelka, Barry Gerson, Paul Sharitis, Ernie Gehr, Hollis Frampton, and Larry Gottheim. The highly academic prose and detailed analyses limit the audience for this very specialized study. Endnotes, a bibliography, and an index are included. Well worth browsing.

Tyler, Parker. SEX PSYCHE ETCETERA IN THE FILM. New York: Horizon Press, 1969. 239pp.
     In his sixth film book, Tyler probes the delicate relationship of ritual and aesthetics, and offers some very controversial opinions about major experimentators like Eisenstein, Chaplin, Warhol, and the film, I AM CURIOUS: YELLOW (1969). Well worth browsing.

*Tyler, Parker. UNDERGROUND FILM: A CRITICAL HISTORY. New York: Grove Press, 1969. Illustrated. 249pp.
     In an attempt to distinguish between experimental and commercial films, Tyler offers a positive and invaluable guide through the AVANT-GARDE history of film. In addition, a selected filmography is included. Well worth browsing.

FILM NOIR

*Crowther, Bruce. FILM NOIR: REFLECTIONS IN A DARK MIRROR.   London: Columbus Books, 1988. Illustrated. 192pp.

*Hirsch, Foster. THE DARK SIDE OF THE SCREEN: FILM NOIR. San Diego: A. S. Barnes and Company, 1981. Illustrated. 231pp.

Karimi, Amir Massoud. TOWARD A DEFINITION OF THE AMERICAN FILM NOIR (1941-1949). New York: Arno Press, 1976. 255pp.

Ottoson, Robert. A REFERENCE GUIDE TO THE AMERICAN FILM NOIR: 1940-1958. Metuchen: The Scarecrow Press, 1981. Illustrated. 290pp.

*Silver, Alain, and Elizabeth Ward. FILM NOIR: AN ENCYCLOPEDIC REFERENCE TO THE AMERICAN FILM STYLE. Woodstock: Overlook Press, 1979. Illustrated.   393pp.

Tuska, Jon. DARK CINEMA: AMERICAN FILM NOIR IN CULTURAL PERSPECTIVE. Westport: Greenwood Press, 1984. 307pp.
     An outgrowth of Tuska's work on FILM NOIR in his book, THE DETECTIVE IN FICTION, this stimulating and informative study pursues the thesis that FILM NOIR is both a screen style and a perspective on human existence. Tuska begins by asserting that the film style's negative perspective can be traced back to Greek and Roman tragedy, and that few people agree on an appropriate definition for the

American film version. For the purposes of his book, he characterizes FILM NOIR as "a mood, a tone, a play of shadows and light, and beyond all these a visual consideration that in its narrative structures embodies a world-view." Among the authors he cites as being fathers to the film style are Dostoyevsky, Nietzsche, Hammett, and Chandler.

Following a meandering discussion on the philosophical roots of FILM NOIR, Tuska divides his study into three major sections: literary antecedents, cinematic antecedents, and American FILM NOIR. The comments are thoughtful, the research comprehensive, and the results generally satisfying. Particularly valuable is the third section, which is subdivided into chapters on the FILM NOIR cannon, NOIR women, NOIR men, and NOIR directors. What adds to the appeal of the book is the author's access to the principal people connected with the films and the insights their recollections provide on events and decisions. While some readers may find the academic tone offsetting, others will appreciate the care the author takes in documenting his observations. Endnotes, a chronology and filmography of FILMS NOIR, a bibliography, and an index are included. Well worth browsing.

STARS AND DIRECTORS

CARROLL BAKER

*Baker, Carroll. BABY DOLL: AN AUTOBIOGRAPHY. Rev. and updated edition. New York: Dell Publishing Company, 1984. Illustrated. 316pp.

ANNE BAXTER

*Baxter, Anne. INTERMISSION: A TRUE STORY. New York: G. P. Putnam's Sons, 1976. Illustrated. 384pp.

STAN BRAKHAGE

Barrett, Gerald R., and Wendy Brabner. STAN BRAKHAGE: A GUIDE TO REFERENCES AND RESOURCES. Boston: G. K. Hall and Company, 1983. 301pp.

Beginning filmmaking in 1952 at nineteen years old, Stan Brakhage had made almost two hundred films at the time this book was written. "His highly personal visions of the self and the world, transmuted to film," Barrett and Brabner point out, "question the conventional assumptions about the nature of vision and the cinematic experience." This pioneering comprehensive study of the artist and his work opens with a biographical portrait of Brakhage's life from his birth as Robert Sanders, orphan, in Kansas City, Missouri, on January 14, 1933, to his sojourn in Lonp Gulch, Colorado, in the early 1980s. Other sections contain a critical survey of his work, an annotated filmography (with synopses and notes), writings about Brakhage, other film-related work, archival sources, and film distributors. Among the conclusions that the authors reach about Brakhage's highly autobiographical films are that they represent his passion for "capturing the essence of a subject," that he edits his work intuitively "during shooting and cutting," and that he "seldom suggest[s] a concern for two-dimensional space for its own sake." An author index and title index are included. Recommended for special collections.

MARLON BRANDO

*Brando, Anna Kashfi, and E. P. Stein. BRANDO FOR BREAKFAST. New York: Berkley Books, 1980. Illustrated. 277pp.

*Carey, Gary. BRANDO. New York: Pocket Books, 1973. Illustrated. 279pp.

Carey, Gary. MARLON BRANDO: THE ONLY CONTENDER. New York: St. Martin's Press, 1985. Illustrated. 276pp.

Downing, David. MARLON BRANDO. New York: Stein and Day Publishers, 1984. Illustrated. 216pp.

*Fiore, Carlo. BUD: THE BRANDO I KNEW--THE UNTOLD STORY OF BRANDO'S PRIVATE LIFE. New York: Dell Publishing Company, 1974. Illustrated. 271pp.

Jordan, Rene. MARLON BRANDO. New York: Galahad Books, 1973. Illustrated. 159pp.

Offen, Ron. BRANDO. Chicago: Henry Regnery, 1973. Illustrated. 222pp.

Shipman, David. BRANDO. Garden City: Doubleday and Company, 1974. Illustrated. 127pp.

Thomas, Bob. MARLON: PORTRAIT OF THE REBEL AS AN ARTIST. New York: Random House, 1973. Illustrated. 277pp.

*Thomas, Terry. THE FILMS OF MARLON BRANDO. Secaucus: The Citadel Press, 1973. Illustrated. 246pp.

MONTGOMERY CLIFT

Bosworth, Patricia. MONTGOMERY CLIFT: A BIOGRAPHY. New York: Harcourt Brace and Jovanovich, 1978. Illustrated. 438pp.

*LaGuardia, Robert. MONTY: A BIOGRAPHY OF MONTGOMERY CLIFT. New York: Arbor House, 1977. Illustrated. 304pp.

DORIS DAY

*Gelb, Alan. THE DORIS DAY SCRAPBOOK. New York: Grosset and Dunlap, 1977. Illustrated. 159pp.

*Morris, George. DORIS DAY. New York: Pyramid Publications, 1976. Illustrated. 159pp.

Hotchner, A. E. DORIS DAY: HER OWN STORY. New York: William Morrow and Company, 1976. Illustrated. 313pp.

*Thomey, Tedd. DORIS DAY. New York: Monarch Books, 1962. Illustrated. 139pp.

Young, Christopher. THE FILMS OF DORIS DAY. Secaucus: The Citadel Press, 1977. Illustrated. 253pp.

JAMES DEAN

*Bast, William. JAMES DEAN: A BIOGRAPHY. New York: Ballantine Books, 1956. Illustrated. 149pp.

*Beath, Warren Newton. THE DEATH OF JAMES DEAN. New York: Grove Press, 1986. Illustrated. 202pp.

*Dalton, David. JAMES DEAN: AMERICAN ICON. New York: St. Martin's Press, 1984. Illustrated. 287pp.

*Dalton, David. JAMES DEAN, THE MUTANT KING: A BIOGRAPHY. San Francisco: Straight Arrow Books, 1974. Illustrated. 358pp.

Herndon, Venable. JAMES DEAN: A SHORT LIFE. Garden City: Doubleday and Company, 1974. Illustrated. 288pp.

*Howlett, John. JAMES DEAN: A BIOGRAPHY. New York: Simon and Schuster, 1975. Illustrated. 191pp.

*Martinetti, Ronald. THE JAMES DEAN STORY. New York: Pinnacle Books, 1975. Illustrated. 185pp.

*Stock, Dennis. JAMES DEAN REVISITED. New York: Penguin Books, 1978. Illustrated. 128pp.

KIRK DOUGLAS

*Douglas, Kirk. THE RAGMAN'S SON: AN AUTOBIOGRAPHY. New York: Simon and Schuster, 1988. Illustrated. 510pp.

*McBride, Joseph. KIRK DOUGLAS. New York: Pyramid Publications, 1976. Illustrated. 160pp.

*Thomas, Tony. THE FILMS OF KIRK DOUGLAS. Introduction Vincente Minnelli. Secaucus: The Citadel Press, 1972. Illustrated. 255pp.

JOHN FORD

*Lyons, Robert, ed. MY DARLING CLEMENTINE: JOHN FORD, DIRECTOR. New Brunswick: Rutgers University Press, 1984. Illustrated. 196pp.

A fine collection of essays coupled with a full transcript of the movie as released in 1946, this welcome publication exemplifies how far the publication of screenplays has come in the last twenty years. The one major drawback is the poor reproduction quality of the visuals. Typical of the book's quality is Lyon's introductory essay on the way in which Ford used history and romance to relate his vision of the American Dream to the western. In addition to showing how the depiction of the Earp family, Doc Holliday, and the Clantons has little to with actual history, Lyons details how Ford recast reality to suit his narrative purposes. Following the continuity script, Lyons provides a collection of material that includes interviews, reviews, and commentaries. The selections are well-chosen, entertaining, and informative. A bibliography and Ford filmography are included, but no index is provided. Recommended for special collections.

SAMUEL FULLER

*Garnham, Nicholas. SAMUEL FULLER. New York: The Viking Press, 1972. Illustrated. 176pp.

Born Samuel Michael Fuller in Worcester, Massachussets, on August 12, 1911, one of America's most provocative AUTEURS tried his hand at crime reporting before becoming a screenwriter in 1936. Over the next six years, he worked the "B"-circuit route, turning out dozens of scripts but no noteworthy films. His distinguished wartime service (1942-45) with the Army's 16th Regiment, 1st Division, was later depicted in his memorable film THE BIG RED ONE (1980). Fuller resumed his screenwriting career in 1946, this time at Warner Bros. (1946-48), making his directorial debut with an independent production, I SHOT JESSE JAMES (1949), followed by THE BARON OF ARIZONA and THE STEEL HELMET (both in 1950). During the early- to mid-1950s, he worked at 20th Century-Fox, turning out films like FIXED BAYONETS (1951), PICKUP ON SOUTH STREET (1953), HELL AND HIGH WATER (1954), and HOUSE OF BAMBOO (1955), while also directing TV programs. In the mid-1950s, he formed his own production company, Globe Enterprises. Among the films he made and released through 20th Century-Fox, RKO, Columbia, Allied Artists, and Warner Bros. were RUN OF THE ARROW, CHINA GATE, FORTY GUNS (all in 1957), THE CRIMSON KIMONO (1959), UNDERWORLD U. S. A. (1960), MERRILL'S MARAUDERS (1961), and SHOCK CORRIDOR (1963). During the 1960s, most of Fuller's time was spent in TV, directing episodes for THE VIRGINIAN, THE DICK POWELL REYNOLDS ALUMINUM SHOW, and THE IRON HORSE. As a result of his fiercely independent views, thirteen years elapsed between the making of SHARK (1967) and release of THE BIG RED ONE (1980). Looking back on Fuller's work, one is struck by his cynical defense of American ideals, the pressures that his protagonists experience in remaining true to their personal values, and the danger that outsiders pose to traditional institutions. While his avid detractors label him a "crude" and "illiterate" director,[724] his passionate defenders point out the complexity of Fuller's action-oriented films and his insistence on showing the price that one pays in remaining part of a group yet true to individual principles.

Garnham's appreciative study ranks Fuller as one of the major American AUTUERS of the transitional years and offers a fast-moving, insightful account of his work. "I must make clear right from the start," the author writes, "what kind

---

[724]   Cited in Gavin Millar, "SAMUEL FULLER," CINEMA: A CRITICAL DICTINARY: THE MAJOR FILMMAKERS--Volume 1, p.403.

of criticism this book contains. Just as Fuller's movies are not cool and objective, so this book does not contain cool, objective criticism . . . I am concerned here not to administer admonitory raps on Fuller's cinematic knuckles, but to exclaim and I hope cause others to exclaim 'Yes, you're right!'" Despite the appreciative nature of the undertaking, Garnham offers a good, overall analysis of Fuller's films rather than a picture-by-picture analysis. "This book," he tells us, "is not a work of evaluation, so much as elucidation." Consequently, the study's topical, rather than chronological,   approach   explores   the   writer-producer-director's   thematic concerns--e.g., individualism, love as a redemptive factor, the nature of society, national identity, and madness--and outlines the pressures that led Fuller to his cinematic biases. A filmography is provided, but no index is included. Well worth browsing.

*Hardy, Phil. SAMUEL FULLER. New York: Praeger Publishers, 1970.   Illustrated. 144pp.

"The idea behind this book," Hardy explains, "is to set Fuller and his films in a context which makes them more accessible to discussion. Some of the ideas considered might seem extraneous to the films and more relevant to a book on contemporary America. However, Fuller is so essentially an American director that a purely cinematic approach to his films would be unprofitable. Yet, Fuller is so much a FILM director that too much context and not enough criticism of the films themselves would inevitably misrepresent his achievements." The author therefore divides his information into five thematic categories: "An American Dream," "Journalism and Style," "An American Reality," "Asia," and "The Violence of Love." With the exception of the chapter on journalism (which deals only with Fuller's 1952, film PARK ROW), each section offers an analysis of several movies together with critical comments on the writer-producer-director's working habits and trademarks. Along with useful visuals and good quotations from Fuller, the well-written narrative presents important observations. A filmography is included, but no bibliography or index is included. Well worth browsing.

*Will, David, and Peter Wollen, eds. SAMUEL FULLER. Edinburgh: Scottish International Review, 1969. Illustrated. 128pp.

Beginning with the reminder that CAHIERS DU CINEMA argued that "the three most important American post-war directors were Orson Welles, Elia Kazan, and Samuel Fuller," Wollen states in the book's introduction that up to 1969, "almost nothing of any value has been written" on Fuller.   This book, he explains, "offer[s] no more than working notes." He then goes on to list the AUTEUR's basic dualistic themes--e.g., "war and marriage, reciprocity of hate and reciprocity of life"--and why they are crucial to understanding Fuller's exploration of the American identity and the internal conflicts that divide the nation. The anthology of film criticism itself offers sixteen terse essays on films from I SHOT JESSE JAMES (1949), to THE NAKED KISS (1963), written by noted authors like Kingsley Canham, David Pirie, Phil Hardy, Colin McArthur, Alan Lovell, Raymond Durgnat, Jacques Bontemps, Jean-Luc Godard, Victor F. Perkins, Thomas Elsaesser, and Peter Wollen. The useful collection ends with an interview Fuller gave to Jean-Louis Noames. A bibliography is included, but no filmography or index is provided. Well worth browsing.

AUDREY HEPBURN

*Woodward, Ian. AUDREY HEPBURN. New York: St. Martin's Press, 1984. Illustrated. 312pp.

ROCK HUDSON

*Bego, Mark. ROCK HUDSON, PUBLIC AND PRIVATE: AN UNAUTHORIZED BIOGRAPHY. New York: Signet, 1986. Illustrated. 189pp.

*Gates, Phyllis, and Bob Thomas. MY HUSBAND, ROCK HUDSON: THE REAL STORY OF ROCK HUDSON'S MARRIAGE TO PHYLLIS GATES. Garden City: Doubleday and Company, 1987. Illustrated. 232pp.

GRACE KELLY

Bradford, Sarah. PRINCESS GRACE. New York: Stein and Day Publishers, 1984. Illustrated. 242pp.

*Spada, James. GRACE: THE SECRET LIVES OF A PRINCESS. Garden City: Doubleday and Company, 1987. Illustrated. 346pp.

GENE KELLY

Hirschhorn, Clive. GENE KELLY: A BIOGRAPHY. Foreword Frank Sinatra. Chicago: Henry Regnery Company, 1974. Illustrated. 335pp.

*Thomas, Terry. THE FILMS OF GENE KELLY: SON AND DANCE MAN. Introduction Fred Astaire. Secaucus: The Citadel Press, 1974. Illustrated. 243pp.

JANET LEIGH

*Leigh, Janet. THERE REALLY WAS A HOLLYWOOD: AN AUTOBIOGRAPHY. Garden City: Doubleday and Company, 1984. Illustrated. 322pp.

JOSEPH LOSEY

*Ciment, Michel. CONVERSATIONS WITH LOSEY. London: Methuen, 1985. Illustrated. 436pp.
　　　The most current and most entertaining of the Losey books, this stimulating set of interviews (taped in Paris and Rome between July 1976 and January 1979) not only updates previous works, but also adds new insights into Losey's thirty films and his uneven career. Ciment does a superb job of stimulating the director's memory of his childhood, his radical theater experiences, life in post-WWII Hollywood, the nature of his screen collaborations with important writers, and his feelings about the many fine performers he has directed. In addition to numerous well reproduced stills, large print, a fast-moving condensation (75 % of the interview material was cut), and a chronological format, the book provides an annotated list of unmade Losey films, a biofilmography, a list of publicity films for British television, and an index. Recommended for special collections.

Hirsch, Foster. JOSEPH LOSEY. Boston: Twayne Publishers, 1980. Illustrated. 256pp.

"What would the superstitious make of the disconcerting discovery," Warren French writes in his foreword, "that those three of this country's handful of imaginative and inventive film directors who were born within a few years of each other in the same chilly state of Wisconsin should have had the most discontinuous careers among their contemporaries because of the difficulties they had in getting their harshly critical, visionary projects funded?" He then adds, "Nicholas Ray, Orson Welles, and Joseph Losey have all sought with the overbearing zeal of Old Testament prophets to use the new art of this century to produce a modern equivalent of Ecclesiastes for our undisciplined, decadent society, and the society, from its sensationalist millionaires who control film production to the mindless audience gorging itself on Coke and popcorn, has responded by frustrating these missionaries' efforts to make thought-provoking pictures, eventually driving all of them into exile and silence." Allusions to Losey's being blacklisted, his going into self-exile in England, and to his puritanical zeal are commonplace not only in Hirsch's work, but also in the writings of others on Losey. The standard commentaries chart the director's life from his birth in La Crosse, Wisconsin, on January 14, 1909, through his academic years at Dartmouth College (1926-1929) and Harvard University (1930), to his involvement in the left-wing theater movement (1931-1948), to his intermittent flirtations with movies during the 1930s and 1940s, and his directorial film debut with THE BOY WITH GREEN HAIR (1948). Considerable space is then given to the effects of the Hollywood witch-hunt, his leaving America in 1951, and the problems that beset Losey in England until his international film success with THE SERVANT (1963). The remainder of the commentaries then debate the art versus commerce issues that have plagued Losey's career ever since.

The advantage of Hirsch's study, however, is its organization and its resource material. In addition to a good chronology, bibliography, filmology, index, and endnotes, the book contains eleven chapters, many of them providing intelligent analyses of Losey's collaboration with Harold Pinter, as well as describing the importance of Brecht on Losey's art and career. Hirsch's writing is clear, detailed, and insightful. More to the point, it is objective and presents a balanced picture of the director's strengths and weaknesses. Recommended for special collections.

*Leahy, James. THE CINEMA OF JOSEPH LOSEY. New York: A. S. Barnes and Company, 1967. Illustrated. 175pp.

At the time it was published, this study offered the best introduction to Joseph Losey's puritanical childhood, his involvment in the left-wing theater movement, and his Hollywood trials. Filled with quotations, arranged in chronological fashion, and complete with an important bibliography and screen credits, Leahy's text highlights the themes of Losey's works and suggests the reasons why the American expatriate prefers to work in England. Although both the Ciment and Hirsch works surpass Leahy's pioneering efforts, this book is still useful in examining the reactions of early scholars to works from THE BOY WITH GREEN HAIR (1948) to ACCIDENT (1967). A filmography and bibliography are included, but no index is provided. Well worth browsing.

*Milne, Tom, ed. LOSEY ON LOSEY. New York: Doubleday and Company, 1968. Illustrated. 192pp.

Written by a writer who has done better work, this hodgepodge of quotations, uneven critical comments, and rambling organization should be tasted rather than digested. Based upon a series of taped interviews done ten days after the London preview of ACCIDENT (1967), the book's seven chapters deal with critical interpretations of Losey's work, problems of expression, Hollywood, stage and screen relationships, continuing themes, collaborators, and the filming of Brecht's GALILEO. In addition to an excellent collection of stills, the book contains a filmography, but no index or bibliography is included. Worth browsing.

ANTHONY MANN

Basinger, Jeanine. ANTHONY MANN. Boston: Twayne Publishers, 1979. Illustrated. 230pp.

A loving and perceptive study of an underrated artist who thrived on low-budget films in the 1950s, this introductory book discusses the majority of Mann's twenty-six films. Basinger's AUTEUR approach acknowledges the contributions of the director's important collaborators (the screenwriters John C. Higgins, Borden Chase, and Philip Yordan, and the cinematographer John Alton), while detailing how Mann perfected his cinematic style. Her primary focus is on his "architectural story line," a narrative form constructed upon "layer upon layer of incident upon incident, while still taking strange turns and angles." Her six stimulating chapters, dealing with key films like WINCHESTER '73 (1950), BEND OF THE RIVER (1952), THE NAKED SPUR (1953), THE FAR COUNTRY, THE MAN FROM LARAMIE (both in 1955), MEN IN WAR (1957), GOD'S LITTLE ACRE, MAN OF THE WEST (both in 1958), and EL CID (1961), outline Mann's recurring themes and formal characteristics. As a result of the author's straightforward writing style, one quickly appreciates Mann's technique of using cinematic composition to underscore the meaning of his heroes' search through rugged terrains in search of wisdom and inner peace.

Although only two films--MEN IN WAR and GOD'S LITTLE ACRE--are discussed in depth, Basinger's work is a welcome addition to Twayne's fine series of books honoring creative artists overlooked by many film histories. In addition to a useful introductory chronology, the author provides a selection of stills, a smattering of endnotes, a good filmography, and a helpful index. Well worth browsing.

MERCEDES MCCAMBRIDGE

McCambridge, Mercedes. THE QUALITY OF MERCY: AN AUTOBIOGRAPHY. New York: Times Books, 1981. Illustrated. 245pp.

RAY MILLAND

Milland, Ray. WIDE-EYED IN BABYLON: AN AUTOBIOGRAPHY. New York: William Morrow and Company, 1974. Illustrated. 264pp.

ROBERT MITCHUM

*Belton, John. ROBERT MITCHUM. New York: Pyramid Publications, 1976. Illustrated. 159pp.

*Marill, Alvin H. ROBERT MITCHUM ON THE SCREEN. South Brunswick: A. S. Barnes and Company, 1978. Illustrated. 246pp.

*Tomkies, Mike. THE ROBERT MITCHUM STORY: "IT SURE BEATS WORKING." New York: Ballantine Books, 1972. Illustrated. 237pp.

MARILYN MONROE

*Carpozi, George, Jr. MARILYN MONROE: HER OWN STORY. New York: Universal-Award House, 1973. Illustrated. 112pp.

Conver, David. FINDING MARILYN: A ROMANCE. New York: Grosset and Dunlap, 1981. Illustrated. 192pp.

*Conway, Michael, and Mark Ricci, eds. THE FILMS OF MARILYN MONROE. Tribute Lee Strasberg and Introductory Essay Mark Harris. New York: The Citadel Press, 1964. Illustrated. 160pp.

Guiles, Fred Lawrence. LEGEND: THE LIFE AND DEATH OF MARILYN MONROE. New York: Stein and Day Publishers, 1984. Illustrated. 501pp.

Guiles, Fred Lawrence. NORMA JEAN: THE LIFE OF MARILYN MONROE. New York: McGraw-Hill Book Company, 1969. Illustrated. 342pp.

Hoyt, Edwin P. MARILYN: THE TRAGIC VENUS. New Edition. Radnor: Chilton Book Company, 1973. Illustrated. 279pp.

Kobal, John, ed. MARILYN MONROE: A LIFE ON FILM. Introduction David Robinson. New York: Hamlyn, 1974. Illustrated. 176pp.

*Lembourn, Hans Jorgen. DIARY OF A LOVER OF MARILYN MONROE. Trans. Hallberg Hallmundsson. New York: Arbor House, 1979. 214pp.

Mailer, Norman. MARILYN: A BIOGRAPHY. New York: Grosset and Dunlap, 1973. Illustrated. 271pp.

Mellen, Joan. MARILYN MONROE. New York: Galahad Books, 1973. Illustrated. 159pp.

*Monroe, Marilyn. MY STORY. New York: Stein and Day, 1974. 143pp.

*Murray, Eunice, with Rose Shade. MARILYN: THE LAST MONTHS. New York: Pyramid Books, 1975. Illustrated. 157pp.

Pepitone, Lena, and William Stadiem. MARILYN MONROE CONFIDENTIAL: AN INTIMATE PERSONAL ACCOUNT. New York: Simon and Schuster, 1979. Illustrated. 251pp.

*Riese, Randall, and Neal Hitchens. THE UNABRIDGED MARILYN: HER LIFE FROM A TO Z. New York: Congdon and Weed, 1987. Illustrated. 578pp.

Rollyson, Carl E., Jr. MARILYN MONROE: A LIFE OF THE ACTRESS. Ann Arbor: UMI Research Press, 1986. Illustrated. 255pp.

*Slatzer, Robert F. THE CURIOUS DEATH OF MARILYN MONROE. New York: Pinnacle Books, 1974. Illustrated. 417pp.

Taylor, Roger G. MARILYN IN ART. Salem: Salem House, 1984. Illustrated.   No pagination.

Weatherby, W. J. CONVERSATIONS WITH MARILYN. New York: Mason/Charter, 1976. 229pp.

MAX OPHULS

*Wexman, Virginia Wright, with Karen Hollinger, eds. "LETTER FROM AN UNKNOWN WOMAN": MAX OPHULS, DIRECTOR. New Brunswick: Rutgers University Press, 1986. Illustrated. 271pp.
    This splendid anthology does far more than provide excellent information on a timeless film ignored in its day and now valued by many modern scholars. The absence of any important book-length studies on the great French formalist filmmaker catapults this modest publication to the forefront of accessible and valuable resources on Ophuls's work and values. The perceptive editor divides her material into four major sections. Part One, "Introduction," provides a first-rate essay by Wexman on how Ophuls used his 1948 film to deal with contemporary history. Karen Hollinger offers a useful biographical sketch. Part Two, "LETTER FROM AN UNKNOWN WOMAN," gives us the cast and credits, continuity script, and notes on its evolution. Part Three, "Contexts," critiques Zweig's novella, and presents important information on the production provided by the screenwriter (Koch), the producer (Houseman), and the director (Ophuls). Part Four, "Reviews and Commentaries," contains the reactions of people like Bosley Crowther, Andrew Sarris, Robin Wood, Stephen Heath, Paul Willemen, and Tania Modleski. A bibliography and a filmography only add to the book's significant contributions to the scarce material available on Ophuls. Regrettably, no index is included. Highly recommended for special collections.

OTTO PREMINGER

Frischauer, Willi. BEHIND THE SCENES OF OTTO PREMINGER: AN UNAUTHORIZED BIOGRAPHY. New York: William Morrow, 1974. Illustrated. 279pp.
    One of the most unlikely Hollywood personalities to emerge as a rebellious soul, Preminger directed thirty-six American films. Among the best remembered are LAURA (1944), FOREVER AMBER, DAISY KENYON (both in 1947), THE MOON IS BLUE (1953), RIVER OF NO RETURN (1954), CARMEN JONES (1954), THE MAN WITH A GOLDEN ARM, THE COURT MARTIAL OF BILLY MITCHELL (both in 1955), SAINT JOAN (1957), PORGY AND BESS, ANATOMY OF A MURDER (both in 1959), EXODUS (1960), ADVISE AND CONSENT (1962), BUNNY LAKE IS MISSING (1965), and TELL ME THAT YOU LOVE ME, JUNIE MOON (1970). Born in Vienna on December 5, 1905, Preminger began his professional career as an actor and director in his native Austria before emigrating to America in the mid-1930s. Americans first grew to known him as the stereotypical Nazi villain in World War II movies. (His last film role was as the Nazi commandant in the 1953 film STALAG 17.) Although he was a liberal throughout his life, Preminger tried to work within the conservative Hollywood system and earned the continuing enmity of critical circles who found his work superficial and sensational, rather than innovative and significant. The literature on film is filled with horror stories about his cruelty to performers, his abusive treatment of underlings, and his determination to turn out pretentious films. Except for the acclaim accorded LAURA, nothing in his early career with 20th Century-Fox suggested the

crusading steps he would take in the postwar period, beginning with FOREVER AMBER and going through his independent productions after 1953.

Frisschauer's biography draws on the author's lifelong friendship with Preminger and focuses on the man rather than the artist. Although references are made to the producer-director's battles with censors, Hollywood witch-hunters, and the film establishment in general, the emphasis is on Preminger's personality and attitudes. We hear about loves, fears, and hates. Interestingly, the one glaring omission is a frank discussion of Preminger's romance with Dorothy Dandridge. The writing is breezy, entertaining, and amusing. In the absence of any documentation, the stories remain good gossip rather than factual accounts. An attractive collection of illustrations, a bibliography, a filmography, and an index are included. Well worth browsing.

*Pratley, Gerald. THE CINEMA OF OTTO PREMINGER. New York: A. S. Barnes and Company, 1971. Illustrated. 192pp.

In journalistic style, Pratley offers a novel guide to Preminger's career. The author (or more accurately editor) takes material that the producer-director wrote, gave during interviews, or had circulated in Hollywood circles and shapes it, along with his own critical commentaries, into two major sections: Preminger's studio years (1931-1952) and his independent years (1953-1971). The first period, covering movies like LAURA (1944), FOREVER AMBER (1947), and WHERE THE SIDEWALK ENDS (1950), is a collection of perspectives on Preminger's experiences with film personalities, specific projects, and particular battles. What detracts from this otherwise stimulating format is a sense of disorganization, especially when considerable space is given to a discussion of behind-the-scenes events during the filming of HURRY SUNDOWN (1966). At the end of the section, the author provides a welcome filmography, complete with numerous comments by the director on the films themselves. The second part, dealing with films like THE MAN WITH A GOLDEN ARM (1955), ANATOMY OF A MURDER (1959), EXODUS (1960), ADVISE AND CONSENT (1962), and TELL ME THAT YOU LOVE ME, JUNIE MOON (1970), is much shorter than Part One and much less stimulating. Except for a good filmography with the Preminger quotations, the section fails badly, especially since almost nothing new is revealed about the producer-director's struggle with the MPAA, his part in fashioning the independent film movement, the role he played in the careers of performers like Dorothy Dandridge and Jean Seberg, and the steps he took to break-down blacklisting in Hollywood. A good concluding chapter and an appendix listing Preminger's stage productions complete the book. The absence of a bibliography or an index in a study of this type is very disappointing. Well worth browsing.

Preminger, Otto. PREMINGER: AN AUTOBIOGRAPHY. Garden City: Doubleday and Company, 1977. Illustrated. 208pp.

Almost anyone who ever heard Preminger tell a story or describe his experiences came away with tremendous respect for his wit and humor. Regrettably, the gifted raconteur is not much in evidence in this otherwise provocative autobiography. The most surprising aspect is the author's unaccustomed modesty. Consider, for example, his account of how he was brought to 20th Century-Fox from Vienna in 1935: "One of Hollywood's most powerful men, Joseph M. Schenk, arrived on a visit to his old friend Julius Steger, who, after making a fortune in the United States, had returned to his native Vienna. He told Schenck about me, the young man who two years before had succeeded the legendary Max Reinhardt as head of the famous Theater in der Josefstadt." Thirty-one chapters tell us about Preminger's problems in learning English; the difficulties in getting established at 20th Century-Fox and winning Darryl F. Zanuck's favor; the importance of his stage productions and personalities like Tallulah Bankhead, John Barrymore, and Katharine Hepburn; what the critical and commercial success of LAURA (1944) did for his career; the goals he set for himself in his major films; and the unique experiences he had with celebrities like Marilyn Monroe, Gypsy Rose Lee, and Howard Hughes. Every now and then, the anecdotes become ugly and ring false.   Typical are Preminger's nasty and less-than-candid stories dealing with Dorothy Dandridge. For those who enjoy gossip and inside stories, this is a real treat. For those who prefer facts, this isn't the place to shop. A filmography and index are included. Well worth browsing.

ANTHONY QUINN

Marill, Alvin H. THE FILMS OF ANTHONY QUINN. Secaucus: The Citadel Press, 1975. Illustrated. 255pp.

Quinn, Anthony. THE ORIGINAL SIN: A SELF-PORTRAIT. Boston: Little, Brown and Company, 1972. Illustrated. 311pp.

NICHOLAS RAY

Allan, Blaine. NICHOLAS RAY: A GUIDE TO REFERENCES AND RESOURCES. Boston: G. K. Hall and Company, 1984. 243pp.
     Few artists in film history have known as much critical recognition and yet been so isolated as Nicholas Ray. Born Raymond Nicholas Kienzle in Galesville, Wisconsin, on August 7, 1911, the great screen rebel began his professional career as an architect and stage director before entering the world of film as an assistant director on Elia Kazan's A TREE GROWS IN BROOKLYN in 1944. Three years later, he made his directorial debut with THEY DRIVE BY NIGHT. Among the more famous of his twenty-two films are KNOCK ON ANY DOOR (1949), IN A LONELY PLACE (1950), JOHNNY GUITAR (1954), and REBEL WITHOUT A CAUSE (1955). His last film was LIGHTNING OVER WATER (1980), released after his death on June 16, 1979.
     Although the primary subject of this study is Nicholas Ray and his films, Allan also discusses the artist who worked in theater, radio, and television before heading to Hollywood and who remained a staunch independent filmmaker through the sixties and the seventies. Allan's thesis that you cannot separate Ray from the movies he directed results in one of this series's most inclusive annotated bibliographies, including entries for film reviews that barely identify Ray as a force in the production of the film. "My purpose in including such reviews," Allan writes, "is simply to provide access to material that demonstrates something of how the films were read in the popular press." The articles, almost exclusively from French and English language publications, are in the book's most important section, "Writings about Nicholas Ray, 1947-1982." Other sections are devoted to a biographical background; a critical survey of his work; a filmography with credits, notes, and synopses; published sources of films directed by Ray; various media, other film work, and writings by Ray; sources for further research; and film distributors. Among the conclusions that Allan reaches about the socially conscious director who made a number of post-WWII Hollywood's most popular "serious movies" is that he was concerned with the "images of the way people live and die; how individuals act and react with others; [and] how an often cruel environment molds our ways of seeing one another and our ways of acting." Moreover, he finds the "gritty social realism" of Ray's early films less stylized than his later works, crediting the director's cinematic techniques to his stage experiences and to the influence of Bertolt Brecht's teachings. A title index and an author index are included. Recommended for special collections.

Kreidl, John Francis. NICHOLAS RAY. Boston: Twayne Publishers, 1977. Illustrated. 230pp.
     Thanks to this welcome introductory discussion of Ray's stormy career, we better appreciate not only the films he made, but also what he tried to achieve in his efforts to advance the art of film. The focus is on the Hollywood years, the making of REBEL

WITHOUT A CAUSE (1955), and Ray's crucial relationship with James Dean. In explaining how Ray's childhood and stage career set the patterns that he would follow in film, Kreidl offers a persuasive case that Ray "deserves credit for pushing (or helping to push) the American cinema from the crude second generational stage he inherited (and Hollywood inherited) from D. W. Griffith to a more advanced form that would later be perfected in Europe as an ontological cinema, a cinema of experience and not just a psychologism or narrative, a true third generation, in the never-too-systematic evolution of the cinema medium." The author notes five major reasons for studying Ray: (1) his contributions to the technical and creative evolution of film, (2) his role as a rebel-within-the-system; (3) his pioneering work in developing a meaningful approach to CinemaScope, (4) his influence on the French New Wave, particularly Francois Truffaut and Jean-Luc Godard, and (5) his status as "an archetypal creator and incarnator of the American 1950s. . . ." In addition to a chronology, endnotes, a filmography, a selective bibliography, and an index, this first and only full-length critical study provides illustrations, intelligent analyses, and an appendix listing Ray's unrealized European projects between 1962 and 1968. Recommended for special collections.

DEBBIE REYNOLDS

Reynolds, Debbie, and David Patrick Columbia. DEBBIE: MY LIFE. New York: William Morrow and Company, 1988. Illustrated. 446pp.

ROBERT ROSSEN

*Casty, Alan. THE FILMS OF ROBERT ROSSEN. New York: The Museum of Modern Art, 1969. Illustrated. 95pp.

Born Robert Rosen in New York City on March 16, 1908, the overlooked and neglected director began his professional career in the theater as a writer and director before becoming a screenwriter for Warner Bros. in the mid-1930s. Like many Eastern intellectuals who migrated to Hollywood, he joined the American Communist party in 1937. Rossen made his directorial film debut with JOHNNY O'CLOCK (1946), followed by such films as BODY AND SOUL (1947) and ALL THE KING'S MEN (1951). In the meantime, he was hounded by HUAC (1947, 1951) and eventually blacklisted (1951-3). After a brief holdout, he capitulated in 1953 and named names. Once reinstated, he made a number of films, the most famous being THE HUSTLER (1961). His early death on December 18, 1966, deprived the screen of a major talent.

In spite of the book's brevity, Casty offers the best source of critical and biographical help on the socially conscious director, who was just beginning to gain the recognition of critics as a result of his final film LILITH (1964). Moreover, as the author explains, ". . . despite his conventional approach, despite his commercial success, despite the blacklist, Rossen produced a body of work that reflected a consistent, deepening, and developing point of view, and a close interrelationship with his life that was unique in American film directors." Endnotes, a filmography, and a bibibliography are included, but no index is provided. Well worth browsing.

GEORGE SANDERS

Sanders, George. MEMOIRS OF A PROFESSIONAL CAD. New York: G. P. Putnam's Sons, 1960. Illustrated. 192pp.

JEAN SEBERG

Richards, David. PLAYED OUT: THE JEAN SEBERG STORY. New York: Random House, 1981. Illustrated. 371pp.

DOUGLAS SIRK

*Halliday, Jon. SIRK ON SIRK. New York: The Viking Press, 1972. Illustrated. 176pp.

Born Hans Detlef Sierck in Hamburg, Germany, in 1900, Douglas Sirk abandoned his interest in art history in favor of the theater before turning to filmmaking for UFA in 1934. Nine films and three years later, he left Nazi Germany, worked in Europe between 1937 and 1939, and then accepted Warner Bros.'s offer to come to Hollywood. When the relationship between Warner Bros. and Sirk ended in 1940, he took up chicken farming for a couple of years. Columbia hired him as a scriptwriter-director in 1942, and the seven films he made between then and 1949, when he left Columbia, made little impression on anyone. After spending a year in Germany, Sirk returned to Hollywood and signed a seven-year contract with Universal. In that period, he made a number of films--e.g., MAGNIFICENT OBSESSION (1954), ALL THAT HEAVEN ALLOWS (1955), WRITTEN ON THE WIND (1956), and IMITATION OF LIFE (1959)--that not only became box-office hits, but also won critical acclaim from serious film students. He retired from film in 1959, eventually settling in Switzerland, and periodically directs plays in a German theater.

The author visited Sirk in 1970 and conducted a series of interviews covering a wide-range of events and periods in the director's life: e.g., the German theater, German films: 1935-1937, France and Holland: 1938-1939, America from 1939 to 1948, America from 1950 to 1959, and the post-Hollywood era. Each of these subjects is covered in individual chapters. Halliday's organization and writing style do a good job of distinguishing Sirk's knowledge of film as an art form from his understanding of movies as a business. A biofilmography and bibliography are included, but there is no index. Well worth browsing.

Stern, Michael. DOUGLAS SIRK. Boston: Twayne Publishers, 1979. Illustrated. 226pp.

The first and only full-length study of Sirk, this thoughtful work examines the problems that the screenwriter-director faced not only in making films but also in getting them distributed. Included in the behind-the-scenes information are details about Sirk's reliance on film neophytes--e.g., Rock Hudson and John Gavin--or over-the-hill stars--e.g., Barbara Stanwyck and Lana Turner--to populate his "filler" films,[725] the skill with which he molded these performers into an impressive stock company, and the steps he took to rework the "women's films" of the 1930s--IMITATION OF LIFE (1934) and MAGNIFICENT OBSESSION (1935)--into modern melodramas. The book's nine chapters give a good overview of Sirk's formal techniques and cinematic style, focusing on his cynical and fatalistic portraits of American life in suburbia in the 1950s. Rather than offering broad strokes on each of the director's twenty-nine American films, Stern isolates specific characteristics of the films and then explains their importance: e.g., "WRITTEN ON THE WIND is discussed as a sexual melodrama and ALL THAT HEAVEN ALLOWS is an example of Sirk's social vision." The later chapters trace Sirk's earlier screen trajectories and demonstrate how they surfaced in his films of the late 1950s. Primary attention is paid to the conditions under which Sirk made his American films and the evolution

---

[725] A "filler" refers to the second-half of a double bill.

of his Hollywood sensibility, ignoring, for the most part, Sirk's relationship to other expatriot filmmakers and his European film roots.

While some readers may object to Stern's narrow focus on specific films, the author's scholarship and wit more than justify a close reading of the material. In addition to a chronology and endnotes, the work includes a collection of stills, a bibliography, a filmography, and an index. Well worth browsing.

MIKE TODD

*Cohn, Art. THE NINE LIVES OF MIKE TODD. New York: Pocket Books, 1959. Illustrated. 344pp.

Todd, Mike, Jr., and Susan McCarthy Todd. A VALUABLE PROPERTY: THE LIFE STORY OF MIKE TODD. Foreword Elizabeth Taylor. New York: Arbor House, 1983. Illustrated. 369pp.

LANA TURNER

*Crane, Cheryl, with Cliff Jahr. DETOUR: A HOLLYWOOD STORY. New York: Arbor House, 1988. Illustrated. 334pp.

*Morella, Joe, and Edward Z. Epstein. LANA: THE PUBLIC AND PRIVATE LIVES OF MISS TURNER. New York: Dell, 1971. 288pp.

*Turner, Lana. LANA: THE LADY, THE LEGEND, AND THE TRUTH. New York: E. P. Dutton, 1982. Illustrated. 311pp.

BILLY WILDER

Dick, Bernard F. BILLY WILDER. Boston: Twayne Publishers, 1980. Illustrated. 188pp.

Born Samuel Wilder in Sucha, in Polish Galacia, on June 22, 1906, the man destined to become one of the masters of dark comedy studied law at the University of Vienna before becoming a journalist in Vienna and Berlin. In 1929, he collaborated on the script of PEOPLE ON SUNDAY/MENSCHEN AM SONNTAG and began a prolific career as a screenwriter in Germany. When Hitler came to power four years later, Wilder moved to Paris and in 1934 emigrated to Hollywood. His famous collaboration with screenwriter Charles Brackett, beginning in 1938 and ending in 1950, resulted in such notable films as NINOTCHKA (1939), HOLD BACK THE DAWN, BALL OF FIRE (both in 1941), THE MAJOR AND THE MINOR (1942), FIVE GRAVES TO CAIRO (1943), THE LOST WEEKEND (1945), and SUNSET BOULEVARD (1950). Following his Hollywood directorial debut with THE MAJOR AND THE MINOR and in addition to the Brackett collaborations, he made important films like DOUBLE INDEMNITY (1944), STALAG 17 (1953), and WITNESS FOR THE PROSECUTION (1958) before teaming up with I. A. L. Diamond in 1957 to create such works as SOME LIKE IT HOT (1959), THE APARTMENT (1960), ONE, TWO, THREE (1961), IRMA LA DOUCE (1963), THE FORTUNE COOKIE (1966), AVANTI! (1972), and FEDORA (1978).

In this welcome introduction to the six-time Academy Award winner, Dick offers us a balanced portrait of Wilder's career from 1929 to 1979. While we're told about his creativity and wit, we're also reminded of his abrasiveness and cruelty. The result is a better appreciation of why many critics have attacked his films as being cold, bitter, and amoral; and Wilder himself as being contemptuous both of his audience and of humanity. Dick's plan is not so much to walk a tightrope between the director's "bad taste" and his charisma, as to describe Wilder's rollercoaster experiences working in Germany, Paris, and Hollywood; and to air the problems that beset the irreverent screenwriter-director, especially during the 1960s and 1970s when critics ignored him and the big studios refused to work with him (e.g., in the late 1970s, every major studio rejected FEDORA, which was finally distributed by United Artists in 1979). From Dick's perspective, "Wilder's is more than a career; it is a microcosm of the American film--from the malts and milkshakes of THE MAJOR AND THE MINOR to the bracing brew of FEDORA." In the author's mind, a number of Wilder's twenty-four films may be failures, but none of them are "really bad" movies. They are all examples of an artist's judgment that results in overreaching and underestimating. The twelve highly informative chapters, arranged topically rather than chronologically, explore the importance of scripts in Wilder's films, but make it clear that he was first a filmmaker who concentrated on images, and secondarily a director who relied on words. Considering the importance of the screenwriters Charles Brackett and I. A. L. Diamond in Wilder's career, it is fascinating to follow Dick's revelations that the scripts rarely were finished before shooting began.

Except for the frustration of not having more discussion on the films and the acts of collaboration, this impressive introductory work continues the high standards of the Twayne series under Warren French's editorial leadership. The standard features--chronology, endnotes, illustrations, filmography, bibliography, and index--are all included. Well worth browsing.

*Madsen, Axel. BILLY WILDER, Bloomington: Indiana University Press, 1969. Illustrated. 168pp.

In this hurried examination of an important Hollywood director, Madsen gives us some general thoughts on films like THE LOST WEEKEND (1945), SUNSET BOULEVARD (1950), WITNESS FOR THE PROSECUTION (1958), SOME LIKE IT HOT (1959), and THE APARTMENT (1960). The focus, however, is on the artist rather than on his creations. At the time of its release, the book's numerous anecdotes offered a valuable behind-the-scenes glimpse of Wilder's work habits and the way in which he harangued his collaborators. While recent publications make Madsen's gossip passe, the book's numerous stills still command attention. A filmography is included, but no index is provided. Worth browsing.

*Seidman, Steve. THE FILM CAREER OF BILLY WILDER. Pleasantville: Redgrave Publishing Company, 1977. 175pp.

Don't be fooled by the typescript into thinking this is a slight work. Seidman's skills as a researcher result in a splendid rebuttal to critics like Andrew Sarris and Manny Farber, who relegated Wilder to the lower depths of film history. The book is divided into ten sections: biographical background; a critical survey of Wilder's works; an annotated filmography; writings about Wilder, 1944-1977; reviews of Wilder's films; writings, performances and other related film activity; archival sources; film distributors; film title index; and author index. The information presented is reliable, the writing, crisp, and the observations, provocative. Recommended for special collections.

Wood, Tom. THE BRIGHT SIDE OF BILLY WILDER, PRIMARILY. Garden City: Doubleday and Company, 1970. Illustrated. 257pp.

This lively and entertaining book treats the behind-the-scenes events of Wilder's productions and personal relations with famous film personalities. The superficial writing style and the uncorroborated anecdotes immediately warn readers that the material is to be taken as a breezy, gossipy biography rather than as a definitive scholarly study. Once those limitations are recognized, some pleasure can be derived from the author's witty observations. A typical example is the book's opening line: "Speaking of Billy Wilder, as who in Hollywood hasn't at one time or another, Harry

Kurnitz remarked after working with him on the movie script of WITNESS FOR THE PROSECUTION that 'beneath his aggressive gruff exterior is pure brillo.'" A filmography and index are included. Worth browsing.

*Zolotow, Maurice. BILLY WILDER IN HOLLYWOOD. New York: G. P. Putnam's Sons, 1977. Illustrated. 364pp.

The best and most authoritative biography on Wilder's American years, this comprehensive and in-depth study should be required reading for anyone who enjoys Hollywood lore. Although no attempt is made to analyze the director's movies, Zolotow's extensive interviews with people who knew and worked with Wilder tell us a great deal of the artist's style and idiosyncracies. Part of the book's charm lies in the delightful anecdotes. For example, Zolotow recounts the time that the cynical Wilder was trying to convince Sam Goldwyn that making a movie about the life of Nijinsky was no problem. After Wilder explained the plot, Goldwyn allegedly replied, "What kind of picture is this? . . . A Man who thinks he's a horse?" To which Wilder responded, "In my version, there's a happy ending, Sam . . . In the final scene we show Nijinsky winning the Kentucky Derby." Another part of the book's significance to film history is the inclusion of revealing insider's stories about important productions, especially the superb chapter on NINOTCHKA (1939). While some critics may deplore Zolotow's neglect of critical analyses,[726] general readers should be more than pleased by the portrait of this controversial artist. An index is included, but no filmography or bibliography. Well worth browsing.

SHELLEY WINTERS

*Winters, Shelley. SHELLEY: ALSO KNOWN AS SHIRLEY. New York: Ballantine Books, 1980. Illustrated. 500pp.

NATALIE WOOD

Harris, Warren G. NATALIE & R. J. : HOLLYWOOD'S STAR-CROSSED LOVERS. New York: Doubleday, 1988. Illustrated. 247pp.

JANE WYMAN

Quirk, Lawrence J. JANE WYMAN, THE ACTRESS AND THE WOMAN: AN ILLUSTRATED BIOGRAPHY. New York: Dembner Books, 1986. Illustrated. 216pp.

FILMS

AVANT-GARDE

STAN BRAKHAGE

THE WAY TO SHADOW GARDEN (U. S.--16mm: 1955, 12 mins., b/w, sound, R-C16, FMC)

---

[726] Roger Greenspun, "A Wilder Life," AMERICAN FILM 2:10 (September 1977):77-8.

Brakhage is an independent filmmaker who worked extensively in 8mm during the fifties and sixties. An example of his use of experimental sound to contrast the tensions between photographic imagery and abstract art, the content of the film concerns the experiences of a disturbed youth moving from a city nightscape to a private room to a garden. In almost all of the artist's films, he challenges our commonly held notions of perception. "Objects," explains Ed Lowry, "remain out of focus, subjects fail to be centered within the frame, scenes are shot with too little or too much light."[727] Other films by this artist can be obtained from the American Federation of the Arts, Films Incorporated, and the Film-Makers' Cooperative.

JAMES BROUGHTON

FOUR IN THE AFTERNOON (U. S.--16mm: 1951, 15 mins., b/w, sound, R-C16, RAD)
   This poetic film presents four different interpretations of love.

LOONY TOM (U. S.--16mm: 1953, 11 mins., b/w, sound, R-C16, RAD)
   Here the San Francisco filmmaker produces a satirical takeoff on the early Charlie Chaplin comedies.

JAMES DAVIS

THROUGH THE LOOKING GLASS (U. S.--16mm: 1954, 10 mins., color, sound, R-RAD)
   Davis seems to be the only filmmaker from the East Coast who has gained recognition for intriguing abstract films. Here the former painter shows some of his skill with illuminated plastics, lights, and colors.

MAYA DEREN

MEDITATION ON VIOLENCE (U. S.--16mm: 1948, 12 mins., b/w, sound, R-C16)
   This poetic dance film by one of the early avant-garde filmmakers is an exciting example of the work produced by independent artists. The action of the film involves visual rhythms and movements corresponding to Chinese boxing.

MESHES OF THE AFTERNOON (U. S.--16mm: 1943, 14 mins., b/w, sound, R-C16)
   A classic of the experimental cinema, this film explores the shades of difference between reality and fantasy.

NORMAN MCLAREN

BLINKETY BLANK (Canada--16mm: 1955, 6 mins., color, sound, R-NFB)

---

[727] Ed Lowry, "Program Notes: Three Films by Brakhage," CINEMATEXAS PROGRAM NOTES 11:2 (October 11, 1976):55. For more information, see Stan Brakhage, "The Art of Vision," FILM CULTURE 30 (Fall 1963):1-99; Jerome Hill, "Brakhage's Eyes," ibid., 52 (Spring 1971):43-7; Ernest Callenbach, "The Films of Stan Brakhage," FILM QUARTERLY 14:3 (Spring 1961):47-8; David James, "The Film-Maker as Romantic Poet: Brakhage and Olson," ibid., 35:3 (Spring 1982):35-43; Paul Arthur, "The Brakhage Lectures," FILM COMMENT 9:1 (January-February 1973):64-5; and Stan Brakhage, "Some Remarks," TAKE ONE 3:1 (September-October 1971):6-9.

McLaren represents a new force in animation, going away from the style of Walt Disney and more toward the techniques developed by UPA. This film is an experiment in intermittent animation and spasmodic imagery.

NEIGHBORS (Canada--16mm: 1953, 9 mins., color, sound, R-NFB)
   An animated film about two individuals who symbolize a breakdown of communications between people.

HOLLYWOOD

GEORGE CUKOR

A DOUBLE LIFE (Universal--16mm: 1947, 103 mins., b/w, sound, R-BUD, CHA, IVY, KIT)
   In this film, the first of seven movies written by the husband-and-wife team of Garson Kanin and Ruth Gordon and directed by Cukor, Ronald Colman gave an Oscar-winning performance as an actor consumed by his stage portrayal of Othello. Miklos Rozsa's music adds considerably to the melodramatic behind-the-scenes depiction of life in the theater. In addition to Coleman, the cast includes Shelley Winters, Philip Loeb,[728] Edmund O'Brien, and Signe Hasso.

ADAM'S RIB (MGM--16mm: 1949, 101 mins., b/w, sound, R-FES, MGM)
   One of the earliest Hollywood attacks on sexism in the post-WWII era, the Kanin-Gordon screenplay deals with two lawyers (Spencer Tracy and Katharine Hepburn) who are also married to each other, battling over the issue of equal rights for women. The defendant is a married woman (Judy Holliday), who is on trial for shooting her adulterous husband (Tom Ewell). The brilliance of the film lies not only in the acting (especially David Wayne's performance as an amorous next door neighbor) and comic situations, but also in the way that the director and script explore the parallels between the two marriages.

JULES DASSIN

THE NAKED CITY (Universal--16mm: 1948, 96 mins., b/w, sound, R-IVY)
   Based upon an unpublished story by Malvin Wald, the Oscar-nominated screenplay by Wald and Albert Maltz helped the director Dassin revolutionize the crime film genre.[729] The New York manhunt by a shrewd, elderly cop (Barry Fitzgerald) for the killer of a beautiful female model was depicted in a semidocumentary style and filmed on over 100 locations throughout Manhattan and Brooklyn by William Daniels. Considerable credit also goes to Mark Hellinger, the producer, who rebelled against

---

[728]   Philip Loeb was one of the first casualties of the blacklisting era and served as the inspiration for the Zero Mostel role in THE FRONT (1976).

[729]   For more information, see *Albert Maltz and Malvin Wald, THE NAKED CITY, ed. Matthew J. Bruccoli (Carbondale: Southern Illinois University Press, 1979); Cynthia Grenier, "Jules Dassin: An Interview," SIGHT AND SOUND 27:3 (Winter 1957-58):141-3; John Francis Lane, "I See Dassin Make the Law," FILMS AND FILMING 4:12 (September 1958):28-9; Jules Dassin, "Style and Instinct: Part 1," ibid., 16:4 (February 1970):22-6; ___, "Style and Instinct: Part 2," ibid., 16:6 (March 1970):66-70; and Rob Edelman, "THE NAKED CITY," THE INTERNATIONAL DICTIONARY OF FILMS AND FILMMAKERS: VOLUME I, pp.309-10.

studio productions and argued for authentic stories shot in realistic formats.   After
proving his point with the hard-hitting prison film, BRUTE FORCE (1947), Hellinger
and Dassin got the go-ahead to expand their on-site shooting with THE NAKED CITY.

JOHN FORD

MY DARLING CLEMENTINE (Fox--16mm: 1946, 97 mins., b/w, sound, R-FNC)
     One of the most mythical of all westerns, the Samuel G. Engel-Winston Miller
screenplay based on a story by Sam Hellman deals with the legendary Wyatt Earp-Doc
Holliday friendship and the gunfight with the Clanton family at the O. K. Corral in
Tombstone, Arizona. Ford's first movie after leaving the military reveals a number
of the effects of World War II had on his cinematic style. On one hand, his emphasis
on the importance of family values remains constant as he contrasts the heroic
Earps--Wyatt (Henry Fonda), Virgil (Tim Holt), Morgan (Ward Bond), James (Don
Garner)--with the villainous Clantons--the father (Walter Brennan), Billy (John
Ireland), Ike (Grant Withers), Sam (Mickey Simpson), Phin (Fred Libby). On the
other hand, family life rapidly disintegrates during the film, so that by the end of
a week (roughly the timespan of the movie) only three Earps and no Clantons are left
alive. The image of the hero also undergoes a transformation from the clear-cut
figures of Ford's pre-WWII days to the vacilating images of Wyatt and Doc Holliday
(Victor Mature), especially in the violent way they settle their disputes. Although a
number of critics attack the film for its technical flaws and for its romantic
storytelling, the film's supporters admire Ford's last optimistic western about the
taming of the frontier.[730]

SAMUEL FULLER

THE STEEL HELMET (Lippert--16mm: 1951, 84 mins., b/w, sound, R-BUD, FNC,
WIL)
     Typical of the action-packed, low-budget independent films that Fuller was
writing, producing, and directing in the early 1950s, this cynical and brutal story
of an American infantry patrol in Korea is not only the first Hollywood film on the
subject but is also the first re-examination of the conventions of the Hollywood World
War II film genre. Fuller has his isolated band of misfits questioning military strategy,
exploring heretofore taboo racial issues concerning black and Nisei soldiers, and
portraying new types of enlisted men in combat. Although the resolution follows
standard Hollywood lines and the production values detract from the film's overall
impact, John Belton speaks for many of Fuller's fans when he writes that the film
"reveals a remarkable refinement of visual style.   The characters' racial and political
biases, which embarrass those critics who mistakenly confuse them with Fuller's own,
set up rigid systems of belief which serve to isolate characters from one another.
Fuller's characters operate on a set of principles so inflexible that change results in
insanity or death rather than flexibility."[731]

---

[730]   For more information see, Courtenay Beinhorn, "Program Notes: MY DARLING
     CLEMENTINE," CINEMATEXAS PROGRAM NOTES 4:37 (March 21, 1973):1-5; Nick Barbaro,
     "Program Notes: MY DARLING CLEMENTINE," ibid., 11:3 (October 21, 1976):1-6; Mark
     Alvey, "Program Notes: MY DARLING CLEMENTINE," ibid., 26:2 (February 29,
     1984):19-30; Stefan Fleischer, "A Study Through Stills of MY DARLING CLEMENTINE,"
     JOURNAL OF MODERN LITERATURE 3:2 (April 1973):241-52; and Douglas Gomery,
     "Mise-En-Scene in John Ford's MY DARLING CLEMENTINE," WIDE ANGLE 2:4 (1978):14-9.

[731]   John Belton, "Are YOU Waving THE Flag at Me?: Samuel Fuller and Politics, THE
     VELVET LIGHT TRAP 14 (Spring 1972):10-1.   For more information, see Arthur

PICKUP ON SOUTH STREET (Fox--16mm: 1953, 80 mins., b/w, sound, R-FNC, WIL)
Operating as writer-director on this adaptation of Dwight Taylor's story about the New York underworld, Fuller fashions a brutal and savage depiction of how communism needs to be fought if America is to survive. The highly controversial merging of the conventions of the gangster film with those of the spy thriller illustrates how Hollywood revised its formulas to satisfy the decade's fears and anxieties. Moreover, the simplistic depiction of communists as mean, violent, and treacherous led many critics to characterize Fuller as someone blind to the complexities of political, social, and moral issues. "For Fuller--and this may be the source of the unfair accusations of fascism levelled at him--there are no [other] versions [of the story]," observes Gavin Millar, "only the truth; the story of the world; no maybes, only right and wrong."[732] Garnham also points out that Fuller's anti-Communist approach is much more complex than critics generally admit. "Communists," he writes, "fulfil two dramatic functions in Fuller's movies. They are often nightmare figures in the minds of the characters, associated directly with mental breakdown . . . [and they] often act as crucial catalysts."[733] In addition to the film's historical value as a unique example of anti-Communist products during the 1950s, it functions as an example of the way that modern filmmakers were examining the pressures and responsibilities of individuals trying to maintain their independence yet reacting to the issues of the day. Good performances are provided by Richard Widmark, Jean Peters, and Thelma Ritter.

HOWARD HAWKS

THE BIG SLEEP (Warner Bros.--16mm: 1946, 114 mins., b/w, sound, R-MGM)
In this very involved but entertaining Raymond Chandler detective story, Philip Marlowe (Bogart) becomes involved with eight murders plus two incredible sisters (Lauren Bacall and Martha Vickers), the greatest two-bit thug in film history (Elisha Cook, Jr.), and the most seductive book-seller (Dorothy Malone) to date. Faulkner

---

Knight, "Sam Fuller: The Gold Beneath the Brass," HOLLYWOOD REPORTER (July 18, 1980):16; Andrew Sarris, "Fuller Up," VILLAGE VOICE 29:3 (January 17, 1984):49; Stig Bjorkman and Mark Shivas, "Samuel Fuller: Two Interviews," MOVIE 17 (Winter 1969-70):25-31; Samuel Fuller, "War That's Fit to Shoot," AMERICAN FILM 2:2 (November 1976):58-62; Bruce Cook, "Sam Fuller Lands with THE BIG RED ONE," ibid., 4:8 (June 1979):20-4, 47; Richard Thompson, "3 x Sam: The Flavor of Ketchup--Sam Fuller Interviewed," FILM COMMENT 13:1 (January-February 1977):25-31; Tom Milne, "Sam Fuller's War," SIGHT AND SOUND 49:4 (Autumn 1980):256-7; Lee Russell, "Samuel Fuller," NEW LEFT REVIEW 23 (January-February 1964):86-9; Peter Wollen, "Notes Towards a Structural Analysis of the Films of Samuel Fuller," CINEMA 3:6 (December 1968):26-9; Kingsley Canham, "The World of Samuel Fuller," FILM 55 (Summer 1969):4-10; and ___, "Samuel Fuller's Action Films," SCREEN 10:6 (November-December 1969):80-92. See also Emil Weiss's documentary FALKENAU, THE IMPOSSIBLE (1988), available in 35mm from the director. For more information on the Weiss film, see Caryn James, "2 Ways Art Gives Shape to Political Horrors," NEW YORK TIMES C (October 5, 1988):23.

[732] Millar, p.402. For more information, see Frank McConnell, "PICKUP ON SOUTH STREET and the Metamorphosis of the Thriller," FILM HERITAGE 8:3 (Spring 1973):9-18; and Colin McArthur, "Samuel Fuller's Gangster Films," ibid., pp.93-101.

[733] Nicholas Garnham, SAMUEL FULLER (New York: The Viking Press, 1971), p.116.

wrote the screenplay,[734] which includes some of the sharpest dialogue and bits of business in film thrillers.

ALFRED HITCHCOCK

DIAL M FOR MURDER (Warner Bros.--16mm: 1954, 105 mins., color, sound, R-FES)
     Frederick Knott's script, adapted from his play, deals with a scheming husband (Ray Milland) who plots to murder his wife (Grace Kelly). In addition to being the first of Kelly's three Hitchcock films--the other two are REAR WINDOW (1954) and TO CATCH A THIEF (1956)--the film is one of the few major works that was originally intended to be released in 3-D. The novelty, however, had worn off by 1954, and the movie was distributed primarily in the standard flat screen format. The film is also a good example of Hitchcock's skill in letting the audience know at the outset who the villain is yet maintaining maximum suspense until the end of the movie. Among the movie's virtues, as Donald Spoto points out, is "its pacing and its refusal to capitulate to the eccentricities of the 3-D process."[735]

REAR WINDOW (Paramount--16mm: 1954, 112 mins, color, sound, R-FES, SWA)
     John Michael Hayes's screenplay, adapted from a novel by Cornell Woolrich, deals with the voyeurism of a press photographer (James Stewart) who has broken his leg and is confined to his second-story apartment. To pass the time, he spies on his neighbors across the courtyard. Although Stewart vicariously becomes involved with a number of different people, the one that interests him most is an adulterer (Raymond Burr),[736] who Stewart thinks has killed his wife. He is unable, however, to convince either his sweetheart (Grace Kelly) or housekeeper (Thelma Ritter) that a crime has been committed. In response to one interviewer's question about Stewart's role, Hitchcock stated that "The audience ARE with Stewart, the identification is direct and therefore they must feel superior to the other characters with him, but the frustration is there all the same. The interesting thing I think about REAR WINDOW is that there's more pure film there, even though it's static, than in many films I've made."[737] Particularly useful in this film is the chance to see why Hitchcock's suspenseful techniques appealed to 1950s' audiences and why feminist critics attack Hitchcock's attitudes on women and marriage.

---

[734] Praxton Davis, "Bogart, Hawks, and THE BIG SLEEP Revisited--Frequently," THE FILM JOURNAL 1:2 (Summer 1971):2-9. In addition, the script is available in FILM SCRIPTS ONE.

[735] Donald Spoto, THE ART OF ALFRED HITCHCOCK: FIFTY YEARS OF HIS MOTION PICTURES (New York: Hopkinson and Blake, 1976), p.235.

[736] A number of commentators suggest that Hitchcock modeled Burr's appearance on David O. Selznick's looks and thus seized an opportunity to caricature his former employer.

[737] Ian Cameron and V. F. Perkins, "Hitchcock," MOVIE 6 (January 1963):6. For other perspectives, see Robert Stam and Roberta Pearson, "Hitchcock's REAR WINDOW: Reflexivity and the Critique of Voyeurism," ENCLITIC, 7:1 (Spring 1983):136-45; R. Barton Palmer, "The Metafictional Hitchcock: The Experience of Viewing and the Viewing of Experience in REAR WINDOW and PSYCHO," ibid., 26:2 (Winter 1986):4-29; and Ruth Perlmutter, "REAR WINDOW: A Construction Story," JOURNAL OF FILM AND VIDEO 37:2 (Spring 1985):53-65.

JOHN HUSTON

THE TREASURE OF THE SIERRA MADRE (Warner Bros.--16mm: 1948, 126 mins., b/w, sound, R-CHA, SWA, UAS)

Huston directed and wrote the screenplay (based on a novel by B. Traven) for this cynical tale of three down-and-out Americans (Humphrey Bogart, Tim Holt, and Walter Huston) searching for gold and finding it in Mexico. Limiting the action to a handful of locations, he does a magnificent job of exploring human nature and the corrupting power of success. No sympathy is extended to the prospectors as they fight against bandits, nature, and themselves. In his first film after leaving the service, Huston did such an outstanding job of examining the power that greed has over the three men, that he won two Oscars (writing and directing), while his father won one for Best Supporting Actor. Interestingly, the film died at the box office and little recognition was given to Alfonso Bedoya's superb performance as the ruthless bandit.

THE AFRICAN QUEEN (United Artists--16mm: 1951, 103 mins., color, sound, R-BUD, CIN, FES, FNC, IMA, IVY, SWA, TWY, WHO)

Scripted by Huston, James Agee, and Peter Viertel (based upon C. S. Forester's novel), this low-key story of a down-and-out skipper (Humphrey Bogart) and an "old-maid" British missionary (Katharine Hepburn) who find love in the Belgian Congo during World War I is one of the great treasures of the 1950s. Not only did Huston's location shooting in the Congo capture the realism of the experience, but also the director's upbeat ending (the last of four climaxes tried in the production) set the perfect mood for the film's touching romance. Nominated for four Oscars, including Best Actress, Best Director, and Best Screenplay (Huston and Agee), it won for Best Actor. Considerable praise also is due to the cinematographer Jack Cardiff.[738]

ELIA KAZAN

BOOMERANG (Fox--16mm: 1947, 88 mins., b/w, sound, R-FNC, TWY

Although Kazan initially showed little interest in Richard Murphy's script, calling it "a routine little drama,"[739] he grew to appreciate the possibilities the story had for semidocumentary filmmaking. Dana Andrews gives one of his finest performances as the honest and relentless district attorney who is unable to prosecute an innocent man for the unsolved murder of a New England priest. The plot, based on an an actual event involving Homer Cummings (attorney general during President Roosevelt's first term), raises important issues on the way law enforcement agencies conduct their investigations.

ON THE WATERFRONT (Columbia--16mm: 1954, 108 mins., b/w, sound, R-BUD, FNC, KIT, ROA, SWA, TWY, WEL, WES, WHO, WIL)

Scripted by Budd Schulberg, this rare film about corruption and brutality on the New York waterfronts is also perceived as a defense by the director Kazan and Schulberg in justifying their cooperation with HUAC. Nominated for Oscars, including Best Supporting Actor (Karl Malden, Lee J. Cobb, and Rod Steiger), and Best

---

[738] For more information, see *Katharine Hepburn, THE MAKING OF "THE AFRICAN QUEEN" OR HOW I WENT TO AFRICA WITH BOGART, BACALL AND HUSTON AND ALMOST LOST MY MIND (New York: Alfred A. Knopf, 1987).

[739] Elia Kazan, A LIFE (New York: Alfred A. Knopf, 1988), p.316.

Scoring of a Dramatic or Comedy Picture (Leonard Bernstein), it won for Best Film, Best Actor (Marlon Brando), Best Supporting Actress (Eva Marie Saint), Best Director, Best Story and Screenplay, Best Cinematograpy (Boris Kaufman), Best Black-and-White Art Direction-Set Direction (Richard Day), and Best Film Editing (Gene Milford).[740]

GENE KELLY AND STANLEY DONEN

SINGIN' IN THE RAIN (MGM--16mm: 1952, 103 mins., color, sound, R-FES, MGM)
     Gene Kelly and Stanley Donen teamed up to direct this superb musical spoof of what happened to Hollywood during the early days of sound. It may well be one of the finest musicals ever made.[741] In addition to a score of marvelous tunes by Nacio Herb Brown and Arthur Freed, there are the inspired performances of Kelly, Debbie Reynolds, Donald O'Connor, and Jean Hagen. It was nominated for two Oscars: Best Supporting Actress (Hagen), and Best Scoring of a Musical Picture (Lennie Hayton).

JOSEPH LOSEY

THE BOY WITH GREEN HAIR (RKO--16mm: 1948, 82 mins., b/w, R-RKO)
     A Dore Schary production with a script by Ben Barzman and Alfred Lewis Levitt, adapted from a story by Betsy Beaton, this low-budget production marks Losey's film debut and reveals a great deal not only about the director's short-lived Hollywood experiences, but also about Hollywood in the post-WWII period. For example, Losey had wanted to do the film in black-and-white, but the studio insisted on technicolor. He had reservations about casting, but the studio forced him to take its contract players. Fortunately, Pat O'Brien, Robert Ryan, and Dean Stockwell worked out well. The original producer for the movie was Adrian Scott, but he was removed from the picture because of the HUAC hearings. And Schary, who was in charge of RKO and in favor of the film, was removed before the picture was released, and Howard Hughes, the new boss, shelved the film for six months because he believed it to be a Communist film. Although the Beaton story was intended to be a fantasy about racial discrimination, Losey turned it into a pacifist allegory on the peace movement. Stockwell stars as a bewildered war orphan sent to live with his grandfather (O'Brien) in a small American town. When the boy's hair suddenly turns green, the bigoted town sees the child as a threat to its security rather than as a reminder to prevent future wars. Although the film's symbolism is awkward and heavy-handed, the movie, as Foster Hirsch explains, foreshadows many of Losey's gifts as a future director: e.g., "the way ideas and states of mind can be communicated visually," "the kind of composition and use of the camera that Losey will develop and refine in his subsequent work," and "the long take and the roving, tracking, inquiring camera that will become Losey's trademarks."[742]

---

[740] Dennis John Hall, "Method Master: Rod Steiger's Career--Part I," FILMS AND FILMING 17:3 (December 1970):28-32; ___, "Part II," ibid., 17:4 (January 1970):28-33; Lindsay Anderson, "The Last Sequence of ON THE WATERFRONT," SIGHT AND SOUND 24:3 (January-February 1955):127-30; and Gary Collins, "Kazan in the Fifties," THE VELVET LIGHT TRAP 11 (Winter 1974):41-5.

[741] Rudy Behlmer, "Gene Kelly," FILMS IN REVIEW 15:1 (January 1964):6-22; John Cutts, "Kelly: Part One . . . Dancer, . . . Director," FILMS AND FILMING 10:11 (August 1964):38-42; and John Cutts, ". . . Part Two," ibid., 10:12 (September 1964):34-7.

[742] Foster Hirsch, JOSEPH LOSEY (Boston: Twayne Publishers, 1980), p.35. For more

JOSEPH L. MANKIEWITZ

ALL ABOUT EVE (Fox--16mm: 1950, 130 mins., b/w, sound, R-FES, FNC)

Based on Mary Orr's short story, "The Wisdom of Eve," Joseph L. Mankiewicz[743] scripted and directed this ironic film of a young woman, Eve Harrington (Anne Baxter), who dreams about becoming a Broadway star. At first, Eve appears innocent to us, but as the story unfolds we come to recognize her true nature. Splendid performances are given by Baxter, as well as Bette Davis and George Sanders.[744] Nominated for an astonishing number of Oscars (fourteen), the picture won six Academy Awards: Best Film, Best Supporting Actor (Sanders), Best Director, Best Screenplay, Best Costume Design (Edith Head and Charles LeMaire), and Best Sound Recording (20th Century-Fox Sound Department).

ANTHONY MANN

WINCHESTER '73 (Universal--16mm: 1950, 92 mins., b/w, R-SWA, WIL)

---

information, see Raymond Durgnat, "The Cubist Puritanism of Joseph Losey," FILM 50 (Winter 1967):10-12; ___, "Losey: Modesty and Eve," FILMS AND FILMING 12:7 (April 1966):26-33; ___, "Losey: Puritan Maids," ibid., 12:8 (May 1966):28-33; Gordon Gow, "Weapons: An Interview with Joseph Losey," ibid., 18: 1 (October 1971):36-41; Gilles Jacob, "Joseph Losey, or the Camera Calls," SIGHT AND SOUND 35:2 (Spring 1966):62-7; Philip Strick, "Mice in the Milk," ibid., 38:2 (Spring 1969):77-9; Richard Combs, "The Country of the Past Revisited: Losey, Galileo, and the Romantic Englishwoman," ibid., 44:3 (Summer 1975):138-43; T. J. Ross, "Notes on an Early Losey," FILM CULTURE 40 (Spring 1966):35-7; Gene D. Phillips, "The Critical Camera of Joseph Losey," CINEMA 4:1 (Spring 1968):22-34; Beverle Houston and Marsha Kinder, "The Losey-Pinter Collaboration," FILM QUARTERLY 32:1 (Fall 1978):17-30; Richard Roud, "The Reluctant Exile: Joseph Losey," SIGHT AND SOUND 48:3 (Summer 1979):145-7, 153; and "Dialogue on Film: Joseph Losey," AMERICAN FILM 4:2 (November 1980):53-60. .

[743] In addition to the material contained in Chapter 5, see John Howard Reid, "Cleo's Joe: Part I--The Typewriter Years," FILMS AND FILMING 9:11 (August 1963):44-8; "Part II--All About Eve and Others," ibid., 9:12 (September 1963):13-6; Gordon Gow, "Cocking A Snook," ibid., 17:2 (November 1970):18-22, 84; Jacques Bontemp and Richard Overstreet, "Measure for Measure: Interview with Joseph L. Mankiewicz," CAHIERS DU CINEMA IN ENGLISH, 8 (May 1966):28-42; John Springer, "The Films of Joseph L. Mankiewicz," FILMS IN REVIEW 22:3 (March 1971):153-7; and Kenneth Geist, "Mankiewicz: The Thinking Man's Director," AMERICAN FILM 3:6 (April 1978):54-60.

[744] For more information, see Farber, p.61; David Shipman, "Whatever Happened to Bette Davis?" FILMS AND FILMING 9:7 (April 1963):8-9; Bette Davis, "What Is a Star?" ibid., 11:12 (September 1965):5-7; Kingsley Canham, Lawrence J. Quirk, "Bette Davis," FILMS IN REVIEW 6:10 (December 1955):481-99; Ann Griffith, "All About Eve," ibid., 1:9 (December 1950):37-8. Gary Carey, "The Lady and the Director: Bette Davis and William Wyler," FILM COMMENT 6:3 (Fall 1970):18-24; Michell Raper, "Mannerisms--in the Grand Manner," FILMS AND FILMING 1:12 (September 1955):7; Peter Baker, "All About Bette," ibid., 2:8 (May 1956):11-3; Ann Guerin, "Bette Davis: Part One," SHOW 2:2 (April 1971):28-30; ___, "Part Two," ibid., 2:3 (May 1972):28-9; "All About Eve," ibid., 15:6 (March 1969):88; Richard Winnington, "All About Eve," SIGHT AND SOUND 19:9 (January 1951):373-4; and DIALOGUE WITH THE WORLD, pp.49-50.

The Robert L. Richards-Borden Chase screenplay adapted from a story by Stuart N. Lake helped pioneer the "adult western," movies that probed the psychological and moral conflicts their protagonists faced on the frontier. Unlike the pre-WWII outdoor films, with uncomplicated heroes defending the community against scoundrels, the new protagonists were neurotic individuals hell-bent on revenge. The Mannian hero, as Jim Kitses explains, is always conscious of his own failings: "The revenge taken by the character is taken upon HIMSELF, a punishment the inner meaning of which is a denial of reason and humanity. In general, all of Mann's heroes behave as if driven by a vengeance they must inflict upon themselves for having once been human, trusting, and therefore vulnerable. Hence the schizophrenic style of the hero, the violent explosions of passion alternating with precarious moments of quiet reflection."[745] In this movie, the first of eight adult westerns directed by Mann and starring James Stewart,[746] the story deals with a tormented cowboy (Stewart) out to kill his brother (Stephen McNally), who murdered their father.

DELBERT MANN

MARTY (United Artists--16mm: 1955, 91 mins., b/w, sound, R-FES, MGM)

This low-budget film momentarily revolutionized the film industry when producers realized that a sensitive and poignant story about a lonely, unappealing New York butcher (Ernest Borgnine) and his search for love with a bashful schoolteacher (Betsy Blair) could draw millions to the box office.[747] The script, adapted from a TV show starring Rod Steiger, gets high marks for its sensitive use of dialogue and true-to-life

---

[745] *Jim Kitses, HORIZONS WEST: ANTHONY MANN, BUD BOETTICHER, SAM PECKINPAH--STUDIES OF AUTHORSHIP WITHIN THE WESTERN (London: British Film Institute, 1969), p.33. For more information on Mann, see Stephen Handzo, "Through the Devil's Door: The Early Westerns of Anthony Mann," BRIGHT LIGHTS 1:4 (Summer 1976):4-15; John Howard Reid, "Mann and His Environment: First Part of an Analysis of Anthony Mann's Work for the Cinema," FILMS AND FILMING 8:4 (January 1962):11-2, 44; ___, "Tension at Twilight: Second Part of an Analysis of Anthony Mann's Work for the Cinema," ibid., 8:5 (February 1962):19-20, 46; Robert Smith, "Mann In the Dark," ibid., 2:1 (Fall 1976):8-15; Christopher Wicking and Barrie Pattison, "Interview With Anthony Mann," SCREEN 10:4 (July-October 1969):32-54; MOVIETONE NEWS, Nos.60-61 (Fall 1978); J. H. Fenwick and Jonathan Green-Armytage, "Now You See It: Landscape and Anthony Mann," SIGHT AND SOUND 34:4 (Autumn 1965):186-9; Jim Kitses, "Borden Chase: An Interview," THE HOLLYWOOD SCREENWRITERS, ed. Richard Corliss (New York: Avon, 1972), pp.147-67; Jean-Claude Missiaen, "A Lesson in Cinema: Interview With Anthony Mann," CAHIERS DU CINEMA IN ENGLISH, No.12 (December 1967):44-51; and Patrick Brion and Olivier Eyquem, "Biofilmography of Anthony Mann," ibid., pp.52-9.

[746] For more information, see William R. Sweigart, "James Stewart," FILMS IN REVIEW 15:10 (December 1964):585-605; Dennis John Hall, "Box Office Drawl: An Analysis of the Films of James Stewart," FILMS AND FILMING 19:3 (December 1972):24-8; and ___, "Portrait in Human Frailty: Concluding an Analysis of the Films of James Stewart," ibid., 19:5 (February 1973):36-40.

[747] John Izod points out that MARTY was the first in a line of TV shows that Hollywood found "bankable" in terms of a pre-sold product. That is, the PARAMOUNT case turned filmmakers away from a heavy reliance on original screenplays, and toward "sources" that the public was familiar with. In this way, the moneymen presumably took less of a gamble with their film investments. See *John Izod, HOLLYWOOD AND THE BOX OFFICE, 1895-1986 (New York: Columbia University Press, 1988), p.154.

situations. Borgnine received an Oscar for Best Actor, and the film, director, and screenwriter (Paddy Chayefsky) were also honored.[748]

VINCENTE MINNELLI

AN AMERICAN IN PARIS (MGM--16mm: 1951, 112 mins., color, sound, R-FNC)
Vincente Minnelli directed his choreographer and star Gene Kelly in a marvelous musical about an ex-GI (Kelly) who decides to stay in Paris and become an artist. While Alan Jay Lerner's screenplay serves as an excuse to involve the audience in Minnelli's favorite theme of art versus life, the purpose of the movie is to showcase Gershwin music and expert dancing. This film contains one of the best ballet sequences ever photographed. The movie was honored with six Oscars, including Best Film, Best Story and Screenplay, Best Color Cinematography (Alfred Gilks and John Alton), Best Art Direction-Set Direction (Cedric Gibbons and Preston Ames), Best Costume Design (Walter Plunkett and Irene Sharaff), and Best Musical Scoring (John Green and Saul Chaplin). At the same time, as Jackie Byers points out, it is important to remember that the ideological underpinnings of Hollywood musicals is to "naturalize and dehistoricize a set of values and beliefs about the world, a world view."[749] Among the elements worth examining in this musical are the attitudes toward women having to work, and the conventions of romantic love.

MAX OPHULS

LETTER FROM AN UNKNOWN WOMAN (Universal--16mm: 1948, 87 mins., b/w, sound, R-BUD, CHA, IMA, KIT; S-NTA)
Produced by John Houseman, scripted by Howard Koch, and based on Stephan Zweig's novella BRIEF EINER UNBEKANNTEN, the classic film, set in Vienna at the turn of the century, tells the story of a callous pianist (Louis Jordan) who seduces an impressionable young woman (Joan Fontaine) and misleads her into thinking she is his one true love. Even after he leaves her, she continues to harbor her misperception. Not only does she bear his child and not tell him, but also she marries another man to provide a proper home for the boy. Years later, the woman encounters the ex-pianist and forsakes her family for him, only to discover the truth about his feelings for her. Disillusioned, she leaves and dies soon after in a typhoid epidemic. He, in turn, learns the truth from a letter she wrote and allows himself to be killed in a duel with her husband. Ophuls's use of costumes, sets, narrative structure, and film technique illustrates his brilliant skill in adapting the work of his collaborators and imbuing it with his unique interpretation of love. Moreover, as Virginia Wright Wexman points out, the film illustrates how Ophuls, working in Hollywood in the late 1940s, "existed in an atmosphere which could only have exacerbated his sense of despair, both about his prospects as German Jew and about the future of technology. Recreating a pivotal moment in turn-of-the-century Vienna allowed him to poeticize that despair if not to master it."[750]

---

[748] See Carolyn Perkins, "Program Notes: MARTY," CINEMATEXAS 6:31 (March 21, 1974):1-6.

[749] Jackie Byers, "Program Notes: AN AMERICAN IN PARIS," CINEMATEXAS PROGRAM NOTES 18:3 (April 30, 1980):94. See also Terry Curtis Fox, "Vincente Minnelli: The Decorative Auteur," VILLAGE VOICE (February 6, 1978):37; Andrew Sarris, "Minnelli's Magic," ibid., (1986):51, 58; and Eric Pace, "Vincente Minnelli Dies; Movie Director was 76," NEW YORK TIMES B (July 27 1986):23.

[750] *Virginia Wright Wexman, ed., with Karen Hollinger, "LETTER FROM AN UNKNOWN WOMAN": MAX OPHULS, DIRECTOR (New Brunswick: Rutgers University Press, 1986),

OTTO PREMINGER

THE MOON IS BLUE (United Artists--16mm: 1953, 90 mins., b/w, sound, R-FNC, WHO)
    In addition to being the first major Hollywood film to be shown successfully without the MPAA's Seal of Approval, this harmless romantic comedy illustrates how directors like Preminger became independent producers and took on the Hollywood establishment. Having staged F. Hugh Herbert's play in 1951, Preminger decided to turn it into his first independent production. In adapting his own work, Hubert's screenplay about a successful architect (William Holden) and his problems with his fiancee (Dawn Addams), an actress (Maggie McNamara), and her father (David Niven) contains six lines of dialogue that offended both the MPAA and the Legion of Decency. Among the words that Preminger, who had complete control of the final version, refused to cut were "virgin," "seduce," and "pregnant."[751]

NICHOLAS RAY

JOHNNY GUITAR (Republic--16mm: 1954, 110 mins., color, sound, R-BUD, FES, IVY, KIT, WHO)
    "Though REBEL [WITHOUT A CAUSE] is Ray's best film," writes John Francis Kreidl, "JOHNNY GUITAR is the film one should see just to get acquainted with Ray's work, for here we see Ray the AUTHOR (as opposed to REBEL, where we see Ray the COLLABORATOR), and in this film Ray's strengths and weaknesses are more vivid and evident than in any other work of his."[752] Set in Arizona in the late 1800s, Phillip Yordan's screenplay, based on Ray Chanslor's novel, tells the story of two ruthless women who battle for power and love in the wild West. At a time when Hollywood seemed ready to write off the western, Ray decided to "break every goddamn rule there was to break in a western."[753] Interestingly, the film was shot in Spain (Ray

---

p.14. After consulting Wright's excellent anthology, see Michael Kerbel, "Letter from An Unknown Woman," FILM COMMENT 7:2 (Summer 1971): 60-1; Roger Greenspun, "Corrections: LETTER FROM AN UNKNOWN WOMAN," ibid., 11:1 (January-February 1975):89-92; and Fred Camper, "Distance and Style: The Visual Rhetoric of Max Ophuls--LETTER FROM AN UNKNOWN WOMAN," MONOGRAM 5 (1974):21-4.

[751] For more information, see Otto Preminger, "Your Taste, My Taste . . ." and the Censor's," FILMS AND FILMING 6:2 (November 1959):7, 31; John Howard Reid, "Both Sides of the Camera," ibid., 7:5 (February 1961):15-6; ___, "Fabulous Saints and Sinners: Second Part of an Analysis of Preminger's Work for the Cinema," ibid., 7:6 (March 1961):31-2, 39; "The Screen Answers Back," ibid., 8:8 (May 1962):18; Andrew Sarris, "Preminger's 2 Periods--Studio and Solo," FILM COMMENT 3:3 (Summer 1965):12-6; "Interview With Otto Preminger," MOVIE 4 (November 1962):18-20; Ian Cameron, et al., "An Interview With Otto Preminger," ibid., 13 (Summer 1965):14-6; Molly Haskell, "Frames: The Quality of Preminger," INTELLECTUAL DIGEST (January 1973):68-70; Andrew Sarris, "Preminger: Two Cheers for the Film-Flam Man," VILLAGE VOICE (May 27, 1986):70; and "Preminger, 80, Dead of Cancer in New York," HOLLYWOOD REPORTER (April 24, 1986):1, 7.

[752] John Francis Kreidl, NICHOLAS RAY (Boston: Twayne Publishers, 1977), p.43.

[753] Michael Goodwin and Naomi Wise, "Nicholas Ray: Rebel!" TAKE ONE 5:6 (January 1977):11. For more information, see Mike Wilmington, "Nicholas Ray: The Years at RKO--Part One," THE VELVET LIGHT TRAP 10 (Fall 1973):46-53; ___, "Nicholas Ray on the Years at RKO," ibid., pp.54-5; ___, "Nicholas Ray: The Years at RKO--Part Two," ibid., 11 (Winter 1974):35-40; Victor Perkins, "The Cinema of

empathised with his peers who were being blacklisted, claiming that his political views had made him "graylisted," and left Hollywood briefly) and is often described as a "political western" containing numerous anti-McCarthy images and statements. At the same time, as Victor F. Perkins comments, Ray's adventurers epitomize the pressure to conform that society imposes on individuals: "Ray's adventurers are adventurers not by choice, like the Hawks or Walsh heroes, but through interior compulsion. They are 'displaced' persons whose isolation is emphasized by their involvement with a group which stands apart from society and often outside the law. Indeed their non-conformism is such that they isolate themselves even from these unconventional groups. . . ."[754] Good performances are turned in by Mercedes McCambridge and Joan Crawford.

ROBERT ROSSEN

aODY AND SOUL (United Artist--16mm: 1947, 104 mins., b/w, sound, R-BUD, IVY, KIT; S-IVY)

John Garfield gives a superb performance as the confused fighter who has to choose between fame and integrity. Based upon actual criminal investigations into corruption in the boxing world, Abraham Polansky's hard-hitting script represents the new direction problem films were taking in the post-war period. The film's impressive pacing earned Francis Lyon and Robert Parrish the 1947 Oscar for Best Editing. That same year, Garfield, Rossen, and Polansky were cited by witch-hunters as "subversives" and, by 1949, the talented trio was blacklisted.[755]

Nicholas Ray," MOVIE READER, ed. Ian Cameron (New York: Praeger, 1972), pp.64-70; Robin Wood, "Film Favorites: BIGGER THAN LIFE," FILM COMMENT 8:3 (September-October 1972):56-61; Nicholas Ray, "Story Into Script," SIGHT AND SOUND 26:2 (Autumn 1956):70-4; Jonathan Rosenbaum, "Circle of Pain: The Cinema of Nicholas Ray," ibid., 42:4 (Autumn 1973):218-21; David Thomson, "In a Lonely Place," ibid., 48:4 (Autumn 1979):215-20; Tom Farrell et al., "Nicholas Ray: The Last Movies," ibid., 50:2 (Spring 1981):92-7; Peter Biskind, "Rebel Without a Cause: Nicholas Ray in the Fifties," FILM QUARTERLY 28:1 (Fall 1974):32-8; Joseph Lederer, "Film as Experience: Nicholas Ray--The Director Turns Teacher," AMERICAN FILM 1:2 (November 1975):60-4; Jay Cocks, "Director In Aspic," TAKE ONE 5:6 (January 1977):17-21; Terry Fox, "Nicholas Ray, Without a Cause," VILLAGE VOICE (July 9, 1979):38; and Alfred E. Clark, "Nicholas Ray, 67; Director of Films," NEW YORK TIMES B (June 18, 1979):13. See also David Helpern, Jr.'s, documentary film about Ray, I'M A STRANGER HERE MYSELF (1974), available in 16mm from FNC.

[754]   V. F. Perkins, "The Cinema of Nicholas Ray," p.69.

[755]   For more information, see Henry Hart, "Notes on Robert Rossen," FILMS IN REVIEW 13:6 (June-July 1962):333-5; Henry Burton, "Notes on Rossen Films," ibid., 335-41; John Springer, "A Rossen Index," ibid., pp.341-2; Andrew Sarris, "Minor Disappointments," FILM CULTURE 28 (Spring 1963):43-4; Saul Cohen, "Robert Rossen and the "New American Gothic," FILM QUARTERLY 20:1 (Fall 1966):22-7; Joan Mellen, "Fascism In the Contemporary Cinema," ibid., 14:4 (Summer 1971):2-19; Alan Casty, "The Films of Robert Rossen," ibid., 20:2 (Winter 1966-67):3-12; ___, "Robert Rossen," CINEMA 4:3 (Fall 1968):18-22; Jean-Louis Noames, "Lessons Learned In Combat: Interview With Robert Rossen," CAHIERS DU CINEMA IN ENGLISH 7 (January 1967): 20-9; Jacques Bontemps, "Reminiscences," ibid., pp.30-1; Jean-Andre Fieschi, "The Unique Film," ibid., pp.32-3; Jean Seberg, "Lilith and I," ibid., pp.34-7; Patrick Brion, "Biofilmography," ibid., pp.38-41; Robert Rossen, "The Face of Independence," FILMS AND FILMING 8:11 (August 1962):7; and Kevin-Gough Yates, "Private Madness and Public Lunacy," ibid., 18:5 (February 1972):26-30.

DOUGLAS SIRK

MAGNIFICENT OBSESSION (Universal--16mm: 1954, 108 mins., color, sound, R-WIL)
Considered by Sirk's supporters to be the turning point in his career, this remake of the 1935 John Stahl tearjerker based upon Lloyd C. Douglas's novel marked the beginning of an important relationship among Sirk, the producer Ross Hunter, and Rock Hudson. Robert Blees's modernistic script, while faithfully following the original film, highlights the cultural changes that had taken place in American films over an eighteen-year period. Hudson, playing the role first created by Robert Taylor, gives a moving perfomance as the reprobate playboy who causes the death of Jane Wyman's husband and then her blindness. Sirk's depiction of Hudson's transformation and the reasons for it is done with rare restraint and tenderness, so much so, that the actor emerged as a major star after the film's release. Wyman is also effective in the Irene Dunne role, particularly in the last half of the film when she and Hudson, now a surgeon, fall in love. Interestingly, a number of film chronologies ignore the artistic and historical importance of the film, choosing instead to dismiss it as a "soap opera." But as Michael Stern points out, the film is essential to understanding the director's formal logic. That is, "The blindness Sirk's characters experience to this grim reality ['a dark, fatalistic vision of a world devoid of tragic dimension and Christian meaning'] is in effect a form of perceptual impotence. Their inability to SEE in the Sirk-created world that all is surface and image is an inability to apprehend the truth of their existence. Whereas in MAGNIFICENT OBSESSION the sexual component of this impotence exists primarily on the subtextual level of the film's classical references, Sirk's later melodramas grow directly out of the sexual implications of the character's struggles."[756]

JOHN STURGES

BAD DAY AT BLACK ROCK (MGM--16mm: 1955, 81 mins., b/w, sound, R-FNC, MGM)
Featuring superb performances by Robert Ryan and Spencer Tracy, this highly unique and suspenseful film raises the issue of what happened to the Nisei (Japanese people who had become American citizens) during World War II. Millard Kaufman's screenplay focuses on the behavior of an entire community trying to cover up its shameful past. Set in a fictional and isolated midwestern town, the plot concerns a one-armed World War II veteran (Tracy) who comes to pay tribute to a fallen comrade and discovers the tragedy that befell his dead Japanese friend's family as a result of racial bigotry. Sturges's superior direction, along with the cinematographer William

---

[756] Michael Stern, DOUGLAS SIRK (Boston: Twayne Publishers, 1979), p.108. For more information, see Special Issue on Sirk in BRIGHT LIGHTS 6:2 (Winter 1977-78); Special Issue on Sirk in SCREEN (Summer 1971); James McCourt, "Douglas Sirk: Melo Maestro," FILM COMMENT 11:6 (November-December 1975):18-21; "Fassbinder on Sirk," trans. Thomas Elsaesser, ibid., 22-4; Laura Mulvey, "Notes on Sirk & Melodrama," MOVIE 25 (Winter 1977-78):53-7; *___ and Jon Halliday, eds. DOUGLAS SIRK: PROGRAM NOTES (Lancashire, England: Edinborough Film Festival 72, 1972); James Harvey, "Sirkumstantial Evidence," FILM COMMENT 14:4 (July-August 1978):52-9; Michael Stern, "Patterns of Power and Potency, Repression and Violence: Sirk's Films of the 1950s," VELVET LIGHT TRAP 16 (Fall 1976):15-21; *Robert Smith and Jeffrey Wise, eds., DOUGLAS SIRK: THE COMPLETE AMERICAN PERIOD (Storrs: University of Connecticut, 1974); and Tim Pulleine, "Stahl into Sirk," MONTHLY FILM BULLETIN (November 1981):236.

C. Mellor's outstanding camerawork, illustrates how movies began developing the art of the film along with widescreens in the early 1950s.[757]

BILLY WILDER

THE LOST WEEKEND (Paramount--16mm: 1945, 101 mins., b/w, sound, R-SWA, WIL)
   Based upon Charles Jackson's novel, the Wilder-Charles Bracket screenplay presents the realistic story of an alcoholic writer (Ray Milland) who finally realizes the horror of what he has become. Except for the distasteful character of a cruel male nurse (played by Frank Faylan), the movie does a good job of showing the problems of dipsomaniacs and the effect it has on their friends. According to one source, Wilder made the movie because of his experiences working with Raymond Chandler on DOUBLE INDEMNITY (1944).[758] Whatever the reason, Wilder proved that downbeat stories could win at the box office and opened up new directions for the postwar Hollywood cinema. At Oscar time, the film picked up awards for Best Picture, Best Actor, and Best Screenplay.

ROBERT WISE

THE DAY THE EARTH STOOD STILL (Fox--16mm: 1951, 92 mins., b/w, sound, R-FES, FNC)
   Edmund A. North's well-conceived screenplay helped make this science-fiction film about a stranger from outer space (Michael Rennie) who comes to warn the world about the dangers of a nuclear competition one of the most popular films of the 1950s.[759] Historically, the film is important because it demonstrates just how big

---

[757] For more information, see John Sturges, "How the West Was Lost," FILMS AND FILMING 9:3 (December 1962):9-10; DuPre Jones, "The Merit of Flying Lead," ibid., 20:4 (January 1974):30-6; ___, "The Power of the Gun," ibid., 20:5 (February 1974):24-9; and Richard Cherry, "Capsule of John Sturges," ACTION 4:6 (November-December 1962):9-11.

[758] *Maurice Zolotow, BILLY WILDER IN HOLLYWOOD (New York: G. P. Putnam's Sons, 1977), p.126. See also Joseph McBride and Michael Wilmington, "The Private Life of Billy Wilder," FILM QUARTERLY 23:4 (Summer 1970):2-9; Stephen Farber, "The Films of Billy Wilder," FILM COMMENT 7:4 (Winter 1971-72):8-22; Andrew Sarris, "Billy Wilder: Closet Romanticist," ibid., 12:4 (July-August 1976):7-9; George Morris, "The Private Films of Billy Wilder," ibid., 15:1 (January-February 1979):33-9; Joseph McBride and Todd McCarthy, "Going for Extra Innings: Billy Wilder Interviewed," ibid., pp.40-8; Douglas McVay, "The Eye of a Cynic: A Monograph on Billy Wilder," FILMS AND FILMING 6:4 (January 1960):11-2, 34-5; Tom Onosko, "Billy Wilder," VELVET LIGHT TRAP 3 (Winter 1971):29-31; "Dialogue on Film: Billy Wilder and I. A. L. Diamond, " AMERICAN FILM 1:9 (July-August 1976):33-48; "Billy Wilder," AFI SOUVENIR EDITION (Washington, D.C.: The American Film Institute, 1986); Charles Higham, "Cast A Cold Eye: The Films of Billy Wilder," SIGHT AND SOUND 32:2 (Spring 1963):83-7, 103; ___, "Meet Whiplash Wilder," ibid., 37:1 (Winter 1967-68):21-3; and Aljean Harmetz, "Seven Years Without Directing, and Billy Wilder is Feeling Itchy," NEW YORK TIMES C (October 3, 1988):21, 24.

[759] In addition to books on science-fiction films discussed in Chapter 2, see Roy Pickard, "The Future . . . A Slight Return," FILMS AND FILMING 17:10 (July 1971):26-31; Ralph Appelbaum, "Audrey Rose: In Search of a Soul," ibid., 24:2 (November 1977):18-22; Samuel Stark, "Robert Wise," FILMS IN REVIEW 14:1 (January 1963):5-22; "Dialogue on Film: Robert Wise," AMERICAN FILM 1:2 (November

studios were using the genre to exploit the cold war era. Not only is the movie's message about ending war indicative of the decade's fear about atomic destruction, but it also illustrates 20th Century-Fox's willingness to invest large sums of money in the production and the era's willingness to upgrade the prestige of the once-ridiculed genre.

WILLIAM WYLER

ROMAN HOLIDAY (Paramount--16mm: 1953, 118 mins., b/w, sound, R-FNC, WHO)
        Scripted by Ian McLellan Hunter and John Dighton, this romantic fantasy about twenty-four hours in the life of a princess (Audrey Hepburn) and an American journalist (Gregory Peck) is Hepburn's screen debut.[760] "Once again," as Michael A. Anderegg points out, "Wyler has chosen and guided his performers in such a way that they become the key element in providing rather slight material with an enduring integrity and charm."[761] Nominated for nine Oscars, including Best Film, Best Supporting Actor (Eddie Albert), Best Director, Best Black-and-White Cinematography (Frank Planer and Henry Alekan), Best Black-and-White Art Direction-Set Direction (Hal Pereira and Walter Tyler), and Best Film Editing (Robert Swink), it won for Best Actress, Best Motion Picture Story (Hunter), and Best Costume Design (Edith Head).

FRED ZINNEMANN

THE SEARCH (MGM--16mm: 1948, 103 mins., b/w/ sound, MGM)
        During its March release, NEW YORK TIMES reviewer Bosley Crowther wrote, "Out of the stuff of one of the saddest and most arresting human dramas of our times--that is the fate of the children of Europe whose homes were wrecked and whose lives were were damaged by the war--Lazar Wechsler, a Swiss film producer, has made a picture which may prudently be said to be as fine, as moving and as challenging as any the contemporary screen provides."[762] Richard Schweizer and

---

1975):33-48; Rui Nogueira, "Robert Wise at RKO," FOCUS ON FILM 12 (Winter 1972):43-50; Allen Eyles, "Robert Wise Filmography (1)," ibid., pp.48-50; Rui Nogueira, "Robert Wise at Fox," ibid., 14 (Spring 1973):47-9; Allen Eyles, "Robert Wise Filmography (2)," ibid., pp.49-50; Rui Nogueira, "Robert Wise Continued," ibid., 16 (Autumn 1973):49-55; Allen Eyles, "Robert Wise Filmography (3), ibid., p.56; Rui Nogueira, "Robert Wise To Date," ibid., 19 (Autumn 1974):52-7; Allen Eyles, "Robert Wise Filmography (4)," ibid., pp.58-9; and "Robert Wise Talks about the New Hollywood," AMERICAN CINEMATOGRAPHER 57:6 (July 1976):770-1, 780, 826.

[760]   Gene Ringgold, "Audrey Hepburn," FILMS IN REVIEW 11:10 (December 1971):585-605.

[761]   Michael A. Anderegg, WILLIAM WYLER (Boston: Twayne, 1979), p.180.

[762]   Bosley Crowther, "THE SEARCH," NEW YORK TIMES 3 (March 24, 1948):3. For more information, see Arthur Knight, "Fred Zinnemann Has Succeeded with New Actors in Real Settings," FILMS IN REVIEW 2:1 (January 1951):21-5; Henry Hart, "Zinnemann on the Verge," ibid., 4:2 (February 1953):80-1; Fred Zinnemann, "From Here to Eternity," ibid., 12:9 (November 1961):564-5; ___, "Some Questions Answered," ACTION 2:3 (May-June 1967):22-3; Colin Young, "The Old Dependables," FILM QUARTERLY 13 :1 (Fall 1959):2-17; "Discussion: Personal Creation In Hollywood--Is it Possible?" ibid., 15:3 (Spring 1962):16-34; Richard Schickel, "Fred Zinnemann: Quiet Man on the Set," SHOW 4 (August 1964):80-1; Fred Zinnemann, "A Conflict of Conscience," FILMS AND FILMING 6:3 (December 1959):7,

David Wechsler's original screenplay uses the heartbreaking search of a Czech mother (Jarmila Novotna) for her son (Ivan Jandl) to depict the plight of refugees in American displaced persons camps in occupied Germany. As a result of Zinnemann's stunning semidocumentary direction, he was elevated to the status of a major director. Immediate recognition was also given to Montgomery Clift, in his screen debut, who played the sympathetic American soldier aiding in the boy's eventual reunion with his mother. Nominated for four Oscars, including Best Actor, Best Director, and Best Screenplay, it won for Best Motion Picture Story.

BUNUEL IN MEXICO

Of all the artists in film, none defies classification more than Bunuel. The Spanish-born filmmaker, who left his homeland in the mid-1920s to explore Surrealistic art in France, was a constant wanderer in the 1930s. First there was an abrreviated period (1930-31) with MGM in Hollywood, followed by a brief return to Spain to make LAND WITHOUT BREAD/LES HURDES (1932). After that, as Bunuel explains, his life took on an aimless quality:

"After LES HURDES, I worked in Paris. I no longer wanted to make films. Thanks to my family, I had enough to live on, but I was rather ashamed of not doing anything. So I worked for two years with Paramount in Paris, doing dubbing, and then went to Spain with Warner Bros. to supervise their co-productions. I did some more dubbing there. Then I began to produce some films with a friend of mine . . . There were four of them; they were of no interest at all . . . Then the Spanish Civil War broke out. I thought this was the end of the world, and that I ought to find something better to do than making films; I offered my services to the Republican Government in Paris. They sent me to Hollywood in 1938 on a 'diplomatic mission' to supervise, as technical adviser, two films that were to be made about the Spanish Republic. Then suddenly the war was over, and there I was, stuck in America without friends or a job. Thanks to Miss Iris Barry, I found employment at the Museum of Modern Art . . . in the end it turned out to be a bureaucratic job . . . [four years later] I was forced to hand in my resignation because I was the director of L'AGE D'OR . . . I was depressed; I had no savings, and . . . then the American Engineering Corps took me on as a commentator for Spanish versions of films made by the American Army."[763]

By 1944, he was producing Spanish versions of Warner Bros. films in Hollywood. But two years of this well-paid but depressing work finally left him eager to leave America altogether. Living on his savings for a short time, he finally decided in 1946 to go to Mexico.

Between 1946 and 1964, Bunuel made twenty films in his new home, eighteen of them in Spanish but employing Mexican performers and technicians. The budgets were

34; ___, "Revelations," ibid., 10:12 (September 1964):5-6; John Howard Reid, "A Man for All Movies: The Films of Fred Zinnemann," ibid., 13: 8 (May 1967):4-11; Alan Stanbrook, "The Films of Fred Zinnemann," ibid., 13: 9 (June 1967):11-5; Gordon Gow, "Individualism Against Machinery: An Interview with Fred Zinnemann," ibid., 24:5 (February 1978):12-7; Gene Phillips, "Fred Zinnemann: An Interview," FOCUS ON FILM 14 (Spring 1973):21-8; and Pat Billings and Allen Eyles, "Fred Zinnemann Filmography," ibid., pp.29-32.

[763] Cited in Buache, pp.40-1.

bare bone and the shooting schedules never longer than twenty-four days.[764] "The simple fact of going to Mexico," explains Francisco Aranda, "was decisive in Bunuel's rediscovery of his road. Not only of the idiom and the race, but the physical types, the dry and dusty landscape, the impassioned speech, the attitudes to life and death, the religious problem, the social structure which he attacked, all combined to restore him to conditions in which he could be himself."[765] Although much of the work he created in this significant period was ordinary and forgettable, at least six films--THE YOUNG AND THE DAMNED/LOS OLVIDADOS (1950), ADVENTURES OF ROBINSON CRUSOE/LAS AVENTURAS DE ROBINSON CRUSOE (1952), THIS STRANGE PASSION (1953), NAZARIN (1959), VIRIDIANA (1961), and THE EXTERMINATING ANGEL/EL ANGEL EXTERMINADOR (1962)--are among the best movies of their generation. The crucial aspect of the Mexican period, however, is that it provided Bunuel with the opportunity to perfect his narrative technique and visual imagery.

BOOKS

*Bunuel, Luis. THREE SCREENPLAYS: VIRIDIANA/THE EXTERMINATING ANGEL/SIMON OF THE DESERT. New York: The Orion Press, 1969. Illustrated. 245pp.

*Bunuel, Luis. THE EXTERMINATING ANGEL, NAZARIN, AND LOS OLVIDADOS: THREE FILMS BY LUIS BUNUEL. Trans. Nicholas Fry. New York: Simon and Schuster, 1972. Illustrated. 299pp.

"Here at last," Ado Kyrou writes in the book's introduction to THE EXTERMINATING ANGEL/EL ANGEL EXTERMINADOR (1962), "is the great liberation. All the chains fall aside and Bunuel rediscovers the freedom of expression of L'AGE D'OR. Rationality, that suppurating wound in our civilisation [sic], and the scourge of the anecdote no longer exist. The surrealist director is once more a man whom nothing alienates, he no longer needs an alibi, he rushes headfirst into the irrational." The three scripts are taken from the scripts originally published by L'AVANT SCENE DU CINEMA, which were based on the filmmaker's original work. Well worth browsing.

FILMS

THE EXTERMINATING ANGEL/EL ANGEL EXTERMINADOR (Mexico--16mm: 1962, 90 mins., b/w, English subtitles, sound, R-BUD; S-FES, FNC, REL)

Scripted by Bunuel, from a treatment by Luis Alcoriza and Bunuel (based on a unpublished play by Jose Bergamin, the plot concerns a group of wealthy guests at a dinner party that keeps them prisoner for a week and turns them into barbarians and cannibals. Francisco Aranda speaks for many fans of this highly complex film when he writes, "In its language, EL ANGEL EXTERMINADOR still remains the most distinctly and complete Surrealist film since L'AGE D'OR, and in the writer's opinion, is second only to that film in Bunuel's whole OEUVRE."[766]

---

[764] Luis Bunuel, MY LAST SIGHT, Trans. Abigail Israel (New York: Alfred A. Knopf, 1983), pp.197-8.

[765] *Francisco Aranda, LUIS BUNUEL: A CRITICAL BIOGRAPHY, trans. and ed. David Robinson (New York: Da Capo Press, 1976), p.130.

[766] Aranda, p.210.

VIRIDIANA (Mexico--16mm: 1961, 90 mins., b/w, English subtitles, sound, R-BUD, COR, EMG, FES, FNC, IMG, KIT)

Scripted by Bunuel and Julio Alejandro, this is a cynical account of a young novitiate whose personal tragedy is told with emotional and forceful cinematic action.[767] "In it," explains Emilio G. Rierra, "Bunuel offers his audience a splendid opportunity for exploring his creative universe and finding enrichment in a fresh point of view, a new outlook on reality."[768]

FRANCE IN THE POSTWAR YEARS (1945-1955)

The French film industry approached the postwar period with mixed emotions. On the one hand, Nazi occupation had kept the nation's theaters in business, film artists who had remained in France had produced some of their best technical work, and clever producers had developed a strong production and distribution organization. Even though the final days of the war had shut the film industry down and the postwar period had caused drastic shortages in materials and electricity to run and heat studios and theaters, the filmmakers themselves were optimistic about the future. The Free French government encouraged such hopes by subsidizing and encouraging quality film productions. As Roy Armes explains, the Committee for the Liberation of the French Cinema, established in 1944, took charge of "restructuring the film industry and carrying out a very partial and inadequate expulsion from the French cinema of those elements deemed to have collaborated with the Germans (among

---

[768]   Emilio G. Riera, "VIRIDIANA," THE WORLD OF LUIS BUNUEL, p.218.

those censured were Arletty, Pierre Fresnay, Sacha Guitry, and Henri-Georges Clouzot)."[769]

The result was that by the end of 1946, French film production nearly equaled that of the pre-WWII period and almost eighty percent of the wartime high of 120 films a year. On the other hand, a production level of roughly ninety films a year hardly sufficed to operate 5,000 French cinemas. Furthermore, the French economy and political system, in serious disarray, needed cash badly. As Georges Sadoul explains,

> A striking characteristic of the post-war French cinema was that its chief men of talent had almost all abandoned production. During the five years since the Liberation (1944-49), Rene Clair, Claude Autant-Lara, Jacques Becker, Jean Gremillon, Julien Duvivier and Marcel Carne had each been able to direct and present one film only in France. Jean Renoir did not return from Hollywood. Robert Bresson had not been able to set his foot in a studio, and Jacques Feyder, returning from Switzerland, died in 1948 without having been able to direct a single film in four years.[770]

Still further, as Dudley Andrew points out, a major debate raged over the direction that the liberated French cinema should take. Certain elements in the country opposed the "international style" (read "Jewish") that had developed in France during the pre-WWII period, while other factions favored "the noble tradition of French culture" or a Marxist commitment to a "realist cinema of social engagement." Almost all the filmmakers opposed the re-establishment of the Hollywood monopoly.[771]

But the French were no match for the wealthy and powerful American film industry. In 1946, President Leon Blum signed a pact with U. S. Secretary of State James F. Byrnes. In hindsight, the Blume-Byrnes Agreement was a mixed blessing. On the positive side, it saturated the French theaters with hundreds of Hollywood movies that were made since the 1930s. These films, created mostly by "assembly line" contract directors, sparked the imagination of a new generation of filmmakers who not only discovered exciting alternatives to France's traditional approach to narrative film, but also found new role models to study in developing fresh directions for French cinema. Unable to get a foothold in the postwar cinema, these young, aspiring artists went to the movie houses and the renovated CINEMATEQUE FRANCAISE to study the techniques and conventions of the American and European filmmakers. Over the next decade, men like Francois Truffaut, Jean Luc-Godard, Claude Chabrol, Jacques Rivette, and Eric Rohmer spent their time critiquing French, Italian, and American films, experimenting with short documentary films, and preparing themselves for a career in theatrical films. On the negative side, the Blum-Byrnes Agreement realigned France's film quota system and left the nation virtually at the mercy of Hollywood. It not only made American films the predominant product in French movie houses but also undercut French film production for several years.[772]

---

[767] David Robinson, "Thank God--I Am Still an Atheist: Luis Bunuel and VIRIDIANA," SIGHT AND SOUND 31:3 (Summer 1962):116-8, 155.

[769] FRENCH CINEMA, p.125. Dudley Andrew claims that the "ignoble process   .   .   . [of] purification   .   .   . affected few in the industry and   .   .   . [was] largely motivated by personal animosities rather than evidence of any real collaboration." See Dudley Andrew, "Postwar French Cinema: Of Waves in the Sea," WORLD CINEMA SINCE 1945, p.171.

[770] FRENCH FILM, p.112.

[771] Nichol, pp.171-2.

[772] For information on how Hollywood used foreign markets to its advantage, see

In fairness to the French government, it tried to soften the impact of the American invasion of backlogged films. As Andrew reports,

Taxes on imported films were levied as always. Profits made by American companies in France were blocked, to be reinvested in France. A law requiring all theaters to screen French films a minimum of four out of every thirteen weeks was enacted, and after strikes and demonstrations in 1948, was renegotiated to five weeks. But these measures were not enough . . . In 1938 French films comprise[d] 65 percent of gross domestic receipts; during the war, 85 percent; but from 1946 to 1954 only 40 percent.[773]

n 1948, the French government encouraged the nation's cinematic climate by naugurating the LOI D'AIDE, an important new film subsidy. Extended and expanded wice in the mid- to late 1950s, the LOI D'AIDE was given in two categories: the AVANCE SUR RECETTES was given to meritorious feature film directors; the PRIMES DE QUALITE, to meritorious short subject directors. Among the struggling artists who benefited from the former were Robert Bresson and Claude Chabrol; among the atter were Georges Franju, Chris Marker, Alain Resnais, and Francois Truffaut. Whether one blames misguided government policies or the badly organized film ndustry for the postwar problems of French filmmakers, it is clear that they had to overcome severe obstacles in their efforts to make worthy films. Seen in this context, heir many successes are all the more impressive.

In addition to a number of noteworthy documentaries--e.g., Henri Cartier-Bresson's REUNION/LE RETOUR and Georges Rouquier's FARREBIQUE (both n 1946); a number of significant feature films were made by five film veterans: Claude Autant-Lara, Jacques Becker, Robert Bresson, Rene Clement, and Jean Cocteau. For he most part, they avoided the realism found in other European countries and oncentrated instead on escapist entertainment. As Wright comments, the "confusion of the immediate post-war situation . . . [encouraged] directors to enjoy and elebrate the return of general freedom, the pleasures of romantic tragedy or of omedy . . . [Moreover, there was a] gradual diminution of the influence of creenwriters . . . [and a shift toward] the AUTEUR concept. . . ."[774]

Autant-Lara, who got his start in silent films with Rene Clair, began the postwar period with THE DEVIL IN THE FLESH/LE DIABLE AU CORPS (1947). Based on Raymond Radiguet's novel about a tragic love affair, the screenplay by Jean Aurenche nd Pierre Bost provided Autant-Lara with the materials to make a daring movie about passion and pain.[775] Over the next seven years, he directed three other noteworthy ilms: KEEP AN EYE ON AMELIA/OCCUPE-TOI D'AMELIE! (1949), THE RED NN/L'AUBERGE ROUGE (1951), and THE GAME OF LOVE/LE BLE EN HERBE (1954). These satirical comedies, relying heavily on the witty and carefully crafted scripts by Aurenche and Bost, eventually made the screenwriters the target of the AUTEURIST critics in the 1950s (more of which later).

Jacques Becker, who broke into film as an assistant to Jean Renoir in the mid-1930s, had had an erratic career throughout most of the early 1940s. But by the end of the Nazi occupation, his second feature film, PARIS FRILLS/FALBALAS (1945),

---

Chapter 3 and Thomas H. Guback, "Hollywood's International Market," THE AMERICAN FILM INDUSTRY, Rev. ed., pp.463-86.

[773]   Andrew, p.172.

[774]   Wright, p.266.

[775]   For more information, see Raymond Durgnat, "The Rebel With Kid Gloves: First Part of an Analysis of Autant-Lara's Work for the Cinema," FILMS AND FILMING 7:1 (October 1960):11, 38; and ___, "Colette--and a Modern Devil: Second Part of an Analysis of Autant-Lara's Work for the Cinema," ibid., 7:2 (November 1960):17, 35, 42.

established his cinematic preoccupation with the everyday activities of ordinary people. As Peter John Dyer observes, Becker, who died at the age of 53 in 1960, "will be remembered in . . . [England] as one of the most accomplished of the generation of French film directors which came to the fore after the Liberation."[776] Like many of his contemporaries, Becker believed in well-crafted films, worked closely with writers and his editor (Marguerite Renoir), and was known, as Andrew notes, for his brilliant direction of actors.[777] Among his most praised works are a trio of psychological comedies: ANTOINE AND ANTOINETTE (1947), RENDEZ-VOUS DE JULLIET (1949), and EDOUARD ET CAROLINE (1951). "Becker's masters," comments Dyer, "were Chaplin and Stroheim, his mentor Renoir. He admired ideas, humour, versatility and invention."[778]

Of the five veteran directors in the postwar period, Robert Bresson clearly was one of the two French filmmakers most admired by emerging directors (the other was Cocteau) and the one with the greatest longevity.[779] Starting in films during the mid-1930s, he directed his first feature film in 1943--ANGELS OF THE STREETS/LES ANGES DU PECHE--and followed soon after with his most memorable occupation film--THE LADIES OF THE BOIS DE BOULOGNE/LES DAMES DU BOIS DE BOULOGNE (1945). Over the next four decades, he would make fewer than ten films--e.g., A CONDEMNED MAN ESCAPES/UN CONDAMNE A MORT S'EST ECHAPPE (1956), PICKPOCKET (1959), THE TRIAL OF JOAN OF ARC/LE PROCES DE JEANNE D'ARC (1961), BALTHAZAR/AU HASARD BALTHAZAR (1966), and L'ARGENT (1983)--but each work would demonstrate not only his total commitment to independent filmmaking, but also his passionate interest in the moral and spiritual dilemmas of ill-fated individuals trying to make sense of inexplicable circumstances. The postwar film that epitomizes Bresson's humanistic style is THE DIARY OF A COUNTRY PRIEST/LE JOURNAL D'UN CURE DE CAMPAGNE (1950). In this tale of a dying priest who is at odds with his congregation, Bresson reveals both the spiritual questioning that preoccupies his characters, and the innovative manner in which the director narrates his metaphysical stories.

Unlike many of his peers who thrived on escapist cinema, Clement responded

---

[776]   Peter John Dyer, "Becker," SIGHT AND SOUND 29:2 (Spring 1960):96.

[777]   Dudley Andrew, "Jacques Becker," THE INTERNATIONAL DICTIONARY OF FILMS AND FILMMAKERS: VOLUME II, p.36.

[778]   Dyer, p.96.

[779]   Some useful articles on Bresson are the following: Roland Monod, "Working with Bresson," SIGHT AND SOUND 28:1 (Summer 1957):30-2; Gavin Lambert, "Notes on Robert Bresson," ibid., 33:1 (July/September 1953):35-39; Tom Milne, "The Two Chambermaids," ibid., 33:4 (Autumn 1964):174-9; Charles Ford, "Robert Bresson," trans. Anne and Thornton K. Brown, FILMS IN REVIEW 10:2 (February 1959):65-7, 79; Jean-Luc Godard and Michel Delahaye, "The Question: Interview With Robert Bresson," CAHIERS DU CINEMA IN ENGLISH 7 (CdC #178, May 1966):5-27; Colin Young, "Conventional-Unconventional," FILM QUARTERLY 13:3 (Spring 1960):4-10; Marjorie Greene, "Robert Bresson," ibid., pp.4-10; Mike Prokosch, "Bresson's Stylistics Revisited," ibid., 25:2 (Winter 1971-72):30-2; Richard Roud, "French Outsider With the Inside Look: A Monograph of Robert Bresson's Early Work," FILMS AND FILMING 6:7 (April 1960):9-10, 35; Donald S. Skoller, "PRAXIS as a Cinematic Principle in Films by Robert Bresson," CINEMA JOURNAL 9:1 (Fall 1969):13-22; and Marvin Zemon, "The Suicide of Robert Bresson," CINEMA (Calif) 6:3 (Spring 1971):37-42.

to the growing demand for a greater realism in the cinema.[780] In his first postwar film, THE BATTLE OF THE RAILS/LA BATAILLE DU RAIL (1945), which he directed and co-authored with Colette Audry, Clement provides a series of semi-documentary episodes about the French Resistance between 1941 and 1944. Although there are striking similarities between it and Rossellini's ROME, OPEN CITY/ROMA, CITTA APERTA (1945)--e.g., use of nonprofessional actors, scenes of tragic deaths, location shooting--the film inspired no neo-realistic movement in France. For the remainder of the decade, Clement worked on other directors' projects, establishing a reputation for painstaking details and tightly written scripts. Then seven years after directing THE BATTLE OF THE RAILS/LA BATAILLE DU RAIL, he released his next film, the memorable FORBIDDEN GAMES/LES JEUX INTERDITS (1952). Again working with a co-authored, disciplined script (this time by Aurenche and Bost), Clement presents the problems of a five-year old girl whose parents are killed in the summer of 1940. Her attempts at dealing with the issues of war and death remain among the most poetical in screen history.   By now, along with Autant-Lara and Becker, Clement personified the postwar French film "tradition of quality" productions known for their expert craftsmanship and reliance on detailed scripts.

Added to this assembly of quality filmmakers was Jean Cocteau, the only artist to mesh his cinematic work with achievements in literature, poetry, painting, sculpture, ballet, and theater. It was his gift for making sight and sound cinematic equals that inspired many disillusioned French novelists in the 1950s to abandon literature in favor of screenwriting and directing. During the Nazi occupation, he had played a major role in developing allegorical and metaphorical themes as a way of allowing his contemporaries to comment on the times. His dialogue for THE PHANTOM BARON/LE BARON FANTOME (1943) and THE LADIES OF THE BOIS DE BOULOGNE/LES DAMES DU BOIS DE BOULOGNE (1945); and his scenario for THE ETERNAL RETURN/L'ETERNAL RETOUR (1943) are all examples of how he sought to isolate himself over a four-year period, as Rene Gilson explains, from being "insulted tirelessly by a certain vermin, and by a political fringe in whose eyes he must have incarnated--more   than   others,   who   did   not   have   this   'dangerous visibility'--individualism, humanism, and liberty."[781] Starting in the postwar period with the breathtaking BEAUTY AND THE BEAST/LA BELLE ET LA BETE (1946), in which Clement functioned as an invaluable technical assistant, Cocteau created several stunning and unusual films: e.g., THE STORM WITHIN/LES PARENTS TERRIBLES (1948), ORPHEUS/ORPHEE (1949), THE STRANGE ONES/LES ENFANTS TERRIBLES (1949),[782] and THE TESTAMENT OF ORPHEUS/LE TESTAMENT D'ORPHEE (1960). "In retrospect," as Roy Armes observes, "he is to be admired for the freedom with which he expressed a wholly personal vision and for his indifference to the given rules of a certain period of French 'quality' filmmaking."[783]

The importance of directors like Autant-Lara, Becker, Bresson, Clement, and Cocteau to the postwar French cinema contributed an additional dimension to the critical-theoretical debates taking place in France between 1946 and 1955. Ever since the early 1940s, as Andrew points out, "cine clubs" had regained their popularity

---

[780]   For more information, see Lotte H. Eisner, "Style of Rene Clement: Part I," FILM CULTURE 12 (September 1957):21; and ___, "Style of Rene Clement: Part II," ibid., 13 (October 1957):11.

[781]   *Rene Gilson, JEAN COCTEAU, trans. Ciba Vaughan (New York: Crown Publishers, 1964), p.24.

[782]   Cocteau originally had written the screenplay as a novel in 1930. Although he updated the script, directed portions of the film, and functioned as the film's narrator, the directorial credits belong to Jean-Pierre Melville.

[783]   Roy Armes, "Jean Cocteau," THE INTERNATIONAL DICTIONARY OF FILMS AND FILMMAKERS: VOLUME II, p.103.

and "the desire to make film study a respectable and indispensable part of French life and culture."[784] These cine-clubs were deeply involved in analyzing the art of the film and the direction that filmmakers like Autant-Lara, Becker, Bresson, Clement, and Cocteau were taking cinema.   Among the more influential cine-club members were notable critics like Andre Bazin, Jean-Georges Auriol, and Alexandre Astruc. Each of them played a major role in redirecting the world's notions on the nature of film.

Astruc led the revolt against sound and dialogue being subservient to screen images. In his famous 1948 article, "The Birth of a New Avant-Garde: LA CAMERA-STYLO," he spoke of the changes that had already begun to reshape the cinema: "It's not just a coincidence that Renoir's LA REGLE DU JEU, Welles's films, and Bresson's LES DAMES DU BOIS DE BOULOGNE, all films which establish the foundations of a new future for the cinema, have escaped the attention of critics, who in any case were not capable of spotting them."[785] Astruc saw in such films a revolutionary change occurring, one that freed the filmmaker from the traditions of the past:

> To come to the point: the cinema is quite simply becoming a means of expression, just as the other arts have been before it, and in particular painting and the novel. After having been successively a fairground attraction, an amusement analogous to boulevard theatre, or a means of preserving the images of an era, it is gradually becoming a language. By language, I mean a form in which and by which an artist can express his thoughts, however abstract they may be, or translate his obsessions exactly as he does in the contemporary essay or novel. That is why I would like to call this new age of cinema the age of CAMERA-STYLO (camera-pen).[786]

In other words, filmmakers should perceive film as the equal of literature, not as its lackey. Only then could a cinematic language emerge that advances the art of the cinema. Astruc's call for a totally independent form of expression that gave equal weight to all aspects of sight and sound became a rallying cry for LE NOUVELLE VAGUE in the 1950s.

Even more influential in the mid- to late-1940s was the restoration, under Auriol's editorship, of the defunct REVUE DU CINEMA.   The magazine had been published between 1929 and 1931, and much of its writings, as Jim Hillier points out, had stressed the important cinematic ideas percolating during the post-WWI period: e.g., the significance of European "art cinema," AVANT-GARDE films, and Hollywood genre films, as well as the relationship of technology to aesthetics.[787] Auriol, along with many illustrious contributors--e.g., Andre Bazin, Jacques Doniol-Valcroze, Lotte Eisner, Henri Langlois, Eric Rohmer, Georges Sadoul--drew attention to the serious side of Hollywood filmmaking, the role that Italian neo-realism was playing in the contemporary film, and the problems inherent in current French cinema.[788]

---

[784]   Dudley Andrew, ANDRE BAZIN, Foreword Francois Truffaut (New York: Oxford University Press, 1978), p.144.

[785]   Alexandre Astruc, "The Birth of a New Avant-Garde: LA CAMERA-STYLO," THE NEW WAVE, ed. Peter Graham (Garden City: Doubleday and Company, 1968), p.17.

[786]   Astruc, pp.17-8.

[787]   Jim Hillier, ed. CAHIERS DU CINEMA: THE 1950s--NEO-REALISM, HOLLYWOOD, NEW WAVE (Cambridge: Harvard University Press, 1985), p.2.

[788]   Rhode points out (p.532) that the programming at the CINEMATEQUE FRANCAISE occasionally created misunderstandings because Langlois "divorced films from

As the theoretical-critical discussions increased in intensity, the most important of all the postwar cine-clubs emerged in 1948, OBJECTIF 48. According to Andrew, it

> was an elegant, influential, and exclusive film club, patronized by the cultured writers and readers of Paris's intellectual journals. While all other film clubs in Paris were occupied with the classics of the art, OBJECTIF 48 was determined to show only current films. It billed itself as a gallery rather than a museum and it hoped to play a decisive role in the direction of the film art industry.[789]

The opening film for the new club was Cocteau's THE STORM WITHIN/LES PARENTS TERRIBLES (1948). During its brief three-year existence, OBJECTIF 48 served as a stimulus for exciting ideas, new friendships, and intriguing projects. Moreover, as Hillier observes, it was from the combination of REVUE DU CINEMA and OBJECTIF 48 that the postwar era's most memorable film periodical, CAHIERS DU CINEMA, not only got its roots, but also many of its most famous contributors.[790]

Founded in 1951 by Bazin and Doniol-Valcroze, the successor to REVUE DU CINEMA (which ceased publication in 1950 and whose guiding light, Auriol, died that same year in a car accident), CAHIERS DU CINEMA began as a movement to recognize the greatness of American filmmaking and to examine seriously the nature of film as art. Defending the value of American films was not, as shown throughout this chapter, a revolutionary idea to French artists and intellectuals. Hollywood had long served as a stimulus to thoughtful filmmaking in France since the birth of moving pictures. What was revolutionary, however, was CAHIER's notions of AUTEURS and MISE EN SCENE.[791] Under the joint editorship of Bazin, Doniol-Valcroze, and Lo Duca, these important discussions became focused in the mid-1950s, when a group of young and unemployed directors--e.g., Eric Rohmer, Claude Chabrol, Jean Domarchi, Jean-Luc Godard, Francois Truffaut, and Jacques Rivette--turned to writing film criticism for the struggling new periodical.

The contributions of CAHIERS DU CINEMA to critical thinking about film as an art form are covered in a number of books and articles, many of which are alluded to in this and other chapters. Here, we need only comment briefly on what the influential periodical advocated in the early 1950s. Building on its ability to accept divergent points of view, the popular journal, citing primarily the works of Hollywood, French, and Italian filmmakers, focused mainly on a formalist perspective developed by Rohmer and Bazin. As Lellis points out, the formalist perspective grew out of three sources: "a philosophic tradition more Platonist than Aristotelian, the importance of painting in the French cultural tradition, and the popularity of

---

their context in culture or time and presented them as an unfolding tapestry, so that it was possible to see them as emanations from some single God-like mind (one reason why the Roman Catholic Andre Bazin and his CAHIERS DU CINEMA followers were inclined to think of the experience in religious terms)."

[789]   ANDRE BAZIN, p.147.

[790]   Hillier, p.3.

[791]   Thomas Elsaesser, "Two Decades in Another Country: Hollywood and the Cinephiles," SUPERCULTURE, C. W. E. Bigsby, ed. (London: Elek, 1975), p.199. Particularly useful is a comparison the author makes between CAHIERS DU CINEMA and another important film periodical, POSITIF, founded in 1952. See also George Lellis, BERTOLT BRECHT: "CAHIERS DU CINEMA" AND CONTEMPORARY FILM THEORY (Ann Arbor: UMI Research Press, 1982); T. L. French, ed., CAHIERS DU CINEMA (New York: The Thousand Eyes, 1977); and Maureen Turim, "The Aesthetic Becomes Political: A History of Film Criticism in CAHIERS DU CINEMA," THE VELVET LIGHT TRAP 9 (Summer 1973):13-7.

phenomenology in French thought at that time."[792] In simplified terms, critics were challenged to identify filmmakers who captured the spiritual essence of life hidden in material existence. The secret lay in looking at how a filmmaker expressed (read MISE EN SCENE) his or her ideas on the themes basic to the arts since the beginning of time: e.g., love, justice, power, greed, and salvation. Led by Rohmer, early CAHIERS DU CINEMA contributors prided themselves on their ability to locate geometric patterns in misperceived works and to show how the filmmakers (e.g., Hawks, Hitchcock, and Renoir) converted these forms into expressions of their moral values. According to Roud, ". . . the [new] French Critics are particularly indifferent to the content of a film . . . The greatest link between all schools of French film criticism is an insistence on the supremacy of form over content."[793] In hindsight, Roud overlooked the magazine's humanistic, Catholic orientation. CAHIERS DU CINEMA's interest in form extended beyond form, beyond a blind commitment to MISE EN SCENE (literally, how the film was staged). While it is true that extremists like the MacMahoniens reduced everything to how the filmmaker handled performers,[794] the majority of CAHIERS DU CINEMA's critics emphasized the filmmaker's conscious decisions to present not only the world around us, but also our moral place in it. This humanistic, Catholic orientation was rejected in the 1960s and replaced by a Marxist, materialistic perspective. Tthat Brechtian-Marxist perspective was brewing in the early days of CAHIERS DU CINEMA; only then did it sidestep the political interpretation that the historical development of film is directly tied to political and economic forces. Instead, the young periodical concentrated on the importance of form in shaping the ideological content of the work of art.

Each of the various strands that had woven itself through the fabric of the French postwar cinema converged in 1954, with Truffaut's seminal CAHIERS DU CINEMA article, "A Certain Tendency of the French Cinema." He began his attack on the cinematic establishment by focusing on leading contemporary screenwriters like Aurenche and Bost, who prided themselves on adapting literary works without being unfaithful to the original sources, "Invention without betrayal." Truffaut acknowledged that these "LITTERATEURS" and their peers (e.g., Jean Ferry, Jacques Sigurd, and Henri Jeanson) had played a major role in establishing the postwar French cinema's "Tradition of Quality" and the reason why it had won so many awards at the Cannes and Venice film festivals. But he insisted that these scenario writers "have made the works they adapt insipid, for EQUIVALENCE is always with us, whether in the form of treason or timidity."[795] What was needed, Truffaut argued, was for filmmakers "to be responsible for the scenarios and dialogues they illustrate."[796] Such personalities would have their own individuality and not be obscured by the nature of the material they create. Moreover, there were

---

[792]   Lellis, pp.15-6. An important reaction to CAHIERS DU CINEMA's ties to painting is found in Richard Roud, "The French Line," SIGHT AND SOUND 29:4 (Autumn 1960):167-71.

[793]   "The French Line," p.167.

[794]   Named for the MacMahonian theater in Paris, the group's leader was Michel Mourlet. For more information, see Lellis, pp.26-8.

[795]   Francois Truffaut, "A Certain Tendency of the French Cinema," CAHIERS DU CINEMA IN ENGLISH 1 (January 1966):33, 35. Originally published in CAHIERS DU CINEMA 31 (1954). For more information on the reaction to the AUTEUR theory, see bibliographical information in THE NEW FILM INDEX, pp.98-9; and Jim Hillier, ed. CAHIERS DU CINEMA: 1960-1968--NEW WAVE, NEW CINEMA, REEVALUATING HOLLYWOOD (Cambridge: Harvard University Press, 1986), p.18-9.

[796]   Truffaut, p.36.

such "AUTEURS" already operating in the cinema and recognized for the control they exercised over their films: e.g., Jacques Becker, Robert Bresson, Jean Cocteau, Abel Gance, Max Ophuls, Jacques Tati, and Jean Renoir. In Truffaut's judgment, these AUTEURS have moved beyond the "psychological realism" of the films made by screenwriters and directors who function as part of a studio system to a bolder and more magnificent plateau.

Truffaut's call for "UN CINEMA D'AUTEURS" was not unique. As Hillier points out, there had been several earlier calls--e.g., Irving Pinchel's November 1946 article in REVUE DU CINEMA, and Jacques Rivette's May 1953 essay on Howard Hawks in CAHIERS DU CINEMA--for an examination of screen authorship.[797] Initially, the focus was on AUTEURISM itself. According to John Caughie,

> The personality of the director, and the consistency within his films, were not, like the explicit subject matter which tended to preoccupy established criticism, simply there as a "given." They had to be sought out, discovered by a process of analysis and attention to a number of films. The recognition that the director was not always able to choose the best subject matter was the concession that AUTEURISM made to the conditions of production.[798]

No matter what genre the director used, his point of view had to be clear to the discerning viewer. To be an AUTEUR, the director had to be greater than the material itself. And not just any perspective was satisfactory. According to John Hess, the CAHIERS crew considered someone an AUTEUR when he or she "expressed an optimistic image of human potentialities within an utterly corrupt society."[799]

It is important to point out that Truffaut's LA POLITIQUE DES AUTEURS was in no way a coherent or sophisticated theory. As Jim Hillier notes, at the same time that Truffaut lauded Hollywood's assembly-line methods he also praised those directors who remained aloof from it. While Truffaut found greatness in film genres that evolved over decades of experimentation and refinement, he was even more impressed with the AUTEURS who imposed their own signature on the genre's conventions. "Only a CONSCIOUS raising of questions about the cinema as a popular art form could begin to reconcile such positions," Hillier explains, "but these were questions rarely addressed directly or seriously by anyone except Bazin."[800] What was significant about the criticism done by Truffaut and the direction he set for CAHIERS DU CINEMA was that it was charting a new direction not only for the French cinema, but also for international film and criticism, one in which artists took responsibility for the total work and critics re-examined the nature of film art.

A particular favorite of the CAHIERS DU CINEMA critics and a man who became a model for the NOUVELLE VAGUE was Jean-Pierre Melville.[801] Born in 1917, the ex-war hero had a brief business career before turning to low-budget filmmaking

---

[797] Hillier, p.5.

[798] John Caughie, ed. THEORIES OF AUTHORSHIP: A READER (London: Routledge and Kegan Paul, 1981), p.11.

[799] John Hess, "Truffaut's Manifesto: Part Two," JUMP CUT 2 (July-August 1974):20. See also John Hess, "LA POLITIQUE DES AUTEURS: Part One--World View as Aesthetic," JUMP CUT 1 (May-June 1974):19-22.

[800] Jim Hillier, ed., CAHIERS DU CINEMA: 1960-1968: NEW WAVE, NEW CINEMA, REEVALUATING HOLLYWOOD (Cambridge: Harvard University Press, 1986), p.4. See also Edward Buscombe, "Ideas on Authorship," SCREEN 14:3 (Autumn 1978):73-85.

[801] For more information, see David Austen, "All Guns and Gangsters: A Report on the Present Situation of the French Cinema, Its Successes, and the People Behind Them ," FILMS AND FILMING 16:9 (June 1970):52-6, 58-60; Roy Armes, "Melville,

during the postwar period. His first feature film, LE SILENCE DE LA MER (1947), dealing with a German officer stationed in occupied France and his tense relationships with an elderly man and his niece, reveals Melville's preoccupation with human communication under stressful conditions. Although he preferred stylistic experiments to an overiding theme throughout his neglected work, Melville, inspired by his love for Hollywood "B" movies of the 1930s, began specializing in gangster movies in the early 1950s.

The result is that his independent theatrical films are noted for their detached and cynical tone. For example, Melville's next film, THE STRANGE ONES/LES ENFANTS TERRIBLES (1949), done in close collaboration with Cocteau, focuses on the problems of a brother and sister having an incestuous relationship and demonstrates his fascination with blending literary sources with cinematic experimentation. Of particular importance, as Armes points out, was Melville's production methods: "use of natural settings, no stars, a minimum crew, no distribution guarantees."[802] Each of these elements, to be discussed later, appealed to the member of the emerging NOUVELLE VAGUE.

In 1949, Melville set up his own studio (destroyed by fire in 1967), giving him the freedom to pursue his stylistic experiments without external interference. Moreover, he was the only filmmaker of his generation who owned his own studios and functioned as his own producer. Among his most noteworthy "B" films are BOB LE FLAMBEUR (1955) and DEUX HOMMES DANS MANHATTAN (1959). In the 1960s, Melville abandoned the low-budget field and turned his attention to expensive productions like LEON MORIN, PRIEST/LEON MORIN, PETRE (1961), LE DOULOS, L'AINE DES FERCHAUX (both in 1963), SECOND WIND/LE DEUXIEME SOUFFLE (1967), LE SAMOURAI (1969), and and LE CERCLE ROUGE (1972). At the time of his death on August 2, 1973, Melville's thrillers were unsurpassed on the continent and his achievements had won him both the CHEVALIER DE LA LEGION D'HONNEUR and CHEVALIER DES ARTS ET DES LETTRES.

Melville's success in the the postwar period, as well as the influence of cine-clubs and serious periodicals encouraged the return of a number of important French filmmakers and the production of memorable works, including Rene Clair--e.g., MAN ABOUT TOWN/LE SILENCE EST D'OR (1947), THE BEAUTY OF THE DEVIL/LA BEAUTE DU DIABLE (1950), THE GRAND MANEUVER/LES GRANDES MANOEUVRES (1956), and THE GATE OF PARIS/PORTE DES LILAS (1957); Henri-Georges Clouzot--e.g., JENNY LAMOUR/QUAI DES ORFEVRES (1947), MANON (1949), and DIABOLIQUE/LES DIABOLIQUES (1955); Max Ophuls--e.g., LA RONDE (1950), THE LOVES OF MADAME DE/MADAME DE . . . (1953), and LOLA MONTES (1955); and Jean Renoir--e.g., FRENCH CAN CAN (1955) and ELENA ET LES HOMMES (1956).

One of France's greatest comedy film artists also emerged during the postwar period: Jacques Tati. A brilliant mime trained in the music halls, he began his interest in screen comedy with a series of comedic shorts in the 1930s and played minor roles in the commercial films of directors like Autant-Lara and Clouzot. Tati made his first feature film, FRANCOIS THE POSTMAN/JOUR DE FETE in 1947, followed by MR. HULOT'S HOLIDAY/LES VACANCES DE MONSIEUR HULOT (1953) and MY UNCLE/MON ONCLE (1958). Despite Tati's limited output (only five feature films in nearly forty years), he holds a unique place in the world of film comedy. As Brent Maddock explains,

---

Jean-Pierre," THE INTERNATIONAL DICTIONARY OF FILMS AND FILMMAKERS: VOLUME II, pp.365-6; Eric Breitbart, "An Interview With Jean-Pierre Melville," FILM CULTURE 35 (Winter 1964):15-9; and Rui Nogueria and Francois Truchaud, "A Samurai in Paris," SIGHT AND SOUND 37:3 (Summer 1968):118-23.

[802] *Roy Armes, FRENCH CINEMA SINCE 1946: VOLUME TWO--THE PERSONAL STYLE (New York: A. S. Barnes and Company, p.36.

Tati, like his predecessors Chaplin and Keaton and unlike most movie funnymen, is a clown, that is a character with an essential or metaphysical base, deriving his comedy talents from outside contemporary or relative ideas of what is funny. Tati's filmic persona is Monsieur Hulot, a character with as universal a basis as Chaplin's tramp.[803]

In commenting patiently but critically on the contemporary scene in France, Tati provides a marvelous example of how film comedy still benefits from the art of the silent film. Moreover, he became another example of the independent artist who created his own work from start to finish in the 1950s.

Thus, by the mid-1950s, the postwar French film industry had overcome the trauma of World War WII and the invasion of Hollywood. It had preserved the talents of a number of memorable filmmakers, developed a handful of new ones, and given birth to an influential school of film criticism. In addition, a growing number of French filmmakers had begun to shift attention away from the "psychological realism" of the postwar period to an emphasis on making films that bore the personality and values of the filmmakers rather than those of studios.

BOOKS

GENERAL

*Armes, Roy. FRENCH CINEMA SINCE 1946: VOLUME ONE--THE GREAT TRADITION. 2nd., enlarged ed. New York: A. S. Barnes and Company, 1970. Illustrated. 176pp.

This is a valuable general introduction to the study of early postwar French filmmaking. Acknowledging a "current state of disagreement among film critics about fundamental aspects of film as an art form," Armes begins his useful survey by stating his two basic premises for the critical judgments used in this book: (1) "insofar as the film is an art the creative personality is the director," and (2) "the film is essentially a narrative medium, like the novel or the play, not simply a visual medium." Armes then goes on to define the French film tradition as "the tradition of Melies rather than that of Lumiere . . . being concerned with the creation of an illusion of reality and having its home therefore in the film studio." After defining formalistic patterns in this studio tradition and observing why French films seem so detached from reality, Armes points out the wide variety of approaches that French filmmakers have taken in opposing "the simple reproduction of reality or of real life" while still searching "for stylization and significance." In discussing the important filmmakers of the early postwar years, the author divides his study into three major groupings. Section One, "Veterans," examines Rene Clair, Jean Renoir, Marcel Carne, Max Ophuls, and Jean Cocteau. Section Two, "Traditionalists," focuses on Henri-Georges Clouzot, Rene Clement, Jacques Becker, and Claude Autant-Lara. Section Three, "Innovators and Independents," deals with Robert Bresson, Jacques Tati, Jean Gremillon, Georges Rouquier, and Roger Leenhardt. A final section provides filmographies and bibliographies. An index is inconcluded. Well worth browsing.

---

[803] Brent Maddock, THE FILMS OF JACQUES TATI (Metuchen: The Scarecrow Press, 1977), p.2. For more information, see Philip Strick, "JOUR DE FETE," FILMS AND FILMING 8:8 (May 1962):19-20, 49, 51-2; Andrew C. Mayer, "The Art of Jacques Tati," QUARTERLY OF FILM, RADIO, AND TELEVISION 10:1 (Fall 1955):19-23; John Simon, "Hulot: Or the Common Man as Observer and Critic," YALE FRENCH REVIEW 23 (1959):18-25; Roy Armes, "The Comic Art of Jacques Tati," SCREEN 11:1 (February 1970):68-80; and Harold Woodside, "Tati Speaks," TAKE ONE 2:6 (1969):6-8.

Hillier, Jim, ed. CAHIERS DU CINEMA: THE 1950s--NEO-REALISM, HOLLYWOOD, NEW WAVE. Cambridge: Harvard University Press, 1985. 312pp.

The first book in a series of splendid anthologies on the most important film periodical of the postwar period, this excellent series places the contributions of CAHIERS DU CINEMA in the social and historical context of its time. Hillier describes, in his introduction, that the magazine had its ideological roots in REVEUE DU CINEMA and that many of the contributors to CAHIERS DU CINEMA first began their critical writings under the editorial guidance of Jean-Georges Auriol in REVUE DU CINEMA. Credit is also given to OBJECTIF '48 as a training ground for the ideas on the AUTEUR theory and MISE EN SCENE. Hillier also draws attention to the relative stability of CAHIERS DU CINEMA's editorial policies in the 1950s: "Bazin, Lo Duca and Doniol-Valcroze continued as joint editors, with Bazin (and perhaps Truffaut) exercising most influence, until early 1957, when Rohmer replaced Lo Duca and began to exert increasing influence, in part just because others were so busy (Truffaut and Godard were also writing for the weekly newspaper ARTS and other publications, while also, like Chabrol, preparing films), in part because of Bazin's illness; Rohmer's position as joint editor with Doniol-Valcroze was then confirmed after Bazin's death in November 1958 and continued until 1963." Hillier is quick to point out, however, that editorial stability is not synonymous with critical homogeneity. He then describes the aesthetic differences at the magazine, but stresses the two major areas of agreement: the AUTEUR theory and MISE EN SCENE. In retrospect, the editor recalls the battles between CAHIERS DU CINEMA's apolitical ideas, and the traditional liberal values in British and American critical circles. The reasons why CAHIERS DU CINEMA had the greatest influence in the 1950s, Hilliers explains is due in part to its responses to the decade's problems with liberal values, and to the fact that the French critics were challenging filmmakers rather than, as their peers were doing, fighting among themselves.

The anthology itself is divided into four major sections, each introduced with valuable and perceptive observations by Hillier. Part One, "French Cinema," provides a context for the critical judgments about American and European cinema, as well as the arguments that the AUTEURISTs were making for changing the direction of French filmmaking. Part Two, "American Cinema," illustrates why CAHIERS DU CINEMA admired Hollywood's "direct engagement with reality." It includes subsections on Nicholas Ray, favorite AUTEURS, and film genres. Part Three, "Italian Cinema," explains why the future filmmakers admired Neo-Realism and especially the works of Rossellini. Part Four, "Polemics," offers a valuable summary of the passionate positions that outraged and excited the magazine's worldwide readership. Hillier points out that beyond the outrageous statements was a deep-felt need to rethink the nature of film history and the course of the commercial cinema. The material is subdivided into two parts: criticism and CinemaScope.

A delight from start to finish, this anthology is filled with marvellous essays and stimulating controversies. Appendices on the magazine's annual "best film" listings from 1955 to 1959, a guide to its issues from nos. 1 to 102, and summary statements on forthcoming books on CAHIERS DU CINEMA are provided, along with an index on names and film titles. Recommended for special collections.

Lowry, Edward. THE FILMOLOGY MOVEMENT AND FILM STUDY IN FRANCE. Ann Arbor: UMI Research Press, 1985. 217pp.

Originally written as a 1982 doctoral dissertation at the University of Texas at Austin, this work is an imaginative and intelligent examination of the French post-WWII period, when a number of intellectuals and scholars set about searching for a comprehensive, systematic approach to film within the academic community. The setting was the Sorbonne, the stimulus was Gilbert Cohen-Seat's influential 1946 tract, ESSAI SUR LES PRINCIPES D'UNE PHILOSOPHIE DU CINEMA. Within months of the publication, an association had been formed at the university, and within a year it was publishing a scholarly journal, LE REVUE INTERNATIONALE DE FILMOLOGIE.

Since the collective efforts produced no major theory or prominent work, the movement itself has been ignored or dismissed as "an obscure tangent of film theory." Lowry's sensitive analysis on what filmology contributed to current film scholarship should change matters. Not only does he argue persuasively that the movement "represents the first major attempt to delineate, structure and institutionalize intellectual concerns about the cinema . . . [but also he makes clear that] its problematic [what Louis Althusser labeled "the particular unit of theoretical formation"] has played a significant role in the formulation of questions which still affect the practice of film scholars and film pedagogy within the Western university." Three of the book's basic themes in defining the filmological problematic are: "(1) the notion of positive science which underlines nearly all of its work; (2) the sense of social mission which surfaces again and again; and (3) its definition in terms of the institutional structure of the university." Lowry divides his material into two major sections. Part One, "A History of Filmology," contains three chapters reviewing the context in which the movement arose, Cohen-Seat's philosophy of cinema, and the initial steps in defining the "new science." Part Two, "Theory and Practice of Filmology," provides five chapters dealing with aesthetic and linguistic considerations, the socio-anthropology of the cinema, psychological considerations, and the author's conclusions. Endnotes, a bibliography, and an index are included. Well worth browsing.

ROBERT BRESSON

*Cameron, Ian, ed. THE FILMS OF ROBERT BRESSON. New York: Praeger Publishers, 1970. Illustrated. 145pp.
One of the screen's great modernist directors, Bresson's minimalist approach to screen language inspired many emerging European directors from the 1950s on, to take complete charge of their work and to restructure traditional approaches to narrative film. Throughout forty years of filmmaking, he personified the independent artist who refused to conform or to stagnate. Although his Spartan style alienated him from mainstream filmmaking, the magnitude of his cinematic explorations in sound and acting to reveal the dichotomy between illusion and reality endeared him to serious artists and intellectuals.
In this uneven and disappointing collection, seven critics (Amedee Ayfre, Raymond Durgnat, Daniel Millar, Leo Murray, Charles Barr, and Phil Hardy) discuss Bresson's major films from ANGELS OF THE STREETS/LES ANGES DU PECHE (1943) to A GENTLE WOMAN/UNE FEMME DOUCE (1969). Originally published in 1969, this American edition contains two additional articles not found in the London edition. The most useful essay is Ayfre's "The Universe of Robert Bresson," examining the director's "mythology." Approaching the subject through categories such as "From Abstraction to Reality," "From Character to Person," "From Loneliness to Communication," and "From Immanence to Transcendence," the author concludes that Bresson is the forerunner of the modern cinema. Among the reasons given are "the extreme importance given to the text and its dissonances with the picture; the entirely new evaluation of the different forms of temporality; the recognized value of empty space and absence; a certain hieratic quality in the acting, the rejection of theatrical performances and traditional dramatisation, not to mention the all too well known 'distanciation' . . . ." A filmography and bibliography are included, but no index. Worth browsing.

Hanlon, Lindley. FRAGMENTS: BRESSON'S FILM STYLE. Rutherford: Associated University Presses, 1986. Illustrated. 240pp.
The first and only full-length study of Bresson in English, this thought-provoking examination looks at five of the director's films: A GENTLE WOMAN/UNE FEMME DOUCE (1969), BALTHAZAR/AU HASARD BALTHAZAR (1966), FOUR NIGHTS OF A DREAMER/QUATRE NUITS D'UN REVEUR (1971), MOUCHETTE (1967), and LANCELOT OF THE LAKE/LANCELOT DU LAC (1974). Using an

interdisciplinary approach that draws on Erich Auerbach's MIMESIS, Angus Fletcher's ALLEGORY: THE THEORY OF A SYMBOLIC MODE, and Roland Barthes's S/Z, Hanlon offers a stimulating discussion of the narrative structures of Bresson's later films. "Bresson designs each narrative element," Hanlon explains, "so that it will acquire its full significance in the edited context where the accumulation of details is organized. Relative to conventional dramatic film narratives, the importance of sound, objects, and glances in Bresson's films is increased. Seldom do sound and image duplicate each other. There is very little exposition of situation, explanation of motive, or clarification of action. Bresson's films proceed without hesitation, deliberately, inexorably toward the revelation of the inner processes of the human spirit." In addition to endnotes, an extensive bibliography, and an index, the book contains an interview with Antoine Monnier, the actor in Bresson's PROBABLY THE DEVIL/LE DIABLE PROBLEMENT (1977). Recommended for special collections.

*Schrader, Paul. TRANSCENDENTAL STYLE IN FILM: OZU, BRESSON, DREYER. Berkeley: University of California Press, 1972. Illustrated. 194pp.

Working on the theory that a common universal style links divergent artists in various cultures, Schrader presents a controversial and challenging analysis of film transcendentalists whose concern is with spiritual art, non-psychological interpretations, and lean techniques. Schrader sees cinematic transcendentalism as one more manifestation of Zen, Byzantine, and Gothic spiritual art. Beginning with the assumption that filmmakers like Ozu, Bresson, and Dreyer are striving to apply transcendental ideas through camera angles, dialogue, music, and editing, the author identifies what he sees as the nature of cinematic transcendental style. Its primary function, Schrader asserts, is "to express the Holy itself (the Transcendent), and not to express or illustrate holy feelings." Avoiding traditional interpretations of reality, the trancendental filmmaker, according to Schrader, "maximizes the mystery of existence" and minimizes "those elements which are primarily expressive of human existence . . . ." That is, he "chooses irrationalism over rationalism, repetition over variation, sacred over profane, the deific over the humanistic, intellectual realism over optical realism, two-dimensional vision over three-dimensional vision, tradition over experiment, anonymity over individualization." In the opening chapter on Ozu, Schrader defines the typical structure of a transcendental film as (1) "The everyday: a meticulous representation of the dull, banal commonplaces of everyday living . . ."; (2) "Disparity: an actual or potential disunity between man and his environment which culminates in a decisive action . . ."; and (3) "Stasis: a frozen view of life which does not resolve the disparity but transcends it."

The strengths and weaknesses of Schrader's debatable theory are evident in his analysis of Bresson's work. On the one hand, he forces us to make important differentiations between superficial films dealing with religious feelings and profound movies examining the integral link of a culture and metaphysical values. On the other hand, forcing all of an artist's works into one mold inevitably leads to oversimplifications and distortions. As Tony Pipola points out, Schrader's approach not only distort's "Bresson's brilliant and lucid narrative style, one which pares away inessentials and uses surface reality to describe the milieu and the obsession of a character . . . [but also distorts] "the filmmaker's over-riding concern for the appropriate CINEMATIC rendering of character states without resorting to the mimetic process of acting: a style which describes the elaborate behavorial patterns of characters (including the detailed attention to the PROCESS of activities which obsess such characters . . .)."[804]

---

[804]   Tony Pipolo, "Squeezing the Wide into a Narrow Temple," VILLAGE VOICE (July 26, 1973):69.

Schrader's detailed analyses provide useful opportunities to consider the nature of the sacred in theatrical films, while reconsidering the work of three important filmmakers. At the same time, his complex, theoretical discussions limit the book's appeal to serious students. Endnotes, a bibliography, and an index is included. Well worth browsing.

Sloan, Joan. ROBERT BRESSON: A GUIDE TO REFERENCES AND RESOURCES. Boston: G. K. Hall and Company, 1983. 231pp.

Comprehensive rather than selective, this important resource provides a first-rate introduction to Bresson's work and reactions to it. Sloan views the director as "a filmmaker's filmmaker," who influenced not only "'art directors' like R. W. Fassbinder, Jean-Luc Godard, and Chantal Akerman, but also people like Walter Hill, Paul Schrader, Kenneth Anger, and Don Siegel . . . ." Her terse biographical overview highlights the important stages in his career, while her perceptive critical study stresses Bresson's distinctions between "cinema" and "cinematography" (the former denotes mechanical reproduction, while the latter involves creative discovery). Sloan's annotated filmography provides synopses, credits on thirteen films from Bresson's first and missing film LES AFFAIRES PUBLIQUES (1934) to PROBABLY THE DEVIL/LE DIABLE PROBLEMENT (1977). The book's most extensive section, "Writings About Bresson," offers an immpressive list of material in English, French, and German, as well as annotations for book-length works in Italian and Spanish. The book concludes with brief sections on Bresson's writings, archival information, distributor listings, and an index. Recommended for special collections.

RENE CLAIR

*Clair, Rene. CLAIR: FOUR SCREENPLAYS--LE SILENCE EST D'OR, LA BEAUTE DU DIABLE, LES BELLES-DE-NUIT, LES GRANDES MANOEUVRES. Trans. Piergiuseppe Bozzetti. New York: The Orion Press, 1970. Illustrated. 439pp.

Each of these four films, made after France was liberated and when Clair found himself once more able to work in his native land, is presented with a foreword, cast and technical credits, script, and commentary. The author's brief reflections add a nice touch to the useful collection. Well worth browsing.

JEAN COCTEAU

*Cocteau, Jean. BEAUTY AND THE BEAST: DIARY OF A FILM. Trans. Ronald Duncan. Introduction George Amberg. New York: Dover Publications, 1972. Illustrated. 142pp.

One of Cocteau's most admired films is discussed in detail in the filmmaker's diary, starting from the day before shooting began (August 26, 1945) and ending on the day following a private screening of the final version of the film (June 1, 1946). The problems with production, the personalities of the performers, and Cocteau's hopes for the project are woven throughout the entertaining and informative pages. The lovely illustrations enhance the experience. Well worth browsing.

*Cocteau, Jean. THREE SCREENPLAYS: ORPHEUS/ THE ETERNAL RETURN/ BEAUTY AND THE BEAST. Trans. Carol Martin-Sperry. New York: Grossman Publishers, 1972. Illustrated. 250pp.

Hammond, Robert M., ed. BEAUTY AND THE BEAST: SCENARIO AND DIALOGS BY JEAN COCTEAU. New York: New York University Press, Illustrated. 441pp.

A helpful introduction by this resourceful scholar provides us with the only accurate and complete text of this rare film. Recommended for special collections.

HENRI LANGLOIS

Roud, Richard. A PASSION FOR FILMS: HENRI LANGLOIS AND THE CINEMATEQUE FRANCAISE. Foreword Francois Truffaut. New York: The Viking Press, 1983. Illustrated. 218pp.

Born on November 12, 1914, the man many filmmakers consider to be a saint because of his unqualified love for film grew up without the benefits of a film library and in a world that often thought of movies as "trash." The 1932 decision by the SALLE DES AGRICULTEURS to abandon its policy of exhibiting classic silent films left France without the opportunity to review the masterpieces of the silent era. According to Langlois, the popularity of sound films in the early 1930s created a demand for CINEMATEQUES (film libraries) in America, Britain, and France: "The last of the film clubs was liquidated, film criticism was paralyzed, everything had fallen to pieces but, before it disappeared, this movement was able to create the cinemateques." The crucial difference between the Museum of Modern Art, the British Film Institute, and Langlois's CINEMATEQUE FRANCAISE, Roud points out, is "that the Cinemateque BEGAN with the idea of showing films as well as preserving them." Working with Jacques Franju, Georges's twin brother, Langlois established the LE CERCLE DU CINEMA in 1935, which changed its name to CINEMATEQUE FRANCAISE in the postwar period. Over the next thirty years, this marvelous film library literally became the school for some of the most famous filmmakers in cinema history: e.g., Bernardo Bertolucci, Claude Chabrol, Jean-Luc Godard, Francois Truffaut, Alain Resnais, Jacques Rivette, and Wim Wenders.

The history of this extraordinary man, his enormous contributions to film history, and his battles with the state are described with wit, candor, and affection. Roud's association with Langlois until the latter's death on January 12, 1977, makes the author's anecdotes about the obsessive and demanding curator not only informative, but also credible. What emerges is a picture of flamboyant personality that would give employees and administrators endless nightmares. Although Roud struggles admirably to present a balanced portrait, he occasionally defends Langlois's biases rather than exposing his shortcomings in terms of spurned directors, aesthetic pretensions, and copyright protection. Nevertheless, as Marcel Ophuls writes in his review of the book, "Richard Roud has written a truly important biography, which cannot fail to be considered a major contribution to film history. . . ."[805] Endnotes and an index are included. Recommended for special collections.

JEAN-PIERRE MELVILLE

*Nogueira, Rui, ed. MELVILLE ON MELVILLE. New York: The Viking Press, 1971. Illustrated. 176pp.

MAX OPHULS

Williams, Alan Larson. MAX OPHULS AND THE CINEMA OF DESIRE: STYLE AND SPECTACLE IN FOUR FILMS, 1948-1955. New York: Arno Press, 1980. 169pp.

---

[805] Marcel Ophuls, "The Passion of Henri Langlois," AMERICAN FILM 8:9 (July-August 1983):52.

Originally written as Williams's 1980 doctoral dissertation at the University of Buffalo, this appreciative study lacks the focus and insights provided in Wexman's superb anthology on LETTER FROM AN UNKNOWN WOMAN. Williams deserves credit, however, for providing a pioneering source of information on a superb director who is unjustly ignored by many scholarly circles. Following two rambling introductory chapters on film theory and its relationship to Ophuls's work and critical reputation, the author discusses six films, not four as stated in the title: LETTER FROM AN UNKNOWN WOMAN (1948), CAUGHT (1949), LA RONDE (1950), LE PLAISIR (1952), MADAME DE . . . (1953), and LOLA MONTES (1955). The material is interesting, if not particularly perceptive. A bibliography is provided, but no filmography or index is included. Worth browsing.

JACQUES TATI

Fischer, Lucy. JACQUES TATI: A GUIDE TO REFERENCES AND RESOURCES. Boston: G. K. Hall and Company, 1983. 160pp.

The most comprehensive study on Tati to-date, this informative and detailed resource presented the author with a number of problems. "Not all of his films are in American distribution," Fisher explains, "nor preserved in archives. Therefore, it is impossible to see his early short films here or his latest work PARADE. Published sources of information on Tati also evidence problematic gaps. Biographies are frequently sketchy and lacking in historical detail. Credits for his early films often fail to specify such things as running time or cast of characters." Thus the value of Fisher's scholarship is in providing the most complete and accurate information in English on Tati. Her opening section dealing with Tati's life and career is one of the most detailed portraits in the invaluable G. K. Hall series. Other sections--e.g., a critical survey, an annoted filmography, writings about Tati, other film-related activities, archival sources, film distributors--also get high marks for thoroughness. In addition to a film title index and an author index, the author includes an appendix containing Bazin's essay "Mr. Hulot and Time." Recommended for special collections.

Maddock, Brent. THE FILMS OF JACQUES TATI. Metuchen: The Scarecrow Press, 1977. 179pp.

"This study," writes Maddock, "attempts to place Tati's work in proper relationship to the early comedy masters, as well as looking at the background of music hall and mime that originally led Tati to films." Maddock begins with a chapter on the film comedian's ties to American comedy films, pointing specifically to his debts to Charlie Chaplin, Buster Keaton, Harry Langdon, and Harold Lloyd. After a brief chapter on Tati's early years, Maddock reviews Tati's early film comedies, and how he created the character of Mr. Hulot, and then proceeds to individual chapters on Tati's major films from MR. HULOT'S HOLIDAY/LES VACANCES DE MONSIEUR HULOT (1953) to TRAFFIC (1971). The book's remaining six chapters discuss how the comedian's films reflect old and new world values, the cinematic world he creates, his comedy style, and his techniques. In the concluding chapter, the author speculates on the different directions Tati is pursuing following the 1973 Swedish TV film, PARADE. A filmography, endnotes, a bibliography, and an index are included. Well worth browsing.

FILMS

ROBERT BRESSON

THE DIARY OF A COUNTRY PRIEST/LE JOURNAL D'UN CURE DE CAMPAGNE (France--16mm: 1951, 95 mins., b/w, English subtitles, sound, R-FNC, TFF; S-REE, TFF)

In this moving story of a country priest's conflict between his abilities and his ambitions, Bresson magnificently adapts Georges Bernanos's novel and captures the isolation and loneliness of an individual in spiritual turmoil. Claude Laydu is perfect as the tragic curate confronting the unknown. The film's innovating technique, as Dudley Andrew comments, "overturns received notions of 'the primacy of the image' and of the 'cinematic story,' abandoning the theatrical, public and architectural ostentation of quality for a fluid, musical interior, and ascetic expression."[806]

RENE CLEMENT

FORBIDDEN GAMES/LES JEUX INTERDITS (France--16mm: 1952, 90 mins., b/w, English subtitles, sound, R-FES, FNC)

With a brilliant script by Jean Aurence and Pierre Bost, this unforgettable story provides a look at what war does to children. Clement's opening scenes of refugees being machine-gunned offers a horrifying contrast between the beauty of nature, and the insanity of human beings. As Colette Audry wrote at the time of the film's release, "Next to this profound and serious life of the children, that of the adults (peasants, priests, nun), all well-meaning people, seem elementary, mechanical, and often ludicrous."[807]

HENRI-GEORGES CLOUZOT

DIABOLIQUE/LES DIABOLIQUES (France--16mm: 1955, 92 mins., b/w, English subtitles, sound, R-BUD, COR, EMG, FES, FNC, IMA, IVY, KIT, TWY; S-IMA, NAT)

Clouzot and Jerome Geronimi adapted Pierre Boileau and Thomas Narcejac's suspenseful novel, CELLE QUI N'ETAIT PLUS into one of the best thrillers of the decade. The cleverly directed murder mystery features Simone Signoret and Vera Clouzot out to kill the sadistic headmaster of a boy's boarding school. The skill with which Clouzot sets the stage for the murder, the recreation of life at a boarding school, and the intricate plot machinations of the script reveal the presence of a master technician.

JEAN COCTEAU

BEAUTY AND THE BEAST/LA BELLE ET LA BETE (France--16mm: 1946, 90 mins., b/w, English subtitles, sound, R-JAN)

In directing his first feature film since the early 1930s, Cocteau adapted the classic LePrince De Beaumont fable about a woman who falls in love with a beast and discovers he is a handsome priest whom she has freed from a horrible curse. The filmmaker gave the strange and haunting tale a unique interpretation of a person's feelings about love, isolation, greed, and self-sacrifice. As Cocteau wrote in his diary of the film, "The postulate of the story requires faith, the faith of childhood. I mean that one must believe implicitly at the very beginning and not question the possibility

---

[806]   Dudley Andrew, "JOURNAL D'UN CURE DE CAMPAGNE," THE INTERNATIONAL DICTIONARY OF FILMS AND FILMMAKERS: VOLUME I, pp.230-1. See also Raymond Durgnat, "DIARY OF A COUNTRY PRIEST," FILMS AND FILMING 13:3 (December 1966):28-32; Jean Douchet, "Bresson on Location," SEQUENCE 13 (1951):6-8; and Richard Roud, "The Early Works of Robert Bresson," FILM CULTURE 20 (1959):44-52.

[807]   Cited in Robin Buss, THE FRENCH THROUGH THEIR FILMS (New York: Ungar Publishing Company, 1988), p.107. See also Dudley Andrew, "LES JEUX INTERDITS," THE DICTIONARY OF FILMS AND FILMMAKERS: VOLUME I, pp.223-4.

that the mere picking of a rose might lead a family into adventure, or that a man can be changed into a beast, and vice versa. Such enigmas offend grown-ups who are readily prejudiced, proud of their doubt, armed with derision. But I have the impudence to believe that the cinema which depicts the impossible is apt to convey conviction, in a way, and may be able to put a 'singular' occurrence into the plural."[808] In addition to magnificent performances by Jean Marais (the Beast) and Josette Day (Beauty), Cocteau got considerable help from the cinematographer Henry Alekan, the composer Georges Auric, and the set designer-costumer Christian Berard.[809]

ORPHEUS/ORPHEE (France--16mm: 1949, 94 mins., b/w, English subtitles, sound, R-JAN)
    Cocteau wrote and directed this strange, haunting film loosely based upon a modern version of the myth of Orpheus and Eurydice. Georges Auric's memorable music, and Nicolas Hayer's bewitching photography contributed to the weird effect of poetry being communicated from another world through a human being to an adoring public. Maris again gives a remarkable performance as the troubled and gifted poet trying to understand the source of his unusual experience.[810]

THE TESTAMENT OF ORPHEUS/LE TESTAMENT D'ORPHEE (France--16mm: 1960, 79 mins., b/w, English subtitles, sound, R-BUD, IMA; S-REE)
    This was Cocteau's last film in the trilogy, with even more mysterious goings on and more controversial results. To a number of critics it remains the artist's summation of his cinematic art.[811]

MAX OPHULS

LOLA MONTES (France--16mm: 1955, 110 mins., cinemascope, color, English subtitles, sound, R-FNC)
    Max Ophuls's last and highly controversial movie depicts the amorous affairs of a famous circus courtesan (Martine Carol), told mostly in flashback, and serves as an attack on the film industry's policies and practices. The screenplay, co-authored by Ophuls and three other writers, and adapted from Cecil St. Laurent's novel, LA

---

[808]   *Jean Cocteau, BEAUTY AND THE BEAST: DIARY OF A FILM, trans.   Ronald Duncan, Introduction George Amberg (New York: Dover Publications, 1972), p.5.

[809]   For more information, see Anthony Slide, FIFTY CLASSIC FRENCH FILMS, 1912-1982: A PICTORIAL RECORD (New York: Dover Publications, 1987), pp.67-9; and Roy Armes, "LA BELLE ET LA BETE," THE INTERNATIONAL DICTIONARY OF FILMS AND FILMMAKERS: VOLUME I, pp.48-9.

[810]   For more information, see Ronald Bowers, "ORPHEE," THE INTERNATIONAL DICTIONARY OF FILMS AND FILMMAKERS: VOLUME I, pp.346-7; Jean R. Debrix, "Cocteau's ORPHEUS Analyzed," trans.   Edith Morgan King, FILMS IN REVIEW 11:6 (June-July 1951):18-23; Raymond Durgnat, "Orphee," FILMS AND FILMING 10:1 (October 1963):45-8; Gavin Lambert, "Cocteau and Orpheus," SEQUENCE 12 (Autumn 1950):20-32; and Robert M. Hammond, "The Mysteries of Cocteau's ORPHEUS," CINEMA JOURNAL 11:2 (Spring 1972):26-33.

[811]   For more information, see Leon Bukowiecki, "Testament," FILMS AND FILMING 8:2 (November 1961):28, 40; Neal Oxenhandler, "On Cocteau," FILM QUARTERLY 18:1 (Fall 1964):12-4; and George Amberg, "The Testament of Jean Cocteau," FILM COMMENT 7:4 (Winter 1971-72):23-7.

VIE EXTRAORDINAIRE DE LOLA MONTES, allowed Ophuls to pursue his lifelong interest in period pieces dealing with women in love and to still experiment with film technique. In this case, his lush production exploiting the costumes, sets, and cinemascope format violently disturbed initial audiences who had expected a spectacle about tragic love affairs between the aristocracy and a common dancer. Instead, as Dennis Nastav, points out, Ophuls demystifies the exhibitionism that engulfs the show business world, turning the film into a "virulent condemnation" on the voyeuristic interests of the public and the producers.[812] Considered today a masterpiece, the cast, in addition to Martine, features Peter Ustinov and a young Oskar Werner.[813]

JACQUES TATI

MR. HULOT'S HOLIDAY/LES VACANCES DE MONSIEUR HULOT (France--16mm: 1953, 85 mins., b/w, sound, dubbed, R-BUD, COR, EMG, FES, IMA, IVY, KIT, WHO; S-EMG, IMA, FES)

The Bernard Maurice-Pierre Aubert-Jacques Tati screenplay introduces the incomparable bourgeoise, pipe-smoking Mr. Hulot to audiences around the world. On the surface, the experiences of an out-of-touch, ambivalent vacationer trying to enjoy his Brittany holiday seem little more than a charming comedy, meticulously crafted, and recalling the great silent comedies. Yhe director Tati stresses visual gags and only has Hulot (played by Tati) speak one word throughout the entire film. On another level, however, Mr. Hulot is a seminal figure in screen comedy. Oblivious to his surroundings and undeterred by the obstacles that confront him, Hulot speaks for all of us who seek a comfortable place in an unfriendly world. As Philip Strick points out, "The revolutionary figure, who meanders through . . . [Tati's] films is, like all clowns a lonely man who tries not to be, a lost soul on the lookout for sanctified ground, a friendly tender-hearted eccentric pathetically convinced that society depends upon him yet ill-equipped to find his place in any aspect of it."[814]

THE SOVIET BLOCK IN THE POSTWAR PERIOD (1945-1955)

---

[812]   Dennis Nastav, "LOLA MONTES," THE INTERNATIONAL DICTIONARY OF FILMS AND FILMMAKERS: VOLUME I, p.265.

[813]   For more information, see Eugene Archer, "Ophuls and the Romantic Tradition," YALE FRENCH STUDIES 17 (1956):3-5; Alan Williams, "The Circles of Desire: Narration and Representation in LA RONDE," FILM QUARTERLY 26:1 (Fall 1973):35-41; Max Ophuls, "My Experience," CAHIERS DU CINEMA IN ENGLISH 1, CdC #81 (January 1966):63-8; Forrest Williams, "The Mastery of Movement: An Appreciation of Max Ophuls," FILM COMMENT 5:4 (Winter 1969):70-4; Eric Rhode, "Max Ophuls," 159-70; Howard Koch, "Script to Screen with Max Ophuls," ibid., 6:4 (Winter 1970-71):40-3; Andrew Sarris, "Max Ophuls: An Introduction," ibid., 7:2 (Summer 1971):56-9; Gary Carey, "Caught," ibid., pp.62-4; William Paul, "The Reckless Moment," ibid., pp.65-66; Foster Hirsch, "MADAME DE," ibid., pp.67-8; and Robin Bean, "Art and Artlessness: Peter Ustinov," FILMS AND FILMING 15:1 (October 1968):4-8.

One result of World War II was that a number of "Eastern European" nations[815] fell under the control of the Soviet Union: e.g., Albania, Bulgaria, Czechoslavakia, the German Democratic Republic, Hungary, Poland, Romania, and Yugoslavia. The history of these national film industries is yet to be fully documented. Nevertheless, as Mira and Antonin J. Liehm observe, the evidence of what these nations contributed to the evolution and development of cinematic art is significant. A key to understanding that contribution is an awareness of the role that the nationalization of an industry plays in the relationship between a filmmaker and a state monopoly:

> Of course, the fact the Eastern European film-maker has no choice, that he cannot select another producer, that he has no possibility of attempting an independent production, that he is faced with a state monopoly, and hence has nowhere to turn--all this intensifies the pressures within a nationalized film industry. And naturally, these pressures also provoke a counter-pressure, which is apparent in the film-makers' efforts to change the situation, in their increased feeling of collective responsibility for the overall state of affairs, in their efforts to achieve a greater decentralization and establish more indpendent production groups, and, ultimately, in the strengthening of the role played by film-makers and their organizations within the entire system.[816]

The story of those national struggles for independent productions is noted in the annotated bibliographies that follow. What is worth mentioning here is that each of the Eastern European nations developed a set of traditions in the years prior to 1945, a set of traditions that had a marked effect on the postwar cinema of the Soviet block nations.

With the exception of Wright's insightful chronicle of film history, most current general film histories either gloss over the conditions that existed in Eastern Europe following World War II or ignore the developments taking place in nationalized cinemas in Albania, Bulgaria, Czechoslavakia, the German Democratic Republic, Hungary, Poland, Romania, and Yugoslavia. These are omissions that future historians need to correct. A case in point is Hungary. As Istvan Nemeskurty notes:

> Liberation was a milestone in Hungarian film history. Cinemas were flooded with new films. The first Soviet films showed the life of a previously unknown, unfamiliar society, in a new and interesting form . . . Bela Balazs came home, founded a journal, gave lectures and began to teach the public how to look at films, and new creative teams how to make films, training the first

---

[814]   "JOUR DE FETE," p.19. For more information, see Dave Kehr, "LES VACANCES DE MONSIEUR HULOT," THE INTERNATIONAL DICTIONARY OF FILMS AND FILMMAKERS: VOLUME I, pp.497-8; and Ristin Thompson, "Parameters of the Open Film: LES VACANCES DE MONSIEUR HULOT," WIDE ANGLE 2:1 (1977):22-30.

[815]   As Mira and Antonin J. Liehm point out, it is more accurate to talk of Eastern and Central Europe than of Eastern European nations. "Early in the century," they explain, "the countries of Eastern and Central Europe could be classified into two clear-cut categories. One of them consisted of Russia, Poland, Bohemia, and Hungary (all countries that were to become republics after World War One), where the values of the Parisian and Viennese film worlds were generally accepted; the other, made up of Bulgaria, Romania, and some sections of what today is Yugoslavia, responded only weakly to signals that came from Western Europe and then frequently faded or died out completely in the stifling native atmosphere." See *Mira Liehm and Antonin J. Liehm, THE MOST IMPORTANT ART: SOVIET AND EASTERN EUROPEAN FILM AFTER 1945 (Berkeley: University of California Press, 1977), p.7.

[816]   Liehm, p.1.

students of film production after 1945, who were to direct their first films in the 'fifties . . . The effect of all this became apparent, first, in the more exacting criticism of reviews and in a better informed public. Progressive films reached Hungary. Untalented craftsmen who had been active during the war years disappeared, yet there was no structural change. From the Liberation to 1948, Hungarian film production was carried on by private enterprise: capitalists could produce films at the state studios.[817]

The three year period before the nationalization of the Hungarian cinema in 1948 and the ten year period that followed provide important information about the social and artistic functions of films in Soviet block contries.

A good starting point for the study of Eastern European filmmaking is the Polish cinema. Most film histories agree that only in Poland were there significant films being made in the immediate postwar period.[818] As Wright points out, there were three basic reasons why the Poles were successful: (1) the nation's fierce sense of independence, (2) the power of the Catholic Church in Poland, and (3) "the making of films about the destruction and suffering in Warsaw and elsewhere, and about the atrocious behaviour of the Germans, could hardly be treated as censorable by the Stalinists. . . ."[819] Following the nationalization of the Polish film industry on December 4, 1945, Oskar Sobanski explains, "The Film Polski State enterprise was the monoplistic producer/distributor/exploiter of films."[820] Aleksander Ford, the general manager of the monopoly, did away with commercial filmmaking and focused attention of social and political issues. Young people's workshops were set up to attract new blood into the cinema. By 1948, the government established the famous Film School at Lodz under the leadership of Jerzy Toeplitz. The artists who emerged from Lodz--e.g., Jerzy Kawalerowicz, Andrzej Munk, Andrzej Wajda, Zbigniew Cybulski; along with the experienced filmmakers--e.g., Jerzy Bossak, Eugene Cekalski, Stanislaus Wohl, Wanda Jakubowska--who had been trained in START (the Society of Devotees of the Artistic Film), a pre-WWII AVANT-GARDE film group, combined to bring worldwide attention to Polish films in the mid-1950s.

BOOKS

GENERAL

*Hibbin, Nina. EASTERN EUROPE: AN ILLUSTRATED GUIDE. New York: A. S. Barnes and Company, 1969. Illustrated. 239pp.

This is a good guide to postwar movies because it is accurate on leading personalities, films, and technicians, and the index and photographs help fill in the gaps. Well worth browsing.

---

[817]   Istvan Nemeskurty, WORD AND IMAGE: HISTORY OF THE HUNGARIAN CINEMA, trans. Zsuzsanna Horn and Fred Macnicol (Chicago: Imported Publications, 1974), p.141.

[818]   The following articles are helpful: Gene Moskowitz, "The Uneasy East: Aleksander Ford and the Polish Cinema," SIGHT AND SOUND 27:3 (Winter 1937-58):136-40; David Robinson, "Better Late Than Never," ibid., 31:2 (Spring 1962):67-70, 103; and Boleslaw Michalek, "The Polish Drama," ibid., 29:4 (Autumn 1960):198-200.

[819]   Wright, pp.410-11.

[820]   Oskar Sobanski, POLISH FEATURE FILMS: A REFERENCE GUIDE 1945-1985 (West Cornwall: Locust Hill Press, 1987),)p.viii.

*Liehm, Mira, and Antonin J. Liehm. THE MOST IMPORTANT ART: SOVIET AND EASTERN EUROPEAN FILM AFTER 1945. Berkeley: University of California Press, 1977. Illustrated. 467pp.

Paul, David W. POLITCS, ART AND COMMITMENT IN THE EAST EUROPEAN CINEMA. New York: St. Martin's Press, 1984. Illustrated. 314pp.

*White, Alistair. NEW CINEMA IN EASTERN EUROPE. New York: E. P. Dutton and Company, 1971. Illustrated. 159pp.

BULGARIA

Holloway, Ronald. THE BULGARIAN CINEMA. Cranbury: Fairleigh Dickinson University Press, 1986. Illustrated. 216pp.

CZECHOSLOVAKIA

Bocek, Jaroslav, et al. MODERN CZECHOSLOVAK FILM 1945-1965. Prague: ARTIA, 1965.

*Broz, Jaroslav. THE PATH OF FAME OF THE CZECHOSLOVAK FILM. Prague: FILMEXPORT, 1967. Illustrated. 112pp.

Dewey, Langdon. OUTLINE OF CZECHOSLOVAKIAN CINEMA. London: Informatics, 1971.

HUNGARY

Nemeskurty, Istvan. WORD AND IMAGE: HISTORY OF THE HUNGARIAN CINEMA. Trans. Zsuzsanna Horn and Fred Macnicol. Chicago: Imported Publications, 1974. Illustrated. 252pp.

POLAND

Banaszkiewicz, Wladyslaw, et al. CONTEMPORARY POLISH CINEMATOGRAPHY. Warsaw: Polona Publishing House, 1962. Illustrated. 175pp.
     Interest for most Americans in Polish cinema began with men like Roman Polanski and Andrzej Wajda, with the excellent Polish animated films and certain key documentaries. The collective authors (seven in all) decided that the foreign audience should know more about Poland's film history and present operating procedures. This book helps us learn about those areas and gives some useful information about important filmmakers. Well worth browsing.

*Coates, Paul. THE STORY OF THE LOST REFLECTION: THE ALIENATION OF THE IMAGE IN WESTERN AND POLISH CINEMA. London: Verso, 1985. 167pp.

*Fuksiewicz, Jacek. FILM AND TELEVISION IN POLAND. Chicago: Imported Publications, 1976. Illustrated. 255pp.

Sobanski, Oskar. POLISH FEATURE FILMS: A REFERENCE GUIDE 1945-1985. West Cornwall: Locust Hill Press, 1987. 335pp.

ANDRZEJ WAJDA

*Michatek, Bolestaw. THE CINEMA OF ANDRZEJ WAJDA. Trans. Edward Rothert. South Brunswick: A. S. Barnes and Company, 1973. Illustrated. 176pp.

Wajda, Andrzej. DOUBLE VISION: MY LIFE IN FILMS. New York: Holt, Rinehart & Winston, 1989. Illustrated.

*Wajda, Andrzej. THREE FILMS BY WAJDA: ASHES AND DIAMONDS, A GENERATION, KANAL. New York: Simon and Schuster, 1973. Illustrated. 239pp.

FILMS

ANDRZEJ WAJDA

A GENERATION/POKOLENIE (Poland--16mm: 1954, 85 mins., b/w, English subtitles, sound, R-FNC)
This significant film marked the screen debuts of the director Wajda, the screenwriter Bohdan Czesko, the cinematographer Jerzy Lipman, the composer Andrzej Markowski, and key members of the cast. In depicting Poland's "lost generation" of the postwar era, the plot divides its characters into stereotypes of good and evil as Wajda explores life in a Communist country during World War II. This film initiates the first part of his trilogy on resistance in Poland. The other two films are KANAL/SEWER (1957) and ASHES AND DIAMONDS/POPIOL I DIAMENT (1958).

YUGOSLAVIA

Goulding, Daniel J. LIBERATED CINEMA: THE YUGOSLAV EXPERIENCE. Bloomington: Indiana University Press, 1985. Illustrated. 190pp.[821]

Holloway, Ronald. Z IS FOR ZAGREB. South Brunswick: A. S. Barnes and Company, 1972. Illustrated. 12899.

JAPAN IN THE POSTWAR PERIOD (1945-1957)

---

[821] For more information, see Andrew Horton, "Satire and Sympathy: A New Wave of Yugoslavian Filmmakers," CINEASTE 11:2 (Spring 1982):18-22; ___, "The New Serbo-Creationism," AMERICAN FILM 11:4 (January-February 1986):24-30; Ronald Holloway, "Social Documentary in Yugoslavia," FILM SOCIETY REVIEW 6:7 (March 1971):42-8; and Andrew Horton, "Yugoslavia: Multi-Faceted Cinema," WORLD CINEMA SINCE 1945, pp.639-60.

The end of World War II on August 14, 1945, gave rise to a second "golden age" for Japanese filmmakers. Part of the reason was that the film industry was in relatively good shape. The studios had survived the destruction of the cities and nearly fifty percent of the movie theaters were functioning. Moreover, the immediate postwar period witnessed an incredible building boom in movie houses, since many people (especially those involved in the thriving black market) considered theaters to be an excellent financial investment. While these fortuitous elements permitted the Japanese film industry to continue production uninterrupted during the transition period, they do not explain why Mellen could justifiably claim that between 1945 and 1962, "the Japanese have produced a body of films and a host of fine directors rivaling, and perhaps surpassing their French, Italian, and American counterparts."[822] How the filmmakers overcame the national trauma brought about by physical exhaustion, mental fatigue, and widespread poverty is still not clearly understood.

A debate rages over the influence of the American occupation on Japanese films. The standard interpretation credits the seven-year period (1945-1952) with democratizing the country and with doing away with feudalistic values in the cinema. In the first stages of the occupation, the filmmakers faced a number of crises, not the least of which was that the Americans permitted only 44% (329 out of 554) of the Japanese films made during the war and immediate postwar period to be shown. Filmmakers also fought with authorities and producers about what type of films should be made. In Jay Leyda's judgment,

> The greatest danger to the postwar Japanese film was neither fiscal nor industrial; Japanese ingenuity can always overcome such common crises. The real threat was the suffocation of new or rebellious artistic tendencies in the postwar film by the tight, successful patterns of the pre-war "sword films," a form precisely as unbending and as satisfying as our "western."[823]

Leyda's basic fear was that the public patronized only tried-and-tested formulas, regardless of their quality, and that Japanese studios had no intention of producing products they didn't think audiences home or abroad would pay to see. It was this reliance on past results rather than on exploring new perspectives that Leyda felt forced filmmakers into non-risk ventures. Anderson and Richie perceived matters differently. "The biggest production problem of the period," they report, "was concerned with scripts, with the worry about what kinds of films would be favored by the Occupation, or SCAP [Supreme Commander for Allied Powers], as General MacArthur's headquarters was called by the allies."[824] Thus, beginning in 1945, Japanese filmmakers not only had to struggle with the postwar problems of outmoded camera equipment, substandard electricity to run the studios, and inadequate supplies of raw film stock, but also with rigid audience expectations and a new set of laws restricting the content of films.

One of the first steps toward resolving the problems was for the SCAP to establish guidelines for the filmmakers to follow. According to one source, "The themes desired [by SCAP] were, in general, those showing a Japan at peace, with industry and agriculture developing productivity, with ex-soldiers being rehabilitated as industrious citizens, and the 'democratization' of Japanese customs, such as formal bowing, which the Americans found peculiarly distasteful and undemocratic."[825] It

---

[822] Mellen, p.1.

[823] Jay Leyda, "Modesty and Pretension in Two New Films," FILM CULTURE 2:4 (1956):3.

[824] Anderson and Richie, p.160.

[825] John Gillett and Roger Manvell, "Japan," THE INTERNATIONAL ENCYCLOPEDIA OF FILM, p.306.

was clear that the oOccupation censors were opposed to films containing religious intolerance, jingoistic ideology, ritual deaths, the mistreatment of wives, and the abuse of children. Ironically, Japanese filmmakers were forced to adopt values that never were imposed on American filmmakers.[826]

The solution to one problem created other problems. For example, one casualty of the new censorship laws was the period drama, well-known for its political perspectives and anti-democratic ideas. Sato argues, however, that "this conscious attempt at Americanization was only partially successful and not completely necessary since after the Occupation the feudalistic period drama was reinstituted."[827] A second casualty was the Japanese apprentice system, requiring young people to make their way through the ranks before being entrusted with the responsibility for directing a film. New "democratic" policies at the major studios made it easier for anyone to become a director. But without adequate training in the industry or an informed awareness of the fickleness of public taste, the younger directors became confused by the demands of the occupation forces and the expectations of the audience.[828]

If you accept Anderson and Richie's perspective on the Occupation film policy, then the work of the Civil Censorship Division of the SCAP and its successor in 1946, the Civil Information and Education Section (CI&E), gets poor grades from the Japanese film establishment. The bureacracy was as officious as the Home Ministry censors, and the types of censorship imposed were oppressive.[829] In addition, Kyoko Hirano points out that the early liberal policies of the SCAP not only destabilized the once-conservative Japanese film industry, but also "nourished Communism."[830] As a result, he adds, the Occupation Forces "changed the course of Japanese reconstruction to a conservative reorganization of Japan based upon the cold war mentality."[831] On the other hand, if you use Kurosawa's reactions as a measuring instrument, CI&E did a first-rate job of breathing new life into the Japanese film industry.[832]

Censorship not withstanding, the Japanese film industry had other major problems as it tried to resume full production in 1946, a year that saw less than seventy indigenous films released as compared to the pre-WWII figures that exceeded six hundred annually since 1927.[833] One of the most destabilizing events during the mid- and late-1940s was a series of devastating labor strikes that virtually drained the major studios--Toho, Daiei, and Shochiku--of their wealth, employees, and goodwill. The ideological battles fought between labor and management during the late 1940s left indelible scars on the film industry for decades to follow.[834] A second unsettling problem was the ferreting out of alleged "war criminals" by various

---

[826]   Tucker, p.34.

[827]   Sato, p.35. For an interesting observation on what types of American films were not exported to Japan during the occupation, see Sato, p.36.

[828]   Anderson and Richie, pp.180-6.

[829]   Anderson and Richie, pp.160-2.

[830]   Kyoko Hirano, "Japan," WORLD CINEMA SINCE 1945, p.382.

[831]   Hirano, p.385.

[832]   SOMETHING LIKE AN AUTOBIOGRAPHY, p.145.

[833]   Cook, p.576.

[834]   One immediate effect of the labor strikes was that disaffected directors like Tadashi Imai and Fumio Kamei formed small independent production companies.

committees of the Japanese film industry. To this day, scholars argue over how much of the search for villains was an act of revenge, rather than an act of justice. A third disruptive problem was the massive influx of foreign films that flooded the Japanese film industry. The imported movies proved to be so popular at the box office, that many exhibitors became reluctant to show Japanese films. A fourth and continuing problem was the rising cost of production, as trade unions, government officials, and film exhibitors sought to exploit the burgeoning Japanese film market through excessive ticket pricing and taxation.

Set against this background, one can readily appreciate Japan's filmmaking accomplishments in the immediate postwar period. The major requirement for success was, of course, flexibility. Evident in many of the films during the late 1940s were attempts by veteran and emerging directors to incorporate Western values into traditional Japanese film genres.[835] Action became a key ingredient in the postwar films, particularly in sophisticated comedies undermining traditional values, gangster films attacking widespread corruption, and melodramas focusing on the problems of widowed mothers rearing rebellious children. Taking their cynical cue from the public's hostility to the discredited policies of the past, and to understandable fears about the future, the successful filmmakers focused on Japan's efforts to rebuild her confidence and stability.

The film emphasis was on becoming independent, thinking for oneself, rather than on passively accepting the values of the past. For example, many of the most successful films reveal a new concern with the image of women and the role of the family in modern Japan, as well as the avoidance of any references to revenge, militarism, and nationalism. Among the most impressive productions were Gosho's ONCE MORE/IMA HITOTABI NO (1947), Imai's GREEN MOUNTAINS/AOI SAMMYUKA (1949), Inagaki's CHILDREN HAND IN HAND/TE O TSUNAGU KORA (1948) and FORGOTTEN CHILDREN/WASURERARETA KORA (1949), Ito's THE CHESS KING/OSHO (1948), Kinoshita's THE GIRL I LOVED/WAGA KOI SESHI OTOME (1946) and APOSTASY/HAKAI (1948), Kinugasa's LORD FOR A NIGHT/ARUYO NO TONOSAMA (1946), Kurosawa's NO REGRETS FOR OUR YOUTH/WAGA SEISHUN NI KUINASHI (1946), ONE WONDERFUL SUNDAY/SUBARASHIKI NICHIYOBI (1947), DRUNKEN ANGEL/YOIDORE TENSHI (1948), and STRAY DOG/NORAINU (1949), Mizoguchi's WOMEN OF THE NIGHT/YORU NO ONNATACHI (1948), Ozu's THE RECORD OF A TENEMENT GENTLEMAN/NAGAYA SHINSHI ROKU (1947) and LATE SPRING/BANSHUN (1949), Shimizu's CHILDREN OF THE BEEHIVE/HACHI NO SU NO KODOMOTACHI (1948), Taniguchi's TO THE END OF THE SILVER-CAPPED MOUNTAINS/GINREI NO HATE (1947), and Yoshimura's THE FELLOWS WHO ATE THE ELEPHANT/ZO O KUTTA RENCHU (1947) and THE DAY OUR LIVES SHINE/WAGA SHOGAI NO KAGAYAKERU (1948). In these films, the artists condemn long-standing values like blind obedience, crowd mentality, and rigidity toward new ideas. Attention is directed to corruption in the postwar era, the plight of orphans, the conflict between generations, and the social and economic roots of prostitution. By the end of the decade, filmmakers were telling their audiences that taking a hard look at the present offered the best chances for a bright future. Clearly, experimentation, fresh perspectives, and optimism were the number one priorities of the new Japanese film industry.

---

[835] Perhaps the most amusing innovation in Japanese films during the postwar period was the fascination with "kissing." According to Hirano (p.385), kissing scenes had been banned up to the end of the Pacific War because they were perceived by the Japanese as not only antithetical to Eastern values, but also indicative of Western decadence. Thus the Japanese film industry, in attempting to prove how democratic it had become under the Occupation, became obsessed with kissing in the postwar movies.

Few people outside of Asia, however, knew about the film renaissance taking place in Japan.[836] Then in 1951, more than a half a century after the Japanese film industry had been operating, world audiences suddenly discovered the glory of the Japanese cinema.[837] Akira Kurosawa's RASHOMON (1950) not only took top honors at the Venice Festival, but Western critics also finally recognized that there was a host of notable Japanese filmmakers, besides Kurosawa, that were being ignored--e.g., Heinosuke Gosho, Kon Ichikawa, Tadashi Imai, Hiroshi Inagaki, Keisuke Kinoshita, Teinosuke Kinugasa, Takiji Kobayashi, Kenji Mizoguchi, Mikio Naruse, Yasujiro Ozu,[838] Kaneto Shindo, and Kimisaburo Yoshimura. In addition, as Wright points out, "Most Japanese directors, and certainly Mizoguchi and Kurosawa, find it easy to move from films of contemporary life to period films and back again; for these two genres were the backbone of Japanese cinema, just as in India there was the two categories of the religious or quasi-religious 'musicals' and the 'social' dramas or comedies."[839]

Following the success of Kurosawa's film, Daie, along with the other five major companies (Toho, Shochiku, Daito, Toei,[840] and Nikkatsu),[841] had moved into the international market. The result was a number of probing films dealing with human tragedies and individual responsibility that appealed to foreign audiences: e.g., Gosha's AN INN IN OSAKA/OSAKA NO YADO (1954), Ichikawa's THE HARP OF BURMA/THE BURMESE HARP/BIRUMA NO TATEGOTO (1956), Imai's MUDDY WATERS/NIGORIE (1953), Inagaki's MUSASHI MIYAMOTO/MIYAMOTO MUSASHI (1954), Kinoshita's A JAPANESE TRAGEDY/NIHON NO HIGEKI 1953) and TWENTY-FOUR EYES/NIJUSHI NO HITOMI (1954), Kurosawa's IKIRU/LIVING (1953), SEVEN SAMURAI/SHICHI-NIN NO SAMURAI (1954), THRONE OF BLOOD/COBWEB

---

[836]   Burch insists (pp.262-90) that the "social-engineering" of the occupation forces resulted in a decline in the quality of Japanese cinema, and not a renaissance.

[837]   Tucker argues (p.39) that Japanese films were better known in Western countries than most film historians acknowledge. Moreover, he claims that RASHOMON (1950) was not well understood either by foreigners or by the Japanese public. For more information on Asian films in general, see David Bordwell, "Our Dream Cinema: Western Historiography and the Japanese Cinema," FILM READER 4, ed. Blaine Allan et al. (Evanston: Northwestern University, 1979), pp.45-62; Alan Stanbrook, "Break with The Past: Part Two," FILMS AND FILMING 6:7 (April 1960):13-4, 30; Larry N. Landrum, "Popular Asian Film: A Checklist of Sources, Part I," JOURNAL OF POPULAR FILM 1:3 (Summer 1972):249-52; and ___, "Popular Asian Film: A Checklist of Sources, Part II," ibid., 1:4 (Fall 1972):338-47.

[838]   Interesting, Roger Greenspun would write in 1972 that "Kenji Mizoguchi (1898-1956) and Yasujiro (1903-1963) still aren't names to conjure with--though one made more than 70, and the other more than 50, feature movies. Both died at the peak of very successful careers, and both surely belong with the supreme masters, not just in Japan but in all film so far." See Roger Greenspun, "Mizoguchi and Ozu--Two Masters from Japan," NEW YORK TIMES D (July 9, 1972):7.

[839]   Wright, p.455.

[840]   Founded in 1947 as Toyoko Film, it evolved into the Toei Motion Picture Company in 1951. According to Svensson (p.99), Toei specialized in short feature films and serials aimed at supplying the low end of Japan's double bill system in the 1950s.

[841]   Although Nikkatsu had given up production during the Pacific War, it still retained control of its vast theater circuit. In 1954, as Svensson notes (p.71), the company resumed filmmaking.

CASTLE/KUMONOSU-JO, THE LOWER DEPTHS/DONZOKO (both in 1957), and THE HIDDEN FORTRESS/KAKUSHI-TORIDE NO SANAKUNIN (1958), Kinugasa's GATE OF HELL/JIGOKUMON (1953), Mizoguchi's THE LIFE OF OHARE/THE LIFE OF A WOMAN/SAIKAKU ICHIDAI (1952), UGETSU MONOGATARI (1953), SANSHO THE BAILIFF/SANSHO DAYU (1954), and RED-LIGHT DISTRICT/AKASEN CHITAI (1956), Naruse's MOTHER/OKAASAN (1952), THE LATE CHRYSANTHEMUM/BANGIKU (1954), FLOATING CLOUDS/UKIGUMO (1955), and FLOWING/NAGARERU (1956), Ozu's TOKYO STORY (1953), Shindo's CHILDREN OF THE ATOMIC BOMB/GENBAKU NO KO (1952), and Yamamura's CRAB-CANNING BOAT/KANIKOSEN (1953). Less significant as art but highly profitable at the box office was Ishiro Honda's internationally acclaimed fantasy film, GODZILLA/GOJIRA (1954).

Of all the directors, two men in particular characterized the era: Akira Kurosawa and Kon Ichikawa. Neither one was new to Japanese film. Both perfectionists came up through the apprentice system in the years prior to the Pacific War. Both admire Western filmmaking but remain committed to preserving the art of Japanese films. Both began as painters and insisted that painting remains the primary influence on their art. Their success lay not only in adapting to the times, but also in adapting Western techniques to their extraordinary cinematic styles.

Clearly, Kurosawa is the better known of the two artists.[842] The most Western of all Japan's directors, his long-standing popularity in America is evident not only in the 1951 Honorary Oscar for RASHOMON and the 1975 Oscar for Best Foreign Film for DERSU UZALA,[843] but also because of the impact that his works have had on numerous Western directors. As David Desser explains, "Kurosawa's influence in the West ranges from the well-known adaptations of his films like THE MAGNIFICENT SEVEN and A FISTFUL OF DOLLARS to more generalized influences on the film styles of many contemporary directors, especially Sam Peckinpah and Walter Hill."[844] In Japan, however, the brilliant director's acclaim has been mixed. According to Greg Mitchell,

Of his twenty-seven movies, all but two made money in Japan, and several even set box-office records. But he has not been an enduring success. He is regarded by the younger directors and critics in Japan [in 1982] as old-fashioned, out of touch, past his prime--though they acknowledge his

---

[842] For the best bibliographical material on Kurosawa, see his autobiography and Patricia Arens, AKIRA KUROSAWA: A GUIDE TO REFERENCES AND RESOURCES (Boston: G. K. Hall, 1979). Particularly useful articles are Jay Leyda, "The Films of Akira Kurosawa," SIGHT AND SOUND 24:2 (October/December 1954):74-8, 112; Donald Richie, "Kurosawa on Kurosawa: Part One," ibid., 33:3 (Summer 1964):108-13; ___, ". . . Part Two," ibid., 33:4 (Autumn 1964):200-203; Douglas McVay, "The Rebel In a Kimono: First Part Of An Analysis Of Kurosawa's Work for The Cinema," FILMS AND FILMING 7:10 (July 1961):9-10, 34; ___, "Samurai and Small Beer: Part Two," ibid., 7:11 (August 1961):15-6; Charles Higham, "Kurosawa's Humanisim," KENYON REVIEW 27:4 (Autumn 1965):737-42; Stuart M. Kaminsky, "The Samurai Film and the Western," THE JOURNAL OF POPULAR FILM (Fall 1972):312-24; Joan Mellen, "The Epic Film of Kurosawa," TAKE ONE 3:4 (June 1972):16-9; and Barbara Wolf, "On Akira Kurosawa," YALE REVIEW 64:2 (1974):218-26.

[843] Kurosawa has also received Best Foreign Film Oscar nominations for DODESKADEN/DODESUKADEN (1970), for SHADOW WARRIOR/KAGEMUSHA (1980), and for Best Director for RAN/CHAOS (1985). For more on SHADOW WARRIOR, see Robert Osborne, "Movie Review: KAGEMUSHA (SHADOW WARRIOR)," THE HOLLYWOOD REPORTER (October 6, 1980):3; and Vincent Canby, "Screen: KAGEMUSHA, Kurosawa's 27TH Film," NEW YORK TIMES C (October 6, 1980):14.

[844] THE SAMURAI FILMS OF AKIRA KUROSAWA, p.2.

achievements: The country's critics recently chose SEVEN SAMURAI and IKIRU, shot in the fifties, as the finest Japanese films ever made.[845]

More to the point, intolerable working conditions and inadequate financing at home resulted in the artist's making just three films--DODESKADEN/DODESUKADEN (1970), DESRSU UZALA (1975), and SHADOW WARRIOR/KAGEMUSHA (1980)--between 1970 and 1980. Of these films, two were made in the Soviet Union.

The basic facts about Kurosawa's life have already been covered in the review of SOMETHING LIKE AN AUTOBIOGRAPHY. Here we need only observe that the immediate postwar period found him in an ideal situation. Not yet having formed a distinctive style, being very much opposed to the Japanese cinematic policies of the war years, and being sympathetic to the SCAP's ideas on abandoning feudal values, he was in a stage of flux and eager to explore different possibilities. As Sato points out, Kurosawa's basic thrust in his first postwar films was to sustain the morale of the Japanese public by demonstrating in a series of films "that the meaning of life is not dictated by the nation but something each individual should discover for himself through suffering."[846] In addition, the director's early postwar films illustrate not only his interest in the rehabilitation of Japanese film genres and their subject matter, but also the filmmaker's problems with critics, censors, and studio bosses.

Re-examining feudalistic values, showing the oppression of the 1930s, and recording the problems of the postwar period, Kurosawa's works also reflect the difficulties filmmakers faced in the mid- to late-1940s. For example, THE MEN WHO TREAD ON THE TIGER'S TAIL/TORO NO O FUMU OTOKOTACHI (1945), a screen adaptation of the exploits of a medieval Japanese folk hero, was banned by the occupation forces because its comic treatment seemed too far to the left. THOSE WHO MAKE TOMORROW/ASU O TSUKURU HITOBITO (1946) was a propaganda film that the director made for Toho's socialist union, but the results of the various strikes rendered the work insignificant. On the other hand, NO REGRETS FOR OUR YOUTH is an extremely important film because it signals Kurosawa's strong social consciousness as well as the era's interest in documenting prewar problems. Filmed during the first two of the three major strikes at Toho, the movie deals with the oppression of a teacher during the 1930s and the refusal by one of his students to forget what happened. ONE WONDERFUL SUNDAY/SUBARASHIKI NICHIYOBI (1947), made without any name players because Toho's top stars had left the company to form a new studio, focuses on the refusal of young people to be defeated by postwar conditions. The unknown cast, the optimistic outlook, and the influence of Western filmmakers on Japanese movies is, as J. B. Hoberman points out, a part of "the same populist ideology found in the postwar films of other defeated Axis powers like Italy and Hungary. . . ."[847] Not until DRUNKEN ANGEL/YOIDORE TENSHI (1948), a film about slum life very much influenced by the director's love for Russian literature, did Kurosawa master a film style that not only enabled his films to appeal both to the West and to the East, but also to give him the recognition and power to make films he wanted to make. While other young directors also wrestled with unsettling labor disputes, the lack of adequate crews and performers, appropriate film content, and finding a suitable style for the era, Kurosawa became the most successful in adapting Western culture to Eastern film genres.

At the same time, however, he continued to reflect the relative instability of filmmakers in the Japanese film industry. For example, the three monumental strikes at Toho during the postwar period forced many artists into establishing their own independent production companies. Kurosawa was no exception. In 1948, he joined

---

[845]   Greg Mitchell, "Kurosawa in Winter," AMERICAN FILM 7:6 April 1982):46.

[846]   Sato, p.116.

[847]   J. Hoberman, "ONE WONDERFUL SUNDAY," VILLAGE VOICE (July 6, 1982):52.

Kajiro Yamamoto and a handful of other Toho expatriates to form The Motion Picture Artists Association (EIGA GEIJUTSUKA KYOKAI). Four years later, the company was taken over by Toho. Meanwhile, Kurosawa found himself making films for Shochiku, Daiei, and Toho in the 1950s.

Now firmly established as one of Japan's great directors, he went on to make such acclaimed films as STRAY DOG/NORAINU (1949), RASHOMON (1950), IKIRU/LIVING (1952), SEVEN SAMURAI/SHICHI-NIN NO SAMURAI (1954), and THRONE OF BLOOD/KUMONOSU-JO/COBWEB CASTLE (1957). Not only did he attain greater freedom in terms of shooting schedules, script control, and editing rights, but he also obtained bigger budgets to make films on a grander scale. What has impressed many critics is the artist's ability to Communicate so effectively with two widely different cultures. For example, Bock points out that "Perhaps most startling of Kurosawa's achievements in a Japanese context . . . have been his innate grasp of a storytelling technique that is not culture bound, and his flair for adapting Western classical literature to the screen."[848] Mellen comments that "He is one of the few artists to achieve international communication while at the same time remaining true to his own highly distinctive and insular national culture."[849] And Richie observes that "Kurosawa is a philospher who works with film, and who affirms that in [mankind's] . . . awareness of oneself and an awareness of the world . . . lies the essential human quality. But, though weak, man can can hope and through this he can prevail."[850]

Regrettably, the West has not delved as critically into Ichikawa's work as it has done to Kurosawa's. The result is that of all the famous Japanese filmmakers, Ichikawa may well be one of the most misunderstood directors of his generation. As Tom Milne observes,

> First impressions can be misleading, and there is something very wrong with the image of Kon Ichikawa--arrived at mainly by way of THE BURMESE HARP, CONFLAGRATION and FIRES ON THE PLAIN--as a man obsessed by human suffering and expressing his pity through a series of long, slow, painful humanistic affirmations. Ichikawa is obsessed by suffering all right, but he is not a humanist in any modern sense of the word ("I look around for some kind of humanism, but I never seem to find it," he himself accurately observes).[851]

The problems go beyond the fact that Ichikawa's works alternate between comedy and tragedy, or that labels tend to gloss over important distinctions between the two. Ichikawa's work, as Bock explains, is associated with terms like "contemporaneity" and "self-exploration" that reflect his "aesthetic consciousness" and "self-expression."[852] Thus one finds in the director's forty-year career visually stunning and ironic films containing relationships between the problems of his cinematic characters who face extraordinary pressures, and the continual probing of Ichikawa's personal values and attitudes. A trademark of his film reflexivity is the

---

[848] Audie E. Bock, "Kurosawa, Akira," THE INTERNATIONAL DICTIONARY OF FILMS AND FILMMAKERS: VOLUME II, p.310.

[849] Mellen, p.42.

[850] *Donald Richie, THE FILMS OF AKIRA KUROSAWA (Berkeley: University of California Press, 1964), p.198.

[851] Tom Milne, "The Skull Beneath the Skin," SIGHT AND SOUND 35:4 (Autumn 1966):185. Interestingly, Cook makes the point (p.583) that Kurosawa has also been falsely labeled as a "humanist" when actually he is a "fatalist, or at least an existentialist, in subtle but thoroughly Japanese terms."

[852] JAPANESE FILM DIRECTORS, p.219.

warmth and sensitivity with which he pursues his themes. As Erens points out, "Kon Ichikawa is noted for a wry humor which often resembles black comedy, for his grim psychological studies, portrayals of misfits and outsiders, and for the visual beauty of his films."[853]

Not much is known about Ichikawa's formative years. Born on November 20, 1915, he had a childhood epitomized by frequent illnesses, a love for drawing, and a passion for movies. Not surprisingly for a man sometimes referred to as "the Japanese Frank Capra," two of Ichikawa's favorite film artists are Charlie Chaplin and Walt Disney. The latter, in particular, has had a profound influence on Ichikawa's career. For example, at age eighteen, finished with school and seeking a profession, he took a job as an animator with J. O., a small film company eventually taken over by Toho. Years later, in describing his work at J. O., Ichikawa told an interviewer, "I did everything--script, music, editing. Not ideologically, but technically, animation has influenced my later movies."[854]

In the tradition of the pre-WWI Japanese film industry, he soon became a screenwriter and an assistant director. As he matured in his craft, Ichikawa claims that in addition to Disney, Chaplin, and the great Japanese filmmakers like Kinoshita, Kurosawa, Mizoguchi, and Ozu, he has been greatly influenced by Jean Renoir, Ernst Lubitsch, Elia Kazan, and the youthful Pier Paolo Pasolini.[855] Interestingly, critical commentaries on Ichikawa are silent on his work during World War II.

Once the war ends, however, we discover the emerging director encountering the same types of problems that Kurosawa had with the SCAP. Depending on the version one reads, Ichikawa either refused or neglected to submit his script for his first feature film, A GIRL AT THE DOJO TEMPLE/MUSUME DOJOJI (1946), to the censors. As a result, they not only banned the film--a puppet movie based upon on a classic Kabuki dance--from being shown, but also confiscated all the prints and destroyed them along with the negative.

Equally noteworthy is Ichikawa's marriage to the talented screenwriter Nato Wada in 1948. They had begun collaborating on films in the mid-1940s, and she was to remain an important influence on his work until her retirement in 1965. Her strong interest in literary adaptations and the fact that many of Ichikawa's films are derived from literary works, as Bock notes, is just one indication of the role that she played in her husband's life.[856] Another indication of her presence is that Ichikawa often cites her in explaining his visual approach to film. For example, he told a group in 1963 that "Simplicity and artistic innovation are the basis of stylistic beauty; as Nato says, they lead to a sense of beauty."[857]

Like the products of many of his peers, Ichikawa's films in the postwar period ridicule human vanities, bemoan contemporary morality, and attack corruption in society. For example, the satirical comedy, MR. POO/PU-SAN (1953), based upon a popular comic strip, begins with the misfortunes of a confused mathematics teacher falsely accused of being a Communist, and ends with the now-fired teacher working

---

[853] Patricia Erens, "Ichikawa, Kon," THE INTERNATIONAL DIRECTORY OF FILMS AND FILMMAKERS: VOLUME II, p.269. For more information, see Donald Richie, "The Several Sides of Kon Ichikawa," SIGHT AND SOUND 35:2 (Spring 1966):84-6; and "The Uniqueness of Kon Ichikawa: A Translated Symposium," trans. Haruji Nakamura and Leonard Schrader Nakamura and Leonard Schrader, CINEMA 6:2 (Fall 1970):30-1.

[854] Cited in Elliot Stein, "Off-Screen: Konography," VILLAGE VOICE (August 2, 1988):64.

[855] Stein, p.64.

[856] JAPANESE FILM DIRECTORS, p.221.

[857] Nakamura and Schrader, p.31.

in a munitions factory, despite the fact that the occupation forces officially banned any type of Japanese rearmament. In attacking the rise of a new militarism and ridiculing modern Japan's values, the director, as Mellen observes, follows a tack taken by another famous Japanese director:

> Like Ozu, Ichikawa in MR. POO . . . focuses on the vulgarization of the Japanese character that has ensued [in the postwar period], a hardening especially apparent in the Japanese woman, who has lost her natural grace and generosity of spirit. In the background of MR. POO looms YAKUZA, gangsters controlling every facet of the postwar society, including the educational system.[858]

Another example of Ichikawa's important satirical comedies is A BILLIONAIRE/OKUMAN CHOJA (1954). In this story of a misguided tax investigator who tries to befriend a family consisting of eighteen children forever neglecting to pay its taxes, the team of Ichikawa and Wada ironically show how the law favors the rich and harms the poor. In the process, the filmmakers inject a strong statement about atomic contamination in postwar Japan. In John Gillett's judgment, the film's "tone is perfectly balanced, taking in startling bizarre situations like the girl who cheerfully constructs a baby atom bomb in her attic and the family, driven by poverty, destroy[ing] themselves with a meal of radioactive tuna fish."[859]

As commented on earlier, Ichikawa's comedies, or as he explains, "his Disney side," are only one of the two types of movies he makes. In 1955, his more somber side was highlighted in THE BURMESE HARP/BIRUMA NO TATEGOTO. The story of a grief-stricken soldier who refuses to return home at the end of the Pacific War and instead dons Buddhist clothes and dedicates himself to burying his dead comrades is but one example of the director's obsessive heroes consumed "with human suffering" and reflecting Ichikawa's "aesthetic consciousness." PUNISHMENT ROOM/SHOKEI NO HEYA (1956) is a fine example of the director's "contemporaneity" and social criticism. Building on the popularity of the novelist Shintaro Ishihara, who in the mid-1950s became the spokesperson for Japan's restless and rebellious youth, Ichikawa turned Shintaro's story about an alienated teenager who rapes his girlfriend and rejects his father into the cornerstone of a new film genre, the TAIYOZOKU ("sun tribe"). These films, as Desser explains, focused on young people "who feel themselves cut off from their past yet [are] part of a new, mythic culture, the culture of youth."[860] ENJO/CONFLAGRATION (1958) is yet another example of Ichikawa's "self-exploration" in films wrestling with contemporary problems. Adapted from a novel by Yukio Mishma and based on an actual event where a young Buddhist novitiate set fire to the famous Golden Pavilion in Kyoto, rather than let it be used for unworthy purposes, the film explores the close relationship between spiritual and economic poverty. "I sympathized with this poor young man," Ichikawa explains, "whose mind had been warped by his horrible background. This was a turning point in my career."[861] The following year, he made his classic film, FIRES ON THE PLAIN/NOBI. In this story about half-crazed soldiers who survive the aftermath of the Pacific War by becoming cannibals, the director described the ultimate horror of war. As he comments, "War is an extreme

---

[858]   Joan Mellen, THE WAVES AT GENJI'S DOOR: JAPAN THROUGH ITS CINEMA (New York: Pantheon Books, 1976), p.222.

[859]   John Gillett, "Kon Ichikawa," CINEMA: A CRITICAL DICTIONARY--THE MAJOR FILM-MAKERS, p.518.

[860]   *David Desser, EROS PLUS MASSACRE: AN INTRODUCTION TO THE JAPANESE NEW WAVE CINEMA (Bloomington: Indiana University Press, 1988), p.40. The term TAIYOZOKU is adapted, in part, from Ishihara's book, TAIYO NO KISETSU/SEASON OF THE SUN.

[861]   Stein, p.64.

situation which can change the nature of man. For this reason, I consider it the greatest sin."[862]

By the end of 1958, the two sides of Ichikawa's film preoccupations were well established. No matter what type of film he made, his protagonist was "essentially an outsider, a man struggling to escape from the world in which he lives, rather than to change it or even accept it as he finds it."[863] Over the next two decades, Ichikawa would continue to criticize the inhumanity of his times and to explore the visual medium. His sense of anguish, as Richie points out, would forever put the filmmaker in conflict with studio heads "who insist that life is fun and humanity happy."[864] Rather than compromise his principles, Ichikawa spent much of his time making television documentaries between 1959 and 1966.

The emphasis in this section on Kurosawa and Ichikawa is not meant to slight other important directors like Mizoguchi, Ozu,[865] or Kinugasa. Rather the point is to use two emerging artists in the postwar era to illustrate the problems of the period and to comment on how Japanese ingenuity overcame them.

By the end of the 1950s, Japan had become one of the largest film-producing nations in the world, turning out more than 500 films a year. The Daiei Motion Picture Company, which had produced RASHOMON, was the nation's most prestigious studio. In 1959, as Hirano points out,

> the number of theaters had increased nearly tenfold since 1945, from 845 to 7,400. Audience attendance reached 1,127,452,000 in 1958, up nearly 50 percent from 1946. The distribution income from Japanese films amounted to . . . $85 million [dollars] . . . in 1959, ten times the 1946 figure. The industry was producing from 208 (1950) to 514 (1956) films every year during the 1950s, compared to 21 in 1945.[866]

Thus the once-ignored Japanese film industry, emerging from the ashes of defeat and provincialism, had become a global power in the film community.[867]

At the same time, the industry's future prospects appeared uncertain. One ominous note was that American films still attracted larger audiences in Japan than did local productions. As a result, the Japanese film industry found itself more and more adapting Hollywood formulas and production schedules rather than adhering to Japanese traditions. What bothered many Japanese filmmakers was the apparent subversion of Eastern culture for profits.[868] A second ominous note was the growing importance of television in the recreational life of the Japanese public. As more and more people came to own TV sets, fewer and fewer people went to the cinema. The

---

[862]   VOICES FROM THE JAPANESE CINEMA, p.125.

[863]   Milne, p. 185.

[864]   "The Several Sides of Kon Ichikawa," p.85.

[865]   For more information, see Donald Richie, "The Later Films of Yasujiro Ozu," FILM QUARTERLY 13:1 (Fall 1959):18-25; and Jean Haponek, "Autumnal Ozu: THE END OF SUMMER," FILAMENT 4 (1984):22-7.

[866]   Hirano, pp.385-6.

[867]   The following articles are helpful: Masayoshi Iwabutchi, "1954 in Japan," SIGHT AND SOUND 24:4 (Spring 1955):202-5; Lindsay Anderson, "Two Inches off the Ground," ibid., 27:3 (Winter 1957-58):131-2, 160; and Clifford V. Harrington, "Japanese Film-Making Today," FILMS IN REVIEW 8:3 (March 1957):102-7.

[868]   THE SAMURAI FILMS OF AKIRA KUROSAWA, pp.43-51.

result was a sharp decline in box-office attendance at the end of the 1950s that never reversed itself.

BOOKS

GENERAL

McDonald, Keiko I. CINEMA EAST: A CRITICAL STUDY OF MAJOR JAPANESE FILMS. Rutherford: Fairleigh Dickinson University Press, 1983. Illustrated. 279pp.

Focusing on the two decades following the end of World War II, McDonald examines a dozen important films that she feels need reconsideration as a result of faulty interpretations by Western critics. The works analyzed range from famous films like RASHOMON (1950), TOKYO STORY/TOKYO MONOGATARI (1953), and UGETSU/UGETSU MONOGATARI (1953) to complex and neglected films like DEATH BY HANGING/KOSHIKEI (1968), DOUBLE SUICIDE/SHINJU TEN NO AMIJIMA (1969), and EROS PLUS MASSACRE/EROSU PURASU GYAKUSATSU (1969). Where McDonald has the advantage over many previous commentators is that she was born in Japan and did her graduate studies in the United States. As a result, she is able to combine her formal training with cultural insights.

The basic thesis concerns the way in which key Japanese directors mastermind the creative tension that exists between a unified work of art and its audiences. McDonald begins by indicating who she feels are the important Japanese filmmakers of the 1950s and 1960s, pointing out their special cinematic interests, and summarizing what major Western scholars have said about the filmmakers. Next, McDonald explains that her experiences in teaching Japanese films to Western audiences have given her an awareness of the types of problems American students encounter when dealing with Eastern mysticism and with the traditional Japanese concept of MUJO ("the mutability of human affairs"). One value of this book, therefore, is that it offers practical advice on how to deal with cross-cultural problems.

McDonald's approach is that of a literary critic who perceives each work as a unified product rather than as an on-going process. In applying that approach, the author directs attention to a film's internal and external structure. The former concentrates on what occurs within the film and among the various parts--e.g., values, mood, choices, characterizations, time, and spatial differentiation. The former relates to the way Japanese directors manipulate their audiences through the use of internal structure. That is, "It entails the protagonist's feelings, degree of involvement, and a notion of good or bad as related to characters, action, and value." To illustrate her point more sharply, McDonald divides her study into seven parts: symbolism, character types, mood, spatial differentiation, time, story, and the rhetoric of film. One of her principal conclusions is that "the major directors discussed in this book use elaborate rhetorical strategies aimed at persuading viewers to bring two worlds together: a 'world out there' in the film-as-presented, and a 'world in here' in the film-as-experienced."

Despite the briefness of the individual chapters and the lackluster illustrations sprinkled throughout the book, the study itself is informative and stimulating. Adding to its value are a bibliography and an index. Well worth browsing.

*Mellen, Joan. VOICES FROM THE JAPANESE CINEMA. New York: Liveright, 1975. Illustrated. 295pp.

Using an interview format, Mellen offers useful observations on fifteen important Japanese filmmakers: Daisuke Ito, Akira Kurosawa, Mme. Kashiko Kawakita, Kaneto Shindo, Tadashi Imai, Kon Ichikawa, Masaki Kobayashi, Setsu Asakura, Hiroshi Teshigahara, Susumu Hani, Sachiko Hidari, Toichiro Narushima, Masahiro Shinoda, Nagisa Oshima, and Shuji Terayama. A long introduction surveys the Japanese renaissance after World War II, the background for the author's contacts with the directors, her general reaction to their criticisms of Japanese culture and authority, the reservations filmmakers have about Western film critics, the special place of women in Japanese society, and the role of documentary films in the postwar era. Each of the main chapters begins with an overview of the director interviewed and includes at least one still and a smattering of footnotes. None of the interviews is particularly long or exceptionally revealing. Collectively, however, they provide a good introduction to the growth of the Japanese film from the occupation to the mid-1970s. An index is provided, but no bibliography. Well worth browsing.

Mellen, Joan. THE WAVES AT GENJI'S DOOR: JAPAN THROUGH ITS CINEMA. New York: Pantheon Books, 1976. Illustrated. 465pp.
     "This book," Mellen explains, "explores Japan through film, its most vital and thriving art. From its beginnings in the 1920s, the Japanese have used their cinema as a rite of passage, a means toward discovering who they are and the kind of culture they have produced as a people." The title is taken from a tenth-century novel about the life of Prince Genji, who saw his traditional values slowly destroyed by changing times and new perspectives. Taking her cue from Genji's experiences, Mellen offers a controversial feminist socio-historical survey of Japanese films, pointing out how more than thirty filmmakers from Mizoguchi, Naruse, and Ozo to Ichikawa, Kurosawa, and Shinoda have treated traditional values. Emphasized in the book's six major sections are the fate of militarism and feudalism, the status of woman and the family, and the attitudes toward the Pacific War and the samurai code. Throughout her provocative study, she attacks Japan's patriarchal system and the oppressive state of women, using the films as a means of exposing the society's repressive values. In analyzing the various cinematic movements, she stresses the importance of history to the Japanese directors, their obsession with the past and with showing its relationship to the present, and the filmmakers' commitment to examining social institutions as a force in shaping the uniqueness of Japanese culture. "Cinema in Japan," she writes, "has become a mirror into the hearts of a people in impatient and, at times, frantic search for values in which to believe."
     Written with a passion that frequently distorts objectivity, this challenging study is a useful step toward understanding the role of film in Japanese society. The difficulty, as Sybil Thornton points out in her devastating review of the book, is that it contains "too many careless mistakes, distortions of films, and an inadequate grasp of Japanese history and the rudiments of Japanese theater. . . ."[869] In addition, the numerous illustrations, poorly reproduced, do little to help the author's cause, and no bibliography is provided. An index is included. Worth browsing.

AKIRA KUROSAWA

*Desser, David. THE SAMURAI FILMS OF AKIRA KUROSAWA. Ann Arbor: UMI Research Press, 1983. Illustrated. 164pp.
     Originally written as a 1981 Ph.D. dissertation for the University of Southern California, this slim volume is packed with information and ideas on how to appreciate not only five of Kurosawa's films, but also the samurai film in general. Desser's splendid introduction outlines a number of impressive objectives (most of which are achieved) that he hopes will provide fresh perspectives on studying Japanese film history. For example, he takes the position "that even though film is a cultural artifact whose political superstucture and cultural climate must be known, it is also a formal-aesthetic system." While other scholars have applied film aesthetics and cultural awareness to the director's work, few have sought to relate the methodology to Kurosawa's fascination with film genres. Desser also concerns himself with new

---

[869]   Sybil Thornton, "Book Review: THE WAVES AT GENJI'S GATE," FILM QUARTERLY 31:2 (Winter 1977-78):58.

approaches to what is meant by the often-used concept that Kurosawa is the most "Western" of Japanese directors. The author, therefore, goes beyond citing specific films that relate the director's work and gives an analysis of key filmic techniques that appear in specific film sequences. Still further, Desser establishes the samurai film as a major film genre; and one comes away with an appreciation of specific works and directors who have occasionally raised the violent formula to an art form. Most important, this study seeks to answer what is the "nature of the themes, motifs, techniques and codes   .   .   .   that Akira Kurosawa adopts from the West? And when they are adopted, what is the significance of the resultant expression?"

Desser's four tightly written, fact-filled chapters follow a logical progression from an examination of the basic foundations of Japanese traditions, up through an understanding of the samurai film, to the study's implications for the samurai films of Kurosawa, and conclude with suggestions on how to apply this approach to other Japanese film genres. Among many intriguing assertions, the author asserts that the Japanese film industry is more dependent on film genres than is Hollywood, that mythologizing history is a key ingredient in both Japanese and American films, that the samurai film can be sub-divided into four subgenres: "(1) The Nostalgic Samurai Drama; (2) the Anti-Feudal Drama; (3) Zen Fighers; (4) the Sword Film," and that the samurai film, the Hollywood Western, and the YAKUZA ("gangster") genre share many common conventions as well as important structural differences. In drawing particular attention to Kurosawa's samurai films--SEVEN SAMURAI/SHICHI-NIN NO SAMURAI (1954), THE HIDDEN FORTRESS/KAKUSHI-TORIDE NO SANAKUNIN (1958), YOJIMBO (1961), SANJURO (1962), and SHADOW WARRIOR/KAGEMUSHA (1980), the author provides considerable information about the way samurai functioned in medieval times, and about the frequent attempts to apply their behavior to the modern era. Especially impressive about Desser's writing style is his ability to deal with structuralist interpretations in a manner easily accessible to readers not comfortable or conversant with concepts of codes and signifiers.

What detracts from this otherwise admirable study is an excessive negativism toward Japanese aesthetics and pioneering films. Also apparent are some questionable interpretations of noted Japanese directors like Ozu and Mizoguchi. For example, Desser remains one of the few historians of Japanese films to argue that neither Ozu or Mizoguchi was affected by Hollywood films. One also can quibble with his treatment of HIGH NOON (1953), an "inferior Western," and RASHOMON (1950), "most assuredly not Japan's hidden idea of itself"; as well as his failure to discuss adequately the influence of John Ford and Jean Renoir on Kurosawa's works.

Those objections aside, this study should be required reading for any examination of the samurai film in general, and Kurosawa's films in particular. The book concludes with valuable footnotes, a good bibliography, and a helpful index. Recommended for special collections.

Erens, Patricia. AKIRA KUROSAWA: A GUIDE TO REFERENCES AND RESOURCES. Boston: G. K. Hall and Company, 1979. 135pp.

An invaluable resource guide, this reference book follows the standard format of the excellent G. K. Hall series edited by Ron Gottesman and includes a critical survey of the subject's work, an annotated filmography, an annotated bibliography about the subject, a list of performances and writings, a list of archival sources, a list of film distributors. Erens's straightforward comments synthesize the important books and articles in English, French, and Japanese. Although problems of accessibility limit the number of references to Japanese journals and newspapers, she does offer a selective list of the key articles by Japanese scholars. Interestingly, citations from American newspapers are limited to just three publications: THE NEW YORK TIMES, THE VILLAGE VOICE, and VARIETY. As she explains, "THE NEW YORK TIMES was chosen because of its accessibility and distribution; THE VILLAGE VOICE because of the prestige of its reviewers; and VARIETY because of its influence upon distribution." Recommended for special collections.

*Kurosawa, Akira. "IKIRU": A FILM. Trans. and introduction Donald Richie. New York: Simon and Schuster, 1969. Illustrated. 88pp.

In addition to the script of the 1952 masterpiece, this useful book contains complete cast and technical credits, a filmography, and numerous illustrations. Richie's five-page introduction stresses the film's theme of one person's search for affirmation. He points out that trying to exist is not enough: ". . . to live, one must live entirely and, at the same time, must give this life whatever meaning it is to have." Recommended for special collections.

*Kurosawa, Akira. "RASHOMON": A FILM. Trans. Donald Richie. New York: Grove Press, 1969. Illustrated. 256pp.

A fine collection of material on Kurosawa's classic film, this book contains the script of the 1950 movie, an introduction by Robert Hughes, nearly 200 frame enlargements from the film, the two short stories by Ryunosuke Akutagawa ("Rashomon" and "In Grove") upon which the film is based, essays by Parker Tyler, James F. Davidson, Donald Richie, and Michael Kanin, and an excerpt from Kanin's script for THE OUTRAGE (1964). Highly recommended for special collections.

*Kurosawa, Akira. "THE SEVEN SAMURAI": A FILM. Trans. and introduction Donald Richie. New York: Simon and Schuster, 1970. Illustrated. 244pp.

Originally, SEVEN SAMURAI ran 200 minutes, but had forty minutes cut from the film before its Japanese release in April, 1954. This valuable edition is based upon the 1954, 160 minute Toho production, since no copy of either the original script or film existed at the time of publication. Also worth noting is that Richie uses the scholarly title SEVEN SAMURAI, not the popular title THE SEVEN SAMURAI, cited by the publisher and used by lay people. In addition to Richie's introduction (reprinted from his THE FILMS OF AKIRA KUROSAWA) and the screenplay, the book provides cast and technical credits and numerous illustrations. Recommended for special collections.

*Richie, Donald. THE FILMS OF AKIRA KUROSAWA. Berkeley: University of California Press, 1964. Illustrated. 218pp.

Probably one of the best studies to date done on any director, Richie analyzes Kurosawa's moral emphasis and his concern with illusion and reality. The brief opening commentary on the director is followed by individual chapters on twenty-three films, from SANSHIRO SUGATA/SUGATA SANSHIRO (1943) to RED BEARD/AKAHIGE (1965). Each chapter is divided into introductory comments, an analysis of the story and treatment, a discussion of the characterizations, and an analysis of the style. In addition to the numerous and stunning illustrations, the author includes a filmography, bibliography, and index. Recommended for special collections.

*Richie, Donald, ed. FOCUS ON "RASHOMON." Englewood Cliffs: Prentice-Hall, 1972. Illustrated. 185pp.

A valuable addition to the Kurosawa material, this handy anthology opens with three brief essays on the director and his work. The bulk of the book is devoted to eight reprinted film reviews, three commentaries on the relevance of RASHOMON to drama and Japanese film, and six essays on the film as a work of art. In addition, there are plot synopses, screen credits, a script extract, the two short stories upon which the film was based, a filmography, a bibliography, and an index. Recommended for special collections.

FILMS

KON ICHIKAWA

FIRES ON THE PLAIN/NOBI (Japan--16mm: 1959, 105 mins., b/w, English subtitles, sound, R-BUD, EMG, FES, FNC, KIT; S-FES)

Based on a novel by Shohei Oaka and scripted by Natto Wada, this story of a Japanese soldier's attempt to survive on Leyte toward the end of the Second World War epitomizes the director's cinematic style and classic commentary on the nature of war. It also captures, as Svensson points out, Ichikawa's fatalistic attitude of life, highlighted by the death of the protagonist, although he survived in the novel.[870] Moreover, as Mellen observes, "The real horror is not the eating of human flesh--which the camera portrays as an aberation of the desperate--but the atrocity of war itself.[871]

TEINOSUKE KINUGASA

GATE OF HELL/JIGOKUMON (Japan--16mm: 1953, 89 mins., color, English subtitles, sound, R-FES, FNC, JAN)

A twelfth-century melodrama about the fate of three individuals caught in a war between rival clans, this unique film impressed audiences worldwide with its exotic settings and its stunning use of color. Kinugasa, the most prolific of his peers during the 1950s, averaging two to three films a year, wrote the screenplay based upon Kan Kikuchi's contemporary drama dealing with love, self-sacrifice, and despair. In addition to winning top honors at the 1954 Venice film festival and two Oscars--one for Best Costume Design and an honorary one for Best Foreign Film, GATE OF HELL, as Timothy Johnson reminds us, was not only the first Japanese color movie exported to the West, but also one of the three films (the other two being RASHOMON and UGETSU) instrumental in getting foreign audiences to appreciate the stature of the Japanese film industry.[872]

AKIRA KUROSAWA

DRUNKEN ANGEL/YOIDORE TENSHI (Japan--16mm: 1948, 102 mins., b/w, English subtitles, sound, R-BUD, FES, FNC)

Based upon an original screenplay by Keinosuke Uekusa and Kurosawa, this extraordinary parable about a two-bit gangster (Toshiro Mifune) dying from tuberculosis and a drunken doctor (Takashi Shimura) who tries to cure him marks the first of many collaborations between Kurosawa and Mifune. It is also noted for the first recognition of Kurosawa's extraordinary cinemtaic skills and superb pacing. Moreover, as Leyda comments, "Though the film's idea springs from one artist's attitude to the corruption and degredation among a defeated people, DRUNKEN ANGEL is not a slumming experience to be added to other exotic dips into alien poverty. Kurosawa's disgust and anger--and hope--bring the film's so very foreign-looking material close to home."[873]

---

[870] Svensson, p.73.

[871] THE WAVES AT GENJI'S DOOR, p.195.

[872] Timothy Johnson, "JIGOKUMON," THE INTERNATIONAL DICTIONARY OF FILMS AND FILMMAKERS: VOLUME I, p.225.

[873] "The Films of Kurosawa," p.77.

RASHOMON (Japan--16mm: 1950, 88 mins., b/w, English subtitles, sound, R-FES, FNC; S-TFF)
    Set in the twelfth century, this feudal tale offers four different interpretations of a bride's rape and the death of her husband in a forest. Each account is presented from the perspective of the person involved and underlines the relative nature of "reality." The editing and photography of the three main sections of the film--the events at the ruined gates, the flashback to the official inquiry into the crime, and the four accounts by the participants--all add to the questioning of reality.[874] Considered by many film historians to be "exotic" and "highly stylized," it embodies the director's fascination in all of his films with the issue of good and evil and how difficult it is to identify the difference between them. Considerable credit for the film's acclaim goes to Kurosawa and his co-screenwriter Shinobu Hashimoto, his cinematographer Kazuo Miyagawa, his sound technician Fumio Hayasaka, and his performers Machika Kyo (the bride), Toshiro Mifune (the bandit), and Masayuki Mori (the murdered groom).

LIVING/IKIRU (Japan--16mm: 1952, 140 mins., b/w, English subtitles, sound, R-FES, FNC)
    This movie is another example of Kurosawa's philosophical bent. The memorable screenplay by Shinobu Hashimoto, Hideo Oguni, and Kurosawa centers on a minor city clerk (Takashi Shimura) dying from cancer, who finds meaning in his life by struggling successfully against the government bureaucracy and finally creating a children's park. The lesson that the protagonist learns by the end of the film is that one has to be responsible to others as well as to himself if his life is to have true significance.[875] As R. Thomas Simone points out in his valuable comparison of the film with Tolstoy's THE DEATH OF IVAN ILLYCH, "Neither Tolstoy nor Kurosawa is a blind optimist, but both give us genuine images of human dignity and heroic actions that lead from despair to hope."[876]

SEVEN SAMURAI/SHICHI-NIN NO SAMURAI (Japan--16mm: 1954, 141 mins., b/w, English subtitles, sound, R-BUD, FNC)
    This epic story of seven RONIN in search of respect and sustenance who defend a village against bandits is considered by many to be one of Kurosawa's masterpieces.[877] In many respects, it epitomizes the Eastern attitude that

---

[874] THE SAMURAI FILMS OF AKIRA KUROSAWA, pp.67-70.

[875] For more information on the film, see Peter John Dyer, "IKIRU," FILMS AND FILMING 5:11 (August 1959):25; William Berhardt, "IKIRU," FILM QUARTERLY 13:4 (Summer 1960):39-41; Robert C. Roman, "IKIRU," FILMS IN REVIEW 11:3 (1960):168; Stanley Kauffmann, "The Fact of Mortality," THE NEW REPUBLIC (March 7, 1960):28, Rpt. A WORLD ON FILM, pp.374-6; and R. Thomas Simone, "The Mythos of 'The Sickness Unto Death': Kurosawa's IKIRU and Tolstoy's THE DEATH OF IVAN ILLYCH," LITERATURE/FILM QUARTERLY 3:1 (Winter 1975):2-12.

[876] Simone, p.12.

[877] For more information, see Peter Barnes, "The Seven Samurai," FILMS AND FILMING 1:7 (April 1955):23; Tony Richard, "Seven Samurai," SIGHT AND SOUND 24:4 (Spring 1955):195-6; Joseph L. Anderson, "When the Twain Meet: Hollywood's Remake of SEVEN SAMURAI," FILM QUARTERLY 15:13 (Spring 1962):55-8; Nathan Glazer, "THE SEVEN SAMURAI," EAST-WEST CENTER REVIEW 1 (July 1964):38-43; S. G. P. Alexander,

self-sacrifice for those who have less is the noblest virtue a human being can demonstrate. It is also a superb illustration of the samurai film convention that forces the characters to choose between "duty" (GIRI) and "human feelings" (NINJO). In making the decision, the protagonists offer us a sharp distinction between concepts of right and wrong, good and bad. Moreover, as Leyda comments, "The film has a beauty all its own, quite dissimilar to Kurosawa's previous work as well as to other Japanese films; it is the beauty of actuality, of tangibility, of the thought behind the faces you see, and of the reasons behind the motions of the bodies."[878]

KENJI MIZOGUCHI

SANSHO THE BAIIFF/SANSHO DAYU (Japan--16mm: 1954, 119 mins., b/w, English subtitles, sound, R-BUD, FES, FNC, KIT)

This highly original film about tyranny in medieval Japan is an excellent example of revisionist history as a means of commenting on present conditions. Adapted by Yahiro Fuji and Yoshikata Yoda from a story by Mori Ogai, the ironic film begins with a provincial governor's being forced into exile because he dared to oppose the slave dealers. The plot centers on the fate of his now-unprotected family. The mother (Kinuyo Tanaka) is coerced into prostitution, while the two children are kidnapped and sold to an evil bailiff. When they reach maturity, Zushio (Yoshiaki Hanayaki) and Anjo (Kyoko Kagawa) have assimilated many of their master's brutal values. Only after recognizing the harm that their cruelty has inflicted on their destitute mother do the son and daughter repent and seek atonement. As usual in a Mizoguchi work, oppressed women function as the basis for reforming people and institutions. But here, as Mellen observes, the director is at his most radical point. The hero finds himself, in the end, unable to do away with the slave system he inherited and learns that "Even the most enlightened feudal ruler will fail, his rebellion merely causing him to be assimilated among the oppressed."[879]

UGETSU/UGETSU MONOGATARI (Japan--16mm: 1953, 96 mins., b/w, English subtitles, sound, R-BUD, EMG, FNC, JAN; S-FES, KIT)

Based upon a collection of stories by Akinari Uyeda, this cinematic allegory of a sixteenth-century potter (Masayuki Mori) and his assistant Tobei (Sakae Ozawa) who seek to exploit the unrest in their wartorn country for their personal gain represents Mizoguchi's flair for historical legends. What happens to the two men and their wives as greed and ambition overcome reason and responsibility is an example of how he used the past to comment on the present. In addition to epitomizing Mizoguchi's lifelong fascination with the fate of women and the repressive nature of fedualistic values, this haunting and poetic film benefits considerably from the superb camerawork of Kazuo Miyagawa.

YASUJIRO OZU

LATE SPRING/BANSHUN (Japan--16mm: 1949, 107 mins., b/w, English subtitles, sound, R-NCE, NYF)

"The Magnificent Seven," SCREEN EDUCATION YEARBOOK (1964):66-8; and Alain Silver, "Samurai," FILM COMMENT 11:5 (September-October 1975):10-15.

[878] "Modesty and Pretension," pp.4-5.

[879] THE WAVES AT GENJI'S DOOR, p.107. For a useful review and bibliography, see Robin Wood, "SANSHO DAYU," THE INTERNATIONAL DICTIONARY OF FILMS AND FILMMAKERS: VOLUME I, pp.410-11.

In keeping with Ozu's belief about accepting life's fortunes, this endearing story focuses on the spiritual strength of a widowed father (Chishu Ryu) who after many years of rearing his daughter realizes that her impending marriage will change forever their relationship. The emphasis is on the parent's ability to understand the way of the world and not lose either his peace of mind or his love for his child. The film also marks the start of Ozu's fruitful collaboration with the screenwriter Kogo Noda and the cinematographer Yuharu Atsuta.

TOKYO STORY/TOKYO MONOGATARI (Japan--16mm: 1953, 139 mins., b/w, subtitles, sound, R-BUD, NCE, NYF)
In this extraordinary analysis of three generations, Ozu demonstrates his continual concern with characters and behavior rather than with plot or action. Noda's sensitive script deals with aging parents who visit their son and his wife in Tokyo. But very quickly the visitors are made to feel unwelcome and to realize that neither their son nor grandaughter has much time to spend with them. Only a widowed daughter-in-law shows the mother any understanding. The couple next visits another son nearby, where the mother becomes fatally ill. The final scene of the children rushing from the funeral only underscores the distance between the family and the widowed parent. Throughout the film, there is Ozu's constant reminder that the best we can do is accept life as it is, rather than question our fate. "This very Japaneseness of Ozu's approach," Richie tells us, "intuitive rather than analytic, the emphasis upon effect rather than cause, emotive rather than intellectual, is what--coupled with his marvelous metamorphosis of the Japanese aesthetic into images visible on film--makes him the most Japanese of all directors."[880]

THE TRANSITION YEARS (1955-1969)

By 1955, the year that television finally displaced film as America's number one form of mass entertainment, the transformation of world film had begun in earnest. Indicative of the metamorphosis was the resurgence of national cinemas, the emphasis on widescreen productions, the revising of long-standing censorship codes, the updating of screen conventions, the rise of new filmmakers trained in TV studios, the box-office appeal of foreign films in American theaters, the spread of multinational productions, the rethinking of film narrative structure, the use of film as a revolutionary tool for change, and the disintegration of major studio systems. Not since the dawn of film had movies been such an international industry. Moreover, the advent of CAHIERS DU CINEMA's AUTEUR theory and an emphasis on MISE EN SCENE had given "insignificant" directors and their much-maligned genres--e.g., westerns, "women's movies," gangster films, horror films, musicals, and science-fiction movies--long overdue respectablity. Instead of denigrating popular culture and "anonymous" contract directors, the new critical emphasis was on independent personalities whose personal credos permeated all their films. By the end of the sixties, many of the most successful films aligned audiences with outsiders who rebelled against corrupt and inept hierarchies. Instead of blaming the establishment for social ills, filmmakers now challenged viewers to take matters into their own hands and to reform society through personal acts.
Collectively, these factors radically changed the nature of the film continuum. First, a polarization developed between the mass film--e.g., Fred Zinnemann's OKLAHOMA (1955), David Lean's LAWRENCE OF ARABIA (1962), and Vittorio Cottafavi's HERCULES AND THE CAPTIVE WOMEN (1963)--and the personal film--e.g., Sidney Lumet's TWELVE ANGRY MEN (1958), Jean-Luc Godard's MY LIFE TO LIVE/VIVRE SA VIE (1962), and Ingmar Bergman's SHAME (1968); in other words,

---

[880]   "The Later Films of Yasujiro Ozu," p.25.

the spectacle theater versus the art house. The former shunned critical commentary, while the latter crusaded for social and political reforms. Second, filmmakers, educators, and critics offered alternatives to traditional Hollywood values by challenging not only classical narrative styles and subject matter, but also the targeting goals of the production process. Filmmakers like John Cassavetes and Alain Resnais experimented with different ways of approaching our depiction of the world around us and our understanding of it. Filmic time, memory, and space became tools in subverting classical story-telling techniques. Other artists challenged the traditional Hollywood standard of excellence by placing greater emphasis on spontaniety and improvisation, rather than on technical perfection and carefully constructed scripts. The result was a much more fragmented audience, fluctuating constantly between a demand for a "new cinema" and a longing for old-fashioned stories. As discussed in Chapter 1, film criticism became more prominent around the world, while in America, higher education finally began to consider film study a respectable intellectual activity. A number of graduates from film programs at NYU, UCLA, and USC--e.g., Francis Ford Coppola, George Lucas, and Martin history but were also in touch with contemporary audiences. These new audiences, in turn, gave rise to a third important trend, a demand for retrospective screenings and "classic" films. No longer were films perceived as products that became obsolete after a six-month run. A fourth development concerned the renewed importance of filmmakers outside the commercial cinema, and the need to establish a film industry independent of big productions and free from debilitating commercial restrictions. In short, the films of the transition years (1955-1969) represent revolutions in taste, conventions, production styles, censorship, distribution formulas, and exhibition patterns.

A survey of the novel approaches by individuals and national cinemas to respond to the cultural, political, technological, and economic forces transforming the art of the film during the transition follows. The major focus here will be on two key film-producing countries: France and the United States. Other nations will be represented by selected annotated bibliographies and filmographies. Because the changes taking place in the United States had the greatest impact on the worldwide film industry, the survey will begin with Hollywood from the mid-1950s to the end of the 1960s.

BOOKS

Aros, Andrew A. A TITLE GUIDE TO THE TALKIES, 1964 THROUGH 1974. Metuchen: The Scarecrow Press, 1977. 336pp.

Following the general format conceived by Richard B. Dimmitt, this valuable companion volume to the earlier works continues to offer information on the original source material of theatrical films. The more than 3,000 entries are alphabetically arranged by film title. The positive feature of this publication is that it makes definitive modifications in the original system by including the names of directors, authors of screenplays, distribution companies, and foreign films. Names of producers, however, have been dropped. A name index is included. Recommended for special collections.

*James, David E. ALLEGORIES OF CINEMA: AMERICAN FILM IN THE SIXTIES. Princeton: Princeton University Press, 1989. Illustrated. 388pp.

Limbacher, James L. FOUR ASPECTS OF THE FILM. New York: Russell and Russell, 1968. Illustrated. 386pp.

One of the best researched, documented, and discussed accounts of the growth of film color, sound, 3-D, and widescreen techniques, this historical survey emphasizes the innovative development of film technology. Besides an erudite commentary, Limbacher provides a valuable collection of diagrams and illustrations, over a hundred pages of useful appendexes listing natural color and tinted films, widescreen films, third-dimensional films, and pioneer sound films.[881] An index is included. Recommended for special collections.

*Samuels, Charles. ENCOUNTERING DIRECTORS. New York: Capricorn, 1972. Illustrated. 255pp.

A disappointing collection of interviews with eleven filmmakers, this book suggests more than it offers. Samuels had originally intended this to be a serious study, but abandoned his research to present instead a chatty account of his talks with Francois Truffaut, Vittorio De Sica, Ingmar Bergman, Federico Fellini, Alfred Hitchcock, Jean-Luc Godard, Jean Renoir, Carol Reed, Michelangelo Antonioni, Rene Clair, and Ermanno Olmi. The profuse illustrations help the book's limited appeal. An index is included. Worth browsing.

UNITED STATES

Between 1955 and 1969, American social and political institutions faced a serious challenge from a growing counterculture, a burgeoning civil rights movement, and an emerging new left. Each group, seeking political and social power to reform racist and sexist policies that made women, minorities, and the poor into second-class citizens in the world's wealthiest and most powerful democratic nation, affected film history. Further dividing the conflicting social and political cultures was an increasing fear about the possibility of a nuclear Armageddon resulting from the ongoing cold war. The Hollywood of the transitional years reflected these political and social tensions, profiting from the emotional needs of its audiences by trying to appeal to all aspects of the cultural spectrum. At the same time, Hollywood, between 1955 and 1969, responded to the political, social, economic, and technological crises gripping the American film industry and impacting on world cinema.[882]

As discussed in Chapters 3 and 5, the process was anything but monolithic. That is, the values of the new left, the "hippies," or the civil libertarians did not displace the conservative, middle-class establishment. Nor did the "emerging culture" become co-opted by the "dominant culture" and lose its force as an agent of social and political reform. Being pragmatic, the patriarchial film industry, like America itself, adjusted to the times. It incorporated into the production, distribution, and exhibition of films many of the oppositional elements advocated by the "emerging cultures."

---

[881] In connection with postwar production, the following three articles are useful: David Paletz and Michael Noorau, "The Exhibitors," FILM QUARTERLY 19:2 (Winter 1965-66):14-40; Arthur Mayer, "Hollywood's Favorite Fable," ibid., 12:2 (Winter 1958):13-20; and Richard Dyer MacCann, "Film and Foreign Policy: The USIA, 1962-1967," CINEMA JOURNAL 9:1 (Fall 1969):23-42.

[882] For more information, see Penelope Houston, "After The Strike," SIGHT AND SOUND 29:3 (Summer 1960):108-12; Axel Madsen, "The Changing of the Guard," ibid., 39:2 (Spring 1970):63-5, 11; Colin Young, "The Hollywood War of Independence," FILM QUARTERLY 12:3 (Spring 1959):4-15; Robert Brustein, "The New Hollywood: Myth and Anti-Myth," ibid., pp.23-31; "Discussion: Personal Creation in Hollywood--Is It Possible? Fred Zinnemann, John Houseman, Irvin Kershner, Kent MacKenzie, Pauline Kael, Colin Young," ibid., 15:3 (Spring 1962):16-34; Harriet R. Polt, "Notes on the New Stylization," ibid., 19:3 (Spring 1966):25-9; Stephen Farber "End of the Road," ibid., 23:2 (Winter 1969-70):3-16; William Johnson, "Hollywood 1965," ibid., 19:1 (Fall 1965):39-51; Richard Dyer MacCann, "From Technology to Adultery," FILMS AND FILMING 9:4 (January 1963):73-7; and George Fenin, "The Face of '63: United States," ibid., 9:6 (March 1963):55-63.

The multi-dimensional nature of the process was evident in the changing structure of Hollywood. By the end of the 1950s, the old studio system had disappeared. Not only were most of the great movie moguls of the past in retirement or dead,[883] but their fabulous studios would soon be taken over by corporate conglomerates and run by chief executive officers who cared more about "package deals" than about creative filmmaking. For example, by the early 1960s, top-flight agents like Lew Wasserman and Ted Ashley were running major studios like Universal Pictures and Warner Bros., respectively. No longer able to control exhibition, recognizing the profound changes that had taken place in lesisure-time values, and acutely aware that young people from thirteen to thirty now made up the majority of filmgoers, the new generation of film moguls reworked the old formulas to incorporate the alternative life-styles and values of those who opposed the simplistic Hollywood pieties of the Motion Picture Code.

Every film genre reflected some aspect of the complex social interaction that was reshaping America's social and political values. For example, science-fiction films from INVASION OF THE BODY SNATCHERS (1956) to PLANET OF THE APES (1968) explored the nation's paranoia about the cold war and the possibility of a nuclear disaster. As discussed elsewhere, romance went out of the optimistic formula and in its place appeared "cynical stories foretelling doomsday happenings."[884] Horror movies from PSYCHO (1960) to ROSEMARY'S BABY (1968) also reflected changes in American attitudes toward parents and children. The militancy of the civil rights movement, the growing generation gap, sexual liberation, political assassinations, and the Vietnam War put an end to the cinematic illusion that pure evil resided solely abroad. The sixties' horror films became one more vehicle by which filmmakers forced us to re-evaluate ourselves instead of others.[885] Westerns from THE FAR COUNTRY (1955) to THE WILD BUNCH (1969) provided a visual trail of pyschological probings of the traditional hero, forcing us to side more often with non-conformists than with upstanding members of the community. The films argued that honor, duty, and justice were as important to outlaws as to respectable citizens.[886] At the same time, films from RIDE THE HIGH COUNTRY (1962) to BUTCH CASSIDY AND THE SUNDANCE KID (1969) mourned the passing of the Western frontier and lamented what civilization had made of America's Garden of Eden. Like the sixties' western, the new gangster films championed an anti-hero who personified the disillusionment with the nation's political and social institutions. From THE KILLING (1956) to MADIGAN (1968), the reworked formula dealing with the dark side of the American Dream took a "realistic" look at the scope of crime and concluded that society's ills--e.g., robberies, prostitution, dope peddling, political corruption, and murders--were not the result of isolated incidents, but rather part of a national and international conspiracy.

That is not to say that Hollywood suddenly abandoned its residual conservative conventions and accepted the values of the counterculture. It didn't. The American film industry remained as traditional in its outlook as it had ever been. No better

---

[883] Jim Hillier offers the important reminder that by the late 1950s, many of Hollywood's established filmmakers and foreign directors were making their last films: e.g., Orson Welles, Fritz Lang, Douglas Sirk, Leo McCarey, Frank Borzage, King Vidor, Charles Chaplin, Raoul Walsh, and Josef von Sternberg. See Jim Hillier, ed. CAHIERS DU CINEMA: 1960-1968--NEW WAVE, NEW CINEMA, REEVALUATING HOLLYWOOD (Cambridge: Harvard University Press, 1986), p.8.

[884] AN ALBUM OF GREAT SCIENCE FICTION FILMS, Rev. ed., p.61.

[885] AN ALBUM OF MODERN HORROR FILMS, p.12.

[886] For more information, see Richard Blumenberg, "The Evolution and Shape of the American Western," WIDE ANGLE 1:1 (1979):30-6; and Ralph Brauer, "Who are Those Guys? The Movie Western During the TV Era," JOURNAL OF POPULAR FILM 2:4 (Fall 1973):389-404, Rpt. FOCUS ON THE WESTERN, pp.118-28.

example of the staying power of residual American values exists than the Hollywood musical. From IT'S ALWAYS FAIR WEATHER (1955) to FUNNY GIRL (1968), Hollywood catered to long-held entertainment values. It is to say that the American film industry could no longer ignore the challenges to those residual values about love, family, and success. To survive, Hollywood had either to discredit the reformist demands, or to find a way to neutralize them. Seen from this perspective, the transformation of the Hollywood genres between 1955 and 1969 results in a series of historical documents that reflect the shift in the doctrines of emerging cultures that began to challenge dominant American values peacefully, but became increasingly militant during the 1960s.

A major contributing factor to the rise of the New Hollywood was the film industry's changing perception of television as a valuable source of revenue. It became strikingly clear that the homilies of the past did better on the home screen, than in the movie houses. The challenge for the film moguls was how to capitalize on this fact by exploiting the virtues of the big screen. The initial solution to financing the new films was to raid studio vaults to supply old films to the TV networks. Few studio executives understood that the massive influx of genre films and their constant, repeated screenings on TV would not only kill off lucrative Hollywood formulas like westerns and gangster films, but would also foster TV clones and force filmmakers into parodying their highly successful genres to keep the formulas commercially viable. No one gave much thought to those issues, especially when the film executives discovered that the showing of relatively current films on TV earned the stations high ratings and opened up new distribution channels for the filmmakers. Moreover, the success of hit shows like WALT DISNEY'S WONDERFUL WORLD OF COLOR and ALFRED HITCHCOCK PRESENTS encouraged film executives to begin producing TV shows. By the middle of the 1960s, Hollywood began making films for television.

Another benefit of the revised attitude toward TV was the emergence of a new corps of writers--e.g., Woody Allen, Robert Alan Arthure, Mel Brooks, Paddy Chayefsky, Horton Foote, Buck Henry, Merle Miller, Rob Reiner, Reginald Rose, and Rod Serling; directors--e.g., Robert Aldrich, John Frankenheimer, George Roy Hill, Norman Jewison, Irvin Kershner, Sidney Lumet, Delbert Mann, Robert Mulligan, Ralph Nelson, and Sam Peckinpah; and performers--e.g., Dick Van Dyke, Clint Eastwood, James Garner, Steve McQueen, Mary Tyler Moore, Burt Reynolds, George C. Scott, and Rod Taylor. Collectively, these individuals helped change the nature of film narratives, the style of film acting, and the conventions of film genres. By the end of the sixties, the boundaries between film and TV (e.g., capital, performers, writers, facilities, and producers) were becoming indistinguishable. At the same time, the influx of new blood into the film industry made the revisionist policies of the new industry easier to achieve.

Another contributing factor to the revolutionary period was the changing attitude toward censorship. If Hollywood had any doubts about the direction the American film industry should be heading, it had only to look at the booming business being done by foreign imports like LA STRADA/THE ROAD (1956), THE SEVENTH SEAL/DET SJUNDE INSERGLET (1957), ROOM AT THE TOP (1959), BREATHLESS/A BOUT DE SOUFFLE, THE ADVENTURE/L'AVVENTURA (both in 1960), THE SWEET LIFE/LA DOLCE VITA, and JULES AND JIM/JULES ET JIM (both in 1961). Language, characterizations, themes, and scenes unthinkable during the studio years from 1922 to 1959 became standard fare in American movies by the end of the 1960s. Films like THE MAN WITH A GOLDEN ARM, BABY DOLL (both in 1956), THE APARTMENT, ELMER GANTRY, PSYCHO (all in 1960), DAYS OF WINE AND ROSES, LOLITA, THE MANCHURIAN CANDIDATE (all in 1962), HUD (1963), FAIL-SAFE, SEVEN DAYS IN MAY, DR. STRANGELOVE OR: HOW I LEARNED TO STOP WORRYING AND LOVE THE BOMB (all in 1964), THE SPY WHO CAME IN FROM THE COLD, THE PAWNBROKER, A PATCH OF BLUE (all in 1965), WHO'S AFRAID OF VIRGINIA WOOLF?, THE PROFESSIONALS (both in 1966), THE GRADUATE, IN THE HEAT OF THE NIGHT, BONNIE AND CLYDE, POINT BLANK (all in 1967), ROSEMARY'S BABY, NIGHT OF THE LIVING DEAD, THE LION IN WINTER, ISADORA, THE PRODUCERS (all in 1968),

THE WILD BUNCH, EASY RIDER, and MIDNIGHT COWBOY (all in 1969) presented images and ideas that not only shocked audiences, but also dramatized the new Hollywood.

Each revolutionary film added to the declining fortunes of censorship groups and codes. As discussed earlier in Chapters 3 and 5, the successors to Hays (Eric Johnston) and Breen (Geoffrey Shurlock) were no match for the changing tastes of the post-WWII generation. Modern audiences responded positively to cynical stories, violent action, full-frontal nudity, and risque dialogue.[887] The uncritical response also gave rise to a sexploitation industry that still flourishes today.[888]

The more aggressive filmmakers challenged the censors in the courts, particularly in the area of prior restraint. One especially important case involved a Baltimore exhibitor named Ronald Freedman, who, as Edward De Grazia and Roger K. Newman explain, "fought with the Maryland board [of censors] for the freedom to show 'exploitation' films with scenes the censors had specifically told him to remove."[889] Using the film, REVENGE AT DAYBREAK (1964)[890] as a test case, the determined Freedman battled the Maryland State Censorship Board and its licensing legislation to the Supreme Court, which ruled in his favor. Justice William J. Brennan, Jr., wrote the Court's unanimous decision in FREEDMAN V. MARYLAND, 380 U. S. 51 (1965), setting forth the principle that "the burden of proving that the film is unprotected expression must rest on the censor. . . ."[891] Although the FREEDMAN Decision, Ira H. Carmen observed in 1966, did not automatically put films on an equal Constitutional footing with publishers of books and pamphlets, or prevent states from pre-screening and rejecting films it found "undesirable," it did force censors across the country to re-examine their due process procedures. The question now was what

---

[887] For an example of how independents cashed in on the new approach to sex in films, see Roger Ebert, "Russ Meyer: King of the Nudies," FILM COMMENT 9:1 (January-February 1973):35-45; Stan Berkowitz, "Sex, Violence and Drugs: All In Good Fun! Russ Meyer Interviewed," ibid., pp.46-51; and Raymond Durgnat, "An Evening With Meyer and Masoch: Aspects of VIXENS and VENUS IN FURS," ibid., pp.52-61.

[888] For more information, see Al Di Lauro and Gerald Rabkin, DIRTY MOVIES: AN ILLUSTRATED HISTORY OF THE STAG FILM 1915-1970, Introduction Kenneth Tynan (New York: Chelsea House, 1976); H. J. Eyesenck and D. K. B. Nias, SEX, VIOLENCE, AND THE MEDIA (London: Maurice Temple Smith, 1978); *Wilson Bryan Key, MEDIA SEXPLOITATION, Introduction Richard D. Zakia (New York: New American Library, 1976); *Michael Milner, SEX ON CELLULOID (New York: Macfadden Books, 1964); *William Rotsler, CONTEMPORARY EROTIC CINEMA (New York: Ballantine Books, 1973); Carolyn See, BLUE MOVIE: PORNOGRAPHY AND THE PORNOGRAPHERS--AN INTIMATE LOOK AT THE TWO-BILLION-DOLLAR FANTASY INDUSTRY (New York: David McKay Company, 1974); Kenneth Turan and Stephen F. Zito, SINEMA: AMERICAN PORNOGRAPHIC FILMS AND THE PEOPLE WHO MAKE THEM (New York: Praeger Publishers, 1974); and *John Warren Wells, DIFFERENT STROKES: OR HOW I (GULP) WROTE, DIRECTED, AND STARRED IN AN X-RATED MOVIE (New York: Dell Publishing Company, 1974). See also Richard Corliss, "Cinema Sex: From THE KISS to DEEP THROAT," FILM COMMENT 9:1 (January-February 1973):4-5; ___, "Radley Metzger: Aristocrat of the Erotic," ibid., pp.18-29; Brendan Gill, "Blue Notes," ibid., 6-11; and Donald Richie, "Sex and Sexism in the Eroduction," ibid., 12-7.

[889] *Edward De Grazia and Roger K. Newman, BANNED FILMS: MOVIES, CENSORS, AND THE FIRST AMENDMENT (New York: R. R. Bowker Company, 1982), p.112.

[890] Originally released in 1954 as DESPERATE DECISION, the film was released in 1964 as REVENGE AT DAYBREAK.

[891] Cited in BANNED FILMS, p.113.

constituted "obscenity," and here the Court had provided no guidelines. In the end, as Carmen explains, ". . . procedural due process will be helpful in checking censors, but the point is that difficulties of this sort exist ONLY for movies and for no other medium of speech or press."[892]

As discussed in Chapter 3, Jack Valenti, the new head of the MPAA, decided not to wait for the Supreme Court to clarify its position and, in 1966, instituted a ratings system based upon age classifications. The 1930s' Production Code Administration thus became the Classification and Ratings Administration. In many respects, film content had long since passed the old taboos by. Heroes no longer were easily distinguishable from villains; crime often went unpunished in sixties' movies; and residual values dealing with marriage, sex, race relations, social and political institutions, law and order, justice, and morality were under heavy attack by civil libertarians and the youth culture.

Not surprisingly, the ratings system needed refining before it could gain industry approval. Meanwhile, the filmmakers were good at improvising interim solutions. For example, when films like ALFIE, GEORGY GIRL, and WHO'S AFRAID OF VIRGINIA WOOLF? (all in 1966) ran into problems with the ratings, the interim solution was a tag, "Suggested for Mature Audiences." As Charles Champlin observes, the interim solution "for the first time acknowledged the new truth about movies: they were no longer necessarily made for a single vast audience; they might, in fact, be inappropriate for an 'immature' patron, no matter how much past twenty-one he or she might be."[893] The new freedom provided by the ratings system was evident not only in the treatment of sex and the use of expletives, but also in the depiction of violence.[894] Beginning with films like BONNIE AND CLYDE and IN COLD BLOOD (both in 1967), filmmakers explored how far they could go in integrating brutality and sadism into the context of their violent themes and stories. Among the more notable examples were THE WILD BUNCH, JOE, and EASY RIDER (all in 1969).

The upheaval of the sixties also changed Hollywood stereotyping. Nowhere was this more evident than in the depiction of minorities and women. Consider the image of African-Americans. As discussed in Chapter 3, the industry had only been able to merchandize one black star during the late 1950s and early 1960s: Sidney Poitier. But by the mid-1960s, a number of noteworthy films like SERGEANT RUTLEDGE (1960), A RAISIN IN THE SUN (1961), TO KILL A MOCKINGBIRD (1962), NOTHING BUT A MAN, and ONE POTATO, TWO POTATO (both in 1964) offered novel black characters who refused to accept subservient roles. These changes became more dramatic once the new ratings system was in place. Films like IN THE HEAT OF THE NIGHT, DUTCHMAN, GUESS WHO'S COMING TO DINNER? (all in 1967), 100 RIFLES, THE SCALPHUNTERS, THE LEARNING TREE, UP TIGHT (all in 1968), THE LIBERATION OF L. B. JONES, and SLAVES (both in 1969) epitomized the direction Hollywood was heading and the difficulties it faced. On the one hand, the film industry was responding to demands that it portray blacks more positively than in the past and create better roles for black performers. On the other hand, many intellectuals and black leaders noted with cynicism that the films were still made primarily by and for white, liberal audiences who had unrealistic goals and naive ideas about black needs. While it was clear that the social and political power that African-Americans exerted on Hollywood in the late 1960s was greater than that of Hispanics or Native Americans, the interactive process that produces popular culture

[892] Ira H. Carmen, MOVIES, CENSORSHIP AND THE LAW (Ann Arbor: University of Michigan Press, 1966), pp.120-1.

[893] *Charles Champlin, THE MOVIES GROW UP 1940-1980 (Chicago: Swallow Press, 1981), p.73.

[894] For a good overview, see "Hollywood: The Shock of Freedom in Films," TIME (December 8, 1967):66-8, 73-4, 76.

was still dominated by a white patriarchy determined to co-opt the needs of the African-American community. And, as discussed in Chapter 3, white Hollywood did just that in the early 1970s.

Another elusive dream deferred in the sixties was the notion of a "New American Cinema," consisting of inexpensive, artistic film productions that resembled the work being done by filmmakers in Britain's Free Cinema and France's LA NOUVELLE VAGUE. The idea gained momentum in 1959, when Jonas Mekas wrote an editorial in FILM CULTURE pleading for a "new generation of filmmakers" who had a distrust of the Hollywood system and its conventions, a commitment to the "emotional and intellectual conditions of their own generation as opposed to the neorealists' preoccupation with materiality," and a desire to make films through "intuition and improvisation, [rather] than by discipline."[895] Pointing to John Cassavetes's SHADOWS (1960) as an example of the new spirit, Mekas argued that low-budget films of quality could be made. As P. Adams Sitney notes, the idea inspired a number of filmmakers--e.g., Shirley Clarke, Robert Frank, Adolfas Mekas--to make feature films, but failed to take into account the crucial aspects of distribution and exhibition. Although the movement was dead by 1963, it did give rise to The Film-Maker's Cooperative. "Through it," Sitney explains, "the film-makers planned to distribute their own films and keep the income, minus a marginal percentage for operational costs."[896] The fact that the cooperative couldn't generate sufficent capital to make underground feature films commercially viable became clear very quickly. The idea, however, helped keep the AVANT-GARDE movement in America alive through the 1960s.[897]

One of the most prominent noncomformists of American film during the sixties was Andy Warhol.[898] His silkscreens, paintings, and wood sculptures of everyday objects like Campbell's soup cans and of personalities like Marilyn Monroe and Elvis

---

[895]   Jonas Mekas, "A Call for a New Generation of Film Makers," FILM CULTURE 19 (1979):1-3. Rpt. *P. Adams Sitney, ed., FILM CULTURE READER (New York: Praeger Publishers, 1970), pp.73-5. See also Jonas Mekas, "New York Letter: Towards a Spontaneous Cinema," SIGHT AND SOUND 28:3-4 (Summer 1959):118-21.

[896]   Sitney, p.71.

[897]   For more information on experimental trends during the transition years, see "Bruce Connor," FILM COMMENT 5:4 (Winter 1969):16-25; Stan Vanderbeek, "The Cinema Dilemma: Films from the Underground," FILM QUARTERLY 14:4 (Summer 1961):5-16; Albert Johnson, "The Dynamic Gesture: New American Independents," ibid., 19:4 (Summer 1966):6-11; David MacDougall, "Prospects of the Ethnographic Film," ibid., 23:2 (Winter 1969-70):16-30; Robert Siegler, "Masquage: The Multi-Image Film," ibid., 21:1 (Fall 1967):2-13; James Lithgow and Colin Heard, "Underground U. S. A. and the Sexploitation Market," FILMS AND FILMING 15:11 (August 1969):18-29; Gordon Gow, "The Underground River: Agnes Varda," ibid., 16:5 (March 1970):6-10; Gordon Gow, "Up from the Underground, Part 1: Curtis Harrington," ibid., 17:11 (August 1971):16-22; and "Part 2: Conrad Rooks," ibid., pp.24-8; and Edgar F. Daniels, "Plain Words on Underground Film Programs," THE JOURNAL OF POPULAR FILM 1:2 (Spring 1972):112-21.

[898]   For more information, see David Ehrenstein, "An Interview with Andy Warhol," FILM CULTURE 40 (Spring 1966):41; Gregory Battcock, "Superstar=Superset," ibid., 45 (Summer 1967):23-32; Andrew M. Lugg, "On Andy Warhol," CINEASTE 1:3 (Winter 1967-68):9-13; ___, "On Andy Warhol" ibid., 1:4 (Spring 1968):12-5;; Gretchen Berg, "Andy," TAKE ONE 1:10 (1968):10-1; ___, "Nothing to Lose: Interview With Andy Warhol," CAHIERS DU CINEMA IN ENGLISH 10 (May 1967):38-43; Andrew Sarris, "The Sub-New York Sensibility," ibid., pp.43-5; Serge Gavronsky, "Warhol's Underground," ibid., pp.46-9; James Stoller, "Beyond Cinema: Notes on Some Films by Andy Warhol," FILM QUARTERLY 20:1 (Fall 1966):35-8; Dennis J. Cipnic, "Andy

Presley earned him the reputation as the "master of pop culture." He became the advocate for representing the commonplace as a major source of contemporary art, for locating a particular image as a symbol for the world around us. By the early 1960s, Warhol turned his brand of expressionism to filmmaking with a number of films--e.g., KISS, SLEEP, HAIRCUT (all in 1963), and EMPIRE (1964)--that recorded ordinary activities and places for a prolonged period of time. While many traditionalists dismiss him as a fraud, others, like John G. Hanhardt, curator of film and Video at the Whitney Museum find Warhol's risk-taking demystification of art compelling and significant. "Often the risk," he explains, "involved what was going to happen or unfold in front of the camera in a time when a lot of people were exploring with drugs, with themselves, with the culture. . . ."[899] Warhol's experiments concerned more than expanding our expectations and how we view the world we lived in. They also challenged Hollywood's perceptions of reality, showing us a violent and sadistic culture that appealed to Warhol and his New York entourage. Although films in the seventies and eighties would appropriate much of the AVANT-GARDE artist's ideas, "Andy Warhol in the early 1960s," as John Russell comments, "was the indispensable man of American art--the one who turned everything upside down and inside out and got away with it."[900]

The post-WWII documentary film movement also contributed to the film revolution. As discussed earlier and in Chapter 2, factual films had become big business in the non-theatrical world. Not only had industry and educational circles opened up new channels of production, distribution, and exhibition, but television had also become an important training ground and market for documentaries. Increased production resulted in more sophisticated equipment. Cheaper and better equipment stimulated new directions for the use and role of documentaries in society. A case in point was the re-emergence of CINEMA-VERITE in the form of "Direct Cinema."[901] Starting in the late 1950s, and led by men like Richard Leacock and Robert Drew, filmmakers became determined to "tell the truth" about how real people lived, worked, and survived. In simplified terms, these artists insisted that the camera not the director was telling "the story." Even here, technical skill was secondary to recording "reality," immediacy was more important than "artistry," and "objectivity" was more desirable than "interpretation." One example of the Direct Cinema movement is Frederick Wiseman's TITICUT FOLLIES (1967), a film made on borrowed funds with portable camera equipment that showed the harrowing existence of the criminally

Warhol: Iconographer," SIGHT AND SOUND 41:3 (Summer 1972):158-61; Rodger Larson, "An Innocence, An Originality, A Clear Eye: A Retrospective Look at the Films of D. W. Griffith and Andy Warhol," THE FILM JOURNAL 1:3-4 (Fall-Winter 1972):80-9; Richard Whitehall, "Whitehall With Warhol," CINEMA (Calif) 3:6 (Winter 1967):20-4; Greg Ford, "You Name It, I'll Eat It: A Monologue Discussion of Morrissey's FLESH, TRASH, HEAT," ibid., 8:1 (Spring 1973):30-7; Ed Lowry, "Warhol, Andy (with Paul Morrissey), THE INTERNATIONAL DICTIONARY OF FILMS AND FILMMAKERS: VOLUME I, pp.573-4; Douglas C. McGill, "Andy Warhol, Pop Artist, Dies," NEW YORK TIMES A (February 23, 1988):1, 16; and "Artist Warhol, 58, Dies of Heart Attack," HOLLYWOOD REPORTER (February 23, 1987):4, 8.

[899]   Cited in Glenn Collins, "Where the Action Was," NEW YORK TIMES H (April 24, 1988):23, 32.

[900]   John Russell, "The Man Who Turned Art Upside Down, Inside Out," NEW YORK TIMES A (February 23, 1987):16.

[901]   For more information on the ties between Direct Cinema and CINEMA-VERITE, see Colin Young, "Cinema of Common Sense," FILM QUARTERLY 17:4 (Summer 1964):26-9, 40; Peter Graham, "CINEMA-VERITE in France," ibid., pp.30-6; and Henry Breitrose, "On the Search for the Real Nitty-Gritty: Problems and Possibilities in CINEMA VERITE," ibid., pp.36-40.

insane imprisoned in the Titicut area of Massachusetts. Another example is Albert and David Maysles's SALESMAN (1969), depicting the commercial underbelly of Bible salesmen traveling along the East Coast from New England to Florida.[902] Although Direct Cinema never achieved the objectivity its advocates desired, it demonstrated the unquestionable power and appeal of factual filmmaking as well as the limitations of theatrical formulas.

The American film industry responded to all these revolutionary trends. But despite all the changes in film content, industry self-censorship, acting styles, corporate reorganizations, and narrative approaches, the end of the sixties saw Hollywood in disarray. No one film was able to ignite lucrative spin-offs, sequels, or remakes, the bread-and-butter of the modern Hollywood. Equally important, few stars were able to overcome a film's structural defects. Corporate studio executives were unable to understand what the public wanted and those who thought they did lost fortunes on box-office disasters like DR. DOLITTLE (1967), STAR!, THE SHOES OF THE FISHERMAN (both in (1968), SWEET CHARITY, PAINT YOUR WAGON, THOSE DARING YOUNG MEN IN THEIR JAUNTY JALOPIES, and HELLO, DOLLY (all in 1969). According to Stephen Farber, studios felt in 1969 that they were

> on the verge of an unprecedented financial disaster. Many have stopped shooting altogether for a period of months. The Paramount lot is to be sold, and MGM and 20th Century-Fox (soon with unwarranted optimism to be renamed 21st Century-Fox) are talking of doing the same. Agencies are desperate--even many of their major stars cannot find work. The boom town is close to becoming a ghost town again.[903]

As the transition years came to an end, box-office receipts were plummeting along with the number of feature films being produced for an ever-decreasing theater audience. "If both the counterculture and the New Left clearly never did triumph or truly alter the nature of American political and social power," explain Al Auter and Leonard Quart, "they nevertheless did change American consciousness. Likewise, the films that followed had to come to terms with the fact that the old conventions and platitudes no longer were totally dominant over the minds and psyches of the American public."[904]

BOOKS

GENERAL

*Baker, Fred, and Ross Firestone, eds. MOVIE PEOPLE: AT WORK IN THE BUSINESS OF FILM. New York: Douglas Book Corporation, 1972. Illustrated. 193pp.

"To explain the living and working realities of feature movie making in America," Baker and Firestone explain, "this book brings together the personal experiences of practitioners of each of the separate skills that interlock to form the total filmmaking enterprise." The book divides the process into three major sections. Section One, "Getting It Together: Pre-Production," presents the opinions of a producer (Roger Lewis) and a distributor (David Picker). Section Two, "Getting It On: Production,"

---

[902] For more information, see Maxine Haleff, "The Maysles Brothers and 'Direct Cinema,'" FILM COMMENT 2:2 (Spring 1964):19-23; and James Blue, "Thoughts on CINEMA VERITE and a Discussion with the Maysles Brothers," ibid., 3:4 (Fall 1965):22-30.

[903] Stephen Farber, "End of the Road," FILM QUARTERLY 23:2 (Winter 1969-70):3.

[904] Al Auster and Leonard Quart, p.12

offers the experiences of directors (Sidney Lumet, and Francis Ford Coppola), screenwriters (Terry Southern and James Salter), an actor (Rod Steiger), an editor (Aram Avakian), and a composer (Quincy Jones). Section Three, "Getting It Out: Release," gives the insights of an exhibitor (Walter Reade, Jr.) and a film critic (Andrew Sarris). Originating from a series of lectures given in 1968, the revised and updated talks reflect the contributors' ongoing evaluations of filmmaking at the end of the 1960s. The book's strength lies more in its collective impressions than in the insights of any one individual. Well worth browsing.

*Billings, Pat, and Allen Eyles. HOLLYWOOD TODAY. New York: A. S. Barnes and Company, 1971. Illustrated. 192pp.
    This handy dictionary provides a biography and filmography of more than 370 film personalities, plus a small collection of illustrative stills. The alphabetically arranged entries offer useful thumbnail profiles and are keyed to performers, producers, and directors who reside primarily in Hollywood. Interestingly, that focus eliminates any entries for people like Marlon Brando, Yul Brynner, and Elizabeth Taylor. A film title index is included. Well worth browsing.

*Higham, Charles, HOLLYWOOD CAMERAMEN: SOURCES OF LIGHT. New York: Doubleday and Company, 1970. Illustrated. 176pp.
    This valuable compendium is a worthwhile introduction to such famous cameramen as James Wong Howe, Lee Garmes, Stanley Cortez, Arthur Miller, Leon Shamroy, Karl Struss, and William Daniels. Higham's introductory essay gives a useful overview of the contributions that cinematographers have given to the American films, pointing out that "With their lighting, either realistic, like Wong Howe's, or painterly, like Lee Garmes's, or symphonic in its range, like Stanley Cortez's, the cameramen have created an American cinema as often bathed in their own vision as in that of a director." The narrative consists of transcribed interviews that omit the question-answer format and include only edited responses. A filmography for each cinematographer is provided, along with a film index. Recommended for special collections.

*Rosenthal, Alan. THE NEW DOCUMENTARY IN ACTION: A CASEBOOK IN FILMMAKING. Berkeley: University of California Press, 1971. Illustrated. 287pp.
    In an attempt to provide some behind-the-scenes information on documentary production, Rosenthal interviewed a number of important people connected with key filmmakers and producers, writers, cameramen, and editors. The result is an excellent text on creative perspectives as seen by Fred Wiseman, Al Maysles, Mort Silverstein, Peter Watkins, and Don Pennebaker. An index is included. Recommended for special collections.

Sherman, Eric, and Martin Rubin. THE DIRECTOR'S EVENT: INTERVIEWS WITH FIVE AMERICAN FILM-MAKERS. New York: Atheneum, 1969. Illustrated. 200pp.
    A worthwhile collection of ideas from and about Budd Boetticher, Peter Bogdanovich, Samuel Fuller, Arthur Penn, and Abraham Polansky, this collection emphasizes the changes taking place with the breakdown of the studio system. Each chapter begins with a brief overview of the director, followed by intriguing observations by the subjects on how they work and the problems they face. Filmographies are provided at the end of the interviews. Well worth browsing.

*Wanger, Walter, and Joe Hyams. MY LIFE WITH CLEOPATRA. New York: Bantam Books, 1963. 182pp.

This producer's view of one of the most widely covered and exploited films of the 1960s supplies a good reason why the Hollywood empire faced ruin in that decade. Well worth browsing.

ROBERT ALDRICH

Arnold, Edwin T., and Eugene L. Miller, Jr. THE FILMS AND CAREER OF ROBERT ALDRICH. Knoxville: The University of Tennessee Press, 1986. Illustrated. 280pp.
    Born in Cranston, Rhode Island, on August 9, 1918, Robert Aldrich, the only son of his wealthy and influential parents, eventually became one of Hollywood's most famous maverick and underrated producer-directors. Although his Economics major at the University of Virginia prepared him to enter the family banking business, Aldrich decided instead to forego graduation and take a job as a production clerk at RKO in 1941. Four years later he moved over to Enterprise Studios, where his day-to-day assignments allowed him opportunities to moonlight as a first assistant director for United Artists. During the 1940s and early 1950s, his progress through the Hollywood ranks brought him in contact with some of the industry's most independent and gifted peronalities: e.g., Charles Chaplin, Jules Dassin, Edward Dmytryk, Ring Lardner, Joseph Losey, Lewis Milestone, Abraham Polansky, Jean Renoir, Robert Rossen, Dalton Trumbo, and William Wellman. Each of these men, especially those who were blacklisted or driven out by the industry's commercial priorities, had a profound effect on Aldrich's cinematic techniques and themes. Television, however, gave him his directorial debut. Between 1950 and 1953, he worked on several TV series, including THE DOCTOR and CHINA SMITH. Aldrich's directorial film debut came with THE BIG LEAGUER in 1953. Considering his training, it's not surprising that his early films--APACHE (1954), KISS ME DEADLY, THE BIG KNIFE (both in 1955), ATTACK! and AUTUMN LEAVES (both in 1956)--offer a set of anti-heroes who symbolize what's wrong with the establishment, rather than with them as individuals. The 1955 creation of Aldrich and Associates, an independent production company, gave the producer-director the leverage to negotiate more favorable contracts, but not the financial security to survive in Hollywood. After Harry Cohn drove him out of the film capital for refusing to follow orders on the making of THE GARMENT INDUSTRY (1957), Aldrich had a five-year stint in Europe--THE ANGRY HILLS, TEN SECONDS TO HELL (both in 1959), THE LAST SUNSET (1961), and SODOM AND GOMORRAH (1963)--before returning to Hollywood in 1962. Acclaimed as a brilliant director by CAHIERS DU CINEMA's Francois Truffaut, Aldrich became even more contemptuous of Hollywood's conventions and teamed up with the screenwriter Lukas Heller to make a number of revisionist genre films: e.g., WHATEVER HAPPENED TO BABY JANE (1962), HUSH . . . HUSH, SWEET CHARLOTTE (1964), THE FLIGHT OF THE PHOENIX (1966), THE DIRTY DOZEN (1967), THE KILLING OF SISTER GEORGE (1968), and TOO LATE THE HERO (1970). The commercial success of these films gave Aldrich the financial stability he had needed. Drawing more on his personal experiences than in the past, and luxuriating in violent action, his sixties' films present outsiders who live in a sick and distorted world where conventional values are ridiculed. Determined to fight the Hollywood establishment, Aldrich revitalized the Aldrich and Associates Company as the Aldrich Studios in 1968 and for the next seven years continued making controversial films. Except for THE LEGEND OF LYLAH CLARE, THE KILLING OF SISTER GEORGE (both in 1968), and THE GREATEST MOTHER OF THEM ALL (1969), Aldrich's movies focused on macho-heroes who cynically exploit society's hypocritical standards and who view women either as sex objects, or superheroines: e.g., THE GRISSOM GANG (1971), ULZANA'S RAID (1972), EMPEROR OF THE NORTH POLE (1973), THE LONGEST YARD (1974), HUSTLE (1975), TWILIGHT'S LAST GLEAMING, and THE CHOIRBOYS (both in 1977). Action rather than ideas dominates the screenplays, designed to appeal to the audience's emotions rather than to its intellect. Although box-office reversals cost him his studio in 1975, Aldrich remained a powerful Hollywood figure during the 1970s. His films symbolized the new Hollywood's preoccupation with film as a reflection of moral depravity rather than movies as a

means to uplift society. Although Aldrich received many awards and honors, including twice being elected President of the Director's Guild, he remained antagonistic to Hollywood's inner circle and an embarrassment to many American critics who deplored his sexist and violent movies. At the time of his death in 1983, he was largely ignored by mainstream studies of the American cinema.

This appreciative and comprehensive biography provides the first in-depth look at Aldrich's career and contributions to film history. Seven well-researched chapters challenge traditional attitudes toward Aldrich's work, emphasizing that he fought for self-respect in a world corrupted by fascist leaders and immoral values. Particular attention is paid to his revisionist perspectives in Hollywood genres like the war film, westerns, melodramas, crime thrillers, and adventure films. In addition to endnotes, illustrations, a filmography, a bibliography, and an index, the authors offer excellent quotations from many sources. One noteworthy example is from Polansky's 1983 eulogy of Aldrich: "He didn't divide the world up into Good and Evil. He didn't see it that simply. He found himself as someone who knew that his idea of himself was why he existed, and that his self-esteem and respect for himself could never be jeopardized--and he could never jeopardize it--by any compromise that involved that deep portion of his nature . . . In the deeper part of human life, one just doesn't want to get things done. One wants to live as things SHOULD BE DONE. And I think he lived that way." Recommended for special collections.

Silver, Alain, and Elizabeth Ward. ROBERT ALDRICH: A GUIDE TO REFERENCES AND RESOURCES. Boston: G. K. Hall and Company, 1979. 172pp.

Originating out of Silver's UCLA master's thesis, "Robert Aldrich: A Critical Study," this pioneering resource guide offers the basic information on the writer-producer-director's career between 1941 and 1977. The authors conclude that "Aldrich's films concentrate on the most basic situation: man attempting to survive in a hostile universe." They find many of his heroes can be "more consistently vicious, self-centered and cynical than any villain." Moreover, because Aldrich's deterministic philosophy has his characters minimizing conventional morality, the authors argue that the "conflicting impulses of nature and society, of real and unreal, of right and wrong, [are resolved] in and through action." The material is presented in a clear, concise, and useful format: a biography, a critical survey of the director's work, a filmography, writings about Aldrich, film-related activities, 16mm distributors, an interview with Aldrich, an author index, and a film title index. Well worth browsing.

WOODY ALLEN

*Adler, Bill, and Jeffrey Feinman. WOODY ALLEN: CLOWN PRINCE OF AMERICAN HUMOR. New York: Pinnacle Books, 1975. Illustrated. 178pp.

Born Allen Stewart Konigsberg in Brooklyn on December 1, 1935, Woody Allen grew up an introvert. By the time he reached high school, Allen had developed a comic wit that got him jobs with New York columnists, ghost writing one-liners for celebrities quoted in the newspapers. The irreverent teenager quickly abandoned any plans for a college education and turned his attention to a professional writing career. During the 1950s, Allen developed his comedic art as a writer for TV celebrities like Pat Boone, Sid Caesar, Art Carney, Buddy Hackett, and Jack Paar. He was particularly influenced during this period by the routines of Mort Sahl. In 1960, Allen gave up writing to become a standup comic. Within three years, he became a comedy sensation on TV shows, on college campuses, and on the nightclub circuit. Allen's screen career began as a screenwriter and actor in WHAT'S NEW, PUSSYCAT? (1964). He then wrote WHAT'S UP, TIGER LILY? (1966), played two parts in CASINO ROYALE (1966), and wrote a Broadway hit, DON'T DRINK THE WATER (1966). His first film as a writer, director, and star was TAKE THE MONEY AND RUN (1969). Since then, he has written, directed, and starred in twelve films: BANANAS (1971), EVERYTHING

YOU ALWAYS WANTED TO KNOW ABOUT SEX (1972), SLEEPER (1973), LOVE AND DEATH (1975), ANNIE HALL (1977), MANHATTAN (1979), STARDUST MEMORIES (1980), A MIDSUMMER NIGHT'S SEX COMEDY (1982), ZELIG (1983), BROADWAY DANNY ROSE (1984), THE PURPLE ROSE OF CAIRO (1985), HANNAH AND HER SISTERS (1986), and RADIO DAYS (1987). Other films he has written and directed are SEPTEMBER, ANOTHER WOMAN (both in 1988), and a short film, OEDIPUS WRECKS, in the film anthology NEW YORK STORIES (1989). In addition, Allen has written one Broadway show that has been adapted for the screen starring Allen--PLAY IT AGAIN, SAM (1972); appeared in THE FRONT (1976), and written and directed two films--INTERIORS (1978) and ANOTHER WOMAN (1988),

In this unauthorized biography, Adler and Feinman focuses on Allen's writings, routines, and acting, rather than on his personal history. The most serious obstacle to appreciating the book's interesting observations is the slick prose. For example, the first page asks the question, "Could this featherweight fellow who looks like a second-best butler when he's dressed up and a College Bowl flunk out when he isn't, could this really be a movie star?" Six uneven chapters saturated with this language and filled with unsupported assertions offset what might have been a useful overview. No bibliography, filmography, or index is included. Approach with caution.

*Allen, Woody. GETTING EVEN. New York: Warner Paperback Library, 1972. 110pp.
The first collection of Allen's pieces for THE NEW YORKER, this anthology contains seventeen entertaining examples of the comic's writing style. Among some of the most enjoyable one-liners are his observations that "death is an acquired trait," "I do not believe in an afterlife, although I'm bringing a change of underwear," and that Mafia families "are actually groups of serious men, whose main joy in life comes from seeing how long certain people can stay under the East River before they start gurgling." Well worth browsing.

Brode, Douglas. WOODY ALLEN: HIS FILMS AND CAREER. Secaucus: Citadel Press, 1985. Illustrated. 256pp.
The most comprehensive study of Allen's career, this intelligent survey updates the standard interpretations of the comic's NEBBISH persona, while drawing parallels between Allen and F. Scott Fitzgerald. An extended introduction reviewing various theories is followed by chapters analyzing nineteen films in which the star appeared, wrote, or directed. Except for the absence of documentation and a bibliography, this well-written and informative work does justice to its many beautifully reproduced illustrations. No index is included. Recommended for special collections.

Guthrie, Lee. WOODY ALLEN: A BIOGRAPHY. New York: Drake Publishers, 1978. Illustrated. 183pp.
A superficial review of Allen's life, this unauthorized biography contains something to annoy almost everyone. A case in point is Guthrie's writing style. "Woody Allen," Guthrie quips, "apparently from the cradle, looked on the world around him and found it totally absurd. In describing its absurdity to us, he also made us see how ridiculous, nutty and wacked-out life really is under that thin veneer known as civilization. And the looniest thing of all is our tendency to take this nuttiness seriously." That is not a problem with this study. Reconstructed conversations, undocumented assertions, and thin analyses litter the book's eight chapters. A filmography and index are included, but no bibliography is provided. Approach with caution.

*Hample, Stuart. NON-BEING AND SOMETHING-NESS: SELECTIONS FROM THE COMIC STRIP "INSIDE WOODY ALLEN." Introduction R. Buckminster Fuller. New York: Random House, 1978. Illustrated. No pagination.

An interesting addition to the Allen mystique, this novel collection of comic strips plays on the comedian's existential speculations. Even the Fuller introduction is in the form of balloon coments, the last one asserting that "Woody Allen has initiated a new era by moving us metaphysically, moving us to learn while smiling, and that is the only lasting way in which we can be mindfully moved to transcend our social inferiority and inherent failure complex to instead exercise our now clearly demonstrated option to make all humanity a lasting physical living success." The syndicated cartoons, appearing in over sixty foreign countries, are amusing but not as thought-provoking as Fuller's. Well worth browsing.

Lax, Eric. ON BEING FUNNY: WOODY ALLEN AND COMEDY. New York: Charterhouse, 1975. Illustrated. 243pp.
Although Allen assisted Lax in his research, this lightweight biography only skims the surface of the artist's ideas and techniques. Lax spent three years in the early 1970s studying the writer-director's routines and films as well as going through some of the subject's personal papers. On the positive side, the research results in a number of intriguing quotations and script excerpts useful to understanding Allen's complex approaches to comedy and drama. Figures are quoted, deals referred to, and controversial decisions explained. On the negative side, nothing is documented and frequently reconstructed conversations challenge the credibility of the interpretations. By sacrificing scholarly standards and opting for a mass market publication, the author misses a significant opportunity to make a valuable contribution to film history. An index is included, but no bibliography or filmography is provided. Well worth browsing.

*Palmer, Myles. WOODY ALLEN: AN ILLUSTRATED BIOGRAPHY. New York: Proteus, 1980. Illustrated. 142pp.
Another breezy survey of Allen's career, this disappointing narrative does come with a good set of candid shots and illustrations. Unfortunately, the skillful selection of pictures frequently is offset by erratic reproduction. A filmography is included, but no bibliography or index is provided. Worth browsing.

Yacowar, Maurice. LOSER TAKE ALL: THE COMIC ART OF WOODY ALLEN. New York: Frederick Ungar Publishing Company, 1979. Illustrated. 243pp.
An outstanding study on all counts, this perceptive analysis of the comedian's techniques and philosophy is the place to start a serious examination of why Allen appeals to the modern generation. Yacowar begins by defining the comic's persona of the "frightened and frustrated SCHLEMIEL": a Jew afflicted "with lust and with inadequacy," "a failed lecher with intellectual pretensions," and a man willing to confess openly "his private fears and failures." The author makes it clear that these characteristics, drawn from aspects of Allen's life, belong as much to the general public as to the comic himself. Yacowar then divides his examination of Allen's persona into four major sections: "The Public Face of Woody Allen" (the monologues and the actor), "Woody in the Theater" (a look at DON'T DRINK THE WATER, PLAY IT AGAIN, SAM, and the one-act plays), "Woody the Writer," (his prose work), and "Woody's Films: Guilt-Edged Cinema" (from WHAT'S UP, TIGER LILY? to MANHATTAN). The writing is crisp, the ideas refreshing, and the material informative. Endnotes, a bibliography, a filmography, and an index are provided. Recommended for special collections.

WARREN BEATTY

*Burke, Jim. WARREN BEATTY. New York: Belmont Tower Books, 1976. Illustrated. 182pp.

Munshower, Suzanne. WARREN BEATTY: HIS LIFE, HIS LOVES, HIS WORK. New York: St. Martin's Press, 1983. Illustrated. 165pp.

*Quirk, Lawrence J. THE FILMS OF WARREN BEATTY. Secaucus: The Citadel Press, 1979. Illustrated. 222pp.

*Thomson, David. WARREN BEATTY AND DESERT EYES: A LIFE AND A STORY. New York: Doubleday and Company, 1987. Illustrated. 399pp.

MEL BROOKS

*Adler, Bill, and Jeffrey Feinman. MEL BROOKS: THE IRREVERENT FUNNYMAN Chicago: Playboy Press, 1976. Illustrated. 190pp.

Born Melvin Kaminsky on June 28, 1926, the youngest of his Russian immigrant parents' four sons developed an iconoclastic sense of humor growing up in the Williamsburg section of Brooklyn. After serving as a combat engineer in World War II (1943-1945), he began a career as a standup comedian in New York's Borscht Belt. He moved to TV in 1950, working as a writer for Sid Caesar's YOUR SHOW OF SHOWS (1950-1954) and CAESAR'S HOUR (1955-1957). A three-year professional drought ended in 1960, when Brooks teamed with Carl Reiner to make a recording of their comedy routines about a 2,000 year old man with a Yiddish accent and an earthy view of life. In 1964, he won an Oscar for his cartoon short, THE CRITIC, and he married the actress Anne Bancroft. A year later, Brooks collaborated with Buck Henry on scripting the hit TV show, GET SMART. Determined not to get in a rut such as he experienced with Caesar, the ambitious comedian accepted an offer from Joseph E. Levine to produce Brooks's novel, SPRINGTIME FOR HITLER, released in 1968 as THE PRODUCERS. Following his screen debut as a writer, director, and actor, Brooks made seven films as a director and writer--THE TWELVE CHAIRS (1970), BLAZING SADDLES, YOUNG FRANKENSTEIN (both in 1974), SILENT MOVIE (1976), HIGH ANXIETY (1977), THE HISTORY OF THE WORLD, PART I (1981), and TO BE OR NOT TO BE (1983).

In this only book-length study of Brooks's career, Adler and Feinman provide a breezy and entertaining review of the comedian's childhood, his cavorting in the Catskills, his experiences on TV, and the reasons why he went into filmmaking. A good feel for Brooks's outrageous humor is conveyed by excerpts from his comic routines, and by cleverly reconstructed conversations. The problem is that nowhere do Adler and Feinman document their sources or offer evidence to support their assertions. In addition, no filmography, bibliography, or index is provided. Well worth browsing.

Holtzman, William. SEESAW: A DUAL BIOGRAPHY OF ANN BANCROFT AND MEL BROOKS. Garden City: Doubleday and Company, 1979. Illustrated. 300pp.

A good analysis on the lives and careers of the two stars, Holtzman offers a very entertaining but undocumented account of a couple who seem to share a lot of laughs. No bibliographies or filmographies are included, but an index is provided. Well worth browsing.

JOHN CASSAVETES

Carney, Raymond. AMERICAN DREAMING: THE FILMS OF JOHN CASSAVETES AND THE AMERICAN EXPERIENCE. Berkeley: University of California Press, 1985. Illustrated. 336pp.

One of the most distinguished actor-directors working in American films between the mid-1950s and the late 1980s, Cassavetes first made his reputation as a leader in alternative cinema. "The types of films we do are different," he once commented. "Commercial movies have no feeling, no sensitivity."[905]In the meantime, his acting credits in Hollywood films like THE DIRTY DOZEN (1967), ROSEMARY'S BABY (1968), WHOSE LIFE IS IT ANYWAY? (1981), and THE TEMPEST (1982) served to underwrite his independent projects. Interestingly, Cassavetes was only one of four actors ever to receive Oscar nominations in three different categories: Best Supporting Actor: THE DIRTY DOZEN (1967); Best Screenwriting: FACES (1968); and Best Director: A WOMAN UNDER THE INFLUENCE (1974). "But it was as a fiercely independent writer and director," as Albin Krebs comments, "who was deeply resentful of big studio interference in the making of his often quirky, mostly improvisational films that Mr. Cassavetes won his measure of fame."[906] His commitment to psychological dramas and brooding stories led some critics to label him "The American Bergman."

Cassavetes was born on December 9, 1929, in New York. He later claimed that his upper-middle class-childhood nurtured his fierce independent spirit as an AVANT-GARDE filmmaker. After getting an acting degree from the American Academy of Dramatic Arts in 1950, he began finding work as a bit player before landing a major role in the 1954 OMNIBUS TV production of Budd Schulberg's PASO DOBLE. Over the next few years, Cassavetes appeared on many of TV's most prestigious shows--e.g., PLAYHOUSE 90, KRAFT TELEVISION THEATER STUDIO ONE--and in a handful of movies--e.g., CRIME IN THE STREETS, EDGE OF THE CITY (both in 1957), and SADDLE THE WIND (1958). He also found time to teach method acting at Burton Lane's Dramatic Workshop in Manhattan. By the late 1950s, he had made up his mind that working in commercial films and TV was not as important to him as writing, directing, and controlling his own films. Before his death on February 3, 1989, Cassavetes made eleven such films: SHADOWS (1960), TOO LATE THE BLUES (1961), FACES (1968), HUSBANDS (1970), MINNIE AND MOSKOWITZ (1971), A WOMAN UNDER THE INFLUENCE (1975), THE KILLING OF A CHINESE BOOKIE (1978), OPENING NIGHT (1978), GLORIA (1980), LOVE STREAMS (1984), and BIG TROUBLE (1986).

Carney's pioneering study, the only in-depth examination of Cassavetes's career, is in the best tradition of the publisher's many splendid film biographies. The author argues persuasively that his subject is one of the most original and imaginative artists working today, this despite the fact that his independent movies remain some of the most ignored and underrated films of the last twenty-five years. Carney sees Cassavetes's films as "inquiries into the trajectory of the American Dream in the local and inevitably hostile environments in which it is forced to express itself in America. They are explorations of the challenges and burdens of the essential American imaginative situation." The author's rich comparisons between the films and the traditional arts serve as underlying themes in the book's eleven stimulating chapters. In addition to providing a wealth of information, fresh insights, and fascinating analyses, Carney makes a strong case for a revival of interest in the work of Cassavetes. Endnotes, a filmography, and an included. Recommended for special collections.

*Cassavetes, John. FACES. Ed., Al Ruban. New York: Signet Books, 1970. Illustrated. 319pp.

---

[905]   Cited in "Actor, Director Cassavetes Dies from Cirrhosis of Liver," BURLINGTON FREE PRESS A (February 4, 1989):4.

[906]   Albin Krebs, "John Cassavetes, Major Director in U. S. Cinema Verite, Dies at 59," NEW YORK TIMES A (February 4, 1989):32. See also Myron Meisel, "Master of Poetic Confusion: John Cassavetes," AMERICAN FILM 14:7 (May 1989):40-3, 56, 58.

In Cassavetes's important introduction to his published script, he describes the events that led to the making of FACES at the end of 1965. The work that had been conceived as a play was transformed into a film "that would allow actors the time and the room to act." Six months later the movie was completed and the final print released in 1968. Al Ruban, who directed the film's photography, does a good editing job of setting the original script alongside the final shooting script to demonstrate what changes were made as the project progressed. Well worth browsing.

ROGER CORMAN

*Di Franco, J. Philip. THE MOVIE WORLD OF ROGER CORMAN. New York: Chelsea House, 1980. Illustrated. 269pp.

Born in Detroit on April 26, 1926, the man some consider to be "the Orson Welles of Z films"[907] was the older of Ann and William Corman's two sons. His father moved the family to Beverly Hills when the future director-producer was a teenager. Although he soon developed a strong love for movies, Corman first graduated from Stanford University with an engineering degree and then served a three-year stint in the Navy before seriously pursuing a career in films. Working his way up from a messenger to a screenwriter, he eventually became an associate producer on Allied Artists's HIGHWAY DRAGNET (1953), a film scripted by Corman. Using his salary from HIGHWAY DRAGNET, the bold Hollywood entrepreneur launched his famous career as a low-budget movie producer. By the mid-1950s he had released his first film, MONSTER FROM THE OCEAN FLOOR (1954), a project completed in less than a week at a cost of $12,000; and had gone into partnership with Sam Arkoff and Jim Nicholson to form the memorable B-production company American International Pictures (AIP). Between 1955 and 1980 (the year that Filmways Pictures bought the company), AIP turned out dozens of sensational screen adaptations of Edgar Allan Poe's works--e.g., THE HOUSE OF USHER (1960), THE PIT AND THE PENDULUM (1961), THE RAVEN (1963), THE MASK OF THE RED DEATH, THE TOMB OF LIGEIA (both in 1964); science fiction fantasies--e.g., THE DAY THE WORLD ENDED (1955), WAR OF THE SATELLITES (1957), THE LITTLE SHOP OF HORRORS, THE LAST WOMAN ON EARTH (both in 1960), THE MAN WITH X-RAY EYES (1963); gangster movies--e.g., MACHINE GUN KELLY (1968), THE ST. VALENTINE'S DAY MASSACRE (1966), BLOODY MAMA (1969); and violent "bike" films--e.g., THE YOUNG RACERS (1962), THE WILD ANGELS (1966), and THE TRIP (1967). Alternating between producing and directing, Corman's improvisational style stressed interesting locations, fresh talent, minimal budgets, and lots of action. Although critics and intellectuals looked down on Corman's quickie exploitation films aimed at the youth market, the films not only did well at the box office, but also served as a training ground for some of Hollywood's most successful artists: e.g., Peter Bogdanovich, Ellen Burstyn, Francis Ford Coppola, Jonathan Demme, Bruce Dern, Robert De Niro, Irvin Kershner, Jack Nicholson, Robert Towne, and Martin Scorsese. By the end of the 1960s, Corman began taking himself more seriously. In 1970, he left AIP to form the powerful and influential distribution and production company, New World Pictures.

Somewhat reminiscent of Corman's high camp, low-budget productions, this profusely illustrated "scrapbook" of the producer-director's work is more fun to look at than to read. Following a brief interview with Corman and some of his "alumni," Di Franco divides his material into several broad sections on Corman's monster movies, his fascination with Poe adaptations, and his cinematic philosophy. The more one knows about the subject, the more enjoyable the experience. A flimsy filmography is included, but no bibliography or index is provided. Worth browsing.

---

[907] Peter John Dyer, "Z Films," SIGHT AND SOUND 33:4 (Autumn 1964):179-81.

McGee, Mark. ROGER CORMAN: THE BEST OF THE CHEAP ACTS.   Jefferson: McFarland, 1988. Illustrated. 261pp.

Naha, Ed. THE FILMS OF ROGER CORMAN: BRILLIANCE ON A BUDGET. New York: Arco Publishing, 1982. Illustrated. 209pp.
     The best and most reliable source of information on the maverick producer and director, this fast-moving and entertaining survey is divided into eleven chapters tracing his rise from a high school film buff to one of the most important producers and distributors of the new Hollywood. Naha covers a lot of ground in rapid-fire prose, but does a good job of introducing the major points about Corman's career and work.   In addition to supplying key credit details and summarizing critical reactions to Corman's prodigious output, the author supplies a range of opinions about Corman's contributions to film history. Two filmographies and an index are included. Well worth browsing.

JANE FONDA

Brough, James. THE FABULOUS FONDAS. New York: David McKay Company, 1973. Illustrated. 296pp.

Carroll, Peter N. FAMOUS IN AMERICA: THE PASSION TO SUCCEED--JANE FONDA, GEORGE WALLACE, PHYLLIS SCHLAFLY, JOHN GLENN. New York: Dutton, 1985. Illustrated. 340pp.

Freedland, Michael. JANE FONDA: A BIOGRAPHY. New York: St. Martin's Press, 1988. Illustrated. 247pp.

*Haddad-Garcia, George. THE FILMS OF JANE FONDA. Secaucus: The Citadel Press, 1981. Illustrated. 256pp.

*Herman, Gary, and David Downing. JANE FONDA: ALL AMERICAN ANTI-HEROINE. New York: Quick Fox, 1980. Illustrated. 144pp.

Kiernan, Thomas. JANE: AN INTIMATE BIOGRAPHY OF JANE FONDA. New York: G. P. Putnam's Sons, 1973. Illustrated. 358pp.

Kiernan, Thomas. JANE FONDA: HEROINE FOR OUR TIME. New York: Delilah Communications, 1982. Illustrated. 320pp.

Spada, James. FONDA: HER LIFE IN PICTURES. Garden City: Doubleday and Company, 1985. Illustrated. 229pp.

*Vadim, Roger. BARDOT DENEUVE FONDA. Trans. Melinda Camber Porter. New York: Simon and Schuster, 1986. Illustrated. 328pp.

PETER FONDA

*Hardin, Nancy, and Marilyn Schlossberg, eds. EASY RIDER: ORIGINAL SCREENPLAY BY PETER FONDA, DENNIS HOPPER, TERRY SOUTHERN. PLUS STILLS, INTERVIEWS AND ARTICLES. New York: Signet Books, 1969. Illustrated. 191pp.

Hollywood's most successful low-budget film, made for less than $376,000 and grossing more than sixty million dollars, remains one of the most controversial films in American film history. This modest publication remains one of the best resources for examining why it became so influential in the late sixties, how it was misunderstood at the time of its release, and the reactions of its creators to the public furor over the film's message. In addition to the script, there is a handful of articles and interviews by and about Peter Fonda, Dennis Hopper, and Jack Nicholson. Regrettably, no bibliography or index is included. Recommended for special collections.

JOHN FRANKENHEIMER

*Pratley, Gerald. THE CINEMA OF JOHN FRANKENHEIMER. New York: A. S. Barnes and Company, 1970. Illustrated. 240pp.

Born in Malba, New York, on February 19, 1930, the man once considered the WUNDERKIND of live television in the 1950s and of commercial filmmaking in the early sixties was brought up in an affluent Manhattan environment. After receiving a high school military education, Frankenheimer, in 1947, tried his hand at acting but met with little encouragement. He then went to Williams College, receiving his Bachelor of Arts degree in 1950. At that point, he was drafted into the U. S. Air Force and served for two years. Following his discharge in 1953, he eventually became an assistant director for CBS in New York, working his way up the TV ladder on THE GARRY MOORE SHOW, LAMP UNTO MY FEET, DANGER, PERSON TO PERSON, and YOU ARE THERE. In 1954, when Sidney Lumet, the director of the Edward R. Murrow hit show, left TV to go into films, Frankenheimer took over the directing chores of PERSON TO PERSON. He soon moved to Hollywood to do his live TV adaptations of the classic works by Hemingway, Faulkner, and Steinbeck for PLAYHOUSE 90. As a result of a 1955 program for the TV series CLIMAX, the twenty-six-year-old Frankenheimer made his directorial film debut with THE YOUNG STRANGERS (1957), an experience so disturbing to him in terms of working with his middle-aged unionized technicians that he refused to direct another film for several years. In the meantime, he continued to perfect his skills doing live TV shows for PLAYHOUSE 90. When live television ended in 1960, however, he turned his attention to commercial filmmaking and directed THE YOUNG SAVAGES. It was followed by such noteworthy productions as THE MANCHURIAN CANDIDATE, ALL FALL DOWN, BIRDMAN OF ALCATRAZ (all in 1962), and SEVEN DAYS IN MAY (1963). The box-office success of these projects enabled him to form John Frankenheimer Productions in 1963. But the changing times forced him to turn away from his personal visions and move toward more spectacular action thrillers. The results not only met with spotty box-office returns, but also received mixed critical reactions: e.g., THE TRAIN (1964), GRAND PRIX, SECONDS (both in 1966), THE FIXER (1968), THE EXTRAORDINARY SEAMAN, THE GYPSY MOTHS (both in 1969), I WALK THE LINE, THE HORSEMAN (both in 1970), IMPOSSIBLE OBJECT/L'IMPOSSIBLE OJECT, THE ICEMAN COMETH (both in 1973), 99 44/100% (1974), THE FRENCH CONNECTION II (1975), BLACK SUNDAY (1976), PROPHECY (1979), THE CHALLENGE (1982), THE HOLCROFT COVENANT (1985), and 52 PICK-UP (1986).

Pratley's important study illustrates Frankenheimer's eclipse starting in the mid-1960s. The only comprehensive examination of the once highly regarded director ends with Frankenheimer's production of THE GYPSY MOTHS. The book's opening chapter talks about its subject's becoming "probably the most important director at work in the American cinema today [1969]" and then goes on to discuss his work in television and film in nineteen appreciative and informative chapters. The most interesting information deals with the writer-producer-director's techniques, and is buttressed by many valuable observations by the artist himself. Unfortunately, neither the author nor the academic community has seen fit to update this pioneering examination. Still further, the book includes no bibliography or index. Well worth browsing.

CHARLTON HESTON

*Druxman, Michael. CHARLTON HESTON. New York: Pyramid Publications, 1976. Illustrated. 159pp.

Heston, Charlton. THE ACTOR'S LIFE: JOURNALS 1956-1976. Ed. Hollis Alpert. New York: E. P. Dutton, 1978. Illustrated. 482pp.

Rovin, Jeff. THE FILMS OF CHARLTON HESTON. Secaucus: The Citadel Press, 1977. Illustrated. 224pp.

*Williams, John. THE FILMS OF CHARLTON HESTON. London: Barnden Castell Williams, 1974. Illustrated. 47pp.

GEORGE ROY HILL

Horton, Andrew. THE FILMS OF GEORGE ROY HILL. New York: Columbia University Press, 1984. Illustrated. 203pp.
      Director of two of the most popular films in movie history, BUTCH CASSIDY AND THE SUNDANCE KID (1969) and THE STING (1973), George Roy Hill was born in Minneapolis on December 20, 1922. He remains one of the few directors who did not make his mark in movies until he was forty years of age. His childhood was spent developing a love for music. After graduating as a music major from Yale University in 1943, he served three years in the Marine Corps as a pilot in the South Pacific during World War II (1943-1945). Following his discharge from the service, he returned to his musical interests by enrolling at Trinity College in Dublin in 1946. It was during this two-and-a-half year period that he decided to pursue a career on the stage. Graduating with a B. Litt. Degree in 1949, Hill returned to America and began acting in earnest, mostly in off-Broadway shows. Before he could gain a strong foothold in the theater, the military recalled him to active duty during the Korean War in 1951. Eighteen months later, Hill was back in New York, only now writing and directing live dramas first for KRAFT TELEVISION THEATER and then PLAYHOUSE 90. He made his directorial stage debut with LOOK HOMEWARD ANGEL in 1957. Five years later, Hill directed his first film, PERIOD OF ADJUSTMENT (1962), an adaptation of the Tennessee Williams's play he had directed on Broadway. In addition to the aforementioned films, his screen credits include TOYS IN THE ATTIC (1963), THE WORLD OF HENRY ORIENT (1964), HAWAII (1966), THOROUGHLY MODERN MILLIE (1967), SLAUGHTERHOUSE FIVE (1972), THE GREAT WALDO PEPPER (1975), SLAPSHOT (1977), A LITTLE ROMANCE (1979), THE WORLD ACCORDING TO GARP (1982), THE LITTLE DRUMMER GIRL (1984), and FUNNY FARM (1988). He received the Oscar for Best Director for THE STING.
      Working on the notion that Hill's films, "directed with a flair for style, are tied to important American themes . . . [that] reflect an ironic, bittersweet vision of life," Horton sets out to defend Hill's films against critics who find his movies "stylish but empty," and the director a man who "rushes from genre to genre for no apparent reason." Horton's pioneering comprehensive study benefits from the

cooperation he received from Hill during the three years devoted to the project, thereby providing us with abundant inside information about people and projects. Too brief to be definitive, the eleven informative and entertaining chapters do a nice job of summarizing the filmmaker's intentions and the critical reactions to them. Endnotes, a filmography, and an index are included. Well worth browsing.

Shores, Edward. GEORGE ROY HILL. Boston: Twayne Publishers, 1983. Illustrated. 163pp.

Narrower in scope than Horton's work, this AUTEURIST study, claims Warren French, created more discussion than any other project in the series, mainly because the company's consultants distrusted Hill's work, dismissing it "as slick commercial productions with little depth . . . ." Shore, however, makes a strong case for his subject, mainly because he skims over Hill's first five films on the grounds that the director didn't have much control over them and instead concentrates on the works from BUTCH CASSIDY AND THE SUNDANCE KID (1969), to A LITTLE ROMANCE (1979). In his concluding chapter, Shore argues that taken collectively, Hill's output amounts to "a loosely structured critique of American social customs that is greater than the sum of its parts." The author's theory is that Hill is challenging people to think more critically about their social beliefs, or else accept the idea that their misperceptions are contributing to America's decline and decay. Even if one questions the strength of the director's philosphical shadings, one comes away respecting Shore's enthusiasm for Hill's technical skill and character development. In addition to a valuable interview with Hill, the book contains a chronology, endnotes, a bibliogaphy, a filmography, and an index. Well worth browsing.

ALFRED HITCHCOCK

*Anobile, Richard J., ed. ALFRED HITCHCOCK'S "PSYCHO." New York: Darian House, 1974. Illustrated. 256pp.

The first in a series of film reconstructions, this book offers an interesting attempt to analyze the secrets of the master of suspense. The version Anobile provides contains a number of shots omitted from the released print. One of the best reasons for examining this useful publication is the illustration of Hitchcock's most shocking and famous montage sequence in which the director uses more than seventy camera setups to depict Anthony Perkins brutally murdering Janet Leigh in a motel shower. While many psychological and feminist critics attack the scene as a culmination of the director's perverted feelings toward women, other observers point out the importance of studying the relationship among the storyboard designs prepared by the title designer Saul Bass, the visual touches added by Hitchcock, and the editing by George Tomasini. Anobile's more than 1,400 frame blow-ups also recall Hitchcock's use of Gothic elements and "doubling" characterizations and events to unify the visual and plot development organically. Especially useful is the chance to study Hitchcock's use of mirrors and bird imagery. Well worth browsing.

*Lehman, Ernest, ed. NORTH BY NORTHWEST. New York: The Viking Press, 1972. Illustrated. 148pp.

Considered by Hitchcock scholars to contain one of the director's most brilliant cinematic chases, as well as a textbook on his use of the "double" motif, NORTH BY NORTHWEST (1959) is also an example of the important contributions of the screenwriter Ernest Lehman to the famous film. Lehman's reputation had been established in the mid-1950s, with scripts LIKE EXECUTIVE SUITE, SABRINA (both in 1954), THE KING AND I, SOMEBODY UP THERE LIKES ME (both in 1956), and SWEET SMELL OF SUCCESS (1957). NORTH BY NORTHWEST was the first of his two collaborations with Hitchcock (the other was the 1976, film FAMILY PLOT). This useful publication contains the original script, including bracketed material that never made it to the theaters. Well worth browsing.

Naremore, James. FILMGUIDE TO "PSYCHO." Bloomington: Indiana University Press, 1973. 87pp.

"PSYCHO," Naremore reminds us, "cost no more than eight hundred thousand dollars to make, and as of 1967 it had grossed fifteen million dollars. It was, however, 'out of the ordinary.' It had no major stars in its cast, it was shot in black-and-white, and it told an extremely desolate story with no appealing characterizations. On the other hand, it offered the public a good scare, and it titillated them with sex and violence." Naremore goes on to describe Hitchcock's speed in shooting the low-budget horror film, the contributions of cinematographer John L. Russell (who received an Oscar nomination), the title designer Saul Bass, the music director Bernard Herrmann, and the screenwriter Joseph Stefano, pointing out that the major credit belongs to Hitchcock's vision and orchestration of their work. Interestingly, Naremore ignores the contributions of Joseph Hurley and Robert Clatworthy, both nominated for Oscars for Best Art Direction-Set Direction. The best sections deal with Naremore's analysis of sound and silence in the film, the relationships between PSYCHO and earlier Hitchcock films, and the use of contrasting plots, characters, and imagery to manipulate the audience's sensibilities. Particularly useful for modern audiences is a comparison between this straightforward commentary and later feminist and psychological critiques that go far more deeply into Hitchcock's conventions and characterizations. In addition to cast and technical credits, analysis, a plot outline, a filmography, and a bibliography, the informative work includes an intriguing summary of critical reactions to the film. Regrettably, there is no index. Well worth browsing.

DUSTIN HOFFMAN

Brode, Douglas. THE FILMS OF DUSTIN HOFFMAN. Secaucus: The Citadel Press, 1983. Illustrated. 224pp.

DENNIS HOPPER

Rodriguez, Elena. DENNIS HOPPER: A MADNESS TO HIS METHOD. New York: St. Martin's Press, 1988. Illustrated. 198pp.

STANLEY KUBRICK

*Agel, Jerome, ed. THE MAKING OF KUBRICK'S "2001." New York: New American Library, 1970. Illustrated. 368pp.

The book by which to begin any serious examination of Kubrick's brilliant film, this in-depth study has something for everyone: behind-the-scenes information on the production, Arthur C. Clarke's short story, "The Sentinel," which was the source for the multi-million dollar film, contemporary film reviews, interviews with key personnel, a reprint of Kubrick's 1968 PLAYBOY interview, analyses of the film, excellent stills, technical information, and complete screen credits. Although the resourceful editor offers no comments throughout the work, he sprinkles the anthology with dozens of outstanding quotations from Kubrick, Clarke, and other noteworthy contributors to the film. For example, the book opens with Clarke's explanation that "2001: A SPACE ODYSSEY is about man's past and future life in space. It's about concern with man's hierarchy in the universe, which is probably pretty low. It's about the reactions of humanity to the discovery of higher intelligence in the universe. We set out with the deliberate intention of creating a myth. The Odyssean parallel was in our minds from the beginning, long before the film's title was chosen." Agel follows that statement with one from Kubrick: "I don't like to talk about 2001 much because it's essentially a nonverbal experience. Less than half the film has dialogue. It attempts to communicate more to the subconscious and to the feelings than it does to the intellect. I think clearly that there's a basic problem with people not paying attention with their eyes. They're listening. And they don't get much from listening to this film. Those who won't believe their eyes won't be able to appreciate this film." The book's two notable omissions are an index and bibliography. Highly recommended for special collections.[908]

*Anon. STANLEY KUBRICK'S CLOCKWORK ORANGE: BASED ON THE NOVEL BY ANTHONY BURGESS. New York: Ballantine Books, 1972. Illustrated. No pagination.
    A frame enlargement continuity of the 1971 film, this publication illustrates the strengths and weaknesses of such an undertaking. The pictures suggest important ideas and recall memorable moments, but the overall experience is disappointing. Worth browsing.

Ciment, Michel. KUBRICK. Trans. Gilbert Adair. New York: Holt, Rinehart and Winston, 1982. Illustrated. 239pp.
    Born in the Bronx, New York City, on July 26, 1928, America's penultimate AUTEUR grew up loving physics, chess, movies, books, and photography. Of particular significance were Kubrick's ties to LOOK magazine, developed during his high school years. After a few months of college, he quit school to work at LOOK as an apprentice photographer in 1946. Kubrick made the transition to films gradually, first by studying Pudovkin's theories and by attending workshops on motion picture technique at the Museum of Modern Art, and then by making short documentary films. In 1950, he produced, wrote, directed, and photographed DAY OF THE FIGHT, which caught the interest of RKO. Over the next few years, sponsored in part by RKO and United Artists, Kubrick made two more documentaries before teaming up with James B. Harris, an independent producer, to form their film company, Harris-Kubrick Productions, in 1955. Their first venture was THE KILLING (1956), followed by PATHS OF GLORY (1958). Now recognized as a "marketable director," Kubrick was asked by his new found friend Kirk Douglas, one of the stars of PATHS OF GLORY, to take over the direction (Anthony Mann quit shortly after beginning the assignment) of Douglas's next film SPARTACUS (1959). Although Kubrick later disassociated himself from the movie, the experience convinced him that his future projects should be completely under his control. Back with Harris-Kubrick Productions, he made LOLITA (1962) in England. Following its release, Kubrick and Harris dissolved their company, and the filmmaker decided to make his home in England and produce his films there. His first solo effort was DR. STRANGELOVE: OR HOW I LEARNED TO STOP WORRYING AND LOVE THE BOMB (1964). Working methodically, Kubrick made only five more films over the next twenty-four years: 2001: A SPACE ODYSSEY (1968), A CLOCKWORK ORANGE (1971), BARRY LYNDON (1975), THE SHINING (1980), and FULL METAL JACKET (1987).
    Cimet's splendid photographic album, filled with stimulating observations on Kubrick's themes and techniques, is divided into seven major sections: Kubrick's films up to THE SHINING, a biographical review, his directing characteristics, reflections on his work habits, his fascination with fantasy films, interviews with Kubrick, and interviews with his colleagues. The comments are intelligent, the interviews informative. "The illustrations (often frame enlargements rather than a set photographer's stills, as was Kubrick's request for his later work)," the author states, "will not only conjure up a shot or lighting effect, a composition or a gesture, but provide a crucial commentary through unexpected analogies or internal rhymes. And the text itself both influenced and was influenced by the choice of photographs."

---

[908] See also Don Daniels, "A Skeleton Key to 2001," SIGHT AND SOUND 40:1 (Winter 1970-71):28-33.

A bibliography and filmography are included, but no index is provided. Recommended for special collections.

Coyle, Wallace. STANLEY KUBRICK: A GUIDE TO REFERENCES AND SOURCES. Boston: G. K. Hall, 1980. 160pp.

The best introduction to Kubrick's work and critical reception, this objective and thoughtful resource guide provides information on every aspect of the controversial director's work: a biographical profile, a critical survey of his films up to THE SHINING (1980), film credits and synopses, writings about and by Kubrick and other film-related activity, archival sources, film distributors, literary works that Kubrick has adapted for the screen, an author index, and a film title index. Coyle's in-depth work synthesizes all of the major perspectives and material available up to the start of the 1980s. In researching his subject, Coyle concludes that Kubrick is very much a self-made artist who taught himself the basics of the filmmaking process. Particularly impressive about the author's style is an ability to inform without narrowing the breadth of possibilities in interpreting Kubrick's genius. Thus we understand why many critics see Kubrick as preoccupied with the alienation of the individual in a technological and dehumanized society, but we also recognize the danger in assuming that such surface observations tell us anything definitive about the artist or his creations. Recommended for special collections.

*Devries, Daniel. THE FILMS OF STANLEY KUBRICK. Grand Rapids: William B. Eerdmans, 1973. 75pp.

More of a quick overview than an in-depth study, this slight book provides a chronological survey of Kubrick's career from FEAR AND DESIRE (1953) to A CLOCKWORK ORANGE (1971). Devries argues that the filmmaker began as a "true screen poet," using his rare talents to communicate visual images that are also the themes of his films--e.g., "man as a loser " and the existence of "a malevolent force" in the universe. But after the appearance of DR. STRANGELOVE, Devries faults Kubrick for becoming too fascinated with technology, rather than with examining humanity.   That is, the artist in creating a personal world on screen forgoes "touch-points between his world and ours" for the freedom "to move at will." The six chapters on films from THE KILLING (1956) to A CLOCKWORK ORANGE (1971) illustrate the author's debatable thesis that Kubrick must rid himself of ".   .   . bad habits [i.e., an inflated opinion of his talents] if he is to make more films that live up to the genius shown in PATHS OF GLORY, DR. STRANGELOVE, and 2001." A bibliography and filmography are included, but no index is provided. Worth browsing.

Kagan, Norman. THE CINEMA OF STANLEY KUBRICK. New York: Holt, Rinehart and Winston, 1972. Illustrated. 204pp.

This academic study of Kubrick's work takes us from his first commercial film, FEAR AND DESIRE (1953), to A CLOCKWORK ORANGE (1971). In eleven stimulating chapters, Kagan provides useful information on Kubrick's working principles, thematic concerns, and production problems, as well as critical reactions to the movies themselves. "This book," Kagan explains, "is based on the auteur theory, which assumes that a film director has the same freedom and control in shaping his creations as do writers, painters, and other artists." Consequently, each of the director's films "gets a very visual dramatized brief treatment, along with story lines, music used, and sound effects, compacted into fifteen or twenty pages." In addition to Kagan's critical analyses, the book also includes a bibliography and filmography. Regrettably, no index is provided. Well worth browsing.

Geduld, Carolyn. FILMGUIDE TO "2001: A SPACE ODYSSEY." Bloomington: Indiana University Press, 1973. 87pp.

A good provocative introduction to the major themes and techniques in this extraordinary film, Geduld asserts that in 2001: A SPACE ODYSSEY, Kubrick renews the whole issue of the essential nature of man in a more exhaustive way [than in his previous works]. He asks historical questions about the separation of feeling and intelligence. How did one come to dominate the other, and where did the other one go'? . . . The basic conflict in the film is between ideas that are philosophical and ideas that are unconscious, as Kubrick believes mythology must be." Whether one agrees with Geduld's perspective is secondary to the handy and succinct material provided in this useful publication: e.g., screen credits, an outline of the film, a biography of the director, a production calendar, an extended analysis, a summary critique, a filmography, and a bibliography. Regrettably, no index is included. Well worth browsing.

Nelson, Thomas Allen. KUBRICK: INSIDE A FILM ARTIST'S MAZE. Bloomington: Indiana University, 1982. Illustrated. 268pp.

The best in-depth study of Kubrick's career, this illuminating and invaluable publication offers a challenging interpretation not only of the artist's work, but also of its critics. Nelson begins by enumerating how almost no one disputes Kubrick's technical genius, but even very few of his admirers know how to deal with his overall work. He points out that the standard approach is to classify Kubrick's films artificially into five spurious categories: "(1) The NOIR Films (KILLER'S KISS, THE KILLING); (2) The Historical/Philosophical Films (PATHS OF GLORY, BARRY LYNDON); (3) The Speculative/Science Fiction Films (FEAR AND DESIRE, 2001); (4) The Contemporary Satiric Films (DR. STRANGELOVE, A CLOCKWORK ORANGE); and (5) The Psychological Films (LOLITA, THE SHINING)." Nelson argues that this generic straightjacket" highlights the complexity of Kubrick's thematic output but little else. He therefore offers a new perspective, one based on relating Pudovkin's aesthetics--e.g., film as a cinematic rather than a photographic art--to Kubrick's application of these theories in his films. That is not to say that the two artists share a common attitude toward montage and certain historical assumptions. They don't. It is to say that Kubrick and Pudovkin share similar working principles: e.g., a passion for an exactness of temporal and spatial directorial construction." Nelson's eight refreshing chapters analyze how Kubrick explored a range of possibilities in changing cinematic form into cinematic meanings. Although Nelson's theoretical discussions are not for neophytes, they should be considered by every serious Kubrick student. Endnotes, a bibliography, and an index are included. Recommended for special collections.

Phillips, Gene D. STANLEY KUBRICK: A FILM ODYSSEY. New York: Popular Library, 1975. Illustrated. 189pp.

An informative and thoughtful analysis of Kubrick's work derived from the author's earlier observations in FILM COMMENT and THE MOVIE MAKERS: ARTISTS IN AN INDUSTRY, this book provides a fast-moving introduction to the director's progress from his years in Hollywood, to his career in England. Phillips divides his study into four major sections, offering not only his critical reactions, but also comments by Kubrick (obtained through a private interview and considerable correspondence). The eight separate chapters on the films from THE KILLING (1956) to the then-uncompleted BARRY LYNDON (1975) are filled with beautifully reproduced stills and candid shots. A filmography and bibliography are provided, but no index is included. Well worth browsing.

Walker, Alexander. STANLEY KUBRICK DIRECTS. New York: Harcourt, Brace, Jovanovich, Inc. 1971. Illustrated. 272pp.

Based upon extended interviews, the book offers a superb visual and printe discussion of the filmmaker's feelings about PATHS OF GLORY (1958), SPARTACL (1960), LOLITA (1962), DR. STRANGELOVE OR: HOW I LEARNED TO STC WORRYING AND LOVE THE BOMB (1964), 2001: A SPACE ODYSSEY (1968), and CLOCKWORK ORANGE (1971). Although the material focuses primarily on the last filr it provides a valuable insight into Kubrick's career and talents. A filmography included, but no bibliography or index is provided. Recommended for speci collections.

RICHARD LEITERMAN

*Reid, Alison, and P. M. Evanchuck. RICHARD LEITERMAN. Ottawa: The Canadir Film Institute, 1978. Illustrated. 120pp.

JACK LEMMON

Baltake, Joe. THE FILMS OF JACK LEMMON. Secaucus: The Citadel Press, 197" Illustrated. 255pp.

Freedland, Michael. JACK LEMMON. New York: St. Martin's Press, 1985. Illustratec 178pp.

*Holtzman, Will. JACK LEMMON. New York: Pyramid Publications, 1977. Illustratec 160pp.

Widener, Don. LEMMON: A BIOGRAPHY. New York: Macmillan Publishing Compan 1975. Illustrated. 247pp.

SIDNEY LUMET

Bowles, Stephen. SIDNEY LUMET: A GUIDE TO REFERENCES AND RESOURCE! Boston: G. K. Hall and Company, 1979. 151pp.
    Born in Philadelphia on June 25, 1924, to the Jewish actor-writer-direct Baruch Lumet and his wife Eugenia, Sidney Lumet moved with his family to New York Lower East Side when he was two years old. At five, he made his stage debut wit his father in Yiddish theater and has been acting or directing ever since. H Broadway debut came at the age of eleven in Sidney Kingsley's DEAD END (1935, After spending five years (1942-1946) in the Signal Corps during World War II, I formed an off-Broadway company and taught acting before turning his attention ' TV in 1950. Starting as an assistant director for CBS shows, he soon became one TV's best directors of live programming for series like YOU ARE THERE, ALCC HOUR, OMNIBUS, KRAFT TELEVISION THEATER, STUDIO ONE, and PLAYHOUS 90. Many of the actors he hired for these live dramas--e.g., Paul Newman, Jam Mason, Ed Asner, and Jack Warden--later starred in his movies. In 1955, Lumet ma his directorial stage debut with an off-Broadway revival of Shaw's THE DOCTOR DILEMMA. About this time, the screenwriter Reginald Rose, who had worked wit Lumet on TV, decided to adapt the writer's TV drama TWELVE ANGRY MEN to tl screen and asked his friend to direct the movie. Following Lumet's directorial fil debut with the acclaimed film in 1957, he became a prolific filmmaker with an unev but overall impressive string of productions dealing with social themes and issue Among his most important works are THE FUGITIVE KIND (1960), A VIEW FROM TH BRIDGE (1961), LONG DAY'S JOURNEY INTO NIGHT (1962), FAIL-SAFE (1964), TH

PAWNBROKER (1965), THE SEA GULL (1968), SERPICO (1974), MURDER ON THE ORIENT EXPRESS (1974), DOG DAY AFTERNOON (1975), NETWORK (1976), EQUUS (1977), PRINCE OF THE CITY (1981), THE VERDICT (1982), DANIEL (1983), and RUNNING ON EMPTY (1988). Although the the tough-minded, socially conscious director has been nominated for five Academy Awards, four for Best Director (1957, 1975, 1976, 1982) and one for Best Screenplay (1981), he has never won an Oscar. Collectively, his films have earned more than forty Oscar nominations.

Bowles's pioneering study of this academically ignored artist is a welcome addition not only because it is the only full-length examination of Lumet's work, but also because it provides useful insights into his social concerns and themes. The standard features of G. K. Hall's significant series--biographical background, critical survey of the director's work, synopses and credits of the films (from TWELVE ANGRY MEN to EQUUS), annotated guide to writings about Lumet, lists of his performances, writings and other related activities, reviews and references, and distributers of Lumet's films--are well-handled and effectively presented. One comes away with a good understanding of the director's personality, the range of careers he has had, and why he feels that movies are "the last and only medium in which it is possible to tell a story of conscience, outside the printed word. A title index and a film index are included. Recommended for special collections.

STEVE MCQUEEN

*Campbell, Joanna. THE FILMS OF STEVE MCQUEEN. London: Barnden Castell Williams, 1973. Illustrated. 47pp.

*McCoy, Malachy. STEVE MCQUEEN: THE UNAUTHORIZED BIOGRAPHY. New York: Signet, 1974. Illustrated. 222pp.

*Nolan, William. STEVE MCQUEEN: STAR ON WHEELS. New York: Medallion Books, 1972. Illustrated. 143pp.

Spiegel, Penina. MCQUEEN: THE UNTOLD STORY OF A BAD BOY IN HOLLYWOOD. Garden City: Doubleday and Company, 1986. Illustrated. 367pp.

*Toffel, Neile McQueen. MY HUSBAND, MY FRIEND. New York: Atheneum, 1986. Illustrated. 327pp.

PATRICIA NEAL

*Burrows, Michael. PATRICIA NEAL AND MARGARET SULLAVAN. London: Primestyle, 1971. Illustrated. 42pp.

Farrell, Barry. PAT AND ROALD. New York: Random House, 1969. Illustrated. 241pp.

Neal, Patricia, and Richard DeNeut. AS I AM: AN AUTOBIOGRAPHY. New York: Simon and Schuster, 1988. Illustrated. 384pp.

PAUL NEWMAN

Godfrey, Lionel. PAUL NEWMAN, SUPERSTAR: A CRITICAL BIOGRAPHY. New York: St. Martin's Press, 1978. Illustrated. 208pp.

Hamblett, Charles. PAUL NEWMAN. Chicago: Henry Regnery, 1975.   Illustrated. 232pp.

*Kerbel, Michael. PAUL NEWMAN. New York: Pyramid Publications, 1974. Illustrated. 158pp.

Quirk, Lawrence J. THE FILMS OF PAUL NEWMAN. Secaucus: The Citadel Press, 1971. Illustrated. 224pp.

*Thompson, Kenneth. THE FILMS OF PAUL NEWMAN. London: Barnden Castell Williams, 1973. Illustrated. 47pp.

MIKE NICHOLS

Schuth, H. Wayne. MIKE NICHOLS. Boston: Twayne Publishers, 1978.   Illustrated. 177pp.

Born Michael Igor Peschkowsky to Jewish parents in Berlin on November 6, 1931, Mike Nichols moved to America with his family in 1939 to escape Nazi persecution. Five years later he was naturalized. Although he considered becoming a physician like his father, Nichols dropped out of medical school to study acting with Lee Strasberg. In part, the decision was encouraged by Elaine May, an aspiring actress he met in 1954.   Together they helped form the Chicago-based improvisational acting company named The Compass Players, which later became The Second City company, that included young performers like Akan Arkin, Shelley Berman, Barbara Harris, and Zohra Lampert. By 1957, Nichols and May had become a sensational comedy team that gained instant fame following a a guest shot on "The Jack Paar Show." Over the next three years, their comedic reputations grew as a result of TV appearances, nightclub performances, and gold records. After a brilliant run on Broadway in AN EVENING WITH   MIKE NICHOLS AND ELAINE MAY, during the 1960-61 season, the couple decided to pursue separate careers. Nichols's directorial stage debut with Neil Simon's BAREFOOT IN THE PARK in 1963 earned the director his first Tony Award. Among other Tony-award shows he has staged are LUV (1964), THE ODD COUPLE (1965), PLAZA SUITE (1968), THE PRISONER OF SECOND AVENUE (1971), ANNIE (1977), and THE REAL THING (1984). The versatile Nichols made his directorial film debut with WHO'S AFRAID OF VIRGINIA WOOLF? in 1966. A year later, he won an Oscar for Best Director for THE GRADUATE. Since then, his film credits include CATCH-22 (1970), CARNAL KNOWLEDGE (1971), THE DAY OF THE DOLPHIN (1973), THE FORTUNE (1975), SILKWOOD (1983), HEARTBURN (1986), BILOXI BLUES, and WORKING GIRL (both in 1988).

Schuth's pioneering study expertly captures the first phase of Nichols's film career (1966-1975), not only tracing his cinematic techniques and their debt to modernist ideas, but also opening new perspectives on several of his underrated and overlooked films. "In this book," the author writes, "I analyze how Nichols articulates ideas through the complex symbol system of film and I explore the consistent themes and elements of style in his work." Building on the premise that all of Nichols's films are essentially about the "tragic nature of the human condition," the author divides his research into nine chapters. After first presenting a biographical overview,

Schuth analyzes the director's first six films in separate chapters, stressing the words, images, and sounds in Nichols's use of the film medium. From Schuth's perspective, Nichols's films stress the importance of the past on the present, how people struggle to survive in a hostile environment, and the importance of sacrificing for friendship. "The sad, pessimistic endings [of his films]," the author concludes, "show that the characters may have gained understanding, but have not gained true freedom." In addition to a valuable AUTEURIST analysis, the book includes a chronology, a bibliography, a filmography, and an index. Recommended for special collections.

JACK NICHOLSON

Brode, Douglas. THE FILMS OF JACK NICHOLSON. Secaucus: The Citadel Press, 1987. Illustrated. 256pp.

*Crane, Robert David, and Christopher Fryer. JACK NICHOLSON: FACE TO FACE. New York: M. Evans and Company, 1975. Illustrated. 192pp.

*Dickens, Norman. JACK NICHOLSON: THE SEARCH FOR A SUPERSTAR. New York: Signet Books, 1975. Illustrated. 182pp.

Downing, David. JACK NICHOLSON: A BIOGRAPHY. New York: Stein and Day, 1984. Illustrated. 195pp.

*Sylvester, Derek. JACK NICHOLSON. New York: Proteus Books, 1982. Illustrated. 95pp.

SAM PECKINPAH

Evans, Max. SAM PECKINPAH: MASTER OF VIOLENCE--BEING THE ACCOUNT OF THE MAKING OF A MOVIE AND OTHER SUNDRY THINGS. Vermillion: University of South Dakota Press, 1972. Illustrated. 92pp.

Born David Samuel Peckinpah in Fresno, California, on February 21, 1925, one of the greatest and most controversial filmmakers who specialized in westerns grew up on a ranch. His childhood ingrained in him a love for the traditional values of courage, loyalty, friendship, and grace under pressure. At the same time, he was fiercely independent and rebellious, so much so that his parents sent the strong-willed teenager to a military school to teach him discipline. After graduation, he enlisted in the Marines and served from 1943 to 1945. He then decided to learn about the theater and received his Bachelor of Arts Degree at Fresno State College and his Master of Arts Degree from the University of Southern California. Now at twenty-five, Peckinpah used his theatrical training to work as a resident director at the Huntington Park Civic Center and as a stage director and TV editor at the CBS studios in California. From 1954 to 1960, he split his time working for Don Siegel on films like RIOT IN CELL BLOCK 11 (1954) and INVASION OF THE BODY SNATCHERS (1956), and writing and directing for TV shows like GUNSMOKE, ROUTE 66, THE DICK POWELL ALUMINUM SHOW, THE RIFLEMAN, and THE WESTERNER. In 1961, he made his directorial screen debut with THE DEADLY COMPANIONS. Among the major productions that followed were RIDE THE HIGH COUNTRY (1962), MAJOR DUNDEE (1966), THE WILD BUNCH (1969), THE BALLAD OF CABLE HOGUE (1970), STRAW DOGS (1971), JUNIOR BONNER, THE GETAWAY (both in 1972), PAT GARRETT AND BILLY THE KID (1974), and THE KILLER ELITE (1975). Throughout this period, Peckinpah obtained a well-deserved reputation for being an extremely

difficult person to work with, most notably during the making of MAJOR DUNDEE and
his brief week before being fired on the production of THE CINCINNATI KID (1964).
To survive professionally in the 1960s, Peckinpah continued his TV work, gaining
high praise for his 1966 adaptation of Katherine Anne Porter's NOON WINE, starring
Jason Robards.   Following the disastrous reception of his film CONVOY in 1978,
Peckinpah suffered a heart attack and remained inactive over the next five years.
The popular reaction to THE OSTERMAN WEEKEND (1983) suggested that he might
be on the comeback trail, but a second heart attack led to his death at fifty-nine
on December 28, 1984.[909]
        Although primarily a book about the making of THE BALLAD OF CABLE HOGUE
(1970), Evans's rambling anecdotal account reflects the feelings that Peckinpah
engendered among his close friends. The author was born the same year as his
subject, and both men respected romantic values and rugged individualism. One gets
a sense of their bond in the author's opening comments: "Among the scores of things
I've heard Sam Peckinpah called are: insane, pure genius, chickenshit, son of a
bitch, true innovator, bloodsucker of other men's works, hell of a good ole boy,
deceitful, loyal, doublecrosser, gentle man who loves children, jealousy ridden ego
maniac, man out of his time, man far ahead of his time, and good outdoor cook. I
intend to go on the record here and now and put it straight once and forever. He
is a little bit of every cockeyed accusation. A lot of people are some of these things.
The difference is he's more of each or less of each than most of us are." Although
Evans merely tantalizes his audience with glimpses of Peckinpah's talents, he does
suggest in his ten breezy disjointed chapters the reason why many critics find THE
BALLAD OF CABLE HOGUE one of his buddy's best films. No bibliography, cast
credits, or index is provided. Worth browsing.

McKinney, Doug. SAM PECKINPAH. Boston: Twayne Publishers, 1979.   Illustrated.
266pp.
        Another fine addition to Twayne's series on underrated film artists, this book
takes a critical look at thirteen of Peckinpah's films (THE OSTERMAN WEEKEND
appeared after the book was done), without degenerating into either a condemnation
of screen violence, or a rhapsodic elegy on the virtues of rugged individualism.
McKinney points out Peckinpah's problems with producers and distributors, the public
misunderstandings over his stated intentions and the finished products, the role of
myth in Peckinpah's stories, and the misperceptions dealing with his controversial
reputation. Following a useful chronology, McKinney offers fifteen detailed chapters
on Peckinpah's life, his films, and thematic concerns. Interestingly, the author
refuses to provide synopses of the films, arguing that they either fail to convey the
spirit of the film, or are unnecssary for those who have seen the work. Among the
book's many noteworthy conclusions is the observation that "While Peckinpah is adept
at depicting action, his films begin with people; central to each of his stories is the
audience's involvement with the characters and their internal conflicts." McKinney
then adds, "Taking that interest in internal conflict and adding it to his respect for
the independent individual, then coloring it with the irony of the ambiguous
experience of appearance versus reality, one arrives at the creation of the Peckinpah
'loser,' the misfit-loner who struggles to make his own way and doesn't always know
why." A bibliography, endnotes, a filmography, and an index complete the study.
Well worth browsing.

---

[909]   For more information, see Bill Desowitz, "Heart Attack 31, 1984):1, 5; and
        Kathleen Murphy, "Obits: Sam Peckinpah--No Bleeding Heart," FILM COMMENT 21:2
        (April 1985):74-5.

Parrill, William. HEROES' TWILIGHT: THE FILMS OF SAM PECKINPAH. Minneapolis: Burgess Publishing Company, 1983. 155pp.

Don't be deceived by the lackluster appearance of this slight publication. Parrill's feisty prose and passionate commitment to Peckinpah result in provocative opinions not only on the director's films, but also on previous commentators. With the exception of glowing comments for Paul Seydor's study, Parrill argues that most writings about the filmmaker are inaccurate. In fact, the most disingenuous information has been provided by the subject himself.   Parrill's remedy is to demonstrate that "Peckinpah's films are romances which embody an unfashionable heroic code which resembles that of Hemingway; that his mastery of film technique, particularly his brilliant use of montage, perfectly expresses that code; and that his later films, far from being contemptible artistic works, are an essential part of his work and a logical outgrowth of his earlier films." Even if one rejects the hyperbolic assertion that Peckinpah is the only contemporary director worthy of being compared favorably with Eisenstein, there are plenty of intriguing observations in the book's twenty-one uneven and brief chapters. A good bibliography and adequate filmography are included, but no index is provided. Well worth browsing.

Seydor, Paul. PECKINPAH: THE WESTERN FILMS. Urbana: University of Illinois Press, 1980. Illustrated. 301pp.

One of the best books on Peckinpah, this exemplary study focuses on six films: THE DEADLY COMPANIONS (1961), RIDE THE HIGH COUNTRY (1962), MAJOR DUNDEE (1966), THE WILD BUNCH (1969), THE BALLAD OF CABLE HOGUE (1970), and PAT GARRETT AND BILLY THE KID (1974). Seydor masterfully recounts the problems that each film created for the director and his employers, explaining that his book is "about trust and betrayal, faith and breach of faith, conflict of commercial interest and artistic integrity, and perhaps it may even be seen to be rather heroic insofar as it contains such elements as legends, or less charitably, bad melodramas are made on." Biographical information is secondary to Seydor's scholarly analyses, starting first with Peckinpah's TV westerns in 1955, and then moving on to feature films. The emphasis is not only on the artist's story-telling skills, but also on his intellectual strengths.   While some may debate the latter, very few serious critics deny the former. The author's seven in-depth, chronological chapters explore Peckinpah's thematic concerns with mythical heroes adrift in a fading frontier and forced into violence by a second-rate sedentary society. Seydor finds Peckinpah's work rooted in American literary traditions from James Fenimore Cooper to Norman Mailer and bolsters his assertions with numerous interviews with Peckinpah and his associates. A bibliography and index are included. Recommended for special collections.

*Simmons, Garner. PECKINPAH: A PORTRAIT IN MONTAGE. Austin: University of Texas Press, 1982. Illustrated. 260pp.

A fast-moving and highly informative overview of Peckinpah's career, this refreshing study is based on dozens of interviews with Peckinpah and his collaborators: e.g., Jason Robards, Steve McQueen, Ali McGraw, Charlton Heston, James Caan, Slim Pickins, Warren Oates, Dustin Hoffman, James Coburn, Strother Martin, and Kris Kristofferson. The fact that the nucleus of the study first served as Simmon's 1975 Ph.D.   dissertation at Northwestern University and then was excerpted periodically for scholarly journals should not deter anyone from reading the revised and expanded version here. The fifteen chronologically arranged chapters incorporate all the facets of Peckinpah's life and career up to the early 1980s, providing a range of opinions almost as funny as they are revealing. For example, Caan's reaction to Peckinpah is that "If we get two more signatures, I'm going to have the man put away." A bibliography and index are included, but no filmography. Recommended for special collections.

ARTHUR PENN

*Cawelti, John G., ed. FOCUS ON "BONNIE AND CLYDE." Englewood Cliffs: Prentice-Hall, 1973. Illustrated. 176pp.
      An outgrowth of revolutionary changes in cinematic technique developed by France's NOUVELLE VAGUE, Arthur Penn's fascination with the legends of the historical Depression outlaws and a desire to modernize the conventions of the Hollywood gangster film led to the making of BONNIE AND CLYDE (1967), one of the most controversial movies of the post-WWII era. Cawelti's first-rate anthology on the film's evolution from idea to finished work provides a look at both sides of the debate. In addition to an interview with the director, cast and credit information, and a handful of mixed reviews, the book provides six stimulating essays--analyzing the film's artistic strengths and weaknesses--and a collection of articles about the life and death of the real Parker and Barrow. Particularly useful is a script excerpt. A filmography, bibliography, and index are included. Recommended for special collections.

Wake, Sandra, and Nicola Hayden, eds. THE "BONNIE AND CLYDE" BOOK. New York: Simon and Schuster, 1972. Illustrated. 223pp.
      The best feature of this film "scrapbook" is the complete film script. Otherwise, the smattering of interviews, articles, and reviews is more effectively grouped and selected in Cawelti's anthology. Well worth browsing.

*Wood, Robin. ARTHUR PENN. New York: Praeger Publishers, 1969. Illustrated. 144pp.
      Born in Philadelphia on September 27, 1922, the second son of emmigrant parents lived three years in Pennsylvania before his mother and father were divorced. For the next eleven years, Penn and his brother lived with their mother in New York. Then in 1936, he moved back to Pennsylvania to live with his father. Later, the sensitive artist would rework the unsettling experiences of his childhood into the complex patriarchial relationships in the his films. Penn developed an interest in drama during the final years of high school. Upon graduation and after his father's death in 1943, the stagestruck young thespian lived briefly in New York. Before he could make any meaningful contacts, however, Penn was drafted into the Army. It was there that he not only developed a significant friendship with Fred Coe (a future collaborator on stage and screen projects), but also became involved with Joshua Logan's Soldiers Show Company, an important group created to entertain the troops overseas. In fact, after Penn left the service in 1945, he managed the group in Paris for a year. The immediate post-WWII period saw him moving back and forth between Europe and America, pursuing his interest in theater. His career took a new direction in 1951, when he got a job as a floor manager for NBC's TV series, THE COLGATE COMEDY HOUR. Working his way up the production ladder, Penn became one of TV's most important directors for prestige series like PHILCO PLAYHOUSE and PLAYHOUSE 90. At the same time, he pursued his love for the theater. While directing Broadway shows like TWO FOR THE SEESAW (1958) and THE MIRACLE WORKER (1959), Penn made his directorial film debut with THE LEFT-HANDED GUN (1958). Fights with the producer and disillusionment over the film process kept him away from moviemaking for the next five years. His successful screen adapation of THE MIRACLE WORKER (1962) proved that he could alternate his interest in drama and television with filmmaking. Among his screen credits are MICKEY ONE (1965), THE CHASE (1966), BONNIE AND CLYDE (1967), ALICE'S RESTAURANT (1969), LITTLE BIG MAN (1970), NIGHT MOVES (1975), THE MISSOURI BREAKS (1976), FOUR FRIENDS (1981), and TARGETS (1985).

Wood's pioneering study offers a valuable analysis of Penn's films from THE LEFT-HANDED GUN to LITTLE BIG MAN. The author draws two important conclusions about the nature of the director's art. One praises "the openness of . . . [Penn's] response to experience, expressed in his ability to feel and communicate contradictory reactions to a given situation simultaneously." The second, his ability to portray tragic individuals who find themselves "in a state of constant conflict between irreconcilable pulls, each of which has its own validity." In addition to the seven separate chapters analyzing specific films, Wood offers a chapter on the problems of editing. The book's two major weaknesses are the poor quality of the visuals and the publication's weak binding. A filmography is included, but no index or bibliography is provided. Well worth browsing.

Zucker, Joel S. ARTHUR PENN: A GUIDE TO REFERENCES AND RESOURCES. Boston: G. K. Hall, 1980. 201pp.
    The most comprehensive resource on an underrated director who has been largely ignored by the scholarly community from the mid-1970s on, this valuable reference work functions better as an annotated bibliography and filmography than as an analytical document. Zucker's format incorporates the standard elements of the G. K. Hall series: e.g., biographical background; critical overview of the subject's work; a filmography with synopses and credits of Penn's nine films and one documentary subject up to 1980; annotations of more than 700 books, essays, articles, reviews, and films in three major languages; films and writings about the director (1952-1978); other film-related activity; archival sources; and film distributors. The weakest sections are those requiring lengthy discussions. For example, Zucker's fine opening comments on the shared eccentricity of Penn's work, "their disruption of genre expectations, their narrative procedures, and their ideological intentions," are never adequately developed in his topical headings--e.g., acting, lighting, sound, myth, violence, the masculine image, figures of authority, marginal groups, ideology, economics, the family, and religion--explaining Penn's formal and thematic accomplishments. On the other hand, the bibliographical section, the main body of the book, is splendid. An author and film index are provided. Recommended for special collections.

SYDNEY POLLACK

Taylor, William R. SYDNEY POLLACK. Boston: Twayne Publisher, 1981. Illustrated. 170pp.
    A consistently successful director whose fourteen films to date have received nearly forty Oscar nominations, Sydney Pollack was born in Lafayette, Indiana, on July 1, 1934, the oldest of his parents' three children. He first came to love drama at South Bend High School. After graduation, he moved to New York and pursued a career in acting. During the early 1950s, Pollack worked primarily in TV and distinguished himself in several TV adaptations of Hemingway's novels directed by John Frankenheimer. When Frankenheimer moved to Hollywood, he hired Pollack as his dialogue coach on THE YOUNG SAVAGES (1961). Pollack eventually became a TV director, earning praise for his work on hit TV series like THE DEFENDERS, BEN CASEY, NAKED CITY, and CHRYSLER THEATER. He made his directorial film debut with THE SLENDER THREAD (1965). His next film, THIS PROPERTY IS CONDEMNED (1966), was the first of six movies he directed starring Robert Redford. The other films are JEREMIAH JOHNSON (1972), THE WAY WE WERE (1973), THREE DAYS OF THE CONDOR (1975), THE ELECTRIC HORSEMAN (1979), and OUT OF AFRICA (1986). In addition, Pollack has directed such noteworthy movies as THE SCALPHUNTERS (1967) and THEY SHOOT HORSES, DON'T THEY? (1969), as well as directing and producing films like BOBBY DEERFIELD (1977), ABSENCE OF MALICE (1983), and TOOTSIE (1985). Still further, he has produced two Willie Nelson films: HONEYSUCKLE ROSE (1980) and SONGWRITER (1984).In 1986, his work on

OUT OF AFRICA won him the Oscar for Best Director (he had been nominated twice before--1969, 1982).

Once again, the invaluable Twayne series provides the only full-length study of a commercially and critically acclaimed director who is overlooked by scholars. As Warren French, the series' editor, points out, "Pollack's films are from one viewpoint difficult to deal with because of a lack of continuity and predictability in his subject matter." Most of Pollack's films since the mid-1970s examine the fragile relationship between men and women of extremely different backgrounds, but at the time this study was being written it seemed to French and to the author Taylor that Pollack could not be pigeonholed in any one category. His films from THE SILENT THREAD to THE ELECTRIC HORSEMAN covered most of the popular Hollywood genres: mysteries, westerns, FILM NOIR, Southern Gothic, and sports romance. Taylor's approach, therefore, is to avoid a chronological review and instead discuss Pollack from the perspective of an AUTEUR. The emphasis is on "the most visible areas of his influence--visual art, American themes, structures, heroes, heroines, and villains. . . ." Each area becomes a separate chapter in the book. Interestingly, Taylor relies heavily on material gleaned from interviews with Pollack and thus provides only three footnotes in the entire study. A bibliography and filmography are included. Recommended for special collections.

ROBERT REDFORD

*Castell, David. THE FILMS OF ROBERT REDFORD. London: Barnden Castell Williams, 1974. Illustrated. 47pp.

*Hanna, David. ROBERT REDFORD. New York: Nordon Publications, 1975. Illustrated. 185pp.

*Reed, Donald A. ROBERT REDFORD: A PHOTOGRAPHIC PORTRAYAL OF THE MAN AND HIS FILMS. Forward Tom Kirk. New York: Popular Library, 1975. Illustrated. 171pp.

Spada, James. THE FILMS OF ROBERT REDFORD. Secaucus: The Citadel Press, 1977. Illustrated. 256pp.

FRANKLIN J. SCHAFFNER

Kim, Erwin. FRANKLIN J. SCHAFFNER. Metuchen: The Scarecrow Press, 1985. Illustrated. 504pp.

Born in Tokyo on May 30, 1920, Franklin, the middle child of missionary parents, lived in Japan until his father died in 1926. His mother then settled the family in Lancaster, Pennsylvania, where Schaffner and his two sisters had a traditional childhood. After graduating from Franklin and Marshall College in 1942, the patriotic young man abandoned his plans for law school and enlisted in the U. S. Navy, serving until 1946. His first job as a civilian was as a fund-raiser and a speech writer for Americans United for World Government, a peace group housed in New York. It not only brought him in contact with many famous literary figures but also landed him a job as an assistant director for THE MARCH OF TIME series. In 1948, Schaffner moved over to CBS and began his illustrious TV career in news and public affairs programming. By 1952, he had worked on every major CBS news program and had become a protege of the distinguished TV producer, Worthington Minor. Over the next decade, Schaffner developed into a key director for TV series like STUDIO ONE, FORD THEATER, PERSON TO PERSON, THE KAISER ALUMINUM HOUR, PLAYHOUSE

90, and THE DEFENDERS. In the mid-1950s, Schaffner became one of three young Turks--the other two being George Roy Hill and Fielder Cook--to join with Minor in forming the famous TV production company Unit Four. By the end of the decade, Schaffner had a solid reputation as "an actor's director."

The transition to film came after Schaffner had directed ADVISE AND CONSENT on Broadway in 1960. That success, plus the fact that he had worked the last three years in Hollywood directing PLAYHOUSE 90 shows, resulted in a contract with 20th Century-Fox. When the first film, A SUMMER WORLD (1961), was aborted, Schaffner returned to TV productions, making his actual directorial film debut in 1963 with THE STRIPPER. His first film success came the following year with THE BEST MAN. Four years would pass before his next success, PLANET OF THE APES (1968), followed by an Oscar for Best Director for PATTON. His other films included NICHOLAS AND ALEXANDRA (1971), PAPILLON (1973), ISLANDS IN THE STREAM (1977), THE BOYS FROM BRAZIL (1978), SPHINX (1981), YES, GIORGIO (1982), and WELCOME HOME (1989). He died on July 2, 1989.[910]

Kim's in-depth and pioneering study of this overlooked and neglected artist is an important contribution not only to understanding Schaffner's evolution from TV to film, but also to appreciating the importance of TV on the film industry during the transition period from the early 1950s to the late 1960s. The author's scholarly insights and hard work in locating details and identifying sources is impressive. Following a good introduction to the subject, Kim divides his material into two major sections: "The Television Career of Franklin J. Schaffner," and "The Film Career of Franklin J. Schaffner." Nowhere else in the current literature can one locate as much useful and intelligent commentary on the development of the director's work, his treatment of actors, and the difficulties he faced in producing his work. A concluding chapter reviews the director's working methods and evaluates his achievements. In addition to important endnotes and an index, Kim provides a videography, filmography, and a bibliography. Highly recommended for special collections.

ALAN SCHNEIDER

*Beckett, Samuel. FILM. With an essay on directing FILM by Alan Schneider. New York: Grove Press, 1969. Illustrated. 96pp.

Written in 1963, Beckett's only venture in filmmaking took place during the summer of 1964. Buster Keaton plays a man plagued by problems of existence as he tries to define himself by relying on self-perception. The scenario of the seventeen-minute, "silent" movie published here is the intended concept for FILM and not exactly what occurred during shooting. The major difference occurs during the opening sequence. In addition to the director Schneider's important comments,[911] there are many beautiful illustrations. Recommended for special collections.

GEORGE C. SCOTT

*Harbinson, Allen. GEORGE C. SCOTT: THE MAN, THE ACTOR, AND THE LEGEND. New York: Pinnacle Books, 1977. Illustrated. 243pp.

---

[910]   Thomas Morgan, "Franklin Schaffner, 69, Oscar-Winning Director," NEW YORK TIMES A (July 4, 1989):9.

[911]   For more information, see Mel Gussow, "Alan Schneider, 66, Director of Beckett Dies," NEW YORK TIMES A (May 5, 1984):1, B6.

ROBERT VAUGHN

Murray, John B. ROBERT VAUGHN: A CRITICAL STUDY. London: Thessaly Press, 1987. Illustrated. 179pp.

ANDY WARHOL

Coplans, John. ANDY WARHOL. Greenwich: New York Graphic Society, 1970. Illustrated. 160pp.
An excellent introduction to the artist's work, this beautiful collection of reproduced pictures and paintings, also includes three useful essays. The best commentary is by Jonas Mekas. Recommended for special collections.

Crone, Rainer. ANDY WARHOL. New York: Praeger, 1970. Illustrated. 331pp.

*Gidal, Peter. ANDY WARHOL. New York: Dutton, 197o. Illustrated. 160pp.

Hackett, Pat, ed. THE ANDY WARHOL DIARIES. New York: Warner Books, 1989. 807pp.

*Koch, Stephen. STARGAZER: ANDY WARHOL'S WORLD AND HIS FILMS. 2nd ed. New York: Charles Scribner's, 1985. Illustrated. 155pp.
Born Andrew Warhola, Jr., in Forest City, Pennsylvania, on August 26, 1928, the son of Czechoslovakian immigrant parents grew up a sickly child preferring toys to friends. He graduated with a B. F. A. from the Carnegie Institute of Technology (now Carnegie Mellon University) in 1949, found work in New York as a commercial artist, and changed his name to Warhol. By the mid-1950s, the obsessed artist began using comic strips as a source for illustrations in his commercial work. As the decade came to a close, Warhol's successful career allowed him to venture into experimental work first with paintings and then silk scren prints. In 1962, the art world and the public heralded him as a pop art genius. A year later, he turned his East Forty-Seventh Street studio into "the Factory," where underground artists joined the celebrity-conscious Warhol in "manufacturing" works of art. That same year, Warhol turned to filmmaking with TARZAN AND JANE REGAINED . . . SORT OF. Among his more noted productions are SLEEP, KISS (both in 1963), EMPIRE (1964), THE CHELSEA GIRLS (1966), and LONESOME COWBOYS (1967). One of Warhol's entourage of hangers-on shot and nearly killed him in 1967, ending the artist's solo film work. After a year-long recovery, Warhol resumed his career but with far less publicity. Although he continued to produce films--e.g., FLESH (1968), TRASH (1970), and HEAT (1973); they were directed by Paul Morrissey, a Factory associate. The two men parted in the mid-1970s. Most of Warhol's remaining years were spent creating silk screen prints of celebrities, writing his memoirs, and doing commissioned projects. He died on February 22, 1987.
Koch's imaginative and stimulating review of Warhol's controversial work stresses the evasive techniques of the master of pop culture. In the author's judgment, Warhol, as an artist, "is a remarkably talented and interesting man who, in his whole public lifetime, has had one, and only one, really interesting idea." Labeling the concept, "visual power," Koch explores how Warhol used images in films and paintings to gain control "over the emotions, over the mind." In the book's fourteen chapters, written in the present tense, one senses the immediacy that personified Warhol's art and the sixties that he captured in his voyeuristic work. Koch pays more attention

to biographical anecdotes and films than to Warhol's paintings and sculpture. A filmography and index are included. Well worth browsing.

*Smith, Patrick S. ANDY WARHOL'S ART AND FILMS. Ann Arbor: UMI Research Press, 1986. Illustrated. 613pp.
     The most extensive and best analysis of Warhol's art and life, this study was originally a 1981 Ph.D. dissertation at Northwestern University. Smith's background as an art historian, coupled with dozens of interviews with key people in the artist's career, helps to makes this extensive collection of information both credible and entertaining. The majority of the material is contained in seven chapters dealing with Warhol's formative years, a critical evaluation of his art and his films, a discussion of his entrepreneurship, the nature of his curious appeal, and a set of conclusions. Just as valuable are transcripts of the author's thirty-seven interviews with people like Jonas Mekas, Ondine (Robert Olivio), Ronald Tavel, Andy Warhol, and Holly Woodlawn. Endnotes, a bibliography, and an index are included. Recommended for special collections.

Violet, Ultra. FAMOUS FOR FIFTEEN MINUTES: MY YEARS WITH ANDY WARHOL. New York: Harcourt, Brace, Jovanovich, 1988. Illustrated. 274pp.

*Warhol, Andy. THE PHILOSOPHY OF ANDY WARHOL (FROM A TO B AND BACK AGAIN). New York: Harcourt, Brace, Jovanovich, 1975. 241pp.

*Wilcock, John. THE AUTOBIOGRAPHY AND SEX LIFE OF ANDY WARHOL. New York: Other Scenes, 1971. Illustrated. No pagination.
     Mainly a series of interviews by Wilcock, the intriguing anthology captures many of Warhol's controversial ideas and much of their effect on people of his generation. Among the noteworthy celebrities included are Nico, Paul Morrissey, Ultra Violet, Ronald Tavel, Viva, and Sam Green. The visuals add to the book's enjoyable tone. No index is included. Well worth browsing.

ORSON WELLES

*Comito, Terry, ed. TOUCH OF EVIL: ORSON WELLES, DIRECTOR. New Brunswick: Rutgers University Press, 1985. Illustrated. 280pp.
     Hollywood folklore is filled with anecdotes about how famous films were conceived and made. This is one of the best. Legend has it that Welles was directing his 1956 Broadway production of KING LEAR when the Universal-producer Albert Zugsmith decided to cast the highly controversial actor-director in the role of the corrupt American cop in a proposed screen adaptation of Whit Masterson's novel, BADGE OF EVIL. The producer then contacted Charlton Heston and offered him the part of the honest narcotics cop. Before agreeing to the role, Heston asked Zugsmith who else was involved with the project and the producer allegedly told him Welles was on board. Misunderstanding the comment, Heston said he would gladly appear in any film that Welles was directing. Thus, according to the legend, Welles took over the project and refashioned the film into TOUCH OF EVIL. Considered by many critics to be one of Welles's great works, the film gets a superb review in this first-rate anthology. Among the many wonderful features of this publication, in addition to the script and the visuals, are a fine biographical sketch of Welles, interviews with Heston and Welles, and contemporary reviews of the film. The best information is supplied by the editor himself in a splendid introduction to the film and its history. Still further, there are perceptive commentaries provided by William Johnson, Jean Collet, and Stephen Heath. A filmography and bibliography are included, but no index is provided. Recommended for special collections.

*Fry, Nicholas, ed. and trans. THE TRIAL: A FILM BY ORSON WELLES. New York: Simon and Schuster, 1970. Illustrated. 176pp.

Over two decades would pass between the release of CITIZEN KANE (1941) and THE TRIAL/LE PROCES (1962), but these two films were the only one that the public saw of Welles's directorial skills as he intended his works to be exhibited. Regrettably, Fry provides little information on how Welles came to make a screen adaptation of the Kafka novel, or what Welles intended the work to represent. The brief reprint from Welles's April 1965 interview in CAHIERS DU CINEMA only suggests what the director-actor had in mind. Nonetheless, the book has value not only for its lovely and numerous visuals but also for the reprinting of the French script that appeared originally in the 1963 L'AVANT SCENE DU CINEMA publication. Well worth browsing.

FREDERICK WISEMAN

*Atkins, Thomas R., ed. FREDERICK WISEMAN. New York: Simon and Schuster, 1976. Illustrated. 134pp.

Born January 1, 1930, the creator of twelve award-winning and controversial documentaries received an LL.B degree from Yale Law School (1954), served two years in the military (1955-1956), and pursued a teaching career in Law (1958-1961) before becoming a film producer with Shirley Clarke's THE COOL WORLD (1963). He made his debut as a producer-director with TITICUT FOLLIES in 1967. Among his other noteworthy films are HIGH SCHOOL (1968), LAW AND ORDER (1969), HOSPITAL (1970), BASIC TRAINING (1971), and CANAL ZONE (1977).

Atkins's useful anthology contains several valuable articles, two helpful interviews, and a handful of reviews. The focus of this introductory volume is on Wiseman's film career from TITICUT FOLLIES to WELFARE (1975). "These films or 'reality fictions,' as he prefers to call them," Atkins explains, "are remarkable not only because of his unusually spare method--all of his films are shot with lightweight, hand-held 16mm equipment on black-and-white film which he edits himself--but also because of the films' extraordinary impact upon viewers and their lasting value both as artistic and social documents." A filmography, bibliography, biographical chronology, rental listing, and index are included. Well worth browsing.

Benson, Thomas W., and Carolyn Anderson. REALITY FILMS: THE FILMS OF FREDERICK WISEMAN. Carbondale: Southern Illinois University Press, 1989. 405pp.

Ellsworth, Liz. FREDERICK WISEMAN: A GUIDE TO REFERENCES AND RESOURCES. Boston: G. K. Hall, 1979. 212pp.

This is the book to read for those interested in beginning a basic study of Wiseman. The opening biographical section is based on a presentation the producer-director made at the 1976 Midwest Film Conference and two interviews (1976 and 1978) the author had with him. Ellsworth's critical evaluation and parts of the annotated filmography (complete with credits and synopses) are derived from her master's thesis at the University of Wisconsin-Madison. Particularly unusual for this highly regarded series are shot lists compiled from repeated viewings of 16mm prints and videotapes of Wiseman's films. A valuable annotated bibliography of writings about the subject covers the major literature published in French, German, and English periodicals and newspapers between 1963 and 1978. In addition to a film index and an author index, the book contains a list of Wiseman's film awards and festival showings, archival sources for further research, and information on film distributors. Recommended for special collections.

FILMS

ROBERT ALDRICH

THE DIRTY DOZEN (MGM--16mm: 1967, 149 mins., color sound, R-FNC)
This raw and fantasized glorification of twelve condemned men who are given a chance for freedom if they destroy a German military resort during the invasion of Normandy is a good example of the brutality and cynicism evident in American films during the late 1960s. In addition, the iconoclastic screenplay by Nunnally Johnson and Lukas Heller, based on the novel by E. M. Nathanson, illustrates the metamorphosis taking place in the conventions of the war film. Unlike the old World War II movies with their cross-section of everyday citizens being turned into gallant warriors fighting for a noble cause, the contemporary war movie attacked military authority and ridiculed traditional codes of conduct. Aldrich's by-now nihilistic style blended perfectly with the cynicism generated by the Vietnam War. As Edward Lowry points out, the film's enormous popularity at the box office resulted not only from its being a superb action film, but also from "the film's uncompromising hopelessness (which can be interpreted both as anti-social and irresponsible by a conservative critic like [Bosley] Crowther and as a glorification of authoritarianism by a liberal critic like [Arthur] Knight) that enabled it to capture, as well as any film of the sixties, the moral stasis of America amidst the debacle of Vietnam."[912] The cast is uniformly effective, with particularly strong performances by Lee Marvin, John Cassavetes, Charles Bronson, Robert Ryan, Donald Sutherland, and Telly Savalas.

KISS ME DEADLY (United Artists--16mm: 1955, 105 mins., b/w, sound, R-MGM)
Although A. I. Bezzerides's screenplay adapted from Mickey Spillane's novel embodied many of Spillane's violent and sexist obssessions, it provided Aldrich with the material that would later endear him to his fans. The story focuses on the sadistic behavior of the detective Mike Hammer (Ralph Meeker) battling killers and foreign agents, thereby allowing the director countless cinematic opportunities to experiment with FILM NOIR conventions, sadistic undercurrents in America during the McCarthy era, and the revisionism evolving in the detective film. For example, Steve Fore argues that the film's protagonist "is the apotheosis of the McCarthy hero, a combination lone avenger and grim reaper. He lives in a black-and-white world untainted by neurosis-inducing ambiguities and constraints on behavior. It is a world filled with evil individuals and conspiracies, yet one in which evil can be purged

---

[912]   Ed Lowry, "Program Notes: THE DIRTY DOZEN," CINEMATEXAS PROGRAM NOTES 23:3 (1982):54. For more information, see Ian Jarvie, "Hysteria and Authoritarianism in the Films of Robert Aldrich," FILM CULTURE 22-23 (Summer 1961):95-111; Robert Aldrich, "What Ever Happened to American Movies?" SIGHT AND SOUND 33:1 (Winter 1963-64):21-2; Richard Coombs, "Worlds Apart: Aldrich Since THE DIRTY DOZEN," ibid., 45:2 (Spring 1976):112-5; Harry Ringel, "Up to Date with Robert Aldrich," ibid., 43:3 (Summer 1974):166-9; Ian Cameron and Mark Shivas "Interview and Filmography," MOVIE 8 (April 1963):8-11; Paul Mayersberg, "Robert Aldrich," ibid., pp.4-5; Pierre Sauvage, "Aldrich Interview," ibid., 23 (Winter 1976-77):50-64; James Silke, ed. "Robert Aldrich," DIALOGUE ON FILM 2 (1972); Alain Silver, "Mr. FILM NOIR Stays at the Table: An Interview With Robert Aldrich," FILM COMMENT 8:1 (Spring 1972):14-23; Stuart Byron, "I Can't Get Jimmy Carter to See My Movie," ibid., 13:2 (March-April 1977):46-52; George Robinson, "Three by Aldrich," VELVET LIGHT TRAP 11 (Winter 1974):46-9; Allen Eyles, "The Private War of Robert Aldrich," FILMS AND FILMING 13:12 (September 1967):4-9; and Harry Ringel, "Robert Aldrich: The Director as Phoenix," TAKE ONE 4:5 (September 1974):9-16.

through the quick and efficient [use] of violence."[913] Although the film did poorly at the box office and was reviled or ignored by contemporary American critics, the CAHIERS DU CINEMA crowd praised its sociopolitical insights. Today, as Edwin T. Arnold and Eugene L. Miller, Jr., assert, it "remains a film which does not date--after twenty-five years it is still a richly imaginative, quirky, and darkly funny work."[914]

WOODY ALLEN

TAKE THE MONEY AND RUN (Palomar--16mm: 1969, 85 mins., color, sound, R-FES, FNC)

The Woody Allen-William Rose screenplay consisted of a series of episodic mishaps in the life of a NEBBISH gangster (Allen) who has pretensions of becoming Public Enemy Number One. Shot in documentary style and parodying the popular CINEMA-VERITE movies of the decade, the comedian's first outing as writer-director-star (also his first complete movie) exemplifies the era's self-reflexive trends and growing criticism of Hollywood genres. Moreover, Allen's ridicule of documentary reporting, as Maurice Yacowar points out, "warns us against the deceptions and seductions of the visual experience."[915]

KENNETH ANGER

SCORPIO RISING (16mm: 1962-63, 31 mins., color, sound, R-FUC)

This underground film made in Brooklyn is one example of how the low-budget movie breaks with the conventions of Hollywood film and uses the old themes for new, dramatic effects.

---

[913] Steve Fore, "Program Notes: KISS ME DEADLY," CINEMATEXAS PROGRAM NOTES 20:2 (March 30, 1981):48-9. For more information, see Robert Lang, "Looking for the 'Great Whatzit': KISS ME DEADLY and FILM NOIR," CINEMA JOURNAL 27:3 (Spring 1988):32-44; and Alain Silver, "KISS ME DEADLY: Evidence of a Style," FILM COMMENT 11:2 (March-April 1975):24-30.

[914] Edwin T. Arnold and Eugene L. Miller, Jr., THE FILMS AND CAREER OF ROBERT ALDRICH (Knoxville: The University of Tennessee Press, 1986), p.45.

[915] Maurice Yacowar, LOSER TAKE ALL: THE COMIC ART OF WOODY ALLEN (New York: Frederick Ungar Publishing Company, 1979), p.127. For more information, see Bernard Drew, ""Woody Allen Is Feeling Better," AMERICAN FILM 2:7 (May 1977):10-5; Bernard Weiner, "The Wooden Acting of Woody Allen," TAKE ONE 3:7 (December 1972):17-9; Ira Halberstadt, "Scenes from a Mind" ibid., 6: 12 (November 1978):16-20; Erik Bork, "Nurturance and Rejection in Woody Allen's INTERIORS and Ingmar Bergman's Melodramas," FILAMENT 5 (1986):11-3; Harry Wasserman, "Woody Allen: Stumbling through the Looking Glass," THE VELVET LIGHT TRAP 7 (Winter 1972-1973):37-40; Leonard Maltin, "Take Woody Allen--Please!" FILM COMMENT 10:2 (March-April 1974):42-5; Michael Dempsey, "The Autobiography of Woody Allen," ibid., 15:3 (May-June 1979):9-16; Maurice Yacowar, "Forms of Coherence In Woody Allen Comedies," WIDE ANGLE 3:2 (1979):34-41; and Gerald Mast, "Allen, Woody," THE INTERNATIONAL DICTIONARY OF FILMS AND FILMMAKERS: VOLUME I, pp.12-4.

JOHN BOORMAN

POINT BLANK (MGM--16mm: 1967, 92 mins., color, sound, R-FNC)
In one of the most unusual and neglected underworld films of the era, the Alexander Jacobs-David Newhouse-Rafe Newhouse screenplay based on a Richard Stark novel focuses on a revengeful hood (Lee Marvin) and his decision to pay back key members of the Organization who have double-crossed him. The director's treatment of the violent action borders more on romance than on reality, showing Marvin's quest as a rite of passage instead of a predictable gangland war. The fact that viewers tend to conentrate only on the gore and not on the character development limited the film's success in the mid-1960s. But, as James Robert Parish and Michael R. Pitts observe, "This was THE film that amazed some viewers, astounded others, annoyed another segment, and led to a loud call for non-violent films."[916]

MEL BROOKS

THE PRODUCERS (Embassy--16mm: 1968, 88 mins., color, sound, R-CIN, FES, FNC, IVY, TWY)
Mel Brooks wrote, directed, and appeared in this farcical tale about a disreputable producer (Zero Mostel) who teams up with a neurotic accountant (Gene Wilder) to hoodwink wealthy old women into backing the worst musical in Broadway history. The duo's selection, SPRINGTIME FOR HITLER, written by an insane neo-Nazi playwright (Kenneth Mars), directed by a disturbed transvestive (Christopher Hewett), and starring an atrocious actor (Dick Shawn) unexpectedly turns into a smash hit. Tried and convicted of fraud, the men end their days in jail, putting together a new scheme to extort their fellow prisoners. Brooks's first feature film contains not only examples of his controversial humor and questionable taste, but also his favorite ploy of matching two unlikely men as partners and then showing how a strong bond of friendship develops. Unlike Woody Allen's films, as Stuart M. Kaminsky observes, where the emphasis is on the protagonist's pathetic circumstances, "Brooks's films reverse the Allen films' endings as the protagonists move into a comic fantasy of friendship."[917] Nominated for two Academy Awards, including Best Supporting Actor (Wilder), THE PRODUCERS won an Oscar for Best Screenplay for material written directly for the screen (Brooks).

---

[916] James Robert Parish and Michael R. Pitts, THE GREAT GANGSTER FILMS (Metuchen: The Scarecrow Press, 1976), p.315. See also David Englebach, "Alex Jacobs: The Best (and Least) Known Screenwriter In Hollywood," MILLIMETER 3:12 (December 1975):20-2, 24, 26, 46-7; Gordon Gow, "Playboy in a Monastery: An Interview With John Bormann," FILMS AND FILMING 18:5 (February 1972):18-22; John Lindsay Brown, "Islands of the Mind," SIGHT AND SOUND 39:1 (Winter 1969-1970):20-3; and David McGillivray, "Review of DELIVERANCE and Filmography of John Boorman," FOCUS ON FILM 11 (Autumn 1972):12-3.

[917] Stuart M. Kaminsky, "Brooks, Mel," THE INTERNATIONAL DICTIONARY OF FILMS AND FILMMAKERS: VOLUME I, p.68. For more information, see Jacoba Atlas, "New Hollywood: Mel Brooks Interviewed," FILM COMMENT 11:2 (March-April 1975):54-7; Gordon Gow, "Fond Salutes and Naked Hate: Mel Brooks Interviewed," FILMS AND FILMING 21:10 (July 1975):10-4; Brad Darrach, "Interview With Mel Brooks," PLAYBOY 22:2 (February 1975):47-9, 52-56, 60-6, 68; Herbert Gold, "Funny Is Money," NEW YORK TIMES MAGAZINE (March 30, 1975):16-7, 19, 21-2, 26, 28, 30-1; Fred Robbins, "What Makes Mel Brooks Run?" SHOW 1:13 (September 17, 1970):12-4; Charles M. Young, "Seven Revelations about Mel Brooks," ROLLING STONE (February 9, 1978):32-6; and Paul D. Zimmerman, "The Mad, Mad World of Mel Brooks," NEWSWEEK (February 17, 1975):54-8, 63.

JOHN CASSAVETES

FACES (Continental--16mm: 1968, 130 mins., b/w, sound, R-CAL)

Writer-director Cassavetes, always concerned with human relations, presents the problems of middle-class men and women in an original, engrossing, and thought-provoking manner. The improvisational film focuses on an unhappily married man (John Marley), who spends one night away from his wife (Lynn Carlin). The situations, conversations, and events suggest the husband's shift from a concern with petty problems, to a better understanding of his life and responsibilities. Gena Rowlands gives a fine performance as the prostitute who provides temporary relief for disillusioned husbands.[918]

SHADOWS (Lion International--16mm: 1960, 81 mins., b/w, sound, R-ROA)

Initiated in 1957 and completed two years later, the movie is not only credited with being the most significant AVANT-GARDE film of the fifties, but also the turning point in Cassavetes's career. The improvisational project, made during the write-director-producer's acting stints on TV and in commercial films, is an outgrowth of a group of young filmmakers rebelling against Hollywood traditions emphasizing commercial success. As Ann Rowe Seaman points out, the New American Cinema Group, which Cassavetes helped form in 1960, rejected the standard production, distribution, and exhibition routes; and instead argued for a new free cinema. This film epitomized the group's principles: "The first version cost only about $15,000; it was free of the clutches of big investors who might interfere with artistic control (small contributions bankrolled SHADOWS); it was a collective artistic enterprise using the talents of the actors as a more direct input than Hollywood usually allowed (for the actors improvised instead of following the script); it was made by a small unpaid crew of volunteers which kept it free of big time union complications; and most of all, it was made with the most pristine of credentials: artistic experimentation, not money, was its goals."[919] The slim plot centers on a black family that includes an older brother who is a jazz musician (Hugh Hurd) and his younger brother (Ben Carruthers) and sister (Lelia Goldoni) who pass for white. Although many contemporary critics attacked the film's "unprofessional" look and its simplistic approach to race relations, Jonas Mekas summed up the general reaction of many sympathetic viewers: "The film's rhythm, its temperament is not that of the ideas in it, but, primarily, their tone of voice, their stammerings, their pauses--their

---

[918]   For more information, see Jonas Mekas, "Notes on the New American Cinema," FILM CULTURE 24 (Spring 1962):8; Andrew Sarris, "Oddities and One-Shots," ibid., 28 (Spring 1963):45; John Cassavetes, "What's Wrong with Hollywood," ibid., 19 (April 1959):4-5; ___, ". . . And the Pursuit of Happiness," FILMS AND FILMING 7:5 (February 1961):7-8, 36; David Austen, "Masks and Faces: An Interview With John Cassavetes," ibid., 14:2 (September 1968):4-6, 8; "John Cassavetes, Peter Falk," DIALOGUE ON FILM 4 (1972):1-23; James Stevenson, "John Cassavetes: Film's Bad Boy," AMERICAN FILM 5:4 (January-February 1980):44-8, 79; "Cassavetes on Cassavetes," MONTHLY FILM BULLETIN 45:533 (June 1978):128; John Russell Taylor, "In the Picture: Cassevetes in London," SIGHT AND SOUND 29:4 (Autumn 1960):177-8; "PLAYBOY Interview: John Cassavetes," PLAYBOY 18:7 (July 1971):55-70, 210-12; and Claire Clouzot, "FACES," FILM QUARTERLY 22:3 (Spring 1969):31-5.

[919]   Ann Rowe Seaman, "Program Notes: SHADOWS," CINEMATEXAS PROGRAM NOTES 10:3 (March 22, 1976):3. For more information, see Clara Hoover, "An Interview With Hugh Hurd," FILM COMMENT 1:4 (1963):24-7; and Albert Johnson, "SHADOWS," FILM QUARTERLY 13:3 (Spring 1960):32-4.

psychological reality as revealed through the most insignificant daily incidents and situations."[920]

ROGER CORMAN

THE LITTLE SHOP OF HORRORS (Allied Artists--16mm: 1960, 73 mins., sound, R-BUD, FES, IVY, KIT)

Charles Griffith's tongue-in-cheek screenplay about a pathetic flowershop clerk (Jonathan Haze) who befriends a strange plant by feeding it human blood and eventually becomes its victim is an excellent spoof of the 1950s' fantasy films about alien visitors. Later made into a hit off-Broadway musical and a 1986 Warner Bros. movie, the original film was directed by Corman as a joke. One of his colleagues dared him to set a production record for quickie movies. Griffith took a week to write the script and Corman shot it in two days. "'It's interesting to note that this movie, in the long run,' Corman explains, "is the one that established me as an underground legend in film circles. This movie had no budget to speak of yet it has made me more fans and friends than some of my bigger pictures."[921]

JOHN FORD

THE MAN WHO SHOT LIBERTY VALANCE (Paramount--16mm: 1962, 122 mins., b/w, sound, R-FNC)

The Willis Goldbeck-James Warner Bellah screenplay adapted from a story by Dorothy M. Johnson and heavily influenced by previous Ford conventions deals with an archetypal relationship among an Eastern lawyer (James Stewart), a rough frontier cowboy (John Wayne), and a vicious killer (Lee Marvin). It not only underscores the director's growing cynicism about frontier myths, but also the changes in Ford macho-conservative westerns. In place of the sweeping panoramas and crowds of people in past films, the action remains primarily confined to rooms and individuals. The plot pays more attention to the fortunes of Wayne and Stewart (appearing for the first time together) than it does to the villainy of Marvin. In large measure, Ford's last great tale about American democracy beautifully balances his conservative philosophy with a respect for the genre that he admired most.[922] As Janey A. Place

---

[920] "Notes on the New American Cinema," p.8.

[921] Ed Naha, THE FILMS OF ROGER CORMAN: BRILLIANCE ON A BUDGET (New York: Chelsea House, 1982), p.142. For more information, see Larry Salvato, "Roger Corman Interview," MILLIMETER 3:12 (December 1975):12-4, 16, 48; Philip Strick, "Ma Barker to Von Richthofen: An Interview With Roger Corman," SIGHT AND SOUND 39:4 (Autumn 1970):179-83; "'Senjamyson': An Interview With Jay Sayer on the Making of THE VIKING WOMEN AND THE SEA SERPENT," TAKE ONE 1:9 (November 9, 1968):8-11; Alan Collins, "A Letter from Roger Corman," ibid., 1:12 (1968):11-2; Joe Medjuck and Alan Collins, "An Interview With Roger Corman," ibid., 2:12 (July-August 1970):6-9; Digby Diehl, "Roger Corman: A Double Life," ACTION 4:4 (July-August 1969):13-4; and David Chute, "The New World of Roger Corman," FILM COMMENT 18:2 (March-April 1982):26-32.

[922] For more information, see Mike Sullivan, "Program Notes: THE MAN WHO SHOT LIBERTY VALANCE," CINEMATEXAS PROGRAM NOTES 5:40 (November 12, 1973):1-6; Ed Lowry, "Program Notes: THE MAN WHO SHOT LIBERTY VALANCE," ibid., 11:3 (November 4, 1976):57-64; Don Hartack, "Program Notes: THE MAN WHO SHOT LIBERTY," ibid., 19:3 (December 10, 1980):75-83; Andrew Sarris, "Cactus Rosebud, or THE MAN WHO SHOT LIBERTY VALANCE," FILM CULTURE 25 (Summer 1962):13-5; David F. Coursen, "John Ford's Wilderness--THE MAN WHO SHOT LIBERTY VALANCE," SIGHT AND SOUND 47:4

points out, the film's themes "are those which have concerned Ford from the very beginning of his career--Eastern versus Western values, transforming the desert of the West into a garden, and creating through progress a society in which law and order are not determined by a gun. The film expresses and affirms all these themes; yet at its core is a deep sorrow for the price the town of Shinbone (and America) had to pay."[923]

THE SEARCHERS (Warners--16mm: 1956, 119 mins., color, sound, R-FES, SWA)
     Probably the most hotly discussed of all Ford films, the Frank S. Nugent screenplay (based on a novel by Alan LeMay) focuses on the ironic alienation of Ethan Edwards (John Wayne) as he searches for his niece Debbie (Natalie Wood), who was abducted as a child by Indians. Synthesizing Ford's humanistic re-evaluation of the frontier myth, begun in the post-WWII period, the obsessive, unpredictable, and brutal Ethan personifies what happens to heroic but violent people trying to survive in a harsh and lonely environment, forced to defend themselves against constant enemies. Although Ford's women represent the civilizing elements that form lasting communities, they only offer strong-minded individuals like Ethan opportunities to defend and to protect them, but not a home or comfort. As Ford observes, "It's the tragedy of a loner . . . a plain loner--could never really be part of a family."[924] In this sense, THE SEARCHERS becomes a brooding and elegaic morality play on violence and changing values.[925]

JOHN FRANKENHEIMER

THE FIXER (MGM--16mm: 1968, 132 mins., color, sound, R-MGM)
     Based upon Bernard Malamud's novel, Dalton Trumbo's fine script centers on a simple Jew (Alan Bates) who becomes a scapegoat in Czarist Russia and how he emerges as an international figure. The location shooting in Budapest was the first filming done by a Hollywood company in a post-WWII Communist country. The recreation of the famous Mendel Beiles case met with mixed reactions at the time of its release, particularly since Trumbo's treatment of what an individual experiences

---

(Autumn 1978):237-41; Robin Wood, "Shall We Gather at the River: The Late Films of John Ford," FILM COMMENT 7:3 (Fall 1971):8-17; David Bordwell, "THE MAN WHO SHOT LIBERTY VALANCE," ibid., pp.18-20; and Nancy Warfield, "THE MAN WHO SHOT LIBERTY VALANCE: A Study of John Ford's Film," THE LITTLE FILM GAZETTE OF N.D.W. 6:1 (August 1975):1-28.

[923] *Janey A. Place, THE WESTERN FILMS OF JOHN FORD (Secaucus: The Citadel Press, 1973), p.216.

[924] *Peter Bogdanovich, JOHN FORD (Berkeley: University of California Press, 1968), pp.92-3.

[925] For more information, see Glenn Lalich, "John Ford's THE SEARCHERS: Capitalist Claptrap,"FILAMENT 4 (1984):50-2; Jeff Shannon, "John Ford's THE SEARCHERS: Heroic Romance," ibid., pp.50-1, 54-6; Ed Lowry, "Program Notes: THE SEARCHERS," CINEMATEXAS PROGRAM NOTES 9:2 (October 2, 1975):27-34; Michael Selig, "Program Notes: THE SEARCHERS," ibid., 16:2 (March 21, 1979):43-50; Lindsay Anderson, "THE SEARCHERS," SIGHT AND SOUND 26:2 (Autumn 1956):94-5; Clay Steinman, "The Method of THE SEARCHERS," JOURNAL OF THE UNIVERSITY FILM ASSOCIATION 28:3 (Summer 1976):19-24; Geoffrey Nowell-Smith, "Six Authors In Pursuit of THE SEARCHERS," SCREEN 17:1 (Spring 1976):26-33; Andrew Sarris, "THE SEARCHERS," FILM COMMENT 7:1 (Spring 1971):58-61; Stuart Byron, "THE SEARCHERS: Cult Movie of the New Hollywood," NEW YORK (March 5, 1979):45-8;

in defense of his principles made some people feel as if the screenwriter was offering a treatise on what he had experienced during the blacklisting years. In fact, Malamud disliked the movie and rejected it publicly. On the other hand, Frankenheimer's direction of this anti-establishment story was a deeply moving experience for him personally. Not only did he relate the movie to his admiration for Robert Kennedy, who was killed the year the movie was released, but he also told Gerald Pratley that "Our film is about the dignity of a human being, about what a man is really capable of, about the growth of a simple human being who never knew he had this strength in him, and suddenly finds it within him."[926]

THE MANCHURIAN CANDIDATE (United Artists--16mm: 1962, 126 mins., b/w, sound, R-CHA, UAS)

Although Frankenheimer considers the film overrated, many of his fans claim it is his best work. George Axelrod's intriguing screenplay based on a Richard Condon novel offers a superb examination of macabre politics that is filled with marvelous moments of suspense, entertainment, and editing. Frank Sinatra stars as an ex-Korean War POW who discovers that a member of his captured patrol (Laurence Harvey), who was awarded the Medal of Honor for his heroic action against the Communists, is actually an unwitting killer in a plan to take over the United States. Among the film's many striking cinematic inventions was the image of a sinister mother (Angela Lansbury) whose maternal cruelty was unparalleled in American film history. The film met with moderate success and for unexplained reasons went out of distribution in 1972. Re-released in 1987, it has developed into a cult movie. At the center of recent critical interest is Frankenheimer's depiction of cold war mentality. On the one hand, Michael Paul Rogin, describing the film as "brilliant" and "self-knowing," claims that it attempted, "with a a political and technical sophistication absent from its models, to initiate a political renewal [about the dangers of Communism]. Instead it was the last cold war movie, for the assassination to which it pointed brought the cold war consensus to an end."[927] On the other hand, Richard Combs argues that, "THE MANCHURIAN CANDIDATE, in the end, is a work of sophisticated primitivism--black humorist Axelrod and Freudian burlesquer

---

[926] *Gerald Pratley, THE CINEMA OF JOHN FRANKENHEIMER (New York: A. S. Barnes, 1970), p.188. For more information, see Paul Filmer, "Three Frankenheimer Films: A Sociological Approach," SCREEN 10:4-5 (July/October 1969):160-73; Charles Higham, "Frankenheimer," SIGHT AND SOUND 37:2 (Spring 1968):91-3; Axel Madsen, "In the Picture: 99 and 44/100% Dead," ibid., 43:1 (Winter 1973-74):26; Richard Combs, "In the Picture: A Matter of Conviction," ibid., 48:4 (Autumn 1979):231; Russell Au Werter, "John Frankenheimer," ACTION 5:3 (May-June 1970):6-9; Bernard Drew, "John Frankenheimer: His Rise and Fall," AMERICAN FILM 2:5 (March 1977):8-16; Bruce Cook, "The War Between the Writers and the Directors: Part II--The Directors," ibid., 4:8 (June 1979):48-53, 61; "Dialogue on Film: John Frankenheimer," ibid., 14:5 (March 1989):20-2,24; Alan Casty, "Realism and Beyond: The Films of John Frankenheimer," FILM HERITAGE 2:2 (Winter 1966-67):21-33; John Frankenheimer, "Seven Ways with SEVEN DAYS IN MAY," FILMS AND FILMING 10:9 (June 1964):9-10; Gordon Gow, "Reflections: An Interview With Alan Bates," ibid., 17:9 (June 1971):22-8; Ralph Appelbaum, "Pop Art Pitfalls: Interview With John Frankenheimer, Part I," ibid., 26:1 (October 1979):10-6; ___, "The Fourth Commitment: Interview With John Frankenheimer, Part II" ibid., 26:2 (November 1979):20-4; and Paul Mayersberg, "John Frankenheimer," MOVIE 5 (December 1962):35.

[927] *Michael Paul Rogin, RONALD REAGAN, THE MOVIE AND OTHER EPISODES IN POLITICAL DEMONOLOGY (Berkeley: University of California Press, 1987), pp.253-4.

Frankenheimer taking on board a political sensibility not unlike that of Samuel Fuller of, say, PARK ROW."[928]

SAMUEL FULLER

UNDERWORLD U. S. A. (Columbia--16mm: 1961: 98 mins., b/w, sound, R-BUD, IMA, KIT, SWA, WEL)

Working under the auspices of Fuller's Globe Enterprises, the writer-producer-director adapted Joseph F. Dineen's SATURDAY EVENING POST articles on modern crime, into a melodramatic analysis of a criminal's rise from childhood, his joining the syndicate, collaborating with Federal authorities, and dying in a shoot-out with the crime lord. According to Fuller, he consciously followed Shakespeare's use of "honest emotions" in writing the contemporary story about "Somebody being jealous of someone, or somebody wants to doublecross someone, or somebody is greedy."[929] Cliff Robertson, in the role originally planned for Bogart, does a good job of demonstrating Dana B. Polan's observation that "Sam Fuller's narratives investigate the ways that belonging to a social group simultaneously functions to sustain and nuture individual identity and, conversely, to pose all sorts of emotional and ideological threats to that identity."[930]

GEORGE ROY HILL

BUTCH CASSIDY AND THE SUNDANCE KID (Fox--16mm: 1969, 112 mins., color, cinemascope, sound, R-FES, FNC)

In this western comedy-drama about two of the West's most vicious gunmen, screenwriter William Goldman presents Butch (Paul Newman) and Sundance (Robert Redford) as two fun-loving outlaws who are forced to leave the closing frontier and flee to Bolivia, where they meet a violent death. The director Hill's careful development and handling of the friendship between the two outlaws is often credited as the start of the "buddy-film cycle" that carried over into the 1970s. The film's humor reflected the public's decreasing interest in serious westerns, and the trend toward parodying the genre's conventions. Nominated for seven Academy Awards, including Best Picture, Best Director (Hill), and Best Sound (William Edmundson and David Dockendorf), it won Oscars for Best Original Story and Screenplay written directly for the screen (Goldman), Best Cinematography (Conrad Hall), Best Original Music (Burt Bacharach), and Best Song (Bacharach and Hal David). In addition to fine performances by Newman and Redford, Katharine Ross is splendid as the understanding and loving Etta Place.[931]

---

[928] Richard Combs, "Retrospective: THE MANCHURIAN CANDIDATE," MONTHLY FILM BULLETIN 55:656 (September 1988):281. See also John Thomas, "John Frankenheimer: The Smile on the Face of the Tiger," FILM QUARTERLY 19:2 (Winter 1965-66):2-13; John Hanhardt, "George Axelrod and THE MANCHURIAN CANDIDATE," FILM COMMENT 6:4 (Winter 1970-71):8-13; J. H. Fenwick, "Black King Takes Two," SIGHT AND SOUND 33:3 (Summer 1964):114-7; and Gordon Gow, "I Was a Young Woman of Parts: An Interview With Angela Lansbury," FILMS AND FILMING 18:3 (December 1971):18-22.

[929] Stig Bjorkman, p.27.

[930] Dana B. Polan, "Fuller, Samuel," THE INTERNATIONAL DICTIONARY OF FILMS AND FILMMAKERS: VOLUME II--DIRECTORS/FILMMAKERS, p.205.

[931] For more information, see Charles Flynn, "Interview With George Roy Hill," FOCUS 6 (Spring 1970):8-11; Laurence Luckinbill, "Oh, You Sundance Kid!" ESQUIRE

THE MAKING OF BUTCH CASSIDY AND THE SUNDANCE KID (EYR-16mm: 1969, 52 mins., color, sound, R-EYR)
    This is a first-rate behind-the-scenes account of a major film production and is a very useful teaching aid.

ALFRED HITCHCOCK

NORTH BY NORTHWEST (MGM--16mm: 1959, 136 mins., color, sound, R-FNC)
    In one of his best films, Hitchcock offers us a fast, action-packed adventure story about a case of mistaken identity when an unsuspecting advertising man (Cary Grant) becomes involved with international spies.   Ernest Lehman's original screenplay, incorporating many of the director's famous touches--e.g., macabre humor, picturesque thrills, the theme of the "wrong man," "icy" blond heroines, exotic locations, and sinister montage effects--provides Hitchcock with numerous opportunities for "pure cinema" and the manipulation of our emotions. Three key scenes in this film illustrate the director's penchant for putting ordinary people in settings exuding respectability and tranquility--e.g., the U. N. building, a corn field, and Mount Rushmore--and then showing how quickly our illusions can deteriorate into chaotic and terrifying experiences.   The loopholes in the plot are overcome by clever editing and non-stop action. As Gordon Gow writes, "This paragon among comedy-thrillers .   .   . is arguably as good an indication as can be found of Alfred Hitchcock's ability to match his sense of humor to his lively suspense tactics."[932]

PSYCHO (Paramount--16mm: 1960, 109 mins., b/w, sound, R-BUD, FES, SWA)
    Considered by many to be Hitchcock's greatest film, Joseph Stefano's screen adaptation of Robert Bloch's novel centers on a schizophrenic young man (Anthony Perkins) who sees the world as his enemy. At the same time, the subplot concerning a woman (Janet Leigh) who steals money from her boss and then meets a violent death introduces a series of Hitchcock conventions dealing with perversity and evil that encourage a multitude of interpetations not only about Hitchcock's treatment of women, but also about the role of women in Hollywood films. On one level, as Jean Douchet points out, Hitchcock's voyeuristic techniques can be seen as his therapeutic attempt to purge us of our sexual repressions and to satisfy our desires to experience frightening experiences without actually being in danger. This approach to catharsis in Hitchcock's universe asserts that "PSYCHO will talk to us about the eternal and the finite, of existence and nothingness, of life and death, but seen in their naked

(October 1970):160-3, 18, 20, 26, 28; Bill Davidson, "The Entertainer," NEW YORK TIMES MAGAZINE (March 16, 1975):18, 68-71, 76; Ralph Appelbaum, "Flying High: An Interview With George Roy Hill," FILMS AND FILMING 25:11 (August 1979): 10-7; Ray Narducy, "Hill, George Roy," THE INTERNATIONAL DICTIONARY OF FILMS AND FILMMAKERS: VOLUME I, p.257; and Michael Shedlin, "Conrad Hall: An Interview," FILM QUARTERLY 24:3 (Spring 1971):2-11.

[932]   Gordon Gow, "The Cult Movies: NORTH BY NORTHWEST," FILMS AND FILMING 21:1 (October 1974):51. For more information, see A. W. Richardson, "NORTH BY NORTHWEST," SCREEN EDUCATION YEARBOOK (1963): pp.45-7; Edward Lowry, Program Notes: NORTH BY NORTHWEST," CINEMATEXAS PROGRAM NOTES 11:3 (November 11, 1978):69-78; and John S. Tumlin, "Audience as Protagonist in Three Hitchcock Films," MIS-EN-SCENE 1 (1969):2-6.

[933]   Jean Douchet, "Hitch and His Public," trans. Vernea Conley, A HITCHCOCK READER, p.15.

truth."[933] Those critics, like Leland Poague, who reject this voyeuristic analysis, and with it Hitchcock's assumed absolute control of our sensibilities, stress the film's "classical narrative" and "focus primarily on the ways in which the classical film narrative alternately effaces or contains the forces and possibilities of the medium --the way cutting, for example, subordinates space to action, subordinates discourse to story; the way the desire for unity or closure 'subordinates impersonal or apersonal causes . . . [to personal causes,' implying thereby that social causes do NOT determine individual actions or narrative outcomes."[934] A third approach, also noted by Poague, points to Hitchcock's films as "submerged in allegories of grace, of mistakes acknowledged, redeemed, and transcended.[935] While critics disagree strenuously about the strengths and weaknesses of the film, few historians disagree with the argument that it marked the beginning of the contemporary horror film and a turning point in Hitchcock's career. In addition to Leigh's Oscar-nominated performance and Perkins's extraordinary acting, there are fine jobs turned in by Martin Balsam and Vera Miles.[936]

VERTIGO (Paramount--16mm: 1958, 127 mins., color, sound, R-SWA)
     Considered by many critics to be Hitchcock's most obsessive film in terms of characterization and plot, the Alec Coppel and Samuel Taylor screenplay (adapted from the novel, D'ENTRE LES MORTS by Pierre Boileau and Thomas Narcejac) focuses on "Scottie" Ferguson (James Stewart), an ex-detective whose acrophobia prevents him from saving Madeleine Elster (Kim Novak), a friend's wife (whom he also loves) from committing "suicide." Several months later, the distraught "Scottie" suddenly sees Judy Barton (Kim Novak), who reminds him of the dead Madeleine. After

---

[934]   Leland Poague, "Links In a Chain: PSYCHO and Film Classicism," A HITCHCOCK READER, eds. Marshall Duetelbaum and Leland Poague (Ames: Iowa State University Press, 1986), pp.340-9. Poague's definition of "classical narrative" and his quotation are from David Bordwell, THE FILMS OF CARL-THEODOR DREYER (Berkely: University of California Press, 1981), p.25.

[935]   Leland Poague, "PSYCHO," THE INTERNATIONAL DICTIONARY OF FILMS AND FILMMAKERS: VOLUME I--FILMS, p.376.

[936]   Rui Nogueira, "PSYCHO, Rosie and a Touch of Orson: Janet Leigh Talks," SIGHT AND SOUND 39:2 (Spring 1970):66-70; Robin Bean, "Pinning Down the Quicksilver: Interview With Anthony Perkins," FILMS AND AND FILMING 11:10 (July 1965):44-9; Robin Wood, "Beauty Bests the Beast," AMERICAN FILM 8:10 (September 1983):62-5; Kevin Gough-Yates, "Private Madness and Public Lunacy," ibid., 18:5 (February 1972):26-30; Chris Secrest, "Program Notes: PSYCHO," CINEMATEXAS PROGRAM NOTES 25:1 (September 28, 1983):65-72; Raymond Bellour, "Psychosis, Neurosis, Perversion," trans. Nancy Huston, CAMERA OBSCURA 3-4 (Summer 1979):104-32, Rpt. A HITCHCOCK READER, pp.311-31; Barbara Klinger, "PSYCHO: The Institutionalization of Female Sexuality," WIDE ANGLE 5:1 (1982):49-55, Rpt. A HITCHCOCK READER, pp.332-39; Richard Corliss, "PSYCHO Therapy," FAVORITE MOVIES, ed. Philip Nobile (New York: Macmillan Company, 1973), pp.213-24; David Thomson, "The Big Hitch: Is the Director a Prisoner of his Own Virtuosity?" FILM COMMENT 15:2 (March-April 1979):26-9; ___, "PSYCHO and the Rollercoaster," OVEREXPOSURES: THE CRISIS IN AMERICAN FILMMAKING (New York: William Morrow and Company, 1981), pp.202-14; Peter Wollen, "Hybrid Plots in PSYCHO," READINGS AND WRITINGS: SEMIOTIC COUNTER STRATEGIES (London: Verso, 1982), pp.34-9; Jacquelyn N. Zita, "Dark Passages: A Feminist Analysis of PSYCHO," THE PARADIGM EXCHANGE, eds. Rene Jara et al. (Minneapolis: The University of Minnesota Press, 1981), pp.77-84; and J. P. Telotte, "Faith and Idolatry In the Horror Film," LITERATURE/FILM QUARTERLY 8:3 (July 1980):143-55.

developing an obsessive relationship with Judy, he proceeds to literally transform her into the dead woman. Eventually "Scottie" becomes convinced that she is Madeleine and takes her back to the scene of the suicide. There he discovers that she actually impersonated the dead woman in order to make Madeleine's murder look like suicide. After admitting her role in the crime, Judy accidentally falls to her death. One major attraction of the plot and the transformation of Judy is that it serves as a blueprint for psychological critics who insist that Hitchcock was infatuated with cool, blond actresses and was forever "making them over" to satisfy his desires. Stewart, in this type of analysis, functions as the director's alter ego. Feminist critics, on the other hand, view the film as an example of Hitchcock's voyeuristic abuses and sexual fantasies. Formalists admire the director's technical virtuosity, Bernard Herrmann's musical score, and the intricate plot development.[937]

DENNIS HOPPER

EASY RIDER (Raybert--16mm: 1969, 95 mins. color, sound, R-FES, FNC, SWA, WHO)
    Set in the late 1960s, the Peter Fonda-Dennis Hopper-Terry Southern screenplay begins with its protagonists, Billy (Fonda) and Wyatt (Hopper), selling cocaine to a big drug dealer in California. The money they make underwrites their picaresque journey across the United States to New Orleans in search of the American Dream. Being dropouts from society and symbolic of the counterculture, Billy and Wyatt epitomize all that a disillusioned youth culture finds repulsive in society's traditional values. Their motorcycle adventures presumably reflect the freedom offered to the "hippie" generation. Their romanticized trip not only brings them in contact with other outcasts living in a commune, but also with the reactionary elements in small-town America. A chance meeting with a disillusioned, alcoholic civil rights lawyer (Jack Nicholson) sets up a short-lived friendship as the three men ride off to find a better life, away from material values and inhibiting social institutions. In the end, before they are killed by rednecks, the men realize that their search for happiness is a naive exercise in lost innocence. Although contemporary audiences at first saw the outcasts as heroes, more careful reflection revealed that they were only modern outlaws whose perverted values predicted their tragic fates. Critics are still debating whether the freshness of the story, the radical approach to film, and the impressive photography of the motorcyclists traveling against the American landscape compensates for the trite messages and the trendy editing.[938]

---

[937]   In addition to the Hitchcock books, see Francis M. Nevins, Jr., "VERTIGO Re-Visited," JOURNAL OF POPULAR CULTURE 2:2 (Fall 1968):321-2; and Virginia Wright Wexman, "The Critic as Consumer: Film Study In the University, VERTIGO, and the Film Canon," FILM QUARTERLY 39:3 (Spring 1986):32-41.

[938]   For more information, see Tony Reif and Iain Ewig, "Fonda," TAKE ONE 2:3 (January-February 1969):6-10; F. Anthony Macklin, "EASY RIDER: The Initiation of Dennis Hopper," FILM HERITAGE 5:1 (Fall 1969):1-12; Harriet Polt, "EASY RIDER," FILM QUARTERLY 23:1 (Fall 1969):22-4; Stephen Farber, "End of the Road," pp.3-16; Frederick Tuten, "EASY RIDER," FILM SOCIETY REVIEW 4:9 (May 1969):35-40; Thomas R. Sullivan, "EASY RIDER: Comic Epic Poem in FILM," JOURNAL OF POPULAR CULTURE 3:4 (Spring 1970):843-50; Mary Rose Sullivan, "EASY RIDER: Critique of the New Hedonism?" WESTERN HUMANITIES REVIEW 24 (1970):179-87; Deborah H. Holdstein, "EASY RIDER," THE INTERNATIONAL DICTIONARY OF FILMS AND FILMMAKERS: VOLUME I--FILMS, pp.137-9; Charles Hampton, "Movies that Play for Keeps," FILM COMMENT 6:3 (Fall 1970):64-9; Paul Warshow, "EASY RIDER," SIGHT AND SOUND 39:1 (Winter 1969-70):36-8; and Jack Barth and Terry Ellis, "EASY RIDER Revisited," PREMIERE 2:9 (May 1989):86-8, 91-2.

NORMAN JEWISON

IN THE HEAT OF THE NIGHT (United Artists--16mm: 1967, 109 mins., color, sound, R-MGM)

Stirling Silliphant's screenplay, based on John Dudley Ball's novel, follows the adventures of Virgil Tibbs (Sidney Poitier), a black Philadelphia homicide detective, passing through Sparta, Mississippi. When a rich industrialist is murdered, the local police bring Tibbs in for routine questioning. Police Chief Bill Gillespie (Rod Steiger) quickly discovers his mistake and is pressured into having Tibbs work with him to solve the crime. By the end of the film, both men overcome their mutual distrust of the other and part friends. The Poitier role synthesizes many of the parts the distinguished actor had played in his career and serves as an excellent example of the controversy surrounding his movie image and its relevance for black audiences. At Oscar time, the film was nominated for six awards, including Best Director (Jewison), and won five: Best Picture, Best Actor (Steiger), Best Screenplay based on material from another medium (Silliphant), Best Editing (Hal Ashby),[939] and Best Sound (Samuel Goldwyn Studio Sound Department). The biggest surprise of the proceedings was that Poitier didn't even get a nomination, even though he had been in two of the most nominated films of the year: GUESS WHO'S COMING TO DINNER? and IN THE HEAT OF THE NIGHT.

THE RUSSIANS ARE COMING, THE RUSSIANS ARE COMING (United Artists--16mm: 1966, 126 mins., color, sound, R-MGM)

William Rose's farcical screenplay based on a Nathaniel Benchley novel depicts what happens to a sleepy New England town when an incompetent Russian captain (Theodore Bikel) accidentally gets his submarine stuck on the beach. He orders his executive officer (Alan Arkin) to take a landing party ashore to get help. The results offer an uneasy blend of good-natured joking about co-existence and serious political posturing. To Jewison's credit, he keeps the farce on a high level and consistently entertaining. Although the film was nominated for four Oscars--Best Picture, Best Actor (Arkin), Best Screenplay based on material from another medium (Rose), and Best Film Editing (Hal Ashby and J. Terry Williams), it won no honors.[940] Nevertheless, it remains a fine example of the commercial filmmaking that kept Hollywood afloat in the late 1960s.

STANLEY KUBRICK

DR. STRANGELOVE OR: HOW I LEARNED TO STOP WORRYING AND LOVE THE BOMB (Columbia--16mm: 1964, 93 mins., b/w, sound, R-FES, SWA)

The greatest film satire to date on nuclear Armageddon, the project began as a serious statement of the possibility of an accidental occurrence triggering the end of civilization. Kubrick and his fellow screenwriters, Terry Southern and Peter George, soon realized that comedy was closer to the truth about people's behavior than anything he could fictionalize. "After all," he explains, "what could be more

---

[939] For more information, see Glenn Collins, "Hal Ashby, 59, an Oscar Winner Whose Films Included SHAMPOO," NEW YORK TIMES B (December 28, 1988):6.

[940] For more information, see John Baxter, "Jewison, Norman," THE INTERNATIONAL DICTIONARY OF FILMS AND FILMMAKERS: VOLUME I, pp.280-1; Gordon Gow, "Confrontations: Norman Jewison Interviewed," FILMS AND FILMING 17:4 (January 1971):20-4; and ___, "Vibrations: An Interview With John Phillip Law," ibid., 18:7 (April 1972):18-22.

absurd than the very idea of two mega-powers willing to wipe out all human life because of an accident, spiced up by political differences that would seem meaningless to people a hundred years from now as the theological conflicts of the Middle Ages appear to us today."[941] The "nightmare comedy" that resulted remains as powerful today as it was a quarter-century ago. Its absurdities about human behavior, its premise that sexual drives operate as the basis of our insane acts, and its visual portrait of technology mishandled by an incompetent power structure are brilliantly edited and superbly photographed. Among the film's many outstanding performances are those given by Peter Sellers, Sterling Hayden, Keenan Wynn, and George C. Scott. Nominated for four Oscars, including Best Picture, Best Actor (Sellers), Best Director, and Best Screenplay based on material from another medium, it won none.

2001: A SPACE ODYSSEY (MGM--16mm: 1968, 138 mins., color, sound, R-MGM)
     One of the most astonishing and complex films in movie history, this technically brilliant adaption of Arthur C. Clarke's short story about our explorations of new frontiers in space and their antecedents in prehistoric human times bewildered audiences and critics when it first appeared.   Considerable praise was lavished on the special effects, the comic images and dialogue, the imaginative computer named HAL, and the creative cutting, but few people then or since understood what Kubrick and his collaborators were doing with the giant monolith or what the film's denouement represented.[942] Nominated for three Oscars, including Best Director, Best Story and

---

[941] Cited in *Joseph Gelmis, THE FILM DIRECTOR AS A SUPERSTAR (Garden City: Doubleday and Company, 1970), p.309. For more information, see Linda Obalil, "Program Notes: DR. STRANGELOVE, OR: HOW I LEARNED TO STOP WORRYING AND LOVE THE BOMB," CINEMATEXAS PROGRAM NOTES 14:4 (May 1, 1978):75-9; Steve Blackburn, ibid., 24:3 (April 18, 1983):5-9; John Gibson, ibid., 25:3 (April 26, 1984):13-8; Stephen Taylor, "DR. STRANGELOVE," FILM COMMENT 2:1 (Winter 1964):40-3; F. Anthony Macklin, "Sex and DR. STRANGELOVE," ibid., 3:3 (Summer 1965):55-7; Jackson Burgess, "DR. STRANGELOVE," FILM QUARTERLY 17:3 (Spring 1964):41-2; ___, "The 'Anti-Militarism' of Stanley Kubrick," ibid., 18:1 (Fall 1964):4-11; Hans Feldmann, "Kubrick and His Discontents," ibid., 30:1 (Fall 1976):12-9; Mark Carducci, "In Search of Stanley Kubrick," MILLIMETER 3:12 (December 1975):32-7, 49-53; Robin Noble, "Killers, Kisses . . . LOLITA: An Analysis of Stanley Kubrick's Work for the Cinema," FILMS AND FILMING 7:3 (December 1960):11-2, 42; Stanley Kubrick, "How I Stopped Worrying and Love the Cinema," ibid., 9:9 (June 1963):12-3; Ryan Forbes, "DR. STRANGELOVE," ibid., 10:5 (February 1964):26; Stanley Kubrick, "Words and Movies," SIGHT AND SOUND 30:1 (Winter 1960-61):14; Tom Milne, "DR. STRANGELOVE," ibid., 33:1 (Winter 1963-64):37-8; Ken Moskowitz, "Clockwork Violence," ibid., 46:1 (Winter 1976-77):22-4, 44; Lyn Tornabene, "Contradicting the Hollywood Image," SATURDAY REVIEW 46:28 (December 1963):19-21; Russell Lee, "Stanley Kubrick," NEW LEFT REVIEW 26 (Summer 1964):71-4; PLAYBOY Interview: Stanley Kubrick," PLAYBOY 15:9 (September 1968):85-6, 88, 90, 92, 94, 96, 158, 180, 182-4, 186, 190, 192, 195; Jack Hofsess, "Mind's Eye," TAKE ONE 3:5 (May-June 1971):28-9; Harriet and Irving Deer, "Kubrick and the Structures of Popular Culture," JOURNAL OF POPULAR FILM 3:3 (Summer 1974):232-44; Paul D. Zimmerman, "Kubrick's Brilliant Vision," NEWSWEEK 79:1 (January 3, 1972):28-33; Jeremy Bernstein, "Profiles: How About a Little Game?" NEW YORKER 42 (November 12, 1966):70-110; and Harlan Kennedy, "Kubrick Goes Gothic," AMERICAN FILM 5:8 (June 1980):49-52.

[942] For more information, see *Arthur C. Clarke, THE LOST WORLDS OF 2001 (New York: Signet, 1972); *___, 2001: A SPACE ODYSSEY, BASED ON A SCREENPLAY BY STANLEY KUBRICK AND ARTHUR C. CLARKE (New York: Signet, 1968); and Adam Eisenberg and Don Shay, "Jupiter Revisited--the Odyssey of '2010'," CINEFEX 20 (January 1985):4-67.

Screenplay written directly for the screen, and Best Art Direction-Set Direction
(Tony Masters, Harry Lange, Ernie Archer), it won none. Nevertheless, it remains
one of the greatest visual experiences in movie history.

SIDNEY LUMET

THE PAWNBROKER (Landau--16mm: 1965, 115 mins., b/w, sound, R-BUD, FNC, IVY,
TWY)
    The David Friedkin-Morton Fine screenplay based on Edward Lewis Wallant's
novel concerns the fate of Sol Nazerman (Rod Steiger), a Holocaust survivor who runs
a pawnshop in Spanish Harlem. Behaving as if his customers are worthless human
beings, fronting for a black gangster named Rodriguez (Brock Peters), and cutting
himself off from any emotional involvement with his hero-worshipping clerk, Jesus
Ortiz (Jaime Sanchez), Nazerman epitomizes a man terrified to face his past, including
the denigration and murder of his family in a Nazi death camp. Among the many
important cinematic breakthroughs in this controversial film is the image of a black
villain consumed with white values, a Holocaust survivor who is is ruthless to people
in general, and the torment of a Jewish mother forced into prostitution by the Nazis.
The film's theme is that no matter how brutal life becomes, we must go on. Lumet's
dramatic editing techniques showing the parallels between the past and the present
caused some critics to dismiss the movie as sensational and melodramatic, even though
Lumet argued that he had no intention of showing Harlem as a modern concentration
camp. In fact, he claims it was just the reverse. "Harlem in the film," Lumet explains,
"is meant to have an enormous life about it with all its sadnesss . . . Life, Harlem,
with its total claustrophobic future with the no-future of it, that brutal horrible way
of living, has actually more life in it than Sol could ever have imagined."[943] The film's
only Oscar nomination was for Best Actor (Steiger), but he lost to Lee Marvin in
CAT BALLOU.

THE MAYSLES BROTHERS

SALESMAN (The Maysles Brothers--16mm: 1969, 90 mins., b/w, sound, R-NTS)
    Shot in Direct Cinema style, this exceptional film captures the frustrations and
life of four traveling door-to-door Bible salesmen. A good deal of the footage focuses
on the most discouraged of the quartet, Paul Brennan, who at fifty-five, finally gives
up and tries to fathom what the future holds for him. "By resolutely refusing to
patronize their subjects," observes Patrick MacFadden," by insisting on the autonomy

---

[943] Sidney Lumet, "Keep Them on the Hook," FILMS AND FILMING 11:1 (October 1964):17.
    For more information, see Sidney Lumet, The Conscience of a Director," NEW YORK
    HERALD TRIBUNE (August 15, 1965):25; "Sidney Lumet," FILMS AND FILMING 11:9 (June
    1965):8-13; Gordon Gow, "What's Real? What's True?" ibid., 21:8 (May 1975):10-6;
    ___, "Colour and Concepts," ibid., 24:8 (May 1978):12-6; Peter Bogdanovich, "An
    Interview With Sidney Lumet," FILM QUARTERLY 14:2 (Winter 1960):18-23; Graham
    Petrie, "The Films of Sidney Lumet: Adaptation as Art," ibid., QUARTERLY 21:2
    (Winter 1967-68):9-18; Gene Moskowitz, "The Tight Close-Up," SIGHT AND SOUND
    28:3-4 (Summer-Autumn 1959):126-30; Stephen Farber, "Lumet In '69," ibid., 38:4
    (Autumn 1969):190-5; Tony Rayns, "Across the Board," ibid., 43:3 (Summer
    1974):147-8; Dan Yakir, "Wiz Kid," FILM COMMENT 14:6 (November-December
    1978):49-54; and Robert Steele, "Another Trip to the Pawnshop," FILM HERITAGE
    1:3 (Spring 1966):15-22.

of the caught moment, the Maysles have elevated the tawdry activities of marginal commerce to the level of metaphor."[944]

MIKE NICHOLS

THE GRADUATE (Avco Embassy--16mm: 1967, 115 mins., color, sound, R-BUD, CIN, FNC, ROA, SWA, TWY, WHO)
   The Calder Willingham-Buck Henry screenplay based on the novel by Charles Webb deals with Benjamin Braddock (Dustin Hoffman), an honor student who graduates from college and returns home to find himself isolated from his parents, their friends, and the California community that he grew up in. The bond that develops between Ben and Elaine Robinson (Katharine Ross), the daughter of the woman he is having an affair with, and one of his parents' best friends (Anne Bancroft), as well as the film's attack on adults in general, struck a responsive chord with young people in the late 1960s, resulting in the film's often being cited as the best example of the generation gap of the period. Although critics continue to debate the effectiveness of the film's biting satire and its questionable morality, Howard Suber points out that the director Nichols superbly manipulated his audiences through the classical principles of structure, theme, and characterization to create a first-rate situation comedy about coming of age.[945] Nominated for seven Academy Awards,

---

[944] Patrick MacFadden, "SALESMAN," FILM SOCIETY REVIEW 4:6 (February 1969):17. For more information, see Bob Sitton, "An Interview: Albert and David Maysles," FILM LIBRARY QUARTERLY 2:3 (Summer 1969):13-8; Calvin Pryluck, "Seeking to Take the Longest Journey: A Conversation With Albert Maysles," JOURNAL OF THE UNIVERSITY FILM ASSOCIATION 28:2 (Spring 1976):9-16; Vincent Canby, "Why, Even You and I Can Be Stars," NEW YORK TIMES D (April 27, 1969):1, 11; Lawrence Van Gelder, "Maysles: Filming the Impossible," ibid., 2 (October 17, 1987):19; David Sargent, "When Does Invasion of Privacy Become Art," VILLAGE VOICE (October 13, 1975):134; and Michael Tolkin, "The Men Who Made 'GREY GARDENS': What Makes the Maysles Run?" ibid., (April 12, 1976): 142, 140-1.

[945] Suber offers his analysis of THE GRADUATE on the Criterion Collection Lasardisc. Not only is this the best source of information on the movie and a wonderful way to study film, but it also offers excellent ideas on film analysis in general. Suber's heavy reliance on Freudian and Jungian interpretations provides a good introduction to the study of screen comedy, making the argument that most successful films use the first hour to have their protagonists react to situations and the last third of the standard ninety-minute movie to have the protagonists seize control of their destiny. The lasardisc also includes screen tests for the role of Benjamin, the producer's notebook, candid photos and wardrobe stills, descriptions of scenes cut from the film, and promotion material. For more information, see Olive Graham, "Program Notes: THE GRADUATE," CINEMATEXAS PROGRAM NOTES 17:3 (December 4, 1979):81-5; Chuck Schapiro, "Program Notes: THE GRADUATE," ibid., 22:1 (January 25, 1982):15-9; Paul Seydor, "The Graduate Flunks Out," FILM SOCIETY REVIEW 5:5 (January 1970):36-44; Charles Webb, "Interview With Mike Nichols," FILM HERITAGE 4:1 (Fall 1968):1-6; Barbara Gelb, "Mike Nichols: The Special Risks and Rewards of the Director's Art," NEW YORK TIMES MAGAZINE (May 27, 1984), pp.20-5, 28-9, 38, 40-3, 45; Mark W. Estrin, "Nichols, Mike," THE INTERNATIONAL DICTIONARY OF FILMS AND FILMMAKERS: VOLUME II, pp.387-8; Renata Adler, YEAR IN THE DARK: JOURNAL OF A FILM CRITIC (New York: Random House, 1969), pp.40-3; Hollis Alpert, "The Graduate," FILM 68-9: AN ANTHOLOGY OF THE NATIONAL SOCIETY OF FILM CRITICS, eds. Hollis Alpert and Andrew Sarris (New York: Simon and Schuster, 1969), pp.235-41; Manny Farber, NEGATIVE SPACE (New York: Praeger Publishers, 1971), p.189, 195-199; Kael, GOING STEADY, pp.124-7; Kauffmann, FIGURES OF LIGHT, pp.34-6, 201; Schickel, pp.160-2; Simon,

including Best Picture, Best Actor (Hoffman), Best Actress (Bancroft), Best Supporting Actress (Ross), Best Cinematographer (Robert L. Surtees), and Best Screenplay based on material from another Medium (Willingham and Henry), it won an Oscar for Best Director (Nichols).

WHO'S AFRAID OF VIRGINIA WOOLF? (Warner Bros.--16mm: 1966, 129 mins., b/w, sound, R-SWA)
Ernest Lehman's screenplay based upon Edward Albee's play revolutionized Hollywood's depiction of marriage, screen dialogue, and film censorship. On one level, the story of a weak history professor (Richard Burton) and his neurotic wife (Elizabeth Tayor) abusing their house guests (George Segal and Sandy Dennis) in order to resolve the older couple's emotional problems strips away many of the illusions people have about love, family, and friendship. On another level, the plight of George and Martha allegorically deals with American history and the need to reverse the negative direction that the nation has taken. Rather than follow the highly symbolic stage version, Nichols stresses the humanity of the characters and thus makes them very accessible to a mass audience. The director's refusal to compromise either with the issues or the dialogue, initially resulted in the MPAA's refusing the film its Seal of Approval. Jack Warner, however, came up with the famous interim solution of tagging the film with "Suggested for Mature Audiences."[946] Nominated for eleven Academy Awards, including Best Picture, Best Actor (Burton), Best Supporting Actor (Segal), Best Screenplay based on material from another medium (Lehman), Best Sound (George R. Groves), Best Film Editing (Sam O'Steen), and Best Original Music (Alex North), it won Oscars for Best Actress (Taylor), Best Supporting Actress (Dennis), Best Black-and-White Cinematography (Haskell Wexler), and Best Black-and-White Costume Design (Irene Sharaff).

SAM PECKINPAH

RIDE THE HIGH COUNTRY (MGM--16mm: 1962, 94 mins., cinemascope or regular, color, sound, R-MGM)
This Peckinpah classic, scripted by N. B. Stone, Jr, sums up thirty years of "B" westerns as Joel McCrae and Randolph Scott play two aging ex-marshals who

---

MOVIES INTO FILM, pp.103-6; Stephen Farber, "The Graduate," FILM QUARTERLY 21:3 (Spring 1968):37-41; Paul Seydor, "The Graduate," FILM SOCIETY REVIEW 5:5 (January 1970):36-44; Robert L. Surtees, "THE GRADUATE'S Photography," FILMS IN REVIEW 19:2 (February 1968):89-95; Adelaide Comerford, "The Graduate," ibid., 19:1 (January 1968):55; Edgar Z. Friedenberg, "The Graduate," NEW YORK REVIEW OF BOOKS 10:6 (March 28, 1968):25-7; Jim Dawson, "The Graduate," SIGHT AND SOUND 37:3 (Summer 1968):158; F. Anthony Macklin, ". . . Benjamin Will Survive: Interview With Charles Webb," FILM HERITAGE 4:1 (Fall 1968):1-6; Jacob Brackman, "The Graduate," THE NEW YORKER (July 27, 1968):34, 42, 46, 48, 50-2, 54-6, 58-66; Barry Day, "It Depends How You Look At It," FILMS AND FILMING 15:2 (November 1968):4-8; and David Austen, "The Graduate," ibid., 15:1 (October 1968):39-40.

[946] For more information, see Alex Plaza, "Program Notes: WHO'S AFRAID OF VIRGINIA WOOLF?" CINEMATEXAS PROGRAM NOTES 18:1 (February 7, 1980):99-107; Ernest Callenbach, "Who's Afraid of Virginia Woolf?" FILM QUARTERLY 20:1 (Fall 1966):45-8; Gordon Gow, "Who's Afraid of Virginia Woolf?" FILMS AND FILMING 12:12 (September 1966):6; Henry Hart, "Who's Afraid of Virginia Woolf?" FILMS IN REVIEW 17:7 (August-September 1966):448-50; James Price, "Who's Afraid of Virginia Woolf?" SIGHT AND SOUND 35:4 (Autumn 1966):198-9; Farber, pp.178-9; Kauffmann, FIGURES OF LIGHT, pp.1-4; Sarris, CONFESSIONS OF A CULTIST, pp.259-62; and Simon, PRIVATE SCREENINGS, pp.235-8.

escort a gold shipment from the mines and reflect on the value of honesty, dedication, and rewards.[947] William Parrill spoke for many people when he wrote that "Above all, it has the kind of divine simplicity which even the greatest of artists only intermittently achieve."[948]

THE WILD BUNCH (Warners--16mm: 1969, 142 mins., color, sound, R-FES)

In one of his best films, Peckinpah presents a violent Western drama about an outlaw gang's final days along the Texas border between Mexico and the United States in the early 1900s. Not only does the Walon Green-Peckinpah screenplay capture the way American westerns had changed in terms of violence, themes, and values since the post-WWII period, but also the movie itself captures the disillusionment prevalent in America at the end of the sixties. At the same time, as Sam Ho points out, "Peckinpah's nobility, integrity and adroitness dominate, and the film emerges as a truly profound personal statement."[949] Outstanding performances are turned in by William Holden as the bandit leader and Emilio Fernandez as the grinning Mexican renegade Mapache. Nominated for two Academy Awards, including Best Story and Screenplay Written Directly for the Screen (story, Walon Green and Roy N. Sickner; screenplay, Green and Peckinpah) and Best Music (Jerry Fielding), it won none.

---

[947] For more information, see John Dupre, "RIDE THE HIGH COUNTRY," SIGHT AND SOUND 31:3 (Summer 1962):146; Richard Whitehall, "Talking With Peckinpah," ibid., 38:4 (Autumn 1969):172-5; Axel Madsen, "Peckinpah In from the Cold," ibid., 36:3 (Summer 1967):123; ___, "Peckinpah In Mexico," ibid., 43:2 (Spring 1974):91; Colin McArthur, "Sam Peckinpah's West," ibid., 36:4 (Autumn 1967):180-3; Nigel Andrews, "Sam Peckinpah: The Survivor and the Individual," ibid., 42:2 (Spring 1973):69-74; "CAHIERS DU Peckinpah," ESQUIRE 59:2 (February 1973):119-23; Winfred Bevins, "The Artistic Vision of Sam Peckinpah," SHOW 2:1 (Spring 1970):37-40; Ernest Callenbach, "A Conversation With Sam Peckinpah," FILM QUARTERLY 17:2 (Winter 1963-64):3-10; Mark Crispin Miller, "In Defense of Sam Peckinpah," ibid., 28:3 (Spring 1975):2-17; S. Neale, "Sam Peckinpah, Robert Ardrey and the Notion of Ideology," FILM FORUM 1 (Spring 1967):107-11; Andrew Tudor, "Figures in a Landscape: Narrative Strategies in MAJOR DUNDEE," ibid., pp.3-18; Arthur G. Pettit, "Nightmare and Nostalgia: The Cinema of Sam Peckinpah," WESTERN HUMANITIES REVIEW 29:2 (Spring 1975):65-74, 92; William Murray, "PLAYBOY Interview: Sam Peckinpah," PLAYBOY 19:8 (August 1972):65-74, 192; "Sam Peckinpah Lets It All Hang Out," TAKE ONE 2:3 (January-February 1969):18-20; Joseph Leydon, "James Coburn: His Life and HARD TIMES," ibid., 4:12 (December 1975):6-8; Louis Garner Simmons, "Sam Peckinpah's Television Work," FILM HERITAGE 10:2 (Winter 1974-75):1-16; and F. A. Macklin, "Mort Sahl Called Me a 1939 American," ibid., 11:4 (Summer 1976):12-26.

[948] *William Parrill, HEROES' TWILIGHT: THE FILMS OF SAM PECKINPAH (Minneapolis: Burgess Publishing Company, 1983), p.11.

[949] Sam Ho, "Program Notes: THE WILD BUNCH," CINEMATEXAS PROGRAM NOTES 24:3 (April 20, 1983)::19. For more information, see John McCarty, "Sam Peckinpah and THE WILD BUNCH," FILM HERITAGE 5:2 (Winter 1969-70):1-10; Cordell Strug, "THE WILD BUNCH and the Problem of Idealist Aesthetics, or How Long Would Sam Peckinpah Last In Plato's Republic?" ibid., 10:2 (Winter 1974-75):17-26; Stephen Farber, "Peckinpah's Return," FILM QUARTERLY 23:1 (Fall 1969):2-11; John Cutts, "Shoot!--Sam Peckinpah," FILMS AND FILMING 16:1 (October 1969):4-6,8; William Blum, "Toward a Cinema of Cruelty," CINEMA JOURNAL 10:2 (Spring 1972):19-33; William Pechter, "Film Favorites: William Pechter on THE WILD BUNCH," FILM COMMENT 6 (Fall 1970):55-7; and Lawrence Shaffer, "THE WILD BUNCH Versus STRAW DOGS," SIGHT AND SOUND 41:3 (Summer 1972):132-3.

ARTHUR PENN

ALICE'S RESTAURANT (MGM--16mm: 1969, 110 mins., color, sound, R-MGM)
  The Vanable Herndon-Arthur Penn screenplay based on a song by Arlo Guthrie, "The Alice Restaurant's Massacre," recreates the singer's attempts to avoid serving in the Vietnam War. The cynical approach to social and political institutions coupled with the bonding that develops among members of the anti-war movement make this social comedy an impressive historical document on the late 1960s. The episodic, narrative style of the film illustrates not only the influences that low-budget European films were having on Hollywood movies, but also the way new directors were reshaping film conventions in favor of anti-heroes opposed to traditional values. The director Penn's sympathetic but critical examination of the lifestyles of Guthrie's friends and supporters earned him an Oscar nomination for Best Director.[950]

BONNIE AND CLYDE (Warner Bros.--16mm: 1967, 111 mins., color, sound, R-FES)
  In one of the most important films of the 1960s, Penn superbly mixes comedy and violence as he re-creates the Depression-era milieu of Bonnie Parker (Faye Dunaway) and Clyde Barrow (Warren Beatty). The David Newman-Robert Benton script reworked a basic plot that had surfaced before in Fritz Lang's YOU ONLY LIVE ONCE (1937) and Nicholas Ray's THEY DRIVE BY NIGHT (1949). In modernizing the story, however, the filmmakers had the benefit of a new ratings system that permitted more realistic treatment of sex and violence, as well as sympathy for outlaws and rebels. While critics disagree strongly over how skillfully Penn crafted his Depression tale of sexual perversion and violent bloodbaths, audiences from the late 1960s to the present find the movie fresh and riveting. "What is most striking in the film," Austar and Quart point out, "is not the pathetic ordinariness of the characters or their psychological or social reality, but their mythic quality."[951] Nominated for ten Academy Awards, including Best Picture, Best Director (Penn), Best Actor (Beatty), Best Actress (Dunaway), Best Supporting Actor (Michael J. Pollard and Gene Hackman), and Best Costume Design (Theodora Van Runkle), it won for Best Supporting Actress (Estelle Parsons), Best Story and Screenplay written directly for the screen (Newman and Benton), and Best Cinematography (Burnett Guffey).

SYDNEY POLLACK

THEY SHOOT HORSES, DON'T THEY? (ABC--16mm: 1969, 129 mins., color, sound, R-FNC)
  The James Poe-Robert E. Thompson screenplay based on Horace McCoy's significant Depression novel uses the disturbing story of desperate people trying to survive by winning a marathon dance contest to draw parallels with American society

---

[950] For more information, see Louis Black, "Program Notes: ALICE'S RESTAURANT," CINEMATEXAS PROGRAM NOTES 18:2 (March 6, 1980):61-9; Robert Seidman and Nicholas Leiber, "Making Peace with the 60s," AMERICAN FILM 7:3 (December 1981):67, 69-71; Wendy Bell, "Arthur Penn: Directing Films and Plays," MIS-EN-SCENE 1 (1976):62-5; Philip Kemp, Penn, Arthur," THE INTERNATIONAL DICTIONARY OF FILMS AND FILMMAKERS: VOLUME II, pp.411-3; Terence Butler, "Arthur Penn: The Flight from Identity," MOVIE 26 (Winter 1978-1979):43-64; and Robin Wood, "Arthur Penn In Canada," ibid., 18 (Winter 1970-1971):26-36.

[951] Auster and Quart, p.10. For more information, see John G. Cawelti, "BONNIE AND CLYDE Revisited: Part One," FOCUS 7 (Spring 1972):13-5, 39; and ___, "BONNIE AND CLYDE Revisited: Part Two," ibid., 8 (Autumn 1972):51-4.

in the Vietnam era. The manipulative and vicious promoter (Gig Young) who exploits the contestants symbolizes how national leaders play on our fears and desires for their own ends. In depicting the disillusionment and destruction of the worldweary heroine (Jane Fonda), the director Pollack describes how people are deceived and betrayed by misdirected ambitions and false hopes. The marathon dance itself becomes a metaphor for the American Dream. Although critics are divided over the film's heavy-handed symbolism, few would deny the movie's value as a historical artifact showing how the Vietnam War directly influenced the content of Hollywood movies in the late 1960s. Nominated for nine Academy Awards, including Best Actress (Fonda), Best Supporting Actress (Susannah York), Best Director (Pollack), Best Screenplay Based on Material from Another Medium (Poe and Thompson), Best Art Direction-Set Decoration (Harry Horner), Film Editing (Frederick Steinkamp), Best Score of a Musical Picture (John Green and Albert Woodbury), and Best Costume Design (Donfeld), it won an Oscar for Best Supporting Actor (Gig Young).[952]

LIONEL ROGOSIN

COME BACK, AFRICA (Rogosin--16mm: 1960, 90 mins., b/w, sound, R-ICS; S-ICS)
    One of the first important films about APARTHEID, this semi-documentary movie about South Africa skillfully blends visuals and music to capture many of the problems of young Africans living in turmoil.[953]

FRANKLIN J. SCHAFFNER

THE BEST MAN (United Artists--16mm: 1964, 80 mins., b/w, sound, R-MGM)
    Gore Vidal's screenplay adapted from his successful Broadway play focuses on a deadlocked U. S. Presidential nominating convention, where the principal opponents--a vacillating ex-secretary of state (Henry Fonda) and a reprehensible Senator (Cliff Robertson)--are seeking the political support of an uncommitted former president (Lee Tracy).[954] The strategies used by both camps and the choices the candidates are forced to make were patterned originally on the campaign practices of Adlai Stevenson and Richard Nixon during the 1950s, but in the early 1960s, after Vidal broke with Bobby Kennedy, the film appeared to have an anti-Kennedy bias in the characterization of the ruthless senator.[955] In addition to a witty, cynical, and absorbing script, Schaffner's favorite film contains excellent examples of clever

---

[952] For more information, see Stephen Farber, "The Monster Marathon," CINEMA (Calif) 6:1 (1970):10-5; Aljean Harmetz, "Sydney Didn't Want to Shoot 'Horses'," NEW YORK TIMES D (March 8, 1970):13; ___, "Gig Finally Made It, Didn't He?" ibid., D (April 26, 1970):16; Patricia Erens, "Sydney Pollack: The Way We Are," FILM COMMENT 11:5 (September-October 1975):24-9; ___, "Pollack, Sydney," THE INTERNATIONAL DICTIONARY OF FILMS AND FILMMAKERS: VOLUME I, pp.420-1; "Dialogue on Film: Sydney Pollack," AMERICAN FILM 3:6 (April 1978):33-48; "Dialogue on Film: Sydney Pollack," ibid., 12: 3 (December 1986):13-5; Axel Madsen, "Pollack's Hollywood History," SIGHT AND SOUND 42:3 (Summer 1973):149; and Michael Buckley, "Gig Young," FILMS IN REVIEW 22:2 (February 1971):66-84.

[953] For information on racism in South African films, see *Keyan Tomaselli, THE CINEMA OF APARTHEID: RACE AND CLASS IN SOUTH AFRICAN FILM (New York: Smyrna Press, 1988).

[954] For more information, see "Dialogue on Film: Gore Vidal," AMERICAN FILM 2:6 (April 1977):33-48.

[955] Erwin Kim, FRANKLIN J. SCHAFFNER (Metuchen: The Scarecrow Press, 1985), pp.176-9.

editing techniques and strong performances. Particular praise for the film's "authentic" look goes to the cinematographer Haskell Wexler.[956] Tracy won the Oscar for Best Supporting Actor.

PLANET OF THE APES (Fox--16mm: 1968, 112 mins., color, sound, R-FNC, WIL)

The Rod Serling-Michael Wilson screenplay adapted from a book by Pierre Boulle deals with the allegorical adventures of four astronauts, led by Charlton Heston, who after flying through thousands of earth years, find themselves marooned on an "unknown" planet ruled by intelligent apes. Believing the astronauts to be a threat to their civilization, the simians systematically set out to kill them. Eventually, Heston confronts the head of the ape society (Maurice Evans) and learns why humans are considered dangerous beasts. In the end, the lone surviving astronaut discovers that the wasteland around him is Earth, and that human beings had set their own destruction in motion through nuclear wars. This extraordinary film not only spawned four sequels and two TV series, but also reflected the era's growing fears about the misuse of nuclear power. Nominated for two Academy Awards, Best Original Score (Jerry Goldsmith) and Best Costume Design (Morton Haack), it won an Honorary Oscar for its outstanding make-up (John Chambers).

STAN VANDERBEEK

A LA MODE (16mm: 1958, 5 mins., b/w, sound, R-FMC, C16)

A filmmaker who works primarily in animation, Vanderbeek describes his film as "A montage of women and appearances, a fantasy about beauty and the female, a formage, a mirage."[957]

BREATHDEATH (16mm: 1964, 15 mins., b/w, sound,

One of his best films. Vanderbeek explains the movie as

. . . a film experiment that deals with the photo reality and the surrealism of life. It is a collage-animation that cuts up photos and newsreel film and reassembles them; producing an image that is a mixture of unexplainable fact (Why is Harpo Marx playing a harp in the middle of a battlefield?) with the inexplicable act (Why is there a battlefield?). It is black comedy that mocks at death . . . a parabolic parable.[958]

---

[956] For more information, see David Wilson, "Franklin Schaffner," SIGHT AND SOUND 35:2 (Spring 1966):73-5; Stanley Lloyd Kaufman, Jr., "The Early Franklin J. Schaffner," FILMS IN REVIEW 20:7 (August-September 1969):409-18; Kenneth Geist, "Chronicler of Power: Interview With Franklin Schaffner," FILM COMMENT 8:3 (September-October 1972):29-36; Dale Monroe, "Franklin Schaffner: From PLANET OF THE APES to PATTON," SHOW 1:10 (August 6, 1970):16-7; Gerald Pratley, "An Interview With Franklin Schaffner," CINEASTE 3:1 (Summer 1969):11-6; and Franklin Schaffner, "The Best and Worst of It," FILMS AND FILMING 11:1 (October 1964):9-11.

[957] FILM-MAKER'S COOPERATIVE CATALOGUE, p.61

[958] ibid., p.62.

ANDY WARHOL

THE CHELSEA GIRLS (Warhol--16mm: 1966, 195 mins., b/w, sound, R-FMC)
Warhol's alternative cinema, stressing ironic relationships between performers and audiences, began to take on commercial overtones with this best known and most popular of his early films. Scripted in part by Ronald Tavel and intended as a further demystification of the illusion of Hollywood glamour, the idea was to show people as they are instead as performers playing a part in a film. The result is a three-hour, fifteen-minute movie containing twelve separate reels, each unedited and of equal length (eight are in color, four in black-and-white), and projecting individual conversations with Warhol's associates. The ideal exhibition is to screen two reels at a time. From the perspective of one Warhol biographer, the film is "a successful effort to ceaselessly play sound against image in an elaborate mechanistic counterpoint."[959]

ORSON WELLES

TOUCH OF EVIL (Universal--16mm: 1958, 108 mins., color, sound, R-SWA)
Directed by Welles and based on his screen adaptation (originally written by Paul Monash) of Whit Masterson's novel, the film focuses on the murder of a local official in a seedy town near the Mexican-American border. When a Mexican investigator (Charlton Heston) arrives to investigate the crime, he quickly discovers that the corrupt American cop (Orson Welles) who runs the town needs a conviction and is willing to pin the murder on the most convenient person around, Heston. The wheeling and dealing that takes place as the innocent cop fights to clear his name and escape Welles's ingenious machinations makes not only for a thrilling story, but also for a beautifully crafted work of art. Particular praise is given to the opening three-minute sequence in which the director Welles establishes the mood and tone of the film. In addition to Russell Mety's impressive photography and Welles's much admired MISE EN SCENE, strong performances are turned in by Heston, Welles, Janet Leigh, Joseph Calleia, Akim Tamiroff, Roy Collins, Dennis Weaver, and Marlene Dietrich.[960]

THE TRIAL/LE PROCES (France--16mm: 1962, 118 mins., b/w, sound, R-BUD, COR, EMG, FES, FNC, IMA, KIT; S-FES, KIT)
Written and directed by Welles, this excellent rendition of the Franz Kafka novel[961] tells a terrifying story about a petty bureaucrat (Anthony Perkins) who wakes up one morning to find himself accused of an unknown crime that he didn't commit and can't avoid being punished for. Interestingly, Welles later explained that in his mind, the man, though innocent of the charges brought against him, was guilty of another crime, of belonging "to something which represents evil and which is a part of him at the same time . . . he belongs to a guilty society, he collaborates

---

[959] *Stephen Koch, STARGAZER: ANDY WARHOL'S WORLD AND HIS FILMS, 2nd ed. (New York: Marion Boyars, 1985), p.64.

[960] In addition to the excellent material available in Terry Comito's anthology, see John Henley, "Program Notes: TOUCH OF EVIL," CINEMATEXAS PROGRAM NOTES 14:4 (April 19, 1978):7-17; and David Rodowick, "Program Notes: TOUCH OF EVIL," ibid., 22:3 (1982):73-9.

[961] For a good discussion of the screen adaptation of the novel, see James Naremore, THE MAGIC WORLD OF ORSON WELLES (New York: Oxford University Press, 1978), pp.233-56.

with it."[962] Useful comparisons can be made between Kafka's nightmarish conventions in the book and film and the various Welles films from CITIZEN KANE (1941) on.

CORNEL WILDE

THE NAKED PREY (Paramount--16mm: 1966, 94 mins., cinemascope and regular, color, sound, R-FNC)

Clint Johnson's screenplay adapted from his own story deals with a white hunter (Cornel Wilde) who is captured by natives in the South African jungle and then given a chance to survive by participating in an ancient tribal ritual. Stripped of his clothes and his weapons, he is given a brief headstart before members of the tribe begin to track him down. At the time of its release, many people found the producer-director Wilde's stunning cinematic exposition of the hunter's battle to survive a riveting experience.[963] But as a result of the emergence of a growing black consciousness in the 1970s, a number of people now see the film as racist. For example, the critic James Murray states, "How one unarmed man . . . could outwit for countless days, on their own terrain, the warriors of an African tribe remains steadfastly beyond my comprehension."[964]

FREDERICK WISEMAN

TITICUT FOLLIES (Evergreen--16mm: 1967, 89 mins., b/w, sound, R-ZIP/L-ZIP)

One of the most haunting and overpowering documentaries of its kind, this revealing look by the producer-director Frederick Wiseman and his cinematographer John Marshall, at Bridgewater State Prison Hospital for the Criminally Insane in Massachusetts, is a shocking condemnation of society's inhumane treatment of the mentally ill. The bulk of the film depicts how the inmates live, the way they are treated, and the attitudes of the medical staff. The film's title refers to the annual recreational show put on by the inmates and some of their attendants. As a result of the controversy generated by the depressing images and information, Wiseman points out, "Three hundred inmates were sent to other institutions, people who had been kept naked for years got clothes, [and] fifty nurses were added down there. . . ."[965]

---

[962]   Cited in *THE TRIAL: A FILM BY ORSON WELLES, trans. Nicholas Fry (New York: Simon and Schuster, 1970), p.9.

[963]   John Coen, "Cornel Wilde: Producer/Director," FILM COMMENT 6:1 (Spring 1970):52-61; and Gordon Gow, "Survival!" FILMS AND FILMING 17:1 (October 1970):4-8, 10.

[964]   James P. Murray, TO FIND AN IMAGE: BLACK FILMS FROM UNCLE TOM TO SUPER FLY (Indianapolis: The Bobbs-Merrill Company, 1973), p.139.

[965]   Donald E. McWilliams, "Frederick Wiseman," FILM QUARTERLY 24:1 (Fall 1970):20. For more information, see Janet Handelman, "An Interview With Frederick Wiseman," FILM LIBRARY QUARTERLY 3:3 (Summer 1970):5-9; Michael Desilets, "Fred Wiseman: TITICUT Revisted," ibid., 4:2 (Spring 1971):29-33, 56; Stephen Mamber, "The New Documentaries of Frederick Wiseman," CINEMA (Calif) 6:1 (1970):33-40; and John Graham, "There Are No Simple Solutions--Frederick Wiseman on Viewing Film," THE FILM JOURNAL 1:1 (Spring 1971):44-7.

FRANCE AND PARALLEL REVOLUTIONS (1955-1969)

In 1958, a French journalist named Francois Giroud coined the expression " LA NOUVELLE VAGUE" (THE NEW WAVE) to describe the exciting and controversial social and political events taking place in French society. But to film historians and critics, LA NOUVELLE VAGUE represents a period in French film history (1958-1963) when nearly 175 directors made their 35mm feature film debuts, ironically at a time when, by 1963, French film attendance fell to a third of its 1957 total of 290 million people.[966] The most significant of the emerging directors were either writers-turned-directors, or filmmakers of documentary shorts who graduated into feature film production. Most of them had spent countless hours watching movies at the CINEMATEQUE FRANCAISE, determined eventually to apply their revolutionary theories to traditional film narratives.[967] "If this movement could be described in one word," Leo Braudy observes, "that word might be 'self-consciousness'--at all levels: a self-consciousness about film history and tradition, a self-consciousness about the act of making a film, a self-consciousness in the audience, which approaches a film more as a cultural artifact than as entertainment for which the mind is turned off, and, perhaps the most important aspect, a self-consciousness about the role of the director, matched with the audience's own increased awareness that the director is a 'star' too."[968]

Exactly who comprised the NOUVELLE VAGUE and the reasons for its controversial and brief existence are still being debated. For example, Eric Breitbart asserts that Jean-Pierre Melville's LE SILENCE DE LA MER (1947) made him "the father of NOUVELLE VAGUE,"[969] while Georges Sadoul claims that Agnes Varda's LA POINTE-COURTE (1955) is "the first film of the French NOUVELLE VAGUE."[970] Burch insists that Jacques Rivette's short film, LA COUP DU BERGER (1956) signaled the

---

[966] Rhode, p.525. Annette Insdorf presents the figures differently, claiming that twenty-four French film directors made their feature film debuts in 1959; forty-three directors in 1960. See Annette Insdorf, FRANCOIS TRUFFAUT (Boston: Twayne Publishers, 1978), p.23.

[967] For more information, see Michel Simon, "Les Enfants Terribles," AMERICAN FILM 10:3 (December 1984):36-9, 42, 86, 91; Jacques Siclier, "New Wave and French Cinema," SIGHT AND SOUND 30:3 (Summer 1961):116-20; Gabriel Pearson and Eric Rhode, "Cinema of Appearance," ibid., 30:4 (Autumn 1961):160-8; Gilles Jacob, "Nouvelle Vague or Jeune Cinema," ibid., 34:1 (Winter 1964-65):4-8; Georges Sadoul, "Notes on a New Generation," ibid., 28:3, 4 (Summer-Autumn 1959):111-6; Noel Burch, "Qu'est-ce que la Nouvelle Vague," FILM QUARTERLY 13:2 (Winter 1959):16-30; Stephen Taylor, "After the Nouvelle Vague," ibid., 18:3 (Spring 1965):5-9; Colin Young, and Gideon Bachmann, "New Wave or Gestures," ibid., 14:3 (Spring 1961):6-14; Eugen Weber, "An Escapist Realism," ibid., 13:2 (Winter 1959):9-16; Peter Graham, "The Face of '63: France," FILMS AND FILMING 9:8 (May 1963):13-22; Raymond Durgnat, "The Decade: France--A Mirror for Marianne," ibid., 9:2 (November 1962):48-55; and David Austen, "All Guns and Gangsters," ibid., pp.52-6, 58-60.

[968] *Leo Braudy, "Introduction," FOCUS ON "SHOOT THE PIANO PLAYER," ed. Leo Braudy (Englewood Cliffs: Prentice-Hall, 1972), p.1.

[969] Breitbart, p.18.

[970] DICTIONARY OF FILMS, p.288.

new direction French films were taking in the mid-1950s.[971] Both Francois Truffaut and James Monocao believe that if the film establishment took documentary shorts more seriously, Alain Resnais would be acclaimed the forerunner of the new movement.[972] Eric Rohmer insists that Claude Chabrol inspired the NOUVELLE VAGUE because (1) he set up his own company, (2) produced his own feature film debut with HANDSOME SERGE/LE BEAU SERGE/BITTER REUNION (1958), and (3) won the AVANCE SUR RECETTES to finance his second film THE COUSINS/LES COUSINS (1959).[973] Jean Rouch, on the other hand, credits Rossellini with playing a key role in getting the New Wave started.[974] No matter which side one takes in the debate, the fact is that by the late 1950s, dozens and dozens of young French filmmakers were making autobiographical, self-conscious films with minimal budgets, unknown performers, and lightweight equipment.

The reasons why this rebellion against the "Tradition of Quality," discussed earlier, occurred when it did are also open to debate. For example, Truffaut feels that "The 'New Wave' was invented not by filmmakers but by journalists on the outside."[975] Ian Cameron insists that

> The French New Wave was less a movement than a situation: for a year or two, conditions favoured the emergence of new directors willing to work on frequently illusory budgets at a time when the established heavyweights were producing poor returns. The boom ground quickly to a halt, though the NOUVELLE VAGUE label hung around for quite a time, particularly in the realm of P. R., and was used by critics in a pejorative way to describe the use of hand-held cameras and jump-cutting in later pictures. The term CINEMA VERITE suffered the same fate at even higher speed.[976]

Rhode, on the other hand, sees the five-year phenomenon growing out of the close links between the youthful directors and the emerging TV generation, both of which had a strong interest in "sexually emancipated women."[977] Jame Monaco dismisses such

---

[971]   "Qu'est-ce que la Nouvelle Vague," p.17.

[972]   *James Monaco, ALAIN RESNAIS (New York: Oxford University Press, 1979), p.18; and Francois Truffaut, THE FILMS IN MY LIFE, trans. Leonard Mayhew (New York: Simon and Schuster, 1975), p.19.

[973]   If not for Chabrol's persistence and success, Rohmer states, ". . . the adventure of the NOUVELLE VAGUE might have stopped there. . . ." Cited in Graham Petrie, "Eric Rohmer: An Interview," FILM QUARTERLY 24:4 (Summer 1971):34.

[974]   According to Rouch, "Before the New Wave, it was forbidden to buy 35mm film without the permission of the Centre du Cinema. When Melville shot LE SILENCE DE LA MER, he had to steal the film. The New Wave was the first reaction to the terrible threat to all art: corporation . . . [Rossellini] came to Paris with his fame . . . and told us: "You can make all the films you want. I'll find you the money in the US or Italy. . . ." Cited in Yakir, p.9.

[975]   Annette Insdorf, "Francois Truffaut on the New mave: Truffaut Looks Back," NEW YORK TIMES H (February 26, 1984):1, 33.

[976]   *Ian Cameron, ed. SECOND WAVE (New York: Praeger Publishers, 1970), p.5.

[977]   Rhode, p.526. The author claims that films like Alexandre Astruc's LES MAUVAISES RECONTRES (1955), Roger Vadim's AND GOD CREATED WOMEN/ET DIEU CREA LA FEMME (1956), and Louis Malle's FRANTIC/ELEVATOR TO THE SCAFFOLD/L'ASCENSEUR POUR L'ECHAFAUD (1957) and THE LOVERS/LES AMANTS (1958) pioneered the New Wave's

perspectives as oversimplifications, arguing instead that by the start of the 1960s, the practical and theoretical issues raised by individual groups had converged. "It becomes evident," he asserts, "that most of New Wave theory, rather than being self-willed, was a natural organic development of the art." According to Monaco, "If CAHIERS DU CINEMA had not existed French film would nevertheless have developed along pretty much the same lines."[978]

These debates notwithstanding, it is clear that at the head of the NOUVELLE VAGUE were a group of ex-critics from the CAHIERS DU CINEMA, whose self-reflexive, personal films exploited the classical conventions of Hollywood "B" movies, and established a dialectical contact between the filmmaker and the audience. At the same time, it is important to stress at the outset, that there were striking political and intellectual differences among the group. Not only did critics like Claude Chabrol, Jean-Luc Godard, Jacques Rivette, Eric Rohmer, and Francois Truffaut have different values and goals, but these differences also became highly politicized in the 1960s. Moreover, as CAHIERS DU CINEMA itself became committed to re-evaluating its application of the AUTEUR theory and the implications for its pantheon of directors, the role that MISE EN SCENE played in the art of the film came to the forefront, forcing the critics-turned-filmmakers to battle among themselves over the issue of "modernism" in the contemporary cinema. As will be discussed later, those battles and the films that resulted had implications far beyond those of the French cinema.[979]

In the beginning, however, their cinematic outlook was indebted, as Annette Insdorf reminds us, to the technological changes taking place during the 1950s:

> The advent of lightweight equipment made it possible to shoot with a handheld camera that is virtually an extension of the filmmaker's body. Less expensive camera methods introduced a visual freedom (for example, the cultivation of cinematic roughness) that permitted more identification between camera and director--and, consequently, between camera and audience.[980]

Whether it was Chabrol's allegiance to Hitchcockian-type thrillers or Truffaut and Godard's love for classic Hollywood genres, the dual vision that linked most of the CAHIERS DU CINEMA filmmakers, as James Monaco explains, was the ability "to parody or comment upon the language they were employing at the same time as they used it to speak of other, more human or political concerns."[981] Paradoxically, as Insdorf points out, the group's "limited knowledge of English made them uniquely equipped to appreciate individual cinematic style: the American films often had no subtitles, thereby inviting a closer look at how meaning is expressed through visual

---

attacks on the dominant hegemony and its puritanical cinema. Astruc's film about the recollections of a woman accused of abortion caters to the audience's impatience with adult hypocrisy, while Vadim's amoral story about an unconscionable woman demonstrates the public's growing fascination with anti-establishment themes. One could also argue that Vadim's success was also due to the appealing personality of the film's star and his new bride, Brigitte Bardot. More enduring in film history was Jeanne Moreau, the star of Malle's two films dealing with the problems of a prostitute and an adulterous wife, respectively.

[978] ALAIN RESNAIS, p.9.

[979] For a useful retrospective on the ex-critics from CAHIERS DU CINEMA, see G. S. Bourdain, "Celebrating France's Directors Who Rode the New Wave," NEW YORK TIMES C (August 11, 1989):1, 14.

[980] FRANCOIS TRUFFAUT, p.23.

[981] ALAIN RESNAIS, p.8.

texture, camera movement, and editing."[982] Consequently, the New Wave was known for its emphasis on visual spontaneity and improvisational techniques, rather than for its concern for film dialogue and plot development.

In many respects, as Burch observes, the journalists-turned-directors were a throwback to France's AVANT-GARDE movement in the 1920s. The basic difference, however, was that the CAHIERS DU CINEMA group focused on "MORAL VALUES," whereas their predecessors focused on "aesthetic problems."[983] The critics-turned-filmmakers--e.g., Chabrol, Godard, Truffaut, Rohmer, and Rivette--initially demonstrated a a pride in French culture, a strong commitment to Christian morality, a love for American FILM NOIR, an aversion to the industry's traditional studio-made products, and a devotion to directors whose personality permeated all their works. This last point is particularly important. CAHIERS DU CINEMA and its major rival, POSITIF, carried on extensive arguments about the significance of the AUTEUR theory.[984] Even the CAHIERS DU CINEMA group themselves disagreed about which filmmakers qualified for the pantheon of film.

No less a figure than Andre Bazin, one of the co-founders of the influential periodical and the spiritual leader of the "young turks," in his seminal 1957 article, "LA POLITIQUE DES AUTEURS," aired his disagreements with his disciples over their failure to anchor their critical judgments within a historical and industrial context. Because of the article's crucial status in film history, it is worth pausing to consider Bazin's arguments. After acknowledging that his journal embraced the AUTEUR theory, the Catholic idealist pointed out that not all of CAHIERS DU CINEMA contributors shared similar enthusiasms for AUTEURS like Alfred Hitchcock, Jean Renoir, Roberto Rossellini, Fritz Lang, Howard Hawks, Vincente Minnelli, Anthony Mann, Orson Welles, Charlie Chaplin, or Nicholas Ray. Bazan made it clear that disagreements about favorite AUTEURS are not synonymous with disagreements about the validity of the AUTEUR theory itself. He saw the former as debatable, the latter was not. Unifying the CAHIERS DU CINEMA critics is their belief that there is "a personal factor in artistic creation" and that it "continues and progresses from one film to the next."[985] The "family quarrel," he explains, is over "the relationship between the work and its creator," not whether a relationship exists.[986] Having addressed the internal disagreements, Bazin then turns to what he sees as the limitations of AUTEURIST criticism: e.g., subjectivity instead of objectivity, overinterpretations resulting from naivete rather than persuasive evidence, and fuzzy distinctions between major and minor works. The problem, Bazin reasons, results from AUTEURIST critics incorrectly presuming that film is like the traditional arts. It isn't. The problem is that the youthful critics overreact to the novelist Jean Giraudoux's

---

[982] FRANCOIS TRUFFAUT, p. 20.

[983] "Qu'est-ce que la Nouvelle Vague," p. 17.

[984] The influential rival of CAHIERS DU CINEMA adamantly opposed the notion of AUTEURISM, the films made by the majority of critics-turned-filmmakers, and the conservative values of Bazin and Rohmer. On the other hand, as Hillier points out, POSITIF warmly embraced the work of the New Left group. See CAHIERS DU CINEMA: 1960-1968--NEW WAVE, NEW CINEMA, REEVALUATING HOLLYWOOD, pp. 14-5. For information on the controversy between the British periodical MOVIE and Pauline Kael over the AUTEUR theory, see Ian Cameron et al. "MOVIE vs. Kael," FILM QUARTERLY 17:1 (Fall 1963):57-64.

[985] Bazin's essay is reprinted in many publications. The citation here are from Andre Bazin, LA POLITIQUES DES AUTEURS," THE NEW WAVE, ed. Peter Graham (Garden City: Doubleday and Company, 1968), p. 151.

[986] Bazin, p. 138.

aphorism that "'There are no works, there are only AUTEURS'."[987] After identifying defects in this extreme polemical position, he points out that movies are industrial products.   That is, filmmakers operating in Hollywood have their work heavily influenced by political, economic, and technical factors. Stressing the necessity of discussing films in an industrial context, Bazin then rejects the notion that great talents grow old. They don't; they just mature. But he offers a crucial caveat. While great artists may not age, the cinema does; and "those who do not know how to grow old WITH it will be overtaken by its evolution."[988] To avoid reducing critical judgments to a single measuring rod or to the alleged superiority of the critic's taste, Bazin points out the importance of genres, particularly in American films. Not only do genres contain conventions established by the audience and by the industry and developed over a prolonged period of time, he argues, but also the existence of conventions is "a base of operations for creative freedom."[989] In short, Bazin applauds the concept of AUTEUR, but asks AUTEUR "of What?"[990]

The AUTEUR theory and Bazin's criticisms of it, as James Monaco explains, provided two vital corrollaries for the CAHIERS filmmakers.   One corollary is the emphasis on "a PERSONAL relationship between filmmaker and film viewer, on movies as "intimate conversations between the people behind the camera and the people in front of the screen."[991] A second corollary of the AUTEUR theory, Monaco argues, is that it turns theatrical filmmaking into a dialectical process. That is, "A movie becomes the sum of a whole set of oppositions: between auteur and genre; between director and audience; between critic and film; between theory and practice; or between 'Method and Sentiment,' in Godard's words."[992] Every prominent member of the   CAHIERS   group--e.g.,   Chabrol,   Godard,   Rivette,   Rohmer,   and Truffaut--incorporated aspects of these values into his works.

The famous film revolution exploded on the international scene at the 1959 Cannes Film Festival, when two of the leading prizes were won by Truffaut's THE FOUR HUNDRED BLOWS/LES QUATRE CENT COUPS, and Resnais's HIROSHIMA MON AMOUR.[993] Not only did these films mark their directors' feature film debuts, but also they, along with Chabrol's second film, THE COUSINS/LES COUSINS (1959), collectively established the NOUVELLE VAGUE as the dominant cinematic mode in

---

[987]   Bazin, p.139.

[988]   Bazin, p.150.

[989]   Bazin, p.154.

[990]   In the 1960s, Andrew Sarris, America's foremost authority on the AUTEUR theory, responded to Bazin's reservations by pointing out three specific criteria for determining who should be considered an AUTEUR: (1) "technical competence," (2) "distinguishable personality," and (3) "tension between a director's personality and his material." See Andrew Sarris, "Notes on the Auteur Theory in 1962," FILM CULTURE 27 (Winter 1962-63):1-8.

[991]   James Monaco, THE NEW WAVE: TRUFFAUT, GODARD, CHABROL, ROHMER, RIVETTE (New York: Oxford University Press, 1976), p.8.

[992]   Monaco, p.8.

[993]   Another notable work at Cannes that year was Marcel Camus's BLACK ORPHEUS/ORFEU NEGRO, winner of the top prize, PALM D'OR. Also of interest is the fact that Truffaut was barred from the Cannes Film Festival the year before because of his savage attacks on the festival in CAHIERS DU CINEMA. Only political influence made his entry in the 1959 festival possible.

France. To understand why and how, let us consider the most prominent members of the New Wave.[994]

Of all the CAHIERS DU CINEMA critics, Claude Chabrol was the first to make his feature film debut.[995] Ironically, as Roger Ebert comments, the intriguing and erratic filmmaker "was the first of the New Wave to be praised, and the first to be dismissed."[996] Even then, the praise never attained the level accorded Godard, Resnais, or Truffaut; while in the mid-1970s, after completing twenty-three feature films and three shorts, as Charles Wolfe points out, Chabrol remained "at best on the periphery of any historical or critical notion in this country of the old New Wave

---

[994] For more information on Jacques Rivette, see Jonathan Rosenbaum et al., "Jacques Rivette," FILM COMMENT 10:5 (September-October 1974):18-24; Louis Marcorelles, "PARIS NOUS APPARTIENT," SIGHT AND SOUND 28:1 (Winter 1958-59):34;   ___, "Interview With Roger Leenhardt and Jacques Rivette," ibid., 32:4 (Autumn 1963):168-173; Elliot Stein, "Suzanne Simonin, Diderot's Nun," ibid., 35:3 (Summer 1966):130-3; Carlos Clarens and Edgardo Cozarinsky, "An Interview with Jacques Rivette," ibid., 43:4 (Autumn 1974):195-8; William Johnson, "Recent Rivette: An Inter-Re-View," FILM QUARTERLY 38:2 (Winter 1974-75):32-9; and Jean-Andre Fieschi, "Jacques Rivette," CINEMA: A CRITICAL DICTIONARY, VOLUME TWO, pp.871-8.

[995] For more information, see Ian Cameron, "The Darwinian World of Claude Chabrol," MOVIE 10 (June 1963):4-9; Jean-Andre Fieschi, "Wait and See: Chabrol's Films Not Yet Shown in Britain," trans. Garry Broughton and Mark Shivas, ibid., pp.10-3; ___ and Mark Shivas, "Interview With Chabrol," trans. Garry Broughton and Mark Shivas, ibid., pp.16-20; Robin Wood, "Chabrol and Truffaut," ibid., 17 (Winter 1969-70):16-24; Michel Ciment et al., "Claude Chabrol Interviewed," trans. Elisabeth Cameron, ibid., 18 (Winter 1970-71):2-9; Michael Walker, "Claude Chabrol into the 'Seventies," ibid., 20 (Spring 1975):44-64; Gordon Gow, "When the New Wave Became Old Hat: The Films of Claude Chabrol," FILMS AND FILMING 13:6 (March 1967):20-6; ___, "When the New Wave Became Old Hat: The Films of Claude Chabrol--Part 2," ibid., 13:7 (April 1967):26-31; Peter Harcourt, "Middle Chabrol," FILM COMMENT 12:6 (November-December 1976):40-5; Rui Nogueira and Nicoletta Zalaffi, "Chabrol," SIGHT AND SOUND 40:1 (Winter 1970-71):2-6; Tom Milne, "Songs of Innocence: Chabrol and Franju," ibid., pp.7-11; ___, "Chabrol's Schizophrenic Spider," ibid., 39:2 (Spring 1970):58-62; Rainer Werner Fassbinder, "Insects in a Glass Case: Random Thoughts on the Films of Claude Chabrol," ibid., 45:4 (Autumn 1976):205-6, 252; Molly Haskell, "The Films of Chabrol--A Priest Among Clowns," VILLAGE VOICE (November 12, 1970):63, 67-8; Charles Wolfe, "Chabrol: The Lyrical Mystery Master," ibid., (September 5, 1974):77, 82; Roger Ebert, "This Man Must Commit Murder," NEW YORK TIMES 2 (November 29, 1970):13; Vincent Canby, "What Has Stephane Audran Got? Glamour," ibid., 2 (January 30, 1972):1, 9; Clyde Haberman, "Chabrol Films a Henry Miller Tale," ibid., C (August 9, 1989):13, 17; Robert Goldberg, "Chabrol Puts de Beauvoir on Film," ibid., 2 (January 15, 1984):1, 19; Robert Giard, "THIS MAN MUST DIE: Chabrol's ILIAD," FILM HERITAGE 6:3 (Spring 1971):26-31; Charles Derry, "Chabrol, Claude," THE INTERNATIONAL DICTIONARY OF FILMS AND FILMMAKERS: VOLUME II, pp.85-9; Charles Berg, "Program Notes: LES BONNES FEMMES," CINEMATEXAS PROGRAM NOTES 5:52 (December 4, 1973):1-5; Carolyn Perkins, "Program Notes: THE LINE OF DEMARCATION," ibid., 6:37 (April 11, 1974):1-6; Nick Barbaro, "Program Notes: LES COUSINS," ibid., 10:4 (April 21, 1976):33-40; and Caryn James, "Thorny Issues from the Seeds of Controversy," NEW YORK TIMES H (May 14, 1989):11, 30.

[996] Ebert, p.13.

and contemporary film."[997] Why? He was clearly a major figure during his days at CAHIERS DU CINEMA, not only playing a significant role in establishing Hitchcock as an AUTEUR and in elevating Hollywood "B" genres to "A" status, but also by playing a crucial role in launching the film careers of Truffaut, Godard, and Rivette. Moreover, Chabrol's early films demonstrate both a masterly handling of New Wave conventions--e.g., fascinating characterizations, lyrical camera movements, intertexual references--and a gift for classical film narrative.

The debate over Chabrol's strength and stature centers on his perceived cinematic flaws. One problem, experienced by Truffaut as well, is that audiences in general find Chabrol's themes and stories "trite" and "superficial." On the other hand, defenders like Charles Derry argue that "Like Balzac, whom he admires, Chabrol attempts, within a popular form, to present a portrait of his society in microcosm."[998] A second problem is that Chabrol's films are attacked as being "derivative," rather than "original." While some critical circles dismiss him as overly imitative of Hitchcock, others accuse him of being "too commercial," "an entertainer," and "a mere technician." Defenders shoot back that Chabrol is as much influenced by Lang and Murnau as he is by Hitchcock; and he never copies, only adapts. Moreover, Peter Harcourt feels that if Chabrol "is the most conventional of the CAHIERS DU CINEMA group of filmmakers, he is also unique in his involvement with the role that children play within a family situation, with the way they understand the adult world."[999] A third problem deals with the range of Chabrol's cynical and cruel pyschopathetic protagonists, whose misguided intentions frequently result in savage and senseless deeds. In response to people who admire Chabrol's "zoological" approach to his subjects, Rainer Werner Fassbinder replies that "Chabrol's viewpoint is not that of the entomologist, as is often claimed, but that of a child who keeps a collection of insects in a glass case and observes with alternating amazement, fear and delight the marvellous behaviour patterns of his tiny creatures."[1000] On the other hand, Jean-Andre Fieschi argues that "Of all the New Wave directors, Chabrol has the greatest facility in inventing and breathing life into his characters, a term both literary and cinematic, since Chabrol's art approaches that of both Hitchcock and Balzac."[1001] A fourth problem concerns the filmmaker's "detached" and "cold-blooded" style. According to Ian Cameron, Chabrol, like Otto Preminger, "shows no desire to make the audience love any of his characters."[1002] Cameron's defense of Chabrol is that he cares greatly for humanity. The misperception occurs because he gives the audience the freedom to make up its own mind about his characters, a position that "is central to his view of the world."[1003] The difficulty in resolving these debates is that both sides contain half-truths.

Born in Paris, on June 24, 1930, Chabrol first studied pharmacy (to please his father, a chemist), then received a law degree, and finally turned his attention to film in the postwar period.   Chabrol's frequent visits to the CINEMATEQUE FRANCAISE and his budding friendship with Truffaut eventually led him to writing

---

[997]   "Chabrol: The Lyrical Mystery Master," p.77.

[998]   "Chabrol, Claude," p.86.

[999]   "Middle Chabrol," p.40.

[1000] Fassbinder, p.205.

[1001] "Wait and See," p.10.

[1002] "The Darwinian World of Claude Chabrol," p.78. This essay has been reprinted in MOVIE READER, pp.78-83. All quotations cited in this chapter from the later edition.

[1003] "The Darwinian World of Claude Chabrol," p.79.

film criticism in the early 1950s, initially for ARTS and then for CAHIERS DU CINEMA. At one point in the mid-1950s, Chabrol even worked as the French publicity director for 20th Century-Fox (a position he later relinquished to Godard). In 1956, he formed AJYM, a film production company, and began funding new filmmakers like Jacques Rivette and Philippe de Broca. By the late 1950s, he was ready for his own film debut.

Chabrol's film career falls into four stages. The first period, from 1958 to 1962, is heavily indebted to his critical appreciation of Hitchcock (enunciated in his 1957 study of Hitchcock, co-authored with Rohmer). As discussed earlier, Chabrol was most impressed with the master of suspense's "moral universe"--e.g., the transference of guilt, the path from temptation to degredation, the importance of absolution in achieving salvation, the danger in judging evil by surface appearances, the fragility of happy and normal lives, and the fascination with the subconscious desires of everyday people. Films like HANDSOME SERGE/LE BEAU SERGE/BITTER REUNION (1958), THE COUSINS/LES COUSINS, A DOUBLE TOUR/WEB OF PASSION/LEDA (both in 1959), and LES BONNES FEMMES (1960) all share an interest in the sordid and dark side of human nature. Hypocrisy runs rampant as a self-righteous young man hurts rather than helps his childhood friend (LE BEAU SERGE), a country boy is shown to be worse than his suave city relative (LES COUSINS), a devoted son turns out to be a murderer (A DOUBLE TOUR), and the romantic escapism of four young Parisian women exposes the dangers of taking surface appearances too literally (LES BONNES FEMMES).[1004] These early works, as Molly Haskell observes, combine "a comic sense of the grotesque with a rage at the world that it should be so steeped in mediocrity."[1005] She perceptively points out that the "feeling of sadness" found in Chabrol's satirical portraits of ordinary people focuses "on the ugliness of mankind, but an ugliness, unlike Swift's, [that] seemed acquired rather than congenital, but no less incurable; and the pain caused seemed out of all proportion . . . to the pettiness of the characters and the pathetic insignificance of their lives."[1006]

Chabrol's fascination with human frailty led him to four disastrous commercial failures over the next two years: LES GODELUREAUX (1961), THE THIRD LOVER/L'OIL DU MALIN, OPHELIA, and BLUEBEARD/LANDRU (all in 1962). Heavily influenced by the works of Fritz Lang, the films explore how people deceive themselves into thinking their actions will bring them satisfaction. The detached and cynical way in which the director's crime stories humorously exposed his protagonists' secret emotions, plus his refusal to judge their actions, made him extremely unpopular with mass audiences.

A desire for commercial success led Chabrol into the second phase of his film career, from 1963 to 1967, known as the "TIGER" period. He blatantly pandered to the lowest common denominator in order to attract a wider following. From THE TIGER LIKES FRESH BLOOD/LE TIGRE AIME LA CHAIR FRAICHE (1964) to THE ROAD TO CORINTH/LA ROUTE DE CORINTHE (1967), the director exploited his craft and alienated himself from serious film circles. In his defense, Chabrol claims that his savage thrillers have redeeming qualities. "No matter how much a scenarist or director

---

[1004] Paul Gegauff, the screenwriter of A DOUBLE TOUR and LES BONNES FEMMES, and Jean Rabier, the cinematographer of LE BEAU SERGE, both became major contributors to Chabrol's films. Another important collaborator is Chabrol's second wife, the actress Stephane Audran.

[1005] "A Priest Among Clowns," p.63.

[1006] "A Priest Among Clowns," p.63.

may seek to distract," he explains, "a thriller must be profound, because it speaks of life and death."[1007]

LES BICHES (1968) inaugurated the third stage of Chabrol's career. Over the next five years, with films like THE UNFAITHFUL WIFE/LA FEMME INFIDELE (1969), THIS MAN MUST DIE/KILLER!/QUE LA BETE MEURE, LA BOUCHER (both in 1969), LA RUPTURE/LE JOUR DES PARQUES (1970), JUSTE AVANT LA NUIT (1971), 10 DAYS WONDER/LA DECADE PRODIGIEUSE (1972), and WEDDING IN BLOOD/LES NOCES ROUGES (1973), the controversial director re-established his critical popularity. For example, Tom Milne states that based on the work from LES BICHES to THIS MAN MUST DIE, Chabrol is "quite simply the best technician in France, EX AEQUO with Jean-Pierre Melville."[1008] In re-evaluating Chabrol, the critical community concentrates on perceived changes in Chabrol's approach to film. "A characteristic of these later films," Haskell believes, "is the contrast between the elaborately cool, controlled style and the violent, threatening instability of the characters and their themes. Chabrol undercuts suspense and attenuates the melodrama through the poise and serenity of the style."[1009] Michael Walker believes that since the late 1950s, the major changes in Chabrol's work demonstrate his artistic growth:

> His attitude toward the majority of characters in his films is less cynical, more sympathetic, and yet at the same time he pushes further into the dark side of their lives to uncover, if not to explore, the dangerous forces which possess and impel them. And no-one escapes critical observation . . . one sees Chabrol 'zeroing in' on the repressive French establishment as THE target.[1010]

Whether one agrees with these perspectives is secondary to the fact that there is near unanimity that the third stage in Chabrol's career is his best.

Since 1974, and the release of NADA, Chabrol's critical reputation has again been the subject of endless debates. Except for A PIECE OF PLEASURE/UNE PARTIE DE PLAISIR (1976) and LES FANTOMES DU CHAPELIER (1982), none of his later work has won him either commercial or critical success. Chabrol himself takes little interest in the attacks. Nearly three decades after his first film, he explains that "I still try to be sensitive to liberty of tone. I still try to direct people as if they were wearing their collars open, not buttoned up."[1011]

On the surface, Eric Rohmer appears to share many similarities with Chabrol. Both men became seriously interested in film in the post-WWII period, both worked as critics for ARTS and CAHIERS DU CINEMA, both loved film history, both helped establish Hitchcock's AUTEUR status, both collaborated with their peers in the production of short subjects, and both made their feature film debuts in the late 1950s. Moreover, both men are criticized for their "detached" filmmaking style and for their total indifference to treating political and social issues in their work. A closer look, however, reveals that Rohmer is not only strikingly different from Chabrol, but also from the rest of the CAHIERS DU CINEMA filmmaking group.[1012]

[1007] Cited in "When the New Wave Becomes Old Hat--Part 2," p.30.

[1008] "Chabrol's Schizophrenic Spider," p.59.

[1009] "A Priest Among Clowns," p.68.

[1010] "Claude Chabrol into the 'Seventies," p.46.

[1011] Cited in Goldberg, p.19.

[1012] For more information, see Carlos Clarens, "Eric Rohmer: L'Amour Sage," SIGHT AND SOUND 39:1 (Winter 1969-70):6-9; Rui Nogueira, "Rohmer Interviewed," ibid., 40:3 (Summer 1971):119-22; Gilbert Adair, "Rohmer's Perceval,"ibid., 47:4 (Autumn

Born Jean-Marie Maurice Scherer in Tulle, on April 4, 1920, Rohmer (who adopted his pseudonym in the mid-1950s, allegedly to conceal his activities from his disapproving family) was ten years older than most of his colleagues in the NOUVELLE VAGUE, and considered by many critics to be the intellectual rival of Bazin, not his successor. Lellis, for example, credits Rohmer, not Bazin, with establishing the classical, humanist tradition that served as the cornerstone of CAHIERS DU CINEMA in its formative stages.[1013] According to C. G. Crisp, "Rohmer's values are based on a profound conservatism .   .   . that can be traced back to the austere, and even Jansenist, forms of Catholicism . . . ."[1014] Those values, when translated to film, create profound differences between Rohmer and the CAHIERS DU CINEMA group. While Rohmer's characters "chose the dream of eternity . . . to gain life," those of Truffaut and Godard lose life by pursuing the world hereafter. While Rohmer's cinematic world is based on "a dream of permanence," Godard's world offers no such possibility, and Truffaut's world provides happiness only to those people who accept life as it is rather than as they want it to be.[1015]

By the time Rohmer joined the CAHIERS DU CINEMA staff in 1951, he was a seasoned schoolteacher and had developed the absolutist social, political, and aesthetic principles that remain with him today. For example, his aesthetics are based more on silent films (particularly Murnau's works) than on the Hollywood genres of the 1930s and 1940s. While his colleagues place directors above studios, Rohmer values directors who benefited from the work patterns fostered by a production-line mentality. Although he shares with Chabrol and Truffaut a love for American genres and for AUTEURs like Hawks, Hitchcock, and Renoir, Rohmer places his emphasis on religious values and on the power of cinematic realism to uncover the glories of God, rather than accept his colleagues' arguments that it is the personalities of the directors and the originality of their films that is crucial. In the 1960s, as Carlos Claren explains, "On the side of what the others termed 'the great naive cinema' (i.e., American), Rohmer was bound to appear somewhat reactionary in his stand against the isolation of the medium, his non-commital attitude to CINEMA VERITE, and his awareness of the parochialism of the New Wave which made dispassionate judgment impossible . . . ."[1016]

Although Rohmer's spiritual and aesthetic principles produced no serious problems for him as long as Bazin was alive (they both shared similar conservative values), Bazin's death in 1958 and the increasing politicization of CAHIERS DU CINEMA made Rohmer's new role as chief editor of the periodical, beginning in 1958, more and more untenable. By the early 1960s, the magazine and its prominent critics-turned-filmmakers were writing Hollywood off, turning their attention to radical forms of filmmaking and away from classical film narratives, and embracing Brecht's Marxist, materialist ideas on a "new cinema." In applying this perspective, the changing CAHIERS DU CINEMA critics reject the notion that humanity functions according to universal truths, arguing further that works espousing such universal truths are ideological tools of the dominant hegemony. Central to Brecht's aesthetics

---

1978):230-4; Molly Haskell, "Eric Rohmer," CINEMA: A CRITICAL DICTIONARY, Volume 2, pp.879-85; "Eric Rohmer: Bibliography," MONTHLY FILM BULLETIN (December 1976):264; Nadja Tesich-Savage, "Rehearsing the Middle Ages," FILM COMMENT 14:5 (September-October 1978):50-6; and Fred Barron, "Eric Rohmer: An Interview," TAKE ONE 4:1 (January 1974):8-10.

[1013] Lellis, p.16.

[1014] *C. G. Crisp, ERIC ROHMER: REALIST AND MORALIST (Bloomington: Indiana University Press, 1988), p.3.

[1015] ERIC ROHMER: REALIST AND MORALIST, p.35.

[1016] Clarens, p.7.

is the notion of the VERFREMDUNG effect, as Lellis explains, "frequently translated in English as the Alienation effect. . . ."[1017] In essence, it states that directors, and stage managers "must make the event strange, must wrench it out of a credible, naturalistic context and produce an effect of heightened theatricality whereby the audience remains constantly aware of the theatrical illusions being presented before it."[1018] The objective is to prevent audiences from becoming passive spectators. In applying the principle to film, artists would be judged on their ability to stimulate the spectator's consciousness rather than his or her feelings. Appealing to the intellect is seen as a greater virtue than arousing meaningless emotions. Rohmer's allegiance to Hollywood, its commitment to traditional storytelling and satisfying the expectations of mass audience, and its reinforcement of humanistic values put him in constant conflict with his colleagues, who now applauded the possibilities that a "new cinema" offered filmmakers. More and more, as Hillier explains, American cinema became important only in its "relationship to the 'new cinema' which, implicitly or explicitly, challenged it."[1019] By 1963, Rohmer resigned (or was removed from) his editorship and had very little connection with CAHIERS DU CINEMA and his editorial successor, Rivette.[1020] Starting in 1964, and continuing to the present, Rohmer spends his time working on his films, doing occasional TV projects, and teaching film appreciation.

Although Rohmer's film career began in 1950, with the 16mm short, JOURNAL D'UN SCELERAT, it wasn't until the end of the decade that he made his feature film debut with SIGN OF THE LION/LE SIGNE DU LION (1959). In addition to taking two years to get distributed, Rohmer's tale about an expatriate American's fall from grace did not garner the attention that the first works of Chabrol, Godard, and Truffaut received; and Rohmer himself did not gain international recognition until the late 1960s, with the release of THE COLLECTOR/LE COLLECTIONNEUSE (1967).[1021] Crisp offers a good explanation why the more youthful ex-critics surpassed their older and more experienced colleague: "The center of Rohmer's life was elsewhere, his interest in the cinema as much theoretical as passionate, and his commitment therefore less total."[1022]

Given the choice of altering his cinematic objectives or adjusting to the demands of the commercial film industry, Rohmer, unlike Chabrol, chose to return to 16mm filmmaking rather than compromise his artistic freedom. He also decided to concentrate on the pre-production process rather than on directing. Interestingly, the man who was part of a movement attacking a literary cinema found himself unable "to shoot with a text devoid of intrinsic literary qualities."[1023] To satisfy his fascination with scenario construction, Rohmer took an unusual step. "Instead of asking myself what

---

[1017] Lellis, pp.10-11.

[1018] Lellis, p.10.

[1019] CAHIERS DU CINEMA: 1960-1968--NEW WAVE, NEW CINEMA, REEVALUATING HOLLYWOOD, p.9.

[1020] ERIC ROHMER: REALIST AND MORALIST, p.17. For short, useful overviews on how the magazine's political views evolved, see Thomas Elsaesser, "French Film Culture and Critical Theory: CINETHIQUE," MONOGRAM 2 (Summer 1971):31-7; William Guynn, "The Political Program of CAHIERS DU CINEMA, 1969-1977," JUMP CUT 17 (1978):32-5; and Maureen Turim, "The Aesthetic Becomes Political: A History of Film Criticism in CAHIERS DU CINEMA," THE VELVET LIGHT TRAP 9 (Summer 1973):13-7.

[1021] Interestingly, no 16mm prints of Rohmer's films before 1970 are available for rental in the United States.

[1022] ERIC ROHMER: REALIST AND MORALIST, p.19.

[1023] "Rohmer's PERCEVAL," p.231.

subjects were most likely to appeal to audiences," he explains, "I persuaded myself that the best thing would be to treat the same subject six times over. In the hope that the sixth time the audience would come to me!"[1024]

The result was CONTES MORAUX, a series of six "moral tales" all growing out of a single theme of a man pursuing and losing a woman, meeting a second woman but still thinking of the first, and then rejecting the second and being reunited with the first woman. The idea initially surfaced in a series of short stories that Rohmer wrote in the 1950s. In explaining the meaning of his film project, he points out that CONTES MORAUX

> doesn't really mean that there's a moral contained in them, even though there might be one and all the characters in these films act according to certain moral ideas that are carefully worked out . . . [and] they try to justify everything in their behavior and that fits the word "moral" in its narrowest sense. But "moral" could also mean that they are people who like to bring their motives, the reasons for their actions, into the open, they try to analyze, they are not people who act without thinking about what they are doing. What matters is what they THINK about their behavior, rather than their behavior. They aren't films of action . . . they are films in which a particular feeling is analyzed and where even the characters themselves analyze their feeling and are very introspective.[1025]

As Clarens observes, the idea is much more complex than it appears, ". . . since the beguiling simplicity of the schema . . . allows a series of permutations subject to social, intellectual, sentimental, and even political variants: a rich gamut of affinity and contradiction, long the common currency of the novel but, so far [1970], only summarily approached by the cinema."[1026]

The "Moral Tales," the first three in black-and white, the last three in color, took more than a decade to complete. LA BOULANGERE DE MONCEAU and LA CARRIERE DE SUZANNE (both in 1964) are the only 16mm films and have never been mass-marketed. These initial works touch lightly on Rohmer's broad theme in that the first film deals with a man pusuing and winning a woman, while the second film has the male reconsidering his relationship with a woman he has rejected once she is pursued by someone else. At this point, Rohmer altered his shooting schedule because the actor Jean-Louis Trintignant was unavailable for the intended third film in the series, MY NIGHT AT MAUD'S/MA NUIT CHEZ MAUD. Filmed and released in 1969, it was shot after THE COLLECTOR/LA COLLECTIONNEUSE (made in 1966 and released in 1967), yet remains the third CONTES MORAUX, with THE COLLECTION the fourth. In telling the story of a religious man (Trintignant) who has to choose between a sensuous divorcee and a devout Catholic woman, Rohmer, working now in 35mm, makes the transition from the tentativeness of his earlier films, to a more detailed look at the temptations we face in a world governed by sensual appetites. THE COLLECTOR/LE COLLECTIONNEUS moves the idea along by having two men choose how they will relate to a promiscuous woman. In the fifth film, CLAIRE'S KNEE/LE GENOU DE CLAIRE (1970), Rohmer focuses on the amorous desires of a French diplomat, whose summer vacation provides him with three very different types of women. The final film in the series, CHLOE IN THE AFTERNOON/L'AMOUR L'APRES-MIDI (1972), presents a romantic husband who deceives himself into thinking that he'd enjoy an extra-marital affair, but quickly changes his mind when a free-spirited woman gives him the opportunity. As Molly Haskell explains,

---

[1024] "Rohmer Interviewed," p.119.

[1025] Petrie, pp.38-9.

[1026] Clarens, p.6.

For Rohmer, love becomes both the trigger and the mirror of human behavior, a vision dense with possibilities that is more often to be found in the novel than in film . . . Rohmer's protagonists define themselves, ethically and morally, by whom they choose to love, by the romantic choices they make--prismatic choices in which place and time and a whole society are refracted.[1027]

Of the six CONTES MOREAUX dealing with corrupting erotic influences in a secular world, the most impressive works are MY NIGHT AT MAUD'S/MA NUIT CHEX MAUD and CLAIRE'S KNEE/LE GRNOU DE CLAIRE. More than exercises about the yearnings of imperfect human beings, they are beautifully crafted tales that demonstrate Rohmer's sensitivity and narrative skills.

Following the completion of the epigrammatic CONTES MORAUX, Rohmer became interested in literary adaptations. This time, instead of focusing on the scenario, he concentrated on the process of directing. First came THE MARQUISE OF O/LA MARQUISE D'O . . . (1975), and then PERCEVAL LE GALLOIS (1979). Despite their visual beauty, the films were box-office failures.

In the 1980s, Rohmer embarked on a new series, "Comedies and Proverbs," pursuing a new interest in "staged" rather than in "narrated" films.[1028] In each work, scripted and directed by Rohmer, the focus is on the romantic and spontaneous problems of young adults trying to reconcile their desires with their moral standards. As Rohmer explains,

"I don't pretend to speak of the Young, just about some young people. I think that in life there are exceptions. In these comedies, I just want to show those exceptions as clearly and as naturally as I can, without any artifice. . . ."[1029]

Working with minimal crews and small budgets, Rohmer to date has completed six films in the series: THE AVIATOR'S WIFE/LA FEMME DE L'AVIATEUR OU ON NE SAURAIT PENSER A RIEN (1981), LE BEAU MARRIAGE (1982), PAULINE AT THE BEACH/PAULINE A LA PLAGE (1983), FULL MOON IN PARIS/LES NUITS DE LA PLEINE LUNE (1984), LE RAYON VERT/SUMMER (1986), and BOYFRIENDS AND GIRLFRIENDS/L'AMI DE MON AMIE (1987).

Critics give different reasons for Rohmer's lackluster commercial success but his unwavering critical popularity. The general complaints deal with the filmmaker's limited subject matter and his obsession with "foolish" people who lead drab lives and persist in sensual pursuits. Their on-going self-analysis and endless conversations not only fail to reflect political and social realities, but also are deadly dull and painfully slow-moving. As Peter Harcourt puts it, Rohmer's films lack "insights," his cinematic dialogue seems "conventionalized and inadequate for what the characters really feel," and his work serves as "apologies (in the classic sense of the term) for the need for repression in middle-class life . . . ."[1030] On the other hand, Rohmer's defenders admire the dedication and imagination that unify his twenty-five films, the thoughtful way in which his characters reflect the evolution of manners and values in a secular world preoccupied with relativism, promiscuity, and consumerism. Sarris, for example, feels that Rhomer's characters are anything but trivial and unimportant, insisting that the problem may be that "Rohmer strikes too close to home for some people with his compassionate but steady ironic gaze at the emotional vulnerability

---

[1027] "Eric Rohmer," p.880.

[1028] ERIC ROHMER: REALIST AND MORALIST, p.88.

[1029] Cited in Paul Chutkow, "Rohmer at Work: Tea for Two," NEW YORK TIMES 2 (July 10, 1988):34.

[1030] "Middle Chabrol," p.45.

that afflicts us all, and the young and untested most of all."[1031] From J. B. Hoberman's perspective in 1988, "Truffaut is dead, Chabrol's become a hack, Rivette seems mired in solipsism. Godard is even more erratic than ever but, on the eve of his seventh decade, Eric Rohmer is the most serenely consistent of New Wave directors."[1032]

If Rohmer remains an anomaly in the NOUVELLE VAGUE, Francois Truffaut represents the central figure in the group of CAHIERS DU CINEMA filmmakers.[1033] Regrettably, his entertaining stories about human beings searching for meaningful and loving relationships often are dismissed as slight amusements rather than appreciated as sensitive and insightful explorations of human experiences. As Eugene P. Walz reminds us, Truffaut has been attacked "for being "too 'Hitchcockian' in the late sixties, . . . too 'Renoirian,' in the seventies, or too derivative in general, even of himself."[1034] The trouble with such judgments, Walz explains, is that they place more emphasis on radical thinking and experimental techniques (which Truffaut admittedly avoids) than on original, superbly crafted portraits of problems faced by "the romantic, the meek, and the marginal."[1035]

[1031] Andrew Sarris, "The Mosaic of Moviegoing," VILLAGE VOICE (November 3, 1987):69.

[1032] J. B. Hoberman, "Suburbs and Proverbs," VILLAGE VOICE (July 19, 1988):60.

[1033] For more information, see Donna Dudinsky, "I Wish: An Interview With Francois Truffaut," TAKE ONE 4:2 (March 1974):8-12; Annette Insdorf, "Francois Truffaut: Feminist Filmmaker?" ibid., 6:2 (January 1978):16-7; "Dialogue on Film: Interview With Francois Truffaut," AMERICAN FILM 1:7 (May 1976):33-40; "Special Truffaut Issue," NY FILM BULLETIN 3:3 (March 1962); Joseph Morgenstern, "Ten Years of Truffaut," NEWSWEEK (March 10, 1969):99-100; Francois Truffaut, "Is Truffaut the Happiest Man on Earth? Yes, ESQUIRE 74 (August 1970):67, 135-6; Louis Marcorelles, "Interview With Truffaut," SIGHT AND SOUND 31:1 (Winter 1961-62):35-7, 48; Julian Jebb, "Truffaut: The Educated Heart," ibid., 41:3 (Summer 1972):144-5; Don Allen, "Truffaut: Twenty Years After," ibid., 48:4 (Autumn 1979):224-28; Neal Oxenhandler, "Truffaut: Heir to Apollinaire," SHENANDOAH 15:2 (Winter 1964):8-13; Geoffrey Nowell-Smith, "Francois Truffaut," NEW LEFT REVIEW 31 (May -June 1965):86-90; Michael Klein, "The Literary Sophistication of Francois Truffaut," FILM COMMENT 3:3 (Summer 1965):24-9; David Bordwell, "Francois Truffaut: A Man Can Serve Two Masters," ibid., 7:1 (Spring 1971):18-23; Annette Insdorf, "THE LITTLE THIEF: Scenes from the Last Truffaut," ibid., 25:1 (January-February 1989):17-22; Paul Ronder, "Francois Truffaut: An Interview," trans. and abridged from CAHIERS DU CINEMA, #138 (December 1962), FILM QUARTERLY 18:1 (Fall 1963):3-13; Judith Shatnoff, "Francois Truffaut: Anarchist Imagination," ibid., 16:3 (Spring 1963):3-11; Beverle Houston and Marsha Kinder, "Truffaut's Gorgeous Killers," ibid., 17:4 (Winter 1973-74):2-10; Sanche de Gramont, "Life Style of Homo Cinematicus," NEW YORK TIMES MAGAZINE (June 15, 1969):12-3, 34, 36, 38, 40, 42, 44; John Hess, "LA POLITIQUE DES AUTEURS: Part One--World View as Aesthetic," JUMP CUT 1 (May-June 1974):19-22; ___, "Part Two--Truffaut's Manifesto," ibid., 2 (July-August 1974):20-2; Adeline R. Tinter, "Truffaut's LA CHAMBRE VERT: Homage to Henry James," LITERATURE/FILM QUARTERLY 8:2 (1980):78-83; Gerald Mast, "Truffaut, Francois," THE INTERNATIONAL DICTIONARY OF FILMS AND FILMMAKERS: VOLUME II, pp.540-2; and ___, "From THE 400 BLOWS to SMALL CHANGE," THE NEW REPUBLIC (April 2, 1977):23-5.

[1034] Eugene P. Walz, FRANCOIS TRUFFAUT: A GUIDE TO REFERENCES AND RESOURCES (Boston: G. K. Hall and Comapny, 1982), p.35.

[1035] Walz, p.36.

Starting with his first feature films like THE 400 BLOWS/LES QUARTES CENTS COUP (1959), SHOOT THE PIANO PLAYER/TIREZ SUR LE PIANISTE (1960), AND JULES AND JIM/JULES ET JIM (1961), working through his middle period with FAHRENHEIT 451 (1966), THE WILD CHILD/L'ENFANT SAUVAGE (1969), and DAY FOR NIGHT/LA NUIT AMERICAINE (1972), and ending with his last films like THE STORY OF ADELE H./L'HISTOIRE D'ADELE H.(1975), SMALL CHANGE/L'ARGENT DE POCHE (1976), and THE LAST METRO/LE DERNIER METRO (1981), Truffaut remained determined not to alienate himself from mass audiences.[1036] If Bazin and Langlois were his critical mentors, Jean Renoir and Alfred Hitchcock were his cinematic mentors. His goal, as Dale Pollock succinctly explains, was "to create a 'cinema of reconciliation' between Renoir's emphasis on man himself, and Hitchcock's obsessions with situations, which came out of the suspense master being 'haunted by the fear of boring the audience.'"[1037] Moreover, Truffaut's unhappy youth not only had left him with many personal scars, but also had served as the source for many of his film ideas. In fact, as Insdorf observes, a central theme in Truffaut's work is verbalized in the words of a kindly schoolteacher in SMALL CHANGE/L'ARGENT DE POCHE (1976): "By a strange sort of balance, those who had a difficult childhood are often better equipped to deal with adult life than those who were protected and loved; it's a kind of law of compensation."[1038]

Born in Paris, on February 2, 1932, the cinematic genius who created twenty-three feature films throughout his traumatic life remains one of the greatest artists of the twentieth century. Truffaut once explained his understanding of the stages that he and other filmmakers generally take in becoming popular directors:

first films are impetuous, a bit experimental, and often have virtuoso tricks since it's sort of an amorous game with the camera . . . [then] the relationship stabilizes, the camera becomes more important, and in general, a young director doesn't easily meet with success because there is invariably a large amount of provocation in his work. Then--his films are seen by a middle-aged public so that the directors are actually successful at 35-40 because at that time their age corresponds more with the median age of the audience and their preoccupations also correspond. Then again, following that stage, in which the director has communicated to a large degree with his public, he should normally detach himself again. That is to say he goes ahead again, because he becomes more abstract, and from that moment on he is lost; that is lost to the industry. But it is from that point on that his pictures become the most fascinating to study.[1039]

Truffaut's contributions, career changes, and ideas have been reported and analyzed in such detail in first-rate books, interviews, and articles by and about him that anything said here is superfluous. His films (almost all low-budget productions) offer invaluable insights into his life; and his evolution from ENFANT TERRIBLE to an internationally acclaimed artist inspired many contemporary film giants, including

---

[1036] Izod points out (p.160) how Truffaut's company, LES FILMS DU CARROSSE, exemplified the difficulty in determining what was a French film and what was an international production, mainly because many of the director's films were underwritten and distributed by United Artists.

[1037] Dale Pollock, "Truffaut Re Renoir, Hitchcock, 'Man' vs 'Situation' Interest," VARIETY (February 28, 1979):41.

[1038] Cited in FRANCOIS TRUFFAUT, p.149.

[1039] R. M. Franchi and Marshall Lewis, p.19.

Francis Ford Coppola, George Lucas, and Steven Spielberg. Sadly, Truffaut died of cancer at the age of fifty-two, on October 21, 1984.[1040]
No figure emerging from the New Wave has had a more revolutionary and controversial career than Jean-Luc Godard. To gauge the extreme reactions to Godard's work, consider Raymond Durgnat's observation that

> Godard wears dark glasses to hide from the world the fact that he's in a permanent state of ocular masturbation, rubbing himself off against anything and everything on which his eye alights. The flickering glance of his camera is the constant dribble of premature ejaculation. It is an unseeing stare.[1041]

Consider next Dudley Andrew's perspective that "Today [1987] Truffaut stands for the sincerity of the Nouvelle Vague; Rohmer for its cool intelligence. Godard, one might think, lit the fuse to set off this volatile concoction."[1042] Finally, consider Robin Wood's assessment that "If influence on the development of world cinema be the criterion, Godard is certainly the most important filmmaker of the past 30 years; he is also one of the most problematic."[1043] Clearly, in discussing Godard, few people take the middle ground.
To understand why the reactions are so extreme, it is instructive to follow Godard's political and social development from being the son of wealthy Swiss parents, to becoming a Maoist Communist from the mid-1960s to the late 1970s. Born in Paris, on December 3, 1930, Godard spent his formative years both in France and in Switzerland. His great loves during childhood were literature and art, not film. Although a Frenchman by virtue of his birth, Godard decided during World War II to become a naturalized Swiss citizen. It was in the postwar period that he developed a passion for movies and an aversion to the values and life-styles of his now-divorced parents. Under the pretext of attending the Sorbonne to study ethnology, Godard used the tuition money he received from his father to indulge his obsession with film and the traditional arts. There was never any doubt that he would become a filmmaker, only when. Not even his father's stopping his son's allowance prevented Godard from pursuing his passion for films. So intent was he that he stole constantly and even spent time in jail to support his bohemian lifestyle.
By the mid-1950s, Godard had not only begun making short films, but had also become an integral part of the CAHIERS DU CINEMA crowd and an unabashed admirer of Truffaut. Like his friends, Godard believed that film criticism and film shorts were the best roads to feature film production. Like his colleagues, Godard took a formalist approach to film criticism, stressing the way that AUTUERS used geometrical patterns to express their ideas. Unlike most of them, however, he was less concerned with the morality found in a filmmaker's MISE EN SCENE, and more interested in a "scientific" approach to "reading" a film's message. If the other critics were obsessed

---

[1040] For more information, see Eric Pace, "Francois Truffaut Dies at 52; Key New Wave Director," NEW YORK TIMES A (October 22, 1984):1, 18; Vincent Canby, "Master of the Movies," ibid., p.A18; ___, "Truffaut: The Man Was Revealed Through His Art," ibid., H (November 4, 1984):19, 22; Andrew Sarris, "Rebels With a Cause," VILLAGE VOICE (August 17, 1985):51; and J. B. Hoberman, "Francois Truffaut, 1932-1984," ibid., (October 30, 1984):67.

[1041] Raymond Durgnat, "Asides on Godard," THE FILMS OF JEAN-LUC GODARD, ed. Ian Cameron (New York: Praeger Publishers, 1970), p.153.

[1042] *Dudley Andrew, ed. BREATHLESS: JEAN-LUC GODARD, DIRECTOR (New Brunswick: Rutgers University Press, 1987), p.4.

[1043] Robin Wood, "Godard, Jean-Luc," THE INTERNATIONAL DICTIONARY OF FILMS AND FILMMAKERS: VOLUME II, p.231.

with the Platonic values, Godard was preoccupied with understanding film as film. It was also during this period that Godard began his lifelong association with film producer Georges de Beauregard, who financed Godard's 35mm film debut with BREATHLESS/A BOUT DE SOUFFLE (1960).

Once his film career was launched, Godard drifted further away from his friends and angrily rejected their humanistic, Catholic theories. In assimilating more and more of Brecht's Marxist, materialistic theories to his own concern with film as a form of communication, Godard nurtured a growing resentment of the production and distribution limitations that the commercial industry placed on the type of films and themes that could be mass distributed. Thus, the more people like Truffaut tried to build close ties between a filmmaker and the audience, the more Godard worked to distance himself from the classic cinema and its conventional values. Influenced in part by his relationship with the actress Anna Karina (whom he married in 1960, and divorced five years later) and in part by Brecht's ideas on using art as a revolutionary tool for reforming society, Godard drifted further and further from conventional narratives and more toward AVANT-GARDE filmmaking. It was at this point that vituperative debates errupted over the filmmaker's values as well as his cinematic art.

Attacking not only traditional cinematic techniques, but also the ideological roots of a "bourgeois capitalistic" film industry, the increasingly political and and cynical Godard began forcing his declining audiences to "use" film to "free" themselves from repressive social values. Relying on a blend of violence, humor, and sex in his idiosyncratic and highly personal films from the mid-1960s on, Godard tries to involve us in "actual" events authentically presented while always making us conscious of the fact that we are watching a movie. Despite his many aborted projects and extremely esoteric works, Godard remains to hard-core cineaphiles, superior to Truffaut in stature, if not equal in popularity. How to evaluate the merits of that argument is difficult because of the nature of Godard's approach to filmmaking. As Sarris points out, ". . . one may argue . . . that Godard's cinema is a diary of his impressions rendered in dialectical sights and sounds."[1044]

[1044] Andrew Sarris, "Dialogue of the Deaf," VILLAGE VOICE (October 15, 1985):59. For more information, see James Price, "A Film Is a Film: Some Notes on Jean-Luc Godard,"EVERGREEN REVIEW 9:38 (November 1965):46-53; Kent E. Carroll, "Film and Revolution: An Interview With Jean-Luc Godard," ibid., 14:83 (October 1970):47-51, 66-8; Judith Goldman, "Godard--Cult or Culture?" FILMS AND FILMING 12:9 (June 1966):36-7; Norman Silverstein, "Godard and Revolution," ibid., 16:9 (June 1970):96-8, 100, 102-5; Annette Michaelson, "Film and the Radical Aspiration," FILM CULTURE 42 (Fall 1966):34-42, 136; Raoul Coutard, "Light of Day," SIGHT AND SOUND 35:1 (Winter 1965-66):9-11; Claire Clouzot, "Godard and the US," ibid., 37:3 (Summer 1968):110-4; Jonathan Rosenbaum, "Theory and Practice: The Criticism of Jean-Luc Godard," ibid., 41:3 (Summer 1972):124-6; David Nicholls, "Godard's WEEKEND: Totem, Taboo and the Fifth Republic," ibid., 49:1 (Winter 1979-80):22-4; Jill Forbes, "Jean-Luc Godard: 2 into 3," ibid., 50:1 (Winter 1980-81):40-5; Jean-Luc Godard, "One or Two Things," ibid., 36:1 (Winter 1966-67):2-6; ___, "Three Thousand Hours of Cinema," CAHIERS DU CINEMA IN ENGLISH 10, CdC 184 (November 1966):10-5; ___, "A Woman Is a Woman," ibid., CdC 98 (August 1959):34-7; ___, et al., "Two Arts in One," ibid., 6, CdC 177 (April 1966):24-33; Michel Delahaye, "Jean-Luc Godard and the Childhood of Art," ibid., CdC 179 (June 1966):18-29; Luc Moullet, "Jean-Luc Godard," ibid., 12, CdC 106 (April 1960):22-33; Jean-Andre Fieschi, "The Difficulty of Being Jean-Luc Godard," ibid., CdC 137 (November 1962):38-43; Raymond Federman, "Jean-Luc Godard and Americanism," FILM HERITAGE 3:3 (Spring 1968):1-10; Joel E. Siegel, "Between Art and Life," ibid., pp.11-22, 47-8; Molly Haskell, "Omegaville," ibid., pp.23-6; John Simon, "Bull In the China Shop: Godard's LA CHINOISE," ibid., pp.35-47; David Cast, "Godard's Truths" ibid., 6:4 (Summer 1971):19-24; Paul J. Sharits, "Red, Blue Godard," FILM QUARTERLY 19:4 (Summer 1966):24-9;

Godard's mercurial career has been covered in such detail that here we need only highlight the different stages it took. The first phase, according to Godard, covered the years from 1949 to 1960, beginning with his endless days watching films at the CINEMATEQUE FRANCAISE, to his writing film criticism for CAHIERS DU CINEMA, and ending with the release of his first feature film, BREATHLESS/A BOUT DE SOUFFLE (1960). The second stage, beginning with A WOMAN IS A WOMAN/UNE FEMME EST UNE FEMME (1961), covers his break with his friends at CAHIERS DU CINEMA over the "bourgeois" films they made, and the start of his experimental interest in film as "research" (documentary) and "spectacle" (fiction). As Alfred Guzzetti explains, the films that Godard made from 1960 to 1967 fall into one of these two categories:

> The mixture of spectacle and research goes far toward defining Godard's style, a style that also mixes the popular with the intellectual, the serious with the comic, the composed with the accidental, the romantic with the witty. The freedom with which Godard combines these opposites points to a central characteristic of his work: a refusal to allow the narrative to determine all of the elements of the film. This attitude manifests itself in complementary ways. On the one hand, the action of the films is frequently interrupted by passages extraneous to the story--characters' remarks to the camera, songs, dances, philosophical discourses, interviews, vaudeville routines, and, in one instance, a recapitulation of the plot for latecomers. On the other [hand], the audience is repeatedly confronted with the formal properties of the sound and image and made to reflect on the mechanisms and processes of the cinema.[1045]

By the mid-1960s, however, Godard began shifting attention away from narrative issues to political and social questions. "One of the major differences between Godard and other political film-makers, and one on which he is keen to insist," explains Colin MacCabe, "is that Godard's political concerns grew out of his work on film and were not imported into filmmaking."[1046] That is, the more he worked in the visual arts the more he grew hostile not only to the system, but also to what the system did to maintain the STATUS QUO. As Julia Lesage observes, "He chafed at the ideological and financial strictures of the film industry, the French governmental system of film finance and censorship, and the Ministry of Culture itself."[1047] In films from LES CARABINIERS/THE SOLDIERS (1963) to TWO OR THREE THINGS I KNOW ABOUT HER/DEUX OU TROIS CHOSES QUE JE SAIS D'ELLE (1967), Godard turns his

---

Ginette Billard, "Interview With Georges de Beauregard," ibid., 20:3 (Spring 1967):20-3; James Roy MacBean, "Politics, Painting and the Language of Signs in Godard's MADE IN USA," ibid., 22:3 (Spring 1969):18-25; Brian Henderson, "Toward a Non-Bourgeois Camera Style," ibid., pp.21-4; ___, "GODARD ON GODARD: Notes for a Reading," ibid., 27:4 (Summer 1974):34-6; Julia Lesage, "Visual Distancing in Godard," WIDE ANGLE 1:3 (1976):4-13; Gretchen Berg, "Fritz Lang on Godard and CONTEMPT," TAKE ONE 2 (June 22, 1969):12-3; Jonathan Cott, "Interview With Godard," ROLLING STONE 35 (June 14, 1969):21-3; Gianni Volpi, "Cinema as a Gun: An Interview With Fernando Solanas," CINEASTE 3:2 (Fall 1969):18-26; 33; and Ron Green, "Programming Works by a Single Filmmaker: Jean-Luc Godard," FILM LIBRARY QUARTERLY 7:3-4 (1974):17-27.

[1045] Alfred Guzzetti, "TWO OR THREE THINGS I KNOW ABOUT HER": ANALYSIS OF A FILM BY GODARD (Cambridge: Harvard University Press, 1981), p.2.

[1046] *Colin MacCabe, GODARD: IMAGES, SOUNDS, POLITICS (Bloomington: Indiana University Press, 1980), p.19.

[1047] Julia Lesage, JEAN-LUC GODARD: A GUIDE TO REFERENCES AND RESOURCES (Boston: G. K. Hall, 1979), p.4.

attention more and more, as Guzzetti explains, "to the demanding process of investigating the world through the agency of pictures and sounds."[1048]

Transforming himself from a "bourgeois" director into a left-wing filmmaker forced Godard to consider how to use the cinema for political acts. According to one source, the filmmaker came to see film in two ways: "A film can be an OBJECT D'ART which presents an aesthetic and/or informative parallel with the world, or it can be a tool with which to alter that world."[1049] By 1967, he had decided to use film as a tool for his political ends. For many Godard scholars, the shooting of WEEKEND/LE WEEK-END in 1967, the battle to reinstate Langlois at the CINEMATEQUE FRANCAISE in February and March of 1968, the student uprising during May and June of that same year, America's role in the Vietnam War, and the filmmaker's growing involvement with Maoist radicals from the miltant French Union of Young Communists, all contributed to his break with conventional AVANT-GARDE filmmaking.

Starting with JOYFUL KNOWLEDGE/LE GAI SAVOIR (1969), Godard committed himself to political militancy and to exploring the role that film could play in revolutionary movements like those espoused by the Black Panther party and Al-Fateh. Joining with the political activitist Jean-Pierre Gorin, he formed the Dziga Vertov Group and made a series of films and TV shows--e.g., BRITISH SOUNDS, PRAVADA, WIND FROM THE EAST/VENT D'EST/VENTTO DELL'EST, STRUGGLE IN ITALY/LOTTE INTALIA/LUTTES EN ITALIE (all shot in 1969), VLADIMIR AND ROSA/VLADIMIR ET ROSA (1970), and LETTER TO JANE/LETTRE A JANE (1972)--that were targeted primarily for radical left-wing audiences and characterized by fragmented images and sounds totally lacking any narrative cohesiveness. According to MacCabe, Godard selected Vertov as his model for two reasons: (1) ". . . he [Vertov] continued, much longer than Eisenstein, to insist that the film-maker's prime concern must be the current state of the class struggle; and . . . (2), his emphasis on the importance of montage before the shooting coincided better with the [Dziga Vertov] group's practice than did notions of montage in Eisenstein's writings."[1050] Although Godard's obsession with restructuring film language impressed selected film critics and intellectuals, his predominantly low-budget 16mm productions consisting of dialogue-monologues, bitter humor, and violent images proved disappointing both to Godard and his extremely limited audiences. In 1973, the Dziga Vertov Group experiment ended.[1051]

Following the box-office failure of his million-dollar, 35mm film, JUST GREAT/TOUT VA BIEN (1972) to make political filmmaking commercially successful,[1052] Godard joined with the feminist Anne-Marie Mieville to form Sonimage, a film company stationed in Switzerland. Out of that partnership came films like HERE AND ELSEWHERE/ICI ET AILEURS, NUMBER TWO/NUMERO DEUX (both in 1975), COMMET CA VA? (1976), and ON AND UNDER COMMUNICATION/SUR ET SOUS LA

[1048] Guzzetti, p.3.

[1049] Michael Goodwin   et al., "The Dziga Vertov Film Group In America: An Interview With Jean-Luc Godard and Jean-Pierre Gorin," TAKE ONE 2:10 (March-April 1970):10.

[1050] MacCabe, p.22. See also Lellis, pp.76-9.

[1051] For more information, see James Roy MacBean "Godard and the Dziga Vertov Group: Film and Dialect," FILM QUARTERLY 26:1 (Fall 1972):30-44; ___, "See You at Mao," ibid., 24:2 (Winter 1970-71):15-23; R. P. Kolkein, "Angle and Reality: Godard and Gorin in America," SIGHT AND SOUND 42:3 (Summer 1973):129-33; and Martin Walsh, "Godard and Me: Jean-Pierre Gorin Talks," TAKE ONE 5:1 (February 2, 1976):14-7.

[1052] Lellis points out (pp.12-3) that Godard modeled his film on Brecht's ideas about revolutionizing the opera and that the film itself "is of prime importance for CAHIERS and the development of its new ideas."

COMMUNICATION (1980). By the 1980s, as MacCabe points out, Godard had turned away from his Maoist preoccupations. The Sonimage films signaled the new direction with their "investigation of the constitutive terms of our subjectivity: the family and the opposition between the city and the country, between factory and landscape."[1053]

Although still interested in the problems of emerging Third World nations and how to use film as a tool of direct communication, Godard also wanted to get back into commercial filmmaking. EVERY MAN FOR HIMSELF/SAUVE QUI PEUT/LA VIE (1980), his first attempt, excited a number of mainstream reviewers, including David Ansen. Describing the fifty-year-old Godard as "mellowed," the NEWSWEEK critic pointed out that the filmmaker who in the 1960s "renounced all vestiges of the commercial cinema and plunged into Maoist didacticism" is back with a film unlike any of his previous works. "The bracing clarity of his vision is unmistakable, and his wonderfully intelligent, funny--and horrific--new movie makes one realize how much he has been missed."[1054] If anyone thought Godard would settle back into routine filmmaking after that, they were brought back to reality with such recent works as HAIL MARY (1985) and KING LEAR (1988). The former is an irreverent and heavy-handed updating of the Annunciation and Nativity stories, dealing with a female gas station attendant's unique pregnancy; and the latter is an inexplicable version of Shakespeare's play that superficially portrays the bard as a punk author looking for his lost works. Summing up the current mainstream thinking about this extraordinary film rebel, Vincent Canby writes, "The most depressing thing about this Godard work [KING LEAR] is that it seems so tired, familiar and out of date."[1055] Roy Armes evaluates Godard's current stage more kindly, saying that ". . . one has the sense of a great director working at less than full power."[1056]

In addition to the CAHIERS DU CINEMA stalwarts and their quest for a new approach to narrative films, LA NOUVELLE VAGUE also gave rise to a second prominent group of filmmakers, the so-called "New Left,"[1057] consisting of filmmakers like Agnes Varda, Chris Marker, and Alain Resnais, who collaborated with intellectual novelists like Jean Cayrol, Marguerite Duras, Alain Robbe-Grillet, Nathalie Sarrayte, and Jorge Semprun.[1058] Unlike the CAHIERS DU CINEMA group and its preoccupation

---

[1053] MacCabe, p.24.

[1054] David Ansen, "Godard's New Wave," NEWSWEEK (October 20, 1984):83.

[1055] Vincent Canby, "Film: Godard In His Mafia KING LEAR," NEW YORK TIMES C (January 22, 1988):6.

[1056] FRENCH FILM, p.276.

[1057] The "New Left" was also called the "Left Bank group," as compared to the CAHIERS group, also known as the "Right Bank group." The terms, as Van Wert notes, alluded to the groups' residences in Paris, as well as their politics. In the formative stages of the NOUVELLE VAGUE, the "New Left" had a strong literary bent and was also referred to as "the literary New Wave" (referring both to a real connection with literature outside of film and to their desire to transpose literary techniques in their films." See William F. Van Wert, THE THEORY AND PRACTICE OF THE "CINE-ROMAN" (New York: Arno Press, 1978), p.3. According to John Francis Kreidl, both revolutionary groups, although taking different approaches to NOUVELLE VAGUE, were friendly to each other. See 8John Francis Kreidl, ALAIN RESNAIS (Boston: Twayne Publishers, 1977), p.39.

[1058] For a general introduction, see Judith Gollub, "French Writers Turned Filmmakers," FILM HERITAGE 4:2 (Winter 1968-69):19-25. For an adverse reaction to the relationship between French novelists and the NOUVELLE VAGUE, see "Qu'est-ce que la Nouvelle Vague," p.19.

with improvisational filmmaking and semi-autobiographical works, the members of the New Left were preoccupied with finding a common ground between literary and cinematic language, as well as investigating the role of film in society. If the CAHIERS DU CINEMA group is noted for its homage to genre conventions and directors, the New Left is famous for its innovative narrative techniques and for the development of LE NOUVEAU ROMAN ("the new novel").

To appreciate the New Left's break with classical film narratives and how it emerged from the group's literary revolt against nineteenth-century traditions, we need to acknowledge the intellectual crisis that key French novelists experienced in the 1950s, and how it gave rise to LE NOUVEAU ROMAN. According to Judith Gollub, youthful novelists like Robbe-Grillet, Duras, and Cayrol were rejecting

> a traditional literature centered on Man, where Nature had been used to echo man's passions . . . [and] any anthropomorphic connotations; they refused psychological analysis, metaphysical background, symbolic meanings; influenced by phenomenology, they limited themselves to describing the world and objects in it. This new school was dubbed the School of the Glance since it purported to show what an objective eye would see.[1059]

Whether one credits the School of the Glance or the AVANT-GARDE movement of the 1920s for the literary uprising, writers like Robbe-Grillet, Duras, and Cayrol endorsed the modernist approach to fiction in general, and to film narrative in particular. Although each author acted independently of the other, as Van Wert points out, they all shared similar characteristics. "The revolution in fiction accompanied by the new novel, . . ." he explains, "[focused on] the difference between definition and process analysis: not what the narrator relates but how he relates it."[1060] In part, this literary and cinematic revolution grew out of the disillusionment that the novelists had with traditional values and institutions. The self-conscious language, the incoherent stories, and the implausible characterizations of LE NOUVEAU ROMAN are directly tied to the authors' attempts to undermine the dominant hegemony. "The disjunction of people and things, as with cubism, in spite of or perhaps because the fragmentation distorts reality," Ben Stoltzfus explains, "reflects the contemporary dissolution of beliefs, the atomicity of perception, the disappearance of the depth of man, the subversion of ideology, and, last, though not least, art's revolutionary potential."[1061]

No one has done more valuable cinematic research on these matters than Van Wert. Here we need only comment on some of his important findings. For example, Van Wert concludes that the authors of "the new novel" argued that they knew little more about the characters or the events in LES NOUVEAU ROMANS than did the audience who "read" them. They told us that their narrators could not be trusted to tell the truth or to explain events. Moreover, these anonymous and fluid characters had a life of their own, as unpredictable and complex as people in real life. Like the reader, the authors were perplexed over what was happening and why and what conclusions, if any, could be drawn about the fate of the characters. In Van Wert's words,

> It's not that their creators are refusing to tell us; it's rather that they, themselves, do not know. Implicit in their not knowing all the answers is of

---

[1059] Gollub, p.21.

[1060] THEORY AND PRACTICE OF THE "CINE-ROMAN," p.62. See also G. S. Bourdain, "Robbe-Grillet on Novels and Films," NEW YORK TIMES C (April 17, 1989):13.

[1061] Ben Stoltzfus, ALAIN ROBBE-GRILLET: THE BODY OF THE TEXT (Rutherford: Fairleigh Dickinson University Press, 1985), p.15.

course the assumption that the work of art cannot be paraphrased or reduced to any empirical meaning or interpretation.[1062]

Led by Robbe-Grillet, the authors of LE NOUVEAU ROMAN turned to the cinema as the ideal place to replace traditional linear stories with a new film narrative that made dialogue equal to imagery, along with giving greater importance to the fallibility of the narrator in explaining events or people. "What is absent in this form of fiction or cinema," Van Wert explains, "is not the vision of a narrator (that, in fact, is in abundance), but the interpretation of that vision."[1063] To make sense of the repetitious dialogue, the confusing points of view, the complex editing, and the depersonalized characters, the viewer has to become a "co-author" with the novelist or filmmaker. In other words, the viewer has to use his or her imagination to "co-create" a meaning for what occurs in the novel or the film.

Because many film critics and historians often use the term "imagination" in a general sense, rather than in its more specific use by the New Left, James Monaco reminds us that Alain Resnais insists on using "imagination" as a description of his work instead of accepting the conventional explanation of "memory."[1064] Taking his cue from the writings of Thomas Hobbes, Resnais considers "imagination" not as something "'realistic' or unrealistic, but simply the sum total of our cognitive dealings with the world around us."[1065] Resnais was not alone in viewing films as a revolutionary way to examine how we perceive the conflict between reality and illusion. Almost every member of the New Left was preoccupied with using cinema to investigate imaginative ways to comprehend reality.

Agnes Varda was the group's pioneering feature film director.[1066] Born in Belgium in 1928, she received her formal education in Paris and became an influential still photographer before making her directorial theatrical film debut with LA POINTE-COURTE in 1955. Based upon William Faulkner's THE WILD PALMS (1935), the filmmaker used the novelist's techniques rather than the content of his unrelated short stories. Varda's objective is to have the audience, as opposed to the filmmaker, supply the relationship between photographic imagery and film "plot." Thus the story of how a unhappy couple rediscover their love for each other as a result of their experiences in a small fishing village affords the twenty-two-year-old filmmaker (and Resnais, her editor) countless opportunities to search for cinematic equivalents to Faulkner's literary style. Another excellent example of Varda's quest for a literary cinema is CLEO FROM 5 TO 7/CLEO DE CINQ A SEPT (1962), a poignant tale of a beautiful woman's fears that she may be dying of cancer. Among Varda's other noteworthy works are short films like OPERA MOUFFE (1958), SALUT LES CUBAINS (1963), and UNCLE YANCO (1967); and feature films like HAPPINESS/LE BONHEUR (1965), BLACK PANTHERS, LION'S LOVE (both in 1968), ONE SINGS, THE OTHER DOESN'T (1979), and VAGABOND/SANS TOIT NI LOI (1986). Throughout her career, France's greatest woman director has aggressively articulated the New Left's

---

[1062] THEORY AND PRACTICE OF THE "CINE-ROMAN," p.68.

[1063] THEORY AND PRACTICE OF THE "CINE-ROMAN," p.71.

[1064] ALAIN RESNAIS, p.11.

[1065] ALAIN RESNAIS, p.13.

[1066] For more information, see Gordon Gow, "The Underground River," FILMS AND FILMMAKING 16:6 (March 1970):6-10; Jacqueline Levitin, "Mother of the New Wave: An Interview With Agnes Varda," WOMEN AND FILM 1:5-6 (1974):62-6, 103; Ying Ying Wu, "Agnes Varda Sings: An Interview," TAKE ONE 5:12 (November 1977):21-3; and Louise Heck-Rabi, "Varda, Agnes," THE INTERNATIONAL DICTIONARY OF FILMMAKERS: VOLUME I, pp.550-1.

opposition to naturalism in film and the group's fascination with restructuring film narrative through the use of time, space, and memory. A life-long feminist and activist, Varda continues to make films that not only appeal to her subjects, but also raise their consciousness. "I still participate in a bourgeois culture," she explains, "in which a film is made by an artist."[1067]

Like Varda, Chris Marker is a life-long political activist.[1068] Born Christian Francois Bouche-Villeneuve in Paris on July 29, 1921, the World War II-Resistance fighter came to film through literature, journalism, and photography. "In a sense," Armes comments, "his films are essays written with words and images on celluloid instead of on paper."[1069] Like his colleagues in the New Left, Marker seeks to understand the world around him in a broader context than our everyday experiences. According to Jacob Gilles,

> One of the keys to Marker might be . . . [his] human sympathy--a sympathy barely masked by the varnish of quirkish ironic humour, which has only to flake off a little to reveal the naked sensibility beneath. Another key is meditation on history--not history in its dusty fixity but life in the process of becoming history and not yet aware of it: the ordinary and everyday seized on the wing without bothering about perspective. . . .[1070]

Opposed to the dominant hegemony, Marker's controversial political films from OLYMPIA (1952) to LE FOND DE L'AIR EST ROUGE (1977) illustrate the New Left's experiments with film narrative. His idiosyncratic editing, which forces viewers to find unique connections among images, sounds, and voice-over commentaries highlights Marker's probing camera and montage effects. One extraordinary example is his twenty-seven-minute science fiction film, LA JETEE (1962). Essentially a compilation of still photographs blended with music and a voice-over narration, the haunting film tells the story of a survivor of World War III who goes back in time to witness his own death. The genius of the film lies in Marker's use of fades, dissolves, and sound effects (there is no dialogue) to animate photographs. Here again, cinematic time, space, and memory play essential roles in shaping the film narrative.

Many of Marker's early films pinpoint his developing cinematic technique. "Differences in his emerging style," Van Wert points out, "were clearly due to differences in subject."[1071] That is, superpowers like the Soviet Union and the United States are attacked in films like LETTER FROM SIBERIA/LETTRE DE SIBERIE (1957) and THE AMERICAN DREAM/L'AMERIQUE REVE (1959), as Marker focuses on the superpowers' "colonialism, lack of culture, eccentricities and stupidities."[1072] On the other hand, emerging nations like Cuba and Israel in films like DESCRIPTION D'UN COMBAT (1960) and CUBA, YES/CUBA SI (1961) are given positive portraits, with Marker stressing "the authenticity of the people within their struggle, emphasizing

---

[1067] Cited in Levitin, p.103.

[1068] For more information, see Jacob Gilles, "Chris Marker and the Mutants," SIGHT AND SOUND 35:4 (Autumn 1966):164-8; Richard Roud, "SLON," ibid., 42:2 (Spring 1973):82-3; Silvio Gaggi, "Marker and Resnais: Myth and Reality," LITERATURE/FILM QUARTERLY 7:1 (1979):11-5; and William F. Van Wert, "Chris Marker: The SLON Films," FILM QUARTERLY 33:3 (Spring 1979):38-46.

[1069] *Roy Armes, FRENCH FILM (New York: E. P. Dutton and Company, 1970), p.135.

[1070] Gilles, p.165.

[1071] "The SLON Films," p.40.

[1072] "The SLON Films," p.41.

their dignity and their grandeur."[1073] Marker's films, mainly documentaries shot around the globe, are also known for their witty and acerbic interviews.   For example, in LE JOLI MAI (1963), he offers a melliflous essay on the meaning of happiness, drawing parallels between France before World War II and after the Algerian war.   As people on screen respond to the interviewer's questions about their hopes and desires, the viewer realizes that the superficial answers about goals and values are part of every generation's search for identity and direction.

The upheaval in French political life during the late 1960s inspired Marker to pioneer a resurgence in cooperative filmmaking. In 1967, he inaugurated a film movement called SLON (SOCIETE POUR LE LANCEMENT DES OUVRES NOUVELLES). The purpose, Richard Roud points out, "was limited: a company--or rather, what the French call an association under the 1901 law--to produce FAR FROM VIETNAM."[1074] Essentially an anthology film attacking America's role in Southeast Asia, FAR FROM VIETNAM/LOIN DU VIETNAM (1967) served as the prototype for Marker's new direction in filmmaking.   After 1968, Van Wert explains, Marker revived the SLON and turned his complete attention to making cooperative films:

> Mediating between film technicians and factory workers, he took film's technology and process out of the studios and movie theaters, allowing the workers to make films about themselves, study the films and form ongoing collectives around such films. In this way Chris Marker, while shrouding himself in an enigmatic obscurity . . . [gave] birth to most of the leading political film collectives still operating in France.[1075]

SLON not only allowed Marker to continue making his political films but also to pursue Astruc's principle of the camera as a pen in creating important visual essays.[1076]

Alain Resnais, perhaps the most intellectual filmmaker of the New Left group, also responded to Astruc's challenge to create an independent cinema.[1077] Like many AVANT-GARDE French filmmakers, he is preoccupied with exploring how film can

---

[1073] "The SLON Films," p.41.

[1074] "SLON," p.82.

[1075] "The SLON Films," p.38.

[1076] Not all of Marker's films are political tracts. For example, his A.K.: THE MAKING OF "RAN" (1985) is a valuable documentary on the cinematic work of Akira Kurosawa.

[1077] For more information, see Alan Stanbrook, "The Time and Space of Alain Resnais," FILMS AND FILMING 10:4 (January 1964):35-8; Adrian Maben, "Alain Resnais: The War Is Over," ibid., 13:1 (October 1966):40-2; Roy Armes, "Resnais and Reality," ibid., 16:8 (May 1970):12-4; Richard Roud, "The Left Bank: Marker, Varda, Resnais," SIGHT AND SOUND 32:1 (Winter 1962-63):24-7; ___, "Memories of Resnais," ibid., 38:3 (Summer 1969):124-9, 162; Francis Lacassin, "Dick Tracy Meets Muriel," ibid., 36:2 (Spring 1967):101-2; Peter Harcourt, "Alain Resnais: 'Memory Is Kept Alive with Dreams,'" FILM COMMENT 9:6 (November-December 1973):47-50; ___, "Alain Resnais: Toward the Certainty of Doubt," ibid., 10:1 (January-February 1974):23-8; James Monaco, "There Isn't Enough Time: An Interview With Alain Resnais," ibid., 11:4 (July-August 1975):38-41; Richard Seaver, "Facts into Fiction: An Interview With Alain Resnais," ibid., pp. 41-4; Raymond Durgnat, "Skin Games," ibid., 17:6 (November-December 1981):28-32; M. B. White, "Resnais, Alain," THE INTERNATIONAL DICTIONARY OF FILMS AND FILMMAKERS: VOLUME II, pp.444-6; and Noel Burch, "A Conversation With Resnais," FILM QUARTERLY 13:3 (Spring 1960):27-9.

express complex and abstract thoughts on the same level with literature. Beginning in the post-WWII period with short films like VAN GOGH (1948) and NIGHT AND FOG/NUIT ET BROUILLARD (1955) and ranging through his feature films from HIROSHIMA MON AMOUR (1959) to MONO (1988), Resnais examines how the imaginative use of time, space, and memory can elevate film narrative to the realm of intellectual thought. "Through editing and an emphasis on formal repetition," M. B. White observes, "Resnais uses the medium to construct the conjunctions of the past and present, fantasy and reality, insisting on the convergence of what are usually considered distict domains of experience."[1078] Like his colleagues in the New Left, his efforts impress serious viewers more than they do the general public.

In many respects, Resnais is both part of, and separate, from his peers. Approaching film more pragmatically than the CAHIERS DU CINEMA group, as James Monaco points out, Resnais nevertheless "felt close to the young theoreticians of CAHIERS in the 1950s."[1079] Although they may have started off in different directions, they found a common ground by the 1960s. If there was one filmmaker in the NOUVELLE VAGUE whom Resnais most resembled, it would probably be Chris Marker. Not only did the two artists collaborate frequently, but also they shared similar thematic concerns. As Silvio Gaggi explains,

> Both filmmakers present sequences of images, words, and music which work together to suggest a conscious groping after its own experience, striving to articulate and order the confusing and often insane events which surround it. While that consciousness seems inextricably involved in the events which define its experience, it is also peculiarly alienated, distanced from those events. Ultimately the most significant similarity between the two filmmakers lies in the nature of the POINT OF VIEW of their films. Both juxtapose image, word, and music to present a multi-layered stream of consciousness roughly suggesting a flux of perception, idea and feeling. In the viewer's experience of these films, photographic images pass before his eyes in a manner analogous to real visual experience. The voice over suggests the movement of articulate thought, an essentially linguistic struggle to comprehend, order and control. And music lies behind it all, suggesting a flow of mood or emotion.[1080]

In other ways, however, Resnais represents a striking departure from the NOUVELLE VAGUE movement. For example, Kreidl insists that Resnais belongs more in the "French intellectual tradition" than in the New Wave movement "because he is at once ultramodern in narrative technique and old-fashioned in image construction."[1081] James Monaco argues that, despite the influence of film history on the New Wave,

> Resnais's consciousness of the cinematic heritage has always been more subtly displayed than say, Godard's or Truffaut's. His cinema is more reserved, and especially in the early years of the movement, notably less ebullient . . .
> Also like his contemporaries, he has been more conscious of the collaborative nature of the filmmaking process . . . Moreover, Resnais's shared attention to the connection between form and content has expressed itself in a more logical and restrained way.[1082]

[1078] White, p.446.

[1079] ALAIN RESNAIS, p.8.

[1080] Gaggi, p.11. For a similar analysis, see Noel Burch, "Four Recent French Documentaries," FILM QUARTERLY 13:1 (Fall 1959):56-61.

[1081] ALAIN RESNAIS, p.5.

[1082] ALAIN RESNAIS, p.10.

Freddy Sweet observes that

> Resnais differs from most directors in two respects. First of all, he refuses
> to make films that are adaptations of novels. Secondly, Resnais seeks major
> French novelists to write screenplays for him. Unlike Godard, Tati, and
> Truffaut, Resnais does not make films generated from his own imagination.
> Unlike Bunuel, Visconti and Richardson, who have adapted novels for cinema,
> Resnais does not begin his film with a published work of fiction. Resnais
> willingly collaborates in the production of a film, but wants the work to be
> original and not to be a transposition from other media.[1083]

Each of these perspectives reinforces Resnais's individuality and the role that "the
new novel" played in his unique career.

Despite the stunning critical success of HIROSHIMA MON AMOUR (1959) and
LAST YEAR AT MARIENBAD/L'ANNEE DERNIERE A MARIENBAD (1961), Resnais has
made fewer than a dozen feature films (depending on how one counts his contributions
to the 1967 anthology film, FAR FROM VIETNAM/LOIN DU VIETNAM in a period of
thirty years. Among his most respected works are MURIEL, OR THE TIME OF A
RETURN/MURIEL, OU LE TEMPS D'UN RETOUR (1963), THE WAR IS OVER/LA
GUERRE EST FINIE (1966), STAVINSKY (1974), and MON ONCLE D'AMERIQUE
(1981).   While critics and historians debate the reason for the limited output,
Resnais's debts to his collaborators, and the influence of Henri Bergson's ideas on
the unique filmmaker, no one denies the value of Resnais's contributions to the
development of film narrative.

Neither the New Right nor the New Left groups had a monopoly on important
artists working in French cinema during this period. Other major new directors

---

[1083] Freddy Sweet, THE FILM NARRATIVES OF ALAIN RESNAIS (Ann Arbor: UMI Press, 1981),
p. 1.

included Marcel Camus, Jacques Demy,[1084] Jacques Doniol-Valcroze, Pierre Etaix, Georges Franju,[1085] Marcel Hanoun, Claude Lelouch,[1086] Louis Malle,[1087] Jean Rouch, Jacques Rozier, and Roger Vadim.[1088] Because of space constraints, let us consider just one director: Rouch.

Often considered one of the two premier pioneers of CINEMA VERITE (the other

---

[1084] For more information, see Jacques Demy, "Lola in Los Angeles," FILMS AND FILMING 16:7 (April 1970):12-6; ___, "I Prefer the Sun to the Rain," FILM COMMENT 3:2 (Spring 1965):61; Graham Petrie, "Jacques Demy: Interview," ibid., 7:4 (Winter 1971-72):46-53; Richard Roud, "Rondo Gallant," SIGHT AND SOUND 33:3 (Summer 1964):136-9; Philip Strick, "Demy Calls the Tune," ibid., 40:4 (Autumn 1971):187; Robin Wood, "Demy, Jacques," THE INTERNATIONAL DICTIONARY OF FILMS AND FILMMAKERS: VOLUME II, pp.128-9; Ginette Billard, "Jacques Demy and His Other World," FILM QUARTERLY 18:1 (Fall 1964):23-7; Marsha Kinder, "Interview With Jacques Demy," FILM HERITAGE 2:3 (Spring 1967):17-24; and Philip K. Scheuer, "Frenchman in Hollywood," ACTION 3:6 (November-December 1968):10-3.

[1085] For more information, see Cynthia Grenier, "Franju," SIGHT AND SOUND 26:4 (Spring 1957):186-90; Tom Milne, "Georges Franju: The Haunted Void," ibid., 44:2 (Spring 1975):68-72; Robin Wood, "Terrible Buildings: The World of Georges Franju," FILM COMMENT 9:6 (November-December 1973):43-6; ___, "Franju, Georges," THE INTERNATIONAL DICTIONARY OF FILMS AND FILMMAKERS: VOLUME II, pp.198-9; and Gordon Gow, "Franju," FILMS AND FILMING 17:11 (August 1971):80.

[1086] For more information, see Peter Lev, "Claude Lelouch Discusses his Work, Francis Lai, Film Distribution, American History and Justice," TAKE ONE 5:10 (July-August 1977):16-20; Allen Eyles, "AND NOW MY LOVE," FOCUS ON FILM 21 (Summer 1975):9-10; and Rob Edelman, "Lelouch, Claude," THE INTERNATIONAL DICTIONARY OF FILMS AND FILMMAKERS: VOLUME II, pp.323-4.

[1087] For more information, see John Culhane, "Louis Malle: An Outsider's Odyssey," NEW YORK TIMES MAGAZINE (April 7, 1985):28-31, 68; Cynthia Grenier, "There's More to Malle Than Sex, Sex, Sex," NEW YORK TIMES 2 (February 6, 1972):15; Leticia Kent, "Malle: PRETTY BABY Could Be Called 'The Apprenticeship of Corruption,'" ibid., D (April 16, 1978):15, 19; Michiko Kakutani, "Louis Malle's Fascination With Life's Turning Points," ibid., 2 (June 28, 1981):1, 15; James Atlas, "The Artistic Recipe for MY DINNER WITH ANDRE," ibid., 2 (February 20, 1982):1, 15; Paul Chutkow, "Louis Malle Diagnoses His MURMUR OF THE HEART," ibid., H (March 9, 1989):15, 20; Marjorie Baumgarten, "Program Notes: ZAZIE DANS LE METRO," CINEMATEXAS PROGRAM NOTES 13:2 (October 20, 1977):61-8; ___, and Ed Lowry, "Program Notes: L'ASCENSEUR POUR L'ECHAFAUD," ibid., 14:1 (January 26, 1978):1-7; Tim O'Malley, "Program Notes: MURMUR OF THE HEART," ibid., 17:2 (October 31, 1979):55-61; Gordon Gow, "Louis Malle's France," FILMS AND FILMING 10:11 (August 1964):14-8; ___, "Like Acid: Interview With Louis Malle," ibid., 22:3 (December 1975):12-6; Dan Yakir, "Louis Malle: From THE LOVERS to PRETTY BABY," FILM QUARTERLY 31:4 (Summer 1978):2-10; Andrew Horton, "Creating a Reality that Doesn't Exist: An Interview With Louis Malle," LITERATURE/FILM QUARTERLY 7:2 (April 1979):86-98; Douglas McVay, "LACOMBE LUCIAN," FOCUS ON FILM 18 (Summer 1974):13-5; Antonio Chemasi, "PRETTY BABY: Love in Storyville," AMERICAN FILM 3:2 (November 1977):8-15; John Baxter, "Malle, Louis," THE INTERNATIONAL DICTIONARY OF FILMS AND FILMMAKERS: VOLUME II, pp.348-50; Lee Russell, "Louis Malle," NEW LEFT REVIEW 30 (March-April 1965):73-6; Eusebio L. Rodrigues, "Phantom India," FILM HERITAGE 9:1 (Fall 1973):23-35; and "Louis Malle on LACOMBE LUCIEN," FILM COMMENT 10:5 (September-October 1974):36-7.

[1088] For more information, see Ginette Billard, "Ban on Vadim," FILMS AND FILMING 6:2 (November 1959):29; Adrian Maben, "Vadim and Zola," ibid., 13:1 (October

being Marker), as well as the leading exponent of ethnographic filmmaking,[1089] Jean Rouch came to film by a circuitous route. Trained as a civil engineer, he was arrested by Nazi occupation troops during Worl War II and forced to work in the French colony of Niger. There he was dismissed by the Vichy governor and deported.[1090] Following World War II, Rouch decided to become an anthropologist, getting his doctorate at the Sorbonne and doing his research in Africa. As his research progressed, Rouch became dissatisfied with his inability through print to communicate his results to the people he studied. Consequently, he turned to filmmaking.[1091] Drawing upon his filmgoing experiences at the CINEMATEQUE FRANCAISE in the late 1930s and teaching himself how to use a Bell and Howell 16mm camera, he explored the advantages of visual anthropology to investigator and subject alike. Rouch's ethnographic studies in Africa during the 1950s convinced him of the need to develop a more flexible and lighter piece of equipment than the camera he was using. Fortunately, the infant medium television had also become interested in using 16mm equipment and had made a number of technical improvements not only in the camera itself, but also in the mechanics of editing and sound mixing. Nevertheless, by the end of the 1950s, Rouch still found 16mm cameras lacking the professional capabilities needed for ethnographic filmmaking.

The important breakthrough both for Rouch and film history came in 1958. Edgar Morin, a friend and sociologist, persuaded Rouch to return to Paris and to make a movie about "his own tribe." Not only did the idea appeal to the filmmaker, but it also gave him the opportunity to work closely with Raoul Coutard, the creator of the new and very impressive Eclair Cameflex 35mm camera,[1092] and Andre Coutant, the manufacturer of the Eclair camera. According to Rouch, the men agreed to design and to build a 16mm version that featured the same capabilities of the 35mm camera--"light, dependable, and steady"--and Rouch would field test it during the shooting of his new film, CHRONICLE OF A SUMMER/CHRONIQUE D'UN ETE

1966):58-9; and John Baxter, "Vadim, Roger," THE INTERNATIONAL DICTIONARY OF FILMS AND FILMMAKERS: VOLUME II, pp.544-5.

[1089] According to David MacDougall, "An ethnographic film may be regarded as any film which seeks to reveal one society to another. It may be concerned with the physical life of a people or with the nature of their social experience. Since they are also the subjects of anthropology, we tend to associate ethnographic film-making with anthropologists, but the two are not invariably linked." See David MacDougall, "Prospects of the Ethnographic Film," FILM QUARTERLY 13:2 (Winter 1969-70):16-30.

[1090] Hamid Naficy, "Jean Rouch: A Personal Perspective," QUARTERLY REVIEW OF FILM STUDIES 4:3 (Summer 1979):339-40.

[1091] For more information, see James Blue, "Jean Rouch In Conversation," FILM COMMENT 4:1-2 (Fall-Winter 1967):80-91; Dan Georgakas, et al. "The Politics of Cultural Anthropolgy: An Interview with Jean Rouch," CINEASTE 8:4 (Summer 1978):16-23; Roger Sandall, "Films by Jean Rouch," FILM QUARTERLY 15:2 (Winter 1961-62):57-9; Dan Yakir, "CINE-TRANSE: The Vision of Jean Rouch," ibid., 31:3 (Spring 1978):2-11; and Fereydoun Hoveyda, "CINEMA VERITE, or Fantastic Realism," CAHIERS DU CINEMA 125 (November 1961), Rpt. CAHIERS DU CINEMA: 1960-1968, pp.248-56.

[1092] Despite his technical genius, Coutard is best known as the cinematographer of JULES AND JIM/JULES ET JIM (1961) and Godard's favorite cameraman on most of the filmmaker's important works from BREATHLESS/A BOUT DE SOUFFLE (1960) to WEEKEND/LE WEEK-END (1967).

[1093] Cited in Georgakas, p.24.

(1961).[1093] The lightweight, dependable, and portable synchronous sound system that resulted from that project, plus the later development of faster film stock, was a crucial step in advancing the art of CINEMA VERITE in France, Free Cinema in Britain, and Direct Cinema in America. According to Rivette, "Rouch is the force behind all French cinema of the past ten years [1968], although few people realize it."[1094]

Since the early 1960s, Rouch has continued his visual anthropolgy in Africa. Being white, a European, and a male have made his African films very controversial works. By openly blending non-fictional material with staged events, Rouch challenges the nature of cinematic reality. Detractors dismiss them as products of an imperialist mind with a colonial vision, pointing out that his ethnographic studies are more myth than fact, and that his work ignores African women completely. Rouch's defenders, however, insist that he not only has added a greater dimension to the anthropology of African tribes, but also helped train a new school of African filmmakers like Mustapha Alassane, Safi Faye, Oumarou Ganda, and Desire Ecare.[1095] Rouch himself explains that cultural traditions in Africa make it impossible for a male, let alone a European male, to do justice to the image of African women.[1096] Nevertheless, the work of Rouch, like that of the Maysles brothers and Frederick Wiseman, continues to raise controversial questions about filming "reality": e.g., the disruptive and distorting role of the camera in shooting the event, the question of individual privacy, the exploitative nature of the filmmaker toward the people being filmed, and the issue of what benefits the distributed film has brought to the subjects themselves.

In hindsight, LA NOUVELLE VAGUE was in a state of flux almost from the moment it burst on the international scene. And why not? The artists who came to filmmaking in the mid- to late 1950s were no ordinary cinephiles. Well-versed in literary and philosophical traditions and obsessed with film history, they saw themselves as the vanguard of a new and revolutionary approach to filmmaking. Moreover, they refused to accept the STATUS QUO. No sooner had they attacked the French film industry's commitment to a literary bias, then they sought to find new ways to make film the equal of the traditional arts in expression and intellect. As the sixties opened, the lines between the classical Hollywood cinema and the "new cinema" advocated by radical filmmakers of the New Right and the New Left was beginning to have an effect on how audiences and critics adjusted to modernism in the cinema. The critical battles over the importance of MISE EN SCENE and AUTEURISM had shifted by the early 1960s, as the debate focused on the relationship between the work of art and the audience. More and more filmmakers began viewing their films as mediating forces between society and the individual. Influenced heavily by the theories of Marxist critics, phenonemologists, and existentialists, the "new cinema" of people like Godard, Resnais, and Rouch sought the audience's active involvement in interpreting physical reality and its relationship to people's lives and circumstances. When Hollywood, once the symbol of CAHIERS DU CINEMA's love affair with AUTEURISM and MISE EN SCENE, refused to accommodate the left's revolutionary ideas about film narrative, type casting, and "distancing," it became a derisive symbol of "naive" filmmaking in comparison to the political goals advocated by the "new cinema." Every major filmmaker, including Truffaut, Rohmer, and Godard, re-evaluated theories that made visuals more important than dialogue in films. From Paul Monaco's perspective, "The New Wave, . . . for all its visual innovativeness, and for all its radical departures in the lengths of shots and scenes as well as the aural components of the soundtrack, nonetheless established the film in a new

[1094] Jacques Rivette, "Time Overflowing: Rivette In Interview With Jacques Aumont, Jean-Louis Comolli, Jean Narboni, Sylvie Pierre (September 1968)," CAHIERS DU CINEMA: 1960-1968, p.320.

[1095] Georgakas, p.17.

[1096] Georgakas, p.21.

relationship to the word, and the serious study and criticism of the cinema, by extension to linguistics."[1097] As the decade drew to a close, the critical emphasis was on developing a "scientific" vocabulary for analyzing how artists set up a scene, filmed it, and cut the pieces.   Those critics who still persisted in exploring a director's personality or his thematic continuity from film to film were deemed "reactionary." Those filmmakers who pushed film language into heretofore unexplored areas of cinematic expression were praised by the French intellectual community. It was as if the artist had to choose between critical respectability or commercial viability. The details of the struggle are evident in the gradually shifting editorial policies of CAHIERS DU CINEMA, with 1968 marking the decisive change from an apolitical, pluralistic periodical to one committed to neo-Marxist, materialistic principles. Whether the search for an effective way to make film the intellectual equivalent of literature was productive is still being debated today. So, too, are the issues of to what degree economics determines a film's ideology and identification with a film character and with the camera's perspective imperceptibly shapes a spectator's values. Thus, as the seventies began, old ideas and old friendships gave way to new directions for the French film as well as for the international film industry.

BOOKS

GENERAL

*Armes, Roy. FRENCH CINEMA SINCE 1946: VOLUME TWO--THE PERSONAL STYLE. 2nd enlarged ed. New York: A. S. Barnes and Company, 1970. Illustrated. 175pp.
     Beginning with the debatable observation that the postwar cinema saw only one director of the first rank (Jacques Tati) appear between 1945 and 1955, Armes describes the period's weaknesses: e.g., a lack of experimentation, a shift away from small films to big-budget productions, and an awareness that "the veteran directors were showing their first signs of lassitude." Armes then outlines the importance of CAHIERS DU CINEMA in developing a new approach to French cinema. He identifies three common features that united the emerging new directors: (1) they made their directorial screen debut at thirty years or younger, (2) almost none of them had followed the standard practice in the French film industry of being an assistant director on a theatrical film, and (3) "most were allowed a free hand to make personal films from the very beginning instead of having to win this freedom by directing first a number of potboilers." Despite the fact that he overlooks Resnais's important work between 1948 and 1957, Armes credits the popularity of the short film during the postwar period as the crucial training ground for these emerging artists and offers a concise survey of its role from 1945 to 1955. Special attention is also paid to the significance of the new French film criticism during this period, particularly in its attacks on the stylized methods of the studio-made film. In the end, he concludes that experiences in short films and concepts gained from the critical study of film as art led the new directors to rethink the nature of film structure.
     Armes develops his theory by dividing his filmmakers into six sections. Section One, "Two Individualists," examines Georges Franju and Jean-Pierre Melville. Section Two, "Critics Incorporated," looks at Claude Chabrol, Francois Truffaut, Jean-Luc Godard, and Jacques Rivette. Section Three, "The Intellectuals," discusses Agnes Varda, Alain Resnais, and Chris Marker. Section Four, "The Professionals," reviews the work of Alexandre Astruc, Roger Vadim, and Louis Malle." Section Five, "Nothing But the Truth," concentrates on Jean Rouch. Section Six, "Into the Sixties," comments on Jacques Demy and Pierre Etaix. In Armes's concluding chapter, he acknowledges the limitations of his classifications but argues that the overriding

---

[1097] RIBBONS IN TIME, p.60.

importance of individualism to French filmmakers prevents their being included in the traditional film categories like genres, unified political positions, or a central theme. He does identify, however, several common characteristics: e.g., the absence of a social and political French cinema, the backgrounds of the directors "are uniformally bourgeois and their culture predominantly Parisian," and the filmmakers concentrate "almost exclusively on the individual and his personal relationships." In addition to an index, the book provides filmographies and bibliographies of the directors up to the mid-sixties. Well worth browsing.

*Cameron, Ian, ed. SECOND WAVE. New York: Praeger Publishers, 1970. Illustrated. 144pp.

In an attempt to assess the impact of the NOUVELLE VAGUE on present-day films, the authors examine the styles of eight unusual contemporary directors who admittedly are reacting to French influences: Dusan Makavejev (Robin Wood), Jerzy Skolimowski (Michael Walker), Nagisa Oshima (Ian Cameron), Ruy Guerra (Michel Ciment), Glauber Rocha (Ciment), Gilles Groulx (Robert Daudelin), Jean Pierre Lefebvre (Jean Chabot), and Jean-Marie Stroub (Andi Engel). Cameron points out in his brief introduction that both the NOUVELLE VAGUE (1959-1960) and the CINEMA VERITE (1962-63) movements led to the establishment of viable alternatives to Hollywood-style products. "In the wake of the New Wave, and provoked to a large extent by the experience of the films themselves," he tells us, "has come more formal discussion about the cinema than there has been since the abortive theorizing of the 'twenties.' This process undermined many of the preconceptions about film which had been accepted equally by the 'commercial' and 'art' cinemas." Set against the background of a "declining" American cinema, the directors discussed in this book represent various approaches to dealing with contemporary conditions in the international film industry and to modern perceptions of reality in the 1960s. The six countries they represent--Brazil, Canada, France, Japan, Poland, and Yugoslavia--are meant to be examples of how other nations were becoming important areas for significant filmmaking. Filmographies of each director are included, but no index is provided. Well worth browsing.

*Graham, Peter, ed. THE NEW WAVE: CRITICAL LANDMARKS. New York: Doubleday and Company, 1968. Illustrated. 184pp.

Attempting to fill in the gaps about the NOUVELLE VAGUE, this pioneering study attempts to "trace the origins of their aesthetics, to indicate the enormous influence of the late Andre Bazin, to give examples of the sort of critcism they were writing before they became directors, and to suggest some of the problems of transition." The ten selections include two interviews with Truffaut, Astruc's "The Birth of a New Avant-Garde: La Camera-Stylo," Bazin's "The Evolution of Film Language" and "LA POLITIQUE DES AUTEURS," Robert Benayoun's "The King Is Naked," critical essays by Claude Chabrol and Jean-Luc Godard, and Gerard Gozlan's two-part essay on Bazin. Regrettably, the editor provides little critical perspective on the material anthologized. Most serious are the book's missing filmographies and poorly reproduced illustrations. Well worth browsing.

Hillier, Jim, ed. CAHIERS DU CINEMA: 1960-1968--NEW WAVE, NEW CINEMA, REEVALUATING HOLLYWOOD. Cambridge: Harvard University Press, 1986. 363pp.

Following Bazin's death in 1958, and running throught the turbulent years of Rohmer's editorship, CAHIERS DU CINEMA moved away from a focus on AUTEURISM and toward a definition of MISE EN SCENE. As Hillier comments in his introduction to this important anthology, "Whereas ideas about authorship were relatively easily admitted, at some level at least, into general critical writing or, more precisely, relatively easily extended into the areas of popular cinema, the ideas about MISE EN SCENE proved more problematic (and, partly in consequence, opened up, ultimately, more important critical issues)." These critical issues--e.g., style, form, content and meaning, the nature of film, the role of the critic--are all addressed in the four major sections of this book. So, too, are misperceptions about the direction of CAHIERS DU CINEMA in the 1960s. For example, Hillier points out that although American cinema continued to be discussed regularly in the pages of the journal, French and European cinema became the primary concerns of the authors.   Also contrary to popular perception, the magazine, during the 1960s, had "very little sense of stability or consensus of values and interests." One figure who did influence the magazine's direction was Brecht. His Marxist, materialist approach to realism and the "public entertainment machine," Hillier stresses, becomes more and more evident from 1960 t0 1968, especially in the writings of Jean-Louis Comolli, Jean Narboni, Louis Marcorelles, Jean-Luc Godard, and Bernard Dort.   Attention is also drawn to the role played by Joseph Losey and Godard in adapting Brecht's ideas to their films, to the reasons why Rohmer left as chief editor, and to the political currents emerging at CAHIERS DU CINEMA after July, 1963.

    In addition to providing a stimulating assortment of articles, interviews, and lively discussions, Hillier offers valuable introductions to each of the book's four major sections. Part One, "New Wave/French Cinema," reviews how CAHIERS DU CINEMA tried to find an audience for neglected or underestimated films like LES BONNES FEMMES (1960) and THE SOLDIERS/LES CARABINIERS (1963); and the increasing friction among the critics-turned-filmmakers over the direction film should take.   Particular attention is given to the importance of LAST YEAR AT MARIENBAD/L'ANNE DERNIERE A MARIENBAD (1959) in focusing debate about "'realism': how to define social reality, the relationship between the individual and society, and how to render that social reality in cinema." Particular attention is also paid to Godard's dialectics. Part Two, "American Cinema: Celebration," examines the "extremism" of the 1959-1961 period, when MISE EN SCENE became king at CAHIERS DU CINEMA. Hillier's review of the heated critical debate in England and America over validating popular films does a fine job of highlighting the arguments about "how" versus "what" in explaining the nature of film criticism. Of special interest is Michel Mourlet's May 1960 article "In Defense of Violence," an essay that not only illustrates the critic's alarming tolerance for violence but also, more importantly, focuses attention on the issue of visual pleasure. Part Three, "American Cinema: Revaluation," superbly captures the mood of change taking place at CAHIERS DU CINEMA during the mid-1960s. Beginning with the December 1963-January 1964 special issue on American Cinema, Hillier illustrates how the critics-turned-filmmakers had grown in their understanding of Hollywood's now-defunct studio system and their realization that their favorite filmmakers were not representative of how the American film industry operated.   A second essay, reassessing Hollywood twenty years after WWII, shifts attention to American cinema in the 1960s, showing why the studio system could never have been useful for LA NOUVELLE VAGUE. Highlighted in this section are the opinions of Comolli, who became the key editorial voice in the mid-1960s. One also gets a sense of how semiotics, Marxist criticism, and psychological interpretations are becoming part of the magazine's new critical vocabulary. Particularly interesting are the attempts by Comolli and Jean Narboni to restructure AUTEUR principles to make AUTEUR favorites like Hawks more palatable to the new critical standards. Part Four, "Towards a New Cinema/New Criticism," contains the largest collection of material and is devoted to examining what is meant by "New Cinema." Again stressing the importance of Brecht and Godard on the evolution of film as well as CAHIERS DU CINEMA in the 1960s, Hillier selects Dort's noted 1960 article, "Towards a Brechtian Criticism of Cinema," to show how the attacks on AUTEURISM and MISE EN SCENE led early on to considerations about film "as a form of mediation on the real world." Regrettably, the editor doesn't include Brecht's 1960 "The Threepenny Lawsuit" essay, in which the German dramatist outlines his arguments against the commercial cinema and insists that economics, not aesthetics, determines the ideological content of a film. Including Hoveyda's 1961 article "Self-Criticism" provides the opportunity to show a growing interest in finding a "more 'scientific' critical language to analyze the cinema's role in dealing with social reality." The famous 1963 interview with Roland Barthes functions both as an illustration of the changes taking place once Rivette replaced Rohmer as chief editor at CAHIERS DU CINEMA and as the jumping off point for the magazine's increasing interest in the application of linguistics to film. Other articles, interviews, and editorials add to our understanding of the periodical's attacks on the modern, political cinema. Cleverly, Hillier concludes this excellent collection with Sylvie Pierre and Jean-Louis Comolli's 1968 article, "Two Faces of FACES," reminding us again how far CAHIERS DU CINEMA had come from the magazine's initial endorsement of American films.

Not only has Hillier done a fine job in selecting and editing the material, but he has also displayed stylistic grace and perceptive insights in providing introductions to these complex matters. As bonuses, he includes a list of the magazine's annual "Best Films" for 1960 through 1968, as well as a guide to CAHIERS DU CINEMA Nos.103-207, January 1960-December 1968, in English translation; a summary of what volume 1 contains and what volumes 3 and 4 will contain, and an index. Highly recommended for special collections.

Lellis, George. BERTOLT BRECHT: "CAHIERS DU CINEMA" AND CONTEMPORARY FILM THEORY. Ann Arbor: UMI Research Press, 1982. 197pp.

Lellis has done a first-rate job of turning his 1976 Ph.D. dissertation for the University of Texas at Austin into a highly informative account of France's most important post-WWII film periodical. Starting with the basic thesis that Brecht's theories of theater primarily influenced the development and evolution of CAHIERS DU CINEMA, the author traces how the magazine's initial apolitical policies changed once it adapted Brecht's aesthetic principles--e.g., the relationship between the artist and the audience--and then applied them to film, the effects of the "Brechtian" editorial slant of CAHIERS DU CINEMA in the 1970s and its "elaborate theoretical system aimed at the almost total revision of existing film theory," and the attempts in the 1980s to return the magazine to its roots in the New Wave. Lellis admits that the post-1968 policies growing out of Brecht's theatrical theories nearly destroyed the magazine's financial base, but points out that in moving to the left, it assumed a leadership role in contemporary Marxist criticism.

Dividing his valuable information into three major parts, Lellis begins with an introductory section summarizing Brecht's theories and the evolution of CAHIERS DU CINEMA's formalist approach. For those readers unfamiliar with Brecht's major preccupations, Lellis reduces them to three key categories: "the form of a work of art is as important to its political meaning as its content; the use of typed actors and characters to produce a genuinely political discourse; the VERFREMDUNG [Alienation] effect." Collectively, they represent Brecht's strong feeling that a new concept of art was needed, one that would change the passive relationship between the audience and the work of art. Although CAHIERS DU CINEMA's early interest in the German dramatist's theories was apolitical (and thus somewhat distorted his ideas), the author explains the significance of Brecht's notion that form determines the political content of a work of art as much as content to the periodical's own concern with form in film. Lellis further divides his analysis into three categories: "the philosophical roots of CAHIERS's formalism; the use of geometric metaphors in some of the critics' writings about film; and the conception of film as an art dealing with physical relationships among the actors presented on the screen."

Part Two, "Brechtian Criticism Before 1968," reviews the influence of the German playwright on CAHIERS DU CINEMA up to the events of May, 1968. Three specific areas are addressed: (1) a chronological look at Brecht's works as performed in French theaters prior to 1960, commenting on the playwright's status in French culture during this period; (2) the role of Jacque Rivette's criticism in linking the "old" and "new" CAHIERS DU CINEMA, pointing out the affinities between Rivette's admiration for the eighteenth century French dramatist Denis Diderot and the links between Diderot and Brecht; and (3) miscellaneous currents at CAHIERS DU CINEMA, suggesting how they helped re-orient the magazine toward Brecht's aesthetics. Particular emphasis is placed on relating Bazin's apolitical aesthetics to Brechtian principles, the contributors' reactions to theories about realism and the importance of illusion in determing cinematic truths, and the influence of Joseph Losey in making

Brechtian ideas palatable to the pluralistic publication. Lellis singles out two specific types of Brechtian criticism found in CAHIERS DU CINEMA prior to 1968: those articles that point directly to Brechtian ideas, working to transfer his dramatic theories to the screen; and those articles that indirectly develop his theories without crediting him openly. The former are represented by the special December 1960 issue on Brecht and the criticisms of Louis Marcorelles and Fereydoun Hoveyda. The latter are represented by the magazine's positive reactions to the films of its ex-critics and to the new Italian cinema of the 1960s. In addition, Lellis identifies two 1966 essays by Michel Mardone and Jean-Louis Comolli that demonstrate the increasing influence of Brecht on CAHIERS DU CINEMA.

Part Three, "Brechtian Criticism After 1968," investigates the political polarization that occurred at CAHIERS DU CINEMA, how it led to alternative theories about film, and the direction that the magazine follows in the 1980s. The shift to the left in 1968, as Lellis explains, was indicative of almost all intellectual French film criticism, "Thus CAHIERS DU CINEMA on the one hand reflects certain trends which are felt more generally in French writing about film; on the other, it proves to be a major force in reformulation of film theory taking place at the time." The author divides his analysis into "theoretical" and "practical" writings. The former includes a discussion of the Dziga Vertov Group and the writings of the magazine's two major theorists in the post-1968 period: Pascal Bonitzer and Jean-Louis Comolli. Among the theoretical issues considered are the rewriting of film history and theory in favor of materialistic principles, the reasons why the history of world film is mainly "the suppression of revolutionary montage," why naturalism operates as a mask for dominant ideology, and the importance of Lacanian psychology. The section of practical writings examines the role of historical movies in articulating "the material and cultural realities by which history is structured," plus the works of three deliberately political filmmakers: Constantin Costa-Gavras, Jean-Marie Straub, and Robert Kramer. The section also includes a detailed examination of CAHIERS DU CINEMA'S reactions to Godard's JUST GREAT/TOUT VA BIEN (1972) and Marin Karmitz's COUP POUR COUP (1971). After explaining the reasons why CAHIERS DU CINEMA began repudiating its neo-Marxist, materialist policies in the mid-1970s and became interested in theories about cinephilia and actors, Lellis discusses how the magazine's contemporary critics try "to reconcile their love of art with their love of politics and the inherent contradiction between cinephilia and political activism." The concluding chapter provides an excellent summary of the author's findings.

Although Lellis's study is limited to Brecht's influence alone, it still provides considerable information on the critical currents operating during nearly forty years of French film history. The writing is crisp, informative, and perceptive. Lellis's conclusions that there is great continuity in the evolution of the magazine's editorial policies, that Brecht is a pivotal figure in the evolutionary process, and that CAHIERS DU CINEMA provided a major alternative to existing film criticism are argued persuasively. Endnotes, a bibliography, and an index are included. Recommended for special collections.

Monaco, James. THE NEW WAVE: TRUFFAUT, GODARD, CHABROL, ROHMER, RIVETTE. New York: Oxford University Press, 1976. Illustrated. 372pp.

A major contribution to understanding the five key figures of the New Wave, this valuable study spends most of its time analyzing the works of Truffaut and Godard, while the remaining ex-CAHIERS DU CINEMA critics get a more limited appraisal. Monaco begins with a useful introduction to the New Wave, a glimpse at its theoretical roots, and a brief discussion of the important ideas developed in CAHIERS DU CINEMA. The primary emphasis in the chapters is on the films of the individual filmmakers, with the author tracing the continuity in each of the director's works and demonstrating the links between the product and its political, social, and economic contexts. This is the book to read if one is interested in beginning a serious study of LA NOUVELLE VAGUE. It contains perceptive insights, a valuable bibliography, and important summaries on the similarities and differences among the directors who helped reshape film history, theory, and criticism during the 1950s and 1960s. An index is included. Highly recommended for special collections.

Porter, Melinda Camber. THROUGH PARISIAN EYES: REFLECTIONS ON CONTEMPORARY FRENCH ARTS AND CULTURE. New York: Oxford University Press, 1986. Illustrated. 244pp.
    A rich collection of more than thirty interviews with artists, phenomenologists, and existentialists who played a major role in the cultural life of France from the post-WWII period to the present, this highly entertaining and informative anthology is delightful reading. The interviews conducted between 1975 and 1985 offer the reflections of key personalities like Jean-Louis Barrault, Peter Brook, Marcel Carne, Costa-Gavras, Marguerite Duras, Louis Malle, Marcel Ophuls, Alain Resnais, Alain Robbe-Grillet, Eric Rohmer, Bernard Tavernier, Francois Truffaut, and Roger Vadim. Rather than present the questions and answers in routine fashion, the ambitious author summarizes her subjects' comments. In addition, Porter does a nice job of grouping her subjects into nine intelligent categories: "History and Responsibility," "The Theatrical Establishment In Renewal," "Foreign Connections," "Communication at the Breaking Point," "Decisive Women," "The Invasion of the Modernist Philosphers," "Freedom Fighters," and "The Sovereignty of the Writer." Don't try guessing who goes where. Get the book and enjoy the stimulating material. An index is included. Well worth browsing.

Van Wert, William F. THE THEORY AND PRACTICE OF THE "CINE-ROMAN." New York: Arno Press, 1978. 382pp.
    One of the most interesting works in the Arno Press series, this reprint of Van Wert[1975 Ph.D. dissertation at Indiana University begins by discussing what distinguished the New Left from the New Right in LA NOUVELLE VAGUE. The latter he sees as heavily influenced by film history, evident in "the tendency in their films toward films-within-the-film, allusions to favorite directors, imitations of those directors' styles and autobiographical (or should we say auto-filmographic) allusions." The New Left, on the other hand, evinced few of these tendencies. Emphasizing the group's search for the cinematic equivalents of literature, Van Wert identifies three stages that members of the New Left followed: "first, the transposition of literary devices into film, which implied adaptations of technique, not content, ... ; second, the recruiting of poets and novelists on the part of Resnais to write directly for film; finally, the passage from screenwriter to director of three of Resnais's collaborators [Cayrol, Duras, and Robbe-Grillet]." The purpose of Van Wert's study is to examine how people like Varda, Resnais, and other members of the New Left developed their "concept of a literary cinema." Their commitment to working in film also influenced literature, in that members of the New Left published many of their film scripts in the form of CINE-ROMAN. According to Van Wert, "These published texts attest to the literary merit of the film texts at the same time that they serve as program notes (like the libretto for an opera) to be used in conjunction with the film." The CINE-ROMAN thus becomes important both as a memory aid and as a study guide to the film. Equally important, the "novel-film" operates as a safeguard against the distortion of the screenwriter's intentions. For example, deletions in a released film remain in the published script; distortions in the film version are explained on the printed page. Five exceptionally well-written chapters amplify Van Wert's ideas on the theory and purpose of the CINE-ROMAN, as well as its relationship to both major groups in LA NOUVELLE VAGUE. Endnotes and bibliographies are included, but no index is provided. Recommended for special collections.

CLAUDE CHABROL

*Wood, Robin, and Michael Walker. CLAUDE CHABROL. New York: Praeger Publishers, 1970. Illustrated. 144pp.

Stressing the influence of Hitchcock on the ex-film critic, Wood and Walker provide the only book-length English-language study of Chabrol as well as a valuable, albeit brief, discussion of his films from 1958 to 1970. Filled with intriguing analyses and stressing the moral consistency in Chabrol's works, Wood and Walker, working continents apart and sharing a common perspective on the value of Chabrol's work, divide the book into a series of independent interpretations of sixteen films. Wood sets the tone with his introductory essay, pointing out that the filmmaker's "great problem as an artist has been the difficulty of affirming belief in anything." Having repudiated the dominant hegemony because of "its materialism, pretensions, and repressiveness," Chabrol's perceived alternatives have proved "self-destructive" or "completely arid." Thus the reason for Chabrol's reaching the "impasse of the 'private-world' artists." Chabrol's search through his films for new and more positive values requires his balancing conflicting values--"hatred and tenderness, disgust and generosity, cynicism and belief." Chabrol's search and balancing act is the central concern of this book.

A little more than half of the chapters are supplied by Wood. Knowing that Chabrol was just emerging from critical disfavor at the time the book was written, Wood hits hard at the virtues of HANDSOME SERGE/LE BEAU SERGE/BITTER REUNION (1958), A DOUBLE TOUR/WEB OF PASSION/LEDA (1959), LES BONNE FEMMES (1960), LES GODELUREAUX (1961), BLUEBEARD/LANDRU (1962), MARIE-CHANTAL CONTRE LE DOCTEUR KHA (1965), THE LINE OF DEMARCATION/LA LIGNE DE DEMARCATION (1966), THE CHAMPAGNE MURDERS/LE SCANDALE (1967), LES BICHES (1968), and THE UNFAITHFUL WIFE/LA FEMME INFIDELE (1969). Walker does the same in his reviews from THE COUSINS/LES COUSINS to LE BOUCHER (1970). Both authors highlight the brutal and cynical aspects of Chabrol's themes, while contrasting his approach between the early and later films. Attention is drawn as well to the bestial and disruptive nature of Chabrol's aesthetics, pointing out the differences among Hitchcock, Chabrol, and Rohmer. Considerable attention is also paid to the importance of Catholicism in Chabrol's work. A filmography is included plus a small number of stills, but no index is provided. Recommended for special collections.

GEORGES FRANJU

*Durgnat, Raymond. FRANJU. Berkeley: University of California Press, 1968. Illustrated. 144pp.

In the only book-length study in English about Franju, Durgnat points out that his subject is a filmmaker difficult to classify: "Georges Franju is sometimes described as a New Wave director. Depending on one's definition of the New Wave, this may be fair enough; he made what is in effect a first short film a year after Resnais' VAN GOGH, and his first feature at the same time as HIROSHIMA MON AMOUR." Durgnat then adds, "In almost every other respect however he is a filmmaker of an older generation." To develop his thesis, Durgnat divides his material into two main sections: "The Artist" and "The Films." The former explains the director's approach as "a synthesis of the compassionate and the steely," while the latter discusses Franju's works from documentary shorts like LE METRO (1934), LES SANG DES BETES (1949), and HOTEL DES INVALIDES (1951) to feature films like THE KEEPERS/LA TETE CONTRE LES MURS (1958), EYES WITHOUT A FACE/LES YEUX SANS VISAGE/THE HORROR CHAMBER OF DR. FAUSTUS (1959), and THOMAS THE IMPOSTER/THOMAS L'IMPOSTEUR (1964). Except for a very slight biography and an overly pedantic discussion of Franju's film technique, Durgnat provides his usual provocative and entertaining observations. We come to know this relatively unknown and unpopular commercial artist who specialized in slow, dismal, pessimistic films that were preoccupied with pain, torture, and death. Yet, Franju is a master of MISE EN SCENE, and Durgnat, in considerable detail, discusses how, why, and where. A filmography and bibliography are included, but no index is provided. Well worth browsing.

JEAN-LUC GODARD

*Andrew, Dudley, ed. BREATHLESS: JEAN-LUC GODARD, DIRECTOR. New Brunswick: Rutgers University Press, 1987. Illustrated. 239pp.

An intelligent and invaluable case study on Godard's first feature film, this informative resource book begins with a literate and sensitive introduction to the controversial filmmaker's role in the New Wave and its influence on BREATHLESS/A BOUT DE SOUFFLE (1960). Andrew points out that Godard's youthful, romantic search for a pure cinema owes a literary debt to writers like Poe, Baudelaire, Rimbaud, Villon, and Sartre; and to other filmmakers like Cocteau, Rossellini, Truffaut, and Visconti. The author credits Sartre with inspiring Godard's basic notion in the 1950s that "Authentic art comes from sincere artists who extend the sacred tradition only when they forget tradition and forge the present with contemporary tools of expression." In describing the impressionable Godard's desire to put on film "the defining characteristics of modern life . . .   speed, boldness, and ingenuity," Andrew discusses how the filmmaker modeled himself after Alfred Hitchcock and Andre Malraux. He is particularly impressed by Godard's use of Hollywood "B" genres (e.g., musicals and westerns) to "address the most serious philosophical issues of the day." Making "authenticity" his standard, the critic-turned-filmmaker adapted Truffaut's idea for a gangster film, to demonstrate Godard's new film aesthetic. Although one can quibble with Andrew's suggestion that Belmondo's performance is the result of a circuitous set of influences that began in the 1930s with the acting style of Gabin, who influenced Bogart and other FILM NOIR stars, who, in turn, influenced Belmondo, the analysis of the film itself is very perceptive and useful. We are given not only technical information, but also examples of Godard's intertexual references to works and directors.

Following a helpful introduction and a brief biographical sketch of the director, the editor divides his material into three sections. The first part provides cast and crew credits, the continuity script, notes on the script, and Truffaut's original treatment. The second part consists of interviews, reviews, and commentaries, including observations by Georges de Beauregard (the film's producer) and Raoul Coutard (the film's cinematographer). The last part gives a filmography and bibliography. Regrettably, there is no index. Recommended for special collections.

*Billard, Pierre, ed. MASCULINE FEMININE: A FILM BY JEAN-LUC GODARD. New York: Grove Press, 1969. Illustrated. 288pp.

Godard's eleventh feature film in seven years and the first of three he completed in 1966, MASCULINE FEMININE/MASCULIN FEMININE deals with Paul (Jean-Pierre Leaud), an ex-soldier who returns to Paris in 1965, trying to rebuild his life. After several attempts at meaningful relationships and at communicating his ideas through the mass media, Paul is found dead either from an accident or from an act of suicide. In providing "a meticulous description of the significant action and a translation of the actual dialogue in the completed film," Billard offers a valuable record of Godard's spontaneous shooting techniques and complex editing style. Supplementary materials are divided into six categories. The first section, "The Starting Point of the Film," examines the loose connection between Maupassant's short stories, "Paul's Mistress" and "The Signal," and the film. Section Two, "Godard's 'Chronicle of a Winter,'" contains the 1965 material that the filmmaker wrote for a pamphlet advertising the film. Section Three, "The 'Script,'" is a summary of Godard's ideas from his personal notebook. Section Four, "Godard Directing," offers two invaluable descriptions of the filmmaker's approach to shooting. Section Five, "Interviews," provides a conversation with Godard and an informative evaluation of him by the leading actress of the film, Chantal Goya. And Section Six, "Reviews," offers more than sixteen reactions from French, British, and American critics. No bibliography or index is included. Recommended for special collections.

*Brown, Royal S., ed. FOCUS ON GODARD. Englewood Cliffs: Prentice-Hall, 1972. Illustrated. 190pp.

Beginning with the assertion that "The recent history of the various revolutionary movements that have taken place within the arts, particularly in France, can best be summed up by the word 'debourgeoisification,'" Brown identifies the broad implications of the concept for understanding Godard's works, particularly in his rejection of materialism and abhorrence toward traditional narrative structure. To illustrate his evenhanded approach to Godard's controversial aesthetics and political positions, Brown divides his anthology into three major sections, containing more than twenty articles, reviews, interviews, and essays (written by authors like Michele Manceaux, Yvonne Baby, Jean Collet, Michel Cournot, Kent E. Carroll, Tom Milne, Gilles Jacob, and Georges Sadoul). Interestingly, some of the best information is supplied by the editor himself. In the perceptive introduction, Brown describes the "predominance of marked dialectic in the French director's work--a dialectic that offers no answers, no solutions within either extreme" and points out the paradoxical and contradictory nature of Godard's films from BREATHLESS/A BOUT DE SOUFFLE (1960) to VLADIMIR AND ROSA/VLADIMIR ET ROSA (1970). Another essay, "Jean-Luc Godard: Nihilism versus Aesthetic Direction," expands on the paradoxical nature of Godard's works, analyzing how his pre-1968 films and their emerging "moral radicalism" led to his revolutionary action films of the late 1960s and early 1970s. Arguing that the filmmaker's distancing techniques conflict with the autobiographical tone of his late films, Brown discusses how "positive" statements emerge from Godard's "oppressive negativism." In Brown's last essay, "LA CHINOISE: Child's Play?" he uses the cinematic relationship between the liberal Yvonne and her radical friends to illustrate the political ambiguities in Godard's attempt to make film a revolutionary political weapon. The range of the director's philosophical and moral positions is addressed throughout the interesting collection. In addition to an annotated chronology, Brown also provides a bibliography, a filmography, and an index. Well worth browsing.

*Cameron, Ian, et al. THE FILMS OF JEAN-LUC GODARD. New York: Praeger Publishers, 1970. Illustrated. 192pp.

In the introduction to this updated and expanded version of the 1967 anthology, Cameron comments on Godard's volatile nature and the enormous contributions that the filmmaker has made in revolutionizing critical consensus. "His work elicits extreme reactions," Cameron tells us, ". . . [from] goofy adulation in some quarters, and elsewhere equally unreasoned hate." The goal of the eighteen articles (written by noted critics like Charles Barr, V. F. Perkins, Jose Luis Guarner, Philip French, Raymond Durgnat, Robin Wood, and Cameron) is to provide a middle ground between polarized positions. The separate chapters analyzing Godard's films from BREATHLESS/A BOUT DE SOUFFLE (1960) to ONE PLUS ONE/SYMPATHY FOR THE DEVIL (1968) examine the controversial characteristics of Godard's sixteen films during the 1960s: e.g., low-budget productions, elliptical filmmaking, assembling cinematic fragments into a simple narrative that not only produces complex results but also reveals the director's personal doubts, and extraordinary use of language to articulate directly Godard's ethical and political values. Two of the best essays are Wood's critique of WEEKEND/LE WEEK-END (1967) and Durgnat's comments on ONE PLUS ONE/SYMPATHY FOR THE DEVIL. A filmography and bibliography are included, but no index is provided. Well worth browsing.

*Collet, Jean. JEAN-LUC GODARD. Trans. Ciba Vaughan. New York: Crown Publishers, 1970. Illustrated. 215pp.

Originally published in the CINEMA D'AUJOURD-HUI series, a third of this English-language edition contains the editor's extented, admiring, and revised introductory essay. Calling his efforts "a preliminary attempt, both fervent and marveling, to approach a body of work, which, at that time [1963], elicited general disdain more than comprehension," Collet hopes that his comments will lead to "a fresh perspective on Godard's films--on his first efforts as well as his most recent work." A key issue the author raises relates to Godard's idea in the 1950s that "True cinema consists only in placing something before the camera. At the cinema, we do not think, we are thought. A poet calls this the takingness of things. That is, not man's taking of things but, rather, things taking, capturing man." The remainder of the essay explores how Godard's doubts and anger grew out of this initial premise of "taking." According to Collet, the way to understand Godard's work is to focus on his dialectical treatment of documentary and fiction.   To develop this perspective, Collet divides the contributions of his collaborators into three major sections. Part One, "Texts and Documents," contains two interviews with Godard. Part Two, "The Work of Jean-Luc Godard," contains screenplay excerpts and presentations from A WOMAN IS A WOMAN/UNE FEMME EST UNE FEMME (1961) to LE WEEK-END/WEEKEND (1967). Part Three, "Critical Spectrum," offers observations by Andre S. Labarthe, Robert Benayoun, Michel Cournot, Marie-Claire Wuilleumier, Alain Jouffroy, and John Simon. The last section, "Witnesses: Notes on Godard," includes comments by Georges de Beauregard, Raoul Coutard, Agnes Guillemot, and Francois Truffaut. A filmography, bibliography, and index are provided. Recommended for special collections.

*GODARD: THREE FILMS--A WOMAN IS A WOMAN, A MARRIED WOMAN, TWO OR THREE THINGS I KNOW ABOUT HER. Trans. Jan Dawson et al. Introduction Alistair Whyte. New York: Harper & Row, 1975. Illustrated. 192pp.
     The three films in this anthology function as a trilogy on several stages in Godard's career when he explored how a Parisian woman lived during a single day and night. As Whyte points out in his introductory remarks, the filmmaker from the start was out to revolutionize the way audiences traditionally watched films. Instead of passively accepting the images and sounds they received in the theater, Godard insisted on involving us with his images, sounds, and messages.   The three films included in this volume were selected because they illustrate both Godard's political perspectives and his cinematic experimentation. A WOMAN IS A WOMAN/UNE FEMME EST FEMME (1961) parodies the Hollywood musical within the context of a humorous love triangle. A MARRIED WOMAN/UNE FEMME MARIEE (1964) also deals with a love triangle, only this time Godard critiques the relationships with "clinical detachment." 2 OR 3 THINGS I KNOW ABOUT HER/2 OU 3 CHOSES QUE JE SAIS D'ELLE (1966) presents a series of episodes dealing with a working-class housewife, and uses bitter satire to ridicule a middle-class society and its repressive values. Each of the films reveals Godard's refusal to portray human relationships as either meaningful or lasting. Moreover, as Whyte observes, "The problems of human relationships are shown to be aggravated by modern society." In addition to the transcripts of the films, this useful publication contains an appendix consisting of critical essays on each of the films. Well worth browsing.

Guzzetti, Alfred. TWO OR THREE THINGS I KNOW ABOUT HER: ANALYSIS OF A FILM BY GODARD. Cambridge: Harvard University Press, 1981. Illustrated. 366pp.
     This shot-by-shot analysis of Godard's 1967 film grows out a series of discussions and seminars that the author participated in at Harvard from 1971 to 1975. To explain his novel approach, Guzzetti first comments on Godard's initial preoccupations with cinema, explaining that for many people that is mainly what the filmmaker is about. The characters in his early films "go to the movies, talk about them, quote them, and live in an environment of movie posters." Those performers--e.g., Jeanne Moreau, Brigitte Bardot, Samuel Fuller, and Fritz Lang--who make cameo appearances in his films from 1961 to 1966, many of which are homages to the works of his favorite AUTEURS--e.g., Hawks, Lubitsch, Dreyer, Rossellini, Lang, and Huston--further reflect Godard's complex intertexual allusions. By the mid-1960s, however, Guzzetti notes the director's emerging biases against traditional narratives and toward political statements. The film under analysis in this book, Godard's thirteenth feature film, signifies for Guzzetti the synthesis of the

director's new feelings about cinema. Without denying Godard's refusal to follow conventional rules and thereby alienating most audiences, the author defends both the filmmaker and his work on the grounds that the experience of the film is valuable to the artist and to the spectator. In making that point, Guzzetti is arguing as much for the serious study of film as an academic subject as for the serious study of Godard's work. Dividing the film's 227 shots into eighteen sequences, the author then proceeds to discuss the work in a detailed and intriguing fashion. The approach may not win many converts for Godard, but it suggests how much we miss in multiple viewings, let alone in a single screening. Well worth browsing.

*Kreidl, John Francis. JEAN-LUC GODARD. Boston: Twayne Publishers, 1980. Illustrated. 273pp.

Lesage, Julia. JEAN-LUC GODARD: A GUIDE TO REFERENCES AND RESOURCES. Boston: G. K. Hall and Company, 1980. 438pp.
    The most complete source of information on Godard, this important reference work tries to be as comprehensive as possible. Part One, "Biographical Background," works on the assumption that "Permeating Godard's entire OUEVRE is the sense of being an outsider, an onlooker, a provincial observer of the mores of large, urban, capitalist centers." Lesage reviews the filmmaker's struggles to escape from his "bourgeois family," his support of "anti-imperalist struggles," his life as a "bohemian cinephile" during the late 1940s and 1950s, and the ties that Godard had to "his fellow film addicts." The comments are perceptive, informative, concise, and interesting. Particularly effective is Lesage's ability to tie Godard's cinematic problems to his personal life and political awakening. My only regret is that in commenting on events like Godard's stormy divorce from Anna Karina and the political friendships he made that same year (1965) "with a group of young people in Paris," Lesage doesn't give us more information. The survey takes us to the late 1970s and to Godard's cooperative filmmaking ventures with Anne-Marie Mieville.
    Part Two, "Critical Survey of Ouevre," tests the author's objectivity in discussing the political filmmaker's "major conflict seen throughout his work: he must stand alone as a creative genius although he has constantly struggled to forge a collective, modernist, politicized art." For example, while other people discuss Godard's alleged misogyny, Lesage cites a handful of films to prove that the filmmaker is very much concerned with the oppression of women. The body of the chapter is divided into ten topical sections: "Critical Approaches to Godard," limiting the spectrum to romantic and political categories; "Godard's Cinematic Technique," stressing the importance of the shot in his work; "Nonpsychological Development of Character," pointing out the filmmaker's strategies in framing and composition to create character motivation or develop the narrative; "Documentary," explaining the importance of the form to reveal the "truth" about the media; "Symbol and Emblem," focusing on the post-1968 films and their concern with abstract social concepts; "The Written Word," describing how print functions in Godard's films from the mid-1960s on; "The Long Take/Color," applauding the virtuosity of Godard's innovative techniques; "Cinematic Reflexivity," reviewing Godard's intertextual references; and "Film and Politics," explaining that "Godard's modernism aims to displace the spectator ideologically, to move her/him away from illusion into a closer relation to social reality." Although one wishes at times that Lesage were more critical of Godard's failings as a communicator, one admires the skill with which she defends the artist and his objectives.
    The most interesting challenge for Lesage appears in Part Three, "The Films: Credits, Notes and Synopsis." She asks, "In writing a synopsis of a film by a director whose work is characterized by disjuncture, what does one summarize?" To her credit, Lesage answers her rhetorical question by providing first-rate summaries not only of the thematic and cinematic structures of the films, but also of their audio and visual structures.

The remaining sections dealing with annotations of articles and interviews by and about Godard reflect the same high standards as other books in this fine series. In addition, Lesage provides sections on screenplays, related activities, archival resources, film distributors, a film title index, and an author index. Recommended for special collections.

*MacCabe, Colin. GODARD: IMAGES, SOUNDS, POLITICS. Bloomington: Indiana University Press, 1980. Illustrated. 175pp.
A cleverly designed book emphasizing the visual aspects of Godard's work, the focus is on the post-1968 films. MacCabe informs us that between 1968 and the publication of this book Godard has finished twelve films, eighteen hours of TV programming, and is working on three projects. The twofold reasons for Godard's abandoning commercial filmmaking, according to the author, are "on the one hand, the financing of films, the methods of production and distribution and, on the other hand, the organization of sounds and images which compose the films themselves." Clearly sympathetic to Godard's experimental work with film language, MacCabe describes the post-1968 period as "perhaps the most conscious and rigorous [investigation into the language of film] in the history of the cinema." Using excerpts from interviews Godard gave to other researchers as well as to MacCabe, the author provides a handful of informative and intriguing chapters on important Godardian concerns: "Money and Montage," "Politics," "Images of Women, Images of Sexuality," "Technology," and "Television." The chapter on women is co-authored with Laura Mulvey; the one on technology is co-authored with Mike Eaton. A filmography concludes the useful publication, but no index is provided. Well worth browsing.

*Mussman, Tony, ed. JEAN-LUC GODARD: A CRITICAL ANTHOLOGY. New York: E. P. Dutton and Company, 1968. Illustrated. 319pp.
This fine compendium of eighteen articles and critical reviews, plus three interviews with Godard, two scenarios, and five commentaries by Godard, offers one of the first important English-language publications critiquing the director's first fifteen films, from BREATHLESS/A BOUT DE SOUFFLE (1960) to WEEKEND/LE WEEK-END (1967). In the editor's opening comments, he argues that Godard's aesthetics always involve "ANALYSIS, REFLECTION, and ACTION." Pointing out that the essay is being written at a time [1967] when the thirty-six year old filmmaker has completed fourteen feature films and ten shorts, yet remains relatively unknown in America, Mussman discusses the reasons for Godard's poor reception outside of Europe: e.g., a heavy emphasis on dialogue, the metaphorical aspects of his fast-moving imagery, and his naive political and social comments. In Godard's defense, the author argues that the films require and deserve several viewings to appreciate the classical aspects of Godard's art and to understand why he is an "action-intellectual." Among the anthology's many noted contributors discussing the nature of Godard's work are Andrew Sarris, Pauline Kael, Susan Sontag, Tom Milne, Robin Wood, Jean Collet, and Godard (very often). Well worth browsing.

*Narboni, Jean, and Tom Milne, eds. and trans. GODARD ON GODARD: CRITICAL WRITINGS BY JEAN-LUC GODARD. Introduction Richard Roud. New York: The Viking Press, 1972. Illustrated. 292pp.
Originally published in French in 1968, this invaluable collection of Godard's critical writings from his initial pieces in LA GAZETTE AU CINEMA, to his articles in CAHIERS DU CINEMA is indicative of both Godard's crusading criticism and cinematic style--e.g., free-flowing associations of wisecracks, personal allusions, and idiosyncratic philosophical speculations. Consider these excerpted comments on Alfred Hitchcock and Ingmar Bergman. On the former, he says, "Let us love Hitchcock when, weary of passing simply for a master of taut style, he takes us the longest way round." On the latter, he comments that "An Ingmar Bergman film is, if you like, one twenty-fourth of a second metamorphosed and expanded over an hour and a half.

It is the world between two blinks of the eyelids, the sadness between two heart-beats, the gaiety between two handclaps." For added spice, there is Godard's opinion of British films, "One really has to rack one's brains to find anything to say about a British film. One wonders why. But that's the way it is. And there isn't even an exception to prove the rule." Thanks to Milne's insightful notes, this publication functions as a commentary on how Godard applied the ideas he wrote about in the 1950s to the films he made in the 1960s. In addition, Milne periodically places a still from a Godard film alongside one from a film the director is copying--e.g., THE LITTLE SOLDIER/LE PETIT SOLDAT (1963) and A TIME TO LOVE AND A TIME TO DIE (1958). As T. A. Gallagher observes, a major value of this welcome publication is that it makes important links between the filmmaker and the critic: "For if in his films Godard has tried to reproduce life as he was experiencing and discovering it, he tried no less in his criticism to communicate his experience and discovery of films."[1098] An index is included. Recommended for special collections.

*Roud, Richard. JEAN-LUC GODARD. New York: Doubleday and Company, 1968. Illustrated. 173pp.
     Proclaiming Godard as the greatest living director (except, perhaps, for Alain Resnais), Roud explains that this book is not an attempt to explain the filmmaker's aims and methods. Such a book, he believes, would only solidify the objections that certain people have to Godard's films with their "contradictory elements, their paradoxes and abrupt alternations." Instead, Roud considers the central role that "dialectics," existentialism, and Hegelian philosphy play in Godard's films. For example, he sees Hegel's theory that "contradictions are the source of all movement and indeed of all life" as forming the basis for Godard's view that "Truth is in all things, even, partly, in error." Moreover, Roud feels that "the whole art of the cinema rests on three polarities, three contradictions, three paradoxes: visual versus narrative, fiction versus documentary, and, perhaps most important, reality versus abstraction." Linking Godard's work to these three paradoxes, the author points to three specific polarities characteristic of the artist's films: "his alternation between a romantic view of life and a naturalistic one, between psychological motivation and pure chance, between the use of stars and non-stars." In the five brief chapters that follow, Roud discusses Godard's moral and political preoccupation in the context of his entire work up to LA CHINOISE, OU PLUTOT A LA CHINOISE (1967). Particular attention is paid to the importance of prostitution in Godard's films. Treating it as both a personal and social subject, he contends that the need to earn money to eat forces us to do things we dislike doing. In Godard's words, "More and more people I see, and I meet many different kinds in the film milieu, . . . don't really enjoy what they are doing. Like prostitutes, they just do it."
     Although Roud's narrative does not go into enough detail to develop his intriguing ideas, it does provide one of the few sources on Godard's short films. A filmography is included, but no bibliography or index is provided. Well worth browsing.

*"LE PETIT SOLDAT": A FILM BY JEAN-LUC GODARD. Trans. Nicholas Garnham. New York: Simon and Schuster, 1971. Illustrated. 96pp.
     In explaining how the film was conceived, Godard writes that he "wanted to achieve the realism, the concreteness that I had missed in A BOUT DE SOUFFLE. The film is based on an idea I had had for a long time: I wanted to say something about brainwashing." Tying that concept to events in the Algerian war, Godard created a story about a French deserter in Switzerland, working as a reporter and

---

[1098] T. A. Gallagher, "'What Lies Between the Objects,'" VILLAGE VOICE (August 24, 1972):51.

secretly operating as an anti-Algerian terrorist, who is forced to kill a man he doesn't know. To explore Godard's intentions in the film, the publisher provides a 1960 interview between the filmmaker and Yvonne Baby, as well as introductory comments by Nicholas Garnham. In addition to the "screenplay," the book includes a Godard filmography. Well worth browsing.

*"WEEKEND" AND "WIND FROM THE EAST": TWO FILMS BY JEAN-LUC GODARD. Trans. Nicholas Fry et al. New York: Simon and Schuster, 1972. Illustrated. 188pp.
     "Since no full script exists for either WEEKEND or WIND FROM THE EAST," the editor tells us, "the versions given in this volume are based in each case on a dialogue transcript combined with descriptive material obtained from a shot-by-shot viewing of the film." Nicholas Fry reconstructed the text of the two films, while Marianne Sinclair translated the dialogue for WEEKEND/LE WEEK-END (1967); and Danielle Adkinson, for WIND FROM THE EAST/VENT D'EST/VENTO DELL'EST (1970). In the introductory article for WEEKEND, Robin Wood discusses Godard's efforts to "face contemporary reality." Pointing out the aesthetic dangers in such a position, Wood describes two factors that are basic to Godard's art: "his habitual policy and practice of distanciation, and his determination to show only what is real." Wood's sensitive and perceptive analysis of the role that humor and violence play in achieving Godard's controversial ends leads the critic to the conclusion that WEEKEND is "the most frightening, exciting and challenging film I have ever seen: the challenge lying in its horrifying optimism." James Roy MacBean's introductory essay to WIND FROM THE EAST explores Godard's contention that bourgeois ideology has disfigured the evolution and development of film right from the beginning. "What Godard attacks in VENT D'EST," the author asserts, "is what he calls 'the bourgeois concept of representation', which encompasses not only a certain acting style but also the traditional relations between image and sound--and ultimately, of course, the relations between the film and the audience." The body of this intelligent essay contrasts the way that the Brazilian filmmaker Glauber Rocha and Godard react to the crises they see in film and society. The publication is worth reading just for these two essays, let alone the transcripts of the films. Recommended for special collections.

CLAUDE LELOUCH

Lev, Peter. CLAUDE LELOUCH, FILM DIRECTOR. Rutherford: Fairleigh Dickinson University Press, 1983. Illustrated. 184pp.
     Ever since the success of A MAN AND A WOMAN/UN HOMME ET UNE FEMME in 1966, Lelouch has become, simultaneously, a popular filmmaker with audiences, and something of an anathema to serious critics. His traditional approach to film narratives, middle-class themes, and the star system in conventional love stories, thrillers, and comedies often overshadows his subtle innovative filmmaking style. Lev's evenhanded study explores Lelouch's personal approach to filmmaking, using ten concise but informative chapters to analyze the director's work over the past forty years. In addition to useful endnotes and an interview with Lelouch, the book includes a filmography, a bibliography, and an index. Well worth browsing.

ALAIN RESNAIS

*Armes, Roy. THE CINEMA OF ALAIN RESNAIS. New York: A. S. Barnes and Company, 1968. Illustrated. 175pp.
     Born in Vannes, Brittany, on June 3, 1922, Resnais's poor health as a child and his isolated environment instilled in him an interesting range of interests: e.g., serious literature, music, comic books, still photography, and 8mm filmmaking. Collectively, these interests play a major role in the director's work after 1947. Frequent visits to Paris and the theater eventually inspired the shy teenager to pursue a career as a stage actor. By his eighteenth birthday, Resnais had moved

to Paris to study acting. His alternating obsessions with drama and filmmaking over the next five years overshadowed his reactions to the Nazi occupation of France and to the resistance movement. Even when he was drafted into the French Army in 1945, Resnais found work in a military theatrical company entertaining the troops. Following his discharge in 1946, Resnais combined his two loves by becoming a film actor. Although the post-WWII period was not a good time for inexperienced filmmakers to find work, it was a superb period for learning about film and for building close ties with other filmmakers. Resnais is a good example why. He began collaborating on noteworthy documentary shorts in 1947, and over the next decade he gained a well-deserved reputation as France's best filmmaker of short subjects. From the outset, he chose to use the scripts of other people rather than to write his own scenarios. Collaboration rather than AUTEURISM became his approach, even though his unique films clearly reveal his controlling personal vision.

Armes's pioneering overview of Resnais's formative film years as an innovative filmmaker of documentary shorts and revolutionary feature films offers a good introduction to Resnais's relationship to his peers, and to his preoccupations in movies. Armes's opening chapter, "The Director's Role," explains why Resnais considers himself a director (METTEUR EN SCENE) rather than an author (AUTEUR). Throughout the book's eight informative chapters, the major emphasis is on Resnais's postwar documentary shorts from VAN GOGH (1948) to LE CHANT DU STYRENE (1958). A filmography and bibliography are provided but no index is included. Well worth browsing.

Etzkowitz, Janice. TOWARD A CONCEPT OF CINEMATIC LITERATURE: AN ANALYSIS of "HIROSHIMA MON AMOUR." New York: Garland Publishing, 1983. 292pp.

Originally written as a 1978 Ph.D. dissertation for Columbia University, this uneven study is slow going, mainly because of the heavy-handed prose and the oversimplified introductory chapters. For example, Etzkowitz begins by making a labored argument that films are "a metamorphosis of literature." In this regard, Etzkowitz takes up the cause of the New Left in identifying cinematic language as the equal of literary language and then applying it to films. She defines the new literary form as that "which communicates through a visual language on celluloid with or without the accompaniment of sound. In its most primitive form it is pure visual expression. In its most complete form it incorporates a multiplicity of languages--visual expression, verbal expression and musical expression--which form the total polymorphic language of the cinema." Despite such a pedantic albatross around her neck, Etzkowitz does a good job of showing the importance of "memory" theories in HIROSHIMA MON AMOUR (1959). In addition to explaining the relationship between "the 'problematic' of the memory process whereby a suppressed memory is brought forth from a state of preconsciousness to a state of consciousness" to its application in the Duras screenplay, she is helpful in describing how the memory process operates dialectically. Curiously, the author makes no references to Bergsonian philosophy in discussing either Proust or Resnais. A bibliography is included, but no index is provided. Worth browsing.

*"LA GUERRE EST FINIE": TEXT BY JORGE SEMPRUN FOR THE FILM BY ALAIN RESNAIS. Trans. Richard Seaver. New York: Grove Press, 1967. Illustrated. 192pp.

Jorge Semprum's imaginative thriller on the long-term effects of the Spanish Civil War on a band of anti-Franco exiles living in France and still actively conspiring against the Spanish dictator has been praised widely as a beautiful love story and as an exciting melodrama. It also shows that critical reactions to Resnais's career based only on his early feature films miss the humanity and wit of the director's style. Regrettably, the publisher did not see fit to include some critical commentary to explain either how the film was crafted, or the types of issues the filmmaker explored in the process. Nevertheless, the script itself and the more than 110 frame enlargements from the film are valuable contributions to appreciating the work. Well worth browsing.

*"HIROSHIMA MON AMOUR": TEXT BY MARGUERITE DURAS FOR THE FILM BY ALAIN RESNAIS. Trans. Richard Seaver. New York: Grove Press, 1961. Illustrated. 112pp.

Awarded the International Critics Prize at the 1959 Cannes Film Festival, this remarkable and heavily stylized film is an early example of how the New Left applied the concepts of LE NOUVEAU ROMAN to film narrative, the difficulty audiences have in absorbing associative editing techniques and appreciating the filmmakers' emphasis on how a film occurs rather than what occurs, and why screenwriters like Duras are receptive to the idea of a CINE-ROMAN. Thus, books like this one that enable interested viewers not only to "read" the film, but also to deal directly with the screenwriter's intentions, become important adjuncts to the film itself. In addition to providing the script of the film, Duras gives us her original synopsis and notes. We get an opportunity to study why the New Left filmmakers insist on the close cooperation between director and screenwriter. Although Duras in her introduction makes no allusions to Resnais's "pictorial" contributions to the script, she does state categorically that her conversations with Resnais and Gerard Jarlot, the film's literary advisor, "were always lucid, demanding, and productive." Of particular importance is her explanation that the passages on Nevers were not in the original screenplay and were added before the December, 1958, shooting occurred. Recommended for special collections.

Kreidl, John Francis. ALAIN RESNAIS. Boston: Twayne Publishers, 1977. Illustrated. 252pp.

Kreidl begins with the popular perspective that Resnais's interest in the aesthetic and intellectual capabilties of film has made him popular in critical circles, but isolated him from mass audiences. Although most of his films from VAN GOGH (1948) to MELO (1988) have won many international awards, Kreidl argues that there is a general misperception that Resnais's cinematic contributions have more to do with technique, than with film narrative. To put matters in better perspective, the author, focusing on Resnais's films from HIROSHIMA MON AMOUR (1959) to PROVIDENCE (1977), sets out to "show why, among all well-respected, world-famous filmmakers, Alain Resnais is the most unique . . . a singular talent, as this book will demonstrate, using his seven feature films as illustrations of his intent, as well as 'reading' them as film texts." Kreidel focuses on two specific ways in which the filmmaker modernized film narrative: (1) in the pre-production process "by using the most modern scripts with multiple metonymic and shifting narrators"; and (2) in the shooting and editing of the narrative, using an achronological approach that relies on "a point-space 'concurrence' left open for the spectator to put in a time-respecting text he makes up." The key to appreciating the filmmaker's art, according to Kreidl, is Resnais's approach to plot. By identifying his three basic themes--"(1) the impossibility of documenting, (2) the presence of the absent, (3) the return of the repressed"--and applying them to the filmmaker's major works over two decades, the author provides valuable insights into why Resnais has made few films in his career, and why screenwriters like Cayrol, Duras, Robbe-Grillet, Sarrayte, and Semprun are vital to his cinematic accomplishments. Endnotes, a bibliography, a filmography, and an index are included. Recommended for special collections.

*"LAST YEAR AT MARIENBAD": TEXT BY ALAIN ROBBE-GRILLET FOR THE FILM BY ALAIN RESNAIS. Trans. Richard Howard. New York: Grove Press, 1962. Illustrated. 168pp.

In the introduction (a reprint from a 1961 SIGHT AND SOUND essay) to this CINE-ROMAN, Robbe-Grillet credits the producers Pierre Courau and Raymont Froment with introducing him to Resnais. The reason he agreed to a meeting, the screenwriter explains, is that he knew the filmmaker's work and recognized in it "my own efforts toward a somewhat ritual deliberation, a certain slowness, a sense of the theatrical, even that occasional rigidity of attitude, that hieratic quality in gesture, word and setting, which suggests both a statue and an opera." Robbe-Grillet also admired Resnais's attempts "to construct a purely mental space and time--those of dreams, perhaps, or of memory, those of any affective life--without worrying too much about the traditional effects, or about an absolute sequence in the narrative." The screenwriter then describes how the two men collaborated on the conception, writing, and shooting of the revolutionary screenplay. In addition to the scenario, the book contains over 140 illustrations. Recommended for special collections.

*Monaco, James. ALAIN RESNAIS. New York: Oxford University Press, 1979. Illustrated. 234pp.

The best English-language study on the noted director, this highly original and absorbing work benefits considerably from Resnais's collaboration with the author. Monaco begins by attacking a number of "critical axioms" that generally prejudice people against Resnais. For example, he claims that the reason why critics like Pauline Kael admire the director's technique or theory, but yet attack him for having "little grasp of character or subject" is due to a misperception about how Resnais consciously tells us a story while also commenting on the story. In addition, Monaco draws an important distinction between the New Wave and contemporary filmmakers, pointing out that the former focus on a humanistic relationship between form and subject matter, while the latter "are content to mimic the past while struggling with it." Still further, Monaco draws a crucial distinction between Resnais and other members of the LA NOUVELLE VAGUE. Pointing out that Resnais was a decade older than many of the CAHIERS DU CINEMA group and had begun making films while they were still children, Monaco explains that Resnais's orientation, unlike that of the CAHIERS DU CINEMA group, is "practical rather than theoretical." That is not to say that Resnais ignores his cinematic heritage. He does not, although he is more subtle about it than are other members of the New Wave. It is to say that he stresses collaboration over AUTEURISM. The most significant attack on the "critical axioms," however, is Monaco's rejection of the notion that Resnais's preoccupation with the themes of "Time" and Memory" renders his films too complex for the public. Not only has Resnais's editing made film more logical and lucid than in the past, Monaco insists, but Resnais's "discontinuous editing" also has more to do with the idea of "imagination" than with "memory." In trying to decipher the world around us and which approach would be most beneficial, Resnais, according to Monaco, produces movies that "far from being the complicated and tortuous intellectual puzzles they are reputed to be, [they] are rather simple, elegant, easily understood--and felt--investigations of the pervasive process of imagination." The nine stimulating and informative chapters that follow review Resnais's career up to PROVIDENCE (1977), making a good argument that the best way to appreciate Resnais's films is to see them as commentaries on the ways stories are told, rather than as stories PER SE. Endnotes, a filmography, and an index are included. Recommended for general collections.

Sweet, Freddy. THE FILM NARRATIVES OF ALAIN RESNAIS. Ann Arbor: UMI Research Press, 1981. 130pp.

"This study," Sweet writes, "will be directed primarily at film structure. Through an analysis of Resnais's feature length films, I will explore the nature, meaning, and techniques of narrative structure. In an exploration of the nature of plot and story, I will discuss not only Resnais's films but also those directed by the authors with whom Resnais worked. At times close attention to the writing of Resnais's scenarists will be helpful in the study of themes and structures. Moreover, it will be necessary to make frequent comparisons with the works of other filmmakers and with novelists like James Joyce and Marcel Proust whose works have had considerable impact on twentieth-century cinema." Sweet also draws attention to the filmmaker's operatic interests and the manner in which Resnais organizes his work into various motifs. Five separate chapters examine Resnais's feature films up to 1968: HIROSHIMA MON AMOUR (1959), L'ANNEE DERNIERE A MARIENBAD/LAST YEAR AT MARIENBAD (1961), MURIEL, OR THE TIME OF A RETURN/MURIEL, OU LE TEMPS D'UN RETOUR (1963), THE WAR IS OVER/LA GUERRE EST FINIE (1966), and JE T'AIME, JE T'AIME (1968). Although originally written as the author's 1973 Ph.D dissertation at the University of Michigan, Sweet's revisions downplay the usual academic prose and offer instead an informative study without being dry or boring. Particularly useful are the sections relating Resnais's fascination with notions about time and space to his repeated interest in themes about "memory, middle-class banality, the relationship of man to his surroundings, the quest for self-knowledge and freedom." Endnotes, a bibliography, and an index are included. Recommended for special collections.

*Ward, John. ALAIN RESNAIS, OR THE THEME OF TIME. New York: Doubleday and Company, 1968. Illustrated. 168pp.
    One of the best of the Cinema One Series, this intelligent study focuses on four major Resnais works: HIROSHIMA MON AMOUR (1959), LAST YEAR AT MARIENBAD/L'ANNEE DERNIERE A MARIENBAD (1961), MURIEL, OR THE TIME OF A RETURN/MURIEL, OU LE TEMPS D'UN RETOUR (1963), and THE WAR IS OVER/LA GUERRE EST FINIE (1966). Ward's basic premise is that Bergson's philosophy operates as the unifying principle in Resnais's idiosyncratic films. The opening chapter, therefore, offers a useful discussion of Bergson's ideas on "mental consciousness." Stressing the philospher's "anti-rational and literary" biases, Ward points out that Bergson's studies led the philosopher to the conclusion that "intellect, which inevitably functioned in a spatial mode, was capable of merely dealing with bits and pieces, and that if it came across a process continuous in time it would proceed to spatialize and so fragment that process." Concluding that intellect inhibited freedom, Bergson championed the concept of intuition, a liberating process that put the physical world (matter) in human rather metaphysical terms. For him, intuition becomes the guide in dealing with the past, present, and future. The concepts are anchored in time, two types in particular: a spatial model (e.g., a clock) and a multi-directional model (intuition). The latter, Ward explains, is not only crucial to understanding LE NOUVEAU ROMAN, but also to appreciating Resnais's films. Drawing further on Bergson's ideas, the author reviews the philospher's discussion of "DURATION, . . . that state in which our present and our past are one. . . ." Of particular relevance to Resnais's films are the notions of "involuntary memory" and "voluntary memory." Both are mental processes that join the past to the present. The former is a habit; the latter, imaginative and creative. When the two function in tandem, "our lives have duration." After explaining why Bergson views Time as destructive, Ward then comments on how Proust applied the philosopher's theories to the novelist's position that "only in art do we discover true reality." For Ward, the two positions--Time as Destroyer (Bergson) and Time as Preserver (Proust)--are central to an analysis of Resnais's major works. The six thoughtful chapters that follow not only offer useful interpretations, but also examine the importance of Resnais's collaborators and his short documentary films. A filmography is provided, but no bibliography or index is included. Well worth browsing.

ALAIN ROBBE-GRILLET

Stoltzfus, Ben. ALAIN ROBBE-GRILLET: THE BODY OF THE TEXT.   Rutherford: Fairleigh Dickinson University Press, 1985. 187pp.
    This is one of those books that at first seems pedantic and pretentious and then suddenly becomes thoughtful and absorbing. Consider your reactions to the author's opening statement: "Throughout this study the designation New Novel ("NOUVEAU ROMAN") refers to Robbe-Grillet's work published between 1953 and 1959, from LES GOMMES to DANS LE LABYRINTHE. The designation New (New) Novel ("NOUVEAU [NOUVEAU] ROMAN") refers to Robbe-Grillet's work published between 1965 and the

present, that is, since LA MAISON DE RENDEZ-VOUS." The next paragraph tells us that the NOUVEAU NOUVEAU ROMAN, characterized by "reflexivity, discontinuity, and archeology," also "emphasizes generative themes, generative numbers, paronomasia, and polysemy." As the author explains, "The designation New (New] Novel ('NOUVEAU [NOUVEAU] ROMAN') thus refers to both periods, and implies that the aesthetic of the first applies to the second, or visa versa." I suspect that by now most readers would conclude that this book is only for a very select audience. They would be wrong. The more one pursues Stoltzfus's concise study of Robbe-Grillet's eleven novels, six films, and a host of other publications and criticism, the more one becomes impressed by the author's gift for making the complex not only accessible to the uninitiated, but also highly enjoyable.   Few English-language studies to date have described as succinctly and effectively the literary and cinematic revolt against traditional narratives. In explaining, for example, that intellectuals generally agree that we are experiencing a crisis in values, Stoltzuf points out that ".   .   . it is normal that the new fiction, whose innovations are in no sense symptomatic of moral and spiritual decadence, should, in addition to speaking of itself, also reflect changing attitudes toward reality and human nature." Thus, the depersonalized, multiple, and anonymous characters in NOUVEAU ROMAN correspond, in part, to the "death of man" syndrome; the NOUVEAU NOUVEAU ROMAN is symptomatic "of the devaluation of the past."

Stoltzufus's seven challenging chapters explore pervasive ideas in Robbe-Grillet's works: generative themes and serial permutations, the revolutionary nature of Robbe-Grillet's aesthetics, the sexuality of the text, the role of specular structures in art and literature to downgrade the importance of reality, the manner in which a dialectical topology establishes binary relationships between external and internal emotions and people, the types of linguistic and emotional labyrinths that we need to escape from, and how play and games help liberate us from our fears and sadistic anxieties. Anchoring his analyses in a Marxian context, the author discusses the links that tie films and novels to music, literature, and structuralist theories. He points out the crucial role that language, myth, and ideology have in Robbe-Grillet's works, how he uses hyperbolic images of sex and violence "in order to expose, undermine, devalue, and neutralize them," and how he "encourages us to think not only about the nature of language but also about the culture behind it--the way of life and forms of life encoded into ideology."

Given a chance, this book should prove stimulating reading to people unfamiliar with the world of Robbe-Grillet. At the very least, one gets a fine sense of what separates the New Left from the CAHIERS group.   Endnotes, a bibliography, and an index are included. Recommended for special collections.

*Van Wert, William F. THE FILM CAREER OF ALAIN ROBBE-GRILLET. Pleasantville: Redgrave Publishing Company, 1977. 208pp.

An outstanding overview of an uncompromising artist, this invaluable resource guide is the first English-language book-length study of Robbe-Grillet's ideas, achievements, and failures. Van Wert focuses almost exclusively on the filmmaker's work in cinema, giving only passing attention to his novels. There are three sensible exceptions: a discussion of Robbe-Grillet's collaboration with Resnais on LAST YEAR AT MARIENBAD/L'ANNEE DERNIERE A MAREINBAD (1961), a review of Robbe-Grillet's ideas on CINE-ROMAN, and a commentary on the relationship between Robbe-Grillet's film techniques and his novels.

Section One, a biographical profile, highlights the significance of the artist's first career as an agricultural engineer, stressing how he later applied his scientific training to the "'objective' descriptions of objects and locales, which would become a trademark of his fiction. . . ." Van Wert then covers Robbe-Grillet's shift to literature in 1953, pointing out that the publication of the novelist's first book by the Editions de Minuit not only led to his career in film but also to the emergence of the CINE-ROMAN. By the time we get to Robbe-Grillet's directorial film debut with THE IMMORTAL ONE/L'IMMORTELLE (1963), Van Wert provides a solid foundation for appreciating Robbe-Grillet's goals and values. The reminder of the insightful chapter includes details on Robbe-Grillet's rejection of nineteenth century literary techniques, why a shift from black-and-white films to color productions with EDEN AND AFTER/L'EDEN ET APRES (1971) altered his ideas on filmmaking, and the various projects that occupied Robbe-Grillet up to the mid-1970s.

Section Two, a critical discussion of the filmmaker's work, summarizes Van Wert's impressive research not only on Robbe-Grillet's career, but also on the CINE-ROMAN. Particular attention is paid to way in which Robbe-Grillet breaks with traditional cinematic language to apply "'the absent-I' point of view" in his novels to his films. Van Wert makes clear that it is not a matter of simple adaptation (Robbe-Grillet never adapts his works) but rather an application of the technique to film narrative. Considerable attention is also paid to defending Robbe-Grillet against the frequent charge that his work is "uneven." Van Wert explains that the filmmaker uses his "stories" and themes as "a pretext for the style, the narrative voice, the elaborately 'objective' descriptions of the obsessively 'subjective' I-void narrators." His emphasis away from an objective camera to a subjective one is premeditated, and thus he consciously creates a disruption between content and form that some critics unfairly label "uneven." To Van Wert's credit, he never downplays the fact that Robbe-Grillet's films are box-office disasters. Just the reverse is true. "Willing to merge the most blatant elements of popular culture with the most formal elements of modern music," Wert tells us, "he persists."

Throughout the remaining sections of the book--e.g., a filmography a listing of writings about Robbe-Grillet; his other performances and related film activities; archival sources; and film distributors--Van Wert continually demonstrates his resourceful and comprehensive research skills. The writing is crisp, clear, and stimulating. A film index is included. Highly recommended for special collections.

ERIC ROHMER

*Crisp, C. G. ERIC ROHMER: REALIST AND MORALIST. Bloomington: Indiana University Press, 1988. 139pp.

An impressive and thought-provoking analysis of Rohmer's work, this AUTEURIST study is the only book-length examination of the French filmmaker's influence on cinematic history. Don't be fooled by the brevity of the publication. It is a comprehensive introduction to Rohmer's critical output between 1948 and 1960 (nearly 250 articles and reviews) and to his more than twenty films from 1950 to 1984. The opening chapter, "Style and Ideology," does a masterly job of explaining not only why Rohmer is unique among the CAHIERS DE CINEMA group, but also why he is often ignored by both the public and by certain critical circles. Crisp begins by pointing out the similarities between Rohmer and Bazin, showing how both men rejected montage theory and practice as the standard for filmmaking, as well as the influence of Catholicism on their thinking. At the same time, the author explains why Rohmer took a more extreme position than Bazin, arguing that while Bazin perceived of "reality" as mainly "representational," Rohmer views it as "a 're-presentation,' which retains all essential aspects of the reality it portrays." Establishing the centrality of Rohmer's credo that "a humble documentary presentation of reality inevitably reveals an inherent order, which speaks of God," Crisp next analyzes why the filmmaker's "interior cinema" creates problems both for Rohmer and his critics. Four specific inconsistencies are identified and then reconciled. For example, the problem of Rohmer's advocating "transparent realism" and still admiring specific AUTEURS like Hitchcock and Minnelli is justified on the grounds that their work was "right-minded." That is, they focused on presenting the world as it is, rather than the way they made it to be. To the charge that Rohmer's admiration for Hollywood genre conventions conflicts with his demand for a realistc cinema, Crisp explains Rohmer's praise as approval for those genres (e.g., westerns) that depict the conflict between good and evil and their support of authority. To the charge that the realistic-oriented Rohmer expresses ambivalence toward literary films, Crisp argues that the filmmaker only objects to those films that make images subordinate to words.

Finally, to the charge that Rohmer's transparent reality is in conflict with his belief in a "moral cinema which shows things not as they are but as they ought to be," Crisp responds that Rohmer's work reveals his obsesesion with resolving the tension between morality and realism. According to the author, "an analysis of Rohmer's critical and theoretical writings is useful not only because it brings to light the correlation between the ideology underlining them and the theme, form, and style of the films he was later to make, but also because it lends weight to the more general conclusion that such theories (and perhaps all aesthetic theories) bear little relationship to the artform around which they are formulated, but on the contrary are much more closely related to the attitudes and values of those who formulate them and whose ideology they externalize around an arbitrarily elected object."

Following up on this superb introduction to Rohmer's values, Crisp offers eleven chapters, charting the filmmaker's evolution from critic to artist. Interestingly, only Chapter Two, "Apprenticeship," is for the general student. Here, as in the previous chapter, the author explains in crisp, intelligent, and perceptive prose the steps that led Rohmer to CAHIERS DU CINEMA and LA NOUVELLE VAGUE. The references are straightforward, generally accurate, and persuasive. In the chapters that follow, however, Crisp makes few concessions to readers unfamiliar with Rohmer's work. The analyses are all predicated on one's having seen the films, no attention is given to plot summaries, and the arguments have to be taken at face value unless one has studied the work. Crisp also disdains using English-language articles and interviews by and about Rohmer, although the author does provide an extensive list of film reviews in English.

In providing a challenging overview of structuralist, psychoanalytical, and ideological perspectives on Rohmer's work, Crisp deserves considerable thanks. It is from this point that future studies dealing with Rohmer's role in postwar-French cinema should begin. Endnotes, a filmography, a bibliography, and an index are included. Recommended for special collections.

"THE MARQUISE OF O": FILM BY ERIC ROHMER, STORY BY HEINRICH VON KLEIST. Trans. Stanley Hochman and Martin Greenberg. New York: The Ungar Publishing Company, 1985. Illustrated. 137pp.

In adapting von Kleist's novel to the screen, Rohmer remains faithful to the author's book. "By means of this work on a classic text," the filmmaker explains in remarks prepared for the release of the film and reprinted in this publication, "we would like to paint the world of another time with the same attention to detail that we had given in our MORAL TALES to the present-day world." The story itself is unusual. A highly virtuous and young widow (Edith Clever) strangely and disturbingly finds herself pregnant. Trying to justify her status to her disturbed parents, she takes an ad in the newspaper and pleads for the unknown father to come forward and exonerate her. To her shock, she learns that her seducer is the count (Bruno Ganz) who had rescued her from being raped by his men. After the marquise had passed out from the ordeal, the Count, in a rare moment of unprincipled behavior, had taken advantage of her. She accepts his proposal of marriage, but refuses to consummate the marriage. The birth of their son and the count's willingness to give his wife and child all his earthly possessions results in a reconciliation and a second, true "marriage." In the book's afterword, Alan Spiegel explains why he considers the film to be the "director's greatest achievement, one of the loveliest, tenderest, most gracious and sagacious works of its decade, a humorous and decorous enchantment from end to end, an uninsistent treasure." The scenario, the bulk of the publication, is based upon Rohmer's German dialogue transcription for synchronization. Combined with scenic and camera-placement directions published in the October 1976 edition of L'AVANT-SCENE DU CINEMA, this is the only available English-language source for studying the written film. Recommended for special collections.

JEAN ROUCH

*Eaton, Mike, ed. ANTHROPOLOGY-REALITY-CINEMA: THE FILMS OF JEAN ROUCH. New York: Zoetrope, 1979.

FRANCOIS TRUFFAUT

*Afron, Mirella Jona, and E. Rubenstein, eds. THE LAST METRO: FRANCOIS TRUFFAUT, DIRECTOR. New Brunswick: Rutgers University Press, 1985. Illustrated. 200pp.

According to Afron, "Francois Truffaut's realization of THE LAST METRO fulfilled a desire nurtured since his elaboration of the script of THE 400 BLOWS in 1958: to make a film that evokes the atmosphere of the Occupation." Because of budgetary matters and a preoccupation with the spirit of the New Wave, Truffaut waited a decade before he approached the subject again, only to put it aside a second time when he heard of Marcel Ophuls's THE SORROW AND THE PITY/LE CHAGRIN ET LA PITIE, released in 1972. The screenplay by Suzanne Schiffmann, Jean-Claude Grumberg, and Truffaut that eventually emerged deals with the problems of a Jewish director of a minor Parisian theater (Heinz Bennett) who goes into hiding during the Nazi occupation, while his wife (Catherine Deneuve) manages the company's affairs. The story of collaborators, the marital problems of the couple, and the ambitions of a young actor (Gerard Depardieu) result in a remarkably warm and sensitive account not only of Parisian life during World War II, but also of French anti-Semitism and personal choices. This splendid publication offers a fine introduction to filmmaking during those years, a complete transcript of the film (including cast and credits), a biographical sketch of Truffaut, an interview with Truffaut by Annette Insdorf, a sampling of contemporary reviews, a filmography, and a bibliography. The comments are interesting, informative, and insightful. Unfortunately, no index is included. Recommended for special collections.

Allen, Don. FRANCOIS TRUFFAUT. New York: The Viking Press, 1974. Illustrated. 176pp. Updated ed. New York: Beaufort Books, 1986. Illustrated. 240pp.

A good job of blending affection and critical judgment, this chronological examination of Truffaut's films from THE MISCHIEF MAKERS/LES MISTONS (1957) to DAY FOR NIGHT/LA NUIT AMERICAINE (1973) works on the assumption that the reader may not be that familiar with the films being analyzed. Consequently, Allen includes plot summaries with his critical commentaries. Each film, with the exception of four Antoine Doniel movies, is discussed in separate chapters. Along with identifying recurring themes and pointing out Truffaut's autobiographical allusions, the film-by-film analyses emphasize the filmmaker's pessimistic view of life, his preoccupation with the search for love, and his "open-ended" approach to storytelling. Although Allen's conclusions that Truffaut was limited in technique and "content mainly to use existing procedures for his own purposes" seem rather narrow, the author deserves credit for writing one of the pioneering studies in the English language on the filmmaker, particularly at a time when Truffaut was ignored by intellectuals and by academic circles.

Allen sets the tone for his sixteen chapters in the opening section, "Grave-digger to Film-maker." Blaming Truffaut the critic for some of the misperceptions about Truffaut the filmmaker, the author discusses why the young, rebellious author was known as "the grave-digger of French cinema." In addition to quoting a number of Truffaut's invectives from essays in CAHIERS DU CINEMA and ARTS, he outlines the angry critic's primary objectives: to demolish the films "of partial creators and production line commercialists with equally militant defense of independent film-makers." One gets a sense of the datedness of the book in reading about Truffaut as a "static" and "remarkably consistent" filmmaker and critic. On the other hand, the opportunity to compare Allen's 1974 judgments with those of his 1985 updated version provides a useful illustration of how the filmmaker's reputation has evolved over a period of eleven years. Curiously, Allen does not document his sources, provide a bibliography, or include an index in either work. Well worth browsing.

*Allen, Don. FINALLY TRUFFAUT. New York: Beaufort Books, 1986. Illustrated. 240pp.
     Proclaiming his affection for Truffaut and the fact that the filmmaker was the one who suggested updating Allen's 1974 edition, the author seems content only to add comments on Truffaut's films after 1973, but not to revise the book's original judgments. Thus, the eight additional chapters provide information on works from THE STORY OF ADELE H./L'HISTORIE D'ADELE H. (1975) to CONFIDENTIALLY YOURS!/VIVEMENT DIMANCHE! (1983). There is also more material on SUCH A GORGEOUS KID/UNE BELLE FILLE COMME MOI (1972) and DAY FOR NIGHT/LA NUIT AMERICAINE (1973), films only briefly commented on in the first edition. Well worth browsing.

*Braudy, Leo, ed. FOCUS ON "SHOOT THE PIANO PLAYER." Englewood Cliffs: Prentice-Hall, 1972. Illustrated. 182pp.
     In the introduction to this valuable anthology, Braudy gives an overview of the New Wave, and points out some of its negative effects. The editor argues that "SHOOT THE PIANO PLAYER was a far greater blow to the received assumptions about film method and subject matter than was THE 400 BLOWS, Truffaut's first film. Although the improvisations, the jump cutting, and the low budget of THE 400 BLOWS illustrated many of the new wave innovations in production method, the film still had a story and a situation that was easy to accept. . . ." To flesh out his opening remarks, Braudy judiciously provides six different interviews with Truffaut, five reviews of the film, six critical essays, a handful of commentaries, script extracts excised from the released film, a filmography, and a bibliography. An index concludes this reliable and readable anthology. Recommended for special collections.

*Crisp, C. G. FRANCOIS TRUFFAUT. New York: Praeger Publishers, 1972. Illustrated. 144pp.
     "The aim of this book," Crisp writes, "is to specify the nature of the decisions taken by Truffaut in the course of his career, together with the motives that guided them." Crisp bases his conclusions on the inordinate number of interviews (mostly in French publications) that Truffaut gave and the honest and candid way in which he decribed his techniques and goals. "Wherever he has stated the relevant facts simply and concisely," Crisp explains, "I have not thought it necessary to pretend that the words are other than his; where he has repeatedly discussed them, in different terms and with different emphases, I have summarized the trend of his arguments as concisely as possible. On the few occasions when he has not, to my knowledge, specified motives or indicated themes, I have tried to fill the gap myself." Although Crisp does an exceptional job in synthesizing the wealth of material provided by Truffaut, it is very disturbing to find that the book contains no footnotes or bibliography for checking the accuracy or context of the quoted material.
     To help prepare us for Truffaut's critical preoccupations and because the artist's unusual childhood bears directly on his work, Crisp begins his useful study with a biographical essay on Truffaut's formative years. Among the key topics raised are the eccentricity of Truffaut's parents, the reasons why he became a delinquent, the importance of film in his early years, the end of his formal schooling at age fourteen, the founding of a cine-club when Truffaut was sixteen, how its badly handled finances led to his being jailed, how this eventually led to Bazin's becoming Truffaut's guardian, the friendships that Truffaut developed with other young film ethusiasts and how they each became film critics at CAHIERS DU CINEMA, Truffaut's diastrous

1951 decision to join the military and the reasons why he served six months in the stockade and received a dishonorable discharge in 1953, the revolutionary impact of Truffaut's 1954 essay "A Certain Tendency of the French Cinema" on the direction of CAHIERS DU CINEMA, the reasons why over a five-year period his hard-hitting reviews, articles, and interviews in CAHIERS DU CINEMA and other French periodicals earned him the animosity of many filmmakers and directors of film festivals, and what led him to try filmmaking in 1954. The next eleven chapters offer individual analyses of Truffaut's feature films from THE 400 BLOWS/LES QUARTRE CENT COUP (1959), to BED AND BOARD/DOMICILE CONJUGAL (1970). Crisp's concise, lucid descriptions of how Truffaut approached his work, and the relationship that the films share with his childhood and critical theories make this book a valuable contribution to our understanding of Truffaut's gifts as an artist and critic. The background material is especially useful and reliable. A filmography is included, but no bibliography or index is provided. Recommended for special collections.

Insdorf, Annette. FRANCOIS TRUFFAUT. Boston: Twayne Publishers, 1978. Illustrated. 250pp.
     Truffaut's favorite book-length study of his work, this affectionate and intelligent publication reviews the filmmaker's career from the perpective of what he called "cinema in the first person singular." The focus is on demonstrating how Truffaut's characters, stories, and events almost always grow out of his personal experiences. Insdorf sees "her role before the reader as continuous with my function before a class: to communicate and justify through close analysis my enthusiasm for the aesthetic and experimental richness of the subject. I address primarily those who are already aware of Truffaut's talent and achievement and wish to explore the thematic and stylistic concerns that have emerged from his films." In Chapter 1, "From 'Cinephile' to 'Cineaste,'" Insdorf comments on the origins of the French New Wave and Truffaut's role as a film critic during the 1950s. Particular attention is paid to the influence of Chaplin and Welles on Truffaut's second film, SHOOT THE PIANO PLAYER/TIREZ SUR LE PIANISTE (1960). Chapter 2, "The Hitchcockian Strain," offers analyses of THE SOFT SKIN/LA PEAU DOUCE (1964), FAHRENHEIT 451 (1966), THE BRIDE WORE BLACK/LA MARIEE ETAINT EN NOIR (1967), and MISSISSIPPI MERMAID/LA SIRENE DU MISSISSIPPI (1969). Although Insdorf spends considerable time describing how Truffaut shared Hitchcock's cinematic objectives for "technical means to emotional ends," she arrives at the perceptive conclusion that the two men have a fundamental difference: Truffaut has a great love for people and human experiences; Hitchcock does not. Consequently, she views the French director's debt to his British mentor to be in the area of technique rather than in content. Chapter 3, "Renoirian Vision," analyzes how Truffaut shares with Renoir a sympathy for their characters' ambitions and misfortunes, especially in STOLEN KISSES/BAISERS VOLES (1968), BED AND BOARD/DOMICILE CONJUGAL (1970), JULES AND JIM/JULES ET JIM (1961), TWO ENGLISH GIRLS/LES DEUX ANGLAISES ET LE CONTINENT (1971), and DAY FOR NIGHT/LA NUIT AMERICAINE (1973). Stressing the absence of heroes or villains in such films, Insdorf identifies a number of characteristics that link the works of the two directors: e.g., the importance of the individual, improvisational shooting, the interaction between characters and nature, a mixture of tenderness and irony, cinematic distancing devices, and the role of art in characters' lives. Especially useful is a thoughtful comparison between Renoir's THE RULES OF THE GAME/LA REGLE DU JEU (1939) and Truffaut's DAY FOR NIGHT/LA NUIT AMERICAINE. Chapter 4, "'Are Women Magic?'" examines Truffaut's "awareness that a multiplicity of selves inhabits even one woman [and] is evident in the doubling that is characteristic of his work." Through her intelligent discussions of films like THE STORY OF ADELE H./L'HISTOIRE D'ADELE H. (1975) and THE MAN WHO LOVED WOMEN/L'HOMME QUI AIMAIT LES FEMMES (1977), the author concludes that the filmmaker's women "are often portrayed as existing less in, of, and for themselves than as realizations of male visions. The men, and the audience, perceive first the image and subsequently the woman who embodies it." Chapter 5, "Les Enfants Terribles," focuses primarily on SMALL CHANGE/L'ARGENT DE POCHE (1976) and

THE WILD CHILD/L' ENFANT SAUVAGE (1969), pointing out that "With neither sentimentality nor condescension, Truffaut captures the need for freedom and tenderness, the spontaneity and the frustrations of being a child in society made by and for adults." The author places considerable importance on the way that Truffaut's child heroes (almost always estranged from their peers and hungering for attention) develop linguistically, explaining that Truffaut is fascinated with language acquisition in childhood. The concluding chapter, "Cinema in the First Person Singular," reviews the autobiographical strands in Truffaut's films, concentrating on his concern for difficult child-father relationships, an evolving interest in literary texts, and an increasing fascination with the cinematic process. Insdorf ends her perceptive study with the observation that Truffaut "has integrated the best part of his masters by becoming a skilled craftsman in the manner of Hitchcock, a humanist poet in the manner of Renoir, and a generous man of letters in the manner of Bazin." Endnotes, a bibliography, a filmography, and an index are included. Recommended for special collections.

*"JULES AND JIM": A FILM BY FRANCOIS TRUFFAUT. Trans. Nicholas Fry. New York: Simon and Schuster, 1968. Illustrated. 104pp.
    Although this publication only includes the script of the classic film and many beautiful illustrations, it is also valuable for the parenthentical shooting suggestions that were used in the finished product. Well worth browsing.

*Petrie, Graham. THE CINEMA OF FRANCOIS TRUFFAUT. New York: A. S. Barnes and Company, 1971. Illustrated. 240pp.
    An affectionate and perceptive study of Truffaut's "open style," Petrie is "interested in how and why one particularly gifted director uses the artistic means at his disposal--camera, editing, music, dialogue, sound effects, silence, colours, settings, objects, gestures, faces, actors, fictional characters and events--and how and why what he does affects us, the viewers." Petrie divides his pioneering book, the first full-length, English-language examination of Truffaut, into five chapters. In Chapter 1, "A Cinema of Discovery," the author discusses the reasons why viewers often have to readjust their preconceptions about people and events in watching a Truffaut film. A major element of the filmmaker's genius, according to Petrie, is that "he is able to re-awaken in us the capacities for joy and tenderness which contemporary life forces us ruthlessly to submerge. . . ." Truffaut does this by subverting our normal expectations about causality and by forcing us to "RECOGNIZE and accept people and things around us rather than SEEING or investigating them." Chapter 2, "Hidden Languages," analyzes Truffaut's unique exploration of non-verbal communication in film. "Truffaut's world," Petrie states, "is one in which places, objects and gestures reveal, and even control, the significance of human behavior and emotion." Chapter 3, "Voices and Reverberations," explores the crucial role that music plays in Truffaut's work from THE MICHIEF MAKERS/LES MISTONS (1957), to MISSISSIPPI MERMAID/LA SIRENE DU MISSISSIPPI (1969). Starting with the premise that he uses music in harmony with settings, characters, and emotions rather than as unobtrusive background sounds, Petrie discusses how Truffaut achieves the lyrical tone of his films. Among the interesting observations is the fact that the filmmaker employs a composer for two consecutive films and then switches to a new composer, that "the orchestration of natural sounds . . . plays a comparatively minor role" in his work, and that many "conversations in Truffaut's films are virtual monologues, the characters arguing with or explaining themselves rather than making any real attempt to complete a dialogue." Chapter 4, "Dream and Reality," explains how Truffaut's world functions as if taking place in a dream. That is, he "gives us a world very like our own world and people with our own weaknesses, desires, obsessions, failures and minor achievements, but he makes us see that world, and hence ourselves, as though for the first time, with the clarity, insight and unpredictability of a dream." In addition to making us sympathetic to anti-social

and/or immoral people, Truffaut also helps us to deal more honestly with our submerged and unconscious desires and feelings. His films, populated by lonely and alienated individuals, teach us not to judge, but rather to understand how failure can affect people's behavior and can result in a search for unusual human relationships. Consider sexual relationships. "Truffaut's men," Petrie explains, "tend to be shy and passive, allowing the women to take the initiative and dominate. The women have vitality, energy, a desire for new experiences which the men usually lack, harassed as they are by a sense of inadequacy and the routines and pressures of daily existence, and possessing often a fundamental gentleness denied the more ruthless females." The concluding chapter, "Styles: LA SIRENE DU MISSISSIPPI," describes the conscious and unconscious collective choices that Truffaut makes in his 1969 film. Emphasis is placed on the fact that he works in an industrial context affected by cultural influences. Thus, Truffaut's work from the mid-1960s on reflects the demands of both the producers and audiences: e.g., "colour, wide-screen or cinemascope, exotic and glamourous settings, star names in the leading roles, and expensive clothes, houses, furniture and cars."

Petrie's intelligent approach to the subject, plus his lucid and informative prose, results in a first-rate examination of Truffaut's major preoccupations in film. A filmography and bibilography are included, but, unfortunately, no index is provided and the book's binding is poor. Recommended for special collections.

Rabourdin, Dominique, ed. TRUFFAUT BY TRUFFAUT. Trans. Robert Erich Wolf. New York: Abrams, 1987. Illustrated. 240pp.

A sheer delight from start to finish, this anthology of Truffaut's writings and remarks is beautifully illustrated and intellectually stimulating. The first of the book's three major sections, "Autobiography," provides a splendid overview of the filmmaker's personal reaction to his childhood, and to the people who influenced his career. Rabourdin skillfully selects Truffaut's responses to interviewers over a thirty-year period and reassembles them in chronological order as if the filmmaker himself were reflecting on his evolution from chronic truant, reform school veteran, cineaste, and military deserter, to film critic and artist. For example, in talking about "the Manifesto of the 121," a political statement signed by intellectuals urging French troops to desert rather than fight in the Algerian War, Truffaut tells us that he "signed that manifesto for a single, very precise reason: it was the first time that a text, one moreover formidably written by Sartre, was encouraging soldiers to desert. That's what pleased me: the very opposite of mobilization." The quote is taken from a February 19, 1968, interview with Pierre Ajame in LA NOUVEL ADAM. Section Two, "The Films In My Life," covers Truffaut's reactions, particularly those recorded in his prefaces to the publication of his completed screenplays in L'AVANT-SCENE CINEMA, to his films from A VISIT/UNE VISIT (1955) to CONFIDENTIALLY YOURS!/VIVEMENT DIMANCHE! (1983). Section Three, "Cinema According to Truffaut: Theory and Practice," is filled with invaluable comments on the filmmaker's reaction to criticisms about his work, his feelings about other members of the New Wave, and his unrealized projects. A chronology, a filmography, a bibliography, and an index add to the book's value as a first-rate introduction to Truffaut. Highly recommended for special collections.

*Roche, Henri-Pierre. JULES AND JIM. Trans. Patrick Evans. New York: Avon Books, 1963. 240pp.

Published in 1953, this autobiographical novel was the author's first book-length work. Roche never saw Truffaut's film adaptation. Just before he died on April 7, 1959, according to the book jacket, the author saw a photograph of Moreau and approved her being cast as Catherine. Truffaut also adapted Roche's second book, DEUX ANGLAIS ET LE CONTINENT (1956). Well worth browsing.

Truffaut, Francois. THE ADVENTURES OF ANTOINE DOINEL: FOUR SCREENPLAYS--THE 400 BLOWS/LOVE AT TWENTY/STOLEN KISSES/BED AND BOARD. Trans. Helen G. Scott. New York: Simon and Schuster, 1972. Illustrated. 320pp.

This superb anthology of four of the five films in the Antoine Doinel cycle (the 1979 concluding episode, LOVE ON THE RUN/L'AMOUR EN FUITE is missing) epitomizes Truffaut's use of his personal experiences to elevate ordinary events into emotionally meaningful stories that enlarge our understanding of human relationships. In the book's important introduction, Truffaut comments that his screen protagonist is the "synthesis of two real-life people: Jean-Pierre Leaud and myself." After describing how they met and what drew him originally to the then fourteen-year-old "antisocial loner," Truffaut explains the parallels between the screen character and the director's own life. He credits Jean Renoir for the younger filmmaker's handling of actors, stating that "It was from Renoir that I learned that actors are always more important than the characters they portray, or, to put it in a different way, that we should always sacrifice the abstract for the concrete." The scripts of the four films dealing with adolescence, love, and maturity come with handsomely reproduced stills, as well as the director's working notes and first treatments. Recommended for special collections.

*Truffaut, Francois. DAY FOR NIGHT: THE COMPLETE SCRIPT OF THE FILM. Trans. Sam Flores. New York: Grove Press, 1975. Illustrated. 175pp.

Truffaut tells us in the book's foreword that he was so exhausted after shooting TWO ENGLISH GIRLS/LES DEUX ANGLAISES ET LE CONTINENT (1971), that he decided to edit the film in Nice, where his children were vacationing. Once there, his daily trips to the editing room took him by an old, abandoned set of the American production of THE MAD WOMAN OF CHAILLOT. The more he saw that big, unused set, the more he thought of its possibilities for a film about the process of filmmaking. Starting with the notion of a movie about the making of a movie, he decided it would be "a FICTIONAL story which would, at the same time, furnish a maximum of FACTUAL INFORMATION. I would not tell ALL the truth about shooting a film," he explains. "That would be impossible. But I would tell ONLY TRUE THINGS: events which happened to me while making other films, or which happened to other filmmakers I knew." In addition to describing how he proceeded, this book provides descriptions of the characters, cast and technical credits, and the completed script. Because the original script had few technical notations, the translator wisely indicates important differences between the published script and the released film. More than fifty lovely stills add to the book's value. Recommended for special collections.

*Truffaut, Francois. THE FILMS IN MY LIFE. Trans. Leonard Mayhew. New York: Simon and Schuster, 1978. 358pp.

A marvelous collection of Truffaut's critical writings between 1954 and 1958, this book provides easy access to many reviews and commentaries discussed in other works but not readily available in one source. The author tells us in his 1975 opening essay, "What Do Critics Dream About?" that as a youthful delinquent who virtually lived in movie theaters, he often "passed up period films, war movies and Westerns because they were more difficult to identify with." He goes on to explain, "That left mysteries and love stories. Unlike most moviegoers my own age, I didn't identify with the heroes, but with the underdog and, in general, with any character who was in the wrong." After listing his favorite AUTEURS and the reasons why they appealed to him, Truffaut comments on why it is foolish to establish a hierarchy of films, his disgust for the contemporary Hollywood emphasis on sex and violence, why critics make a mistake in discussing a filmmaker's intentions, the superiority of American critics over their European counterparts, and why artists generally don't take critics too seriously. "The main complaint against some critics--and a certain type of criticism," he writes, "is that too seldom do they speak about CINEMA as such." To illustrate his position, Truffaut gives us nearly one-sixth of his total critical output, divided into six sections. Interestingly, only a handful of his negative reviews are included. Reflecting on his transformation once he began making films, Truffaut wants to be positive about the medium he adores. Section 1, "The Big Secret," covers filmmakers who successfully made the transition from silent to sound films: e.g., Jean Vigo, Abel Gance, Jean Renoir, Carl Th. Dreyer, Ernst Lubitsch, Charlie Chaplin, Luis Bunuel, John Ford, Frank Capra, Howard Hawks, Josef von Sternberg, and Alfred Hitchcock. A number of the essays are original and in the case of Ford indicate Truffaut's re-evaluation of an artist he once disliked.   Sections 2 and 3, "The Generation of the Talkies: The Americans" and "The Generation of the Talkies: The French," provide opinions on artists like Robert Aldrich, Billy Wilder, George Cukor, Elia Kazan, Nicholas Ray, Frank Tashlin, Robert Wise, Claude Autant-Lara, Jacques Becker, Robert Bresson, Jules Dassin, Sacha Guitry, and Max Ophuls. Anticipating the reader's desire for an honest reaction to those men and the times, Truffaut includes his few negative essays. Section 4, "Hurrah for the Japanese Cinema," focuses on four directors: Kenji Mizoguchi, Kon Ichikawa, Yasushi Nakahira, and Keisuke Kinoshita. Section 5, "Some Outsiders," deals with artists like Ingmar Bergman, Norman MacLaren, Federico Fellini, Roberto Rossellini, Orson Welles, Humphrey Bogart, and James Dean. The concluding section, "My Friends In the New Wave," offers the book's major surprises. Truffaut argues that he wants, first of all, to reaffirm his status as a New Wave director and to defend the movement as an important phase in film history. Secondly, he wants to focus on the important films that played a crucial role in the development of LA NOUVELLE VAGUE. Third, Truffaut freely admits that a number of the "occasional pieces" about the filmmakers are less-than-objective, designed to help in launching their careers rather than in judging their works. Nevertheless, it's a delight to re-read his views on filmmakers like Alain Resnais, Agnes Varda, Roger Vadim, Louis Malle, Jean-Luc Godard, and Claude Berri. An index is included. Highly recommended for special collections.

*Truffaut, Francois. "SMALL CHANGE": A FILM NOVEL. Trans. Anselm Hollo. New York: Grove Press, 1976. Illustrated. 190pp.
      In the introduction to this CINE-ROMAN, Truffaut tells us that he originally intended to make an episodic film about childhood, but instead created a "collective chronicle" about ten small children (ranging from infancy to early adolescence) and what happens to them between the last month of a school year, and the summer holiday in a children's camp. Their adventures, he explains, are illustrative of the formative years--"from the first feeding bottle to the first loving kiss--the different stages of passage from early childhood to adolescence." Perhaps the most impressive aspect of Truffaut's cinematic achievement is the authenticity of the children's experiences, especially those of his two leads, Julian (Philippe Goldman) and Patrick (Geory Desmouchceaux).   Except for the introduction and numerous illustrations, the publication provides only the novel and not cast and credits, notes on the production, or critical insights. Well worth browsing.

*Truffaut, Francois. "THE STORY OF ADELE H.": THE COMPLETE SCRIPT OF THE FILM. Ed. Helen G. Scott. English dialogue Jan Dowson. New York: Grove Press, 1976. Illustrated. 191pp.
      In this CINE-ROMAN, Truffaut tells us that his interest in the project began when he read Frances Vernor Guille's biography of Victor Hugo's second daughter, the unwanted and emotionally disturbed Adele. Three other films occupied his attention before he, Jean Gruault, and Suzanne Schiffman began scripting Adele's misadventures. The finished script begins in 1863, with Adele's arrival in Halifax in pursuit of the cold-blooded British Lieutenant Pinson, a man who romanced and then deserted Adele, followed by the desperate woman's attempts to win his love, and culminates with an epilogue explaining that Adele spent the last forty years of her life in an insane asylum. "I felt," Truffaut informs us, "it would be a fascinating challenge to concentrate on a single character, obsessed by a one-way passion." In

addition to the script of this extraordinary tale, Truffaut provides us with a note on Guille, cast and credits, and over 125 illustrations from the film. Well worth browsing.

*Truffaut, Francois, and Jean Gruault. "THE WILD CHILD": A SCREENPLAY. Trans. Linda Lewin and Christine Lemery. New York: Washington Square Press, 1973. Illustrated. 189pp.

In this CINE-ROMAN, Lewin begins with a brief biographical sketch of Truffaut, followed by the filmmaker's explanation of how the movie was made. Among the many important insights Truffaut provides, two are especially interesting. First, he points out the connections between this work and two of his previous films: THE 400 BLOWS/LES QUATRE CENT COUP (1959) and FAHRENHEIT 451 (1966). All three films, he tells us, are "built on a major frustration." Secondly, in condensing Dr. Jean Itard's research with a "wild boy" named Victor of Aveyron from seven years (1801-1807) to a nine-month period, Truffaut crystalizes his notion of how Itard approached his work as well as Truffaut's relationship to the film and the effect that the project had on him. "The experience has left me," he writes, "with the impression not of having acted a role [Truffaut plays Itard in the film], but simply of having directed the film IN FRONT of the camera and not, as usual, FROM BEHIND it." In addition to the screenplay and over eighty illustrations, the publication includes cast and credits. Well worth browsing.

Walz, Eugene P. FRANCOIS TRUFFAUT: A GUIDE TO REFERENCES AND RESOURCES. Boston: G. K. Hall and Company, 1982. 319pp.

An impressive scholarly undertaking, this extensive resource guide reflects the sizable challenge that Walz faced in categorizing Truffaut's prodigious output of writings, interviews, and notes on his twenty-three feature films. For example, the accessibility and availability of the filmmaker's screenplays enable Walz to offer only minimal notations and plot summaries in his section on Truffaut's films. In handling the enormous number of reviews, Walz decides to list them by language (e.g., English, French) rather than chronologically or alphabetically, the titles and page numbers are omitted, and the most important material is placed first.

The opening section, "Biographical Background," is a model of conciseness, with useful topical headings--"CINEPHILE," "CRITIC," and "CINEASTE"--identifying the major features of Truffaut's career. In outlining the facts, Walz also comments about Truffaut's observations. For example, in dealing with the filmmaker's childhood, the author points out that Truffaut's reflections indicate "barely a ripple of happiness." In discussing the filmmaker's meteoric and controversial critical career, Walz not only highlights Truffaut's objectives but also identifies by number the annotated references in the book's sections on writings about and by Truffaut. In discussing Truffaut's ideas on films, Walz makes frequent allusions to the filmmaker's work.

The second section, "Critical Survey," provides a first-rate summary of the critical reactions to Truffaut's films. Divided into four topical headings, the first part deals with "Characters: Solitary, Immature, Myopic," pointing out that the isolation of Truffaut's protagonists results from uncertain love relationships, poor family experiences, and ill-conceived intentions. The second part, "Themes: Love, Death, Art," traces the consistency in Truffaut's work, while making useful distinctions between love that is "provisional (temporary) or definitive (permanent)." The third part, "The Truffaut Touch," stresses the filmmaker's concern with emotions rather than intellect and describes the nature of his "first-person confidential tone." The fourth part, "Conclusion: Not Just an Artist," comments on his dedication and discipline, pointing out that his commitment to being a "'popular artist' . . . is not a compromise but a challenge."

The other sections of this important reference guide contain the standard G. K. Hall material in annotated entries on writings by and about the subject, 16mm distributors, other related film activities, and archival sources. In addition, Walz includes an appendix listing the films screened by The American Film Institute for its 1979 retrospective on Truffaut, plus three separate indexes (author, film title, and AUTEUR). The more one uses the book, the more one appreciates the love and care that went into it. Highly recommended for special collections.

FILMS

CLAUDE CHABROL

LES BICHES (France--16mm: 1968, 97 mins., color, English subtitles, sound, R-FNC)
In this strange and elegant film, co-authored by Chabrol and Paul Gegauff, and photographed by Jean Rabier, the director focuses on the complicated relationship among three unusual people: a rich lesbian photographer (Stephane Andran), her female lover (Jacqueline Sassard), and the disrupting architect (Jan-Louis Trintignant) who eventually seduces both women. Describing this intriguing love triangle as "an archetypal French Film," Roy Armes asserts that not only is this Chabrol's "best film [up to 1968]," but also LES BICHES signals "a return to the sources of his inspiration after a long desert of commercial film-making for producers he despises".[1099]

JEAN-LUC GODARD

ALPHAVILLE (France--16mm: 1965, 100 mins., b/w, English subtitles, sound, R-BUD, FES, IMA; S-FES, REE)
Here is Godard for mass audiences, mixing literary allusions, science fiction, gangsters, and social satire. Eddie Constantine and Anna Karina star.[1100]

BREATHLESS/A BOUT DE SOUFFLE (France--16mm: 1959, 89 mins., b/w, English subtitles, sound, R-FES, IMA, TFF, IVY; S-FES, IVY, TFF)
Directed and written by Godard, based upon an original idea by Truffaut, the plot concerns a cynical gangster (Jean-Paul Belmondo) who casually steals a car and murders a cop. On the run in Paris, the angry fugitive tries to persuade his American sweetheart (Jean Seberg) to escape with him to Italy. At first, she agrees but then decides to inform on him. The film ends with the police killing the confused gangster in a street shoot-out. Noted for its exciting editing, intextexual references, clever plot manipulations, and stunning performance by Belmondo, the existential film, dedicated to Monogram Pictures (a master of "B" productions), is considered by admirers like Kreidl to be even more innovative than CITIZEN KANE, claiming that Godard's movie "changed film narratology."[1101]

[1099] Roy Armes, "Review of LES BICHES," SCREEN 10:2 (March-April 1969):81. For more information, see Don Allen, "Claude Chabrol," SCREEN 11:1 (February 1970):55-65; and Roy Armes, "Rejoinder," pp.66-7.

[1100] Richard Roud, "Anguish: Alphaville," SIGHT AND SOUND 34:4 (Autumn 1965):164-6; and Jack Edmund Nolan, "Eddie Constantine," FILMS IN REVIEW 19:7 (August-September 1968):431-44.

[1101] JEAN-LUC GODARD, p.98. For more information, see David Shipman, "Belmondo," FILMS AND FILMING 10:11 (August 1964):7-11; Arlene Croce "Breathless," FILM QUARTERLY 14:3 (Spring 1961):54-6; Marie-Claire Ropars, "The Graphic In Filmic Writing: A BOUT DE SOUFFLE or the Erratic Alphabet," ENCLITIC 6 (Fall 1981/Winter 1982):147-161; Pamela Falkenberg, "Hollywood and the 'Art Cinema' as a Bipolar

CHRIS MARKER

LE JOLI MAI (France--16mm: 1963, 124 mins., b/w, sound, R-NCE)
Directed by Marker, this film focuses on Paris in May of 1962, at the end of the Algerian war and the first peaceful period in France's history since the late 1930s. Part One of the CINEMA VERITE film's two parts probes the hopes and ambitions of ordinary people: e.g., workers, a salesman, and a housewife. Part Two takes the discussion out of the personal, Parisian context and places it in the framework of the nation's political and and social unrest. Marker's use of newsreel footage and the observations of foreign vistors on France gives the film, as Sharon Lee points out, "a bittersweet quality . . . [that] evokes the troubles of the past and present and hopes for a better future."[1102] In the French version Yves Montand does the voice-over commentary; in the American version, Simone Signoret.

ALAIN RESNAIS

HIROSHIMA MON AMOUR (France--(16mm: 1959, 88 mins., b/w, English subtitles, sound, R-BUD, FES, FNC, IMA, KIT, REE, TFF; S-TFF)
Working closely with the screenwriter Marguerite Duras, Resnais "modernizes" film narrative with a highly original story about a brief love affair between a French actress (Emmanuelle Riva) and a Japanese architect (Eiji Okada). Instead of the traditional linear unfolding of the pair's relationship, Resnais relies on montage effects using sight and sound to draw the audience into making associations between the unnamed woman's tragic experience at the end of the Nazi occupation in her hometown of Nevers, and the architect's remembrance of what the atom bomb did to his hometown of Hiroshima. Although the characterizations are less than satisfactory, Resnais's discontinuous editing, the striking photography of the cinematographers Sascha Vierny and Michio Takahashi, and the valuable musical score provided by Giovanni Fucso result in a remarkable set of images and time leaps that effectively illustrate the theories of LE NOUVEAU ROMAN. The value of the film, as David Hansard suggests, is that it "represents the initial formulation of the central notion in the Resnais OUEVRE, a notion that for Resnais establishes the starting point of the dialection: the illusion of time."[1103]

LAST YEAR AT MARIENBAD/L'ANNEE DERNIERE A MARIENBAD (France--16mm: 1961, 93 mins., b/w, English subtitles, sound, R-BUD, COR, FES, IMA, KIT, MAC, WHO; S-COR, REL)

Modeling System: A BOUT DE SOUFFLE and BREATHLESS," WIDE ANGLE 7:3 (1985):44-53; and Chris Secrest, "Program Notes: BREATHLESS," CINEMATEXAS PROGRAM NOTES 22:2 (November 24, 1981):69-74.

[1102] Sharon Lee, "LE JOLI MAI," THE INTERNATIONAL DICTIONARY OF FILMS AND FILMMAKERS: VOLUME I, p.228.

[1103] David Hansard, "Program Notes: HIROSHIMA MON AMOUR," CINEMATEXAS PROGRAM NOTES 13:2 (October 13, 1977):42. For more information, see Gregory Sanders, "Program Notes: HIROSHIMA MON AMOUR," CINEMATEXAS PROGRAM NOTES 5:54 (December 6, 1973):1-5; Louis Marcorelles, "Rebel With a Camera," SIGHT AND SOUND 39:1 (Winter 1959-60):12-4; Henri Colpi, "Editing HIROSHIMA MON AMOUR," ibid., pp.14-6; Richard Roud, "Conversation With Marguerite Duras," ibid., pp.16-7; and William F. Van Wert, "The Cinema of Marguerite Duras: Sound and Voice in a Closed Room," FILM QUARTERLY 33:1 (Fall 1979):22-9.

Resnais's application of modernist concepts of time, space, and memory on film narrative produced one of the most controversial and challenging films of LA NOUVELLE VAGUE.[1104] Set in a spacious, Baroque hotel somewhere in Germany, the film presents three main and depersonalized characters: a beautiful heroine A; her admirer, X; and A's older male companion, or husband, M. The action centers on X's arguing with A that they had an affair the previous "year" at Marienbad, that she required he wait a "year" until they met again, and that A must forsake M and go off with X. The difficulty is that we have no way of knowing what is actually happening. Both Resnais and Robbe-Grillet, his screenwriter, offer no help in determining who is telling the truth. Moreover, the past and present appear as one, with no clue as to what is real or imaginary, fact or fiction. Through a clever use of flashbacks and flashforwards, Resnais forces us to create our own interpretation of what is taking place and why. The stylized acting, the theatrical look of the setting, and the construction of the "plot" contribute to the filmmakers' preoccupation with forcing the viewer to focus on how the film is being made rather than on what is taking place. According to Neal Oxenhandler, the film "is, first of all, the revelation of a method or strategy of a tremendously well-organized and brillantly executed esthetic maneuver."[1105] On the other hand, many viewers find the film a boring, pretentious exercise in cinematic experimentation. In defense of his script, Robbe-Grillet argues that "MARIENBAD is as opaque as the moments we live through in the climaxes of our feeling, in our loves, in our whole emotional life. So to reproach the film for its lack of clarity is really to reproach human feelings for their obscurity."[1106]

JEAN ROUCH

CHRONICLE OF A SUMMER/CHRONIQUE D'UN ETE (France--16mm: 1961, 90 mins, b/w, subtitles, sound, R-COR)

Co-directed by Jean Rouch and Edgar Morin, the sociological study of the attitudes of French workers and students to the end of the Algerian war during the summer of 1960 marked a new stage in film history. Not only did the French filmmaker and his sociological colleague tackle a subject other members of LA NOUVELLE VAGUE stayed away from, but they also pioneered the use of a new lightweight synchronous sound system that made CINEMA VERITE possible and practical. A number of questions have been raised about the film's integrity, particularly since the sociologist Morin misled Rouch about the background of the people interviewed, never telling him they were all part of a Marxist group. Rouch, on the other hand, defends the

---

[1104] For more information, see Alain Robbe-Grillet, "L'ANNEE DERNIERE A MARIENBAD," SIGHT AND SOUND 30:4 (Autumn 1961):176-9; Penelope Houston, "Resnais: L'ANNEE DERNIERE A MARIENBAD," ibid., 31:1 (Winter 1961-62):26-8; Jacques Brunius, "Every Year in Marienbad or The Discipline of Uncertainty," ibid., 31:3 (Summer 1962):122-7, 153; Alain Resnais, "Trying To Understand My Own Film," FILMS AND FILMING 8:5 (February 1962):9-10, 41; Lorrie Oshatz, "Program Notes: L'ANNEE DERNIERE A MARIENBAD," CINEMATEXAS PROGRAM NOTES 14:3 (March 30, 1978):15-9; Neal Oxenhandler, "MARIENBAD Revisited," FILM QUARTERLY 17:1 (Fall 1963):30-5; Richard Blumenberg, "Ten Years After Marienbad," CINEMA JOURNAL 10:2 (Spring 1971):40-3; Roy Armes, "Ricardou and LAST YEAR AT MARIENBAD," QUARTERLY REVIEW OF FILM STUDIES 5:1 (Winter 1980):1-17; and Joseph Milicia, "L'ANNEE DERNIERE A MARIENBAD," THE INTERNATIONAL DICTIONARY OF FILMS AND FILMMAKERS--VOLUME I, pp.30-2.

[1105] Oxenhandler, p.33.

[1106] "Last Words on Last Year: A Discussion with Alain Resnais and Alain Robbe-Grillet," FILMS AND FILMING 8:6 (March 1962):39-40.

film on the grounds that it deals with a specific group at a specific time in French history that would have made it dangerous to be more open about its political values.[1107] Tom Milne sums up the reactions of many viewers when he describes the film as "a fascinating experience, but one which leaves words like truth and reality open for definition."[1108]

FRANCOIS TRUFFAUT

DAY FOR NIGHT/LE NUIT AMERICAINE (France--16mm: 1973, 116 mins., color, English subtitles, color, R-FES, SWA)

Co-scripted by Truffaut, Louis Richard, and Suzanne Schiffman, this memorable movie about the making of a movie gets its title from the cinematic use of a filter to shoot a night scene during the day. Truffaut's emphasis is more on the interpersonal relationships among Ferrand, the director (Truffaut), his cast, and his crew, than upon the completion of MEET PAMELA, the film-within-the-film. The "doubling" of the characters and events, operating as reflections of Truffaut's preoccupation with searches for identity, are evident from the opening shots to the closing sequence. Highly entertaining, insightful, and absorbing, the film may be the best fictional account of what takes place on and off the set of a standard film project. In an insightful comparison between Truffaut's film and Renoir's THE RULES OF THE GAME/LA REGLE DU JEU (1939), Insdorf reminds us that both works reflect their directors' personal values and style, and that for Truffaut, the production synthesized the "thematic and stylistic preoccupations that he had been developing through twelve years of filmmaking."[1109] In addition, a major reason for the film's winning the New York Critic's Best Film award and the Oscar for Best Foreign Film is the movie's outstanding cast that includes not only Truffaut, but also Jacqueline Bisset, Jean-Pierre Leaud, Valentine Cortese, and Jean-Pierre Aumont.

THE 400 BLOWS/LES QUATRE CENT COUPS (France--16mm: 1959, 98 mins., b/w, English subtitles, sound, R-JAN, NEC)

Scripted by Truffaut and Marcel Moussy, this remarkable film in which Truffaut cast Jean-Pierre Leaud, a rebellious youngster-turned-film actor, to depict the hardships of adolescence is often described as completely autobiographical of Truffaut's childhood, a charge he denies. The story of Antoine Doniel, an unwanted and unloved child who is neglected by his parents and abused by his teacher, traces the lonely child's experiences from truancy and delinquency, to his being sent to jail for stealing, and ends with his escape to an unknown future. "If there was a thesis behind our film," Truffaut explains, "it would be this: adolescence leaves pleasant

---

[1107] Cited in Georgakas, p.18. For more information, see David Gerard, "CHRONICLE OF A SUMMER," FILMS AND FILMING 8:11 (August 1962):33; Tom Milne, "CHRONICLE OF A SUMMER," SIGHT AND SOUND 31:3 (Summer 1962):144-5; and John Baxter, "CHRONIQUE D'UN ETE," THE INTERNATIONAL DICTIONARY OF FILMS AND FILMMAKERS: VOLUME I, pp.94-5.

[1108] Milne, 145.

[1109] FRANCOIS TRUFFAUT, p.95. For more information, see Vincent Canby, "Night or Day, Truffaut's the One," NEW YORK TIMES D (October 7, 1973):1, 31; Judy Klemesrud, "'It's My Fault--I Never Followed the Rules,'" ibid., D (February 17, 1974):17, 22; and Joanna Ney, "Night and Day, Truffaut Is the One," VILLAGE VOICE (January 24, 1974):87.

memories only for adults who can't remember."[1110] Among the many remarkable aspects of this classic film are the insightful portraits of abused children, oppressive classrooms, and selfish parents. Truffaut's forceful and sensitive direction result in a movie about the roots of juvenile delinquency that still stands as an excellent case study on the subject. At the same time, as Lealand Poague points out, the film reveals how indebted Truffaut's approach was to artists like Jean Vigo, Roberto Rossellini, Jean Renoir, Alfred Hitchcock, and Orson Welles.[1111]

JULES AND JIM/JULES ET JIM (France--16mm: 1961, 104 mins., b/w, English subtitles, sound, R-FNC, NEC)
    Co-authored by Truffaut and Jean Gruault, the screenplay, adapted from Henri-Pierre Roche's novel, chronicles a triangular love story of two friends, Jules (Oskar Werner) and Jim (Henri Serre), and the woman (Jeanne Moreau) who personsifies a statue both men love. In many respects, the affairs of these three unusual people over a twenty-year period, and how Truffaut makes us sympathetic to their disturbing life-styles is reminiscent of Jean Renoir's A DAY IN THE COUNTRY/UNE PARTIE DE CAMPAGNE (1936). Moreover, in typical Truffaut style, he not only refuses to pass judgment on their amoral behavior, but also demonstrates his admiration for rebellious characters who search for friendship and love. The Don Quixote-Sancho Panza relationship between the two men is secondary to Moreau's brilliant performance as Catherine, a woman who loves freedom more than life itself.[1112] As Insdorf points out, the film heroine is "the definitive Truffaut goddess--all things to all men--but inherent in such a 'reflected' identity is the ravenous need for the attention to which she has been accustomed."[1113]

SHOOT THE PIANO PLAYER/TIREZ SUR LE PIANISTE (France--16mm: 1960, 84 mins., b/w, English subtitles, sound, R-BUD, EMG, FES, FNC, KIT, NCE, TFF, WHO; S-REE, TFF)
    Truffaut's second film, co-scripted with Marcel Moussy and based on the novel DOWN THERE by David Goodis, deals with a once-famous concert pianist (Charles Anznavour), whose wife committed suicide and left him bitter and disillusioned.

[1110] Cited in Dominique Rabourdin, ed. TRUFFAUT BY TRUFFAUT, trans. Robert Erich Wolf (New York: Harry N. Abrams, 1987), p.57.

[1111] Leland Poague, "LES QUATRE CENT COUPS," THE DICTIONARY OF FILMS AND FILMMAKERS: VOLUME I, p.382. For more information, see Jacob Gilles, "The 400 Blows of Francois Truffaut," SIGHT AND SOUND 37:4 (Autumn 1968):190-1; James Monaco, "Jean-Pierre Leaud: Coming of Age," trans. Catherine Verret TAKE ONE 5:4 (October 1976):16-20; Guido DeVita, "Program Notes: LES QUATRE CENT COUPS," CINEMATEXAS PROGRAM NOTES 14:1 (February 2, 1978):35-41; and Marie Mohoney, "Program Notes: LES QUATRE CENT COUPS," ibid., 22:2 (March 24, 1982):23-9.

[1112] For more information, see Alan Stanbrook, "The Stars They Couldn't Photograph," FILMS AND FILMING 9:5 (February 1963):10-4; Roger Greenspun, "Elective Affinities: Aspects of JULES AND JIM," ibid., 32:2 (Spring 1963):78-82; Francois Truffaut, "JULES AND JIM: Sex and Life," ibid., 8:10 (July 1962):19; "Dialogue on Film: An Interview With Jeanne Moreau," AMERICAN FILM 1:7 (May 1976):41-8; Barbara Coffey, "Art and Film in Francois Truffaut's JULES AND JIM and TWO ENGLISH GIRLS," FILM HERITAGE 9:3 (Spring 1974):1-11; Debbie Burk, "Program Notes: JULES AND JIM," CINEMATEXAS PROGRAM NOTES 4:38 (March 22, 1973):1-5; Joe Rape, "Program Notes: JULES AND JIM," ibid., 12:3 (April 26, 1977):1-4; and Marie Mohoney, "Program Notes: JULES AND JIM," ibid., 22:2 (April 20, 1982):79-84.

[1113] FRANCOIS TRUFFAUT, p.114.

Having changed his name and seeking anonymity in a seamy bistro, the timid piano player suddenly has to befriend his two older brothers, both criminals, who are being pursued by gangsters whom they have double-crossed. By the end of the film, the melancholy piano player has lost his brothers, accidentally killed the bar owner, had his mistress murdered accidentally by the mobsters, and is once more eking out a living playing in the demimonde bar. The film's appeal, however, has less to do with its plot and more with its visual pace and musical score. Truffaut's obvious tribute to the Hollywood "B" gangster films,[1114] his ironic characters and events, and his spontaneous and improvisational cutting demonstrate not only his penchant for burlesquing Hollywood conventions, but also his admiration for AUTEURS like Chaplin and Welles. For example, the name that the piano player assumes is Charlie Koher, a tribute to Chaplin. Interestingly, the picture did terribly at the box office when it first appeared. Not until the success of JULES ET JIM/JULES AND JIM a year later did the film get worldwide distribution. J. Hoberman speaks for many cineastes when he writes that "Funny, passionate, and idiosyncratic, the film is suffused with an almost unbearably sensual melancholy; even more than Godard's BREATHLESS, it epitomized the spirit of the early new wave."[1115]

AGNES VARDA

CLEO FROM 5 TO 7/CLEO DE CINQ A SEPT (France--16mm: 1961, 90 mins., Color sequences, b/w, English subtitles, sound, R-NYF)
        Working on the premise that the events in the film would be presented in their real timespan, the writer-director Varda opens with the film's only color sequence showing Cleo (Corinne Marchand) having her fortune told with tarot cards. The remaining hour and half follows the popular singer as she waits for news from her doctors telling her whether she has cancer. The cinematic plan is to focus on how the idea of death alters Cleo's personality and provides her with a clearer understanding of who she is and why. While contemporary critics like Hollis Alpert found the idea more intriguing than its execution on screen,[1116] Stanley Kauffmann attacks the movie as "archetypal New Wave nonsense, full of cinematic blabber intended and taken as new wisdom made accessible by new approaches to film. . . ,"[1117] and Gordon Gow finds the film's mood "suspended deftly between the documentary idiom and the poetic strain . . . [although he considers the film]

[1114] In a discussion following a screening of the film, Truffaut said that the film is "a RESPECTFUL PASTICHE of the Hollywood B-films from which I learned so much." See Francois Truffaut, "Should Films Be Politically Committed?" FOCUS ON "SHOOT THE PIANO PLAYER," p.135. He has also claimed that the film's theme is "The love and relations between men and women . . . [and what unifies the story] is the theme of love." Cited in Yvonne Baby, "I Want to Treat SHOOT THE PIANO PLAYER Like a Tale by Perrault: An Interview With Francois Truffaut," FOCUS ON SHOOT THE PIANO PLAYER, p.23.

[1115] "Francois Truffaut, 1932-1984," p.67. For more information, see Valentin Almendarez, "Program Notes: SHOOT THE PIANO PLAYER," CINEMATEXAS PROGRAM NOTES 7:41 (November 12, 1974):1-6; Nina Nichols, "Program Notes: SHOOT THE PIANO PLAYER," ibid., 17:3 (November 27, 1979):53-9; and Dudley Andrew, "TIREZ SUR LE PIANISTE," THE INTERNATIONAL DICTIONARY OF FILMS AND FILMMAKERS: VOLUME I, pp.476-7.

[1116] Hollis Alpert, "Movies by Metronome," SATURDAY REVIEW (August 4, 1962):14.

[1117] Stanley Kauffmann, "Women Growing," THE NEW REPUBLIC (October 8, 1977):26-7.

overpraised and   .   .   .   barely [standing] up to a second viewing."[1118] With all its flaws, the film is a fine example of New Left practices in the early 1960s.[1119]

A SELECTED COUNTRY-BY-COUNTRY LISTING OF SOURCE MATERIALS

ARGENTINA

BOOKS

*Barnard, Tim, ed. ARGENTINE CINEMA. Toronto: Nightwood Editions, 1986. Illustrated. 177pp.[1120]

AUSTRALIA

BOOKS

*Baxter, John. THE AUSTRALIAN CINEMA. Sydney: Pacific Books, 1970. Illustrated. 118pp.

McFarlane, Brian. AUSTRALIAN CINEMA. New York: Columbia university Press, 1988. Illustrated. 237pp.

*McFarlane, Brian. WORDS AND IMAGES: AUSTRALIAN NOVELS INTO FILM. London: Martin Secker and Warburg, 1983. Illustrated. 210pp.

Pike, Andrew, and Ross Cooper. AUSTRALIAN FILM 1900-1977: A GUIDE TO FEATURE FILM PRODUCTION. Sydney: Oxford University Press and the Australian Film Institute, 1980.

*Reade, Eric. HISTORY AND HEARTBURN: THE SAGA OF AUSTRALIAN FILM 1896-1978. Rutherford: Fairleigh Dickinson University Press, 1981. Illustrated. 353pp.

[1118] "The Underground River," p.8.

[1119] For more information, see "CLEO DE 5 a 7: Script Excerpt," trans. Raymond Durgnat, FILMS AND FILMING 9:3 (December 1962):22-3 .

[1120] See also Domingo Di Nubila, "Argentina Way--Part One," FILMS AND FILMING 7:3 (December 1961):16, 39; ___, ". . . Part Two," ibid., 7:4 (January 1961):41-2; Peter Baker, "Argentina Way," ibid., 6:8 (May 1960):8-9, 33; James Roy MacBean, "LA HORA DE LOS HORNOS," FILM QUARTERLY 24:1 (Fall 1970):31-7; ___, trans., "Fernando Solanas: An Interview," ibid., pp.37-43; and Nicholas E. Meyer, "Argentina," WORLD CINEMA SINCE 1975, pp.22-34.

Shirley, Graham, and Brian Adams. AUSTRALIAN CINEMA: THE FIRST EIGHTY YEARS. Sydney: Oxford University Press and the Australian Film Institute, 1980. Illustrated. 325pp.

Stratton, David. THE LAST NEW WAVE: THE AUSTRALIAN FILM REVIVAL.   New York: Ungar Publishing, 1981. Illustrated. 356pp.

Tulloch, John. LEGENDS ON THE SCREEN: THE AUSTRALIAN NARRATIVE CINEMA 1919-1929. Sydney: Currency Press and the Australian Film Institute, 1981.

*Tulloch, John. AUSTRALIAN CINEMA: INDUSTRY, NARRATIVE AND MEANING. Winchester: George Allen & Unwin, 1982. 272pp.

*White, David. AUSTRALIAN MOVIES TO THE WORLD: THE INTERNATIONAL SUCCESS OF AUSTRALIAN FILMS SINCE 1970. Melbourne: Fontana Australia, 1984. Illustrated. 143pp.

BALKAN CINEMA

BOOKS

*Stoil, Michael J. BALKAN CINEMA: EVOLUTION AFTER THE REVOLUTION. Ann Arbor: UMI Research Press, 1982. Illustrated. 160pp.

BRAZIL

BOOKS

Hollyman, Burnes Saint Patrick. GLAUBER ROCHA AND THE CINEMA NOVO: A STUDY OF HIS WRITINGS AND FILMS. New York: Garland Publishing, 1983. 213pp.[1121]

*Johnson, Randal. CINEMA NOVO X 5: MASTERS OF CONTEMPORARY BRAZILIAN CINEMA. Austin: University of Texas, 1984. Illustrated. 246pp.

[1121] For more information, see Gary Crowdus and William Starr, Cinema Novo vs. Cultural Colonialism: An Interview With Glauber Rocha," CINEASTE 4:1 (Summer 1970):2-9;; Allan Francovich, "BLACK GOD AND WHITE DEVIL," FILM QUARTERLY 23:2 (Winter 1969-1970):59-62; Gordon Hitchens, "The Way to make a Future: A Conversation With Glauber Rocha," ibid., 24:1 (Fall 1970):27-30; Robert Stam, "Slow Fade to Afro: The Black Presence In Brazilian Cinema," ibid., 36:2 (Winter 1982-1983):16-32; Hans Proppe and Susan Tarr, "Cinema Novo: Pitfalls of Cultural Nationalism," JUMP CUT 10/11 (June 1976):45-8; Patricia Aufderheide, "Will Success Spoil Brazilian Cinema?" AMERICAN FILM 8:5 (March 1983):65-70; ___, "Brazil," WORLD CINEMA SINCE 1945, pp.70-85; ___, "Memories of Prison: An Interview With Nelson Pereira Dos Santos," CINEASTE 14:2 (1985):23-4; and Robert Stam and Ismail Xavier,"MEMORIES OF PRISON," ibid., pp.21-2.

Johnson, Randal. FILM INDUSTRY IN BRAZIL: CULTURE AND THE STATE. Pittsburgh: University of Pittsburgh Press, 1987. 265pp.

*Johnson, Randal, and Robert Stam, eds. BRAZILIAN CINEMA. Rutherford: Fairleigh Dickinson University Press, 1982. Illustrated. 373pp.

BRITAIN

BOOKS

GENERAL

*Auty, Martyn, and Nick Roddick, eds. BRITISH CINEMA NOW. London: British Film Institute, 1985. Illustrated. 168pp.[1122]

The Monopolies Commission. FILMS: A REPORT ON THE SUPPLY OF FILMS FOR EXHIBITION IN CINEMAS. London: Her Majesty's Stationary Office, 1967.

*Perry, George. LIFE OF PYTHON. Boston: Little, Brown and Company, 1983. Illustrated. 192pp.

LINDSAY ANDERSON

*Sussex, Elizabeth. LINDSAY ANDERSON. New York: Praeger Publisher, 1969. Illustrated. 96pp.
    This rather shallow text fails to present a serious critical study and background material about the enterprising Anderson. The quotations, narrative, general information, and photographs tease you with thoughts of what might have been, had more time and effort gone into the text. Worth browsing.

[1122] The following articles are helpful: Penelope Houston, "The Undiscovered Country," SIGHT AND SOUND 25:1 (Summer 1955):10-14; ___, "Time of Crisis," ibid., 27:4 (Spring 1958):166-75; ___, "Whose Crisis," ibid., 33:1 (Winter 1963-64):26-8, 50; ___, "Seventy," ibid., 39:1 (Winter 1969-70):2-5; Richard Roud, "Britain In America," ibid., 26:3 (Winter 1956-57):119-23; John Berger, "Look at Britain," ibid., 27:1 (Summer 1957):12-4; John Gillett, "State of the Studios," ibid., 33:2 (Spring 1964):54-61; Kenneth Cavander et al., "British Feature Directors: An Index to Their Work," ibid., 27:6 (Autumn 1958):289-304; Penelope Houston and Duncan Crow, "Into the Sixties," ibid., 29:1 (Winter 1959-60):4-8; Derek Hill, "A Writer's Wave," ibid., 29:2 (Spring 1960):56-60; John Russell Taylor, "Backing Britain, ibid., 38:3 (Summer 1969):112-5; Jan Dawson and Claire Johnston, "More British Sounds," ibid., 39:3 (Summer 1970):144-7; Ian Jarvie, "Media and Manners: Film and Society In Some Current British Films," FILM QUARTERLY 22:3 (Spring 1969):11-7; and Ian Johnson, "The Decade: Britain--We're All Right Jack," FILMS AND FILMING 8:12 (September 1962):44-8.

PETER O'TOOLE

Wapshott, Nicholas. PETER O'TOOLE: A BIOGRAPHY. New York: Beaufort Books, 1983. Illustrated. 239pp.

FILMS

LINDSAY ANDERSON

THIS SPORTING LIFE (Britain--16mm: 1963, 129 mins., b/w, sound, R-BUD, FNC, KIT)
Produced by Karel Reisz and Albert Fennell, scripted by David Story (who adapted his novel), and directed by Anderson, the film is a a realistic story of an ambitious rugby player (Richard Harris) who refuses to let anything interfere with his ambitions. According to Ronald Bowers, the film fails to sustain its image as the best of the "Angry Young Men" school of filmmaking that dominated the early 1960s, but "was a major step away from the restrained, tight-upper-lip tradition of film-making in England. . . ."[1123] It was nominated for two Oscars: Best Actor and Best Actress (Rachel Roberts).

DONALD CAMMELL AND NICOLAS ROEG

PERFORMANCE (Britain--16mm: 1970, 110 min, color, sound, R-FNC, SWA, TWY)
Cammell not only co-directed with his photographer Roeg, but also wrote the screenplay for this superb movie about a rock singer (Mick Jagger) who retires to an obscure house and takes for a tenant a gangster (James Fox) hiding out from members of his own gang and the police. Eventually, the men's personalities exert reciprocal influence on them, creating fascinating character studies for the screen. As Jan Dawson points out, the film's brilliant, often confusing, notion of intermingling indenties, results in a film, "relying entirely on what it shows, what we see, to suggest the workings of less visible forces."[1124] Jagger sings on the sound track as well.

LEWIS GILBERT

ALFIE (Britain--16mm: 1966, 114 mins., cinemascope, color, sound, R-FNC, WHO)
Scripted by Bill Naughton and based on his play, wiith Lewis Gilbert directing, this exceptional film portrays Alfie (Michael Caine), the cad, who suddenly loses his touch with women and sinks into despair. In its day, the bitter-comedy did a superb

---

[1123] Ronald Bowers, "THIS SPORTING LIFE," THE INTERNATIONAL DICTIONARY OF FILMS AND FILMMAKERS: VOLUME I, p.474. For other views, see Robert Vas, "Arrival and Departure," SIGHT AND SOUND 32:2 (Spring 1963):56-59; Tom Milne, "THIS SPORTING LIFE," ibid., 31:3 (Summer 1962):112-15; and Ernest Callenbach, "THIS SPORTING LIFE," FILM QUARTERLY 17:4 (Summer 1964):45-48.

[1124] Jan Dawson, "PERFORMANCE," MONTHLY FILM BULLETIN 38:445 (February 1971):28. For other perspectives, see Philip French, "Performance," SIGHT AND SOUND 40:2 (Spring 1971):67-69; Foster Hirsch, "Underground Chic: Performance," FILM HERITAGE 6:3 (Spring 1971):1-6, 36; and Gordon Gow, "Identity: An Interview With Nicholas Roeg," FILMS AND FILMING 18:4 (January 1972):18-24.

job of presenting a popular anti-hero for contemporary society. It was nominated for five Oscars: Best Film, Best Actor, Best Supporting Actress (Vivien Merchant), Best Screenplay--Based on Material from Another Medium, and Best Musical Song ("Alfie"--Music: Burt Bacharach; Lyrics: Hal David).[1125]

RICHARD LESTER

HELP! (Britain--16mm: 1965, 90 mins., color sound, S-Video cassette)
    This mad and delightful film tries every type of cutting and camera technique that comes to mind so that the Beatles can sing and romp through the world in entertaining fashion.[1126]

JOSEPH LOSEY

ACCIDENT (Britain--16mm: 1967, 105 mins., color, sound, R-FNC)
    Scripted by Harold Pinter and based on a novel by Nicholas Mosley, with Losey directing, this fascinating screenplay deals with a neurotic teacher and father (Dirk Bogarde) who tries extramarital relations and nearly destroys himself. The film was the second of Losey's works with Pinter--the other two are THE SERVANT (1963) and THE GO-BETWEEN (1970)--and, as Foster Hirsch observes, a remarkable illustration of how artists can collaborate successfully on adapting novels to the screen.[1127] In addition to a fine performance by Harris, Stanley Baker is outstanding as the jealous colleague.[1128]

THE SERVANT (Britain--16mm: 1963, 115 mins., b/w, sound, R-FNC, JAN)
    The same team of Losey, Pinter, and Bogarde presents an extraordinary tale of depravity as a weak aristocrat (James Fox) becomes a pawn of a degenerate servant (Bogarde). It remains a fascinating study of corruption. In addition to fine performances Fox and Bogarde, there is a stunning bit of acting by Sarah Miles, who, according to Losey, was miscast and should have had the leading female role.[1129]

[1125] David Austen, "Playing Dirty: Michael Caine--Part One," FILMS AND FILMING 15:7 (April 1969):4-8, 10; David Austen, ". . . . Part Two," ibid., 15:8 (May 1969):15-18; and Stephen Farber, "ALFIE," FILM QUARTERLY 20:3 (Spring 1967):42-46.

[1126] Robin Bean, "Keeping Up With The Beatles," FILMS AND FILMING 10:5 (February 1964):9-12.

[1127] JOSEPH LOSEY, p.92. For more information, see Penelope Houston and John Gillett, "Conversation With Nicholas Ray and Joseph Losey," SIGHT AND SOUND 30:4 (Autumn 1961):182-7; John Russell Taylor, "ACCIDENT," ibid., 35:4 (Autumn 1966):179-84; Tom Milne, "ACCIDENT," ibid., 36:2 (Spring 1967):56-9; Raymond Durgnat, "Losey: Modesty and Eve--Part One," FILMS AND FILMING 12:7 (April 1966):26-33; ___, ". . . Part Two," ibid., 12:8 (May 1966):28-33.

[1128] For more information, see Margaret Tarratt and Kevin Gough-Yates, "Playing the Game: Stanley Baker," FILMS AND FILMING 16:11 (August 1970):30-4.

[1129] CONVERSATIONS WITH LOSEY, p.226. See also Richard Whitehall, "Dirk Bogarde," FILMS AND FILMING 10:2 (November 1963):13-6.

KAREL REISZ

SATURDAY NIGHT AND SUNDAY MORNING (Britain--16mm: 1961, 90 mins., b/w, sound, R-BUD, COR)
    Scripted by Alan Sillitoe and based on his novel, Reisz makes his directorial debut with this exceptional film about the life and loves of a blue-collar cad (Albert Finney) from the English industrial world. The pseudo-documentary approach, depicting working-class conditions in modern factory towns underscored the unrest and rebellious nature of the "angry young men" school of filmmaking. The film's appeal today rests on the performances of Finney and Rachel Roberts, who plays his pathetic wife.

TONY RICHARDSON

THE ENTERTAINER (Britain--16mm: 1960, 97 mins., b/w, sound, R-BUD)
    Richardson does a fine job with the John Osborne-Nigel Kneale screenplay (adapted from Osborne's stage play) about an egocentric, second-rate song-and-dance man (Laurence Olivier) whose sick ambitions destroy him in the end. Olivier's success with the stage play initially overshadowed his brilliant performance later in the screen adaptation. Today, however, it stands as one of his greatest screen roles. As Foster Hirsch points out, "Submerging himself beneath the character's pained, grinning mask, Olivier erases his own mannerisms, and we respond to Archie's failure rather than to Olivier's brilliance."[1130] The great actor lost the Oscar for Best Actor to Burt Lancaster in ELMER GANTRY.

CANADA

*Beattie, Eleanor. A HANDBOOK OF CANADIAN FILM. Toronto: Take One, 1973. Illustrated. 280pp.[1131]

*Harcourt, Peter. JEAN PIERRE LEFEBVRE. Ottawa: Canadian Film Institute, 1981. Illustrated. 178pp.

*Morris, Peter. EMBATTLED SHADOWS: A HISTORY OF CANADIAN CINEMA 1895-1939. Montreal: McGill-Queen's University Press, 1978. Illustrated. 350pp.

Pratley, Gerald. TORN SPROCKETS: THE UNCERTAIN PROJECTION OF THE CANADIAN FILM. Newark: Uinversity of Delaware Press, 1987. Illustrated. 330pp.

*Reid, Alison, and P. M. Evanchuck. RICHARD LEITERMAN. Ottawa: The Canadian

---

[1130] Foster Hirsch, LAURENCE OLIVIER (Boston: Twayne Publishers, 1979), p.146.

[1131] For a good overview of the activities of the National Film Board, see John Curtin, "Canada Celebrates a Mission In Film," NEW YORK TIMES H (April 30, 1989):17, 21. See also Bruce Cook, "The Canadian Dilemma: A Problem of Identity," AMERICAN FILM 1:2 (November 1975):20-4.

Film Institute, 1978. Illustrated. 120pp.

CHILE

BOOKS

Garcia Marquez, Gabriel. CLANDESTINE IN CHILE: THE ADVENTURES OF MIGUEL LITTIN. New York: Henry Holt and Company, 1986. 116pp.

CHINA

Clark, Paul. CHINESE CINEMA: CULTURE & POLITICS SINCE 1949. New York: Cambridge University Press, 1987. Illustrated. 243pp.[1132]

Leyda, Jay. DIANYING: AN ACCOUNT OF FILMS AND THE FILM AUDIENCE IN CHINA. Illustrated. 515pp.

Semsel, George Stephen, ed. CHINESE FILM: THE STATE OF THE ART IN THE PEOPLE'S REPUBLIC. New York: Praeger, 1987. Illustrated. 191pp.

CUBA

BOOKS

*Chanan, Michael. THE CUBAN IMAGE: CINEMA AND CULTURAL POLITICS IN CUBA. Bloomington: Indiana University Press, 1986. Illustrated. 314pp.[1133]

Myerson, Michael, ed. MEMORIES OF UNDERDEVELOPMENT: THE REVOLUTIONARY

[1132] For useful articles, see Mark J. Scher, "Film In China," FILM COMMENT 5:2 (Spring 1969):8-21; Leonard Rubenstein, "Report From China," FILM SOCIETY REVIEW 7:1 (September 1971):36-9; ___, "Red China," ibid., 7:2 (October 1971):40-3; ___, "Revolution in China," ibid., 7:3 (November 1971):37-42; ___, "China: The Red Sons," ibid., 7:4 (December 1971):41-4; Joseph Gross, "One Man's China: An Interview With Felix Greene," CINEASTE 14:4 (1986):26-8; "Special Issue on China," WIDE ANGLE 11:2 (1989); Esther Yau, "China," WORLD CINEMA SINCE 1945, pp.116-39; and Ian Jarvie, "Recent Books on Chinese Films," JOURNAL OF POPULAR FILM 3:4 (Fall 1974):351-5.

[1133] For some useful articles, see Nestor Almendros, "The Cinema in Cuba," FILM CULTURE 9 ((1956):21; Andi Engel, "Solidarity and Violence," SIGHT AND SOUND 38:4 (Autumn 1969):196-200; William Johnson, "Report From Cuba," FILM QUARTERLY 15:2 (Winter 1961-62):42-9; Thomas Guitierrez Alea, "I Wasn't Always a Filmmaker," CINEASTE 14:1 (1985):36-9 ; Dan Georgakas and Gary Crowdus, "Parting of the Ways: An Interview With Jesus Diaz," ibid., 15:4 (1987):22; Enrique Fernandez, "Parting of the Ways: A Cuban-American View," ibid., pp.23, 39; Fausto Canel, "Cowardly Cuban Film Critics?" ibid., 16:1-2 (1987-88):7; Dennis West, "Reconciling Entertainment and Thought: An Interview With Julio Garcia Espinosa," ibid., pp.20-6, 89; ___, "Cuba," WORLD CINEMA SINCE 1945, pp.140-53; and Pat Aufderheide, "Red Harvest," AMERICAN FILM 9:5 9:5 (March 1984):28-32, 34.

FILMS OF CUBA. New York: Grossman, 1973.

CZECHOSLOVAKIA

BOOKS

Hames, Peter. THE CZECHOSLOVAK NEW WAVE. Berkeley: University of California Press, 1985. Illustrated. 322pp.

Liehm, Antonin J. CLOSELY WATCHED FILMS: THE CZECHOSLOVAK EXPERIENCE. White Plains: International Arts and Sciences Press, 1974. Illustrated. 485pp.

MILOS FORMAN

*Liehm, Antonin J. THE MILOS FORMAN STORIES. White Plains: International Arts and Sciences Press, 1975. Illustrated. 191pp.

JIRI MENZEL

*Menzel, Jiri, and Bohumil Hrabal. CLOSELY WATCHED TRAINS. New York: Simon and Schuster, 1971. Illustrated. 144pp.

Skvorecky, Josef. JIRI MENZEL AND THE HISTORY OF CLOSELY WATCHED TRAINS. Boulder: East European Monographs, 1982. Illustrated.

FILMS

MILOS FORMAN

THE LOVES OF A BLONDE/LASKEY JEDNE PLAVOVLASKY (Czechoslovakia--16mm: 1965, 88 mins., b/w, sound, English subtitles, R-FNC)
    The writer-director Milos Forman created this comic tale of two young people in love. Originally perceived as pornographic by Czechoslovakian officials, the "New Wave" film is considered today one of the first Czechoslovakian works to bring recognition to the emerging industry, mainly because of its "mixture of 'realist" observation, humanity, and humor."[1134]

[1134] Peter Hames, THE CZECHOSLOVAK NEW WAVE. Berkeley: University of California Press, 1985), p.1. For more information, see Claire Clouzot, "Loves of a Blonde," FILM QUARTERLY 21:1 (Fall 1967):47-8; James Conaway, "Milos Forman's America Is Like Kafka's--Basically Comic," THE NEW YORK TIMES MAGAZINE (July 11, 1971), pp.8-12; and Gordon Gow, "A Czech In New York: An Interview With Milos Forman," FILMS AND FILMING 17:12 (September 1971):20-4. See also Peter John Dyer, "Star-Crossed In Prague," SIGHT AND SOUND 35:1 (Winter 1965-66):34-5; Antonin Liehm, "A Reckoning of the Miracle: An Analysis of Czechoslovak Cinematography," Q%M COMMENT 5:1 (Fall 1968):64-9; Kirk Bond, "The New Czech Film," ibid., pp.70-8; Jan Zalman, "Question Marks on the New Czechoslovak Cinema," FILM QUARTERLY 21:2 (Winter 1967-68):18-27; Jaroslav Broz, "Here Come the Czechs: Grass Roots," FILM AND

JAN KADAR

THE SHOP ON MAIN STREET/OBCHOD NA KORZE (Czechoslovakia--16mm: 1965, 128 mins., b/w, English subtitles, sound, R-FNC, NLC)
Jan Kadar and Elmer Klos co-directed this screen masterpiece on the moral dilemma that simple people face in war. Memorable performances by Ida Kaminska and Josef Kroner. It won the Oscar for Best Foreign Film.

JIRI MENZEL

CLOSELY WATCHED TRAINS/OSTRE SLEDOVANE VLAKY (Czechoslovakia--16mm: 1966, 89 mins., b/w, English subtitles, sound, R-FNC)
Menzel directed and co-authored with Bohumil Hrabal the screenplay (based on Hrabal's novel) of this masterly tragic-comic depiction of youthful resistance fighters during World War II. Impeccably cast, beautifully photographed, and impressively edited, it is one of the postwar period's outstanding films. It won the Oscar for the Best Foreign Film.

GERMANY

BOOKS

*Corrigan, Timothy. NEW GERMAN FILM: THE DISPLACED IMAGE.   Austin: University of Texas Press, 1983. Illustrated. 213pp.
An AUTEURIST approach to the contemporary German cinema, this book stresses the historical, cultural, and aesthetic foundations of important directors like Rainer Werner Fassbinder, Werner Herzog, Wim Wenders, Volker Schlondorff, Hans-Jurgen Syberberg, and Alexander Kluge.[1135] Endnotes, a filmography, a bibliography, and an index are included. Recommended for special collections

*Pflaum, Hans Gunther, and Hans Helmut Prinzler. CINEMA IN THE FEDERAL REPUBLIC OF GERMANY: THE NEW GERMAN FILM ORIGINS AND PRESENT SITUATION--A HANDBOOK. Bonn: Inter Nationes, 1983. Illustrated. 180pp.

FILMING 11:9 (June 1965):39-42; Robin Bates, "The Ideological Foundations of the Czech New Wave," JOURNAL OF THE UNIVERSITY FILM ASSOCIATION 29:3 (Summer 1977):37-42; and Josef Skvorecky, "Czechoslovakia," WORLD CINEMA SINCE 1945, pp.154-69.

[1135] Some useful articles on the history of German films are the following: Louis Marcorelles, "Glimpses of the Nazi Cinema (1933-1945)," SIGHT AND SOUND 25:2 (Autumn 1955):65-9; Enno Patalas, "The German Wasteland," ibid., 26:1 (Summer 1956):24-7; Robert Vas, "Fifteen Years After: Notes from West Germany," ibid., 30:4 (Autumn 1961):201-4; "Young German Film" FILM COMMENT 6:1 (Spring 1970):32-44; Ulrich Gregor, "The German Film In 1964: Stuck at Zero," FILM QUARTERLY 18:2 (Winter 1964):7-21; Robin Bean, "The Face of '63: Germany," FILMS AND FILMING 9:9 (June 1963):41-8; ___, "Hands Up, Hans!," ibid., 11:1 (October 1964):53-7; Eric Rentschler, "Germany: The Past that Will Not Go Away," WORLD CINEMA SINCE 1945, pp.208-51; Gerald Clarke, "Seeking Planets That Do Not Exist," TIME (March 20, 1978):51-3, Robert Acker, "The Major Directions of German Feminist Cinema," LITERATURE/FILM QUARTERLY 13:4 (1985):245-9; and Kent Casper and Susan Linville, "Nazi Reframes: Negative Stereotyping In American Reviews of New German Films," ibid., pp.250-7.

*Phillips, Klaus, ed. NEW GERMAN FILMMAKERS FROM OBERHAUSEN THROUGH THE 1970s. New York: Frederick Unger Publishing Company, 1984. Illustrated. 462pp.

*Rentschler, Eric. WEST GERMAN FILM IN THE COURSE OF TIME: REFLECTIONS ON THE TWENTY YEARS SINCE OBERHAUSEN. Bedford Hills: Redgrave Publishing Company, 1984. 260pp.

RAINER WERNER FASSBINDER

*Iden, Peter, et al. FASSBINDER. Trans. Ruth McCormick. New York: Tanam Press, 1981. Illustrated. 249pp.

*Rayns, Tony, ed. FASSBINDER. London: British Film Institute, 1976. 61pp.

*Rheuban, Joyce, ed. THE MARRIAGE OF MARIA BRAUN: RAINER WERNER FASSBINDER, DIRECTOR. New Brunswick: Rutgers University Press, 1986. Illustrated. 275pp.

WERNER HERZOG

*Corrigan, Timothy, ed. THE FILMS OF WERNER HERZOG: BETWEEN MIRAGE AND HISTORY. New York: Methuen, 1987. Illustrated. 232pp.

Herzog, Werner. SCREENPLAYS: AGUIRRE, THE WRATH OF GOD; EVERY MAN FOR HIMSELF AND GOD AGAINST ALL; LAND OF SILENCE AND DARKNESS. Trans. Alan Greenberg and Martje Herzog. New York: Tanam Press, 1980. 205pp.

*Herzog, Werner. OF WALKING IN ICE: MUNICH-PARIS 11/23 TO 12/14, 1974. New York: Tanam Press, 1980. 90pp.

GREECE

BOOKS

Schuster, Mel. THE CONTEMPORARY GREEK CINEMA. Metuchen: The Scarecrow Press, 1979. Illustrated. 360pp.

HUNGARY

BOOKS

*Petrie, Graham. HUNGARIAN CINEMA TODAY: HISTORY MUST ANSWER TO THE

MAN. New York: Zoetrope, 1978. Illustrated. 284pp.[1136]

INDIA

BOOKS

*Barnouw, Erik and Subrahmanyam Krishnaswamy. INDIAN FILM. New York: Columbia University Press, 1963. New York: Oxford University Press, 1980. Illustrated. 327pp. Second Edition.
    India, one of the largest filmmaking countries in the world, has her filmmakers treated sympathetically and perceptively in this standard book. For many who have never been to India, this text offers some interesting observations as well as some significant information on the start of Indian filmmaking, the influence of mythology on her artists, and a very helpful chapter on Satyajit Ray. Production statistics, a chronology, interviews, a bibliography, and an index are included. Recommended for special collections.

Vasudev, Aruna, and Philippe Lenglet, eds. INDIAN CINEMA SUPERBAZAAR. New York: Advent Books, 1983. Illustrated. 384pp.

ISMAIL MERCHANT

*Ivory, James. TWO FILMS: SAVAGES, SHAKESPEARE WALLAH. New York: Grove Press, 1973. Illustrated. 152pp.

*Pym, John. THE WANDERING COMPANY: TWENTY-ONE YEARS OF MERCHANT IVORY FILMS. Comments James Ivory. New York: Museum of Modern Art, 1983. Illustrated. 102pp.

SATYAJIT RAY

Das Gupta, Chidananda. THE CINEMA OF SATYAJIT RAY. New York: Advent Books, 1980. Illustrated. 88pp.

Seton, Marie. PORTRAIT OF A DIRECTOR: SATYAJIT RAY. Bloomington: Indiana University Press, 1971. Illustrated. 350pp.
    In this superbly written and exhaustive study of the famed Indian director, Seton, as always in her work, offers a critical and biographical examination of the man, his films, and his unique cinematic contributions, particularly his additions to

---

[1136] For some useful articles, see J. Hoberman, "New Kid on Bloc," AMERICAN FILM 9:2 (November 1983):52-7, 87; Louis Marcorelles, "Hungarian Cinema: The Fight for Freedom," SIGHT AND SOUND 26:3 (Winter 1956-57):124-30; Robert Vas, "Yesterday and Tomorrow: New Hungarian Films," ibid., 29:1 (Winter 1959-60):1-34; David Robinson, "Quite Apart from Miklos Jansso . . . Some Notes on the New Hungarian Cinema," ibid., 39:2 (Spring 1970):84-9; and John Mosier, "Hungary," WORLD CINEMA SINCE 1945, pp.287-300.

the documentary and the neo-realistic traditions. Many useful stills and a helpful index are included.[1137] Recommended for special collections.

SPECIAL ISSUE ON SATYAJIT RAY, MONTAGE 5-6 (July 1966).
Up to the Seton book, this was the best available source on the man who put Indian films on a world circuit. There are useful articles by Ray on his work as well as essays by his collaborators. Well worth browsing.

*Wood, Robin. THE APU TRILOGY. New York: Praeger Publishers, 1971. Illustrated. 96pp.
This book provides a good study of the three films that catapulted Ray to international fame. Wood's comments are stimulating, perceptive, and entertaining. Stills and a helpful bibliography are included, but no index is provided.[1138]

FILMS

SATYAJIT RAY

PATHER PANCHALI (India--16mm: 1956, 112 mins., b/w, English subtitles, sound, R-BUD; S-FES, FNC)
This cinematic poem of the life of a poor but dedicated Indian scholar and his family struggling to survive in a tiny Bengali hamlet was the first film to bring Ray justly deserved fame. It was awarded a significant prize at the 1956 Cannes Film Festival. Nevertheless, Ray's cinematic record of the social and economic problems existing in India made Indian officials hesitant about encouraging future productions, especially for distribution outside of India.

THE WORLD OF APU (India--16mm: 1960, 103 mins., b/w, English subtitles, sound, R-BUD, EMG, FES, FNC; S-FES)
In this final part of the film trilogy, Ray reaches his greatest heights as he poignantly and magnificently follows the difficult life of Apu, the now grown-up son of the poor scholar's family, whose meager living and happy marriage are tragically disrupted by his wife's death in childbirth. The movie ends on an optimistic note as

---

[1137] The following articles are useful: Eric Rhode, "Satyajit Ray: A Study," SIGHT AND SOUND 30:3 (Summer 1961):132-36; Marie Seton, "Kanchenjunga: Satyajit Ray at Work on His Film," ibid., 31:2 (Spring 1962):73-5, Folke Isaksson, "Conversation With Satyajit Ray," ibid., 39:3 (Summer 1970):114-20; Satyajit Ray, "From Film to Film," CAHIERS DU CINEMA IN ENGLISH 3, CdC #175 (February 1966):12-9, 62-3; James Blue, "Satyajit Ray: An Interview," FILM COMMENT 4:4 (Summer 1968):4-17; Barbara Crossette, "Satyajit Ray Gives Ibsen a Bengali Spin, ..." NEW YORK TIMES H (May 7, 1989):15, 21; and Andrew Robinson, ". . . . And Reflects on Life and Art," ibid., pp.15, 19. Robinson, Andrew

[1138] The following articles offer some help: Marie Seton, "Journey Through India," SIGHT AND SOUND 26:4 (Spring 1957):198-202; Chidananda Das Gupta, "Indian Cinema Today," FILM QUARTERLY 22:4 (Summer 1969):27-35; and Sanjoy Hazarika, "An American Star of the Hindi Screen,"

the bereaved husband finally becomes reconciled to the child.

ISRAEL

BOOKS

Arzooni, O. G. J. THE ISRAELI FILM: SOCIAL AND CULTURAL INFLUENCES 1912-1973. New York: Garland Publishing, 1983. 387pp.[1139]

ITALY

BOOKS

GENERAL

Michalczyk, John J. THE ITALIAN POLITICAL FILMMAKERS. Rutherford: Fairleigh Dickinson University Press, 1986. Illustrated. 325pp.

Witcombe, R. T. THE NEW ITALIAN CINEMA: STUDIES IN DANCE AND DESPAIR. New York: Oxford University Press, 1982. Illustrated. 294pp.

MICHELANGELO ANTONIONI

*Antonioni, Michelangelo. SCREENPLAYS OF MICHELANGELO ANTONIONI: IL GRIDO/L'AVVENTURA/LA NOTTE//L'ECLISSE. Introduction Michelangelo Antonioni. New York: Orion Press, 1963.[1140] Illustrated. 361pp.

*Antonioni, Michelangelo, et al. L'AVVENTURA. New York: Grove Press, 1969. Illustrated. 288pp.

*Antonioni, Michelangelo, and Tonino Guerra. BLOW-UP (1966). New York: Simon and Schuster, 1971. Illustrated. 119pp.

[1139] For some useful articles, see Ella Shohat, "The Return of the Repressed: The Palestinian Wave in Recent Israeli Cinema," CINEASTE 15:3 (1987):10-7; ___, "Israel," WORLD CINEMA SINCE 1945, pp.330-46; and Patricia Erens, "Israeli Cinema," FILM COMMENT 18:1 (January-February 1981):60-6.

[1140] The following articles on Italian Cinema are useful: Merando Morandini, "The Year of LA DOLCE VITA," SIGHT AND SOUND 29:3 (Summer 1960):123-7; Giulio Cesare Castello, "Cinema Italiano 1962," trans. Isabel Quigley, ibid., 32:1 (Winter 1962-63):28-33; Geoffrey Nowell-Smith, "Italy Sotto Voce," ibid., 37:3 (Summer 1968):145-7; John Francis Lane, "A Case of Artistic Inflation," ibid., 32:3 (Summer 1963):130-5; ___, "The Face of '63: Italy," FILMS AND FILMING 9:7 (April 1963):11-21; ___, "Italy's Angry Young Directors," ibid., 15:1 (October 1968):74-80; ___, "A Style is Born," ibid., 5:7 (April 1959):13-5, 32; and Peter Bondanella, "Italy," WORLD CINEMA SINCE 1945, pp.347-79.

*Huss, Roy, ed. FOCUS ON "BLOW-UP." Englewood Cliffs: Prentice-Hall, 1971. Illustrated. 171pp.
     This valuable anthology of the film, in addition to a variety of critical reviews, includes an outline of the film, three sequences and shot analyses, and a filmography. Well worth browsing.

ATILIO BERTOLUCCI

Kline, T. Jefferson. BERTOLUCCI'S DREAM LOOM: A PSYCHOANALYTIC STUDY OF CINEMA. Amherst: University of Massachusetts Press, 1987. Illustrated. 206pp.

FEDERICO FELLINI

*Affron, Charles, ed. 8 1/2: FEDERICO FELLINI, DIRECTOR. New Brunswick: Rutgers University Press, 1987. Illustrated. 288pp.

Benderson, Albert Edward. CRITICAL APPROACHES TO FEDERICO FELLINI'S 8 1/2. New York: Arno Press, 1974. 239pp.

Boyer, Deena. THE TWO HUNDRED DAYS OF 8 1/2. Trans. Charles Lam Markmann. Afterword Dwight Macdonald. New York: The Macmillan Company, 1964. Illustrated. 218pp. New York: Garland Publishing, 1978. New Introduction Deena Boyer. Illustrated. 218pp.
     This diary of the day-by-day shooting of the film is a film buff's bargain, filled with anecdotes and behind-the-scenes stills.   Considering the movie, the book is lacking in depth and serious insights. Worth browsing.

*Grazzini, Giovanni, ed. FEDERICO FELLINI: COMMENTS ON FILM.   Trans. Joseph Henry. Carbondale: Southern Illinois University Press, 1989. Illustrated. 232pp.

Hughes, Eileen Lanouette.   ON   THE   SET   OF   FELLINI'S   SATYRICON: A BEHIND-THE-SCENES DIARY. New York: William Morrow and Company, 1971. Illustrated. 248pp.
     One of the best books of its kind, this fast-reading and entertaining account of the movie is a superb bedside companion and a useful source for behind-the-camera comments and details. Well worth browsing.

*Perry, Ted. FILMGUIDE TO "8 1/2." Bloomington: Indiana University Press, 1975. 89pp.

*Taylor, John Russell. CINEMA EYE CINEMA EAR: SOME KEY FILM-MAKERS OF THE SIXTIES. New York: Hill and Wang, 1964. 294pp.
     Here is a basic and valuable introduction to some of the best filmmakers: Antonioni, Bunuel, Bergman, Bresson, Hitchcock, Truffaut, and Godard. But the best essay is on Fellini. It is original, insightful, and essential. Well worth browsing.

*Fellini, Federico. LA DOLCE VITA. Trans. Oscar DeLiso and Bernard Shir-Cliff. New York: Ballantine Books, 1961. Illustrated. 276pp.

Fellini, Federico. JULIET OF THE SPIRITS. Ed. Tullio Kezich. Trans. Howard Greenfield. Transcription John Cohen. New York: Ballantine Books, 1966. Illustrated. 318pp.

*Fellini, Federico. THREE SCREENPLAYS: I VITELLONI/IL BIDONE/THE TEMPTATIONS OF DOCTOR ANTONIO. Trans. Judith Green. New York: The Orion Press, 1970. Illustrated. 287pp.

SERGIO LEONE

Cumbo, Robert C. ONCE UPON A TIME: THE FILMS OF SERGIO LEONE. Methuen: The Scarecrow Press, 1987. Illustrated. 266pp.[1141]

PIER PAOLA PASOLINI

Pasolini, Pier Paolo. HERETICAL EMPIRICISM. Ed. Louise K. Barnett. Trans. Ben Lawton and Louise K. Barnett. Bloomington: Indiana University Press, 1988. 319pp.

*Pasolini, Pier Paolo. OEDIPUS REX. Trans. John Mathews. New York: Simon and Schuster, 1971. Illustrated. 150pp.

*Pasolini, Pier Paolo. THE POETICS OF HERESY. Ed. Beverly Allen. Saratoga, Calif.: ANMA Libri and Company, 1982. Illustrated. 138pp.

*Pasolini, Pier Paolo. POEMS. Ed. and trans. Norman MacAfee, with Luciano Martinengo. Introduction Enzo Siciliano. New York: Vintage Books, 1982. 233pp.

Siciliano, Enzo. PASOLINI: A BIOGRAPHY. Trans. John Shepley. New York: Random House, 1982. Illustrated. 435pp.

Snyder, Stephen. PIER PAOLO PASOLINI. Boston: Twayne Publishers, 1980. Illustrated. 199pp.

*Stack, Oswald. PASOLINI ON PASOLINI: INTERVIEWS. Bloomington: Indiana University Press, 1969. Illustrated. 176pp.
    During two weeks in Rome in 1968, Stack interviewed the talented director and the results are a valuable collection of information on his career, theories, and filmography.[1142] Well worth browsing.

[1141] See Peter B. Flint, "Sergio Leone, 67, Italian Director Who Revitalized Westerns," NEW YORK TIMES B (May 1, 1989):8.

[1142] Roy Armes, "Pasolini," FILMS AND FILMING 17:9 (June 1971):55-58.

Van Watson, William. PIER PAOLO PASOLINI AND THE THEATRE OF THE WORD. Ann Arbor: UMI Research Press, 1989. 166pp.

GILLO PONTECORVO

*Mellen, Joan. FILMGUIDE TO "THE BATTLE OF ALGIERS." Bloomington: Indiana University Press, 1973. 82pp.

*Solinas, PierNico, ed. GILLO PONTECORVO'S "THE BATTLE OF ALGIERS": A FILM WRITTEN BY FRANCO SOLINAS. New York: Charles Scribner's Sons, 1973. Illustrated. 206pp.

LUCHINO VISCONTI

*Visconti, Luchino. THREE SCREENPLAYS: WHITE NIGHTS/ROCCO AND HIS BROTHERS/THE JOB. Trans. Judith Green. New York: The Orion Press, 1970. Illustrated. 313pp.

LINA WERTMULLER

Wertmuller, Lina. THE SCREENPLAYS OF LINA WERTMULLER: THE SEDUCTION OF MIMI, LOVE AND ANARCHY, SWEPT AWAY, SEVEN BEAUTIES. Trans. Steven Wagner. Introduction John Simon. New York: Quadrangle, 1977. Illustrated. 334pp.

FRANCO ZEFFIRELLI

Zeffirelli, Franco. ZEFFIRELLI: THE AUTOBIOGRAPHY OF FRANCO ZEFFIRELLI. London: Weidenfeld & Nicolson, 1986. Illustrated. 358pp.

FILMS

MICHELANGELO ANTONIONI

THE ADVENTURE/L'AVVENTURA (16mm: 1960, 145 mins., b/w, English subtitles, sound, R-FNC; S-FES, FNC, REE)
    Antonioni directed and co-authored with Elio Bartolini and Tonino Guerra (based on an original story by Antonioni) this unusual tale of an unsuccessful search for a lost friend. As Andrew Tudor points out, "A sense of the alienation of people from their environment and from each other is conveyed in every stark composition, in every camera movement."[1143] The film not only played a major role in the screen relationship of the director and his star, Monica Vitti, but also in Antonioni's future films about human paradoxes.[1144]

[1143] Andrew Tudor, "L'AVVENTURA," THE INTERNATIONAL DICTIONARY OF FILMS AND FILMMAKERS: VOLUME I, p.43

[1144] John Francis Lane, "Oh! Oh! Antonioni," FILMS AND FILMING 9:3 (December 1962):58-66.

BLOW-UP (MGM--16mm: 1966, 108 mins., color, sound, R-FNC, MGM)
    In his first English film, Antonioni explored different kinds of visual reality by focusing attention on a peculiar weekend in the life of a fashionable London photographer. The screenplay by Antonioni and Tonino Guerra (based on a short story by Julio Cortazar) reworked many of the thematic elements from THE ADVENTURE/L'AVVENTURA: e.g., the differences between perception and reality, the sense of alienation in contemporary life, and the distractions that occupy human beings. Strong performances are given by David Hemmings and Vanessa Redgrave.[1145]

RED DESERT/IL DESERTO ROSSO (Italy--16mm: 1964, 116 mins., color, English subtitles, sound, R-FNC)
    This is another clinical study, starring Monica Vitti, of a woman confused, trapped, and neurotic in an industrial society.[1146] Particularly important, as Peter Bondanella observes, the "color photography prempts the central function of traditional plot and character."[1147] In addition to being Antonioni's first color film, it was a fine example of how popular Italian "Art" films were becoming in the international market.

MARIO BELLOCCHIO

CHINA IS NEAR/LA CINA E VICINA (Italy--16mm: 1968, 108 mins., b/w, English subtitles, sound, R-COR, SWA)
    Typical of many Italian political filmmakers, Bellocchio has spent much of his career making films, directing stage plays, and working in TV. In his second film, co-scripted with Elda Tattloli (who also starred in the movie), the director told the story of an egocentric woman, her two brothers, and a dangerous romance. This revolutionary film about left-wing politics was temporarily banned in Italy.[1148] Today, as R. T. Witcombe notes, it "remains impressive for its verbal and visual humour and great clarity of psychological observation."[1149]

[1145] For more information, see Carey Harrison, "Blow-Up," SIGHT AND SOUND 36:2 (Spring 1967):60-2; Arthur Knight, "Blow-Up," FILM HERITAGE 2:3 (Spring 1967):3-6; Hubert Meeker, "Blow-Up," ibid., pp.7-15; Bosley Crowther, "Blow-Up," THE GREAT FILMS, pp.242-46; and Max Kozloff, "The Blow-Up," FILM QUARTERLY 20:3 (Spring 1967):28-31.

[1146] For more information, see Michele Manceaux, "In The RED DESERT," SIGHT AND SOUND 33:3 (Summer 1964):118-9; Richard Roud and Penelope Houston, "The RED DESERT," ibid., 34:2 (Spring 1965):76-81, 103; and Colin Young, "RED DESERT," FILM QUARTERLY 19:1 (Fall 1965):51-4.

[1147] "Italy," p.358.

[1148] For more information, see Claire Clouzot, "CHINA IS NEAR," FILM QUARTERLY 22:1 (Fall 1968):70-2; and William Starr et al., "Mario Bellocchio: An Interview," FILM SOCIETY REVIEW 7:5 (January 1972):33-40. The script is available from Grossman Publishers in New York.

[1149] R. T. Witcombe, THE NEW ITALIAN CINEMA: STUDIES IN DANCE AND DESPAIR (New York: Oxford University Press, 1982), p.46.

BERNARDO BERTOLUCCI

THE CONFORMIST/IL CONFORMISTA (Italy--16mm: 1970, 115 mins., color, English subtitles, sound, R-FNC)

In a tightly constructed film adapted from Alberto Moravia's novel, screenwriter-director Bertolucci magnificently manipulates time to show a fascist secret agent (Jean-Louis Trintignant) involved in three murders and his eventual reactions years later as he watches the end of the Fascist party in Italy.[1150] What we get, explains Jan Dawson, both visually and viscerally, "is a demonstration of how style, architectural and rhetorical, seduces intelligence."[1151]

VITTORIO DE SICA

THE GARDEN OF THE FINZI-CONTINIS/IL GIARDINO DEI FINZI-CONTINI (Italian-German--16mm: 1970, 103 mins., color, English subtitles, sound, R-FES)

Adapted from Giorgio Bassani's novel, De Sica's thoughtful and depressing film follows the adolescent love in the late 1930s of a middle-class Jewish boy (Lino Capolichio) for the aristocratic and beautiful Jewess, Micol (Dominique Sanda). Neither the boy's parents nor the wealthy Finzi-Continis family can avoid at the end their eventual arrest by Mussolini's Fascist government. In between we are shown a remarkable recreation of a frightening era which might yet occur again. It won the 1971 Oscar for Best Foreign Film.

TWO WOMEN (16mm: 1961, 105 mins., b/w, English subtitles, sound, R-FNC)

Scripted by Cesare Zavattini and Vittorio De Sica (and based on Alberto Moravia's 1957 novel LA CIOCIARA), this film deals with a widow (Sophia Loren) and her teenage daughter (Eleonora Brown) who try desperately to stay alive in Italy toward the end of World War II. De Sica's direction stresses the human problems that confront the lonely woman as she struggles to be both a parent and a provider. Loren won the Oscar for the year's Best Actress.

FEDERICO FELLINI

THE SWEET LIFE/LA DOLCE VITA (Italy--16mm: 1961, 180 mins., b/w, English subtitles, sound, R-FES, FNC)

In its initial release, this was a sensational and significant expose of Roman high society that centered on the news-gathering activities of a scandal magazine reporter (Marcello Mastroianni) searching for smut. Scripted by Fellini, Ennio Flaiano, Tullio Pinelli, and Brunello Rondi, this satirical work took aim at the values and behavior of the PAPARAZZI (photographers) as they hound celebrities and expoit their human failings. Nominated for four Oscars, including Best Director, Best Screenplay Written

---

[1150] For more information, see Richard Roud, "Fathers and Sons," SIGHT AND SOUND 40:2 (Spring 1971):60-4; Marilyn Goldin, "Bertolucci on THE CONFORMIST," ibid., pp.64-6; and Amos Vogel, "Bernardo Bertolucci: An Interview," FILM COMMENT 7:3 (Fall 1971):24-9.

[1151] Jan Dawson, "CONFORMISTA, IL (THE CONFORMIST)," MONTHLY FILM BULLETIN 38:455 (December 1971):238.

Directly for the Screen, and Best Black-and-White Art Direction-Set Direction (Piero Gherardi), it won for Best Black-and-White Costume Design (Piero Gheradi).[1152]

8 1/2/OTTO E MEZZO (Italy--16mm: 1963, 135 mins., b/w, plus color, English subtitles, sound, R-AUD)

This extraordinary autobiographical film explores the psychological and actual world of a famous Italian film director (Marcello Mastroianni) who seeks rest at a spa as he is preparing for a new movie. Scripted by Fellini, Ennio Flaiano, Tullio Pinelli, and Brunello Rondi, this visually brilliant film remains not only Fellini's most discussed film, but also a magnificent commentary on filmmaking. Critics continually debate the merits of the filmmaker's camerawork and thematic preoccupations. Fellini explains the work by saying, "It seems to me that this must be my MYTHOS: to try and throw off my back the upbringing I have had; that is to say, to try and uneducate myself in order to recapture a virginal availability and a new type of personal, individual education."[1153] Nominated for three Oscars, including Best Director and Best Screenplay Written Directly for the Screen, it won for Best Black-and-White Costume Design (Piero Gheradi).

FELLINI SATYRICON (Italy--16mm: 1969, 136 mins., color, English subtitles, sound, R-MGM)

In this stunning commentary on one man's struggle to survive, Fellini follows the adventures of a young and serious Roman (Martin Potter) who faces death-defying challenges successfully because he understands his own strengths and weaknesses[1154] Scripted by Fellini and Bernardino Zapponi, this depiction of the excesses of ancient Rome, as Mike Wellington observes, "attains neither analytical depth nor polemical pointedness but rests more metaphysically on the destiny of wounded conscience."[1155] Fellini lost the Oscar for Best Director to Franklin J. Schaffner (PATTON).

PIER PAOLO PASOLINI

THE GOSPEL ACCORDING TO ST. MATTHEW/IL VANGELO SECONDO MATTEO (France--16mm: 1964, 136 mins., b/w, dubbed, sound R-BUD, COR, FES, FNC, IMA, KIT; S-FES, REE)

Told in the CINEMA VERITE style, this Biblical depiction of Jesus (Enrique Irazoqui) as a magnificent revolutionary figure remains one of the most stunning religious films ever made. In defending himself against charges that the movie is a Marxist picture, the screenwriter-director states, "My film is a reaction against the

---

[1152] Joseph McBride, "The Director as Superstar," SIGHT AND SOUND 41:2 (Spring 1972):78-81.

[1153] Cited in *Ted Perry, FILMGUIDE TO "8 1/2." Bloomington: Indiana University Press, 1975), p.5.

[1154] For some useful perspectives, see Joseph O'Mealy, "Fellini Satyricon: A Structural Analysis," FILM HERITAGE 6:4 (Summer 1971):25-9; and Marsha Kinder and Beverle Houston, "SATYRICON," CLOSE-UP: A CRITICAL PERSPECTIVE ON FILM (New York: Harcourt Brace Jovanovich, Inc., 1972), pp.313-9.

[1155] Mike Wellington, "FELLINI-SATYRICON," MONTHLY FILM BULLETIN 37 (October 1970):200.

conformity of Marxism. The mystery of life and death and of suffering--and particularly of religion--is something Marxists do not want to consider."[1156]

GILLO PONTECORVO

THE BATTLE OF ALGIERS/LA BATTAGLIA DI ALGERI (Italy--16mm: 1967, 120 mins., b/w, English subtitles, sound, R-FNC, TFF; S-TFF)
   This extremely powerful film of the Algerian uprising against the French between 1954 and 1957 is a model for mixing documentary technique with a fictional narrative. Scripted by Pontecorvo and Franco Solinas, it represents the screenwriter-director's feelings about oppression not only in Algeria but throughout the Third World. As Joan Mellon points out, "Pontecorvo's approach to the political and ideological realities of the Algerian War is lyrical rather than analytical. He is not concerned with providing a how-to primer of urban guerrilla warfare, as some black revolutionary groups have concluded, but rather with presenting the example of the Algerians to inspire oppressed peoples."[1157] The film was nominated for two Oscars: Best Director and Best Story and Screenplay Written Directly for the Screen.

BURN! (United Artists--16mm: 1970, 115 mins., color, sound, R-MGM)
   In this fascinating attempt to make a contemporary statement on black Caribbean heritage and the modern struggle for freedom, Pontecorvo tells a mid-ninteeth-century story of a Caribbean Bolivar (Evaristo Marquez) who is first used and then destroyed by a British secret agent (Marlon Brando).[1158]

JAPAN

BOOKS

*Desser, David. EROS PLUS MASSACRE: AN INTRODUCTION TO THE JAPANESE NEW WAVE CINEMA. Bloomington: Indiana University Press, 1988. Illustrated. 239pp..[1159]

[1156] Cited in Stephen Snyder, PIER PAOLO PASOLINI (Boston: Twayne Publishers, 1980), p.59. For other perspectives, see Pier Paolo Pasolini, "The Cinema of Poetry," CAHIERS DU CINEMA IN ENGLISH CDC #171 (October 1965):34-43; "Pier Paolo Pasolini: An Epical-Religious View of the World," FILM QUARTERLY 18:4 (Summer 1965):31-45; and James Blue, "Pier Paolo Pasolini: An Interview," FILM COMMENT 3:4 (Fall 1965):24-32.

[1157] *Joan Mellen, FILMGUIDE TO "THE BATTLE OF ALGIERS." Bloomington: Indiana University Press, 1973), p.24. See also Marsha Kinder and Beverle Houston, "THE BATTLE OF ALGIERS," CLOSE-UP: A CRITICAL PERSPECTIVE ON FILM, pp.332, 334-37.

[1158] David Wilson, "Politics and Pontecorvo," SIGHT AND SOUND 40:3 (Summer 1971):160-1.

[1159] The following articles are helpful: Donald Richie, "Japan: The Younger Talents," SIGHT AND SOUND 29:2 (Spring 1960):78-81; ___, "A Personal Record," FILM QUARTERLY 14:1 (Fall 1960):20-30; ___, "The Face of '63: Japan," FILMS AND FILMING 9:10 (July 1963):15-8, 35-6; S. K. Oberbeck, "Samurai to Shomin-geki," NEWSWEEK 124 (May 11, 1970):96-8; James Blue, "Susumu Hani," FILM COMMENT 5:2 (Spring 1969):24-36; William Johnson, "Ichikawa and the Wanderers," ibid., 11:5

FILMS

KON ICHIKAWA

TOKYO OLYMPIAD/TOKYO ORIMPIKKU (Japan--16mm: 1965, 93 mins., color, sound, R-FNC)
     This extraordinary sports film stresses the humanity, rather than the competitive nature, of the 1964 Olympic Games. The people who financed the project were incensed at Ichikawa's neglect of the athletic drama, while scholars and serious film students marvel at the director's wry look at the events and participants. "Whereas Leni Riefenstahl crafted her 1936 OLYMPIA to thrill viewers with the individual victor's triumph of will," comments Georgia Brown, "TOKYO OLYMPIAD uses its own splendid widescreen cinematography to defeat our usual lust for victory."[1160] Unfortunately, the only circulating print is this considerably shortened version. Nevertheless, one can still admire the director's unique blend of comedy and drama in depicting the athletes' humanity.

HIROSHI TESHIGAHARA

WOMAN IN THE DUNES/SUNA NO ONNA (Japan--16mm: 1964, 130 mins., b/w, English subtitles, sound, R-BUD, COR, IMA, WHO)
     Based upon Kobo Abe's allegorical novel, this haunting film explores one man's values of life, freedom, and love as he is held prisoner with a woman at the bottom of a sandpit in a remote desert area. "To the Western youth audience of the 1960s," David Desser explains, "when the film achieved its cult status, the film encapsulated their own feelings of meaninglessness and entrapment."[1161]

LATIN AMERICA

BOOKS

*Burns, E. Bradford. LATIN AMERICA CINEMA: FILM AND HISTORY. Los Angeles: UCLA Latin American Center, 1975. Illustrated. 137pp.

*Burton, Julianne. THE NEW LATIN AMERICAN CINEMA--AN ANNOTATED BIBLIOGRAPHY OF SOURCES IN ENGLISH, SPANISH, AND PORTUGESE: 1960-1980.

(September-October 1975):16-20; Kyoko Hirano, "Japan," WORLD CINEMA SINCE 1945, pp.380-423; Vincent Canby, "Japan: Bullish on Pandas and Pets," NEW YORK TIMES H (November 6, 1988):11, 20; ___, "Japan's Best Movies Don't Travel Well," ibid., H (November 11, 1988):1, 13; and ___, "What's So Funny About Japan? THE NEW YORK TIMES MAGAZINE (June 18, 1989):26-8, 42

[1160] Georgia Brown, "It's How You Play the Game," VILLAGE VOICE (August 2, 1988):64.

[1161] EROS PLUS MASSACRE: AN INTRODUCTION TO THE JAPANESE NEW WAVE CINEMA, p.78. For another perspective, see Judith Shatnoff, "Woman In The Dunes," FILM QUARTERLY 18:2 (Winter 1964):43-6.

New York: Smyrna Press, 1983. 80pp.[1162]

MEXICO

BOOKS

*Mora, Carl J. MEXICAN CINEMA: REFLECTIONS OF A SOCIETY 1896-1980. Berkeley: University of California Press, 1982. Illustrated. 287pp.[1163]

Nevares, Beatriz Reyes. THE MEXICAN CINEMA: INTERVIEWS WITH THIRTEEN DIRECTORS. Introduction E. Bradford Burns. Trans. Carl J. Mora and Elizabeth Gard. Alburquerque: The University of New Mexico Press, 1976. Illustrated. 176pp.

MIDDLE EAST

BOOKS

Landau, Jacob M. STUDIES IN THE ARAB THEATER AND CINEMA.   Philadelphia: University of Pennsylvania Press, 1958. Illustrated. 290pp.[1164]

McClintock, Marsha Hamilton. THE MIDDLE EAST AND NORTH AFRICA ON FILM: AN ANNOTATED FILMOGRAPHY. New York: Garland Press, 1982. 542pp.

*Sadoul, George. THE CINEMA IN THE ARAB COUNTRIES. Beirut: Interarab Centre of Cinema & Television, 1966. 310pp.

THE NETHERLANDS

BOOKS

Cowie, Peter. DUTCH CINEMA: AN ILLUSTRATED HISTORY. South Brunswick: A.

[1162] For addition information, see Daniel Appleman, "A Bibliography of Latin American Cinema," JOURNAL OF THE UNIVERSITY FILM ASSOCIATION 28:2 (Spring 1976):41-7; Julianne Burton, "Latin America: On the Periphery of the Periphery," WORLD CINEMA SINCE 1945, pp.424-46; and Howard Dratch and Barbara Margolis, "Film and Revolution in Nicaragua: An Interview With Incine Filmmakers, CINEASTE 15:3 (1987):27-9.

[1163] For useful articles, see Manuel Michel, "Mexican Cinema: A Panoramic View," trans. Neal Oxenhandler, FILM QUARTERLY 18:4 (Summer 1965):46-55; Jesus Salvador Trevino, "The New Mexican Cinema," ibid., and Dennis West, "Mexico: From the Golden Age to the Present," WORLD CINEMA SINCE 1945, pp.447-65.

[1164] For some useful articles, see Miriam Rosen, "Festivals," CINEASTE 15:4 (1987):30-1; and Lizabeth Malkmus, "The 'New' Egyptian Cinema: Adapting Genre Conventions to a Changing Society," ibid., 16:3 (1988):30-3.

S. Barnes and Company, 1979. Illustrated. 154pp.[1165]

POLAND

BOOKS

GENERAL

*Michatek, Bolestaw, and Frank Turaj. THE MODERN CINEMA OF POLAND. Bloomington: Indiana University Press, 1988. Illustrated. 205pp.[1166]

ROMAN POLANSKI

*Butler, Ivan. THE CINEMA OF ROMAN POLANSKI. New York: A. S. Barnes and Company, 1970. Illustrated. 192pp.

Kiernan, Thomas. THE ROMAN POLANSKI STORY. New York: Delilah/Grove Press, 1980. Illustrated. 262pp.

Leaming, Barbara. POLANSKI: THE FILMMAKER AS A VOYEUR--A BIOGRAPHY. New York: Simon and Schuster, 1981. Illustrated. 220pp.

Polanski, Roman. POLANSKI BY POLANSKI. New York: William Morrow and Company, 1984. Illustrated. 461pp.

*Polanski, Roman. POLANSKI: THREE FILM SCRIPTS--KNIFE IN THE WATER, REPULSION, CUL-DE-SAC. Introduction Boleslaw Sulik. New York: Harper & Row, 1975. Illustrated. 214pp.

FILMS

ROMAN POLANSKI

KNIFE IN THE WATER/NOZ W WODZIE (Poland--16mm: 1962, 95 mins., b/w, English subtitles, sound, R-BUD, EMG, FES, FNC, IMA, KIT, ROA; S-FES, IMA, REE, TFF)

[1165] For some useful articles, see Peter Cowie, "Dutch Films," FILM QUARTERLY 19:2 (Winter 1965-66):41-6; and Elaine Mancini, "The Netherlands," WORLD CINEMA SINCE 1945, pp.466-75.

[1166] The following articles are helpful: David Stewart Hull, "New Films From Poland," FILM QUARTERLY 14:3 (Spring 1961):24-29; Mira Coopman, "Report From Poland," FILMS AND FILMING 10:4 (January 1964):47-51; Lawrence Weschler, "Poland's Banned Films," CINEASTE 13:3 (1984):11; David Paul, "The Esthetics of Courage," ibid., 14:4 (1986):16-22; Annette Insdorf, "For Polish Film, A Mood of Cautious Optimism," NEW YORK TIMES H (July 23, 1989):20; and John Mosier, "Poland," WORLD CINEMA SINCE 1945, pp.476-89.

Scripted by Polanski (born Jerzy [Yurek] Skolimowski) and Jakub Goldberg, the story focuses on a couple having marital problems who pick up a hitchhiker and take him for a weekend on their yacht. The director Polanski develops this simple relationship into a tightly knit film filled with tension, sexual symbolism, and meaningful personal relationships. Commenting on the filmmaker's impressive and controversial feature film debut, Ivan Butler takes issue with critics who objected to Polanski's detached style: "But the mere fact that he refrains from soliciting our sympathy and directing it toward any particular one of his three characters, and yet has us, by the end of the story, deeply interested, involved in their situation . . . is a surer sign of 'compassion' than any easy loading of the scales would be."[1167] The film was nominated for the Best Foreign Film of 1963, but lost to 8 1/2/OTTO E MEZZO.

ANDRZEJ WAJDA

ASHES AND DIAMONDS/POPIOL I DIAMENT (Poland--16mm: 1959, 105 mins., b/w, English subtitles, sound, R-FNC, JAN)

Rarely has anyone been as effective as Wajda in capturing the the disillusionment and horror that follow a town's revenge on its former Quislings. Collaborating with screenwriter Jerzy Andrzejewski (who adapted his novel for the conclusion of Wajda's trilogy), he used the recent political turmoil in Poland to provide a historical perspective on the surrender of the Germans and the first day of Peace in his homeland on May 8th, 1945. The film is particularly effective in showing how the times destroy a young idealist (Zbigniew Cybulski) in war-torn Poland.[1168] "If Wajda succeeded in ASHES AND DIAMOND in articulating the popular feeling," writes Boleslaw Sulik, "the emotional contradictions of his time, his debt to Cybluski [who identified totally with his character] is incalculabe."[1169]

KANAL/SEWER (Poland--16mm: 1957, 96 mins., b/w, English subtitles, sound, R-JAN)

Scripted by Jerzy Stefan (and based on his short story), this grim film traces the parallels between discouraged soldiers existing in Poland's sewers and the nation's personal dejection. Wajda focuses on the courage of the home army as it tries to combat both the physical and emotional horrors in the last years of World War II. "Made with overpowering visual force," Bolestaw Michatek explains, "KANAL straddles a gulf between the realism of actual events with characters who are reasonably faithful

---

[1167] *Ivan Butler, THE CINEMA OF ROMAN POLANSKI (New York: A. S. Barnes, 1970), p.42. See also Michel Delahaye and Jean-Andre Fieschi, "Landscape of a Mind: Interview With Roman Polanski," CAHIERS DU CINEMA IN ENGLISH 3, CdC #175 (February 1966):28-35; Harrison Engle, "Roman Polanski In New York," FILM COMMENT 5:1 (Fall 1968):4-11; Gordon Gow, "Satisfaction--A Most Unpopular Feeling," FILMS AND FILMING 15:7 (April 1969):15-8; and Krzysztof-Teodor Toeplitz, "Jerzy Skolimowski: Portrait of a Debutant Director," FILM QUARTERLY 26:2 (Fall 1967):25-31.

[1168] Eric Rhode, "Andrzej Wajda," TOWER OF BABEL, pp.171-90. For related material, see Annette Insdorf, "Andrzej Wajda, Director With Double Vision," NEW YORK TIMES H (July2, 1989):5, 29.

[1169] *Boleslaw Sulik, "Introduction," THREE FILMS OF WAJDA: ASHES AND DIAMONDS/ A GENERATION/ KANAL (New York: Simon and Schuster, 1973), p.25.

portraits of the mentality and attitudes of the time, and an almost abstract vision of a sealed world whose inhabitants are doomed to extinction."[1170]

SOVIET UNION

BOOKS

GENERAL

Dolmatovskaya, Galina, and Irina Shilova. WHO'S WHO IN THE SOVIET CINEMA: SEVENTY DIFFERENT PORTRAITS. Trans. L. Shakanov, ed. Vladislav Kostin. Chicago: Imported Publications, 1979. Illustrated. 685pp.

A reference guide to contemporary Soviet filmmaking, the book is divided into two main sections. The first part, compiled by Dolmatovskaya, lists thirty-five directors and provides biographical data, professional development, critical commentary, and a filmography. Included as well are a few illustration's from the subject's films, plus a snapshot picture of the director. The second part, compiled by Shilova, lists the performers alphabetically and provides similar information. The writing itself is on a film buff level. Until more detailed information appears, this interesting volume is an important resource. Recommended for special collections.

Golovskoy, Val S., with John Rimberg. BEHIND THE SOVIET SCREEN: THE MOTION-PICTURE INDUSTRY IN THE USSR 1972-1982. Trans. Steven Hill. Ann Arbor: Ardis, 1986. 144pp.

The best contemporary evaluation on the day-to-day operations of the Soviet cinema, this succinct study traces not only the process of filmmaking from pre-production to post-production planning, but also examines the role of government, unions, and personalities in the structure of the film industry. Particular attention is paid to the role of Goskino in Moscow in the book's ten interesting chapters. Rimberg, in an afterword, points out that production in the Soviet Union stands at an all-time high, with nearly 150 movies produced annually. He also notes that "there is no film industry person in the Soviet Union who is really among the governing elite--no Ronald Reagan equivalent." Moreover, he finds the modern film industry operation on a three-prong model of party-filmmakers-audience. "The Communist Party," he explains, "has power over resources, positions and personnel, especially 'at the top.' The film-makers have talent, knowledge of their craft, and professional dedication, all sources of power. The film audiences, especially the 20 percent of the population which accounts for 80 percent of the ticket sales, have discretionary time and money, a willingness to suspend disbelief and the reality principle and the desire to keep their eyes open in the presence of a motion picture on the screen." Ten appendexes are included, but regrettably no index. Well worth browsing.[1171]

[1170] *Bolestaw Michatek, THE CINEMA OF ANDRZEJ WAJDA, trans. Edward Rothert. (South Brunswick: A. S. Barnes and Company, 1973), p.29.

[1171] Some useful articles on contemporary Soviet films are the following: Nina Hibbin, "Ivan The Magnificent," FILMS AND FILMING 9:5 (February 1963):56-61; ___, "See No Evil," ibid., 12:5 (February 1966):43-6; ___, "Living on with Lenin," ibid., 16:10 (July 1970):25-26; Peter Baker, "The Other Side of the Curtain," ibid., 7:6 (March 1961):8-9, 34; Peter John Dyer, "Russian Youth in an Uproar," ibid., 5:11 (August 1959):12-4, 32-33; Sergei Gerasimov, "Socialist Realism and the Soviet Cinema," ibid., 5:3 (December 1958):11-2, 33; Y. Varshavsky, "From

ANDREY TARKOVSKY

Tarkovsky, Andrey. SCULPTING IN TIME: REFLECTIONS ON THE CINEMA. Trans.
Kitty Hunter-Blair. New York: Alfred A. Knopf, 1987. Illustrated. 256pp.

SPAIN

BOOKS

Schwartz, Ronald. SPANISH FILM DIRECTORS (1950-1985): 21 PROFILES. Metuchen:
THe Scarecrow Press, 1986. Illustrated. 253pp.[1172]

SWEDEN

BOOKS

INGMAR BERGMAN

Bergman, Ingmar. THE MAGIC LANTERN: AN AUTOBIOGRAPHY. Trans. Joan Tate.
New York: Viking, 1988. Illustrated. 308pp.
    Born in Uppsala, Sweden[1173] on July 14, 1918, Ingmar Bergman's father was a
stern Lutheran clergyman whose religious teachings and behavior had a profound

---

Generation to Generation," ibid., 13:11 (August 1967):42-46; Vladimir Baskakov,
"After The Revolution," ibid., 16:1 (October 1969):62-8; John Gillett, "Between
The Acts," SIGHT AND SOUND 25:4 (Spring 1956):201-4; Cynthia Grenier, "Soviet
Cinema: The New Way," ibid., 27:5 (Summer 1958):236-37; Robert Vas, "Sunflowers
and Commissars," ibid., 31:3 (Summer 1962):148-51; John Gillett, "Round About
Moscow," ibid., 32:4 (Autumn 1963):987-9; David Robinson, "Russia Revisited,"
ibid., 29:2 (Spring 1960):70-75; Joseph L. Anderson, "Soviet Films Since
1945--Part One," FILMS IN REVIEW 4:1 (January 1953):7-14; ___, "Soviet Films
Since 1945--Part Two," ibid., 4:2 (February 1953):64-73; Stephen P. Hlll, "Soviet
Film Criticism," FILM QUARTERLY 14:1 (Fall 1960):31-40; ---, "The Soviet Film
Today," ibid., 20:4 (Summer 1967):33-52; Felicity Barringer, "Glasnost in Wide
Screen: Hush, Hush, Old Stalinist," NEW YORK TIMES A (November 25, 1988:1, 8;
___, "Soviet Documentaries that Face Up to Reality," ibid., C (March 29,
1989):17; Glenn Collins, "Soviet Actress Talks About Sex and Symbolism," ibid.,
c (March 30, 1989):17; Kathleen R. Conniff, "Soviet Directors Mix Illusion and
Reality," ibid., H (July 16, 1989):5-6; Louis Menashe, "Glasnost In the Soviet
Union," CINEASTE 16:1-2 (1987-88):28-33; and Leo Hecht, "Union of Soviet
Socialist Republics," WORLD CINEMA SINCE 1945, pp.558-86.

[1172] For some useful articles, see Juan Cobos, "The Decade: Spain," FILMS AND FILMING
9:4 (January 1963):67-71; ___, "The Face of '63: The Spanish Influence," ibid.,
10:1 (October 1963):39-43; Virginia Higginbotham, "Spain: Spanish Film Under
Franco--Do Not Disturb," WORLD CINEMA SINCE 1945, pp.499-513; and David E. Pitt,
"Films Reflect a Brash New Spain," NEW YORK TIMES H (September 18, 1988):1, 28.

[1173] For some useful articles on modern Swedish cinema, see Vernon Young, "After
Bergman," SIGHT AND SOUND 32:2 (Spring 1963):96-9; Peter Cowie, "Swedish Films
at Sorrento," FILM COMMENT 6:2 (Summer 1970):22-5; Frederic Fleischer, "Export
or Die," ibid., pp.36-7, Rune Waldekranz, "Young Swedish Cinema: In Relation to

effect not only on Bergman's life, but also on his films. Growing up a sickly, insecure, and neurotic child, he often turned to Swedish literature for inspiration and serenity. It was during his stay at Stockholm University (1938-1940) that he decided to pursue a career in drama. Developing his stage skills first in student productions and then moving into AVANT-GARDE theater and opera, Bergman also took advantage of the screenwriting program initiated by SVENSK FILMINDUSTRI in the early 1940s. His first screen credit was for TORMENT/FRENZY/HETS (1944). More important was the significant relationship he developed with the film's director, Alf Sjoberg. From the mid-1940s until the mid-1980s, Bergman divided his time among films, stage plays, and operas. In each area, his temper tantrums, often bizarre moods, and frequent callous treatment of cast and crew made him an artist not only respected but feared. Starting in the seventies, he became inolved with television productions. By the end of World War II, Bergman was a well-known theater director, a respected screenwriter, and an emerging film director (he had made his debut with the 1946 film CRISIS/KRIS). His first critically acclaimed international film was THE CLOWN'S EVENING/THE NAKED NIGHT/SAWDUST AND TINSEL/GYCKLARNAS AFTON (1953). His first commercially successful international film was SMILES OF A SUMMER NIGHT/SOMMARNATTENS LEENDE (1955). Over his distinguished career, he has made more than fifty films, including such masterpieces as THE SEVENTH SEAL/DET SJUNDE INSEGLET, WILD STRAWBERRIES/SMULTRONSTALLET (both in 1957), THE MAGICIAN/THE FACE/ANSIKTET (1958), THE VIRGIN SPRING/JUNGFRUKALLAN (1959), THROUGH A GLASS DARKLY/SASOM I EN SPEGEL (1961), THE SILENCE/TYSTNADEN (1962), PERSONA (1966), SHAME/SKAMMEN (1968), and CRIES AND WHISPERS/VISKNINGAR OCH ROP (1973). His final film was the brilliant FANNY AND ALEXANDER/FANNY OCH ALEXANDER (1982). In addition to relying heavily on the cinematography of Sven Nykvist (Bergman's constant cameraman since 1963), the great filmmaker has often relied on a select group of performers: e.g., Bibi Andersson, Harriet Andersson, Gunnar Bjornstrand, Max von Sydow, Ingril Thulin, and Liv Ullmann.

Bergman's eloquent personal account of his turbulent childhood, his stormy careers in theater, opera, television, and films, his feelings about art and human relationships, and his five wives is fascinating from start to finish.[1174] A chronology by Peter Cowie and an index are included. Highly recommended for special collections.

Swedish Film Tradition," ibid., pp.38-43; Ann Morrissett, "The Swedish Paradox," SIGHT AND SOUND 30:4 (Autumn 1961):192-4, 207; ---, "Sweden: Paradise or Paradox," FILM QUARTERLY 15:1 (Fall 1961):22-9; Frederick J. Marker and Lise-Lone Marker, "Sweden: Past and Present," WORLD CINEMA SINCE 1945, pp.514-41; and Jorn Donner, "The Rule of Nobody: Myth and Reality In Swedish Cinema," CHAPLIN/25th Anniversary Issue (194):79-83.

[1174] The following articles are helpful: Erik Ulrichsen, "Ingmar Bergman and the Devil," SIGHT AND SOUND 27:5 (Summer 1958):224-30; Jean-Luc Godard, "Bergmanorama," CAHIERS DU CINEMA IN ENGLISH I, CdC #85 (January 1966):56-62; Ingmar Bergman, "The Serpent's Skin," ibid., II, CdC #188 (March 1967):24-9; Jean-Louis Comolli, "The Phantom of Personality," ibid., pp.30-3; Birgitta Steene, "Images and Words In Ingmar Bergman's Films," CINEMA JOURNAL 10:1 (Fall 1970):23-33; ___, "The Isolated Hero of Ingmar Bergman," FILM COMMENT 3:2 (Spring 1965):68-78; Ingmar Bergman, "My Three Powerfully Effective Commandments," trans. P. E. Burke and Lennart Swahn, ibid., 6:2 (Summer 1970):8-20; David Madden, "THE VIRGIN SPRING: Anatomy of a Mythic Image," FILM HERITAGE 2:2 (Winter 1966-67):2-20; Robert Rossen, "The Relationship of Ingmar Bergman to E. T. A. Hoffmann," ibid., 6:1 (Spring 1970):26-31; Eugene Archer, "The Rock of Life," FILMS IN REVIEW 12:4 (Summer 1959):3-16; Jerry Vermilye, "An Ingmar Bergman Film Index," ibid., 12:5 (May 1961):280-92; Art Carduner, "Nobody Has Any Fun in Bergman's Movies," FILM SOCIETY REVIEW 7:5 (January 1972):27-32; Maaret Koskinen, "The Typically Swedish In Ingmar Bergman," CHAPLIN/25th Anniversary Issue (1984):5-11; Egil Tornqvist, "The Little World and the Big:

*Bergman, Ingmar. FOUR SCREENPLAYS OF INGMAR BERGMAN: SMILES OF A SUMMER NIGHT/THE SEVENTH SEAL/WILD STRAWBERRIES/THE MAGICIAN. Trans. Lars Malstrom and David Kushner. New York: Secker and Warburg. 1960. Illustrated. 384pp. New York: Garland Publishing, 1985. 384pp.

In the preface to this valuable publication, Carl Anders Dymling, the president of SVENSK FILMINDUSTRI and one of Bergman's three noted producers (the other two are Lorens Marmstedt and Rune Waldekranz), explains how he was responsible for bringing the filmmaker into the movie business in 1942. Bergman than follows with introductory comments on the art of the film. Well worth browsing.

*Bergman, Ingmar. SCENES FROM A MARRIAGE. Trans. Alan Blair. New York: Bantam Books, 1974. Illustrated. 213pp.

Bergman provides an introduction to the six scenes in this powerful 1973 made-for-TV film. Well worth browsing.

*Bergman, Ingmar. FACE TO FACE. Trans. Alan Blair. New York: Pantheon Books, 1976. Illustrated. 118pp.

The publication includes Bergman's letter to the cast and crew prior to their beginning production on the 1976 made-for-TV film. Well worth browsing.

*Bergman, Ingmar. FOUR STORIES: "THE TOUCH," "CRIES AND WHISPERS," "THE HOUR OF THE WOLF," AND "THE PASSION OF ANNA." Trans. Alan Blair. Garden City: Anchor Press/Doubleday, 1976. Illustrated. 168pp.

A wonderful example of how Bergman first writes a short story or a novella and then circulates it among the people who are going to collaborate on the proposed film. Recommended for special collections.

*Bergman, Ingmar. THE SERPENT'S EGG. Trans. Alan Blair. New York: Pantheon Books, 1977. Illustrated. 124pp.

*Bergman, Ingmar. FROM THE LIFE OF THE MARIONETTES. Trans. Alan Blair. New York: Pantheon Books, 1980. Illustrated. 99pp.

*Bergman, Ingmar. FANNY AND ALEXANDER. Trans. Alan Blair. New York: Pantheon Books, 1982. Illustrated. 217pp.

Although it contains no introductory material, this publication of the screenplay of Bergman's last and most ambitious film provides a good opportunity to review the filmmaker's thoughts about his childhood, his parents, and religion. The world of reality and imagination created in the film is lost on the printed page, but not the underlying themes of the film. Recommended for special collections.

Bergom-Larsson, Maria. INGMAR BERGMAN AND SOCIETY. Trans. Barrie Saleman. South Brunswick: A. S. Barnes and Company, 1978. Illustrated. 127pp.

Concerning Ingmar Bergman's FANNY AND ALEXANDER," ibid., pp.12-20; and SPECIAL ISSUE ON BERGMAN, ibid., (1984).

*Bjorkman, Stig, et al. BERGMAN ON BERGMAN: INTERVIEWS WITH BERGMAN. Trans. Paul Britten Austin. New York: Simon and Schuster, 1973. Illustrated. 288pp.

Based upon a series of separate four hour interviews with Bergman from January 1968 to April 1970, this book contains the filmmaker's comments on his life and films. The fifty hours of conversation range from pleasant reflections to genuine insights into Bergman's films. A filmography and index are included. Well worth browsing.

Blake, Richard Aloysius. THE LUTHERAN MILIEU OF THE FILMS OF INGMAR BERGMAN. New York: Arno Press, 1978. 333pp.

Originally written as Blake's 1972 Ph.D. dissertation for Northwestern University, this study compares the work of Ingmar Bergman to that of Martin Luther's. "The fact that both men have produced an immense amount," Blake explains, "does not facilitate matters, since both resist fossilized concepts and both struggle to develop their ideas from one work to the next. Luther, for his part, thinks in terms of antitheses, like faith and love, man condemned and man justified, freedom and bondage, and although he himself keeps alive the precarious balance in his own thought, he is easily quoted out of context as holding a lopsided position. Indeed, in various circumstances he does stress different sides of his paradoxes. Bergman, on the other hand, subordinates his philosophical position to the demands of drama, with the result that his ideas are not as clearly articulated as a textbook proposition. Like Luther, his ideas show the mark of development from the 'angry young man' phase of his youth to the present, when as an artist of international reputation he enjoys the benefits of his society and freedom from critical and financial adversity." Blake divides his study into seven sections: an introduction reviewing the history and relationship among the Church, Sweden, Bergman, and Luther; five chapters on "Sin and Guilt: A Philosophy of Man," "Silence and Wrath: An Understanding of God," "Faith and Reconciliation: Man's Way to God," "Love and Sexuality: Man's Need for Man," and "Society and Institutions: Man's Relationship to Men"; and a summary chapter. A filmography and bibliography are included, but no index is provided. Well worth browsing.

*Cowie, Peter. INGMAR BERGMAN: A MONOGRAPH, MOTION 4 (March 1962).

This is a brief sketch of Bergman's life, with a commentary that shows the regard that many people have for the great Swedish director. Worth browsing.

Cowie, Peter. INGMAR BERGMAN: A CRITICAL BIOGRAPHY. New York: Simon and Schuster, 1983. Illustrated. 397pp.

*Donner, Jorn. THE PERSONAL VISION OF INGMAR BERGMAN. Trans. Holger Lundbergh. Bloomington: Indiana University Press, 1966. Illustrated. 276pp. Retitled THE FILMS OF INGMAR BERGMAN: FROM "TORMENT" TO "ALL THESE WOMEN." New York: Dover Publications, 1972. Illustrated. 276pp.

A critical analysis by a Swedish critic on Bergman's existential tendencies in filmmaking, the study's major drawback is the eclectic organization of its examination of the filmmaker's work. The material is arranged chronologically, covering the years from 1944 to 1964, and the emphasis is on Bergman's ideas and techniques in his major films. Plot summaries, thematic concerns, and specific influences on the filmmaker throughout his life are provided in eleven highly speculative chapters. A bibliography and index are included. Well worth browsing.

*Gado, Frank. THE PASSION OF INGMAR BERGMAN. Durham: Duke University Press, 1986. Illustrated. 547pp.

"Over four decades," Gado observes, "Bergman's fictions have displayed remarkable variety: their settings range from the newly Christianized Sweden of the thirteenth century to the war-ravaged landscape of a near future; their protagonists, from adolescents struggling for a place in the bewildering world of adults to a man revisiting his youth in the course of weighing his life's worth; their styles, from low and high comedy to slow-moving modern versions of religious drama." Gado's superb study emphasizes not only Bergman's recurring (and, at times, contradictory) motifs--"the search for God or the flight from God; the pleading for the alienated artist or the attack on art for its vapidity; the horror over the apocalyptic disintegration of our society or the morbid fascination with its decline; the veneration of the Female or the essential misogyny in his portrayal of women; the rejection of bourgeois values or the nostalgia for the vanished milieu they once governed"--but also the links between the films and Bergman's personal history. Nine eloquently written chapters discuss in detail the scope of Bergman's contributions to art and culture in the latter half of the twentieth century. A filmography, endnotes, and an index are included. Highly recommended for special collections.

Gibson, Arthur. THE SILENCE OF GOD: CREATIVE RESPONSE TO THE FILMS OF INGMAR BERGMAN. New York: Harper & Row, 1969. Illustrated. 171pp.
        Throughout seven of Bergman's major films--THE SEVENTH SEAL/DET SJUNDE INSEGLET (1957), WILD STRAWBERRIES/SMULTRONSTALLET (1957), THE MAGICIAN/THE FACE/ANSIKTET (1958), THROUGH A GLASS DARKLY/SASOM I EN SPEGEL (1961), WINTER LIGHT/THE COMMUNICANTS/NATTVARDSGASTERNA (1963), THE SILENCE/TYSTNADEN (1963), PERSONA (1966)--the question of God's silence remains uppermost in this critic's mind. "This book," Gibson argues, "is the answer of one   .   .   .   human being, preoccupied with the problem and the phenomenon of modern atheism, to that other human being who exposed on film his own inner vision." By providing us with a reflective analysis of each film, Gibson offers some fascinating and significant insights into Bergman's approach to film. Endnotes are provided, but no index is included. Well worth browsing.

*Gill, Jerry H. INGMAR BERGMAN AND THE SEARCH FOR MEANING. Grand Rapids: William B. Eerdmans Publishing Company, 1969. 45pp.
        This ambitious assistant professor of philosophy tries to analyze Bergman's attitudes toward an ideal community implied in THE SEVENTH SEAL/DET SJUNDE INSEGLET, WILD STRAWBERRIES/SMULTRONSTALLET, THROUGH A GLASS DARKLY/SASOM I EN SPEGEL, WINTER LIGHT/THE COMMUNICANTS/NATTVARDSGASTERNA, and THE SILENCE/TYSTNADEN. A good idea, but this can not be accomplished in such a brief study. Worth browsing.

*Isaksson, Ulla. THE VIRGIN SPRING. New York: Ballantine Books, 1960. Illustrated. 114pp.

*Jones, G. William, ed. TALKING WITH INGMAR BERGMAN. Foreword Eugene Bonelli. Preface Charles Champlin. Dallas: Southern Methodist University Press, 1983. Illustrated. 101pp.
        In 1981, Bergman visited SMU to receive the first Algur H. Meadows Award for Excellence in the Arts, and to participate in a series of seminars on his work. This transcription of the only English-seminars the brilliant director has done is filled with interesting and anecdotal information from several hours of candid conversations. Well worth browsing.

*Kaminsky, Stuart M., with Joseph F. Hill, eds. INGMAR BERGMAN: ESSAYS IN CRITICISM. New York: Oxford University Press, 1975. Illustrated. 340pp.

Kaminsky and Hall divide their material into two major sections: an overview of Bergman's career and perspectives on his films. Except for Stanley Kauffmann's hostile reaction to THE VIRGIN SPRING/JUNGFRUKALLAN, all of the analyses are positive. "The concern of the collection," the editors explain, ". . . is not so much that you will come to love the films of Ingmar Bergman, but that you will, to a great extent, understand them." A filmography is included, but no index is provided.

Livingston, Paisley. INGMAR BERGMAN AND THE RITUALS OF ART. Ithica: Cornell University Press, 1982. Illustrated. 291pp.

While most commentaries dwell on Bergman's pessimism and his absorption with personal and unresolved crises, this study focuses on the postive aspects of the filmmaker's thematic concerns. "It is the premise of this book," Livingston writes, ". . . that the insights and innovations Bergman offers have never been adequately explored and that his films are far from exhausted." His career "is a sustained interrogation of conflict and crisis, neither a series of frenzied and gratuitous revolts nor an agonized, purely symptomatic chorus of desperate cries." Livingston's five thoughtful chapters increase our understanding of conflict in various aspects of society, focusing on his attempts to break with traditional screen narratives and symbols. Endnotes, a filmography, a bibliography, and an index are included. Recommended for special collections.

Manvell, Roger. INGMAR BERGMAN: AN APPRECIATION. New York: Arno Press, 1980. 114pp.

Marker, Lise-Lone, and Frederick J. Marker. INGMAR BERGMAN: FOUR DECADES IN THE THEATER. New York: Cambridge University Press, 1982. Illustrated. 262pp.

Mosley, Philip. INGMAR BERGMAN: THE CINEMA AS MISTRESS. Boston: Marion Boyars, 1981. Illustrated. 192pp.

*Petric, Vlada, ed. FILMS AND DREAMS: AN APPROACH TO BERGMAN. South Salem: Redgrave Publishing Company, 1981. Illustrated. 263pp.

Following an introductory essay orienting readers to recent theories in the psychophysiology of dreams and a history of films from the turn-of-the-century to the eighties, this stimulating anthology offers thirteen theoretical and analytical essays on dream imagery in Bergman's films. The concluding piece is a chronology of Bergman's life and career. This work is for the very serious student, not for the film buff. A bibliography is provided, but no index is included. Well worth browsing.

Simon, John. INGMAR BERGMAN DIRECTS. New York: Harcourt Brace Jovanovich, 1972. Illustrated. 315pp.

Without question, this study of four key Bergman films--THE CLOWN'S EVENING/THE NAKED NIGHT/SAWDUST AND TINSEL/GYCKLARNAS AFTON, SMILES OF A SUMMER NIGHT/SOMMARNATTENS LEENDE, WINTER LIGHT/THE COMMUNICANTS/NATTVARDSGASTERNA, and PERSONA--is a superb illustration of Simon's impressive critical powers and standards. It is also an excellent model for analyzing films. Beginning with an interview with Bergman, followed by a critical overview, the author offers four meticulous analyses of the films, relying heavily on more than 400 frame enlargements to support his conclusions. A filmography of the films is included, but no bibliography or index is provided. Highly recommended for special collections.

Sjoman, Vilgot. L136: DIARY WITH INGMAR BERGMAN. Trans. Alan Blair.   Ann Arbor: Karoma Publishers, 1978. 243pp.
    A   detailed   diary   of   the   production   of   WINTER   LIGHT/THE COMMUNICANTS/NATTVARDSGASTERNA,   this   book   provides   many   fascinating insights into Bergman's approach to the project and his relationship with the cast and crew. Well worth browsing.

*Steene,   Birgitta,   ed.   FOCUS   ON   "THE   SEVENTH   SEAL."   Englewood   Cliffs: Prentice-Hall, 1972. Illustrated. 182pp.
    This excellent anthology contains serious essays, critical reviews, commentaries, an outline, a script extract and WOOD PAINTING: A MORALITY PLAY, plus a filmography and bibliography. Recommended for special collections.

Steene, Birgitta. INGMAR BERGMAN. New York: Twayne Publishers, 1968.   158pp. New York: St. Martin's Press, 1974.
    This comprehensive and insightful book is an expansion of Steene's FILM COMMENT article and is a good source of information on Bergman's early theater training, where he directed and studied. Ten of the book's twelve chapters analyze his films. A bibliography and index are included. Recommended for special collections.

*Wood, Robin. INGMAR BERGMAN. New York: Praeger Publishers, 1969. Illustrated. 192pp.
    One of the best books in the Praeger Film Library series, this critical and appreciative study offers the best succinct examination of the Swedish director's films. As always, Wood's perceptive comments reveal new insights into neglected areas of technique and screen conventions. Ten chapters chronologically examine the films and false perceptions about their content and meaning. A filmography and bibliography are included, but no index is provided. Recommended for special collections.

*Young, Vernon. CINEMA BOREALIS: INGMAR BERGMAN AND THE SWEDISH ETHOS. New York: Avon Books, 1971. Illustrated. 331pp.
    Focusing on attempts to minimize Bergman's debts to his heritage and to label him an "intellectual director" unappealing to mass audiences, this study argues that Bergman is not only a product of his native roots, but also a very sensitive director in tune with the public and eager to communicate with it. Seven provocative chapters do a fine job of softening the mystique of the great artist. Endnotes, a bibliography, a filmography, and an index are included. Well worth browsing.

FILMS

INGMAR BERGMAN

THE SEVENTH SEAL/DET SJUNDE INSEGLET (Sweden--16mm: 1957, 96 mins., b/w, English subtitles, sound, R-FES, FNC, IMA, JAN)
    Written and directed by Bergman, this low-budget film made in thirty-two days is an allegorical story of a knight's search for the meaning of life and presents marvelous metaphorical images of suffering, fear, and optimism. As Birgitta Steene

observes, the film's "visual splendor has not faded even if its philosophical theme has tended to become overexposed by content-oriented critics."[1175]

WILD STRAWBERRIES/SMULTRONSTALLET (Sweden--16mm: 1957, 90 mins., b/w, English subtitles, sound, R-FNC, JAN, IMA, KIT; S-FES, TFF)
   Bergman offers a memorable story of a septuagenarian doctor (Victor Sjostrom) who recalls his past experiences as he journeys to receive an honorary degree from his university. As Roger Manvell aptly states, "WILD STRAWBERRIES is to Ingmar Bergman what KING LEAR was to Shakespeare--a study in old age and the need for an old man to discover the errors and inhuman deeds of his life and, as he cannot mend them, his own fallibility.[1176]

CARL THEODOR DREYER

GERTRUD (Denmark--16mm: 1964, 115 mins., b/w, English subtitles, sound, R-BUD, COR, FES, IMA, KIT; S-FES, IMA, TFF)
   Dreyer's last film is a controversial screenplay about one woman's determination, in middle age, to live her life according to her desires.[1177] Nina Pens Rhode gives a memorable performance as the retired singer who choses to abandon her marriage for love and freedom.[1178]

SWITZERLAND

BOOKS

Leach, Jim. A POSSIBLE CINEMA: THE FILMS OF ALAIN TANNER. Metuchen: The Scarecrow Press, 1984. Illustrated. 201pp.

THIRD WORLD NATIONS

BOOKS

*Armes, Roy. THIRD WORLD FILMMAKING AND THE WEST. Berkeley: University of

---

[1175] *Birgitta Steene, "FOCUS ON "THE SEVENTH SEAL," (Englewood Cliffs: Prentice-Hall, 1972), p.4. See also Darryl Wimberly, "Program Notes: THE SEVENTH SEAL," CINEMATEXAS PROGRAM NOTES 13:1 (September 15, 1977):43-51; Roger Manvell, "DET SJUNDE INSEGLET," THE INTERNATIONAL DICTIONARY OF FILMS AND FILMMAKERS: VOLUME I, pp.432-5; ___, "The Seventh Seal," SCREEN EDUCATION YEARBOOK (1966):95-9; and Peter Cowie, "Great Films of the Century: THE SEVENTH SEAL," FILMS AND FILMING 9:4 (January 1963):44-6.

[1176] Roger Manvell, "SMULTRONSTALLET," THE INTERNATIONAL DICTIONARY OF FILMS AND FILMMAKERS: VOLUME I, p.435. See also Eleanor McCann, "The Rhetoric of WILD STRAWBERRIES," SIGHT AND SOUND 30:1 (Winter 1960-61):44-6.

[1178] For more information, see Elliott Stein, "GERTRUD," SIGHT AND SOUND 34:2 (Spring 1965):56-8; Carl Lerner, "My Way of Working Is Iin Relation to the Future: A Conversation With Carl Dreyer," FILM COMMENT 4:1 (Fall 1966):62-7; Kirk Bond, "The Basic Demand of Life for Love," ibid., pp.67-9; Don Skoller, "To Rescue GERTRUD," ibid., pp.70-6; and Elsa Gress Wright, "GERTRUD," FILM QUARTERLY 9:3 (Spring 1966):36-40.

California Press, 1987. Illustrated. 381pp.

THE CONTEMPORARY CINEMA

Ever since films became an industry, it has been clear that the history of American movies and world cinema has been not only cyclical, but also chaotic. No one has given a better succinct overview of how American film history evolved than has Gerald Mast. Describing Hollywood's historical cyclical process as "periods of adventurous imagination and innovation . . . succeeded by periods of stabilization and formula which have then been succeeded by periods of innovation, and so forth,"[1179] the gifted film historian looked back on a number of controversies and artistic developments that brought Hollywood to the seventies. For example, unrest in Europe during the teens not only had affected the content and length of American feature films, but had also shaped the role that Hollywood would play in world cinema. As Mast observes, one of America's most adventurous decades had started "with unchartered artistic and commercial seas but ended with a clearly drawn map of movie art and commerce that has survived to the present day."[1180] For many critics and film scholars, the health of a national cinema would henceforth be judged by the innovative and adventuresome energy of its filmmakers. The industry's reliance on low-risk, high-profit movies, however, would be seen as a period of stagnation and decline. The rise of Hollywood formula films in the 1920s and 1930s not only influenced the state of national cinemas but also the careers of international directors. In each instance, imagination and experimentation were coupled with industrial insecurity and a codification of screen conventions. The end of World War II intensified worldwide competition for profits, performers, and prestige. At the same time, national cinemas struggled against the commercial dangers posed by new forms of entertainment, technology, and censorship. As always, demands for novelty produced structural changes and management shake-ups in the film industry . And as always, these events frightened investors, who then insisted on low-risk, high-profit ventures, with pundits predictably predicting the demise of Hollywood. By the end of the 1960s, Hollywood was dependent on foreign markets for at least half of its profits, while directors around the world conceived of their products either as copies of American formulas, or as reactions against the "Hollywood model." In the meantime, the lines between national products and international collaborations became increasingly blurred.

What follows is a brief commentary on the film capital's trials and tribulations from 1970 to 1989. Its purpose is threefold: (1) to indicate a new era of imagination and adventure in Hollywood and to suggest the problems it poses for the future, (2) to identify some of the major personalities and their debts to the past, and (3) to provide resources for future study. Unlike previous sections, this one does not contain an annotated bibliography and filmography. Circumstances that I could not

---

[1177] For more information, see Carl Dreyer, "Film Style," FILMS IN REVIEW 3:1 (January 1952):15-21; ___, "Thoughts on My Craft," SIGHT AND SOUND 25:1 (Winter 1955-56):128-9; Tom Milne, "Darkness and Light: Carl Dreyer," 34:4 (Autumn 1965):167-72; Dale S. Drum, "Carl Dreyer's Shorts," FILMS IN REVIEW 20:1 (January 1969):34-41; and Michel Delahaye, "Between Heaven and Hell: Interview With Carl Dreyer," CAHIERS DU CINEMA IN ENGLISH 4, CdC #170 (September 1965):7-17.

[1179] Gerald Mast, "The Cycles and Gyres of Hollywood History," THE NEW REPUBLIC (January 1, 8, 1977):21. For another perspective on recent developments in world cinema, see J. Hoberman, "1975-1985: Ten Years that Shoot the World," AMERICAN FILM 10:8 (June 1985):34-9, 42-9, 52-9.

[1180] "The Cycles and Gyres of Hollywood History," p.21.

control made it impossible to collect and include the information. Hopefully, future editions of FILM STUDY: AN ANAYLTICAL BIBLIOGRAPHY will correct what occasioned this curtailed conclusion.

UNITED STATES

As the seventies opened, Hollywood was an industry in turmoil. A national recession, coupled with rising film costs, shrinking profits, and diminishing ticket sales, found the film capital in a siege mentality. As TIME reported, ". . . the 1970 statistics are terrifying: the films [M*A*S*H, PATTON, and AIRPORT] that are still earning heavy profits consititute a mere skeleton crew."[1181] On the other hand, the Hollywood blockbuster mentality of the sixties had resulted in a series of recent "trendy megaton disasters"--e.g., SWEET CHARITY, PAINT YOUR WAGON (both in 1969), and ON A CLEAR DAY YOU CAN SEE FOREVER (1970)--and "overpriced losers"--e.g., SCROOGE, DIRTY DINGUS MAGEE, and TORA! TORA! TORA! (all in 1970).[1182] The one bright spot, according to TIME, was the enormous popularity of LOVE STORY (1970), a film that rekindled the industry's "ties to romanticism" and to mass-appeal, big-budgeted entertainment.[1183]

To survive, Hollywood addressed the issues of production costs, film conventions, and audience expectations. Seven companies--e.g., 20th Century-Fox, United Artists, Warner Bros., Universal, Columbia Pictures, Paramount Pictures, and Disney--controlled the production and distribution process in the seventies. As discussed in Chapter 3, the obsession of these companies with mass-appeal, big-budgeted films had put the industry into the red, and seriously reduced the number of films being made. It had also kept the companies' competitors at bay, allowing the majors to determine what films were made and shown. To offset their economic problems, the majors revised their distribution policies, abandoned their heavy reliance on best-sellers and hit plays as the sources of important films, and forced the television networks, cable TV owners, independents, and exhibitors to share the risks of the filmmaking business. The focus was on finding new ways to gain a greater handle on the youth market. Thus, as the seventies began, Richard Corliss reminds us, Hollywood was "in a productive, promising turmoil, with young filmmakers leaping the barricades to take over the moguls' offices, foreign directors testing their skills against a new language (English) and, sometimes, a crazy new country (America), and the old men of the studio running for cover."[1184] Moreover, as William Paul observes, the New Hollywood turned its attention to "lists of 'bankable' stars, trend-spotting, demographic studies--all of which . . . [added] up to a clear admission of failure, a loss of the intuitive certainty about its audience that old Hollywood had: what brought the audience into a theater, what it wanted when it got there, what would surprise it."[1185]

By the summer of 1971, TIME reported a number of changes in the way Hollywood did business:

[1181] "Ali McGraw: A Return to Basics," TIME (January 11, 1971):41.

[1182] "Ali McGraw," p.45.

[1183] "Ali McGraw," p.45.

[1184] Richard Corliss, "We Lost It at the Movies: The Generation that Grew Up on THE GRADUATE Took Over Hollywood--And Went Into Plastics," FILM COMMENT 16:1 (January-February 1980):34.

[1185] William Paul, "Hollywood Harakiri: On the Decline of an Industry and an Art," FILM COMMENT 13:2 (March-April 1977):41.

Discotheques are closing, servants are being let go, and psychiatrists have more leisure time. Private jets and yachts are up for grabs. Hostesses are turning from expensive fresh-flower arrangements to polished fruit to adorn their tables.[1186]

As discussed in Chapters 3 and 5, some of the majors not only began selling their studio lots to real estate developers, but also began merging their production facilities. According to TIME, unemployment in the craft unions was at eighty percent, fewer than sixteen percent (110 out of 634) of the screenwriters had jobs, and ninety percent of the Screen Actors Guild (23,000 members) were out of work.[1187] Many producers, stars, screenwriters, and financiers had turned to TV for jobs and investments instead of relying on the commercial film industry for income. The switch not only affected what types of films were being made, but also what types of values the film industry espoused.

One cinematic approach advocated exploiting the new freedom provided by the ratings system. Nudity, explicit sex, and vulgarity became the order of the day. Except for rare films like CARNAL KNOWLEDGE (1971), LAST TANGO IN PARIS (1973), and SHAMPOO (1975), Hollywood appealed to the public's fascination for uninhibted sexual fantasies, regardless of quality, taste, or reason. As discussed in Chapter 3, this lust for profits gave rise not only to the controversial "Blaxpolitation" films, but also to the popularity of "pornography" films like DEEP THROAT (1972). Not surprisingly, the media had a field day when former First Lady Jacqueline Kennedy went to see what Linda Lovelace was doing about her unique "medical" problem. By 1973, the Supreme Court stepped in and issued guidelines on how communities could protect themselves against "obscene" films and periodicals.[1188]

Hollywood's cynicism also capitalized on the nation's political turmoil over the Watergate scandal. Once it became clear that Richard Nixon had abused his presidential prerogatives, the film capital upgraded its exploitation of widespread public paranoia. Films like WUSA (1970), THE FRENCH CONNECTION, THE ANDERSON TAPES, KLUTE, DIRTY HARRY (all in 1971), THE GODFATHER (1972), THE PARALLEX VIEW, THE GODFATHER, PART II (both in 1974), THREE DAYS OF THE CONDOR (1975), and THE OMEN (1976) emphasized the fact that politicians, corporate executives, and gangsters operated in much the same manner. Anyone who believed differently, the filmmakers told us, was naive and ignorant. To appreciate the power of these new morality tales, it helps to remember that the best of them--THE FRENCH CONNECTION, THE GODFATHER, and THE GODFATHER PART II--were given Oscars as the year's top film. In fact, THE GODFATHER PART II became the only sequel in film history to win that honor.

Yet another example of Hollywood's cynicism was its ability to incorporate modern

---

[1186] "Hollywood (Hot Dog) Days," TIME (August 23, 1971):46.

[1187] "Hollywood (Hot) Dog Days," p.46.

[1188] For a useful overview of the problems, see Ted Morgan, "United States Versus the Princes of Porn," THE NEW YORK TIMES MAGAZINE (March 6, 1977):16-7, 26, 28, 30, 33-4, 36-7; and Carlos Clarens, "The Artist as Pornographer: Borowcyzk Interviewed," FILM COMMENT 12:1 (January-February 1976):44-7.

paranoia into the nostalgia craze started with BONNIE AND CLYDE (1967),[1189] and accelerated with LOVE STORY and PATTON (both in 1970).[1190] The shrewd filmmakers, playing on the public's increasing anxiety fueled by Nixon's perceived misconduct and the Vietnam War, revised screen conventions about the nation's past and played on the collective desire for bittersweet memories about our loss of innocence. Films like THE GODFATHER and THE GODFATHER PART II weren't the only ones justifying new interpretations of modern America's intolerable moral dilmema. Revisionist film history was also apparent in films like THE BALLAD OF CABLE HOGUE, LITTLE BIG MAN, SOLDIER BLUE (all in 1970), THE LAST PICTURE SHOW, MCCABE AND MRS. MILLER (both in 1971), BUCK AND THE PREACHER, THE CANDIDATE, RAGE, SLAUGHTERHOUSE FIVE, THE TRIAL OF THE CATONSVILLE NINE (all in 1972), PAPER MOON, AMERICAN GRAFFITI, THE WAY WE WERE (all in 1973), THE GREAT GATSBY, and CHINATOWN (both in 1974).

Still another example of Hollywood's willingness to mix public paranoia with cinematic escapism was the rise of the "disaster" film. In movies like THE POSEIDON ADVENTURE (1972), EARTHQUAKE, and THE TOWERING INFERNO (both in 1974), filmmakers highlighted how greedy entrepreneurs and distraught individuals contributed to the danger to public health and safety. Although basically an updating of the GRAND HOTEL formula of the 1930s, the new screen conventions featured big stars facing modern horrors and experiencing spectacular deaths. The message was that no one was safe. Disaster could strike anyone, anywhere, and anytime.

Given the nation's cynicism toward its public institutions and their leadership, it's not surprising that American films also became more self-reflexive. As Robert B. Ray points out, "Between 1966 and 1980, an enormous number of films depended on their audiences' ability to recognize them as overt parodies, 'corrected' genre

---

[1189] Paul Monaco argues that a period of "collective nostalgia" gripped the United States from the late 1960s to the mid-1980s. One reason for America's desire to look back on its past in an emotional and uncritical way was linked to the "emergence of a self-conscious youth counterculture." These baby-boomers born in the postwar period, raised in the upward mobility-family consciousness of the fifties, and disillusioned by the political and social turmoil of the sixties (the turning point being President Kennedy's assassination in November 1963), turned against the "crass, superficial, and plastic values of their parents' generation, often citing their felt affinity to their grandparents generation." Another reason Monaco gives for the nation's desire for "memory without pain" was its anxiety over its sense of loss and feelings of declining self-worth. Asserting that America's general values are tied to "youth, beauty or handsomeness, productivity and accomplishment, and the acquisition of material goods," Monaco emphasizes the importance of nostalgia in preserving "the sense of continuity and personal self-importance simultaneously." Monaco considers BONNIE AND CLYDE the seminal film in characterizing the new morality and in capturing the baby boomers' desires to view the past nostalgically rather than critically. Other key films are PATTON (1970), SAVE THE TIGER, AMERICAN GRAFFITI (both in 1973), THE LORDS OF FLATBUSH (1974), NATIONAL LAMPOON'S ANIMAL HOUSE, THE BUDDY HOLLY STORY (both in 1978), THE GREAT SANTINI (1980), and THE BIG CHILL (1983). See RIBBONS IN TIME, pp.93-125. For a current example of cinematic nostalgia, see Aljean Harmetz, "The High Price of Nostalgia for Things Cinematic," NEW YORK TIMES C (May 23, 1989):15.

[1190] Interestingly, a number of Hollywood movies during this period focused more on male bonding than on traditional male-female romances. For a good overview, see Aljean Harmetz, "Boy Meets Boy--Or Where the Girls Aren't," NEW YORK TIMES 2 (January 20, 1974):1, 11. See also Charles Michener, with Martin Kasindorf, "Old Movies Come Alive," NEWSWEEK (May 31, 1976):48-54.

pictures, or exaggerated camp versions of Hollywood's traditional morality."[1191] In an attempt to deal with the nation's anxieties and appeal to its collective nostalgia, the filmmakers found it profitable to ridicule and to challenge Hollywood's mythmaking conventions. Moreover, Ray explains,

> The period's growing self-consciousness about the received American myths also promoted a new kind of star, who in classic Hollywood might have operated only in the margins of straight genre movies. Elliot Gould, Walter Matthau, Dustin Hoffman, Al Pacino, Robert De Niro, Woody Allen, Gene Wilder, Gene Hackman, Mel Brooks, Jack Nicholson, Jane Fonda, Goldie Hawn, and Jill Clayburgh were all essentially character actors whose self-reflexive, self-doubting personae contrasted sharply with the confident, natural imperturbability of Cooper, Grant, Gable, and Wayne. While the Classic stars had depended on the cumulative power of typecasting and genre conventions, these new performers specialized in playing against the expectations created either by a film's nominal genre or by their own previous roles.[1192]

Some of the best films mocking Hollywood's conventions in the early seventies are M*A*S*H (1970), BANANAS, LITTLE BIG MAN (both in 1971), SLEUTH, PLAY IT AGAIN, SAM (both in 1972), THE LONG GOODBYE (1973), BLAZING SADDLES, YOUNG FRANKENSTEIN, THE THREE MUSKETEERS, and PHANTOM OF THE PARADISE (all in 1974).[1193]

A good source for evaluating how well Hollywood's new policies worked is A. D. Murphy's report on the major film stories of 1973. After noting the nation's economic woes and its links to the film industry's continuing problems, the astute commentator outlined ten significant trends: (1) a contracting spectrum of theatrical films, (2) confusion over what constitutes legal obscenity, (3) declining domestic box-office returns, (4) setbacks in new markets for films, (5) the disappointing results of new franchising concepts, (6) the plight of Columbia Pictures and its blockbuster film policies, (7) the damaging writer's strike and Hollywood labor unrest, (8) the rise of new distribution patterns (e.g., four-walling and the American Film Theatre experiment), (9) new production patterns and affiliations that result in shared risks, and (10) the transfer of major theater circuits into private ownerships.[1194] In Murphy's judgment, "The American film industry, rocked by economic upheaval in the 1969-71 period, in 1973 continued in what reasonably appears to be the final phases of its shakeout."[1195] In short, the majors were on a rocky road to recovery.

Murphy's reasoning was confirmed the following year, when U.S. NEWS AND

[1191] *Robert B. Ray, A CERTAIN TENDENCY OF THE HOLLYWOOD CINEMA, 1930-1980 (Princeton: Princeton University Press, 1985), p.257. For a brief update, see Vincent Canby, "Comedy That Smirks at Itself," NEW YORK TIMES H (April 16, 1989):1, 22.

[1192] Ray, p.260.

[1193] For a more complete list, see Ray, pp.257-60.

[1194] A. D. Murphy, "Big Film Trend Stories of '73," VARIETY (January 9, 1974):11, 64.

[1195] Murphy, p.11. Elsewhere, Murphy cautioned the industry to watch out for periodic recessions every three or four years. That is, boom periods often result in overconfident studio heads' and new companies' increasing production schedules. "The resulting flood of product," the brilliant statistician warned, "dilutes the marketplace." Then the studios start cutting back. Cited in Anne Thompson, "Industry: Tenth Annual Grosses Gloss," FILM COMMENT 22:2 (March-April 1986):64.

WORLD REPORT asserted that film attendance was the highest it had been since 1966.[1196] In addition to crediting Hollywood with satisfying America's desires to escape from its economic troubles, the periodical pointed to a new wave of directors as the main architects of Hollywood's resurgence. For the most part, U.S. NEWS AND WORLD REPORT was right. A number of new personalities had come on the scene and were reshaping Hollywood film history. Along with "old-timers" like Woody Allen, Mel Brooks, Blake Edwards, and Robert Altman, newcomers like Peter Bogdanovich,[1197] William Friedkin,[1198] and Alan Pakula[1199] had received their training in TV before coming to film. Other notable talents were emerging from the ranks of film editors: e.g., Hal Ashby[1200] and Ralph Bakshi.[1201] In addition, there were new screenwriters like Paul Schrader,[1202] Willard Huyck, Gloria Katz, Joan Tewkesbury,[1203] and Robert

---

[1196] "New 'Great Era' for Movies: What's Behind the Comeback," U.S. NEWS AND WORLD REPORT (March 17, 1975):52. See also Joseph McBride, "The Glory That Was Hollywood: The Babylon of the West Is Being Revisited by Every Filmmaker In Town. Why?" AMERICAN FILM 1:3 (December 1975):52-6.

[1197] For more information, see Gordon Gow, "Without a Dinosaur: Peter Bogdanovich Interviewed," FILMS AND FILMING 18:9 (June 1972):18-22; "Dialogue on Film: Peter Bogdanovich," AMERICAN FILM 3:3 (December-January 1978):35-50; "Dialogue on Film: Peter Bogdanovich," John Baxter, "Bogdanovich, Peter," THE INTERNATIONAL DICTIONARY OF FILMS AND FILMMAKERS: VOLUME II, pp.53-5.

[1198] For more information, see "Dialogue on Film: William Friedkin," AMERICAN FILM 3:4 (February-March 1974):1-36; Ralph Applebaum, "Tense Situation: Interview With William Friedkin," FILMS AND FILMING 25:6 (March 1979):12-9; and Ray Narducy, "Friedkin, William," THE INTERNATIONAL DICTIONARY OF FILMS AND FILMMAKERS: VOLUME II, pp.202-3.

[1199] For more information, see "Dialogue on Film: Alan J. Pakula," AMERICAN FILM 4:3 (December-January 1979):33-44; "Dialogue on Film: Alan J. Pakula," ibid., 9:2 (November 1985):13, 76-7; Tom Milne, "Not a Garbo or a Gilbert in the Bunch: Alan Pakula Talks With Tom Milne," SIGHT AND SOUND 41:2 (Spring 1972):32-7; Gordon Gow, "Unlikely Elements: Alan J. Pakula Interviewed," FILMS AND FILMING 19:3 (December 1972):14-8; and Deborah H. Holdstein, "Pakula, Alan J.," THE INTERNATIONAL DICTIONARY OF AMERICAN FILMS AND FILMMAKERS: VOLUME II, p.402.

[1200] For more information, see "Dialogue on Film: Hal Ashby," AMERICAN FILM 5:7 (May 1980):53-60; Ralph Applebaum, "Positive Thinking: Hal Ashby," FILMS AND FILMING 24:10 (July 1978):10-6; and Ray Narducy, "Ashby, Hal," THE INTERNATIONAL DICTIONARY OF FILMS AND FILMMAKERS: VOLUME II, pp.27-8.

[1201] For more information, see Linda J. Obalil, "Bakshi, Ralph," THE INTERNATIONAL DICTIONARY OF FILMS AND FILMMAKERS: VOLUME II, pp.34-5.

[1202] For more information, see Stephen Rebello, "CAT PEOPLE: Paul Schrader Changes Spots," AMERICAN FILM 7:6 (April 1982):38-40, 42-5; Jay Scott, "He Who Treads the Tiger's Tale," ibid., 10:5 (March 1985):36-40; "Dialogue on Film: Paul Schrader," ibid., 14:9 (July-August 1989):16-21; Charles Higham, "When I do It, It's Not Gore, Says Writer Paul Schrader," NEW YORK TIMES D (February 5, 1978):15, 22; and Anthony T. Allegro, "Schrader, Paul," THE INTERNATIONAL DICTIONARY OF FILMS AND FILMMAKERS: VOLUME II, pp.483-5.

[1203] For more information, see "Dialogue of Film: Joan Tewkesbury," AMERICAN FILM 4:5 (March 1979):35-46.

[1204] For more information, see "Dialogue on Film: Robert Towne," AMERICAN FILM 1:3

Towne.[1204] But far more important were the university-trained writer-directors like Francis Ford Coppola,[1205] Steven Spielberg,[1206] Brian De Palma,[1207] George Lucas,[1208] John Milius,[1209] and Martin Scorsese.[1210]

(December 1975):33-48. See also L. M. Kit Carson, "It's Here! Hollywood's Ninth Era!" ESQUIRE (February 1975):65-75.

[1205] For more information, see Joseph McBride, "Coppola, Inc.," AMERICAN FILM 1:2 (November 1975):14-8; Audie Bock, "Zoetrope and APOCALYPSE NOW," ibid., 4:10 (September 1979):55-60; Mike Bygrave and Joan Goodman, "Meet Me In Las Vegas," ibid., 7:1 (October 1981):38-43, 84; Jill Kearney, "The Road Warrior," ibid., 13:8 (June 1988):20-6, 52-3; Richard Koszarski, "The Youth of Francis Ford Coppola," FILM IN REVIEW 19:9 (November 1968):529-36; Lynda Miles, "The Zoetrope Saga," SIGHT AND SOUND 51:2 (Spring 1982):91-3; Marjorie Rosen, "Francis Ford Coppola Interviewed," FILM COMMENT 10:4 (July-August 1974):43-9; and Rob Edelman, "Coppola, Francis Ford," THE INTERNATIONAL DICTIONARY OF FILMS AND FILMMAKERS: VOLUME II, pp.107-8.

[1206] For more information, see Bruce Cook, "Close Encounters With Steven Spielberg," AMERICAN FILM 3:2 (November 1977):24-9; "Dialogue on Film: Steven Spielberg," ibid., 13:8 (June 1988):12, 14-6; Todd McCarthy, "Sand Castles: Steven Spielberg Interviewed," FILM COMMENT 18:3 (May-June 1982):53-9; Richard Coombs, "Primal Scream: An Interview With Steven Spielberg," SIGHT AND SOUND 46:2 (Spring 1977):111-3; Richard Corliss, "Steve's Summer Magic: E. T. And POLTERGEIST--Two From The Heart," TIME (May 31, 1982):54-60; ___, "I Dream for a Living: Steven Spielberg, the Prince of Hollywood, Is Still a Little Boy at Heart," ibid., (July 15, 1985):54-61; Steven Spielberg, "The Autobiography of Peter Pan," ibid., pp.62-3; "RAIDERS OF THE LOST ARK and How it Was Filmed," AMERICAN CINEMATOGRAPHER 62:11 (November 1981):1096-1110; Susan Royal, "Steven Spielberg In His Adventures on Earth," PREMIERE (July 10, 1982):17-25; Nancy Griffin, "Manchild In the Promised Land," ibid., 2:10 (June 1985):86-90, 93-4; Charles Derry, "Spielberg, Steven," THE INTERNATIONAL DICTIONARY OF FILMS AND FILMMAKERS: VOLUME II, pp.511-2; Glenn Collins, "New Departures for Two Major Directors," NEW YORK TIMES H (December 15, 1985):1, 23; Myra Folsberg, "Spielberg at 40: The Man and The Child," ibid., H (January 10, 1988):1, 30; and Vincent Canby, "Spielberg's Elixir Shows Signs of Mature Magic," ibid., H (June 18, 1989):15-6.

[1207] For more information, see Bruce Weber, "Cool Head, Hot Images," THE NEW YORK TIME MAGAZINE (May 21, 1989):24-7, 105, 116-7, 126; Royal S. Brown, "Considering De Palma," AMERICAN FILM 2:9 (July-August 1977):54-61; Georgia A. Brown, "Obsession," ibid., 9:3 (December 1983):28-34; and Tom Snyder, "De Palma, Brian," THE INTERNATIONAL DICTIONARY OF FILMS AND FILMMAKERS: VOLUME II, pp.129-30.

[1208] For more information, see Stephen Zito, "George Lucas Goes Far Out," AMERICAN FILM 2:6 (April 1977):8-13; Aljean Harmetz, "George Lucas--Burden of Dreams," ibid., 8:8 (June 1983):30-9; ___, "But Can Hollywood Live Without George Lucas?" NEW YORK TIMES C (July 13, 1981):11; Donald Goddard, "From AMERICAN GRAFFITI to Outer Space," ibid., D (September 12, 1978):15; Janet Maslin, "How Old Movie Serials Inspired Lucas and Spielberg," ibid., H (June 7, 1981):1, 19; David A. Kaplan, "Secret Lair of the Jedi, the Grail and the Green Slimers," NEW YORK TIMES H (July 2, 1989):9, 16; Mike Grossberg, "Program Notes: THX 1138," CINEMATEXAS PROGRAM NOTES 9:3 (November 5, 1975):69-74; Stephen Farber, "George Lucas: The Stinky Kid Hits the Big Time," FILM QUARTERLY 27:3 (Spring 1974):2-9; B. H. Fairchild, "Songs of Innocence and Experience: The Blakean Vision of George Lucas," LITERATURE/FILM QUARTERLY 7:2 (1979):112-9; Thomas Snyder, "Lucas, George," THE INTERNATIONAL DICTIONARY OF FILMS AND FILMMAKERS: VOLUME

In essence, the seventies were the first moviemaking generation that had many of its most important artists trained in graduate film programs at UCLA, USC, and NYU. Like their peers in LA NOUVELLE VAGUE, these new "movie brats" cherished the old Hollywood "B" productions and poverty row serials.[1211] Coppola led the way, first working as a screenwriter for Roger Corman[1212] and Seven-Arts in the sixties. He wrote and directed his first major theatrical film, YOU'RE A BIG BOY NOW! in 1966. The film also earned him his graduate degree from UCLA. He then went to work for Warner Bros., making films like FINIAN'S RAINBOW (1968) and THE RAIN PEOPLE (1969). By the end of the sixties, he had enough clout and money to open a production center in San Francisco, where he nurtured other newcomers like Lucas, Milius, Huyck, and Katz. In 1970, because he was allegedly the only Italian film director currently working in Hollywood, Paramount studio head Bob Evans signed the young director to THE GODFATHER. The success of that film opened the door for the other youngsters, and by the mid-1970s they had made such notable films as Coppola's THE CONVERSATION and THE GODFATHER PART II (both in 1974), Lucas's AMERICAN GRAFFITI (1973), Spielberg's JAWS (1975), Scorsese's MEAN STREETS (1973) and ALICE DOESN'T LIVE HERE ANYMORE (1974), Brian De Palma's SISTERS (1973) and PHANTOM OF THE PARADISE (1974), and Milius's DILLINGER (1973) and THE WIND AND THE LION (1975). Over the next fifteen years, the fate and fortunes of these men encapsulated the trends, glories, and failures of modern Hollywood.

Equally influential was the new breed of studio bosses and producers. For example, a number of former talent agents were now running major studios and supervising TV programming: e.g., Lew Wasserman, chairperson of Universal; Ted Ashley, chairperson of Warner Bros.; David Begelman, president of Columbia Pictures; Patrick Kelly, chairperson of First Artists; and Barry Diller, president of ABC-TV.[1213] Each of these men would play a crucial role in moving the movies more into the escapist traditions of the past and away from the social-consciousness mood of the sixties. The emphasis would be on go-for-broke productions that reworked old formulas or exploited the emerging special-effects breakthroughs in spectacular productions.

Although many pundits now believed Hollywood was back in stride, Jack Valenti's

---

II, pp.341-3; and Robert Goldberg, "Back to the Future," PREMIERE 1:10 (June 1988):42-4, 48, 50.

[1209] For more information, see Kirk Honeycutt, "Milius the Barbarian," AMERICAN FILM 7:7 (May 1982):32-7; and John Gallagher, "John Milius," FILMS IN REVIEW 32:6 (June-July 1982):357-61.

[1210] After consulting Weiss, see Thomas Wiener, "Martin Scorsese Fights Back," AMERICAN FILM 6:2 (November 1980):30-4, 75; Carrie Rickey, "Marty," ibid., 8:2 (November 1982):66-73; and Chris Holdenfield, "The Art of Noncompromise: You've Got to Love Something Enough to Kill It," ibid., 14:5 (March 1989):46-51.

[1211] For another perspective, see Mike Bygrave and Joan Goodman, "First-Time Directors: A New Breed," AMERICAN FILM 6:4 (January-February 1984):22-6.

[1212] Corman allowed Coppola to write and direct DEMENTIA 13 in 1963.

[1213] Thomas M. Pryor, "Agent Power Now Rules Hollywood: No Film Czars to Snub Them," VARIETY (January 9, 1974):9. See also Robert Lindsay, "The New Tycoons of Hollywood," THE NEW YORK TIMES MAGAZINE (August 7, 1977):12-6, 18, 20, 22-3. For an update on the importance of the Hollywood agent, see L. J. Davis, "Hollywood's Most Secret Agent," THE NEW YORK TIMES MAGAZINE (July 9, 1989):24-7, 51-2, 54, 74-5.

economic summary of theatrical films in 1975 suggested otherwise.[1214] On the one hand, he applauded the fact that box-office figures were the best in twelve years, film production was up ninteeen percent over the previous year, adult (eighteen and older) admissions were on the rise (from seventy-four percent to eighty-one percent), and college-educated audiences had reached an all-time high of thirty-six percent. On the other hand, Hollyood's most resourceful cheerleader agonized over the rise in production and distribution costs, the seven percent drop in teenage (twelve to seventeen) admissions (from twenty-six to nineteen percent), and the "economic and political difficulties triggered by anti-Americanism, rising nationalism, rampant inflation and an aching business recession."[1215] Valenti also agonized over the potential restraints that might be placed on film exhibition. For example, in one 1975 case, the Supreme Court ruled that a Jacksonville, Florida, ordinance against a drive-in whose nudity on the screen was visible off the grounds was unconstitutional. The justices left open the possibility, however, that certain types of obscenity legislation against drive-ins might be acceptable. "The issue is of major significance," Valenti explained, "because drive-ins constitute 26% or 3,800 of the 14,650 theatres in the U. S."[1216] In another key court case, the U. S. Court of Appeals let stand a lower court dismissal of a law suit challenging the PG rating assigned PAPILLON (1973). The plaintiff had claimed that the rating didn't adequately warn parents of the film's objectionable material. In ruling in favor of the defendant, the courts continued to support the MPAA's ratings. It was clear, however, that such cases posed challenges to the freedom of the screen.

Other problems were also apparent in 1975. As discussed in Chapter 3, many people were complaining that movies had abandoned their "day-dream" role in society and had put too much money and time into overblown films that settled for immediate, immature gratification. More to the point, Hollywood suffered the first of its modern recessions. Between late 1975 and early 1977, the industry was once again in a state of turmoil.

To bolster its dwindling receipts and stagnant audience numbers, Hollywood offered the public a range of options. The winners at the box office would set in motion the beginning of a pattern of sequels, remakes, and spinoffs that are still the mainstream of modern Hollywood movies. For example, the film capital, enjoying America's Bicentennial, resurrected its traditional values in films like ALL THE PRESIDENT'S MEN and ROCKY (both in 1976). The latter, a low-budget film, not only established the unknown screenwriter and actor Sylvester Stallone as a major force in contemporary films, but also made him the catalyst for a renaissance in violent and reactionary values. Although Stallone would only succeed in two roles (Rocky and Rambo), his box-office appeal created a horde of films about macho-heroes who thrived on physical stamina and illiteracy. His macho image blazed the trail for actors like Chuck Norris, Arnold Schwarzenegger, and Charles Bronson in movies about Fascists taking on urban hoods and foreign enemies.[1217] Social Consciousness was a second option, as in NETWORK and TAXI DRIVER. Despite their critical success, they spawned few spin-offs over the next decade, either because the nation was not in

---

[1214] In analyzing the statistics about film lengths and shots, it is valuable to read Barry Salt, "Statistical Style Analysis of Motion Pictures," FILM QUARTERLY 28:1 (Fall 1974):13-22.

[1215] Jack Valenti, "1975 Film Biz: At 12-Year High; Some Big Buts," VARIETY (January 7, 1976):5, 64.

[1216] Valenti, p.64.
Some Big Buts

[1217] For a useful perspective, see J. Hoberman, "The Fascist Guns In the West," AMERICAN FILM 9:5 (March 1986):42-6, 48.

the mood to examine its shortcomings, or because the public preferred its violence in action-packed, non-challenging movies filled with comic-book heroes and simplistic plots. A third option was to give free rein to a number of film veterans, whose significant public following still made them bankable. Among the noteworthy success stories were George Roy Hill's SLAUGHTERHOUSE FIVE (1972) and THE STING (1973), Alfred Hitchcock's FRENZY (1972), John Huston's THE LIFE AND TIMES OF JUDGE ROY BEAN, FAT CITY (both in 1972), and THE MAN WHO WOULD BE KING (1975), Stanley Kubrick's A CLOCKWORK ORANGE (1971), David Lean's DR. ZHIVAGO (1970), Sidney Lumet's SERPICO (1973) and DOG DAY AFTERNOON (1975), Sydney Pollack's JEREMIAH JOHNSON (1972) and THE WAY WE WERE (1973), Martin Ritt's SOUNDER (1972) and THE FRONT (1976), Don Siegel's DIRTY HARRY (1971) and THE SHOOTIST (1976), and Fred Zinnemann's THE DAY OF THE JACKAL (1973). The problem was that either these artists were too old or too independent to rely on.

The issue of which direction to choose was settled in 1977. Not since 1939 had Hollywood been so in touch with the public consciousness. There was a film for everyone and dozens to imitate in the upcoming decade. Exhibitors and critics are still debating the wisdom of the decisions based on the year's hit films. For example, the success of JULIA raised false hopes for films about female bonding. NEWSWEEK reported that the film "supposedly signals a new deal for women in films, in which they'll no longer be satellites to men but suns and stars in their own right."[1218] It never happened. Except for a handful of good films about female bonding--e.g., THE TURNING POINT (1977), GIRLFRIENDS (1978), RICH AND FAMOUS (1981), TERMS OF ENDEARMENT (1983), and BEACHES (1988), Hollywood remains committed to the satellite system, rather than to independently orbiting women. SATURDAY NIGHT FEVER offered a more promising hope by bringing back Hollywood musicals, albeit in a new form and with a different slant. Within a year, Hollywood had released four major rock musicals: THE WIZ, SGT. PEPPER'S LONELY HEARTS CLUB BAND, GREASE, and HAIR. Since then, we've had impressive works like ALL THAT JAZZ (1979), FAME (1980), ZOOT SUIT, PENNIES FROM HEAVEN (both in 1981), FLASHDANCE (1983), FOOTLOOSE (1984), and DIRTY DANCING (1987).[1219] Nevertheless, flops like ONE FROM THE HEART (1982), A CHORUS LINE (1985), and LITTLE SHOP OF HORRORS (1986) have convinced modern filmmakers that musicals are box-office poison.[1220]

By far the most revolutionary event of the year and the one that did capture the interest and pocketbooks of Hollywood was the renaissance of science-fiction films. Not only did spectacular works like STAR WARS and CLOSE ENCOUNTERS OF THE THIRD KIND set in motion a craze for special effects films, but they also reinforced the idea that heroes existed and prevailed.[1221] Essentially poverty row formulas with mega-bucks budgets, these recycled escapist films of the 1930s and 1940s appealed to the nation's longing for simpler times and clear-cut messages of good and evil. Film fanatics like Lucas and Spielberg had proved that modern audiences shared their love affair with the time-honored conventions of horror, science fiction, and adventure stories. Among the most successful spin-offs, sequels, and remakes

---

[1218] Jack Kroll et al., "Hollywood's New Heroines," NEWSWEEK (October 10, 1977):78.

[1219] For a useful overview, see Dave Kehr, "Can't Stop the Musicals," AMERICAN FILM 9:7 (May 1984):33-7.

[1220] For a good perspective, see Thomas Wiener, "The Rise and Fall of the Rock Film: Part I," AMERICAN FILM 1:2 (November 1975):25-9; and ___, "The Rise and Fall of the Rock Film: Part II--From WOODSTOCK to STARDUST, The Parade's Gone By," ibid., 1:3 (December 1975):58-63.

[1221] For a good overview, see Michael Wood, "Kiss Tomorrow Goodbye," AMERICAN FILM 2:6 (April 1977):14-7; and Donald Chase, "War of the Wizards," ibid., 7:8 (June 1982):52-9.

inspired by the SFX hits of 1977 are SUPERMAN (1978), ALIEN, STAR TREK: THE MOTION PICTURE (both in 1979), THE EMPIRE STRIKES BACK, THE SHINING, ALTERED STATES (all in 1980), RAIDERS OF THE LOST ARK (1981), E. T.: THE EXTRA-TERRESTRIAL, BLADE RUNNER, STAR TREK II: THE WRATH OF KAHN, POLTERGEIST, TRON (all in 1982), INDIANA JONES AND THE TEMPLE OF DOOM, ROMANCING THE STONE, STAR TREK III: THE SEARCH FOR SPOCK, GHOSTBUSTERS, CONAN THE DESTROYER, THE TERMINATOR, STARMAN, 2010 (all in 1984), LADYHAWKE, COCOON, BACK TO THE FUTURE, THE EMERALD FOREST, RETURN OF THE JEDI (all in 1985), ALIENS, THE FLY, PEGGY SUE GOT MARRIED, STAR TREK IV: THE VOYAGE HOME (all in 1986), and INDIANA JONES AND THE LAST CRUSADE (1989). This list does not include the eight versions of FRIDAY THE 13th, the fifth STAR TREK film, THE KARATE KID, and HALLOWEEN, and the current sequels to BACK TO THE FUTURE and GHOSTBUSTERS.[1222]

The big fear in 1977, however, was the escalating cost of film production.[1223] Ever since the phenomenal success of movies like JAWS and STAR WARS, film companies had been gambling with ever-increasing budgets on the premise that it just takes one film to hit the jackpot. After all, as Vincent Canby observes, "Producer Richard Zanuck's share of the profits from JAWS reportedly represents more money than his father, Darryl, made during a lifetime as one of Hollywood's most successful producers."[1224] The influential critic also points out the dangers in assuming that being a successful filmmaker is a guarantee against box-office failure. For example, George Lucas made AMERICAN GRAFFITI (1973) and bombed with LUCKY LADY (1975), William Friedkin made THE EXORCIST (1973) and overproduced SORCERER (1977), and Bernardo Bertolucci created a sensation with LAST TANGO IN PARIS (1973) and suffered a financial disaster with 1900 (1977).[1225] As Canby explains, few people in the industry worried about Hollywood's expenditures' exceeding the rate of inflation or the fact that more movies were failing at the box office than in the past, so long as when you had a box-office hit, it broke the profit records. While critics like Canby worried about the escalating production costs and the industry's return to extravagant filmmaking, the filmmakers exuded a new sense of self-confidence.

Hollywood even felt secure enough to examine the Vietnam War in the seventies. Although it had stayed away from the controversial war in the sixties (see Chapter 2), America's disastrous exit from Vietnam in 1973 created a need to mask the nation's scars and to restore its tarnished pride. At first, the film capital began identifying villains in films like COMING HOME, THE DEER HUNTER, THE BOYS IN COMPANY C, GO TELL THE SPARTANS (all in 1978), FRIENDLY FIRE, and APOCALYPSE NOW (both in 1979). But President Reagan's stunning election in 1980 convinced Hollywood that a more conservative approach to the horrors of the Vietnam War would do better at the box office. That is, films should emphasize what the divisive conflict did to our men and women in combat and the viciousness of the enemy they fought. To test the commercial waters, the film industry released sophomoric films like FIRST BLOOD (1982), UNCOMMON VALOR, MISSING IN ACTION (both in 1983), and RAMBO: FIRST

[1222] For a good overview of the sequels, remakes, and spinoffs that appeared in the summer of 1989, see Aljean Harmetz, "Boom Summer for Sequels," NEW YORK TIMES C (May 3, 1989):19; and Betsy Sharkey, "Return of the Return of the Summer Sequel," AMERICAN FILM 14:8 (June 1989):40-1.

[1223] For a current update on the budget problems, see Alex Gibney and Anne Thompson, "Make Money, Not War," FILM COMMENT 23:6 (December 1987):17-22.

[1224] Vincent Canby, "Somebody Must Put a Lid on Budgets," NEW YORK TIMES D (November 27, 1977):11.

[1225] "Somebody Must Put a Lid on Budgets," p.11.

BLOOD PART II (1985). Then came more serious examinations in films PLATOON (1986), FULL METAL JACKET, GOOD MORNING, VIETNAM, and HAMBURGER HILL (all in 1987).

Thus the end of the seventies saw a confident Hollywood, bolstered by a number of box-office hits, drawing more and more people to movie houses. The filmmakers now felt it was time to devote more attention to comedy films, a genre seriously ignored during most of the decade. According to Aljean Harmetz, the industry put nearly a third of its upcoming product in upbeat comic movies. "Definitely consigned to the 1980 dustbin are gang movies, sentimental looks at the lives of blue-collar workers and love stories in which the heroines are crippled, deaf or dying of some unnamed disease."[1226] This formula would be taken over by the TV industry in the eighties, as viewers found themselves being offered "Disease of the Week" made-for-TV movies on a regular basis. But Hollywood had other concerns as it opened the eighties with its second eighteen-month recession in six years. Fortunately, theatrical releases were now only part of the profits being made as a result of the new channels of production, distribution, and exhibition provided by network television, cable channels, and the emerging videocassette industry.[1227]

In 1980, Hollywood got another of its cyclical surprises. The constant escalation of big-budget productions and runaway costs resulted in one of the American film industry's biggest box-office disasters, Michael Cimino's HEAVEN'S GATE (1980). Not only did the film eventually cause the demise of United Artists as a major force in the industry since 1953, but it also sent the shakers and movers back to their strategy boards to rethink production policies.[1228] ISHTAR (1986) would have the same effect in the mid-1980s. As a result, the decade of the eighties witnessed a polarization between the spectacle film--e.g., E. T.: THE EXTRA-TERRESTRIAL (1982), INDIANA JONES AND THE TEMPLE OF DOOM (1985), and ALIENS (1986)--and the low-budget production--e.g., BROADCAST NEWS, GOOD MORNING, VIETNAM (both in 1986), and MOONSTRUCK (1987).[1229]

By the mid-1980s, with the industry in its third eighteen-month recession, Hollywood seemed more and more committed to the concept of the mega-buck hit. Success had allowed new companies like Orion and Tri-Star to challenge the dominance of the six majors, with companies like Cannon, New World, New Line, De Laurentis Entertainment Group, Atlantic Releasing, and Island coming on strong.[1230] But the overall industry picture was far less positive. As Anne Thompson points out, a handful of films--BEVERLY HILLS COP, WITNESS, BACK TO THE FUTURE, FIRST BLOOD (RAMBO), JAGGED EDGE, and COMMANDO--accounted for most of the industry's profits for the year, with only six of ninety-one pictures released between Labor Day and Christmas grossing over fifteen million dollars.[1231] But Christmas hits like ROCKY IV, OUT OF AFRICA, THE COLOR PURPLE, SPIES LIKE US, THE JEWEL

[1226] Aljean Harmetz, "Hollywood Is Taking Aim at the Funny Bone," NEW YORK TIMES H (August 5, 1979):1, 3.

[1227] For another perspective, see "Summing Up the Seventies," AMERICAN FILM 5:3 (December 1979):24-32, 50-65.

[1228] In addition to FINAL CUT, see Michael Dempsey, "After the Fall: Post-Cimino Hollywood," AMERICAN FILM 6:10 (September 1981):50-4.

[1229] For useful perspectives, see Vincent Canby, "Sometimes 'Small' Movies Can Be Very Big," NEW YORK TIMES H (January 22, 1989):1, 9; and David Thomson, "The Real Crisis In American Films," AMERICAN FILM 6:8 (June 1981):41-5.

[1230] Anne Thompson, "Industry: The 12th Annual Grosses," FILM COMMENT 23:2 (March-April 1987):62.

[1231] "Industry: Tenth Annual Grosses," p.64.

OF THE NILE, WHITE NIGHTS, and 101 DALMATIANS appeared to justify the studios' big-picture perspective. The resourceful Thompson did note, however, that Universal's Marvin Antonowsky now felt it was time that Hollywood move more toward the adult market, not only because the baby boomers were fast approaching middle age, but also because well-crafted stories like OUT OF AFRICA, JAGGED EDGE, PRIZZI'S HONOR, and MASK were doing respectable box-office business.[1232] Another important link between baby boomers and film profits was the increasing importance of hit films featuring former members of the controversial TV show SATURDAY NIGHT LIVE. Racist and sexist in content, the immensely popular show had launched the careers of Eddie Murphy, John Belushi, Bill Murray,[1233] and Chevy Chase, all of whom had a wide following at the box office.[1234] The challenge for Hollywood was to maintain its relationship with its primary audience (twelve to seventeen) and to increase its appeal to audiences over thirty.[1235]

As 1986 demonstrated, the challenge was more difficult than it seemed; BOXOFFICE reported that the industry wasn't very effective with its summer releases. Except for hit films like TOP GUN, BACK TO SCHOOL, THE KARATE KID II, and FERRIS BUELLER'S DAY OFF, revenues dropped by sixteen million dollars (from $463 million to $447 million) from the previous year. Industry hopes rose, however, in the fall as surprise hits like CROCODILE DUNDEE and STAND BY ME drew impressive crowds to theaters across the country. Nevertheless, by the end of the year, the total box-office drop for 1986 amounted to eleven percent (over 110 million tickets). As a result, management and structural shakeups occurred at MGM/UA, Columbia Pictures, and Universal. More disturbing to exhibitors was a three-year industry study that concluded home video was damaging the exhibition business.[1236] Still further, the Justice Department increased its war on "product-splitting," and the MPPA finally agreed to add PG-13 to its Rating System to satisfy angry groups who claimed parents weren't being given enough information on film content.[1237] Perhaps the most alarming news to small exhibitors was the fact that the majors were once more moving into the exhibition market, buying up large theater chains.[1238]

[1232] "Industry: Tenth Annual Grosses," p.64. See also Stephen Farber, "The Return of the Grown-up Movie," AMERICAN FILM 7:3 (December 1981):46-8, 50-3, 76.

[1233] For a useful overview, see Timothy White, "The Rumpled Anarchy of Bill Murray," THE NEW YORK TIMES MAGAZINE (November 20, 1988):38-9, 52, 54, 56, 94, 106.

[1234] "Industry: Tenth Annual Grosses," pp.64-5.

[1235] For a useful perspective on reactions to films in the mid-1980s, see Jill Kearney, "What's Wrong With Today's Films?" AMERICAN FILM 11:7 (May 1986):53-6.

[1236] In addition to Chapter 3, see Janet Maslin, "Mysteries of Cassette Love," NEW YORK TIMES H (March 5, 1989):11; Philip Kopper, "Movie Theater of the Future: The Home?" AMERICAN FILM 3:3 (December-January 1978):16-21; Patrick McGilligan, "Movies Are Better Than Ever--On Television," ibid., 5:5 (March 1980):50-4; Karen Stabiner, "The Shape of Theaters to Come," ibid., 7:10 (September 1982):50-3, 56; and Laurence Jarvik and Nancy Strickland, "TV Movies--Better Than the Real Thing (Are You Kidding?)," ibid., 14:3 (December 1988):40-3, 56.

[1237] For a good overview of the controversy surrounding G and PG films, see Bruce A. Austin et al., "M. P. A. A. Ratings and the Box Office: Some Tantalizing Statistics," FILM QUARTERLY 35:2 (Winter 1981-1982):28-30.

[1238] "1986 Chronology of Major Industry Events," BOXOFFICE 123:4 (April 1987):13-4.

As discussed in Chapter 3, Hollywood insiders took the bad news calmly. Realizing that the recession would soon run its course, they continued to pour money into high-concept, big-budget remakes, sequels, and spinoffs. The majors concentrated on the formula films, inching their way more into the adult market, while the smaller companies experimented with speciality films like A ROOM WITH A VIEW and MY BEAUTIFUL LAUNDRETTE. No one doubted, as Thompson reports, that key changes in production policies had to be implemented. The surprise successes of STAND BY ME and CROCODILE DUNDEE had demonstrated three things: "(1) the historical strength of the fish-out-of-water genre; (2) the potency of a well-liked TV personality; and (3) the appeal of the laconic hero-outsider who has warmth, charm and vulnerability and who one-ups the city sophisticates."[1239]

By 1987, the results of the switching, shifting, and stylistic machinations in products, personnel, and technology had resulted in record-breaking box-office profits, and the majors were once more in firm control of the industry. "The trick for the studios," Thompson explains," which most of them pulled off, was to churn out modest hits that earned more than $15 million in domestic rentals."[1240] In other words, the strategy of appealing to both a youth-oriented and an adult market was finally in place.[1241] Along with the sequels, spinoffs, and remakes are low-budget, risky products like HOLLYWOOD SHUFFLE, LA BAMBA, HOOSIERS, RAISING ARIZONA, RADIO DAYS, SOMEONE TO WATCH OVER ME, 84 CHARING CROSS ROAD, THE STEPFATHER, and WISH YOU WERE HERE. Not all of these critically noteworthy films did well at the box office. But thanks to the ancillary markets (especially videocassettes), such films not only get made and seen, but others like them are now possible.

As box-office and production records continued to fall in 1988, the majors tightened their grip on the film industry. The biggest news was that the videocassette industry now surpassed the theaters as the main source of profits, although videocassette sales still depended on a film's getting a good theatrical release. The most disappointing news was that filmmaking by Disney and Paramount, the industrial leaders, had become matter-of-fact. According to Thompson, "They manufacture their product almost as other giant corporations do, drafting and marketing each movie to a targeted audience."[1242] On the other hand, she pointed out that original and clever films likes WHO KILLED ROGER RABBIT?, A FISH CALLED WANDA, BEETLEJUICE, and BULL DURHAM offered hope for a more flexible cinematic future.

As the eighties draw to a close, Hollywood continues its love affair with the "yuppie" generation, insisting that the Eisenhower years are still in vogue. This nostalgic view of the fifties--i.e., we are still a mighty nation endowed with extraordinary moral values--has resulted in a number of notable changes in film content. The most obvious change since the decade began is that the film industry has become more conservative.[1243] In place of the nudity and clinical sex of the

---

[1239] "Industry: The 12th Annual Grosses Gloss,"p.64.

[1240] Anne Thompson, "Industry: The 13 Annual Grosses Gloss," FILM COMMENT 24:2 (March-April 1988):56. For an overview of the problems of independents, see Debra Goldman, "Indie Boom Turns Bust PREMIERE 2:9 (May 1989):31-4.

[1241] For more information, see Debra Goldman, "Business for Art's Sake," AMERICAN FILM 12:6 (April 1987):44-8; and Stephen Holden, "How Rock is Changing Hollywood's Tune," ibid., H (July 16, 1989):1, 18-9.

[1242] Anne Thompson, "Industry: The 14th Annual Grosses Gloss," FILM COMMENT 25:2 (March-April 1989):70. See also William Severini Kowinski, "The Malling of the Movies," AMERICAN FILM 8:10 (September 1983):52-3, 55-6.

[1243] For a useful perspective on modern formula filmmaking, see Anna McDonnell, ". . . Happily Ever After," AMERICAN FILM 12:4 (January-February 1987):42-6.

seventies are traditional romances like MYSTIC PIZZA, CROSSING DELANCEY, WORKING GIRL, and COMING TO AMERICA (all in 1988). Even promiscuous sex has become unpopular, most notably with James Bond limiting his sexual exploits to just one woman in NEVER SAY NEVER (1988). And if there are still meandering husbands who think that an occasional fling is not so terrible, we have pictures like FATAL ATTRACTION and SOMEONE TO WATCH OVER ME (both in 1987).[1244] Given the fear over the AIDS epidemic[1245] and the problem with the growing number of divorced children, the moviegoing public has embraced these neo-conservative values. Hollywood has also resumed its interest in adapting Broadway productions, thanks to the success of ventures like AMADEUS, A SOLDIER'S STORY (both in 1984), and AGNES OF GOD (1985).[1246] Moreover, by the end of the Reagan years, even the Soviet Union is emerging as a potential ally for the nineties. In place of films like RED DAWN and MOSCOW ON THE HUDSON (both in 1984), Hollywood has jumped on the national bandwagon with films like RAMBO IV and RED HEAT (both in 1988). The filmmakers are recycling their cold war anti-Soviet propaganda into anti-war films and stories about detente.

At the center of the modern Hollywood is the notion that filmmakers produce films they enjoy rather than trying to outguess the audience's expectations.[1247] On the one hand, people like Spielberg argue that he is remaking the types of films that he enjoyed in his youth at the movie theaters and on TV. On the other hand, marketing research is bigger than ever, trying to find out what titles, stars, and stories most appeal to mass audiences. The youth-oriented genre movies of the seventies have given way to modest productions that rely on topical scripts to capture the flavor of the times.

Hollywood's cyclical nature also continues. Audiences continue to fluctuate, periods of recession are followed by successful seasons; executives continue to play the corporate chairs game, while the majors reorganize themselves to offset box-office flops;[1248] technology still spurs dramatic changes in content and form; the market

---

[1244] For another perspective, see Julia Cameron, "What's Love Got to Do with It?: A Kiss Is Still a Kiss, But the Rules Have Changed," AMERICAN FILM 14:6 (April 1989):30-3, 58-9.

[1245] For a useful perspective, see Michael Kimmelman, "Bitter Harvest: AIDS and the Arts," NEW YORK TIMES H (March 19, 1989):1, 6.

[1246] For a good overview, see Don Shewey, "Hollywood Does Broadway," AMERICAN FILM 12:2 (November 1986):37-9, 42.

[1247] If you enjoy predictions, see "Into the '90s: The Future of Talking Pictures," AMERICAN FILM 14:4 (January-February 1989):24-39, 52.

[1248] One of the biggest stories of 1989 was Time Inc.'s acquistion of Warner Communications and the aborted attempt by Paramount Communications Inc. to block the merger. The new company is called Time Warner. For more information, see Floyd Norris, "Time Inc. and Warner to Merge, Creating Largest Media Company," NEW YORK TIMES A (March 5, 1989):1, 30; ___, "Time and Warner Look to Europe and Pacific," ibid., D (March 7, 1989):22; ___," In The Time Inc. Game, Warner Head Has Aces," ibid., D (June 8, 1989):1, 23; ___, "Battle for Time Inc.: Bottom Line Is Cash," ibid., A (June 9, 1989):1, D5; ___, "In Time Inc. Battle, All Eyes On the Courts," ibid., D (June 19, 1989):1, 4; Geraldine Fabrikant, "A Frustrated Warner Head Sees His Dream Threatened," ibid., D (June 12, 1989):1, 3; ___, "United Artists Sale Backed," ibid., D (April 18, 1989):24; Stephen Labaton, "Court Declines to Block Time Inc. Meeting," ibid., D (June 29, 1989):1-2; Robert J. Cole, "Paramount Bids for Time Inc.; Battle With Warner Is Likely," ibid., A (June 7, 1989):1, D5; ___, "Paramount Bid Lifts Time by $44," ibid., D (June 8,

continues to determine the supply and demand of film production; and film attendance remains as unpredictable as ever. Despite the conservative mood of the current film industry where fewer than one percent of the films released in a single year make a profit at the box office, filmmakers are still willing to gamble big--e.g., in 1988, the average film cost $18 million dollars, with an additional $4 million for promotion--to make a fortune. Consider the case of the ten box-office hit films of 1987: BEVERLY HILLS COP II, PLATOON, FATAL ATTRACTION, THREE MEN AND A BABY, THE UNTOUCHABLES, THE SECRET OF MY SUCCESS, STAKEOUT, LETHAL WEAPON, THE WITCHES OF EASTWICK, and DRAGNET. Their overwhelming success will probably result in a slew of sequels.

There are, however, ominous signs in the entertainment industry.[1249] For example, ABC suffered a $40-million loss because of the epic mini-series, WAR AND REMEMBRANCE (1988-1989). The longest running and most costly TV series (close to thirty hours, shown on twelve different nights, and produced for $110 million) has convinced TV producers that in the future they would only back major film projects if the film didn't exceed eight hours.[1250] Perhaps the most startling news is that Japan may soon take over many of Hollywood's studios. "Cash-rich and eager

1989):1, 23; ___, "Time Inc.'s Board Plots A Defense," ibid., D (June 9, 1989):1, 4; ___, "Time Inc. and Warner Prepare a Counterattack," ibid., D (June 12, 1989):3; ___, "Time Inc., Rejecting Bid by Paramount, Will Pursue Warner," ibid., A (June 17, 1989):1, B42; ___, "Paramount Faults Time Over Stockholder Data," ibid., D (June 23, 1989):15; ___, "Paramount Raises Bid For Time," ibid., B (June 24, 1989):31, 33; ___, "Time Turns Paramount Bid Down," ibid., D (June 27, 1989):1, 21; ___," "Skirting a Time Inc. Barrier, Paramount Lines Up 7 Banks," ibid., D (June 30, 1989):1, 5; ___, "Paramount Delay Cited by Citibank," ibid., D (July 7, 1989):1, 5; ___, "Time Case Is Dividing Wall Street," ibid., D (July 17, 1989):1-2; Geraldine Fabrikant, "Paramount Adds to Bid for Time," ibid., D (July 11, 1989):1, 18; ___, "Decision on Time by Friday Seen," ibid., D (July 12, 1989):1, 17; ___, "A Delaware Court Refuses to Block Time-Warner Link," ibid., A (July 15, 1989):1, 44; ___, "Warner Is Acquired by Time Inc. Within Hours of Court Approval," ibid., A (July 25, 1989):1, D23; ___, "Despite Defeat, Paramount Is Expected to Persevere," ibid., D (July 26, 1989):1, 16; ___, "Assessing Time Warner Data Offer a Glimpse," ibid., D (July 27, 1989):9; and ___, "Behind a Corporate Courtship," ibid., F (August 13, 1989):1, 12. A second major story was the Sony Corporation's acquisition of Columbia Pictures Entertainment Inc. For more information, see Geraldine Fabrikant, "Deal Is Expected For Sony to Buy Columbia Pictures," NEW YORK TIMES A (September 26, 1989):1, D8; ___, "Producer Likely to Head Sony-Owned Columbia," ibid., D (September 27, 1989):1, 12; ___, "Sale to Sony Approved by Columbia Pictures," ibid., D (September 28, 1989):9; and David E. Sanger, "Sony Has High Hopes for Columbia Pictures," ibid., pp.D1, 9. For information on other recent developments, see Michael Lev, "MGM/UA Accepts New Quintex Bid," NEW YORK TIMES A (September 16, 1989):37; Richard W. Stevenson, "Deal for MGM/UA Assets," ibid., D (April 3, 1989):7; ___, "Paramount Pictures' Success Key to Revamping at G&W," ibid., D (April 11, 1989):1, 8; ___, "Not Just Another Charlie Bluhdorn," ibid., F (June 11, 1989):1, 9; N. R. Kleinfield, "Steve Ross's Days of Deal-Making," ibid., p.9; "Hollywood Spent More for TV Ads Last Year," ibid., D (April 6, 1989):23; Geraldine Fabrikant, "New Allies for Studios In Challenge of Networks," ibid., D (April 17, 1989):11; and Aljean Harmetz, "A Revamping of Fox Film Puts Emphasis on Movies," ibid., D (July13, 1989):1, 20.

[1249] For a brief look at conditions for experimental films, see Caryn James, "Avant-Garde Films in Struggle to Stay Alive," NEW YORK TIMES C (June 29, 1989):17.

[1250] For more details, see Bill Carter, "A Mini-Series Teaches ABC Hard Lessons," NEW YORK TIMES D (May 4, 1989):1, 10.

for new investments," NEWSWEEK points out, "the Japanese want a piece of America's
$4 billion-a-year movie business."[1251]

The major industrial debates of the decade focus on whether the Hollywood
mentality has inhibited the art of filmmaking. One issue deals with such questions
as "Are pictures less complex today than in the past, are filmmakers opting for easier
challenges than their predecessors, and are the movies more simplistic in their themes
than during the sixties and early seventies? Put another way, does Hollywood's
obessession with spinoffs, sequels, and remakes define a new era in Hollywood
history, or is it still the same old approach to the business of motion pictures?[1252]
Another issue relates to the conglomerate nature of the American film industry.
Because the chief executive officers of the big companies like Paramount, Universal,
and Warner Bros. are no longer the flamboyant showpeople of the past who adored
the filmmaking game, are they less interested in making good films and more interested
in the financial gains associated with mega-hits?[1253] The answer may well depend on
how sentimental the questioner is about the factory products turned out by Harry
Cohn, Jack L. Warner, Louis B. Mayer, David O. Selznick, and Darryl F. Zanuck.
Still another issue centers on the strength of the star system.[1254] With superstars
like Stallone, Eastwood, Newman, Streisand, Redford, Jane Fonda, Hoffman, Pacino,
Tom Cruise, and Murphy getting multi-million-dollar contracts with hefty shares in
the profits, industry insiders and film critics are at odds over the wisdom of such
deals. Can the stars insure a film's success, as they did in the past; or do they
make the difference in the size of a film's profit IF the film is already a good project
that needs an additional lift in being made, and receives worldwide distribution in
movie theaters, on TV, and in the videocassette market? A fourth issue raises the
future of Hollywood itself as the film capital of the world.[1255] The on-going escalation
of production budgets resulting, in part, from the enormous costs of making a film
in California has increased the attraction of making movies not only outside the United
States, but also in different parts of the country. Observers are asking if movies
like THREE MEN AND A BABY, THE SECRET OF MY SUCCESS, STAKEOUT,
COCOON, FATAL ATTRACTION (all in 1987), THE ACCUSED, CROSSING DELANCEY,
and BETRAYED (all in 1988) suffered in quality or impact because they were made
outside the California environment? A fifth issue relates to the changing status in

---

[1251] Joshua Hammer et al., "Next Stop, Tinseltown," NEWSWEEK (March 20, 1989):48. See
also Richard W. Stevenson, "Hollywood Entices Japanese,' NEW YORK TIMES D
(October 4, 1988):1, 7; and ___, "Japanese Put Up $100 Million to Back Films in
Hollywood," ibid., A (August 21, 1989):1, D4.

[1252] For some insights into the problem of sequels and the financial health of film
companies, see Aljean Harmetz, "Waking From a New 'Nightmare' to New Profits,"
NEW YORK TIMES C (July 13, 1989):17, 24; ___, "BATMAN Sets Sales Record: 4100
Million in 10 Days," ibid., A (July 4, 1989):25; and ___, "Movie Studios Prepare
for a Record Summer," ibid., C (June 21, 1989):17.

[1253] Interestingly, Joe Roth, an independent producer and director, was made head of
20th Century-Fox's new filmmaking unit, Fox Film Corporation, in 1989. The last
time a director headed a major film studio was in 1935, when Ernst Lubitsch took
over Paramount Pictures. For more information, see "A Revamping of Fox Film Puts
Emphasis on Movies," pp.1, 20.

[1254] For an interesting perspective on nepotism in recent films, see Andrea King, "The
N Word," THE HOLLYWOOD REPORTER (February 24, 1989):20-2, 65, 85-7.

[1255] For an interesting wrinkle, see Vincent Canby, "Ici Se Habla Euro-English," NEW
YORK TIMES H (June 4, 1989):1, 19; and Antoine De Clermont-Tonnerre et al.,
"'Euro-English' Movies: More British Than Not," ibid., H (June 25, 1989):3.

theater ownership. As Damon Wright points, "Before the mid-1980s, none of the seven major studios owned theater interests. Today, four of them do. . . ."[1256] How will this affect the current building boom in theater construction, how will it influence the way films are booked, how will it change the management of movie houses, and how will it provide more technological breakthroughs in the screening of films?

Concern is also being raised about subject matter, particularly about the setbacks women and minorities are suffering in roles and images. For example, Elayne Rapping reports "What women have actually achieved--an amazing amount in twenty years--is everywhere being undermined, distorted, co-opted."[1257] Pointing to films like JUST BETWEEN FRIENDS (1982), VIOLETS ARE BLUE (1986), PLENTY, JAGGED EDGE, HANNAH AND HER SISTERS, BABY BOOM, FATAL ATTRACTION, SOMEONE TO WATCH OVER ME, MOONSTRUCK, (all in 1987), THE GOOD MOTHER, RUNNING ON EMPTY, BROADCAST NEWS, and CROSSING DELANCEY (all in 1988), Hollywood has been telling women that freedom isn't as glamorous as the feminist movement suggested, that women really don't enjoy the business world, and that the true answer to a woman's happiness is a good man and a healthy family.

The perceptive critic also identifies problems with the current crop of youth-oriented films. Placing some of the blame on the techno-sociological phenomenon of adults' preferring to watch TV rather than go to a movie theater, Rapping explains why Hollywood has put considerable emphasis on making films geared to teenagers and young adults. The content of films like FAST TIMES AT RIDGEMONT HIGH (1982), RISKY BUSINESS (1983), RECKLESS (1984), AT CLOSE RANGE (1986) and THE RIVER'S EDGE (1987) is much different, however, from the "rebellion films" of the fifties and sixties. The youth cult films of the eighties, she observes,

> take place in a clautrophobic world inhabited and negotiated entirely by kids, and informed by their very shallow, very limited sense of emotional and social reality. Parents are either wholly absent or hopelessly out of it, giving dated, barely tolerated advice about things they don't understand in any way. The anger of James Dean is as foreign to these kids as is the rebelliousness of the kids in THE BLACKBOARD JUNGLE or THE WILD ONE."[1258]

To a large degree, the films of the eighties not only limit an adolescent's options, but also suggest few alternatives to a nihlistic existence.

The approaches to the study of film more than match the changes taking place in the industry. A new generation of scholars, steeped in the traditions of the 1960s, argue that race, gender, and class determine a film's content and form. Whether trained in Marxist, psychological, or feminist criticism, the determinists reject the notion that artists transcended their race, sex, or backgrounds to film universal statements about humanity. As in the traditional arts, film educators are debating the nature of film canons and what is basic in a film education.

[1256] Damon Wright, "What's New at the Movies," NEW YORK TIMES F (July 23, 1989):13.

[1257] Elayne Rapping, "Liberation in Chains: 'The Woman Question' In Hollywood," CINEASTE 17:1 (1989):8. See also Lynne Jackson with Karen Jaehne, "Eavesdropping on Female Voices: A Who's Who of Contemporary Women Filmmakers," CINEASTE 16:1-2 (1987-88):38-43; Aljean Harmetz, "2 Women Succeeded as Producers, But Easy Street Is Down the Road," NEW YORK TIMES C (September 14, 1988):19, 21; ___, "Report Cites Unequal Pay for Female Writers," ibid., C (May 25, 1989):25; and Caryn James, "Are Feminist Heroines An Endangered Species?" ibid., H (July 16, 1989):15, 20.

[1258] Elayne Rapping, "Hollywood's Youth Cult Films," CINEASTE 16:1-2 (1987-88):15. For another perspective, see Jay Scott, "The Wild Ones," AMERICAN FILM 8:6 (April 1983):30-5, 64-5.

BOOKS

GENERAL

*Taylor, John Russell. DIRECTORS AND DIRECTIONS: CINEMA FOR THE SEVENTIES. New York: Hill and Wang, 1975. 327pp.

DIRECTORS AND STARS

WOODY ALLEN

*Allen, Woody. FOUR FILMS OF WOODY ALLEN: ANNIE HALL, INTERIORS, MANHATTAN, STARDUST MEMORIES. New York: Random House, 1982. Illustrated. 389pp.

*Allen, Woody. THREE FILMS OF WOODY ALLEN: ZELIG, BROADWAY DANNY ROSE, THE PURPLE ROSE OF CAIRO. New York: Random House, 1987. Illustrated. Illustrated. 475pp.

*Allen, Woody. HANNAH AND HER SISTERS. New York: Random House, 1987. Illustrated. 188pp.

*Anobile, Richard J., ed. WOODY ALLEN'S "PLAY IT AGAIN, SAM." New York: Grosset and Dunlap, 1972. Illustrated. 192pp.

FRANCIS FORD COPPOLA

*Chaillet, Jean-Paul, and Elizabeth Vincent. FRANCIS FORD COPPOLA. Trans. Denise Raab Jacobs. New York: St. Martin's Press, 1984. Illustrated. 124pp.

Chowan, Jeffrey. HOLLYWOOD AUTEUR: FRANCIS COPPOLA. New York: Praeger, 1988. Illustrated. 231pp.

Johnson, Robert K. FRANCIS FORD COPPOLA. Boston: Twayne Publishers, 1977. Illustrated. 199pp.

BRIAN DE PALMA

Bouzereau, Laurent. THE DE PALMA CUT: THE FILMS OF AMERICA'S MOST CONTROVERSIAL DIRECTOR. New York: Dembner Books, 1988. Illustrated. 176pp.

*Dworkin, Susan. DOUBLE DE PALMA: A FILM STUDY WITH BRIAN DE PALMA. New York: Newmarket Press, 1984. Illustrated. 215pp.

GEORGE LUCAS

Pollack, Dale. SKYWALKING: THE LIFE AND FILMS OF GEORGE LUCAS. New York: Harmony Books, 1983. Illustrated. 304pp.

MIKE NICHOLS

*Feiffer, Jules. CARNAL KNOWLEDGE: A SCREENPLAY. New York: Farrar, Straus and Giroux, 1971. Illustrated. 118pp.

NICOLAS ROEG

Feineman, Neil. NICOLAS ROEG. Boston: Twayne Publishers, 1978.   Illustrated. 153pp.

MARTIN SCORSESE

Bliss, Michael. MARTIN SCORSESE AND MICHAEL CIMINO. Metuchen: The Scarecrow Press, 1985. Illustrated. 301pp.

*Kelly, Mary Pat. MARTIN SCORSESE: THE FIRST DECADE. New York: Redgrave Publishing Company, 1980. Illustrated. 206pp.

Weiss, Marion. MARTIN SCORSESE: A GUIDE TO REFERENCES AND RESOURCES. Boston: G. K. Hall, 1987. 137pp.

SISSY SPACEK

Emerson, Mark, and Eugene E. Pfaff, Jr. COUNTRY GIRL: THE LIFE OF SISSY SPACEK. New York: St. Martin's Press, 1988. Illustrated. 202pp.

STEVEN SPIELBERG

*Crawley, Tony. THE STEVEN SPIELBERG STORY: THE MAN BEHIND THE MOVIES. New York: Quill, 1983. Illustrated. 160pp

Mott, Donald R., and Cheryl McAllister Saunders. STEVEN SPIELBERG.   Boston: Twayne Publishers, 1986. 199pp.

Sinyard, Neil. THE FILMS OF STEVEN SPIELBERG. London: Bison Books, 1986. Illustrated. 128pp.

JOHN WATERS

Waters, John. CRACKPOT: THE OBSESSIONS OF JOHN WATERS. New York: Macmillan

Publishing Company, 1986. 144pp.

EPILOGUE

In looking back on the seven approaches to film study synthesized in this book, one senses the author's arrogance in attempting such a project, but also the enormous gaps in discussions of theories, personalities, national cinemas, and significant events. Clearly, this sweeping overview has only skimmed the surface of the cinema's power to influence historical events, to shape the collective consciousness, and to entertain mass audiences throughout the twentieth century. The issue of art versus industry continues to dominate intellectual debates and commercial decisions. To paraphrase a scene from Shaw's SAINT JOAN, when the maid asks the lord of the manor for arms to free France, the evolution of motion pictures seems crazy, but look where the sane leaders of nations have brought us.

The history of film throughout the world reveals that in almost every case, dominant cultural forces control the content and direction that film industries take. Invariably, there arise artists whose vision of the world and its contemporary values challenges the STATUS QUO. But if one thing is clear in film history, it is that the audience remains the major factor in demanding and determining the major directions the commercial film industry will take. Without mass acceptance, important works that challenge our values and shape our decisions are ignored, and the artists themselves are driven to despair and exile. It behooves each of us, therefore, not only to understand the role that these inspired individuals play in our lives, but also to appreciate the necessity for educating the public to its responsiblities for providing an environment where such artists can work and flourish. At the very least, our institutions of learning must encourage cultural diversity and intellectual curiosity so that conflicting points of view are not only heard, but also debated. At the very best, we should honor and support those who seek to make film assume its destiny as the universal language.